sixth edition

Survey of Accounting

sixth edition

Survey of Accounting

Thomas P. Edmonds
University of Alabama—Birmingham

Christopher T. Edmonds
University of Alabama—Birmingham

Mark A. Edmonds
University of Alabama—Birmingham

Jennifer E. Edmonds
University of Alabama—Birmingham

Philip R. Olds
Virginia Commonwealth University

Mc
Graw
Hill

SURVEY OF ACCOUNTING

Published by McGraw-Hill Education, 2 Penn Plaza, New York, NY 10121. Copyright © 2021 by McGraw-Hill Education. All rights reserved. Printed in the United States of America. No part of this publication may be reproduced or distributed in any form or by any means, or stored in a database or retrieval system, without the prior written consent of McGraw-Hill Education, including, but not limited to, in any network or other electronic storage or transmission, or broadcast for distance learning.

Some ancillaries, including electronic and print components, may not be available to customers outside the United States.

This book is printed on acid-free paper.

1 2 3 4 5 6 7 8 9 LWI 24 23 22 21 20

ISBN 978-1-260-57529-3
MHID 1-260-57529-2

Cover Image: © bybostanci/Getty Images

This book is dedicated to our students, whose questions have so frequently caused us to reevaluate our method of presentation that they have, in fact, become major contributors to the development of this text.

Courtesy of Thomas Edmonds

Thomas P. Edmonds

Thomas P. Edmonds, Ph.D., is Professor Emeritus in the Department of Accounting at the University of Alabama at Birmingham (UAB). He has been actively involved in teaching accounting principles throughout his academic career. Dr. Edmonds has coordinated the accounting principles courses at the University of Houston and UAB. He has taught introductory accounting in mass sections and in distance learning programs. He has received five prestigious teaching awards, including the Alabama Society of CPAs Outstanding Educator Award, the UAB President's Excellence in Teaching Award, and the distinguished Ellen Gregg Ingalls Award for excellence in classroom teaching. He has written numerous articles that have appeared in many publications, including *Issues in Accounting,* the *Journal of Accounting Education, Advances in Accounting Education, Accounting Education: A Journal of Theory, Practice and Research,* the *Accounting Review, Advances in Accounting,* the *Journal of Accountancy, Management Accounting,* the *Journal of Commercial Bank Lending,* the *Banker's Magazine,* and the *Journal of Accounting, Auditing, and Finance.* Dr. Edmonds has served as a member of the editorial board for *Advances in Accounting: Teaching and Curriculum Innovations* and *Issues in Accounting Education.* He has published five textbooks, five practice problems (including two computerized problems), and a variety of supplemental materials including study guides, work papers, and solutions manuals. Dr. Edmonds's writing is influenced by a wide range of business experience. He is a successful entrepreneur. He has worked as a management accountant for Refrigerated Transport, a trucking company. Dr. Edmonds also worked in the not-for-profit sector as a commercial lending officer for the Federal Home Loan Bank. In addition, he has acted as a consultant to major corporations, including First City Bank of Houston (now Citi Bank), AmSouth Bank in Birmingham (now Regions Bank), Texaco, and Cortland Chemicals. Dr. Edmonds began his academic training at Young Harris Community College in Young Harris, Georgia. He received a B.B.A. degree with a major in finance from Georgia State University in Atlanta, Georgia. He obtained an M.B.A. degree with a concentration in finance from St. Mary's University in San Antonio, Texas. His Ph.D. degree with a major in accounting was awarded by Georgia State University. Dr. Edmonds's work experience and academic training have enabled him to bring a unique user perspective to this textbook.

Courtesy of Christopher Edmonds

Christopher T. Edmonds

Christopher T. Edmonds, PhD, is an Associate Professor in the Department of Accounting and Finance at the UAB Collat School of Business. He is the course coordinator for the face-to-face and online principles of accounting courses. Dr. Edmonds specializes in teaching and developing engaging face-to-face and online introductory accounting courses. He is a frequent speaker at conferences and universities on best teaching practices and has delivered over 25 professional teaching workshops. His passion for helping students learn inspired him to create hundreds of short videos teaching the fundamental concepts of accounting. This work led to the publication of the first interactive video textbook for introductory accounting. Dr. Edmonds has received seven prestigious teaching awards including the UAB President's Outstanding Teaching Award, UAB Faculty Student Success Award, UAB Transformative Online Course Award, UAB Loudell Ellis Robinson Classroom Teaching Award, UAB Disability Support Recognition Award, and the Virginia Tech Favorite Faculty Award. He has published four textbooks and has written numerous articles that have appeared in publications, including *The Accounting Review, Journal of Accounting and Public Policy, Issues in Accounting Education, Advances in Accounting Education, Advances in Accounting,* and *Review of Quantitative Finance and Accounting.* He currently serves on several editorial boards. Dr. Edmonds started his career as a web application developer creating software solutions to put newspapers online. He began his academic training at Colorado State University. He obtained an MBA from UAB. His PhD with a major in accounting was awarded by Virginia Polytechnic Institute and State University. Check out his blog at **www.accountingstepbystep.com.**

Mark A. Edmonds

Mark A. Edmonds, Ph.D., CPA, is an Assistant Professor in the Department of Accounting and Finance at the University of Alabama at Birmingham. He has taught principles and advanced accounting classes in face-to-face, flipped, and online formats. He is the recipient of the Loudell Ellis Robinson excellence in teaching award. Dr. Edmonds began his career providing assurance services for the internationally recognized accounting firm Ernst & Young. At the conclusion of his professional service, he obtained his Ph.D. from Southern Illinois University Carbondale. He serves as the education adviser on the board of the Institute of Internal Auditors Birmingham Chapter. Dr. Edmonds's research focuses on alternative learning strategies and auditor decision making.

Courtesy of Mark Edmonds

Jennifer E. Edmonds

Jennifer Echols Edmonds, Ph.D., is an Associate Professor at the University of Alabama at Birmingham (UAB) Collat School of Business. Her primary teaching areas are financial and managerial accounting. She has experience teaching in the Undergraduate, MAC, and MBA programs and currently serves as the course coordinator for the managerial accounting sequence at UAB. She has received the UAB Loudell Ellis Robinson Classroom Teaching Award, as well as teaching grants from Deloitte, UAB, and Virginia Tech. She created teaching resources for incorporating International Financial Reporting Standards into Intermediate Accounting. The teaching resources were published online at the American Accounting Association. Dr. Edmonds is also active in the research community. She has published articles in prominent journals such as *Journal of Accounting and Public Policy, Advances in Accounting, Research in Accounting Regulation,* and *The CPA Journal.* Dr. Edmonds received a bachelor's degree in accounting from Birmingham-Southern College and completed her master's and Ph.D. degrees in accounting at Virginia Polytechnic Institute and State University.

Courtesy of Jennifer Edmonds

Philip R. Olds

Professor Olds is Associate Professor of Accounting at Virginia Commonwealth University (VCU). He serves as the coordinator of the introduction to accounting courses at VCU. Professor Olds received his A.S. degree from Brunswick Junior College in Brunswick, Georgia (now Costal Georgia College). He received a B.B.A. in accounting from Georgia Southern College (now Georgia Southern University), and his M.P.A. and Ph.D. degrees are from Georgia State University. After graduating from Georgia Southern, he worked as an auditor with the U.S. Department of Labor in Atlanta, Georgia. A former CPA in Virginia, Professor Olds has published articles in various professional journals and presented papers at national and regional conferences. He also served as the faculty adviser to the VCU chapter of Beta Alpha Psi for five years. In 1989, he was recognized with an Outstanding Faculty Vice-President Award by the national Beta Alpha Psi organization. Professor Olds has received both the Distinguished Teaching Award and the Distinguished Service Award from the VCU School of Business. Most recently, he received the university's award for maintaining High Ethical and Academic Standards While Advocating for Student-Athletes and Their Quest Towards a Degree.

Courtesy of Philip Olds

NOTE FROM THE AUTHORS

● SET B EXERCISES AND PROBLEMS NOW AVAILABLE

What's new? We have added an additional set of exercises and problems to the end-of-chapter materials. Now you can work on your favorite exercises and problems in class and then assign mirror image exercises and problems for homework. The new Set B is available through the *Connect* website. It is designed to maximize usefulness in multiple applications.

As many students choose to adopt the electronic version of textbooks, instructors are beginning to face a situation where students do not have textbooks available in the classroom. Accordingly, working on a particular exercise or problem in class can be frustrating when students do not have access to the exercises and problems. To resolve this issue, we offer a *student version* of the Set B exercises and problems along with **Active Learning Worksheets** as chapter by chapter downloadable Word documents. These documents show each exercise and problem with a corresponding working paper directly below it. Simply download, or have your students download, the Set B exercises, problems, and accompanying Active Learning Worksheets. Students can print out the exercises and problems you assign and bring them to class. An example of the student version of Exercise 1-1B *appears* as follows.

Exercise 1-1B   *The role of accounting in society*   LO 1-1

Resource owners provide three types of resources to conversion agents that transform the resources into products or services that satisfy consumer demands.

Required

Identify the three types of resources. Write a brief memo explaining how resource owners select the particular conversion agents to which they will provide resources. Your memo should include answers to the following questions: If you work as a private accountant, what role would you play in the allocation of resources? Which professional certification would be most appropriate to your career?

We also provide an *instructor version* of the Active Learning Worksheets. The instructor version is identical—page for page—to the student version. Organized like the student version, the corresponding solutions are shown directly below each of the Set B exercises and problems. It is no longer necessary to flip back and forth between an exercise in the textbook and the answer shown separately in a solutions manual. Now both the exercise and the solution are together in a single document. The matching of exercises and problems with solutions makes it easy for instructors to toggle between the exercise and the solution when making classroom presentations.

The instructor version of the Active Learning Worksheets is provided in an electronic format using Microsoft Word documents. The active learning sheets provide innovative opportunities to improve classroom presentations. Just open a Word document and display any Set B exercise or problem along with the corresponding solutions. With a couple of keystrokes, the you can hide any portion of a solution. The hidden data can be made to reappear as the instructor discusses the solution. Not only will you avoid the annoying chalk dust, but your students will appreciate a presentation that perfectly matches their.

Since Set B is composed in Microsoft Word you can easily "cut and paste" the materials to customize content for your particular course. Your customized materials can be delivered to students via electronic files or printouts. We also provide a video to show how easy it is to use these solutions in class. In less than a minute you will learn how to hide and retrieve data from the Set B solutions.

Using Analytics to Improve Video Quality

We know that there are a lot of videos out there, but all videos are not equal. In order for a video to be successful, students must watch it. If students stop watching in the early stages of a video, you know that they are not getting the content exposure they need and you can rest assured that failure is just around the corner. Based on this rationale, we have implemented a continuous quality improvement program for the videos that accompany our texts. Specifically, we analyze drop and finish rates to determine which videos are working and which ones are not. A typical analytical report is shown here:

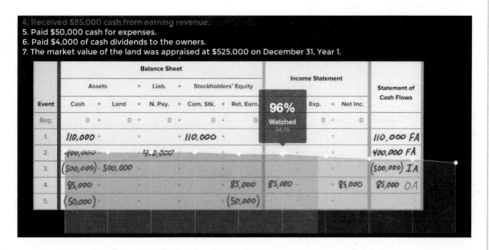

This report shows that the video kept 96 percent of students tuned-in at the halfway point and 85 percent of students completed the entire video. While there is always room for improvement, this video produced a high-quality result. We completed an extensive analysis of all Survey 5e videos and replaced select videos that had a finish rate of less than 80 percent. The results of this analysis lead us to create new and/or improved videos for learning objectives 1-1, 3-1, 3-2, 3-3, 3-4, 3-5, 3-7, 5-1, 5-2, 5-3, 6-1, 6-5, and 6-7.

If you have questions or comments regarding the new Set B exercises and problems, please contact Mark Edmonds at medmonds@gmail.com.

If you have questions or comments regarding the lecture videos, please contact Chris Edmonds at cedmonds@gmail.com.

HOW DOES EDMONDS

The Curious Accountant

General Dynamics Corporation is an aerospace and defense company that provides both products and services in business aviation; combat vehicles, weapons systems, and munitions; shipbuilding; and communications and information technology. Its products include Gulfstream business jet airplanes. Its largest customer is the U.S. Government. In 2017, 61 percent of its revenue came from sales to the U.S. government, and another 11 percent came from sales to governments of other countries. The remaining 28 percent of its revenues were from commercial customers.

Suppose the U.S. government contracted with General Dynamics to purchase four Gulfstream airplanes at a total cost of $200 million. Assume the government offers to pay for the airplanes the day they are delivered (a cash purchase) or 30 days later (a purchase on account). Assume that General Dynamics is absolutely sure the government will pay its account when due.

Do you think the company should care whether the government pays for the services upon delivery or 30 days later? Why? (Answer on page 165.)

Answers to The Curious Accountant

General Dynamics would definitely prefer to make the sale to the government in cash rather than on account. Even though it may be certain to collect its accounts receivable, the sooner the company gets its cash, the sooner the cash can be reinvested.

The interest cost related to a small accounts receivable of $50 that takes 40 days to collect may seem immaterial. At 3 percent, the lost interest amounts to $.16. However, when one considers that General Dynamics had approximately $3.6 billion of accounts receivable on December 31, 2017, and took an average of 43 days to collect them, the cost of financing receivables for a real-world company becomes apparent. At 3 percent, the cost of waiting 43 days to collect $3.6 billion of cash is $12.7 million ($3.6 billion × .03 × 43/365). For a full year, the cost to General Dynamics would be $108 million ($3.6 billion × .03). In 2017, the weighted-average interest rate on General Dynamic's debt was approximately 2.6 percent.

FOCUS ON INTERNATIONAL ISSUES

LIFO IN OTHER COUNTRIES

This chapter introduced a rather strange inventory cost flow assumption called LIFO. As explained, the primary advantage of LIFO is to reduce a company's income taxes. Given the choice, companies that use LIFO to reduce their taxes would probably prefer to use another method when preparing their GAAP-based financial statements, but the IRS does not permit this. Thus, they are left with no choice but to use the seemingly counterintuitive LIFO assumption for GAAP as well as tax reporting.

What happens in countries other than the United States? International Financial Reporting Standards (IFRS) do not allow the use of LIFO. Most industrialized nations are now using IFRS. You can see the impact of this disparity if you review the annual report of a U.S. company that uses LIFO *and* has significant operations in other countries. Very often it will explain that LIFO is used to calculate inventory (and cost of goods sold) for domestic operations, but another method is used for activities outside the United States.

For example, here is an excerpt from **General Electric**'s 2017 Form 10-K, Note 1.

All inventories are stated at the lower of cost or realizable values. Cost for a significant portion of GE U.S. inventories is determined on a last-in, first-out (LIFO) basis. Cost of other GE inventories is determined on a first-in, first-out (FIFO) basis. LIFO was used for 34% and 32% of GE inventories at December 31, 2017 and 2016, respectively.*

If the company has its headquarters in the United States, why not simply use LIFO in its foreign operations? In addition to having to prepare financial statements for the United States, the company probably has to prepare statements for its local operations using the reporting standards of the local country.

Prior to the establishment of IFRS each country was responsible for issuing its own, local GAAP. Even then, most countries did not allow for the use of LIFO.

*2017. General Electric Company Form 10-K. General Electric Company.

Real-World Examples

The text provides a variety of thought-provoking, real-world examples of financial and managerial accounting as an essential part of the management process. The names of the real-world companies used in these examples are highlighted in blue font to facilitate their identification.

The Curious Accountant

Each chapter opens with a short vignette that sets the stage and helps pique student interest. These pose a question about a real-world accounting issue related to the topic of the chapter. The answer to the question appears in a separate sidebar a few pages further into the chapter.

Focus on International Issues

These boxed inserts expose students to international issues in accounting.

"The Curious Accountant and Real-World Examples, all make the text better and would make it a pleasure to teach from."

VIVIAN WINSTON, INDIANA UNIVERSITY

Check Yourself

These short question/answer features occur at the end of each main topic and ask students to stop and think about the material just covered. The answer follows to provide immediate feedback before students go on to a new topic.

> ☑ **CHECK YOURSELF 2.1**
>
> During Year 1, Anwar Company earned $345,000 of revenue on account and collected $320,000 cash from accounts receivable. Anwar paid cash expenses of $300,000 and cash dividends of $12,000. Determine the amount of net income Anwar should report on the Year 1 income statement and the amount of cash flow from operating activities Anwar should report on the Year 1 statement of cash flows.
>
> **Answer** Net income is $45,000 ($345,000 revenue − $300,000 expenses). The cash flow from operating activities is $20,000, the amount of revenue collected in cash from customers (accounts receivable) minus the cash paid for expenses ($320,000 − $300,000). Dividend payments are classified as financing activities and do not affect the determination of either net income or cash flow from operating activities.

Reality Bytes

This feature provides examples or expansions of the topics presented by highlighting companies and showing how they use the accounting concepts discussed in the chapter to make business decisions.

> **REALITY BYTES**
>
> Good inventory management is essential for merchandising and manufacturing companies. Even if a company uses a perpetual inventory system, the amount of inventory believed to be on hand may be incorrect because of lost, damaged, or stolen goods, so a physical count is still required. Unfortunately, counting inventory is not a revenue-generating activity. If a company's employees are used to conduct the physical count, it takes time that may be better used for other activities. In fact, it may be so time-consuming that the business must close temporarily so employees will have the time to complete the inventory count.
>
> To avoid this problem many businesses hire outside companies to count their inventory. These outside vendors can bring in a large crew of specially trained workers and complete a count very quickly. There are many companies that provide inventory counting services, but RIGIS, LLC claims to be the world's largest. RIGIS reports that its 34,000 employees have counted over 400 billion items in the more than 4 million inventory counts it has conducted since beginning operations in 1958. On second thought, counting inventory is a revenue-producing activity if you are a company that counts inventory for others.
>
>
> Digital Vision/Photodisc/Getty Images

A Look Back/A Look Forward

Students need a roadmap to make sense of where the chapter topics fit into the whole picture. A Look Back reviews the chapter material, and a Look Forward introduces new material to come in the next chapter.

> **« A Look Back**
>
> Financial statement analysis involves many factors, among them user characteristics, information needs for particular types of decisions, and how financial information is analyzed. Analytical techniques include *horizontal, vertical,* and *ratio analysis.* Users commonly calculate ratios to measure a company's liquidity, solvency, and profitability. The specific ratios presented in this chapter are summarized in Exhibit 9.6. Although ratios are easy to calculate and provide useful insights into business operations, when interpreting analytical results, users should consider limitations resulting from differing industry characteristics, differing economic conditions, and the fundamental accounting principles used to produce reported financial information.

> **» A Look Forward**
>
> This chapter concludes the financial accounting portion of the text. Beginning with Chapter 10, we introduce various topics related to managerial accounting. Managerial accounting focuses on meeting the accounting information needs of decision makers inside, rather than outside, a company. In addition to financial statement data, inside users require detailed, forward-looking information that includes nonfinancial as well as financial components. We begin with a chapter that discusses the value management accounting adds to the decision-making process.

"The Reality Bytes and Check Yourself sections in the chapters enhance the presentation."

ROBERT PATTERSON, PENN STATE-ERIE

"I like the Check Yourself examples."

BRUCE DARLING, UNIVERSITY OF OREGON

HOW ARE CHAPTER CONCEPTS

Regardless of the instructional approach, there is no shortcut to learning accounting. Students must practice to master basic accounting concepts. The text includes a prodigious supply of practice materials and exercises and problems.

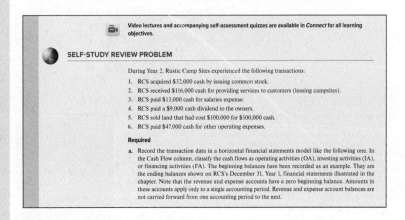

Video lectures and accompanying self-assessment quizzes are available in *Connect* for all learning objectives.

SELF-STUDY REVIEW PROBLEM

During Year 2, Rustic Camp Sites experienced the following transactions:

1. RCS acquired $32,000 cash by issuing common stock.
2. RCS received $116,000 cash for providing services to customers (leasing campsites).
3. RCS paid $13,000 cash for salaries expense.
4. RCS paid a $9,000 cash dividend to the owners.
5. RCS sold land that had cost $100,000 for $100,000 cash.
6. RCS paid $47,000 cash for other operating expenses.

Required

a. Record the transaction data in a horizontal financial statements model like the following one. In the Cash Flow column, classify the cash flows as operating activities (OA), investing activities (IA), or financing activities (FA). The beginning balances have been recorded as an example. They are the ending balances shown on RCS's December 31, Year 1, financial statements illustrated in the chapter. Note that the revenue and expense accounts have a zero beginning balance. Amounts in these accounts apply only to a single accounting period. Revenue and expense account balances are not carried forward from one accounting period to the next.

Self-Study Review Problem

These sections offer problems and solutions of major chapter concepts.

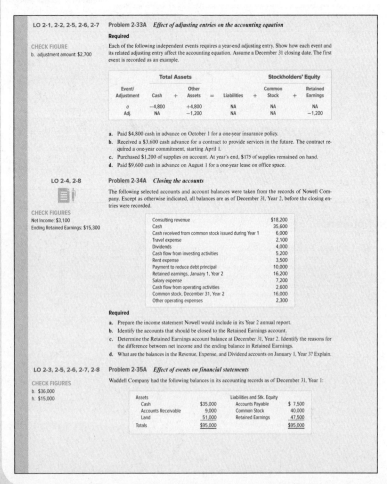

LO 2-1, 2-2, 2-5, 2-6, 2-7

CHECK FIGURE
b. adjustment amount: $2,700

Problem 2-33A *Effect of adjusting entries on the accounting equation*

Required

Each of the following independent events requires a year-end adjusting entry. Show how each event and its related adjusting entry affect the accounting equation. Assume a December 31 closing date. The first event is recorded as an example.

| Event/ | Total Assets | | | | Stockholders' Equity | |
Adjustment	Cash	+	Other Assets	= Liabilities +	Common Stock	+ Retained Earnings
a	−4,800		+4,800	NA	NA	NA
Adj.	NA		−1,200	NA	NA	−1,200

a. Paid $4,800 cash in advance on October 1 for a one-year insurance policy.
b. Received a $3,600 cash advance for a contract to provide services in the future. The contract required a one-year commitment, starting April 1.
c. Purchased $1,200 of supplies on account. At year's end, $175 of supplies remained on hand.
d. Paid $9,600 cash in advance on August 1 for a one-year lease on office space.

LO 2-4, 2-8

CHECK FIGURES
Net Income: $3,100
Ending Retained Earnings: $15,300

Problem 2-34A *Closing the accounts*

The following selected accounts and account balances were taken from the records of Nowell Company. Except as otherwise indicated, all balances are as of December 31, Year 2, before the closing entries were recorded.

Consulting revenue	$18,200
Cash	35,600
Cash received from common stock issued during Year 1	6,000
Travel expense	2,100
Dividends	4,000
Cash flow from investing activities	5,200
Rent expense	3,500
Payment to reduce debt principal	10,000
Retained earnings, January 1, Year 2	16,200
Salary expense	7,200
Cash flow from operating activities	2,600
Common stock, December 31, Year 2	16,000
Other operating expenses	2,300

Required

a. Prepare the income statement Nowell would include in its Year 2 annual report.
b. Identify the accounts that should be closed to the Retained Earnings account.
c. Determine the Retained Earnings account balance at December 31, Year 2. Identify the reasons for the difference between net income and the ending balance in Retained Earnings.
d. What are the balances in the Revenue, Expense, and Dividend accounts on January 1, Year 3? Explain.

LO 2-3, 2-5, 2-6, 2-7, 2-8

CHECK FIGURES
b. $36,000
h. $15,000

Problem 2-35A *Effect of events on financial statements*

Waddell Company had the following balances in its accounting records as of December 31, Year 1:

Assets		Liabilities and Stk. Equity	
Cash	$35,000	Accounts Payable	$ 7,500
Accounts Receivable	9,000	Common Stock	40,000
Land	51,000	Retained Earnings	47,500
Totals	$95,000		$95,000

Exercise and Problem Sets

• Check figures

The figures provide a quick reference for students to check on their progress in solving the problem.

REINFORCED?

Analyze, Think, Communicate (ATC)

Each chapter includes an innovative section titled Analyze, Think, Communicate (ATC). This section contains:

- Business application cases related to the annual report for Target Company

- **Writing Assignments**

- **Group Exercises**

- **Ethics Cases**

- **Internet Assignments**

- **Real Company Examples**

- **Target Corp.**

ANALYZE, THINK, COMMUNICATE

ATC 4-1 Business Application Case *Understanding real-world annual reports*

Obtain the Target Corporation's annual report for its 2018 fiscal year (year ended February 2, 2019) at http://investors.target.com using the instructions in Appendix A, and use it to answer the following questions:

Required

a. Instead of "Cash," the company's balance sheet uses the account name "Cash and cash equivalents." How does the company define cash equivalents?
b. The annual report has two reports in which management is clearly identified as having responsibility for the company's financial reporting and internal controls. What are the names of these reports and on what pages are they located?

ATC 4-2 Group Assignment *Bank reconciliations*

The following cash and bank information is available for three companies on June 30:

Cash and Adjustment Information	Peach Co.	Apple Co.	Pear Co.
Unadjusted cash balance per books, 6/30	$45,620	$32,450	$23,467
Outstanding checks	1,345	2,478	2,540
Service charge	50	75	35
Balance per bank statement, 6/30	48,632	37,176	24,894
Credit memo for collection of notes receivable	4,500	5,600	3,800
NSF check	325	145	90
Deposits in transit	2,500	3,200	4,800
Credit memo for interest earned	42	68	12

ATC 4-3 Research Assignment *Investigating cash and management issues at Smucker's*

Using the most current Form 10-K available on EDGAR, or the company's website, answer the following questions about the J. M. Smucker Company. Instructions for using EDGAR are in Appendix A. *Note: In some years the financial statements, footnotes, etc., portion of Smucker's annual report have been located at the end of the Form 10-K, in or just after "Item 15."*

Required

a. Instead of "Cash," the company's balance sheet uses the account name "Cash and cash equivalents." How does the company define cash equivalents?
b. The annual report has two reports in which management clearly acknowledges its responsibility for the company's financial reporting and internal controls. What are the names of these reports and on what pages are they located?

ATC 4-4 Writing Assignment *Internal control procedures*

Sarah Johnson was a trusted employee of Evergreen Trust Bank. She was involved in everything. She worked as a teller, she accounted for the cash at the other teller windows, and she recorded many of the transactions in the accounting records. She was so loyal that she never would take a day off, even when she was really too sick to work. She routinely worked late to see that all the day's work was posted into the accounting records. She would never take even a day's vacation because they might need her at the bank. Adam and Jammie, CPAs, were hired to perform an audit, the first complete audit that had been done in several years. Johnson seemed somewhat upset by the upcoming audit. She said that everything had been properly accounted for and that the audit was a needless expense. When Adam and Jammie examined some of the bank's internal control procedures, it discovered problems. In fact, as the audit progressed, it became apparent that a large amount of cash was missing. Numerous adjustments had been made to customer accounts with credit memorandums, and many of the transactions had been posted several days late. In addition, there were numerous cash payments for "office expenses." When the audit was complete, it was determined that more than $100,000 of funds was missing or improperly accounted for. All fingers pointed to Johnson. The bank's president, who was a close friend of Johnson, was bewildered. How could this type of thing happen at this bank?

Required

Prepare a written memo to the bank president, outlining the procedures that should be followed to prevent this type of problem in the future.

ATC 4-5 Ethical Dilemma *I need just a little extra money*

John Riley, a certified public accountant, has worked for the past eight years as a payroll clerk for Southeast Industries, a small furniture manufacturing firm in the Northeast. John recently experienced unfortunate circumstances. His teenage son required major surgery and the medical bills not covered by John's insurance have financially strained John's family.

John works hard and is a model employee. Although he received regular performance raises during his first few years with Southeast, John's wages have not increased in three years. John asked his supervisor, Bill Jameson, for a raise. Bill agreed that John deserved a raise, but told him he could not currently approve one because of sluggish sales.

A disappointed John returned to his duties while the financial pressures in his life continued. Two weeks later, Larry Tyler, an assembly worker at Southwest, quit over a dispute with management. John

---

"I like the real life examples; I like the Analyze, Think, and Communicate."

DEBBIE GAHR, WAUKESHA COUNTY TECHNICAL COLLEGE

WHAT WE DID TO MAKE IT BETTER!

As discussed in the "Note from the Authors," this text adds a Set B of exercises and problems. The new Set B is accompanied by **instructor** and student **Active Learning Worksheets**. (For more details refer to the "Note from the Authors.") This edition also includes new and improved lecture video content. Data analytics were used to identify areas of underperforming video content. As a result, an already high-quality **video textbook** was made even better. (Again, the details are explained more fully in the "Note from the Authors.")

We also added two new appendices. Appendix C provides the financial statements and other selected data from the annual report of Target Corporation. You no longer have to send your students to the Internet to find the essential elements of the Company's annual report. Instead, this information is now incorporated directly in the text. Appendix D provides coverage of data analytics including coverage of key features of Tableau big data software. This appendix includes a simple exercise that requires students to use the power of Tableau to solve a business problem.

Finally, we made improvements to the statements model that is used throughout the text. The first row of the model now includes the titles of each statement. This change will improve the students' ability to identify the particular statements that are affected by accounting events.

The revision also includes many more changes aimed at improving clarity and maintaining currency. A chapter-by-chapter list of these updates is provided as follows.

● CHAPTER-SPECIFIC CHANGES

Chapter 1 An Introduction to Accounting

- Revised *Curious Accountant* 1 & 2 content.
- Revised *Focus on International Issues* text box that includes IFRS coverage.
- New *Reality Bytes* feature.
- Updated exercises, problems, and cases.

Chapter 2 Accounting for Accruals and Deferrals

- Updated *Curious Accountant* content.
- Revised *Reality Bytes* feature.
- Updated Exhibit 2.8 with new real-world data.
- Updated exercises, problems, and cases.

Chapter 3 Accounting for Merchandising Businesses

- Updated *Curious Accountant* content.
- Updated Exhibit 3.1 with new real-world data.
- Updated exercises, problems, and cases.

Chapter 4 Internal Control, Accounting for Cash, and Ethics

- Revised *Curious Accountant* content.
- Updated exercises, problems, and cases.

Chapter 5 Accounting for Receivables and Inventory Cost Flow

- Revised *Curious Accountant* content.
- Revised *Reality Bytes* feature.
- Updated exercises, problems, and cases.

Chapter 6 Accounting for Long-Term Operational Assets

- Updated *Curious Accountant* content.
- Updated Exhibit 6.8 with new real-world data.
- Updated exercises, problems, and cases.

Chapter 7 Accounting for Liabilities

- Revised *Curious Accountant* content.
- Updated *Reality Bytes* feature.
- Updated exercises, problems, and cases.

Chapter 8 Proprietorships, Partnerships, and Corporations

- Revised *Curious Accountant* content.
- Revised *Reality Bytes* feature.
- Updated *Focus on International Issues* text box that includes IFRS coverage.
- Updated exercises, problems, and cases.

Chapter 9 Financial Statement Analysis

• Revised *Curious Accountant* content.
• Updated *Reality Bytes* feature.
• Updated exercises, problems, and cases.

Chapter 10 An Introduction to Management Accounting

• Revised *Curious Accountant* content.
• Updated exercises, problems, and cases.

Chapter 11 Cost Behavior, Operating Leverage, and Profitability Analysis

• Revised *Curious Accountant* content.
• Updated *Reality Bytes* feature.
• Updated exercises, problems, and cases.

Chapter 12 Cost Accumulation, Tracing, and Allocation

• Updated *Reality Bytes* feature.
• Updated exercises, problems, and cases.

Chapter 13 Relevant Information for Special Decisions

• Revised *Curious Accountant* content.
• Updated *Reality Bytes 1* feature.

• New *Reality Bytes 2* feature.
• Updated exercises, problems, and cases.

Chapter 14 Planning for Profit and Cost Control

• Updated *Curious Accountant* content.
• Updated *Reality Bytes* feature.
• Updated *Focus on International Issues* text box that includes IFRS coverage.
• Updated exercises, problems, and cases.

Chapter 15 Performance Evaluation

• Revised *Curious Accountant* content.
• Revised *Reality Bytes* feature.
• Updated exercises, problems, and cases.

Chapter 16 Planning for Capital Investments

• Updated *Curious Accountant* content.
• Updated *Reality Bytes* feature.
• Updated exercises, problems, and cases.

You're in the driver's seat.

Want to build your own course? No problem. Prefer to use our turnkey, prebuilt course? Easy. Want to make changes throughout the semester? Sure. And you'll save time with Connect's auto-grading too.

65%
Less Time Grading

Laptop: McGraw-Hill; Woman/dog: George Doyle/Getty Images

They'll thank you for it.

Adaptive study resources like SmartBook® 2.0 help your students be better prepared in less time. You can transform your class time from dull definitions to dynamic debates. Find out more about the powerful personalized learning experience available in SmartBook 2.0 at **www.mheducation.com/highered/ connect/smartbook**

Make it simple, make it affordable.

Connect makes it easy with seamless integration using any of the major Learning Management Systems— Blackboard®, Canvas, and D2L, among others—to let you organize your course in one convenient location. Give your students access to digital materials at a discount with our inclusive access program. Ask your McGraw-Hill representative for more information.

Padlock: Jobalou/Getty Images

Solutions for your challenges.

A product isn't a solution. Real solutions are affordable, reliable, and come with training and ongoing support when you need it and how you want it. Our Customer Experience Group can also help you troubleshoot tech problems— although Connect's 99% uptime means you might not need to call them. See for yourself at **status. mheducation.com**

Checkmark: Jobalou/Getty Images

FOR STUDENTS

Effective, efficient studying.

Connect helps you be more productive with your study time and get better grades using tools like SmartBook 2.0, which highlights key concepts and creates a personalized study plan. Connect sets you up for success, so you walk into class with confidence and walk out with better grades.

Study anytime, anywhere.

Download the free ReadAnywhere app and access your online eBook or SmartBook 2.0 assignments when it's convenient, even if you're offline. And since the app automatically syncs with your eBook and SmartBook 2.0 assignments in Connect, all of your work is available every time you open it. Find out more at **www.mheducation.com/readanywhere**

> *"I really liked this app—it made it easy to study when you don't have your text-book in front of you."*
>
> - Jordan Cunningham, Eastern Washington University

No surprises.

The Connect Calendar and Reports tools keep you on track with the work you need to get done and your assignment scores. Life gets busy; Connect tools help you keep learning through it all.

Calendar: owattaphotos/Getty Images

Learning for everyone.

McGraw-Hill works directly with Accessibility Services Departments and faculty to meet the learning needs of all students. Please contact your Accessibility Services office and ask them to email accessibility@mheducation.com, or visit **www.mheducation.com/about/accessibility** for more information.

Top: Jenner Images/Getty Images, Left: Hero Images/Getty Images. Right: Hero Images/Getty Images

HOW CAN TECHNOLOGY HELP

Online Assignments

Connect helps students learn more efficiently by providing feedback and practice material when and where they need it. *Connect* grades homework automatically and students benefit from the immediate feedback that they receive, particularly on any questions they may have missed. Also, select questions have been redesigned to test students' knowledge more fully. They now include tables for students to work through rather than requiring that all calculations be done offline.

End-of-chapter questions in *Connect* include:

- Exercises
- Problems
- Multiple-Choice Questions
- Analyze, Think, Communicate

Lecture Videos

One or more lecture videos are available for every learning objective introduced throughout the text. The videos have been developed by a member of the author team and have the touch and feel of a live lecture. The videos are accompanied by a set of self-assessment quizzes. Students can watch the videos and then test themselves to determine if they understand the material presented in the video. Students can repeat the process, switching back and forth between the video and self-assessment quizzes, until they are satisfied that they understand the material.

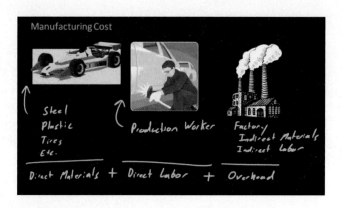

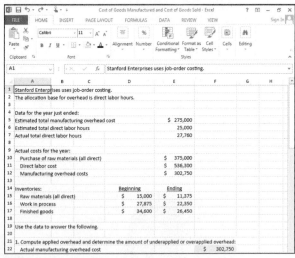

Source: Microsoft Corporation.

Guided Examples

The Guided Examples in *Connect* provide a narrated, animated, step-by-step walk-through of select exercises similar to those assigned. These short presentations can be turned on or off by instructors and provide reinforcement when students need it most.

Excel Simulations

Simulated Excel Questions, assignable within *Connect*, allow students to practice their Excel skills—such as basic formulas and formatting—within the content of survey of accounting. These questions feature animated, narrated Help and Show Me tutorials (when enabled), as well as automatic feedback and grading for both students and professors.

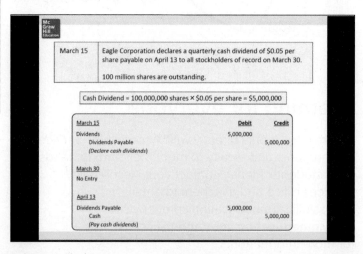

IMPROVE STUDENT SUCCESS?

McGRAW-HILL CUSTOMER EXPERIENCE

At McGraw-Hill, we understand that getting the most from new technology can be challenging. That's why our services don't stop after you purchase our products. You can e-mail our Product Specialists 24 hours a day to get product training online. Or search our knowledge bank of Frequently Asked Questions on our support website. For Customer Support, call **800-331-5094** or visit www.mhhe.com/support. One of our Technical Support Analysts will be able to assist you in a timely fashion.

> "A well-designed textbook with a variety of in-class and online activities and practice problems. Also has a nice accompanying website that students can access. Clear examples, good Excel practice exercises, nice structure. The Instructor's Manual and the text are tightly integrated and well laid out (the instructor can easily and quickly choose practice activities for in-class assignments and homework).
>
> KRISTEN BALL, DODGE CITY COMMUNITY COLLEGE

Assurance of Learning Ready

Many educational institutions today are focused on the notion of assurance of learning, an important element of some accreditation standards. *Survey of Accounting*, 6e, is designed specifically to support your assurance of learning initiatives with a simple, yet powerful, solution. Each test bank question for *Survey of Accounting*, 6e, maps to a specific chapter learning outcome/objective listed in the text. You can use our test bank software, EZ Test, and *Connect* to easily query for learning outcomes/objectives that directly relate to the learning objectives for your course. You can then use the reporting features of EZ Test and *Connect* to aggregate student results in similar fashion, making the collection and presentation of assurance of learning data simple and easy.

AACSB Statement

McGraw-Hill Education is a proud corporate member of AACSB International. Recognizing the importance and value of AACSB accreditation, we have sought to recognize the curricula guidelines detailed in AACSB standards for business accreditation by connecting selected questions in Edmonds 6e with the general knowledge and skill guidelines found in the AACSB standards. The statements contained in Edmonds 6e are provided only as a guide for the users of this text. The AACSB leaves content coverage and assessment clearly within the realm and control of individual schools, the mission of the school, and the faculty. The AACSB does also charge schools with the obligation of doing assessment against their own content and learning goals. While Edmonds 6e and its teaching package make no claim of any specific AACSB qualification or evaluation, we have labeled selected questions according to the eight general knowledge and skills areas. The labels or tags within Edmonds 6e are as indicated. There are, of course, many more within the test bank, the text, and the teaching package that might be used as a "standard" for your course. However, the labeled questions are suggested for your consideration.

ACKNOWLEDGMENTS

We would like to express our appreciation to the people who have provided assistance in the development of this textbook.

We recognize the following instructors for their invaluable feedback and involvement in the development of *Survey of Accounting*, Sixth Edition. We are thankful for their feedback and suggestions.

Reviewers

Our appreciation to those who reviewed the current and previous editions:

Wafeek Abdelsayed, *Southern Connecticut State University*

Patricia Abels, *University of Findlay*

Khaled Abdou, *Penn State University–Berks Campus*

Mollie Adams, *Virginia Polytechnic Institute*

Gary Ames, *Brigham Young University–Idaho*

David Bukovinsky, *Wright State University*

Susan Cain, *Southern Oregon University*

Alvaro Carreras, *Barry University*

Thomas Casey, *DeVry University–Tinley Park*

Suzanne Cercone, *Keystone College*

Al Chen, *North Carolina State University*

Cheryl Corke, *Genesee Community College*

Terry Dancer, *Arkansas State University*

Bruce Darling, *University of Oregon*

Harry Davis, *Baruch College*

Julie Dilling, *Fox Valley Technical College*

Timothy Dimond, *Northern Illinois University*

Edwin A. Doty, Jr., *East Carolina University*

Andrew Faber, *Tiffin University*

Barbara Fox, *Northern Illinois University*

Debbie Gahr, *Waukesha County Technical College*

Dana Garner, *Virginia Polytechnic Institute*

John Giles, *North Carolina State University*

Gladys Gomez, *University of Mary Washington*

Robert Holtfreter, *Central Washington University*

Harry Hughes, *University of Tennessee–Knoxville*

Kim Hurt, *Central Community College*

Constance Hylton, *George Mason University*

Ronald Jastrzebski, *Penn State University–Berks Campus*

Ann Kakouras, *Virginia Western Community College*

Tammy Kowalczyk, *Appalachian State University*

Nancy Lynch, *West Virginia University–Morgantown*

Susan Lynn, *Houston Baptist University*

John Markert, *Utica College*

Gwendolyn McFadden-Wade, *North Carolina A&T State University*

Christopher McKittrick, *North Carolina State University*

Roger McMillian, *Mineral Area College*

Melanie Middlemist, *Colorado State University*

Linda Miller, *Northeast Community College*

Gay Mills, *Amarillo College*

Richard Newmark, *University of Northern Colorado*

Brian O'Doherty, *East Carolina State University*

Sandra Owen, *Indiana University–Bloomington*

Lolita Paff, *Penn State University–Berks Campus*

Robert Patterson, *Penn State–Erie, the Behrend College*

Vanda Pauwels, *Texas Tech University*

Therese Rice, *North Hennepin Community College*

Daniel Ricigliano, *Buffalo State College*

Jacci Rodgers, *Oklahoma City University*

Shiv Sharma, *Robert Morris University*

Jim Shelton, *Harding University*

George Smith, *Newman University*

Hans Sprohge, *Wright State University*

Bill Stahlin, *Stevens Institute of Technology*

Lynn Trent, *Golden Gate University*

Jill Trucke, *University of Nebraska–Lincoln*

Stephanie Weiss, *Coker College*

George Wilson, *Northern Michigan University*

Vivian Winston, *Indiana University–Bloomington*

Jan Workman, *East Carolina University*

We would like to thank Helen Roybark and Beth Kobylarz for their review work on the text for the sixth edition. Special thanks to the talented people who prepared the supplements. These take a great deal of time and effort to write and we appreciate their efforts. We want to thank Debby Bloom of Florida Institute of Technology for preparing the PowerPoints Jeannie Folk and Barbara Muller for the Test Bank; and Helen Roybark and Kristine Palmer for accuracy checking the text and solutions manual. Thank you to Beth Kobylarz and Patricia Lopez for their *Connect* reviews. Thank you to Molly Brown of James Madison University for reviewing the *Connect* Video Lecture assignments for accuracy and consistency. A special thanks to Linda Bell of William Jewell College for her contribution to the Financial Statement Analysis material that appears in the Instructor Manual and Instructor Library.

In addition to the helpful and generous colleagues listed, we thank the entire McGraw-Hill Education *Survey of Accounting*, 6e, team, including Tim Vertovec, Steve Schuetz, Erin Quinones, Danielle McLimore, Fran Simon, Jill Eccher, Brian Nacik, Kevin Moran, Xin Lin, and Matt Diamond. We deeply appreciate the long hours that you committed to the formation of a high-quality text.

Thomas P. Edmonds • Christopher T. Edmonds • Mark A. Edmonds • Jennifer E. Edmonds • Philip R. Olds

BRIEF CONTENTS

CONTENTS

© B. O'Kane/Alamy Stock Photo

Damian Dovarganes/AP Images

jvdwolf/123RF

Chapter 4   Internal Controls, Accounting for Cash, and Ethics   130

idp geneva collection/Alamy Stock Photo

Chapter 5   Accounting for Receivables and Inventory Cost Flow   162

Stephen Reynolds

Chapter 6   **Accounting for Long-Term Operational Assets   206**

Ken Wolter/123RF

Chapter 7   Accounting for Liabilities   246

Stockbyte/Getty Images

Chapter 8   Proprietorships, Partnerships, and Corporations   292

Worawee Meepian/Shutterstock

Chapter 9   Financial Statement Analysis   326

Mike Davies/Alamy Stock Photo

Chapter 10 An Introduction to Management Accounting 364

chrisdorney/Shutterstock

Chapter 11 Cost Behavior, Operating Leverage, and Profitability Analysis 406

Ariel Skelley/Blend Images

nattul/Shutterstock

Tim Clayton/Corbis/Getty Images

Ken Wolter/Shutterstock

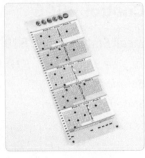

sixth edition

Survey of Accounting

CHAPTER 1

An Introduction to Accounting

LEARNING OBJECTIVES

After you have mastered the material in this chapter, you will be able to:

SECTION 1: COLLECTING AND ORGANIZING INFORMATION

LO 1-1   Identify the ways accounting benefits society.

LO 1-2   Identify reporting entities.

LO 1-3   Identify the elements of the accounting equation.

LO 1-4   Show how business events affect the accounting equation.

LO 1-5   Interpret information shown in an accounting equation.

LO 1-6   Classify business events as asset source, use, or exchange transactions.

SECTION 2: REPORTING INFORMATION

LO 1-7   Prepare an income statement, a statement of changes in stockholders' equity, and a balance sheet.

LO 1-8   Prepare a statement of cash flows.

LO 1-9   Distinguish between permanent and temporary accounts.

LO 1-10   Record business events using a horizontal financial statements model.

 Video lectures and accompanying self-assessment quizzes are available in Connect for all learning objectives.

 Set B exercises and problems are available in Additional Student Resources.

The Curious Accountant

Who owns **Apple, Inc.**? Who owns the **American Cancer Society** (ACS)? Many people and organizations other than owners are interested in the operations of Apple and the ACS. These parties are called *stakeholders*. Among others, they include lenders, employees, suppliers, customers, benefactors, research institutions, local governments, cancer victims, lawyers, bankers, financial analysts, and government agencies such as the Internal Revenue Service and the Securities and Exchange Commission. Organizations communicate information to stakeholders through *financial reports*.

Mirko Vitali/123RF

How do you think the financial reports of Apple differ from those of the ACS? (Answer on page 24.)

SECTION 1:

COLLECTING AND ORGANIZING INFORMATION

Why should you study accounting? You should study accounting because it can help you succeed in business. Businesses use accounting to keep score. Imagine trying to play football without knowing how many points a touchdown is worth. Like sports, business is competitive. If you do not know how to keep score, you are not likely to succeed.

Accounting is an information system that reports on the economic activities and financial condition of a business or other organization. Do not underestimate the importance of accounting information. If you had information that enabled you to predict business success, you could become a very wealthy Wall Street investor. Communicating economic information is so important that accounting is frequently called the *language of business*.

ROLE OF ACCOUNTING IN SOCIETY

LO 1-1

Identify the ways accounting benefits society.

How should society allocate its resources? Should we spend more to harvest food or cure disease? Should we build computers or cars? Should we invest money in IBM or General Motors? Accounting provides information that helps answer such questions.

Accounting Facilitates Resource Allocation

Suppose you want to start a business. You may have heard the adage "you have to have money to make money." In fact, you will need more than just money to start and operate a business. You will likely need such resources as equipment, land, materials, and employees. If you do not have these resources, how can you get them? In the United States, you compete for resources in open markets.

A **market** is a group of people or entities organized to exchange items of value. The market for business resources involves three distinct participants: consumers, businesses, and resource owners. *Consumers* use resources. Resources are frequently not in a form consumers want. For example, nature provides trees but consumers want furniture. Businesses transform resources such as trees into desirable products such as furniture. *Resource owners* control the distribution of resources to businesses. Thus, resource owners provide resources (inputs) to businesses that provide goods and services (outputs) to consumers.

For example, a home builder (a business) transforms labor and materials (inputs) into houses (output) that consumers use. The transformation adds value to the inputs, creating outputs worth more than the sum of the inputs. For example, a house that required $220,000 of materials and labor to build could have a market value of $250,000.

Common terms for the added value created in the transformation process include **profit, income,** or **earnings.** Accountants measure the added value as the difference between the cost

David Buffington/Photodisc/Getty Images

of a product or service and the selling price of that product or service. The profit on the house described previously is $30,000, the difference between its $220,000 cost and $250,000 market value.

Businesses that successfully and efficiently (at low cost) satisfy consumer preferences are rewarded with high earnings. These earnings are shared with resource owners, so businesses that exhibit high earnings potential are more likely to compete successfully for resources.

Return to the original question. How can you get the resources you need to start a business? You must go to open markets and convince resource owners that you can produce profits. Exhibit 1.1 illustrates the market trilogy involved in resource allocation.

The specific resources businesses commonly use to satisfy consumer demand are financial resources, physical resources, and labor resources.

Financial Resources

Businesses need **financial resources** (money) to get started and to operate. *Investors* and *creditors* provide financial resources.

- **Investors** provide financial resources in exchange for ownership interests in businesses. Owners expect businesses to return to them a share of the business, including a portion of earned income.

- **Creditors** lend financial resources to businesses. Instead of a share of the business, creditors expect the businesses to repay borrowed resources plus a specified fee called **interest.**

Investors and creditors prefer to provide financial resources to businesses with high earnings potential because such companies are better able to share profits and make interest payments. Profitable businesses are also less likely to experience bankruptcy.

Physical Resources

In their most primitive form, **physical resources** are natural resources. Physical resources often move through numerous stages of transformation. For example, standing timber may be successively transformed into harvested logs, raw lumber, and finished furniture. Owners of physical resources seek to sell those resources to businesses with high earnings potential because profitable businesses are able to pay higher prices and make repeat purchases.

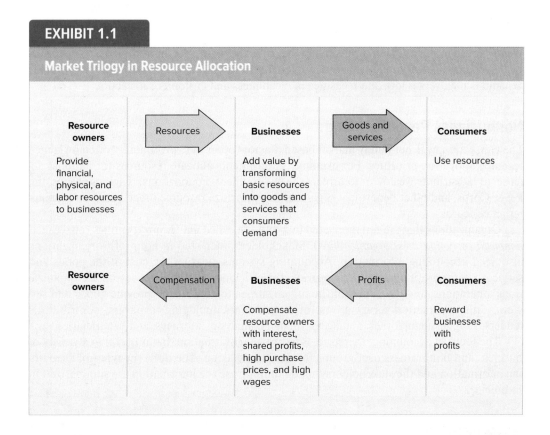

EXHIBIT 1.1

Market Trilogy in Resource Allocation

Resource owners — Resources → **Businesses** — Goods and services → **Consumers**

Provide financial, physical, and labor resources to businesses

Add value by transforming basic resources into goods and services that consumers demand

Use resources

Resource owners ← Compensation — **Businesses** ← Profits — **Consumers**

Compensate resource owners with interest, shared profits, high purchase prices, and high wages

Reward businesses with profits

Labor Resources

Labor resources include both intellectual and physical labor. Like other resource providers, workers prefer businesses that have high income potential because these businesses are able to pay higher wages and offer continued employment.

Accounting Provides Information

How do providers of financial, physical, and labor resources identify businesses with high profit potential? Investors, creditors, and workers rely heavily on accounting information to evaluate which businesses are worthy of receiving resources. In addition, other people and organizations have an interest in accounting information about businesses. The many **users** of accounting information are commonly called **stakeholders.** Stakeholders include resource providers, financial analysts, brokers, attorneys, government regulators, and news reporters.

The link between businesses and those stakeholders who provide resources is direct: businesses pay resource providers. Resource providers use accounting information to identify companies with high earnings potential because those companies are more likely to return higher profits, make interest payments, repay debt, pay higher prices, and provide stable, high-paying employment.

The link between businesses and other stakeholders is indirect. Financial analysts, brokers, and attorneys may use accounting information when advising their clients. Government agencies may use accounting information to assess companies' compliance with income tax laws and other regulations. Reporters may use accounting information in news reports.

Types of Accounting Information

Stakeholders such as investors, creditors, lawyers, and financial analysts exist outside of and separate from the businesses in which they are interested. The accounting information these *external users* need is provided by **financial accounting.** In contrast, the accounting information needed by *internal users,* stakeholders such as managers and employees who work within a business, is provided by **managerial accounting.**

The information needs of external and internal users frequently overlap. For example, external and internal users are both interested in the amount of income a business earns. Managerial accounting information, however, is usually more detailed than financial accounting reports. For example, investors are concerned about the overall profitability of Wendy's versus Burger King; whereas a Wendy's regional manager is interested in the profits of individual Wendy's restaurants. In fact, a regional manager is also interested in nonfinancial measures, such as the number of employees needed to operate a restaurant, the times at which customer demand is high versus low, and measures of cleanliness and customer satisfaction.

Nonbusiness Resource Usage

The U.S. economy is not purely market based. Factors other than profitability often influence resource allocation priorities. For example, governments allocate resources for national defense, to redistribute wealth, or to protect the environment. Foundations, religious groups, the Peace Corps, and other benevolent organizations prioritize resource usage based on humanitarian concerns.

Organizations that are not motivated by profit are called **not-for-profit entities** (also called *nonprofit* or *nonbusiness organizations*). Stakeholders interested in nonprofit organizations also need accounting information. Accounting systems measure the cost of the goods and services not-for-profit organizations provide, the efficiency and effectiveness of the organizations' operations, and the ability of the organizations to continue to provide goods and services. This information serves a host of stakeholders, including taxpayers, contributors, lenders, suppliers, employees, managers, financial analysts, attorneys, and beneficiaries.

The focus of accounting, therefore, is to provide information that is useful to a variety of business and nonbusiness user groups for decision making. The different types of accounting information and the stakeholders that commonly use the information are summarized in Exhibit 1.2.

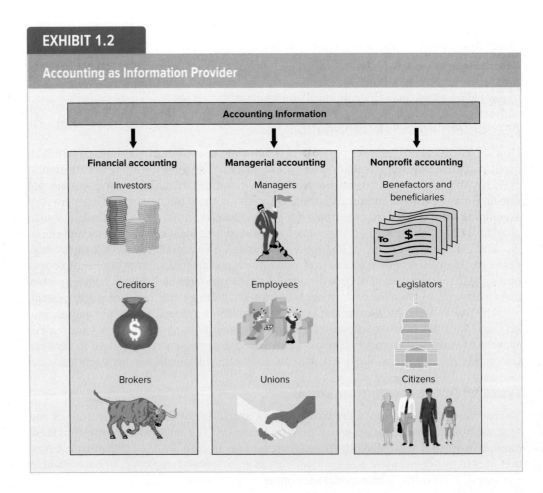

EXHIBIT 1.2

Accounting as Information Provider

Accounting Information

Financial accounting	Managerial accounting	Nonprofit accounting
Investors	Managers	Benefactors and beneficiaries
Creditors	Employees	Legislators
Brokers	Unions	Citizens

Accounting Improves Communication

Suppose a store sells an MP3 player in December to a customer who agrees to pay for it in January. Should the business *recognize* (report) the sale as a December transaction or as a January transaction? It really does not matter as long as the storeowner discloses the rule the decision is based on and applies it consistently to other transactions. Because businesses may use different reporting rules, however, clear communication also requires full and fair disclosure of the accounting rules chosen.

Communicating business results would be simpler if each type of business activity were reported using only one measurement method. World economies and financial reporting practices, however, have not evolved uniformly. Even in highly sophisticated countries such as the United States, companies exhibit significant diversity in reporting methods. Providers of financial reports assume that users are educated about accounting practices.

The **Financial Accounting Standards Board (FASB)**[1] is a privately funded organization with the primary authority for establishing accounting standards in the United States. The measurement rules established by the FASB are called **generally accepted accounting principles (GAAP)**. Financial reports issued to the public must follow GAAP. This textbook introduces these principles so you will be able to understand business activity reported by companies in the United States.

Companies are not required to follow GAAP when preparing *management accounting* reports. Although there is considerable overlap between financial and managerial accounting, managers are free to construct internal reports in whatever fashion best suits the effective operation of their companies.

Lars Niki

FOCUS ON INTERNATIONAL ISSUES

IS THERE GLOBAL GAAP?

As explained in this chapter, accounting is a measurement and communication discipline based on rules referred to as *generally accepted accounting principles (GAAP)*. The rules described in this text are based on GAAP used in the United States, but what rules do the rest of the world use? Is there a global GAAP, or does each country establish its own unique GAAP?

Until recently, each country developed its own unique GAAP. Global companies were required to prepare multiple sets of financial statements to satisfy each country's GAAP. The use of multiple accounting standards across the globe made comparing company performance difficult and expensive. To address the need for a common set of financial standards, the International Accounting Standards Committee was formed in 1973. The committee was reorganized as the **International Accounting Standards Board (IASB)** in 2001. The IASB issues **International Financial Reporting Standards (IFRS)**, which are rapidly gaining support worldwide. In 2005, companies in the countries who were members of the European Union were required to use the IFRS as established by the IASB, which is headquartered in London. Today, over 100 countries require or permit companies to prepare their financial statements using IFRS. However, the United States is not one of them.

Jeremy Graham/dbimages/Alamy

Throughout this text, where appropriate, we will note the differences between U.S. GAAP and IFRS. However, by the time you graduate, it is likely that among the major industrialized nations there will be a global GAAP.

[1]The FASB consists of seven full-time members appointed by the supporting organization, the Financial Accounting Foundation (FAF). The FAF membership is intended to represent the broad spectrum of individuals and institutions that have an interest in accounting and financial reporting. FAF members include representatives of the accounting profession, industry, financial institutions, the government, and the investing public.

Accounting Provides Jobs

What do accountants do? Accountants identify, record, analyze, and communicate information about the economic events that affect organizations. They may work in either public accounting or private accounting.

Public Accounting

You are probably familiar with the acronym *CPA*. CPA stands for certified *public* accountant. Public accountants provide services to various clients. They are usually paid a fee that varies depending on the service provided. Services typically offered by public accountants include (1) audit services, (2) tax services, and (3) consulting services.

- *Audit services* involve examining a company's accounting records in order to issue an opinion about whether the company's financial statements conform to generally accepted accounting principles. The auditor's opinion adds credibility to the statements, which are prepared by the company's management.
- *Tax services* include both determining the amount of tax due and tax planning to help companies minimize tax expense.
- *Consulting services* cover a wide range of activities that include everything from installing sophisticated computerized accounting systems to providing personal financial advice.

All public accountants are not certified. Each state government, as well as Washington, DC, and four U.S. territories, establishes certification requirements applicable in that jurisdiction. Although the requirements vary from jurisdiction to jurisdiction, CPA candidates normally must have a college education, pass a demanding technical examination, and obtain work experience relevant to practicing public accounting.

Private Accounting

Accountants employed in the private sector usually work for a specific company or non-profit organization. Private-sector accountants perform a wide variety of functions for their employers. Their duties include classifying and recording transactions, billing customers and collecting amounts due, ordering merchandise, paying suppliers, preparing and analyzing financial statements, developing budgets, measuring costs, assessing performance, and making decisions.

Private accountants may earn any of several professional certifications. For example, the Institute of Management Accountants issues the *Certified Management Accounting* (*CMA*) designation. The Institute of Internal Auditors issues the *Certified Internal Auditor* (*CIA*) designation. These designations are widely recognized indicators of technical competence and integrity on the part of individuals who hold them. All professional accounting certifications call for meeting education requirements, passing a technical examination, and obtaining relevant work experience.

REPORTING ENTITIES

LO 1-2

Identify reporting entities.

Think of accountants in the same way you would think of news reporters. A news reporter gathers and discloses information about some person, place, or thing. Likewise, an accountant gathers and discloses financial information about specific people or businesses. The people or businesses accountants report on are called **reporting entities.** When studying accounting you should think of yourself as the accountant. Your first step is to identify the person or business on which you are reporting. This is not always as easy as it may seem. To illustrate, consider the following scenario.

Jason Winston recently started a business. During the first few days of operation, Mr. Winston transferred cash from his personal account into a business account for a company he named Winston Enterprises. Mr. Winston's brother, George, invested cash in Winston Enterprises for which he received an ownership interest in the company. Winston Enterprises borrowed cash from First Federal Bank. The company then paid cash to purchase a building from Commercial Properties, Inc. Winston Enterprises earned cash revenues from its customers and paid its employees cash for salaries expense.

How many reporting entities are described in this scenario? Assuming all of the customers are counted as a single entity and all of the employees are counted as a single entity, there are a total of seven entities named in the scenario. These entities include (1) Jason Winston, (2) Winston Enterprises, (3) George Winston, (4) First Federal Bank, (5) Commercial Properties, Inc., (6) the customers, and (7) the employees. A separate set of accounting records would be maintained for each entity.

Your ability to learn accounting will be greatly influenced by how you approach the entity concept. Based on your everyday experiences, you likely think from the perspective of a customer. In contrast, this text is written from the perspective of a business entity. These opposing perspectives dramatically affect how you view business events. For example, as a customer you consider a sales discount a great bargain. The view is different from the perspective of the business granting the discount. A sales discount means an item did not sell at the expected price. To move the item, the business had to accept less money than it originally planned to receive. From this perspective, a sales discount is not a good thing. To understand accounting, train yourself to interpret transactions from the perspective of a business rather than a consumer. Each time you encounter an accounting event ask yourself, how does this affect the business?

 CHECK YOURSELF 1.1

In a recent business transaction, land was exchanged for cash. Did the amount of cash increase or decrease?

Answer   The answer depends on the reporting entity to which the question pertains. One entity sold land. The other entity bought land. For the entity that sold land, cash increased. For the entity that bought land, cash decreased.

CREATING AN ACCOUNTING EQUATION

The Accounting Equation is composed of three **elements** called assets, liabilities, and stockholders' equity. Stockholders' equity may be subdivided into two additional elements called common stock and retained earnings. Each of these elements is discussed in this section of the chapter.

Businesses use resources to conduct their operations. For example, Carmike Cinemas, Inc. uses buildings, seating, screens, projection equipment, vending machines, cash registers, and so on in order to earn money from ticket sales. The resources a business uses to earn money are called **assets.** So, where do businesses get assets? There are three distinct sources.

First, a business can borrow assets from creditors. Usually a business acquires cash from creditors and then uses the cash to purchase the assets it needs to conduct its operations. When a business receives cash from creditors it accepts an obligation to return the cash to the creditors at some future date. In accounting terms, the obligations a business has to its creditors are called **liabilities.**

The second source of assets is investors. When a business acquires assets from investors, it commits to keep the assets safe and to use the assets in a manner that benefits the investors. The business also grants the investor an ownership interest in the business, thereby allowing the investor (owner) to share in the profits earned by the business. The specific commitments made to the investors are described in certificates called **common stock.** In accounting terms investors are called **stockholders.** Further, the business's commitment to the stockholders is called **stockholders' equity.**

LO 1-3

 Identify the elements of the accounting equation.

The third source of assets is operations. Businesses use assets in order to produce higher amounts of other assets. For example, Best Buy may sell a TV that cost the company $500 for $600. The $100 difference between the sales price and the cost of the TV results in an increase in Best Buy's total assets. This explains how operations can be a source of assets. Of course operations may also result in a decrease in assets. If Best Buy has to discount the sales price of the TV to $450 in order to sell it, the company's total assets decrease by $50.

Net increases in assets generated from operations are commonly called *earnings* or *income*. Net decreases in assets caused by operations are called *losses*. As a result of their ownership status, the stockholders reap the benefits and suffer the sacrifices that a business experiences from its operations. A business may distribute all or part of the assets generated through operations to the shareholders. The distribution of assets generated through earnings is called a **dividend**.

Notice that paying dividends is an option—not a legal requirement. Instead of paying dividends, a business may retain the assets it generates through operations. If a business retains the assets, it commits to use those assets for the benefit of the stockholders. This increase in the business's commitments to its stockholders is normally called **retained earnings.** Also, note that earnings that have been retained in the past can be used to pay dividends in the future. However, a company that does not have current or prior retained earnings cannot pay dividends.

As a result of providing assets to a business, the creditors and investors are entitled to make potential **claims**[2] on the assets owned by the business. The relationship between a business's assets and the claims on its assets is frequently expressed in an equality called the **accounting equation.** Based on the relationships described, the accounting equation can be developed as follows:

Assets =   Claims

Assets = Liabilities   +   Stockholders' equity

Assets = Liabilities   +   Common stock + Retained earnings

☑ CHECK YOURSELF 1.2

Gupta Company has $250,000 of assets, $60,000 of liabilities, and $90,000 of common stock. What percentage of the assets was provided by retained earnings?

Answer   First, determine the dollar amount of retained earnings:

Assets = Liabilities + Common stock + Retained earnings
Retained earnings = $250,000 − $60,000 − $90,000
Retained earnings = $100,000

Second, determine the percentage:

Percentage of assets provided by retained earnings = Retained earnings/Total assets
Percentage of assets provided by retained earnings = $100,000/$250,000 = 40%

RECORDING BUSINESS EVENTS UNDER AN ACCOUNTING EQUATION

LO 1-4

Show how business events affect the accounting equation.

Detailed information about the accounting equation is maintained in records commonly called **accounts.** For example, information regarding *assets* may be organized in separate accounts for cash, equipment, buildings, land, and so forth. The types and number of accounts used by a business depend on the information needs of its stakeholders. Some businesses provide very detailed information; others report highly summarized information. The more detail desired, the greater number of accounts needed. Think of accounts like the notebooks

---

[2]A claim is a legal action to obtain money, property, or the enforcement of a right against another party.

students keep for their classes. Some students keep detailed notes about every class they take in a separate notebook. Other students keep only the key points for all of their classes in a single notebook. Similarly, some businesses use more accounts than other businesses.

Diversity also exists regarding the names used for various accounts. For example, employee pay may be called salaries, wages, commissions, and so forth. Do not become frustrated with the diversity of terms used in accounting. Remember, accounting is a language. The same word can have different meanings. Similarly, different words can be used to describe the same phenomenon. The more you study and use accounting, the more familiar it will become to you.

Companies typically report about business activity occurring over a span of time called an **accounting period**. The typical accounting period for a complete set of financial statements and disclosures is one year. However, in addition to a comprehensive annual report, the Securities and Exchange Commission requires public companies to issue abbreviated reports on a quarterly basis. The length of the accounting period used in this text is normally one year.

Companies experience numerous accounting events during a typical accounting period. An **accounting event** is an economic occurrence that changes an enterprise's assets, liabilities, or stockholders' equity. A **transaction** is a particular kind of event that involves transferring something of value between two entities. Examples of transactions include acquiring assets from owners, borrowing money from creditors, and purchasing or selling goods and services. The following section of the text explains how several different types of accounting events affect a company's accounting equation.

Asset Source Transactions

As previously mentioned, businesses obtain assets (resources) from three sources. They acquire assets from owners (stockholders); they borrow assets from creditors; and they earn assets through profitable operations. Asset source transactions increase total assets and total claims. A more detailed discussion of the effects of asset source transactions is provided as follows.

EVENT 1   Rustic Camp Sites (RCS) was formed on January 1, Year 1, when it acquired $120,000 cash from issuing common stock.

When RCS issued stock, it received cash and gave each investor (owner) a stock certificate as a receipt. Since this transaction provided $120,000 of assets (cash) to the business, it is an **asset source transaction.** It increases the business's assets (cash) and its stockholders' equity (common stock).

Accounting Equation								
Assets			=	**Liab.**	+	**Stockholders' Equity**		
Cash	+	**Land**	=	**N. Pay.**	+	**Com. Stk.**	+	**Ret. Earn.**
120,000	+	NA	=	NA	+	120,000	+	NA

Notice the elements have been divided into accounts. For example, the element *assets* is divided into a Cash account and a Land account. Do not be concerned if some of these account titles are unfamiliar. They will be explained as new transactions are presented. Recall that the number of accounts a company uses depends on the nature of its business and the level of detail management needs to operate the business. For example, Costco would have an account called Cost of Goods Sold although GEICO Insurance would not. Why? Because Costco sells goods (merchandise) but GEICO does not.

Also, notice that a stock issue transaction affects the accounting equation in two places, both under an asset (cash) and also under the source of that asset (common stock). All transactions affect the accounting equation in at least two places. It is from this practice that the **double-entry bookkeeping** system derives its name.

EVENT 2   RCS acquired an additional $400,000 of cash by borrowing from a creditor.

This transaction is also an *asset source transaction.* It increases assets (cash) and liabilities (notes payable). The account title Notes Payable is used because the borrower (RCS) is required to issue a promissory note to the creditor (a bank). A promissory note describes, among other things, the amount of interest RCS will pay and for how long it will borrow the money.[3] The effect of the borrowing transaction on the accounting equation is indicated as follows:

Accounting Equation								
Assets			=	Liab.	+	Stockholders' Equity		
Cash	+	Land	=	N. Pay.	+	Com. Stk.	+	Ret. Earn.
400,000	+	NA	=	400,000	+	NA	+	NA

Asset Exchange Transactions

Businesses frequently trade one asset for another asset. In such cases, the amount of one asset decreases and the amount of the other asset increases. Total assets are unaffected by asset exchange transactions. Event 3 is an asset exchange transaction.

EVENT 3   RCS paid $500,000 cash to purchase land.

This asset exchange transaction reduces the asset account Cash and increases the asset account Land. The amount of total assets is not affected. An **asset exchange transaction** simply reflects changes in the composition of assets. In this case, the company traded cash for land. The amount of cash decreased by $500,000 and the amount of land increased by the same amount.

Accounting Equation								
Assets			=	Liab.	+	Stockholders' Equity		
Cash	+	Land	=	N. Pay.	+	Com. Stk.	+	Ret. Earn.
(500,000)	+	500,000	=	NA	+	NA	+	NA

Another Asset Source Transaction

EVENT 4   RCS obtained $85,000 cash by leasing campsites to customers.

The *economic benefit* a company derives from providing goods and services to its customers is called **revenue**. In this example the economic benefit is an increase in the asset cash. Businesses may receive other benefits that will be discussed later. However, at this point we will limit our definition of revenue to being *an increase in assets* that results from providing goods and services to customers. For this event the increase in the asset account Cash is balanced by an increase in the stockholders' equity account (retained earnings). The effects on the accounting equation are as follows:

Accounting Equation								
Assets			=	Liab.	+	Stockholders' Equity		
Cash	+	Land	=	N. Pay.	+	Com. Stk.	+	Ret. Earn.	Acct. Title
85,000	+	NA	=	NA	+	NA	+	85,000	Revenue

Note carefully that the $85,000 shown in the retained earnings column is *not* in the Retained Earnings account. It is in the Revenue account. It will be transferred to the Retained Earnings account at the end of the accounting period. Transferring the Revenue account balance to the Retained Earnings account is part of a process called *closing the accounts.*

---

[3]For simplicity, the computation of interest is ignored in this chapter. Interest computation is discussed in the appendix to Chapter 2 and in subsequent chapters.

Asset Use Transactions

Businesses use assets for a variety of purposes. For example, assets may be used to pay off liabilities or they may be transferred to owners. Assets may also be used in the process of generating earnings. All **asset use transactions** decrease the total amount of assets and the total amount of claims on assets (liabilities or stockholders' equity).

EVENT 5   RCS paid $50,000 cash for operating expenses such as salaries, rent, and interest. RCS could establish a separate account for each type of expense. However, the management team does not currently desire this level of detail. Remember, the number of accounts a business uses depends on the level of information managers need to make decisions.

An economic sacrifice a business incurs in the process of generating revenue is called an **expense**. In this example, the economic sacrifice is a decrease in the asset Cash. While expenses may result in other types of sacrifice, at this point we will limit our definition of expense to being a *use of assets* that is necessary to generate revenue. For this event the decrease in the asset account is balanced by a decrease in the amount of stockholders' equity (retained earnings). The effects on the accounting equation are as follows:

Accounting Equation									
Assets			=	Liab.	+	Stockholders' Equity			
Cash	+	Land	=	N. Pay.	+	Com. Stk.	+	Ret. Earn.	Acct. Title
(50,000)	+	NA	=	NA	+	NA	+	(50,000)	Expense

Like revenues, expenses are not recorded directly into the Retained Earnings account. The $50,000 of expense is recorded in the Expense account. It will be transferred to the Retained Earnings account at the end of the accounting period as part of the closing process. The current balance in the Retained Earnings account is zero.

EVENT 6   RCS paid $4,000 in cash dividends to its owners.

To this point operating RCS has caused the amount of total assets to increase by $35,000 ($85,000 of revenue − $50,000 of operating expenses). Since the owners bear the risk and reap the rewards of operating the business, the $35,000 increase in assets benefits them. RCS can use the additional assets to grow the business or the company can transfer the earned assets to the owners. If a business transfers some or all of its earned assets to owners, the transfer is called a **dividend.** The $4,000 dividend paid by RCS reduces the asset account Cash and the amount of stockholders' equity (retained earnings). The effects on the accounting equation are as follows:

Accounting Equation									
Assets			=	Liab.	+	Stockholders' Equity			
Cash	+	Land	=	N. Pay.	+	Com. Stk.	+	Ret. Earn.	Acct. Title
(4,000)	+	NA	=	NA	+	NA	+	(4,000)	Dividends

Like revenues and expenses, dividends are not recorded directly into the Retained Earnings account. The $4,000 dividend is recorded in the Dividends account. It will be transferred to retained earnings at the end of the accounting period as part of the closing process. The current balance in the Retained Earnings account is zero.

EVENT 7   The land that RCS paid $500,000 to purchase had an appraised market value of $525,000 on December 31, Year 1.

Although the appraised value of the land is higher than the original cost, RCS will not increase the amount recorded in its accounting records above the land's $500,000 historical cost. In general, accountants do not recognize changes in market value. The **historical cost concept** requires that most assets be reported at the amount paid for them (their historical cost) regardless of increases in market value.

Surely investors would rather know what an asset is worth instead of how much it originally cost. So why do accountants maintain records and report financial information based on historical cost? Accountants rely heavily on verification. Information is considered to be more useful if it can be independently verified. For example, two people looking at the legal documents associated with RCS's land purchase will both conclude that RCS paid $500,000 for the land. That historical cost is a verifiable fact. The appraised value, in contrast, is an opinion. Even two persons who are experienced appraisers are not likely to come up with the same amount for the land's market value. Accountants do not report market values in financial statements because such values are not reliable.

There are exceptions to the application of the historical cost rule. When market value can be clearly established, GAAP not only permits but requires its use. For example, securities that are traded on the New York Stock Exchange must be shown at market value rather than historical cost. We will discuss other notable exceptions to the historical cost principle later in the text. However, as a general rule you should assume that assets shown in a company's financial statements are valued at historical cost.

Summary of Transactions

The complete collection of a company's accounts is called the **general ledger.** A summary of the accounting events and the general ledger accounts is shown in Exhibit 1.3. The color coding for the numbers shown under the accounting equation will be explained in a subsequent section of this chapter. The Revenue, Expense, and Dividend account data appear in the retained earnings column. These account titles are shown immediately to the right of the dollar amounts listed in the retained earnings column.

EXHIBIT 1.3

Accounting Events

1.	RCS issued common stock, acquiring $120,000 cash from its owners.
2.	RCS borrowed $400,000 cash.
3.	RCS paid $500,000 cash to purchase land.
4.	RCS received $85,000 cash from earning revenue.
5.	RCS paid $50,000 cash for expenses.
6.	RCS paid dividends of $4,000 cash to the owners.
7.	The land that RCS paid $500,000 to purchase had an appraised market value of $525,000 on December 31, Year 1.

General Ledger Accounts Organized under the Accounting Equation

	Assets			=	Liabilities	+	Stockholders' Equity		
Event No.	Cash	+	Land	=	Notes Payable	+	Common Stock	+	Retained Earnings	Other Account Titles
Beg. bal.	0		0		0		0		0	
1.	120,000						120,000			
2.	400,000				400,000					
3.	(500,000)		500,000							
4.	85,000								85,000	Revenue
5.	(50,000)								(50,000)	Expense
6.	(4,000)								(4,000)	Dividend
7.	NA		NA		NA		NA		NA	
	51,000	+	500,000	=	400,000	+	120,000	+	31,000	

INTERPRETING INFORMATION SHOWN IN THE ACCOUNTING EQUATION

Before showing how financial information is reported to stakeholders, we highlight some interesting features of the accounting equation.

LO 1-5

Interpret information shown in an accounting equation.

The Left versus the Right Side of the Accounting Equation

To illustrate the relationship between the left and right sides of the accounting equation, assume Educate Inc. begins an accounting period with balances shown in the following accounting equation:

Accounting Equation								
Assets			=	Liabilities	+	Common Stock	+	Retained Earnings
Cash		Land						
2,000	+	0	=	1,200	+	500	+	300

Now assume that Educate Inc. uses all of its cash to purchase land. Immediately after this purchase, the company's accounting equation is as follows:

Accounting Equation								
Assets			=	Liabilities	+	Common Stock	+	Retained Earnings
Cash		Land						
0	+	2,000	=	1,200	+	500	+	300

At this point the company has zero cash. This highlights the fact that the amounts in liabilities, common stock, and retained earnings do not represent cash. Instead they represent the sources of the company's assets. Indeed, the right side of the accounting equation could be expressed as percentages instead of dollars. Specifically, the equation could be written as follows:

Accounting Equation								
Assets			=	Liabilities.	+	Common Stock	+	Retained Earnings
Cash		Land						
0	+	2,000	=	60%	+	25%	+	15%

This equation shows that 60 percent of Educate's assets came from creditors, 25 percent came from owners, and 15 percent from prior period earnings. However, this does not explain what has happened to the company's assets since they were acquired. Specifically, the right side of the equation does not show that the company acquired cash and then used the cash to purchase land. The right side identifies the sources of assets, not their composition.

Cash and Retained Earnings

While the amount of retained earnings does not represent the amount of cash a company has on hand, it does limit the amount of cash that can be used to pay dividends. To illustrate, assume Creative Associates begins an accounting period with balances shown in the following accounting equation:

Accounting Equation								
Assets			=	Liabilities	+	Common Stock	+	Retained Earnings
Cash		Land						
400	+	1,900	=	700	+	1,000	+	600

Given that the company has $600 in retained earnings, can the company pay a $500 cash dividend? The answer is no. Remember, there is no cash in retained earnings. The only cash the company has is listed on the left side of the equation. In this case, the maximum cash dividend that can be paid is $400 because that is all the cash the company has. Suppose Creative Associates decides it no longer needs the land and sells it for $1,900 cash. After this event, the accounting equation appears as follows:

Accounting Equation								
Assets		=	Liabilities	+	Common Stock	+	Retained Earnings	
Cash	Land							
2,300	+	0	=	700	+	1,000	+	600

Given that Creative Associates now has $2,300 in cash, can the company pay a $700 dividend? The answer is no. Based on the information in the accounting equation, Creative Associates has retained only $600 of its earnings. Since dividends are a distribution of assets that were generated through earnings, the maximum dividend Creative can distribute at this time is $600. In summary, the payment of dividends is limited by both the amount of cash and the amount of retained earnings. In other words, to pay a cash dividend a company must have both cash and retained earnings.

Business Liquidations Resulting from Net Losses

If a business ceases to operate, its remaining assets are sold and the sale proceeds are returned to the creditors and investors through a process called business **liquidation**. Creditors have priority in business liquidations. This means the business uses its assets first to settle the obligations to the creditors. Any assets remaining after the creditors have been paid are then distributed to the investors.

To illustrate, assume Cruz Company was started on January 1, Year 1, when it acquired $200 cash from creditors and $100 cash from investors. Equation 1 shows Cruz's financial position immediately after these events.

EQUATION 1

Accounting Equation						
Assets	=	Liabilities	+	Common Stock	+	Retained Earnings
300	=	200	+	100	+	0

Assume Cruz had a net operating loss of $75 during Year 1. At the beginning of Year 2, Cruz's accounting equation is as follows:

Accounting Equation						
Assets	=	Liabilities	+	Common Stock	+	Retained Earnings
225	=	200	+	100	+	(75)

If Cruz is forced to liquidate at this point, the creditors would receive $200 and the owners (investors) would receive only $25.

Return to the original scenario shown in Equation 1 where Cruz acquires $200 cash from creditors and $100 cash from investors. Now suppose instead of experiencing a $75 loss Cruz experiences a $120 loss. In this scenario, Cruz's accounting equation at the beginning of Year 2 is as follows:

Accounting Equation						
Assets	=	Liabilities	+	Common Stock	+	Retained Earnings
180	=	200	+	100	+	(120)

If Cruz is forced to liquidate at this point, the investors would receive zero and the creditors would receive only $180 even though the business owes them $200. Simply stated, Cruz cannot distribute assets that it does not have. This case shows that creditors as well as investors are at risk of losing some or all of the resources they provide to businesses. However, creditors are at lesser risk because they are first in line to receive assets in case of liquidation.

In practice, the relationships between creditors and investors are determined by complex legal documents that may conflict with the general conditions described. We will discuss some of these exceptions in later chapters.

Business Liquidations Resulting from the Mismanagement of Assets

It is interesting to note that even profitable companies can be forced to liquidate. To illustrate, assume Bandera Company acquires $300 cash from creditors and $500 cash from investors and earns $200 of net income during its first year of operations. Also assume Bandera pays $950 to purchase land. Based on these events, Bandera would have the following accounting equation at the beginning of its second year of operation.

Accounting Equation								
Assets			=	Liabilities	+	Common Stock	+	Retained Earnings
Cash		Land						
50	+	950	=	300	+	500	+	200

At this point, if the liabilities come due and the creditors demand payment, Bandera could be forced into bankruptcy. Assuming the land could not be sold immediately, Bandera has only $50 cash available to settle a $300 debt. A company must properly manage its assets as well as its liabilities and stockholders' equity in order to remain a going concern.

The **going concern** doctrine assumes that a business is able to continue its operations into the foreseeable future. Many procedures and practices used by accountants are based on a going concern assumption. If a company's going concern status becomes uncertain, accountants are required to notify creditors and investors.

Two Views of the Right Side of the Accounting Equation

Another important point to recognize is that there are two views of the right side of the accounting equation. One view is that the right side shows the sources of assets. Clearly, when a company borrows money from a bank the business receives an asset, cash. Therefore, we say creditors are a source of assets. However, borrowing money creates an obligation for the business to return the amount borrowed to creditors. Thus, we can view the liabilities of a company as its obligations to return assets to its creditors. In summary, liabilities can be viewed as sources of assets or, alternatively, as obligations of the business.

Similarly, a business may acquire assets from its owners by issuing stock or it may earn assets through its operations. Therefore, common stock and retained earnings can be viewed as sources of assets. However, the business has a **stewardship** function, which means that it has a duty to protect and use the assets for the benefit of the owners. As a result, common stock and retained earnings can be viewed as sources of assets or, alternatively, as commitments to the investors. In summary, the right side of the accounting equation can be viewed either as sources of assets or as the obligations and commitments of the business.

RECAP: TYPES OF TRANSACTIONS

The transactions described previously have each been classified into one of three categories: (1) asset source transactions, (2) asset exchange transactions, and (3) asset use transactions. A fourth category, claims exchange transactions, is introduced in a later chapter. In summary:

■ *Asset source transactions* increase the total amount of assets and increase the total amount of claims. In its first year of operation, RCS acquired assets from three sources: first,

LO 1-6

 Classify business events as asset source, use, or exchange transactions.

from owners (Event 1); next, by borrowing (Event 2); and finally, through earnings activities (Event 4). Each of these events affects the accounting equation as shown here.

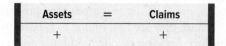

- *Asset exchange transactions* decrease one asset and increase another asset. The total amount of assets is unchanged by asset exchange transactions. RCS experienced one asset exchange transaction; it used cash to purchase land (Event 3). This event affects the accounting equation as shown here.

- *Asset use transactions* decrease the total amount of assets and the total amount of claims. RCS used assets to pay expenses (Event 5) and to pay dividends (Event 6). Each of these events affects the accounting equation as shown here.

As you proceed through this text, practice classifying transactions into one of the four categories. Businesses engage in thousands of transactions every day. It is far more effective to learn how to classify the transactions into meaningful categories than to attempt to memorize the effects of thousands of transactions.

The Curious Accountant

JHVEPhoto/Shutterstock

The RCS case includes only seven business events, one of which is not recognized in the ledger accounts. These events are assumed to have taken place over the course of a year. In contrast, real-world companies engage in thousands, even millions, of transactions in a single day. For example, think of the number of sales events eBay processes in a day or how many tickets Priceline.com sells. Presenting this many events in accounting equation format would produce such a volume of data that users would be overwhelmed with details. To facilitate communication, accountants summarize and organize the transaction data into reports called *financial statements*. This section discusses the information contained in financial statements and explains how they are prepared. While the RCS illustration contains only a few transactions, the financial statements prepared for this company contain the same basic content as those of much larger companies.

Accounting information is normally presented to external users in four general-purpose **financial statements**. The information in the ledger accounts is used to prepare these financial statements. The data in the ledger accounts in Exhibit 1.3 are color-coded to help you understand the source of information in the financial statements. The numbers in *green* are used in the *statement of cash flows*. The numbers in *red* are used to prepare the *balance sheet*. Finally, the numbers in *blue* are used to prepare the *income statement*. The numbers reported in the statement of changes in stockholders' equity have not been color coded because they appear in more than one statement. The next section explains how the information in the accounts is presented in financial statements.

PREPARING AN INCOME STATEMENT, A STATEMENT OF CHANGES IN STOCKHOLDERS' EQUITY, AND A BALANCE SHEET

Section 1 of this chapter focused on how accountants collect information about business events. Section 2 focuses on how that information is *reported* to stakeholders. Information is normally reported annually in four financial statements including the (1) income statement, (2) statement of changes in stockholders' equity, (3) balance sheet, and (4) statement of cash flows. To illustrate the reporting process we return to the Rustic Camp Sites example summarized in Exhibit 1.3. You should reacquaint yourself with this exhibit before reading about the statements that are shown in Exhibit 1.4.

LO 1-7

Prepare an income statement, a statement of changes in stockholders' equity, and a balance sheet.

Income Statement and the Matching Concept

The **income statement** matches revenue (benefits) with the expenses (sacrifices) that were incurred to generate the revenue. If revenues exceed expenses, the difference is called **net income**. If expenses are greater than revenues, the difference is called **net loss**. The practice of pairing revenues with expenses on the income statement is called the **matching concept**. The primary components of the income statement including revenue, expense, and net income are sometimes called the elements of the income statement.

The income statement in Exhibit 1.4 shows that RCS earned $85,000 of revenue and incurred $50,000 of expenses resulting in net income of $35,000. Using our definition of revenue as increases in assets and expenses as decreases in assets, we can conclude that the net income figure of $35,000 represents an increase in the total amount of RCS's assets.[4]

Observe the phrase *For the Year Ended December 31, Year 1* in the heading of the income statement. The income statement is a report about the company's operations that occurred over a span of time called the accounting period. While accounting periods of one year are normal for external financial reporting, income can be measured weekly, monthly, quarterly, semiannually, or using any other desired time period. Accordingly, the terminology used to describe the date should clearly indicate the time period covered by the statement.

[4]The definitions for revenue and expense are expanded in subsequent chapters as additional relationships among the elements of financial statements are introduced.

EXHIBIT 1.4 Financial Statements

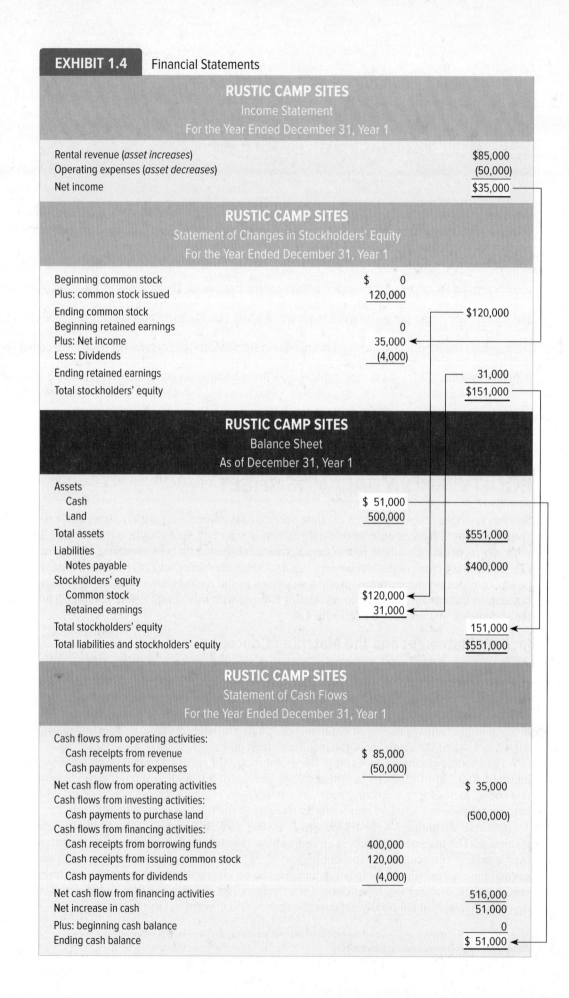

RUSTIC CAMP SITES
Income Statement
For the Year Ended December 31, Year 1

Rental revenue (*asset increases*)	$85,000
Operating expenses (*asset decreases*)	(50,000)
Net income	$35,000

RUSTIC CAMP SITES
Statement of Changes in Stockholders' Equity
For the Year Ended December 31, Year 1

Beginning common stock	$ 0	
Plus: common stock issued	120,000	
Ending common stock		$120,000
Beginning retained earnings	0	
Plus: Net income	35,000	
Less: Dividends	(4,000)	
Ending retained earnings		31,000
Total stockholders' equity		$151,000

RUSTIC CAMP SITES
Balance Sheet
As of December 31, Year 1

Assets		
Cash	$ 51,000	
Land	500,000	
Total assets		$551,000
Liabilities		
Notes payable		$400,000
Stockholders' equity		
Common stock	$120,000	
Retained earnings	31,000	
Total stockholders' equity		151,000
Total liabilities and stockholders' equity		$551,000

RUSTIC CAMP SITES
Statement of Cash Flows
For the Year Ended December 31, Year 1

Cash flows from operating activities:		
Cash receipts from revenue	$ 85,000	
Cash payments for expenses	(50,000)	
Net cash flow from operating activities		$ 35,000
Cash flows from investing activities:		
Cash payments to purchase land		(500,000)
Cash flows from financing activities:		
Cash receipts from borrowing funds	400,000	
Cash receipts from issuing common stock	120,000	
Cash payments for dividends	(4,000)	
Net cash flow from financing activities		516,000
Net increase in cash		51,000
Plus: beginning cash balance		0
Ending cash balance		$ 51,000

Notice that the cash RCS paid to its stockholders is not reported as an expense on the income statement because the dividends were not incurred for the purpose of generating revenue. For example, a company pays employees so that they will work to produce revenue. Since the salary payment was made for the purpose of producing revenue, it is called an expense. In contrast, a business pays dividends to reward stockholders for the investment they made in the business. The stockholders are not being paid to produce revenue. A business first determines how much income it has earned and then decides how much of that income it will distribute to reward stockholders. The portion of earnings (income) distributed to owners is called a dividend. In summary, dividends are paid after the amount of income is determined. Therefore, dividends are not included on the income statement.

☑ CHECK YOURSELF 1.3

Mahoney, Inc. was started when it issued common stock to its owners for $300,000. During its first year of operation Mahoney received $523,000 cash for services provided to customers. Mahoney paid employees $233,000 cash. Advertising costs paid in cash amounted to $102,000. Other cash operating expenses amounted to $124,000. Finally, Mahoney paid a $25,000 cash dividend to its stockholders. What amount of net income would Mahoney report on its earnings statement?

Answer   The amount of net income is $64,000 ($523,000 Revenue − $233,000 Salary Expense − $102,000 Advertising Expense − $124,000 Other Operating Expenses). The cash received from issuing stock is not revenue because it was not acquired from earnings activities. In other words, Mahoney did not work (perform services) for this money; it was contributed by owners of the business. The dividends are not expenses because the decrease in cash was not incurred for the purpose of generating revenue. Instead, the dividends represent a transfer of wealth to the owners.

Statement of Changes in Stockholders' Equity

The **statement of changes in stockholders' equity** shown in Exhibit 1.4 explains the effects of transactions on stockholders' equity during the accounting period. It starts with the beginning balance in the common stock account. In the case of RCS, the beginning balance in the common stock account is zero because the company did not exist before the Year 1 accounting period. The $120,000 of stock issued during the accounting period is added to the beginning balance to determine the ending balance in the common stock account.

In addition to reporting the changes in common stock, the statement describes the changes in retained earnings for the accounting period. RCS had no beginning balance in retained earnings. During the period, the company earned $35,000 and paid $4,000 in dividends to the stockholders, producing an ending retained earnings balance of $31,000 ($0 + $35,000 − $4,000). Since stockholders' equity consists of common stock and retained earnings, the ending total stockholders' equity balance is $151,000 ($120,000 + $31,000). This statement is also dated with the phrase *For the Year Ended December 31, Year 1* because it describes what happened to stockholders' equity only for the Year 1 accounting period.

Balance Sheet

The **balance sheet** draws its name from the accounting equation. Total assets balance with (equal) liabilities plus stockholders' equity. The Year 1 balance sheet for RCS is shown in Exhibit 1.4. In this case, total assets equal total liabilities plus stockholders' equity ($551,000 = $400,000 + $151,000). Also, like the accounting equation, the key components of the balance sheet (assets, liabilities, and stockholders' equity) are called the elements of the balance sheet.

The order in which assets are shown in the balance sheet is important. Assets are displayed in the balance sheet based on their level of liquidity. Financial **liquidity** is measured by how fast an asset can be converted to cash. Since in the normal course of business, inventory can be sold for cash quicker than land can be sold, inventory is considered to be more liquid than land. On the balance sheet the most liquid asset, cash, is listed first, and the remaining assets are listed in the order of how rapidly they are normally converted into cash.

Observe carefully that the balance sheet is dated with the phrase *As of December 31, Year 1*, indicating that it describes the company's financial condition at a specific *point in time*. To distinguish between *span of time* versus *point in time* statements, it may be helpful to draw a parallel to how income is reported for individuals. Most people think of income in annual terms. For example, when you start work your salary will be stated in terms of how much you will earn per year. For budgeting purposes you may also consider how much income you earn per month or per week. As these examples suggest, income is always measured in relation to some *span of time*. In contrast, the amount of your assets and liabilities is cumulative. For example, the amount of cash you own today (at this specific *point in time*) is equal to all of the cash you have collected minus all of the cash you have disbursed throughout your entire life.

For financial reporting purposes the income statement, statement of changes in stockholders' equity, and the statement of cash flows provide information about events that occurred over some *span of time*. In contrast, the balance sheet provides information about conditions that exist at a specific *point in time*.

☑ CHECK YOURSELF 1.4

To gain a clear understanding of the balance sheet, try to create one that describes your personal financial condition. First list your assets, then your liabilities. Determine the amount of your equity by subtracting your liabilities from your assets.

Answer   Answers for this exercise will vary depending on the particular assets and liabilities each student identifies. Common student assets include automobiles, computers, stereos, TVs, phones, furniture, clothes, and textbooks. Common student liabilities include car loans, mortgages, student loans, and credit card debt. The difference between the assets and the liabilities is the equity.

PREPARING THE STATEMENT OF CASH FLOWS

LO 1-8

Prepare a statement of cash flows.

The **statement of cash flows** explains how a company obtained and used *cash* during the accounting period. Receipts of cash are called *cash inflows,* and payments are *cash outflows.* The statement classifies cash receipts (inflows) and payments (outflows) into three categories: financing activities, investing activities, and operating activities.

Businesses normally start with an idea. Implementing the idea usually requires cash. For example, suppose you decide to start an apartment rental business. First, you would need cash to finance acquiring the apartments. Acquiring cash to start a business is a financing activity. **Financing activities** include obtaining cash (inflow) from owners or paying cash (outflow) to owners (dividends). Financing activities also include borrowing cash (inflow) from creditors and repaying the principal (outflow) to creditors. In contrast, interest paid to creditors is an expense, and therefore, the associated cash flow is reported in the operating activities section of the statement of cash flows.

After obtaining cash from financing activities, you would invest the money by building or buying apartments. **Investing activities** involve paying cash (outflow) to purchase long-term assets or receiving cash (inflow) from selling long-term assets. Long-term assets are normally used for more than one year. Cash outflows to purchase land or cash inflows from selling a building are examples of investing activities.

After investing in the productive assets (apartments), you would engage in operating activities. **Operating activities** involve receiving cash (inflow) from revenue and paying cash (outflow) for expenses. Note that cash spent to purchase short-term assets such as office supplies is reported in the operating activities section because the office supplies would likely be used (expensed) within a single accounting period.

The primary cash inflows and outflows related to the types of business activity introduced in this chapter are summarized in Exhibit 1.5. The exhibit will be expanded as additional types of events are introduced in subsequent chapters.

The statement of cash flows for Rustic Camp Sites in Exhibit 1.4 shows that the amount of cash increased by $51,000 during the year. The beginning balance in the Cash account was zero; adding the $51,000 increase to the beginning balance results in a $51,000 ending balance. Notice that the $51,000 ending cash balance on the statement of cash flows is the same as the amount of cash reported in the asset section on the December 31 year-end balance sheet.

The statement of cash flows in Exhibit 1.4 is dated with the phrase *For the Year Ended December 31, Year 1*. Specifically, this statement of cash flows explains what caused the balance in the Cash account to increase by $51,000 during the Year 1 accounting period. The next statement of cash flows will explain what happens to the Cash account during the Year 2 accounting period and so on with subsequent accounting periods.

In summary, the balance sheet shows the amounts that exist in the accounts at the end of each accounting period, while the income statement, the statement of changes in stockholders' equity, and the statement of cash flows explain what caused the account balances to change from one accounting period to the next. To reflect these differences, balance sheets are dated with a phrase that begins with "As of" while the other statements are dated with a phrase that begins with "For the Period Ended."

Take note that information in one statement may relate to information in another statement. For example, the amount of net income reported on the income statement also appears on the statement of changes in stockholders' equity. Accountants use the term **articulation** to describe the interrelationships among the various elements of the financial statements. The key articulated relationships in RCS's financial statements are highlighted with the arrows shown in Exhibit 1.4.

EXHIBIT 1.5

Classification Scheme for Statement of Cash Flows

Cash flows from operating activities:
    Cash receipts (inflows) from customers
    Cash payments (outflows) to suppliers

Cash flows from investing activities:
    Cash receipts (inflows) from the sale of long-term assets
    Cash payments (outflows) for the purchase of long-term assets

Cash flows from financing activities:
    Cash receipts (inflows) from borrowing funds
    Cash receipts (inflows) from issuing common stock
    Cash payments (outflows) to repay borrowed funds
    Cash payments (outflows) for dividends

☑ CHECK YOURSELF 1.5

Classify each of the following cash flows as an operating activity, investing activity, or financing activity.

1. Acquired cash from owners.
2. Borrowed cash from creditors.
3. Paid cash to purchase land.
4. Earned cash revenue.
5. Paid cash for salary expenses.
6. Paid cash dividend.
7. Paid cash for interest.

Answer (1) financing activity; (2) financing activity; (3) investing activity; (4) operating activity; (5) operating activity; (6) financing activity; (7) operating activity.

Answers to The Curious Accountant

Anyone who owns stock in Apple owns a part of the company. Accordingly, Apple has many owners. In contrast, nobody actually owns the American Cancer Society (ACS). The ACS has a board of directors that is responsible for overseeing its operations, but the board is not its owner.

Ultimately, the purpose of a business entity is to increase the wealth of its owners. To this end, it "spends money to make money." The expense that Apple incurs for research is a cost incurred in the hope that it will generate revenues when it sells smartphones and tablets. The financial statements of a business show, among other things, whether and how the company made a profit during the current year. For example, Apple's income statements show that in 2018 it spent $14.2 billion on research and development, and generated $265.6 billion in revenues.

The ACS is a not-for-profit entity. It operates to provide services to society at large, not to make a profit. It cannot increase the wealth of its owners, because it has no owners. When the ACS spends money to assist cancer patients, it does not spend this money in the expectation that it will generate revenues. The revenues of the ACS come from contributors who wish to support efforts related to fighting cancer. Because the ACS does not spend money to make money, it has no reason to prepare an *income statement* like that of Apple. The ACS's statement of activities shows how much revenue was received from contributions versus from "investment income."

Not-for-profit entities do prepare financial statements that are similar in appearance to those of commercial enterprises. The financial statements of not-for-profit entities are called the *statement of financial position,* the *statement of activities,* and the *cash flow statement.*

DISTINGUISH BETWEEN PERMANENT AND TEMPORARY ACCOUNTS

LO 1-9

Distinguish between permanent and temporary accounts.

In practice the information about revenues, expenses, and dividends is *not* recorded directly into the Retained Earnings account. Instead information is recorded in separate Revenue, Expense, and Dividend accounts during the accounting period. Keeping these accounts separate permits the capture of information that pertains to a specific accounting period. This information is needed to prepare the income statement and the statement of changes in stockholders' equity. At the end of the accounting period, after the statements are prepared, the information is transferred from the separate accounts to the Retained Earnings account.

The process of transferring information from the revenue, expense, and dividend accounts to the Retained Earnings account is called **closing**. Since the Revenue, Expense, and Dividend information is held in the accounts temporarily, these accounts are called **temporary accounts**. At the beginning of each new accounting period, the temporary accounts have zero balances. In contrast, the Retained Earnings account balance carries forward from one accounting period to the next. Since this account is not closed, it is called a **permanent account**.

Since Rustic Camp Sites (RCS) started its business on January 1, Year 1, it had a zero beginning balance in retained earnings. Recall that during Year 1 RCS recognized $85,000 of revenue, $50,000 of expenses, and $4,000 of dividends. On December 31, Year 1, the *before-closing* Retained Earnings accounts would have a zero balance because the revenue, expenses, and dividends would have been recorded in the temporary accounts. During the closing process RCS would transfer the balances in the Revenue, Expense, and Dividend accounts to the Retained Earnings account. Therefore, the *after-closing* balance in the Retained Earnings account would be $31,000 ($85,000 – $50,000 – $4,000) while the Revenue, Expense, and Dividend accounts would have zero balances after closing.

 CHECK YOURSELF 1.6

After closing on December 31, Year 1, Walston Company had $4,600 of assets, $2,000 of liabilities, $700 of common stock, and $1,900 of retained earnings. During January of Year 2, Walston earned $750 of revenue and incurred $300 of expense. Assume no other transactions occur during Year 2. Walston closes its books each year on December 31.

1. Determine the balance in the Retained Earnings account as of January 1, Year 2.
2. Determine the balance in the Retained Earnings account as of January 31, Year 2.
3. Determine the balance in the Retained Earnings account as of January 1, Year 3.
4. Determine the balance in the Revenue and Expense accounts as of January 1, Year 3.

Answer

1. The balance in the Retained Earnings account on January 1, Year 2, is the same as it was on December 31, Year 1. This year's ending balance becomes next year's beginning balance. Therefore, the balance in the Retained Earnings account on January 1, Year 2, is $1,900.

2. The balance in the Retained Earnings account on January 31, Year 2, is still $1,900. The revenue earned and expenses incurred during January are not recorded in the Retained Earnings account. Instead, they are recorded in the Year 2 temporary Revenue and Expense accounts. Balances in these temporary accounts will be closed to retained earnings at the end of the accounting period (December 31, Year 2).

3. On December 31, Year 2 the balances in the Revenue and Expense accounts would have been transferred (i.e., closed) into the Retained Earnings account. This process increased the Retained Earnings account by $450 ($750 Revenue – $300 Expense). Therefore the December 31, Year 2 ending balance in the Retained Earnings account is $2,350 ($1,900 beginning balance + $450 net income). The balance in the Retained Earnings account on January 1, Year 3 is the same as it was on December 31, Year 2, that is $2,350. In other words, last year's ending balance becomes this year's beginning balance.

4. The balance in the Revenue and Expense accounts on January 1, Year 3, is zero. The balances in these accounts were transferred (i.e., closed) to the Retained Earnings account on December 31, Year 2.

THE HORIZONTAL FINANCIAL STATEMENTS MODEL

Financial statements are the scorecard for business activity. If you want to succeed in business, you must know how your business decisions affect your company's financial statements. This text uses a **horizontal statements model** to help you understand how business events affect financial statements. This model shows a set of financial statements horizontally across a single page of paper. The balance sheet is displayed first, adjacent to the income statement, and then the statement of cash flows. Because the effects of equity transactions can be analyzed by referring to certain balance sheet columns, and because of limited space, the statement of changes in stockholders' equity is not shown in the horizontal statements model.

The model frequently uses abbreviations. For example, activity classifications in the statement of cash flows are identified using OA for operating activities, IA for investing

LO 1-10

 Record business events using a horizontal financial statements model.

activities, and FA for financing activities. NC designates the net change in cash. The statements model uses NA when an account is not affected by an event. The background of the *balance sheet* is red, the *income statement* is blue, and the *statement of cash flows* is green. To demonstrate the usefulness of the horizontal statements model, we use it to display the seven accounting events that RCS experienced during its first year of operation (Year 1).

1. RCS acquired $120,000 cash from the issuance of common stock.
2. RCS borrowed $400,000 cash.
3. RCS paid $500,000 cash to purchase land.
4. RCS received $85,000 cash from earning revenue.
5. RCS paid $50,000 cash for expenses.
6. RCS paid $4,000 of cash dividends to the owners.
7. The market value of the land owned by RCS was appraised at $525,000 on December 31, Year 1.

Event No.	Balance Sheet									Income Statement						Statement of Cash Flows	
	Assets			=	Liab.	+	Stockholders' Equity										
	Cash	+	Land	=	N. Pay.	+	Com. Stk.	+	Ret. Earn.	Rev.	−	Exp.	=	Net Inc.			
Beg. bal.	0	+	0	=	0	+	0	+	0	0	−	0	=	0		NA	
1.	120,000	+	NA	=	NA	+	120,000	+	NA	NA	−	NA	=	NA		120,000	FA
2.	400,000	+	NA	=	400,000	+	NA	+	NA	NA	−	NA	=	NA		400,000	FA
3.	(500,000)	+	500,000	=	NA	+	NA	+	NA	NA	−	NA	=	NA		(500,000)	IA
4.	85,000	+	NA	=	NA	+	NA	+	85,000	85,000	−	NA	=	85,000		85,000	OA
5.	(50,000)	+	NA	=	NA	+	NA	+	(50,000)	NA	−	50,000	=	(50,000)		(50,000)	OA
6.	(4,000)	+	NA	=	NA	+	NA	+	(4,000)	NA	−	NA	=	NA		(4,000)	FA
7.	NA	+	NA	=	NA	+	NA	+	NA	NA	−	NA	=	NA		NA	
Totals	51,000	+	500,000	=	400,000	+	120,000	+	31,000	85,000	−	50,000	=	35,000		51,000	NC

Recognize that statements models are learning tools. Because they are helpful in understanding how accounting events affect financial statements, they are used extensively in this book. However, the models omit many of the details used in published financial statements. For example, the horizontal model shows only a partial set of statements. Also, since the statements are presented in aggregate, the description of dates (i.e., "as of" versus "for the period ended") does not distinguish periodic from cumulative data.

Real-World Financial Reports

As previously indicated, organizations exist in many different forms, including *business* entities and *not-for-profit* entities. Business entities are typically service, merchandising, or manufacturing companies. **Service businesses,** which include doctors, attorneys, accountants, dry cleaners, and housekeepers, provide services to their customers. **Merchandising businesses,** sometimes called *retail* or *wholesale companies,* sell goods to customers that other entities make. **Manufacturing businesses** make the goods that they sell to their customers.

Some business operations include combinations of these three categories. For example, an automotive repair shop might change oil (service function), sell parts such as oil filters (retail function), and rebuild engines (manufacturing function). The nature of the reporting entity affects the form and content of the information reported in an entity's financial statements. For example, governmental entities provide statements of activities while business entities provide income statements. Similarly, income statements of retail companies show an expense item called *cost of goods sold,* but service companies that do not sell goods have no such item in their income statements. You should expect some diversity when reviewing real-world financial statements.

Throughout this book we usually present income statements that end with "Net income." Due to an accounting rule that became effective at the end of 2009, income statements of large, real-world companies often appear to have three lines for net income. The partial income statements for Merck & Company, a large pharmaceutical company, shown in Exhibit 1.6, illustrate this issue. Notice that the third line from the bottom of the statement is called "Net income." However, "Net income attributable to noncontrolling interest" is subtracted from this first net income to arrive at "Net income attributable to Merck & Co., Inc." The illustrations in this text always assume that there is no net income attributable to noncontrolling interests; therefore, our examples simply end with the term "Net income."

EXHIBIT 1.6	Real-World Financial Reporting

MERCK & CO., INC. AND SUBSIDIARIES
Consolidated Statement of Income (partial)
Years Ended December 31
($ in millions except per share amounts)

	2017	2016	2015
Sales	$ 40,122	$39,807	$ 39,498
Costs, expenses, and other			
Materials and production	12,775	13,891	14,934
Marketing and administrative	9,830	9,762	10,313
Research and development	10,208	10,124	6,704
Restructuring costs	776	651	619
Other (income) expense, net	12	720	1,527
	33,601	35,148	34,097
Income before taxes	6,521	4,659	5,401
Taxes on income	4,103	718	942
Net income	2,418	3,941	4,459
Less: Net income attributable to noncontrolling interests	24	21	17
Net income attributable to Merck & Co., Inc.	$ 2,394	$ 3,920	$ 4,442

Some real-world companies with complex operations report information related to *comprehensive income.* Comprehensive income is determined by adding or subtracting certain items to or from net income. A description of the items used to determine comprehensive income is complex and beyond the scope of this course. Even so, the reader should be aware that companies that must report comprehensive income may do so in one of two ways. First, comprehensive income items can be added to the bottom of the primary statement of earnings. Alternatively, a separate statement showing the determination of comprehensive income can be presented immediately following the primary statement of earnings. If a company chooses to report comprehensive income in a separate statement, the company's annual report will contain five financial statements. This text limits coverage to the four financial statements that traditionally appear in real-world annual reports. The optional statement of comprehensive income is not covered.

Annual Report for Target Corporation

Organizations normally provide information, including financial statements, to *stakeholders* yearly in a document known as an **annual report.** The annual report for Target Corporation is referred to in some of the end-of-chapter assignments, and it is worth your while to review it as an example of a real-world annual report. This report can be found online at http:// investors.target.com. On the web page that appears, under the "Investors" link at the top of the page, click on "sec filings." Next, under "filter by form type," select "Annual filings" and then select the most recent "10-K" form from the list that appears. This will provide a PDF version of the company's "Form 10-K." This report includes the company's financial statements (see pages 35–39 of the 2018 annual report). Immediately following the statements are a set of notes that provide additional details about the items described in the statements (see pages 40–63 of the 2018 annual report). The annual report contains the *auditors' report,* which is discussed in a later chapter. Annual reports also include written commentary describing management's assessment of significant events that affected the company during the reporting period. This commentary is called *management's discussion and analysis (MD&A).* Appendix C contains excerpts from Target's 2018 Form 10-K, including its financial statements and reports from its independent registered public accounting firm.

Todd Pearson/Digital Vision/PunchStock   Andrew Resek/McGraw-Hill Education   Monty Rakusen/Getty Images

REALITY BYTES

The Snapchat application for smartphones was launched in 2011, and was being used widely by 2012. On February 2, 2017 the parent company of Snapchat, Snap, Inc. announced formally that it planned to become a public company through an initial public offering of its stock, commonly referred to as an IPO.

The company's IPO in 2017 was one of the most highly anticipated new stock offerings of the past several years. However, the documents filed by the company with the Securities and Exchange Commission showed that while its revenues were growing rapidly, its net losses were also growing. In fact, the company had never made a profit, and its cumulative losses through 2017 were $4.7 billion. Even so, *The Wall Street Journal* reported that the price of the company's stock at its IPO was expected to indicate that the value of the company was around $25 billion. Clearly, investors' primary focus was not on past earnings.

baloon111/123RF

Investors frequently use more information than just what is reported in a company's annual report. The annual report focuses on historical data, but investors are more interested in the future than the past. The historical information contained in the annual report is important because the past is frequently a strong predictor of what will occur in the future, but it does not provide a complete picture of a company's prospects.

A new company that has never earned a profit, like Snap, may have an idea that is so innovative that investors rush to buy its stock, even though they believe it will be a few years before the company has positive earnings. Although Snap has consistently reported losses in the past, it has become one of the leading providers of social media technology. Investors and creditors may also be motivated by nonfinancial considerations such as social consciousness, humanitarian concerns, or personal preferences. People who buy stock in the Green Bay Packers, the only publicly traded NFL team, are motivated by team spirit, not profit.

While accounting information is very important, it is only part of the information pool that investors and creditors use to make decisions.

The U.S. Securities and Exchange Commission (SEC) requires public companies to file an annual report in a document known as a Form 10-K. The SEC is discussed in more detail later. Even though the annual report is usually flashier (contains more color and pictures) than the 10-K, the 10-K is normally more comprehensive with respect to content. As a result, the 10-K report frequently substitutes for the annual report, but the annual report cannot substitute for the 10-K. In an effort to reduce costs, many companies, including Target Corporation, now use the 10-K report as their annual report.

Special Terms in Real-World Reports

The financial statements of real-world companies include numerous items relating to advanced topics that are not covered in introductory accounting textbooks, especially the first chapter of an introductory accounting textbook. Do not, however, be discouraged from browsing through real-world annual reports. You will significantly enhance your learning if you look at many annual reports and attempt to identify as many items as you can. As your accounting knowledge grows, you will likely experience increased interest in real-world financial reports and the businesses they describe.

We encourage you to look for annual reports in the library or ask your employer for a copy of your company's report. The Internet is another excellent source for obtaining annual reports. Most companies provide links to their annual reports on their home pages. Look for links labeled "about the company" or "investor relations" or other phrases that logically lead to the company's financial reports. The best way to learn accounting is to use it. Accounting is the language of business. Learning the language will serve you well in almost any area of business that you pursue.

A Look Back <<

This chapter introduced the role of accounting in society and business: to provide information helpful to operating and evaluating the performance of organizations. Accounting is a measurement discipline. To communicate effectively, users of accounting must agree on the rules of measurement. *Generally accepted accounting principles (GAAP)* constitute the rules used by the accounting profession in the United States to govern financial reporting. GAAP is a work in progress that continues to evolve.

This chapter has identified five elements of a balance sheet *(assets, liabilities, stockholders' equity, common stock, and retained earnings)* and three elements of an income statement *(revenue, expenses, and net income)*. Four basic financial statements appear in the reports of public companies: the *balance sheet,* the *income statement,* the *statement of changes in stockholders' equity,* and the *statement of cash flows.* The chapter discussed the form and content of each statement as well as the interrelationships among the statements.

This chapter introduced a *horizontal financial statements model* as a tool to help you understand how business events affect a set of financial statements. This model is used throughout the text. You should carefully study this model before proceeding to the next chapter.

A Look Forward >>

To keep matters as simple as possible and to focus on the interrelationships among financial statements, this chapter considered only cash events. Obviously, many real-world events do not involve an immediate exchange of cash. For example, customers use telephone service throughout the month without paying for it until the next month. Such phone usage represents an expense in one month with a cash exchange in the following month. Events such as this are called *accruals.* Understanding the effects that accrual events have on the financial statements is included in the next chapter.

Video lectures and accompanying self-assessment quizzes are available in *Connect* for all learning objectives.

 ## SELF-STUDY REVIEW PROBLEM

During Year 2, Rustic Camp Sites experienced the following transactions:

1. RCS acquired $32,000 cash by issuing common stock.
2. RCS received $116,000 cash for providing services to customers (leasing campsites).
3. RCS paid $13,000 cash for salaries expense.
4. RCS paid a $9,000 cash dividend to the owners.
5. RCS sold land that had cost $100,000 for $100,000 cash.
6. RCS paid $47,000 cash for other operating expenses.

Required

a. Record the transaction data in a horizontal financial statements model like the following one. In the Cash Flow column, classify the cash flows as operating activities (OA), investing activities (IA), or financing activities (FA). The beginning balances have been recorded as an example. They are the ending balances shown on RCS's December 31, Year 1, financial statements illustrated in the chapter. Note that the revenue and expense accounts have a zero beginning balance. Amounts in these accounts apply only to a single accounting period. Revenue and expense account balances are not carried forward from one accounting period to the next.

	Balance Sheet								Income Statement					Statement of Cash Flows
	Assets			= Liab.	+	Stockholders' Equity								
Event No.	Cash	+	Land	= N. Pay.	+	Com. Stk.	+	Ret. Earn.	Rev.	−	Exp.	=	Net Inc.	
Beg. bal.	51,000	+	500,000	= 400,000	+	120,000	+	31,000	NA	−	NA	=	NA	NA

b. Explain why there are no beginning balances in the income statement columns.
c. What amount of net income will RCS report on the Year 2 income statement?
d. What amount of total assets will RCS report on the December 31, Year 2, balance sheet?
e. What amount of retained earnings will RCS report on the December 31, Year 2, balance sheet?
f. What amount of net cash flow from operating activities will RCS report on the Year 2 statement of cash flows?

Solution

a.

	Balance Sheet								Income Statement					Statement of Cash Flows	
Event No.	Assets			= Liab.	+	Stockholders' Equity									
	Cash	+	Land	= N. Pay.	+	Com. Stk.	+	Ret. Earn.	Rev.	−	Exp.	=	Net Inc.		
Beg. bal.	51,000	+	500,000	= 400,000	+	120,000	+	31,000	NA	−	NA	=	NA	NA	
1.	32,000	+	NA	= NA	+	32,000	+	NA	NA	−	NA	=	NA	32,000	FA
2.	116,000	+	NA	= NA	+	NA	+	116,000	116,000	−	NA	=	116,000	116,000	OA
3.	(13,000)	+	NA	= NA	+	NA	+	(13,000)	NA	−	13,000	=	(13,000)	(13,000)	OA
4.	(9,000)	+	NA	= NA	+	NA	+	(9,000)	NA	−	NA	=	NA	(9,000)	FA
5.	100,000	+	(100,000)	= NA	+	NA	+	NA	NA	−	NA	=	NA	100,000	IA
6.	(47,000)	+	NA	= NA	+	NA	+	(47,000)	NA	−	47,000	=	(47,000)	(47,000)	OA
Totals	230,000	+	400,000	= 400,000	+	152,000	+	78,000	116,000	−	60,000	=	56,000	179,000	NC*

*The letters NC on the last line of the column designate the net change in cash.

b. The revenue and expense accounts are temporary accounts used to capture data for a single accounting period. They are closed (amounts removed from the accounts) to retained earnings at the end of the accounting period and therefore always have zero balances at the beginning of the accounting cycle.

c. RCS will report net income of $56,000 on the Year 2 income statement. Compute this amount by subtracting the expenses from the revenue ($116,000 Revenue − $13,000 Salaries expense − $47,000 Other operating expense).

d. RCS will report total assets of $630,000 on the December 31, Year 2, balance sheet. Compute total assets by adding the cash amount to the land amount ($230,000 Cash + $400,000 Land).

e. RCS will report retained earnings of $78,000 on the December 31, Year 2, balance sheet. Compute this amount using the following formula: Beginning retained earnings + Net income − Dividends = Ending retained earnings. In this case, $31,000 + $56,000 − $9,000 = $78,000.

f. Net cash flow from operating activities is the difference between the amount of cash collected from revenue and the amount of cash spent for expenses. In this case, $116,000 cash inflow from revenue − $13,000 cash outflow for salaries expense − $47,000 cash outflow for other operating expenses = $56,000 net cash inflow from operating activities.

KEY TERMS

Accounting 3
Accounting equation 10
Accounting event 11
Accounting period 11
Accounts 10
Annual report 27
Articulation 23
Asset exchange
   transaction 12
Asset source transaction 11
Asset use transaction 13
Assets 9
Balance sheet 20
Claims 10
Closing (the books) 24
Common stock 9
Creditors 4
Dividend 13
Double-entry accounting
   (bookkeeping) 11

Earnings 4
Elements 9
Expenses 13
Financial accounting 5
Financial Accounting
   Standards Board
   (FASB) 7
Financial resources 4
Financial statements 19
Financing activities 22
General ledger 14
Generally accepted accounting
   principles (GAAP) 7
Going concern 17
Historical cost concept 13
Horizontal statements
   model 25
Income 4
Income statement 19
Interest 4

International Accounting
   Standards Board
   (IASB) 7
International Financial
   Reporting Standards
   (IFRS) 7
Investing activities 22
Investors 4
Labor resources 5
Liabilities 9
Liquidation 16
Liquidity 20
Managerial accounting 5
Manufacturing
   businesses 26
Market 4
Matching concept 19
Merchandising
   businesses 26
Net income 19

Net loss 19
Not-for-profit entities 6
Operating activities 22
Permanent accounts 24
Physical resources 4
Profit 4
Reporting entities 8
Retained earnings 10
Revenue 12
Service businesses 26
Stakeholders 5
Statement of cash flows 22
Statement of changes in
   stockholders' equity 20
Stewardship 17
Stockholders 9
Stockholders' equity 9
Temporary accounts 24
Transaction 11
Users 5

QUESTIONS

1. Explain the term *stakeholder*. Distinguish between stakeholders with a direct versus an indirect interest in the companies that issue financial reports.

2. Why is accounting called the *language of business*?

3. What is the primary mechanism used to allocate resources in the United States?

4. In a business context, what does the term *market* mean?

5. What market trilogy components are involved in the process of transforming resources into finished products?

6. Give an example of a financial resource, a physical resource, and a labor resource.

7. What type of income or profit does an investor expect to receive in exchange for providing financial resources to a business? What type of income does a creditor expect from providing financial resources to an organization or business?

8. How do financial and managerial accounting differ?

9. Describe a not-for-profit or nonprofit enterprise. What is the motivation for this type of entity?

10. What are the U.S. rules of accounting information measurement called?

11. Explain how a career in public accounting differs from a career in private accounting.

12. What are the three elements of the accounting equation?

13. What role do assets play in business profitability?

14. To whom do the assets of a business belong?

15. Describe the differences between creditors and investors.

16. Name the accounting term used to describe a business's obligations to creditors.

17. What is the accounting equation? Describe each of its three elements.

18. Who ultimately bears the risk and collects the rewards associated with operating a business?

19. What does a *double-entry bookkeeping system* mean?

20. How does acquiring capital from owners affect the accounting equation?

21. What is the difference between assets that are acquired by issuing common stock and those that are acquired using retained earnings?

22. How does earning revenue affect the accounting equation?

23. What are the three primary sources of assets?

24. What is the source of retained earnings?

25. How does distributing assets (paying dividends) to owners affect the accounting equation?

26. What are the similarities and differences between dividends and expenses?

27. What four general-purpose financial statements do business enterprises use?

28. Which of the general-purpose financial statements provides information about the enterprise at a specific designated date?

29. What causes a net loss?

30. What three categories of cash receipts and cash payments do businesses report on the statement of cash flows? Explain the types of cash flows reported in each category.

31. How are asset accounts usually arranged in the balance sheet?

32. Discuss the term *articulation* as it relates to financial statements.

33. How do temporary accounts differ from permanent accounts? Name three temporary accounts. Is retained earnings a temporary or a permanent account?

34. What is the historical cost concept and how does it relate to verifiability?

35. Identify the three types of accounting transactions discussed in this chapter. Provide an example of each type of transaction, and explain how it affects the accounting equation.

36. What type of information does a business typically include in its annual report?

37. What is U.S. GAAP? What is IFRS?

SECTION 1 EXERCISES—SERIES A

 An electronic auto-gradable version of the Series A Exercises is available in Connect. A PDF version of Series B Exercises is in Connect under the "Additional Student Resources" tab. Solutions to the Series B Exercises are available in Connect under the "Instructor Library" tab. Instructor and student Workpapers for the Series B Exercises are available in Connect under the "Instructor Library" and "Additional Student Resources" tabs respectively.

LO 1-1

Exercise 1-1A   *The role of accounting in society*

Free economies use open markets to allocate resources.

Required

Identify the three participants in a free business market. Write a brief memo explaining how these participants interact to ensure that goods and services are distributed in a manner that satisfies customers. Your memo should include answers to the following questions: If you work as a public accountant, what role would you play in the allocation of resources? Which professional certification would be most appropriate to your career?

LO 1-1

Exercise 1-2A   *Careers in accounting*

While public and private accounting overlap, various professional certifications are designed to attest to competency for specific areas of interest.

Required

a. Name the most common professional certification held by public accountants. Describe the general requirements for attaining this certification.

b. Name two types of professional certification, other than CPA, held by private accountants. Describe the general requirements for attaining these certifications.

LO 1-2

Exercise 1-3A   *Identifying the reporting entities*

Karen White helped organize a charity fund to help cover the medical expenses of a friend of hers who was seriously injured in a bicycle accident. The fund was named Vicky Hill Recovery Fund (VHRF). Karen contributed $1,000 of her own money to the fund. The $1,000 was paid to WKUX, a local radio station that designed and played an advertising campaign to educate the public as to the need for help. The campaign resulted in the collection of $20,000 cash. VHRF paid $12,000 to Mercy Hospital to cover Vicky's outstanding hospital cost. The remaining $8,000 was contributed to the National Cyclist Fund.

Required

Identify the entities that were mentioned in the scenario and explain what happened to the cash accounts of each entity that you identify.

Exercise 1-4A   *Key definitions and missing information in the accounting equation*

LO 1-3

Required

a. Match the terms (identified as a through g) with the definitions and phrases (marked 1 through 7). For example, the term "a. Assets" matches with definition "7. Economic resources that will be used by a business to produce revenue."

a. Assets	1. Individuals or institutions that have contributed assets or services to a business in exchange for an ownership interest in the business.
b. Common Stock	2. Common Stock + Retained Earnings.
c. Creditors	3. Certificates that evidence ownership in a company.
d. Liability	4. Assets – Liabilities – Common Stock.
e. Retained Earnings	5. An obligation to pay cash in the future.
f. Stockholders	6. Individuals or institutions that have loaned goods or services to a business.
g. Stockholders' Equity	7. Economic resources that will be used by a business to produce revenue.

b. Calculate the missing amounts in the following table:

Company	Assets	=	Liabilities	+	Stockholders' Equity Common Stock	+	Stockholders' Equity Retained Earnings
A	$?		$25,000		$ 48,000		$50,000
B	40,000		?		7,000		30,000
C	75,000		15,000		?		42,000
D	125,000		45,000		60,000		?

Exercise 1-5A   *Effect of events on the accounting equation*

LO 1-4

Olive Enterprises experienced the following events during Year 3:

1. Acquired cash from the issue of common stock.
2. Paid cash to reduce the principal on a bank note.
3. Sold land for cash at an amount equal to its cost.
4. Provided services to clients for cash.
5. Paid utilities expenses with cash.
6. Paid a cash dividend to the stockholders.

Required

Explain how each of the events would affect the accounting equation by writing the letter I for increase, the letter D for decrease, and NA for does not affect under each of the elements of the accounting equation. If an event increases one account and decreases another account equally within the same element, record I/D. The first event is shown as an example.

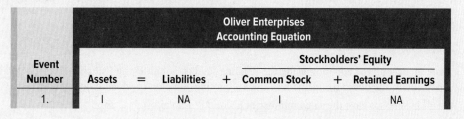

Event Number	Assets	=	Liabilities	+	Stockholders' Equity Common Stock	+	Stockholders' Equity Retained Earnings
1.	I		NA		I		NA

LO 1-4

Exercise 1-6A   *Effect of transactions on the accounting equation*

At the beginning of Year 2, Better Corp.'s accounting equation showed the following accounts and balances:

	Assets		**= Liabilities**	**+ Stockholders' Equity**		**Acct. Titles for RE**
Event	**Cash**	**Land**	**Notes Payable**	**Common Stock**	**Retained Earnings**	
1/1/Year 2	10,000	20,000	12,000	7,000	11,000	

Better Corp. completed the following transactions during Year 2:

1. Purchased land for $5,000 cash.
2. Acquired $25,000 cash from the issue of common stock.
3. Received $75,000 cash for providing services to customers.
4. Paid cash operating expenses of $42,000.
5. Borrowed $10,000 cash from the bank.
6. Paid a $5,000 cash dividend to the stockholders.
7. Determined that the market value of the land purchased in event 1 is $35,000.

Required

a. Record the transactions in the accounting equation for Year 2. Record the amounts of revenue, expense, and dividends in the Retained Earnings column. Provide the appropriate titles for these accounts in the last column of the table.

b. As of December 31, Year 2, determine the total amount of assets, liabilities, and stockholders' equity and present this information in the form of an accounting equation.

c. What is the amount of total assets, liabilities, and stockholders' equity as of January 1, Year 3?

LO 1-3, 1-4

Exercise 1-7A   *Missing information and recording events*

As of December 31, Year 2, Moss Company had total cash of $195,000, notes payable of $90,500, and common stock of $84,500. During Year 3, Moss earned $42,000 of cash revenue, paid $24,000 for cash expenses, and paid a $3,000 cash dividend to the stockholders.

Required

a. Determine the amount of retained earnings as of December 31, Year 2.

b. Create an accounting equation and record the beginning account balances under the appropriate headings.

c. Record the revenue, expense, and dividend events under the appropriate headings of the accounting equation created in Requirement *b*.

d. Prove the equality of the accounting equation as of December 31, Year 3.

e. Identify the beginning and ending balances in the Cash and Common Stock accounts. Explain why the beginning and ending balances in the Cash account are different, but the beginning and ending balances in the Common Stock account remain the same.

LO 1-3, 1-4

Exercise 1-8A   *Account titles and the accounting equation*

The following account titles were drawn from the general ledger of Holt Food Supplies, Incorporated (HFSI): Computers, Operating Expenses, Rent Revenue, Building, Cash, Notes Payable, Land, Utilities Payable, Utilities Expense, Trucks, Gasoline Expense, Retained Earnings, Supplies, Accounts Payable, Office Furniture, Salaries Expense, Common Stock, Service Revenue, Interest Expense, Dividends, Supplies Expense.

Required

a. Create an accounting equation using the headings assets, liabilities, and stockholders' equity. List each account title under the element of the accounting equation to which it belongs.

b. Will all businesses have the same number of accounts? Explain your answer.

Exercise 1-9A   *Interpreting the accounting equation*   LO 1-5

Jones Enterprises was started when it acquired $6,000 cash from creditors and $10,000 from owners. The company immediately purchased land that cost $12,000.

Required

a. Record the events under an accounting equation.
b. After all events have been recorded, Jones's obligations to creditors represent what percent of total assets?
c. After all events have been recorded, Jones's stockholders' equity represents what percentage of total assets?
d. Assume the debt is due. Given that Jones has $10,000 in stockholders' equity, can the company repay the creditors at this point? Why or why not?

Exercise 1-10A   *Interpreting the accounting equation*   LO 1-5

The financial condition of White Co. Inc. is expressed in the following accounting equation:

Accounting Equation						
Assets		=	Liabilities	+	Common stock	+	Retained earnings
Cash	Land					
$1,800	+ $12,000 =		$6,000	+	$5,000	+	$2,800

Required

a. Are dividends paid to creditors or investors? Explain why.
b. How much cash is in the Retained Earnings account?
c. Determine the maximum dividend White Co. Inc. can pay.
d. If the obligation to creditors is due, can White Co. Inc. repay the loan? Why or why not?
e. Suppose the land sinks into the sea as a result of an earthquake and a resulting tsunami. The business is then liquidated. How much cash will creditors receive? How much cash will investors receive? (Assume there are no legal fees or other costs of liquidation.)

Exercise 1-11A   *Differences between interest and dividends*   LO 1-5

The following account balances were drawn from the financial records of Kent Company (KC) as of January 1, Year 5: Assets, $35,000; Liabilities, $6,000; Common Stock, $12,000; and Retained Earnings, $17,000. KC has agreed to pay the creditors $400 of interest per year. Further, KC agrees that for the Year 5 fiscal year any annual earnings remaining after the interest charges will be paid out as dividends to the owners.

Required

a. Assuming KC earns a before interest expense recognition profit of $1,600 during Year 5, determine the amount of interest and dividends paid.
b. Assuming KC earns a before interest expense recognition profit of $900 during Year 5, determine the amount of interest and dividends paid.
c. Assuming KC earns a before interest expense recognition profit of $300 during Year 5, determine the amount of interest and dividends paid.

Exercise 1-12A   *Distribution in a business liquidation*   LO 1-5

Assume that Harris Company acquires $3,600 cash from creditors and $4,200 cash from investors.

Required

a. Explain the primary differences between investors and creditors.
b. If Harris has net income of $2,000 and then liquidates, what amount of cash will the creditors receive? What amount of cash will the investors receive?
c. If Harris has a net loss of $2,000 cash and then liquidates, what amount of cash will the creditors receive? What amount of cash will the investors receive?
d. If Harris has a net loss of $4,900 cash and then liquidates, what amount of cash will the creditors receive? What amount of cash will the investors receive?

LO 1-6

Exercise 1-13A   *Classifying events as asset source, use, or exchange*

Nevada Companies experienced the following events during its first year of operations:

1. Acquired $1,000 cash from the issue of common stock.
2. Paid $24 cash for utilities expense.
3. Paid a $1,500 cash dividend to the stockholders.
4. Provided boarding services for $6,000 cash.
5. Purchased additional land for $2,500 cash.
6. Determined the market value of the land to be $24,000 at the end of the accounting period.
7. Acquired an additional $16,000 cash from the issue of common stock.
8. Paid $3,500 cash for salary expense.
9. Borrowed $10,000 cash from New South Bank.
10. Paid $6,000 cash to purchase land.
11. Provided additional boarding services for $10,500 cash.

Required

Classify each event as an asset source, use, or exchange transaction or as not applicable (NA).

SECTION 2 EXERCISES—SERIES A

LO 1-7

Exercise 1-14A   *Missing information for determining net income*

The December 31, Year 4, balance sheet for Deen Company showed total stockholders' equity of $156,000. Total stockholders' equity increased by $65,000 between December 31, Year 4, and December 31, Year 5. During Year 5, Deen Company acquired $20,000 cash from the issue of common stock. The company paid a $5,000 cash dividend to the stockholders during Year 5.

Required

Determine the amount of net income or loss Deen reported on its Year 5 income statement. (*Hint:* Remember that stock issues, net income, and dividends all change total stockholders' equity.)

LO 1-7

Exercise 1-15A   *Preparing an income statement and a balance sheet*

Mijka Company was started on January 1, Year 1. During Year 1, the company experienced the following three accounting events: (1) earned cash revenues of $28,600, (2) paid cash expenses of $13,200, and (3) paid a $1,500 cash dividend to its stockholders. These were the only events that affected the company during Year 1.

Required

a. Create an accounting equation and record the effects of each accounting event under the appropriate general ledger account headings.
b. Prepare an income statement, statement of changes in stockholders' equity, and a balance sheet dated December 31, Year 1, for Mijka Company.
c. Explain why the income statement uses different terminology to date the income statement than is used to date the balance sheet.

LO 1-7

Exercise 1-16A   *Historical cost versus market value*

Lakeside, Inc. purchased land in January, Year 3 at a cost of $250,000. The estimated market value of the land is $425,000 as of December 31, Year 8.

Required

a. Name the December 31, Year 8, financial statement(s) on which the land will be shown.
b. At what dollar amount will the land be shown in the financial statement(s)?
c. Name the key concept that will be used in determining the dollar amount that will be reported for land that is shown in the financial statement(s).

Exercise 1-17A *Statement of cash flows*

On January 1, Year 2, Moore, a fast-food company, had a balance in its Cash account of $45,800. During the Year 2 accounting period, the company had (1) net cash inflow from operating activities of $24,800, (2) net cash outflow for investing activities of $16,000, and (3) net cash outflow from financing activities of $6,800.

Required

a. Prepare a statement of cash flows.

b. Provide a reasonable explanation as to what may have caused the net cash inflow from operating activities.

c. Provide a reasonable explanation as to what may have caused the net cash outflow from investing activities.

d. Provide a reasonable explanation as to what may have caused the net cash outflow from financing activities.

Exercise 1-18A *Prepare a statement of cash flows*

All-Star Automotive Company experienced the following accounting events during Year 3:

1. Performed services for $25,000 cash.
2. Purchased land for $6,000 cash.
3. Hired an accountant to keep the books.
4. Received $50,000 cash from the issue of common stock.
5. Borrowed $5,000 cash from State Bank.
6. Paid $14,000 cash for salary expense.
7. Sold land for $9,000 cash.
8. Paid $10,000 cash on the loan from State Bank.
9. Paid $2,800 cash for utilities expense.
10. Paid a cash dividend of $5,000 to the stockholders.

Required

a. Indicate how each of the events would be classified on the statement of cash flows as operating activities (OA), investing activities (IA), financing activities (FA), or not applicable (NA).

b. Prepare a statement of cash flows for Year 3. Assume All-Star Automotive Company had a beginning cash balance of $9,000 on January 1, Year 3.

Exercise 1-19A *Preparing financial statements*

Dakota Company experienced the following events during Year 2:

1. Acquired $30,000 cash from the issue of common stock.
2. Paid $12,000 cash to purchase land.
3. Borrowed $10,000 cash.
4. Provided services for $20,000 cash.
5. Paid $1,000 cash for utilities expense.
6. Paid $15,000 cash for other operating expenses.
7. Paid a $2,000 cash dividend to the stockholders.
8. Determined that the market value of the land purchased in Event 2 is now $12,700.

Required

a. The January 1, Year 2, general ledger account balances are shown in the following accounting equation. Record the eight events in the appropriate general ledger accounts. Record the amounts of revenue, expense, and dividends in the Retained Earnings column. Provide the appropriate titles for these accounts in the last column of the table. The first event is shown as an example.

	DAKOTA COMPANY Accounting Equation					
	Assets		= Liabilities	+	Stockholders' Equity	Acct. Titles for RE
Event	Cash	Land	Notes Payable		Common Stock Retained Earnings	
1/1/Year 2	2,000	12,000	0		6,000 8,000	
1.	30,000				30,000	

b. Prepare an income statement, statement of changes in equity, year-end balance sheet, and statement of cash flows for the Year 2 accounting period.

c. Determine the percentage of assets that were provided by retained earnings. Round to three decimal places. How much cash is in the retained earnings account?

LO 1-2, 1-6, 1-8

Exercise 1-20A   *Relating accounting events to entities*

Riley Company paid $60,000 cash to purchase land from Smally Company in Year 2. Smally originally paid $60,000 for the land.

Required

a. Was this event an asset source, use, or exchange transaction for Riley Company?

b. Was this event an asset source, use, or exchange transaction for Smally Company?

c. Was the cash flow an operating, investing, or financing activity on Riley Company's Year 2 statement of cash flows?

d. Was the cash flow an operating, investing, or financing activity on Smally Company's Year 2 statement of cash flows?

LO 1-5, 1-6, 1-7, 1-8

Exercise 1-21A   *Preparing financial statements—retained earnings emphasis*

On January 1, Year 3, the following information was drawn from the accounting records of Carter Company: cash of $800; land of $3,500; notes payable of $600; and common stock of $1,000.

Required

a. Determine the amount of retained earnings as of January 1, Year 3.

b. After looking at the amount of retained earnings, the chief executive officer (CEO) wants to pay a $1,000 cash dividend to the stockholders. Can the company pay this dividend? Why or why not?

c. As of January 1, Year 3, what percentage of the assets were acquired from creditors? Round to three decimal places.

d. As of January 1, Year 3, what percentage of the assets were acquired from investors? Round to three decimal places.

e. As of January 1, Year 3, what percentage of the assets were acquired from retained earnings? Round to three decimal places.

f. Create an accounting equation using percentages instead of dollar amounts on the right side of the equation.

g. During Year 3, Carter Company earned cash revenue of $1,800, paid cash expenses of $1,200, and paid a cash dividend of $500. Prepare an income statement, statement of changes in stockholders' equity, a balance sheet, and a statement of cash flows dated December 31, Year 3. (*Hint:* It is helpful to record these events under an accounting equation before preparing the statements.)

h. Comment on the terminology used to date each statement.

i. An appraiser determines that as of December 31, Year 3, the market value of the land is $4,200. How will this fact change the financial statements?

j. What is the balance in the Revenue account on January 1, Year 4?

Exercise 1-22A   *Preparing financial statements—cash flow emphasis*   LO 1-7, 1-8

As of January 1, Year 2, Room Designs, Inc. had a balance of $9,900 in Cash, $3,500 in Common Stock, and $6,400 in Retained Earnings. These were the only accounts with balances in the ledger on January 1, Year 2. Further analysis of the company's cash account indicated that during the Year 2 accounting period, the company had (1) net cash inflow from operating activities of $9,800, (2) net cash outflow for investing activities of $16,500, and (3) net cash inflow from financing activities of $11,000. All revenue and expense events were cash events. The following accounts and balances represent the general ledger of Room Designs, Inc. as of December 31, Year 2, before closing.

ROOM DESIGNS, INC.
General Ledger

Assets	=	Liabilities	+	Stockholders' Equity	

Cash		**Notes Payable**		**Common Stock**		**Revenue**
Bal. 14,200		Bal. 9,000		Bal. 7,500		Bal. 18,100

Land				**Retained Earnings**		**Expenses**
Bal. 16,500				Bal. 6,400		Bal. 8,300

						Dividends
						Bal. 2,000

Required

a. Assume that the net cash inflow from financing activities of $11,000 was caused by three events. Based on the information given, identify these events and determine the cash flow associated with each event.

b. What did the company purchase that resulted in the cash outflow from investing activities?

c. Prepare an income statement, statement of changes in stockholders' equity, balance sheet, and statement of cash flows.

Exercise 1-23A   *Retained earnings and the closing process*   LO 1-9

As of December 31, Year 3, Flowers Company had total assets of $130,000, total liabilities of $50,000, and common stock of $70,000. The company's Year 3 income statement contained revenue of $30,000 and expenses of $18,000. The Year 3 statement of changes in stockholders' equity stated that $3,000 of dividends were paid to investors.

Required

a. Determine the before-closing balance in the Retained Earnings account on December 31, Year 3.

b. Determine the after-closing balance in the Retained Earnings account on December 31, Year 3.

c. Determine the before-closing balances in the Revenue, Expense, and Dividend accounts on December 31, Year 3.

d. Determine the after-closing balances in the Revenue, Expense, and Dividend accounts on December 31, Year 3.

e. Explain the difference between common stock and retained earnings.

f. On January 1, Year 4, Flowers Company raised $30,000 by issuing additional common stock. Immediately after the additional capital was raised. Flowers reported total stockholders' equity of $110,000. Are the stockholders of Flowers in a better financial position than they were on December 31, Year 3?

LO 1-9

Exercise 1-24A *The closing process*

Sammy's Pizza opened on January 1, Year 1. Sammy's reported the following for cash revenues and cash expenses for the Years 1 to 3:

	Cash Revenues	Cash Expenses
Year 1	$20,000	$11,000
Year 2	$30,000	$14,000
Year 3	$40,000	$22,000

Required

a. What would Sammy's Pizza report for net income and retained earnings for the Years 1, 2, and 3?

b. Explain the difference between net income and retained earnings.

c. Assume that Sammy's Pizza paid a $5,000 dividend to stockholders in Year 2. What would Sammy's Pizza report for net income and retained earnings for Year 2 and Year 3?

LO 1-9

Exercise 1-25A *Retained earnings and the closing process*

Critz Company was started on January 1, Year 1. During the month of January, Critz earned $7,500 of revenue and incurred $4,800 of expenses. During the remainder of Year 1, Critz earned $86,000 and incurred $51,000 of expenses. Critz closes its books on December 31 of each year.

Required

a. Determine the balance in the Retained Earnings account as of January 31, Year 1.

b. Determine the balance in the Revenue and Expense accounts as of January 31, Year 1.

c. Determine the balance in the Retained Earnings account as of December 31, Year 1, before closing.

d. Determine the balances in the Revenue and Expense accounts as of December 31, Year 1, before closing.

e. Determine the balance in the Retained Earnings account as of January 1, Year 2.

f. Determine the balance in the Revenue and Expense accounts as of January 1, Year 2.

LO 1-10

Exercise 1-26A *Types of transactions and the horizontal statements model*

The Candle Shop experienced the following events during its first year of operations:

1. Acquired cash by issuing common stock.
2. Paid a cash dividend to the stockholders.
3. Paid cash for operating expenses.
4. Borrowed cash from a bank.
5. Provided services and collected cash.
6. Purchased land with cash.
7. Determined that the market value of the land is higher than the historical cost.

Required

a. Indicate whether each event is an asset source, use, or exchange transaction.

b. Use a horizontal statements model to show how each event affects the balance sheet, income statement, and statement of cash flows. Indicate whether the event increases (I), decreases (D), or does not affect (NA) each element of the financial statements. Also, in the Cash Flows column, classify the cash flows as operating activities (OA), investing activities (IA), or financing activities (FA). The first transaction is shown as an example.

	Balance Sheet										Income Statement					Statement of Cash Flows
Event No.	Cash	+	Land	=	N. Pay.	+	C. Stock.	+	Ret. Ear.		Rev.	−	Exp.	=	Net Inc.	
1.	1	+	NA	=	NA	+	1	+	NA		NA	−	NA	=	NA	1 FA

Exercise 1-27A   *International Financial Reporting Standards*

LO IFRS

Corrugated Boxes Inc. is a U.S.-based company that develops its financial statements under GAAP. The total amount of the company's assets shown on its balance sheet was approximately $305 million. The president of Corrugated is considering the possibility of relocating the company to a country that practices accounting under IFRS. The president has hired an international accounting firm to determine what the company's statements would look like if they were prepared under IFRS. One striking difference is that under IFRS the assets shown on the balance sheet would be valued at approximately $345 million.

Required

a. Would Corrugated Boxes's assets really be worth $40 million more if it moves its headquarters?

b. Discuss the underlying conceptual differences between U.S. GAAP and IFRS that cause the difference in the reported asset values.

SECTIONS 1 AND 2 PROBLEMS—SERIES A

 An electronic auto-gradable version of the Series A Problems is available in Connect. A PDF version of Series B Problems is in Connect under the "Additional Student Resources" tab. Solutions to the Series B Problems are available in Connect under the "Instructor Library" tab. Instructor and student Workpapers for the Series B Problems are available in Connect under the "Instructor Library" and "Additional Student Resources" tabs respectively.

Problem 1-28A   *Accounting's role in not-for-profits*

LO 1-1

Beverly Moore is struggling to pass her introductory accounting course. Beverly is intelligent but she likes to party. Studying is a low priority for Beverly. When one of her friends tells her that she is going to have trouble in business if she doesn't learn accounting, Beverly responds that she doesn't plan to go into business. She says that she is arts oriented and plans someday to be a director of a museum. She is in the school of business to develop her social skills, not her quantitative skills. Beverly says she won't have to worry about accounting, since museums are not intended to make a profit.

Required

a. Write a brief memo explaining whether you agree or disagree with Beverly's position regarding accounting and not-for-profit organizations.

b. Distinguish between financial accounting and managerial accounting.

c. Identify some of the stakeholders of not-for-profit institutions that would expect to receive financial accounting reports.

d. Identify some of the stakeholders of not-for-profit institutions that would expect to receive managerial accounting reports.

Problem 1-29A   *Accounting entities*

LO 1-2

The following business scenarios are independent from one another:

1. Bob Wilder starts a business by transferring $10,000 from his personal checking account into a checking account for his business, Wilder Co.

2. A business that Sam Pace owns earns $4,600 of cash revenue from customers.

3. Jim Sneed borrows $30,000 from the National Bank and uses the money to purchase a car from Iuka Ford.

4. Oz Company pays its five employees $2,500 each to cover their salaries.

5. Gil Roberts loans his son Jim $5,000.

6. Game, Inc. paid $100,000 cash to purchase land from Atlanta Land Co.

7. Rob Moore and Gil Thomas form the MT partnership by contributing $20,000 each from their personal bank accounts to a partnership bank account.

8. Stephen Woo pays cash to purchase $5,000 of common stock that is issued by Izzard, Inc.

9. Natural Stone pays a $5,000 cash dividend to each of its seven shareholders.

10. Billows, Inc. borrowed $5,000,000 from the National Bank.

CHECK FIGURE
1. Entities mentioned: Bob Wilder and Wilder Co.

Required

a. For each scenario, create a list of all the entities that are mentioned in the description.

b. Describe what happens to the cash account of each entity that you identified in Requirement *a*.

LO 1-3

Problem 1-30A   *Matching key terms with definitions*

Required

Match the terms (identified as a through p) with the definitions and phrases (marked 1 through 16). For example the term "a. Assets" matches with definition "15. Equal to liabilities plus stockholders' equity."

a. Assets	1. The economic benefit (increase in assets) gained by providing goods or services to customers.
b. Common Stock	2. Investors who purchase common stock.
c. Creditors	3. The economic sacrifice (decrease in assets) incurred in the process of providing goods or services to customers.
d. Dividend	4. Created when a company borrows money from a bank.
e. General Ledger	5. Assets minus liabilities and retained earnings.
f. Expense	6. Occurs when expenses exceed revenues during the year.
g. Financing Activity	7. Individuals or institutions that have loaned goods or services to a business.
h. Investing Activity	8. Complete set of accounts used in accounting systems.
i. Liability	9. Occurs when revenue exceeds expenses during the year.
j. Net Income	10. Assets minus liabilities.
k. Net Loss	11. The section of the statement of cash flows that reflects cash paid for expenses.
l. Operating Activity	12. The section of the statement of cash flows that reflects cash collected from the issue of stock.
m. Retained Earnings	13. The section of the statement of cash flows that reflects cash paid to purchase land.
n. Revenue	14. The item shown on the statement of changes in stockholders' equity that represents a transfer of wealth from a business to its owners.
o. Stockholders	15. Equal to liabilities plus stockholders' equity.
p. Stockholders' Equity	16. A stockholders' equity account that contains the amount of net income earned minus dividends paid since the inception of the business.

LO 1-6

Problem 1-31A   *Classifying events as asset source, use, or exchange*

The following unrelated events are typical of those experienced by business entities:

1. Acquire cash by issuing common stock.
2. Pay cash for operating expenses.
3. Agree to represent a client in an IRS audit and to receive payment when the audit is complete.
4. Receive cash for services that have been performed.
5. Pay employees salary with cash.
6. Pay back a bank loan with cash.
7. Pay interest on the bank loan with cash.
8. Transfer cash from a checking account to a money market account.
9. Sell land for cash at its original cost.
10. Pay a cash dividend to stockholders.
11. Learn that a financial analyst determined the company's price-earnings ratio to be 26.
12. Borrow cash from a bank.
13. Pay office supplies expense.
14. Make plans to purchase office equipment at a future date.
15. Trade a used car for a computer with the same value.

Required

Identify each of the events as an asset source, use, or exchange transaction. If an event would not be recorded under generally accepted accounting principles, identify it as not applicable (NA). Also indicate for each event whether total assets would increase, decrease, or remain unchanged. Organize your answer according to the following table. The first event is shown in the table as an example.

Event No.	Type of Event	Effect on Total Assets
1	Asset source	Increase

Problem 1-32A   *Relating titles and accounts to financial statements*

LO 1-3, 1-7, 1-8

Required

Identify the financial statements on which each of the following items (titles, date descriptions, and accounts) appears by placing a check mark in the appropriate column. If an item appears on more than one statement, place a check mark in every applicable column.

Item	Income Statement	Statement of Changes in Stockholders' Equity	Balance Sheet	Statement of Cash Flows
Financing activities				
Ending common stock				
Interest expense				
As of (date)				
Land				
Beginning cash balance				
Notes payable				
Beginning common stock				
Service revenue				
Utility expense				
Stock issued				
Operating activities				
For the period ended (date)				
Net income				
Investing activities				
Net loss				
Ending cash balance				
Salary expense				
Consulting revenue				
Dividends				

Problem 1-33A   *Preparing financial statements for two complete accounting cycles*

LO 1-3, 1-4, 1-5, 1-7, 1-8, 1-9

Mark's Consulting experienced the following transactions for Year 1, its first year of operations, and Year 2. *Assume that all transactions involve the receipt or payment of cash.*

Transactions for Year 1

1. Acquired $20,000 by issuing common stock.
2. Received $35,000 cash for providing services to customers.

CHECK FIGURES
a. Net Income Year 1: $13,000
b. Retained Earnings Year 2: $33,500

3. Borrowed $25,000 cash from creditors.
4. Paid expenses amounting to $22,000.
5. Purchased land for $30,000 cash.

Transactions for Year 2

Beginning account balances for Year 2 are:

Cash	$28,000
Land	30,000
Notes payable	25,000
Common stock	20,000
Retained earnings	13,000

1. Acquired an additional $24,000 from the issue of common stock.
2. Received $95,000 for providing services.
3. Paid $15,000 to creditors to reduce loan.
4. Paid expenses amounting to $71,500.
5. Paid a $3,000 dividend to the stockholders.
6. Determined that the market value of the land is $47,000.

Required

a. Write an accounting equation, and record the effects of each accounting event under the appropriate headings for each year. Record the amounts of revenue, expense, and dividends in the Retained Earnings column. Provide appropriate titles for these accounts in the last column of the table.

b. Prepare an income statement, statement of changes in stockholders' equity, year-end balance sheet, and statement of cash flows for each year.

c. Determine the amount of cash that is in the Retained Earnings account at the end of Year 1 and Year 2.

d. Compare the information provided by the income statement with the information provided by the statement of cash flows. Point out similarities and differences.

e. Determine the balance in the Retained Earnings account immediately after Event 2 in Year 1 is recorded and after Event 2 in Year 2 is recorded.

LO 1-5, 1-7, 1-8, 1-9

Problem 1-34A   *Interrelationships among financial statements*

Prat Corp. started the Year 2 accounting period with $30,000 of assets (all cash), $12,000 of liabilities, and $13,000 of common stock. During the year, the Retained Earnings account increased by $7,550. The bookkeeper reported that Prat paid cash expenses of $26,000 and paid a $2,000 cash dividend to the stockholders, but she could not find a record of the amount of cash that Prat received for performing services. Prat also paid $3,000 cash to reduce the liability owed to the bank, and the business acquired $4,000 of additional cash from the issue of common stock.

Required

CHECK FIGURE
a. Net Income Year 2: $9,550
   Total Assets: $38,550

a. Prepare an income statement, statement of changes in stockholders' equity, period-end balance sheet, and statement of cash flows for the Year 2 accounting period. (*Hint:* Determine the amount of beginning retained earnings before considering the effects of the current period events. It also might help to record all events under an accounting equation before preparing the statements.)

b. Determine the percentage of total assets that were provided by creditors, investors, and earnings. Round to three decimal places.

c. Determine the balance in the Revenue, Expense, and Dividends accounts as of January 1, Year 3.

LO 1-3, 1-4, 1-5, 1-6, 1-7, 1-8, 1-9, 1-10

Problem 1-35A   *Recording events in a horizontal statements model*

Maben Company was started on January 1, Year 1, and experienced the following events during its first year of operation:

CHECK FIGURES
a. Net Income: $23,000
e. Net Cash Flow from Operating Activities: $23,000

1. Acquired $30,000 cash from the issue of common stock.
2. Borrowed $40,000 cash from National Bank.
3. Earned cash revenues of $48,000 for performing services.
4. Paid cash expenses of $25,000.

5. Paid a $1,000 cash dividend to the stockholders.
6. Acquired an additional $20,000 cash from the issue of common stock.
7. Paid $10,000 cash to reduce the principal balance of the bank note.
8. Paid $53,000 cash to purchase land.
9. Determined that the market value of the land is $75,000.

Required

a. Record the preceding transactions in the horizontal statements model. Also, in the Cash Flows column, classify the cash flows as operating activities (OA), investing activities (IA), or financing activities (FA). The first event is shown as an example.

	Balance Sheet								Income Statement					Statement of Cash Flows
Event No.	Cash	+	Land	=	N. Pay.	+	C. Stock.	+	Ret. Ear.	Rev.	−	Exp.	=	Net Inc.	
1.	30,000	+	NA	=	NA	+	30,000	+	NA	NA	−	NA	=	NA	30,000 FA

b. Determine the amount of total assets that Maben would report on the December 31, Year 1, balance sheet.
c. Identify the asset source transactions and related amounts for Year 1.
d. Determine the net income that Maben would report on the Year 1 income statement. Explain why dividends do not appear on the income statement.
e. Determine the net cash flows from operating activities, financing activities, and investing activities that Maben would report on the Year 1 statement of cash flows.
f. Determine the percentage of assets that were provided by investors, creditors, and earnings. Round to three decimal places.
g. What is the balance in the Retained Earnings account immediately after Event 3 is recorded?

ANALYZE, THINK, COMMUNICATE

ATC 1-1 Business Applications Case *Understanding real-world annual reports*

Required

Obtain the Target Corporation's annual report for its 2018 fiscal year (year ended February 2, 2019) at http://investors.target.com using the instructions in Appendix A, and use it to answer the following questions:

a. What was Target's net income for 2018 (the year ended February 2, 2019)?
b. Did Target's net income increase or decrease from 2017 to 2018, and by how much?
c. What was Target's accounting equation for 2018?
d. Which of the following had the largest percentage change from 2017 to 2018: net sales; cost of sales; or selling, general, and administrative expenses? Show all computations.

ATC 1-2 Group Assignment *Missing information*

The following selected financial information is available for HAS, Inc. Amounts are in millions of dollars.

Income Statements	Year 6	Year 5	Year 4	Year 3
Revenue	$ 860	$ 1,520	$ (a)	$ 1,200
Cost and expenses	(a)	(a)	(2,400)	(860)
Income from continuing operations	(b)	450	320	(a)
Unusual items	-0-	175	(b)	(b)
Net income	$ 20	$ (b)	$ 175	$ 300
				(continued)

Balance Sheets	Year 6	Year 5	Year 4	Year 3
Assets				
Cash and marketable securities	$ 350	$ 1,720	$ (c)	$ 940
Other assets	1,900	(c)	2,500	(c)
Total assets	2,250	$ 2,900	$ (d)	$ 3,500
Liabilities	$ (c)	$ (d)	$ 1,001	$ (d)
Stockholders' equity				
Common stock	880	720	(e)	800
Retained earnings	(d)	(e)	800	(e)
Total stockholders' equity	1,520	1,345	(f)	2,200
Total liabilities and stockholders' equity	$ 2,250	$ (f)	$ 3,250	$ 3,500

Required

a. Divide the class into groups of four or five students each. Organize the groups into four sections. Assign Task 1 to the first section of groups, Task 2 to the second section, Task 3 to the third section, and Task 4 to the fourth section.

Group Tasks

(1) Fill in the missing information for Year 3.

(2) Fill in the missing information for Year 4.

(3) Fill in the missing information for Year 5.

(4) Fill in the missing information for Year 6.

b. Each section should select two representatives. One representative is to put the financial statements assigned to that section on the board, underlining the missing amounts. The second representative is to explain to the class how the missing amounts were determined.

c. Each section should list events that could have caused the unusual items category on the income statement.

ATC 1-3 Research Assignment *Finding real-world accounting information*

This chapter introduced the basic four financial statements companies use annually to keep their stakeholders informed of their accomplishments and financial situation. Complete the following requirements using the most recent financial statements available on the McDonald's Corporation's website. Obtain the online statements by following the steps given. (The formatting of the company's website may have changed since these instructions were written.)

1. Go to www.mcdonalds.com.
2. Click on the "Investors Relations" link at the bottom of the page.
3. Using the "INVESTORS" link at the top of the page, click on "Financial Information."
4. Under the list of "Annual Reports" select the most recent annual report available.
5. Go to the company's financial statements that have begun around page 30 of the annual report in recent years.

Required

a. What was the company's net income in each of the last three years?

b. What amount of total assets did the company have at the end of the most recent year?

c. How much retained earnings did the company have at the end of the most recent year?

d. For the most recent year, what was the company's cash flow from operating activities, cash flow from investing activities, and cash flow from financing activities?

ATC 1-4 Writing Assignment *Portions of financial statements defined*

Sam and his sister Blair both attend the state university. As a reward for their successful completion of the past year (Sam had a 3.2 GPA in business, and Blair had a 3.7 GPA in art), their father gave each of them 100 shares of The Walt Disney Company stock. They have just received their first annual report. Blair does not understand what the information means and has asked Sam to explain it to her. Sam is currently taking an accounting course, and she knows he will understand the financial statements.

Required

Assume that you are Sam. Write Blair a memo explaining the following financial statement items to her. In your explanation, describe each of the two financial statements and explain the financial information each contains. Also define each of the terms listed for each financial statement and explain what it means.

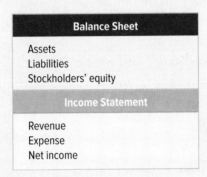

Balance Sheet
Assets
Liabilities
Stockholders' equity
Income Statement
Revenue
Expense
Net income

Accounting for Accruals and Deferrals

LEARNING OBJECTIVES

After you have mastered the material in this chapter, you will be able to:

SECTION 1: SHOW HOW ACCRUALS AFFECT FINANCIAL STATEMENTS

LO 2-1   Show how receivables affect financial statements.

LO 2-2   Show how payables affect financial statements.

LO 2-3   Prepare financial statements that include accruals.

LO 2-4   Identify the steps in the accounting cycle.

SECTION 2: SHOW HOW DEFERRALS AFFECT FINANCIAL STATEMENTS

LO 2-5   Show how accounting for supplies affects financial statements.

LO 2-6   Show how accounting for prepaid items affects financial statements.

LO 2-7   Show how accounting for unearned revenues affects financial statements.

LO 2-8   Prepare financial statements that include deferrals.

LO 2-9   Classify accounting events into one of four categories.

 Video lectures and accompanying self-assessment quizzes are available in Connect *for all learning objectives.*

 Set B exercises and problems are available in Additional Student Resources.

SHOW HOW ACCRUALS AFFECT FINANCIAL STATEMENTS

Suppose a painting company signs a contract to paint a house. Two weeks after signing the contract a painter starts the job. The job is completed in one week. The company sends the client a bill a few days after the job is complete. The company receives payment from the client 10 days after the bill was sent. Should the paint company recognize revenue on the day the contract was signed, when the work started, when the work was finished, when the bill was sent, or when the cash was collected? To provide guidance in answering such questions the Financial Accounting Standards Board (FASB) issued Accounting Standards Codification 606, which provides the following core principal:

> [A]n entity should recognize revenue to depict the transfer of promised goods or services to customers in an amount that reflects the consideration to which the entity expects to be entitled in exchange for those goods or services.

In lay terms this means that revenue should be recognized in the period in which it is earned regardless of whether cash has or has not been collected. More specifically, companies may recognize revenue in the income statement in a different accounting period than the period in which they collect the related cash. Furthermore, companies frequently make cash payments for expenses in accounting periods other than the periods in which the expenses are recognized in the income statement. Recognizing revenue when it is earned and expenses when they are incurred, regardless of when cash changes hands, is commonly called **accrual accounting.**

To illustrate, assume Johnson Company provides services to customers in Year 1 but collects cash for those services in Year 2. When should Johnson recognize the services revenue?

First, note that accrual accounting is not used by all companies. Indeed, many small private companies use cash basis accounting. Users of *cash basis* accounting recognize (report) revenues and expenses in the period in which cash is collected or paid. Under cash basis accounting Johnson would recognize the revenue in Year 2 when it collects the cash. In contrast, users of accrual accounting recognize revenues and expenses in the period in which they occur, regardless of when cash is collected or paid. Under accrual accounting Johnson would recognize the revenue in Year 1 (the period in which it performed the services) even though it does not collect the cash until Year 2.

Accrual accounting is required by generally accepted accounting principles (GAAP). Virtually all major companies operating in the United States use it. Its two distinguishing features are called *accruals* and *deferrals*.

- The term **accrual** describes a revenue or an expense event that is recognized *before* cash is exchanged. Johnson's recognition of revenue in Year 1 that is related to cash collected in Year 2 is an example of an accrual.

■ The term **deferral** describes a revenue or an expense event that is recognized *after* cash has been exchanged. Suppose Johnson pays cash in Year 1 to purchase office supplies it uses in Year 2. In this case the cash payment occurs in Year 1, although supplies expense is recognized in Year 2. This example is a deferral.

The Curious Accountant

© B. O'Kane/Alamy Stock Photo

On September 15, 2020, Mary Garcia purchased a subscription to *Parents* magazine for her daughter, who is expecting her first child. She paid $12 for a one-year subscription to the **Meredith Corporation**, the company that publishes 25 major magazines, including *Better Homes and Gardens, People, Shape,* and *Martha Stewart Living*. The company also owns 17 television stations. Mary's daughter will receive her first issue of the magazine in October.

How should Meredith Corporation account for the receipt of this cash? How would this event be reported on its December 31, 2020, financial statements? (Answer on page 68.)

ACCOUNTING FOR RECEIVABLES

LO 2-1

Show how receivables affect financial statements.

This section of the text describes seven events experienced by Cato Consultants, a training services company that uses accrual accounting.

EVENT 1   Cato Consultants was started on January 1, Year 1, when it acquired $5,000 cash by issuing common stock.

The issue of stock for cash is an **asset source transaction.** It increases the company's assets (cash) and its stockholders' equity (common stock). The transaction does not affect the income statement. The cash inflow is classified as a financing activity (acquisition from owners). These effects are shown in the following financial statements model:

Balance Sheet						Income Statement						Statement of Cash Flows
Assets	=	Liab.	+	Stockholders' Equity								
Cash	=			Com. Stk.	+	Ret. Earn.	Rev.	−	Exp.	=	Net Inc.	
5,000	=	NA	+	5,000	+	NA	NA	−	NA	=	NA	5,000 FA

Recognizing Accounts Receivable

EVENT 2   During Year 1, Cato Consultants provided $84,000 of consulting services to its clients. The business has completed the work and sent bills to the clients, but not yet collected any cash. This type of transaction is frequently described as providing services *on account.*

Accrual accounting requires companies to recognize revenue in the period in which the work is done regardless of when cash is collected. In this case, revenue is recognized in Year 1 even though cash has not been collected. Recall that revenue represents the economic benefit that results in an increase in assets from providing goods and services to customers. The specific asset that increases is called **Accounts Receivable.** The balance in Accounts Receivable represents the amount of cash the company expects to collect in the future. Since the revenue recognition causes assets (accounts receivable) to increase, it is classified as an asset source transaction. Its effect on the financial statements follows:

Balance Sheet									Income Statement					Statement of Cash Flows
Assets			=	Liab.	+	Stockholders' Equity								
Cash	+	Accts. Rec.	=			Com. Stk.	+	Ret. Earn.	Rev.	−	Exp.	=	Net Inc.	
NA	+	84,000	=	NA	+	NA	+	84,000	84,000	−	NA	=	84,000	NA

Notice that the event affects the income statement but not the statement of cash flows. The statement of cash flows will be affected in the future when cash is collected.

EVENT 3   Cato collected $60,000 cash from customers in partial settlement of its accounts receivable.

The collection of an account receivable is an **asset exchange transaction.** One asset account (Cash) increases and another asset account (Accounts Receivable) decreases. The amount of total assets is unchanged. The effect of the $60,000 collection of receivables on the financial statements is as follows:

Balance Sheet									Income Statement					Statement of Cash Flows
Assets			=	Liab.	+	Stockholders' Equity								
Cash	+	Accts. Rec.	=			Com. Stk.	+	Ret. Earn.	Rev.	−	Exp.	=	Net Inc.	
60,000	+	(60,000)	=	NA	+	NA	+	NA	NA	−	NA	=	NA	60,000 OA

Notice that collecting the cash did not affect the income statement. The revenue was recognized when the work was done (see Event 2). Revenue would be double counted if it were recognized again when the cash is collected. The statement of cash flows reflects a cash inflow from operating activities.

Other Events

EVENT 4   Cato paid the instructor $10,000 for teaching training courses (salary expense).

Cash payment for salary expense is an **asset use transaction.** Both the asset account Cash and the stockholders' equity account Retained Earnings decrease by $10,000. Recognizing the expense decreases net income on the income statement. Since Cato paid cash for the expense, the statement of cash flows reflects a cash outflow from operating activities. These effects on the financial statements follow:

Balance Sheet									Income Statement					Statement of Cash Flows
Assets			=	Liab.	+	Stockholders' Equity								
Cash	+	Accts. Rec.	=			Com. Stk.	+	Ret. Earn.	Rev.	−	Exp.	=	Net Inc.	
(10,000)	+	NA	=	NA	+	NA	+	(10,000)	NA	−	10,000	=	(10,000)	(10,000) OA

EVENT 5   Cato paid $2,000 cash for advertising costs. The advertisements were shown in Year 1.

Cash payments for advertising expenses are asset use transactions. Both the asset account Cash and the stockholders' equity account Retained Earnings decrease by $2,000. Recognizing the expense decreases net income on the income statement. Since the expense was paid with cash, the statement of cash flows reflects a cash outflow from operating activities. These effects on the financial statements follow:

Balance Sheet								Income Statement					Statement of Cash Flows
Assets		=	Liab.	+	Stockholders' Equity								
Cash	+ Accts. Rec.	=			Com. Stk.	+	Ret. Earn.	Rev.	−	Exp.	=	Net Inc.	
(2,000)	+ NA	=	NA	+	NA	+	(2,000)	NA	−	2,000	=	(2,000)	(2,000) OA

EVENT 6   Cato signed contracts for $42,000 of consulting services to be performed in Year 2.

The $42,000 for consulting services to be performed in Year 2 is not recognized in the Year 2 financial statements. Revenue is recognized for work actually completed, *not* work expected to be completed. This event does not affect any of the financial statements.

Balance Sheet								Income Statement					Statement of Cash Flows
Assets		=	Liab.	+	Stockholders' Equity								
Cash	+ Accts. Rec.	=			Com. Stk.	+	Ret. Earn.	Rev.	−	Exp.	=	Net Inc.	
NA	+ NA	=	NA	+	NA	+	NA	NA	−	NA	=	NA	NA

ACCOUNTING FOR PAYABLES (ADJUSTING THE ACCOUNTS)

It is impractical to record many business events as they occur. For example, Cato incurs salary expense continually as the instructor teaches courses. Imagine the impossibility of trying to record salary expense second by second! Companies normally record transactions when it is most convenient. The most convenient time to record many expenses is when they are paid. Often, however, a single business transaction pertains to more than one accounting period. To provide accurate financial reports in such cases, companies may need to recognize some expenses before paying cash for them. Expenses that are recognized before cash is paid are called **accrued expenses.** The accounting for Event 7 illustrates the effect of recognizing accrued salary expense.

EVENT 7   At the end of Year 1, Cato recorded accrued salary expense of $6,000 (the salary expense is for courses the instructor taught in Year 1 that Cato will pay cash for in Year 2).

Accrual accounting requires that companies recognize expenses in the period in which they are incurred regardless of when cash is paid. Cato must recognize all salary expense in the period in which the instructor worked (Year 1) even though Cato will not pay the instructor again until Year 2. Cato must also recognize the obligation (liability) it has to pay the instructor. To accurately report all Year 1 salary expense and year-end obligations, Cato must record the unpaid salary expense and salary liability before preparing its financial statements. The entry to recognize the accrued salary expense is called an **adjusting entry.** Like all adjusting entries, it is only to update the accounting records; it does not affect cash.

This adjusting entry decreases stockholders' equity (Retained Earnings) and increases a liability account called **Salaries Payable.** The balance in the Salaries Payable account represents the amount of cash the company is obligated to pay the instructor in the future. The effect of the expense recognition on the financial statements follows:

Balance Sheet									Income Statement				Statement of Cash Flows
Assets			=	Liab.	+	Stockholders' Equity							
Cash	+	Accts. Rec.	=	Sal. Pay.	+	Com. Stk.	+	Ret. Earn.	Rev.	−	Exp.	=	Net Inc.	
NA	+	NA	=	6,000	+	NA	+	(6,000)	NA	−	6,000	=	(6,000)	NA

This event is a **claims exchange transaction.** The claims of creditors (liabilities) increase and the claims of stockholders (retained earnings) decrease. Total claims remain unchanged. The salary expense is reported on the income statement. The statement of cash flows is not affected.

Be careful not to confuse liabilities with expenses. Although liabilities may increase when a company recognizes expenses, liabilities are not expenses. Liabilities are obligations. They can arise from acquiring assets as well as recognizing expenses. For example, when a business borrows money from a bank, it recognizes an increase in assets (cash) and liabilities (notes payable). The borrowing transaction does not affect expenses.

 CHECK YOURSELF 2.1

During Year 1, Anwar Company earned $345,000 of revenue on account and collected $320,000 cash from accounts receivable. Anwar paid cash expenses of $300,000 and cash dividends of $12,000. Determine the amount of net income Anwar should report on the Year 1 income statement and the amount of cash flow from operating activities Anwar should report on the Year 1 statement of cash flows.

Answer   Net income is $45,000 ($345,000 revenue − $300,000 expenses). The cash flow from operating activities is $20,000, the amount of revenue collected in cash from customers (accounts receivable) minus the cash paid for expenses ($320,000 − $300,000). Dividend payments are classified as financing activities and do not affect the determination of either net income or cash flow from operating activities.

Summary of Events and General Ledger

The previous section of this chapter described seven events Cato Consultants experienced during the Year 1 accounting period. These events are summarized in Exhibit 2.1. The associated general ledger accounts are also shown in the exhibit. The information in these accounts is used to prepare the financial statements. The revenue and expense items appear in the Retained Earnings column with their account titles immediately to the right of the dollar amounts. The amounts are color-coded to help you trace the data to the financial statements. Data in red appear on the balance sheet, data in blue on the income statement, and data in green on the statement of cash flows.

EXHIBIT 2.1

Transaction Data for Year 1 Recorded in General Ledger Accounts

1	Cato Consultants acquired $5,000 cash by issuing common stock.
2	Cato provided $84,000 of consulting services on account.
3	Cato collected $60,000 cash from customers in partial settlement of its accounts receivable.
4	Cato paid $10,000 cash for salary expense
5	Cato paid $2,000 cash for Year 1 advertising costs.
6	Cato signed contracts for $42,000 of consulting services to be performed in Year 2.
7	Cato recognized $6,000 of accrued salary expense.

	Assets			=	Liabilities	+	Stockholders' Equity			
Event No.	Cash	+	Accounts Receivable	=	Salaries Payable	+	Common Stock	+	Retained Earnings	Other Account Titles
Beg. bal.	0		0		0		0		0	
1	5,000						5,000			
2			84,000						84,000	Consulting revenue
3	60,000		(60,000)							
4	(10,000)								(10,000)	Salary expense
5	(2,000)								(2,000)	Advertising expense
6										
7					6,000				(6,000)	Salary Expense
End bal.	53,000	+	24,000	=	6,000	+	5,000	+	66,000	

PREPARING FINANCIAL STATEMENTS

LO 2-3

Prepare financial statements that include accruals.

The financial statements for Cato Consultants's Year 1 accounting period are represented in a vertical statements model in Exhibit 2.2. A vertical statements model arranges a set of financial statement information vertically on a single page. Like horizontal statements models, vertical statements models are learning tools. They illustrate interrelationships among financial statements. The models do not, however, portray the full, formal presentation formats companies use in published financial statements. For example, statements models may use summarized formats with abbreviated titles and dates. As you read the following explanations of each financial statement, trace the color-coded financial data from Exhibit 2.1 to Exhibit 2.2.

Income Statement

The income statement reflects accrual accounting. Consulting revenue represents the price Cato charged for all the services it performed in Year 1, even though Cato had not received cash by the end of the year for some of the services performed. Expenses include all costs incurred to produce revenue, whether paid for by year-end or not. We can now expand the definition of expenses introduced in Chapter 1. Expenses were previously defined as assets consumed in the process of generating revenue. Cato's adjusting entry to recognize accrued salaries expense did not reflect consuming assets. Instead of a decrease in assets, Cato recorded an increase in liabilities (salaries payable). An **expense** can therefore be more precisely defined as *a decrease in assets or an increase in liabilities resulting from operating activities undertaken to generate revenue.*

EXHIBIT 2.2   Vertical Statements Model

CATO CONSULTANTS
Financial Statements*
Income Statement
For the Year Ended December 31, Year 1

Consulting revenue	$84,000
Salary expense	(16,000)
Advertising expense	(2,000)
Net income	$66,000

Statement of Changes in Stockholders' Equity
For the Year Ended December 31, Year 1

Beginning common stock	$ 0	
Plus: Common stock issued	5,000	
Ending common stock		$ 5,000
Beginning retained earnings	0	
Plus: Net income	66,000	
Less: Dividends	0	
Ending retained earnings		66,000
Total stockholders' equity		$71,000

Balance Sheet
As of December 31, Year 1

Assets		
Cash	$53,000	
Accounts receivable	24,000	
Total assets		$77,000
Liabilities		
Salaries payable		$ 6,000
Stockholders' equity		
Common stock	$ 5,000	
Retained earnings	66,000	
Total stockholders' equity		71,000
Total liabilities and stockholders' equity		$77,000

Statement of Cash Flows
For the Year Ended December 31, Year 1

Cash flows from operating activities		
Cash receipts from customers	$60,000	
Cash payments for salary expense	(10,000)	
Cash payments for advertising expenses	(2,000)	
Net cash flow from operating activities		$48,000
Cash flow from investing activities		0
Cash flows from financing activities		
Cash receipt from issuing common stock	5,000	
Net cash flow from financing activities		5,000
Net change in cash		53,000
Plus: Beginning cash balance		0
Ending cash balance		$53,000

*In real-world annual reports, financial statements are normally presented separately with appropriate descriptions of the date to indicate whether the statement applies to the entire accounting period or a specific point in time.

Statement of Changes in Stockholders' Equity

The statement of changes in stockholders' equity reports the effects on stockholders' equity of issuing common stock, earning net income, and paying dividends to stockholders. It identifies how stockholders' equity increased and decreased during the period as a result of transactions with stockholders and operating the business. In the Cato case, the statement shows that stockholders' equity increased when the business acquired $5,000 cash by issuing common stock. The statement also reports that stockholders' equity increased by $66,000 from earning income and that none of the $66,000 of net earnings was distributed to owners (no dividends were paid). Stockholders' equity at the end of the year is $71,000 ($5,000 + $66,000).

Balance Sheet

The balance sheet discloses an entity's assets, liabilities, and stockholders' equity at a particular point in time. As of December 31, Year 1, Cato Consultants had total assets of $77,000 ($53,000 cash + $24,000 accounts receivable). These assets are equal to the obligations and commitments Cato has to its creditors and investors. Specifically, Cato has a $6,000 obligation (liability) to creditors, with the remaining $71,000 of assets available to support commitments (stockholders' equity) to stockholders.

Statement of Cash Flows

The statement of cash flows explains the change in cash from the beginning to the end of the accounting period. It can be prepared by analyzing the Cash account. Since Cato Consultants was established in Year 1, its beginning cash balance was zero. By the end of the year, the cash balance was $53,000. The statement of cash flows explains this increase. The Cash account increased because Cato collected $60,000 from customers and decreased because Cato paid $12,000 for expenses. As a result, Cato's net cash inflow from operating activities was $48,000. Also, the business acquired $5,000 cash through the financing activity of issuing common stock, for a cumulative cash increase of $53,000 ($48,000 + $5,000) during Year 1.

Comparing Cash Flow from Operations with Net Income

The amount of net income measured using accrual accounting differs from the amount of cash flow from operating activities. For Cato Consulting in Year 1, the differences are summarized as follows:

	Accrual Accounting	Cash Flow
Consulting revenue	$84,000	$60,000
Salary expense	(16,000)	(10,000)
Advertising expense	(2,000)	(2,000)
Net income	$66,000	$48,000

Many students begin their first accounting class with the misconception that revenue and expense items are cash equivalents. The Cato illustration demonstrates that a company may recognize a revenue or expense without a corresponding cash collection or payment in the same accounting period.

STEPS IN AN ACCOUNTING CYCLE

The Closing Process

At the end of the accounting cycle the balances in the temporary accounts (revenue, expense, and dividends) are transferred (closed) to the permanent account, Retained Earnings. Exhibit 2.3 shows the Year 1 closing entries and the after-closing general ledger account balances.

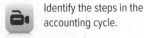

LO 2-4

Identify the steps in the accounting cycle.

EXHIBIT 2.3

Cato Corporation, Year 1 Closing Process

Panel 1 Closing Entries

C1   Transfers the balance from the Consulting Revenue account to the Retained Earnings account.
C2   Transfers the balance from the Salary Expense account to the Retained Earnings account.
C3   Transfers the balance from the Advertising Expense account to the Retained Earnings account.

Panel 2 General Ledger Accounts after Closing

Assets		=	Liabilities		+	Permanent Equity		+	Temporary Equity	
Cash			**Salaries Payable**			**Common Stock**			**Consulting Revenue**	
Bal.	0		(6) Adj.	6,000		Bal.	0		(2)	84,000
(1)	5,000		Bal.	6,000		(1)	5,000		Bal.	84,000
(3)	60,000					Bal.	5,000		Cl.1	(84,000)
(4)	(10,000)								Bal.	0
(5)	(2,000)					**Retained Earnings**				
Bal.	53,000					Bal.	0		**Salary Expense**	
						Cl.1	84,000		(4)	(10,000)
Accounts Receivable						Cl.2	(16,000)		(6) Adj.	(6,000)
(2)	84,000					Cl.3	(2,000)		Bal.	16,000
(3)	(60,000)					Bal.	66,000		Cl.2	16,000
Bal.	24,000								Bal.	0
									Advertising Expense	
									(5)	(2,000)
									Bal.	(2,000)
									Cl.3	2,000
									Bal.	0

FOCUS ON INTERNATIONAL ISSUES

As explained in Chapter 1, companies in the United States must follow GAAP, as established by the Financial Accounting Standards Board (FASB), while most of the remainder of the world follows International Financial Reporting Standards (IFRS), which are established by the International Accounting Standards Board (IASB). Although there are some significant differences between GAAP and IFRS, it is the goal of the two rule-making bodies to have as much uniformity as possible. The process of trying to achieve this goal is often referred to as "convergence."

One very clear example of the attempt at convergence relates to revenue recognition. On May 28, 2014, both boards issued a converged standard related to how companies should recognize revenue earned from contract agreements. The FASB issued ASU 2014-09 (Topic 606) and the IASB issued IFRS 15. Both statements were titled "Revenue from Contracts with Customers." Although the wording of the two pronouncements was not exactly the same, the requirements were. For example, both statements list the same five-step process to be used to determine when revenue should be recognized:

1. Identify the contract(s) with a customer.
2. Identify the performance obligations in the contract.
3. Determine the transaction price.
4. Allocate the transaction price to the performance obligations in the contract.
5. Recognize revenue when (or as) the entity satisfies a performance obligation.

Although the five steps are worded exactly the same in the two pronouncements, the wording that explains each of these steps is a bit different. Keep in mind that while differences between U.S. GAAP and IFRS exist, the two rule-making bodies are working diligently to keep these differences to a minimum. Therefore, the accounting that you learn in the United States is very relevant to the financial reporting of companies throughout the world.

EXHIBIT 2.4

The Accounting Cycle

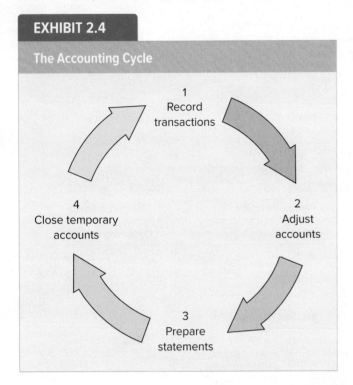

1 Record transactions

2 Adjust accounts

3 Prepare statements

4 Close temporary accounts

After the Year 1 year-end closing the Consulting Revenue and Salary Expense accounts have a zero balance. These temporary accounts are now ready to capture the revenue and expense information for the Year 2 accounting period. At the end of Year 2 they will be closed again. This process will continue for every accounting cycle throughout the life of the business. In other words, the revenue and expense accounts hold information temporarily (for a single accounting period), thereby facilitating the preparation of the annual statements. While not included in this illustration, the Dividend account has these same temporary properties. Notice that after closing, the balance in the Retained Earnings account is equal to the amount shown in the year-end balance sheet. This equality affirms the fact that all temporary accounts have been closed correctly.

An accounting cycle, which is represented graphically in Exhibit 2.4, involves several steps. The four steps identified to this point are (1) recording transactions, (2) adjusting the accounts, (3) preparing financial statements, and (4) closing the temporary accounts. The first step occurs continually throughout the accounting period. Steps 2, 3, and 4 normally occur at the end of the accounting period.

The Matching Concept

Cash basis accounting can distort reported net income because it sometimes fails to match expenses with the revenues they produce. To illustrate, consider the $6,000 of accrued salary expense that Cato Consultants recognized at the end of Year 1. The instructor's teaching produced revenue in Year 1. If Cato waited until Year 2 (when it paid the instructor) to recognize $6,000 of the total $16,000 salary expense, then $6,000 of the expense would not be matched with the revenue it generated. By using accrual accounting, Cato recognized all the salary expense in the same accounting period in which the consulting revenue was recognized. A primary goal of accrual accounting is to appropriately match expenses with revenues, the **matching concept.**

Appropriately matching expenses with revenues can be difficult even when using accrual accounting. For example, consider Cato's advertising expense. Money spent on advertising may generate revenue in future accounting periods as well as in the current period. A prospective customer could save an advertising brochure for several years before calling Cato for training services. It is difficult to know when and to what extent advertising produces revenue. When the connection between an expense and the corresponding revenue is vague, accountants commonly match the expense with the period in which it is incurred. Cato matched (recognized) the entire $2,000 of advertising cost with the Year 1 accounting period even though some of that cost might generate revenue in future accounting periods. Expenses that are matched with the period in which they are incurred are frequently called **period costs.**

Matching is not perfect. Although it would be more accurate to match expenses with revenues than with periods, there is sometimes no obvious direct connection between expenses and revenue. Accountants must exercise judgment to select the accounting period in which to recognize revenues and expenses.

SECTION 2:

SHOW HOW DEFERRALS AFFECT FINANCIAL STATEMENTS

As previously discussed, cash may be exchanged before revenue or expense is recognized. In this case the business defers recognition. This section introduces three common deferrals.

SECOND ACCOUNTING CYCLE

The effects of Cato Consultants's Year 2 events are as follows:

EVENT 1   Cato pays $6,000 to the instructor to settle the salaries payable obligation.

Cash payments to creditors are asset use transactions. When Cato pays the instructor, both the asset account Cash and the liability account Salaries Payable decrease. The event does not affect the income statement. The salary expense was recognized in Year 1 when the instructor taught the classes. Since the cash was paid for salaries of employees that operate the business, the cash outflow is classified as an operating activity. The effects on the financial statements are shown in the following financial statements model.

Balance Sheet							Income Statement				Statement of Cash Flows
Assets	=	Liab.	+		Stk. Equity						
Cash	=	Sal. Pay.	+	C. Stk.	+	R. Earn.	Rev.	−	Exp.	=	Net Inc.	
(6,000)	=	(6,000)	+	NA	+	NA	NA	−	NA	=	NA	(6,000) OA

ACCOUNTING FOR SUPPLIES

EVENT 2   Cato purchases $800 of supplies on account.

The purchase of supplies on account is an asset source transaction. The asset account Supplies and the liability account Accounts Payable increase. Note that this event does not affect the income statement. Expense recognition is deferred until the supplies are used. Also, the statement of cash flows is not affected because the company did not spend cash to purchase the supplies. These effects are shown in the following financial statements model:

LO 2-5

Show how accounting for supplies affects financial statements.

Balance Sheet							Income Statement				Statement of Cash Flows
Assets	=	Liab.	+		Stk. Equity						
Supplies	=	Acct. Pay.	+	C. Stk.	+	R. Earn.	Rev.	−	Exp.	=	Net Inc.	
800	=	800	+	NA	+	NA	NA	−	NA	=	NA	NA

Year-End Adjustment for Supplies

ADJ.1   After determining through a physical count that it has $150 of unused supplies on hand as of December 31, Cato recognizes supplies expense.

If a company were to attempt to record supplies expense each time a pencil, piece of paper, envelope, or other supply item were used, the cost of such tedious recordkeeping would far outweigh its benefits. Instead, accountants transfer to expense the total cost of all supplies used during the entire accounting period in a single year-end adjusting entry. The cost of supplies used is determined as follows:

Beginning balance of supplies	$ 0
Plus: Supplies purchases	800
Supplies available for use	800
Less: Ending balance of supplies	(150)
Supplies used	$ 650

Recognizing Cato's supplies expense is an asset use transaction. The asset account Supplies and the stockholders' equity account Retained Earnings decrease. The recognition of supplies expense would cause the amount of net income shown on the income statement to decrease. Since the expense recognition did not involve the payment of cash, the statement of cash flows is not affected.

Balance Sheet							Income Statement				Statement of Cash Flows
Assets	=	Liab.	+		Stk. Equity						
Supplies	=	Acct. Pay.	+	C. Stk.	+	R. Earn.	Rev.	−	Exp.	=	Net Inc.	
(650)	=	NA	+	NA	+	(650)	NA	−	650	=	(650)	NA

✓ CHECK YOURSELF 2.2

Treadmore Company started the Year 2 accounting period with $580 of supplies on hand. During Year 2, the company paid cash to purchase $2,200 of supplies. A physical count of supplies indicated that there were $420 of supplies on hand at the end of Year 2. Treadmore pays cash for supplies at the time they are purchased. Based on this information alone, determine the amount of supplies expense to be recognized on the income statement and the amount of cash flow to be shown in the operating activities section of the statement of cash flows.

Answer   The amount of supplies expense recognized on the income statement is the amount of supplies that were used during the accounting period. This amount is computed as follows:

$580 Beginning balance + $2,200 Supplies purchases = $2,780 Supplies available for use

$2,780 Supplies available for use − $420 Ending supplies balance = $2,360 Supplies used

The cash flow from operating activities is the amount of cash paid for supplies during the accounting period. In this case, Treadmore paid $2,200 cash to purchase supplies. This amount would be shown as a cash outflow.

ACCOUNTING FOR PREPAID ITEMS

EVENT 3   On March 1, Cato pays $12,000 cash to lease office space for one year beginning immediately.

Accrual accounting draws a distinction between the terms cost and expense. A **cost** might be either an asset or an expense. If a company has already consumed a purchased resource in the process of earning revenue, the cost of the resource is an expense. For example, companies

LO 2-6

Show how accounting for prepaid items affects financial statements.

normally pay for electricity the month after using it. The cost of electric utilities is therefore usually recorded as an expense. In contrast, if a company purchases a resource it will use in the future to generate revenue, the cost of the resource represents an asset. Accountants record such a cost in an asset account and defer recognizing an expense until the resource has been used to produce revenue. Deferring the expense recognition provides more accurate matching of revenues and expenses.

The cost of the office space described in Event 3 is an asset. It is recorded in the asset account Prepaid Rent. Cato expects to benefit from incurring this cost by using the office to generate revenue over the next 12 months. Expense recognition is deferred until Cato actually uses the office space to help generate revenue. Other commonly deferred expenses include prepaid insurance and prepaid taxes. As these titles imply, deferred expenses are frequently called **prepaid items**. Exhibit 2.5 illustrates the relationship between costs, assets, and expenses.

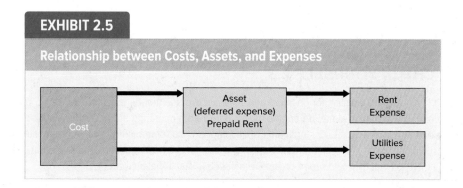

EXHIBIT 2.5

Relationship between Costs, Assets, and Expenses

Purchasing prepaid rent is an asset exchange transaction. The asset account Cash decreases and the asset account Prepaid Rent increases. The amount of total assets is not affected. Note that this event does not affect the income statement. Expense recognition is deferred until the office space is used. Since the cash outflow was incurred to purchase prepaid rent (a short-term asset) that will be used to operate the business, it is classified as an operating activity on the statement of cash flows. The effects of this transaction on the financial statements are shown here:

Balance Sheet								Income Statement				Statement of Cash Flows
Assets		=	Liab.	+	Stk. Equity							
Cash	+ Prepaid Rent	=			Com. Stk.	+	Ret. Earn.	Rev.	− Exp.	=	Net Inc.	
(12,000)	+ 12,000	=	NA	+	NA	+	NA	NA	− NA	=	NA	(12,000) OA

Year-End Adjustment for Prepaid Rent

ADJ.2 **Cato recognizes rent expense for the office space used during the Year 2 accounting period.**

At the end of Year 2, Cato is required to expense the amount of office space that has been used. Recall that Cato paid $12,000 on March 1, Year 2, to rent office space for one year (see Event 3). The portion of the lease cost that represents using office space from March 1 through December 31 is computed as follows:

$12,000 Cost of annual lease ÷ 12 Months = $1,000 Cost per month

$1,000 Cost per month × 10 Months used = $10,000 Rent expense

Recognizing the rent expense decreases the asset account Prepaid Rent and the amount of stockholders' equity. The expense reduces net income shown on the income statement and ultimately the amount of stockholders' equity (retained earnings) shown on the balance sheet. The statement of cash flows is not affected. Recall that the cash flow effect was recorded in Event 3. The effects on the financial statements are as follows:

Balance Sheet										Income Statement					Statement of Cash Flows
Assets			=	Liab.	+		Stk. Equity								
Cash	+	Prepaid Rent	=				Com. Stk.	+	Ret. Earn.	Rev.	−	Exp.	=	Net Inc.	
NA	+	(10,000)	=	NA	+		NA	+	(10,000)	NA	−	10,000	=	(10,000)	NA

Note that while $12,000 cash was paid for rent, only $10,000 of that amount is recognized as an expense in Year 2. The deferral of the additional $2,000 causes a difference between the amounts of cash flow from operating activities versus the amount of net income reported in Year 2.

☑ CHECK YOURSELF 2.3

Rujoub Inc. paid $18,000 cash for one year of insurance coverage that began on November 1, Year 1. Based on this information alone, determine the cash flow from operating activities that Rujoub would report on the Year 1 and Year 2 statements of cash flows. Also, determine the amount of insurance expense Rujoub would report on the Year 1 income statement and the amount of prepaid insurance (an asset) that the company would report on the December 31, Year 1, balance sheet.

Answer   Since Rujoub paid all of the cash in Year 1, the Year 1 statement of cash flows would report an $18,000 cash outflow from operating activities. The Year 2 statement of cash flows would report zero cash flow from operating activities. The expense would be recognized in the periods in which the insurance is used. In this case, insurance expense is recognized at the rate of $1,500 per month ($18,000 ÷ 12 months). Rujoub used two months of insurance coverage in Year 1 and therefore would report $3,000 (2 months × $1,500) of insurance expense on the Year 1 income statement. Rujoub would report a $15,000 (10 months × $1,500) asset, prepaid insurance, on the December 31, Year 1, balance sheet. The $15,000 of prepaid insurance would be recognized as insurance expense in Year 2 when the insurance coverage is used.

ACCOUNTING FOR UNEARNED REVENUE

EVENT 4   Cato receives $18,000 cash in advance from Westberry Company for consulting services Cato agrees to perform over a one-year period beginning June 1, Year 2.

LO 2-7

Show how accounting for unearned revenues affects financial statements.

Cato must defer (delay) recognizing any revenue until it performs the consulting services (does the work) for Westberry. From Cato's point of view, the deferred revenue is a liability because Cato is obligated to perform services in the future. The liability is called **unearned revenue.** The asset account Cash and the liability account Unearned Revenue both increase.

The cash receipt is an asset source transaction. Collecting the cash has no effect on the income statement. The revenue will be reported on the income statement after Cato performs the services. The statement of cash flows reflects a cash inflow from operating activities. The effects of this transaction on the financial statements are shown here:

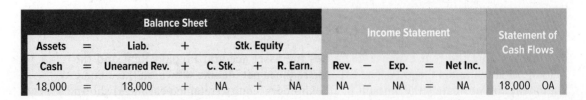

Balance Sheet								Income Statement					Statement of Cash Flows
Assets	=	Liab.	+		Stk. Equity								
Cash	=	Unearned Rev.	+	C. Stk.	+	R. Earn.		Rev.	−	Exp.	=	Net Inc.	
18,000	=	18,000	+	NA	+	NA		NA	−	NA	=	NA	18,000 OA

Year-End Adjustment for Unearned Revenue

ADJ. 3   Cato recognizes the portion of the unearned revenue it earned during the accounting period.

The $18,000 cash advance requires Cato to provide consulting services from June 1, Year 2, to May 31, Year 3. By December 31, Cato has earned 7 months (June 1 through December 31) of the revenue related to this contract. Rather than recording the revenue continuously as the consulting services are being performed, Cato can simply recognize the amount earned in a single adjustment to the accounting records *at the end of the accounting period*. The amount of the adjustment is computed as follows:

$18,000 ÷ 12 months = $1,500 revenue earned per month

$1,500 × 7 months = $10,500 revenue to be recognized in Year 2

The adjusting entry moves $10,500 from the liability Unearned Revenue account to the Consulting Revenue account. This adjusting entry is a claims exchange event. Assets are not affected. On the balance sheet the liabilities decrease and stockholders' equity (retained earnings) increases. Cash flow is not affected by the adjustment. Recall that the impact on cash occurred previously when Cato received the cash from Westberry in Event 4. The effects of this transaction on the financial statements are as follows:

Balance Sheet								Income Statement					Statement of Cash Flows
Assets	=	Liab.	+		Stk. Equity								
Cash	=	Unearned Rev.	+	C. Stk.	+	R. Earn.		Rev.	−	Exp.	=	Net Inc.	
NA	=	(10,500)	+	NA	+	10,500		10,500	−	NA	=	10,500	NA

Recall that revenue was previously defined as an economic benefit a company obtains by providing customers with goods and services. In this case the economic benefit is a decrease in the liability account Unearned Revenue. **Revenue** can therefore be more precisely defined as *an increase in assets or a decrease in liabilities that a company obtains by providing customers with goods or services.*

 CHECK YOURSELF 2.4

Sanderson & Associates received a $24,000 cash advance as a retainer to provide legal services to a client. The contract called for Sanderson to render services during a one-year period beginning October 1, Year 1. Based on this information alone, determine the cash flow from operating activities Sanderson would report on the Year 1 and Year 2 statements of cash flows. Also determine the amount of revenue Sanderson would report on the Year 1 and Year 2 income statements.

Answer Since Sanderson collected all of the cash in Year 1, the Year 1 statement of cash flows would report a $24,000 cash inflow from operating activities. The Year 2 statement of cash flows would report zero cash flow from operating activities. Revenue is recognized in the period in which it is earned. In this case, revenue is earned at the rate of $2,000 per month ($24,000 ÷ 12 months = $2,000 per month). Sanderson rendered services for three months in Year 1 and nine months in Year 2. Sanderson would report $6,000 (3 months × $2,000) of revenue on the Year 1 income statement and $18,000 (9 months × $2,000) of revenue on the Year 2 income statement.

Other Year 2 Events

Cato also experienced the following events during Year 2. The effects of these types of events on the accounting equation and the financial statements have been covered in previous sections of Chapters 1 and 2 and will not be repeated here. However, the transaction data have been recorded in the general ledger accounts shown in Exhibit 2.6. To confirm your understanding you should trace each transaction to the appropriate ledger accounts. The information in the ledger accounts has been labeled with the event or adjusting entry number to simplify the tracing process.

EVENT 5   Provided $96,400 of consulting services on account.

EVENT 6   Collected $105,000 cash from customers as partial settlement of accounts receivable.

EVENT 7   Paid $32,000 cash for salary expense.

EVENT 8   Incurred $21,000 of other operating expenses on account.

EVENT 9   Paid $18,200 in partial settlement of accounts payable.

EVENT 10 Paid $79,500 to purchase land it planned to use in the future as a building site for its home office.

EVENT 11 Paid $21,000 in cash dividends to its stockholders.

EVENT 12 Acquired $2,000 cash from issuing additional shares of common stock.

ADJ. 4   Recognized $4,000 of accrued salary expense.

Summary of Events and General Ledger

The 12 events and 4 adjusting entries Cato Consultants experienced during Year 2 are summarized in Exhibit 2.6. Recall that all adjustments are made at the end of the accounting period so that all account balances are updated prior to their use in preparing the financial statements. Notice that the Year 2 beginning balances shown in the general ledger accounts are derived from the Year 1 ending balances shown in Exhibit 2.3. Likewise, the Year 2 ending balances will become the Year 3 beginning balances. However, the Revenue, Expense, and Dividend account balances do not carry forward because they are designed to capture transaction data for a single accounting period. Therefore, the balances in these accounts are transferred to the Retained Earnings account at the end of the accounting period through the closing process. Prior to closing, the balances in the ledger accounts shown in Exhibit 2.6 are used to prepare the Year 2 financial statements shown in Exhibit 2.7.

EXHIBIT 2.6

Ledger Accounts with Year 2 Transaction Data

1. Cato paid $6,000 to the instructor to settle the salaries payable obligation.
2. Cato purchased $800 of supplies on account.
3. On March 1, Cato paid $12,000 cash to lease office space for one year.
4. Cato received $18,000 cash in advance from Westberry Company for consulting services to be performed for one year beginning June 1.
5. Cato provided $96,400 of consulting services on account.
6. Cato collected $105,000 cash from customers as partial settlement of accounts receivable.
7. Cato paid $32,000 cash for salary expense.
8. Cato incurred $21,000 of other operating expenses on account.
9. Cato paid $18,200 in partial settlement of accounts payable.
10. Cato paid $79,500 to purchase land it planned to use in the future as a building site for its home office.
11. Cato paid $21,000 in cash dividends to its stockholders.
12. Cato acquired $2,000 cash from issuing additional shares of common stock.

The year-end adjustments are:

Adj. 1   After determining through a physical count that it had $150 of unused supplies on hand as of December 31, Cato recognized supplies expense.

Adj. 2   Cato recognized rent expense for the office space used during the accounting period.

Adj. 3   Cato recognized the portion of the unearned revenue it earned during the accounting period.

Adj. 4   Cato recognized $4,000 of accrued salary expense.

| Assets | | | = | Liabilities | + | Stockholders' Equity | |

Cash

Bal.	53,000
(1)	(6,000)
(3)	(12,000)
(4)	18,000
(6)	105,000
(7)	(32,000)
(9)	(18,200)
(10)	(79,500)
(11)	(21,000)
(12)	2,000
Bal.	9,300

Accounts Receivable

Bal.	24,000
(5)	96,400
(6)	(105,000)
Bal.	15,400

Supplies

Bal.	0
(2)	800
Adj. 1	(650)
Bal.	150

Prepaid Rent

Bal.	0
(3)	12,000
Adj. 2	(10,000)
Bal.	2,000

Land

Bal.	0
(10)	79,500
Bal.	79,500

Accounts Payable

Bal.	0
(2)	800
(8)	21,000
(9)	(18,200)
Bal.	3,600

Unearned Revenue

Bal.	0
(4)	18,000
Adj. 3	(10,500)
Bal.	7,500

Salaries Payable

Bal.	6,000
(1)	(6,000)
Adj. 4	4,000
Bal.	4,000

Common Stock

Bal.	5,000
(12)	2,000
Bal.	7,000

Retained Earnings

Bal.	66,000

Dividends

Bal.	0
(11)	(21,000)
Bal.	(21,000)

Consulting Revenue

Bal.	0
(5)	96,400
Adj. 3	10,500
Bal.	106,900

Other Operating Expenses

Bal.	0
(8)	(21,000)
Bal.	(21,000)

Salary Expense

Bal.	0
(7)	(32,000)
Adj. 4	(4,000)
Bal.	(36,000)

Rent Expense

Bal.	0
Adj. 2	(10,000)
Bal.	(10,000)

Supplies Expense

Bal.	0
Adj. 1	(650)
Bal.	(650)

PREPARING FINANCIAL STATEMENTS

Financial statement users obtain helpful insights by analyzing company trends over multiple accounting cycles. Exhibit 2.7 presents for Cato Consultants a multicycle **vertical statements model** of Year 1 and Year 2 accounting data. To conserve space, we have combined all the expenses for each year into single amounts labeled "Operating Expenses," determined as follows:

LO 2-8

Prepare financial statements that include deferrals.

	Year 1	Year 2
Other operating expenses	$ 0	$21,000
Salary expense	16,000	36,000
Rent expense	0	10,000
Advertising expense	2,000	0
Supplies expense	0	650
Total operating expenses	$18,000	$67,650

Similarly, we combined the cash payments for operating expenses on the statement of cash flows as follows:

	Year 1	Year 2
Supplies and other operating expenses	$ 0	$18,200*
Salary expense	10,000	38,000
Rent expense	0	12,000
Advertising expense	2,000	0
Total cash payments for operating expenses	$12,000	$68,200

*Amount paid in partial settlement of accounts payable

Recall that the level of detail reported in financial statements depends on user information needs. Most real-world companies combine many account balances together to report highly summarized totals under each financial statement caption. Before reading further, trace the remaining financial statement items from the ledger accounts in Exhibit 2.6 to where they are reported in Exhibit 2.7.

The vertical statements model in Exhibit 2.7 shows significant interrelationships among the financial statements. For each year, trace the amount of net income from the income statement to the statement of changes in stockholders' equity. Next, trace the ending balances of common stock and retained earnings reported on the statement of changes in stockholders' equity to the stockholders' equity section of the balance sheet. Also, confirm that the amount of cash reported on the balance sheet equals the ending cash balance on the statement of cash flows.

Other relationships connect the two accounting periods. For example, trace the ending retained earnings balance from the Year 1 statement of stockholders' equity to the beginning retained earnings balance on the Year 2 statement of stockholders' equity. Also, trace the ending cash balance on the Year 1 statement of cash flows to the beginning cash balance on the Year 2 statement of cash flows. Finally, confirm that the change in cash between the Year 1 and Year 2 balance sheets ($53,000 − $9,300 = $43,700 decrease) agrees with the net change in cash reported on the Year 2 statement of cash flows.

Closing for the Year 2 Accounting Period

At the end of the Year 2 accounting period the Revenue, Expense, and Dividend accounts would be closed to the Retained Earnings Account. After the closing entries are posted, the balance in the Retained Earnings account is $84,250, which is equal to the amount of retained earnings shown on the Year 2 balance sheet. The after-closing balances in the Revenue, Expense, and Dividend accounts will be zero, which makes them ready to capture information that pertains only to the Year 3 accounting period.

EXHIBIT 2.7	Vertical Statements Model

CATO CONSULTANTS
Financial Statements
Income Statements
For the Years Ended December 31

	Year 1	Year 2
Consulting revenue	$84,000	$106,900
Operating expenses	(18,000)	(67,650)
Net income	$66,000	$ 39,250

(continued)

EXHIBIT 2.7   *Concluded*

Statements of Changes in Stockholders' Equity
For the Years Ended December 31

	Year 1	Year 2
Beginning common stock	$ 0	$ 5,000
Plus: Common stock issued	5,000	2,000
Ending common stock	5,000	7,000
Beginning retained earnings	0	66,000
Plus: Net income	66,000	39,250
Less: Dividends	0	(21,000)
Ending retained earnings	66,000	84,250
Total stockholders' equity	$71,000	$ 91,250

Balance Sheets
As of December 31

	Year 1	Year 2
Assets		
Cash	$53,000	$ 9,300
Accounts receivable	24,000	15,400
Supplies	0	150
Prepaid rent	0	2,000
Land	0	79,500
Total assets	$77,000	$106,350
Liabilities		
Accounts payable	$ 0	$ 3,600
Unearned revenue	0	7,500
Salaries payable	6,000	4,000
Total liabilities	6,000	15,100
Stockholders' equity		
Common stock	5,000	7,000
Retained earnings	66,000	84,250
Total stockholders' equity	71,000	91,250
Total liabilities and stockholders' equity	$77,000	$106,350

Statements of Cash Flows
For the Years Ended December 31

	Year 1	Year 2
Cash Flows from Operating Activities		
Cash receipts from customers	$60,000	$123,000
Cash payments for operating expenses	(12,000)	(68,200)
Net cash flow from operating activities	48,000	54,800
Cash Flows from Investing Activities		
Cash payment to purchase land	0	(79,500)
Cash Flows from Financing Activities		
Cash receipts from issuing common stock	5,000	2,000
Cash payments for dividends	0	(21,000)
Net cash flow from financing activities	5,000	(19,000)
Net change in cash	53,000	(43,700)
Plus: Beginning cash balance	0	53,000
Ending cash balance	$53,000	$ 9,300

REALITY BYTES

WHY DID THAT BIG EXPENSE CAUSE THE STOCK PRICE TO RISE?

If you follow business news, which you should if you are a business major, you have probably heard about a company reporting a big write-off of assets, sometimes called a "special charge." Such an announcement sends a signal to readers that the company's earnings will decrease as a result of the write-off. However, in many cases, this seemingly bad news does not cause the company's stock price to fall; in fact, it sometimes causes it to increase. Why?

Linda Parton/Shutterstock

Consider the following January 27, 2018, announcement from General Motors Company (GM) related to its plans to close several plants and eliminate almost 15,000 jobs:

On November 20, 2018, the General Motors Company . . . Board of Directors approved a plan to accelerate the Company's transformation for the future (the "Plan"). The Plan is expected to strengthen the Company's core business, capitalize on the future of personal mobility, and drive significant cost efficiencies, and it consists, in relevant part, of (i) restructuring the Global Product Development Group, (ii) realigning current manufacturing capacity and utilization, and (iii) reducing salaried and contract staff and capital expenditures. These actions are expected to be substantially completed by the end of 2019.

The Company expects to record pre-tax charges of $3.0 billion to $3.8 billion related to these actions, including up to $1.8 billion of non-cash accelerated asset write-downs and pension charges, and up to $2.0 billion of employee-related and other cash-based expenses.

Despite this seemingly bad financial news about a reduction in earnings of over $3 billion, GM's stock price increased by 4.8 percent on the day of the announcement, while the overall market was up only 1.5 percent.

There are at least a couple of reasons why this seeming bad news may have a positive impact on a company's stock price. First, while write-offs do decrease earnings, they often do not decrease the company's cash flows, and cash flow is at least as important to investors as earnings. Much of GM's special charge did not increase its cash outflows.

The second reason that writing off assets can have a positive effect on a company's stock price is because extra expenses that are recognized today may mean there will be less expenses recognized in the future; thus, future earnings will be higher than they otherwise would have been. This subject will be explained further in later chapters, but keep in mind that investors are more interested in the future than they are in the past, so lower current earnings that lead to higher future earnings is often viewed as good news.

So, when you hear a company make a big announcement about its business, always ask yourself two questions: How does this event affect cash flows? And, how will this event affect future earnings?

Answers to The Curious Accountant

Because the Meredith Corporation receives cash from customers before actually sending any magazines to them, the company has not earned any revenue when it receives the cash. Meredith has a liability called *unearned revenue*. If Meredith closed its books on December 31, then $3 of the subscription would be recognized as revenue in 2020. The remaining $9 would appear on the balance sheet as a liability.

Meredith actually ends its accounting year on June 30 each year. The June 30, 2018, balance sheet for the company is presented in Exhibit 2.8. The liability for unearned revenue was $484.5 million ($360.4 + $124.1)—which represented about 9.5 percent (484.5 ÷ 5,107.1) of total liabilities.

Will Meredith need cash to pay these subscription liabilities? Not exactly. The liabilities will not be paid directly with cash. Instead, they will be satisfied by providing magazines to the subscribers. However, Meredith will need cash to pay for producing and distributing the magazines supplied to the customers. Even so, the amount of cash required to provide magazines will probably differ significantly from the amount of unearned revenues. In most cases, subscription fees do not cover the cost of producing and distributing magazines. By collecting significant amounts of advertising revenue, publishers can provide magazines to customers at prices well below the cost of publication. The amount of unearned revenue is not likely to coincide with the amount of cash needed to cover the cost of satisfying the company's obligation to produce and distribute magazines. Even though the association between unearned revenues and the cost of providing magazines to customers is not direct, a knowledgeable financial analyst can use the information to make estimates of future cash flows and revenue recognition.

EXHIBIT 2.8	Balance Sheet for Meredith Corporation

MEREDITH CORPORATION AND SUBSIDIARIES
Consolidated Balance Sheets
As of June 30 (amounts in millions)

	2018	2017
Assets		
Current assets		
Cash and cash equivalents	$ 437.6	$ 22.3
Accounts receivable (net of allowances of $14.4 in 2018 and $8.0 in 2017)	542.0	289.1
Inventories	44.2	21.9
Current portion of subscription acquisition costs	118.1	145.0
Current portion of broadcast rights	9.8	7.8
Other current assets	713.1	—
Assets held for sale	114.3	19.3
Total current assets	1,979.1	505.4
Property, plant, and equipment		
Land	$ 24.6	$ 24.7
Buildings and improvements	153.5	153.7
Machinery and equipment	359.8	316.6
Leasehold improvements	177.4	14.3
Capitalized software	125.9	38.5
Construction in progress	20.2	1.7
Total property, plant, and equipment	861.4	549.5
Less accumulated depreciation	(377.6)	(359.7)
Net property, plant, and equipment	483.8	189.8
Subscription acquisition costs	61.1	79.7
Broadcast rights	18.9	21.8
Other assets	263.3	69.6
Intangible assets, net	2,005.2	955.9
Goodwill	1,915.8	907.5
Total assets	$6,727.2	$2,729.7
Liabilities and shareholders' equity		
Current liabilities		
Current portion of long-term debt	$ 17.7	$ 62.5
Current portion of long-term broadcast rights payable	8.9	9.2
Accounts payable	194.7	66.6
Accrued expenses		
Compensation and benefits	122.3	69.0
Distribution expenses	10.0	5.3
Other taxes and expenses	277.9	28.1
Total accrued expenses	410.2	102.4
Current portion of unearned revenues	360.4	219.0
Liabilities associated with assets held for sale	198.4	—
Total current liabilities	1,190.3	459.7
Long-term debt	3,117.9	635.7
Long-term broadcast rights payable	20.8	22.5
Unearned revenues	124.1	106.5
Deferred income taxes	437.0	384.7
Other noncurrent liabilities	217.0	124.6
Total liabilities	5,107.1	1,733.7
Redeemable convertible Series A preferred stock, par value $1 per share, $1,000 per share liquidation preference	522.6	—
Shareholders' equity		
Series preferred stock, par value $1 per share	—	—
Common stock, par value $1 per share	39.8	39.4
Class B stock, par value $1 per share, convertible to common stock	5.1	5.1
Additional paid-in capital	199.5	54.8
Retained earnings	889.8	915.7
Accumulated other comprehensive (loss)	(36.7)	(19.0)
Total shareholders' equity	1,097.5	996.0
Total liabilities and shareholders' equity	$6,727.2	$2,729.7

TRANSACTION CLASSIFICATION

LO 2-9

Classify accounting events into one of four categories.

Chapters 1 and 2 introduced four types of transactions. Although businesses engage in an infinite number of different transactions, all transactions fall into one of four types. By learning to identify transactions by type, you can understand how unfamiliar events affect financial statements. The four types of transactions are

1. *Asset source transactions:* An asset account increases, and a corresponding claims account increases.

2. *Asset use transactions:* An asset account decreases, and a corresponding claims account decreases.

3. *Asset exchange transactions:* One asset account increases, and another asset account decreases.

4. *Claims exchange transactions:* One claims account increases, and another claims account decreases.

You should review the classifications for the Year 1 and Year 2 transactions for Cato Consultants that are shown in Exhibit 2.9. The column titled "Type" uses the following abbreviations: Asset Source is "AS"; Asset Use is "AU"; Asset Exchange is "AE"; Claims Exchange is "CE"; and Not Applicable is "NA."

EXHIBIT 2.9

Event Classification for Cato Consultants' Year 1 Transactions

Event	Description	Type
1	Cato Consultants acquired $5,000 cash by issuing common stock.	AS
2	Cato provided $84,000 of consulting services on account.	AS
3	Cato collected $60,000 cash from customers in partial settlement of its accounts receivable.	AE
4	Cato paid $10,000 cash for salary expense.	AU
5	Cato paid $2,000 cash for Year 1 advertising costs.	AU
6	Cato signed contracts for $42,000 of consulting services to be performed in Year 2.	NA
7 Adj.	Cato recognized $6,000 of accrued salary expense.	CE
Cl. 1,2,3	Closing entries.	CE

Event Classification for Cato Consultants' Year 2 Transactions

Event	Description	Type
1	Cato pays $6,000 to the instructor to settle the salaries payable obligation.	AU
2	Cato purchases $800 of supplies on account.	AS
Adj. 1	After determining through a physical count that it has $150 of unused supplies on hand as of December 31, Cato recognizes supplies expense.	AU
3	On March 1, Cato pays $12,000 cash to lease office space for one year beginning immediately.	AE
Adj. 2	Cato recognizes rent expense for the office space used during the Year 2 accounting period.	AU
4	Cato receives $18,000 cash in advance from Westberry Company for consulting services Cato agrees to perform over a one-year period beginning June 1, Year 2.	AS
Adj. 3	Cato recognizes the portion of the unearned revenue it earned during the accounting period.	CE
5	Provided $96,400 of consulting services on account.	AS
6	Collected $105,000 cash from customers as partial settlement of accounts receivable.	AE
7	Paid $32,000 cash for salary expense.	AU
8	Incurred $21,000 of other operating expenses on account.	CE
9	Paid $18,200 in partial settlement of accounts payable.	AU
10	Paid $79,500 to purchase land it planned to use in the future as a building site for its home office.	AE
11	Paid $21,000 in cash dividends to its stockholders.	AU
12	Acquired $2,000 cash from issuing additional shares of common stock.	AS
Adj. 4	Recognized $4,000 of accrued salary expense.	CE
Cl.	Closing entries.	CE

This chapter introduced the *accrual accounting* concept. Accrual accounting causes the amount of revenues and expenses reported on the income statement to differ significantly from the amount of cash flow from operating activities reported on the statement of cash flows because of timing differences. These differences are readily apparent when relevant events are recorded in a horizontal financial statements model. To review, study the following transactions and the corresponding statements model. Set up a statements model on a piece of paper and try to record the effects of each event before reading the explanation.

Events

1. Provided $600 of services on account.
2. Collected $400 cash from accounts receivable.
3. Accrued $350 of salary expense.
4. Paid $225 cash in partial settlement of salaries payable.

Event No.	Balance Sheet								Income Statement					Statement of Cash Flows	
	Cash	+	Accts. Rec.	=	Sal. Pay.	+	Ret. Earn.		Rev.	−	Exp.	=	Net Inc.		
1	NA	+	600	=	NA	+	600		600	−	NA	=	600	NA	
2	400	+	(400)	=	NA	+	NA		NA	−	NA	=	NA	400	OA
3	NA	+	NA	=	350	+	(350)		NA	−	350	=	(350)	NA	
4	(225)	+	NA	=	(225)	+	NA		NA	−	NA	=	NA	(225)	OA
Totals	175	+	200	=	125	+	250		600	−	350	=	250	175	NC

Notice the $250 of net income differs from the $175 cash flow from operating activities. The entries in the statements model demonstrate the reasons for the difference. Although $600 of revenue is recognized, only $400 of cash was collected. The remaining $200 will be collected in the future and is currently shown on the balance sheet as Accounts Receivable. Also, although $350 of salary expense is recognized, only $225 was paid in cash. The remaining $125 will be paid in the future. This obligation is shown as Salaries Payable on the balance sheet. Study these relationships carefully to develop a clear understanding of how accrual accounting affects financial reporting.

Also, the definitions of revenue and expense have been expanded. The complete definitions of these two elements are as follows:

1. **Revenue:** Revenue is the *economic benefit* derived from operating the business. Its recognition is accompanied by an increase in assets or a decrease in liabilities resulting from providing products or services to customers.

2. **Expense:** An expense is an *economic sacrifice* incurred in the process of generating revenue. Its recognition is accompanied by a decrease in assets or an increase in liabilities resulting from consuming assets and services in an effort to produce revenue.

A Look Forward >>

Chapters 1 and 2 focused on businesses that generate revenue by providing services to their customers. Examples of these types of businesses include consulting, real estate sales, medical services, and legal services. The next chapter introduces accounting practices for businesses that generate revenue by selling goods. Examples of these companies include Walmart, Abercrombie & Fitch, Office Depot, and Lowes.

Video lectures and accompanying self-assessment quizzes are available in *Connect* for all learning objectives.

SELF-STUDY REVIEW PROBLEM

Gifford Company experienced the following accounting events during Year 1:

1. Started operations on January 1 when it acquired $20,000 cash by issuing common stock.
2. Earned $18,000 of revenue on account.
3. On March 1 collected $36,000 cash as an advance for services to be performed in the future.
4. Paid cash operating expenses of $17,000.
5. Paid a $2,700 cash dividend to stockholders.
6. On December 31, Year 1, adjusted the books to recognize the revenue earned by providing services related to the advance described in Event 3. The contract required Gifford to provide services for a one-year period starting March 1.
7. Collected $15,000 cash from accounts receivable.

Gifford Company experienced the following accounting events during Year 2:

1. Recognized $38,000 of cash revenue.
2. On April 1, paid $12,000 cash for an insurance policy that provides coverage for one year beginning immediately.
3. Collected $2,000 cash from accounts receivable.
4. Paid cash operating expenses of $21,000.
5. Paid a $5,000 cash dividend to stockholders.
6. On December 31, Year 2, adjusted the books to recognize the remaining revenue earned by providing services related to the advance described in Event 3 of Year 1.
7. On December 31, Year 2, Gifford adjusted the books to recognize the amount of the insurance policy used during Year 2.

Required

a. Record the events in a financial statements model like the following one. The first event is recorded as an example.

	Balance Sheet								Income Statement			Statement of Cash Flows
	Assets			=	Liab.	+	Stk. Equity					
Event No.	Cash	+ Accts. Rec.	+ Prep. Ins.	=	Unearn. Rev.	+	Com. Stk.	+ Ret. Earn.	Rev.	− Exp.	= Net Inc.	
1	20,000 +	NA	+ NA	=	NA	+	20,000	+ NA	NA	− NA	= NA	20,000 FA

b. What amount of revenue would Gifford report on the Year 1 income statement?
c. What amount of cash flow from customers would Gifford report on the Year 1 statement of cash flows?
d. What amount of unearned revenue would Gifford report on the Year 1 and Year 2 year-end balance sheets?
e. What are the Year 2 opening balances for the revenue and expense accounts?
f. What amount of total assets would Gifford report on the December 31, Year 1, balance sheet?
g. What obligations and commitments would Gifford report on the December 31, Year 2, balance sheet?

Solution to Requirement *a*

The financial statements model follows:

Event No.	Balance Sheet														Income Statement						Statement of Cash Flows	
	Assets					=	Liab.	+	Stk. Equity						Rev.	−	Exp.	=	Net Inc.			
	Cash	+	Accts. Rec.	+	Prep. Ins.	=	Unearn. Rev.	+	Com. Stk.	+	Ret. Earn.											
Year 1																						
1	20,000	+	NA	+	NA	=	NA	+	20,000	+	NA				NA	−	NA	=	NA		20,000	FA
2	NA	+	18,000	+	NA	=	NA	+	NA	+	18,000				18,000	−	NA	=	18,000		NA	
3	36,000	+	NA	+	NA	=	36,000	+	NA	+	NA				NA	−	NA	=	NA		36,000	OA
4	(17,000)	+	NA	+	NA	=	NA	+	NA	+	(17,000)				NA	−	17,000	=	(17,000)		(17,000)	OA
5	(2,700)	+	NA	+	NA	=	NA	+	NA	+	(2,700)				NA	−	NA	=	NA		(2,700)	FA
6*	NA	+	NA	+	NA	=	(30,000)	+	NA	+	30,000				30,000	−	NA	=	30,000		NA	
7	15,000	+	(15,000)	+	NA	=	NA	+	NA	+	NA				NA	−	NA	=	NA		15,000	OA
Bal.	51,300	+	3,000	+	NA	=	6,000	+	20,000	+	28,300				48,000	−	17,000	=	31,000		51,300	NC
	Asset, liability, and stockholders' equity account balances carry forward														Rev. & exp. accts. are closed							
Year 2																						
Bal.	51,300	+	3,000	+	NA	=	6,000	+	20,000	+	28,300				NA	−	NA	=	NA		NA	
1	38,000	+	NA	+	NA	=	NA	+	NA	+	38,000				38,000	−	NA	=	38,000		38,000	OA
2	(12,000)	+	NA	+	12,000	=	NA	+	NA	+	NA				NA	−	NA	=	NA		(12,000)	OA
3	2,000	+	(2,000)	+	NA	=	NA	+	NA	+	NA				NA	−	NA	=	NA		2,000	OA
4	(21,000)	+	NA	+	NA	=	NA	+	NA	+	(21,000)				NA	−	21,000	=	(21,000)		(21,000)	OA
5	(5,000)	+	NA	+	NA	=	NA	+	NA	+	(5,000)				NA	−	NA	=	NA		(5,000)	FA
6*	NA	+	NA	+	NA	=	(6,000)	+	NA	+	6,000				6,000	−	NA	=	6,000		NA	
7†	NA	+	NA	+	(9,000)	=	NA	+	NA	+	(9,000)				NA	−	9,000	=	(9,000)		NA	
Bal.	53,300	+	1,000	+	3,000	=	0	+	20,000	+	37,300				44,000	−	30,000	=	14,000		2,000	NC

*Revenue is earned at the rate of $3,000 ($36,000/12 months) per month. Revenue recognized in Year 1 is $30,000 ($3,000 × 10 months). Revenue recognized in Year 2 is $6,000 ($3,000 × 2 months).

†Insurance expense is incurred at the rate of $1,000 ($12,000/12 months) per month. Insurance expense recognized in Year 2 is $9,000 ($1,000 × 9 months).

Solutions to Requirements *b–g*

b. Gifford would report $48,000 of revenue in Year 1 ($18,000 revenue on account plus $30,000 of the $36,000 of unearned revenue).

c. The cash inflow from customers in Year 1 is $51,000 ($36,000 when the unearned revenue was received plus $15,000 collection of accounts receivable).

d. The December 31, Year 1, balance sheet will report $6,000 of unearned revenue, which is the amount of the cash advance less the amount of revenue recognized in Year 1 ($36,000 − $30,000). The December 31, Year 2, unearned revenue balance is zero.

e. Since revenue and expense accounts are closed at the end of each accounting period, the beginning balances in these accounts are always zero.

f. Assets on the December 31, Year 1, balance sheet are $54,300 [Gifford's cash at year-end plus the balance in accounts receivable ($51,300 + $3,000)].

g. Since all unearned revenue would be recognized before the financial statements were prepared at the end of Year 2, there would be no liabilities on the Year 2 balance sheet. In this case, all of the assets are committed to the investors.

KEY TERMS

Accounts receivable 51	Asset exchange	Cost 60	Revenue 63
Accrual 49	transaction 51	Deferral 50	Salaries payable 53
Accrual accounting 49	Asset source transaction 50	Expense 54	Unearned revenue 62
Accrued expenses 52	Asset use transaction 51	Matching concept 58	Vertical statements
Adjusting entry 53	Claims exchange	Period costs 58	model 65
	transaction 53	Prepaid items 61	

QUESTIONS

1. What does accrual accounting attempt to accomplish?

2. Define *recognition*. How is it independent of collecting or paying cash?

3. What does the term *deferral* mean?

4. If cash is collected in advance of performing services, when is the associated revenue recognized?

5. What does the term *asset source transaction* mean?

6. What effect does the issue of common stock have on the accounting equation?

7. How does the recognition of revenue on account (accounts receivable) affect the income statement compared to its effect on the statement of cash flows?

8. Give an example of an asset source transaction. What is the effect of this transaction on the accounting equation?

9. When is revenue recognized under accrual accounting?

10. Give an example of an asset exchange transaction. What is the effect of this transaction on the accounting equation?

11. What is the effect on the right side of the accounting equation when cash is collected in advance of performing services?

12. What does the term *unearned revenue* mean?

13. What effect does expense recognition have on the accounting equation?

14. What does the term *claims exchange transaction* mean?

15. What type of transaction is a cash payment to creditors? How does this type of transaction affect the accounting equation?

16. When are expenses recognized under accrual accounting?

17. Why may net cash flow from operating activities on the cash flow statement be different from the amount of net income

reported on the income statement?

18. What is the relationship between the income statement and changes in assets and liabilities?

19. How does net income affect the stockholders' claims on the business's assets?

20. What is the difference between a cost and an expense?

21. When does a cost become an expense? Do all costs become expenses?

22. How and when is the cost of the *supplies used* recognized in an accounting period?

23. What does the term *expense* mean?

24. What does the term *revenue* mean?

25. What is the purpose of the statement of changes in stockholders' equity?

26. What is the main purpose of the balance sheet?

27. Why is the balance sheet dated *as of* a specific date when the income statement, statement of changes in stockholders' equity, and statement of cash flows are dated with the phrase *for the period ended*?

28. In what order are assets listed on the balance sheet?

29. What does the statement of cash flows explain?

30. What does the term *adjusting entry* mean? Give an example.

31. What types of accounts are closed at the end of the accounting period? Why is it necessary to close these accounts?

32. Give several examples of period costs.

33. Give an example of a cost that can be directly matched with the revenue produced by an accounting firm from preparing a tax return.

34. List and describe the four stages of the accounting cycle discussed earlier in this chapter.

SECTION 1 EXERCISES—SERIES A

connect An electronic auto-gradable version of the Series A Exercises is available in Connect. A PDF version of Series B Exercises is in Connect under the "Additional Student Resources" tab. Solutions to the Series B Exercises are available in Connect under the "Instructor Library" tab. Instructor and student Workpapers for the Series B Exercises are available in Connect under the "Instructor Library" and "Additional Student Resources" tabs respectively.

Where applicable in all exercises, round computations to the nearest dollar.

LO 2-1

Exercise 2-1A *Effect of collecting accounts receivable on the accounting equation and financial statements*

Holloway Company earned $18,000 of service revenue on account during Year 1. The company collected $14,000 cash from accounts receivable during Year 1.

Required

Based on this information alone, determine the following for Holloway Company. (*Hint:* Record the events in general ledger accounts under an accounting equation before satisfying the requirements.)

a. The balance of the accounts receivable that would be reported on the December 31, Year 1, balance sheet.

b. The amount of net income that would be reported on the Year 1 income statement.

c. The amount of net cash flow from operating activities that would be reported on the Year 1 statement of cash flows.

d. The amount of retained earnings that would be reported on the Year 1 balance sheet.

e. Why are the answers to Requirements *b* and *c* different?

Exercise 2-2A   *Effect of accrued expenses on the accounting equation and financial statements*

LO 2-2, 2-3

During Year 1, Chung Corporation earned $8,000 of cash revenue and accrued $5,000 of salaries expense.

Required

(*Hint:* Record the events in general ledger accounts under an accounting equation before satisfying the requirements.) Based on this information alone:

a. Prepare the December 31, Year 1, balance sheet.

b. Determine the amount of net income that Chung would report on the Year 1 income statement.

c. Determine the amount of net cash flow from operating activities that Chung would report on the Year 1 statement of cash flows.

d. Why are the answers to Requirements *b* and *c* different?

Exercise 2-3A   *Effect of accruals on the financial statements*

LO 2-1, 2-2, 2-3

Milea Inc. experienced the following events in Year 1, its first year of operations:

1. Received $20,000 cash from the issue of common stock.
2. Performed services on account for $56,000.
3. Paid the utility expense of $2,500.
4. Collected $48,000 of the accounts receivable.
5. Recorded $10,000 of accrued salaries at the end of the year.
6. Paid a $2,000 cash dividend to the stockholders.

Required

a. Record the events in general ledger accounts under an accounting equation. In the last column of the table, provide appropriate account titles for the Retained Earnings amounts. The first transaction has been recorded as an example.

					Milea Inc.			
					Accounting Equation			
		Assets	=	Liabilities	+	Stockholders' Equity		Acct. Titles for Ret. Earn.
Event No.	Cash	Accounts Receivable		Salaries Payable		Common Stock	Retained Earnings	
1.	20,000					20,000		

b. Prepare the income statement, statement of changes in stockholders' equity, balance sheet, and statement of cash flows for the Year 1 accounting period.

c. Why is the amount of net income different from the amount of net cash flow from operating activities?

LO 2-1, 2-2

Exercise 2-4A *Effect of accounts receivable and accounts payable transactions on financial statements*

The following events apply to Lewis and Harper, a public accounting firm, for the Year 1 accounting period:

1. Performed $70,000 of services for clients on account.
2. Performed $40,000 of services for cash.
3. Incurred $36,000 of other operating expenses on account.
4. Paid $10,000 cash to an employee for salary.
5. Collected $47,000 cash from accounts receivable.
6. Paid $16,000 cash on accounts payable.
7. Paid an $8,000 cash dividend to the stockholders.
8. Accrued salaries were $2,000 at the end of Year 1.

Required

a. Show the effects of the events on the financial statements using a horizontal statements model like the following one. In the Cash Flow column, use OA to designate operating activity, IA for investing activity, FA for financing activity, and NC for net change in cash. Use NA to indicate the element is not affected by the event. The first event is recorded as an example.

			Balance Sheet						Income Statement				Statement of Cash Flows
			Assets	=	Liabilities	+	Equity						
Event No.	Cash	+	Accts. Rec.	=	Accts. Pay.	+	Sal. Pay	+	Ret. Earn.	Rev.	−	Exp.	=	Net Inc.	
1.	NA	+	70,000	=	NA	+	NA	+	70,000	70,000	−	NA	=	70,000	NA

b. What is the amount of total assets at the end of Year 1?
c. What is the balance of accounts receivable at the end of Year 1?
d. What is the balance of accounts payable at the end of Year 1?
e. What is the difference between accounts receivable and accounts payable?
f. What is net income for Year 1?
g. What is the amount of net cash flow from operating activities for Year 1?

LO 2-1, 2-2

Exercise 2-5A *Missing information related to accruals*

Castile Inc. had a beginning balance of $4,000 in its Accounts Receivable account. The ending balance of Accounts Receivable was $4,500. During the period, Castile recognized $68,000 of revenue on account. Castile's Salaries Payable account has a beginning balance of $2,600 and an ending balance of $1,500. During the period, the company recognized $46,000 of accrued salary expense.

Required

a. Based on the information provided, determine the amount of net income.
b. Based on the information provided, determine the amount of net cash flow from operating activities.

LO 2-1, 2-2, 2-4

Exercise 2-6A *Effect of accruals on the financial statements*

Cordell Inc. experienced the following events in Year 1, its first year of operation:

1. Received $40,000 cash from the issue of common stock.
2. Performed services on account for $82,000.
3. Paid a $6,000 cash dividend to the stockholders.
4. Collected $76,000 of the accounts receivable.
5. Paid $53,000 cash for other operating expenses.
6. Performed services for $19,000 cash.
7. Recognized $3,500 of accrued utilities expense at the end of the year.

Required

a. Identify the events that result in revenue or expense recognition.

b. Based on your response to Requirement *a*, determine the amount of net income reported on the Year 1 income statement.

c. Identify the events that affect the statement of cash flows.

d. Based on your response to Requirement *c*, determine the amount of cash flow from operating activities reported on the Year 1 statement of cash flows.

e. What is the before- and after-closing balance in the Service Revenue account? What other accounts would be closed at the end of the accounting cycle?

f. What is the balance of the Retained Earnings account that appears on the Year 1 balance sheet?

Exercise 2-7A   *Net income versus changes in cash*

LO 2-1, 2-2

In Year 1, Lee Inc. billed its customers $62,000 for services performed. The company collected $51,000 of the amount billed. Lee incurred $39,000 of other operating expenses on account. Lee paid $31,000 of the accounts payable. Lee acquired $40,000 cash from the issue of common stock. The company invested $21,000 cash in the purchase of land.

Required

(*Hint:* Identify the six events described in the paragraph and record them in general ledger accounts under an accounting equation before attempting to answer the questions.) Use the preceding information to answer the following questions:

a. What amount of revenue will Lee report on the Year 1 income statement?

b. What amount of cash flow from revenue will be reported on the statement of cash flows?

c. What is the net income for the period?

d. What is the net cash flow from operating activities for the period?

e. Why is the amount of net income different from the net cash flow from operating activities for the period?

f. What is the amount of net cash flow from investing activities?

g. What is the amount of net cash flow from financing activities?

h. What amounts of total assets, liabilities, and equity will be reported on the year-end balance sheet?

SECTION 2 EXERCISES

Exercise 2-8A   *Supplies and the financial statements model*

LO 2-5

Pizza Express Inc. began the Year 2 accounting period with $2,500 cash, $1,400 of common stock, and $1,100 of retained earnings. Pizza Express was affected by the following accounting events during Year 2:

1. Purchased $3,600 of supplies on account.

2. Earned and collected $12,300 of cash revenue.

3. Paid $2,700 cash on accounts payable.

4. Adjusted the records to reflect the use of supplies. A physical count indicated that $250 of supplies was still on hand on December 31, Year 2.

Required

a. Show the effects of the events on the financial statements using a horizontal statements model like the following one. In the Cash Flows column, use OA to designate operating activity, IA for investing activity, FA for financing activity, and NC for net change in cash. Use NA to indicate accounts not affected by the event. The beginning balances are entered in the following example:

	Balance Sheet									Income Statement					Statement of Cash Flows
	Assets			=	Liab.	+	Stk. Equity								
Event No.	Cash	+	Supplies	=	Accts. Pay.	+	Com. Stk	+	Ret. Earn.	Rev.	−	Exp.	=	Net Inc.	
Beg. bal.	2,500	+	0	=	0	+	1,400	+	1,100	0	−	0	=	0	0

b. Explain the difference between the amount of net income and amount of net cash flow from operating activities.

LO 2-5, 2-8

Exercise 2-9A   *Supplies on financial statements*

Yard Professionals Inc. experienced the following events in Year 1, its first year of operation:

1. Performed services for $35,000 cash.
2. Purchased $6,000 of supplies on account.
3. A physical count on December 31, Year 1, found that there was $1,800 of supplies on hand.

Required

Based on this information alone:

a. Record the events under an accounting equation.
b. Prepare an income statement, balance sheet, and statement of cash flows for the Year 1 accounting period.
c. What is the balance in the Supplies account as of January 1, Year 2?
d. What is the balance in the Supplies Expense account as of January 1, Year 2?

LO 2-5, 2-6

Exercise 2-10A   *Asset versus expense*

A cost can be either an asset or an expense.

Required

a. Distinguish between a cost that is an asset and a cost that is an expense.
b. List three costs that are assets.
c. List three costs that are expenses.

LO 2-6, 2-8

Exercise 2-11A   *Prepaid items on financial statements*

Life, Inc., experienced the following events in Year 1, its first year of operation:

1. Performed counseling services for $36,000 cash.
2. On February 1, Year 1, paid $18,000 cash to rent office space for the coming year.
3. Adjusted the accounts to reflect the amount of rent used during the year.

Required

Based on this information alone:

a. Record the events under an accounting equation.
b. Prepare an income statement, balance sheet, and statement of cash flows for the Year 1 accounting period.
c. Ignoring all other future events, what is the amount of rent expense that would be recognized in Year 2?

LO 2-6

Exercise 2-12A   *Effect of an error on financial statements*

On April 1, Year 2, Maine Corporation paid $18,000 cash in advance for a one-year lease on an office building. Assume that Maine records the prepaid rent as an asset and that the books are closed on December 31.

Required

a. Show the payment for the one-year lease and the related adjusting entry to recognize rent expense in the accounting equation.
b. Assume that Maine Corporation failed to record the adjusting entry to reflect using the office building. How would the error affect the company's Year 2 income statement and balance sheet?

Exercise 2-13A Unearned items on financial statements

Yard Designs (YD) experienced the following events in Year 1, its first year of operation:

1. On October 1, Year 1, YD collected $54,000 for consulting services it agreed to provide during the coming year.
2. Adjusted the accounts to reflect the amount of consulting service revenue recognized in Year 1.

Required

Based on this information alone:

a. Record the events under an accounting equation.
b. Prepare an income statement, balance sheet, and statement of cash flows for the Year 1 accounting period.
c. Ignoring all other future events, what is the amount of service revenue that would be recognized in Year 2?

Exercise 2-14A Unearned revenue defined as a liability

Lan, an accounting major, and Pat, a marketing major, are watching a *Matlock* rerun on late-night TV. Of course, there is a murder and the suspect wants to hire Matlock as the defense attorney. Matlock will take the case but requires an advance payment of $150,000. Pat remarks that Matlock has earned a cool $150,000 without lifting a finger. Lan tells Pat that Matlock has not earned anything but has a $150,000 liability. Pat asks, "How can that be?"

Required

Assume you are Lan. Explain to Pat why Matlock has a liability and when Matlock would actually earn the $150,000.

Exercise 2-15A Supplies, unearned revenue, and the financial statements model

Hart, Attorney at Law, experienced the following transactions in Year 1, the first year of operations:

1. Accepted $36,000 on April 1, Year 1, as a retainer for services to be performed evenly over the next 12 months.
2. Performed legal services for cash of $54,000.
3. Purchased $2,800 of office supplies on account.
4. Paid $2,400 of the amount due on accounts payable.
5. Paid a cash dividend to the stockholders of $5,000.
6. Paid cash for operating expenses of $31,000.
7. Determined that at the end of the accounting period $200 of office supplies remained on hand.
8. On December 31, Year 1, recognized the revenue that had been earned for services performed in accordance with Transaction 1.

Required

Show the effects of the events on the financial statements using a horizontal statements model like the following one. In the Cash Flows column, use the initials OA to designate operating activity, IA for investing activity, FA for financing activity, and NC for net change in cash. Use NA to indicate accounts not affected by the event. The first event has been recorded as an example.

Event No.			Balance Sheet						Income Statement					Statement of Cash Flows
	Assets		=	Liabilities		+	Stk. Equity		Rev.	−	Exp.	=	Net Inc.	
	Cash	+ Supplies	=	Accts. Pay.	+ Unearn. Rev.	+	Ret. Earn.							
1	36,000	+ NA	=	NA	+ 36,000	+	NA		NA	− NA	=	NA		36,000 OA

LO 2-7

Exercise 2-16A *Unearned revenue and the financial statements model*

Clark Bell started a personal financial planning business when he accepted $36,000 cash as advance payment for managing the financial assets of a large estate. Bell agreed to manage the estate for a one-year period beginning June 1, Year 1.

Required

a. Show the effects of the advance payment and revenue recognition on the Year 1 financial statements using a horizontal statements model like the following one. In the Cash Flows column, use OA to designate operating activity, IA for investing activity, FA for financing activity, and NC for net change in cash. Use NA if the account is not affected.

	Balance Sheet					Income Statement			Statement of Cash Flows
	Assets	=	Liab.	+	Stk. Equity				
Event	Cash	=	Unearn. Rev.	+	Ret. Earn.	Rev. − Exp. = Net Inc.			

b. How much revenue would Bell recognize on the Year 2 income statement?

c. What is the amount of cash flow from operating activities in Year 2?

LO 2-6, 2-7

Exercise 2-17A *Prepaid versus unearned, the entity concept*

On October 1, Year 2, Stokes Company paid Eastport Rentals $4,800 for a 12-month lease on warehouse space.

Required

a. Record the deferral and the related December 31, Year 2, adjustment for Stokes Company in the accounting equation.

b. Record the deferral and the related December 31, Year 2, adjustment for Eastport Rentals in the accounting equation.

LO 2-1, 2-2, 2-5, 2-6, 2-7

Exercise 2-18A *Identifying deferral and accrual events*

Required

Identify each of the following events as an accrual, a deferral, or neither:

a. Paid cash in advance for a one-year insurance policy.

b. Paid cash to settle an account payable.

c. Collected accounts receivable.

d. Paid cash for current salaries expense.

e. Paid cash to purchase supplies.

f. Provided services on account.

g. Provided services and collected cash.

h. Paid cash to purchase land.

i. Recognized accrued salaries at the end of the accounting period.

j. Paid a cash dividend to the stockholders.

k. Recognized accrued interest revenue at the end of the period.

l. Collected cash for services to be provided in the future.

LO 2-1, 2-2, 2-5, 2-6, 2-7

Exercise 2-19A *Revenue and expense recognition*

Required

a. Describe an expense recognition event that results in an increase in liabilities.

b. Describe an expense recognition event that results in a decrease in assets.

c. Describe a revenue recognition event that results in a decrease in liabilities.

d. Describe a revenue recognition event that results in an increase in assets.

Exercise 2-20A   Closing entries

Love Company's accounting records show an after-closing balance of $42,100 in its Retained Earnings account on December 31, Year 5. During the Year 5 accounting cycle, Love earned $19,400 of revenue, incurred $9,800 of expense, and paid $500 of dividends. Revenues and expenses were recognized evenly throughout the accounting period.

Required

a. Determine the balance in the Retained Earnings account as of January 1, Year 6.

b. Determine the balance in the temporary accounts as of January 1, Year 5.

c. Determine the after-closing balance in the Retained Earnings account as of December 31, Year 4.

d. Determine the balance in the Retained Earnings account as of June 30, Year 5.

Exercise 2-21A   Adjusting the accounts

Norell Inc. experienced the following accounting events during its Year 2 accounting period:

1. Recognized revenue on account.

2. Issued common stock.

3. Paid cash to purchase supplies.

4. Collected a cash advance for services that will be provided during the coming year.

5. Paid a cash dividend to the stockholders.

6. Paid cash for an insurance policy that provides coverage during the next year.

7. Collected cash from accounts receivable.

8. Paid cash for operating expenses.

9. Paid cash to settle an account payable.

10. Paid cash to purchase land.

Required

a. Identify the events that would require a year-end adjusting entry.

b. Are adjusting or closing entries recorded first? Why?

Exercise 2-22A   Closing the accounts

The following information was drawn from the accounting records of Wyckoff Company as of December 31, Year 2, before the temporary accounts had been closed. The Cash balance was $3,600, and Notes Payable amounted to $4,000. The company had revenues of $7,500 and expenses of $3,400. The company's Land account had a $8,000 balance. Dividends amounted to $1,000. The balance of the Common Stock account was $2,000.

Required

a. Identify which accounts would be classified as permanent and which accounts would be classified as temporary.

b. Assuming that Wyckoff's beginning balance (as of January 1, Year 2) in the Retained Earnings account was $2,500, determine its balance after the temporary accounts were closed at the end of Year 2.

c. What amount of net income would Wyckoff Company report on its Year 2 income statement?

d. Explain why the amount of net income differs from the amount of the ending Retained Earnings balance.

e. What are the balances in the revenue, expense, and dividend accounts on January 1, Year 3?

Exercise 2-23A   Closing accounts and the accounting cycle

Required

a. Identify which of the following accounts are temporary (will be closed to Retained Earnings at the end of the year) and which are permanent:

  (1) Other Operating Expenses

  (2) Utilities Expense

(3) Retained Earnings

(4) Salaries Expense

(5) Land

(6) Dividends

(7) Service Revenue

(8) Cash

(9) Salaries Payable

(10) Common Stock

b. List and explain the four stages of the accounting cycle. Which stage must be first? Which stage is last?

LO 2-8

Exercise 2-24A   *Matching concept*

Companies make sacrifices known as *expenses* to obtain benefits called *revenues*. The accurate measurement of net income requires that expenses be matched with revenues. In some circumstances, matching a particular expense directly with revenue is difficult or impossible. In these circumstances, the expense is matched with the period in which it is incurred.

Required

a. Identify an expense that could be matched directly with revenue.

b. Identify a period expense that would be difficult to match with revenue. Explain why.

LO 2-8

Exercise 2-25A   *Classifying events on the statement of cash flows*

The following transactions pertain to the operations of Ewing Company for Year 1:

1. Acquired $30,000 cash from the issue of common stock.
2. Provided $65,000 of services on account.
3. Paid $22,000 cash on accounts payable.
4. Performed services for $8,000 cash.
5. Collected $51,000 cash from accounts receivable.
6. Incurred $37,000 of operating expenses on account.
7. Paid $6,500 cash for one year's rent in advance.
8. Paid a $4,000 cash dividend to the stockholders.
9. Paid $1,200 cash for supplies to be used in the future.
10. Recognized $3,100 of accrued salaries expense.

Required

a. Classify the cash flows from these transactions as operating activities (OA), investing activities (IA), or financing activities (FA). Use NA for transactions that do not affect the statement of cash flows.

b. Prepare a statement of cash flows. (There is no beginning cash balance.)

LO 2-8

Exercise 2-26A   *Relationship of accounts to financial statements*

Required

Identify whether each of the following items would appear on the income statement (IS), statement of changes in stockholders' equity (SE), balance sheet (BS), or statement of cash flows (CF). Some items may appear on more than one statement; if so, identify all applicable statements. If an item would not appear on any financial statement, label it NA.

a. Supplies

b. Cash Flow from Financing Activities

c. "As of" Date Notation

d. Ending Retained Earnings

e. Net Income

f. Dividends

g. Net Change in Cash

h. "For the Period Ended"

i. Land

j. Ending Common Stock

k. Salaries Expense

l. Prepaid Rent

m. Accounts Payable

n. Total Assets

o. Salaries Payable

p. Insurance Expense

q. Notes Payable

r. Accounts Receivable

s. Interest Receivable

t. Interest Revenue

u. Rent Expense

v. Price/Earnings Ratio

w. Taxes Payable

x. Unearned Revenue

y. Service Revenue

z. Cash Flow from Investing Activities

aa. Consulting Revenue

bb. Utilities Expense

cc. Operating Income

dd. Total Liabilities

ee. Operating Cycle

ff. Cash Flow from Operating Activities

gg. Operating Expenses

hh. Supplies Expense

ii. Beginning Retained Earnings

jj. Beginning Common Stock

kk. Prepaid Insurance

ll. Salary Expense

mm. Beginning Cash Balance

nn. Ending Cash Balance

Exercise 2-27A *Identifying transaction type and effect on the financial statements*

LO 2-1, 2-2, 2-5, 2-6, 2-7, 2-9

Required

Identify whether each of the following transactions is an asset source (AS), asset use (AU), asset exchange (AE), or claims exchange (CE). Also show the effects of the events on the financial statements using the horizontal statements model. Indicate whether the event increases (I), decreases (D), or does not affect (NA) each element of the financial statements. If an event increases one account and decreases another account equally within the same element, record I/D. In the Cash Flows column, designate the cash flows as operating activities (OA), investing activities (IA), or financing activities (FA). The first two transactions have been recorded as examples.

| Event | Type of Event | Balance Sheet | | | | | | | Income Statement | | | | | | Statement of Cash Flows |
		Assets	=	Liabilities	+	Common Stock	+	Retained Earnings	Rev.	−	Exp.	=	Net Inc.	
a	AS	I		NA		NA		I	I		NA		I	I OA
b	AS	I		I		NA		NA	NA		NA		NA	NA

a. Provided services and collected cash.

b. Purchased supplies on account to be used in the future.

c. Paid cash in advance for one year's rent.

d. Paid cash to purchase land.

e. Paid a cash dividend to the stockholders.

f. Received cash from the issue of common stock.

g. Paid cash on accounts payable.

h. Collected cash from accounts receivable.

i. Received cash advance for services to be provided in the future.

j. Incurred other operating expenses on account.

k. Performed services on account.

l. Adjusted books to reflect the amount of prepaid rent expired during the period.

m. Paid cash for operating expenses.

n. Adjusted the books to record the supplies used during the period.

o. Recorded accrued salaries.

p. Paid cash for salaries accrued at the end of a prior period.

q. Recorded accrued interest revenue earned at the end of the accounting period.

Exercise 2-28A *Effect of accounting events on the income statement and statement of cash flows*

Required

Explain how each of the following events or series of events and the related adjusting entry will affect the amount of *net income* and the amount of *cash flow from operating activities* reported on the year-end financial statements. Identify the direction of change (increase, decrease, or NA) and the amount of the change. Organize your answers according to the following table. The first event is recorded as an example. If an event does not have a related adjusting entry, record only the effects of the event.

Event/Adjustment	Net Income Direction of Change	Net Income Amount of Change	Cash Flows from Operating Activities Direction of Change	Cash Flows from Operating Activities Amount of Change
a	NA	NA	Decrease	$9,000
Adj	Decrease	$2,250	NA	NA

a. Paid $9,000 cash on October 1 to purchase a one-year insurance policy.

b. Purchased $2,000 of supplies on account. Paid $500 cash on accounts payable. The ending balance in the Supplies account, after adjustment, was $300.

c. Provided services for $10,000 cash.

d. Collected $2,400 in advance for services to be performed in the future. The contract called for services to start on May 1 and to continue for one year.

e. Accrued salaries amounting to $5,600.

f. Sold land that cost $3,000 for $3,000 cash.

g. Acquired $15,000 cash from the issue of common stock.

h. Earned $12,000 of revenue on account. Collected $8,000 cash from accounts receivable.

i. Paid cash operating expenses of $4,500.

Exercise 2-29A *Transactions that affect the elements of financial statements*

Required

Give an example of a transaction that will:

a. Increase an asset and increase stockholders' equity (asset source event).

b. Decrease an asset and decrease stockholders' equity (asset use event).

c. Increase an asset and decrease another asset (asset exchange event).

d. Decrease a liability and increase stockholders' equity (claims exchange event).

e. Increase a liability and decrease stockholders' equity (claims exchange event).

f. Increase an asset and increase a liability (asset source event).

g. Decrease an asset and decrease a liability (asset use event).

Exercise 2-30A *Identifying source, use, and exchange transactions*

Required

Indicate whether each of the following transactions is an asset source (AS), asset use (AU), asset exchange (AE), or claims exchange (CE) transaction.

a. Acquired cash from the issue of stock.

b. Paid a cash dividend to the stockholders.

c. Paid cash on accounts payable.

d. Incurred other operating expenses on account.

e. Paid cash for rent expense.

f. Performed services for cash.

g. Performed services for clients on account.

h. Collected cash from accounts receivable.

i. Received cash for services to be performed in the future.

j. Purchased land with cash.

Exercise 2-31A   *Identifying asset source, use, and exchange transactions*

LO 2-9

Required

a. Name an asset use transaction that will *not* affect the income statement.

b. Name an asset exchange transaction that will affect the statement of cash flows.

c. Name an asset source transaction that will *not* affect the income statement.

d. Name an asset source transaction that will *not* affect the statement of cash flows.

e. Name an asset source transaction that will affect the income statement.

SECTIONS 1 AND 2 PROBLEMS—SERIES A

 An electronic auto-gradable version of the Series A Problems is available in Connect. A PDF version of Series B Problems is in Connect under the "Additional Student Resources" tab. Solutions to the Series B Problems are available in Connect under the "Instructor Library" tab. Instructor and student Workpapers for the Series B Problems are available in Connect under the "Instructor Library" and "Additional Student Resources" tabs respectively.

Problem 2-32A   *Recording events in a horizontal statements model*

LO 2-1, 2-2, 2-6, 2-7

The following events pertain to Super Cleaning Company:

1. Acquired $10,000 cash from the issue of common stock.

2. Provided $15,000 of services on account.

3. Provided services for $5,000 cash.

4. Received $2,800 cash in advance for services to be performed in the future.

5. Collected $12,200 cash from the account receivable created in Event 2.

6. Paid $1,900 for cash expenses.

7. Performed $1,400 of the services agreed to in Event 4.

8. Incurred $3,600 of expenses on account.

9. Paid $4,800 cash in advance for one-year contract to rent office space.

10 Paid $2,800 cash on the account payable created in Event 8.

11. Paid a $1,500 cash dividend to the stockholders.

12. Recognized rent expense for nine months' use of office space acquired in Event 9.

Required

Show the effects of the events on the financial statements using a horizontal statements model like the following one. In the Cash Flows column, use the letters OA to designate operating activity, IA for investing activity, FA for financing activity, and NC for net change in cash. Use NA to indicate accounts not affected by the event. The first event is recorded as an example.

	Balance Sheet								Income Statement				Statement of Cash Flows
	Assets			=	Liabilities	+		Stk. Equity					
Event No.	Cash +	Accts. Rec. +	Prep. Rent =	Accts. Pay. +	Unearn. Rev. +		Common Stock +	Ret. Earn.	Rev. −	Exp. =	Net Inc.		
1	10,000 +	NA +	NA =	NA +	NA +		10,000 +	NA	NA −	NA =	NA		10,000 FA

LO 2-1, 2-2, 2-5, 2-6, 2-7

Problem 2-33A *Effect of adjusting entries on the accounting equation*

Required

Each of the following independent events requires a year-end adjusting entry. Show how each event and its related adjusting entry affect the accounting equation. Assume a December 31 closing date. The first event is recorded as an example.

	Total Assets				**Stockholders' Equity**		
Event/ Adjustment	Cash	+	Other Assets	= Liabilities	+	Common Stock	+ Retained Earnings
a	−4,800		+4,800	NA		NA	NA
Adj.	NA		−1,200	NA		NA	−1,200

a. Paid $4,800 cash in advance on October 1 for a one-year insurance policy.

b. Received a $3,600 cash advance for a contract to provide services in the future. The contract required a one-year commitment, starting April 1.

c. Purchased $1,200 of supplies on account. At year's end, $175 of supplies remained on hand.

d. Paid $9,600 cash in advance on August 1 for a one-year lease on office space.

LO 2-4, 2-8

Problem 2-34A *Closing the accounts*

The following selected accounts and account balances were taken from the records of Nowell Company. Except as otherwise indicated, all balances are as of December 31, Year 2, before the closing entries were recorded.

Consulting revenue	$18,200
Cash	35,600
Cash received from common stock issued during Year 1	6,000
Travel expense	2,100
Dividends	4,000
Cash flow from investing activities	5,200
Rent expense	3,500
Payment to reduce debt principal	10,000
Retained earnings, January 1, Year 2	16,200
Salary expense	7,200
Cash flow from operating activities	2,600
Common stock, December 31, Year 2	16,000
Other operating expenses	2,300

Required

a. Prepare the income statement Nowell would include in its Year 2 annual report.

b. Identify the accounts that should be closed to the Retained Earnings account.

c. Determine the Retained Earnings account balance at December 31, Year 2. Identify the reasons for the difference between net income and the ending balance in Retained Earnings.

d. What are the balances in the Revenue, Expense, and Dividend accounts on January 1, Year 3? Explain.

LO 2-3, 2-5, 2-6, 2-7, 2-8

Problem 2-35A *Effect of events on financial statements*

Waddell Company had the following balances in its accounting records as of December 31, Year 1:

Assets		Liabilities and Stk. Equity	
Cash	$35,000	Accounts Payable	$ 7,500
Accounts Receivable	9,000	Common Stock	40,000
Land	51,000	Retained Earnings	47,500
Totals	$95,000		$95,000

The following accounting events apply to Waddell Company's Year 2 fiscal year:

Jan.   1   Acquired $20,000 cash from the issue of common stock.
Feb.   1   Paid $6,000 cash in advance for a one-year lease for office space.
Mar.   1   Paid a $2,000 cash dividend to the stockholders.
April 1   Purchased additional land that cost $15,000 cash.
May   1   Made a cash payment on accounts payable of $5,500.
July   1   Received $9,600 cash in advance as a retainer for services to be performed monthly over the
           coming year.
Sept. 1   Sold land for $30,000 cash that had originally cost $30,000.
Oct.   1   Purchased $2,500 of supplies on account.
Dec. 31   Earned $58,000 of service revenue on account during the year.
      31   Received cash collections from accounts receivable amounting to $46,000.
      31   Incurred other operating expenses on account during the year that amounted to $28,000.
      31   Recognized accrued salaries expense of $6,500.
      31   Had $50 of supplies on hand at the end of the period.
      31   The land purchased on April 1 had a market value of $20,000.
      31   Recognized $500 of accrued interest revenue.

Required

Based on the preceding information, answer the following questions for Waddell Company. All questions pertain to the Year 2 financial statements. (*Hint:* Enter items in general ledger accounts under the accounting equation before answering the questions.)

a. Based on the preceding transactions, identify two additional adjustments and describe them.
b. What amount would Waddell report for land on the balance sheet?
c. What amount of net cash flow from operating activities would be reported on the statement of cash flows?
d. What amount of rent expense would be reported on the income statement?
e. What amount of total liabilities would be reported on the balance sheet?
f. What amount of supplies expense would be reported on the income statement?
g. What amount of unearned revenue would be reported on the balance sheet?
h. What amount of net cash flow from investing activities would be reported on the statement of cash flows?
i. What amount of total expenses would be reported on the income statement?
j. What amount of service revenue would be reported on the income statement?
k. What amount of cash flows from financing activities would be reported on the statement of cash flows?
l. What amount of net income would be reported on the income statement?
m. What amount of retained earnings would be reported on the balance sheet?

Problem 2-36A   *Identifying and arranging elements on financial statements*

LO 2-8

The following accounts and balances were drawn from the records of Barker Company at December 31, Year 2:

CHECK FIGURES
a. Net Income $18,500
b. Total Assets $93,200

Supplies	$ 1,000	Beginning retained earnings	$ 9,300
Cash flow from investing act.	(5,200)	Cash flow from financing act.	(5,000)
Prepaid insurance	1,200	Rent expense	2,500
Service revenue	65,200	Dividends	3,000
Other operating expenses	41,000	Cash	48,000
Supplies expense	1,100	Accounts receivable	14,200
Insurance expense	2,100	Prepaid rent	4,800
Beginning common stock	40,000	Unearned revenue	6,400
Cash flow from operating act.	15,600	Land	24,000
Common stock issued	5,000	Accounts payable	17,000

Required

Use the accounts and balances from Barker Company to construct an income statement, statement of changes in stockholders' equity, balance sheet, and statement of cash flows (show only totals for each activity on the statement of cash flows).

Problem 2-37A   *Missing information in financial statements*

Required

Fill in the blanks (indicated by the alphabetic letters in parentheses) in the following financial statements. Assume the company started operations January 1, Year 1, and all transactions involve cash.

	For the Years		
	Year 1	Year 2	Year 3
Income Statements			
Revenue	$ 700	$ 1,300	$ 2,000
Expense	(a)	(700)	(1,300)
Net income	$ 200	$ (m)	$ 700
Statement of Changes in Stockholders' Equity			
Beginning common stock	$ 0	$ (n)	$ 6,000
Plus: Common stock issued	5000	1,000	2,000
Ending common stock	5,000	6,000	(t)
Beginning retained earnings	0	100	200
Plus: Net income	(b)	(0)	700
Less: Dividends	(c)	(500)	(300)
Ending retained earnings	100	(p)	600
Total stockholders' equity	$ (d)	$ 6,200	$ 8,600
Balance Sheets			
Assets			
Cash	$ (e)	$ (q)	$ (u)
Land	0	(r)	8,000
Total assets	$ (f)	$11,200	$10,600
Liabilities	$ (g)	$ 5,000	$ 2,000
Stockholders' equity			
Common stock	(h)	(s)	8,000
Retained earnings	(i)	200	600
Total stockholders' equity	(j)	6,200	8,600
Total liabilities and stockholders' equity	$8,100	$11,200	$10,600
Statements of Cash Flows			
Cash flows from operating activities			
Cash receipts from customers	$ (k)	$ 1,300	$ (v)
Cash payments for expenses	(l)	(700)	(w)
Net cash flows from operating activities	200	600	700
Cash flows from investing activities			
Cash payments for land	0	(8,000)	0
Cash flows from financing activities			
Cash receipts from loan	3,000	3,000	0
Cash payments to reduce debt	0	(1,000)	(x)
Cash receipts from stock issue	5,000	1,000	(y)
Cash payments for dividends	(100)	(500)	(z)
Net cash flows from financing activities	7,900	2,500	(1,300)
Net change in cash	8,100	(4,900)	(600)
Plus: Beginning cash balance	0	8,100	3,200
Ending cash balance	$8,100	$ 3,200	$ 2,600

Problem 2-38A   *Events for two complete accounting cycles*

LO 2-1, 2-2, 2-3, 2-4, 2-5, 2-6, 2-7, 2-8, 2-9

Alcorn Service Company was formed on January 1, Year 1.

Events Affecting the Year 1 Accounting Period

1. Acquired $20,000 cash from the issue of common stock.
2. Purchased $800 of supplies on account.
3. Purchased land that cost $14,000 cash.
4. Paid $800 cash to settle accounts payable created in Event 2.
5. Recognized revenue on account of $10,500.
6. Paid $3,800 cash for other operating expenses.
7. Collected $7,000 cash from accounts receivable.

Information for Year 1 Adjusting Entries

8. Recognized accrued salaries of $3,600 on December 31, Year 1.
9. Had $100 of supplies on hand at the end of the accounting period.

Events Affecting the Year 2 Accounting Period

1. Acquired $15,000 cash from the issue of common stock.
2. Paid $3,600 cash to settle the salaries payable obligation.
3. Paid $9,000 cash in advance to lease office space.
4. Sold the land that cost $14,000 for $14,000 cash.
5. Received $6,000 cash in advance for services to be performed in the future.
6. Purchased $2,400 of supplies on account during the year.
7. Provided services on account of $24,500.
8. Collected $12,600 cash from accounts receivable.
9. Paid a cash dividend of $2,000 to the stockholders.
10. Paid other operating expenses of $2,850.

Information for Year 2 Adjusting Entries

11. The advance payment for rental of the office space (see Event 3) was made on March 1 for a one-year term.
12. The cash advance for services to be provided in the future was collected on October 1 (see Event 5). The one-year contract started on October 1.
13. Had $300 of supplies remaining on hand at the end of the period.
14. Recognized accrued salaries of $4,800 at the end of the accounting period.
15. Recognized $500 of accrued interest revenue.

Required

a. Identify each event affecting the Year 1 and Year 2 accounting periods as asset source (AS), asset use (AU), asset exchange (AE), or claims exchange (CE). Record the effects of each event under the appropriate general ledger account headings of the accounting equation.

b. Prepare an income statement, statement of changes in stockholders' equity, balance sheet, and statement of cash flows for Year 1 and Year 2, using the vertical statements model.

CHECK FIGURES
Net Income, Year 1: $2,400
Net Income, Year 2: $9,150

ANALYZE, THINK, COMMUNICATE

ATC 2-1   Business Applications Case   *Understanding real-world annual reports*

Required

Obtain the Target Corporation's annual report for its 2018 fiscal year (year ended February 2, 2019) at http://investors.target.com using the instructions in Appendix A, and use it to answer the following questions:

a. Which accounts on Target's balance sheet are accrual-type accounts?

b. Which accounts on Target's balance sheet are deferral-type accounts?

c. Compare Target's 2018 *net earnings* (the year ended February 2, 2019) to its 2017 *cash provided by operating activities*. Which is larger?

d. First, compare Target's 2017 net income to its 2018 net income. Next, compare Target's 2017 cash provided by operating activities to its 2018 cash provided by operating activities. Which changed the most from 2017 to 2018, net earnings or cash provided by operating activities?

ATC 2-2   Group Assignment   *Financial reporting and market evaluation*

The following financial highlights were drawn from the December 31, 2017 annual report of ExxonMobil Corporation and the September 29, 2018 annual report of Apple Inc.

	ExxonMobil	Apple
Revenue	$244.4 Billion	$265.6 Billion
Net income	$ 19.7 Billion	$ 59.5 Billion
Cash and short-term investments	$ 3.1 Billion	$ 66.3 Billion

Even so, as of December 3, 2018, Wall Street valued ExxonMobil at $337 billion and Apple at $849 billion.

Divide the class into groups of four or five students.

Required

Have the members of each group reach a consensus response for each of the following tasks. Each group should elect a spokesperson to represent the group.

Group Tasks

(1) Determine the amount of expenses incurred by each company.

(2) Speculate as to why investors would be willing to pay more for Apple than ExxonMobil.

ATC 2-3   Research Assignment   *Identifying accruals and deferrals at Netflix*

This chapter defined and discussed accrual and deferral transactions. Complete the requirements below using the most recent financial statements available on the Internet for Netflix, Inc. Obtain the statements by following the steps below. (Be aware that the formatting of the company's website may have changed since these instructions were written.)

1. Go to www.netflix.com.

2. Click on "Investor Relations," which is at the bottom of the page in very small print.

3. Click on the "Annual Reports and Proxies" link at the bottom of the page.

4. Click on the "20xx Annual Report." Use the PDF version of the annual report.

5. Find the company's balance sheet and complete the following requirements. In recent years this has been shown toward the end of the Form 10-K section of the company's annual report, on page 43. The "Index" near the beginning of the report can help you locate the financial statements.

Required

a. Make a list of all the accounts on the balance sheet that you believe are accrual-type accounts.

b. Make a list of all the accounts on the balance sheet that you believe are deferral-type accounts.

ATC 2-4   Writing Assignment   *Revenue Recognition and Matching*

Glenn's Cleaning Services Company is experiencing cash flow problems and needs a loan. Glenn has a friend who is willing to lend him the money he needs provided she can be convinced that he will be able to repay the debt. Glenn has assured his friend that his business is viable, but his friend has asked to see the company's financial statements. Glenn's accountant produced the following financial statements:

Income Statement	
Service Revenue	$ 38,000
Operating Expenses	(70,000)
Net Loss	$(32,000)

Balance Sheet	
Assets	$85,000
Liabilities	$35,000
Stockholders' Equity	
Common Stock	82,000
Retained Earnings	(32,000)
Total Liabilities and Stockholders' Equity	$85,000

Glenn made the following adjustments to these statements before showing them to his friend. He recorded $82,000 of revenue on account from Barrymore Manufacturing Company for a contract to clean its headquarters office building that was still being negotiated for the next month. Barrymore had scheduled a meeting to sign a contract the following week, so Glenn was sure that he would get the job. Barrymore was a reputable company, and Glenn was confident that he could ultimately collect the $82,000. Also, he subtracted $30,000 of accrued salaries expense and the corresponding liability. He reasoned that since he had not paid the employees, he had not incurred any expense.

Required

a. Reconstruct the income statement and balance sheet as they would appear after Glenn's adjustments.

b. Write a brief memo explaining how Glenn's treatment of the expected revenue from Barrymore violated the revenue recognition concept.

c. Write a brief memo explaining how Glenn's treatment of the accrued salaries expense violates the matching concept.

CHAPTER 3

Accounting for Merchandising Businesses

LEARNING OBJECTIVES

After you have mastered the material in this chapter, you will be able to:

LO 3-1   Record and report on inventory transactions using the perpetual system.

LO 3-2   Show how purchase returns and allowances affect financial statements.

LO 3-3   Show how purchase discounts affect financial statements.

LO 3-4   Show how transportation costs affect financial statements.

LO 3-5   Show how inventory shrinkage affects financial statements.

LO 3-6   Calculate gains and losses and show how they are presented on a multistep income statement.

LO 3-7   Determine the amount of net sales.

LO 3-8   Use common size financial statements to evaluate managerial performance.

LO 3-9   Identify the primary features of the periodic inventory system. (Appendix)

Video lectures and accompanying self-assessment quizzes are available in Connect *for all learning objectives.*

Set B exercises and problems are available in Additional Student Resources.

CHAPTER OPENING

Previous chapters have discussed accounting for service businesses. These businesses obtain revenue by providing some kind of service such as medical or legal advice to their customers. Other examples of service companies include dry cleaning companies, residential and business cleaning service companies, and car washes. This chapter introduces accounting practices for merchandising businesses. **Merchandising businesses** generate revenue by selling goods. They buy the merchandise they sell from companies called suppliers. The goods purchased for resale are called **merchandise inventory.** Merchandising businesses include **retail companies** (companies that sell goods to the final consumer) and **wholesale companies** (companies that sell to other businesses). Sears, JCPenney, Target, and Sam's Club are real-world merchandising businesses.

The Curious Accountant

Damian Dovarganes/AP Images

Katie recently purchased a new Ford automobile from a dealer near her home. When she told her friend George that she was able to purchase the car for $1,000 less than the sticker price, George told her that she had gotten a lousy deal. "Everybody knows there is a huge markup on cars," George said. "You could have gotten a much lower price if you'd shopped around."

Katie responded, "If there is such a big profit margin on cars, why did so many of the car manufacturers get into financial trouble?" George told her that she was confusing the maker of the car with the dealer. George argued that although the manufacturers may not have high profit margins, the dealers do, and told her again that she had paid too much.

Exhibit 3.1 presents the income statements for AutoNation, Inc. and Ford Motor Company. Based on these statements, do you think either Katie or George is correct? For example, if you pay $20,000 for a vehicle from a dealership operated by AutoNation, the largest auto retailer in the United States, how much did the car cost the company? Also, how much did it cost Ford Motor Company to make the car? (Answers on page 111.)

EXHIBIT 3.1	Comparative Income Statements

AUTONATION, INC.
Consolidated Statements of Income (Partial)
For the Years Ended December 31
(In millions, except per share data)

	2017	2016	2015
Revenue:			
New vehicle	$12,180.8	$12,255.8	$11,995.0
Used vehicle	4,878.4	4,995.3	4,768.7
Parts and service	3,398.3	3,321.4	3,082.8
Finance and insurance, net	939.2	894.6	868.7
Other	137.9	141.9	146.8
Total revenue	21,534.6	21,609.0	20,862.0
Cost of Sales:			
New vehicle	11,592.4	11,620.0	11,321.9
Used vehicle	4,563.2	4,677.7	4,415.0
Parts and service	1,907.6	1,886.7	1,744.8
Other	112.4	111.4	118.8
Total cost of sales	18,175.6	18,295.8	17,600.5
Gross Profit:			
New vehicle	588.4	635.8	673.1
Used vehicle	315.2	317.6	353.7
Parts and service	1,490.7	1,434.7	1,338.0
Finance and insurance	939.2	894.6	868.7
Other	25.5	30.5	28.0
Total gross profit	3,359.0	3,313.2	3,261.5
Selling, general & administrative expenses	2,436.2	2,349.4	2,263.5
Depreciation and amortization	158.6	143.4	127.4
Franchise rights impairment	—	—	15.4
Other expenses (income), net	(79.2)	(69.1)	(17.9)
Operating income	843.4	889.5	873.1
Nonoperating income (expense) items:			
Floorplan interest expense	(97.0)	(76.5)	(58.3)
Other interest expense	(120.2)	(115.5)	(90.9)
Interest income	1.0	1.1	0.1
Other income (losses), net	9.3	3.7	(1.3)
Income (loss) from continuing operations before income taxes	636.5	702.3	722.7
Income tax provision	201.5	270.6	279.0
Net income from continuing operations	435.0	431.7	443.7
Loss from discontinued operations, net of income taxes	(0.4)	(1.2)	(1.1)
Net income	$ 434.6	$ 430.5	$ 442.6

FORD MOTOR COMPANY AND SUBSIDIARIES
Consolidated Income Statements (Partial)
For the Years Ended December 31
(In millions except per share amounts)

	2017	2016	2015
Sales and revenues			
Automotive sales	$ 145,653	$ 141,546	$ 140,566
Financial Services revenues	11,113	10,253	8,992
Other	10	1	—
Total sales and revenues	156,776	151,800	149,558

(continued)

	2017	2016	2015
Costs and expenses			
Cost of sales	131,332	126,183	124,446
Selling, administrative and other expenses	11,527	10,972	10,763
Financial Services interest, operating, and other services	9,104	8,904	7,368
Total costs and expenses	151,963	146,059	142,577
Interest expense on Automotive debt	1,133	894	773
Non–Financial Services interest income and other income (loss), net	3,060	(269)	1,854
Financial Services other income/(loss), net	207	438	372
Equity in income of affiliated companies	1,201	1,780	1,818
Income before income taxes	8,148	6,796	10,252
Provision for/(Benefit from) income taxes	520	2,189	2,881
Net income	7,628	4,607	7,371
Less: Income/(Loss) attributable to noncontrolling interests	26	11	(2)
Net income attributable to Ford Motor Company	$ 7,602	$ 4,596	$ 7,373

ACCOUNTING FOR INVENTORY TRANSACTIONS

Companies report inventory costs on the balance sheet in the asset account Merchandise Inventory. All costs incurred to acquire merchandise and ready it for sale are included in the inventory account. Examples of inventory costs include the price of goods purchased, shipping and handling costs, transit insurance, and storage costs. Since inventory items are referred to as products, inventory costs are frequently called **product costs.**

Costs that are not included in inventory are usually called **selling and administrative costs.** Examples of selling and administrative costs include advertising, administrative salaries, sales commissions, insurance, and interest. Since selling and administrative costs are usually recognized as expenses *in the period* in which they are incurred, they are sometimes called **period costs.** In contrast, product costs are expensed when inventory is sold regardless of when it was purchased. In other words, product costs are matched directly with sales revenue, while selling and administrative costs are matched with the period in which they are incurred.

LO 3-1

Record and report on inventory transactions using the perpetual system.

Allocating Inventory Cost between Asset and Expense Accounts

The cost of inventory that is available for sale during a specific accounting period is determined as follows:

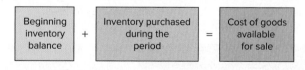

Beginning inventory balance + Inventory purchased during the period = Cost of goods available for sale

The **cost of goods available for sale** is allocated between the asset account Merchandise Inventory and an expense account called **Cost of Goods Sold.** The cost of inventory items that have not been sold (Merchandise Inventory) is reported as an asset on the balance sheet, and the cost of the items sold (Cost of Goods Sold) is expensed on the income statement. This allocation is depicted graphically as follows:

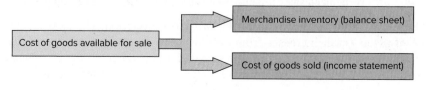

Cost of goods available for sale → Merchandise inventory (balance sheet) / Cost of goods sold (income statement)

The difference between the sales revenue and the cost of goods sold is called **gross margin** or **gross profit.** The selling and administrative expenses (period costs) are subtracted from gross margin to obtain the net income.

Exhibit 3.1 displays income statements from the annual reports of AutoNation and Ford. For each company, review the most current income statement and determine the amount of gross margin. You should find a gross profit of $2,988.7 for AutoNation and a gross margin of $12,266 ($135,782 − $123,516) for Ford (auto sales only).

Perpetual Inventory System

Most modern companies maintain their inventory records using the **perpetual inventory system,** so called because the inventory account is adjusted perpetually (continually) throughout the accounting period. Each time merchandise is purchased, the inventory account is increased; each time it is sold, the inventory account is decreased. The following illustration demonstrates the basic features of the perpetual inventory system.

June Gardener loved plants and grew them with such remarkable success that she decided to open a small retail plant store. She started June's Plant Shop (JPS) on January 1, Year 1. The following discussion explains and illustrates the effects of the five events the company experienced during its first year of operation.

Effects of Year 1 Events on Financial Statements

EVENT 1   JPS acquired $15,000 cash by issuing common stock.

This event is an asset source transaction. It increases both assets (cash) and stockholders' equity (common stock). The income statement is not affected. The statement of cash flows reflects an inflow from financing activities. These effects are shown here.

Balance Sheet									Income Statement			Statement of Cash Flows	
Assets				=	Liab.	+	Stk. Equity						
Cash	+	Inventory	+	Land	=	Accts. Pay.	+	Com. Stk.	+	Ret. Earn.	Rev. − Exp. = Net Inc.		
15,000	+	NA	+	NA	=	NA	+	15,000	+	NA	NA − NA = NA	15,000	FA

EVENT 2   JPS purchased merchandise inventory for $14,000 cash.

This event is an asset exchange transaction. One asset, cash, decreases and another asset, merchandise inventory, increases; total assets remain unchanged. Because product costs are expensed when inventory is sold, not when it is purchased, the event does not affect the income statement. The cash outflow, however, is reported in the operating activities section of the statement of cash flows. These effects are illustrated as follows.

Balance Sheet									Income Statement			Statement of Cash Flows	
Assets				=	Liab.	+	Stk. Equity						
Cash	+	Inventory	+	Land	=	Accts. Pay.	+	Com. Stk.	+	Ret. Earn.	Rev. − Exp. = Net Inc.		
(14,000)	+	14,000	+	NA	=	NA	+	NA	+	NA	NA − NA = NA	(14,000)	OA

EVENT 3A   JPS recognized sales revenue from selling inventory for $12,000 cash.

The revenue recognition is the first part of a two-part transaction. The *sales part* represents a source of assets (cash increases from earning sales revenue). Both assets (cash) and stockholders' equity (retained earnings) increase. Sales revenue on the income statement increases. The $12,000 cash inflow is reported in the operating activities section of the statement of cash flows. These effects are shown in the following financial statements model:

Balance Sheet											Income Statement					Statement of Cash Flows	
Assets				=	Liab.	+	Stk. Equity										
Cash	+	Inventory	+	Land	=	Accts. Pay.	+	Com. Stk.	+	Ret. Earn.	Rev.	−	Exp.	=	Net Inc.		
12,000	+	NA	+	NA	=	NA	+	NA	+	12,000	12,000	−	NA	=	12,000	12,000	OA

EVENT 3B   JPS recognized $8,000 of cost of goods sold.

The expense recognition is the second part of the two-part transaction. The *expense part* represents a use of assets. Both assets (merchandise inventory) and stockholders' equity (retained earnings) decrease. An expense account, Cost of Goods Sold, is reported on the income statement. This part of the transaction does not affect the statement of cash flows. A cash outflow occurred when the goods were bought, not when they were sold. These effects are shown here.

Balance Sheet											Income Statement					Statement of Cash Flows
Assets				=	Liab.	+	Stk. Equity									
Cash	+	Inventory	+	Land	=	Accts. Pay.	+	Com. Stk.	+	Ret. Earn.	Rev.	−	Exp.	=	Net Inc.	
NA	+	(8,000)	+	NA	=	NA	+	NA	+	(8,000)	NA	−	8,000	=	(8,000)	NA

EVENT 4   JPS paid $1,000 cash for selling and administrative expenses.

This event is an asset use transaction. The payment decreases both assets (cash) and stockholders' equity (retained earnings). The increase in selling and administrative expenses decreases net income. The $1,000 cash payment is reported in the operating activities section of the statement of cash flows. These effects are illustrated as follows.

Balance Sheet											Income Statement					Statement of Cash Flows	
Assets				=	Liab.	+	Stk. Equity										
Cash	+	Inventory	+	Land	=	Accts. Pay.	+	Com. Stk.	+	Ret. Earn.	Rev.	−	Exp.	=	Net Inc.		
(1,000)	+	NA	+	NA	=	NA	+	NA	+	(1,000)	NA	−	1,000	=	(1,000)	(1,000)	OA

EVENT 5   JPS paid $5,500 cash to purchase land for a place to locate a future store.

Buying the land increases the Land account and decreases the Cash account on the balance sheet. The income statement is not affected. The statement of cash flow shows a cash outflow to purchase land in the investing activities section of the statement of cash flows. These effects are shown as follows.

Balance Sheet											Income Statement					Statement of Cash Flows	
Assets				=	Liab.	+	Stk. Equity										
Cash	+	Inventory	+	Land	=	Accts. Pay.	+	Com. Stk.	+	Ret. Earn.	Rev.	−	Exp.	=	Net Inc.		
(5,500)	+	NA	+	5,500	=	NA	+	NA	+	NA	NA	−	NA	=	NA	(5,500)	IA

Financial Statements for Year 1

JPS's financial statements for Year 1 are shown in Exhibit 3.2. JPS had no beginning inventory in its first year, so the cost of merchandise inventory available for sale was $14,000 (the amount of inventory purchased during the period). Recall that JPS must allocate the

EXHIBIT 3.2

Financial Statements

12/31/Year 1 Income Statement	
Sales revenue	$12,000
Cost of goods sold	(8,000)
Gross margin	4,000
Less: Operating exp.	
Selling &	
admin. exp.	(1,000)
Net income	$ 3,000

12/31/Year 1 Balance Sheet		
Assets		
Cash	$ 6,500	
Merchandise inventory	6,000	
Land	5,500	
Total assets		$18,000
Liabilities		$ 0
Stockholders' equity		
Common stock	$15,000	
Retained earnings	3,000	
Total stockholders' equity		18,000
Total liab. and stk. equity		$18,000

12/31/Year 1 Statement of Cash Flows		
Operating activities		
Inflow from customers	$12,000	
Outflow for inventory	(14,000)	
Outflow for selling &		
admin. exp.	(1,000)	
Net cash outflow for		
operating activities		$ (3,000)
Investing activities		
Outflow to purchase land		(5,500)
Financing activities		
Inflow from stock issue		15,000
Net change in cash		6,500
Plus: Beginning cash balance		0
Ending cash balance		$ 6,500

Cost of Goods (Inventory) Available for Sale between the *Cost of Goods Sold* ($8,000) and the ending balance ($6,000) in the *Merchandise Inventory* account. The cost of goods sold is reported as an expense on the income statement and the ending balance of merchandise inventory is reported as an asset on the balance sheet. The difference between the sales revenue ($12,000) and the cost of goods sold ($8,000) is labeled *gross margin* ($4,000) on the income statement.

 CHECK YOURSELF 3.1

Phambroom Company began Year 2 with $35,600 in its Inventory account. During the year, it purchased inventory costing $356,800 and sold inventory that had cost $360,000 for $520,000. Based on this information alone, determine (1) the inventory balance as of December 31, Year 2, and (2) the amount of gross margin Phambroom would report on its Year 2 income statement.

Answer

1. $35,600 Beginning inventory + $356,800 Purchases = $392,400 Goods available for sale
   $392,400 Goods available for sale − $360,000 Cost of goods sold = $32,400 Ending inventory
2. Sales revenue − Cost of goods sold = Gross margin $520,000 − $360,000 = $160,000

TRANSACTIONS RELATED TO INVENTORY PURCHASES

Purchasing inventory often involves (1) returning inventory or receiving purchase allowances (cost reductions), (2) taking purchase discounts (also called cash discounts), (3) incurring transportation costs, and (4) recognizing inventory shrinkage. During its second accounting cycle, JPS encountered these kinds of events. The final account balances at the end of the Year 1 fiscal year become the beginning balances for Year 2: Cash, $6,500; Merchandise Inventory, $6,000; Land, $5,500; Common Stock, $15,000; and Retained Earnings, $3,000.

Effects of Year 2 Events on Financial Statements

JPS experienced the following events during its Year 2 accounting period. The effects of each of these events are explained and illustrated in the following discussion.

EVENT 1   JPS borrowed $4,000 cash by issuing a note payable.

JPS borrowed the money to enable it to purchase a plot of land for a site for a store it planned to build in the near future. Borrowing the money increases the Cash account and the Note Payable account on the balance sheet. The income statement is not affected. The statement of cash flow shows a cash flow from financing activities. These effects are shown as follows.

Balance Sheet													Income Statement					Statement of Cash Flows
Assets				=	Liabilities		+	Stk. Equity										
Cash	+	Inventory	+	Land	=	Accts. Pay.	+	Notes Pay.	+	Com. Stk.	+	Ret. Earn.	Rev.	−	Exp.	=	Net Inc.	
4,000	+	NA	+	NA	=	NA	+	4,000	+	NA	+	NA	NA	−	NA	=	NA	4,000 FA

EVENT 2   JPS purchased on account merchandise inventory with a list price of $11,000.

The inventory purchase increases both assets (merchandise inventory) and liabilities (accounts payable) on the balance sheet. The income statement is not affected until later, when inventory is sold. Since the inventory was purchased on account, there was no cash outflow. These effects are shown here.

Balance Sheet													Income Statement					Statement of Cash Flows
Assets				=	Liab.		+	Stk. Equity										
Cash	+	Inventory	+	Land	=	Accts. Pay.	+	Notes Pay.	+	Com. Stk.	+	Ret. Earn.	Rev.	−	Exp.	=	Net Inc.	
NA	+	11,000	+	NA	=	11,000	+	NA	+	NA	+	NA	NA	−	NA	=	NA	NA

ACCOUNTING FOR PURCHASE RETURNS AND ALLOWANCES

EVENT 3   JPS returned some of the inventory purchased in Event 2. The list price of the returned merchandise was $1,000.

To promote customer satisfaction, many businesses allow customers to return goods for reasons such as wrong size, wrong color, wrong design, or even simply because the purchaser changed his mind. The effect of a purchase return is the *opposite* of the original purchase. For JPS the **purchase return** decreases both assets (merchandise inventory) and liabilities (accounts payable). There is no effect on either the income statement or the statement of cash flows. These effects are shown as follows.

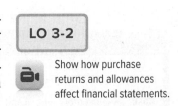

LO 3-2

Show how purchase returns and allowances affect financial statements.

Balance Sheet													Income Statement					Statement of Cash Flows
Assets				=	Liab.		+	Stk. Equity										
Cash	+	Inventory	+	Land	=	Accts. Pay.	+	Notes Pay.	+	Com. Stk.	+	Ret. Earn.	Rev.	−	Exp.	=	Net Inc.	
NA	+	(1,000)	+	NA	=	(1,000)	+	NA	+	NA	+	NA	NA	−	NA	=	NA	NA

Sometimes dissatisfied buyers will agree to keep goods instead of returning them if the seller offers to reduce the price. Such reductions are called allowances. **Purchase allowances** affect the financial statements the same way purchase returns do.

PURCHASE DISCOUNTS

EVENT 4   JPS received a cash discount on goods purchased in Event 2. The credit terms were 2/10, n/30.

LO 3-3

Show how purchase discounts affect financial statements.

To encourage buyers to pay promptly, sellers sometimes offer **cash discounts.** To illustrate, assume JPS purchased the inventory in Event 2 under terms **2/10, n/30** (two-ten, net thirty). These terms mean the seller will allow a 2 percent cash discount if the purchaser pays cash within 10 days from the date of purchase. The amount not paid within the first 10 days is due at the end of 30 days from date of purchase. Recall that JPS returned $1,000 of the inventory purchased in Event 1 leaving a $10,000 balance ($11,000 list price − $1,000 purchase return). If JPS pays for the inventory within 10 days, the amount of the discount is $200 ($10,000 × 0.02).

When cash discounts are applied to purchases they are called **purchases discounts.** When they are applied to sales, they are called sales discounts. Sales discounts will be discussed later in the chapter. A *purchase discount* reduces the cost of the inventory and the associated account payable on the balance sheet. A purchase discount does not directly affect the income statement or the statement of cash flow. These effects are shown here.

Balance Sheet										Income Statement				Statement of Cash Flows
Assets			=	Liab.		+	Stk. Equity							
Cash	+ Inventory +	Land	=	Accts. Pay.	+ Notes Pay.	+	Com. Stk.	+	Ret. Earn.	Rev.	− Exp.	=	Net Inc.	
NA	+ (200) +	NA	=	(200)	+ NA	+	NA	+	NA	NA	− NA	=	NA	NA

If JPS paid the account payable after 10 days, there would be no purchase discount. In this case, the balances in the Inventory and Account Payable accounts would remain at $10,000.

EVENT 5   JPS paid the $9,800 balance due on the account payable.

The remaining balance in the accounts payable is $9,800 ($10,000 list price − $200 purchase discount). Paying cash to settle the liability reduces cash and accounts payable on the balance sheet. The income statement is not affected. The cash outflow is shown in the operating section of the statement of cash flows. These effects are shown as follows.

Balance Sheet										Income Statement				Statement of Cash Flows
Assets			=	Liab.		+	Stk. Equity							
Cash	+ Inventory +	Land	=	Accts. Pay.	+ Notes Pay.	+	Com. Stk.	+	Ret. Earn.	Rev.	− Exp.	=	Net Inc.	
(9,800)	+ NA +	NA	=	(9,800)	+ NA	+	NA	+	NA	NA	− NA	=	NA	(9,800) OA

The Cost of Financing Inventory

Suppose you buy inventory this month and sell it next month. Where do you get the money to pay for the inventory at the time you buy it? One way to finance the purchase is to buy it on account and withhold payment until the last day of the term for the account payable. For example, suppose you buy inventory under terms 2/10, net/30. Under these circumstances you could delay payment for 30 days after the day of purchase. This way you may be able to collect enough money from the inventory you sell to pay for the inventory you purchased.

REALITY BYTES

Many real-world companies have found it more effective to impose a penalty for late payment than to use a cash discount to encourage early payment. The invoice from Arley Water Works is an example of the penalty strategy. Notice that the amount due, if paid by the due date, is $18.14. A $1.88 late charge is imposed if the bill is paid after the due date. The $1.88 late charge is in fact interest. If Arley Water Works collects the payment after the due date, the utility will receive cash of $20.02. The collection will increase cash ($20.02), reduce accounts receivable ($18.14), and increase interest revenue ($1.88).

Refusing the discount allows you the time needed to generate the cash necessary to pay off the liability (account payable). Unfortunately, this is usually a very expensive way to finance the purchase of inventory.

While the amount of a cash discount may appear small, the discount period is short. With respect to the terms 2/10, net/30, you can pay on the 10th day and still receive the discount, you obtain financing for only 20 days (30-day full credit term − 10-day discount term). In other words, you must forgo a 2 percent discount to obtain a loan with a 20-day term. What is the size of the discount in annual terms? The answer is determined by the following formula.

$$\text{Annual rate} = \text{Discount rate} \times (365 \text{ days} \div \text{Term of the loan})$$

$$\text{Annual rate} = 2\% \times (365 \div 20)$$

$$\text{Annual rate} = 36.5\%$$

This means that a 2 percent discount rate for 20 days is equivalent to a 36.5 percent annual rate of interest. So, if you do not have the money to pay the account payable, but can borrow money from a bank at less than 36.5 percent annual interest, you should borrow the money and pay off the account payable within the discount period.

ACCOUNTING FOR TRANSPORTATION COSTS

EVENT 6   The shipping terms for the inventory purchased in Event 2 were FOB shipping point. JPS paid the freight company $300 cash for delivering the merchandise.

The terms **FOB shipping point** and **FOB destination** identify whether the buyer or the seller is responsible for transportation costs. If goods are delivered FOB shipping point, the buyer is responsible for the freight cost. If goods are delivered FOB destination, the seller is responsible. When the buyer is responsible, the freight cost is called **transportation-in.** When the seller is responsible, the cost is called **transportation-out.** The following table summarizes freight cost terms:

Show how transportation costs affect financial statements.

Responsible Party	Buyer	Seller
Freight terms	FOB shipping point	FOB destination
Account title	Merchandise inventory	Transportation-out

Event 6 indicates the inventory was delivered FOB shipping point, so JPS (the buyer) is responsible for the $300 freight cost. Since incurring transportation-in costs is necessary to obtain inventory, these costs are added to the inventory account. The freight cost increases one asset account (Merchandise Inventory) and decreases another asset account (Cash). The income statement is not affected by this transaction because transportation-in costs are not expensed when they are incurred. Instead they are expensed as part of *cost of goods sold* when the inventory is sold. However, the cash paid for transportation-in costs is reported as an outflow in the operating activities section of the statement of cash flows. The effects of *transportation-in costs* are shown here.

Balance Sheet								Income Statement			Statement of Cash Flows
Assets			=	Liab.		+	Stk. Equity				
Cash	+ Inventory +	Land	=	Accts. Pay. +	Notes Pay. +		Com. Stk. +	Ret. Earn.	Rev. −	Exp. = Net Inc.	
(300) +	300 +	NA	=	NA +	NA +		NA +	NA	NA −	NA = NA	(300) OA

✓ CHECK YOURSELF 3.2

Tsang Company purchased $32,000 of inventory on account with payment terms of 2/10, n/30 and freight terms FOB shipping point. Freight costs were $1,100. Tsang obtained a $2,000 purchase allowance because the inventory was damaged upon arrival. Tsang paid for the inventory within the discount period. Based on this information alone, determine the balance in the inventory account.

Answer

List price of inventory	$32,000
Plus: Transportation-in costs	1,100
Less: Purchase returns and allowances	(2,000)
Less: Purchase discount [($32,000 − $2,000) × 0.02]	(600)
Balance in inventory account	$30,500

EVENT 7A   JPS recognized $24,750 of revenue on the cash sale of merchandise that cost $11,500.

The sale increases assets (cash) and stockholders' equity (retained earnings). The revenue recognition increases net income. The $24,750 cash inflow from the sale is reported in the operating activities section of the statement of cash flows. These effects are shown as follows.

Balance Sheet								Income Statement			Statement of Cash Flows
Assets			=	Liab.		+	Stk. Equity				
Cash	+ Inventory +	Land	=	Accts. Pay. +	Notes Pay. +		Com. Stk. +	Ret. Earn.	Rev. −	Exp. = Net Inc.	
24,750 +	NA +	NA	=	NA +	NA +		NA +	24,750	24,750 −	NA = 24,750	24,750 OA

EVENT 7B   JPS recognized $11,500 of cost of goods sold.

When goods are sold, the product cost—*including a proportionate share of transportation-in and adjustments for purchase returns and allowances*—is transferred from the Merchandise

Inventory account to the expense account, Cost of Goods Sold. Recognizing cost of goods sold decreases both assets (merchandise inventory) and stockholders' equity (retained earnings). The expense recognition for cost of goods sold decreases net income. Cash flow is not affected. These effects are shown here.

Balance Sheet										Income Statement				Statement of Cash Flows
Assets			=	Liab.			+	Stk. Equity						
Cash	+ Inventory +	Land	=	Accts. Pay.	+	Notes Pay.	+	Com. Stk.	+	Ret. Earn.	Rev. −	Exp.	= Net Inc.	
NA	+ (11,500) +	NA	=	NA	+	NA	+	NA	+	(11,500)	NA −	(11,500)	= (11,500)	NA

EVENT 8   JPS paid $450 cash for freight costs on inventory delivered to customers.

Assume the merchandise sold in Event 7A was shipped FOB destination. Also assume JPS paid the freight cost in cash. FOB destination means the seller is responsible for the freight cost, which is called transportation-out. Transportation-out is reported on the income statement as an operating expense in the section below gross margin. The cost of freight on goods shipped to customers is incurred *after* the goods are sold. It is not part of the costs to obtain goods or ready them for sale. Recognizing the expense of transportation-out reduces assets (cash) and stockholders' equity (retained earnings). Operating expenses increase and net income decreases. The cash outflow is reported in the operating activities section of the statement of cash flows. These effects are shown as follows.

Balance Sheet										Income Statement				Statement of Cash Flows
Assets			=	Liab.			+	Stk. Equity						
Cash	+ Inventory +	Land	=	Accts. Pay.	+	Notes Pay.	+	Com. Stk.	+	Ret. Earn.	Rev. −	Exp.	= Net Inc.	
(450)	+ NA +	NA	=	NA	+	NA	+	NA	+	(450)	NA −	450	= (450)	(450) OA

If the terms had been FOB shipping point, the customer would have been responsible for the transportation cost and JPS would not have recorded an expense.

EVENT 9   JPS paid $5,000 cash for selling and administrative expenses.

The effect on the balance sheet is to decrease both assets (cash) and stockholders' equity (retained earnings). Recognizing the selling and administrative expenses decreases net income. The $5,000 cash outflow is reported in the operating activities section of the statement of cash flows. These effects are shown here.

Balance Sheet										Income Statement				Statement of Cash Flows
Assets			=	Liab.			+	Stk. Equity						
Cash	+ Inventory +	Land	=	Accts. Pay.	+	Notes Pay.	+	Com. Stk.	+	Ret. Earn.	Rev. −	Exp.	= Net Inc.	
(5,000)	+ NA +	NA	=	NA	+	NA	+	NA	+	(5,000)	NA −	5,000	= (5,000)	(5,000) OA

EVENT 10   JPS paid $360 cash for interest expense on the note described in Event 1.

The effect on the balance sheet is to decrease both assets (cash) and stockholders' equity (retained earnings). Recognizing the interest expense decreases net income. The $360 cash outflow is reported in the operating activities section of the statement of cash flows. These effects are shown as follows.

Balance Sheet												Income Statement				Statement of Cash Flows	
Assets			=	Liab.			+	Stk. Equity									
Cash	+	Inventory	+	Land	=	Accts. Pay.	+	Notes Pay.	+	Com. Stk.	+	Ret. Earn.	Rev.	−	Exp.	=	Net Inc.	
(360)	+	NA	+	NA	=	NA	+	NA	+	NA	+	(360)	NA	−	360	=	(360)	(360) OA

ACCOUNTING FOR INVENTORY SHRINKAGE

LO 3-5

Show how inventory shrinkage affects financial statements.

EVENT 11   JPS took a physical count of its inventory and found $4,100 of inventory on hand.

Most merchandising companies experience some level of inventory **shrinkage,** a term that reflects decreases in inventory for reasons other than sales to customers. Inventory may be stolen by shoplifters, damaged by customers or employees, or even simply lost or misplaced. Since the *perpetual* inventory system is designed to record purchases and sales of inventory as they occur, the balance in the merchandise inventory account represents the amount of inventory that *should* be on hand at any given time. For example, based on the previous transactions, the book balance of the JPS's Inventory account can be computed as follows:

Beginning balance	$ 6,000
Purchases	11,000
Purchase returns	(1,000)
Purchase discounts	(200)
Transportation-in	300
Goods available for sale	16,100
Cost of goods sold	(11,500)
Ending balance	$ 4,600

Assume that JPS takes a physical count of its inventory on hand and finds that it has only $4,100 of inventory. By comparing the $4,600 book balance in the Merchandise Inventory account with the $4,100 of actual inventory counted, we determine that the Company has experienced $500 of shrinkage. Under these circumstances JPS must make an adjusting entry to write down the Inventory account so the amount reported on the financial statements agrees with the amount actually on hand at the end of the period. The write-down decreases both assets (inventory) and stockholders' equity (retained earnings). The write-down increases expenses and decreases net income. Cash flow is not affected. The effects on the statements are as follows.

Balance Sheet												Income Statement				Statement of Cash Flows	
Assets			=	Liab.			+	Stk. Equity									
Cash	+	Inventory	+	Land	=	Accts. Pay.	+	Notes Pay.	+	Com. Stk.	+	Ret. Earn.	Rev.	−	Exp.	=	Net Inc.	
NA	+	(500)	+	NA	=	NA	+	NA	+	NA	+	(500)	NA	−	500	=	(500)	NA

Theoretically, inventory losses are operating expenses. However, because such losses are normally immaterial in amount, they are usually added to cost of goods sold for external reporting purposes.

REALITY BYTES

Good inventory management is essential for merchandising and manufacturing companies. Even if a company uses a perpetual inventory system, the amount of inventory believed to be on hand may be incorrect because of lost, damaged, or stolen goods, so a physical count is still required. Unfortunately, counting inventory is not a revenue-generating activity. If a company's employees are used to conduct the physical count, it takes time that may be better used for other activities. In fact, it may be so time-consuming that the business must close temporarily so employees will have the time to complete the inventory count.

To avoid this problem many businesses hire outside companies to count their inventory. These outside vendors can bring in a large crew of specially trained workers and complete a count very quickly. There are many companies that provide inventory counting services, but RIGIS, LLC claims to be the world's largest. RIGIS reports that its 34,000 employees have counted over 400 billion items in the more than 4 million inventory counts it has conducted since beginning operations in 1958. On second thought, counting inventory is a revenue-producing activity if you are a company that counts inventory for others.

Digital Vision/Photodisc/Getty Images

RECOGNIZING GAINS AND LOSSES

EVENT 12   JPS sold the land that had cost $5,500 for $6,200 cash.

When JPS sells merchandise inventory for more than it cost, the difference between the sales revenue and the cost of the goods sold is called the *gross margin*. In contrast, when JPS sells land for more than it cost, the difference between the sales price and the cost of the land is called a **gain.** Why is one called *gross margin* and the other a *gain*? The terms are used to alert financial statement users to the fact that the nature of the underlying transactions is different.

JPS's primary business is selling inventory, not land. The term *gain* indicates profit resulting from transactions that are not likely to regularly recur. Similarly, had the land sold for less than cost the difference would have been labeled **loss** rather than expense. This term also indicates the underlying transaction is not from normal, recurring operating activities. Gains and losses are shown separately on the income statement to communicate the expectation that they are nonrecurring.

The presentation of gains and losses in the income statement is discussed in more detail in a later section of the chapter. At this point note that the sale increases cash, decreases land, and increases retained earnings on the balance sheet. The income statement shows a gain on the sale of land and net income increases. The $6,200 cash inflow is shown as an investing activity on the statement of cash flows. These effects are shown as follows.

LO 3-6

Calculate gains and losses and show how they are presented on a multistep income statement.

Balance Sheet											Income Statement						Statement of Cash Flows
Assets			=	Liab.			+	Stk. Equity									
Cash	+	Inventory	+	Land	=	Accts. Pay.	+	Notes Pay.	+	Com. Stk.	+	Ret. Earn.	Gain.	−	Exp.	=	Net Inc.	
6,200	+	NA	+	(5,500)	=	NA	+	NA	+	NA	+	700	700	−	NA	=	700	6,200 IA

For your convenience, the Year 2 transactions and their financial statement effects for JPS are summarized in Exhibit 3.3.

EXHIBIT 3.3

Summary of Year 2 Events and Their Financial Statement Effects

Accounting Events

Event 1   JPS borrowed $4,000 cash by issuing a note payable.
Event 2   JPS purchased on account merchandise inventory with a list price of $11,000.
Event 3   JPS returned some of the inventory purchased in Event 2. The list price of the returned merchandise was $1,000.
Event 4   JPS received a cash discount on goods purchased in Event 2. The credit terms were 2/10, n/30.
Event 5   JPS paid the $9,800 balance due on the account payable.
Event 6   The inventory purchased in Event 2 was delivered FOB shipping point. JPS paid the freight company $300 cash for delivering the merchandise.
Event 7a   JPS recognized $24,750 of revenue on the cash sale of merchandise that cost $11,500.
Event 7b   JPS recognized $11,500 of cost of goods sold.
Event 8   JPS paid $450 cash for freight costs on inventory delivered to customers.
Event 9   JPS paid $5,000 cash for selling and administrative expenses.
Event 10   JPS paid $360 cash for interest expense on the note payable described in Event 1.
Event 11   JPS took a physical count of its inventory and found $4,100 of inventory on hand.
Event 12   JPS sold the land that had cost $5,500 for $6,200 cash.

Financial Statement Effects

Event No.	Cash	+	Inventory	+	Land	=	Accts. Pay.	+	Notes Pay.	+	Com. Stk.	+	Ret. Earn.	Rev./ Gain	−	Exp./ Loss	=	Net Inc.	Statement of Cash Flows
Beg. Bal.	6,500	+	6,000	+	5,500	=	NA	+	NA	+	15,000	+	3,000	NA	−	NA	=	NA	6,500
1.	4,000	+	NA	+	NA	=	NA	+	4,000	+	NA	+	NA	NA	−	NA	=	NA	4,000 FA
2.	NA	+	11,000	+	NA	=	11,000	+	NA	+	NA	+	NA	NA	−	NA	=	NA	NA
3.	NA	+	(1,000)	+	NA	=	(1,000)	+	NA	+	NA	+	NA	NA	−	NA	=	NA	NA
4.	NA	+	(200)	+	NA	=	(200)	+	NA	+	NA	+	NA	NA	−	NA	=	NA	NA
5.	(9,800)	+	NA	+	NA	=	(9,800)	+	NA	+	NA	+	NA	NA	−	NA	=	NA	(9,800) OA
6.	(300)	+	300	+	NA	=	NA	+	NA	+	NA	+	NA	NA	−	NA	=	NA	(300) OA
7a.	24,750	+	NA	+	NA	=	NA	+	NA	+	NA	+	24,750	24,750	−	NA	=	24,750	24,750 OA
7b.	NA	+	(11,500)	+	NA	=	NA	+	NA	+	NA	+	(11,500)	NA	−	11,500	=	(11,500)	NA
8.	(450)	+	NA	+	NA	=	NA	+	NA	+	NA	+	(450)	NA	−	450	=	(450)	(450) OA
9.	(5,000)	+	NA	+	NA	=	NA	+	NA	+	NA	+	(5,000)	NA	−	5,000	=	(5,000)	(5,000) OA
10.	(360)	+	NA	+	NA	=	NA	+	NA	+	NA	+	(360)	NA	−	360	=	(360)	(360) OA
11.	NA	+	(500)	+	NA	=	NA	+	NA	+	NA	+	(500)	NA	−	500	=	(500)	NA
12.	6,200	+	NA	+	(5,500)	=	NA	+	NA	+	NA	+	700	700	−	NA	=	700	6,200 IA
End	25,540	+	4,100	+	0	=	0	+	4,000	+	15,000	+	10,640	25,450	−	17,810	=	7,640	25,540

Multistep Income Statement

The information shown in the horizontal financial statements model in Exhibit 3.3 is used to prepare the financial statements in Exhibits 3.4, 3.6, and 3.7. JPS's Year 2 income statement is shown in Exhibit 3.4. Observe the form of this statement carefully. It is more informative than one that simply subtracts expenses from revenues. First, it compares sales revenue with the cost of the goods that were sold to produce that revenue. The difference between the sales revenue and the cost of goods sold is called *gross margin*. Next, the operating expenses are subtracted from the gross margin to determine the *operating income*. **Operating income** is the amount of income that is generated from the normal recurring operations of a business.

Items that are not expected to recur on a regular basis are subtracted from the operating income to determine the amount of *net income*.[1]

Income statements that show these additional relationships are called **multistep income statements.** Income statements that display a single comparison of all revenues minus all expenses are called **single-step income statements.** To this point in the text we have shown only single-step income statements to promote simplicity. However, the multistep form is used more frequently in practice. Exhibit 3.5 shows the percentage of Dow Jones Industrial companies that use the multistep versus the single-step format. Go to Exhibit 3.1 and identify the company that presents its income statement in the multistep format. You should have identified AutoNation as the company using the multistep format. Ford's statement is shown in the single-step format.

Note that interest is reported as a *nonoperating* item on the income statement in Exhibit 3.4. In contrast, it is shown in the *operating* activities section of the statement of cash flows in Exhibit 3.7. When the FASB issued Statement of Financial Accounting Standard (SFAS) 95, it required interest to be reported in the operating activities section of the statement of cash flows. There was no corresponding requirement for the treatment of interest on the income statement. Prior to SFAS 95, interest was considered to be a nonoperating item. Most companies continued to report interest as a nonoperating item on their income statements even though they were required to change how it was reported on the statement of cash flows. As a result, there is frequent inconsistency in the way interest is reported on the two financial statements.

Also note that while the gain on the sale of land is shown on the income statement, it is not included in the operating activities section of the statement of cash flows. Since the gain is a nonoperating item, it is included in the cash inflow from the sale of land shown in the investing activities section. In this case the full cash inflow from the sale of land ($6,200) is shown in the investing activities section of the statement of cash flows in Exhibit 3.7. Finally, note that the ending inventory balance is shown on the balance sheet in Exhibit 3.6.

EXHIBIT 3.4	
JUNE'S PLANT SHOP	
Income Statement	
For the Period Ended December 31, Year 2	
Sales revenue	$ 24,750
Cost of goods sold*	(12,000)
Gross margin	12,750
Less: Operating expenses	
Selling and administrative expense	(5,000)
Transportation-out	(450)
Operating income	7,300
Nonoperating items	
Interest expense	(360)
Gain on the sale of land	700
Net income	$ 7,640

*$11,500 inventory sold + $500 shrinkage.

EXHIBIT 3.5

Income Statement Format Used by U.S. Companies

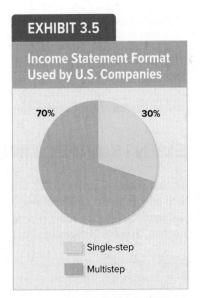

70%   30%

Single-step

Multistep

The chart is based on data drawn from recent annual reports published by the 30 companies that comprise the Dow Jones Industrial Average.

[1]Revenue and expense items with special characteristics may be classified as discontinued or extraordinary items. These items are shown separately just above net income regardless of whether a company uses a single-step or multistep format. Further discussion of these items is beyond the scope of this text.

EXHIBIT 3.6

JUNE'S PLANT SHOP
Balance Sheet
As of December 31, Year 2

Assets		
Cash	$25,540	
Merchandise inventory	4,100	
Total assets		$29,640
Liabilities		
Notes payable		$ 4,000
Stockholders' equity		
Common stock	$15,000	
Retained earnings	10,640	
Total stockholders' equity		25,640
Total liabilities and stockholders' equity		$29,640

EXHIBIT 3.7

JUNE'S PLANT SHOP
Statement of Cash Flows
For the Period Ended December 31, Year 2

Operating activities		
Inflow from customers	$ 24,750	
Outflow for inventory*	(10,100)	
Outflow for transportation-out	(450)	
Outflow for selling and administrative expense	(5,000)	
Outflow for interest expense	(360)	
Net cash outflow for operating activities		$ 8,840
Investing activities		
Inflow from sale of land		6,200
Financing activities		
Inflow from issue of note payable		4,000
Net change in cash		19,040
Plus beginning cash balance		6,500
Ending cash balance		$25,540

*Net cash paid to purchase inventory $9,800 + transportation-in $300 = $10,100

EVENTS AFFECTING SALES

LO 3-7

Determine the amount of net sales.

To this point we assumed JPS did not offer cash discounts to its customers. However, sales, as well as purchases of inventory, can be affected by returns, allowances, and discounts. **Sales discounts** are price reductions offered by sellers to encourage buyers to pay promptly. To illustrate, assume JPS engaged in the following selected events during January, Year 3.

EVENT 1A   JPS sold on account merchandise with a list price of $8,500. Payment terms were 1/10, n/30. The merchandise had cost JPS $4,000.

The sale increases both assets (accounts receivable) and shareholders' equity (retained earnings). Recognizing revenue increases net income. The statement of cash flows is not affected. The effects on the financial statements follow:

Balance Sheet											Income Statement				Statement of Cash Flows
Assets				=	Liab.	+	Stk. Equity									
Cash	+	Accts. Rec.	+	Inventory	=	Note Pay.	+	Com. Stk.	+	Retained Earnings	Rev.	−	Exp.	=	Net Inc.	
NA	+	8,500	+	NA	=	NA	+	NA	+	8,500	8,500	−	NA	=	8,500	NA

EVENT 1B   JPS recognized $4,000 of cost of goods sold.

Recognizing the expense decreases assets (merchandise inventory) and stockholders' equity (retained earnings). Cost of goods sold increases and net income decreases. Cash flow is not affected. The effects on the financial statements follow:

Balance Sheet									Income Statement			Statement of Cash Flows
Assets			=	Liab.	+	Stk. Equity						
Cash	+	Accts. Rec.	+ Inventory =	Note Pay.	+ Com. Stk.	+	Retained Earnings		Rev. −	Exp. =	Net Inc.	
NA	+	NA	+ (4,000) =	NA	+ NA	+	(4,000)		NA −	4,000 =	(4,000)	NA

Accounting for Sales Returns and Allowances

EVENT 2A   A customer from Event 1A returned inventory with a $1,000 list price. The merchandise had cost JPS $450.

The sales return decreases both assets (accounts receivable) and stockholders' equity (retained earnings) on the balance sheet. Sales and net income decrease. Cash flow is not affected. The effects on the financial statements follow:

Balance Sheet									Income Statement			Statement of Cash Flows
Assets			=	Liab.	+	Stk. Equity						
Cash	+	Accts. Rec.	+ Inventory =	Note Pay.	+ Com. Stk.	+	Retained Earnings		Rev. −	Exp. =	Net Inc.	
NA	+	(1,000)	+ NA =	NA	+ NA	+	(1,000)		(1,000) −	NA =	(1,000)	NA

EVENT 2B   The cost of the goods ($450) is returned to the inventory account.

Since JPS got the inventory back, the sales return increases both assets (merchandise inventory) and stockholders' equity (retained earnings). The expense (cost of goods sold) decreases and net income increases. Cash flow is not affected. The effects on the financial statements follow:

Balance Sheet									Income Statement			Statement of Cash Flows
Assets			=	Liab.	+	Stk. Equity						
Cash	+	Accts. Rec.	+ Inventory =	Note Pay.	+ Com. Stk.	+	Retained Earnings		Rev. −	Exp. =	Net Inc.	
NA	+	NA	+ 450 =	NA	+ NA	+	450		NA −	(450) =	450	NA

Accounting for Sales Discounts

EVENT 3   JPS collected the balance of the accounts receivable generated in Event 1A. Recall the goods were sold under terms 1/10, net/30.

ALTERNATIVE 1   The collection occurs before the discount period has expired (within 10 days from the date of the sale).

JPS would give the buyer a 1 percent discount. Given the original sales amount of $8,500 and a sales return of $1,000, the amount of the discount is $75 [($8,500 − $1,000) × 0.01]. The sales discount reduces the amount of accounts receivable and retained earnings on the balance sheet. It also reduces the amount of revenue and the net income shown on the balance sheet. It does not affect the statement of cash flows. The effects on the financial statements follow:

Balance Sheet										Income Statement					Statement of Cash Flows
Assets				=	Liab.	+	Stk. Equity								
Cash	+	Accts. Rec.	+	Inventory =	Note Pay.	+	Com. Stk.	+	Retained Earnings	Rev.	−	Exp.	=	Net Inc.	
NA	+	(75)	+	NA =	NA	+	NA	+	(75)	(75)	−	NA	=	(75)	NA

The balance due on the account receivable is $7,425 ($8,500 original sales − $1,000 sales return − $75 discount). The collection increases the Cash account and decreases the Accounts Receivable account. The income statement is not affected. The cash inflow is shown in the operating activities section of the statement of cash flows. The effects on the financial statements follow:

Balance Sheet										Income Statement					Statement of Cash Flows
Assets				=	Liab.	+	Stk. Equity								
Cash	+	Accts. Rec.	+	Inventory =	Accts. Pay.	+	Com. Stk.	+	Retained Earnings	Rev.	−	Exp.	=	Net Inc.	
7,425	+	(7,425)	+	NA =	NA	+	NA	+	NA	NA	−	NA	=	NA	7,425 OA

Net Sales

The gross amount of sales minus **sales returns and allowance** and sales discounts is commonly called **net sales.** Companies are not required by GAAP to show sales returns and allowance and sales discount on their income statement. Indeed, most companies show only the amount of *net sales* on the income statement. In this case, the net sales amount to $7,425 ($8,500 original sales − $1,000 sales return − $75 discount).

ALTERNATIVE 2   The collection occurs after the discount period has expired (after 10 days from the date of the sale).

Under these circumstances there is no sales discount. The amount collected is $7,500 ($8,500 original sale − $1,000 sales return). Net sales shown on the income statement would also be $7,500.

COMMON SIZE FINANCIAL STATEMENTS

LO 3-8

Use common size financial statements to evaluate managerial performance.

How good is a $1,000,000 increase in net income? The answer is not clear because there is no indication as to the size of the company. A million dollar increase may be excellent for a small company but would be virtually meaningless for a company the size of Exxon. To enable meaningful comparisons analysts prepare **common size financial statements.** Common size statements display information in percentages as well as absolute dollar amounts.

To illustrate, we expand the income statements for JPS to include percentages. The results are shown in Exhibit 3.8. The percentage data are computed by defining net sales as the base figure, or 100 percent. The other amounts on the statements are then shown as a percentage of net sales. For example, the *cost of goods sold percentage* is the dollar amount of *cost of goods sold* divided by the dollar amount of *net sales,* which produces a percentage of 66.7 percent ($8,000 ÷ $12,000) for Year 1 and 48.5 percent ($12,000 ÷ $24,750) for Year 2. Other income statement items are computed using the same approach.

EXHIBIT 3.8	Common Size Financial Statements

JUNE'S PLANT SHOP
Income Statement
For the Period Ended

	Year 1		Year 2	
Net sales*	$12,000	100.0%	$24,750	100.0%
Cost of goods sold	(8,000)	66.7	(12,000)	48.5
Gross margin	4,000	33.3	12,750	51.5
Less: Operating expenses				
Selling and administrative expense	(1,000)	8.3	(5,000)	20.2
Transportation-out			(450)	1.8
Operating income	3,000	25.0	7,300	29.5
Nonoperating items				
Interest expense			(360)	(1.5)
Gain on the sale of land			700	2.8
Net income	$ 3,000	25.0	$ 7,640	30.9

*Since JPS did not offer sales discounts or have sales returns and allowances during Year 1 or Year 2, the amount of sales revenue is equal to the amount of net sales. We use the term *net sales* here because it is more commonly used in business practice. Percentages do not add exactly because they have been rounded.

These common size statements provide insight into the company's operating strategy. For example, assume JPS relocated its store in an upscale mall in early Year 2. Management realized that the company would have to pay more for operating expenses but believed those expenses could be offset by charging significantly higher prices. The common size income statement confirms that the company's goals were accomplished. Note that the gross margin increased from 33.3 percent of sales to 51.5 percent, confirming that the company was able

Answers to The Curious Accountant

As data from the income statement for AutoNation show, automobile dealers do not have big markups on the cars they sell. The new vehicles the company sold for $12,180.8 million in 2017 cost the company $11,592.4 to purchase, resulting in a gross margin of $588.4, or 4.8 percent. In other words, if you bought an "average" car from AutoNation for $20,000, the company's gross profit on it was only $960 ($20,000 × .048), meaning it paid Ford $19,040 ($20,000 − $960). Furthermore, the company still had other expenses to pay besides its cost of goods sold. In 2017, only 2.0 percent of each dollar of AutoNation's sales was net profit ($434.6 ÷ $21,534.6). Remember, the amount shown for sales on AutoNation's income statement is based on what customers actually paid for the cars the company sold, not the "sticker price."

Meanwhile, if Ford sold the car to AutoNation for $19,040, it earned a 10.5 percent gross margin on the sale, or $1,866 [$14,321 ÷ $145,653 = 9.8%; ($145,653 − $131,332 = $14,321)] [$19,040 × .098 = $1,866]. Like AutoNation, Ford still had other expenses to pay for besides the cost of goods sold. In 2017, Ford earned 4.8 percent of net profit on each dollar of sales ($7,602 ÷ $156,776).

Most consumers significantly overestimate the profit margins of the companies from which they buy goods. Retailers, especially, operate with small profit margins, so inventory management is very important to their success.

to increase prices. Also, note that operating expenses increased. Selling and administrative expense increased from 8.3 percent of sales to 20.2 percent. Also, the company experienced a new expense, transportation out, for delivering merchandise to its customers. These increases in expenses confirm the fact that JPS is paying more for rental space and providing additional services to its customers. The common size statements, therefore, support the conclusion that JPS's increase in net income from $3,000 to $7,640 was a result of management's new operating strategy. As a side note, the new operating strategy may also explain why JPS sold its land in late Year 2. Considering the success the company experienced at the new location, there was no motive to build a store on the land.

A Look Back

Merchandising companies earn profits by selling inventory at prices that are higher than the cost paid for the goods. Merchandising companies include *retail companies* (companies that sell goods to the final consumer) and *wholesale companies* (companies that sell to other merchandising companies). The products sold by merchandising companies are called *inventory.* The costs to purchase inventory, to receive it, and to ready it for sale are *product costs,* which are first accumulated in an inventory account (balance sheet asset account) and then recognized as cost of goods sold (income statement expense account) in the period in which goods are sold. Purchases and sales of inventory can be recorded continually as goods are bought and sold (perpetual system) or at the end of the accounting period (periodic system, discussed in the chapter appendix).

Accounting for inventory includes the treatment of cash discounts, transportation costs, and returns and allowances. The cost of inventory is the list price less any purchase returns and allowances and purchase discounts, plus transportation-in costs. The cost of freight paid to acquire inventory (*transportation-in*) is considered a product cost. The cost of freight paid to deliver inventory to customers (*transportation-out*) is a selling expense. *Sales returns and allowances* and *sales discounts* are subtracted from sales revenue to determine the amount of *net sales* reported on the income statement. Purchase returns and allowances reduce product cost. Theoretically, the cost of lost, damaged, or stolen inventory is an operating expense. However, because these costs are usually immaterial in amount, they are typically included as part of cost of goods sold on the income statement.

Some companies use a *multistep income statement* that reports product costs separately from selling and administrative costs. Cost of goods sold is subtracted from sales revenue to determine *gross margin.* Selling and administrative expenses are subtracted from gross margin to determine income from operations. Other companies report income using a *single-step format* in which the cost of goods sold is listed along with selling and administrative items in a single expense category that is subtracted in total from revenue to determine income from operations.

Managers of merchandising businesses operate in a highly competitive environment. They must manage company operations carefully to remain profitable. *Common size financial statements* (statements presented on a percentage basis) and ratio analysis are useful monitoring tools. Common size financial statements permit ready comparisons among different-size companies. Although a $1 million increase in sales may be good for a small company and bad for a large company, a 10 percent increase can apply to any size company.

A Look Forward

To this point, the text has explained the basic accounting cycle for service and merchandising businesses. Future chapters more closely address specific accounting issues. For example, in Chapter 5 you will learn how to deal with inventory items that are purchased at differing prices. Other chapters will discuss a variety of specific practices that are widely used by real-world companies.

APPENDIX

Periodic Inventory System

Under certain conditions, it is impractical to record inventory sales transactions as they occur. Consider the operations of a fast-food restaurant. To maintain perpetual inventory records, the restaurant would have to transfer from the Inventory account to the Cost of Goods Sold account the *cost* of each hamburger, order of fries, soft drink, or other food items as they were sold. Obviously, recording the cost of each item at the point of sale would be impractical without using highly sophisticated computer equipment (recording the selling price the customer pays is captured by cash registers; the difficulty lies in capturing inventory cost).

LO 3-9

Identify the primary features of the periodic inventory system (Appendix).

The **periodic inventory system** offers a practical solution for recording inventory transactions in a low-technology, high-volume environment. Inventory costs are recorded in a Purchases account at the time of purchase. Purchase returns and allowances and transportation-in are recorded in separate accounts. No entries for the cost of merchandise purchases or sales are recorded in the Inventory account during the period. The cost of goods sold is determined at the end of the period as shown in Exhibit 3.9.

The perpetual and periodic inventory systems represent alternative procedures for recording the same information. The amounts of cost of goods sold and ending inventory reported in the financial statements will be the same regardless of the method used.

The **schedule of cost of goods sold** presented in Exhibit 3.9 is used for internal reporting purposes. It is normally not shown in published financial statements. The amount of cost of goods sold is reported as a single line item on the income statement. The income statement in Exhibit 3.4 will be the same whether JPS maintains perpetual or periodic inventory records.

EXHIBIT 3.9

Schedule of Cost of Goods Sold for Year 2	
Beginning inventory	$ 6,000
Purchases	11,000
Purchase returns and allowances	(1,000)
Purchase discounts	(200)
Transportation-in	300
Cost of goods available for sale	16,100
Ending inventory	(4,100)
Cost of goods sold	$12,000

Advantages and Disadvantages of the Periodic System versus the Perpetual System

The chief advantage of the periodic method is recording efficiency. Recording inventory transactions occasionally (periodically) requires less effort than recording them continually (perpetually). Historically, practical limitations offered businesses like fast-food restaurants or grocery stores no alternative to using the periodic system. The sheer volume of transactions made recording individual decreases to the Inventory account balance as each item was sold impossible. Imagine the number of transactions a grocery store would have to record every business day to maintain perpetual records.

Although the periodic system provides a recordkeeping advantage over the perpetual system, perpetual inventory records provide significant control advantages over periodic records. With perpetual records, the book balance in the Inventory account should agree with the amount of inventory in stock at any given time. By comparing that book balance with the results of a physical inventory count, management can determine the amount of lost, damaged, destroyed, or stolen inventory. Perpetual records also permit more timely and accurate reorder decisions and profitability assessments.

When a company uses the *periodic* inventory system, lost, damaged, or stolen merchandise is automatically included in cost of goods sold. Because such goods are not included in the year-end physical count, they are treated as sold regardless of the reason for their absence. Since the periodic system does not separate the cost of lost, damaged, or stolen merchandise from the cost of goods sold, the amount of any inventory shrinkage is unknown. This feature is a major disadvantage of the periodic system. Without knowing the amount of inventory losses, management cannot weigh the costs of various security systems against the potential benefits.

Advances in such technology as electronic bar code scanning and increased computing power have eliminated most of the practical constraints that once prevented merchandisers with high-volume, low dollar-value inventories from recording inventory transactions on a continual basis. As a result, use of the perpetual inventory system has expanded rapidly in recent years and continued growth can be expected. This text, therefore, concentrates on the perpetual inventory system.

Video lectures and accompanying self-assessment quizzes are available in *Connect* for all learning objectives.

SELF-STUDY REVIEW PROBLEM

Academy Sales Company (ASC) started the Year 2 accounting period with the balances given in the financial statements model shown as follows. During Year 2, ASC experienced the following business events:

1. Purchased $16,000 of merchandise inventory on account, terms 2/10, n/30.
2. The goods that were purchased in Event 1 were delivered FOB shipping point. Freight costs of $600 were paid in cash by the responsible party.
3. Returned $500 of goods purchased in Event 1.
4. (a) Recorded the cash discount on the goods purchased in Event 1.
   (b) Paid the balance due on the account payable within the discount period.
5. (a) Recognized $21,000 of cash revenue from the sale of merchandise.
   (b) Recognized $15,000 of cost of goods sold.
6. The merchandise in Event 5a was sold to customers FOB destination. Freight costs of $950 were paid in cash by the responsible party.
7. Paid cash of $4,000 for selling and administrative expenses.
8. Sold the land for $5,600 cash.

Required

a. Record these transactions in a financial statements model like the one shown as follows.

	Balance Sheet											Income Statement						Statement of Cash Flows
Event No.	Cash	+	Inventory	+	Land	=	Accts. Pay.	+	Com. Stk.	+	Ret. Earn.	Rev./ Gain	−	Exp.	=	Net Inc.		
Bal.	25,000	+	3,000	+	5,000	=	−0−	+	18,000	+	15,000	NA	−	NA	=	NA		NA

b. Prepare a schedule of cost of goods sold (Appendix).
c. Prepare a multistep income statement. Include common size percentages on the income statement.
d. ASC's gross margin percentage in Year 1 was 22 percent. Based on the common size data in the income statement, did ASC raise or lower its prices in Year 2 (Appendix)?
e. Assuming a 10 percent rate of growth, what is the amount of net income expected for Year 3?

Solution

a.

	Balance Sheet											Income Statement					Statement of Cash Flows
Event No.	Cash	+	Inventory	+	Land	=	Accts. Pay.	+	Com. Stk.	+	Ret. Earn.	Rev./ Gain	−	Exp.	=	Net Inc.	
Bal.	25,000	+	3,000	+	5,000	=	−0−	+	18,000	+	15,000	NA	−	NA	=	NA	NA
1		+	16,000			=	16,000	+		+			−		=		
2	(600)	+	600			=		+		+			−		=		(600) OA
3		+	(500)			=	(500)	+		+			−		=		
4a		+	(310)			=	(310)	+		+			−		=		
4b	(15,190)	+				=	(15,190)	+		+			−		=		(15,190) OA
5a	21,000	+				=		+		+	21,000	21,000	−		=	21,000	21,000 OA
5b		+	(15,000)			=		+		+	(15,000)		−	15,000	=	(15,000)	
6	(950)	+				=		+		+	(950)		−	950	=	(950)	(950) OA
7	(4,000)	+				=		+		+	(4,000)		−	4,000	=	(4,000)	(4,000) OA
8	5,600	+			(5,000)	=		+		+	600	600	−		=	600	5,600 IA
Bal.	30,860	+	3,790		−0−	=	−0−	+	18,000	+	16,650	21,600	−	19,950	=	1,650	5,860 NC

b.

ACADEMY SALES COMPANY	
Schedule of Cost of Goods Sold	
For the Period Ended December 31, Year 2	
Beginning inventory	$ 3,000
Plus purchases	16,000
Less: Purchase returns and allowances	(500)
Less: Purchases discounts	(310)
Plus: Transportation-in	600
Goods available for sale	18,790
Less: Ending inventory	3,790
Cost of goods sold	$15,000

c.

ACADEMY SALES COMPANY		
Income Statement*		
For the Period Ended December 31, Year 2		
Net sales	$21,000	100.0%
Cost of goods sold	(15,000)	71.4
Gross margin	6,000	28.6
Less: Operating expenses		
Selling and administrative expense	(4,000)	19.0
Transportation-out	(950)	4.5
Operating income	1,050	5.0
Nonoperating items		
Gain on the sale of land	600	2.9
Net income	$ 1,650	7.9

*Percentages do not add exactly because they have been rounded.

d. All other things being equal, the higher the gross margin percentage, the higher the sales prices. Since the gross margin percentage increased from 22 percent to 28.6 percent, the data suggest that Academy raised its sales prices.

e. $1,155 [$1,050 + (0.10 × $1,050)]. Note that the gain is not expected to recur.

KEY TERMS

Cash discount 100
Common size financial statements 110
Cost of goods available for sale 95
Cost of Goods Sold 95
FOB (free on board) destination 101
FOB (free on board) shipping point 101
Gain 105
Gross margin 96
Gross profit 96

Loss 105
Merchandise inventory 92
Merchandising businesses 92
Multistep income statement 107
Net sales 110
Operating income (or loss) 106
Period costs 95
Periodic inventory system 113

Perpetual inventory system 96
Product costs 95
Purchase allowances 99
Purchase discount 100
Purchase returns 99
Retail companies 93
Sales discount 108
Sales returns and allowances 110
Schedule of cost of goods sold 113

Selling and administrative costs 95
Shrinkage 104
Single-step income statement 107
Transportation-in (freight-in) 101
Transportation-out (freight-out) 101
2/10, n/30 100
Wholesale companies 93

QUESTIONS

1. Define *merchandise inventory*. What types of costs are included in the Merchandise Inventory account?

2. What is the difference between a product cost and a selling and administrative cost?

3. How is the cost of goods available for sale determined?

4. What portion of cost of goods available for sale is shown on the balance sheet? What portion is shown on the income statement?

5. When are period costs expensed? When are product costs expensed?

6. If PetCo had net sales of $600,000, goods available for sale of $450,000, and cost of goods sold of $375,000, what is its gross margin? What amount of inventory will be shown on its balance sheet?

7. Describe how the perpetual inventory system works. What are some advantages of using the perpetual inventory system? Is it necessary to take a physical inventory when using the perpetual inventory system?

8. What are the effects of the following types of transactions on the accounting equation? Also identify the financial statements that are affected. (Assume that the perpetual inventory system is used.)
   a. Acquisition of cash from the issue of common stock.
   b. Contribution of inventory by an owner of a company.
   c. Purchase of inventory with cash by a company.
   d. Sale of inventory for cash.

9. Northern Merchandising Company sold inventory that cost $12,000 for $20,000 cash. How does this event affect the accounting equation? What financial statements and accounts are affected? (Assume that the perpetual inventory system is used.)

10. If goods are shipped FOB shipping point, which party (buyer or seller) is responsible for the shipping costs?

11. Define *transportation-in*. Is it a product or a period cost?

12. Quality Cellular Co. paid $80 for freight on merchandise that it had purchased for resale to customers (transportation-in) and paid $135 for freight on merchandise delivered to customers (transportation-out). The $80 payment is added to what account? The $135 payment is added to what account?

13. Why would a seller grant an allowance to a buyer of his merchandise?

14. Dyer Department Store purchased goods with the terms 2/10, n/30. What do these terms mean?

15. Eastern Discount Stores incurred a $5,000 cash cost. How does the accounting for this cost differ if the cash were paid for inventory versus commissions to sales personnel?

16. What is the purpose of giving a cash discount to charge customers?

17. Define *transportation-out*. Is it a product cost or a period cost for the seller?

18. Ball Co. purchased inventory with a list price of $4,000 with the terms 2/10, n/30. What amount will be added to the Merchandise Inventory account?

19. Explain the difference between purchase returns and sales returns. How do purchase returns affect the financial statements of both buyer and seller? How do sales returns affect the financial statements of both buyer and seller?

20. Explain the difference between gross margin and a gain.

21. What is the difference between a multistep income statement and a single-step income statement?

22. What is the advantage of using common size income statements to present financial information for several accounting periods?

23. What is the purpose of preparing a schedule of cost of goods sold?

24. Explain how the periodic inventory system works. What are some advantages of using the periodic inventory system? What are some disadvantages of using the periodic inventory system? Is it necessary to take a physical inventory when using the periodic inventory system?

25. Why does the periodic inventory system impose a major disadvantage for management in accounting for lost, stolen, or damaged goods?

EXERCISES—SERIES A

McGraw Hill **connect** An electronic auto-gradable version of the Series A Exercises is available in Connect. A PDF version of Series B Exercises is in Connect under the "Additional Student Resources" tab. Solutions to the Series B Exercises are available in Connect under the "Instructor Library" tab. Instructor and student Workpapers for the Series B Exercises are available in Connect under the "Instructor Library" and "Additional Student Resources" tabs respectively.

When the instructions for *any* exercise or problem call for the preparation of an income statement, use the *multistep format* unless otherwise indicated.

LO 3-1

Exercise 3-1A *Determining the cost of financing inventory*

On January 1, Year 1, Jana started a small flower merchandising business that she named Jana's Flowers. The company experienced the following events during the first year of operation:

1. Started the business by issuing common stock for $30,000 cash.
2. Paid $19,000 cash to purchase inventory.

3. Sold merchandise that cost $10,000 for $21,000 on account.
4. Collected $16,000 cash from accounts receivable.
5. Paid $3,750 for operating expenses.

Required

a. Organize ledger accounts under an accounting equation and record the events in the accounts.
b. Prepare an income statement, a balance sheet, and a statement of cash flows.
c. Since Jana sold inventory for $21,000, she will be able to recover more than half of the $30,000 she invested in the stock. Do you agree with this statement? Why or why not?

Exercise 3-2A   *Comparing a merchandising company with a service company*   LO 3-1

The following information is available for two different types of businesses for the Year 1 accounting year. Hopkins CPAs is a service business that provides accounting services to small businesses. Sports Clothing is a merchandising business that sells sports clothing to college students.

Data for Hopkins CPAs

1. Borrowed $90,000 from the bank to start the business.
2. Provided $60,000 of services to clients and collected $50,000 cash.
3. Paid salary expense of $32,000.

Data for Sports Clothing

1. Borrowed $90,000 from the bank to start the business.
2. Purchased $60,000 inventory for cash.
3. Inventory costing $26,000 was sold for $50,000 cash.
4. Paid $8,000 cash for operating expenses.

Required

a. Prepare an income statement, balance sheet, and statement of cash flows for each of the companies.
b. Which of the two businesses would have product costs? Why?
c. Why does Hopkins CPAs not compute gross margin on its income statement?
d. Compare the assets of both companies. What assets do they have in common? What assets are different? Why?

Exercise 3-3A   *Effect of inventory transactions on financial statements: Perpetual system*   LO 3-1

Dan Watson started a small merchandising business in Year 1. The business experienced the following events during its first year of operation. Assume that Watson uses the perpetual inventory system.

1. Acquired $30,000 cash from the issue of common stock.
2. Purchased inventory for $18,000 cash.
3. Sold inventory costing $15,000 for $32,000 cash.

Required

a. Record the events in a statements model like the one shown here.

Balance Sheet							Income Statement			Statement of Cash Flows
Assets			=	Stk. Equity						
Cash	+	Inv.	=	Com. Stk.	+	Ret. Earn.	Rev.	− Exp.	= Net Inc.	

b. Prepare an income statement for Year 1 (use the multistep format).
c. What is the amount of total assets at the end of the period?

LO 3-1

Exercise 3-4A   *Effect of inventory transactions on the income statement and statement of cash flows: Perpetual system*

During Year 1, Hardy Merchandising Company purchased $40,000 of inventory on account. Hardy sold inventory on account that cost $24,500 for $38,000. Cash payments on accounts payable were $22,000. There was $26,000 cash collected from accounts receivable. Hardy also paid $5,100 cash for operating expenses. Assume that Hardy started the accounting period with $20,000 in both cash and common stock.

Required

a. Identify the events described in the preceding paragraph and record them in a horizontal statements model like the following one.

Balance Sheet									Income Statement				Statement of Cash Flows
Assets				=	Liab.	+	Stk. Equity						
Cash	+	Accts. Rec.	+	Inv.	=	Accts. Pay.	+	Com. Stk.	+	Ret. Earn.	Rev. − Exp. = Net Inc.		
20,000	+	NA	+	NA	=	NA	+	20,000	+	NA	NA − NA = NA		NA

b. What is the balance of accounts receivable at the end of Year 1?

c. What is the balance of accounts payable at the end of Year 1?

d. What are the amounts of gross margin and net income for Year 1?

e. Determine the amount of net cash flow from operating activities.

f. Explain why net income and retained earnings are the same for Hardy.

g. Normally would these amounts be the same? Why or why not?

LO 3-1

Exercise 3-5A   *Recording inventory transactions in a financial statements model*

Milo Clothing experienced the following events during Year 1, its first year of operation:

1. Acquired $30,000 cash from the issue of common stock.

2. Purchased inventory for $15,000 cash.

3. Sold inventory costing $9,000 for $20,000 cash.

4. Paid $1,500 for advertising expense.

Required

Record the events in a statements model like the one shown here.

Balance Sheet							Income Statement			Statement of Cash Flows
Assets			=	Stk. Equity						
Cash	+	Inv.	=	Com. Stk.	+	Ret. Earn.	Rev.	− Exp.	= Net Inc.	

LO 3-2, 3-3

Exercise 3-6A   *Purchase Discounts and Purchase Returns*

On April 6, Home Furnishings purchased $25,200 of merchandise from Una's Imports, terms 2/10, n/45. On April 8, Home Furnishings returned $2,400 of the merchandise to Una's Imports for credit. Home Furnishings paid cash for the merchandise on April 15.

Required

a. What is the amount that Home Furnishings must pay Una's Imports on April 15?

b. Record the events in a horizontal statements model like the following one.

Balance Sheet								Income Statement			Statement of Cash Flows
Assets			=	Liab.	+	Stk. Equity					
Cash	+	Inv.	=	Accts. Pay.	+	C. Stock.	+	Ret. Earn.	Rev.	− Exp. = Net Inc.	

c. How much must Home Furnishings pay for the merchandise purchased if the payment is not made until April 20?

d. Record the payment in event (c) in a horizontal statements model like the previous one.

e. Why would Home Furnishings want to pay for the merchandise by April 15?

Exercise 3-7A   *Effect of purchase returns and allowances and freight costs on the financial statements: Perpetual system*   LO 3-2, 3-3, 3-4

The beginning account balances for Terry's Auto Shop as of January 1, Year 2, follow:

Account Titles	Beginning Balances
Cash	$16,000
Inventory	8,000
Common stock	20,000
Retained earnings	4,000

The following events affected the company during the Year 2 accounting period:

1. Purchased merchandise on account that cost $15,000.
2. The goods in Event 1 were purchased FOB shipping point with freight cost of $800 cash.
3. Returned $2,600 of damaged merchandise for credit on account.
4. Agreed to keep other damaged merchandise for which the company received a $1,100 allowance.
5. Sold merchandise that cost $15,000 for $31,000 cash.
6. Delivered merchandise to customers in Event 5 under terms FOB destination with freight costs amounting to $500 cash.
7. Paid $8,000 on the merchandise purchased in Event 1.

Required

a. Organize appropriate ledger accounts under an accounting equation. Record the beginning balances and the transaction data in the accounts.

b. Prepare an income statement and a statement of cash flows for Year 2.

c. Explain why a difference does or does not exist between net income and net cash flow from operating activities.

Exercise 3-8A   *Accounting for product costs: Perpetual inventory system*   LO 3-2, 3-3, 3-4

Which of the following would be *added* to the Inventory account for a merchandising business using the perpetual inventory system?

Required

a. Transportation-out.
b. Purchase discount.
c. Transportation-in.
d. Purchase of a new computer to be used by the business.
e. Purchase of inventory.
f. Allowance received for damaged inventory.

Exercise 3-9A   *Effect of product cost and period cost: Horizontal statements model*   LO 3-1, 3-2, 3-4

The Pet Store experienced the following events for the Year 1 accounting period:

1. Acquired $60,000 cash from the issue of common stock.
2. Purchased $65,000 of inventory on account.
3. Received goods purchased in Event 2 FOB shipping point; freight cost of $900 paid in cash.

4. Sold inventory on account that cost $38,000 for $71,000.

5. Freight cost on the goods sold in Event 4 was $620. The goods were shipped FOB destination. Cash was paid for the freight cost.

6. Customer in Event 4 returned $4,200 worth of goods that had a cost of $2,150.

7. Collected $58,300 cash from accounts receivable.

8. Paid $59,200 cash on accounts payable.

9. Paid $2,600 cash for advertising expense.

10. Paid $3,100 cash for insurance expense.

Required

a. Which of these events affect period (selling and administrative) costs? Which result in product costs? If neither, label the transaction NA.

b. Record each event in a horizontal statements model like the following one. The first event is recorded as an example.

Balance Sheet									Income Statement			Statement of Cash Flows
Assets			=	Liab.	+	Stk. Equity						
Cash	+ Accts. Rec.	+ Inv.	=	Accts. Pay.	+	C. Stk.	+ Ret. Earn.		Rev. – Exp.	= Net Inc.		
60,000	+ NA	+ NA	=	NA	+	60,000	+ NA		NA – NA	= NA		60,000 FA

LO 3-4

Exercise 3-10A *Understanding the freight terms* **FOB shipping point** *and* **FOB destination**

Required

For each of the following events, indicate whether the freight terms are FOB destination or FOB shipping point.

a. Sold merchandise and the buyer paid the freight costs.

b. Purchased merchandise and the seller paid the freight costs.

c. Sold merchandise and paid the freight costs.

d. Purchased merchandise and paid the freight costs.

LO 3-1, 3-2, 3-3, 3-4

Exercise 3-11A *Determining the effect of inventory transactions on the horizontal statements model: Perpetual system*

Bali Sales Company experienced the following events:

1. Purchased merchandise inventory for cash.

2. Purchased merchandise inventory on account.

3. Returned merchandise purchased on account.

4. Sold merchandise inventory for cash. Label the revenue recognition 4a and the expense recognition 4b.

5. Paid cash on accounts payable not within the discount period.

6. Sold merchandise inventory on account. Label the revenue recognition 6a and the expense recognition 6b.

7. Paid cash for selling and administrative expenses.

8. Paid cash for transportation-in.

9. Collected cash from accounts receivable.

10. Paid cash for transportation-out.

Required

Identify each event as asset source (AS), asset use (AU), asset exchange (AE), or claims exchange (CE). Also explain how each event affects the financial statements by placing a + for increase, – for decrease, or NA for not affected under each of the components in the following statements model. Assume the use of the perpetual inventory system. The first event is recorded as an example.

Event No.	Event Type	Balance Sheet					Income Statement				Statement of Cash Flows
		Assets	=	Liab.	+	Stk. Equity	Rev.	−	Exp.	= Net Inc.	
1	AE	+ −	=	NA	+	NA	NA	−	NA	= NA	− OA

Exercise 3-12A   *Inventory financing costs*

LO 3-2, 3-4

Bill Norman comes to you for advice. He has just purchased a large amount of inventory with the terms 2/10, n/30. The amount of the invoice is $310,000. He is currently short of cash but has decent credit. He can borrow the money needed to settle the account payable at an annual interest rate of 7 percent. Bill is sure he will have the necessary cash by the due date of the invoice but not by the last day of the discount period.

Required

a. Convert the discount rate into an annual interest rate.

b. Make a recommendation regarding whether Bill should borrow the money and pay off the account payable within the discount period.

Exercise 3-13A   *Effect of shrinkage: Perpetual system*

LO 3-5

Ho Designs experienced the following events during Year 1, its first year of operation:

1. Started the business when it acquired $70,000 cash from the issue of common stock.
2. Paid $41,000 cash to purchase inventory.
3. Sold inventory costing $37,500 for $56,200 cash.
4. Physically counted inventory showing $3,200 inventory was on hand at the end of the accounting period.

Required

a. Determine the amount of the difference between book balance and the actual amount of inventory as determined by the physical count.

b. Explain how differences between the book balance and the physical count of inventory could arise. Why is being able to determine whether differences exist useful to management?

Exercise 3-14A   *Comparing gross margin and gain on sale of land*

LO 3-6

Lopez Sales Company had the following balances in its accounts on January 1, Year 2:

Cash	$42,000
Merchandise Inventory	36,000
Land	50,000
Common Stock	70,000
Retained Earnings	58,000

Lopez experienced the following events during Year 2:

1. Sold merchandise inventory that cost $22,000 for $40,500.
2. Sold land that cost $30,000 for $46,000.

Required

a. Determine the amount of gross margin recognized by Lopez.

b. Determine the amount of the gain on the sale of land recognized by Lopez.

c. Comment on how the gross margin versus the gain will be recognized on the income statement.

d. Comment on how the gross margin versus the gain will be recognized on the statement of cash flows.

LO 3-6

Exercise 3-15A *Single-step and multistep income statements*

The following information was taken from the accounts of Green Market, a delicatessen, at December 31, Year 2. The accounts are listed in alphabetical order, and each has a normal balance.

Accounts payable	$ 800
Accounts receivable	2,250
Advertising expense	600
Cash	1,850
Common stock	2,000
Cost of goods sold	2,950
Interest expense	120
Merchandise inventory	1,250
Prepaid rent	720
Retained earnings 1/1/Year 2	2,610
Sales revenue	5,600
Salaries expense	960
Rent expense	510
Gain on sale of land	200

Required

First, prepare an income statement for the year using the single-step approach. Then prepare another income statement using the multistep approach.

LO 3-2, 3-3, 3-4, 3-6, 3-7

Exercise 3-16A *Effect of sales returns and allowances and freight costs on the financial statements: Perpetual system*

Powell Company began the Year 3 accounting period with $40,000 cash, $86,000 inventory, $60,000 common stock, and $66,000 retained earnings. During Year 3, Powell experienced the following events:

1. Sold merchandise costing $58,000 for $99,500 on account to Prentise Furniture Store.
2. Delivered the goods to Prentise under terms FOB destination. Freight costs were $900 cash.
3. Received returned goods from Prentise. The goods cost Powell $4,000 and were sold to Prentise for $5,900.
4. Granted Prentise a $3,000 allowance for damaged goods that Prentise agreed to keep.
5. Collected partial payment of $81,000 cash from accounts receivable.

Required

a. Record the events in a statements model like the one shown as follows.

Balance Sheet							Income Statement			Statement of Cash Flows
Assets			=	Stk. Equity						
Cash	+ Accts. Rec.	+ Inv.	= Com. Stk.	+ Ret. Earn.			Rev.	− Exp.	= Net Inc.	

b. Prepare an income statement, a balance sheet, and a statement of cash flows.

c. Why would Prentise agree to keep the damaged goods? Who benefits more?

LO 3-3, 3-6

Exercise 3-17A *Effect of purchase discounts on financial statements: Perpetual system*

Expert Computers was started in Year 1. The company experienced the following accounting events during its first year of operation:

1. Started business when it acquired $40,000 cash from the issue of common stock.
2. Purchased merchandise with a list price of $32,000 on account, terms 2/10, n/30.

3. Paid off one-half of the accounts payable balance within the discount period.

4. Sold merchandise on account for $28,000. Credit terms were 1/20, n/30. The merchandise had cost Expert Computers $16,000.

5. Collected cash from the account receivable within the discount period.

6. Paid $2,100 cash for operating expenses.

7. Paid the balance due on accounts payable. The payment was not made within the discount period.

Required

a. Record the events in a horizontal statements model like the following one.

Balance Sheet							Income Statement			Statement of Cash Flows
Assets			=	Liab.	+	Stk. Equity				
Cash +	Accts. Rec. +	Inv. =		Accts. Pay. +	Com. Stk. +	Ret. Earn.	Rev. −	Exp. =	Net Inc.	

b. What is the amount of gross margin for the period? What is the net income for the period?

c. Why would Expert Computers sell merchandise with the terms 1/20, n/30?

d. What do the terms *2/10, n/30* in Event 2 mean to Expert Computers?

Exercise 3-18A   *Using common size statements and ratios to make comparisons*   LO 3-8

At the end of Year 5 the following information is available for Billings and Phoenix companies:

	Billings	Phoenix
Sales	$3,000,000	$3,000
Cost of goods sold	1,800,000	2,100
Operating expenses	960,000	780
Total assets	3,750,000	3,750
Stockholders' equity	1,000,000	1,200

Required

a. Prepare common size income statements for each company.

b. One company is a high-end retailer, and the other operates a discount store. Which is the discounter? Support your selection by referring to the common size statements.

Exercise 3-19A   *Effect of inventory transactions on the income statement and balance sheet: Periodic system (Appendix)*   LO 3-9

Bill Rose owns Rose Sporting Goods. At the beginning of the year, Rose Sporting Goods had $18,000 in inventory. During the year, Rose Sporting Goods purchased inventory that cost $66,000. At the end of the year, inventory on hand amounted to $28,500.

Required

Calculate the following:

a. Cost of goods available for sale during the year.

b. Cost of goods sold for the year.

c. Amount of inventory would Rose Sporting Goods report on the year-end balance sheet.

Exercise 3-20A   *Determining cost of goods sold: Periodic system (Appendix)*   LO 3-9

Tippah Antiques uses the periodic inventory system to account for its inventory transactions. The following account titles and balances were drawn from Tippah's records for Year 2: beginning balance in inventory, $42,000; purchases, $128,000; purchase returns and allowances, $12,000; sales, $520,000;

sales returns and allowances, $3,900; freight-in, $1,000; and operating expenses, $130,000. A physical count indicated that $26,000 of merchandise was on hand at the end of the accounting period.

Required

a. Prepare a schedule of cost of goods sold.

b. Prepare a multistep income statement.

PROBLEMS—SERIES A

Mc Graw Hill connect An electronic auto-gradable version of the Series A Problems is available in Connect. A PDF version of Series B Problems is in Connect under the "Additional Student Resources" tab. Solutions to the Series B Problems are available in Connect under the "Instructor Library" tab. Instructor and student Workpapers for the Series B Problems are available in Connect under the "Instructor Library" and "Additional Student Resources" tabs respectively.

Problem 3-21A *Identifying product and period costs*

Required

Indicate whether each of the following costs is a product cost or a period (selling and administrative) cost:

a. Goods purchased for resale.

b. Salaries of salespersons.

c. Advertising costs.

d. Transportation-out.

e. Interest on a note payable.

f. Salary of the company president.

g. Transportation-in.

h. Insurance on the office building.

i. Office supplies.

LO 3-2, 3-3

CHECK FIGURES
a. Ending Cash: $51,098
b. Net Income: $13,550

Problem 3-22A *Effect of purchase returns and allowances and purchase discounts on the financial statements: Perpetual system*

The following events were completed by Dana's Imports in September, Year 1:

Sept.	1	Acquired $50,000 cash from the issue of common stock.
	1	Purchased $28,000 of merchandise on account with terms 2/10, n/30.
	5	Paid $600 cash for freight to obtain merchandise purchased on September 1.
	8	Sold merchandise that cost $15,000 to customers for $31,000 on account, with terms 2/10, n/30.
	8	Returned $600 of defective merchandise from the September 1 purchase to the supplier.
	10	Paid cash for the balance due on the merchandise purchased on September 1.
	20	Received cash from customers of September 8 sale in settlement of the account balances, but not within the discount period.
	30	Paid $2,450 cash for selling expenses.

Required

a. Record each event in a statements model like the following one. The first event is recorded as an example.

Balance Sheet										Income Statement			Statement of Cash Flows
Assets				=	Liab.	+	Stk. Equity						
Cash	+	Accts. Rec.	+	Inv.	=	Accts. Pay.	+	Com. Stk.	+	Ret. Earn.	Rev.	−	Exp. = Net Inc.	
50,000	+	NA	+	NA	=	NA	+	50,000	+	NA	NA	−	NA = NA	50,000 FA

b. Prepare an income statement for the month ending September 30.

c. Prepare a statement of cash flows for the month ending September 30.

d. Explain why there is a difference between net income and cash flow from operating activities.

Problem 3-23A *Identifying freight costs*

LO 3-4

Required

For each of the following events, determine the amount of freight paid by The Box Company. Also indicate whether the freight cost would be classified as a product or period (selling and administrative) cost.

CHECK FIGURE

Event (b): NA

Cost: $0

a. Purchased inventory with freight costs of $650. The goods were shipped FOB shipping point.

b. Sold merchandise to a customer. Freight costs were $310. The goods were shipped FOB shipping point.

c. Purchased merchandise inventory with freight costs of $1,500. The merchandise was shipped FOB destination.

d. Shipped merchandise to customers, freight terms FOB destination. The freight costs were $520.

Problem 3-24A *Preparing a schedule of cost of goods sold and multistep and single-step income statements: Periodic system (Appendix)*

LO 3-2, 3-6, 3-9

The following account titles and balances were taken from the adjusted trial balance of King Co. for Year 2. The company uses the periodic inventory system.

CHECK FIGURES

Cost of Goods Available for Sale: $100,900

Net Income: $15,100

Account Title	Balance
Sales returns and allowances	$ 3,500
Miscellaneous expense	900
Transportation-out	2,200
Sales	156,300
Advertising expense	6,200
Salaries expense	21,000
Transportation-in	3,800
Purchases	88,000
Interest expense	250
Merchandise inventory, January 1	11,200
Rent expense	12,000
Merchandise inventory, December 31	10,700
Purchase returns and allowances	2,100
Loss on sale of land	3,100
Utilities expense	1,850

Required

a. Prepare a schedule to determine the amount of cost of goods sold.

b. Prepare a multistep income statement.

c. Prepare a single-step income statement.

Problem 3-25A *Basic transactions for three accounting cycles: Perpetual system*

LO 3-6

Blooming Flower Company was started in Year 1 when it acquired $60,000 cash from the issue of common stock. The following data summarize the company's first 3 years' operating activities. Assume that all transactions were cash transactions.

	Year 1	Year 2	Year 3
Purchases of inventory	$50,000	$60,000	$ 85,000
Sales	68,000	85,000	130,000
Cost of goods sold	34,000	43,000	71,000
Selling and administrative expenses	29,000	35,000	42,000

Required

Prepare an income statement (use multistep format) and balance sheet for each fiscal year. (*Hint:* Record the transaction data for each accounting period in the accounting equation before preparing the statements for that year.)

LO 3-2, 3-3, 3-4, 3-5, 3-6, 3-7

Problem 3-26A *Comprehensive cycle problem: Perpetual system*

At the beginning of Year 2, the Redd Company had the following balances in its accounts:

Cash	$16,900
Inventory	25,000
Common stock	30,000
Retained earnings	11,900

During Year 2, the company experienced the following events:

1. Purchased inventory that cost $15,200 on account from Ross Company under terms 1/10, n/30. The merchandise was delivered FOB shipping point. Freight costs of $200 were paid in cash.

2. Returned $800 of the inventory that it had purchased because the inventory was damaged in transit. The seller agreed to pay the return freight cost.

3. Paid the amount due on its account payable to Ross Company within the cash discount period.

4. Sold inventory that had cost $18,000 for $32,000 on account, under terms 2/10, n/45.

5. Received merchandise returned from a customer. The merchandise originally cost $800 and was sold to the customer for $1,500 cash. The customer was paid $1,500 cash for the returned merchandise.

6. Delivered goods FOB destination in Event 4. Freight costs of $140 were paid in cash.

7. Collected the amount due on the account receivable within the discount period.

8. Took a physical count indicating that $21,100 of inventory was on hand at the end of the accounting period.

Required

a. Identify these events as asset source (AS), asset use (AU), asset exchange (AE), or claims exchange (CE).

b. Record each event in a statements model like the following one.

	Balance Sheet								Income Statement			Statement of Cash Flows
	Assets			=	Liab.	+	Stk. Equity					
Event	Cash	+ Accts. Rec.	+ Inv.	=	Accts. Pay.	+	Com. Stk.	+ Ret. Earn.	Rev.	− Exp.	= Net Inc.	

c. Prepare a multistep income statement, a statement of changes in stockholders' equity, a balance sheet, and a statement of cash flows.

LO 3-8

Problem 3-27A *Using common size income statements to make comparisons*

The following income statements were drawn from the annual reports of Toner Sales Company:

	Year 2*	Year 3*
Net sales	$200,000	$200,000
Cost of goods sold	(90,000)	(80,000)
Gross margin	110,000	120,000
Less: Operating expense		
Selling and administrative expenses	(60,000)	(50,000)
Net income	$ 50,000	$ 70,000

*All dollar amounts are reported in thousands.

The president's message in the company's annual report stated that the company had implemented a strategy to increase market share by spending more on advertising. The president indicated that prices held steady and sales grew as expected. Write a memo indicating whether you agree with the president's statements. How has the strategy affected profitability? Support your answer by measuring growth in sales and selling expenses. Also prepare common size income statements and make appropriate references to the differences between Year 2 and Year 3.

Problem 3-28A   *Comprehensive cycle problem: Periodic system (Appendix)*   LO 3-9

The following listing of accounts pertains to Benji's Grocery as of January 1, Year 2:

Account Title	Beginning Balances
Cash	$64,000
Accounts receivable	12,000
Merchandise inventory	90,000
Accounts payable	7,500
Common stock	89,000
Retained earnings	69,500

The following events occurred in Year 2. Assume that Benji's uses the periodic inventory method.

CHECK FIGURES
a. Ending Cash: $161,994
b. Cost of Goods Sold: $262,986

1. Purchased land for $30,000 cash.
2. Purchased merchandise on account for $230,000, terms 1/10, n/45.
3. Paid freight of $2,100 cash on merchandise purchased FOB shipping point.
4. Returned $8,600 of defective merchandise purchased in Event 2.
5. Sold merchandise for $186,000 cash.
6. Sold merchandise on account for $236,000, terms 2/10, n/30.
7. Paid cash within the discount period on accounts payable due on merchandise purchased in Event 2.
8. Paid $28,500 cash for selling expenses.
9. Collected $156,000 of the accounts receivable from Event 6 within the discount period.
10. Collected $56,000 of the accounts receivable but not within the discount period.
11. Paid $17,100 of other operating expenses.
12. A physical count indicated that $48,300 of inventory was on hand at the end of the accounting period.

Required

a. Record these transactions in a horizontal statements model like the following one.

	Balance Sheet								Income Statement			Statement of Cash Flows
	Assets				= Liab. +		Stk. Equity					
Event	Cash +	Accts. Rec. +	Mdse. Inv. +	Land =	Accts. Pay. +	Com. Stock +	Ret. Earn.	Rev. −	Exp. =	Net Inc.		

b. Prepare a schedule of cost of goods sold and an income statement.

ANALYZE, THINK, COMMUNICATE

ATC 3-1   Business Application Case   *Understanding real-world annual reports*

Obtain the Target Corporation's annual report for its 2018 fiscal year (year ended February 2, 2019) at http://investors.target.com using the instructions in Appendix A, and use it to answer the following questions:

Target Corporation

Required

a. What percentage of Target's *Total Revenues* end up as net earnings?
b. What percentage of Target's *Sales* go to pay for the costs of the goods being sold?

c. What costs does Target include in its Cost of Sales account?

d. When does Target recognize revenue from the sale of gift cards?

ATC 3-2   Group Exercise   *Multistep income statement*

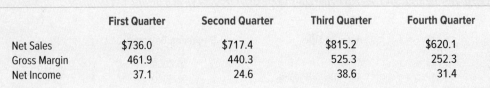

The following quarterly information is given for Raybon for the year ended Year 2 (amounts shown are in millions):

	First Quarter	Second Quarter	Third Quarter	Fourth Quarter
Net Sales	$736.0	$717.4	$815.2	$620.1
Gross Margin	461.9	440.3	525.3	252.3
Net Income	37.1	24.6	38.6	31.4

Required

a. Divide the class into groups and organize the groups into four sections. Assign each section financial information for one of the quarters.

   (1) Each group should compute the cost of goods sold and operating expenses for the specific quarter assigned to its section and prepare a multistep income statement for the quarter.

   (2) Each group should compute the gross margin percentage and cost of goods sold percentage for its specific quarter.

   (3) Have a representative of each group put that quarter's sales, cost of goods sold percentage, and gross margin percentage on the board.

Class Discussion

b. Have the class discuss the change in each of these items from quarter to quarter and explain why the change might have occurred. Which was the best quarter and why?

ATC 3-3   Research Assignment   *Analyzing Amazon.com's income statement*

Complete the following requirements using the most recent financial statements available [20xx] on Amazon.com's corporate website. Obtain the statements on the Internet by following the steps given. (Be aware that the formatting of the company's website may have changed since these instructions were written.)

■ Go to www.amazon.com.

■ At the bottom of the screen, under "Get to Know Us," click on "Investor Relations."

■ Annual reports, proxies and shareholders' letters.

■ Click on "20xx Annual Report" (the most recent year).

Read the following sections of the annual report:

■ The income statement, which Amazon.com calls the "Consolidated Statement of Operations."

■ In the footnotes section, "Note 1—Description of Business and Accounting Policies," read the subsections titled "*Revenue*" and "*Cost of Sales.*"

Required

a. What percentage of Amazon's sales end up as net income?

b. What percentage of Amazon's sales go to pay for the costs of the goods being sold?

c. What specific criteria are necessary before Amazon will recognize a sale as having been completed and record the related revenue?

d. How does Amazon account for (report on its income statement) the shipping costs it incurs to ship goods to its customers?

ATC 3-4 Written Assignment, Critical Thinking *Effect of sales returns on financial statements*

Bell Farm and Garden Equipment reported the following information for Year 2:

Net Sales of Equipment	$2,450,567
Other Income	6,786
Cost of Goods Sold	1,425,990
Selling, General, and Administrative Expense	325,965
Net Operating Income	$ 705,398

Selected information from the balance sheet as of December 31, Year 2, follows:

Cash and Marketable Securities	$113,545
Inventory	248,600
Accounts Receivable	82,462
Property, Plant, and Equipment—Net	335,890
Other Assets	5,410
Total Assets	$785,907

Assume that a major customer returned a large order to Bell on December 31, Year 2. The amount of the sale had been $146,800 with a cost of sales of $94,623. The return was recorded in the books on January 1, Year 3. The company president does not want to correct the books. He argues that it makes no difference as to whether the return is recorded in Year 2 or Year 3. Either way, the return has been duly recognized.

Required

a. Assume that you are the CFO for Bell Farm and Garden Equipment Co. Write a memo to the president explaining how omitting the entry on December 31, Year 2, could cause the financial statements to be misleading to investors and creditors. Explain how omitting the return from the customer would affect net income and the balance sheet.

b. Why might the president want to record the return on January 1, Year 3, instead of December 31, Year 2?

CHAPTER 4

Internal Controls, Accounting for Cash, and Ethics

LEARNING OBJECTIVES

After you have mastered the material in this chapter, you will be able to:

LO 4-1   Identify the key elements of a strong system of internal control.

LO 4-2   Identify special internal controls for cash.

LO 4-3   Prepare a bank reconciliation.

LO 4-4   Identify the role of ethics in the accounting profession.

LO 4-5   Identify the auditor's role in financial reporting.

 Video lectures and accompanying self-assessment quizzes are available in Connect *for all learning objectives.*

 Set B exercises and problems are available in Additional Student Resources.

CHAPTER OPENING

In the first three chapters, we covered the basics of the accounting system. By now you should understand how basic business events affect financial statements and how the accounting cycle works. Accounting is an elegant system that when implemented correctly provides meaningful information to investors and other stakeholders. However, without effective control, the accounting system can be manipulated in ways that may overstate business performance. This can lead investors to make bad decisions, which can result in huge losses when the true performance is revealed. This chapter discusses the importance of internal control systems. The chapter also discusses accounting for cash, an area where good internal controls are critical. The chapter concludes with a discussion on the importance of ethical conduct in the accounting profession.

The Curious Accountant

jvdwolf/123RF

When many people think about the threats to a company's financial resources they imagine someone trying to steal its cash or other assets, or a hacker trying to drain its bank account. Although these are legitimate threats, the biggest threats facing business often come from within.

Consider the case of the Volkswagen AG (VW) emissions scandal that became widely known to the public in September 2015, when the Environmental Protection Agency (EPA) filed charges claiming VW had intentionally installed software to provide inaccurate results related to mileage and emissions performance in some of its vehicles with diesel engines. Within months of the charges by the EPA, VW admitted that its emissions-defeating software had been installed on about 11 million vehicles worldwide.

Companies' responsibilities under the Sarbanes–Oxley Act (SOX) are discussed later in this chapter. Do you think SOX was intended to require companies to protect their customers from the type of cyber-security frauds reported here? If not, are there other aspects of financial accounting systems that should protect a company's customers? (Answer on page 142.)

KEY FEATURES OF INTERNAL CONTROL SYSTEMS

LO 4-1

Identify the key elements of a strong system of internal control.

During the early 2000s, a number of accounting-related scandals cost investors billions. In 2001, Enron's share price went from $85 to $0.30 after it was revealed that the company had billions of dollars in losses that were not reported on the financial statements. Several months later, WorldCom reported an $11 billion accounting fraud, which included hundreds of millions in personal loans to then CEO, Bernie Ebbers.

The Enron and WorldCom accounting scandals had such devastating effects that they led Congress to pass the Sarbanes–Oxley Act of 2002 (SOX). SOX requires public companies to evaluate their *internal control* and to publish those findings with their SEC filings. **Internal control** is the process designed to ensure reliable financial reporting, effective and efficient operations, and compliance with applicable laws and regulations. Safeguarding assets against theft and unauthorized use, acquisition, or disposal is also part of internal control.

Section 404 of Sarbanes–Oxley requires a statement of management's responsibility for establishing and maintaining adequate internal control over financial reporting by public companies. This section includes an assessment of the controls and the identification of the framework used for the assessment. The Committee of Sponsoring Organizations of the Treadway Commission (COSO) identified a framework in 1992. In 2013, the Committee superseded that framework with an updated framework contained in a document titled *Internal Control–Integrated Framework*. The 2013 framework is the de facto standard by which SOX compliance is judged. COSO's framework recognizes five interrelated components including:

1. *Control Environment.* The integrity and ethical values of the company, including its code of conduct, involvement of the board of directors, and other actions that set the tone of the organization.

2. *Risk Assessment.* Management's process of identifying potential risks that could result in misstated financial statements and developing actions to address those risks.

3. *Control Activities.* These are the activities usually thought of as "the internal controls." They include such things as segregation of duties, account reconciliations, and information processing controls that are designed to safeguard assets and enable an organization to timely prepare reliable financial statements.

4. *Information and Communication.* The internal and external reporting process, and includes an assessment of the technology environment.

5. *Monitoring.* Assessing the quality of a company's internal control over time and taking actions as necessary to ensure it continues to address the risks of the organization.

In 2017, COSO updated the 2004 framework to help entities design and implement effective enterprise-wide approaches to risk management. The updated document is titled *ERM Framework: Enterprise Risk Management (ERM)–Integrating with Strategy and Performance.* The ERM framework introduces an enterprise-wide approach to risk management as well as concepts such as risk appetite, risk tolerance, and portfolio view. While SOX applies only to U.S. public companies, the ERM framework has been adopted by both public and private organizations around the world.

This new document builds on its predecessor, *Enterprise Risk Management–Integrated Framework*, one of the most widely recognized and applied risk management frameworks in the world. The updated edition is designed to help organizations create, preserve, and realize value while improving their approach to managing risk. Accordingly, the 2004 *Enterprise Risk Management–Integrated Framework* and the 2013 *Internal Control–Integrated Framework* are considered to be complementary.

While a detailed discussion of the COSO documents is beyond the scope of this text, the following overview of the more common *control activities* of the internal control framework is insightful.

Separation of Duties

The likelihood of fraud or theft is reduced if collusion is required to accomplish it. Clear **separation of duties** is frequently used as a deterrent to corruption. When duties are separated, the work of one employee can act as a check on the work of another employee. For example, a person selling seats to a movie may be tempted to steal money received from customers who enter the theater. This temptation is reduced if the person staffing the box office is required to issue tickets that a second employee collects as people enter the theater. If ticket stubs collected by the second employee are compared with the cash receipts from ticket sales, any cash shortages would become apparent. Furthermore, friends and relatives of the ticket agent could not easily enter the theater without paying. Theft or unauthorized entry would require collusion between the ticket agent and the usher who collects the tickets. Both individuals would have to be dishonest enough to steal, yet trustworthy enough to convince each other they would keep the embezzlement secret. Whenever possible, the functions of *authorization, recording,* and *custody of assets* should be performed by separate individuals.

Quality of Employees

A business is only as good as the people it employs. Cheap labor is not a bargain if the employees are incompetent. Employees should be properly trained. In fact, they should be trained to perform a variety of tasks. The ability of employees to substitute for one another prevents disruptions when co-workers are absent because of illnesses, vacations, or other commitments. The capacity to rotate jobs also relieves boredom and increases respect for the contributions of other employees. Every business should strive to maximize the productivity of every employee. Ongoing training programs are essential to a strong system of internal control.

Bonded Employees

The best way to ensure employee honesty is to hire individuals with *high levels of personal integrity.* Employers should screen job applicants using interviews, background checks, and recommendations from prior employers or educators. Even so, screening programs may fail to identify character weaknesses. Further, unusual circumstances may cause honest employees to go astray. Therefore, employees in positions of trust should be bonded. A **fidelity bond** provides insurance that protects a company from losses caused by employee dishonesty.

Required Absences

Employees should be required to take regular vacations and their duties should be rotated periodically. Employees may be able to cover up fraudulent activities if they are always present at work. Consider the case of a parking meter collection agent who covered the same route for several years with no vacation. When the agent became sick, a substitute collected more money each day than the regular reader usually reported. Management checked past records and found that the ill meter reader had been understating the cash receipts and pocketing the difference. If management had required vacations or rotated the routes, the embezzlement would have been discovered much earlier.

Procedures Manual

Appropriate accounting procedures should be documented in a **procedures manual.** The manual should be routinely updated. Periodic reviews should be conducted to ensure that employees are following the procedures outlined in the manual.

Authority and Responsibility

Employees are motivated by clear lines of authority and responsibility. They work harder when they have the authority to use their own judgment and they exercise reasonable caution when they are held responsible for their actions. Businesses should prepare an **authority manual** that establishes a definitive *chain of command.* The authority manual should guide both specific and general authorizations. **Specific authorizations** apply to specific positions within the organization. For example, investment decisions are authorized at the division level while hiring decisions are authorized at the departmental level. In contrast, **general authority** applies across different levels of management. For example, employees at all levels may be required to fly coach or to make purchases from specific vendors.

Prenumbered Documents

How would you know if a check were stolen from your checkbook? If you keep a record of your check numbers, the missing number would tip you off immediately. Businesses also use prenumbered checks to avoid the unauthorized use of their bank accounts. In fact, prenumbered forms are used for all important documents such as purchase orders, receiving reports, invoices, and checks. To reduce errors, prenumbered forms should be as simple and easy to use as possible. Also, the documents should allow for authorized signatures. For example, credit sales slips should be signed by the customer to clearly establish who made the purchase, reducing the likelihood of unauthorized transactions.

Physical Control

Employees walk away with billions of dollars of business assets each year. To limit losses, companies should establish adequate physical control over valuable assets. For example, inventory should be kept in a storeroom and not released without proper authorization. Serial numbers on equipment should be recorded along with the name of the individual who is responsible for the equipment. Unannounced physical counts should be conducted randomly to verify the presence of company-owned equipment. Certificates of deposit and marketable securities should be kept in fireproof vaults. Access to these vaults should be limited to authorized personnel. These procedures protect the documents from fire and limit access to only those individuals who have the appropriate security clearance to handle the documents.

In addition to safeguarding assets, there should be physical control over the accounting records. The accounting journals, ledgers, and supporting documents should be kept in a fireproof safe. Only personnel responsible for recording transactions in the journals should have access to them. With limited access, there is less chance that someone will change the records to conceal fraud or embezzlement.

Performance Evaluations

Because few people can evaluate their own performance objectively, internal controls should include independent verification of employee performance. For example, someone other than the person who has control over inventory should take a physical count of inventory. Internal and external audits serve as independent verification of performance. Auditors should evaluate the effectiveness of the internal control system as well as verify the accuracy of the accounting records. In addition, the external auditors attest to the company's use of generally accepted accounting principles in the financial statements.

Limitations

A system of internal controls is designed to prevent or detect errors and fraud. However, no control system is foolproof. Internal controls can be circumvented by collusion among employees. Two or more employees working together can hide embezzlement by covering for each other. For example, if an embezzler goes on vacation, fraud will not be reported by a replacement who is in collusion with the embezzler. Similarly, internal controls can be compromised by management override. For example, a manager may order an employee to ignore certain internal control procedures. This may be done with deceitful intent or innocently with good intentions. Indeed, human error is a common cause of internal control failure. No system can prevent all fraud. However, a good system of internal controls minimizes illegal or unethical activities by reducing temptation and increasing the likelihood of early detection.

 CHECK YOURSELF 4.1

Identify 10 features of an internal control system.

Answer

The 10 features follow:

1. Separating duties so that fraud or theft requires collusion.
2. Hiring and training competent employees.

3. Bonding employees to recover losses through insurance.

4. Requiring employees to be absent from their jobs so that their replacements can discover errors or fraudulent activity that might have occurred.

5. Establishing proper procedures for processing transactions.

6. Establishing clear lines of authority and responsibility.

7. Using prenumbered documents.

8. Implementing physical controls such as locking cash in a safe.

9. Conducting performance evaluations through independent internal and external audits.

10. No control system is foolproof. Internal controls can be circumvented by a variety of actions such as collusion among employees.

ACCOUNTING FOR CASH

For financial reporting purposes, **cash** generally includes currency and other items that are payable *on demand,* such as checks, money orders, bank drafts, and certain savings accounts. Savings accounts that impose substantial penalties for early withdrawal should be classified as *investments* rather than cash. Postdated checks or IOUs represent *receivables* and should not be included in cash. As illustrated in Exhibit 4.1, most companies combine currency and other payable on demand items in a single balance sheet account with varying titles.

Companies must maintain a sufficient amount of cash to pay employees, suppliers, and other creditors. When a company fails to pay its legal obligations, its creditors can force the company into bankruptcy. Even so, management should avoid accumulating more cash than is needed. The failure to invest excess cash in earning assets reduces profitability. Cash inflows and outflows must be managed to prevent a shortage or surplus of cash.

LO 4-2

Identify special internal controls for cash.

Controlling Cash

Controlling cash, more than any other asset, requires strict adherence to internal control procedures. Cash has universal appeal. A relatively small suitcase filled with high-denomination currency can represent significant value. Furthermore, the rightful owner of currency is difficult to prove. In most cases, possession constitutes ownership. As a result, cash is highly susceptible to theft and must be carefully protected. Cash is most susceptible to embezzlement when it is received or disbursed. The following controls should be employed to reduce the likelihood of theft.

Cash Receipts

A record of all cash collections should be prepared immediately upon receipt. The amount of cash on hand should be counted regularly. Missing amounts of money can be detected by comparing the actual cash on hand with the book balance. Employees who receive cash should give customers a copy of a written receipt. Customers usually review their receipts to ensure they have gotten credit for the amount paid and call any errors to the receipts clerk's attention. This not only reduces errors but also provides a control on the clerk's honesty. Cash receipts should be deposited in a bank on a timely basis. Cash collected late in the day should be deposited in a night depository. Every effort should be made to minimize the amount of cash on hand. Keeping large amounts of cash on hand not only increases the risk of loss from theft but also places employees in danger of being harmed by criminals who may be tempted to rob the company.

Cash Payments

To effectively control cash, a company should make all disbursements using checks, thereby providing a record of cash payments. All checks should be prenumbered, and unused checks should be locked up. Using prenumbered checks allows companies to easily identify lost or stolen checks by comparing the numbers on unused and canceled checks with the numbers used for legitimate disbursements.

EXHIBIT 4.1

Balance Sheet Classifications That Include the Word *Cash*

3%
7%
7%
83%

- Cash and cash equivalents
- Cash and equivalents
- Cash
- Cash and marketable securities

Note: The chart is based on data drawn from the recent annual reports published by the 30 companies that comprise the Dow Jones Industrial Average.

REALITY BYTES

THE COST OF PROTECTING CASH

Could you afford to buy a safe like the one shown here? The vault is only one of many expensive security devices used by banks to safeguard cash. By using checking accounts, companies are able to avoid many of the costs associated with keeping cash safe. In addition to providing physical control, checking accounts enable companies to maintain a written audit trail of cash receipts and payments. Checking accounts represent the most widely used internal control device in modern society. It is difficult to imagine a business operating without the use of checking accounts.

Bettmann/Getty Images

The duties of approving disbursements, signing checks, and recording transactions should be separated. If one person is authorized to approve, sign, and record checks, he or she could falsify supporting documents, write an unauthorized check, and record a cover-up transaction in the accounting records. By separating these duties, the check signer reviews the documentation provided by the approving individual before signing the check. Likewise, the recording clerk reviews the work of both the approving person and the check signer when the disbursement is recorded in the accounting records. Thus, writing unauthorized checks requires trilevel collusion.

Supporting documents with authorized approval signatures should be required when checks are presented to the check signer. For example, a warehouse receiving order should be matched with a purchase order before a check is approved to pay a bill from a supplier. Before payments are approved, invoice amounts should be checked and payees verified as valid vendors. Matching supporting documents with proper authorization discourages employees from creating phony documents for a disbursement to a friend or fictitious business. Also, the approval process serves as a check on the accuracy of the work of all employees involved.

Supporting documents should be marked *Paid* when the check is signed. If the documents are not indelibly marked, they could be retrieved from the files and resubmitted for a duplicate, unauthorized payment. A payables clerk could collude with the payee to split extra cash paid out by submitting the same supporting documents for a second payment.

All spoiled and voided checks should be defaced and retained. If defaced checks are not retained, an employee could steal a check and then claim that it was written incorrectly and thrown away. The clerk could then use the stolen check to make an unauthorized payment.

Checking Account Documents

The previous section explained the need for businesses to use checking accounts. A description of four main types of forms associated with a bank checking account follows.

Signature Card

A bank **signature card** shows the bank account number and the signatures of the people authorized to sign checks. The card is retained in the bank's files. If a bank employee is unfamiliar with the signature on a check, he or she can refer to the signature card to verify the signature before cashing the check.

Deposit Ticket

Each deposit of cash or checks is accompanied by a **deposit ticket,** which normally identifies the account number and the name of the account. The depositor lists the individual amounts of currency, coins, and checks, as well as the total deposited, on the deposit ticket.

Bank Check

A written check affects three parties: (1) the person or business writing the check (the *payer*); (2) the bank on which the check is drawn; and (3) the person or business to whom the check is payable (the *payee*). Companies often write **checks** using multicopy, prenumbered forms, with the name of the issuing business preprinted on the face of each check. A remittance notice is usually attached to the check forms. This portion of the form provides the issuer space to record what the check is for (e.g., what invoices are being paid), the amount being disbursed, and the date of payment. When signed by the person whose signature is on the signature card, the check authorizes the bank to transfer the face amount of the check from the payer's account to the payee.

Bank Statement

Periodically, the bank sends the depositor a **bank statement.** The bank statement is presented from the bank's point of view. Checking accounts are liabilities to a bank because the bank is obligated to pay back the money that customers have deposited in their accounts. Therefore, in the bank's accounting records a customer's checking account has a *credit* balance. As a result, **bank statement debit memos** describe transactions that reduce the customer's account balance (the bank's liability). **Bank statement credit memos** describe activities that increase the customer's account balance (the bank's liability). Since a checking account is an asset (cash) to the depositor, a *bank statement debit memo* requires a *credit entry* to the cash account on the depositor's books. Likewise, when a bank tells you that it has credited your account, you will debit your cash account in response.

Bank statements normally report (a) the balance of the account at the beginning of the period; (b) additions for customer deposits made during the period; (c) other additions described in credit memos (e.g., for interest earned); (d) subtractions for the payment of checks drawn on the account during the period; (e) other subtractions described in debit memos (e.g., for service charges); (f) a running balance of the account; and (g) the balance of the account at the end of the period. The sample bank statement in Exhibit 4.2 illustrates these items. Normally, the canceled checks or copies of them are enclosed with the bank statement.

RECONCILING THE BANK ACCOUNT

Usually the ending balance reported on the bank statement differs from the balance in the depositor's cash account as of the same date. The discrepancy is normally attributable to timing differences. For example, a depositor deducts the amount of a check from its cash account when it writes the check. However, the bank does not deduct the amount of the check from the depositor's account until the payee presents it for payment, which may be days, weeks, or even months after the check is written. As a result, the balance on the depositor's books is lower than the balance on the bank's books. Companies prepare a **bank reconciliation** to explain the differences between the cash balance reported on the bank statement and the cash balance recorded in the depositor's accounting records.

LO 4-3

Prepare a bank reconciliation.

Determining True Cash Balance

A bank reconciliation normally begins with the cash balance reported by the bank, which is called the **unadjusted bank balance.** The adjustments necessary to determine the amount of cash that the depositor actually owns as of the date of the bank statement are then added to and subtracted from the unadjusted bank balance. The final total is the **true cash balance.** The true cash balance is independently reached a second time by making adjustments to the **unadjusted book balance.** The bank account is reconciled when the true cash balance

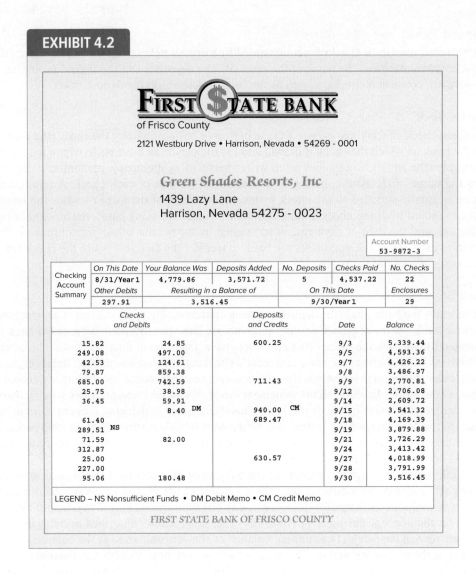

EXHIBIT 4.2

FIRST **$** **TATE BANK**
of Frisco County

2121 Westbury Drive • Harrison, Nevada • 54269 - 0001

Green Shades Resorts, Inc

1439 Lazy Lane
Harrison, Nevada 54275 - 0023

Account Number
53-9872-3

Checking Account Summary	On This Date	Your Balance Was	Deposits Added	No. Deposits	Checks Paid	No. Checks
	8/31/Year 1	4,779.86	3,571.72	5	4,537.22	22
	Other Debits	Resulting in a Balance of		On This Date		Enclosures
	297.91	3,516.45		9/30/Year 1		29

Checks and Debits			Deposits and Credits		Date	Balance
15.82	24.85		600.25		9/3	5,339.44
249.08	497.00				9/5	4,593.36
42.53	124.61				9/7	4,426.22
79.87	859.38				9/8	3,486.97
685.00	742.59		711.43		9/9	2,770.81
25.75	38.98				9/12	2,706.08
36.45	59.91				9/14	2,609.72
	8.40 DM		940.00 CM		9/15	3,541.32
61.40			689.47		9/18	4,169.39
289.51 NS					9/19	3,879.88
71.59	82.00				9/21	3,726.29
312.87					9/24	3,413.42
25.00			630.57		9/27	4,018.99
227.00					9/28	3,791.99
95.06	180.48				9/30	3,516.45

LEGEND – NS Nonsufficient Funds • DM Debit Memo • CM Credit Memo

FIRST STATE BANK OF FRISCO COUNTY

determined from the perspective of the unadjusted *bank* balance agrees with the true cash balance determined from the perspective of the unadjusted *book* balance. The procedures a company uses to determine the *true cash balance* from the two different perspectives are outlined here.

Adjustments to the Bank Balance

A typical format for determining the true cash balance beginning with the unadjusted bank balance is

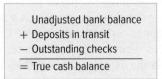

Unadjusted bank balance
+ Deposits in transit
− Outstanding checks
= True cash balance

Deposits in Transit. Companies frequently leave deposits in the bank's night depository or make them on the day following the receipt of cash. Such deposits are called **deposits in transit.** Because these deposits have been recorded in the depositor's accounting records but have not yet been added to the depositor's account by the bank, they must be added to the unadjusted bank balance.

Outstanding Checks. These are disbursements that have been properly recorded as cash deductions on the depositor's books. However, the bank has not deducted the amounts from the depositor's bank account because the checks have not yet been presented by the payee to the bank for payment; that is, the checks have not cleared the bank. **Outstanding checks** must be subtracted from the unadjusted bank balance to determine the true cash balance.

Adjustments to the Book Balance

A typical format for determining the true cash balance beginning with the unadjusted book balance is as follows:

```
        Unadjusted book balance
      + Accounts receivable collections
      + Interest earned
      - Bank service charges
      - Non-sufficient-funds (NSF) checks
      ───────────────────────────────────
      = True cash balance
```

Accounts Receivable Collections. To collect cash as quickly as possible, many companies have their customers send payments directly to the bank. The bank adds the collection directly to the depositor's account and notifies the depositor about the collection through a credit memo that is included on the bank statement. The depositor adds the amount of the cash collections to the unadjusted book balance in the process of determining the true cash balance.

Interest Earned. Banks pay interest on certain checking accounts. The amount of the interest is added directly to the depositor's bank account. The bank notifies the depositor about the interest through a credit memo that is included on the bank statement. The depositor adds the amount of the interest revenue to the unadjusted book balance in the process of determining the true cash balance.

Service Charges. Banks frequently charge depositors fees for services performed. They may also charge a penalty if the depositor fails to maintain a specified minimum cash balance throughout the period. Banks deduct such fees and penalties directly from the depositor's account and advise the depositor of the deduction through a debit memo that is included on the bank statement. The depositor deducts such **service charges** from the unadjusted book balance to determine the true cash balance.

Non-Sufficient-Funds (NSF) Checks. **Non-sufficient-funds (NSF) checks** are checks that a company obtains from its customers and deposits in its checking account. However, when the checks are submitted to the customers' banks for payment, the banks refuse payment because there is insufficient money in the customers' accounts. When such checks are returned, the amounts of the checks are deducted from the company's bank account balance. The company is advised of NSF checks through debit memos that appear on the bank statement. The depositor deducts the amounts of the NSF checks from the unadjusted book balance in the process of determining the true cash balance.

Correction of Errors

In the course of reconciling the bank statement with the cash account, the depositor may discover errors in the bank's records, the depositor's records, or both. If an error is found on the bank statement, an adjustment for it is made to the unadjusted bank balance to determine the true cash balance, and the bank should be notified immediately to correct its records. Errors made by the depositor require adjustments to the book balance to arrive at the true cash balance.

Certified Checks

A **certified check** is guaranteed for payment by a bank. Whereas a regular check is deducted from the customer's account when it is presented for payment, a certified check is deducted from the customer's account when the bank certifies that the check is good. Certified checks, therefore, *have* been deducted by the bank in determining the unadjusted bank balance, whether they have cleared the bank or remain outstanding as of the date of the bank statement. Since certified checks are deducted both from bank and depositor records immediately, they do not cause differences between the depositor and bank balances. As a result, certified checks are not included in a bank reconciliation.

Illustrating a Bank Reconciliation

The following example illustrates preparing the bank reconciliation for Green Shades Resorts, Inc. (GSRI). The bank statement for GSRI is displayed in Exhibit 4.2. Exhibit 4.3 illustrates the completed bank reconciliation. The items on the reconciliation are described as follows.

Adjustments to the Bank Balance

As of September 30, Year 1, the bank statement showed an unadjusted balance of $3,516.45. A review of the bank statement disclosed three adjustments that had to be made to the unadjusted bank balance to determine GSRI's true cash balance.

1. Comparing the deposits on the bank statement with deposits recorded in GSRI's accounting records indicated there was $724.11 of deposits in transit.

2. An examination of the returned checks disclosed that the bank had erroneously deducted a $25 check written by Green Valley Resorts from GSRI's bank account. This amount must be added back to the unadjusted bank balance to determine the true cash balance.

3. The checks returned with the bank statement were sorted and compared to the cash records. Three checks with amounts totaling $235.25 were outstanding.

After these adjustment are made, GSRI's true cash balance is determined to be $4,030.31.

EXHIBIT 4.3

GREEN SHADES RESORTS, INC.
Bank Reconciliation
September 30, Year 1

Unadjusted bank balance, September 30, Year 1	$3,516.45
Add: Deposits in transit	724.11
Bank error: Check drawn on Green Valley Resorts charged to GSRI	25.00
Less: Outstanding checks	

Check No.	Date	Amount
639	Sept. 18	$ 13.75
646	Sept. 20	29.00
672	Sept. 27	192.50

Total	(235.25)
True cash balance, September 30, Year 1	$4,030.31
Unadjusted book balance, September 30, Year 1	$3,361.22
Add: Receivable collected by bank	940.00
Error made by accountant (Check no. 633 recorded as $63.45 instead of $36.45)	27.00
Less: Bank service charges	(8.40)
NSF check	(289.51)
True cash balance, September 30, Year 1	$4,030.31

Adjustments to the Book Balance

As indicated in Exhibit 4.3, GSRI's unadjusted book balance as of September 30, Year 1, was $3,361.22. This balance differs from GSRI's true cash balance because of four unrecorded accounting events:

1. The bank collected a $940 account receivable for GSRI.
2. GSRI's accountant made a $27 recording error.
3. The bank charged GSRI an $8.40 service fee.
4. GSRI had deposited a $289.51 check from a customer who did not have sufficient funds to cover the check.

Two of these four adjustments increase the unadjusted cash balance. The other two decrease the unadjusted cash balance. After the adjustments have been recorded, the cash account reflects the true cash balance of $4,030.31 ($3,361.22 unadjusted cash balance + $940.00 receivable collection + $27.00 recording error − $8.40 service charge − $289.51 NSF check). Because the true balance determined from the perspective of the bank statement agrees with the true balance determined from the perspective of GSRI's books, the bank statement has been successfully reconciled with the accounting records.

Updating GSRI's Accounting Records

Each of the adjustments to the book balance must be recorded in GSRI's financial records. The effects of each adjustment on the financial statements are as follows.

ADJUSTMENT 1 *Recording the $940 receivable collection increases cash and reduces accounts receivable.*

The event is an asset exchange transaction. The effect of the collection on GSRI's financial statements is

Balance Sheet						Income Statement				Statement of Cash Flows
Assets			=	Liab.	+ Stk. Equity					
Cash	+	Accts. Rec.				Rev.	− Exp.	=	Net Inc.	
940	+	(940)	=	NA	+ NA	NA	− NA	=	NA	940 OA

ADJUSTMENT 2 *Assume the $27 recording error occurred because GSRI's accountant accidentally transposed two numbers when recording check no. 633 for utilities expense.*

The check was written to pay utilities expense of $36.45 but was recorded as a $63.45 disbursement. Since cash payments are overstated by $27.00 ($63.45 − $36.45), this amount must be added back to GSRI's cash balance and deducted from the utilities expense account, which increases net income. The effects on the financial statements are

Balance Sheet				Income Statement				Statement of Cash Flows
Assets	=	Liab.	+ Stk. Equity					
Cash	=		Ret. Earn.	Rev.	− Exp.	=	Net Inc.	
27	=	NA	+ 27	NA	− (27)	=	27	27 OA

ADJUSTMENT 3 *The $8.40 service charge is an expense that reduces assets, stockholders' equity, net income, and cash.*

The effects are

Balance Sheet				Income Statement				Statement of Cash Flows
Assets	=	Liab.	+ Stk. Equity					
Cash	=		Ret. Earn.	Rev.	− Exp.	=	Net Inc.	
(8.40)	=	NA	+ (8.40)	NA	− 8.40	=	(8.40)	(8.40) OA

ADJUSTMENT 4   *The $289.51 NSF check reduces GSRI's cash balance.*

When it originally accepted the customer's check, GSRI increased its cash account. Because there is not enough money in the customer's bank account to pay the check, GSRI didn't actually receive cash so GSRI must reduce its cash account. GSRI will still try to collect the money from the customer. In the meantime, it will show the amount of the NSF check as an account receivable. The adjusting entry to record the NSF check is an asset exchange transaction. Cash decreases and accounts receivable increases. The effect on GSRI's financial statements is

Balance Sheet						Income Statement			Statement of Cash Flows	
Assets		=	Liab.	+	Stk. Equity					
Cash	+ Accts. Rec.					Rev. −	Exp. =	Net Inc.		
(289.51)	+ 289.51	=	NA	+	NA	NA −	NA =	NA	(289.51)	OA

Answers to The Curious Accountant

The Sarbanes–Oxley Act (SOX) places a lot of emphasis on companies having a good system of internal controls, primarily to ensure proper financial reporting. But SOX was intended mostly to protect a company's investors, not its customers. Fraud involving stealing customers' credit card information is not a financial reporting issue. However, as this chapter has explained, good internal controls are about more than accurate financial reporting; they should also protect the company's resources, and customers are a major company resource.

The fraud that occurred at Volkswagen was bad for customers and the environment, but it was very costly to the company and its investors. By early 2017, *The Wall Street Journal* estimated that the emissions scandal would ultimately cost VW over $25 billion in direct compensation to car owners and fines to governments. As for stock investors, in the four years from February 2015, until December 2018, VW's stock price fell by about 18 percent. However, during this same period, the stock prices of Ford, General Motors, and Toyota also fell by an average of 18 percent. And, while these three automakers' sales increased by an average of 2.4 percent from 2014 through 2017, VW's increased by 14 percent. So, VW's program of buying back the affected cars at a fair price and firing the individuals involved in the scandal seemed to have satisfied its customers. In addition to the financial cost of fines and reparations, the scandal had human costs. By late 2018, eight current and former VW executives had been indicted in the United States, and one, Oliver Schmidt, had pled guilty and been sentenced to seven years in prison. VW's former CEO, Martin Winterkorn, had been indicted in Germany.

The problem at VW did not occur overnight, nor was it the work of one employee. VW initiated its "clean diesel" program in 2008, and as early as 2009, emissions-defeating devices had already been installed in cars. The problems even went beyond VW. Bosch, a parts supplier for VW, was also alleged to have known about the scheme, and Bosch agreed to pay $327.5 million to settle claims that it assisted in developing the software used to defeat emissions tests. One element of good internal control is to have a separation of duties so that if one person is behaving inappropriately, another is likely to see the misbehavior and take corrective action. This system does not work if many high-level employees are all willing to participate in the inappropriate behavior. Even the best systems of internal controls still rely on people.

Source: The emissions testing problems for VW vehicles was reported widely in the press. Many of the specifics for this Curious Accountant were from online postings of *The Wall Street Journal* dated January 9, 11, and 27, 2017, and the companies' public financial reporting.

☑ CHECK YOURSELF 4.2

The following information was drawn from Reliance Company's October bank statement. The unadjusted bank balance on October 31 was $2,300. The statement showed that the bank had collected a $200 account receivable for Reliance. The statement also included $20 of bank service charges for October and a $100 check payable to Reliance that was returned NSF. A comparison of the bank statement with company accounting records indicates that there was a $500 deposit in transit and $1,800 of checks outstanding at the end of the month. Based on this information, determine the true cash balance on October 31.

Answer   Since the unadjusted book balance is not given, start with the unadjusted bank balance to determine the true cash balance. The collection of the receivable, the bank service charges, and the NSF check are already recognized in the unadjusted bank balance, so these items are not used to determine the true cash balance. Determine the true cash balance by adding the deposit in transit to and subtracting the outstanding checks from the unadjusted bank balance. The true cash balance is $1,000 ($2,300 unadjusted bank balance + $500 deposit in transit − $1,800 outstanding checks).

IMPORTANCE OF ETHICS

The chapter began with a discussion of the importance of internal control systems in preventing accounting scandals. After the Enron and WorldCom scandals and the passage of the Sarbanes–Oxley Act, much more attention has been paid to establishing effective internal control systems. However, despite this increase in legislation and awareness, accounting scandals continue to occur. In 2008, Lehman Brothers declared bankruptcy after it was discovered that the company had kept more than $50 billion in loans off the balance sheet by classifying them as sales. Several months later, Bernie Madoff used a Ponzi scheme to leave his investors with more than $21.2 billion in cash losses. These examples illustrate that legislation alone will not prevent accounting scandals. To prevent a scandal it is necessary to develop a culture that fosters and promotes ethical conduct.

LO 4-4

Identify the role of ethics in the accounting profession.

The accountant's role in society requires trust and credibility. Accounting information is worthless if the accountant is not trustworthy. Similarly, tax and consulting advice is useless if it comes from an incompetent person. The high ethical standards required by the profession state "a certified public accountant assumes an obligation of self-discipline above and beyond requirements of laws and regulations." The **American Institute of Certified Public Accountants (AICPA)** requires its members to comply with the **Code of Professional Conduct.** Section I of the Code includes six articles that are summarized in Exhibit 4.4. The importance of ethical conduct is universally recognized across a broad spectrum of accounting organizations. The Institute of Management Accountants requires its members to follow a set of Standards of Ethical Conduct. The Institute of Internal Auditors also requires its members to subscribe to the organization's Code of Ethics.

Common Features of Criminal and Ethical Misconduct

Unfortunately, it takes more than a code of conduct to stop fraud. People frequently engage in activities that they know are unethical or even criminal. The auditing profession has identified three elements that are typically present when fraud occurs:

1. The availability of an opportunity.
2. The existence of some form of pressure leading to an incentive.
3. The capacity to rationalize.

EXHIBIT 4.4

Articles of AICPA Code of Professional Conduct

Article I Responsibilities
In carrying out their responsibilities as professionals, members should exercise sensitive professional and moral judgments in all their activities.

Article II The Public Interest
Members should accept the obligation to act in a way that will serve the public interest, honor the public trust, and demonstrate commitment to professionalism.

Article III Integrity
To maintain and broaden public confidence, members should perform all professional responsibilities with the highest sense of integrity.

Article IV Objectivity and Independence
A member should maintain objectivity and be free of conflicts of interest in discharging professional responsibilities. A member in public practice should be independent in fact and appearance when providing auditing and other attestation services.

Article V Due Care
A member should observe the profession's technical and ethical standards, strive continually to improve competence and the quality of services, and discharge professional responsibility to the best of the member's ability.

Article VI Scope and Nature of Services
A member in public practice should observe the principles of the Code of Professional Conduct in determining the scope and nature of services to be provided.

Reprinted with permission of Articles of AICPA Code of Professional Conduct

The three elements are frequently arranged in the shape of a triangle as shown in Exhibit 4.5.

Opportunity is shown at the head to the triangle because without opportunity fraud could not exist. The most effective way to reduce opportunities for ethical or criminal misconduct is to implement an effective set of internal controls. *Internal controls* are policies

EXHIBIT 4.5

The Fraud Triangle

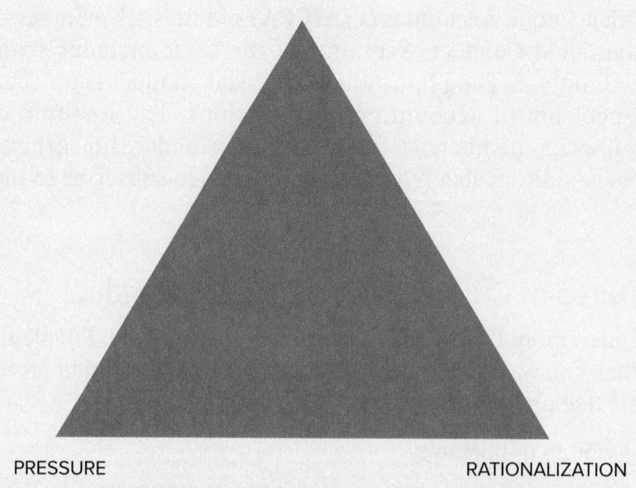

Donald R. Cressey, Other People's Money (Montclair: Patterson Smith, 1973).

and procedures that a business implements to reduce opportunities for fraud and to ensure that its objectives will be accomplished. Specific controls are tailored to meet the individual needs of particular businesses. For example, banks use elaborate vaults to protect cash and safety deposit boxes, but universities have little use for this type of equipment. Even so, many of the same procedures are used by a wide variety of businesses. The internal control policies and procedures that have gained widespread acceptance are discussed in a subsequent chapter.

Only a few employees turn to the dark side even when internal control is weak and opportunities abound. So, what causes one person to commit fraud and another to remain honest? The second element of the fraud triangle recognizes **pressure** as a key ingredient of misconduct. A manager who is told "either make the numbers or you are fired" is more likely to cheat than one who is told to "tell it like it is." Pressure can come from a variety of sources.

- Personal vices such as drug addiction, gambling, and promiscuity.
- Intimidation from superiors.
- Personal debt from credit cards, consumer and mortgage loans, or poor investments.
- Family expectations to provide a standard of living that is beyond one's capabilities.
- Business failure caused by poor decision making or temporary factors such as a poor economy.
- Loyalty or trying to be agreeable.

The third and final element of the fraud triangle is **rationalization.** Few individuals think of themselves as evil. They develop rationalizations to justify their misconduct. Common rationalizations include the following:

- Everybody does it.
- They are not paying me enough. I'm only taking what I deserve.
- I'm only borrowing the money. I'll pay it back.
- The company can afford it. Look what it is paying the officers.
- I'm taking what my family needs to live like everyone else.

Most people are able to resist pressure and the tendency to rationalize ethical or legal misconduct. However, some people will yield to temptation. What can accountants do to protect themselves and their companies from unscrupulous characters? The answer lies in personal integrity. The best indicator of personal integrity is past performance. Accordingly, companies must exercise due care in performing appropriate background investigations before hiring people to fill positions of trust.

Ethical misconduct is a serious offense in the accounting profession. A single mistake can destroy an accounting career. If you commit a white-collar crime, you normally lose the opportunity to hold a white-collar job. Second chances are rarely granted; it is extremely important that you learn how to recognize and avoid the common features of ethical misconduct. To help you prepare for the real-world situations you are likely to encounter, we include ethical dilemmas in the end-of-chapter materials. When working with these dilemmas, try to identify the (1) opportunity, (2) pressure, and (3) rationalization associated with the particular ethical situation described. If you are not an ethical person, accounting is not the career for you.

ROLE OF THE INDEPENDENT AUDITOR

As previously explained, financial statements are prepared in accordance with certain rules called *generally accepted accounting principles (GAAP)*. Thus, when General Electric publishes its financial statements, it is saying, "here are our financial statements prepared according to GAAP." How can a financial analyst know that a company really did follow GAAP? Analysts and other statement users rely on **audits** conducted by **certified public accountants (CPAs).**

LO 4-5

Identify the auditor's role in financial reporting.

The primary roles of an independent auditor (CPA) are summarized below:

1. Conducts a financial audit (a detailed examination of a company's financial statements and underlying accounting records).

2. Assumes both legal and professional responsibilities to the public as well as to the company paying the auditor.

3. Determines if financial statements are *materially* correct rather than *absolutely* correct.

4. Presents conclusions in an audit report that includes an opinion as to whether the statements are prepared in conformity with GAAP. In rare cases, the auditor issues a disclaimer.

5. Maintains professional confidentiality of client records. The auditor is not, however, exempt from legal obligations such as testifying in court.

The Financial Statement Audit

What is an audit? There are several types of audits. The type most relevant to this course is a **financial statement audit**. The financial audit is a detailed examination of a company's financial statements and the documents that support those statements. It also tests the reliability of the accounting system used to produce the financial reports. A financial audit is conducted by an **independent auditor,** who must be a CPA.

The term *independent auditor* typically refers to a *firm* of certified public accountants. CPAs are licensed by state governments to provide services to the public. They are to be as independent of the companies they audit as is reasonably possible. To help ensure independence, CPAs may not be employees of the companies they audit. Further, they cannot have investments in the companies they audit. Although CPAs are paid by the companies they audit, the audit fee may not be based on the outcome of the audit.

Independent auditors are chosen by, paid by, and can be fired by their client companies, but the auditors are primarily responsible to *the public.* In fact, auditors have a legal responsibility to those members of the public who have a financial interest in the company being audited. If investors in a company lose money, they sometimes sue the independent auditors in an attempt to recover their losses, especially if the losses were related to financial failure. A lawsuit against auditors will succeed only if the auditors failed in their professional responsibilities when conducting the audit. Auditors are not responsible for the success or failure of a company. Instead, they are responsible for the appropriate reporting of that success or failure. While recent debacles such as Bernard Madoff Investments produce spectacular headlines, auditors are actually not sued very often, considering the number of audits they perform.

Materiality and Financial Audits

Auditors do not guarantee that financial statements are absolutely correct—only that they are *materially* correct. This is where things get a little fuzzy. What is a *material error*? The concept of materiality is subjective. If Walmart inadvertently overstated its sales by $1 million, would this be material? In 2017, Walmart had approximately $495 billion of sales! A $1 million error in computing sales at Walmart is like a $1 error in computing the pay of a person who makes $495,000 per year—not material at all! An error, or other reporting problem, is **material** if knowing about it would influence the decisions of an *average prudent investor.*

Financial audits are not directed toward the discovery of fraud. Auditors are, however, responsible for providing *reasonable assurance* that statements are free from material misstatements, whether caused by errors or fraud. Also, auditors are responsible for evaluating whether internal control procedures are in place to help prevent material misstatements due to fraud. If fraud is widespread in a company, normal audit procedures should detect it.

Accounting majors take at least one and often two or more courses in auditing to understand how to conduct an audit. An explanation of auditing techniques is beyond the scope of this course, but at least be aware that auditors do not review how the company accounted for every transaction. Along with other methods, auditors use statistics to choose representative samples of transactions to examine.

Types of Audit Opinions

Once an audit is complete, the auditors present their conclusions in a report that includes an *audit opinion.* There are three basic types of audit opinions.

An **unqualified opinion,** despite its negative-sounding name, is the most favorable opinion auditors can express. It means the auditor believes the financial statements are in compliance with GAAP without qualification, reservation, or exception. Most audits result in unqualified opinions because companies correct any reporting deficiencies the auditors find before the financial statements are released.

The most negative report an auditor can issue is an **adverse opinion.** An adverse opinion means that one or more departures from GAAP are so material that the financial statements do not present a fair picture of the company's status. The auditor's report explains the unacceptable accounting practice(s) that resulted in the adverse opinion being issued. Adverse opinions are very rare because public companies are required by law to follow GAAP.

A **qualified opinion** falls between an unqualified and an adverse opinion. A qualified opinion means that for the most part, the company's financial statements are in compliance with GAAP, but the auditors have reservations about something in the statements. The auditors' report explains why the opinion is qualified. A qualified opinion usually does not imply a serious accounting problem, but users should read the auditors' report and draw their own conclusions.

If an auditor is unable to perform the audit procedures necessary to determine whether the statements are prepared in accordance with GAAP, the auditor cannot issue an opinion on the financial statements. Instead, the auditor issues a **disclaimer of opinion.** A disclaimer means that the auditor is unable to obtain enough information to confirm compliance with GAAP.

Regardless of the type of report they issue, auditors are only expressing their judgment about whether the financial statements present a fair picture of a company. They do not provide opinions regarding the investment quality of a company.

The ultimate responsibility for financial statements rests with the executives of the reporting company. Just like auditors, managers can be sued by investors who believe they lost money due to improper financial reporting. This is one reason all business persons should understand accounting fundamentals.

Confidentiality

The **confidentiality** rules in the AICPA's code of ethics for CPAs prohibits auditors from *voluntarily disclosing* information they have acquired as a result of their accountant–client relationships. However, accountants may be required to testify in a court of law. In general, federal law does not recognize an accountant–client privilege as it does with attorneys and clergy. Some federal courts have taken exception to this position, especially as it applies to tax cases. State law varies with respect to accountant–client privilege. Furthermore, if auditors terminate a client relationship because of ethical or legal disagreements and they are subsequently contacted by a successor auditor, they may be required to inform the successor of the reasons for the termination. In addition, auditors must consider the particular circumstances of a case when assessing the appropriateness of disclosing confidential information. Given the diverse legal positions governing accountant–client confidentiality, auditors should seek legal counsel prior to disclosing any information obtained in an accountant–client relationship.

To illustrate, assume that Joe Smith, CPA, discovers that his client Jane Doe is misrepresenting information reported in her financial statements. Smith tries to convince Doe to correct the misrepresentations, but she refuses to do so. Smith is required by the code of ethics to terminate his relationship with Doe. However, Smith is not permitted to disclose Doe's dishonest reporting practices unless he is called on to testify in a legal hearing or to respond to an inquiry by Doe's successor accountant.

With respect to the discovery of significant fraud, the auditor is required to inform management at least one level above the position of the employee who is engaged in the fraud and to notify the board of directors of the company. Suppose that Joe Smith, CPA, discovers that Jane Doe, employee of Western Company, is embezzling money from Western. Smith is required to inform Doe's supervisor and to notify Western's board of directors. However, Smith is prohibited from publicly disclosing the fraud.

A Look Back

The policies and procedures used to provide reasonable assurance that the objectives of an enterprise will be accomplished are called *internal controls*. While the mechanics of internal control systems vary from company to company, the more prevalent features include the following.

1. *Separation of duties.* Whenever possible, the functions of authorization, recording, and custody should be exercised by different individuals.

2. *Quality of employees.* Employees should be qualified to competently perform the duties that are assigned to them. Companies must establish hiring practices to screen out unqualified candidates. Furthermore, procedures should be established to ensure that employees receive appropriate training to maintain their competence.

3. *Bonded employees.* Employees in sensitive positions should be covered by a fidelity bond that provides insurance to reimburse losses due to illegal actions committed by employees.

4. *Required absences.* Employees should be required to take extended absences from their jobs so that they are not always present to hide unscrupulous or illegal activities.

5. *Procedures manual.* To promote compliance, the procedures for processing transactions should be clearly described in a manual.

6. *Authority and responsibility.* To motivate employees and promote effective control, clear lines of authority and responsibility should be established.

7. *Prenumbered documents.* Prenumbered documents minimize the likelihood of missing or duplicate documents. Prenumbered forms should be used for all important documents such as purchase orders, receiving reports, invoices, and checks.

8. *Physical control.* Locks, fences, security personnel, and other physical devices should be employed to safeguard assets.

9. *Performance evaluations.* Because few people can evaluate their own performance objectively, independent performance evaluations should be performed. Substandard performance will likely persist unless employees are encouraged to take corrective action.

Because cash is such an important business asset and because it is tempting to steal, much of the discussion of internal controls in this chapter focused on cash controls. Special procedures should be employed to control the receipts and payments of cash. One of the most common control policies is to use *checking accounts* for all payments except petty cash disbursements.

A *bank reconciliation* should be prepared each month to explain differences between the bank statement and a company's internal accounting records. A common reconciliation format determines the true cash balance based on both bank and book records. Items that typically appear on a bank reconciliation include the following:

Unadjusted bank balance	xxx	Unadjusted book balance	xxx
Add		Add	
Deposits in transit	xxx	Interest revenue	xxx
		Collection of receivables	xxx
Subtract		Subtract	
Outstanding checks	xxx	Bank service charges	xxx
		NSF checks	xxx
True cash balance	xxx	True cash balance	xxx

Agreement of the two true cash balances provides evidence that accounting for cash transactions has been accurate.

The chapter discussed the importance of ethics in the accounting profession. The *American Institute of Certified Public Accountants* requires all of its members to comply with the *Code of Professional Conduct.* Situations where *opportunity, pressure,* and *rationalization* exist can lead employees to conduct unethical acts, which, in cases like Enron, have destroyed the organization. Finally, the chapter discussed the auditor's role in financial reporting, including the materiality concept and the types of audit opinions that may be issued.

A Look Forward

The next chapter focuses on more specific issues related to accounts receivables and inventory. Accounting for receivables and payables was introduced in Chapter 2, using relatively simple illustrations. For example, we assumed that customers who purchased services on account always paid their bills. In real business practice, some customers do not pay their bills. Among other topics, Chapter 5 examines how companies account for uncollectible accounts receivable.

Accounting for inventory was discussed in Chapter 3. However, we assumed that all inventory items were purchased at the same price. This is unrealistic given that the price of goods is constantly changing. Chapter 5 discusses how to account for inventory items that are purchased at different times and different prices.

 Video lectures and accompanying self-assessment quizzes are available in *Connect* for all learning objectives.

 SELF-STUDY REVIEW PROBLEM

The following information pertains to Terry's Pest Control Company (TPCC) for July:

1. The unadjusted bank balance at July 31 was $870.
2. The bank statement included the following items:
   (a) A $60 credit memo for interest earned by TPCC.
   (b) A $200 NSF check made payable to TPCC.
   (c) A $110 debit memo for bank service charges.
3. The unadjusted book balance at July 31 was $1,400.

4. A comparison of the bank statement with company accounting records disclosed the following:

   (a) A $400 deposit in transit at July 31.

   (b) Outstanding checks totaling $120 at the end of the month.

Required

Prepare a bank reconciliation.

Solution

TERRY'S PEST CONTROL COMPANY	
Bank Reconciliation	
July 31	
Unadjusted bank balance	$ 870
Add: Deposits in transit	400
Less: Outstanding checks	(120)
True cash balance	$1,150
Unadjusted book balance	$1,400
Add: Interest revenue	60
Less: NSF check	(200)
Less: Bank service charges	(110)
True cash balance	$1,150

KEY TERMS

Adverse opinion 147

American Institute of Certified Public Accountants (AICPA) 143

Audit 145

Authority manual 133

Bank reconciliation 137

Bank statement 137

Bank statement credit memo 137

Bank statement debit memo 137

Cash 135

Certified check 139

Certified public accountant (CPA) 145

Checks 137

Code of Professional Conduct 143

Confidentiality 147

Deposits in transit 138

Deposit ticket 137

Disclaimer of opinion 147

Fidelity bond 133

Financial statement audit 146

General authority 133

Independent auditor 146

Internal controls 132

Material 146

Non-sufficient-funds (NSF) check 139

Opportunity 144

Outstanding checks 139

Pressure 145

Procedures manual 133

Qualified opinion 147

Rationalization 145

Separation of duties 132

Service charges 139

Signature card 136

Specific authorizations 133

True cash balance 137

Unadjusted bank balance 137

Unadjusted book balance 137

Unqualified opinion 147

QUESTIONS

1. What motivated Congress to pass the Sarbanes–Oxley Act (SOX) of 2002?

2. Define the term *internal control*.

3. Explain the relationship between SOX and COSO.

4. Name and briefly define the five components of COSO's internal control framework.

5. Explain how COSO's *Enterprise Risk Management–An Integrated Framework* project relates to COSO's *Internal Control–An Integrated Framework* project.

6. List several control activities of an effective internal control system.

7. What is meant by *separation of duties*? Give an illustration.

8. What are the attributes of a high-quality employee?

9. What is a fidelity bond? Explain its purpose.

10. Why is it important that every employee periodically take a leave of absence or vacation?

11. What are the purpose and importance of a procedures manual?

12. What is the difference between specific and general authorizations?

13. Why should documents (checks, invoices, receipts) be prenumbered?

14. What procedures are important in the physical

control of assets and accounting records?

15. What is the purpose of independent verification of performance?

16. What items are considered cash?

17. Why is cash more susceptible to theft or embezzlement than other assets?

18. Giving written copies of receipts to customers can

help prevent what type of illegal acts?

19. What procedures can help protect cash receipts?

20. What procedures can help protect cash disbursements?

21. What effect does a debit memo in a bank statement have on the Cash account? What effect does a credit memo in a bank statement have on the Cash account?

22. What information is normally included in a bank statement?

23. Why might a bank statement reflect a balance that is larger than the balance recorded in the depositor's books? What could cause the bank balance to be smaller than the book balance?

24. What is the purpose of a bank reconciliation?

25. What is an outstanding check?

26. What is a deposit in transit?

27. What is a certified check?

28. How is an NSF check accounted for in the accounting records?

29. Name and comment on the three elements of the fraud triangle.

30. What are the six articles of ethical conduct set out under section I of the AICPA's Code of Professional Conduct?

EXERCISES—SERIES A

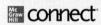 An electronic auto-gradable version of the Series A Exercises is available in Connect. A PDF version of Series B Exercises is in Connect under the "Additional Student Resources" tab. Solutions to the Series B Exercises are available in Connect under the "Instructor Library" tab. Instructor and student Workpapers for the Series B Exercises are available in Connect under the "Instructor Library" and "Additional Student Resources" tabs respectively.

Exercise 4-1A   *SOX and COSO's internal control frameworks*   LO 4-1

Required

a. Discuss the requirements of Section 404 of the Sarbanes–Oxley Act and how it relates to COSO.

b. These rules apply to what type of companies?

Exercise 4-2A   *Control activities of a strong internal control system*   LO 4-1

Required

List and describe nine activities of a strong internal control system discussed in the chapter.

Exercise 4-3A   *Internal controls for small businesses*   LO 4-1

Stan Oden is opening a new business that will sell sporting goods. It will initially be a small operation, and he is concerned about the security of his assets. He will not be able to be at the business all of the time and will have to rely on his employees and internal control procedures to ensure that transactions are properly accounted for and assets are safeguarded. He will have a store manager and two other employees who will be sales personnel and stock personnel and who will also perform any other duties necessary. Stan will be in the business on a regular basis. He has come to you for advice.

Required

Write a memo to Stan outlining the procedures that he should implement to ensure that his store assets are protected and that the financial transactions are properly recorded.

Exercise 4-4A   *Internal controls to prevent theft*   LO 4-1

Sally Knox worked as the parts manager for East River Automobiles, a local automobile dealership. Sally was very dedicated and never missed a day of work. Since East River was a small operation, she was the only employee in the parts department. Her duties consisted of ordering parts for stock and as needed for repairs, receiving the parts and checking them in, distributing them as needed to the shop or to customers for purchase, and keeping track of and taking the year-end inventory of parts. East River decided to expand and needed to secure additional financing. The local bank agreed to a loan contingent on an audit of the dealership. One requirement of the audit was to oversee the inventory count of both automobiles and parts on hand. Sally was clearly nervous, explaining that she had just inventoried all parts in the parts department. She supplied the auditors with a detailed list. The inventory showed parts on hand worth $225,000. The auditors decided they needed to verify a substantial part of the inventory. When the auditors began their counts, a pattern began to develop. Each type of part seemed to be one or two items short when the actual count was taken. This raised more concern. Although Sally assured the auditors the parts were just misplaced, the auditors continued the count. After completing the count of parts on hand, the auditors could document only $155,000 of actual parts. Suddenly, Sally quit her job and moved to another state.

Required

a. What do you suppose caused the discrepancy between the actual count and the count that Sally had supplied?

b. What procedures could be put into place to prevent this type of problem?

LO 4-1

Exercise 4-5A   *Internal control procedures to prevent embezzlement*

Anna Chun was in charge of the returns department at The Luggage Company. She was responsible for evaluating returned merchandise. She sent merchandise that was reusable back to the warehouse, where it was restocked in inventory. Chun was also responsible for taking the merchandise that she determined to be defective to the city dump for disposal. She had agreed to buy a friend a tax planning program at a discount through her contacts at work. That is when the idea came to her. She could simply classify one of the reusable returns as defective and bring it home instead of taking it to the dump. She did so and made a quick $150. She was happy, and her friend was ecstatic; he was able to buy a $400 software package for only $150. He told his friends about the deal, and soon Chun had a regular set of customers. She was caught when a retail store owner complained to the marketing manager that his pricing strategy was being undercut by The Luggage Company's direct sales to the public. The marketing manager was suspicious because The Luggage Company had no direct marketing program. When the outside sales were ultimately traced back to Chun, the company discovered that it had lost over $10,000 in sales revenue because of her criminal activity.

Required

Identify an internal control procedure that could have prevented the company's losses. Explain how the procedure would have stopped the embezzlement.

LO 4-2

Exercise 4-6A   *Internal controls for cash*

Required

List and discuss effective internal control procedures that apply to cash.

LO 4-3

Exercise 4-7A   *Treatment of NSF check*

Han's Supplies' bank statement contained a $270 NSF check that one of its customers had written to pay for supplies purchased.

Required

a. Show the effects of recognizing the NSF check on the financial statements by recording the appropriate amounts in a horizontal statements model like the following one.

Balance Sheet						Income Statement			Statement of Cash Flows
Assets		=	Liab.	+	Stk. Equity				
Cash	+	Accts. Rec.				Rev.	−	Exp.	=	Net Inc.	

b. Is the recognition of the NSF check on Han's books an asset source, use, or exchange transaction?

c. Suppose the customer redeems the check by giving Han $290 cash in exchange for the bad check. The additional $20 paid a service fee charged by Han. Show the effects on the financial statements in the horizontal statements model in Requirement *a*.

d. Is the receipt of cash referenced in Requirement *c* an asset source, use, or exchange transaction?

Exercise 4-8A   *Adjustments to the balance per books*   LO 4-3

Required

Identify which of the following items are added to or subtracted from the unadjusted *book balance* to arrive at the true cash balance. Distinguish the additions from the subtractions by placing a + beside the items that are added to the unadjusted book balance and a − beside those that are subtracted from it. The first item is recorded as an example.

Reconciling Items	Book Balance Adjusted?	Added or Subtracted?
Credit memo	Yes	+
Interest revenue		
Deposits in transit		
Debit memo		
Service charge		
Charge for printing new checks		
NSF check from customer		
Notes receivable collected by bank		
Outstanding checks		

Exercise 4-9A   *Adjustments to the balance per bank*   LO 4-3

Required

Identify which of the following items are added to or subtracted from the unadjusted *bank balance* to arrive at the true cash balance. Distinguish the additions from the subtractions by placing a + beside the items that are added to the unadjusted bank balance and a − beside those that are subtracted from it. The first item is recorded as an example.

Reconciling Items	Bank Balance Adjusted?	Added or Subtracted?
Bank service charge	No	NA
Outstanding checks		
Deposits in transit		
Debit memo		
Credit memo		
Certified check		
Petty cash voucher		
NSF check from customer		
Interest revenue		

Exercise 4-10A   *Adjusting the cash account*   LO 4-3

As of June 30, Year 2, the bank statement showed an ending balance of $19,500. The unadjusted Cash account balance was $15,200. The following information is available:

1. Deposit in transit, $2,400.
2. Credit memo in bank statement for interest earned in June, $30.
3. Outstanding check, $6,690.
4. Debit memo for service charge, $20.

Required

Determine the true cash balance by preparing a bank reconciliation as of June 30, Year 2, using the preceding information.

LO 4-3

Exercise 4-11A   *Determining the true cash balance, starting with the unadjusted bank balance*

The following information is available for Trinkle Company for the month of June:

1. The unadjusted balance per the bank statement on June 30 was $81,500.
2. Deposits in transit on June 30 were $3,150.
3. A debit memo was included with the bank statement for a service charge of $40.
4. A $5,611 check written in June had not been paid by the bank.
5. The bank statement included a $950 credit memo for the collection of a note. The principal of the note was $900, and the interest collected amounted to $50.

Required

Determine the true cash balance as of June 30. (*Hint:* It is not necessary to use all of the preceding items to determine the true balance.)

LO 4-3

Exercise 4-12A   *Determining the true cash balance, starting with the unadjusted book balance*

Nickleson Company had an unadjusted cash balance of $7,750 as of May 31. The company's bank statement, also dated May 31, included a $72 NSF check written by one of Nickleson's customers. There were $700 in outstanding checks and $950 in deposits in transit as of May 31. According to the bank statement, service charges were $50, and the bank collected a $800 note receivable for Nickleson. The bank statement also showed $13 of interest revenue earned by Nickleson.

Required

Determine the true cash balance as of May 31. (*Hint:* It is not necessary to use all of the preceding items to determine the true balance.)

LO 4-4

Exercise 4-13A   *AICPA Code of Professional Conduct*

Required

Name and provide a brief explanation of the six Principles of Professional Conduct of the AICPA Code of Professional Conduct.

LO 4-4

Exercise 4-14A   *AICPA Code of Professional Conduct*

Raula Kato discovered a material reporting error in the accounting records of Sampoon, Inc. (SI) during the annual audit. The error was so significant that it will certainly have an adverse effect on the price of the client's stock, which is actively traded on the western stock exchange. After talking to his close friend, and president of SI, Kato agreed to withhold the information until the president had time to sell his SI stock. Kato leaked the information to his parents so that they could sell their shares of stock as well. The reporting matter was a relatively complex issue that involved recently issued reporting standards. Kato told himself that if he were caught he would simply plead ignorance. He would simply say that he did not have time to keep up with the rapidly changing standards and he would be off the hook.

Required

a. Write a memo that identifies specific articles of the AICPA Code of Professional Conduct that were violated by Kato.
b. Would pleading ignorance relieve Kato from his audit responsibilities?

LO 4-4

Exercise 4-15A   *Fraud triangle*

John Simmons is a CPA with a secret. His secret is that he gambles on sports. John knows that his profession disapproves of gambling, but considers the professional standards to be misguided in his case. John really doesn't consider his bets to be gambling because he spends a lot of time studying sports facts. He believes that he is simply making educated decisions based on facts. He argues that using sports facts to place bets is no different than using accounting information to buy stock.

Required

Use the fraud triangle as a basis to comment on John Simmons's gambling activities.

Exercise 4-16A   *Materiality and the auditor*

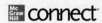

LO 4-5

Sarah Bale is an auditor. Her work at two companies disclosed inappropriate recognition of revenue. Both cases involved dollar amounts in the $100,000 range. In one case, Bale considered the item material and required her client to restate earnings. In the other case, Bale dismissed the misstatement as being immaterial.

Required

Write a memo that explains how a $100,000 misstatement of revenue is acceptable for one company but unacceptable for a different company.

PROBLEMS—SERIES A

Mc Graw Hill connect An electronic auto-gradable version of the Series A Problems is available in Connect. A PDF version of Series B Problems is in Connect under the "Additional Student Resources" tab. Solutions to the Series B Problems are available in Connect under the "Instructor Library" tab. Instructor and student Workpapers for the Series B Problems are available in Connect under the "Instructor Library" and "Additional Student Resources" tabs respectively.

Problem 4-17A   *Using internal controls to restrict illegal or unethical behavior*

LO 4-1

Required

For each of the following fraudulent acts, describe one or more internal control procedures that could have prevented (or helped prevent) the problems.

a. Everyone in the office has noticed what a dedicated employee Carley Trap is. She never misses work, not even for a vacation. Trap is in charge of the petty cash fund. She transfers funds from the company's bank account to the petty cash account on an as-needed basis. During a surprise audit, the petty cash fund was found to contain fictitious receipts. Over a three-year period, Trap had used more than $4,000 of petty cash to pay for personal expenses.

b. Doug Clampet was hired as the vice president of the manufacturing division of a corporation. His impressive resume listed a master's degree in business administration from a large state university and numerous collegiate awards and activities, when in fact Clampet had only a high school diploma. In a short time, the company was in poor financial condition because of his inadequate knowledge and bad decisions.

c. Stone Manufacturing has good internal control over its manufacturing materials inventory. However, office supplies are kept on open shelves in the employee break room. The office supervisor has noticed that he is having to order paper, tape, staplers, and pens with increasing frequency.

Problem 4-18A   *Bank reconciliation and internal control*

LO 4-2, 4-3

Following is a bank reconciliation for Zocar Enterprises for June 30, Year 2.

CHECK FIGURE
True Cash Balance, June 30, Year 2: $2,093

	Cash Account	Bank Statement
Balance as of 6/30/Year 2	$ 1,918	$ 3,000
Deposit in transit		600
Outstanding checks		(1,507)
Note collected by bank	2,000	
Bank service charge	(25)	
NSF check	(1,800)	
Adjusted cash balance as of 6/30/Year 2	$ 2,093	$ 2,093

When reviewing the bank reconciliation, Zocar's auditor was unable to locate any reference to the NSF check on the bank statement. Furthermore, the clerk who reconciles the bank account and records the adjusting entries could not find the actual NSF check that should have been included in the bank statement. Finally, there was no specific reference in the accounts receivable supporting records identifying a party who had written a bad check.

Required

a. Prepare the adjustments that the clerk would have made to record the NSF check.

b. Assume that the clerk who prepares the bank reconciliation and records the adjustments also makes bank deposits. Explain how the clerk could use a fictitious NSF check to hide the theft of cash.

c. How could Zocar avoid the theft of cash that is concealed by the use of fictitious NSF checks?

LO 4-3

CHECK FIGURE
True Cash Balance, August 31,
Year 3: $14,920

Problem 4-19A   *Preparing a bank reconciliation*

Rick Hall owns a card shop, Hall's Cards. The following cash information is available for the month of August, Year 3.

As of August 31, the bank statement shows a balance of $16,140. The August 31 unadjusted balance in the Cash account of Hall's Cards is $14,100. A review of the bank statement revealed the following information:

1. A deposit of $4,150 on August 31, Year 3, does not appear on the August bank statement.

2. It was discovered that a check to pay for baseball cards was correctly written and paid by the bank for $4,500 but was recorded on the books as $5,400.

3. When checks written during the month were compared with those paid by the bank, three checks amounting to $5,370 were found to be outstanding.

4. A debit memo for $80 was included in the bank statement for the purchase of a new supply of checks.

Required

Prepare a bank reconciliation at the end of August showing the true cash balance.

LO 4-3

CHECK FIGURE
Unadjusted Cash Balance,
May 31, Year 2: $8,510

Problem 4-20A   *Missing information in a bank reconciliation*

The following data apply to Pro Beauty Supply Inc. for May, Year 2:

1. Balance per the bank on May 31, $9,150.

2. Deposits in transit not recorded by the bank, $1,510.

3. Bank error; check written by Best Beauty Supply was charged to Pro Beauty Supply's account, $560.

4. The following checks written and recorded by Pro Beauty Supply were not included in the bank statement:

3013	$ 510
3054	640
3056	1,520

5. Note collected by the bank, $500.

6. Service charge for collection of note, $20.

7. The bookkeeper recorded a check written for $320 to pay for the May utilities expense as $230 in the cash disbursements journal.

8. Bank service charge in addition to the note collection fee, $40.

9. Customer checks returned by the bank as NSF, $310.

Required

Determine the amount of the unadjusted cash balance per Pro Beauty Supply's books.

Problem 4-21A *Adjustments to the cash account based on the bank reconciliation*

Required

Determine whether the following items included in Wong Company's January bank reconciliation will require adjustments on Wong's books and indicate the amount of any necessary adjustment.

a. Service charges of $50 for the month of January were listed on the bank statement.

b. The bank charged a $250 check drawn on Wing Restaurant to Wong's account. The check was included in Wong's bank statement.

c. A check of $62 was returned to the bank because of insufficient funds and was noted on the bank statement. Wong received the check from a customer and thought that it was good when it was deposited into the account.

d. A $990 deposit was recorded by the bank as $980.

e. Four checks totaling $810 written during the month of January were not included with the January bank statement.

f. A $75 check written to Office Max for office supplies was recorded in the general journal as $57.

g. The bank statement indicated that the bank had collected a $450 note for Wong.

h. Wong recorded $900 of receipts on January 31 that were deposited in the night depository of the bank. These deposits were not included in the bank statement.

Problem 4-22A *Bank reconciliation and adjustments to the cash account*

The following information is available for Pyle Garage for March, Year 2:

BANK STATEMENT
HAZARD STATE BANK
215 MAIN STREET
HAZARD, GA 30321

Pyle Garage	Account number
629 Main Street	62-00062
Hazard, GA 30321	March, Year 2

Beginning balance 3/1/Year 2	$15,000.00
Total deposits and other credits	7,000.00
Total checks and other debits	6,000.00
Ending balance 3/31/Year 2	16,000.00

Checks and Debits		Deposits and Credits	
Check No.	Amount	Date	Amount
1462	$1,163.00	March 1	$1,000.00
1463	62.00	March 2	1,340.00
1464	1,235.00	March 6	210.00
1465	750.00	March 12	1,940.00
1466	1,111.00	March 17	855.00
1467	964.00	March 22	1,480.00
DM	15.00	CM	175.00
1468	700.00		

The following is a list of checks and deposits recorded on the books of Pyle Garage for March, Year 2:

Date	Check No.	Amount of Check	Date	Amount of Deposit
March 1	1463	$ 62.00	March 1	$1,340.00
March 5	1464	1,235.00	March 5	210.00
March 6	1465	750.00		
March 9	1466	1,111.00	March 10	1,940.00
March 10	1467	964.00		
March 14	1468	70.00	March 16	855.00
March 19	1469	1,500.00	March 19	1,480.00
March 28	1470	102.00	March 29	2,000.00

Other Information

1. Check no. 1462 was outstanding from February.
2. A credit memo for collection of accounts receivable was included in the bank statement.
3. All checks were paid at the correct amount.
4. The bank statement included a debit memo for service charges.
5. The February 28 bank reconciliation showed a deposit in transit of $1,000.
6. Check no. 1468 was for the purchase of equipment.
7. The unadjusted Cash account balance at March 31 was $16,868.

Required

a. Prepare the bank reconciliation for Pyle Garage at the end of March.
b. Explain how the adjustments described affect the cash account.

LO 4-4

Problem 4-23A   *Fraud triangle*

Sam Sharp is an accountant with a shady past. Suffice it to say that he owes some very unsavory characters a lot of money. Despite his past, Sam works hard at keeping up a strong professional image. He is a manager at Flowers and Associates, a fast-growing CPA firm. Sam is highly regarded around the office because he is a strong producer of client revenue. Indeed, on several occasions he exceeded his authority in establishing prices with clients. This is typically a partner's job, but who could criticize Sam, who is most certainly bringing in the business. Indeed, Sam is so good that he is able to pull off the following scheme. He bills clients at inflated rates and then reports the ordinary rate to his accounting firm. Say, for example, the normal charge for a job is $2,500. Sam will smooth talk the client, then charge him $3,000. He reports the normal charge of $2,500 to his firm and keeps the extra $500 for himself. He knows it isn't exactly right. Even so, his firm gets its regular charges and the client willingly pays for the services rendered. He thinks to himself, as he pockets his ill-gotten gains, who is getting hurt, anyway?

Required

The text discusses three common features (conditions) that motivate ethical misconduct. Identify and explain each of the three features as they appear in the given scenario.

LO 4-5

Problem 4-24A   *Confidentiality and the auditor*

Cal Lopez discovered significant fraud in the accounting records of a high-profile client. The story has been broadcast on national airways. Lopez was unable to resolve his remaining concerns with the company's management team and ultimately resigned from the audit engagement. Lopez knows that he will be asked by several interested parties, including his friends and relatives, the successor auditor, and prosecuting attorneys in a court of law, to tell what he knows. He has asked you for advice.

Required

Write a memo that explains Lopez's disclosure responsibilities to each of the interested parties.

LO 4-5

Problem 4-25A   *Auditor responsibilities*

You have probably heard it is unwise to bite the hand that feeds you. Independent auditors are chosen by, paid by, and can be fired by the companies they audit. What keeps the auditor independent? In other words, what stops an auditor from blindly following the orders of a client?

Required

Write a memo that explains the reporting responsibilities of an independent auditor.

Problem 4-26A *Types of audit reports*

LO 4-5

Connie Stevens is a partner of a regional accounting firm. Stevens was hired by a client to audit the company's books. After extensive work, Stevens determined that she was unable to perform the appropriate audit procedures.

Required

a. Name the type of audit report that Stevens should issue with respect to the work that she did accomplish.

b. If Stevens had been able to perform the necessary audit procedures, there are three types of audit reports that she could have issued depending on the outcome of the audit. Name and describe these three types of audit reports.

ANALYZE, THINK, COMMUNICATE

ATC 4-1 Business Application Case *Understanding real-world annual reports*

Obtain the Target Corporation's annual report for its 2018 fiscal year (year ended February 2, 2019) at http://investors.target.com using the instructions in Appendix A, and use it to answer the following questions:

Required

a. Instead of "Cash," the company's balance sheet uses the account name "Cash and cash equivalents." How does the company define cash equivalents?

b. The annual report has two reports in which management is clearly identified as having responsibility for the company's financial reporting and internal controls. What are the names of these reports and on what pages are they located?

ATC 4-2 Group Assignment *Bank reconciliations*

The following cash and bank information is available for three companies on June 30:

Cash and Adjustment Information	Peach Co.	Apple Co.	Pear Co.
Unadjusted cash balance per books, 6/30	$45,620	$32,450	$23,467
Outstanding checks	1,345	2,478	2,540
Service charge	50	75	35
Balance per bank statement, 6/30	48,632	37,176	24,894
Credit memo for collection of notes receivable	4,500	5,600	3,800
NSF check	325	145	90
Deposits in transit	2,500	3,200	4,800
Credit memo for interest earned	42	68	12

Required

a. Organize the class into three sections and divide each section into groups of three to five students. Assign Peach Co. to section 1, Apple Co. to section 2, and Pear Co. to section 3.

Group Tasks

(1) Prepare a bank reconciliation for the company assigned to your group.

(2) Select a representative from a group in each section to put the bank reconciliation on the board.

Class Discussion

   b. Discuss the cause of the difference between the unadjusted cash balance and the ending balance for the bank statement. Also, discuss types of adjustment that are commonly made to the bank balance and types of adjustment that are commonly made to the unadjusted book balance.

ATC 4-3   Research Assignment   *Investigating cash and management issues at Smucker's*

Using the most current Form 10-K available on EDGAR, or the company's website, answer the following questions about the J. M. Smucker Company. Instructions for using EDGAR are in Appendix A. *Note: In some years the financial statements, footnotes, etc., portion of Smucker's annual report have been located at the end of the Form 10-K, in or just after "Item 15."*

Required

   a. Instead of "Cash," the company's balance sheet uses the account name "Cash and cash equivalents." How does the company define cash equivalents?

   b. The annual report has two reports in which management clearly acknowledges its responsibility for the company's financial reporting and internal controls. What are the names of these reports and on what pages are they located?

ATC 4-4   Writing Assignment   *Internal control procedures*

Sarah Johnson was a trusted employee of Evergreen Trust Bank. She was involved in everything. She worked as a teller, she accounted for the cash at the other teller windows, and she recorded many of the transactions in the accounting records. She was so loyal that she never would take a day off, even when she was really too sick to work. She routinely worked late to see that all the day's work was posted into the accounting records. She would never take even a day's vacation because they might need her at the bank. Adam and Jammie, CPAs, were hired to perform an audit, the first complete audit that had been done in several years. Johnson seemed somewhat upset by the upcoming audit. She said that everything had been properly accounted for and that the audit was a needless expense. When Adam and Jammie examined some of the bank's internal control procedures, it discovered problems. In fact, as the audit progressed, it became apparent that a large amount of cash was missing. Numerous adjustments had been made to customer accounts with credit memorandums, and many of the transactions had been posted several days late. In addition, there were numerous cash payments for "office expenses." When the audit was complete, it was determined that more than $100,000 of funds was missing or improperly accounted for. All fingers pointed to Johnson. The bank's president, who was a close friend of Johnson, was bewildered. How could this type of thing happen at this bank?

Required

Prepare a written memo to the bank president, outlining the procedures that should be followed to prevent this type of problem in the future.

ATC 4-5   Ethical Dilemma   *I need just a little extra money*

John Riley, a certified public accountant, has worked for the past eight years as a payroll clerk for Southeast Industries, a small furniture manufacturing firm in the Northeast. John recently experienced unfortunate circumstances. His teenage son required major surgery and the medical bills not covered by John's insurance have financially strained John's family.

   John works hard and is a model employee. Although he received regular performance raises during his first few years with Southeast, John's wages have not increased in three years. John asked his supervisor, Bill Jameson, for a raise. Bill agreed that John deserved a raise, but told him he could not currently approve one because of sluggish sales.

   A disappointed John returned to his duties while the financial pressures in his life continued. Two weeks later, Larry Tyler, an assembly worker at Southwest, quit over a dispute with management. John conceived an idea. John's duties included not only processing employee terminations but also approving timecards before paychecks were issued and then distributing the paychecks to firm personnel. John decided to delay processing Tyler's termination, to forge timecards for Tyler for the next few weeks, and to cash the checks himself. Since he distributed paychecks, no one would find out, and John reasoned that he was really entitled to the extra money anyway. In fact, no one did discover his maneuver and John stopped the practice after three weeks.

Required

a. Does John's scheme affect Southeast's balance sheet? Explain your answer.

b. Review the AICPA's Articles of Professional Conduct and comment on any of the standards that have been violated.

c. Identify the three elements of unethical and criminal conduct recognized in the fraud triangle.

CHAPTER 5

Accounting for Receivables and Inventory Cost Flow

LEARNING OBJECTIVES

After you have mastered the material in this chapter, you will be able to:

LO 5-1	Use the percent of revenue method to account for uncollectible accounts expense.
LO 5-2	Use the percent of receivables method to estimate the uncollectible accounts expense.
LO 5-3	Use aging of accounts receivable to estimate the uncollectible accounts expense.
LO 5-4	Show how accounting for notes receivable and accrued interest affects financial statements.
LO 5-5	Show how accounting for credit card sales affects financial statements.
LO 5-6	Show how different inventory cost flow methods (specific identification, FIFO, LIFO, and weighted average) affect financial statements.

 Video lectures and accompanying self-assessment quizzes are available in Connect *for all learning objectives.*

 Set B exercises and problems are available in Additional Student Resources.

CHAPTER OPENING

Many people buy on impulse. If they must wait, the desire to buy wanes. To take advantage of impulse buyers, most merchandising companies offer customers credit because it increases their sales. A disadvantage of this strategy occurs when some customers are unable or unwilling to pay their bills. Nevertheless, the widespread availability of credit suggests that the advantages of increased sales outweigh the disadvantages of some uncollectible accounts.

When a company allows a customer to "buy now and pay later," the company's right to collect cash in the future is called an **account receivable**. Typically, amounts due from individual accounts receivable are relatively small and the collection period is short. Most accounts receivable are collected within 30 days. When a longer credit term is needed or when a receivable is large, the seller usually requires the buyer to issue a note reflecting a credit agreement between the parties. The note specifies the maturity date, interest rate, and other credit terms. Receivables evidenced by such notes are called **notes receivable.** Accounts and notes receivable are reported as assets on the balance sheet.

The Curious Accountant

idp geneva collection/Alamy Stock Photo

General Dynamics Corporation is an aerospace and defense company that provides both products and services in business aviation; combat vehicles, weapons systems, and munitions; shipbuilding; and communications and information technology. Its products include Gulfstream business jet airplanes. Its largest customer is the U.S. Government. In 2017, 61 percent of its revenue came from sales to the U.S. government, and another 11 percent came from sales to governments of other countries. The remaining 28 percent of its revenues were from commercial customers.

Suppose the U.S. government contracted with General Dynamics to purchase four Gulfstream airplanes at a total cost of $200 million. Assume the government offers to pay for the airplanes the day they are delivered (a cash purchase) or 30 days later (a purchase on account). Assume that General Dynamics is absolutely sure the government will pay its account when due.

Do you think the company should care whether the government pays for the services upon delivery or 30 days later? Why? (Answer on page 165.)

ESTIMATING UNCOLLECTIBLE ACCOUNTS EXPENSE* USING THE PERCENT OF REVENUE METHOD

LO 5-1

Use the percent of revenue method to account for uncollectible accounts expense.

Most companies do not expect to collect the full amount (face value) of their accounts receivable. Even carefully screened credit customers sometimes don't pay their bills. The **net realizable value (NVR)** of accounts receivable represents the amount of receivables a company estimates it will actually collect. The net realizable value is the *face value* less an *allowance for doubtful accounts.*

The **allowance for doubtful accounts** represents a company's estimate of the amount of uncollectible receivables. To illustrate, assume a company with total accounts receivable of $50,000 estimates that $2,000 of its receivables will not be collected. The net realizable value of receivables is computed as follows:

Accounts receivable	$50,000
Less: Allowance for doubtful accounts	(2,000)
Net realizable value of receivables	$48,000

A company cannot know today, of course, the exact amount of the receivables it will not be able to collect in the future. The *allowance for doubtful accounts* and the *net realizable value* are necessarily *estimated amounts.* The net realizable value, however, more closely measures the cash that will ultimately be collected than does the face value. To avoid overstating assets, companies report receivables on their balance sheets at the net realizable value.

Reporting accounts receivable in the financial statements at net realizable value is commonly called the **allowance method of accounting for uncollectible accounts.** As indicated previously, the allowance method requires accountants to estimate the amount of uncollectible accounts. How do accountants make these estimates? One approach is to base the estimates on a percentage of revenue. The following section of this chapter illustrates accounting for uncollectible accounts when the percentage of revenue approach is employed.

Accounting Events Affecting the Year 1 Period

Allen's Tutoring Services (ATS) is a small company that provides tutoring services to college students. ATS started operations on January 1, Year 1. During Year 1, ATS experienced three types of accounting events. These events are discussed as follows.

EVENT 1   Revenue Recognition
Allen's Tutoring Services (ATS) recognized $3,750 of service revenue earned on account during Year 1.

This is an asset source transaction. ATS obtained assets (accounts receivable) by providing services to customers. Both assets and stockholders' equity (retained earnings) increase. The event increases revenue and net income. Cash flow is not affected. The effects on the financial statements are shown here:

Balance Sheet				Income Statement				Statement of Cash Flows
Assets	=	Liab.	+	Stk. Equity				
Accts. Rec.	=			Ret. Earn.	Rev.	−	Exp.	=	Net Inc.	
3,750	=	NA	+	3,750	3,750	−	NA	=	3,750	NA

*In practice the estimated amount of *uncollectible accounts expense* is frequently called *bad debts expense*. While frequently used, the term bad debts expense is a misnomer because it is a receivable rather than a debt that has turned bad. To avoid confusion in the early stages of the learning process the author team has chosen to use the term uncollectible accounts expense, which more accurately describes the true nature of the expense being recognized.

Answers to The Curious Accountant

General Dynamics would definitely prefer to make the sale to the government in cash rather than on account. Even though it may be certain to collect its accounts receivable, the sooner the company gets its cash, the sooner the cash can be reinvested.

The interest cost related to a small accounts receivable of $50 that takes 40 days to collect may seem immaterial. At 3 percent, the lost interest amounts to $.16. However, when one considers that General Dynamics had approximately $3.6 billion of accounts receivable on December 31, 2017, and took an average of 43 days to collect them, the cost of financing receivables for a real-world company becomes apparent. At 3 percent, the cost of waiting 43 days to collect $3.6 billion of cash is $12.7 million ($3.6 billion × .03 × 43/365). For a full year, the cost to General Dynamics would be $108 million ($3.6 billion × .03). In 2017, the weighted-average interest rate on General Dynamic's debt was approximately 2.6 percent.

EVENT 2   Collection of Receivables
ATS collected $2,750 cash from accounts receivable in Year 1.

This event is an asset exchange transaction. The asset cash increases; the asset accounts receivable decreases. Total assets remain unchanged. Net income is not affected because the revenue was recognized in the previous transaction. The cash inflow is reported in the operating activities section of the statement of cash flows. The effects on the financial statements are shown here:

Balance Sheet						Income Statement			Statement of Cash Flows
Assets			= Liab.	+	Stk. Equity	Rev. −	Exp.	= Net Inc.	
Cash	+	Accts. Rec.							
2,750	+	(2,750)	= NA	+	NA	NA −	NA	= NA	2,750 OA

EVENT 3   Recognizing Uncollectible Accounts Expense
ATS recognized uncollectible accounts expense for accounts expected to be uncollectible in the future.

While ATS has collected cash for some of the revenue earned in Year 1, some of the remaining receivables may never be collected. ATS will not know the *actual amount* of uncollectible accounts until Year 2 when the customers fail to pay. However, the company can estimate the amount of revenue that it expects will be uncollectible. The *estimated amount* of uncollectible accounts can then be recognized as an expense on the Year 1 income statement. Recognizing the estimated **uncollectible accounts expense** (frequently called *bad debts expense*) improves the matching of revenues and expenses and therefore increases the accuracy of the financial statements.

Many accountants determine the estimated amount of uncollectible accounts expense by taking a percentage of revenue. This approach is commonly called the **percent of revenue method.** The percentage used to make the estimate is usually based on the company's past collection experiences. However, the percentage may be adjusted for anticipated future circumstances. For example, the percentage may be reduced if the company plans to adopt more rigorous credit approval standards. Alternatively, the percentage may be increased if economic forecasts signal an economic downturn that would make customer defaults more likely.

Since this is ATS's first year of operation, there is no prior experience for determining the estimated percentage of uncollectible accounts. Instead ATS will have to base its estimate on industry averages. To illustrate the accounting procedures for recognizing uncollectible accounts expense, assume that ATS estimates that 2 percent of revenue will be uncollectible. Under these circumstances, ATS would recognize $75 ($3,750 of revenue × 2%) of uncollectible accounts expense on the Year 1 income statement.

The estimated amount of uncollectible accounts expense is recognized in a year-end adjusting entry. The adjusting entry reduces the net realizable value of receivables, stockholders' equity, and the amount of reported net income. The statement of cash flows is not affected. The effects on the financial statements are shown here:

Balance Sheet					Income Statement					Statement of Cash Flows
Assets	=	Liab.	+	Stk. Equity						
NRV Accts. Rec.	=			Ret. Earn.	Rev.	−	Exp.	=	Net Inc.	
(75)	=	NA	+	(75)	NA	−	75	=	(75)	NA

The Accounts Receivable account is not reduced directly because none of the receivables have *actually* been determined to be uncollectible. The decrease in the net realizable value of receivables represents an *estimate* of what will be uncollectible some time in the future. To distinguish the actual balance in accounts receivable from the net realizable value, accountants use a **contra asset account** called Allowance for Doubtful Accounts. The allowance account is called a *contra account* because it is subtracted from the balance in the Accounts Receivable account to determine the net realizable value of receivables that is shown on the balance sheet. The net realizable value of receivables for ATS is determined as follows.

Accounts receivable	$1,000*
Less: Allowance for doubtful accounts	(75)
Net realizable value of receivables	$ 925

*($3,750 revenue on account − $2,750 of collections).

Generally accepted accounting principles require disclosure of both the net realizable value and the amount of the allowance account. Many companies disclose these amounts directly in the balance sheet in a manner similar to that shown in the previous text box. Other companies disclose allowance information in the notes to the financial statements.

Analysis of Year 1 Financial Statements

Exhibit 5.1, Panel A shows a summary of the Year 1 transactions for ATC. Panel B contains the financial statements. While the illustration does not show the Year 1 year-end closing entries, recall that the closing entries will transfer the amounts from the revenue and expense accounts to the Retained Earnings account. The balance in the Retained Earnings account after closing will be $3,675, as reported on the year-end balance sheet.

As previously indicated, estimating uncollectible accounts improves the usefulness of the Year 1 financial statements in two ways. First, the balance sheet reports the amount of cash ($1,000 − $75 = $925) the company actually expects to collect (net realizable value of accounts receivable). Second, the income statement provides a clearer picture of managerial performance because it better *matches* the uncollectible accounts expense with the revenue it helped produce. The statements in Exhibit 5.1 show that the cash flow from operating activities ($2,750) differs from net income ($3,675). The statement of cash flows reports only cash collections, whereas the income statement reports revenues earned on account less the estimated amount of uncollectible accounts expense.

EXHIBIT 5.1

The Big Picture

Panel A Transactions Summary

Event 1   ATS earned $3,750 of revenue on account.

Event 2   ATS collected $2,750 cash from accounts receivable.

Event 3   ATS adjusted its accounts to reflect management's estimate that uncollectible accounts expense would be $75.

Panel B Financial Statements for Year 1

Income Statement			Balance Sheet				Statement of Cash Flows	
Service revenue	$3,750		Assets				**Operating Activities**	
Uncollectible accts. exp.	(75)		Cash		$2,750		Inflow from customers	$2,750
Net income	$3,675		Accounts receivable	$1,000			**Investing Activities**	0
			Less: Allowance	(75)			**Financing Activities**	0
			Net realizable value		925		Net change in cash	2,750
			Total assets		$3,675		Plus: Beginning cash balance	0
			Stockholders' equity				Ending cash balance	$2,750
			Retained earnings		$3,675			

☑ CHECK YOURSELF 5.1

Pamlico Inc. began operations on January 1, Year 1. During Year 1, it earned $400,000 of revenue on account. The company collected $370,000 of accounts receivable. At the end of the year, Pamlico estimates uncollectible accounts expense will be 1 percent of revenue. Based on this information alone, what is the net realizable value of accounts receivable as of December 31, Year 1?

Answer   Accounts receivable at year-end are $30,000 ($400,000 sales on account − $370,000 collection of receivables). The recognition of uncollectible accounts expense would result in a $4,000 ($400,000 × 0.01) balance in the allowance account. The net realizable value of accounts receivable is therefore $26,000 ($30,000 − $4,000).

Accounting Events Affecting the Year 2 Period

To further illustrate accounting for uncollectible accounts, we discuss six accounting events affecting Allen's Tutoring Services (ATS) during Year 2.

EVENT 1   Write-Off of Uncollectible Accounts Receivable
ATS wrote off $70 of uncollectible accounts receivable.

This is an asset exchange transaction. The amount of the uncollectible accounts is removed from the Accounts Receivable account and from the Allowance for Doubtful Accounts account. Since the balances in both the Accounts Receivable and the Allowance accounts decrease, the net realizable value of receivables—and therefore total assets—remains unchanged. This impact is represented by a zero under the NRV Accts. Rec. title shown in the following statements model below. The write-off does not affect the income statement. Since the uncollectible accounts expense was recognized in the previous year, the expense would be double counted if it were recognized again at the time an uncollectible account is written off. Finally, the statement of cash flows is not affected by the write-off. The effects on the financial statements are shown here:

Balance Sheet					Income Statement				Statement of
Assets	=	Liab.	+	Stk. Equity					Cash Flows
NRV Accts. Rec.				Ret. Earn.	Rev.	−	Exp.	=	Net Inc.
0	=	NA	+	NA	NA	−	NA	=	NA	NA

The computation of the *net realizable value,* before and after the write-off, is shown as follows.

	Before Write-Off	After Write-Off
Accounts receivable	$1,000	$930
Less: Allowance for doubtful accounts	(75)	(5)
Net realizable value	$ 925	$925

EVENT 2   Revenue Recognition
ATS provided $10,000 of tutoring services on account during Year 2.

Assets (accounts receivable) and stockholders' equity (retained earnings) increase. Recognizing revenue increases net income. Cash flow is not affected. The effects on the financial statements are shown here:

Balance Sheet				Income Statement			Statement of Cash Flows
Assets	=	Liab.	+ Stk. Equity				
Accts. Rec.	=		Ret. Earn.	Rev.	− Exp.	= Net Inc.	
10,000	=	NA	+ 10,000	10,000	− NA	= 10,000	NA

EVENT 3   Collection of Accounts Receivable
ATS collected $8,430 cash from accounts receivable.

The balance in the Cash account increases, and the balance in the Accounts Receivable account decreases. Total assets are unaffected. Net income is not affected because revenue was recognized previously. The cash inflow is reported in the operating activities section of the statement of cash flows. The effects on the financial statements are shown here:

Balance Sheet					Income Statement			Statement of Cash Flows
Assets		=	Liab.	+ Stk. Equity				
Cash	+ Accts. Rec.				Rev.	− Exp.	= Net Inc.	
8,430	+ (8,430)	=	NA	+ NA	NA	− NA	= NA	8,430 OA

EVENT 4   Recovery of an Uncollectible Account: Reinstate Receivable
ATS recovered a receivable that it had previously written off.

Occasionally, a company receives payment from a customer whose account was previously written off. In such cases, the customer's account should be reinstated and the cash received should be recorded the same way as any other collection on account. The account receivable is reinstated because a complete record of the customer's payment history may be useful if the customer requests credit again at some future date. To illustrate, assume that ATS received a $10 cash payment from a customer whose account had previously been written off. The first step is to **reinstate** the account receivable by reversing the previous write-off. The balances in the Accounts Receivable and the Allowance accounts increase. Since the Allowance is a contra asset account, the increase in it offsets the increase in the Accounts Receivable account, and total assets are unchanged. Net income and cash flow are unaffected. The effects on the financial statements are shown here:

Balance Sheet				Income Statement			Statement of Cash Flows
Assets	=	Liab.	+ Stk. Equity				
NRV Accts. Rec.			0	Rev.	− Exp.	= Net Inc.	
0	=	NA	+ NA	NA	− NA	= NA	NA

EVENT 5   Recovery of an Uncollectible Account: Collection of Receivable
ATS recorded collection of the reinstated receivable.

The collection of $10 is recorded like any other collection of a receivable account. Cash increases, and Accounts Receivable decreases. The effects on the financial statements are shown here:

Balance Sheet							Income Statement					Statement of Cash Flows	
Assets			=	Liab.	+	Stk. Equity							
Cash	+	Accts. Rec.					Rev.	−	Exp.	=	Net Inc.		
10	+	(10)	=	NA	+	NA	NA	−	NA	=	NA	10	OA

EVENT 6   Adjustment for Recognition of Uncollectible Accounts Expense
Using the percent of revenue method, ATS recognized uncollectible accounts expense for Year 2.

Assuming management continues to estimate uncollectible accounts expense at 2 percent of revenue, ATS will recognize $200 ($10,000 revenue × 0.02) of uncollectible accounts expense in a year-end adjusting entry. The effects on the financial statements are shown here:

Andrey Popov/Shutterstock

Balance Sheet					Income Statement					Statement of Cash Flows
Assets	=	Liab.	+	Stk. Equity						
NRV Accts. Rec.	=			Ret. Earn.	Rev.	−	Exp.	=	Net Inc.	
(200)	=	NA	+	(200)	NA	−	200	=	(200)	NA

Analysis of the Year 2 Financial Statements

Panel A of Exhibit 5.2 shows a summary of the Year 2 accounting events for ATS. Panel B contains the financial statements. Exhibit 5.2 does not include the closing entries. Closing the accounts will transfer the amounts from the revenue and expense accounts to the Retained Earnings account, resulting in a $13,475 ending balance in this account as shown on the Year 2 balance sheet.

Exhibit 5.2 Panel B displays the Year 2 financial statements. The amount of uncollectible accounts expense ($200) differs from the ending balance of the Allowance account ($215). The balance in the Allowance account was $15 before the Year 2 adjusting entry for uncollectible accounts expense was recorded. At the end of Year 1, Allen's Tutoring Services estimated there would be $75 of uncollectible accounts as a result of Year 1 credit sales. Actual write-offs, however, amounted to $70 and $10 of that amount was recovered, indicating the actual uncollectible accounts expense for Year 1 was only $60. Hindsight shows the expense for Year 1 was overstated by $15. However, if no estimate had been made, the amount of uncollectible accounts expense would have been understated by $60. In some accounting periods estimated uncollectible accounts expense will likely be overstated; in others it may be understated. The allowance method cannot produce perfect results, but it does improve the accuracy of the financial statements.

Since no dividends were paid, retained earnings at the end of Year 2 equals the December 31, Year 1, retained earnings plus Year 2 net income (that is, $3,675 + $9,800 = $13,475). Again, the cash flow from operating activities ($8,440) differs from net income ($9,800) because the statement of cash flows does not include the effects of revenues earned on account or the recognition of uncollectible accounts expense.

EXHIBIT 5.2

The Big Picture

Panel A Transactions Summary

Event 1   ATS wrote off $70 of uncollectible accounts receivable.
Event 2   ATS earned $10,000 of revenue on account.
Event 3   ATS collected $8,430 cash from accounts receivable.
Event 4   ATS reinstated a $10 account receivable it had previously written off.
Event 5   ATS recorded the collection of $10 from the reinstated receivable referenced in Event 4.
Event 6   ATS adjusted its accounts to recognize $200 of uncollectible accounts expense.

Panel B Financial Statements for Year 2

Income Statement		Balance Sheet			Statement of Cash Flows	
Service revenue	$10,000	Assets			**Operating Activities**	
Uncollectible accts. exp.	(200)	Cash		$11,190	Inflow from customers	$ 8,440
Net income	$ 9,800	Accounts receivable	$2,500		**Investing Activities**	0
		Less: Allowance	(215)		**Financing Activities**	0
		Net realizable value		2,285	Net change in cash	8,440
		Total assets		$13,475	Plus: Beginning cash balance	2,750
		Stockholders' equity			Ending cash balance	$11,190
		Retained earnings		$13,475		

☑ CHECK YOURSELF 5.2

Maher Company had beginning balances in Accounts Receivable and Allowance for Doubtful Accounts of $24,200 and $2,000, respectively. During the accounting period Maher earned $230,000 of revenue on account and collected $232,500 of cash from receivables. The company also wrote off $1,950 of uncollectible accounts during the period. Maher estimates uncollectible accounts expense will be 1 percent of credit sales. Based on this information, what is the net realizable value of receivables at the end of the period?

Answer   The balance in the Accounts Receivable account is $19,750 ($24,200 + $230,000 − $232,500 − $1,950). The amount of uncollectible accounts expense for the period is $2,300 ($230,000 × 0.01). The balance in the Allowance for Doubtful Accounts is $2,350 ($2,000 − $1,950 + $2,300). The net realizable value of receivables is therefore $17,400 ($19,750 − $2,350).

ESTIMATING UNCOLLECTIBLE ACCOUNTS EXPENSE USING THE PERCENT OF RECEIVABLES METHOD

LO 5-2

Use the percent of receivables method to estimate the uncollectible accounts expense.

Some accountants believe they can better estimate the amount of uncollectible expense by basing their estimates on a percentage of accounts receivable rather than a percentage of revenue. This approach is commonly called the **percent of receivables method** of estimating uncollectible accounts expense. The approach focuses on estimating the most accurate balance for the Allowance for Doubtful Accounts account that appears on the year-end balance sheet.

To illustrate, assume that before adjusting its accounts on December 31, Year 1, Pyramid Corporation had a $56,000 balance in its Accounts Receivable account and a $500 credit balance in its Allowance for Doubtful Accounts account. Further assume that Pyramid estimates it will be unable to collect 6 percent of its accounts receivable. In other words, Pyramid estimates that $3,360 ($56,000 × 0.06) of the accounts receivable will be uncollectible. Accordingly, the balance in the Allowance for Doubtful Accounts account that appears on the December 31, Year 1, balance sheet must be $3,360.

Since the Allowance account currently has a $500 balance, Pyramid must add $2,860 ($3,360 − $500) to the Allowance account before preparing the financial statements. Pyramid must recognize a corresponding amount ($2,860) of uncollectible accounts expense. In other words, *the amount of the uncollectible accounts expense is determined by calculating the amount necessary to achieve the required ending balance in the Allowance account.* The effects of recognizing the expense are shown here:

Balance Sheet				Income Statement				Statement of Cash Flows
Assets	=	Liab.	+ Stk. Equity					
NRV Accts. Rec.	=		Ret. Earn.	Rev. −	Exp. =	Net Inc.		
(2,860)	=	NA	+ (2,860)	NA −	2,860 =	(2,860)		NA

☑ CHECK YOURSELF 5.3

During Year 1, Oron Company earned $100,000 of revenue. Before adjusting its accounts on December 31, Year 1, Oron had a $20,000 balance in its Accounts Receivable account and a $50 credit balance in its Allowance for Doubtful Accounts account. Determine the amount of uncollectible accounts expense Oron will recognize on its Year 1 income statement assuming the company estimates uncollectible accounts expense to be 4 percent of receivables.

Answer The ending balance in the Allowance for Doubtful Accounts account after the adjusting entries are posted to the ledger accounts is an $800 ($20,000 accounts receivable × 0.04) balance. Since there is an unadjusted balance of $50 in the Allowance account, the adjusting entry must include a $750 increase to the Allowance account. A corresponding $750 increase to the Uncollectible Accounts Expense account would be required. Accordingly, the amount of uncollectible expense recognized on the Year 1 income statement is $750.

AGING ACCOUNTS RECEIVABLE

History suggests that an account receivable that is past its due date is less likely to be collected than one that is not yet currently due. The longer an account receivable remains past due, the less likely it is to be collected. Accordingly, the accuracy of the amount of estimated uncollectible expense can be improved by **aging of accounts receivable,** which involves applying higher uncollectible percentage estimates to older receivables. To illustrate, assume that Pyramid Corporation prepared the aging of accounts receivable schedule shown in Exhibit 5.3.

LO 5-3

Use aging of accounts receivable to estimate the uncollectible accounts expense.

EXHIBIT 5.3

PYRAMID CORPORATION
Accounts Receivable Aging Schedule
December 31, Year 1

Customer Name	Total Balance	Current	Number of Days Past Due			
			0–30	31–60	61–90	Over 90
J. Davis	$ 6,700	$ 6,700				
B. Diamond	4,800	2,100	$ 2,700			
K. Eppy	9,400	9,400				
B. Gilman	2,200				$1,000	$1,200
A. Kelly	7,300	7,300				
L. Niel	8,600	1,000	6,000	$ 1,600		
L. Platt	4,600			4,600		
J. Turner	5,500			3,000	2,000	500
H. Zachry	6,900		3,000	3,900		
Total	$56,000	$26,500	$11,700	$13,100	$3,000	$1,700

EXHIBIT 5.4

Balance Required in the Allowance for Doubtful Accounts at December 31, Year 1			
Number of Days Past Due	Receivables Amount	Percentage Likely to Be Uncollectible	Required Allowance Account Balance
Current	$26,500	0.01	$ 265
0–30	11,700	0.05	585
31–60	13,100	0.10	1,310
61–90	3,000	0.25	750
Over 90	1,700	0.50	850
Total	$56,000		$3,760

The amount of accounts receivable that is estimated to be uncollectible (the ending balance in the Allowance for Doubtful Accounts account) is determined by applying different percentages to each category in the aging schedule. The percentage for each category is based on a company's previous collection experience for each of the categories. The percentages become progressively higher as the accounts become older. Exhibit 5.4 illustrates computing the ending balance required for Pyramid Corporation's December 31, Year 1, balance sheet.

The computations in Exhibit 5.4 show that the *ending balance* in the Allowance for Doubtful Accounts account shown must be $3,760. Since Pyramid has an unadjusted $500 balance in its Allowance account, the amount of uncollectible expense to be recognized is $3,260 ($3,760 required ending balance − $500 current unadjusted balance). Except for the amount of the estimated expense, the effects on the financial statement would be the same as previously shown. Remember that aging is designed to improve the estimated amount of uncollectible accounts expense. It does not affect how the recognition of the expense affects the financial statements.

Matching Revenues and Expenses versus Asset Measurement

The *percent of revenue* method, with its focus on determining the uncollectible accounts expense, is often called the income statement approach. The *percent of receivables* method, focused on determining the best estimate of the allowance balance, is frequently called the balance sheet approach. Which estimating method is better? In any given year, the results will vary slightly between approaches. In the long run, however, the percentages used in either approach are based on a company's actual history of uncollectible accounts. Accountants routinely revise their estimates as more data become available, using hindsight to determine if the percentages should be increased or decreased. Either approach provides acceptable results.

ACCOUNTING FOR NOTES RECEIVABLE (PROMISSORY NOTES)

LO 5-4

Show how accounting for notes receivable and accrued interest affects financial statements.

Companies typically do not charge their customers interest on accounts receivable that are not past due. When a company extends credit for a long time or when the amount of credit it extends is large, however, the cost of granting free credit and the potential for disputes about payment terms both increase. To address these concerns, the parties frequently enter into a credit agreement, the terms of which are legally documented in a **promissory note.**

To illustrate, assume Allen's Tutoring Services (ATS) loans some of its idle cash to an individual, Stanford Cummings, so Cummings can buy a car. ATS and Cummings agree that Cummings will repay the money borrowed plus interest at the end of one year. Also, to secure the debt Cummings provides collateral by agreeing to allow ATS to hold the title to the car. Exhibit 5.5 illustrates a promissory note that outlines this credit agreement. For ATS, the credit arrangement represents a *note receivable.*

EXHIBIT 5.5

Promissory Note

Promissory Note

$15,000   (3)   *November 1, Year 1*

Amount   **Date**

For consideration received, Stanford Cummings **hereby promises to pay to the order of:**

_____ Allen's Tutoring Services (2) _____

_____ Fifteen thousand and no/100 _____ **Dollars**

payable on _____ October 31, Year 2 (5) _____

plus interest thereon at the rate of _6_ **percent per year.** (4)

Collateral Description _____ Automobile title (6) _____

Signature _____ *Stanford Cummings* (1) _____

Features of this note are discussed as follows. Each feature is cross-referenced with a number that corresponds to an item on the promissory note in Exhibit 5.5. Locate each feature in Exhibit 5.5 and read the corresponding description of the feature given.

1. Maker—The person responsible for making payment on the due date is the **maker** of the note. The maker may also be called the *borrower* or *debtor.*

2. Payee—The person to whom the note is made payable is the **payee.** The payee may also be called the *creditor* or *lender.* The payee loans money to the maker and expects the return of the principal and the interest due.

3. Principal—The amount of money loaned by the payee to the maker of the note is the **principal.**

4. Interest—The economic benefit earned by the payee for loaning the principal to the maker is **interest,** which is normally expressed as an annual percentage of the principal amount. For example, a note with a 6 percent interest rate requires interest payments equal to 6 percent of the principal amount every year the loan is outstanding.

5. Maturity Date—The date on which the maker must repay the principal and make the final interest payment to the payee is the **maturity date.**

6. Collateral—Assets belonging to the maker that are assigned as security to ensure that the principal and interest will be paid when due are called **collateral.** In this example, if Cummings fails to pay ATS the amount due, ownership of the car Cummings purchased will be transferred to ATS.

How Accounting for Notes Receivable Affects Financial Statements

We illustrate accounting for notes receivable using the credit agreement evidenced by the promissory note in Exhibit 5.5. Allen's Tutoring Services engaged in many transactions during Year 1; we discuss here only transactions directly related to the note receivable.

EVENT 1   **Loan of Money**

The note shows that ATS loaned $15,000 to Stanford Cummings on November 1, Year 1. This event is an asset exchange. The asset account Cash decreases and the asset account Notes Receivable increases. The income statement is not affected. The statement of cash flows shows a cash outflow for investing activities. The effects on the financial statements are shown as follows.

Date	Balance Sheet								Income Statement				Statement of Cash Flows
	Assets				=	Liab.	+	Stk. Equity					
	Cash	+	Notes Rec.	+	Int. Rec.	=		Ret. Earn.	Rev.	−	Exp.	=	Net Inc.	
11/01/Year 1	(15,000)	+	15,000	+	NA	=	NA	+	NA	NA	−	NA	=	NA	(15,000) IA

EVENT 2   Accrual of Interest

For ATS, loaning money to the maker of the note, Stanford Cummings, represents investing in the note receivable. Cummings will repay the principal ($15,000) plus interest of 6 percent of the principal amount (0.06 × $15,000 = $900), or a total of $15,900, on October 31, Year 2, one year from the date he borrowed the money from ATS.

Conceptually, lenders *earn* interest continually even though they do not *collect* cash payment for it every day. Each day, the amount of interest due, called **accrued interest,** is greater than the day before. Companies would find it highly impractical to attempt to record (recognize) accrued interest continually as the amount due increased.

Businesses typically solve the record-keeping problem by only recording accrued interest when it is time to prepare financial statements or when it is due. At such times, the accounts are *adjusted* to reflect the amount of interest currently due. For example, ATS recorded the asset exchange immediately upon investing in the note receivable on November 1, Year 1. ATS did not, however, recognize any interest earned on the note until the balance sheet date, December 31, Year 1. At year-end ATS made an entry to recognize the interest it had earned during the previous two months (November 1 through December 31). This entry is an **adjusting entry** because it adjusts (updates) the account balances prior to preparing financial statements.

ATS computed the amount of accrued interest by multiplying the principal amount of the note by the annual interest rate and by the length of time for which the note has been outstanding.

$$\text{Principal} \times \text{Annual interest rate} \times \text{Time outstanding} = \text{Interest revenue}$$
$$\$15,000 \times \quad 0.06 \quad \times \quad (2/12) \quad = \quad \$150$$

ATS recognized the $150 of interest revenue in Year 1 although ATS will not collect the cash until Year 2. This practice illustrates the **matching concept.** Interest revenue is recognized in (matched with) the period in which it is earned regardless of when the related cash is collected. The adjustment is an asset source transaction. The asset account Interest Receivable increases, and the stockholders' equity account Retained Earnings increases. The income statement reflects an increase in revenue and net income. The statement of cash flows is not affected because ATS will not collect cash until the maturity date (October 31, Year 2). The effects on the financial statements are shown as follows.

Date	Balance Sheet								Income Statement				Statement of Cash Flows
	Assets				=	Liab.	+	Stk. Equity					
	Cash	+	Notes Rec.	+	Int. Rec.	=		Ret. Earn.	Rev.	−	Exp.	=	Net Inc.	
12/31/Year 1	NA	+	NA	+	150	=	NA	+	150	150	−	NA	=	150	NA

EVENT 3   Collection of Principal and Interest on the Maturity Date

ATS collected $15,900 cash on the maturity date. The collection included $15,000 for the principal plus $900 for the interest. Recall that ATS previously accrued interest in the December 31, Year 1, adjusting entry for the two months in Year 1 that the note was outstanding. Since year-end, ATS has earned an additional 10 months of interest revenue, ATS must recognize this interest revenue before recording the cash collection. The amount of interest earned in Year 2 is computed as follows.

$$\text{Principal} \times \text{Annual interest rate} \times \text{Time outstanding} = \text{Interest revenue}$$
$$\$15,000 \times \quad 0.06 \quad \times \quad (10/12) \quad = \quad \$750$$

The effects on the financial statements are shown as follows.

	Balance Sheet							Income Statement			Statement of Cash Flows
	Assets			=	Liab.	+	Stk. Equity				
Date	Cash	+ Notes Rec.	+ Int. Rec.	=			Ret. Earn.	Rev. – Exp.	=	Net Inc.	
10/31/Year 2	NA	+ NA	+ 750	=	NA	+	750	750 – NA	=	750	NA

The total amount of accrued interest is now $900 ($150 accrued in Year 1 plus $750 accrued in Year 2). The $15,900 cash collection is an asset exchange transaction. The asset account Cash increases and two asset accounts, Notes Receivable and Interest Receivable, decrease. The income statement is not affected. The statement of cash flows shows a $15,000 inflow from investing activities (recovery of principal) and a $900 inflow from operating activities (interest collection). The effects on the financial statements are shown as follows.

	Balance Sheet							Income Statement			Statement of Cash Flows
	Assets			=	Liab.	+	Stk. Equity				
Date	Cash	+ Notes Rec.	+ Int. Rec.	=			Ret. Earn.	Rev. – Exp.	=	Net Inc.	
10/31/Year 2	15,900	+ (15,000)	+ (900)	=	NA	+	NA	NA – NA	=	NA	15,000 IA 900 OA

Financial Statements

The financial statements reveal key differences between the timing of revenue recognition and the exchange of cash. These differences are highlighted as follows.

	Year 1	Year 2	Total
Interest revenue recognized	$150	$750	$900
Cash inflow from operating activities	0	900	900

Accrual accounting calls for recognizing revenue in the period in which it is earned regardless of when cash is collected.

Income Statement

Although generally accepted accounting principles require reporting receipts of or payments for interest on the statement of cash flows as operating activities, they do not specify how to classify interest on the income statement. In fact, companies traditionally report interest on the income statement as a nonoperating item. Interest is therefore frequently reported in two different categories within the same set of financial statements.

Balance Sheet

As with other assets, companies report interest receivable and notes receivable on the balance sheet in order of their liquidity. **Liquidity** refers to how quickly assets are expected to be converted to cash during normal operations. In the preceding example, ATS expects to convert its accounts receivable to cash before it collects the interest receivable and notes receivable. Companies commonly report interest and notes receivable after accounts receivable. Exhibit 5.6 shows a partial balance sheet for Southern Company to illustrate the presentation of receivables.

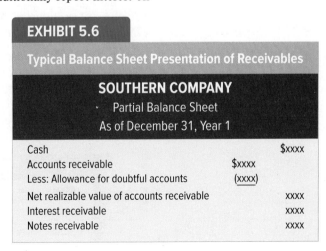

EXHIBIT 5.6

Typical Balance Sheet Presentation of Receivables

SOUTHERN COMPANY
Partial Balance Sheet
As of December 31, Year 1

Cash		$xxxx
Accounts receivable	$xxxx	
Less: Allowance for doubtful accounts	(xxxx)	
Net realizable value of accounts receivable		xxxx
Interest receivable		xxxx
Notes receivable		xxxx

☑ CHECK YOURSELF 5.4

On October 1, Year 1, Mei Company accepted a promissory note for a loan it made to the Asia Pacific Company. The note had a $24,000 principal amount, a four-month term, and an annual interest rate of 4 percent. Determine the amount of interest revenue and the cash inflow from operating activities Mei will report in its Year 1 and Year 2 financial statements.

Answer   The computation of accrued interest revenue is shown as follows. The interest rate is stated in annual terms even though the term of the note is only four months. Interest rates are commonly expressed as an annual percentage regardless of the term of the note. The *time outstanding* in the following formulas is therefore expressed as a fraction of a year. Mei charged annual interest of 4 percent, but the note was outstanding for only 3/12 of a year in Year 1 and 1/12 of a year in Year 2.

Year 1
Principal × Annual interest rate × Time outstanding = Interest revenue
$24,000 ×   0.04   ×   (3/12)   = $240

Year 2
Principal × Annual interest rate × Time outstanding = Interest revenue
$24,000 ×   0.04   ×   (1/12)   = $80

In Year 1, Mei's cash inflow from interest will be zero.
In Year 2, Mei will report a $320 ($240 + $80) cash inflow from operating activities for interest.

ACCOUNTING FOR CREDIT CARD SALES

LO 5-5

Show how accounting for credit card sales affects financial statements.

Maintaining accounts and notes receivable is expensive. In addition to uncollectible accounts expense, companies extending credit to their customers incur considerable costs for such clerical tasks as running background checks and maintaining customer records. Many businesses find it more efficient to accept third-party credit cards instead of offering credit directly to their customers. Credit card companies service the merchant's credit sales for a fee that typically ranges between 2 and 8 percent of gross sales.

The credit card company provides customers with plastic cards that permit cardholders to charge purchases at various retail outlets. When a sale takes place, the seller records the transaction on a receipt the customer signs. The receipt is forwarded to the credit card company, which immediately pays the merchant.

The credit card company deducts its service fee from the gross amount of the sale and pays the merchant the net balance (gross amount of sale less credit card fee) in cash. The credit card company collects the gross sale amount directly from the customer. The merchant avoids the risk of uncollectible accounts as well as the cost of maintaining customer credit records. To illustrate, assume that Allen's Tutoring Service experiences the following events.

EVENT 1   Recognition of Revenue and Expense on Credit Card Sales
ATS accepts a credit card payment for $1,000 of services rendered.

Assume the credit card company charges a 5 percent fee for handling the transaction ($1,000 × 0.05 = $50). ATS's income increases by the amount of revenue ($1,000) and decreases by the amount of the credit card expense ($50). Net income increases by $950. The event increases an asset, accounts receivable, due from the credit card company, and stockholders' equity (retained earnings) by $950 ($1,000 revenue − $50 credit card expense). Cash flow is not affected. These effects are shown here.

Event No.	Balance Sheet						Income Statement						Statement of Cash Flows
	Assets	=	Liab.	+	Stk. Equity								
	Accts. Rec.	=			Ret. Earn.		Rev.	−	Exp.	=	Net Inc.		
1	950	=	NA	+	950		1,000	−	50	=	950		NA

EVENT 2   Collection of Credit Card Receivable
The collection of the receivable due from the credit card company is recorded like any other receivable collection.

When ATS collects the net amount of $950 ($1,000 − $50) from the credit card company, one asset account (Cash) increases and another asset account (Accounts Receivable) decreases. Total assets are not affected. The income statement is not affected. A $950 cash inflow is reported in the operating activities section of the statement of cash flows. These effects are illustrated as follows.

Event No.	Balance Sheet					Income Statement				Statement of Cash Flows
	Assets		=	Liab.	+ Stk. Equity					
	Cash	+ Accts. Rec.				Rev.	− Exp.	= Net Inc.		
2	950	+ (950)	=	NA	+ NA	NA	− NA	= NA		950 OA

As mentioned earlier, two costs of extending credit to customers are bad debts expense and record-keeping costs. These costs can be significant. Large companies spend literally millions of dollars to buy the equipment and pay the staff necessary to operate entire departments devoted to managing accounts receivable. Further, there is an implicit interest charge associated with extending credit. When a customer is permitted to delay payment, the creditor forgoes the opportunity to invest the amount the customer owes.

INVENTORY COST FLOW METHODS

LO 5-6

Show how different inventory cost flow methods (specific identification, FIFO, LIFO, and weighted average) affect financial statements.

In Chapter 3, we used the simplifying assumption that identical inventory items cost the same amount. In practice, businesses often pay different amounts for identical items. Suppose The Mountain Bike Company (TMBC) sells high-end Model 201 helmets. Even though all Model 201 helmets are identical, the price TMBC pays for each helmet frequently changes.

Assume TMBC purchases one Model 201 helmet at a cost of $100. Two weeks later, TMBC purchases a second Model 201 helmet. Because the supplier has raised prices, the second helmet costs $110. If TMBC sells one of its two helmets, should it record $100 or $110 as cost of goods sold? The following section of this chapter discusses several acceptable alternative methods for determining the amount of cost of goods sold under generally accepted accounting principles.

Recall that when goods are sold, product costs flow (are transferred) from the Inventory account to the Cost of Goods Sold account. Four acceptable methods for determining the amount of cost to transfer are (1) specific identification; (2) first-in, first-out (FIFO); (3) last-in, first-out (LIFO); and (4) weighted average.

Specific Identification

Suppose TMBC tags inventory items so that it can identify which one is sold at the time of sale. TMBC could then charge the actual cost of the specific item sold to cost of goods sold. Recall that the first inventory item TMBC purchased cost $100 and the second item cost $110. Using **specific identification,** cost of goods sold would be $100 if the first item purchased were sold or $110 if the second item purchased were sold.

When a company's inventory consists of many low-priced, high-turnover goods, the record keeping necessary to use specific identification isn't practical. Imagine the difficulty of recording the cost of each specific food item in a grocery store. Another disadvantage of the specific identification method is the opportunity for managers to manipulate the income statement. For example, TMBC can report a lower cost of goods sold by selling the first instead of the second item. Specific identification is, however, frequently used for high-priced, low-turnover inventory items such as automobiles. For big-ticket items like cars, customer demands for specific products limit management's ability to select which merchandise is sold, and volume is low enough to manage the record keeping.

First-In, First-Out (FIFO)

The **first-in, first-out (FIFO) cost flow method** requires that the cost of the items purchased *first* be assigned to cost of goods sold. Using FIFO, TMBC's cost of goods sold is $100.

Last-In, First-Out (LIFO)

The **last-in, first-out (LIFO) cost flow method** requires that the cost of the items purchased *last* be charged to cost of goods sold. Using LIFO, TMBC's cost of goods sold is $110.

Weighted Average

To use the **weighted-average cost flow method,** first calculate the average cost per unit by dividing the *total cost* of the inventory available by the *total number* of units available. In the case of TMBC, the average cost per unit of the inventory is $105 [($100 + $110) ÷ 2]. Cost of goods sold is then calculated by multiplying the average cost per unit by the number of units sold. Using weighted average, TMBC's cost of goods sold is $105 ($105 × 1).

Physical Flow

The preceding discussion pertains to the flow of *costs* through the accounting records, *not* the actual **physical flow of goods.** Goods usually move physically on a FIFO basis, which means that the first items of merchandise acquired by a company (first-in) are the first items sold to its customers (first-out). The inventory items on hand at the end of the accounting period are typically the last items in (the most recently acquired goods). If companies did not sell their oldest inventory items first, inventories would include dated, less marketable merchandise. *Cost flow,* however, can differ from *physical flow.* For example, a company may use LIFO or weighted average for financial reporting even if its goods flow physically on a FIFO basis.

Effect of Cost Flow on Financial Statements

Effect on Income Statement

The cost flow method a company uses can significantly affect the gross margin reported in the income statement. To demonstrate, assume that TMBC sold the inventory item discussed previously for $120. The amounts of gross margin using the FIFO, LIFO, and weighted-average cost flow assumptions are shown in the following table.

	FIFO	LIFO	Weighted Average
Sales	$120	$120	$120
Cost of goods sold	(100)	(110)	(105)
Gross margin	$ 20	$ 10	$ 15

Even though the physical flow is assumed to be identical for each method, the gross margin reported under FIFO is double the amount reported under LIFO. Companies experiencing identical economic events (same units of inventory purchased and sold) can report significantly different results in their financial statements. Meaningful financial analysis requires an understanding of financial reporting practices.

Effect on Balance Sheet

Because total product costs are allocated between cost of goods sold and ending inventory, the cost flow method a company uses affects its balance sheet as well as its income statement. Because FIFO transfers the first cost to the income statement, it leaves the last cost on the balance sheet. Similarly, by transferring the last cost to the income statement, LIFO leaves the first cost in ending inventory. The weighted-average method bases both cost of goods sold and ending inventory on the average cost per unit. To illustrate, the ending inventory TMBC would report on the balance sheet using each of the three cost flow methods is shown in the following table.

	FIFO	LIFO	Weighted Average
Ending inventory	$110	$100	$105

The FIFO, LIFO, and weighted-average methods are all used extensively in business practice. The same company may even use one cost flow method for some of its products and different cost flow methods for other products. Exhibit 5.7 illustrates the relative use of the different cost flow methods among the 30 companies that comprise the Dow Jones Industrial Average.

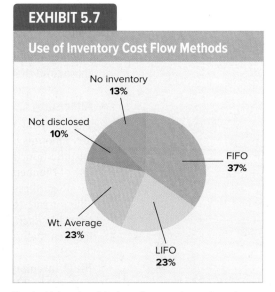

EXHIBIT 5.7

Use of Inventory Cost Flow Methods

No inventory 13%
Not disclosed 10%
FIFO 37%
Wt. Average 23%
LIFO 23%

The chart is based on data drawn from recent annual reports published by the 30 companies that comprise the Dow Jones Industrial Average. The category titled "Not disclosed" consisted of companies with relatively small quantities of inventory.

☑ CHECK YOURSELF 5.5

Nash Office Supply (NOS) purchased two Model 303 copiers at different times. The first copier purchased cost $400 and the second copier purchased cost $450. NOS sold one of the copiers for $600. Determine the gross margin on the sale and the ending inventory balance assuming NOS accounts for inventory using (1) FIFO, (2) LIFO, and (3) weighted average.

Answer

	FIFO	LIFO	Weighted Average
Sales	$600	$600	$600
Cost of goods sold	(400)	(450)	(425)
Gross margin	$200	$150	$175
Ending inventory	$450	$400	$425

Multiple Layers with Multiple Quantities

The previous example illustrates different **inventory cost flow methods** using only two cost layers ($100 and $110) with only one unit of inventory in each layer. Actual business inventories are considerably more complex. Most real-world inventories are composed of multiple cost layers with different quantities of inventory in each layer. The underlying allocation concepts, however, remain unchanged.

For example, a different inventory item TMBC carries in its stores is a bike called the Eraser. TMBC's beginning inventory and two purchases of Eraser bikes are described as follows.

Jan. 1	Beginning inventory	10 units @ $200	=	$ 2,000
Mar. 18	First purchase	20 units @ $220	=	4,400
Aug. 21	Second purchase	25 units @ $250	=	6,250
Total cost of the 55 bikes available for sale				$12,650

The accounting records for the period show that TMBC paid cash for all Eraser bike purchases and that it sold 43 bikes at a cash price of $350 each.

Allocating Cost of Goods Available for Sale

The following discussion shows how to determine the cost of goods sold and ending inventory amounts under FIFO, LIFO, and weighted average. We show all three methods to demonstrate how they affect the financial statements differently; TMBC would actually use only one of the methods.

Regardless of the cost flow method chosen, TMBC must allocate the cost of goods available for sale ($12,650) between cost of goods sold and ending inventory. The amounts assigned to each category will differ depending on TMBC's cost flow method. Computations for each method are shown as follows.

FIFO Inventory Cost Flow. Recall that TMBC sold 43 Eraser bikes during the accounting period. The FIFO method transfers to the Cost of Goods Sold account the *cost of the first 43 bikes* TMBC had available to sell. The first 43 bikes acquired by TMBC were the 10 bikes in the beginning inventory (these were purchased in the prior period) plus the 20 bikes purchased in March and 13 of the bikes purchased in August. The expense recognized for the cost of these bikes ($9,650) is computed as follows.

Jan. 1	Beginning inventory	10 units @ $200	=	$2,000
Mar. 18	First purchase	20 units @ $220	=	4,400
Aug. 21	Second purchase	13 units @ $250	=	3,250
Total cost of the 43 bikes sold				$9,650

Because TMBC had 55 bikes available for sale it would have 12 bikes (55 available − 43 sold) in ending inventory. The cost assigned to these 12 bikes (the ending balance in the Inventory account) equals the cost of goods available for sale minus the cost of goods sold shown as follows.

Cost of goods available for sale	$12,650
Cost of goods sold	(9,650)
Ending inventory balance	$ 3,000

We show the allocation of the cost of goods available for sale between cost of goods sold and ending inventory graphically here:

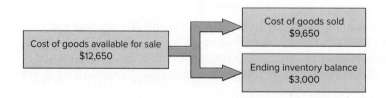

LIFO Inventory Cost Flow. Under LIFO, the cost of goods sold is the cost of the last 43 bikes acquired by TMBC, computed as follows.

Aug. 21	Second purchase	25 units @ $250 =	$ 6,250
Mar. 18	First purchase	18 units @ $220 =	3,960
	Total cost of the 43 bikes sold		$10,210

The LIFO cost of the 12 bikes in ending inventory is computed as follows.

Cost of goods available for sale	$12,650
Cost of goods sold	(10,210)
Ending inventory balance	$ 2,440

We show the allocation of the cost of goods available for sale between cost of goods sold and ending inventory graphically here.

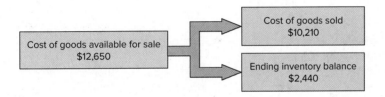

Weighted-Average Cost Flow. The weighted-average cost per unit is determined by dividing the *total cost of goods available for sale* by the *total number of units* available for sale. For TMBC, the weighted-average cost per unit is $230 ($12,650 ÷ 55). The weighted-average cost of goods sold is determined by multiplying the average cost per unit by the number of units sold ($230 × 43 = $9,890). The cost assigned to the 12 bikes in ending inventory is $2,760 (12 × $230).

We show the allocation of the cost of goods available for sale between cost of goods sold and ending inventory graphically as follows.

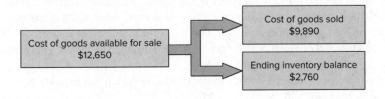

Effect of Cost Flow on Financial Statements

Exhibit 5.8 displays partial financial statements for TMBC. This exhibit includes only information pertaining to the Eraser bikes inventory item described. Other financial statement data are omitted.

Recall that assets are reported on the balance sheet in order of liquidity (how quickly they are expected to be converted to cash). Because companies frequently sell inventory on account, inventory is less liquid than accounts receivable. As a result, companies commonly report inventory below accounts receivable on the balance sheet.

EXHIBIT 5.8

TMBC COMPANY
Comparative Financial Statements

Partial Income Statements

	FIFO	LIFO	Weighted Average
Sales	$15,050	$15,050	$15,050
Cost of goods sold	(9,650)	(10,210)	(9,890)
Gross margin	5,400	4,840	5,160

Partial Balance Sheets

	FIFO	LIFO	Weighted Average
Assets			
Cash	$ xx	$ xx	$ xx
Accounts receivable	xx	xx	xx
Inventory	3,000	2,440	2,760

Partial Statements of Cash Flows

	FIFO	LIFO	Weighted Average
Operating Activities			
Cash inflow from customers	$15,050	$15,050	$15,050
Cash outflow for inventory	(10,650)	(10,650)	(10,650)

Exhibit 5.8 demonstrates that the amounts reported for gross margin on the income statement and inventory on the balance sheet differ significantly. The cash flow from operating activities on the statement of cash flows, however, is identical under all three methods. Regardless of cost flow reporting method, TMBC paid $10,650 cash ($4,400 first purchase + $6,250 second purchase) to purchase inventory and received $15,050 cash for inventory sold.

The Impact of Income Tax

Based on the financial statement information in Exhibit 5.8, which cost flow method should TMBC use? Most people initially suggest FIFO because FIFO reports the highest gross margin and the largest balance in ending inventory. However, other factors are relevant. FIFO produces the highest gross margin; it also produces the highest net income and the highest income tax expense. In contrast, LIFO results in recognizing the lowest gross margin, lowest net income, and the lowest income tax expense.

Will investors favor a company with more assets and higher net income or one with lower tax expense? Recognize that specific identification, FIFO, LIFO, and weighted average are *different methods of reporting the same information.* TMBC experienced only one set of events pertaining to Eraser bikes. Exhibit 5.8 reports those same events three different ways. However, if the FIFO reporting method causes TMBC to pay more taxes than the LIFO method, using FIFO will cause a real reduction in the value of the company. Paying more money in taxes leaves less money in the company. Knowledgeable investors would be more attracted to TMBC if it uses LIFO because the lower tax payments allow the company to keep more value in the business.

Research suggests that, as a group, investors are knowledgeable. They make investment decisions based on economic substance regardless of how information is reported in financial statements.

The Income Statement versus the Tax Return

In some instances companies may use one accounting method for financial reporting and a different method to compute income taxes (the tax return must explain any differences). With respect to LIFO, however, the Internal Revenue Service requires that companies using LIFO for income tax purposes must also use LIFO for financial reporting. A company could not, therefore, get both the lower tax benefit provided by LIFO and the financial reporting advantage offered under FIFO.

Inflation versus Deflation

Our illustration assumes an inflationary environment (rising inventory prices). In a deflationary environment, the impact of using LIFO versus FIFO is reversed. LIFO produces tax advantages in an inflationary environment, while FIFO produces tax advantages in a deflationary environment. Companies operating in the computer industry where prices are falling would obtain a tax advantage by using FIFO. In contrast, companies that sell medical supplies in an inflationary environment would obtain a tax advantage by using LIFO.

Full Disclosure and Consistency

Generally accepted accounting principles allow each company to choose the inventory cost flow method best suited to its reporting needs. Because results can vary considerably among methods, however, the GAAP principle of **full disclosure** requires that financial statements disclose the method chosen. In addition, so that a company's financial statements are comparable from year to year, the GAAP principle of **consistency** generally requires that companies use the same cost flow method each period. The limited exceptions to the consistency principle are described in more advanced accounting courses.

 CHECK YOURSELF 5.6

The following information was drawn from the inventory records of Fields, Inc.:
Assume that Fields sold 900 units of inventory.

Beginning inventory	200 units @ $20
First purchase	400 units @ $22
Second purchase	600 units @ $24

1. Determine the amount of cost of goods sold using FIFO.

2. Would using LIFO produce a higher or lower amount of cost of goods sold? Why?

Answer

1. Cost of goods sold using FIFO

Beginning inventory	200 units @ $20	=	$ 4,000
First purchase	400 units @ $22	=	8,800
Second purchase	300 units @ $24	=	7,200
Total cost of goods sold			$20,000

2. The inventory records reflect an inflationary environment of steadily rising prices. Since LIFO charges the latest costs (in this case the highest costs) to the income statement, using LIFO would produce a higher amount of cost of goods sold than would using FIFO.

REALITY BYTES

As previously noted in this chapter, the main incentive for a company to use the LIFO inventory assumption is to reduce, or at least defer, payment of income taxes. But, how much are U.S. companies really saving in taxes by using LIFO?

Some companies make it easy to estimate the amount of their taxes deferred by LIFO. Although Kroger Company uses the LIFO method for most of its merchandise inventory, it provides the difference between its ending inventory as measured by LIFO versus FIFO on its balance sheet. It refers to this difference as a "LIFO reserve." As of February 3, 2018, this reserve was $1,248 million. The federal income tax rate is currently 21 percent. So, multiplying $1,248 million by .21 suggests Kroger has been able to defer paying about $262 million in federal income taxes by using LIFO versus FIFO.

Jonathan Weiss/123RF

What about the tax savings for all of the companies in the United States who use LIFO? Various researchers have attempted to answer this question; one such recent study was authored by Daniel Tinkelman and Christine Tan. Their research used data from the IRS. These data revealed that while only about 1 percent of all U.S. companies use LIFO for most of their inventories, about 14 percent of the inventory on U.S. companies' balance sheets are measured with LIFO. Recall from Exhibit 5.7 that 35 percent of the large companies in the Dow Jones Industrial Average use LIFO. Tinkelman and Tan's analysis suggest that if LIFO method were no longer allowed by the IRS, companies would have to pay an additional $11 billion to $14 billion in taxes.

Sources: Kroger's Form 10-K and "Estimating the Potential Revenue Impact of Taxing LIFO Reserves in the Current Low Commodity Price Environment," *Journal of the American Taxation Association*, published online, January 2018.

FOCUS ON INTERNATIONAL ISSUES

LIFO IN OTHER COUNTRIES

This chapter introduced a rather strange inventory cost flow assumption called LIFO. As explained, the primary advantage of LIFO is to reduce a company's income taxes. Given the choice, companies that use LIFO to reduce their taxes would probably prefer to use another method when preparing their GAAP-based financial statements, but the IRS does not permit this. Thus, they are left with no choice but to use the seemingly counterintuitive LIFO assumption for GAAP as well as tax reporting.

What happens in countries other than the United States? International Financial Reporting Standards (IFRS) do not allow the use of LIFO. Most industrialized nations are now using IFRS. You can see the impact of this disparity if you review the annual report of a U.S. company that uses LIFO *and* has significant operations in other countries. Very often it will explain that LIFO is used to calculate inventory (and cost of goods sold) for domestic operations, but another method is used for activities outside the United States.

Weng lei-Imaginechina/AP Images

For example, here is an excerpt from General Electric's 2017 Form 10-K, Note 1.

> All inventories are stated at the lower of cost or realizable values. Cost for a significant portion of GE U.S. inventories is determined on a last-in, first-out (LIFO) basis. Cost of other GE inventories is determined on a first-in, first-out (FIFO) basis. LIFO was used for 34% and 32% of GE inventories at December 31, 2017 and 2016, respectively.*

If the company has its headquarters in the United States, why not simply use LIFO in its foreign operations? In addition to having to prepare financial statements for the United States, the company probably has to prepare statements for its local operations using the reporting standards of the local country.

Prior to the establishment of IFRS each country was responsible for issuing its own, local GAAP. Even then, most countries did not allow for the use of LIFO.

*2017. General Electric Company Form 10-K. General Electric Company.

A Look Back

We first introduced accounting for receivables in Chapter 2. This chapter presented additional complexities related to accounts receivable, such as the *allowance method of accounting for uncollectible accounts.* The allowance method improves matching of expenses with revenues. It also provides a more accurate measure of the value of accounts receivable on the balance sheet.

Under the allowance method, estimated uncollectible accounts expense is recorded in an adjusting entry at the end of the period in which a company has made credit sales. There are two methods commonly used to estimate the amount of uncollectible accounts expense: the percent of revenue method and the percent of receivables method. With the percent of revenue method, uncollectible accounts expense is measured as a percent of the period's sales. With the percent of receivables method, a company analyzes its accounts receivable at the end of the period, usually classifying them by age, to estimate the amount of the accounts receivable balance that is likely to be uncollectible. The balance in the Allowance for Doubtful Accounts account is then adjusted to equal the estimated amount of uncollectible accounts. Uncollectible accounts expense decreases the net realizable value of receivables (accounts receivable − allowance for doubtful accounts), stockholders' equity, and net income.

The allowance method of accounting for uncollectible accounts is conceptually superior to the *direct write-off method,* in which uncollectible accounts expense is recognized when an account is determined to be uncollectible. The direct write-off method fails to match revenues with expenses and overstates accounts receivable on the balance sheet. It is easier to use, however, and is permitted by generally accepted accounting principles if the amount of uncollectible accounts expense is immaterial.

The chapter also introduced notes receivable and accounting for *accrued interest.* When the term of a promissory note extends over more than one accounting period, companies must record adjusting entries to recognize interest in the appropriate accounting period, even if the cash exchange of interest occurs in a different accounting period.

We also discussed accounting for credit card sales, a vehicle that shifts uncollectible accounts expense to the credit card issuer. Many companies find the benefits of accepting major credit cards to be worth the credit card expense consequently incurred. Finally, we addressed the costs of making credit sales. In addition to uncollectible accounts expense, interest is a major cost of financing receivables.

This chapter also discussed the inventory cost flow methods of first-in, first-out (FIFO); last-in, first-out (LIFO); weighted average; and specific identification. Under FIFO, the cost of the items purchased first is reported on the income statement, and the cost of the items purchased last is reported on the balance sheet. Under LIFO, the cost of the items purchased last is reported on the income statement, and the cost of the items purchased first is reported on the balance sheet. Under the weighted-average method, the average cost of inventory is reported on both the income statement and the balance sheet. Finally, under specific identification the actual cost of goods is reported on the income statement and the balance sheet.

A Look Forward

Chapter 6 discusses accounting for long-term assets such as buildings and equipment. As with inventory cost flow, GAAP allows companies to use different accounting methods to report on similar types of business events. Life would be easier for accounting students if all companies used the same accounting methods. However, the business world is complex. For the foreseeable future, people are likely to continue to have diverse views as to the best way to account for a variety of business transactions. To function effectively in today's business environment, it is important for you to be able to recognize differences in reporting practices.

Video lectures and accompanying self-assessment quizzes are available in *Connect* for all learning objectives.

SELF-STUDY REVIEW PROBLEM 1

During Year 2, Calico Company experienced the following accounting events:

1. Provided $120,000 of services on account.
2. Collected $85,000 cash from accounts receivable.
3. Wrote off $1,800 of accounts receivable that were uncollectible.
4. Loaned $3,000 to an individual, Emma Gardner, in exchange for a note receivable.
5. Paid $90,500 cash for operating expenses.
6. Estimated that uncollectible accounts expense would be 2 percent of revenue earned on account. Recorded the year-end adjusting entry.
7. Recorded the year-end adjusting entry for accrued interest on the note receivable (see Event 4). Calico made the loan on August 1. It had a six-month term and a 6 percent rate of interest.

Calico's ledger balances on January 1, Year 2, were as follows:

	Balance Sheet												
Event No.	Assets								= Liab. +		Equity		
	Cash	+	NRV Accts. Rec.	+	Notes Rec.	+	Int. Rec.	=		+	Com. Stk.	+	Ret. Earn.
Bal.	12,000		15,800	+	NA	+	NA	=	NA	+	20,000	+	7,800

Required

a. Record the Year 2 events in ledger accounts under an accounting equation like the one shown above.
b. Determine net income for Year 2.
c. Determine net cash flow from operating activities for Year 2.
d. Determine the net realizable value of accounts receivable at December 31, Year 2.
e. What amount of interest revenue will Calico recognize on its note receivable in Year 3?

Solution to Requirement *a*

	Balance Sheet												
Event No.	Assets								= Liab. +		Equity		
	Cash	+	NRV Accts. Rec.	+	Notes Rec.	+	Int. Rec.	=		+	Com. Stk.	+	Ret. Earn.
Bal.	12,000	+	15,800	+	NA	+	NA	=	NA	+	20,000	+	7,800
1	NA	+	120,000	+	NA	+	NA	=	NA	+	NA	+	120,000
2	85,000	+	(85,000)	+	NA	+	NA	=	NA	+	NA	+	NA
3	NA	+	0	+	NA	+	NA	=	NA	+	NA	+	NA
4	(3,000)	+	NA	+	3,000	+	NA	=	NA	+	NA	+	NA
5	(90,500)	+	NA	+	NA	+	NA	=	NA	+	NA	+	(90,500)
6	NA	+	(2,400)	+	NA	+	NA	=	NA	+	NA	+	(2,400)
7	NA	+	NA	+	NA	+	75*	=	NA	+	NA	+	75
Totals	3,500	+	48,400	+	3,000	+	75	=	NA	+	20,000	+	34,975

*$3,000 × 0.06 × 5/12 = $75.

Solution to Requirements *b–e*

b. Net income is $27,175 ($120,000 − $90,500 − $2,400 + $75).
c. Net cash flow from operating activities is an outflow of $5,500 ($85,000 − $90,500).
d. The net realizable value of accounts receivable is $48,400 ($51,200 − $2,800).
e. In Year 3, Calico will recognize interest revenue for one month: $3,000 × 0.06 × 1/12 = $15.

Video lectures and accompanying self-assessment quizzes are available in *Connect* for all learning objectives.

SELF-STUDY REVIEW PROBLEM 2

Erie Jewelers sells gold earrings. Its beginning inventory of Model 407 gold earrings consisted of 100 pairs of earrings at $50 per pair. Erie purchased two batches of Model 407 earrings during the year. The first batch purchased consisted of 150 pairs at $53 per pair; the second batch consisted of 200 pairs at $56 per pair. During the year, Erie sold 375 pairs of Model 407 earrings.

Required

Determine the amount of product cost Erie would allocate to cost of goods sold and ending inventory assuming that Erie uses (a) FIFO, (b) LIFO, and (c) weighted average.

Solution to Requirements *a–c*

Goods Available for Sale				
Beginning inventory	100	@	$50	=	$ 5,000
First purchase	150	@	53	=	7,950
Second purchase	200	@	56	=	11,200
Goods available for sale	450				$24,150

a. FIFO

Cost of Goods Sold	Pairs		Cost per Pair		Cost of Goods Sold
From beginning inventory	100	@	$50	=	$ 5,000
From first purchase	150	@	53	=	7,950
From second purchase	125	@	56	=	7,000
Total pairs sold	375				$19,950

Ending inventory = Goods available for sale − Cost of goods sold
Ending inventory = $24,150 − $19,950 = $4,200

b. LIFO

Cost of Goods Sold	Pairs		Cost per Pair		Cost of Goods Sold
From second purchase	200	@	$56	=	$11,200
From first purchase	150	@	53	=	7,950
From beginning inventory	25	@	50	=	1,250
Total pairs sold	375				$20,400

Ending inventory = Goods available for sale − Cost of goods sold
Ending inventory = $24,150 − $20,400 = $3,750

c. Weighted average

Goods available for sale ÷ Total pairs = Cost per pair
$24,150   ÷   450   = $53.6667

Cost of goods sold 375 units @ $53.6667 = $20,125
Ending inventory   75 units @ $53.6667 = $4,025

KEY TERMS

Account receivable 162
Accrued interest 174
Adjusting entry 174
Aging of accounts
    receivable 171
Allowance for doubtful
    accounts 164
Allowance method of
    accounting for uncollectible
    accounts 164
Bad debts expense   165

Collateral 173
Consistency 183
Contra asset account 166
First-in, first-out (FIFO) cost
    flow method 178
Full disclosure 183
Interest 173
Inventory cost flow
    methods 179
Last-in, first-out (LIFO) cost
    flow method 178

Liquidity 175
Maker 173
Matching concept 174
Maturity date 173
Net realizable value 164
Notes receivable 163
Payee 173
Percent of receivables
    method 170
Percent of revenue
    method 165

Physical flow of goods 178
Principal 172
Promissory note 172
Reinstate 168
Specific identification 177
Uncollectible accounts
    expense 165
Weighted-average cost flow
    method 178

QUESTIONS

1. What is the difference between accounts receivable and notes receivable?

2. What is the *net realizable value* of receivables?

3. What type of account is the Allowance for Doubtful Accounts?

4. What are two ways in which estimating uncollectible accounts improves the accuracy of the financial statements?

5. When using the allowance method, why is uncollectible accounts expense an estimated amount?

6. What is the most common format for reporting accounts receivable on the balance sheet? What information does this method provide beyond showing only the net amount?

7. Why is it necessary to reinstate a previously written-off account receivable before the collection is recorded?

8. What are some factors considered in estimating the amount of uncollectible accounts receivable?

9. What is the effect on the accounting equation of recognizing uncollectible accounts expense?

10. What is the effect on the accounting equation of writing off an uncollectible account receivable when the allowance method is used?

11. How does the recovery of a previously written-off account affect the income statement when the allowance method is used? How does the recovery of a previously written-off account affect the statement of cash flows when the allowance method is used?

12. What is the advantage of using the allowance method of accounting for uncollectible accounts?

13. How do companies determine the percentage estimate of uncollectible accounts when using the percent of revenue method?

14. What is an advantage of using the percent of receivables method of estimating uncollectible accounts expense?

15. What is "aging of accounts receivable"?

16. What is a promissory note?

17. Define the following terms:
    a. Maker
    b. Payee
    c. Principal
    d. Interest
    e. Maturity date
    f. Collateral

18. What is the formula for computing interest revenue?

19. What is accrued interest?

20. How does the accrual of interest revenue or expense illustrate the matching concept?

21. Assets are listed on the balance sheet in the order of their liquidity. Explain this statement.

22. When is an adjusting entry for accrued interest generally recorded?

23. Assume that on July 1, Year 1 Big Corp. loaned Little Corp. $12,000 for a period of one year at 6 percent interest. What amount of interest revenue will Big report for Year 1? What amount of cash will Big receive upon maturity of the note?

24. In which section of the statement of cash flows will Big report the cash collected in Question 23?

25. Why is it generally beneficial for a business to accept major credit cards as payment for goods and services even when the fee charged by the credit card company is substantial?

26. What types of costs do businesses avoid when they accept major credit cards as compared with handling credit sales themselves?

27. Name and describe the four cost flow methods discussed in this chapter.

28. What are some advantages and disadvantages of the specific identification method of accounting for inventory?

29. What are some advantages and disadvantages of using the FIFO method of inventory valuation?

30. What are some advantages and disadvantages of using the LIFO method of inventory valuation?

31. In an inflationary period, which inventory cost flow method will produce the highest net income? Explain.

32. In an inflationary period, which inventory cost flow method will produce the largest amount of total assets on the balance sheet? Explain.

33. What is the difference between the flow of costs and the physical flow of goods?

34. Does the choice of cost flow method (FIFO, LIFO, or weighted average) affect the statement of cash flows? Explain.

35. Assume that Key Co. purchased 1,000 units of merchandise in its first year of operations for $25 per unit. The company sold 850 units for $40. What is the amount of cost of goods sold using FIFO? LIFO? Weighted average?

36. Assume that Key Co. purchased 1,500 units of merchandise in its second year of operation for $27 per unit. Its beginning inventory was determined in Question 35. Assuming that 1,500 units are sold, what is the amount of cost of goods sold using FIFO? LIFO? Weighted average?

37. Refer to Questions 35 and 36. Which method might be preferable for financial statements? For income tax reporting? Explain.

38. In an inflationary period, which cost flow method, FIFO or LIFO, produces the larger cash flow? Explain.

39. Which inventory cost flow method produces the highest net income in a deflationary period?

EXERCISES—SERIES A

Mc Graw Hill connect   An electronic auto-gradable version of the Series A Exercises is available in Connect. A PDF version of Series B Exercises is in Connect under the "Additional Student Resources" tab. Solutions to the Series B Exercises are available in Connect under the "Instructor Library" tab. Instructor and student Workpapers for the Series B Exercises are available in Connect under the "Instructor Library" and "Additional Student Resources" tabs respectively.

Exercise 5-1A   *Accounting for uncollectible accounts: Allowance method*   LO 5-1

Holmes Cleaning Service began operation on January 1, Year 1. The company experienced the following events for its first year of operations:

Events Affecting Year 1:

1. Provided $84,000 of cleaning services on account.
2. Collected $76,000 cash from accounts receivable.
3. Paid salaries of $28,500 for the year.
4. Adjusted the accounts to reflect management's expectations that uncollectible accounts expense would be $1,650. The expense was determined using the percent of revenue method.

Required

a. Organize the transaction data in accounts under on accounting equation.

b. Prepare an income statement, a balance sheet, and a statement of cash flows for Year 1.

Exercise 5-2A   *Analysis of financial statement effects of accounting for uncollectible*   LO 5-1
                      accounts under the allowance method

Businesses using the allowance method for the recognition of uncollectible accounts expense commonly experience four accounting events:

1. Recognition of uncollectible accounts expense through a year-end adjusting entry.
2. Write-off of uncollectible accounts.
3. Recognition of revenue on account.
4. Collection of cash from accounts receivable.

Required

Show the effect of each event on the elements of the financial statements, using a horizontal statements model like the one shown here. Use the following coding scheme to record your answers: increase is +, decrease is −, not affected is NA. In the cash flow column, indicate whether the item is an operating activity (OA), investing activity (IA), or financing activity (FA). The first transaction is entered as an example.

Event No.	Balance Sheet			Income Statement			Statement of Cash Flows
	Assets	= Liab.	+ Stk. Equity	Rev.	– Exp.	= Net Inc.	
1	–	NA	–	NA	+	–	NA

LO 5-1

Exercise 5-3A *Analyzing account balances for a company using the allowance method of accounting for uncollectible accounts*

The following account balances come from the records of Ourso Company:

	Beginning Balance	Ending Balance
Accounts Receivable	$2,800	$3,600
Allowance for Doubtful Accounts	280	350

During the accounting period, Ourso recorded $14,000 of sales revenue on account. The company also wrote off a $150 account receivable.

Required

a. Determine the amount of cash collected from receivables.

b. Determine the amount of uncollectible accounts expense recognized during the period.

LO 5-1

Exercise 5-4A *Effect of recognizing uncollectible accounts expense on financial statements: Percent of revenue allowance method*

Rosie Dry Cleaning was started on January 1, Year 1. It experienced the following events during its first two years of operation:

Events Affecting Year 1

1. Provided $45,000 of cleaning services on account.
2. Collected $39,000 cash from accounts receivable.
3. Adjusted the accounting records to reflect the estimate that uncollectible accounts expense would be 1 percent of the cleaning revenue on account.

Events Affecting Year 2

1. Wrote off a $300 account receivable that was determined to be uncollectible.
2. Provided $62,000 of cleaning services on account.
3. Collected $61,000 cash from accounts receivable.
4. Adjusted the accounting records to reflect the estimate that uncollectible accounts expense would be 1 percent of the cleaning revenue on account.

Required

a. Organize the transaction data in accounts under an accounting equation.

b. Determine the following amounts:
   (1) Net income for Year 1.
   (2) Net cash flow from operating activities for Year 1.
   (3) Balance of accounts receivable at the end of Year 1.
   (4) Net realizable value of accounts receivable at the end of Year 1.

c. Repeat Requirement *b* for the Year 2 accounting period.

Exercise 5-5A *Analyzing financial statement effects of accounting for uncollectible accounts using the percent of revenue allowance method*   **LO 5-1**

Grover Inc. uses the allowance method to account for uncollectible accounts expense. Grover Inc. experienced the following four accounting events in Year 1:

1. Recognized $92,000 of revenue on account.
2. Collected $78,000 cash from accounts receivable.
3. Wrote off uncollectible accounts of $720.
4. Recognized uncollectible accounts expense. Grover estimated that uncollectible accounts expense will be 1 percent of sales on account.

Required

Show the effect of each event on the elements of the financial statements, using a horizontal statements model like the one shown here. Use + for increase, − for decrease, and NA for not affected. In the cash flow column, indicate whether the item is an operating activity (OA), investing activity (IA), or financing activity (FA). The first transaction is entered as an example.

Event No.	Balance Sheet					Income Statement					Statement of Cash Flows
	Assets	=	Liab.	+	Stk. Equity	Rev.	−	Exp.	=	Net Inc.	
1	+		NA		+	+		NA		+	NA

Exercise 5-6A *Effect of recovering a receivable previously written off*   **LO 5-1**

The accounts receivable balance for Renue Spa at December 31, Year 1, was $61,000. Also on that date, the balance in the Allowance for Doubtful Accounts was $3,750. Total retained earnings at the end of Year 1 was $53,500. During Year 2, $2,100 of accounts receivable were written off as uncollectible. In addition, Renue unexpectedly collected $500 of receivables that had been written off in a previous accounting period. Services provided on account during Year 2 were $215,000, and cash collections from receivables were $218,000. Uncollectible accounts expense was estimated to be 2 percent of the sales on account for the period.

Required

a. Organize the information in accounts under an accounting equation.
b. Based on the preceding information, compute (after year-end adjustment):
   (1) Balance of Allowance for Doubtful Accounts at December 31, Year 2.
   (2) Balance of Accounts Receivable at December 31, Year 2.
   (3) Net realizable value of Accounts Receivable at December 31, Year 2.
c. What amount of uncollectible accounts expense will Renue Spa record for Year 2?
d. Explain how the $500 recovery of receivables affected the accounting equation.

Exercise 5-7A *Accounting for uncollectible accounts: Percent of revenue allowance method*   **LO 5-1**

Joey's Bike Shop sells new and used bicycle parts. Although a majority of its sales are cash sales, it makes a significant amount of credit sales. During Year 1, its first year of operations, Joey's Bike Shop experienced the following:

Sales on account	$260,000
Cash sales	580,000
Collections of accounts receivable	235,000
Uncollectible accounts charged off during the year	1,250

Required

Assume that Joey's Bike Shop uses the allowance method of accounting for uncollectible accounts and estimates that 1 percent of its sales on account will not be collected. Answer the following questions:

a. What is the Accounts Receivable balance at December 31, Year 1?

b. What is the ending balance of Allowance for Doubtful Accounts at December 31, Year 1, after all entries and adjusting entries are posted?

c. What is the amount of uncollectible accounts expense for Year 1?

d. What is the net realizable value of accounts receivable at December 31, Year 1?

LO 5-1

Exercise 5-8A   Determining account balances: Allowance method of accounting for uncollectible accounts

During the first year of operation, Year 1, Direct Service Co. recognized $290,000 of service revenue on account. At the end of Year 1, the accounts receivable balance was $46,000. For this first year in business, the owner believes uncollectible accounts expense will be about 1 percent of sales on account.

Required

a. What amount of cash did Direct Service collect from accounts receivable during Year 1?

b. Assuming Direct Service uses the allowance method to account for uncollectible accounts, what amount should Direct Service record as uncollectible accounts expense for Year 1?

c. What is the net realizable value of receivables at the end of Year 1?

d. Show the effects of the given transactions on the financial statements by recording the appropriate amounts in a horizontal statements model like the one shown here. In the Cash Flow column, indicate whether the item is an operating activity (OA), investing activity (IA), or financing activity (FA). Use NA for not affected.

Balance Sheet						Income Statement						Statement of Cash Flows
Assets			=	Liab.	+	Stk. Equity						
Cash	+	NRV Accts. Rec.	=				Rev.	−	Exp.	=	Net Inc.	

LO 5-2

Exercise 5-9A   Effect of recognizing uncollectible accounts on the financial statements: Percent of receivables allowance method

Leach Inc. experienced the following events for the first two years of its operations:

Year 1:

1. Issued $10,000 of common stock for cash.

2. Provided $78,000 of services on account.

3. Provided $36,000 of services and received cash.

4. Collected $69,000 cash from accounts receivable.

5. Paid $38,000 of salaries expense for the year.

6. Adjusted the accounting records to reflect uncollectible accounts expense for the year. Leach estimates that 5 percent of the ending accounts receivable balance will be uncollectible.

Year 2:

1. Wrote off an uncollectible account for $650.

2. Provided $88,000 of services on account.

3. Provided $32,000 of services and collected cash.

4. Collected $81,000 cash from accounts receivable.

5. Paid $65,000 of salaries expense for the year.

6. Adjusted the accounts to reflect uncollectible accounts expense for the year. Leach estimates that 5 percent of the ending accounts receivable balance will be uncollectible.

Required

a. Organize the transaction data in accounts under an accounting equation.

b. Prepare the income statement, statement of changes in stockholders' equity, balance sheet, and statement of cash flows for Year 1.

c. What is the net realizable value of the accounts receivable at December 31, Year 1?

d. Repeat Requirements *a, b,* and *c* for Year 2.

Exercise 5-10A   *Accounting for uncollectible accounts: Use of an aging schedule*   LO 5-2, 5-3

Roth Service Co. experienced the following transactions for Year 1, its first year of operations:

1. Provided $110,000 of services on account.
2. Collected $89,000 cash from accounts receivable.
3. Paid $41,000 of salaries expense for the year.
4. Roth adjusted the accounts using the following information from an accounts receivable aging schedule:

Number of Days Past Due	Amount	Percent Likely to Be Uncollectible	Allowance Balance
Current	$9,500	0.01	
0–30	4,000	0.05	
31–60	2,500	0.10	
61–90	2,000	0.30	
Over 90 days	3,000	0.50	

Required

a. Organize the information in accounts under an accounting equation.

b. Prepare the income statement for Roth Service Co. for Year 1.

c. What is the net realizable value of the accounts receivable at December 31, Year 1?

Exercise 5-11A   *Accounting for notes receivable*   LO 5-4

Rainey Enterprises loaned $20,000 to Small Co. on June 1, Year 1, for one year at 6 percent interest.

Required

Show the effects of the following transactions in a horizontal statements model like the one shown here.

(1) The loan to Small Co.

(2) The adjusting entry at December 31, Year 1.

(3) The adjusting entry and collection of the note on June 1, Year 2.

	Balance Sheet							Income Statement				Statement of Cash Flows
	Assets				=	Liab.	+	Stk. Equity				
Date	Cash	+	Notes Rec.	+	Int. Rec.	=		Ret. Earn.	Rev.	−	Exp.	=	Net Inc.	

Exercise 5-12A   *Notes receivable–accrued interest*   LO 5-4

On May 1, Year 1, Benz's Sandwich Shop loaned $10,000 to Mark Henry for one year at 6 percent interest.

Required

Answer the following questions:

a. What is Benz's interest income for Year 1?

b. What is Benz's total amount of receivables at December 31, Year 1?

c. How will the loan and interest be reported on Benz's Year 1 statement of cash flows?

d. What is Benz's interest income for Year 2?

e. What is the total amount of cash that Benz's will collect in Year 2 from Mark Henry?

f. How will the loan and interest be reported on Benz's Year 2 statement of cash flows?

g. What is the total amount of interest that Benz's earned on the loan to Mark Henry?

LO 5-1, 5-4

Exercise 5-13A *Comprehensive single-cycle problem*

The following post-closing trial balance was drawn from the accounts of Little Grocery Supplier (LGS) as of December 31, Year 1:

Cash	$ 9,000
Accounts Receivable	41,000
Allowance for Doubtful Accounts	2,500
Inventory	78,000
Accounts Payable	21,000
Common Stock	50,000
Retained Earnings	54,500

Transactions for Year 2

1. Acquired an additional $20,000 cash from the issue of common stock.
2. Purchased $85,000 of inventory on account.
3. Sold inventory that cost $91,000 for $160,000. Sales were made on account.
4. The company wrote off $900 of uncollectible accounts.
5. On September 1, LGS loaned $18,000 to Eden Co. The note had an 8 percent interest rate and a one-year term.
6. Paid $19,000 cash for operating expenses.
7. The company collected $161,000 cash from accounts receivable.
8. A cash payment of $92,000 was paid on accounts payable.
9. The company paid a $5,000 cash dividend to the stockholders.
10. Uncollectible accounts are estimated to be 1 percent of sales on account.
11. Recorded the accrued interest at December 31, Year 2 (see item 5).

Required

a. Organize the transaction data in accounts under an accounting equation.

b. Prepare an income statement, a statement of changes in stockholders' equity, a balance sheet, and a statement of cash flows for Year 2.

LO 5-5

Exercise 5-14A *Effect of credit card sales on financial statements*

Ultra Day Spa provided $120,000 of services during Year 1. All customers paid for the services with credit cards. Ultra submitted the credit card receipts to the credit card company immediately. The credit card company paid Ultra cash in the amount of face value less a 5 percent service charge.

Required

a. Record the credit card sales and the subsequent collection of accounts receivable in a horizontal statements model like the one shown here. In the Cash Flow column, indicate whether the item is an operating activity (OA), investing activity (IA), or financing activity (FA). Use NA to indicate that an element is not affected by the event.

Balance Sheet					Income Statement			Statement of
Assets		=	Liab.	+	Stk. Equity			Cash Flows
Cash	+	Accts. Rec.			Rev.	−	Exp.	=	Net Inc.	

b. Based on this information alone, answer the following questions:

   (1) What is the amount of total assets at the end of the accounting period?

   (2) What is the amount of revenue reported on the income statement?

   (3) What is the amount of cash flow from operating activities reported on the statement of cash flows?

   (4) What costs would a business incur if it maintained its own accounts receivable? What cost does a business incur by accepting credit cards?

Exercise 5-15A   *Recording credit card sales*   LO 5-5

Luna Company accepted credit cards in payment for $6,000 of services performed during July. The credit card company charged Luna a 4 percent service fee; it paid Luna as soon as it received the invoices.

Required

Based on this information alone, what is the amount of net income earned during the month of July?

Exercise 5-16   *Effect of inventory cost flow assumption on financial statements*   LO 5-6

Required

For each of the following situations, indicate whether FIFO, LIFO, or weighted average applies:

a. In a period of falling prices, net income would be highest.

b. In a period of falling prices, the unit cost of goods would be the same for ending inventory and cost of goods sold.

c. In a period of rising prices, net income would be highest.

d. In a period of rising prices, cost of goods sold would be highest.

e. In a period of rising prices, ending inventory would be highest.

Exercise 5-17A   *Allocating product cost between cost of goods sold and ending inventory*   LO 5-6

Jones Co. started the year with no inventory. During the year, it purchased two identical inventory items at different times. The first purchase cost $1,060 and the other, $1,380. Jones sold one of the items during the year.

Required

Based on this information, how much product cost would be allocated to cost of goods sold and ending inventory on the year-end financial statements, assuming use of

a. FIFO?

b. LIFO?

c. Weighted average?

Exercise 5-18A   *Allocating product cost between cost of goods sold and ending inventory:*   LO 5-6
            Multiple purchases

Cortez Company sells chairs that are used at computer stations. Its beginning inventory of chairs was 100 units at $60 per unit. During the year, Cortez made two batch purchases of this chair. The first was a 150-unit purchase at $68 per unit; the second was a 200-unit purchase at $72 per unit. During the period, it sold 270 chairs.

Required

Determine the amount of product costs that would be allocated to cost of goods sold and ending inventory, assuming that Cortez uses

a. FIFO.

b. LIFO.

c. Weighted average.

LO 5-6

Exercise 5-19A   *Effect of inventory cost flow (FIFO, LIFO, and weighted average) on gross margin*

The following information pertains to Mason Company for Year 2:

Beginning inventory	90 units @ $40
Units purchased	310 units @ $45

Ending inventory consisted of 30 units. Mason sold 370 units at $90 each. All purchases and sales were made with cash. Operating expenses amounted to $4,100.

Required

a. Compute the gross margin for Mason Company using the following cost flow assumptions: (1) FIFO, (2) LIFO, and (3) weighted average.

b. What is the amount of net income using FIFO, LIFO, and weighted average? (Ignore income tax considerations.)

c. Determine the cash flow from operating activities, using each of the three cost flow assumptions listed in Requirement *a*. Ignore the effect of income taxes. Explain why these cash flows have no differences.

LO 5-6

Exercise 5-20A   *Effect of inventory cost flow on ending inventory balance and gross margin*

The Shirt Shop had the following transactions for T-shirts for Year 1, its first year of operations:

Jan. 20	Purchased 400 units @ $ 8	=	$3,200
Apr. 21	Purchased 200 units @ $10	=	2,000
July 25	Purchased 280 units @ $13	=	3,640
Sept. 19	Purchased 90 units @ $15	=	1,350

During the year, The Shirt Shop sold 810 T-shirts for $20 each.

Required

a. Compute the amount of ending inventory The Shirt Shop would report on the balance sheet, assuming the following cost flow assumptions: (1) FIFO, (2) LIFO, and (3) weighted average, rounded to two decimal places.

b. Compute the difference in gross margin between the FIFO and LIFO cost flow assumptions.

LO 5-6

Exercise 5-21A   *Income tax effect of shifting from FIFO to LIFO*

The following information pertains to the inventory of Parvin Company:

Jan. 1	Beginning inventory	400 units @ $30
Apr. 1	Purchased	2,000 units @ $35
Oct. 1	Purchased	600 units @ $38

During the year, Parvin sold 2,700 units of inventory at $90 per unit and incurred $41,500 of operating expenses. Parvin currently uses the FIFO method but is considering a change to LIFO. All transactions are cash transactions. Assume a 30 percent income tax rate. Parvin started the period with cash of $75,000, inventory of $12,000, common stock of $50,000, and retained earnings of $37,000.

Required

a. Prepare income statements using FIFO and LIFO.

b. Determine the amount of income tax that Parvin would pay using each cost flow method.

c. Determine the cash flow from operating activities under FIFO and LIFO.

d. Why is the cash flow from operating activities different under FIFO and LIFO?

PROBLEMS—SERIES A

Mc Graw Hill connect An electronic auto-gradable version of the Series A Problems is available in Connect. A PDF version of Series B Problems is in Connect under the "Additional Student Resources" tab. Solutions to the Series B Problems are available in Connect under the "Instructor Library" tab. Instructor and student Workpapers for the Series B Problems are available in Connect under the "Instructor Library" and "Additional Student Resources" tabs respectively.

Problem 5-22A   *Accounting for uncollectible accounts—two cycles using the percent of revenue allowance method*

LO 5-1

The following transactions apply to Jova Company for Year 1, the first year of operation:

1. Issued $10,000 of common stock for cash.
2. Recognized $210,000 of service revenue earned on account.
3. Collected $162,000 from accounts receivable.
4. Paid operating expenses of $125,000.
5. Adjusted accounts to recognize uncollectible accounts expense. Jova uses the allowance method of accounting for uncollectible accounts and estimates that uncollectible accounts expense will be 1 percent of sales on account.

CHECK FIGURES
c. Ending Accounts Receivable, Year 1: $48,000
d. Net Income, Year 2: $113,400

The following transactions apply to Jova for Year 2:

1. Recognized $320,000 of service revenue on account.
2. Collected $335,000 from accounts receivable.
3. Determined that $2,150 of the accounts receivable were uncollectible and wrote them off.
4. Collected $800 of an account that had previously been written off.
5. Paid $205,000 cash for operating expenses.
6. Adjusted the accounts to recognize uncollectible accounts expense for Year 2. Jova estimates uncollectible accounts expense will be 0.5 percent of sales on account.

Required

Complete the following requirements for Year 1 and Year 2. Complete all requirements for Year 1 prior to beginning the requirements for Year 2.

a. Identify the type of each transaction (asset source, asset use, asset exchange, or claims exchange).
b. Show the effect of each transaction on the elements of the financial statements, using a horizontal statements model like the one shown here. Use + for increase, − for decrease, and NA for not affected. Also, in the Cash Flow column, indicate whether the item is an operating activity (OA), investing activity (IA), or financing activity (FA). The first transaction is entered as an example. (*Hint:* Closing entries do not affect the statements model.)

	Balance Sheet					Income Statement				Statement of Cash Flows
Event No.	Assets	=	Liab.	+	Stk. Equity	Rev.	−	Exp.	=	Net Inc.	
1	+		NA		+	+		NA		+	NA

c. Organize the transaction data in accounts under an accounting equation.
d. Prepare the income statement, statement of changes in stockholders' equity, balance sheet, and statement of cash flows.

Problem 5-23A   *Determining account balances: Percent of revenue method of accounting for uncollectible accounts*

LO 5-1

The following information is available for Quality Book Sales's sales on account and accounts receivable:

CHECK FIGURE
a. Net Realizable Value: $65,040

Accounts Receivable Balance, January 1, Year 2	$ 78,500
Allowance for Doubtful Accounts, January 1, Year 2	4,710
Sales on Account, Year 2	550,000
Collections of Accounts Receivable, Year 2	556,000

After several collection attempts, Quality Book Sales wrote off $2,850 of accounts that could not be collected. Quality Book Sales estimates that 0.5 percent of sales on account will be uncollectible.

Required

a. Compute the following amounts:

   (1) Using the allowance method, the amount of uncollectible accounts expense for Year 2.

   (2) Net realizable value of receivables at the end of Year 2.

b. Explain why the uncollectible accounts expense amount is different from the amount that was written off as uncollectible.

LO 5-2

Problem 5-24A *Determination of account balances—percent of receivables allowance method of accounting for uncollectible accounts*

During the first year of operation, Year 1, McGinnis Appliance recognized $275,000 of service revenue on account. At the end of Year 1, the accounts receivable balance was $55,300. Even though this is his first year in business, the owner believes he will collect all but about 3 percent of the ending balance.

Required

CHECK FIGURE
c. Net Realizable Value: $53,641

a. What amount of cash was collected by McGinnis during Year 1?

b. Assuming the use of an allowance system to account for uncollectible accounts, what amount should McGinnis record as uncollectible accounts expense in Year 1?

c. What is the net realizable value of receivables at the end of Year 1?

d. Show the effect of these transactions on the financial statements by recording the appropriate amounts in a horizontal statements model like the one shown here. When you record amounts in the Cash Flow column, indicate whether the item is an operating activity (OA), investing activity (IA), or financing activity (FA). The letters NA indicate that an element is not affected by the event.

Balance Sheet					Income Statement			Statement of Cash Flows
Assets		= Liab.	+	Stk. Equity				
Cash	+ NRV Accts. Rec.				Rev.	− Exp.	= Net Inc.	

LO 5-2, 5-3

Problem 5-25A *Accounting for uncollectible accounts: Percent of receivables allowance method*

Sage Inc. experienced the following transactions for Year 1, its first year of operations:

CHECK FIGURE
b. Net income: $61,430
Total assets: $133,430

1. Issued common stock for $50,000 cash.
2. Purchased $140,000 of merchandise on account.
3. Sold merchandise that cost $110,000 for $250,000 on account.
4. Collected $236,000 cash from accounts receivable.
5. Paid $118,000 on accounts payable.
6. Paid $50,000 of salaries expense for the year.
7. Paid other operating expenses of $28,000.
8. Sage adjusted the accounts using the following information from an accounts receivable aging schedule:

Number of Days Past Due	Amount	Percent Likely to Be Uncollectible	Allowance Balance
Current	$10,000	0.01	
0–30	2,000	0.05	
31–60	1,200	0.10	
61–90	500	0.20	
Over 90 days	300	0.50	

Required

a. Organize the transaction data in accounts under an accounting equation.

b. Prepare the income statement, statement of changes in stockholders' equity, balance sheet, and statement of cash flows for Sage Inc. for Year 1.

c. What is the net realizable value of the accounts receivable at December 31, Year 1?

Problem 5-26A *Accounting for notes receivable and uncollectible accounts using the percent of sales allowance method*   LO 5-1, 5-4

The following transactions apply to Hooper Co. for Year 1, its first year of operations:

1. Issued $60,000 of common stock for cash.
2. Provided $90,000 of services on account.
3. Collected $78,000 cash from accounts receivable.
4. Loaned $20,000 to Mosby Co. on November 30, Year 1. The note had a one-year term to maturity and a 6 percent interest rate.
5. Paid $26,000 of salaries expense for the year.
6. Paid a $2,000 dividend to the stockholders.
7. Recorded the accrued interest on December 31, Year 1 (see item 4).
8. Estimated that 1 percent of service revenue will be uncollectible.

Required

a. Show the effects of these transactions in a horizontal statements model like the one shown as follows.

	Balance Sheet								Income Statement			Statement of Cash Flows
	Assets					Stk. Equity						
Event	Cash	+	NRV Accts. Rec.	+	Notes Rec.	+	Int. Rec.	=	Com. Stk.	+	Ret. Earn.	Rev. − Exp. = Net Inc.

b. Prepare the income statement, balance sheet, and statement of cash flows for Year 1.

Problem 5-27A *Multistep income statement and balance sheet*   LO 5-4

CHECK FIGURES
Total Current Assets: $264,900
Total Current Liabilities: $106,400

Required

Use the following information to prepare a multistep income statement and a classified balance sheet for Chun Equipment Co. for Year 2. (*Hint:* Some of the items will *not* appear on either statement, and ending retained earnings must be calculated.)

Salaries expense	$ 41,200	Interest receivable (short term)	$ 2,100
Common stock	90,000	Beginning retained earnings	120,100
Notes receivable (short term)	15,000	Operating expenses	45,000
Allowance for doubtful accounts	6,500	Cash flow from investing activities	(91,600)
Accumulated depreciation	12,000	Prepaid rent	16,100
Notes payable (long term)	26,000	Land	35,000
Salvage value of equipment	6,000	Cash	26,700
Interest payable (short term)	1,900	Inventory	105,000
Uncollectible accounts expense	9,600	Accounts payable	48,000
Supplies	14,500	Interest expense	1,300
Office equipment	57,000	Salaries payable	14,500
Interest revenue	2,000	Unearned revenue	42,000
Sales revenue	340,000	Cost of goods sold	225,000
Dividends	10,000	Accounts receivable	92,000
Rent expense	7,500		

LO 5-4

Problem 5-28A   *Missing information*

The following information comes from the accounts of James Company:

Account Title	Beginning Balance	Ending Balance
Accounts Receivable	$36,000	$34,000
Allowance for Doubtful Accounts	1,800	1,600
Note Receivable	40,000	40,000
Interest Receivable	1,400	4,200

Required

a. There were $190,000 of sales on account during the accounting period. Write-offs of uncollectible accounts were $1,450. What was the amount of cash collected from accounts receivable? What amount of uncollectible accounts expense was reported on the income statement? What was the net realizable value of receivables at the end of the accounting period?

b. The note receivable has a two-year term with a 7 percent interest rate. What amount of interest revenue was recognized during the period? How much cash was collected from interest?

LO 5-2, 5-5

Problem 5-29A   *Accounting for credit card sales and uncollectible accounts: Percent of receivables allowance method*

Northwest Sales had the following transactions in Year 1:

CHECK FIGURE
b. Net Income: $280,300
Total Assets: $480,300

1. Acquired $200,000 cash from the issue of common stock.
2. Purchased $900,000 of merchandise for cash in Year 1.
3. Sold merchandise that cost $710,000 for $1,200,000 during the year under the following terms:

$520,000	Cash sales
380,000	Credit card sales (The credit card company charges a 4 percent service fee.)
300,000	Sales on account

4. Collected all the amount receivable from the credit card company.
5. Collected $210,000 of accounts receivable.
6. Paid selling and administrative expenses of $190,000.
7. Determined that 5 percent of the ending accounts receivable balance would be uncollectible.

Required

a. Record these events in a horizontal statements model like the following one. When you record amounts in the Cash Flow column, indicate whether the item is an operating activity (OA), an investing activity (IA), or a financing activity (FA). The letters NA indicate that an element is not affected by the event.

	Balance Sheet						Income Statement			Statement of Cash Flows
	Assets			=	Stk. Equity					
Event	Cash +	NRV Accts. Rec. +	Mdse. Inv. =	Com. Stk. +	Ret. Earn.		Rev. −	Exp. =	Net Inc.	

b. Prepare an income statement, a statement of changes in stockholders' equity, a balance sheet, and a statement of cash flows for Year 1.

LO 5-1, 5-4, 5-5

Problem 5-30A   *Effect of transactions on the elements of financial statements*

Required

Identify each of the following independent transactions as asset source (AS), asset use (AU), asset exchange (AE), or claims exchange (CE). Also explain how each event affects assets, liabilities, stockholders' equity, net income, and cash flow by placing a + for increase, − for decrease, or NA for not affected under each of the categories. The first event is recorded as an example.

Event	Type of Event	Assets	Liabilities	Common Stock	Retained Earnings	Net Income	Cash Flow
a	AS	+	NA	NA	+	+	NA

a. Provided services on account.
b. Wrote off an uncollectible account (use the allowance method).
c. Loaned cash to H. Phillips for one year at 6 percent interest.
d. Collected cash from customers paying their accounts.
e. Paid cash for land.
f. Sold merchandise at a price above cost. Accepted payment by credit card. The credit card company charges a service fee. The receipts have not yet been forwarded to the credit card company.
g. Provided services for cash.
h. Paid cash for operating expenses.
i. Paid cash for salaries expense.
j. Recovered an uncollectible account that had been previously written off (assume the allowance method is used to account for uncollectible accounts).
k. Paid cash to creditors on accounts payable.
l. Recorded three months of accrued interest on the note receivable (see item c).
m. Submitted receipts to the credit card company (see item f) and collected cash.
n. Sold land at its cost.

Problem 5-31A Comprehensive accounting cycle problem (uses percent of revenue allowance method)

LO 5-1, 5-4, 5-5

The following trial balance was prepared for Tile, Etc., Inc. on December 31, Year 1, after the closing entries were posted:

CHECK FIGURES
Net Income: $490,300
Total Assets: $1,102,300

Account Title	
Cash	$110,000
Accounts Receivable	125,000
Allowance for Doubtful Accounts	18,000
Inventory	425,000
Accounts Payable	95,000
Common Stock	450,000
Retained Earnings	97,000

Tile, Etc. had the following transactions in Year 2:

1. Purchased merchandise on account for $580,000.
2. Sold merchandise that cost $420,000 for $890,000 on account.
3. Sold for $245,000 cash merchandise that had cost $160,000.
4. Sold merchandise for $190,000 to credit card customers. The merchandise had cost $96,000. The credit card company charges a 4 percent fee.
5. Collected $620,000 cash from accounts receivable.
6. Paid $610,000 cash on accounts payable.
7. Paid $145,000 cash for selling and administrative expenses.
8. Collected cash for the full amount due from the credit card company (see item 4).
9. Loaned $60,000 to J. Parks. The note had an 8 percent interest rate and a one-year term to maturity.
10. Wrote off $7,500 of accounts as uncollectible.
11. Made the following adjusting entries:
    (a) Recorded uncollectible accounts expense estimated at 1 percent of sales on account.
    (b) Recorded seven months of accrued interest on the note at December 31, Year 2 (see item 9).

Required

a. Organize the transaction data in accounts under an accounting equation.
b. Prepare an income statement, a statement of changes in stockholders' equity, a balance sheet, and a statement of cash flows for Year 2.

LO 5-6

Problem 5-32A *Effect of different inventory cost flow methods on financial statements*

The accounting records of Wall's China Shop reflected the following balances as of January 1, Year 2:

Cash	$80,100
Beginning inventory	33,000 (220 units @ $150)
Common stock	50,000
Retained earnings	63,100

The following five transactions occurred in Year 2:

1. First purchase (cash)   150 units @ $155
2. Second purchase (cash)   160 units @ $160
3. Sales (all cash)   410 units @ $320
4. Paid $38,000 cash for salaries expense
5. Paid cash for income tax at the rate of 25 percent of income before taxes

Required

a. Compute the cost of goods sold and ending inventory, assuming (1) FIFO cost flow, (2) LIFO cost flow, and (3) weighted-average cost flow. Compute the income tax expense for each method.
b. Use a vertical model to show the Year 2 income statement, balance sheet, and statement of cash flows under FIFO, LIFO, and weighted average. (*Hint:* Record the events under an accounting equation before preparing the statements.)

LO 5-6

Problem 5-33A *Effect of FIFO versus LIFO on income tax expense*

The Brick Company had cash sales of $280,000 for Year 1, its first year of operation. On April 2, the company purchased 210 units of inventory at $390 per unit. On September 1, an additional 160 units were purchased for $425 per unit. The company had 110 units on hand at the end of the year. The company's income tax rate is 40 percent. All transactions are cash transactions.

Required

a. The preceding paragraph describes five accounting events: (1) a sales transaction, (2) the first purchase of inventory, (3) a second purchase of inventory, (4) the recognition of cost of goods sold expense, and (5) the payment of income tax expense. Record the amounts of each event in horizontal statements models like the following ones, assuming first a FIFO and then a LIFO cost flow.

Effect of Events on Financial Statements
Panel 1: FIFO Cost Flow

	Balance Sheet					Income Statement					Statement of Cash Flows
Event No.	Cash	+	Inventory	=	Ret. Earn.	Rev.	−	Exp.	=	Net Inc.	

Panel 2: LIFO Cost Flow

	Balance Sheet					Income Statement					Statement of Cash Flows
Event No.	Cash	+	Inventory	=	Ret. Earn.	Rev.	−	Exp.	=	Net Inc.	

b. Compute net income using FIFO.

c. Compute net income using LIFO.

d. Explain the difference, if any, in the amount of income tax expense incurred using the two cost flow assumptions.

e. How does the use of FIFO versus the LIFO cost flow assumptions affect the statement of cash flows?

ANALYZE, THINK, COMMUNICATE

ATC 5-1   Business Application Case   *Understanding real-world annual reports*

Obtain the Target Corporation's annual report for its 2018 fiscal year (year ended February 2, 2019) at http://investors.target.com using the instructions in Appendix A, and use it to answer the following questions. Round answers to one decimal place.

Required

a. What percentage of Target's total assets was comprised of inventory?

b. What cost flow method did Target use to account for its inventory?

ATC 5-2   Group Assignment   *Inventory cost flow*

The accounting records of Robin Co. showed the following balances at January 1, Year 2:

Cash	$30,000
Beginning inventory (100 units @ $50, 70 units @ $55)	8,850
Common stock	20,000
Retained earnings	18,850

Transactions for Year 2 were as follows:

Purchased 100 units @ $54 per unit.
Purchased 250 units @ $58 per unit.
Sold 220 units @ $80 per unit.
Sold 200 units @ $90 per unit.
Paid operating expenses of $3,200.
Paid income tax expense. The income tax rate is 30%.

Required

a. Organize the class into three sections, and divide each section into groups of three to five students. Assign each section one of the cost flow methods, FIFO, LIFO, or weighted average. The company uses the perpetual inventory system.

Group Tasks

Determine the amount of ending inventory, cost of goods sold, gross margin, and net income after income tax for the cost flow method assigned to your section. Also prepare an income statement using that cost flow assumption.

Class Discussion

b. Have a representative of each section put its income statement on the board. Discuss the effect that each cost flow method has on assets (ending inventory), net income, and cash flows. Which method is preferred for tax reporting? For financial reporting? What restrictions are placed on the use of LIFO for tax reporting?

ATC 5-3   Research Assignment   *Analyzing two real-world companies' accounts receivable*

Using the most current annual reports or the Forms 10-K for Chipolte Mexican Grill, Inc. and Whirlpool, which manufactures appliances, complete the following requirements. To obtain the Forms 10-K, use either the EDGAR system following the instructions in Appendix A or the companies' websites. The annual reports can be found on the companies' websites.

Required

a. For each company, compute accounts receivable as a percentage of revenue. Show your computations.

b. Which company appears to be making more of its sales on account? Explain your answer.

c. Try to provide a logical explanation as to why one of these companies is making more of its sales on account than the other.

ATC 5-4   Writing Assignment   *Cost of charge sales*

Paul Smith is opening a plumbing supply store in University City. He plans to sell plumbing parts and materials to both wholesale and retail customers. Since contractors (wholesale customers) prefer to buy parts and materials and pay at the end of the month, Paul expects he will have to offer charge accounts. He plans to offer charge sales to the wholesale customers only and to require retail customers to pay with either cash or credit cards. Paul wondered what expenses his business would incur relative to the charge sales and the credit cards.

Required

a. What issues will Paul need to consider if he allows wholesale customers to buy plumbing supplies on account?

b. Write a memo to Paul Smith outlining the potential cost of accepting charge customers. Discuss the difference between the allowance method for uncollectible accounts and the direct write-off method. Also discuss the cost of accepting credit cards.

ATC 5-5   Ethical Dilemma   *How bad can it be?*

Alonzo Saunders owns a small training services company that is experiencing growing pains. The company has grown rapidly by offering liberal credit terms to its customers. Although his competitors require payment for services within 30 days, Saunders permits his customers to delay payment for up to 90 days. Saunders's customers thereby have time to fully evaluate the training that employees receive before they must pay for that training. Saunders guarantees satisfaction. If a customer is unhappy, the customer does not have to pay. Saunders works with reputable companies, provides top-quality training, and rarely encounters dissatisfied customers.

The long collection period, however, has created a cash flow problem. Saunders has a $100,000 accounts receivable balance, but needs cash to pay current bills. He has recently negotiated a loan agreement with National Bank of Brighton County that should solve his cash flow problems. The loan agreement requires that Saunders pledge the accounts receivable as collateral for the loan. The bank agreed to loan Saunders 70 percent of the receivables balance, thereby giving him access to $70,000 cash. Saunders is satisfied with this arrangement because he estimates he needs approximately $60,000.

On the day Saunders was to execute the loan agreement, he heard a rumor that his biggest customer was experiencing financial problems and might declare bankruptcy. The customer owed Saunders $45,000. Saunders promptly called the customer's chief accountant and learned "off the record" that the rumor was true. The accountant told Saunders that the company's net worth was negative and most of its assets were pledged as collateral for bank loans. In his opinion, Saunders was unlikely to collect the balance due. Saunders's immediate concern was the impact the circumstances would have on his loan agreement with the bank.

Saunders uses the direct write-off method to recognize uncollectible accounts expense. Removing the $45,000 receivable from the collateral pool would leave only $55,000 of receivables, reducing the available credit to \$38,500 (\$55,000 × 0.70). Even worse, recognizing the uncollectible accounts expense would so adversely affect his income statement that the bank might further reduce the available credit by reducing the percentage of receivables allowed under the loan agreement. Saunders will have to attest to the quality of the receivables at the date of the loan but reasons that since the information he obtained about the possible bankruptcy was "off the record" he is under no obligation to recognize the uncollectible accounts expense until the receivable is officially uncollectible.

Required

a. How are income and assets affected by the decision not to act on the bankruptcy information?

b. Review the AICPA's Articles of Professional Conduct (see Chapter 4) and comment on any of the standards that would be violated by the actions Saunders is contemplating.

c. How do the elements of the fraud triangle (see Chapter 4) apply to this case?

CHAPTER 6

Accounting for Long-Term Operational Assets

LEARNING OBJECTIVES

After you have mastered the material in this chapter, you will be able to:

LO 6-1 Identify and determine the cost of long-term operational assets.

LO 6-2 Calculate straight-line depreciation and show how it affects financial statements.

LO 6-3 Calculate double-declining-balance depreciation and show how it affects financial statements.

LO 6-4 Calculate units-of-production depreciation and show how it affects financial statements.

LO 6-5 Show how gains and losses on disposals of long-term operational assets affect financial statements.

LO 6-6 Show how revising estimates affects financial statements.

LO 6-7 Show how continuing expenditures for operational assets affect financial statements.

LO 6-8 Show how expense recognition for natural resources (depletion) affects financial statements.

LO 6-9 Identify and determine the cost of intangible assets.

LO 6-10 Show how the amortization of intangible assets affects financial statements.

LO 6-11 Show how expense recognition choices and industry characteristics affect financial performance measures.

 Video lectures and accompanying self-assessment quizzes are available in Connect *for all learning objectives.*

 Set B exercises and problems are available in Additional Student Resources.

CHAPTER OPENING

Companies use assets to produce revenue. Some assets, like inventory or office supplies, are called **current (short-term)** assets because they are used relatively quickly (within a single accounting period). Other assets, like equipment or buildings, are used for extended periods of time (two or more accounting periods). These assets are called **long-term operational assets.**[1] Accounting for long-term assets raises several questions. For example, what is the cost of the asset? Is it the list price only or should the cost of transportation, transit insurance, setup, and so on be added to the list price? Should the cost of a long-term asset be recognized as expense in the period the asset is purchased or should the cost be expensed over the useful life of the asset? What happens in the accounting records when a long-term asset is retired from use? This chapter answers these questions. It explains accounting for long-term operational assets from the date of purchase through the date of disposal.

[1]Classifying assets as current versus long term is explained in more detail in Chapter 7.

The Curious Accountant

Stephen Reynolds

Most companies have various types of long-term assets that they use to operate their business. Common types of long-term assets include buildings, machinery, and equipment. But there are other types as well. A major category of long-term assets for a mining company is the mineral reserves from which they extract ore.

Freeport-McMoRan Copper & Gold, Inc. (referred to as FCX) is one of the largest mining operations in the world. It produces copper, gold, and molybdenum from 12 major mines located on four continents. As of December 31, 2017, it owned proven mineral reserves that cost $4.0 billion, and buildings, machinery, and equipment that cost $23.4 billion.

How do you think the way a mining company uses its buildings and equipment differs from the way it uses its mineral reserves, and how will these differences affect the way the company accounts for these assets? (Answer on page 222.)

LONG-TERM OPERATIONAL ASSETS

Long-term assets may be tangible or intangible. **Tangible assets** have a physical presence; they can be seen and touched. Tangible assets include equipment, machinery, land, and natural resources. In contrast, intangible assets have no physical form. Although they may be represented by physical documents, **intangible assets** are, in fact, rights or privileges. They cannot be seen or touched. For example, a patent represents an exclusive legal *privilege* to produce and sell a particular product. It protects inventors by making it illegal for others to profit by copying their inventions. Although a patent may be represented by legal documents, the privilege is the actual asset. Because the privilege cannot be seen or touched, the patent is an intangible asset.

Tangible Long-Term Assets

Tangible long-term assets are classified as (1) property, plant, and equipment or (2) natural resources.

Property, Plant, and Equipment

Property, plant, and equipment is sometimes called *plant assets* or *fixed assets.* Examples of property, plant, and equipment include furniture, cash registers, machinery, delivery trucks, computers, mechanical robots, buildings, and land. The level of detail used to account for these assets varies. One company may include all office equipment in one account, whereas another company might divide office equipment into computers, desks, chairs, and so on. The term used to recognize expense for property, plant, and equipment is **depreciation.**

Land is not subject to depreciation. Land has an infinite life. It is not worn out or consumed as it is used. When buildings or other assets are purchased simultaneously with land, the amount paid must be divided between the land and the other assets because of the nondepreciable nature of the land.

Natural Resources

Mineral deposits, oil and gas reserves, timber stands, coal mines, and stone quarries are examples of **natural resources.** Conceptually, natural resources are inventories. When sold, the cost of these assets is frequently expensed as *cost of goods sold.* Although inventories are usually classified as short-term assets, natural resources are normally classified as long term because the resource deposits generally have long lives. For example, it may take decades to extract all of the diamonds from a diamond mine. The term used to recognize expense for natural resources is **depletion.**

Intangible Assets

Intangible assets fall into two categories, those with *identifiable useful lives* and those with *indefinite useful lives.*

Intangible Assets with Identifiable Useful Lives

Intangible assets with identifiable useful lives include patents and copyrights. These assets may become obsolete (a patent may become worthless if new technology provides a superior product) or may reach the end of their legal lives. The term used when recognizing expense for intangible assets with identifiable useful lives is called **amortization.**

Intangible Assets with Indefinite Useful Lives

The benefits of some intangible assets may extend so far into the future that their useful lives cannot be estimated. For how many years will the Coca-Cola trademark attract customers?

When will the value of a McDonald's franchise end? There are no answers to these questions. Intangible assets such as renewable franchises, trademarks, and goodwill have indefinite useful lives. The costs of such assets are not expensed unless the value of the assets becomes impaired.

Determining the Cost of Long-Term Assets

The **historical cost concept** requires that an asset be recorded at the amount paid for it. This amount includes the purchase price plus any costs necessary to get the asset in the location and condition for its intended use. Common cost components are:

- *Buildings:* (1) purchase price, (2) sales taxes, (3) title search and transfer document costs, (4) realtor's and attorney's fees, and (5) remodeling costs.
- *Land:* (1) purchase price, (2) sales taxes, (3) title search and transfer document costs, (4) realtor's and attorney's fees, (5) costs for removal of old buildings, and (6) grading costs.
- *Equipment:* (1) purchase price (less discounts), (2) sales taxes, (3) delivery costs, (4) installation costs, and (5) costs to adapt for intended use.

The cost of an asset does not include payments for fines, damages, and so on that could have been avoided.

 CHECK YOURSELF 6.1

Sheridan Construction Company purchased a new bulldozer that had a $260,000 list price. The seller agreed to allow a 4 percent cash discount in exchange for immediate payment. The bulldozer was delivered FOB shipping point at a cost of $1,200. Sheridan hired a new employee to operate the dozer for an annual salary of $36,000. The employee was trained to operate the dozer for a one-time training fee of $800. The cost of the company's theft insurance policy increased by $300 per year as a result of adding the dozer to the policy. The dozer had a five-year useful life and an expected salvage value of $26,000. Determine the asset's cost.

Answer

List price	$260,000
Less: Cash discount ($260,000 × 0.04)	(10,400)
Shipping cost	1,200
Training cost	800
Total asset cost (amount capitalized)	$251,600

Basket Purchase Allocation

Acquiring a group of assets in a single transaction is known as a **basket purchase.** The total price of a basket purchase must be allocated among the assets acquired. Accountants commonly allocate the purchase price using the **relative fair market value method.** To illustrate, assume that Beatty Company purchased land and a building for $240,000 cash. A real estate appraiser determined the fair market value of each asset to be as follows:

Building	$270,000
Land	90,000
Total	$360,000

The appraisal indicates that the land is worth 25 percent ($90,000 ÷ $360,000) of the total value and the building is worth 75 percent ($270,000 ÷ $360,000). Using these percentages, the actual purchase price is allocated as follows:

Building	0.75 × $240,000 =	$180,000
Land	0.25 × $240,000 =	60,000
Total		$240,000

METHODS OF RECOGNIZING DEPRECIATION EXPENSE

The life cycle of an operational asset involves (1) acquiring the funds to buy the asset, (2) purchasing the asset, (3) using the asset, and (4) retiring (disposing of) the asset. These stages are illustrated in Exhibit 6.1. The stages involving (1) acquiring funds and (2) purchasing assets have been discussed previously. This section of the chapter describes how accountants recognize the *use* of assets (Stage 3). As they are used, assets suffer from wear and tear called *depreciation*. Ultimately, assets depreciate to the point that they are no longer useful in the process of earning revenue. This process usually takes several years. The amount of an asset's cost that is allocated to expense during an accounting period is called **depreciation expense.**

An asset that is fully depreciated by one company may still be useful to another company. For example, a rental car that is no longer useful to Hertz may still be useful to a local delivery company. As a result, companies are frequently able to sell their fully depreciated assets to other companies or individuals. The expected market value of a fully depreciated asset is called its **salvage value.** The total amount of depreciation a company recognizes for an asset, its **depreciable cost,** is the difference between its original cost and its salvage value.

For example, assume a company purchases an asset for $5,000. The company expects to use the asset for 5 years (the **estimated useful life**) and then to sell it for $1,000 (salvage value). The depreciable cost of the asset is $4,000 ($5,000 − $1,000). The portion of the depreciable cost ($4,000) that represents its annual usage is recognized as depreciation expense.

Accountants must exercise judgment to estimate the amount of depreciation expense to recognize each period. For example, suppose you own a personal computer. You know how much the computer cost, and you know you will eventually need to replace it. How would you determine the amount the computer depreciates each year you use it? Businesses may use any of several acceptable methods to estimate the amount of depreciation expense to recognize each year.

The method used to recognize depreciation expense should match the asset's usage pattern. More expense should be recognized in periods when the asset is used more and less in periods when the asset is used less. Because assets are used to produce revenue, matching expense recognition with asset usage also matches expense recognition with revenue recognition. Three alternative methods for recognizing depreciation expense are (1) straight-line, (2) double-declining-balance, and (3) units-of-production.

The *straight-line* method produces the same amount of depreciation expense each accounting period. *Double-declining-balance,* an accelerated method, produces more depreciation expense in the early years of an asset's life, with a declining amount of expense in later years. *Units-of-production* produces varying amounts of depreciation expense in different accounting periods (more in some accounting periods and less in others). Exhibit 6.2 shows the relative use of different depreciation methods by U.S. companies.

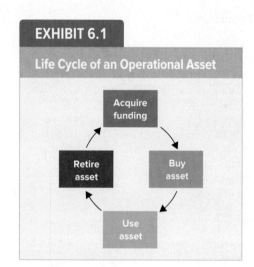

EXHIBIT 6.1

Life Cycle of an Operational Asset

Acquire funding

Buy asset

Use asset

Retire asset

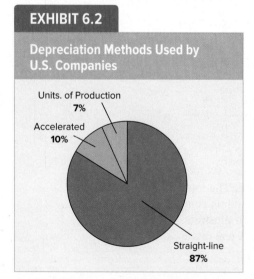

EXHIBIT 6.2

Depreciation Methods Used by U.S. Companies

Units. of Production 7%

Accelerated 10%

Straight-line 87%

The chart is based on data drawn from recent annual reports published by the 30 companies that comprise the Dow Jones Industrial Average. The percentages add to more than 100 percent because one company used two depreciation methods and therefore was included in two categories.

Dryden Enterprises Illustration

To illustrate the different depreciation methods, consider a van purchased by Dryden Enterprises. Dryden plans to use the van as rental property. The van had a list price of $23,500. Dryden obtained a 10 percent cash discount from the dealer. The van was delivered FOB shipping point, and Dryden paid an additional $250 for transportation costs. Dryden also paid $2,600 for a custom accessory package to increase the van's appeal as a rental vehicle. The cost of the van is computed as follows:

List price	$23,500	
Less: Cash discount	(2,350)	$23,500 × 0.10
Plus: Transportation costs	250	
Plus: Cost of customization	2,600	
Total	$24,000	

The van has an estimated *salvage value* of $4,000 and an *estimated useful life* of four years. The following section examines three different patterns of expense recognition for this van.

STRAIGHT-LINE DEPRECIATION

The first scenario assumes the van purchased by Dryden Enterprises is used evenly over its four-year life. The revenue from renting the van is assumed to be $8,000 per year. The matching concept calls for the expense recognition pattern to match the revenue stream. Since the same amount of revenue is recognized in each accounting period, Dryden should use **straight-line depreciation** because it produces equal amounts of depreciation expense each year.

LO 6-2

Calculate straight-line depreciation and show how it affects financial statements.

The first phase of the asset life cycle is to acquire funds to purchase the asset. Assume Dryden acquired $25,000 cash on January 1, Year 1, by issuing common stock. The effects on the financial statements are shown here:

Balance Sheet							Income Statement						Statement of Cash Flows
Assets			=	Stk. Equity									
Cash	+	Book Value of Van	=	Com. Stk.	+	Ret. Earn.	Rev.	−	Exp.	=	Net Inc.		
25,000	+	NA	=	25,000	+	NA	NA	−	NA	=	NA	25,000	FA

The second phase of the life cycle is to purchase the van. Assume Dryden bought the van on January 1, Year 1, using funds from the stock issue. The cost of the van, previously computed, was $24,000 cash. The effects on the financial statements are shown here:

Balance Sheet							Income Statement						Statement of Cash Flows
Assets			=	Stk. Equity									
Cash	+	Book Value of Van	=	Com. Stk.	+	Ret. Earn.	Rev.	−	Exp.	=	Net Inc.		
(24,000)	+	24,000	=	NA	+	NA	NA	−	NA	=	NA	(24,000)	IA

Dryden used the van by renting it to customers. The rent revenue each year is $8,000 cash. The effects on the financial statements are shown here:

Balance Sheet							Income Statement						Statement of Cash Flows
Assets			=	Stk. Equity									
Cash	+	Book Value of Van	=	Com. Stk.	+	Ret. Earn.	Rev.	−	Exp.	=	Net Inc.		
8,000	+	NA	=	NA	+	8,000	8,000	−	NA	=	8,000	8,000	OA

Although illustrated only once, these effects occur four times—once for each year Dryden earns revenue by renting the van.

At the end of each year, Dryden adjusts its accounts to recognize depreciation expense. The amount of depreciation recognized using the straight-line method is calculated as follows:

$$\text{(Asset cost} - \text{Salvage value)} \div \text{Useful life} = \text{Depreciation expense}$$
$$(\$24,000 - \$4,000) \div 4 \text{ years} = \$5,000 \text{ per year}$$

Recognizing depreciation expense is an asset use transaction that reduces assets and stockholders' equity. The asset reduction is reported using a **contra asset account** called **Accumulated Depreciation.** Like other contra asset accounts, the Accumulated Depreciation account has a balance that is opposite from the balance in the associated asset account. The **book value** of a long-term tangible asset is determined by subtracting the balance in the Accumulated Depreciation account from the balance in the associated asset account. The book value may also be called the **carrying value.**

While recognizing depreciation expense decreases net income, it *does not affect cash flow.* The $24,000 cash outflow occurred in January Year 1 when Dryden purchased the van. In contrast, the $5,000 depreciation expense is recognized each year as the van is used. The effects of recognizing depreciation expense on December 31, Year 1, are shown here:

Balance Sheet							Income Statement				Statement of Cash Flows
Assets			=	Stk. Equity							
Cash	+	Book Value of Van	=	Com. Stk.	+	Ret. Earn.	Rev.	−	Exp.	=	Net Inc.	
NA	+	(5,000)	=	NA	+	(5,000)	NA	−	5,000	=	(5,000)	NA

The book value of the van as of December 31, Year 1, is $19,000, computed as shown here:

Van	$24,000
Accumulated depreciation	(5,000)
Book value	$19,000

Depreciation expense is recognized each year the van is used. Like other expense accounts, the Depreciation Expense account is a temporary account that is closed to retained earnings at the end of each accounting cycle. In other words, each year $5,000 is recognized in the Depreciation Expense account and then closed to the Retained Earnings account. As a result, the Depreciation Expense account will never have a balance that is larger than $5,000.

In contrast, the Accumulated Depreciation account is a permanent account. As its name implies, the total amount in the Accumulated Depreciation account increases (accumulates) each time depreciation expense is recognized. For example, at the end of Year 2 Dryden will recognize $5,000 of depreciation expense and the balance in the Accumulated Depreciation account will increase to $10,000. At the end of Year 3 Dryden will recognize $5,000 of depreciation expense and increase the balance in the Accumulated Depreciation account to $15,000, and so on.

Effects on the Financial Statements

Exhibit 6.3 displays a vertical statements model that shows the financial results for the Dryden illustration from Year 1 through Year 4. Study the exhibit until you understand how all the figures were derived. The amount of depreciation expense ($5,000) reported on the income statement is constant each year from Year 1 through Year 4. The amount of accumulated depreciation reported on the balance sheet grows from $5,000 to $10,000, to $15,000, and finally to $20,000. The Accumulated Depreciation account is a *contra asset account* that is subtracted from the Van account in determining total assets.

EXHIBIT 6.3	Financial Statements under Straight-Line Depreciation

DRYDEN ENTERPRISES
Financial Statements

	Year 1	Year 2	Year 3	Year 4
Income Statements				
Rent revenue	$ 8,000	$ 8,000	$ 8,000	$ 8,000
Depreciation expense	(5,000)	(5,000)	(5,000)	(5,000)
Net income	$ 3,000	$ 3,000	$ 3,000	$ 3,000
Balance Sheets				
Assets				
Cash	$ 9,000	$17,000	$25,000	$33,000
Van	24,000	24,000	24,000	24,000
Accumulated depreciation	(5,000)	(10,000)	(15,000)	(20,000)
Total assets	$28,000	$31,000	$34,000	$37,000
Stockholders' equity				
Common stock	$25,000	$25,000	$25,000	$25,000
Retained earnings	3,000	6,000	9,000	12,000
Total stockholders' equity	$28,000	$31,000	$34,000	$37,000
Statements of Cash Flows				
Operating Activities				
Inflow from customers	$ 8,000	$ 8,000	$ 8,000	$ 8,000
Investing Activities				
Outflow to purchase van	(24,000)			
Financing Activities				
Inflow from stock issue	25,000			
Net Change in Cash	9,000	8,000	8,000	8,000
Beginning cash balance	0	9,000	17,000	25,000
Ending cash balance	$ 9,000	$17,000	$25,000	$33,000

Notice the differences between cash flow from operating activities and the income statement. For example, in Year 1 Dryden paid $24,000 cash to purchase the van. However, only $5,000 of this cost is shown as an operating expense on the income statement. Further, there is no effect on cash flow from operating activities. Instead the entire $24,000 cash outflow is shown as an investing activity. These differences highlight the fact that cash flow from operating activities and the income statement are purposefully designed to inform users about different aspects of the business' operations.

DOUBLE-DECLINING-BALANCE DEPRECIATION

For the second scenario, assume demand for the Dryden Enterprises van is strong when it is new, but fewer people rent the van as it ages. As a result, the van produces smaller amounts of revenue as time goes by. To match expenses with revenues, it is reasonable to recognize more depreciation expense in the van's early years and less as it ages.

Double-declining-balance depreciation produces a large amount of depreciation in the first year of an asset's life and progressively smaller levels of expense in each succeeding year. Since the double-declining-balance method recognizes depreciation expense more rapidly than the straight-line method does, it is called an **accelerated**

LO 6-3

Calculate double-declining-balance depreciation and show how it affects financial statements.

Car Collection/Alamy Stock Photo

depreciation method. Depreciation expense recognized using double-declining-balance is computed in three steps.

1. *Determine the straight-line rate.* Divide one by the asset's useful life. Since the estimated useful life of Dryden's van is four years, the straight-line rate is 25 percent (1 ÷ 4) per year.
2. *Determine the double-declining-balance rate.* Multiply the straight-line rate by 2 (double the rate). The double-declining-balance rate for the van is 50 percent (25 percent × 2).
3. *Determine the depreciation expense.* Multiply the double-declining-balance rate by the book value of the asset *at the beginning of the period* (recall that book value is historical cost minus *accumulated depreciation*). The following table shows the amount of depreciation expense Dryden will recognize over the van's useful life (Year 1–Year 4).

Year	Book Value at Beginning of Period	×	Double the Straight-Line Rate	=	Annual Depreciation Expense	
Year 1	($24,000 − $ 0)	×	0.50	=	$12,000	
Year 2	(24,000 − 12,000)	×	0.50	=	6,000	
Year 3	(24,000 − 18,000)	×	0.50	=	~~3,000~~	2,000
Year 4	(24,000 − 20,000)	×	0.50	=	~~2,000~~	0

Regardless of the depreciation method used, *an asset cannot be depreciated below its salvage value.* This restriction affects depreciation computations for the third and fourth years. Because the van had a cost of $24,000 and a salvage value of $4,000, the total amount of depreciable cost (historical cost − salvage value) is $20,000 ($24,000 − $4,000). Since $18,000 ($12,000 + $6,000) of the depreciable cost is recognized in the first two years, only $2,000 ($20,000 − $18,000) remains to be recognized after the second year. Depreciation expense recognized in the third year is therefore $2,000 even though double-declining-balance computations suggest that $3,000 should be recognized. Similarly, zero depreciation expense is recognized in the fourth year even though the computations indicate a $2,000 charge.

Effects on the Financial Statements

Exhibit 6.4 displays financial statements for the life of the asset assuming Dryden uses double-declining-balance depreciation. The illustration assumes a cash revenue stream of $15,000, $9,000, $5,000, and $3,000 for Year 1, Year 2, Year 3, and Year 4, respectively. Trace the depreciation expense from the previous table to the income statements. Reported depreciation expense is greater in the earlier years and smaller in the later years of the asset's life.

EXHIBIT 6.4	Financial Statements under Double-Declining-Balance Depreciation

DRYDEN ENTERPRISES
Financial Statements

	Year 1	Year 2	Year 3	Year 4
Income Statements				
Rent revenue	$15,000	$ 9,000	$ 5,000	$ 3,000
Depreciation expense	(12,000)	(6,000)	(2,000)	0
Net income	$ 3,000	$ 3,000	$ 3,000	$ 3,000
Balance Sheets				
Assets				
Cash	$16,000	$25,000	$30,000	$33,000
Van	24,000	24,000	24,000	24,000
Accumulated depreciation	(12,000)	(18,000)	(20,000)	(20,000)
Total assets	$28,000	$31,000	$34,000	$37,000
Stockholders' equity				
Common stock	$25,000	$25,000	$25,000	$25,000
Retained earnings	3,000	6,000	9,000	12,000
Total stockholders' equity	$28,000	$31,000	$34,000	$37,000
Statements of Cash Flows				
Operating Activities				
Inflow from customers	$15,000	$ 9,000	$ 5,000	$ 3,000
Investing Activities				
Outflow to purchase van	(24,000)			
Financing Activities				
Inflow from stock issue	25,000			
Net Change in Cash	16,000	9,000	5,000	3,000
Beginning cash balance	0	16,000	25,000	30,000
Ending cash balance	$16,000	$25,000	$30,000	$33,000

The double-declining-balance method smoothes the amount of net income reported over the asset's useful life. In the early years, when heavy asset use produces higher revenue, depreciation expense is also higher. Similarly, in the later years, lower levels of revenue are matched with lower levels of depreciation expense. Net income is constant at $3,000 per year.

The depreciation method a company uses *does not* affect how it acquires the financing, invests the funds, and retires the asset. For Dryden's van, the accounting effects of these life cycle phases are the same as under the straight-line approach. Similarly, the *recording procedures* are not affected by the depreciation method. Different depreciation methods affect only the amounts of depreciation expense recorded each year, not which accounts are used. The general journal entries are therefore not illustrated for the double-declining-balance or the units-of-production depreciation methods.

 CHECK YOURSELF 6.2

Olds Company purchased an asset that cost $36,000 on January 1, Year 1. The asset had an expected useful life of five years and an estimated salvage value of $5,000. Assuming Olds uses the double-declining-balance method, determine the amount of depreciation expense and the amount of accumulated depreciation Olds would report on the Year 3 financial statements.

(continued)

Answer

Year	Book Value at Beginning of Period	×	Double the Straight-Line Rate*	=	Annual Depreciation Expense
Year 1	($36,000 − $ 0)	×	0.40	=	$14,400
Year 2	(36,000 − 14,400)	×	0.40	=	8,640
Year 3	(36,000 − 23,040)	×	0.40	=	5,184
Total accumulated depreciation at December 31, Year 3					$28,224

*Double-declining-balance rate = 2 × Straight-line rate = 2 × (1 ÷ 5 years) = 0.40

UNITS-OF-PRODUCTION DEPRECIATION

LO 6-4

Calculate units-of-production depreciation and show how it affects financial statements.

Suppose rental demand for Dryden's van depends on general economic conditions. In a robust economy, travel increases, and demand for renting vans is high. In a stagnant economy, demand for van rentals declines. In such circumstances, revenues fluctuate from year to year. To accomplish the matching objective, depreciation should also fluctuate from year to year. A method of depreciation known as **units-of-production depreciation** accomplishes this goal by basing depreciation expense on actual asset usage.

Computing depreciation expense using units-of-production begins with identifying a measure of the asset's productive capacity. For example, the number of miles Dryden expects its van to be driven may be a reasonable measure of its productive capacity. If the depreciable asset were a saw, an appropriate measure of productive capacity could be the number of board feet the saw was expected to cut during its useful life. In other words, the basis for measuring production depends on the nature of the depreciable asset.

To illustrate computing depreciation using the units-of-production depreciation method, assume that Dryden measures productive capacity based on the total number of miles the van will be driven over its useful life. Assume Dryden estimates this productive capacity to be 100,000 miles. The first step in determining depreciation expense is to compute the cost per unit of production. For Dryden's van, this amount is total depreciable cost (historical cost − salvage value) divided by total units of expected productive capacity (100,000 miles). The depreciation cost per mile is therefore $0.20 [($24,000 cost − $4,000 salvage) ÷ 100,000 miles]. Annual depreciation expense is computed by multiplying the cost per mile by the number of miles driven. Odometer readings indicate the van was driven 40,000 miles, 20,000 miles, 30,000 miles, and 15,000 miles in Year 1, Year 2, Year 3, and Year 4, respectively. Based on these data, Dryden developed the following schedule of depreciation charges.

Year	Cost per Mile (a)	Miles Driven (b)	Depreciation Expense (a × b)
Year 1	$0.20	40,000	$8,000
Year 2	0.20	20,000	4,000
Year 3	0.20	30,000	6,000
Year 4	0.20	15,000	~~3,000~~ 2,000

As pointed out in the discussion of the double-declining-balance method, an asset cannot be depreciated below its salvage value. Since $18,000 of the $20,000 ($24,000 cost − $4,000 salvage) depreciable cost is recognized in the first three years of using the van, only $2,000 ($20,000 − $18,000) remains to be charged to depreciation in the fourth year, even though the depreciation computations suggest the charge should be $3,000. As the preceding table indicates, the general formula for computing units-of-production depreciation is

$$\frac{\text{Cost} - \text{Salvage value}}{\text{Total estimated units of production}} \times \begin{array}{c}\text{Units of production}\\\text{in current}\\\text{year}\end{array} = \begin{array}{c}\text{Annual}\\\text{depreciation}\\\text{expense}\end{array}$$

EXHIBIT 6.5	Financial Statements under Units-of-Production Depreciation

DRYDEN ENTERPRISES
Financial Statements

	Year 1	Year 2	Year 3	Year 4
Income Statements				
Rent revenue	$11,000	$ 7,000	$ 9,000	$ 5,000
Depreciation expense	(8,000)	(4,000)	(6,000)	(2,000)
Net income	$ 3,000	$ 3,000	$ 3,000	$ 3,000
Balance Sheets				
Assets				
Cash	$12,000	$19,000	$28,000	$33,000
Van	24,000	24,000	24,000	24,000
Accumulated depreciation	(8,000)	(12,000)	(18,000)	(20,000)
Total assets	$28,000	$31,000	$34,000	$37,000
Stockholders' equity				
Common stock	$25,000	$25,000	$25,000	$25,000
Retained earnings	3,000	6,000	9,000	12,000
Total stockholders' equity	$28,000	$31,000	$34,000	$37,000
Statements of Cash Flows				
Operating Activities				
Inflow from customers	$11,000	$ 7,000	$ 9,000	$ 5,000
Investing Activities				
Outflow to purchase van	(24,000)			
Financing Activities				
Inflow from stock issue	25,000			
Net Change in Cash	12,000	7,000	9,000	5,000
Beginning cash balance	0	12,000	19,000	28,000
Ending cash balance	$12,000	$19,000	$28,000	$33,000

Effects on the Financial Statements

Exhibit 6.5 displays financial statements that assume Dryden uses units-of-production depreciation. The exhibit assumes a cash revenue stream of $11,000, $7,000, $9,000, and $5,000 for Year 1, Year 2, Year 3, and Year 4, respectively. Trace the depreciation expense from the schedule above to the income statements. Depreciation expense is greater in years the van is driven more and smaller in years the van is driven less, providing a reasonable matching of depreciation expense with revenue produced. Net income is again constant at $3,000 per year.

ACCOUNTING FOR THE DISPOSAL OF LONG-TERM OPERATIONAL ASSETS

Regardless of which method of depreciation a company chooses to use, the van will ultimately cease to be useful for the purpose of generating revenue. At this point, the company will have to dispose of the asset. To illustrate accounting for the disposal of the asset, assume Dryden Enterprises retires the van from service and sells it on January 1, Year 5, for $4,500 cash. On this date, the van's book value is $4,000 ($24,000 cost − $20,000 accumulated

LO 6-5

Show how gains and losses on disposals of long-term operational assets affect financial statements.

depreciation). Under these circumstances, Dryden would recognize a $500 gain ($4,500 sales price − $4,000 book value) on the sale.

Gains are *like* revenues in that they increase assets or decrease liabilities. Gains are *unlike* revenues in that gains result from peripheral (incidental) transactions rather than routine operating activities. Dryden is not in the business of selling vans. Dryden's normal business activity is renting vans. Because selling vans is incidental to Dryden's normal operations, gains are reported separately, after operating income, on the income statement.

If Dryden had sold the asset for less than book value, the company would have recognized a loss on the asset disposal. Losses are similar to expenses in that they decrease assets or increase liabilities. However, like gains, losses result from peripheral transactions. Losses are reported as nonoperating items on the income statement.

The effects of the asset disposal on the financial statements are shown here.

Balance Sheet						Income Statement					Statement of Cash Flows
Assets			=	Stk. Equity							
Cash	+	Book Value of Van	=	Com. Stk.	+	Ret. Earn.	Rev. or Gain	−	Exp. or Loss	=	Net Inc.	
4,500	+	(4,000)	=	NA	+	500	500	−	NA	=	500	4,500 IA

Total assets increase by $500 because the amount of cash collected is more than the book value of the van. The gain causes the amount of net income and ultimately stockholders' equity to increase. The amount of the gain is not reported on the statement of cash flows. Instead, the entire $4,500 is shown in the statement of cash flows as an inflow from investing activities. Since selling vans is not part of Dryden's normal operations, the gain will be reported separately, after operating income, on the income statement.

Comparing the Depreciation Methods

The total amount of depreciation expense Dryden recognized using each of the three methods was $20,000 ($24,000 cost − $4,000 salvage value). The different methods affect the *timing*, but not the *total amount*, of expense recognized. The different methods simply assign the $20,000 to different accounting periods. Exhibit 6.6 presents graphically the differences among the three depreciation methods discussed previously. A company should use the method that most closely matches expenses with revenues.

EXHIBIT 6.6

Depreciation Expense under Different Depreciation Methods

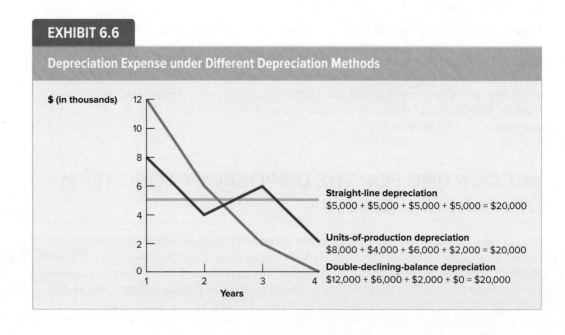

Straight-line depreciation
$5,000 + $5,000 + $5,000 + $5,000 = $20,000

Units-of-production depreciation
$8,000 + $4,000 + $6,000 + $2,000 = $20,000

Double-declining-balance depreciation
$12,000 + $6,000 + $2,000 + $0 = $20,000

REVISION OF ESTIMATES

In order to report useful financial information on a timely basis, accountants must make many estimates of future results, such as the salvage value and useful life of depreciable assets and uncollectible accounts expense. Estimates are frequently revised when new information surfaces. Because revisions of estimates are common, generally accepted accounting principles call for incorporating the revised information into present and future calculations. Prior reports are not corrected.

To illustrate, assume that McGraw Company purchased a machine on January 1, Year 1, for $50,000. McGraw estimated the machine would have a useful life of 8 years and a salvage value of $3,000. Using the straight-line method, McGraw determined the annual depreciation charge as follows:

$$(\$50,000 - \$3,000) \div 8 \text{ years} = \$5,875 \text{ per year}$$

At the beginning of the fifth year, accumulated depreciation on the machine is $23,500 ($5,875 × 4). The machine's book value is $26,500 ($50,000 − $23,500). At this point, what happens if McGraw changes its estimates of useful life or the salvage value? Consider the following revision examples independently of each other.

LO 6-6

Show how revising estimates affects financial statements.

Revision of Life

Assume McGraw revises the expected life to 14, rather than 8, years. The machine's *remaining* life would then be 10 more years instead of 4 more years. Assume salvage value remains $3,000. Depreciation for each remaining year is:

$$(\$26,500 \text{ book value} - \$3,000 \text{ salvage}) \div 10\text{-year remaining life} = \$2,350$$

Revision of Salvage

Alternatively, assume the original expected life remained 8 years, but McGraw revised its estimate of salvage value to $6,000. Depreciation for each of the remaining four years would be

$$(\$26,500 \text{ book value} - \$6,000 \text{ salvage}) \div 4\text{-year remaining life} = \$5,125$$

The revised amounts are determined for the full year, regardless of when McGraw revised its estimates. For example, if McGraw decides to change the estimated useful life on October 1, Year 4, the change would be effective as of January 1, Year 4. The year-end adjusting entry for depreciation would include a full year's depreciation calculated on the basis of the revised estimated useful life.

CONTINUING EXPENDITURES FOR PLANT ASSETS

Most plant assets require additional expenditures for maintenance or improvement during their useful lives. Accountants must determine if these expenditures should be expensed or capitalized (recorded as assets).

LO 6-7

Show how continuing expenditures for operational assets affect financial statements.

Costs That Are Expensed

Maintenance costs are the costs of routine maintenance and minor repairs that are incurred to *keep* an asset in good working order. These costs are expensed in the period in which they are incurred.

With respect to the previous example, assume McGraw spent $500 for routine lubrication and to replace minor parts. The effects on the financial statements follow.

Balance Sheet					Income Statement					Statement of Cash Flows	
Assets	=		Stk. Equity								
Cash	=	Com. Stk.	+	Ret. Earn.	Rev.	−	Exp.	=	Net Inc.		
(500)	=	NA	+	(500)	NA	−	500	=	(500)	(500)	OA

Costs That Are Capitalized

Substantial amounts spent to improve the quality or extend the life of an asset are described as **capital expenditures.** Capital expenditures are accounted for in one of two ways, depending on whether the cost incurred *improves the quality* or *extends the life* of the asset.

Improving Quality

Expenditures such as adding air conditioning to an existing building or installing a trailer hitch on a vehicle improve the quality of service these assets provide. If a capital expenditure improves an asset's quality, the amount is added to the historical cost of the asset. The additional cost is expensed through higher depreciation charges over the asset's remaining useful life.

To demonstrate, return to the McGraw Company example. Recall that the machine originally cost $50,000, had an estimated salvage value of $3,000, and had a predicted life of 8 years. Recall further that accumulated depreciation at the beginning of the fifth year is $23,500 ($5,875 × 4), so the book value is $26,500 ($50,000 − $23,500). Assume McGraw makes a major expenditure of $4,000 in the machine's fifth year to improve its productive capacity. The effects on the financial statements are shown next:

Balance Sheet							Income Statement					Statement of Cash Flows	
	Assets		=		Stk. Equity								
Cash	+	Book Value of Mach.	=	Com. Stk.	+	Ret. Earn.	Rev.	−	Exp.	=	Net Inc.		
(4,000)	+	4,000	=	NA	+	NA	NA	−	NA	=	NA	(4,000)	IA

After recording the expenditure, the machine account balance is $54,000 and the asset's book value is $30,500 ($54,000 − $23,500). The depreciation charges for each of the remaining 4 years are

$$(\$30{,}500 \text{ book value} - \$3{,}000 \text{ salvage}) \div 4\text{-year remaining life} = \$6{,}875$$

Extending Life

Expenditures such as replacing the roof of an existing building or putting a new engine in an older vehicle extend the useful life of these assets. If a capital expenditure extends the life of an asset rather than improving the asset's quality of service, accountants view the expenditure as canceling some of the depreciation previously charged to expense. The event is still an asset exchange; cash decreases, and the book value of the machine increases. However, the increase in the book value of the machine results from reducing the balance in the contra asset account, Accumulated Depreciation.

To illustrate, assume that instead of increasing productive capacity, McGraw's $4,000 expenditure had extended the useful life of the machine by 2 years. The effects on the financial statements are shown next:

Balance Sheet							Income Statement					Statement of Cash Flows	
	Assets		=		Stk. Equity								
Cash	+	Book Value of Mach.	=	Com. Stk.	+	Ret. Earn.	Rev.	−	Exp.	=	Net Inc.		
(4,000)	+	4,000	=	NA	+	NA	NA	−	NA	=	NA	(4,000)	IA

After the expenditure is recorded, the book value is the same as if the $4,000 had been added to the Machine account ($50,000 cost − $19,500 adjusted balance in Accumulated Depreciation = $30,500). Depreciation expense for each of the remaining 6 years follows:

($30,500 book value − $3,000 salvage) ÷ 6-year remaining life = $4,583

☑ CHECK YOURSELF 6.3

On January 1, Year 1, Dager Inc. purchased an asset that cost $18,000. It had a five-year useful life and a $3,000 salvage value. Dager uses straight-line depreciation. On January 1, Year 3, it incurred a $1,200 cost related to the asset. With respect to this asset, determine the amount of expense and accumulated depreciation Dager would report in the Year 3 financial statements under each of the following assumptions.

1. The $1,200 cost was incurred to repair damage resulting from an accident.
2. The $1,200 cost improved the operating capacity of the asset. The total useful life and salvage value remained unchanged.
3. The $1,200 cost extended the useful life of the asset by one year. The salvage value remained unchanged.

Answer

1. Dager would report the $1,200 repair cost as an expense. Dager would also report depreciation expense of $3,000 [($18,000 − $3,000) ÷ 5]. Total expenses related to this asset in Year 3 would be $4,200 ($1,200 repair expense + $3,000 depreciation expense). Accumulated depreciation at the end of Year 3 would be $9,000 ($3,000 depreciation expense × 3 years).
2. The $1,200 cost would be capitalized in the asset account, increasing both the book value of the asset and the annual depreciation expense.

	After Effects of Capital Improvement
Amount in asset account ($18,000 + $1,200)	$19,200
Less: Salvage value	(3,000)
Accumulated depreciation on January 1, Year 3	(6,000)
Remaining depreciable cost before recording Year 3 depreciation	$10,200
Depreciation for Year 3 ($10,200 ÷ 3 years)	$ 3,400
Accumulated depreciation at December 31, Year 3 ($6,000 + $3,400)	$ 9,400

3. The $1,200 cost would be subtracted from the Accumulated Depreciation account, increasing the book value of the asset. The remaining useful life would increase to four years, which would decrease the depreciation expense.

	After Effects of Capital Improvement
Amount in asset account	$18,000
Less: Salvage value	(3,000)
Accumulated depreciation on January 1, Year 3 ($6,000 − $1,200)	(4,800)
Remaining depreciable cost before recording Year 3 depreciation	$10,200
Depreciation for Year 3 ($10,200 ÷ 4 years)	$ 2,550
Accumulated depreciation at December 31, Year 3 ($4,800 + $2,550)	$ 7,350

NATURAL RESOURCES

The cost of natural resources includes not only the purchase price but also related items such as the cost of exploration, geographic surveys, and estimates. The process of expensing natural resources is commonly called depletion.[2] The most common method used to calculate depletion is units-of-production.

To illustrate, assume Apex Coal Mining paid $4,000,000 cash to purchase a mine with an estimated 16,000,000 tons of coal. The unit depletion charge is

$$\$4,000,000 \div 16,000,000 \text{ tons} = \$0.25 \text{ per ton}$$

If Apex mines 360,000 tons of coal in the first year, the depletion charge is

$$360,000 \text{ tons} \times \$0.25 \text{ per ton} = \$90,000$$

The depletion of a natural resource has the same effect on the accounting equation as other expense recognition events. Assets (in this case, a *coal mine*) and stockholders' equity decrease. The depletion expense reduces net income. The effects on the financial statements follow.

Balance Sheet								Income Statement						Statement of Cash Flows	
Assets			=		Stk. Equity										
Cash	+	Coal Mine	=	Com. Stk.	+	Ret. Earn.		Rev.	−	Exp.	=	Net Inc.			
(4,000,000)	+	4,000,000	=	NA	+	NA		NA	−	NA	=	NA		(4,000,000)	IA
NA	+	(90,000)	=	NA	+	(90,000)		NA	−	90,000	=	(90,000)		NA	

Answers to The Curious Accountant

As assets lose their productive capacity, either from being used or due to obsolescence, the asset account is reduced and an expense account is increased. Assets such as buildings and equipment may decline faster if they are used, but, due to obsolescence, they usually continue to decline even if they are not used. For this reason, a time-based depreciation method, such as straight-line or double-declining-balance, is almost always used for buildings and more often than not for equipment. In contrast, a mineral reserve does not lose its capacity unless ore is extracted. After all, the gold FCX is mining today has been in the earth for millions of years. For this reason, companies typically use the units-of-production method to calculate depletion on mineral reserves. In both cases, the objective should be to achieve the best matching of expenses incurred with the revenues they generate.

INTANGIBLE ASSETS

Intangible assets provide rights, privileges, and special opportunities to businesses. Common intangible assets include trademarks, patents, copyrights, franchises, and goodwill. Some of the unique characteristics of these intangible assets are described in the following sections.

Trademarks

A **trademark** is a name or symbol that identifies a company or a product. Familiar trademarks include the Polo emblem, the name *Coca-Cola*, and the Nike slogan, "Just do it." Trademarks are registered with the federal government and have an indefinite legal lifetime.

[2]In practice, the depletion charge is considered a product cost and allocated between inventory and cost of goods sold. This text uses the simplifying assumption that all resources are sold in the same accounting period in which they are extracted. The full depletion charge is therefore expensed in the period in which the resources are extracted.

The costs incurred to design, purchase, or defend a trademark are capitalized in an asset account called Trademarks. Companies want their trademarks to become familiar but also face the risk of a trademark being used as the generic name for a product. To protect a trademark, companies in this predicament spend large sums on legal fees and extensive advertising programs to educate consumers. Well-known trademarks that have been subject to this problem include Coke, Xerox, Kleenex, and Vaseline.

Patents

A **patent** grants its owner an exclusive legal right to produce and sell a product that has one or more unique features. Patents issued by the U.S. Patent Office have a legal life of 20 years. Companies may obtain patents through purchase, lease, or internal development. The costs capitalized in the Patent account are usually limited to the purchase price and legal fees to obtain and defend the patent. The research and development costs that are incurred to develop patentable products are usually expensed in the period in which they are incurred.

FOCUS ON INTERNATIONAL ISSUES

As you have learned, U.S. GAAP requires companies to use historical cost when accounting for property, plant, and equipment (PPE). Once a company begins depreciating its buildings and equipment, expenses increase (due to depreciation expense), which causes net income and retained earnings to decrease. This, of course, ignores the revenue the company hopes to generate by using the asset.

Under IFRS a company has two options regarding accounting of PPE. First, it can use a historical cost accounting method that is virtually identical to that required by U.S. GAAP. Second, it can use the "revaluation model," which reports PPE at its fair value. There can be different ways of determining fair value, but the preferred approach is to base fair value on a market-based appraisal, performed by professional appraisers. These revaluations must be conducted frequently enough that the fair value of an asset is not materially different from its recorded book value.

Basically, the revaluation model works as follows. The company periodically compares the current book value of its PPE to the fair value at that same date. This fair value relates to the value of the used asset, not the amount required to replace it with a new asset. If the fair value of an asset is higher than its currently recorded book value, the recorded amount for the asset is increased, which increases total assets. However, the increase in the asset's fair value is *not* reported on the company's income statement, as would a gain from selling the asset. Rather, the increase is reported in a special section of stockholders' equity, which balances the increase that was recorded for assets. However, if the new fair value is *lower* than the asset's current book value, the decrease is charged to net income, as well as to assets. This is another example of the conservatism principle at work. Not surprisingly, there are exceptions to these rules. Once a new fair value is established, future depreciation expense is based on these values.

Aspen Stock/Pixtal/age fotostock

One concern might be that companies, hoping to manipulate earnings, would pick and choose some assets to account for under historical costs and others to account for under the revaluation model. This is not permitted. Although a company does not have to use a single method for all its assets, it must use a single method for all the assets in a given class of assets. For example, historical costs could be used for all factory equipment, and the revaluation model used for all its buildings.

As significant as the difference between the historical cost method and the fair value approach might be, the majority of companies continue to use historical costs to account for long-term operational assets. Professors H. B. Christensen and V. Nikolaev conducted a study of the use of revaluation accounting for nonfinancial assets by companies in Germany and the United Kingdom. Their research found that only 3.2 percent of the 1,539 companies surveyed used the revaluation model for property, plant, and equipment.

Source: Christensen, Hans B, and Nikolaev, Valeri V. Does Fair Value Accounting for Non-Financial Assets Pass the Market Test? Chicago, IL, The University of Chicago Booth School of Business, 2009.

Copyrights

A **copyright** protects writings, musical compositions, works of art, and other intellectual property for the exclusive benefit of the creator or persons assigned the right by the creator. The cost of a copyright includes the purchase price and any legal costs associated with obtaining and defending the copyright. Copyrights granted by the federal government extend for the life of the creator plus 70 years. A radio commercial could legally use a Bach composition as background music; it could not, however, use the theme song from the movie *The Matrix* without obtaining permission from the copyright owner. The cost of a copyright is often expensed early because future royalties may be uncertain.

Franchises

Franchises grant exclusive rights to sell products or perform services in certain geographic areas. Franchises may be granted by governments or private businesses. Franchises granted by governments include federal broadcasting licenses. Private business franchises include fast-food restaurant chains and brand labels such as Healthy Choice. The legal and useful lives of a franchise are frequently difficult to determine. Judgment is often crucial to establishing the estimated useful life for franchises.

Goodwill

Goodwill is the value attributable to favorable factors such as reputation, location, and superior products. Consider the most popular restaurant in your town. If the owner sells the restaurant, do you think the purchase price would be simply the total value of the chairs, tables, kitchen equipment, and building? Certainly not, because much of the restaurant's value lies in its popularity; in other words, its ability to generate a high return is based on the goodwill (reputation) of the business.

REALITY BYTES

In 2017, Reckitt Benckiser Group, PLC reported that it had paid $17.9 billion to acquire Mead Johnson Nutrition Co. (M-J), even though the company's assets were reported on its December 31, 2016, balance sheet to be only $4.1 billion. Reckitt is a British-based company that owns numerous consumer brands, including Air Wick, French's, Lysol, and Dr. Scholl's. M-J's brands include Enfamil infant formulas. Why would Reckitt pay the owners of M-J over four times the value of the assets shown on the company's balance sheet?

Reckitt was willing to pay well above the book value of the assets for several reasons. First, the value of the assets on M-J's balance sheet represented the historical cost of the assets. The current market value of these assets was probably higher than their historical cost, especially for intangible assets such as its trademarks and research in progress. Second, Reckitt believed that the two companies combined could operate at a lower cost than the two could as separate companies,

Jill Braaten/McGraw-Hill Education

thus increasing the total earnings they could generate. It estimated these savings would be over $200 million per year by the third year after the acquisition. Third, M-J had a bigger presence than Reckitt in developing markets, especially China, so this would make it easier to get Reckitt's existing products into those markets. Finally, Reckitt probably believed that M-J had *goodwill* that enables a company to use its assets in a manner that will generate above-average earnings. In other words, Reckitt was paying for a hidden asset not shown on M-J's balance sheet.

Source: 2016. Annual Report and Financial Statements, Reckitt Benckiser Group plc (RB).

Calculating goodwill can be complex; here we present a simple example to illustrate how it is determined. Suppose the accounting records of a restaurant named Bendigo's show the following:

$$\text{Assets} = \text{Liabilities} + \text{Stockholders' Equity}$$
$$\$200,000 = \$50,000 + \$150,000$$

Assume a buyer agrees to purchase the restaurant by paying the owner $300,000 cash and assuming the existing liabilities. In other words, the restaurant is purchased at a price of $350,000 ($300,000 cash + $50,000 assumed liabilities). Now assume that the assets of the business (tables, chairs, kitchen equipment, etc.) have a fair market value of only $280,000. Why would the buyer pay $350,000 to purchase assets with a market value of $280,000? Obviously, the buyer is purchasing more than just the assets. The buyer is purchasing the business's goodwill. The amount of the goodwill is the difference between the purchase price and the fair market value of the assets. In this case, the goodwill is $70,000 ($350,000 − $280,000). The effects of the purchase on the financial statements of the buyer follow.

Balance Sheet								Income Statement					Statement of Cash Flows
Assets				=	Liab.	+	Stk. Equity						
Cash	+	Rest. Assets	+	Goodwill	=				Rev.	−	Exp.	=	Net Inc.	
(300,000)	+	280,000	+	70,000	=	50,000	+	NA	NA	−	NA	=	NA	(300,000) IA

The fair market value of the restaurant assets represents the historical cost to the new owner. It becomes the basis for future depreciation charges.

EXPENSE RECOGNITION FOR INTANGIBLE ASSETS

As mentioned earlier, intangible assets fall into two categories, those with *identifiable useful lives* and those with *indefinite useful lives.* Expense recognition for intangible assets depends on which classification applies.

LO 6-10

Show how the amortization of intangible assets affects financial statements.

Expensing Intangible Assets with Identifiable Useful Lives

The costs of intangible assets with identifiable useful lives are normally expensed on a straight-line basis using a process called *amortization.* An intangible asset should be amortized over the shorter of two possible time periods: (1) its legal life or (2) its useful life.

To illustrate, assume that Flowers Industries purchased a newly granted patent for $44,000 cash. Although the patent has a legal life of 20 years, Flowers estimates that it will be useful for only 11 years. The annual amortization charge is therefore $4,000 ($44,000 ÷ 11 years). The effects on the financial statements follow.

Balance Sheet							Income Statement					Statement of Cash Flows
Assets			=	Stk. Equity								
Cash	+	Patent	=	Com. Stk.	+	Ret. Earn.	Rev.	−	Exp.	=	Net Inc.	
(44,000)	+	44,000	=	NA	+	NA	NA	−	NA	=	NA	(44,000) IA
NA	+	(4,000)	=	NA	+	(4,000)	NA	−	4,000	=	(4,000)	NA

Impairment Losses for Intangible Assets with Indefinite Useful Lives

Intangible assets with indefinite useful lives must be tested for impairment annually. The impairment test consists of comparing the fair value of the intangible asset to its carrying value (book value). If the fair value is less than the book value, an impairment loss must be recognized.

To illustrate, return to the example of the Bendigo's restaurant purchase. Recall that the buyer of Bendigo's paid $70,000 for goodwill. Assume the restaurant experiences a significant decline in revenue because many of its former regular customers are dissatisfied with the food prepared by the new chef. Suppose the decline in revenue is so substantial that the new owner believes the Bendigo's name is permanently impaired. The owner decides to hire a different chef and change the name of the restaurant. In this case, the business has suffered a permanent decline in value of goodwill. The company must recognize an impairment loss.

The restaurant's name has lost its value, but the owner believes the location continues to provide the opportunity to produce above-average earnings. Some, but not all, of the goodwill has been lost. Assume the fair value of the remaining goodwill is determined to be $40,000. The impairment loss to recognize is $30,000 ($70,000 − $40,000). The loss reduces the intangible asset (goodwill), stockholders' equity (retained earnings), and net income. The statement of cash flows would not be affected. The effects on the financial statements follow.

Balance Sheet						Income Statement						Statement of Cash Flows
Assets	=	Liab.	+	Stk. Equity								
Goodwill	=			Ret. Earn.		Rev.	−	Exp./Loss	=	Net Inc.		
(30,000)	=	NA	+	(30,000)		NA	−	30,000	=	(30,000)		NA

Balance Sheet Presentation

This chapter has explained accounting for the acquisition, expense recognition, and disposal of a wide range of long-term assets. Exhibit 6.7 illustrates typical balance sheet presentation of many of the assets discussed.

EXHIBIT 6.7

Balance Sheet Presentation of Operational Assets

Partial Balance Sheet

Long-Term Assets			
Plant and equipment			
Buildings	$4,000,000		
Less: Accumulated depreciation	(2,500,000)	$1,500,000	
Equipment	1,750,000		
Less: Accumulated depreciation	(1,200,000)	550,000	
Total plant and equipment			$2,050,000
Land			850,000
Natural resources			
Mineral deposits (Less: Depletion)		2,100,000	
Oil reserves (Less: Depletion)		890,000	
Total natural resources			2,990,000
Intangibles			
Patents (Less: Amortization)		38,000	
Goodwill		175,000	
Total intangible assets			213,000
Total long-term assets			$6,103,000

EFFECT OF JUDGMENT AND ESTIMATION

LO 6-11

Show how expense recognition choices and industry characteristics affect financial performance measures.

Many people believe that the numbers shown in financial statements are exact. In fact, financial statement data are influenced by judgment and estimates. The following section describes some of the common opinions and estimates used in financial reports.

Judgment in Financial Reporting

Managers may have differing opinions about which allocation method (straight-line, accelerated, or units-of-production) best matches expenses with revenues. As a result, one company may use straight-line depreciation while another company in similar circumstances uses double-declining-balance. Because the allocation method a company uses affects the amount of expense it recognizes, analysts reviewing financial statements must consider the accounting procedures companies use in preparing the statements.

Assume that two companies, Alpha and Zeta, experience identical economic events in Year 1 and Year 2. Both generate revenue of $50,000 and incur cost of goods sold of $30,000 during each year. In Year 1, each company pays $20,000 for an asset with an expected useful life of five years and no salvage value. How will the companies' financial statements differ if one uses straight-line depreciation and the other uses the double-declining-balance method? To answer this question, first compute the depreciation expense for both companies for Year 1 and Year 2.

If Alpha Company uses the straight-line method, depreciation for Year 1 and Year 2 is

$$(\text{Cost} - \text{Salvage}) \div \text{Useful life} = \text{Depreciation expense per year}$$
$$(\$20{,}000 - \$0) \div 5 \text{ years} = \$4{,}000$$

In contrast, if Zeta Company uses the double-declining-balance method, Zeta recognizes the following amounts of depreciation expense for Year 1 and Year 2.

	(Cost − Accumulated Depreciation)	×	2 × (Straight-Line Rate)	=	Depreciation Expense
Year 1	($20,000 − $ 0)	×	[2 × (1 ÷ 5)]	=	$8,000
Year 2	($20,000 − $8,000)	×	[2 × (1 ÷ 5)]	=	$4,800

Based on these computations, the income statements for the two companies are:

Income Statements				
	Year 1		**Year 2**	
	Alpha Co.	Zeta Co.	Alpha Co.	Zeta Co.
Sales	$50,000	$50,000	$50,000	$50,000
Cost of goods sold	(30,000)	(30,000)	(30,000)	(30,000)
Gross margin	20,000	20,000	20,000	20,000
Depreciation expense	(4,000)	(8,000)	(4,000)	(4,800)
Net income	$16,000	$12,000	$16,000	$15,200

The relevant sections of the balance sheets are

Plant Assets				
	Year 1		**Year 2**	
	Alpha Co.	Zeta Co.	Alpha Co.	Zeta Co.
Assets	$20,000	$20,000	$20,000	$20,000
Accumulated depreciation	(4,000)	(8,000)	(8,000)	(12,800)
Book value	$16,000	$12,000	$12,000	$ 7,200

The depreciation method is not the only aspect of expense recognition that can vary between companies. Companies may also make different assumptions about the useful lives and salvage values of long-term operational assets. Thus, even if the same depreciation method is used, depreciation expense may still differ.

Because the depreciation method and the underlying assumptions regarding useful life and salvage value affect the determination of depreciation expense, they also affect the amounts of net income, retained earnings, and total assets.

To promote meaningful analysis, public companies are required to disclose all significant accounting policies used to prepare their financial statements. This disclosure is usually provided in the notes that accompany the financial statements.

Effect of Industry Characteristics

As indicated in previous chapters, industry characteristics affect financial performance measures. For example, companies in manufacturing industries invest heavily in machinery while insurance companies rely more on human capital. Manufacturing companies therefore have relatively higher depreciation charges than insurance companies. To illustrate how the type of industry affects financial reporting, examine Exhibit 6.8. This exhibit compares the ratio of sales to property, plant, and equipment for two companies in each of three different industries. These data are for 2017.

EXHIBIT 6.8

Industry Data Reflecting the Use of Long-Term Tangible Assets

Industry	Company	Sales ÷ Property, Plant, and Equipment
Cable Companies	Comcast Corporation	2.20
	Verizon Communications	1.21
Airlines	Alaska Air Group	1.26
	Southwest Airlines	1.14
Employment Agencies	Kelly Services	62.42
	Manpower, Inc.	133.38

The table indicates that for every $1.00 invested in property, plant, and equipment, Kelly Services produced $62.42 of sales. In contrast, Verizon Communications and Alaska Air Group produced only $1.21 and $1.26, respectively, for each $1.00 they invested in operational assets. Does this mean the management of Kelly is doing a better job than the management of Verizon Communications or Alaska Air Group? Not necessarily. It means that these companies operate in different economic environments. In other words, it takes significantly more equipment to operate a cable company or an airline than it takes to operate an employment agency.

A Look Back

This chapter explains that the primary objective of recognizing depreciation is to match the cost of a long-term tangible asset with the revenues the asset is expected to generate. The matching concept also applies to natural resources (depletion) and intangible assets (amortization). The chapter explains how alternative methods can be used to account for the same event (e.g., straight-line versus double-declining-balance depreciation). Companies experiencing exactly the same business events could produce different financial statements. The alternative accounting methods for depreciating, depleting, or amortizing assets include the (1) straight-line, (2) double-declining-balance, and (3) units-of-production methods.

The *straight-line method* produces equal amounts of expense in each accounting period. The amount of the expense recognized is determined using the formula [(cost − salvage) ÷ number of years of useful life]. The *double-declining-balance method* produces proportionately larger amounts of expense in the early years of an asset's useful life and increasingly smaller amounts of expense in the later years of the asset's useful life. The formula for calculating double-declining-balance depreciation is [book value at beginning of period × (2 × the straight-line rate)]. The *units-of-production method* produces expense in direct proportion to the number of units produced during an accounting period. The formula for the amount of expense recognized each period is [(cost − salvage) ÷ total estimated units of production = allocation rate × units of production in current accounting period].

This chapter showed how to account for *changes in estimates* such as the useful life or the salvage value of a depreciable asset. Changes in estimates do not affect the amount of depreciation recognized previously. Instead, the remaining book value of the asset is expensed over its remaining useful life.

After an asset has been placed into service, companies typically incur further costs for maintenance, quality improvement, and extensions of useful life. *Maintenance costs* are expensed in the period in which they are incurred. *Costs that improve the quality* of an asset are added to the cost of the asset, increasing the book value and the amount of future depreciation charges. *Costs that extend the useful life* of an asset are subtracted from the asset's Accumulated Depreciation account, thereby increasing the book value of the asset.

A Look Forward

In Chapter 7 we move from the assets section of the balance sheet to issues in accounting for liabilities.

 Video lectures and accompanying self-assessment quizzes are available in *Connect* for all learning objectives.

 ## SELF-STUDY REVIEW PROBLEM

The following information pertains to a machine purchased by Bakersfield Company on January 1, Year 1:

Purchase price	$ 63,000
Delivery cost	$ 2,000
Installation charge	$ 3,000
Estimated useful life	8 years
Estimated units the machine will produce	130,000
Estimated salvage value	$ 3,000

The machine produced 14,400 units during Year 1 and 17,000 units during Year 2.

Required

Determine the depreciation expense Bakersfield would report for Year 1 and Year 2 using each of the following methods:

a. Straight-line.
b. Double-declining-balance.
c. Units-of-production.

Solution to Requirements *a–c*

a. Straight-line

Purchase price	$63,000	
Delivery cost	2,000	
Installation charge	3,000	
Total cost of machine	68,000	
Less: Salvage value	(3,000)	
	$65,000	÷ 8 = $8,125 Depreciation per year
Year 1	$ 8,125	
Year 2	$ 8,125	

b. Double-declining-balance

			Accumulated Depreciation					Annual
Year	Cost	—	at Beginning of Year	×	2 × S-L Rate	=		Depreciation
Year 1	$68,000	—	$ 0	×	(2 × 0.125)	=		$17,000
Year 2	68,000	—	17,000	×	(2 × 0.125)	=		12,750

c. Units-of-production

(1) (Cost − Salvage value) ÷ Estimated units of production = Depreciation cost per unit produced

$$\frac{\$68,000 - \$3,000}{130,000} = \$0.50 \text{ per unit}$$

(2) Cost per unit × Annual units produced = Annual depreciation expense

Year 1 $0.50 × 14,400 = $7,200

Year 2   0.50 × 17,000 = 8,500

KEY TERMS

Accelerated depreciation
  method 213
Accumulated
  Depreciation 212
Amortization 208
Basket purchase 209
Book value 212
Capital expenditures (on an
  existing asset) 220
Carrying value 212
Contra asset account 212

Copyright 224
Current (short-term)
  asset 206
Depletion 208
Depreciable cost 210
Depreciation 208
Depreciation expense 210
Double-declining-balance
  depreciation 213
Estimated useful life 210
Franchise 224

Goodwill 224
Historical cost
  concept 229
Intangible assets 208
Long-term operational
  assets 207
Maintenance costs 219
Natural resources 208
Patent 223
Property, plant, and
  equipment 208

Relative fair market value
  method 209
Salvage value 210
Straight-line
  depreciation 211
Tangible assets 208
Trademark 222
Units-of-production
  depreciation 216

QUESTIONS

1. What is the difference between the functions of long-term operational assets and investments?

2. What is the difference between tangible and intangible assets? Give an example of each.

3. What is the difference between goodwill and specifically identifiable intangible assets?

4. Define *depreciation*. What kind of asset depreciates?

5. When are natural resources expensed?

6. Is land a depreciable asset? Why or why not?

7. Define *amortization*. What kind of assets are *amortized*?

8. Explain the historical cost concept as it applies to long-term operational assets. Why is the book value of an asset likely to be different from the current market value of the asset?

9. What different kinds of expenditures might be included in the recorded cost of a building?

10. What is a basket purchase of assets? When a basket purchase is made, how is cost assigned to individual assets?

11. What are the stages in the life cycle of a long-term operational asset?

12. Explain straight-line, units-of-production, and double-declining-balance depreciation. When is it appropriate to use each of these depreciation methods?

13. What effect does the recognition of depreciation expense have on total assets? On total stockholders' equity?

14. Does the recognition of depreciation expense affect cash flows? Why or why not?

15. MalMax purchased a depreciable asset. What would be the difference in total assets at the end of the first year if MalMax chooses straight-line depreciation versus double-declining-balance depreciation?

16. John Smith mistakenly expensed the cost of a long-term tangible fixed asset. Specifically, he charged the cost of a truck to a delivery expense account. How will this error affect the income statement and the balance sheet in the year in which the mistake is made?

17. What is *salvage value*?

18. What type of account (classification) is Accumulated Depreciation?

19. How is the book value of an asset determined?

20. Why is depreciation that has been recognized over the life of an asset shown in a contra account? Why not just reduce the asset account?

21. Assume that a piece of equipment cost $5,000 and had accumulated depreciation of $3,000. What is the book value of the equipment? Is the book value equal to the fair market value of the equipment? Explain.

22. Why would a company choose to depreciate one piece of equipment using the double-declining-balance method and another piece of equipment using straight-line depreciation?

23. Why may it be necessary to revise the estimated life of a plant asset? When the estimated life is revised, does it affect the amount of depreciation per year? Why or why not?

24. How are capital expenditures made to improve the quality of a capital asset accounted for? Would the answer change if the expenditure extended the life of the asset but did not improve quality? Explain.

25. When a long-term operational asset is sold at a gain, how is the balance sheet affected? Is the statement of cash flows affected? If so, how?

26. Define *depletion*. What is the most commonly used method of computing depletion?

27. List several common intangible assets. How is the life determined that is to be used to compute amortization?

28. How can judgment and estimation affect information reported in the financial statements?

EXERCISES—SERIES A

connect All applicable Exercises in Series A are available in *Connect*. A Series B version of these Exercises can also be found in *Additional Student Resources and solutions can be found in the Instructor Library.*

Unless specifically included, ignore income tax considerations in all exercises and problems.

Exercise 6-1A *Long-term operational assets used in a business*   LO 6-1

Required

Give some examples of long-term operational assets that each of the following companies is likely to own: *(a)* Caterpillar, *(b)* Amtrak, *(c)* Facebook, and *(d)* Bank of America Corp.

Exercise 6-2A *Identifying long-term operational assets*   LO 6-1

Required

Which of the following items should be classified as long-term operational assets?

a. Prepaid insurance
b. Coal mine
c. Office equipment
d. Accounts receivable
e. Supplies
f. Copyright

g. Delivery van
h. Land used in the business
i. Goodwill
j. Cash
k. Filing cabinet
l. Tax library of accounting firm

Exercise 6-3A *Classifying tangible and intangible assets*   LO 6-1

Required

Identify each of the following long-term operational assets as either tangible (T) or intangible (I):

a. Pizza oven
b. Land
c. Franchise
d. Filing cabinet
e. Copyright
f. Silver mine

g. Office building
h. Drill press
i. Patent
j. Oil well
k. Desk
l. Goodwill

Exercise 6-4A *Determining the cost of an asset*   LO 6-1

Southwest Milling Co. purchased a front-end loader to move stacks of lumber. The loader had a list price of $140,000. The seller agreed to allow a 4 percent discount because Southwest Milling paid cash.

Delivery terms were FOB shipping point. Freight cost amounted to $1,200. Southwest Milling had to hire a specialist to calibrate the loader. The specialist's fee was $1,800. The loader operator is paid an annual salary of $60,000. The cost of the company's theft insurance policy increased by $800 per year as a result of acquiring the loader. The loader had a four-year useful life and an expected salvage value of $6,000.

Required

Determine the amount to be capitalized in the asset account for the purchase of the front-end loader.

LO 6-1

Exercise 6-5A *Allocating costs on the basis of relative market values*

Carver Inc. purchased a building and the land on which the building is situated for a total cost of $700,000 cash. The land was appraised at $320,000 and the building at $480,000.

Required

a. What is the accounting term for this type of acquisition?

b. Determine the amount of the purchase cost to allocate to the land and the amount to allocate to the building.

c. Would the company recognize a gain on the purchase? Why or why not?

d. Record the purchase in a statements model like the following one.

Balance Sheet						Income Statement			Statement of Cash Flows
Assets			= Liab.	+	Stk. Equity				
Cash	+ Land	+ Building				Rev.	− Exp.	= Net Inc.	

LO 6-1

Exercise 6-6A *Allocating costs for a basket purchase*

Pitney Co. purchased an office building, land, and furniture for $500,000 cash. The appraised value of the assets was as follows:

Land	$180,000
Building	300,000
Furniture	120,000
Total	$600,000

Required

a. Compute the amount to be recorded on the books for each asset.

b. Record the purchase in a horizontal statements model like the following one.

Balance Sheet							Income Statement			Statement of Cash Flows
Assets				= Liab.	+	Stk. Equity				
Cash	+ Land	+ Building	+ Furn.				Rev.	− Exp.	= Net Inc.	

LO 6-2

Exercise 6-7A *Effect of depreciation on the accounting equation and financial statements*

The following events apply to Gulf Seafood for the Year 1 fiscal year:

1. The company started when it acquired $60,000 cash by issuing common stock.
2. Purchased a new cooktop that cost $40,000 cash.
3. Earned $72,000 in cash revenue.
4. Paid $25,000 cash for salaries expense.
5. Adjusted the records to reflect the use of the cooktop. Purchased on January 1, Year 1, the cooktop has an expected useful life of four years and an estimated salvage value of $4,000. Use straight-line depreciation. The adjusting entry was made as of December 31, Year 1.

Required

a. Record the previous transactions in a horizontal statements model like the following one.

Balance Sheet					Income Statement			Statement of Cash Flows
Assets		=	Stk. Equity					
Cash	+ Book Value of Cooktop	= Com. Stk.	+ Ret. Earn.		Rev.	− Exp.	= Net Inc.	

b. What amount of depreciation expense would Gulf Seafood report on the Year 1 income statement?

c. What amount of accumulated depreciation would Gulf Seafood report on the December 31, Year 2, balance sheet?

d. Would the cash flow from operating activities be affected by depreciation in Year 1?

Exercise 6-8A *Effect of double-declining-balance depreciation on financial statements*   LO 6-3

Golden Manufacturing Company started operations by acquiring $150,000 cash from the issue of common stock. On January 1, Year 1, the company purchased equipment that cost $120,000 cash, had an expected useful life of six years, and had an estimated salvage value of $4,000. Golden Manufacturing earned $72,000 and $83,000 of cash revenue during Year 1 and Year 2, respectively. Golden Manufacturing uses double-declining-balance depreciation.

Required

a. Record the previous transactions in a horizontal statements model like the following one.

Balance Sheet					Income Statement			Statement of Cash Flows
Assets		=	Stk. Equity					
Cash	+ Book Value of Equip.	= Com. Stk.	+ Ret. Earn.		Rev.	− Exp.	= Net Inc.	

b. Prepare income statements, balance sheets, and statements of cash flows for Year 1 and Year 2. Use a vertical statements format.

Exercise 6-9A *Computing and recording straight-line versus double-declining-balance depreciation*   LO 6-2, 6-3

At the beginning of Year 1, Copeland Drugstore purchased a new computer system for $52,000. It is expected to have a five-year life and a $7,000 salvage value.

Required

a. Compute the depreciation for each of the five years, assuming that the company uses

(1) Straight-line depreciation.

(2) Double-declining-balance depreciation.

b. Record the purchase of the computer system and the depreciation expense for the first year under straight-line and double-declining-balance methods in a financial statements model like the following one.

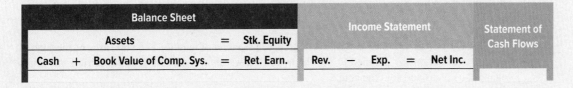

Balance Sheet				Income Statement			Statement of Cash Flows
Assets		= Stk. Equity					
Cash	+ Book Value of Comp. Sys.	= Ret. Earn.		Rev.	− Exp.	= Net Inc.	

LO 6-3, 6-4, 6-5

Exercise 6-10A   *Double-declining-balance and units-of-production depreciation: Gain or loss on disposal*

Exact Photo Service purchased a new color printer at the beginning of Year 1 for $38,000. The printer is expected to have a four-year useful life and a $3,500 salvage value. The expected print production is estimated at 1,500,000 pages. Actual print production for the four years was as follows:

Year 1	390,000
Year 2	410,000
Year 3	420,000
Year 4	300,000
Total	1,520,000

The printer was sold at the end of Year 4 for $1,650.

Required

a. Compute the depreciation expense for each of the four years, using double-declining-balance depreciation.

b. Compute the depreciation expense for each of the four years, using units-of-production depreciation.

c. Calculate the amount of gain or loss from the sale of the asset under each of the depreciation methods.

LO 6-2, 6-5

Exercise 6-11A   *Events related to the acquisition, use, and disposal of a tangible plant asset: Straight-line depreciation*

City Taxi Service purchased a new auto to use as a taxi on January 1, Year 1, for $36,000. In addition, City paid sales tax and title fees of $1,200 for the vehicle. The taxi is expected to have a five-year life and a salvage value of $4,000.

Required

a. Using the straight-line method, compute the depreciation expense for Year 1 and Year 2.

b. Assume the auto was sold on January 1, Year 3, for $21,000. Determine the amount of gain or loss that would be recognized on the asset disposal.

LO 6-5

Exercise 6-12A   *Effect of the disposal of plant assets on the financial statements*

Uno Company sold office equipment with a cost of $23,000 and accumulated depreciation of $12,000 for $14,000.

Required

a. What is the book value of the asset at the time of sale?

b. What is the amount of gain or loss on the disposal?

c. How would the sale affect net income (increase, decrease, no effect) and by how much?

d. How would the sale affect the amount of total assets shown on the balance sheet (increase, decrease, no effect) and by how much?

e. How would the event affect the statement of cash flows (inflow, outflow, no effect) and in what section?

LO 6-5

Exercise 6-13A   *Effect of gains and losses on the accounting equation and financial statements*

On January 1, Year 1, Prairie Enterprises purchased a parcel of land for $28,000 cash. At the time of purchase, the company planned to use the land for a warehouse site. In Year 3, Prairie Enterprises changed its plans and sold the land.

Required

a. Assume that the land was sold for $29,500 in Year 3.

   (1) Show the effect of the sale on the accounting equation.

   (2) What amount would Prairie report on the Year 3 income statement related to the sale of the land?

   (3) What amount would Prairie report on the Year 3 statement of cash flows related to the sale of the land?

b. Assume that the land was sold for $24,000 in Year 3.

   (1) Show the effect of the sale on the accounting equation.

   (2) What amount would Prairie report on the Year 3 income statement related to the sale of the land?

   (3) What amount would Prairie report on the Year 3 statement of cash flows related to the sale of the land?

Exercise 6-14A *Revision of estimated useful life*

LO 6-2, 6-6

On January 1, Year 1, Poultry Processing Company purchased a freezer and related installation equipment for $42,000. The equipment had a three-year estimated life with a $3,000 salvage value. Straight-line depreciation was used. At the beginning of Year 3, Poultry Processing revised the expected life of the asset to four years rather than three years. The salvage value was revised to $2,000.

Required

Compute the depreciation expense for each of the four years, Year 1 to Year 4.

Exercise 6-15A *Distinguishing between maintenance cost and capital expenditures*

LO 6-7

Bill's Wrecker Service has just completed a minor repair on a tow truck. The repair cost was $1,550, and the book value prior to the repair was $6,500. In addition, the company spent $12,000 to replace the roof on a building. The new roof extended the life of the building by five years. Prior to the roof replacement, the general ledger reflected the Building account at $85,000 and related Accumulated Depreciation account at $32,000.

Required

After the work was completed, what book value should appear on the balance sheet for the tow truck and the building?

Exercise 6-16A *Effect of maintenance cost versus capital expenditures on financial statements*

LO 6-7

Sellers Construction Company purchased a compressor for $28,000 cash. It had an estimated useful life of four years and a $4,000 salvage value. At the beginning of the third year of use, the company spent an additional $6,000 related to the equipment. The company's financial condition just prior to this expenditure is shown in the following statements model.

Balance Sheet						Income Statement				Statement of Cash Flows
Assets			=	Stk. Equity						
Cash	+	Book Value of Compressor	=	Com. Stk.	+	Ret. Earn.	Rev.	− Exp.	= Net Inc.	
45,000	+	16,000	=	40,000	+	21,000	NA	− NA	= NA	NA

Required

Record the $6,000 expenditure in the statements model under each of the following *independent* assumptions:

a. The expenditure was for routine maintenance.

b. The expenditure extended the compressor's life.

c. The expenditure improved the compressor's operating capacity.

LO 6-2, 6-7

Exercise 6-17A *Effect of maintenance cost versus capital expenditures on financial statements*

On January 1, Year 2, Webb Construction Company overhauled four cranes, resulting in a slight increase in the life of the cranes. Such overhauls occur regularly at two-year intervals and have been treated as maintenance expense in the past. Management is considering whether to capitalize this year's $22,000 cash cost in the Cranes asset account or to expense it as a maintenance expense. Assume that the cranes have a remaining useful life of two years and no expected salvage value. Assume straight-line depreciation.

Required

a. Determine the amount of additional depreciation expense Webb would recognize in Year 2 and Year 3 if the cost were capitalized in the Cranes account.

b. Determine the amount of expense Webb would recognize in Year 2 and Year 3 if the cost were recognized as maintenance expense.

c. Determine the effect of the overhaul on cash flow from operating activities for Year 2 and Year 3 if the cost were capitalized and expensed through depreciation charges.

d. Determine the effect of the overhaul on cash flow from operating activities for Year 2 and Year 3 if the cost were recognized as maintenance expense.

LO 6-8

Exercise 6-18A *Computing and recording depletion expense*

Colorado Mining paid $600,000 to acquire a mine with 40,000 tons of coal reserves. The following statements model reflects Colorado Mining's financial condition just prior to purchasing the coal reserves. The company extracted 15,000 tons of coal in Year 1 and 18,000 tons in Year 2.

Balance Sheet						Income Statement			Statement of Cash Flows
Assets		=	Stk. Equity						
Cash	+ Coal Res.	= Com. Stk.	+ Ret. Earn.			Rev. − Exp.	= Net Inc.		
800,000 +	NA	= 800,000	+ NA			NA − NA	= NA		NA

Required

a. Compute the depletion charge per unit.

b. Record the acquisition of the coal reserves and the depletion expense for Years 1 and 2 in a financial statements model like the preceding one.

LO 6-9, 6-10

Exercise 6-19A *Computing and recording the amortization of intangibles*

Dynamo Manufacturing paid cash to acquire the assets of an existing company. Among the assets acquired were the following items:

Patent with 4 remaining years of legal life	$40,000
Goodwill	35,000

Dynamo's financial condition just prior to the acquisition of these assets is shown in the following statements model.

Balance Sheet						Income Statement			Statement of Cash Flows
Assets			= Liab.	+ Stk. Equity					
Cash	+ Patent	+ Goodwill				Rev. − Exp.	= Net Inc.		
90,000 +	NA	+ NA	= NA	+ 90,000		NA − NA	= NA		NA

Required

a. Compute the annual amortization expense for these items.

b. Record the acquisition of the intangible assets and the related amortization expense for Year 1 in a horizontal statements model like the one previously shown.

Exercise 6-20A   Computing and recording goodwill

Arizona Corp. acquired the business Data Systems for $320,000 cash and assumed all liabilities at the date of purchase. Data's books showed tangible assets of $260,000, liabilities of $40,000, and stock-holders' equity of $220,000. An appraiser assessed the fair market value of the tangible assets at $250,000 at the date of acquisition. Arizona Corp.'s financial condition just prior to the acquisition is shown in the following statements model.

Balance Sheet								Income Statement				Statement of Cash Flows
Assets				=	Liab.	+	Stk. Equity	Rev.	−	Exp.	= Net Inc.	
Cash	+	Tang. Assets	+ Goodwill									
450,000	+	NA	+ NA	=	NA	+	450,000	NA	−	NA	= NA	NA

Required

a. Compute the amount of goodwill acquired.

b. Record the acquisition in a financial statements model like the preceding one.

Exercise 6-21A   Performing ratio analysis using real-world data

Electronic Arts, Inc. (commonly known as EA Sports) develops, markets, and publishes electronic games. Union Pacific Corporation is one of the largest railway networks in the nation, with 32,122 miles of railroads. The following data were taken from one of the companies' December 31, 2017, annual reports. Revealing which data relate to which company was intentionally omitted. The dollar amounts are in millions.

	Company 1	Company 2
Sales	$21,240	$5,150
Depreciation costs	2,105	136
Net earnings	10,712	1,043
Current assets	4,006	6,004
Property, plant, and equipment	51,605	453
Total assets	57,806	8,584

Required

a. Calculate depreciation costs as a percentage of sales for each company. (Round to three decimal places.)

b. Calculate property, plant, and equipment as a percentage of total assets for each company. (Round to three decimal places.)

c. Based on the information now available to you, decide which data relate to which company. Explain the rationale for your decision.

d. Which company appears to be using its assets most efficiently? Explain your answer.

PROBLEMS—SERIES A

connect All applicable Problems in Series A are available in *Connect*. A Series B version of these Problems can also be found in *Additional Student Resources and solutions can be found in the Instructor Library.*

Problem 6-22A   Accounting for acquisition of assets, including a basket purchase

Trinkle Company made several purchases of long-term assets during the year. The details of each purchase are presented here.

CHECK FIGURES
Total cost of equipment: $62,800
Cost allocated to copier: $16,500

New Office Equipment

1. List price: $60,000; terms: 2/10, n/30; paid within the discount period.
2. Transportation-in: $1,500.
3. Installation: $2,500.

4. Cost to repair damage during unloading: $650.
5. Routine maintenance cost after eight months: $350.

Basket Purchase of Copier, Computer, and Scanner for $30,000 with Fair Market Values

1. Copier, $22,000.
2. Computer, $10,000.
3. Scanner, $8,000.

Land for New Warehouse with an Old Building Torn Down

1. Purchase price, $250,000.
2. Demolition of building, $18,000.
3. Lumber sold from old building, $6,000.
4. Grading in preparation for new building, $22,000.
5. Construction of new building, $510,000.

Required

In each of these cases, determine the amount of cost to be capitalized in the asset accounts.

LO 6-2, 6-3, 6-4

Problem 6-23A *Calculating depreciation expense using three different methods*

CHECK FIGURES

b. Depreciation Expense, Year 1: $29,600

c. Depreciation Expense, Year 2: $19,000

Banko Inc. manufactures sporting goods. The following information applies to a machine purchased on January 1, Year 1:

Purchase price	$ 70,000
Delivery cost	$ 3,000
Installation charge	$ 1,000
Estimated life	5 years
Estimated units	140,000
Salvage estimate	$ 4,000

During Year 1, the machine produced 36,000 units and during Year 2, it produced 38,000 units.

Required

Determine the amount of depreciation expense for Year 1 and Year 2 using each of the following methods:

a. Straight-line.
b. Double-declining-balance.
c. Units of production.

LO 6-2, 6-3, 6-4

Problem 6-24A *Determining the effect of depreciation expense on financial statements*

CHECK FIGURES

a. Company A, Net Income: $28,750

c. Company C, Highest Book Value: $16,700

Three different companies each purchased trucks on January 1, Year 1, for $50,000. Each truck was expected to last four years or 200,000 miles. Salvage value was estimated to be $5,000. All three trucks were driven 66,000 miles in Year 1, 42,000 miles in Year 2, 40,000 miles in Year 3, and 60,000 miles in Year 4. Each of the three companies earned $40,000 of cash revenue during each of the four years. Company A uses straight-line depreciation, company B uses double-declining-balance depreciation, and company C uses units-of-production depreciation.

Required

Answer each of the following questions. Ignore the effects of income taxes.

a. Which company will report the highest amount of net income for Year 1?
b. Which company will report the lowest amount of net income for Year 4?
c. Which company will report the highest book value on the December 31, Year 3, balance sheet?
d. Which company will report the highest amount of retained earnings on the December 31, Year 4, balance sheet?
e. Which company will report the lowest amount of cash flow from operating activities on the Year 3 statement of cash flows?

Problem 6-25A *Accounting for depreciation over multiple accounting cycles:*
Straight-line depreciation

LO 6-2, 6-5

CHECK FIGURES
Net Income, Year 1: $16,100
Total Assets, Year 4: $137,900

Bensen Company began operations when it acquired $60,000 cash from the issue of common stock on January 1, Year 1. The cash acquired was immediately used to purchase equipment for $50,000 that had a $10,000 salvage value and an expected useful life of four years. The equipment was used to produce the following revenue stream (assume all revenue transactions are for cash). At the beginning of the fifth year, the equipment was sold for $8,800 cash. Bensen uses straight-line depreciation.

	Year 1	Year 2	Year 3	Year 4	Year 5
Revenue	$26,100	$28,500	$32,000	$31,300	$0

Required

Prepare income statements, statements of changes in stockholders' equity, balance sheets, and statements of cash flows for each of the five years. Present the statements in the form of a vertical statements model.

Problem 6-26A *Effect of straight-line versus double-declining-balance depreciation*
on the recognition of expense and gains or losses

LO 6-2, 6-3, 6-5

CHECK FIGURES
a. Depreciation Expense, Year 2: $7,000
b. Depreciation Expense, Year 2: $9,600

Becker Office Service purchased a new computer system on January 1, Year 1, for $40,000. It is expected to have a five-year useful life and a $5,000 salvage value. Becker Office Service expects to use the computer system more extensively in the early years of its life.

Required

a. Calculate the depreciation expense for each of the five years, assuming the use of straight-line depreciation.

b. Calculate the depreciation expense for each of the five years, assuming the use of double-declining-balance depreciation.

c. Would the choice of one depreciation method over another produce a different amount of cash flow for any year? Why or why not?

d. Assume that Becker Office Service sold the computer system at the end of the fourth year for $15,000. Compute the amount of gain or loss using each depreciation method.

Problem 6-27A *Computing and recording units-of-production depreciation*

LO 6-4, 6-5

Sabel Co. purchased assembly equipment for $500,000 on January 1, Year 1. Sabel's financial condition immediately prior to the purchase is shown in the following horizontal statements model.

Balance Sheet							Income Statement			Statement of Cash Flows
Assets			=	Stk. Equity						
Cash	+	Book Value of Equip.	=	Com. Stk.	+	Ret. Earn.	Rev.	− Exp.	= Net Inc.	
800,000	+	NA	=	800,000	+	NA	NA	− NA	= NA	NA

The equipment is expected to have a useful life of 200,000 miles and a salvage value of $20,000. Actual mileage was as follows:

Year 1	56,000
Year 2	61,000
Year 3	42,000
Year 4	36,000
Year 5	10,000

CHECK FIGURES
a. Depreciation Expense, Year 1: $134,400
c. Gain on Sale: $600

Required

a. Compute the depreciation for each of the five years, assuming the use of units-of-production depreciation.

b. Assume that Sabel earns $230,000 of cash revenue during Year 1. Record the purchase of the equipment and the recognition of the revenue and the depreciation expense for the first year in a financial statements model like the preceding one.

c. Assume that Sabel sold the equipment at the end of the fifth year for $20,600. Calculate the amount of gain or loss on the sale.

LO 6-6

Problem 6-28A   *Revision of estimated useful life of tangible assets*

Banger Co. purchased delivery equipment for $56,000 on January 1, Year 1. Banger estimated that the delivery equipment would have a life of five years and a $6,000 salvage value. Banger uses the straight-line method to compute the depreciation expense. At the beginning of Year 4, Banger revised the useful life of the delivery equipment to be a total of seven years. The estimated salvage value was not changed. Compute the depreciation expense for each of the seven years.

LO 6-6

Problem 6-29A   *Revision of estimated salvage value*

Delta Machine Company purchased a computerized assembly machine for $135,000 on January 1, Year 1. Delta Machine Company estimated that the machine would have a life of four years and a $25,000 salvage value. Delta Machine Company uses the straight-line method to compute depreciation expense. At the beginning of Year 3, Delta discovered that the machine was quickly becoming obsolete and would have little value at the end of its useful life. Consequently, Delta Machine Company revised the estimated salvage to only $5,000. It did not change the estimated useful life of the machine. Compute the depreciation expense for each of the four years.

LO 6-1, 6-3, 6-7

CHECK FIGURES
b. Net Income, Year 1: $48,520
   Total Assets, Year 3: $242,591

Problem 6-30A   *Purchase and use of tangible asset: Three accounting cycles, double-declining-balance depreciation*

The following transactions pertain to Accounting Solutions Inc. Assume the transactions for the purchase of the computer and any capital improvements occur on January 1 each year.

Year 1

1. Acquired $80,000 cash from the issue of common stock.
2. Purchased a computer system for $35,000. It has an estimated useful life of five years and a $5,000 salvage value.
3. Paid $2,450 sales tax on the computer system.
4. Collected $65,000 in fees from clients.
5. Paid $1,500 in fees for routine maintenance to service the computers.
6. Recorded double-declining-balance depreciation on the computer system for Year 1.

Year 2

1. Paid $1,000 for repairs to the computer system.
2. Bought off-site backup services to maintain the computer system, $1,500.
3. Collected $68,000 in fees from clients.
4. Paid $1,500 in fees to service the computers.
5. Recorded double-declining-balance depreciation for Year 2.

Year 3

1. Paid $6,000 to upgrade the computer system, which extended the total life of the system to six years. The salvage value did not change.
2. Paid $1,200 in fees to service the computers.
3. Collected $70,000 in fees from clients.
4. Recorded double-declining-balance depreciation for Year 3.

Required

a. Record the previous transactions in a horizontal statements model like the following one.

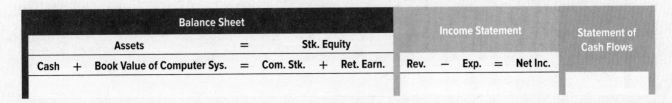

Balance Sheet						Income Statement			Statement of Cash Flows
Assets		=	Stk. Equity						
Cash	+ Book Value of Computer Sys.	=	Com. Stk.	+	Ret. Earn.	Rev.	− Exp.	= Net Inc.	

b. Use a vertical model to present financial statements for Year 1, Year 2, and Year 3.

Problem 6-31A   *Recording continuing expenditures for plant assets*

Morris Inc. recorded the following transactions over the life of a piece of equipment purchased in Year 1:

Jan. 1, Year 1   Purchased equipment for $90,000 cash. The equipment was estimated to have a five-year life and $5,000 salvage value and was to be depreciated using the straight-line method.

Dec. 31, Year 1   Recorded depreciation expense for Year 1.

Sept. 30, Year 2   Undertook routine repairs costing $900.

Dec. 31, Year 2   Recorded depreciation expense for Year 2.

Jan. 1, Year 3   Made an adjustment costing $2,500 to the equipment. It improved the quality of the output but did not affect the life and salvage value estimates.

Dec. 31, Year 3   Recorded depreciation expense for Year 3.

June 1, Year 4   Incurred $850 cost to oil and clean the equipment.

Dec. 31, Year 4   Recorded depreciation expense for Year 4.

Jan. 1, Year 5   Had the equipment completely overhauled at a cost of $9,000. The overhaul was estimated to extend the total life to seven years. The salvage value did not change.

Dec. 31, Year 5   Recorded depreciation expense for Year 5.

Oct. 1, Year 6   Received and accepted an offer of $19,000 for the equipment.

Required

a. Use a horizontal statements model like the following one to show the effects of these transactions on the elements of the financial statements. Use + for increase, − for decrease, and NA for not affected. The first event is recorded as an example.

	Balance Sheet					Income Statement	Statement of Cash Flows
Date	Assets	=	Liabilities	+	Stk. Equity	Net Inc.	
Jan. 1, Year 1	+ −	=	NA	+	NA	NA	− IA

b. Determine the amount of depreciation expense to be reported on the income statements for Years 1 through 5.

c. Determine the book value (cost − accumulated depreciation) Morris will report on the balance sheets at the end of Year 1 through Year 5.

d. Determine the amount of the gain or loss Morris will report on the disposal of the equipment on October 1, Year 6.

Problem 6-32A   *Accounting for continuing expenditures*

Tower Company owned a service truck that was purchased at the beginning of Year 1 for $31,000. It had an estimated life of three years and an estimated salvage value of $4,000. Tower company uses

LO 6-2, 6-5, 6-7

CHECK FIGURES
b. Year 3 Depreciation Expense: $17,833
d. Gain on Sale: $2,820

LO 6-2, 6-7

CHECK FIGURE
New Depreciation Expense: $8,000

straight-line depreciation. Its financial condition as of January 1, Year 3, is shown in the following financial statements model.

Balance Sheet						Income Statement			Statement of Cash Flows
Assets		=	Stk. Equity						
Cash	+	Book Value of Truck	=	Com. Stk.	+	Ret. Earn.	Rev.	−	Exp.	=	Net Inc.	
20,000	+	13,000	=	9,000	+	24,000	NA	−	NA	=	NA	NA

In Year 3, Tower Company spent the following amounts on the truck:

Jan. 4   Overhauled the engine for $6,000. The estimated life was extended one additional year, and the salvage value was revised to $3,000.

July 6   Obtained oil change and transmission service, $250.

Aug. 7   Replaced the fan belt and battery, $350.

Dec. 31   Purchased gasoline for the year, $7,500.

31   Recognized Year 3 depreciation expense.

Required

Record the Year 3 transactions in a statements model like the preceding one.

LO 6-8

Problem 6-33A   *Accounting for depletion*

CHECK FIGURES
a. Silver Mine Depletion, Year 1: $210,000
c. Total Natural Resources: $4,844,000

Flannery Company engages in the exploration and development of many types of natural resources. In the last two years, the company has engaged in the following activities:

Jan. 1, Year 1   Purchased for $1,500,000 a silver mine estimated to contain 100,000 tons of silver ore.

July 1, Year 1   Purchased for $1,700,000 a tract of timber estimated to yield 1,000,000 board feet of lumber, and the residual value of the land was estimated at $100,000.

Feb. 1, Year 2   Purchased for $2,700,000 a gold mine estimated to yield 50,000 tons of gold-veined ore.

Sept. 1, Year 2 Purchased oil reserves for $1,300,000. The reserves were estimated to contain 270,000 barrels of oil, of which 10,000 would be unprofitable to pump.

Required

a. Determine the amount of depletion expense that would be recognized on the Year 1 income statement for each of the two reserves, assuming 14,000 tons of silver were mined and 500,000 board feet of lumber were cut.

b. Determine the amount of depletion expense that would be recognized on the Year 2 income statement for each of the four reserves, assuming 20,000 tons of silver are mined, 300,000 board feet of lumber are cut, 4,000 tons of gold ore are mined, and 50,000 barrels of oil are extracted.

c. Prepare the portion of the December 31, Year 2, balance sheet that reports natural resources.

LO 6-9

Problem 6-34A   *Accounting for intangible assets*

Mitre Company acquired Midwest Transportation Co. for $1,400,000. The fair market values of the assets acquired were as follows. No liabilities were assumed.

Equipment	$510,000
Land	150,000
Building	520,000
Franchise (10-year life)	40,000

Required

Calculate the amount of goodwill purchased.

Problem 6-35A *Accounting for goodwill*

Rossie Equipment Manufacturing Co. acquired the assets of Alba Inc., a competitor, in Year 3. It recorded goodwill of $70,000 at acquisition. Because of defective machinery Alba had produced prior to the acquisition, it has been determined that all of the acquired goodwill has been permanently impaired.

Required

Explain how the recognition of the impairment of the goodwill will affect the Year 3 balance sheet, income statement, and statement of cash flows.

Problem 6-36A *Performing ratio analysis using real-world data*

Companies in the coal mining business use a lot of property, plant, and equipment. Not only is there the significant investment they must make in the equipment used to extract and process the coal, but they must also purchase the rights to the coal reserves themselves.

Goodyear Tire & Rubber Company, Inc. is the largest tire manufacturer in North America. Chesapeake Energy Corporation claims to be the largest private-sector coal company in the world. The following information was taken from these companies' December 31, 2017, annual reports. All dollar amounts are in millions.

	Chesapeake Energy	Goodyear Tire
Sales	$9,496	$15,377
Depreciation and depletion costs	995	781
Property, plant, and equipment		
(net of accumulated depreciation)	10,680	7,451
Total assets	12,425	17,064
Depreciation method	Straight-line and units of production	Straight-line
Estimated life of assets:		
Buildings	10 to 39 years	3 to 45 years
Machinery and equipment	3 to 20 years	3 to 40 years

Required

a. Calculate depreciation costs as a percentage of sales for each company. (Round to three decimal places.)

b. Calculate buildings, property, plant, and equipment as a percentage of total assets for each company. (Round to three decimal places.)

c. Based only on the percentages calculated in Requirements *a* and *b*, which company appears to be using its assets most efficiently? Explain your answer.

d. Identify some of the problems a financial analyst encounters when trying to compare the use of long-term assets of Chesapeake versus Goodyear.

ANALYZE, THINK, COMMUNICATE

ATC 6-1 Business Applications Case *Understanding real-world annual reports*

Required

Obtain the Target Corporation's annual report for its 2018 fiscal year (year ended February 2, 2019) at http://investors.target.com using the instructions in Appendix A, and use it to answer the following questions.

a. What method of depreciation does Target use?

b. What types of intangible assets does Target have?

c. What are the estimated lives that Target uses for the various types of long-term assets?

d. As of February 2, 2019, what is the original cost of Target's Land; Buildings and improvements; and Fixtures and equipment?

e. What was Target's depreciation expense and amortization expense for 2018 (see the footnotes)?

ATC 6-2   Group Assignment   *Different depreciation methods*

Sweet's Bakery makes cakes, pies, and other pastries that it sells to local grocery stores. The company experienced the following transactions during the Year 1:

1. Started business by acquiring $60,000 cash from the issue of common stock.
2. Purchased bakery equipment for $46,000 with a four-year life and a $6,000 salvage value.
3. Had cash sales in Year 1 amounting to $42,000.
4. Paid $8,200 of cash for supplies which were all used during the year to make baked goods.
5. Paid other operating expenses of $12,000 for Year 1.

Required

a. Organize the class into two sections and divide each section into groups of three to five students. Assign each section a depreciation method: straight-line or double-declining-balance.

Group Task

Prepare an income statement and a balance sheet using the preceding information and the depreciation method assigned to your group.

Class Discussion

b. Have a representative of each section put its income statement on the board. Are there differences in net income? How will these differences in the amount of depreciation expense change over the life of the equipment?

ATC 6-3   Research Assignment   *Comparing Microsoft's and Intel's operational assets*

Companies in different industries often use different proportions of current versus long-term assets to accomplish their business objective. The technology revolution resulting from the silicon microchip has often been led by two well-known companies: Microsoft and Intel. Although often thought of together, these companies are really very different. Using either the most current Forms 10-K or annual reports for Microsoft Corporation and Intel Corporation, complete the following requirements. To obtain the Forms 10-K, use either the EDGAR system following the instructions in Appendix A or the company's website. Microsoft's annual report is available on its website; Intel's annual report is its Form 10-K.

Required

a. Fill in the missing data in the following table. The percentages must be computed; they are not included in the companies' 10-Ks. (*Note:* The percentages for current assets and property, plant, and equipment will not sum to 100.)

	Current Assets	Property, Plant, and Equipment	Total Assets
Microsoft			
Dollar Amount	$	$	$
% of Total Assets	%	%	100%
Intel			
Dollar Amount	$	$	$
% of Total Assets	%	%	100%

b. Briefly explain why these two companies have different percentages of their assets in current assets versus property, plant, and equipment.

ATC 6-4   Writing Assignment   *Impact of historical cost on asset presentation on the balance sheet*

Assume that you are examining the balance sheets of two companies and note the following information.

	Company A	Company B
Equipment	$1,130,000	$900,000
Accumulated Depreciation	(730,000)	(500,000)
Book Value	$ 400,000	$400,000

Maxie Smith, a student who has had no accounting courses, remarks that Company A and Company B have the same amount of equipment.

Required

In a short paragraph, explain to Maxie that the two companies do not have equal amounts of equipment. You may want to include in your discussion comments regarding the possible age of each company's equipment, the impact of the historical cost concept on balance sheet information, and the impact of different depreciation methods on book value.

ATC 6-5   Ethical Dilemma   *What's an expense?*

Several years ago, Wilson Blowhard founded a communications company. The company became successful and grew by expanding its customer base and acquiring some of its competitors. In fact, most of its growth resulted from acquiring other companies. Mr. Blowhard is adamant about continuing the company's growth and increasing its net worth. To achieve these goals, the business's net income must continue to increase at a rapid pace.

If the company's net worth continues to rise, Mr. Blowhard plans to sell the company and retire. He is, therefore, focused on improving the company's profit any way he can.

In the communications business, companies often use the lines of other communications companies. This line usage is a significant operating expense for Mr. Blowhard's company. Generally accepted accounting principles require operating costs like line use to be expensed as they are incurred each year. Each dollar of line cost reduces net income by a dollar.

After reviewing the company's operations, Mr. Blowhard concluded that the company did not currently need all of the line use it was paying for. It was really paying the owner of the lines now so that the line use would be available in the future for all of Mr. Blowhard's expected new customers. Mr. Blowhard instructed his accountant to capitalize all of the line cost charges and depreciate them over 10 years. The accountant reluctantly followed Mr. Blowhard's instructions, and the company's net income for the current year showed a significant increase over the prior year's net income. Mr. Blowhard had found a way to report continued growth in the company's net income and increase the value of the company.

Required

a. How does Mr. Blowhard's scheme affect the amount of income that the company would otherwise report in its financial statements and how does the scheme affect the company's balance sheet? Explain your answer.

b. Review the AICPA's Articles of Professional Conduct (see Chapter 4) and comment on any of the standards that were violated.

c. Review the fraud triangle discussed in Chapter 4 and comment on the features of the fraud triangle that are evident in this case.

CHAPTER 7

Accounting for Liabilities

LEARNING OBJECTIVES

After you have mastered the material in this chapter, you will be able to:

LO 7-1 Show how notes payable and related interest expense affect financial statements.

LO 7-2 Show how sales tax liabilities affect financial statements.

LO 7-3 Define contingent liabilities and show how they are reported in financial statements.

LO 7-4 Show how warranty obligations affect financial statements.

LO 7-5 Show how installment notes affect financial statements.

LO 7-6 Show how a line of credit affects financial statements.

LO 7-7 Show how bonds issued at face value affect financial statements.

LO 7-8 Using the straight-line method show how bonds issued at a discount affect financial statements.

LO 7-9 Using the straight-line method show how bonds issued at a premium affect financial statements.

LO 7-10 Distinguish between current and noncurrent assets and liabilities on a classified balance sheet.

LO 7-11 Using the effective interest rate method show how bonds issued at a discount affect financial statements. (Appendix)

LO 7-12 Using the effective interest rate method show how bonds issued at a premium affect financial statements. (Appendix)

 Video lectures and accompanying self-assessment quizzes are available in Connect *for all learning objectives.*

 Set B exercises and problems are available in Additional Student Resources.

CHAPTER OPENING

Chapter 2 discussed several types of liabilities with known amounts due, including accounts payable, salaries payable, and unearned revenue. This chapter introduces other liabilities with known amounts due: notes payable, sales taxes payable, lines of credit, and bond liabilities. We also discuss contingent liabilities, which are obligations with estimated amounts due.

The Curious Accountant

Ken Wolter/123RF

In 2017, Dell Technologies, Inc. reported a net loss of $3.9 billion. The previous year it had reported a loss of $1.7 billion. The company had $2.4 billion of interest expense in 2017.

With such huge losses on its income statement, do you think Dell was able to make the interest payments on its debt? If so, how? (Answer on page 255.)

CURRENT LIABILITIES

This section of the chapter discusses a variety of current liabilities. Current liabilities are payable within one year or the operating cycle, whichever is longer.

ACCOUNTING FOR NOTES PAYABLE

LO 7-1

Show how notes payable and related interest expense affect financial statements.

Our discussion of promissory notes in Chapter 5 focused on the payee, the company with a note receivable on its books. In this chapter we focus on the maker of the note, the company with a note payable on its books. Because the maker of the note issues (gives) the note to the payee, the maker is sometimes called the **issuer**.

To illustrate, assume that on September 1, Year 1, Herrera Supply Company (HSC) borrowed $90,000 from the National Bank. As evidence of the debt, Herrera issued a **note payable** that had a one-year term and an annual interest rate of 9 percent.

Issuing the note is an asset source transaction. The asset account Cash increases and the liability account Notes Payable increases. The income statement is not affected. The statement of cash flows shows a $90,000 cash inflow from financing activities. The effects on the financial statements are as follows.

	Balance Sheet							Income Statement			Statement of Cash Flows
	Assets	=	Liabilities			+	Stk. Equity				
Date	Cash	=	Notes Pay.	+	Int. Pay.	+	Com. Stk.	+	Ret. Earn.	Rev. − Exp. = Net Inc.	
09/01/Year 1	90,000	=	90,000	+	NA	+	NA	+	NA	NA − NA = NA	90,000 FA

On December 31, Year 1, HSC would recognize four months (September 1 through December 31) of accrued interest expense. The accrued interest is $2,700 [$90,000 × 0.09 × (4 ÷ 12)]. Recognizing the accrued interest expense increases the liability account Interest Payable and decreases retained earnings. It is a claims exchange event. The income statement would report interest expense although HSC had not paid any cash for interest in Year 1. The effects on the financial statements are as follows.

	Balance Sheet							Income Statement			Statement of Cash Flows
	Assets	=	Liabilities			+	Stk. Equity				
Date	Cash	=	Notes Pay.	+	Int. Pay.	+	Com. Stk.	+	Ret. Earn.	Rev. − Exp. = Net Inc.	
12/31/Year 1	NA	=	NA	+	2,700	+	NA	+	(2,700)	NA − 2,700 = (2,700)	NA

HSC would record three events on August 31, Year 2 (the maturity date). The first event recognizes $5,400 of interest expense that accrued in Year 2 from January 1 through August 31 [$90,000 × 0.09 × (8 ÷ 12)]. The effects on the financial statements are as follows.

	Balance Sheet							Income Statement			Statement of Cash Flows
	Assets	=	Liabilities			+	Stk. Equity				
Date	Cash	=	Notes Pay.	+	Int. Pay.	+	Com. Stk.	+	Ret. Earn.	Rev. − Exp. = Net Inc.	
08/31/Year 2	NA	=	NA	+	5,400	+	NA	+	(5,400)	NA − 5,400 = (5,400)	NA

The second event recognizes HSC's cash payment for interest on August 31, Year 2. This event is an asset use transaction that reduces both the Cash and Interest Payable accounts for the total amount of interest due, $8,100 [$90,000 × 0.09 × (12 ÷ 12)]. The interest payment includes the four months' interest accrued in Year 1 and the eight months accrued in Year 2 ($2,700 + $5,400 = $8,100). There is no effect on the income statement because HSC recognized the interest expense in two previous entries. The statement of cash flows would report an $8,100 cash outflow from operating activities. The effects on the financial statements follow.

	Balance Sheet									Income Statement					Statement of Cash Flows	
	Assets	=	Liabilities			+	Stk. Equity									
Date	Cash	=	Notes Pay.	+	Int. Pay.	+	Com. Stk.	+	Ret. Earn.	Rev.	−	Exp.	=	Net Inc.		
08/31/Year 2	(8,100)	=	NA	+	(8,100)	+	NA	+	NA	NA	−	NA	=	NA	(8,100)	OA

The third event on August 31, Year 2, reflects repaying the principal. This event is an asset use transaction. The Cash account and the Notes Payable account each decrease by $90,000. There is no effect on the income statement. The statement of cash flows would show a $90,000 cash outflow from financing activities. Recall that paying interest is classified as an operating activity even though repaying the principal is a financing activity. The effects on the financial statements are as follows.

	Balance Sheet									Income Statement					Statement of Cash Flows	
	Assets	=	Liabilities			+	Stk. Equity									
Date	Cash	=	Notes Pay.	+	Int. Pay.	+	Com. Stk.	+	Ret. Earn.	Rev.	−	Exp.	=	Net Inc.		
08/31/Year 2	(90,000)	=	(90,000)	+	NA	+	NA	+	NA	NA	−	NA	=	NA	(90,000)	FA

☑ CHECK YOURSELF 7.1

On October 1, Year 1, Mellon Company issued an interest-bearing note payable to Better Banks Inc. The note had a $24,000 principal amount, a four-month term, and an annual interest rate of 4 percent. Determine the amount of interest expense and the cash outflow from operating activities Mellon will report in its Year 1 and Year 2 financial statements.

Answer   The computation of accrued interest expense is shown as follows. Unless otherwise specified, the interest rate is stated in annual terms even though the term of the note is only four months. Interest rates are commonly expressed as an annual percentage regardless of the term of the note. The *time outstanding* in the following formulas is therefore expressed as a fraction of a year. Mellon paid interest at an annual rate of 4 percent, but the note was outstanding for only 3/12 of a year in Year 1 and 1/12 of a year in Year 2.

Year 1

Principal × Annual interest rate × Time outstanding = Interest expense

$24,000 ×   0.04   ×   (3/12)   = $240

Year 2

Principal × Annual interest rate × Time outstanding = Interest expense

$24,000 ×   0.04   ×   (1/12)   = $80

Mellon will report a $320 ($240 + $80) cash outflow from operating activities for interest in Year 2.

ACCOUNTING FOR SALES TAX

LO 7-2

Most states require retail companies to collect a sales tax on items sold to their customers. The retailer collects the tax from its customers and remits the tax to the state at regular intervals. The retailer has a current liability for the amount of sales tax collected but not yet paid to the state.

Show how sales tax liabilities affect financial statements.

To illustrate, assume Herrera Supply Company (HSC) sells merchandise to a customer for $2,000 cash plus tax in a state where the sales tax rate is 6 percent. The effects on the financial statements are shown as follows.[1]

Balance Sheet						Income Statement					Statement of Cash Flows
Assets	=	Liab.	+	Stk. Equity							
Cash	=	Sales Tax Pay.	+	Com. Stk.	+	Ret. Earn.	Rev.	−	Exp.	=	Net Inc.	
2,120	=	120	+	NA	+	2,000	2,000	−	NA	=	2,000	2,120 OA

Remitting the tax (paying cash to the tax authority) is an asset use transaction. Both the Cash account and the Sales Tax Payable account decrease. The effects on the financial statements are as follows.

Balance Sheet						Income Statement					Statement of Cash Flows
Assets	=	Liab.	+	Stk. Equity							
Cash	=	Sales Tax Pay.	+	Com. Stk.	+	Ret. Earn.	Rev.	−	Exp.	=	Net Inc.	
(120)	=	(120)	+	NA	+	NA	NA	−	NA	=	NA	(120) OA

CONTINGENT LIABILITIES

LO 7-3

Define contingent liabilities and show how they are reported in financial statements.

A **contingent liability** is a potential obligation arising from a past event. The amount or existence of the obligation depends on some future event. A pending lawsuit, for example, is a contingent liability. Depending on the outcome, a defendant company could be required to pay a large monetary settlement or could be relieved of any obligation. Generally accepted accounting principles require that companies classify contingent liabilities into three different categories depending on the likelihood of their becoming actual liabilities. The categories and the accounting for each are described as follows.

1. If the likelihood of a future obligation arising is *probable* (likely) and its amount can be *reasonably estimated,* a liability is recognized in the financial statements. Contingent liabilities in this category include warranties, vacation pay, and sick leave.

2. If the likelihood of a future obligation arising is *reasonably possible* but not likely or if it is probable but *cannot be reasonably estimated,* no liability is reported on the balance sheet. The potential liability is, however, disclosed in the notes to the financial statements. Contingent liabilities in this category include legal challenges, environmental damages, and government investigations.

3. If the likelihood of a future obligation arising is *remote,* no liability need be recognized in the financial statements or disclosed in the notes to the statements.[2]

Determining whether a contingent liability is probable, reasonably possible, or remote requires professional judgment. Even seasoned accountants seek the advice of attorneys, engineers, insurance agents, and government regulators before classifying significant contingent liabilities. Professional judgment is also required to distinguish between contingent liabilities and **general uncertainties**. All businesses face uncertainties such as competition and damage from floods or storms. Such uncertainties are not contingent liabilities, however, because they do not arise from past events.

Exhibit 7.1 summarizes the three categories of contingent liabilities and the accounting for each category.

---

[1]The entry to record cost of goods sold for this sale is intentionally omitted.

[2]Companies may, if desired, voluntarily disclose contingent liabilities classified as remote.

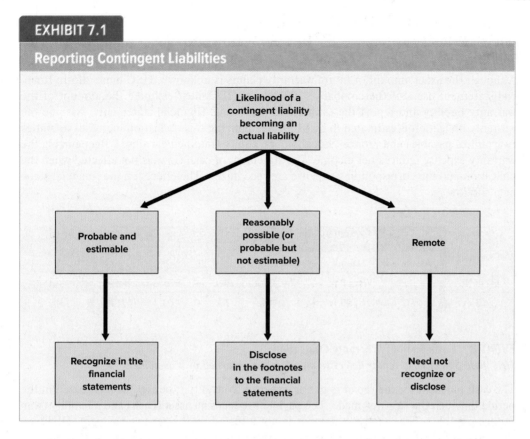

EXHIBIT 7.1

Reporting Contingent Liabilities

WARRANTY OBLIGATIONS

To attract customers, many companies guarantee their products or services. Such guarantees are called **warranties.** Warranties take many forms. Usually, they extend for a specified period of time. Within this period, the seller promises to replace or repair defective products without charge. Although the amount and timing of warranty obligations are uncertain, warranties usually represent liabilities that must be reported in the financial statements.

 Show how warranty obligations affect financial statements.

    To illustrate accounting for warranty obligations, assume Herrera Supply Company (HSC) had cash of $2,000, inventory of $6,000, common stock of $5,000, and retained earnings of $3,000 on January 1, Year 2. The Year 2 accounting period is affected by three accounting events: (1) sale of merchandise under warranty; (2) recognition of warranty obligations to customers who purchased the merchandise; and (3) settlement of a customer's warranty claim.

EVENT 1   Sale of Merchandise
HSC sold for $7,000 cash merchandise that had cost $4,000.

In the following statements model, revenue from the sale is referenced as 1a and the cost of the sale as 1b. The effects of the sales transaction on the financial statements are shown as follows.

	Balance Sheet						Income Statement					Statement of Cash Flows
	Assets		=	Liab.	+	Stk. Equity						
Event No.	Cash	+ Inventory	=			Ret. Earn.	Rev.	−	Exp.	=	Net Inc.	
1a	7,000	+ NA	=	NA	+	7,000	7,000	−	NA	=	7,000	7,000 OA
1b	NA	+ (4,000)	=	NA	+	(4,000)	NA	−	4,000	=	(4,000)	NA

EVENT 2   Recognition of Warranty Expense
HSC guaranteed the merchandise sold in Event 1 to be free from defects for one year following the date of sale.

Although the exact amount of future warranty claims is unknown, HSC must inform financial statement users of the company's obligation. HSC must estimate the amount of the warranty liability and report the estimate in the Year 2 financial statements. Assume the warranty obligation is estimated to be $100. Recognizing this obligation increases liabilities (warranties payable) and reduces stockholders' equity (retained earnings). Recognizing the warranty expense reduces net income. The statement of cash flows is not affected when the obligation and the corresponding expense are recognized. The effects on the financial statements follow.

	Balance Sheet						Income Statement					Statement of Cash Flows
	Assets	=	Liab.	+	Stk. Equity							
Event No.			Warr. Pay.	+	Ret. Earn.	Rev.	−	Exp.	=	Net Inc.		
2	NA	=	100	+	(100)	NA	−	100	=	(100)		NA

EVENT 3   Settlement of Warranty Obligation
HSC paid $40 cash to repair defective merchandise returned by a customer.

The cash payment for the repair is not an expense. Warranty expense was recognized in the period in which the sale was made. The payment reduces an asset (cash) and a liability (warranties payable). The income statement is not affected by the repairs payment. However, there is a $40 cash outflow reported in the operating activities section of the statement of cash flows. The effects on the financial statements follow.

	Balance Sheet						Income Statement					Statement of Cash Flows
	Assets	=	Liab.	+	Stk. Equity							
Event No.	Cash	=	Warr. Pay.	+	Ret. Earn.	Rev.	−	Exp.	=	Net Inc.		
3	(40)	=	(40)	+	NA	NA	−	NA	=	NA		(40) OA

Financial Statements

The financial statements for HSC's Year 2 accounting period are shown in Exhibit 7.2.

EXHIBIT 7.2

Financial Statements for Year 2

Income Statement			Balance Sheet			Statement of Cash Flows	
Sales revenue	$7,000		Assets			**Operating Activities**	
Cost of goods sold	(4,000)		Cash	$ 8,960		Inflow from customers	$7,000
Gross margin	3,000		Inventory	2,000		Outflow for warranty	(40)
Warranty expense	(100)		Total assets	$10,960		Net inflow from	
Net income	$2,900		Liabilities			operating activities	6,960
			Warranties payable	$ 60		**Investing Activities**	0
			Stockholders' equity			**Financing Activities**	0
			Common stock	5,000		Net change in cash	6,960
			Retained earnings	5,900		Plus: Beginning cash balance	2,000
			Total liab. and stockholders' equity	$10,960		Ending cash balance	$8,960

REALITY BYTES

Many of the items we purchase come with a manufacturer's warranty, but companies that sell electronics and electrical appliances often offer to sell you an extended warranty that provides protection after the manufacturer's warranty has expired. Why do they offer this option to customers, and how do these warranties differ from the standard manufacturers' warranties?

Companies such as Best Buy offer to sell customers extended warranties because they make a significant profit on them. If you buy an extended warranty from Best Buy, the retailer is not actually the one who is promising to repair your product; that will be done by a third party. Best Buy simply receives a commission for selling the warranty. In 2018 such commissions accounted for 2.0 percent of the company's total revenues, and since it had to incur very little expense to earn these revenues, they are mostly profit.

The typical manufacturer's warranty, as you have learned in this chapter, is an expense recognized at the time of the sale. However, companies that provide extended warranties must recognize the warranty revenue over the life of the warranty, not immediately upon sale. Remember, this is referring to the third-party warranty provider, not Best Buy. Since Best Buy is simply earning a commission from selling the warranty, it gets to recognize all of the revenue at the time of the sale.

Digital Vision/SuperStock

☑ CHECK YOURSELF 7.2

Flotation Systems, Inc. (FSI) began operations in Year 1. Its sales were $360,000 in Year 1 and $410,000 in Year 2. FSI estimates the cost of its one-year product warranty will be 2 percent of sales. Actual cash payments for warranty claims amounted to $5,400 during Year 1 and $8,500 during Year 2. Determine the amount of warranty expense that FSI would report on its Year 1 and Year 2 income statements. Also, determine the amount of warranties payable FSI would report on its Year 1 and Year 2 balance sheet.

Answer   FSI would report Warranty Expense on the December 31, Year 1, income statement of $7,200 ($360,000 × 0.02). Warranty Expense on the December 31, Year 2, income statement is $8,200 ($410,000 × 0.02).

FSI would report Warranties Payable on the December 31, Year 1, balance sheet of $1,800 ($7,200 − $5,400). Warranties Payable on the December 31, Year 2, balance sheet is $1,500 ($1,800 + $8,200 − $8,500).

Accounting for Long-Term Debt

Most businesses finance their investing activities with long-term debt. Recall that current liabilities mature within one year or a company's operating cycle, whichever is longer. Other liabilities are **long-term liabilities**. Long-term debt agreements vary with respect to requirements for paying interest charges and repaying principal (the amount borrowed). Interest payments may be due monthly, annually, at some other interval, or at the maturity date. Interest charges may be based on a **fixed interest rate** that remains constant during the term of the loan or may be based on a **variable interest rate** that fluctuates up or down during the loan period.

Principal repayment is generally required either in one lump sum at the maturity date or in installments that are spread over the life of the loan. For example, each monthly payment on your car loan probably includes both paying interest and repaying some of the principal.

Repaying a portion of the principal with regular payments that also include interest is often called loan **amortization**.[3] This section explains accounting for interest and principal with respect to the major forms of long-term debt financing.

INSTALLMENT NOTES PAYABLE

LO 7-5

Show how installment notes affect financial statements.

Loans that require payments of principal and interest at regular intervals (amortizing loans) are typically represented by **installment notes**. The terms of installment notes usually range from two to five years. To illustrate accounting for installment notes, assume Blair Company was started on January 1, Year 1, when it borrowed $100,000 cash from the National Bank. In exchange for the money, Blair issued the bank a five-year installment note with a 9 percent fixed interest rate. The effects on the financial statements are as follows.

Balance Sheet								Income Statement						Statement of Cash Flows
Assets	=	Liab.	+			Stk. Equity								
Cash	=	Note Pay.	+	Com. Stk.	+	Ret. Earn.		Rev.	−	Exp.	=	Net Inc.		
100,000	=	100,000	+	NA	+	NA		NA	−	NA	=	NA		100,000 FA

The loan agreement required Blair to pay five equal installments of $25,709[4] on December 31 of each year from Year 1 through Year 5. Exhibit 7.3 shows the allocation of each payment between principal and interest. When Blair pays the final installment, both the principal and interest will be paid in full. The amounts shown in Exhibit 7.3 are computed as follows.

1. The Interest Expense (Column D) is computed by multiplying the Principal Balance on Jan. 1 (Column B) by the interest rate. For example, interest expense for Year 1 is $100,000 × 0.09 = $9,000; for Year 2 it is 83,291 × 0.09 = $7,496; and so on.

2. The Principal Repayment (Column E) is computed by subtracting the Interest Expense (Column D) from the Cash Payment on Dec. 31 (Column C). For example, the Principal

---

EXHIBIT 7.3

Amortization Schedule for Installment Note Payable

Accounting Period Column A	Principal Balance on Jan. 1 Column B	Cash Payment on Dec. 31 Column C	Interest Expense Column D	Principal Repayment Column E	Principal Balance on Dec. 31 Column F
Year 1	$100,000	$25,709	$9,000	$16,709	$83,291
Year 2	83,291	25,709	7,496	18,213	65,078
Year 3	65,078	25,709	5,857	19,852	45,226
Year 4	45,226	25,709	4,070	21,639	23,587
Year 5	23,587	25,710*	2,123	23,587	0

*All computations are rounded to the nearest dollar. To fully liquidate the liability, the final payment is one dollar more than the others because of rounding differences.

[3]In Chapter 6 the term *amortization* described the expense recognized when the *cost of an intangible asset* is systematically allocated to expense over the useful life of the asset. This chapter shows that the term *amortization* refers more broadly to a variety of allocation processes. Here it means the systematic process of allocating the *principal repayment* over the life of a loan.

[4]The amount of the annual payment is determined using the present value concepts presented in a later chapter. Usually the lender (bank or other financial institution) calculates the amount of the payment for the customer. In this chapter we provide the amount of the annual payment.

Answers to The Curious Accountant

Even though Dell Technologies reported a $3.9 billion loss in 2017, it was able to make the interest payments on its debt with no difficulty for two reasons. First, interest is paid with cash, not accrual earnings. Some of the expenses on the company's income statement did not require the use of cash in 2017. For example, Dell reported a depreciation and amortization expense of $8.6 billion, which did not require cash payments.

Second, the net loss the company incurred was *after* the interest expense of $2.4 billion had been deducted. The company's statement of cash flows shows that net cash flow from operating activities in 2017, *after making interest payments,* was a positive $6.8 billion. The capacity of operations to support interest payments is measured by the amount of earnings before interest deductions. For example, look at the 2018 income statement for Blair Company in Exhibit 7.4. This statement shows only $3,000 of net income, but $12,000 of cash revenue was available for the payment of interest. Similarly, Dell's 2017 net loss is not an indication of the company's ability to pay interest in the short run of earnings before interest deductions.

Repayment for Year 1 is $25,709 − $9,000 = $16,709; for Year 2 it is $25,709 − $7,496 = $18,213; and so on.

3. The Principal Balance on Dec. 31 (Column F) is computed by subtracting the Principal Repayment (Column E) from the Principal Balance on Jan. 1 (Column B). For example, the Principal Balance on Dec. 31 for Year 1 is $100,000 − $16,709 = $83,291; on December 31, Year 2, the principal balance is $83,291 − $18,213 = $65,078; and so on. The Principal Balance on Dec. 31 (ending balance) for Year 1 ($83,291) is also the Principal Balance on Jan. 1 (beginning balance) for Year 2; the principal balance on December 31, Year 2, is the principal balance on January 1, Year 3; and so on.

Although the amounts for interest expense and principal repayment differ each year, the effects of the annual payment on the financial statements are the same. On the balance sheet, assets (cash) decrease by the total amount of the payment; liabilities (note payable) decrease by the amount of the principal repayment; and stockholders' equity (retained earnings) decreases by the amount of interest expense. Net income decreases from recognizing interest expense. On the statement of cash flows, the portion of the cash payment applied to interest is reported in the operating activities section and the portion applied to principal is reported in the financing activities section. The effects of the December 31, Year 1 payment on the financial statements are as follows.

Balance Sheet							Income Statement			Statement of Cash Flows
Assets	=	Liab.	+	Stk. Equity						
Cash	=	Note Pay.	+	Com. Stk.	+	Ret. Earn.	Rev.	− Exp.	= Net Inc.	
(25,709)	=	(16,709)	+	NA	+	(9,000)	NA	− 9,000	= (9,000)	(9,000) OA (16,709) FA

Exhibit 7.4 displays income statements, balance sheets, and statements of cash flows for Blair Company for the accounting periods Year 1 through Year 5. The illustration assumes that Blair earned $12,000 of rent revenue each year. Because some of the principal is repaid each year, the note payable amount reported on the balance sheet and the amount of the interest expense on the income statement both decline each year.

EXHIBIT 7.4

BLAIR COMPANY
Financial Statements

	Year 1	Year 2	Year 3	Year 4	Year 5
Income Statements					
Rent revenue	$ 12,000	$12,000	$12,000	$12,000	$12,000
Interest expense	(9,000)	(7,496)	(5,857)	(4,070)	(2,123)
Net income	$ 3,000	$ 4,504	$ 6,143	$ 7,930	$ 9,877
Balance Sheets					
Assets					
Cash	$ 86,291	$72,582	$58,873	$45,164	$31,454
Liabilities					
Note payable	$ 83,291	$65,078	$45,226	$23,587	$ 0
Stockholders' equity					
Retained earnings	3,000	7,504	13,647	21,577	31,454
Total liabilities and stk. equity	$ 86,291	$72,582	$58,873	$45,164	$31,454
Statements of Cash Flows					
Operating Activities					
Inflow from customers	$ 12,000	$12,000	$12,000	$12,000	$12,000
Outflow for interest	(9,000)	(7,496)	(5,857)	(4,070)	(2,123)
Investing Activities	0	0	0	0	0
Financing Activities					
Inflow from note issue	100,000	0	0	0	0
Outflow to repay note	(16,709)	(18,213)	(19,852)	(21,639)	(23,587)
Net change in cash	86,291	(13,709)	(13,709)	(13,709)	(13,710)
Plus: Beginning cash balance	0	86,291	72,582	58,873	45,164
Ending cash balance	$ 86,291	$72,582	$58,873	$45,164	$31,454

☑ CHECK YOURSELF 7.3

On January 1, Year 1, Krueger Company issued a $50,000 installment note to State Bank. The note had a 10-year term and an 8 percent interest rate. Krueger agreed to repay the principal and interest in 10 annual payments of $7,451.47 at the end of each year. Determine the amount of principal and interest Krueger paid during the first and second year that the note was outstanding.

Answer

Accounting Period	Principal Balance January 1 A	Cash Payment December 31 B	Applied to Interest C = A × 0.08	Applied to Principal B − C
Year 1	$50,000.00	$7,451.47	$4,000.00	$3,451.47
Year 2	46,548.53	7,451.47	3,723.88	3,727.59

LINE OF CREDIT

LO 7-6

Show how a line of credit affects financial statements.

A **line of credit** enables a company to borrow or repay funds as needed. For example, a business may borrow $50,000 one month and make a partial repayment of $10,000 the next month. Credit agreements usually specify a limit on the amount that can be borrowed. Exhibit 7.5 shows that credit agreements are widely used.

Interest rates on lines of credit normally vary with fluctuations in some designated interest rate benchmark such as the rate paid on U.S. Treasury bills. For example, a company may pay 4 percent interest one month and 4.5 percent the next month, even if the principal balance remains constant.

Lines of credit typically have one-year terms. Although they are classified on the balance sheet as short-term liabilities, lines of credit are frequently extended indefinitely by simply renewing the credit agreement.

To illustrate accounting for a line of credit, assume Lagoon Company owns a wholesale jet-ski distributorship. In the spring, Lagoon borrows money using a line of credit to finance building up its inventory. Lagoon repays the loan over the summer months using cash generated from jet-ski sales. Borrowing or repaying events occur on the first of the month. Interest payments occur at the end of each month. Exhibit 7.6 presents all Year 1 line of credit events.

Each borrowing event (March 1, April 1, and May 1) is an asset source transaction. Both cash and the line of credit liability increase. Each repayment (June 1, July 1, and August 1) is an asset use transaction. Both cash and the line of credit liability decrease. Each month's interest expense is an asset use transaction. Assets (cash) and stockholders' equity (retained earnings) decrease, as does net income. The effects of the events on the financial statements are shown in Exhibit 7.7.

EXHIBIT 7.5

Percentage of Dow Companies Disclosing Credit Agreements

The chart is based on data drawn from recent annual reports published by the 30 companies that comprise the Dow Jones Industrial Average.

EXHIBIT 7.6

Summary of Year 1 Line of Credit Events

Date	Amount Borrowed (repaid)	Loan Balance at End of Month	Effective Interest Rate per Month (%)	Interest Expense (rounded to nearest $1)
Mar. 1	$ 20,000	$ 20,000	0.09 ÷ 12	$150
Apr. 1	30,000	50,000	0.09 ÷ 12	375
May 1	50,000	100,000	0.105 ÷ 12	875
June 1	(10,000)	90,000	0.10 ÷ 12	750
July 1	(40,000)	50,000	0.09 ÷ 12	375
Aug. 1	(50,000)	0	0.09 ÷ 12	0

EXHIBIT 7.7

Date	Balance Sheet					Income Statement					Statement of Cash Flows	
	Assets	=	Liabilities	+	Stk. Equity	Rev.	−	Exp.	=	Net Inc.		
Mar. 1	20,000	=	20,000	+	NA	NA	−	NA	=	NA	20,000	FA
31	(150)	=	NA	+	(150)	NA	−	150	=	(150)	(150)	OA
Apr. 1	30,000	=	30,000	+	NA	NA	−	NA	=	NA	30,000	FA
30	(375)	=	NA	+	(375)	NA	−	375	=	(375)	(375)	OA
May 1	50,000	=	50,000	+	NA	NA	−	NA	=	NA	50,000	FA
31	(875)	=	NA	+	(875)	NA	−	875	=	(875)	875	OA
June 1	(10,000)	=	(10,000)	+	NA	NA	−	NA	=	NA	(10,000)	FA
30	(750)	=	NA	+	(750)	NA	−	750	=	(750)	(750)	OA
July 1	(40,000)	=	(40,000)	+	NA	NA	−	NA	=	NA	(40,000)	FA
31	(375)	=	NA	+	(375)	NA	−	375	=	(375)	(375)	OA
Aug. 1	(50,000)	=	(50,000)	+	NA	NA	−	NA	=	NA	(50,000)	FA
31	NA	=	NA	+	NA	NA	−	NA	=	NA	NA	

BOND LIABILITIES

Many companies borrow money directly from the public by selling **bond certificates,** otherwise called *issuing* bonds. Bond certificates describe a company's obligation to pay interest and to repay the principal. The seller, or **issuer,** of a bond is the borrower; the buyer of a bond, or **bondholder,** is the lender.

From the issuer's point of view, a bond represents an obligation to pay a sum of money to the bondholder on the bond's maturity date. The amount due at maturity is the **face value** of the bond. Most bonds also require the issuer to make cash interest payments based on a **stated interest rate** at regular intervals over the life of the bond. Exhibit 7.8 shows a typical bond certificate.

EXHIBIT 7.8

Bond Certificate

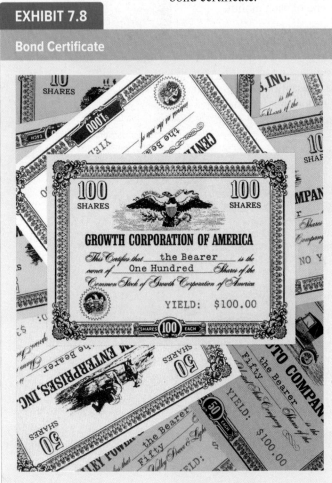

CSA Images/Getty Images

Advantages of Issuing Bonds

Bond financing offers companies the following advantages:

1. Bonds usually have longer terms than notes issued to banks. While typical bank loan terms range from 2 to 5 years, bonds normally have 20-year terms to maturity. Longer terms to maturity allow companies to implement long-term strategic plans without having to worry about frequent refinancing arrangements.

2. Bond interest rates may be lower than bank interest rates. Banks earn profits by borrowing money from the public (depositors) at low interest rates, then loaning that money to companies at higher rates. By issuing bonds directly to the public, companies can pay lower interest costs by eliminating the intermediary (banks).

BONDS ISSUED AT FACE VALUE

Assume Marsha Mason needs cash in order to seize a business opportunity. Mason knows of a company seeking a plot of land on which to store its inventory of crushed stone. Mason also knows of a suitable tract of land she could purchase for $100,000. The company has agreed to lease the land it needs from Mason for $12,000 per year. Mason lacks the funds to buy the land.

Some of Mason's friends recently complained about the low interest rates banks were paying on certificates of deposit. Mason suggested that her friends invest in bonds instead of CDs. She offered to sell them bonds with a 9 percent stated interest rate. The terms specified in the bond agreement Mason drafted included making interest payments in cash on December 31 of each year, a five-year term to maturity, and pledging the land as collateral for the bonds.[5] Her friends were favorably impressed, and Mason issued the bonds to them in exchange for cash on January 1, Year 1.

Mason used the bond proceeds to purchase the land and immediately contracted to lease it for five years. On December 31, Year 5, the maturity date of the bonds, Mason sold the land for its $100,000 book value and used the proceeds from the sale to repay the bond liability.

[5]In practice, bonds are usually issued for much larger sums of money, often hundreds of millions of dollars. Also, terms to maturity are normally long, with 20 years being common. Using such large amounts for such long terms is unnecessarily cumbersome for instructional purposes. The effects of bond issues can be illustrated efficiently by using smaller amounts of debt with shorter maturities, as assumed in the case of Marsha Mason.

Mason's business venture involved six distinct accounting events:

1. Received $100,000 cash from issuing five-year bonds at face value.
2. Invested proceeds from the bond issue to purchase land for $100,000 cash.
3. Earned $12,000 cash revenue annually from leasing the land.
4. Paid $9,000 annual interest on December 31 of each year.
5. Sold the land for $100,000 cash.
6. Repaid the bond principal to bondholders.

Effect of Events on Financial Statements

EVENT 1   Issue Bonds for Cash
Issuing bonds is an asset source transaction.

Assets (cash) and liabilities (bonds payable) increase. Net income is not affected. The $100,000 cash inflow is reported in the financing activities section of the statement of cash flows. These effects are shown here.

Balance Sheet					Income Statement				Statement of Cash Flows
Assets	=	Liab.	+	Stk. Equity					
Cash	=	Bonds Pay.			Rev.	−	Exp.	=	Net Inc.	
100,000	=	100,000	+	NA	NA	−	NA	=	NA	100,000 FA

EVENT 2   Investment in Land
Paying $100,000 cash to purchase land is an asset exchange transaction.

The asset cash decreases and the asset land increases. The income statement is not affected. The cash outflow is reported in the investing activities section of the statement of cash flows. These effects are illustrated as follows.

Balance Sheet							Income Statement				Statement of Cash Flows
Assets			=	Liab.	+	Stk. Equity					
Cash	+	Land					Rev.	−	Exp.	=	Net Inc.	
(100,000)	+	100,000	=	NA	+	NA	NA	−	NA	=	NA	(100,000) IA

EVENT 3   Revenue Recognition
Recognizing $12,000 cash revenue from renting the property is an asset source transaction.

This event is repeated each year from Year 1 through Year 5. The event increases assets and stockholders' equity. Recognizing revenue increases net income. The cash inflow is reported in the operating activities section of the statement of cash flows. These effects follow:

Balance Sheet					Income Statement				Statement of Cash Flows
Assets	=	Liab.	+	Stk. Equity					
Cash	=			Ret. Earn.	Rev.	−	Exp.	=	Net Inc.	
12,000	=	NA	+	12,000	12,000	−	NA	=	12,000	12,000 OA

EVENT 4   Expense Recognition
Mason's $9,000 ($100,000 × 0.09) cash payment represents interest expense.

This event is also repeated each year from Year 1 through Year 5. The interest payment is an asset use transaction. Cash and stockholders' equity (retained earnings) decrease. The expense recognition decreases net income. The cash outflow is reported in the operating activities section of the statement of cash flows. These effects follow:

Balance Sheet				Income Statement			Statement of Cash Flows
Assets	=	Liab.	+ Stk. Equity				
Cash	=		Ret. Earn.	Rev. —	Exp. =	Net Inc.	
(9,000)	=	NA	+ (9,000)	NA —	9,000 =	(9,000)	(9,000) OA

EVENT 5   Sale of Investment in Land
Selling the land for cash equal to its $100,000 book value is an asset exchange transaction.

Cash increases and land decreases. Because there was no gain or loss on the sale, the income statement is not affected. The cash inflow is reported in the investing activities section of the statement of cash flows. These effects follow:

Balance Sheet					Income Statement			Statement of Cash Flows
Assets			= Liab.	+ Stk. Equity				
Cash	+	Land			Rev. —	Exp. =	Net Inc.	
100,000	+	(100,000)	= NA	+ NA	NA —	NA =	NA	100,000 IA

EVENT 6   Payoff of Bond Liability
Repaying the face value of the bond liability is an asset use transaction.

Cash and bonds payable decrease. The income statement is not affected. The cash outflow is reported in the financing activities section of the statement of cash flows.

Balance Sheet				Income Statement			Statement of Cash Flows
Assets	=	Liab.	+ Stk. Equity				
Cash	=	Bonds Pay.		Rev. —	Exp. =	Net Inc.	
(100,000)	=	(100,000)	+ NA	NA —	NA =	NA	(100,000) FA

Financial Statements

Exhibit 7.9 displays Mason Company's financial statements. For simplicity, the income statement does not distinguish between operating and nonoperating items. Rent revenue and interest expense are constant across all accounting periods, so Mason recognizes $3,000 of net income in each accounting period. On the balance sheet, cash increases by $3,000 each year because cash revenue exceeds cash paid for interest. Land remains constant each year at its $100,000 historical cost until it is sold in Year 5. Similarly, the bonds payable liability is reported at $100,000 from the date the bonds were issued in Year 1 until they are paid off on December 31, Year 5.

Compare Blair Company's income statements in Exhibit 7.4 with Mason Company's income statements in Exhibit 7.9. Both Blair and Mason borrowed $100,000 cash at a

EXHIBIT 7.9

Mason Company Financial Statements

	Bonds Issued at Face Value				
	Year 1	Year 2	Year 3	Year 4	Year 5
Income Statements					
Rent revenue	$ 12,000	$ 12,000	$ 12,000	$ 12,000	$ 12,000
Interest expense	(9,000)	(9,000)	(9,000)	(9,000)	(9,000)
Net income	$ 3,000	$ 3,000	$ 3,000	$ 3,000	$ 3,000
Balance Sheets					
Assets					
Cash	$ 3,000	$ 6,000	$ 9,000	$ 12,000	$ 15,000
Land	100,000	100,000	100,000	100,000	0
Total assets	$103,000	$106,000	$109,000	$112,000	$ 15,000
Liabilities					
Bonds payable	$100,000	$100,000	$100,000	$100,000	$ 0
Stockholders' equity					
Retained earnings	3,000	6,000	9,000	12,000	15,000
Total liabilities and stockholders' equity	$103,000	$106,000	$109,000	$112,000	$ 15,000
Statements of Cash Flows					
Operating Activities					
Inflow from customers	$ 12,000	$ 12,000	$ 12,000	$ 12,000	$ 12,000
Outflow for interest	(9,000)	(9,000)	(9,000)	(9,000)	(9,000)
Investing Activities					
Outflow to purchase land	(100,000)				
Inflow from sale of land					100,000
Financing Activities					
Inflow from bond issue	100,000				
Outflow to repay bond liab.					(100,000)
Net change in cash	3,000	3,000	3,000	3,000	3,000
Plus: Beginning cash balance	0	3,000	6,000	9,000	12,000
Ending cash balance	$ 3,000	$ 6,000	$ 9,000	$ 12,000	$ 15,000

9 percent stated interest rate for five-year terms. Blair, however, repaid its liability under the terms of an installment note while Mason did not repay any principal until the end of the five-year bond term. Because Blair repaid part of the principal balance on the installment loan each year, Blair's interest expense declined each year. The interest expense on Mason's bond liability, however, remained constant because the full principal amount was outstanding for the entire five-year bond term.

Effect of Semiannual Interest Payments

The previous examples assumed that interest payments were made annually. In practice, most bond agreements call for interest to be paid semiannually, which means that interest is paid in cash twice each year. If Marsha Mason's bond certificate had stipulated semiannual interest payments, her company would have paid $4,500 ($100,000 × 0.09 = $9,000 ÷ 2 = $4,500) cash to bondholders for interest on June 30 and December 31 of each year.

AMORTIZATION OF A BOND DISCOUNT USING THE STRAIGHT-LINE METHOD

LO 7-8

Using the straight-line method show how bonds issued at a discount affect financial statements.

Return to the Mason Company illustration with one change. Assume Mason's bond certificates have a 9 percent stated rate of interest printed on them. Suppose Mason's friends find they can buy bonds from another entrepreneur willing to pay a higher rate of interest. They explain to Mason that business decisions cannot be made on the basis of friendship. Mason provides a counteroffer. There is no time to change the bond certificates, so Mason offers to accept $95,000 for the bonds today and still repay the full face value of $100,000 at the maturity date. The $5,000 difference is called a **bond discount**. Mason's friends agree to buy the bonds for $95,000.

Effective Interest Rate

The bond discount increases the interest Mason must pay. First, Mason must still make the annual cash payments described in the bond agreement. In other words, Mason must pay cash of $9,000 (0.09 × $100,000) annually even though she actually borrowed only $95,000. Second, Mason will have to pay back $5,000 more than she received ($100,000 − $95,000). The extra $5,000 (bond discount) is additional interest. Although the $5,000 of additional interest is not paid until maturity, when spread over the life of the bond, it amounts to $1,000 of additional interest expense per year.

The actual rate of interest that Mason must pay is called the **effective interest rate**. A rough estimate of the effective interest rate for the discounted Mason bonds is 10.5 percent [($9,000 annual stated interest + $1,000 annual amortization of the discount) ÷ $95,000 amount borrowed]. Selling the bonds at a $5,000 discount permits Mason to raise the 9 percent stated rate of interest to an effective rate of roughly 10.5 percent. Deeper discounts would raise the effective rate even higher. Shallower discounts would reduce the effective rate of interest. Mason can set the effective rate of interest to any level desired by adjusting the amount of the discount.

Bond Prices

It is common business practice to use discounts to raise the effective rate of interest above the stated rate. Bonds frequently sell for less than face value. Bond prices are normally expressed *as a percentage of the face value.* For example, Mason's discounted bonds sold for 95, meaning the bonds sold at 95 percent of face value ($100,000 × 0.95 = $95,000). Amounts of less than 1 percentage point are usually expressed as a fraction. Therefore, a bond priced at 98 3/4 sells for 98.75 percent of face value.

Effect of Events on Financial Statements

To illustrate accounting for bonds issued at a discount, return to the Mason Company example using the assumption the bonds are issued for 95 instead of face value. We examine the same six events using this revised assumption. This revision changes some amounts reported on the financial statements. For example, Event 1 in Year 1 reflects receiving only $95,000 cash from the bond issue. Because Mason had only $95,000 available to invest in land, the illustration assumes that Mason acquired a less desirable piece of property which generated only $11,400 of rent revenue per year.

EVENT 1   Bonds with a face value of $100,000 are issued at 95.

Because Mason must pay the face value at maturity, the $100,000 face value of the bonds is recorded in the Bonds Payable account. The $5,000 discount is recorded in a separate contra liability account called **Discount on Bonds Payable**. Shown as follows, the contra account is subtracted from the face value to determine the **carrying value** (book value) of the bond liability on January 1, Year 1.

Bonds payable	$100,000
Less: Discount on bonds payable	(5,000)
Carrying value	$ 95,000

The bond issue is an asset source transaction. Both assets and total liabilities increase by $95,000. Net income is not affected. The cash inflow is reported in the financing activities section of the statement of cash flows. The effects on the financial statements are shown here.

Balance Sheet				Income Statement			Statement of Cash Flows
Assets	=	Liabilities	+ Stk. Equity				
Cash	=	Carrying Value of Bond Liability	Stk. Equity	Rev. −	Exp. =	Net Inc.	
95,000	=	95,000	+ NA	NA −	NA =	NA	95,000 FA

EVENT 2   Paid $95,000 cash to purchase land.

The asset cash decreases and the asset land increases. The income statement is not affected. The cash outflow is reported in the investing activities section of the statement of cash flows. The effects on the financial statements are shown here.

Balance Sheet						Income Statement			Statement of Cash Flows
Assets			=	Liab.	+ Stk. Equity				
Cash	+	Land				Rev. −	Exp. =	Net Inc.	
(95,000)	+	95,000	=	NA	+ NA	NA −	NA =	NA	(95,000) IA

EVENT 3   Recognized $11,400 cash revenue from renting the land.

This event is repeated each year from Year 1 through Year 5. The event is an asset source transaction that increases assets and stockholders' equity. Recognizing revenue increases net income. The cash inflow is reported in the operating activities section of the statement of cash flows. The effects on the financial statements are shown here.

Balance Sheet				Income Statement			Statement of Cash Flows
Assets	=	Liab.	+ Stk. Equity				
Cash	=		Ret. Earn.	Rev. −	Exp. =	Net Inc.	
11,400	=	NA	+ 11,400	11,400 −	NA =	11,400	11,400 OA

EVENT 4   Recognized interest expense. The interest cost of borrowing has two components: the $9,000 paid in cash each year and the $5,000 discount paid at maturity.

Using **straight-line amortization,** the amount of the discount recognized as expense in each accounting period is $1,000 ($5,000 discount ÷ 5 years). Mason will therefore recognize $10,000 of interest expense each year ($9,000 at the stated interest rate plus $1,000 amortization of the bond discount). On the balance sheet, the asset cash decreases by $9,000, the carrying value of the bond liability increases by $1,000 (through a decrease in the bond discount), and retained earnings (interest expense) decreases by $10,000. The effects on the financial statements are shown here.

Balance Sheet				Income Statement			Statement of Cash Flows
Assets	=	Liabilities	+ Stk. Equity				
Cash	=	Carrying Value of Bond Liability	+ Ret. Earn.	Rev. − Exp.	= Net Inc.		
(9,000)	=	1,000	+ (10,000)	NA − 10,000	= (10,000)		(9,000) OA

EVENT 5　Sold the land for cash equal to its $95,000 book value.

Cash increases and land decreases. Because there was no gain or loss on the sale, the income statement is not affected. The cash inflow is reported in the investing activities section of the statement of cash flows. The effects on the financial statements are shown here.

Balance Sheet				Income Statement			Statement of Cash Flows
Assets	=	Liab.	+ Stk. Equity				
Cash	+	Land		Rev. − Exp.	= Net Inc.		
95,000	+	(95,000)	= NA + NA	NA − NA	= NA		95,000 IA

EVENT 6　Paid the bond liability.

Cash and bonds payable decrease. The income statement is not affected. For reporting purposes, the cash outflow is separated into two parts on the statement of cash flows: $95,000 of the cash outflow is reported in the financing activities section because it represents repaying the principal amount borrowed; the remaining $5,000 cash outflow is reported in the operating activities section because it represents the interest arising from issuing the bonds at a discount. In practice, the amount of the discount is frequently immaterial and is combined in the financing activities section with the principal repayment. The effects on the financial statements are shown here.

Balance Sheet				Income Statement			Statement of Cash Flows
Assets	=	Liab.	+ Stk. Equity				
Cash	=	Bonds Pay.		Rev. − Exp.	= Net Inc.		
(100,000)	=	(100,000)	+ NA	NA − NA	= NA		(95,000) FA (5,000) OA

Financial Statements

Exhibit 7.10 displays Mason Company's financial statements assuming the bonds were issued at a discount. Contrast the net income reported in Exhibit 7.10 (bonds issued at a discount) with the net income reported in Exhibit 7.9 (bonds sold at face value). Two factors cause the net income in Exhibit 7.10 to be lower. First, because the bonds were sold at a discount, Mason Company had less money to spend on its land investment. It bought less desirable land which generated less revenue. Second, the effective interest rate was higher than the stated rate, resulting in higher interest expense. Lower revenues coupled with higher expenses result in less profitability.

On the balance sheet, the carrying value of the bond liability increases each year until the maturity date, December 31, Year 5, when it is equal to the $100,000 face value of the bonds (the amount Mason is obligated to pay). Because Mason did not pay any dividends, the retained

EXHIBIT 7.10

Mason Company Financial Statements

Bonds Issued at a Discount

	Year 1	Year 2	Year 3	Year 4	Year 5
Income Statements					
Rent revenue	$ 11,400	$ 11,400	$ 11,400	$ 11,400	$ 11,400
Interest expense	(10,000)	(10,000)	(10,000)	(10,000)	(10,000)
Net income	$ 1,400	$ 1,400	$ 1,400	$ 1,400	$ 1,400
Balance Sheets					
Assets					
Cash	$ 2,400	$ 4,800	$ 7,200	$ 9,600	$ 7,000
Land	95,000	95,000	95,000	95,000	0
Total assets	$ 97,400	$ 99,800	$102,200	$104,600	$ 7,000
Liabilities					
Bonds payable	$100,000	$100,000	$100,000	$100,000	$ 0
Discount on bonds payable	(4,000)	(3,000)	(2,000)	(1,000)	0
Carrying value of bond liab.	96,000	97,000	98,000	99,000	0
Stockholders' equity					
Retained earnings	1,400	2,800	4,200	5,600	7,000
Total liabilities and stockholders' equity	$ 97,400	$ 99,800	$102,200	$104,600	$ 7,000
Statements of Cash Flows					
Operating Activities					
Inflow from customers	$ 11,400	$ 11,400	$ 11,400	$ 11,400	$ 11,400
Outflow for interest	(9,000)	(9,000)	(9,000)	(9,000)	(14,000)
Investing Activities					
Outflow to purchase land	(95,000)				
Inflow from sale of land					95,000
Financing Activities					
Inflow from bond issue	95,000				
Outflow to repay bond liab.					(95,000)
Net change in cash	2,400	2,400	2,400	2,400	(2,600)
Plus: Beginning cash balance	0	2,400	4,800	7,200	9,600
Ending cash balance	$ 2,400	$ 4,800	$ 7,200	$ 9,600	$ 7,000

earnings of $7,000 on December 31, Year 5, is equal to the total amount of net income reported over the five-year period ($1,400 × 5). All earnings were retained in the business.

Several factors account for the differences between net income and cash flow. First, although $10,000 of interest expense is reported on each income statement, only $9,000 of cash was paid for interest each year until Year 5, when $14,000 was paid for interest ($9,000 based on the stated rate + $5,000 for discount). The $1,000 difference between interest expense and cash paid for interest in Year 1, Year 2, Year 3, and Year 4 results from amortizing the bond discount. The cash outflow for the interest related to the discount is included in the $100,000 payment made at maturity on December 31, Year 5. Even though $14,000 of cash is paid for interest in Year 5, only $10,000 is recognized as interest expense on the income statement that year. Although the total increase in cash over the five-year life of the business ($7,000) is equal to the total net income reported for the same period, there are significant timing differences between when the interest expense is recognized and when the cash outflows occur to pay for it.

✓ CHECK YOURSELF 7.4

On January 1, Year 1, Moffett Company issued bonds with a $600,000 face value at 98. The bonds had a 9 percent annual interest rate and a 10-year term. Interest is payable in cash on December 31 of each year. What amount of interest expense will Moffett report on the Year 3 income statement? What carrying value for bonds payable will Moffett report on the December 31, Year 3, balance sheet?

Answer The bonds were issued at a $12,000 ($600,000 × 0.02) discount. The discount will be amortized over the 10-year life at the rate of $1,200 ($12,000 ÷ 10 years) per year. The amount of interest expense for Year 3 is $55,200 ($600,000 × 0.09 = $54,000 annual cash interest + $1,200 discount amortization).

The carrying value of the bond liability is equal to the face value less the unamortized discount. By the end of Year 3, $3,600 of the discount will have been amortized ($1,200 × 3 years = $3,600). The unamortized discount as of December 31, Year 3, will be $8,400 ($12,000 − $3,600). The carrying value of the bond liability as of December 31, Year 3, will be $591,600 ($600,000 − $8,400).

AMORTIZATION OF A BOND PREMIUM USING THE STRAIGHT-LINE METHOD

LO 7-9

Using the straight-line method show how bonds issued at a premium affect financial statements.

When bonds are sold for more than their face value, the difference between the amount received and the face value is called a **bond premium**. Bond premiums reduce the effective interest rate. For example, assume Mason Company issued its 9 percent bonds at 105, receiving $105,000 cash on the issue date. The company is still only required to repay the $100,000 face value of the bonds at the maturity date. The $5,000 difference between the amount received and the amount repaid at maturity reduces the total amount of interest expense. The premium is recorded in a separate liability account called **Premium on Bonds Payable**. This account is reported on the balance sheet as an addition to Bonds Payable, increasing the carrying value of the bond liability. On the issue date, the bond liability would be reported on the balance sheet as follows.

Bonds payable	$100,000
Plus: Premium on bonds payable	5,000
Carrying value	$105,000

The entire $105,000 cash inflow is reported in the financing activities section of the statement of cash flows even though the $5,000 premium is conceptually an operating activities cash flow because it pertains to interest. In practice, premiums are usually so small they are immaterial and the entire cash inflow is normally classified as a financing activity. The effects on the financial statements are shown here.

	Balance Sheet			Income Statement			Statement of Cash Flows
	Assets =	Liabilities	+ Stk. Equity				
Date	Cash =	Carrying Value of Bond Liability		Rev. −	Exp. =	Net Inc.	
Jan. 1	105,000 =	105,000	+ NA	NA −	NA =	NA	105,000 FA
Dec. 31	(9,000)	(1,000)	(8,000)		8,000	(8,000)	9,000 OA

The Market Rate of Interest

When a bond is issued, the effective interest rate is determined by current market conditions. Market conditions are influenced by many factors such as the state of the economy, government policy, and the law of supply and demand. These conditions are collectively reflected in the **market rate of interest**. The *effective rate of interest* investors are willing to accept *for a particular bond* equals the *market rate of interest* for other investments with similar levels of risk at the time the bond is issued. When the market rate of interest is higher than the stated rate of interest, bonds will sell at a discount to increase the effective rate of interest to the market rate. When the market rate is lower than the stated rate, bonds will sell at a premium so as to reduce the effective rate to the market rate.

Security for Loan Agreements

In general, large loans with long terms to maturity pose more risk to lenders (creditors) than small loans with short terms. To reduce the risk that they won't get paid, lenders frequently require borrowers (debtors) to pledge designated assets as **collateral** for loans. For example, when a bank makes a car loan, it usually retains legal title to the car until the loan is fully repaid. If the borrower fails to make the monthly payments, the bank repossesses the car, sells it to someone else, and uses the proceeds to pay the original owner's debt. Similarly, assets like accounts receivable, inventory, equipment, buildings, and land may be pledged as collateral for business loans.

In addition to requiring collateral, creditors often obtain additional protection by including **restrictive covenants** in loan agreements. Such covenants may restrict additional borrowing, limit dividend payments, or restrict salary increases. If the loan restrictions are violated, the borrower is in default and the loan balance is due immediately.

Finally, creditors often ask key personnel to provide copies of their personal tax returns and financial statements. The financial condition of key executives is important because they may be asked to pledge personal property as collateral for business loans, particularly for small businesses.

CURRENT VERSUS NONCURRENT

Because meeting obligations on time is critical to business survival, financial analysts and creditors are interested in whether companies will have enough money available to pay bills when they are due. Most businesses provide information about their bill-paying ability by classifying their assets and liabilities according to liquidity. The more quickly an asset is converted to cash or consumed, the more *liquid* it is. Assets are usually divided into two major classifications: *current* and *noncurrent*. Current items are also referred to as *short term* and noncurrent items as *long term*.

A **current (short-term) asset** is expected to be converted to cash or consumed within one year or an operating cycle, whichever is longer. An **operating cycle** is defined as the average time it takes a business to convert cash to inventory, inventory to accounts receivable, and accounts receivable back to cash. For most businesses, the operating cycle is less than one year. As a result, the one-year rule normally prevails with respect to classifying assets as current. The current assets section of a balance sheet typically includes the following items:

LO 7-10

Distinguish between current and noncurrent assets and liabilities on a classified balance sheet.

```
Current Assets
    Cash
    Marketable securities
    Accounts receivable
    Short-term notes receivable
    Interest receivable
    Inventory
    Supplies
    Prepaid items
```

Given the definition of current assets, it seems reasonable to assume that **current (short-term) liabilities** would be those due within one year or an operating cycle, whichever is longer. This assumption is usually correct. However, an exception is made for long-term renewable debt. For example, consider a liability that was issued with a 20-year term to maturity. After 19 years, the liability becomes due within one year and is, therefore, a current liability. Even so, the liability will be classified as long term if the company plans to issue new long-term debt and to use the proceeds from that debt to repay the maturing liability. This situation is described as *refinancing short-term debt on a long-term basis*. In general, if a business does not plan to use any of its current assets to repay a debt, that debt is listed as long term even if it is due within one year. The current liabilities section of a balance sheet typically includes the following items:

> Current Liabilities
>   Accounts payable
>   Short-term notes payable
>   Wages payable
>   Taxes payable
>   Interest payable

Balance sheets that distinguish between current and noncurrent items are called **classified balance sheets**. To enhance the usefulness of accounting information, most real-world balance sheets are classified. Exhibit 7.11 displays an example of a classified balance sheet.

EXHIBIT 7.11

LIMBAUGH COMPANY
Classified Balance Sheet
As of December 31, Year 1

Assets

Current Assets		
Cash	$ 20,000	
Accounts receivable	35,000	
Inventory	230,000	
Prepaid rent	3,600	
Total current assets		$288,600
Property, Plant, and Equipment		
Office equipment	$ 80,000	
Less: Accumulated depreciation	(25,000)	55,000
Building	340,000	
Less: Accumulated depreciation	(40,000)	300,000
Land		120,000
Total property, plant, and equipment		475,000
Total assets		$763,600

Liabilities and Stockholders' Equity

Current Liabilities		
Accounts payable	$ 32,000	
Notes payable	120,000	
Salaries payable	32,000	
Unearned revenue	9,800	
Total current liabilities		$193,800
Long-Term Liabilities		
Note payable		100,000
Total liabilities		293,800
Stockholders' Equity		
Common stock	200,000	
Retained earnings	269,800	469,800
Total liabilities and stockholders' equity		$763,600

FOCUS ON INTERNATIONAL ISSUES

WHY ARE THESE BALANCE SHEETS BACKWARD?

As discussed in earlier chapters, most industrialized countries require companies to use international financial accounting standards (IFRS), which are similar to the GAAP used in the United States. The globalization of accounting standards should, therefore, make it easier to read a company's annual report regardless of its country or origin. However, there are still language differences between companies; German companies prepare their financial reports using IFRS, but in German, while the UK companies use English.

Suppose language is not an issue. For example, companies in the United States, England, and even India prepare their annual reports in English. Thus, one would expect to find few differences between financial reports prepared by companies in these countries. However, if a person who learned accounting in the United States looks at the balance sheet of a UK company he or she might think the statement is a bit "backward," and if he or she reviews the balance sheet of an Indian company the person may find it to be upside down.

Like U.S. companies, UK companies report assets at the top, or left, of the balance sheet, and liabilities and stockholders' equity on the bottom or right. However, unlike the United States, UK companies typically show long-term assets before current assets. Even more different are balance sheets of Indian companies, which begin with stockholders' equity and liabilities at the top or left, and then show assets on the bottom or right. Like the UK statements, those in India show long-term assets before current assets. Realize that most of the accounting rules established by IFRS or U.S. GAAP deal with measurement issues. Assets can be measured using the same rules but be disclosed in different manners. IFRS require companies to classify assets and liabilities as current versus noncurrent, but the order in which these categories are listed on the balance sheet is not specified.

Kevin Burke/Passage
Unreleased/Getty Images

For an example of a financial statement for a UK company, go to www.itvplc.com. Click on "Investors" and then "Annual Report." For an example of an Indian company's annual report, go to www.colgate.co.in. Click on "For Investors" and then "Annual Report."

A Look Back

Chapter 7 discussed accounting for current liabilities and long-term debt. Current liabilities are obligations due within one year or the company's operating cycle, whichever is longer. The chapter expanded the discussion of promissory notes begun in Chapter 5. Chapter 5 introduced accounting for the note payee, the lender; Chapter 7 discussed accounting for the note maker (issuer), the borrower. Notes payable and related interest payable are reported as liabilities on the balance sheet. Chapter 7 also discussed accounting for the contingent liability and warranty obligations.

Long-term notes payable mature in two to five years and usually require payments that include a return of principal plus interest. *Lines of credit* enable companies to borrow limited amounts on an as-needed basis. Although lines of credit normally have one-year terms, companies frequently renew them, extending the effective maturity date to the intermediate range of five or more years. Interest on a line of credit is normally paid monthly. Long-term debt financing for more than 10 years usually requires issuing *bonds*.

A Look Forward

A company seeking long-term financing might choose to use debt, such as the types of bonds or term loans that were discussed in this chapter. Owners' equity is another source of long-term financing. Several equity alternatives are available, depending on the type of business organization the owners choose to establish. For example, a company could be organized as a sole proprietorship, partnership, or corporation. Chapter 8 presents accounting issues related to equity transactions for each of these types of business structures.

APPENDIX

Amortization of a Discount Using the Effective Interest Rate

LO 7-11

Using the effective interest rate method show how bonds issued at a discount affect financial statements.

To this point we have demonstrated the straight-line method for amortizing bond discounts and premiums. While this method is easy to understand, it is inaccurate because it does not show the correct amount of interest expense incurred during each accounting period. To illustrate, return to the case of Mason Company demonstrated in Exhibit 7.10. Recall that the exhibit shows the effects of accounting for a $100,000 face value bond with a 9 percent stated rate of interest that was issued at a price of 95. The carrying value of the bond liability on the January 1, Year 1, issue date was $95,000. The bond discount was amortized using the straight-line method.

Recall that the straight-line method amortizes the discount equally over the life of the bond. Specifically, there is a $5,000 discount that is amortized over a five-year life resulting in a $1,000 amortization per year. As the discount is amortized the bond liability (carrying value of the bond) increases. The carrying value of the bond liability shown in Exhibit 7.10 increases as follows.

Accounting Period	Year 1	Year 2	Year 3	Year 4
Carrying value as of December 31	$96,000	$97,000	$98,000	$99,000

While the carrying value of the bond liability increases steadily, the straight-line method recognizes the same amount of interest expense ($9,000 stated rate of interest + $1,000 discount amortization = $10,000 interest expense) per year. This straight-line recognition pattern is irrational because the amount of interest expense recognized should increase as the carrying value of the bond liability increases. A more accurate recognition pattern can be accomplished by using an approach called the **effective interest rate method**.

Amortizing Bond Discounts

The effective interest rate is determined by the price that the buyer of a bond is willing to pay on the issue date. In the case of Mason Company the issue price of $95,000 for bonds with a $100,000 face value, a 9 percent stated rate of interest, and a five-year term produces an effective interest rate of approximately 10.33 percent.[6] Since the effective interest rate is based on the market price of the bonds on the day of issue, it is sometimes called *the market rate of interest.*

Interest recognition under the effective interest method is accomplished as follows:

1. Determine the cash payment for interest by multiplying the stated rate of interest times the face value of the bonds.

2. Determine the amount of interest expense by multiplying the effective rate of interest times the carrying value of the bond liability.

---

[6]In practice the effective rate of interest is calculated using software programs, interest formulas, or interest tables.

EXHIBIT 7.12

Amortization Schedule for Bond Discount

	(A) Cash Payment	(B) Interest Expense	(C) Discount Amortization	(D) Carrying Value
January 1, Year 1				$ 95,000
December 31, Year 1	$ 9,000	$ 9,814	$ 814	95,814
December 31, Year 2	9,000	9,898	898	96,712
December 31, Year 3	9,000	9,990	990	97,702
December 31, Year 4	9,000	10,093	1,093	98,795
December 31, Year 5	9,000	10,205	1,205	100,000
Totals	$45,000	$50,000	$5,000	

(A) Stated rate of interest times the face value of the bonds ($100,000 × 0.09).
(B) Effective interest rate times the carrying value at the beginning of the period. For the Year 1 accounting period the amount is $9,814 ($95,000 × 0.1033).
(C) Interest Expense − Cash Payment. For Year 1 the discount amortization is $814 ($9,814 − $9,000 = $814).
(D) Carrying value at beginning of period plus portion of discount amortized. For the accounting period ending December 31, Year 1, the amount is $95,814 ($95,000 + $814).

3. Determine the amount of the amortization of the bond discount by subtracting the cash payment from the interest expense.
4. Update the carrying value of the liability by adding the amount of the discount amortization to the amount of the carrying value at the beginning of the accounting period.

Applying these procedures to the Mason Company illustration produces the amortization schedule shown in Exhibit 7.12.

The recognition of interest expense at the end of each accounting period has the following effects on the financial statements. On the balance sheet, assets decrease, liabilities increase, and retained earnings decrease. On the income statement, expenses increase and net income decreases. There is a cash outflow in the operating activities of the statement of cash flows. The effects on the financial statements are shown here.

Balance Sheet						Income Statement			Statement of Cash Flows
Assets	=	Liabilities	+	Stk. Equity					
Cash	=	Carrying Value of Bond Liab.	+	Ret. Earn.	Rev.	−	Exp.	= Net Inc.	
(9,000)	=	814	+	(9,814)	NA	−	9,814	= (9,814)	(9,000) OA

Exhibit 7.13 shows the financial statements for Mason Company for Year 1 through Year 5. The statements assume the same events as described as those used to construct Exhibit 7.10. These events are summarized as follows.

1. Mason issues a $100,000 face value bond with a 9 percent stated rate of interest. The bond has a 5-year term and is issued at a price of 95. Annual interest is paid with cash on December 31 of each year.
2. Mason uses the proceeds from the bond issue to purchase land.
3. Leasing the land produces rent revenue of $11,400 cash per year.
4. On the maturity date of the bond, the land is sold and the proceeds from the sale are used to repay the bond liability.

EXHIBIT 7.13

Financial Statements

Under the Assumption That Bonds Are Issued at a Discount

	Year 1	Year 2	Year 3	Year 4	Year 5
Income Statements					
Rent revenue	$ 11,400	$ 11,400	$ 11,400	$ 11,400	$ 11,400
Interest expense	(9,814)	(9,898)	(9,990)	(10,093)	(10,205)
Net income	$ 1,586	$ 1,502	$ 1,410	$ 1,307	$ 1,195
Balance Sheets					
Assets:					
Cash	$ 2,400	$ 4,800	$ 7,200	$ 9,600	$ 7,000
Land	95,000	95,000	95,000	95,000	
Total assets	$ 97,400	$ 99,800	$102,200	$104,600	$ 7,000
Liabilities					
Bond payable	$100,000	$100,000	$100,000	$100,000	$ 0
Discount on bonds payable	(4,186)	(3,288)	(2,298)	(1,205)	0
Carrying value of bond liab.	95,814	96,712	97,702	98,795	0
Stockholders' Equity					
Retained earnings	1,586	3,088	4,498	5,805	7,000
Total liabilities and stk. equity	$ 97,400	$ 99,800	$102,200	$104,600	$ 7,000
Statements of Cash Flows					
Operating Activities					
Inflow from customers	$ 11,400	$ 11,400	$ 11,400	$ 11,400	$ 11,400
Outflow for interest	(9,000)	(9,000)	(9,000)	(9,000)	(14,000)
Investing Activities					
Outflow to purchase land	(95,000)				
Inflow from sale of land					95,000
Financing Activities					
Inflow from bond issue	95,000				
Outflow to repay bond liab.					(95,000)
Net change in cash	2,400	2,400	2,400	2,400	(2,600)
Beginning cash balance	0	2,400	4,800	7,200	9,600
Ending cash balance	$ 2,400	$ 4,800	$ 7,200	$ 9,600	$ 7,000

The only difference between the two exhibits is that Exhibit 7.10 was constructed assuming that the bond discount was amortized using the straight-line method while Exhibit 7.13 assumes that the discount was amortized using the effective interest rate method.

Notice that interest expense under the effective interest rate method (Exhibit 7.13) increases each year while interest expense under the straight-line method (Exhibit 7.10) remains constant for all years. This result occurs because the effective interest rate method amortizes increasingly larger amounts of the discount (see Column C of Exhibit 7.12) as the carrying value of the bond liability increases. In contrast, the straight-line method amortized the bond discount at a constant rate of $1,000 per year over the life of the bond. Even so, total amount of interest expense recognized over the life of the bond is the same ($50,000) under both methods. Since the effective interest rate method matches the interest expense with the carrying value of the bond liability, it is the theoretically preferred approach. Indeed, accounting standards require the use of the effective interest rate method when the differences between it and the straight-line method are material.

The amortization of the discount affects the carrying value of the bond as well as the amount of interest expense. Under the effective interest method the rate of growth of the carrying value of the bond increases as the maturity date approaches. In contrast, under the straight-line method the rate of growth of the carrying value of the bond remains constant at $1,000 per year throughout the life of the bond.

Finally, notice that cash flow is not affected by the method of amortization. The exact same cash flow consequences occur under both the straight-line (Exhibit 7.10) and the effective interest rate method (Exhibit 7.13).

AMORTIZATION OF A PREMIUM USING THE EFFECTIVE INTEREST RATE

Bond premiums can also be amortized using the effective interest rate method. To illustrate, assume United Company issued a $100,000 face value bond with a 10 percent stated rate of interest. The bond had a 5-year term. The bond was issued at a price of $107,985. The effective rate of interest is 8 percent. United's accountant prepared the amortization schedule shown in Exhibit 7.14.

The recognition of interest expense at the end of each accounting period has the following effects on the financial statements. On the balance sheet assets decrease, liabilities decrease, and retained earnings decrease. On the income statement expenses increase and net income decreases. There is a cash outflow in the operating activities of the statement of cash flows. The effects on the financial statements are shown here.

LO 7-12

Using the effective interest rate method show how bonds issued at a premium affect financial statements.

Balance Sheet				Income Statement				Statement of Cash Flows
Assets	=	Liabilities	+ Stk. Equity					
Cash	=	Carrying Value of Bond Liab.	+ Ret. Earn.	Rev.	− Exp.	= Net Inc.		
								(8,639) OA
(10,000)	=	(1,361)	+ (8,639)	NA	− 8,639	= (8,639)		(1,361) FA

EXHIBIT 7.14

Amortization Schedule for Bond Premium

	(A) Cash Payment	(B) Interest Expense	(C) Premium Amortization	(D) Carrying Value
January 1, Year 1				$107,985
December 31, Year 1	$ 10,000	$ 8,639	$1,361	106,624
December 31, Year 2	10,000	8,530	1,470	105,154
December 31, Year 3	10,000	8,413	1,587	103,567
December 31, Year 4	10,000	8,285	1,715	101,852
December 31, Year 5	10,000	8,148	1,852	100,000
Totals	$50,000	$42,015	$7,985	

(A) Stated rate of interest times the face value of the bonds ($100,000 × 0.10).

(B) Effective interest times the carrying value at the beginning of the period. For the Year 1 accounting period the amount is $8,639 ($107,985 × 0.08).

(C) Cash Payment − Interest Expense. For Year 1 the premium amortization is $1,361 ($10,000 − $8,639 = $1,361).

(D) Carrying value at beginning of period minus the portion of premium amortized. For the accounting period ending December 31, Year 1, the amount is $106,624 ($107,985 − 1,361).

Video lectures and accompanying self-assessment quizzes are available in *Connect* for all learning objectives.

SELF-STUDY REVIEW PROBLEM

Perfect Picture Inc. (PPI) experienced the following transactions during Year 2. The transactions are summarized (transaction data pertain to the full year) and limited to those that affect the company's current liabilities.

1. PPI had cash sales of $820,000. The state requires that PPI charge customers an 8 percent sales tax (ignore cost of goods sold).
2. PPI paid the state sales tax authority $63,000.
3. On March 1, PPI issued a note payable to the County Bank. PPI received $50,000 cash (principal balance). The note had a one-year term and a 6 percent annual interest rate.
4. On December 31, PPI recognized accrued interest on the note issued in Event 3.
5. On December 31, PPI recognized warranty expense at the rate of 3 percent of sales.
6. PPI paid $22,000 cash to settle warranty claims.
7. On January 1, Year 1, PPI issued a $100,000 installment note. The note had a 10-year term and an 8 percent interest rate. PPI agreed to repay the principal and interest in 10 annual interest payments of $14,902.94 at the end of each year. While the note was issued in Year 1, the effects of interest appear in the Year 2 balance sheet.

Required

Prepare the liabilities section of the December 31, Year 2, balance sheet.

Solution

PERFECT PICTURE INC.	
Partial Balance Sheet	
December 31, Year 2	
Current Liabilities	
Sales tax payable	$ 2,600
Notes payable	50,000
Interest payable	2,500
Warranties payable	2,600
Installment note payable	85,642
Total liabilities	$143,342

Explanations for amounts shown in the balance sheet:

1. Sales Tax Payable: $820,000 × 0.08 = $65,600 Amount Due − $63,000 Amount Paid = $2,600 Liability as of December 31, Year 2.
2. Note Payable: $50,000 Borrowed with no repayment.
3. Interest Payable: $50,000 × 0.06 × 10/12 = $2,500.
4. Warranty Payable: $820,000 × 0.03 = $24,600 Estimated Warranty Liability − $22,000 Cash Paid to Settle Warranty Claims = $2,600 Remaining Liability.
5. Installment Note Payable:

Accounting Period	Principal Bal. January 1 A	Cash Payment December 31 B	Applied to Interest $C = A \times 0.08$	Applied to Principal B − C
Year 1	$100,000.00	$14,902.94	$8,000.00	$6,902.94
Year 2	93,097.06	14,902.94	7,447.76	7,455.18
Year 3*	85,641.88			

*The amount due on December 31, Year 2, is the same as the amount due on January 1, Year 3. The amount shown on the balance sheet has been rounded to the nearest dollar.

KEY TERMS

Amortization 254
Bond certificate 258
Bond discount 262
Bond premium 266
Bondholder 258
Carrying value 263
Classified balance sheet 268
Collateral 267
Contingent liability 250

Current (short-term)
  asset 267
Current (short-term)
  liability 267
Discount on bonds
  payable 262
Effective interest
  rate 262
Effective interest rate
  method 270

Face value 258
Fixed interest rate 253
General uncertainties 250
Installment note 254
Issuer 258
Line of credit 257
Long-term liabilities 253
Market rate of
  interest 266
Note payable 248

Operating cycle 267
Premium on bonds
  payable 266
Restrictive covenants 267
Stated interest rate 258
Straight-line
  amortization 263
Variable interest rate 253
Warranties 251

QUESTIONS

1. What type of transaction is a cash payment to creditors? How does this type of transaction affect the accounting equation?

2. What is a current liability? Distinguish between a current liability and a long-term debt.

3. How does recording accrued interest affect the accounting equation?

4. Who is the maker of a note payable?

5. How does the going concern assumption discussed in Chapter 1 affect the way liabilities are reported in the financial statements?

6. Why is it necessary to make an adjustment at the end of the accounting period for unpaid interest on a note payable?

7. Assume that on October 1, Year 1 Big Company borrowed $10,000 from the local bank at 6 percent interest. The note is due on October 1, Year 2. How much interest does Big pay in Year 1? How much interest does Big pay in Year 2? What amount of cash does Big pay back in Year 2?

8. When a business collects sales tax from customers, is it revenue? Why or why not?

9. What is a contingent liability?

10. List the three categories of contingent liabilities.

11. Are contingent liabilities recorded on a company's books? Explain.

12. What is the difference in accounting procedures for a liability that is probable and estimable and one that is reasonably possible but not estimable?

13. What type of liabilities are not recorded on a company's books?

14. What does the term *warranty* mean?

15. What effect does recognizing future warranty obligations have on the balance sheet? On the income statement?

16. When is warranty cost reported on the statement of cash flows?

17. What is the difference between classification of a note as short term or long term?

18. At the beginning of year 1, B Co. has a note payable of $72,000 that calls for an annual payment of $16,246, which includes both principal and interest. If the interest

rate is 8 percent, what is the amount of interest expense in year 1 and in year 2? What is the balance of the note at the end of year 2?

19. What is the purpose of a line of credit for a business? Why would a company choose to obtain a line of credit instead of issuing bonds?

20. What are the primary sources of debt financing for most large companies?

21. What are some advantages of issuing bonds versus borrowing from a bank?

22. What are some disadvantages of issuing bonds?

23. Why can a company usually issue bonds at a lower interest rate than the company would pay if the funds were borrowed from a bank?

24. If Roc Co. issued $100,000 of 5 percent, 10-year bonds at the face amount, what is the effect of the issuance of the bonds on the financial statements? What amount of interest expense will Roc Co. recognize each year?

25. What mechanism is used to adjust the stated interest

rate to the market rate of interest?

26. When the effective interest rate is higher than the stated interest rate on a bond issue, will the bond sell at a discount or premium? Why?

27. What type of transaction is the issuance of bonds by a company?

28. What factors may cause the effective interest rate and the stated interest rate to be different?

29. If a bond is selling at 97½, how much cash will the company receive from the sale of a $1,000 bond?

30. How is the carrying value of a bond computed?

31. Gay Co. has a balance in the Bonds Payable account of $25,000 and a balance in the Discount on Bonds Payable account of $5,200. What is the carrying value of the bonds? What is the total amount of the liability?

32. When the effective interest rate is higher than the stated interest rate, will interest expense be higher or lower than the amount of interest paid?

33. What is a classified balance sheet?

EXERCISES—SERIES A

LO 7-1

Exercise 7-1A   *Recognizing accrued interest expense*

Abardeen Corporation borrowed $90,000 from the bank on October 1, Year 1. The note had an 8 percent annual rate of interest and matured on March 31, Year 2. Interest and principal were paid in cash on the maturity date.

Required

a. What amount of cash did Abardeen pay for interest in Year 1?
b. What amount of interest expense was recognized on the Year 1 income statement?
c. What amount of total liabilities was reported on the December 31, Year 1, balance sheet?
d. What total amount of cash was paid to the bank on March 31, Year 2, for principal and interest?
e. What amount of interest expense was reported on the Year 2 income statement?

LO 7-1

Exercise 7-2A   *Effects of recognizing accrued interest on financial statements*

Bill Darby started Darby Company on January 1, Year 1. The company experienced the following events during its first year of operation:

1. Earned $16,200 of cash revenue.
2. Borrowed $12,000 cash from the bank.
3. Adjusted the accounting records to recognize accrued interest expense on the bank note. The note, issued on September 1, Year 1, had a one-year term and an 8 percent annual interest rate.

Required

a. What is the amount of interest expense in Year 1?
b. What amount of cash was paid for interest in Year 1?
c. Use a horizontal statements model to show how each event affects the balance sheet, income statement, and statement of cash flows. Indicate whether the event increases (I), decreases (D), or does not affect (NA) each element of the financial statements. In the Cash Flows column, designate the cash flows as operating activities (OA), investing activities (IA), or financing activities (FA). The first transaction has been recorded as an example.

Event No.	Cash	=	Notes Pay.	+	Int. Pay.	+	Com. Stk.	+	Ret. Earn.	Rev.	−	Exp.	=	Net Inc.	Statement of Cash Flows
1	I	=	NA	+	NA	+	NA	+	I	I	−	NA	=	I	I OA

LO 7-2

Exercise 7-3A   *Recording sales tax*

Vail Book Mart sells books and other supplies to students in a state where the sales tax rate is 8 percent. Vail engaged in the following transactions during the year. Sales tax of 8 percent is collected on all sales.

1. Book sales, not including sales tax, for the year amounted to $250,000 cash.
2. Cash sales of miscellaneous items for the year were $85,000, not including tax.
3. Cost of goods sold was $190,000 for the year.
4. Paid $117,000 in operating expenses for the year.
5. Paid the sales tax collected to the state agency.

Required

a. What is the total amount of sales tax Vail Book Mart collected and paid for the year?
b. What is the Vail Book Mart's net income for the year?

Exercise 7-4A   *Recognizing sales tax payable*   LO 7-2

The following selected transactions apply to Topeca Supply for November and December, Year 1. November was the first month of operations. Sales tax is collected at the time of sale but is not paid to the state sales tax agency until the following month.

1. Cash sales for November, Year 1 were $165,000 plus sales tax of 7 percent.
2. Topeca Supply paid the November sales tax to the state agency on December 10, Year 1.
3. Cash sales for December, Year 1 were $180,000 plus sales tax of 7 percent.

Required

a. Show the effect of the above transactions on a statements model like the one shown as follows.

Balance Sheet							Income Statement				Statement of Cash Flows
Assets	=	Liabilities	+		Stk. Equity						
Cash	=	Sales Tax Pay.	+	Com. Stk.	+	Ret. Earn.	Rev.	−	Exp.	=	Net Inc.	

b. What was the total amount of sales tax paid in Year 1?
c. What was the total amount of sales tax collected in Year 1?
d. What is the amount of the sales tax liability as of December 31, Year 1?
e. On which financial statement will the sales tax liability appear?

Exercise 7-5A   *Contingent liabilities*   LO 7-3

The following three independent sets of facts relate to contingent liabilities:

1. In November of the current year an automobile manufacturing company recalled all pickup trucks manufactured during the past two years. A flaw in the battery cable was discovered and the recall provides for replacement of the defective cables. The estimated cost of this recall is $2 million.
2. The EPA has notified a company of violations of environmental laws relating to hazardous waste. These actions seek cleanup costs, penalties, and damages to property. The company is reasonably certain there will be cost associated with the cleanup, but cannot estimate the amount. The cleanup cost could be as high as $4,000,000 or as little as $500,000 and insurance could reimburse all or part of the cost. There is no way to more accurately estimate the cost to the company at this time.
3. Holland Company does not carry property damage insurance because of the cost. The company has suffered substantial losses each of the past three years. However, it has had no losses for the current year. Management thinks this is too good to be true and is sure there will be significant losses in the coming year. However, the exact amount cannot be determined.

Required

a. Discuss the various categories of contingent liabilities.
b. For each item given determine the correct accounting treatment.

Exercise 7-6A   *Effect of warranties on income and cash flow*   LO 7-4

To support herself while attending school, Daun Deloch sold stereo systems to other students. During the first year of operations, Deloch purchased the stereo systems for $140,000 and sold them for $250,000 cash. She provided her customers with a one-year warranty against defects in parts and labor. Based on industry standards, she estimated that warranty claims would amount to 2 percent of sales. During the year she paid $2,820 cash to replace a defective tuner.

Required

a. Prepare an income statement and a statement of cash flows for Deloch's first year of operation.
b. Explain the difference between net income and the amount of cash flow from operating activities.

Exercise 7-7A   *Effect of warranty obligations and payments on financial statements*   LO 7-4

The Chair Company provides a 120-day parts-and-labor warranty on all merchandise it sells. The Chair Company estimates the warranty expense for the current period to be $2,650. During the period a customer returned a product that cost $1,830 to repair.

Required

a. Show the effects of these transactions on the financial statements using a horizontal statements model like the example shown here. Use a + to indicate increase, a − for decrease, and NA for not affected. In the Cash Flow column, indicate whether the item is an operating activity (OA), investing activity (IA), or financing activity (FA).

Balance Sheet					Income Statement			Statement of Cash Flows
Assets	=	Liab.	+	Equity	Rev.	−	Exp.	=	Net Inc.	

b. Discuss the advantage of estimating the amount of warranty expense.

LO 7-1, 7-5

Exercise 7-8A   *Principle due at maturity versus installments*

Sanders Co. is planning to finance an expansion of its operations by borrowing $150,000. City Bank has agreed to loan Sanders the funds. Sanders has two repayment options: (1) to issue a note with the principal due in 10 years and with interest payable annually or (2) to issue a note to repay $15,000 of the principal each year along with the annual interest based on the unpaid principal balance. Assume the interest rate is 8 percent for each option.

Required

a. What amount of interest will Sanders pay in Year 1
   (1) Under option 1?
   (2) Under option 2?
b. What amount of interest will Sanders pay in Year 2
   (1) Under option 1?
   (2) Under option 2?
c. Explain the advantage of each option.

LO 7-5

Exercise 7-9A   *Financial statement effects of an installment note*

Dan Dayle started a business by issuing an $80,000 face value note to First State Bank on January 1, Year 1. The note had an 8 percent annual rate of interest and a five-year term. Payments of $20,037 are to be made each December 31 for five years. Round answers to nearest whole dollar.

Required

a. What portion of the December 31, Year 1, payment is applied to
   (1) Interest expense?
   (2) Principal?
b. What is the principal balance on January 1, Year 2?
c. What portion of the December 31, Year 2, payment is applied to
   (1) Interest expense?
   (2) Principal?

LO 7-5

Exercise 7-10A   *Amortization of a long-term loan*

A partial amortization schedule for a 10-year note payable that Mabry Company issued on January 1, Year 1, is shown as follows.

Accounting Period	Principal Balance January 1	Cash Payment	Applied to Interest	Applied to Principal
Year 1	$200,000	$27,174	$12,000	$15,174
Year 2	184,826	27,174	11,090	16,084
Year 3	168,742	27,174	10,125	17,049

Required

a. What rate of interest is Mabry Company paying on the note?

b. Using a financial statements model like the one shown, record the appropriate amounts for the following two events:

(1) January 1, Year 1, issue of the note payable.

(2) December 31, Year 1, payment on the note payable.

Event No.	Balance Sheet					Income Statement				Statement of Cash Flows
	Assets	=	Liab.	+	Stk. Equity	Rev.	−	Exp.	= Net Inc.	
1										

c. If the company earned $62,000 cash revenue and paid $45,000 in cash expenses in addition to the interest in Year 1, what is the amount of each of the following?

(1) Net income for Year 1.

(2) Cash flow from operating activities for Year 1.

(3) Cash flow from financing activities for Year 1.

d. What is the amount of interest expense on this loan for Year 4?

Exercise 7-11A   *Accounting for a line of credit*

Colson Company has a line of credit with Federal Bank. Colson can borrow up to $800,000 at any time over the course of the calendar year. The following table shows the prime rate expressed as an annual percentage along with the amounts borrowed and repaid during the first four months of the year. Colson agreed to pay interest at an annual rate equal to 2 percent above the bank's prime rate. Funds are borrowed or repaid on the first day of each month. Interest is payable in cash on the last day of the month. The interest rate is applied to the outstanding monthly balance. For example, Colson pays 6 percent (4 percent + 2 percent) annual interest on $80,000 for the month of January.

Month	Amount Borrowed or (Repaid)	Prime Rate for the Month
January	$80,000	4.0%
February	50,000	4.25
March	(30,000)	4.5
April	20,000	4.25

Required

a. Compute the amount of interest that Colson will pay on the line of credit for the first four months of the year. Round answers to nearest whole dollar.

b. Compute the amount of Colson's liability at the end of each of the first four months.

Exercise 7-12A   *Effect of a line of credit on financial statements*

Boyd Company has a line of credit with State Bank. Boyd can borrow up to $400,000 at any time over the course of the calendar year. The following table shows the prime rate expressed as an annual percentage along with the amounts borrowed and repaid during the year. Boyd agreed to pay interest at an annual rate equal to 2 percent above the bank's prime rate. Funds are borrowed or repaid on the first day of each month. Interest is payable in cash on the last day of the month. The interest rate is applied to the outstanding monthly balance. For example, Boyd pays 7 percent (5 percent + 2 percent) annual interest on $100,000 for the month of January.

Month	Amount Borrowed or (Repaid)	Prime Rate for the Month
January	$100,000	5%
February	70,000	6
March	(30,000)	7
April through October	No change	No change
November	(50,000)	6
December	(40,000)	5

Boyd earned $45,000 of cash revenue during the year.

Required

Show the effects of these transactions on the financial statements using a horizontal statements model like the one shown here. Use a + to indicate increase, a − for decrease, and NA for not affected. In the Cash Flow column, indicate whether the item is an operating activity (OA), investing activity (IA), or financing activity (FA).

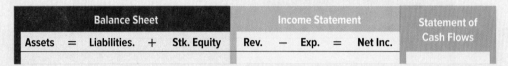

What is the total amount of interest expense paid for the year? Round answers to nearest whole dollar.

LO 7-7

Exercise 7-13A   Two complete accounting cycles: Bonds issued at face value with annual interest

Doyle Company issued $500,000 of 10-year, 7 percent bonds on January 1, Year 1. The bonds were issued at face value. Interest is payable in cash on December 31 of each year. Doyle immediately invested the proceeds from the bond issue in land. The land was leased for an annual $125,000 of cash revenue, which was collected on December 31 of each year, beginning December 31, Year 1.

Required

a. Organize the transaction data in accounts under the accounting equation for Year 1 and Year 2.
b. Prepare the income statement, balance sheet, and statement of cash flows for Year 1 and Year 2.

LO 7-7

Exercise 7-14A   Annual versus semiannual interest for bonds issued at face value

Milan Company issued bonds with a face value of $200,000 on January 1, Year 1. The bonds had a 7 percent stated rate of interest and a six-year term. The bonds were issued at face value. Interest is payable on an annual basis.

Required

a. What total amount of interest will Milan Company pay in Year 1 if bond interest is paid annually each December 31?
b. What total amount of interest will Milan Company pay in Year 1 if bond interest is paid semiannually each June 30 and December 31?
c. Write a memo explaining which option Milan would prefer.

LO 7-8

Exercise 7-15A   Straight-line amortization of a bond discount

Diaz Company issued $180,000 face value of bonds on January 1, Year 1. The bonds had a 7 percent stated rate of interest and a five-year term. Interest is paid in cash annually, beginning December 31, Year 1. The bonds were issued at 98. The straight-line method is used for amortization.

Required

a. Use a financial statements model like the following one to demonstrate how (1) the January 1, Year 1, bond issue and (2) the December 31, Year 1, recognition of interest expense, including the amortization of the discount and the cash payment, affect the company's financial statements. Use + for increase, − for decrease, and NA for not affected.

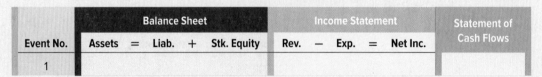

b. Determine the carrying value (face value less discount or plus premium) of the bond liability as of December 31, Year 1.
c. Determine the amount of interest expense reported on the Year 1 income statement.
d. Determine the carrying value (face value less discount or plus premium) of the bond liability as of December 31, Year 2.
e. Determine the amount of interest expense reported on the Year 2 income statement.

Exercise 7-16A *Stated rate of interest versus the market rate of interest*   LO 7-7, 7-8, 7-9

Required

Indicate whether a bond will sell at a premium (P), discount (D), or face value (F) for each of the following conditions.

a. _____ The stated rate of interest is higher than the market rate.
b. _____ The market rate of interest is equal to the stated rate.
c. _____ The market rate of interest is less than the stated rate.
d. _____ The stated rate of interest is less than the market rate.
e. _____ The market rate of interest is higher than the stated rate.

Exercise 7-17A *Determining cash receipts from bond issues*   LO 7-8, 7-9

Required

Compute the cash proceeds from bond issues under the following terms. For each case, indicate whether the bonds sold at a premium or discount.

a. Pear, Inc. issued $400,000 of 10-year, 8 percent bonds at 103.
b. Apple, Inc. issued $200,000 of five-year, 12 percent bonds at 97½.
c. Cherry Co. issued $100,000 of five-year, 6 percent bonds at 102¼.
d. Grape, Inc. issued $120,000 of four-year, 8 percent bonds at 96.

Exercise 7-18A *Determining the amount of bond premiums and discounts*   LO 7-8, 7-9

Required

For each of the following situations, calculate the amount of bond discount or premium, if any.

a. Gray Co. issued $80,000 of 6 percent bonds at 101¼.
b. Bush, Inc. issued $200,000 of 10-year, 6 percent bonds at 97½.
c. Oak, Inc. issued $100,000 of 20-year, 6 percent bonds at 103.
d. Willow Co. issued $180,000 of 15-year, 7 percent bonds at 99.

Exercise 7-19A *Identifying bond premiums and discounts*   LO 7-8, 7-9

Required

In each of the following situations, state whether the bonds will sell at a premium or discount.

a. Valley issued $300,000 of bonds with a stated interest rate of 7 percent. At the time of issue, the market rate of interest for similar investments was 6 percent.
b. Spring issued $220,000 of bonds with a stated interest rate of 5 percent. At the time of issue, the market rate of interest for similar investments was 6 percent.
c. River Inc. issued $150,000 of callable bonds with a stated interest rate of 5 percent. The bonds were callable at 102. At the date of issue, the market rate of interest was 6 percent for similar investments.

Exercise 7-20A *Straight-line amortization of a bond premium*   LO 7-9

The Square Foot Grill, Inc. issued $200,000 of 10-year, 6 percent bonds on January 1, Year 1, at 102. Interest is payable in cash annually on December 31. The straight-line method is used for amortization.

Required

a. Use a financial statements model like the following one to demonstrate how (1) the January 1, Year 1, bond issue and (2) the December 31, Year 1, recognition of interest expense, including the amortization of the premium and the cash payment, affects the company's financial statements. Use + for increase, − for decrease, and NA for not affected.

Event	Balance Sheet					Income Statement				Statement of
No.	Assets	=	Liab.	+	Equity	Rev.	−	Exp.	= Net Inc.	Cash Flows
1										

b. Determine the carrying value (face value less discount or plus premium) of the bond liability as of December 31, Year 1.

c. Determine the amount of interest expense reported on the Year 1 income statement.

d. Determine the carrying value of the bond liability as of December 31, Year 2.

e. Determine the amount of interest expense reported on the Year 2 income statement.

LO 7-1, 7-2, 7-4, 7-10

Exercise 7-21A *Current liabilities*

The following transactions apply to Ozark Sales for Year 1:

1. The business was started when the company received $50,000 from the issue of common stock.
2. Purchased equipment inventory of $380,000 on account.
3. Sold equipment for $510,000 cash (not including sales tax). Sales tax of 8 percent is collected when the merchandise is sold. The merchandise had a cost of $330,000.
4. Provided a six-month warranty on the equipment sold. Based on industry estimates, the warranty claims would amount to 2 percent of sales.
5. Paid the sales tax to the state agency on $400,000 of the sales.
6. On September 1, Year 1, borrowed $50,000 from the local bank. The note had a 4 percent interest rate and matured on March 1, Year 2.
7. Paid $6,200 for warranty repairs during the year.
8. Paid operating expenses of $78,000 for the year.
9. Paid $250,000 of accounts payable.
10. Recorded accrued interest on the note issued in transaction no. 6. Round answer to nearest whole dollar.

Required

a. Record the given transactions in a horizontal statements model like the following one.

	Balance Sheet									Income Statement			Statement of Cash Flows
	Assets	=	Liabilities					+	Stk. Equity				
				Sales									
Event	Cash +	Mdse. Inv. =	Acct. Pay. +	Tax Pay. +	War. Pay. +	Int. Pay. +	Notes Pay. +	Com. Stock +	Ret. Earn.	Rev. −	Exp. =	Net Inc.	

b. Prepare the income statement, balance sheet, and statement of cash flows for Year 1.

c. What is the total amount of current liabilities at December 31, Year 1?

LO 7-10

Exercise 7-22A *Preparing a classified balance sheet*

Required

Use the following information to prepare a classified balance sheet for Alpha Co. at the end of Year 1.

Accounts receivable	$26,500
Accounts payable	12,200
Cash	20,500
Common stock	30,000
Land	10,000
Long-term notes payable	17,500
Merchandise inventory	26,300
Retained earnings	23,600

LO 7-11

Exercise 7-23A *Effective interest amortization of a bond discount*

On January 1, Year 1, Parker Company issued bonds with a face value of $80,000, a stated rate of interest of 8 percent, and a five-year term to maturity. Interest is payable in cash on December 31 of each year. The effective rate of interest was 9 percent at the time the bonds were issued. The bonds sold for $76,888. Parker used the effective interest rate method to amortize the bond discount.

Required

a. Prepare an amortization table like the one that follows. Round answers to nearest whole dollar.

	Cash Payment	Interest Expense	Discount Amortization	Carrying Value
January 1, Year 1				76,888
December 31, Year 1	6,400	6,920	520	77,408
December 31, Year 2	?	?	?	?
December 31, Year 3	?	?	?	?
December 31, Year 4	?	?	?	?
December 31, Year 5	?	?	?	?
Totals	32,000	35,112	3,112	

b. What item(s) in the table would appear on the Year 4 balance sheet?
c. What item(s) in the table would appear on the Year 4 income statement?
d. What item(s) in the table would appear on the Year 4 statement of cash flows?

Exercise 7-24A   *Effective interest amortization of a bond discount (Appendix)*

LO 7-12

On January 1, Year 1, Hart Company issued bonds with a face value of $60,000, a stated rate of interest of 8 percent, and a five-year term to maturity. Interest is payable in cash on December 31 of each year. The effective rate of interest was 9 percent at the time the bonds were issued. The bonds sold for $57,666. Hart used the effective interest rate method to amortize the bond discount. Round all answers to nearest whole dollar.

a. Determine the amount of the discount on the day of issue.
b. Determine the amount of interest expense recognized on December 31, Year 1.
c. Determine the carrying value of the bond liability on December 31, Year 1.

Exercise 7-25A   *Effective interest versus straight-line amortization*

LO 7-8, 7-9, 7-11, 7-12

On January 1, Year 1, the Christie Companies issued bonds with a face value of $500,000, a stated rate of interest of 10 percent, and a 20-year term to maturity. Interest is payable in cash on December 31 of each year. The effective rate of interest was 8 percent at the time the bonds were issued.

Required

Write a brief memo explaining whether the effective interest rate method or the straight-line method will produce the highest amount of interest expense recognized on the Year 1 income statement.

PROBLEMS—SERIES A

connect An electronic auto-gradable version of the Series A Problems is available in Connect. A PDF version of Series B Problems is in Connect under the "Additional Student Resources" tab. Solutions to the Series B Problems are available in Connect under the "Instructor Library" tab. Instructor and student Workpapers for the Series B Problems are available in Connect under the "Instructor Library" and "Additional Student Resources" tabs respectively.

Problem 7-26A   *Effect of accrued interest on financial statements*

LO 7-1

Malco Enterprises issued $10,000 of common stock when the company was started. In addition, Malco borrowed $36,000 from a local bank on July 1, Year 1. The note had a 6 percent annual interest rate and a one-year term to maturity. Malco Enterprises recognized $72,500 of revenue on account in Year 1 and $85,200 of revenue on account in Year 2. Cash collections of accounts receivable were $61,300 in Year 1 and $71,500 in Year 2. Malco paid $39,000 of other operating expenses in Year 1 and $45,000 of other operating expenses in Year 2. Malco repaid the loan and interest at the maturity date.

CHECK FIGURES
b. $22,300
c. $1,080

Required

a. Organize the information in accounts under an accounting equation.

b. What amount of net cash flow from operating activities would be reported on the Year 1 cash flow statement?

c. What amount of interest expense would be reported on the Year 1 income statement?

d. What amount of total liabilities would be reported on the December 31, Year 1, balance sheet?

e. What amount of retained earnings would be reported on the December 31, Year 1, balance sheet?

f. What amount of cash flow from financing activities would be reported on the Year 1 statement of cash flows?

g. What amount of interest expense would be reported on the Year 2 income statement?

h. What amount of cash flows from operating activities would be reported on the Year 2 cash flow statement?

i. What amount of assets would be reported on the December 31, Year 2, balance sheet?

LO 7-1, 7-2

CHECK FIGURE
Net Income, Year 1: $65,750

Problem 7-27A   *Accounting for short-term debt and sales tax—two accounting cycles*

The following transactions apply to Walnut Enterprises for Year 1, its first year of operations:

1. Received $50,000 cash from the issue of a short-term note with a 6 percent interest rate and a one-year maturity. The note was made on April 1, Year 1.

2. Received $130,000 cash plus applicable sales tax from performing services. The services are subject to a sales tax rate of 6 percent.

3. Paid $62,000 cash for other operating expenses during the year.

4. Paid the sales tax due on $110,000 of the service revenue for the year. Sales tax on the balance of the revenue is not due until Year 2.

5. Recognized the accrued interest at December 31, Year 1.

The following transactions apply to Walnut Enterprises for Year 2:

1. Paid the balance of the sales tax due for Year 1.

2. Received $201,000 cash plus applicable sales tax from performing services. The services are subject to a sales tax rate of 6 percent.

3. Repaid the principal of the note and applicable interest on April 1, Year 2.

4. Paid $102,500 of other operating expenses during the year.

5. Paid the sales tax due on $185,000 of the service revenue. The sales tax on the balance of the revenue is not due until Year 3.

Required

a. Organize the transaction data in accounts under an accounting equation.

b. Prepare an income statement, a statement of changes in stockholders' equity, a balance sheet, and a statement of cash flows for Year 1 and Year 2.

LO 7-3

Problem 7-28A   *Contingent liabilities*

Required

a. Give an example of a contingent liability that is probable and reasonably estimable. How would this type of liability be shown in the accounting records?

b. Give an example of a contingent liability that is reasonably possible or probable but not reasonably estimable. How would this type of liability be shown in the accounting records?

c. Give an example of a contingent liability that is remote. How is this type of liability shown in the accounting records?

LO 7-1, 7-2, 7-3, 7-4

CHECK FIGURES
a. (2) $1,600, Interest Expense, Year 1
b. $22,600, Current Liabilities, 12/31/Year 1

Problem 7-29A   *Current liabilities*

The following selected transactions were taken from the books of Ripley Company for Year 1:

1. On February 1, Year 1, borrowed $70,000 cash from the local bank. The note had a 6 percent interest rate and was due on June 1, Year 1.

2. Cash sales for the year amounted to $240,000 plus sales tax at the rate of 7 percent.

3. Ripley provides a 90-day warranty on the merchandise sold. The warranty expense is estimated to be 1 percent of sales.

4. Paid the sales tax to the state sales tax agency on $210,000 of the sales.

5. Paid the note due on June 1 and the related interest.

6. On November 1, Year 1, borrowed $20,000 cash from the local bank. The note had a 6 percent interest rate and a one-year term to maturity.

7. Paid $2,100 in warranty repairs.

8. A customer has filed a lawsuit against Ripley for $1 million for breach of contract. The company attorney does not believe the suit has merit.

Required

a. Answer the following questions:

   (1) What amount of cash did Ripley pay for interest during Year 1?

   (2) What amount of interest expense is reported on Ripley's income statement for Year 1?

   (3) What is the amount of warranty expense for Year 1?

b. Prepare the current liabilities section of the balance sheet at December 31, Year 1.

c. Show the effect of these transactions on the financial statements using a horizontal statements model like the following one. Use + for increase, − for decrease, and NA for not affected. In the Cash Flow column, indicate whether the item is an operating activity (OA), investing activity (IA), or financing activity (FA). The first transaction has been recorded as an example.

Balance Sheet			Income Statement				Statement of Cash Flows
Assets	=	Liabilities	+	Equity	Rev.	−	Exp.	=	Net Inc.	
+		+		NA	NA		NA		NA	+ FA

Problem 7-30A *Effect of an installment note on financial statements*

LO 7-5

On January 1, Year 1, Brown Co. borrowed cash from First Bank by issuing a $100,000 face value, four-year term note that had an 8 percent annual interest rate. The note is to be repaid by making annual cash payments of $30,192 that include both interest and principal on December 31 of each year. Brown used the proceeds from the loan to purchase land that generated rental revenues of $52,000 cash per year.

CHECK FIGURES
a. Year 1 Ending Principal Balance: $77,808
c. Year 1 Net Income: $44,000

Required

a. Prepare an amortization schedule for the four-year period. Round answers to nearest whole dollar.

b. Organize the information in accounts under an accounting equation.

c. Prepare an income statement, a balance sheet, and a statement of cash flows for each of the four years.

d. Does cash outflow from operating activities remain constant or change each year? Explain.

Problem 7-31A *Accounting for an installment note payable*

LO 7-5

The following transactions apply to Pecan Co. for Year 1, its first year of operations:

1. Received $100,000 cash in exchange for issuance of common stock.

2. Secured a $300,000 five-year installment loan from State Bank. The interest rate is 5 percent and annual payments are $69,292.

3. Purchased land for $100,000.

4. Provided services for $260,000.

5. Paid other operating expenses of $150,000.

6. Paid the annual payment on the loan. Round answers to nearest whole dollar.

Required

a. Organize the transaction data in accounts under an accounting equation.

b. Prepare an income statement and balance sheet for Year 1.

c. What is the interest expense for Year 2? Year 3?

Problem 7-32A   *Accounting for a line of credit*

Elite Boat Sales uses a line of credit to help finance its inventory purchases. Elite Boat Sales sells boats and equipment and uses the line of credit to build inventory for its peak sales months, which tend to be clustered in the summer months. Account balances at the beginning of Year 2 were as follows.

Cash	$120,000
Inventory	225,000
Common stock	185,000
Retained earnings	160,000

Elite Boat Sales experienced the following transactions for April, May, and June Year 2:

1. April 1, Year 2, obtained approval for a line of credit of up to $700,000. Funds are to be obtained or repaid on the first day of each month. The interest rate is the bank prime rate plus 1 percent.
2. April 1, Year 2, borrowed $190,000 on the line of credit. The bank's prime interest rate is 5 percent for April.
3. April 15, purchased inventory on account, $210,000.
4. April 31, paid other operating expenses of $105,000.
5. In April, sold inventory for $420,000 on account. The inventory had cost $250,000.
6. April 30, paid the interest due on the line of credit.
7. May 1, borrowed $230,000 on the line of credit. The bank's prime rate is 6 percent for May.
8. May 1, paid the accounts payable from transaction 3.
9. May 10, collected $380,000 of the sales on account.
10. May 20, purchased inventory on account, $230,000.
11. May sales on account were $510,000. The inventory had cost $305,000.
12. May 31, paid the interest due on the line of credit.
13. June 1, repaid $150,000 on the line of credit. The bank's prime rate is 6 percent for June.
14. June 5, paid $280,000 of the accounts payable.
15. June 10, collected $630,000 from accounts receivable.
16. June 20, purchased inventory on account, $375,000.
17. June sales on account were $605,000. The inventory had cost $370,000.
18. June 30, paid the interest due on the line of credit.

Required

a. What is the amount of interest expense for April? May? June?
b. What amount of cash was paid for interest in April? May? June?

Problem 7-33A   *Effect of a line of credit on financial statements*

Mott Company has a line of credit with Bay Bank. Mott can borrow up to $400,000 at any time over the course of the calendar year. The following table shows the prime rate expressed as an annual percentage along with the amounts borrowed and repaid during the year. Mott agreed to pay interest at an annual rate equal to 1 percent above the bank's prime rate. Funds are borrowed or repaid on the first day of each month. Interest is payable in cash on the last day of the month. The interest rate is applied to the outstanding monthly balance. For example, Mott pays 6 percent (5 percent + 1 percent) annual interest on $60,000 for the month of January.

Month	Amount Borrowed or (Repaid)	Prime Rate for the Month, %
January	$60,000	5%
February	40,000	5
March	(30,000)	6
April through October	No change	No change
November	(20,000)	6
December	(10,000)	5

Mott earned $25,000 of cash revenue during the year.

Required

a. Organize the information in accounts under an accounting equation. Round interest amount to nearest whole dollar.

b. Prepare an income statement, balance sheet, and statement of cash flows for the year.

c. Write a memo discussing the advantages to a business of arranging a line of credit.

Problem 7-34A   *Effect of debt transactions on financial statements*

LO 7-1, 7-6, 7-7

Required

Show the effect of each of the following independent accounting events on the financial statements using a horizontal statements model like the following one. Use + for increase, − for decrease, and NA for not affected. The first event is recorded as an example.

Event No.	Balance Sheet			Income Statement			Statement of Cash Flows
	Assets	= Liab.	+ Stk. Equity	Rev.	− Exp.	= Net Inc.	
a	+	+	NA	NA	NA	NA	+ FA

a. Issued a bond at face value.

b. Borrowed funds using a line of credit.

c. Made an interest payment for funds that had been borrowed against a line of credit.

d. Made a cash payment on a note payable for both interest and principal.

e. Made an interest payment on a bond that had been issued at face value.

Problem 7-35A   *Straight-line amortization of a bond premium*

LO 7-9

Pine Land Co. was formed when it acquired cash from the issue of common stock. The company then issued bonds at a premium on January 1, Year 1. Interest is payable annually on December 31 of each year, beginning December 31, Year 1. On January 2, Year 1, Pine Land Co. purchased a piece of land and leased it for an annual rental fee. The rent is received annually on December 31, beginning December 31, Year 1. At the end of the eight-year period (December 31, Year 8), the land was sold at a gain, and the bonds were paid off. A summary of the transactions for each year follows.

Year 1

1. Acquired cash from the issue of common stock.
2. Issued eight-year bonds.
3. Purchased land.
4. Received land rental income.
5. Recognized interest expense including the straight-line amortization of the premium and made the cash payment for interest on December 31.

Year 2–Year 7

6. Received land rental income.
7. Recognized interest expense including the straight-line amortization of the premium and made the cash payment for interest on December 31.

Year 8

8. Sold land at a gain.
9. Retired bonds at face value.

Required

Identify each of these nine transactions as asset source (AS), asset use (AU), asset exchange (AE), or claims exchange (CE). Explain how each event affects assets, liabilities, stockholders' equity, net income, and cash flow by placing a + for increase, − for decrease, or NA for not affected under each of the categories. In the Cash Flow column, indicate whether the item is an operating activity (OA), investing activity (IA), or financing activity (FA). The first event is recorded as an example.

Event No.	Type of Event	Balance Sheet					Income Statement	Statement of Cash Flows
		Assets	= Liabilities	+	Common Stock	+ Retained Earnings	Net Income	
1	AS	+	NA		+	NA	NA	+ FA

Problem 7-36A *Straight-line amortization of a bond discount*

During Year 1 and Year 2, Kale Co. completed the following transactions relating to its bond issue. The company's fiscal year ends on December 31.

Year 1

Mar. 1 Issued $200,000 of 8 year, 6 percent bonds for $194,000. The semiannual cash payment for interest is due on March 1 and September 1, beginning September Year 1.

Sept. 1 Recognized interest expense including the amortization of the discount and made the semiannual cash payment for interest.

Dec. 31 Recognized accrued interest expense including the amortization of the discount.

Year 2

Mar. 1 Recognized interest expense including the amortization of the discount and made the semiannual cash payment for interest.

Sept. 1 Recognized interest expense including the amortization of the discount and made the semiannual cash payment for interest.

Dec. 31 Recognized accrued interest expense including the amortization of the discount.

Required

a. When the bonds were issued, was the market rate of interest more or less than the stated rate of interest? If the bonds had sold at face value, what amount of cash would Kale Co. have received?
b. Prepare the liabilities section of the balance sheet at December 31, Year 1 and Year 2.
c. Determine the amount of interest expense Kale would report on the income statements for Year 1 and Year 2.
d. Determine the amount of interest Kale would pay to the bondholders in Year 1 and Year 2.

Problem 7-37A *Multistep income statement and classified balance sheet*

Required

Use the following information to prepare a multistep income statement and a classified balance sheet for Eller Equipment Company for Year 1. (*Hint:* Some of the items will *not* appear on either statement, and ending retained earnings must be calculated.)

Salaries expense	$ 72,000	Beginning retained earnings	$134,150
Common stock	50,000	Warranties payable (short term)	2,500
Notes receivable (short term)	10,000	Gain on sale of equipment	8,500
Allowance for doubtful accounts	6,500	Operating expenses	96,000
Accumulated depreciation	42,300	Cash flow from investing activities	125,000
Notes payable (long term)	80,000	Prepaid rent	14,000
Salvage value of building	6,000	Land	70,000
Interest payable (short term)	1,500	Cash	26,300
Uncollectible accounts expense	7,150	Inventory	110,500
Supplies	1,800	Accounts payable	32,000
Equipment	97,500	Interest Expense	8,600
Interest revenue	3,600	Salaries payable	5,200
Sales revenue	510,000	Unearned revenue	26,300
Dividends	11,500	Cost of goods sold	310,000
Warranty expense	9,600	Accounts receivable	56,000
Interest receivable (short term)	600	Depreciation expense	1,000

Problem 7-38A   *Effective interest amortization for a bond premium (Appendix)*   LO 7-12

On January 1, Year 1, Reese Incorporated issued bonds with a face value of $120,000, a stated rate of interest of 8 percent, and a five-year term to maturity. Interest is payable in cash on December 31 of each year. The effective rate of interest was 7 percent at the time the bonds were issued. The bonds sold for $124,920. Reese used the effective interest rate method to amortize bond premium.

Required

a. Prepare an amortization table, shown as follows. Round interest expense amounts to nearest whole dollar.

	Cash Payment	Interest Expense	Premium Amortization	Carrying Value
January 1, Year 1				124,920
December 31, Year 1	9,600	8,744	856	124,064
December 31, Year 2	?	?	?	?
December 31, Year 3	?	?	?	?
December 31, Year 4	?	?	?	?
December 31, Year 5	?	?	?	?
Totals	48,000	43,080	4,920	

b. What item(s) in the table would appear on the Year 3 balance sheet?

c. What item(s) in the table would appear on the Year 3 income statement?

d. What item(s) in the table would appear on the Year 3 statement of cash flows?

ANALYZE, THINK, COMMUNICATE

ATC 7-1   **Business Application Case**   *Understanding real-world annual reports*

Obtain the Target Corporation's annual report for its 2018 fiscal year (year ended February 2, 2019) at http://investors.target.com using the instructions in Appendix A, and use it to answer the following questions. You will need to read carefully the company's Consolidated Statements of Financial Position (balance sheets) as well as notes 8, 14, and 16.

Target Corporation

Required

a. What percentage of Target's assets was being financed with liabilities (versus shareholders' equity)?

b. How does Target account for bank overdrafts, and how much overdrafts did it have as of February 2, 2019?

c. What was the average interest rate that Target paid on its borrowings?

d. Target reported Accrued and Other Liabilities of $4,201 as of February 2, 2019. What was the largest subcategory of liabilities included in this account?

ATC 7-2   **Group Assignment**   *Missing information*

The following three companies issued the following bonds:

1. Lot, Inc. issued $100,000 of 8 percent, five-year bonds at 102¼ on January 1, Year 1. Interest is payable annually on December 31.

2. Max, Inc. issued $100,000 of 8 percent, five-year bonds at 98 on January 1, Year 1. Interest is payable annually on December 31.

3. Par, Inc. issued $100,000 of 8 percent, five-year bonds at 104 on January 1, Year 1. Interest is payable annually on December 31.

Required

a. Organize the class into three sections and divide each section into groups of three to five students. Assign each of the sections one of the companies.

Group Tasks

(1) Compute the following amounts for your company (use straight-line amortization):

(a) Cash proceeds from the bond issue.

(b) Interest paid in Year 1.

(c) Interest expense for Year 1.

(2) Prepare the liabilities section of the balance sheet as of December 31, Year 1.

Class Discussion

b. Have a representative of each section put the liabilities section for its company on the board.

c. Is the amount of interest expense different for the three companies? Why or why not?

d. Is the amount of interest paid different for each of the companies? Why or why not?

e. Is the amount of total liabilities different for each of the companies? Why or why not?

ATC 7-3   Research Assignment   *Analyzing two real-world companies' use of liabilities*

Complete the requirements below using the most current annual reports or the Forms 10-K for Toll Brothers, Inc., a large home-building company, and Dominion Energy, Inc., one of the nation's leading generators of energy. To obtain the Forms 10-K, use either the EDGAR system following the instructions in Appendix A or the companies' websites. The annual reports can be found on the companies' websites.

Required

a. Which of these two companies is using debt to finance its assets the most? Show your computations.

b. Toll Brothers has some lines of credit called a "Credit Facility." How much money is available to under this line of credit?

ATC 7-4   Writing Assignment   *Definition of elements of financial statements*

Shake Shack, Inc. began operations in 2014, and it incorporated in Delaware in Year 1. In February, 2015 it went public with its initial public offering of common stock. By December 31, 2017 it was operating 159 restaurants. At the end of 2017, it had total assets of $470.6 million, long-term debt of $212.1 million, and total liabilities of $246.1 million. Shake Shack's income before interest and taxes in 2017 was $33.8 million. Its average interest rate on long-term debt was less than 1.0 percent.

Required

a. Assuming Shake Shack incurs interest expense mostly on its long-term debt, how much interest did the company incur in 2017, assuming the average interest rate remains at 1.0 percent?

b. Does the debt seem excessive compared with the amount of 2017 net income before interest and taxes? Explain.

c. Assuming Shake Shack pays tax at the rate of 25 percent, what amount of tax will the company pay in 2017?

d. Assume you are the president of the company. Write a memo to the shareholders explaining why Shake Shack would want to finance so much of its assets with debt rather than stockholders' equity.

ATC 7-5   Ethical Dilemma   *Sometimes debt is not debt*

David Sheridan was a well-respected CPA in his mid-fifties. After spending 10 years at a national accounting firm, he was hired by Global, Inc., a multinational corporation headquartered in the United States. He patiently worked his way up to the top of Global's accounting department, and in the early 1990s, took over as chief financial officer for the company. As the Internet began to explode, management at Global, Inc. decided to radically change the nature of its business to one of e-commerce. Two years after the transition, Internet commerce began to slow down, and Global was in dire need of cash in order to continue operations. Management turned to the accounting department.

Global, Inc. needed to borrow a substantial amount of money but couldn't afford to increase the amount of liabilities on the balance sheet for fear of the stock price dropping and banks demanding repayment of existing loans. David discovered a way that would allow the company to raise the needed cash to continue operations without having to report the long-term notes payable on the balance sheet. Under an obscure rule, companies can set up separate legal organizations that do not have to be reported on the parent company's financial statements, if a third party contributes just 3 percent of the start-up capital. David called a friend, Brian Johnson, and asked him to participate in a business venture with Global. Brian agreed, and created a special purpose entity with Global named BrianCo. For his participation, Brian was awarded a substantial amount of valuable Global stock. Brian went to a bank and used the stock as collateral to borrow a large sum of money for BrianCo. Then, Global sold some of its poor or underperforming assets to BrianCo for the cash that Brian borrowed. In the end, Global got rid of bad assets, received the proceeds of the long-term note payable, and did not have to show the liability on the balance sheet. Only the top executives and the accountants that worked closely with David knew of the scheme, and they planned to use this method only until the e-commerce portion of Global became profitable again.

Required

a. How did David's scheme affect the overall appearance of Global's financial statements? Why was this important to investors and creditors?

b. Review the AICPA's Articles of Professional Conduct (see Chapter 4) and comment on any of the standards that have been violated.

c. Name the features of the fraud triangle and explain how they materialize in this case.

CHAPTER 8

Proprietorships, Partnerships, and Corporations

LEARNING OBJECTIVES

After you have mastered the material in this chapter, you will be able to:

LO 8-1	Identify the primary characteristics of sole proprietorships, partnerships, and corporations.
LO 8-2	Identify the characteristics of capital stock.
LO 8-3	Differentiate between common and preferred stock.
LO 8-4	Show how issuing different classes of stock affects financial statements.
LO 8-5	Show how treasury stock affects financial statements.
LO 8-6	Show how declaring and paying cash dividends affect financial statements.
LO 8-7	Show how stock dividends and stock splits affect financial statements.
LO 8-8	Show how the appropriation of retained earnings affects financial statements.
LO 8-9	Show how accounting information is used to make stock investment decisions.

 Video lectures and accompanying self-assessment quizzes are available in Connect for all learning objectives.

 Set B exercises and problems are available in Additional Student Resources.

CHAPTER OPENING

You want to start a business. How should you structure it? Should it be a sole proprietorship, partnership, or corporation? Each form of business structure presents advantages and disadvantages. For example, a sole proprietorship allows maximum independence and control while partnerships and corporations allow individuals to pool resources and talents with other people. This chapter discusses these and other features of the three primary forms of business structure.

The Curious Accountant

Stockbyte/Getty Images

Imagine your rich uncle rewarded you for doing well in your first accounting course by giving you $10,000 to invest in the stock of one company. After reviewing many recent annual reports, you narrowed your choice to two companies with the following characteristics.

Mystery Company A: This company began operations in 2007, and began selling its stock to the public on March 23, 2018. It has lost money every year it has been in existence. In 2017 alone, its losses were $112 million, and by December 31, 2017, it had total life-time losses of approximately $1.1 billion. Even so, the company provides services that are used by millions of individuals every day. At its current price of $23, you could buy 435 shares. A friend tells you that a person whose head was "in the clouds" anyway would be crazy not to buy this company's stock.

Mystery Company B: This company has been in existence since 1837, and has been incorporated since 1905. It has made a profit and paid dividends for as long as anyone can remember. In its 2018 fiscal-year alone, its net earnings were $9.8 billion, and it paid dividends of $7.1 billion. Almost every home in America uses one or more of its products or services. Its stock is selling for about $94 per share, so you can buy 106 shares. Your friend says that owning this company's stock would be about as exciting as brushing your teeth.

The names of the real-world companies described are disclosed later. Based on the information provided, which company's stock would you buy? (Answer on page 296.)

FORMS OF BUSINESS ORGANIZATIONS

LO 8-1

Identify the primary characteristics of sole proprietorships, partnerships, and corporations.

Sole proprietorships are owned by a single individual who is responsible for making business and profit distribution decisions. If you want to be the absolute master of your destiny, you should organize your business as a proprietorship. Establishing a sole proprietorship is usually as simple as obtaining a business license from local government authorities. Usually no legal ownership agreement is required.

Partnerships allow persons to share their talents, capital, and the risks and rewards of business ownership. Because two or more individuals share ownership, partnerships require clear agreements about how authority, risks, and profits will be shared. Prudent partners minimize misunderstandings by hiring attorneys to prepare a **partnership agreement** that defines the responsibilities of each partner and describes how income or losses will be divided. Because the measurement of income affects the distribution of profits, partnerships frequently hire accountants to ensure that records are maintained in accordance with generally accepted accounting principles (GAAP). Partnerships (and sole proprietorships) also may need professional advice to deal with tax issues.

A **corporation** is a separate legal entity created by the authority of a state government. The paperwork to start a corporation is complex. For most laypersons, engaging professional attorneys and accountants to assist with the paperwork is well worth the fees charged.

Each state has separate laws governing establishing corporations. Many states follow the standard provisions of the Model Business Corporation Act. All states require the initial application to provide **articles of incorporation,** which normally include the following information: (1) the corporation's name and proposed date of incorporation; (2) the purpose of the corporation; (3) the location of the business and its expected life (which can be *perpetuity,* meaning *endless*); (4) provisions for capital stock; and (5) the names and addresses of the members of the first board of directors, the individuals with the ultimate authority for operating the business. If the articles are in order, the state establishes the legal existence of the corporation by issuing a charter of incorporation. The charter and the articles are public documents.

Advantages and Disadvantages of Different Forms of Business Organization

Each form of business organization presents a different combination of advantages and disadvantages. Persons wanting to start a business or invest in one should consider the characteristics of each type of business structure.

Regulation

Few laws specifically affect the operations of proprietorships and partnerships. Corporations, however, are usually heavily regulated. The extent of government regulation depends on the size and distribution of a company's ownership interests. Ownership interests in corporations are normally evidenced by **stock certificates.**

Ownership of corporations can be transferred from one individual to another through exchanging stock certificates. As long as the exchanges (buying and selling of shares of stock, often called *trading*) are limited to transactions between individuals, a company is defined as a **closely held corporation.** However, once a corporation reaches a certain size, it may list its stock on a stock exchange such as the New York Stock Exchange or the NASDAQ. Trading on a stock exchange is limited to the stockbrokers who are members of the exchange. These brokers represent buyers and sellers who are willing to pay the brokers commissions for exchanging stock certificates on their behalf. Although closely held corporations are relatively free from government regulation, companies whose stock is publicly traded on the exchanges by brokers are subject to extensive regulation.

The extensive regulation of trading on stock exchanges began in the 1930s. The stock market crash of 1929 and the subsequent Great Depression led Congress to pass the **Securities Act of 1933** *and* **Securities Exchange Act of 1934** to regulate issuing stock and to govern the exchanges. The 1934 act also created the Securities and Exchange Commission (SEC) to enforce the securities laws. Congress gave the SEC legal authority to establish accounting principles for corporations that are registered on the exchanges. However, the SEC has generally deferred its rule-making authority to private sector accounting bodies such as the Financial Accounting Standards Board (FASB), effectively allowing the accounting profession to regulate itself.

A number of high-profile business failures around the turn of the last century raised questions about the effectiveness of self-regulation and the usefulness of audits to protect the public. The Sarbanes–Oxley Act of 2002 was adopted to address these concerns. The act creates a five-member Public Company Accounting Oversight Board (PCAOB) with the authority to set and enforce auditing, attestation, quality control, and ethics standards for auditors of public companies. The PCAOB is empowered to impose disciplinary and remedial sanctions for violations of its rules, securities laws, and professional auditing and accounting standards. Public corporations operate in a complex regulatory environment that requires the services of attorneys and professional accountants.

Double Taxation

Corporations pay income taxes on their earnings and then owners pay income taxes on distributions (dividends) received from corporations. As a result, distributed corporate profits are taxed twice—first when income is reported on the corporation's income tax return and a second time when distributions are reported on individual owners' tax returns. This phenomenon is commonly called **double taxation** and is a significant disadvantage of the corporate form of business organization.

To illustrate, assume Glide Corporation earns pretax income of $100,000. Glide is in a 21 percent tax bracket. The corporation itself will pay income tax of $21,000 ($100,000 × 0.21). Next, assume that the corporation distributes the after-tax income of $79,000 ($100,000 − $21,000) to individual stockholders who are in a personal federal income tax bracket of 22 percent. The $79,000 dividend will be reported on the stockholders' individual income tax returns, requiring tax payments of $17,380 ($79,000 × 0.22). Ultimately, total income tax of $38,380 ($21,000 + $17,380) is paid on the $100,000 of income earned by the corporation. In contrast, consider a proprietorship that is owned by an individual in a 22 percent federal income tax bracket. If the proprietorship earns and distributes $100,000 profit, the total tax would be only $22,000 ($100,000 × 0.22).

Double taxation can be a burden for small companies. To reduce that burden, tax laws permit small closely held corporations to elect "S Corporation" status. S Corporations are taxed as proprietorships or partnerships. Also, many states have recently enacted laws permitting the formation of **limited liability companies (LLCs),** which offer many of the benefits of corporate ownership yet are in general taxed as partnerships. Because proprietorships and partnerships are not separate legal entities, company earnings are taxable to the owners rather than the company itself.

Limited Liability

Given the disadvantages of increased regulation and double taxation, why would anyone choose the corporate form of business structure over a partnership or proprietorship? A major reason is that the corporate form limits an investor's potential liability as an owner of a business venture. Because a corporation is legally separate from its owners, creditors cannot claim owners' personal assets as payment for the company's debts. Also, plaintiffs must sue the corporation, not its owners. The most that owners of a corporation can lose is the amount they have invested in the company (the value of the company's stock).

Unlike corporate stockholders, the owners of proprietorships and partnerships are *personally liable* for actions they take in the name of their companies. In fact, partners are responsible not only for their own actions but also for those taken by any other partner on behalf of the partnership. The benefit of **limited liability** is one of the most significant reasons the corporate form of business organization is so popular.

Continuity

Unlike partnerships or proprietorships, which terminate with the departure of their owners, a corporation's life continues when a shareholder dies or sells his or her stock. Because of **continuity** of existence, many corporations formed in the 1800s still thrive today.

Answers to The Curious Accountant

Mystery Company A is Dropbox, Inc., as of December 12, 2018. For its initial public offering on March 23, 2018, its stock was priced at $21 per share; by the end of the day it was selling for $28.48. Nine months later, the stock was trading at $22.81, a decline of 20 percent.

Mystery Company B is Procter & Gamble Company, as of December 12, 2018. It manufactures and sells numerous personal care and household care products, including toothpaste, shampoo, and laundry detergent. During the nine months of trading when Dropbox's stock price declined by 20 percent, Procter & Gamble's stock price increased by 24 percent, from $75.91 to $94.03. Of course, only the future will reveal which company is the better investment in the long run.

Transferability of Ownership

The **transferability** of corporate ownership is easy. An investor simply buys or sells stock to acquire or give up an ownership interest in a corporation. Hundreds of millions of shares of stock are bought and sold on the major stock exchanges each day.

Transferring the ownership of proprietorships is much more difficult. To sell an ownership interest in a proprietorship, the proprietor must find someone willing to purchase the entire business. Because most proprietors also run their businesses, transferring ownership also requires transferring management responsibilities. Consider the difference in selling $1 million of ExxonMobil stock versus selling a locally owned gas station. The stock could be sold on the New York Stock Exchange within minutes. In contrast, it could take years to find a buyer who is financially capable of and interested in owning and operating a gas station.

Transferring ownership in partnerships can also be difficult. As with proprietorships, ownership transfers may require a new partner to make a significant investment and accept management responsibilities in the business. Further, a new partner must accept and be accepted by the other partners. Personality conflicts and differences in management style can cause problems in transferring ownership interests in partnerships.

Management Structure

Partnerships and proprietorships are usually managed by their owners. Corporations, in contrast, have three tiers of management authority. The *owners* (**stockholders**) represent the highest level of organizational authority. The stockholders *elect* a **board of directors** to oversee company operations. The directors then *hire* professional executives to manage the company on a daily basis. Because large corporations can offer high salaries and challenging career opportunities, they can often attract superior managerial talent.

While the management structure used by corporations is generally effective, it sometimes complicates dismissing incompetent managers. The chief executive officer (CEO) is usually a member of the board of directors and is frequently influential in choosing other board members. The CEO is also in a position to reward loyal board members. As a result, board members may be reluctant to fire the CEO or other top executives even if the individuals are performing poorly. Corporations operating under such conditions are said to be experiencing **entrenched management.**

Ability to Raise Capital

Because corporations can have millions of owners (shareholders), they have the opportunity to raise huge amounts of capital. Few individuals have the financial means to build and operate a telecommunications network such as AT&T or a marketing distribution system such as Walmart. However, by pooling the resources of millions of owners through public stock and bond offerings, corporations generate the billions of dollars of capital needed for such massive investments. In contrast, the capital resources of proprietorships and partnerships are limited to a relatively small number of private owners. Although proprietorships and partnerships can also obtain resources by borrowing, the amount creditors are willing to lend them is usually limited by the size of the owners' net worth.

Appearance of Capital Structure in Financial Statements

The ownership interest (equity) in a business is composed of two elements: (1) owner/investor contributions and (2) retained earnings. The way these two elements are reported in the financial statements differs for each type of business structure (proprietorship, partnership, or corporation).

Presentation of Equity in Proprietorships

Owner contributions and retained earnings are combined in a single capital account on the balance sheets of proprietorships. To illustrate, assume that Worthington Sole Proprietorship was started on January 1, Year 1, when it acquired a $5,000 capital contribution from its owner, Phil Worthington. During the first year of operation, the company generated $4,000 of cash revenues, incurred $2,500 of cash expenses, and distributed $1,000 cash to the owner. Exhibit 8.1 displays Year 1 financial statements for Worthington's company. Note on the *capital statement* that distributions are called **withdrawals.** Verify that the $5,500 balance in the capital account on the balance sheet includes the $5,000 owner contribution and the retained earnings of $500 ($1,500 net income − $1,000 withdrawal).

EXHIBIT 8.1

WORTHINGTON SOLE PROPRIETORSHIP
Financial Statements
As of December 31, Year 1

Income Statement		Capital Statement		Balance Sheet	
Revenue	$4,000	Beginning capital balance	$ 0	Assets	
Expenses	2,500	Plus: Investment by owner	5,000	Cash	$5,500
Net income	$1,500	Plus: Net income	1,500	Owners' Equity	
		Less: Withdrawal by owner	(1,000)	Worthington, capital	$5,500
		Ending capital balance	$5,500		

☑ CHECK YOURSELF 8.1

Weiss Company was started on January 1, Year 1, when it acquired $50,000 cash from its owner(s). During Year 1, the company earned $72,000 of net income. Explain how the equity section of Weiss's December 31, Year 1, balance sheet would differ if the company were a proprietorship versus a corporation.

Answer *Proprietorship* records combine capital acquisitions from the owner and earnings from operating the business in a single capital account. In contrast, *corporation* records separate capital acquisitions from the owners and earnings from operating the business. If Weiss were a proprietorship, the equity section of the year-end balance sheet would report a single capital component of $122,000. If Weiss were a corporation, the equity section would report two separate equity components, most likely common stock of $50,000 and retained earnings of $72,000.

Presentation of Equity in Partnerships

The financial statement format for reporting partnership equity is similar to that used for proprietorships. Contributed capital and retained earnings are combined. However, a separate capital account is maintained for each partner in the business to reflect each partner's ownership interest.

To illustrate, assume that Sara Slater and Jill Johnson formed a partnership on January 1, Year 1. The partnership acquired $2,000 of capital from Slater and $4,000 from Johnson.

EXHIBIT 8.2

SLATER AND JOHNSON PARTNERSHIP
Financial Statements
As of December 31, Year 1

Income Statement		Capital Statement		Balance Sheet	
Revenue	$5,000	Beginning capital balance	$ 0	Assets	
Expenses	3,000	Plus: Investment by owners	6,000	Cash	$7,400
Net income	$2,000	Plus: Net income	2,000	Owners' Equity	
		Less: Withdrawal by owners	(600)	Slater, capital	$2,700
		Ending capital balance	$7,400	Johnson, capital	4,700
				Total capital	$7,400

The partnership agreement called for each partner to receive an annual distribution equal to 10 percent of her capital contribution. Any further earnings were to be retained in the business and divided equally between the partners. During Year 1, the company earned $5,000 of cash revenue and incurred $3,000 of cash expenses, for net income of $2,000 ($5,000 − $3,000). As specified by the partnership agreement, Slater received a $200 ($2,000 × 0.10) cash withdrawal and Johnson received $400 ($4,000 × 0.10). The remaining $1,400 ($2,000 − $200 − $400) of income was retained in the business and divided equally, adding $700 to each partner's capital account.

Exhibit 8.2 displays financial statements for the Slater and Johnson partnership. Again, note that distributions are called *withdrawals*. Also find on the balance sheet a *separate capital account* for each partner. Each capital account includes the amount of the partner's contributed capital plus her proportionate share of the retained earnings.

Presentation of Equity in Corporations

Corporations have more complex capital structures than proprietorships and partnerships. Explanations of some of the more common features of corporate capital structures and transactions follow.

CHARACTERISTICS OF CAPITAL STOCK

LO 8-2

Identify the characteristics of capital stock.

Stock issued by corporations may have a variety of different characteristics. For example, a company may issue different classes of stock that grant owners different rights and privileges. Also, the number of shares a corporation can legally issue may differ from the number it actually has issued. Further, a corporation can even buy back its own stock. Finally, a corporation may assign different values to the stock it issues. Accounting for corporate equity transactions is discussed in the next section of the text.

Par Value

Many states require assigning a **par value** to stock. Historically, par value represented the maximum liability of the investors. Par value multiplied by the number of shares of stock issued represents the minimum amount of assets that must be retained in the company as protection for creditors. This amount is known as **legal capital.** To ensure that the amount of legal capital is maintained in a corporation, many states require that purchasers pay at least the par value for a share of stock initially purchased from a corporation. To minimize the amount of assets that owners must maintain in the business, many corporations issue stock with very low par values, often $1 or less. Therefore, *legal capital* as defined by par value has come to have very little relevance to investors or creditors. As a result, many states allow corporations to issue no-par stock.

FOCUS ON INTERNATIONAL ISSUES

PICKY, PICKY, PICKY . . .

Considering the almost countless number of differences that could exist between U.S. GAAP and IFRS, it is not surprising that some of those that do exist relate to very specific issues. Consider the case of the timing of stock splits.

Assume a company that ends its fiscal year on December 31, 2019, declares a 2-for-1 stock split on January 15, 2020, before it has issued its 2019 annual report. Should the company apply the effects of the stock split retroactively to its 2019 financial statements, or begin showing the effects of the split on its 2020 statements? Under U.S. GAAP the split must be applied retroactively to the 2019 statements since they had not been issued at the time of the split. Under IFRS the 2019 statements would not show the effects of the split, but the 2020 statements would. By the way, an event that occurs between a company's fiscal year-end and the date its annual report is released is called a *subsequent event* by accountants.

Obviously no one can know every GAAP rule, much less all of the differences between GAAP and IFRS. This is why it is important to learn how to find answers to specific accounting questions as well as to develop an understanding of the basic accounting rules. Most important, if you are not sure you know the answer, do not assume you do.

Steve Allen/Stockbyte/Getty Images

Stated Value

No-par stock may have a stated value. Like par value, **stated value** is an arbitrary amount assigned by the board of directors to the stock. It also has little relevance to investors and creditors. Stock with a par value and stock with a stated value are accounted for exactly the same way. When stock has no par or stated value, accounting for it is slightly different. These accounting differences are illustrated later in this chapter.

Other Valuation Terminology

The price an investor must pay to purchase a share of stock is the **market value.** The sales price of a share of stock may be more or less than the par value. Another term analysts frequently associate with stock is *book value.* **Book value per share** is calculated by dividing total stockholders' equity (assets — liabilities) by the number of shares of stock owned by investors. Book value per share differs from market value per share because stockholders' equity is measured in historical dollars and market value reflects investors' estimates of a company's current value.

Stock: Authorized, Issued, and Outstanding

As part of the regulatory function, states approve the maximum number of shares of stock corporations are legally permitted to issue. This maximum number is called **authorized stock.** Authorized stock that has been sold to the public is called **issued stock.** When a corporation buys back some of its issued stock from the public, the repurchased stock is called **treasury stock.** Treasury stock is still considered to be issued stock, but it is no longer outstanding. **Outstanding stock** (total issued stock minus treasury stock) is stock owned by investors outside the corporation. For example, assume a company that is authorized to issue 150 shares of stock issues 100 shares to investors, and then buys back 20 shares of treasury stock. There are 150 shares authorized, 100 shares issued, and 80 shares outstanding. Panel A of Exhibit 8.3 shows the percentage of Dow 30 companies that show treasury stock in their financial statements.

COMMON VERSUS PREFERRED STOCK

The corporate charter defines the number of shares of stock authorized, the par value or stated value (if any), and the classes of stock that a corporation can issue. Most stock issued is either *common* or *preferred.*

LO 8-3

Differentiate between common and preferred stock.

Common Stock

All corporations issue **common stock**. Common stockholders bear the highest risk of losing their investment if a company is forced to liquidate. On the other hand, they reap the greatest rewards when a corporation prospers. Common stockholders generally enjoy several rights, including (1) the right to buy and sell stock, (2) the right to share in the distribution of profits, (3) the right to share in the distribution of corporate assets in the case of liquidation, (4) the right to vote on significant matters that affect the corporate charter, and (5) the right to participate in the election of directors.

Preferred Stock

Many corporations issue **preferred stock** in addition to common stock. Holders of preferred stock receive certain privileges relative to holders of common stock. In exchange for special privileges in some areas, preferred stockholders give up rights in other areas. Preferred stockholders usually have no voting rights and the amount of their dividends is usually limited. Preferences granted to preferred stockholders include the following:

1. *Preference as to assets.* Preferred stock often has a liquidation value. In case of bankruptcy, preferred stockholders must be paid the liquidation value before any assets are distributed to common stockholders. However, preferred stockholder claims still fall behind creditor claims.

2. *Preference as to dividends.* Preferred shareholders are frequently guaranteed the right to receive dividends before common stockholders. The amount of the preferred dividend is normally stated on the stock certificate. It may be stated as a dollar value (say, $5) per share or as a percentage of the par value. Most preferred stock has **cumulative dividends,** meaning that if a corporation is unable to pay the preferred dividend in any year, the dividend is not lost but begins to accumulate. Cumulative dividends that have not been paid are called **dividends in arrears**. When a company pays dividends, any preferred stock arrearages must be paid before any other dividends are paid. Noncumulative preferred stock is not often issued because preferred stock is much less attractive if missed dividends do not accumulate.

To illustrate the effects of preferred dividends, consider Dillion, Incorporated, which has the following shares of stock outstanding:

> Preferred stock, 4%, $10 par, 10,000 shares
> Common stock, $10 par, 20,000 shares

Assume the preferred stock dividend has not been paid for two years. If Dillion pays $22,000 in dividends, how much will each class of stock receive? It depends on whether the preferred stock is cumulative.

Allocation of Distribution for Cumulative Preferred Stock

	To Preferred	To Common
Dividends in arrears	$ 8,000	$ 0
Current year's dividends	4,000	10,000
Total distribution	$12,000	$10,000

Allocation of Distribution for Noncumulative Preferred Stock

	To Preferred	To Common
Dividends in arrears	$ 0	$ 0
Current year's dividends	4,000	18,000
Total distribution	$4,000	$18,000

EXHIBIT 8.3

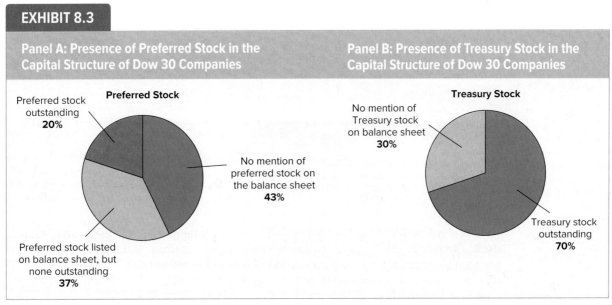

| Panel A: Presence of Preferred Stock in the Capital Structure of Dow 30 Companies | Panel B: Presence of Treasury Stock in the Capital Structure of Dow 30 Companies |

Preferred Stock

Preferred stock outstanding **20%**

No mention of preferred stock on the balance sheet **43%**

Preferred stock listed on balance sheet, but none outstanding **37%**

Treasury Stock

No mention of Treasury stock on balance sheet **30%**

Treasury stock outstanding **70%**

The chart is based on data drawn from recent annual reports published by the 30 companies that comprise the Dow Jones Industrial Average.

The total annual dividend on the preferred stock is $4,000 (0.04 × $10 par × 10,000 shares). If the preferred stock is cumulative, the $8,000 in arrears must be paid first. Then $4,000 for the current year's dividend is paid next. The remaining $10,000 goes to common stockholders. If the preferred stock is noncumulative, the $8,000 of dividends from past periods is ignored. This year's $4,000 preferred dividend is paid first, with the remaining $18,000 going to common.

Other features of preferred stock may include the right to participate in distributions beyond the established amount of the preferred dividend, the right to convert preferred stock to common stock or to bonds, and the potential for having the preferred stock called (repurchased) by the corporation. Detailed discussion of these topics is left to more advanced courses. Panel B of Exhibit 8.3 shows the percentage of Dow 30 companies that show preferred stock in their financial statements.

Other Classes of Stock

There can be different classes of common or preferred stock. For example, a company could issue class A common stock that provides its stockholders with rights to vote in the elections of the members of the board of directors. The same company could also issue class B common stock that does not provide voting rights. In conclusion, a company can have many classes of stock with each type offering the shareholders a different set of rights and privileges.

ACCOUNTING FOR STOCK TRANSACTIONS ON THE DAY OF ISSUE

Issuing stock with a par or stated value is accounted for differently from issuing no-par stock. For stock with either a par or stated value, the total amount acquired from the owners is divided between two separate stockholders' equity accounts. The amount of the par or stated value is recorded in the stock account. Any amount received above the par or stated value is recorded in an account called **Paid-in Capital in Excess of Par (or Stated) Value.**

LO 8-4

Show how issuing different classes of stock affects financial statements.

Issuing Par Value Stock

To illustrate the issue of common stock with a par value, assume that Nelson Incorporated is authorized to issue 250 shares of common stock. During Year 1, Nelson issued 100 shares of

$10 par common stock for $22 per share. The event increases assets and stockholders' equity by $2,200 ($22 × 100 shares). The increase in stockholders' equity is divided into two parts, $1,000 of par value ($10 per share × 100 shares) and $1,200 ($2,200 − $1,000) received in excess of par value. The income statement is not affected. The $2,200 cash inflow is reported in the financing activities section of the statement of cash flows. The effects on the financial statements follow:

Balance Sheet						Income Statement				Statement of Cash Flows
Assets	=	Liab.	+		Stk. Equity					
Cash	=			Com. Stk.	+ PIC in Excess	Rev.	− Exp.	= Net Inc.		
2,200	=	NA	+	1,000	+ 1,200	NA	− NA	= NA		2,200 FA

The *legal capital* of the corporation is $1,000, the total par value of the issued common stock. The number of shares issued can be easily verified by dividing the total amount in the common stock account by the par value ($1,000 ÷ $10 = 100 shares).

Stock Classification

Assume Nelson Incorporated obtains authorization to issue 400 shares of class B, $20 par value common stock. The company issues 150 shares of this stock at $25 per share. The event increases assets and stockholders' equity by $3,750 ($25 × 150 shares). The increase in stockholders' equity is divided into two parts, $3,000 of par value ($20 per share × 150 shares) and $750 ($3,750 − $3,000) received in excess of par value. The income statement is not affected. The $3,750 cash inflow is reported in the financing activities section of the statement of cash flows. The effects on the financial statements follow:

Balance Sheet						Income Statement				Statement of Cash Flows
Assets	=	Liab.	+		Stk. Equity					
Cash	=			Com. Stk.	+ PIC in Excess	Rev.	− Exp.	= Net Inc.		
3,750	=	NA	+	3,000	+ 750	NA	− NA	= NA		3,750 FA

As the preceding event suggests, companies can issue numerous classes of common stock. The specific rights and privileges for each class are described in the individual stock certificates.

Stock Issued at Stated Value

Assume Nelson is authorized to issue 300 shares of a third class of stock, 7 percent cumulative preferred stock with a stated value of $10 per share. Nelson issued 100 shares of the preferred stock at a price of $22 per share. The effects on the financial statements are identical to those described for the issue of the $10 par value common stock.

Balance Sheet						Income Statement				Statement of Cash Flows
Assets	=	Liab.	+		Stk. Equity					
Cash	=			Pfd. Stk.	+ PIC in Excess	Rev.	− Exp.	= Net Inc.		
2,200	=	NA	+	1,000	+ 1,200	NA	− NA	= NA		2,200 FA

Stock Issued with No Par Value

Assume that Nelson Incorporated is authorized to issue 150 shares of a fourth class of stock. This stock is no-par common stock. Nelson issues 100 shares of this no-par stock at $22 per

EXHIBIT 8.4

NELSON INCORPORATED
Balance Sheet
As of December 31, Year 1

Assets	
Cash	$15,350
Stockholders' equity	
Preferred stock, $10 stated value, 7% cumulative,	
300 shares authorized, 100 issued and outstanding	$ 1,000
Common stock, $10 par value, 250 shares authorized,	
100 issued and outstanding	1,000
Common stock, class B, $20 par value, 400 shares	
authorized, 150 issued and outstanding	3,000
Common stock, no par, 150 shares authorized,	
100 issued and outstanding	2,200
Paid-in capital in excess of stated value—preferred	1,200
Paid-in capital in excess of par value—common	1,200
Paid-in capital in excess of par value—class B common	750
Total paid-in capital	10,350
Retained earnings	5,000
Total stockholders' equity	$15,350

share. The entire amount received ($22 × 100 = $2,200) is recorded in the stock account. The effects on the financial statements follow:

Balance Sheet						Income Statement				Statement of Cash Flows
Assets	=	Liab.	+		Stk. Equity					
Cash	=			Com. Stk.	+	PIC in Excess	Rev.	−	Exp.	=	Net Inc.	
2,200	=	NA	+	2,200	+	NA	NA	−	NA	=	NA	2,200 FA

Financial Statement Presentation

Exhibit 8.4 displays Nelson Incorporated's balance sheet after the four stock issuances described previously. The exhibit assumes that Nelson earned and retained $5,000 of cash income during Year 1. The stock accounts are presented first, followed by the paid-in capital in excess of par (or stated) value accounts. A wide variety of reporting formats is used in practice. For example, another popular format is to group accounts by stock class, with the paid-in capital in excess accounts listed with their associated stock accounts. Alternatively, many companies combine the different classes of stock into a single amount and provide the detailed information in notes to the financial statements.

TREASURY STOCK

When a company buys its own stock, the stock purchased is called *treasury stock*. Why would a company buy its own stock? Common reasons include (1) to have stock available to give employees pursuant to stock option plans, (2) to accumulate stock in preparation for a merger or business combination, (3) to reduce the number of shares outstanding in order to increase earnings per share, (4) to keep the price of the stock high when it appears to be falling, and (5) to avoid a hostile takeover (removing shares from the open market reduces the opportunity for outsiders to obtain enough voting shares to gain control of the company).

LO 8-5

Show how treasury stock affects financial statements.

Conceptually, purchasing treasury stock is the reverse of issuing stock. When a business issues stock, the assets and stockholders' equity of the business increase. When a business buys treasury stock, the assets and stockholders' equity of the business decrease. To illustrate, return to the Nelson Incorporated example. Assume that in Year 2 Nelson paid $20 per share to buy back 50 shares of the $10 par value common stock that it originally issued at $22 per share. The purchase of treasury stock is an asset use transaction. Assets and stockholders' equity decrease by the cost of the purchase ($20 × 50 shares = $1,000). The income statement is not affected. The cash outflow is reported in the financing activities section of the statement of cash flows. The effects on the financial statements follow:

Balance Sheet								Income Statement						Statement of Cash Flows
Assets	=	Liab.	+			Stk. Equity								
Cash	=			Other Equity Accts.	−	Treasury Stk.		Rev.	−	Exp.	=	Net Inc.		
(1,000)	=	NA	+	NA	−	1,000		NA	−	NA	=	NA		(1,000) FA

The Treasury Stock account is a contra stockholders' equity account. It is deducted from the other stockholders' equity accounts in determining total stockholders' equity. In this example, the Treasury Stock account contains the full amount paid ($1,000). The original issue price and the par value of the stock have no effect on the Treasury Stock account. Recognizing the full amount paid in the treasury stock account is called the **cost method of accounting for treasury stock** transactions. Although other methods could be used, the cost method is the most common.

Assume Nelson reissues 30 shares of treasury stock at a price of $25 per share. As with any other stock issue, the sale of treasury stock is an asset source transaction. In this case, assets and stockholders' equity increase by $750 ($25 × 30 shares). The income statement is not affected. The cash inflow is reported in the financing activities section of the statement of cash flows. The effects on the financial statements follow:

Balance Sheet										Income Statement					Statement of Cash Flows
Assets	=	Liab.	+				Stk. Equity								
Cash	=			Other Equity Accounts	−	Treasury Stock	+	PIC from Treasury Stk.		Rev.	−	Exp.	=	Net Inc.	
750	=	NA	+	NA	−	(600)	+	150		NA	−	NA	=	NA	750 FA

The decrease in the Treasury Stock account increases stockholders' equity. The $150 difference between the cost of the treasury stock ($20 per share × 30 shares = $600) and the sales price ($750) is *not* reported as a gain. The sale of treasury stock is a capital acquisition, not a revenue transaction. The $150 is additional paid-in capital. *Corporations do not recognize gains or losses on the sale of treasury stock.*

After selling 30 shares of treasury stock, 20 shares remain in Nelson's possession. These shares cost $20 each, so the balance in the Treasury Stock account is now $400 ($20 × 20 shares). Treasury stock is reported on the balance sheet directly below retained earnings. Although this placement suggests that treasury stock reduces retained earnings, the reduction actually applies to the entire stockholders' equity section. Exhibit 8.5 shows the presentation of treasury stock in the balance sheet.

 CHECK YOURSELF 8.2

On January 1, Year 2, Janell Company's Common Stock account balance was $20,000. On April 1, Year 2, Janell paid $12,000 cash to purchase some of its own stock. Janell resold this stock on October 1, Year 2, for $14,500. What is the effect on the company's cash and stockholders' equity from both the April 1 purchase and the October 1 resale of the stock?

(continued)

Answer The April 1 purchase would reduce both cash and stockholders' equity by $12,000. The treasury stock transaction represents a return of invested capital to those owners who sold stock back to the company.

The sale of the treasury stock on October 1 would increase both cash and stockholders' equity by $14,500. The difference between the sales price of the treasury stock and its cost ($14,500 − $12,000) represents additional paid-in capital from treasury stock transactions. The stockholders' equity section of the balance sheet would include Common Stock, $20,000, and Additional Paid-in Capital from Treasury Stock Transactions, $2,500.

CASH DIVIDENDS

Cash dividends are affected by three significant dates: *the declaration date, the date of record, and the payment date.* Assume that on October 15, Year 2, the board of Nelson Incorporated declared a 7 percent cash dividend on the 100 outstanding shares of its $10 stated value preferred stock. The dividend will be paid to stockholders of record as of November 15, Year 2. The cash payment will be made on December 15, Year 2.

LO 8-6

Show how declaring and paying cash dividends affect financial statements.

Declaration Date

Although corporations are not required to declare dividends, they are legally obligated to pay dividends once they have been declared. They must recognize a liability on the **declaration date** (in this case, October 15, Year 2). The increase in liabilities is accompanied by a decrease in retained earnings. The income statement and statement of cash flows are not affected. The effects on the financial statements of *declaring* the $70 (0.07 × $10 × 100 shares) dividend follow:

Balance Sheet						Income Statement				Statement of Cash Flows
Assets	=	Liab.	+	Stk. Equity						
Cash	=	Div. Pay.	+	Com. Stk.	+ Ret. Earn.	Rev.	− Exp.	= Net Inc.		
NA	=	70	+	NA	+ (70)	NA	− NA	= NA		NA

REALITY BYTES

As you have learned, dividends, unlike interest on bonds, do not have to be paid. In fact, a company's board of directors must vote to pay dividends before they can be paid. Even so, once a company establishes a practice of paying a dividend of a given amount each period, usually quarterly, the company is reluctant to not pay the dividend. The amount of dividends that companies pay, relative to their earnings, varies widely.

Large, well-established companies usually do pay dividends, while young, growing companies often do not. Consider the 30 companies that make up the Dow Jones Industrial Average. In 2017, all of these companies paid dividends. VISA paid out the lowest percentage of its earnings in dividends (18.6 percent). At the other extreme was Chevron, which paid dividends of $.84 per share even though it reported a net loss of $0.72 per share. The average percentage of earnings paid out as dividends for all 30 companies in the Dow was about 58 percent in 2017, but seven of the companies paid out more in dividends than they earned in profit.

Uladzik Kryhin/Shutterstock

For comparison, consider two large, relatively young, technology companies: Alphabet, the parent company of Google, and Facebook. Although both of these companies have had positive earnings in recent years—Google alone had $12.7 billion of earnings in 2017—neither has ever paid a dividend to its common shareholders. They are using their cash to grow their businesses, often by purchasing other companies.

Date of Record

Cash dividends are paid to investors who owned the preferred stock on the **date of record** (in this case November 15, Year 2). Any stock sold after the date of record but before the payment date (in this case December 15, Year 2) is traded **ex-dividend,** meaning the buyer will not receive the upcoming dividend. The date of record is merely a cutoff date. It does not affect the financial statements.

Payment Date

Nelson actually paid the cash dividend on the **payment date.** This event has the same effect as paying any other liability. Assets (cash) and liabilities (dividends payable) both decrease. The income statement is not affected. The cash outflow is reported in the financing activities section of the statement of cash flows. The effects of the cash payment on the financial statements follow:

Balance Sheet								Income Statement					Statement of Cash Flows
Assets	=	Liab.	+		Stk. Equity								
Cash	=	Div. Pay.	+	Com. Stk.	+	Ret. Earn.		Rev.	−	Exp.	=	Net Inc.	
(70)	=	(70)	+	NA	+	NA		NA	−	NA	=	NA	(70) FA

STOCK DIVIDENDS AND SPLITS

Stock Dividends

Dividends are not always paid in cash. Companies sometimes choose to issue **stock dividends,** wherein they distribute additional shares of stock to the stockholders. To illustrate, assume that Nelson Incorporated decided to issue a 10 percent stock dividend on its class B, $20 par value common stock. Because dividends apply to outstanding shares only, Nelson will issue 15 (150 outstanding shares × 0.10) additional shares of class B stock.

Assume the new shares are distributed when the market value of the stock is $30 per share. As a result of the stock dividend, Nelson will transfer $450 ($30 × 15 new shares) from retained earnings to paid-in capital.[1] The stock dividend is an equity exchange transaction. The income statement and statement of cash flows are not affected. The effects of the stock dividend on the financial statements follow:

Balance Sheet								Income Statement					Statement of Cash Flows
Assets	=	Liab.	+			Stk. Equity							
				Com. Stk.	+	PIC in Excess	+	Ret. Earn.	Rev.	−	Exp.	=	Net Inc.	
NA	=	NA	+	300	+	150	+	(450)	NA	−	NA	=	NA	NA

Stock dividends have no effect on assets. They merely increase the number of shares of stock outstanding. Because a greater number of shares represents the same ownership interest in the same amount of assets, the market value per share of a company's stock normally declines when a stock dividend is distributed. A lower market price makes the stock more affordable and may increase demand for the stock, which benefits both the company and its stockholders.

Stock Splits

A corporation may also reduce the market price of its stock through a **stock split.** A stock split replaces existing shares with a greater number of new shares. Any par or stated value of

---

[1]The accounting here applies to small stock dividends. Accounting for large stock dividends is explained in a more advanced course.

the stock is proportionately reduced to reflect the new number of shares outstanding. For example, assume Nelson Incorporated declared a 2-for-1 stock split on the 165 outstanding shares (150 originally issued + 15 shares distributed in a stock dividend) of its $20 par value, class B common stock. Nelson notes in the accounting records that the 165 old $20 par shares are replaced with 330 new $10 par shares. Investors who owned the 165 shares of old common stock would now own 330 shares of the new common stock.

Stock splits have no effect on the dollar amounts of assets, liabilities, and stockholders' equity. They affect only the number of shares of stock outstanding. In Nelson's case, the ownership interest that was previously represented by 165 shares of stock is now represented by 330 shares. Because twice as many shares now represent the same ownership interest, the market value per share should be one-half as much as it was prior to the split. However, as with a stock dividend, the lower market price will probably stimulate demand for the stock. As a result, doubling the number of shares will likely reduce the market price to slightly more than one-half of the pre-split value. For example, if the stock were selling for $30 per share before the 2-for-1 split, it might sell for $15.50 after the split.

APPROPRIATION OF RETAINED EARNINGS

The board of directors may restrict the amount of retained earnings available to distribute as dividends. The restriction may be required by credit agreements, or it may be discretionary. A retained earnings restriction, often called an *appropriation,* is an equity exchange event. It transfers a portion of existing retained earnings to **Appropriated Retained Earnings.** Total retained earnings remains unchanged. To illustrate, assume that Nelson appropriates $1,000 of retained earnings for future expansion. The income statement and the statement of cash flows are not affected. The effects on the financial statements of appropriating $1,000 of retained earnings follow:

Show how the appropriation of retained earnings affects financial statements.

Balance Sheet							Income Statement			Statement of Cash Flows
Assets	=	Liab.	+	Stk. Equity						
				Com. Stk. +	Ret. Earn. +	App. Ret. Earn.	Rev. −	Exp. =	Net Inc.	
NA	=	NA	+	NA −	(1,000) +	1,000	NA −	NA =	NA	NA

Financial Statement Presentation

The Year 1 and Year 2 events for Nelson Incorporated are summarized as follows. Events 1 through 8 are cash transactions. The results of the Year 1 transactions (nos. 1–5) are reflected in Exhibit 8.4. The results of the Year 2 transactions (nos. 6–9) are shown in Exhibit 8.5.

1. Issued 100 shares of $10 par value common stock at a market price of $22 per share.
2. Issued 150 shares of class B, $20 par value common stock at a market price of $25 per share.
3. Issued 100 shares of $10 stated value, 7 percent cumulative preferred stock at a market price of $22 per share.
4. Issued 100 shares of no-par common stock at a market price of $22 per share.
5. Earned and retained $5,000 cash from operations.
6. Purchased 50 shares of $10 par value common stock as treasury stock at a market price of $20 per share.
7. Sold 30 shares of treasury stock at a market price of $25 per share.
8. Declared and paid a $70 cash dividend on the preferred stock.
9. Issued a 10 percent stock dividend on the 150 shares of outstanding class B, $20 par value common stock (15 additional shares). The additional shares were issued when the market price of the stock was $30 per share. There are 165 (150 + 15) class B common shares outstanding after the stock dividend.

EXHIBIT 8.5

NELSON INCORPORATED
Balance Sheet
As of December 31, Year 2

Assets		
Cash		$21,030
Stockholders' equity		
Preferred stock, $10 stated value, 7% cumulative,		
300 shares authorized, 100 issued and outstanding	$1,000	
Common stock, $10 par value, 250 shares authorized,		
100 issued, and 80 outstanding	1,000	
Common stock, class B, $10 par, 800 shares authorized,		
330 issued and outstanding	3,300	
Common stock, no par, 150 shares authorized,		
100 issued and outstanding	2,200	
Paid-in capital in excess of stated value—preferred	1,200	
Paid-in capital in excess of par value—common	1,200	
Paid-in capital in excess of par value—class B common	900	
Paid-in capital in excess of cost of treasury stock	150	
Total paid-in capital		$10,950
Retained earnings		
Appropriated	1,000	
Unappropriated	9,480	
Total retained earnings		10,480
Less: Treasury stock, 20 shares @ $20 per share		(400)
Total stockholders' equity		$21,030

10. Issued a 2-for-1 stock split on the 165 shares of class B, $20 par value common stock. After this transaction, there are 330 shares outstanding of the class B common stock with a $10 par value.

11. Appropriated $1,000 of retained earnings.

The illustration assumes that Nelson earned net income of $6,000 in Year 2. The ending retained earnings balance is determined as follows: Beginning Balance $5,000 − $70 Cash Dividend − $450 Stock Dividend + $6,000 Net Income = $10,480 Ending Balance ($1,000 appropriated and $9,480 unappropriated).

INVESTING IN CAPITAL STOCK

LO 8-9

Show how accounting information is used to make stock investment decisions.

Stockholders may benefit in two ways when a company generates earnings. The company may distribute the earnings directly to the stockholders in the form of dividends. Alternatively, the company may retain some or all of the earnings to finance growth and increase its potential for future earnings. If the company retains earnings, the market value of its stock should increase to reflect its greater earnings prospects. How can analysts use financial reporting to help assess the potential for dividend payments or growth in market value?

Receiving Dividends

Is a company likely to pay dividends in the future? The financial statements can help answer this question. They show if dividends were paid in the past. Companies with a history of paying dividends usually continue to pay dividends. Also, to pay dividends in the future, a company must have sufficient cash and retained earnings. These amounts are reported on the balance sheet and the statement of cash flows.

Increasing the Price of Stock

Is the market value (price) of a company's stock likely to increase? Increases in a company's stock price occur when investors believe the company's earnings will grow. Financial statements provide information that is useful in predicting the prospects for earnings growth. Here also, a company's earnings history is an indicator of its growth potential. However, because published financial statements report historical information, investors must recognize their limitations. Investors want to know about the future. Stock prices are therefore influenced more by forecasts than by history.

For example:

- On December 14, 2018, Costco Wholesale Corporation announced that revenues for the quarter ended November 25, 2018, were 10.2 percent higher than for the same quarter of the previous year, and its earnings were up 19.9 percent. In reaction to this seemingly good news, the price of its stock *fell* by 4.9 percent. Why did the market respond in this way? Even though the quarterly earnings per share (EPS) of $1.61 were higher than last year, analysts had expected Costco's EPS to be $1.62, and they were concerned that increased competition would reduce the rate of Costco's future growth.

- On November 27, 2018, salesforce.com, Inc. announced that EPS for the quarter ended October 31, 2018 were 65 percent lower than for the previous quarter, and 4.3 percent lower than for the same quarter of 2017. The market's reaction to this seemingly negative news was to *increase* the price of the company's stock by 7.4 percent. The market reacted this way because even though earnings were down significantly, total revenues increased by around 26 percent from the prior year, and 3.4 percent from the previous quarter.

In each case, investors reacted to the potential for earnings growth rather than the historical earnings reports. Because investors find forecasted statements more relevant to decision making than historical financial statements, most companies provide forecasts in addition to historical financial statements.

The value of a company's stock is also influenced by nonfinancial information that financial statements cannot provide. For example, suppose ExxonMobil announced in the middle of its fiscal year that it had just discovered substantial oil reserves on property to which it held drilling rights. Consider the following questions:

- What would happen to the price of ExxonMobil's stock on the day of the announcement?
- What would happen to ExxonMobil's financial statements on that day?

The price of ExxonMobil's stock would almost certainly increase as soon as the discovery was made public. However, nothing would happen to its financial statements on that day. There would probably be very little effect on its financial statements for that year. Only after the company begins to develop the oil field and sell the oil will its financial statements reflect the discovery. Changes in financial statements tend to lag behind the announcements companies make regarding their earnings potential.

Stock prices are also affected by general economic conditions and consumer confidence as well as the performance measures reported in financial statements. For example, the stock prices of virtually all companies declined sharply immediately after the September 11, 2001, terrorist attacks on the World Trade Center and the Pentagon. Historically based financial statements are of little benefit in predicting general economic conditions or changes in consumer confidence.

Exercising Control through Stock Ownership

The more influence an investor has over the operations of a company, the more the investor can benefit from owning stock in the company. For example, consider a power company that needs coal to produce electricity. The power company may purchase some common stock in a coal mining company to ensure a stable supply of coal. What percentage of the mining company's stock must the power company acquire to exercise significant influence over the mining company? The answer depends on how many investors own stock in the mining company and how the number of shares is distributed among the stockholders.

The greater its number of stockholders, the more *widely held* a company is. If stock ownership is concentrated in the hands of a few persons, a company is *closely held.* Widely held companies can generally be controlled with smaller percentages of ownership than closely held companies. Consider a company in which no existing investor owns more than 1 percent of the voting stock. A new investor who acquires a 5 percent interest would immediately become, by far, the largest shareholder and would likely be able to significantly influence board decisions. In contrast, consider a closely held company in which one current shareholder owns 51 percent of the company's stock. Even if another investor acquired the remaining 49 percent of the company, that investor could not control the company.

Financial statements contain some, but not all, of the information needed to help an investor determine ownership levels necessary to permit control. For example, the financial statements disclose the total number of shares of stock outstanding, but they normally contain little information about the number of shareholders and even less information about any relationships between shareholders. Relationships between shareholders are critically important because related shareholders, whether bound by family or business interests, might exercise control by voting as a block. For publicly traded companies, information about the number of shareholders and the identity of some large shareholders is disclosed in reports filed with the Securities and Exchange Commission.

A Look Back

Starting a business requires obtaining financing; it takes money to make money. Although some money may be borrowed, lenders are unlikely to make loans to businesses that lack some degree of owner financing. Equity financing is therefore critical to virtually all profit-oriented businesses. This chapter has examined some of the issues related to accounting for equity transactions.

The idea that a business must obtain financing from its owners was one of the first events presented in this textbook. This chapter discussed the advantages and disadvantages of organizing a business as a sole proprietorship versus a partnership versus a corporation. These advantages and disadvantages include the following:

1. *Double taxation*—Income of corporations is subject to double taxation, but that of proprietorships and partnerships is not.

2. *Regulation*—Corporations are subject to more regulation than are proprietorships and partnerships.

3. *Limited liability*—An investor's personal assets are not at risk as a result of owning corporate securities. The investor's liability is limited to the amount of the investment. In general, proprietorships and partnerships do not offer limited liability. However, laws in some states permit the formation of limited liability companies, which operate like proprietorships and partnerships yet place some limits on the personal liability of their owners.

4. *Continuity*—Proprietorships and partnerships dissolve when one of the owners leaves the business. Corporations are separate legal entities that continue to exist regardless of changes in ownership.

5. *Transferability*—Ownership interests in corporations are easier to transfer than those of proprietorships or partnerships.

6. *Management structure*—Corporations are more likely to have independent professional managers than are proprietorships or partnerships.

7. *Ability to raise capital*—Because they can be owned by millions of investors, corporations have the opportunity to raise more capital than proprietorships or partnerships.

Corporations issue different classes of common stock and preferred stock as evidence of ownership interests. In general, *common stock* provides the widest range of privileges including the right to vote and participate in earnings. *Preferred stockholders* usually give up the right to vote in exchange for preferences such as the right to receive dividends or assets upon liqui-dation before common stockholders. Stock may have a *par value* or *stated value,* which relates to legal requirements governing the amount of capital that must be maintained in the corpo-ration. Corporations may also issue *no-par stock,* avoiding some of the legal requirements that pertain to par or stated value stock.

Stock that a company issues and then repurchases is called *treasury stock.* Purchasing treasury stock reduces total assets and stockholders' equity. Reselling treasury stock repre-sents a capital acquisition. The difference between the reissue price and the cost of the trea-sury stock is recorded directly in the stockholders' equity accounts. Treasury stock transactions do not result in gains or losses on the income statement.

Companies may issue *stock splits* or *stock dividends.* These transactions increase the num-ber of shares of stock without changing the net assets of a company. The per share market value usually drops when a company issues stock splits or dividends.

A Look Forward

Financial statement analysis is so important that Chapter 9 is devoted solely to a detailed discussion of this subject. The chapter covers vertical analysis (analyzing relationships within a specific statement) and horizontal analysis (analyzing relationships across ac-counting periods). Finally, the chapter discusses limitations associated with financial state-ment analysis.

 Video lectures and accompanying self-assessment quizzes are available in *Connect* for all learning objectives.

 ## SELF-STUDY REVIEW PROBLEM

Edwards Inc. experienced the following events:

1. Issued common stock for cash.
2. Declared a cash dividend.
3. Issued noncumulative preferred stock for cash.
4. Appropriated retained earnings.
5. Distributed a stock dividend.
6. Paid cash to purchase treasury stock.
7. Distributed a 2-for-1 stock split.
8. Issued cumulative preferred stock for cash.
9. Paid a cash dividend that had previously been declared.
10. Sold treasury stock for cash at a higher amount than the cost of the treasury stock.

Required

Show the effect of each event on the elements of the financial statements using a horizontal statements model like the one shown here. Use + for increase, − for decrease, and NA for not affected. In the Cash Flow column, indicate whether the item is an operating activity (OA), investing activity (IA), or a financing activity (FA). The first transaction is entered as an example.

	Balance Sheet				Income Statement					Statement of Cash Flows
Event	Assets	=	Liab.	+	Stk. Equity	Rev.	−	Exp.	=	Net Inc.	
1	+		NA		+	NA		NA		NA	+ FA

Solution to Self-Study Review Problem

	Balance Sheet			Income Statement			Statement of Cash Flows
Event	Assets =	Liab. +	Stk. Equity	Rev. −	Exp. =	Net Inc.	
1	+	NA	+	NA	NA	NA	+ FA
2	NA	+	−	NA	NA	NA	NA
3	+	NA	+	NA	NA	NA	+ FA
4	NA	NA	− +	NA	NA	NA	NA
5	NA	NA	− +	NA	NA	NA	NA
6	−	NA	−	NA	NA	NA	− FA
7	NA	NA	NA	NA	NA	NA	NA
8	+	NA	+	NA	NA	NA	+ FA
9	−	−	NA	NA	NA	NA	− FA
10	+	NA	+	NA	NA	NA	+ FA

KEY TERMS

Appropriated retained earnings 307
Articles of incorporation 294
Authorized stock 299
Board of directors 296
Book value per share 299
Closely held corporation 294
Common stock 300
Continuity 295
Corporation 294

Cost method of accounting for treasury stock 304
Cumulative dividends 300
Date of record 306
Declaration date 305
Dividends in arrears 300
Double taxation 295
Entrenched management 296
Ex-dividend 306
Issued stock 299
Legal capital 298

Limited liability 295
Limited liability company (LLC) 295
Market value 299
Outstanding stock 299
Paid-in capital in excess of par (or stated) value 301
Partnership agreement 294
Partnership 294
Par value 294
Payment date 306
Preferred stock 300

Securities Act of 1933 and Securities Exchange Act of 1934 294
Sole proprietorship 294
Stated value 299
Stock certificate 294
Stock dividend 306
Stockholders 296
Stock split 306
Transferability 296
Treasury stock 299
Withdrawals 297

QUESTIONS

1. What are the three major forms of business organizations? Describe each.
2. How are sole proprietorships formed?
3. Discuss the purpose of a partnership agreement. Is such an agreement necessary for partnership formation?
4. What is meant by the phrase *separate legal entity*? To which type of business organization does it apply?
5. What is the purpose of the articles of incorporation? What information do they provide?
6. What is the function of the stock certificate?
7. What prompted Congress to pass the Securities Act of 1933 and the Securities Exchange Act of 1934? What is the purpose of these laws?
8. What are the advantages and disadvantages of the corporate form of business organization?
9. What is a limited liability company? Discuss its advantages and disadvantages.
10. How does the term *double taxation* apply to corporations? Give an example of double taxation.
11. What is the difference between contributed capital and retained earnings for a corporation?
12. What are the similarities and differences in the equity structure of a sole proprietorship, a partnership, and a corporation?
13. Why is it easier for a corporation to raise large amounts of capital than it is for a partnership?
14. What is the meaning of each of the following terms with respect to the corporate form of organization:
(a) Legal capital
(b) Par value of stock
(c) Stated value of stock
(d) Market value of stock
(e) Book value of stock
(f) Authorized shares of stock
(g) Issued stock
(h) Outstanding stock
(i) Treasury stock
(j) Common stock
(k) Preferred stock
(l) Dividends

15. What is the difference between cumulative preferred stock and noncumulative preferred stock?

16. What is no-par stock? How is it recorded in the accounting records?

17. Assume that Best Co. has issued and has outstanding 1,000 shares of $100 par value, 10 percent, cumulative preferred stock. What is the dividend per share? If the preferred dividend is two years in arrears, what total amount of dividends must be paid before the common shareholders can receive any dividends?

18. If Best Co. issued 10,000 shares of $20 par value

common stock for $30 per share, what amount is added to the Common Stock account? What amount of cash is received?

19. What is the difference between par value stock and stated value stock?

20. Why might a company repurchase its own stock?

21. What effect does the purchase of treasury stock have on the stockholders' equity of a company?

22. Assume that Day Company repurchased 1,000 of its own shares for $30 per share and sold the shares two weeks later for $35 per share. What is the amount of gain on the sale? How is it reported on the balance

sheet? What type of account is Treasury Stock?

23. What is the importance of the declaration date, record date, and payment date in conjunction with corporate dividends?

24. What is the difference between a stock dividend and a stock split?

25. Why would a company choose to distribute a stock dividend instead of a cash dividend?

26. What is the primary reason that a company would declare a stock split?

27. If Best Co. had 10,000 shares of $20 par value common stock outstanding and declared a 5-for-1 stock

split, how many shares would then be outstanding and what would be their par value after the split?

28. When a company appropriates retained earnings, does the company set aside cash for a specific use? Explain.

29. What is the largest source of financing for most U.S. businesses?

30. What is meant by *equity financing*? What is meant by *debt financing*?

31. What is a widely held corporation? What is a closely held corporation?

32. What are some reasons that a corporation might not pay dividends?

EXERCISES—SERIES A

An electronic auto-gradable version of the Series A Exercises is available in Connect. A PDF version of Series B Exercises is in Connect under the "Additional Student Resources" tab. Solutions to the Series B Exercises are available in Connect under the "Instructor Library" tab. Instructor and student Workpapers for the Series B Exercises are available in Connect under the "Instructor Library" and "Additional Student Resources" tabs respectively.

Exercise 8-1A *Characteristics of sole proprietorships, partnerships, and corporations*   LO 8-1

The three primary types of business organization are proprietorship, partnership, and corporation. Each type has characteristics that distinguish it from the other types. In the left column of the following table write the name of the type of business organization that is most likely to possess the characteristic that is described in the right column of the table. The first item is shown as an example.

Business Type	Characteristic
Proprietorship	Owned and operated by a single individual
	Subject to double taxation
	Has a retained earnings account on its balance sheet
	One owner may be held personally liable for actions taken on behalf of the business by different owner
	Profits benefit a single individual
	Frequently uses legal agreements to define profit distribution for two or more owners
	Most highly regulated form of business
	The business dissolves with the death of its only owner
	Offers the least capacity to raise capital
	Provides the best opportunity to benefit a few people
	Has only one capital account on its balance sheet
	Provides for easy transfer of ownership
	Offers the highest level of control over operating decisions
	Has multiple capital accounts but no retained earnings account on its balance sheet
	Provides the greatest capacity to raise capital
	Least regulated form of business
	Usually operated by a professional management team that is separated from the owners
	Has two or more owners who are not stockholders

Exercise 8-2A *Effect of accounting events on the financial statements of a sole proprietorship*

A sole proprietorship was started on January 1, Year 1, when it received $60,000 cash from Marlin Jones, the owner. During Year 1, the company earned $35,300 in cash revenues and paid $16,200 in cash expenses. Jones withdrew $1,000 cash from the business during Year 1.

Required

Prepare the income statement, capital statement (statement of changes in equity), balance sheet, and statement of cash flows for Jones's Year 1 fiscal year.

Exercise 8-3A *Effect of accounting events on the financial statements of a partnership*

Faith Busby and Jeremy Beatty started the B&B partnership on January 1, Year 1. The business acquired $44,000 cash from Busby and $66,000 from Beatty. During Year 1, the partnership earned $42,000 in cash revenues and paid $18,400 for cash expenses. Busby withdrew $2,000 cash from the business, and Beatty withdrew $2,500 cash. The net income was allocated to the capital accounts of the two partners in proportion to the amounts of their original investments in the business.

Required

Prepare an income statement, capital statement (statement of changes in equity), balance sheet, and statement of cash flows for B&B's Year 1 fiscal year.

Exercise 8-4A *Effect of accounting events on the financial statements of a corporation*

Astro Corporation was started with the issue of 2,000 shares of $5 par stock for cash on January 1, Year 1. The stock was issued at a market price of $12 per share. During Year 1, the company earned $31,000 in cash revenues and paid $17,100 for cash expenses. Also, a $2,000 cash dividend was paid to the stockholders.

Required

Prepare an income statement, statement of changes in stockholders' equity, balance sheet, and statement of cash flows for Astro Corporation's Year 1 fiscal year.

Exercise 8-5A *Characteristics of capital stock*

The stockholders' equity section of Creighton Company's balance sheet is shown as follows.

CREIGHTON COMPANY As of December 31, Year 1	
Stockholders' equity	
Preferred stock, $10 stated value, 7% cumulative, 300 shares authorized, 50 issued and outstanding	$ 500
Common stock, $10 par value, 250 shares authorized, 100 issued and outstanding	1,000
Common stock, class B, $20 par value, 400 shares authorized, 150 issued and outstanding	3,000
Common stock, no par, 150 shares authorized, 100 issued and outstanding	2,200
Paid-in capital in excess of stated value—preferred	600
Paid-in capital in excess of par value—common	1,200
Paid-in capital in excess of par value—class B common	750
Retained earnings	7,000
Total stockholders' equity	$16,250

Required

a. Assuming the preferred stock was originally issued for cash, determine the amount of cash that was collected when the stock was issued.

b. Based on the class B common stock alone, determine the amount of the company's legal capital.

c. Based on the class B common stock alone, determine the minimum amount of assets that must be retained in the company as protection for creditors.

d. Determine the number of shares of class B common stock that are available to sell as of December 31, Year 1.

e. Assuming Creighton purchases treasury stock consisting of 25 shares of its no par common stock on January 1, Year 2, determine the amount of the no-par common stock that would be outstanding immediately after the purchase.

f. Based on the stockholders' equity section shown, can you determine the market value of the preferred stock? If yes, what is the market value of one share of this stock?

Exercise 8-6A *Effect of issuing common stock on the balance sheet*

Newly formed S&J Iron Corporation has 50,000 shares of $10 par common stock authorized. On March 1, Year 1, S&J Iron issued 6,000 shares of the stock for $16 per share. On May 2, the company issued an additional 10,000 shares for $18 per share. S&J Iron was not affected by other events during Year 1.

Required

a. Record the transactions in a horizontal statements model like the following one. In the Cash Flow column, indicate whether the item is an operating activity (OA), investing activity (IA), or financing activity (FA). Use NA to indicate that an element was not affected by the event.

Balance Sheet					Income Statement			Statement of Cash Flows
Assets =	Liab. +	Stk. Equity						
Cash =	+	Com. Stk. +	PIC in Excess		Rev. −	Exp. =	Net Inc.	

b. Determine the amount S&J Iron would report for common stock on the December 31, Year 1, balance sheet.

c. Determine the amount S&J Iron would report for paid-in capital in excess of par.

d. What is the total amount of capital contributed by the owners?

e. What amount of total assets would S&J Iron report on the December 31, Year 1, balance sheet?

Exercise 8-7A *Recording and reporting common and preferred stock transactions*

Eastport Inc. was organized on June 5, Year 1. It was authorized to issue 300,000 shares of $10 par common stock and 50,000 shares of 5 percent cumulative class A preferred stock. The class A stock had a stated value of $50 per share. The following stock transactions pertain to Eastport Inc.:

1. Issued 15,000 shares of common stock for $12 per share.
2. Issued 5,000 shares of the class A preferred stock for $51 per share.
3. Issued 60,000 shares of common stock for $15 per share.

Required

Prepare the stockholders' equity section of the balance sheet immediately after these transactions have been recognized.

LO 8-3

Exercise 8-8A *Accounting for cumulative preferred dividends*

When Crossett Corporation was organized in January, Year 1, it immediately issued 4,000 shares of $50 par, 6 percent, cumulative preferred stock and 50,000 shares of $20 par common stock. Its earnings history is as follows: Year 1, net loss of $35,000; Year 2, net income of $125,000; Year 3, net income of $215,000. The corporation did not pay a dividend in Year 1.

Required

a. How much is the dividend arrearage as of January 1, Year 2?
b. Assume that the board of directors declares a $40,000 cash dividend at the end of Year 2 (remember that the Year 1 and Year 2 preferred dividends are due). How will the dividend be divided between the preferred and common stockholders?

LO 8-3

Exercise 8-9A *Cash dividends for preferred and common shareholders*

Weaver Corporation had the following stock issued and outstanding at January 1, Year 2:

1. 150,000 shares of $1 par common stock.
2. 15,000 shares of $100 par, 6 percent, noncumulative preferred stock.

On June 10, Weaver Corporation declared the annual cash dividend on its 15,000 shares of preferred stock and a $0.50 per share dividend for the common shareholders. The dividend will be paid on July 1 to the shareholders of record on June 20.

Required

Determine the total amount of dividend to be paid to the preferred shareholders and common shareholders.

LO 8-4

Exercise 8-10A *Effect of no-par common and par preferred stock on the horizontal statements model*

Mercury Corporation issued 6,000 shares of no-par common stock for $45 per share. Mercury also issued 3,000 shares of $50 par, 5 percent noncumulative preferred stock at $52 per share.

Required

Record these events in a horizontal statements model like the following one. In the cash flow column, indicate whether the item is an operating activity (OA), investing activity (IA), or financing activity (FA). Use NA to indicate that an element was not affected by the event.

Balance Sheet					Income Statement			Statement of
Assets =	Stk. Equity							Cash Flows
Cash =	Pfd. Stk. +	Com. Stk. +	PIC in Excess		Rev. −	Exp. =	Net Inc.	

LO 8-4

Exercise 8-11A *Issuing stock for cash*

Tom Yuppy, a wealthy investor, paid $20,000 for 1,000 shares of $10 par common stock issued to him by Leuig Corp. A month later, Leuig Corp. issued an additional 2,000 shares of stock to Yuppy for $25 per share.

Required

Show the effect of the two stock issues on Leuig's books in a horizontal statements model like the following one. In the Cash Flow column, indicate whether the item is an operating activity (OA), investing activity (IA), or financing activity (FA). Use NA to indicate that an element was not affected by the event.

Balance Sheet					Income Statement			Statement of
Assets	=	Stk. Equity						Cash Flows
Cash +	Land =	Com. Stk. +	PIC in Excess		Rev. −	Exp. =	Net Inc.	

Exercise 8-12A   *Treasury stock transactions*   LO 8-5

Elroy Corporation repurchased 4,000 shares of its own stock for $30 per share. The stock has a par of $10 per share. A month later Elroy resold 900 shares of the treasury stock for $32 per share.

Required

What is the balance of the Treasury Stock account after these transactions are recognized?

Exercise 8-13A   *Recording and reporting treasury stock transactions*   LO 8-5

The following information pertains to JAE Corp. at January 1, Year 2:

Common stock, $10 par, 20,000 shares authorized,	
2,000 shares issued and outstanding	$20,000
Paid-in capital in excess of par, common stock	15,000
Retained earnings	82,000

JAE Corp. completed the following transactions during Year 2:

1. Issued 3,000 shares of $10 par common stock for $25 per share.
2. Repurchased 500 shares of its own common stock for $26 per share.
3. Resold 200 shares of treasury stock for $30 per share.

Required

a. How many shares of common stock were outstanding at the end of the period?
b. How many shares of common stock had been issued at the end of the period?
c. Organize the transactions data in accounts under the accounting equation.
d. Prepare the stockholders' equity section of the balance sheet reflecting these transactions. Include the number of shares authorized, issued, and outstanding in the description of the common stock.

Exercise 8-14A   *Effect of cash dividends on financial statements*   LO 8-6

On May 1, Year 3, Love Corporation declared a $50,000 cash dividend to be paid on May 31 to shareholders of record on May 15.

Required

Record the events occurring on May 1 and May 31 in a horizontal statements model like the following one. In the Cash Flow column, indicate whether the item is an operating activity (OA), investing activity (IA), or financing activity (FA).

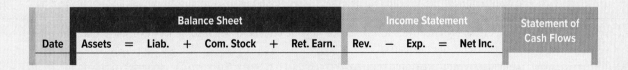

	Balance Sheet						Income Statement				Statement of Cash Flows
Date	Assets	=	Liab.	+	Com. Stock	+	Ret. Earn.	Rev.	−	Exp. = Net Inc.	

Exercise 8-15A   *Accounting for stock dividends*   LO 8-7

Beacon Corporation issued a 5 percent stock dividend on 30,000 shares of its $10 par common stock. At the time of the dividend, the market value of the stock was $15 per share.

Required

a. Compute the amount of the stock dividend.

b. Show the effects of the stock dividend on the financial statements using a horizontal statements model like the following one.

Balance Sheet						Income Statement				Statement of Cash Flows
Assets	=	Liab.	+ Com. Stk.	+ PIC in Excess	+ Ret. Earn.	Rev.	− Exp.	= Net Inc.		

LO 8-7

Exercise 8-16A   *Determining the effects of stock splits on the accounting records*

The market value of Yeates Corporation's common stock had become excessively high. The stock was currently selling for $240 per share. To reduce the market price of the common stock, Yeates declared a 3-for-1 stock split for the 100,000 outstanding shares of its $10 par value common stock.

Required

a. How will Yeates Corporation's books be affected by the stock split?

b. Determine the number of common shares outstanding and the par value after the split.

c. Explain how the market value of the stock will be affected by the stock split.

LO 8-8

Exercise 8-17A   *Determining how the appropriation of retained earnings affects financial statements*

On December 30, Billy's Boat Yard (BBY) had $90,000 of cash, $20,000 of liabilities, $30,000 of common stock, and $40,000 of unrestricted retained earnings. On December 31, BBY appropriated retained earnings in the amount of $18,000 for a future remodeling project.

Required

a. Record the December 31 appropriation in the following statements model:

Balance Sheet							Income Statement				Statement of Cash Flows
				Stk. Equity							
Assets	=	Liab.	+ C. Stk	+ Ret. Earn.	+ App. Ret. Earn.		Rev.	− Exp.	= Net Inc.		

b. Determine the amount of dividends that BBY can pay immediately after the December 31 appropriation.

c. Determine the total amount of retained earnings immediately after the December 31 appropriation.

d. Determine the total amount of cash immediately after the December 31 appropriation.

LO 8-9

Exercise 8-18A   *Corporate announcements*

Discount Drugs (one of the three largest drug makers) just reported that its Year 2 third quarter profits are essentially the same as the Year 1 third quarter profits. In addition to this announcement, the same day, Discount Drugs also announced that the Food and Drug Administration has just approved a new drug used to treat high blood pressure that Discount Drugs developed. This new drug has been shown to be extremely effective and has few or no side effects. It will also be less expensive than the other drugs currently on the market.

Required

Using this information, answer the following questions:

a. What do you think will happen to the stock price of Discount Drugs on the day these two announcements are made? Explain your answer.

b. How will the balance sheet be affected on that day by these announcements?

c. How will the income statement be affected on that day by these announcements?

d. How will the statement of cash flows be affected on that day by these announcements?

PROBLEMS—SERIES A

 An electronic auto-gradable version of the Series A Problems is available in Connect. A PDF version of Series B Problems is in Connect under the "Additional Student Resources" tab. Solutions to the Series B Problems are available in Connect under the "Instructor Library" tab. Instructor and student Workpapers for the Series B Problems are available in Connect under the "Instructor Library" and "Additional Student Resources" tabs respectively.

Problem 8-19A   *Different forms of business organization*

LO 8-1

Cal Cagle was working to establish a business enterprise with four of his wealthy friends. Each of the five individuals would receive a 20 percent ownership interest in the company. A primary goal of establishing the enterprise was to minimize the amount of income taxes paid. Assume that the five investors are in a 35 percent personal tax bracket and that the corporate tax rate is 25 percent. Also assume that the new company is expected to earn $220,000 of cash income before taxes during its first year of operation. All earnings are expected to be immediately distributed to the owners.

Required

Calculate the amount of after-tax cash flow available to each investor if the business is established as a partnership versus a corporation. Write a memo explaining the advantages and disadvantages of these two forms of business organization. Explain why a limited liability company may be a better choice than either a partnership or a corporation.

Problem 8-20A   *Effect of business structure on financial statements*

LO 8-1

CHECK FIGURES
a. Net Income: $16,900
b. Cascade Capital: $72,900

Cascade Company was started on January 1, Year 1, when it acquired $60,000 cash from the owners. During Year 1, the company earned cash revenues of $35,000 and incurred cash expenses of $18,100. The company also paid cash distributions of $4,000.

Required

Prepare a Year 1 income statement, capital statement (statement of changes in equity), balance sheet, and statement of cash flows under each of the following assumptions. (Consider each assumption separately.)

a. Cascade is a sole proprietorship owned by Carl Cascade.

b. Cascade is a partnership with two partners, Carl Cascade and Beth Cascade. Carl Cascade invested $24,000 and Beth Cascade invested $36,000 of the $60,000 cash that was used to start the business. Beth was expected to assume the vast majority of the responsibility for operating the business. The partnership agreement called for Beth to receive 60 percent of the profits and Carl to get the remaining 40 percent. With regard to the $4,000 distribution, Beth withdrew $2,400 from the business and Carl withdrew $1,600.

c. Cascade is a corporation. It issued 5,000 shares of $5 par common stock for $60,000 cash to start the business.

Problem 8-21A   *Cash dividends: Common and preferred stock*

LO 8-3, 8-6

Nowell Inc. had the following stock issued and outstanding at January 1, Year 2:

1. 150,000 shares of no-par common stock.

2. 30,000 shares of $50 par, 4 percent, cumulative preferred stock. (Dividends are in arrears for one year, Year 1.)

On March 8, Year 2, Nowell declared a $175,000 cash dividend to be paid March 31 to shareholders of record on March 20.

Required

What amount of dividends will be paid to the preferred shareholders versus the common shareholders?

LO 8-4, 8-5

CHECK FIGURES
Total Paid-In Capital: $74,240
Total Stockholders' Equity: $156,400

Problem 8-22A   *Recording and reporting treasury stock transactions*

The following information pertains to Ming Corp. at January 1, Year 2:

Common stock, $10 par, 50,000 shares authorized,	
3,000 shares issued and outstanding	$30,000
Paid-in capital in excess of par, common stock	12,000
Retained earnings	46,000

Ming Corp. completed the following transactions during Year 2:

1. Issued 2,000 shares of $10 par common stock for $16 per share.
2. Repurchased 500 shares of its own common stock for $18 per share.
3. Resold 120 shares of treasury stock for $20 per share.
4. Earned $85,000 of cash revenue.
5. Paid $42,000 of cash operating expenses.

Required

Prepare the stockholders' equity section of the year-end balance sheet.

LO 8-3, 8-4, 8-5, 8-6

CHECK FIGURES
b. Preferred Stock, Year 1: $50,000
c. Common Shares Outstanding,
    Year 2: 35,100

Problem 8-23A   *Recording and reporting stock transactions and cash dividends across two accounting cycles*

Sun Corporation received a charter that authorized the issuance of 100,000 shares of $10 par common stock and 50,000 shares of $50 par, 5 percent cumulative preferred stock. Sun Corporation completed the following transactions during its first two years of operation:

Year 1

Jan.   5   Sold 6,000 shares of the $10 par common stock for $15 per share.
       12   Sold 1,000 shares of the 5 percent preferred stock for $55 per share.
Apr.   5   Sold 30,000 shares of the $10 par common stock for $21 per share.
Dec. 31   During the year, earned $150,000 in cash revenue and paid $88,000 for cash operating expenses.
       31   Declared the cash dividend on the outstanding shares of preferred stock for Year 1. The dividend will be paid on February 15 to stockholders of record on January 10, Year 2.

Year 2

Feb. 15   Paid the cash dividend declared on December 31, Year 1.
Mar.   3   Sold 15,000 shares of the $50 par preferred stock for $53 per share.
May   5   Purchased 900 shares of the common stock as treasury stock at $24 per share.
Dec. 31   During the year, earned $210,000 in cash revenues and paid $98,000 for cash operating expenses.
       31   Declared the annual dividend on the preferred stock and a $0.50 per share dividend on the common stock.

Required

a. Organize the transaction data in accounts under an accounting equation.
b. Prepare the stockholders' equity section of the balance sheet at December 31, Year 1.
c. Prepare the balance sheet at December 31, Year 2.

LO 8-3, 8-4, 8-6, 8-7

CHECK FIGURES
b. Total Paid-In Capital:
    $1,084,500,
    Retained Earnings: $8,500

Problem 8-24A   *Recording and reporting stock dividends*

Burk Corp. completed the following transactions in Year 1, the first year of operation:

1. Issued 30,000 shares of $10 par common stock for $15 per share.
2. Issued 6,000 shares of $100 par, 5 percent, preferred stock at $101 per share.
3. Paid the annual cash dividend to preferred shareholders.

4. Issued a 5 percent stock dividend on the common stock. The market value at the dividend declaration date was $19 per share.

5. Later that year, issued a 2-for-1 split on the 31,500 shares of outstanding common stock.

6. Earned $165,000 of cash revenues and paid $98,000 of cash operating expenses.

Required

a. Record each of these events in a horizontal statements model like the following one. In the Cash Flow column, indicate whether the item is an operating activity (OA), investing activity (IA), or financing activity (FA). Use NA to indicate that an element is not affected by the event.

Balance Sheet						Income Statement			Statement of Cash Flows
Assets = Liab. +			Stk. Equity			Rev. −	Exp. =	Net Inc.	
	Pfd. Stk. +	Com. Stk. +	PIC in Excess PS +	PIC in Excess CS +	Ret. Earn.				

b. Prepare the stockholders' equity section of the balance sheet at the end of Year 1.

Problem 8-25A *Analyzing the stockholders' equity section of the balance sheet*

LO 8-2, 8-4, 8-5, 8-7

The stockholders' equity section of the balance sheet for Mann Equipment Co. at December 31, Year 2, is as follows.

CHECK FIGURES
a. Par value per share: $20
b. Dividend per share: $1.20

Stockholders' Equity		
Paid-in capital		
Preferred stock, ? par value, 6% cumulative, 100,000 shares authorized, 10,000 shares issued and outstanding	$ 200,000	
Common stock, $10 stated value, 200,000 shares authorized, 100,000 shares issued and ?? shares outstanding	1,000,000	
Paid-in capital in excess of par—Preferred	25,000	
Paid-in capital in excess of stated value—Common	500,000	
Total paid-in capital		$1,725,000
Retained earnings		420,000
Treasury stock, 1,000 shares		(13,000)
Total stockholders' equity		$2,132,000

Note: The market value per share of the common stock is $42, and the market value per share of the preferred stock is $26.

Required

a. What is the par value per share of the preferred stock?

b. What is the dividend per share on the preferred stock?

c. What is the number of common stock shares outstanding?

d. What was the average issue price per share (price for which the stock was issued) of the common stock?

e. Explain the difference between the average issue price and the market price of the common stock.

f. If Mann Equipment Company declared a 2-for-1 stock split on the common stock, how many shares would be outstanding after the split? What amount would be transferred from the Retained Earnings account because of the stock split? Theoretically, what would be the market price of the common stock immediately after the stock split?

Problem 8-26A   *Treasury stock transactions and appropriation of retained earnings*

Choctaw Co. completed the following transactions in Year 1, the first year of operation:

1. Issued 20,000 shares of $10 par common stock for $10 per share.
2. Issued 3,000 shares of $20 stated value preferred stock for $20 per share.
3. Purchased 1,000 shares of common stock as treasury stock for $12 per share.
4. Declared a $2,000 cash dividend on preferred stock.
5. Sold 500 shares of treasury stock for $14 per share.
6. Paid $2,000 cash for the preferred dividend declared in Event 4.
7. Earned cash revenues of $78,000 and incurred cash expenses of $41,000.
8. Appropriated $8,000 of retained earnings.

Required

a. Organize the transaction in accounts under an accounting equation.
b. Prepare the stockholders' equity section of the balance sheet as of December 31, Year 1.

Problem 8-27A   *Effects of equity transactions on financial statements*

The following events were experienced by Sequoia, Inc.:

1. Issued cumulative preferred stock for cash.
2. Issued common stock for cash.
3. Issued noncumulative preferred stock for cash.
4. Paid cash to purchase treasury stock.
5. Sold treasury stock for an amount of cash that was more than the cost of the treasury stock.
6. Declared a cash dividend.
7. Declared a 2-for-1 stock split on the common stock.
8. Distributed a stock dividend.
9. Appropriated retained earnings.
10. Paid a cash dividend that was previously declared.

Required

Show the effect of each event on the elements of the financial statements using a horizontal statements model like the following one. Use + for increase, − for decrease, and NA for not affected. In the Cash Flow column indicate whether the item is an operating activity (OA), investing activity (IA), or financing activity (FA). The first transaction is entered as an example.

Event No.	Balance Sheet				Income Statement			Statement of Cash Flows
	Assets	=	Liab.	+ Stk. Equity	Rev. −	Exp. =	Net Inc.	
1	+	NA		+	NA	NA	NA	+ FA

Problem 8-28A   *Using accounting information to make investment decisions*

Sea Coast Plumbing Company (SCPC) is a national company that provides residential plumbing services. SCPC is considering making a substantial investment in Rakeland Distributors, Inc. (RDI). RDI sells plumbing supplies throughout the United States.

Required

a. Identify two financial benefits that SCPC could receive from an investment in RDI.
b. What types of information would be helpful in evaluating SCPC's investment opportunity?
c. Speculate as to how owning RDI stock could benefit SCPC's capacity to conduct its operations.

ANALYZE, THINK, COMMUNICATE

ATC 8-1   Business Applications Case   *Understanding real-world annual reports*

Obtain the Target Corporation's annual report for its 2018 fiscal year (year ended February 2, 2019) at http://investors.target.com using the instructions in Appendix A, and use it to answer the following questions.

Required

a. What is the par value per share of Target's stock?

b. How many shares of Target's common stock were *outstanding* as of February 2, 2019?

c. Target's annual report provides some details about the company's executive officers. How many are identified? What is their minimum, maximum, and average age?

d. Target's balance sheet does not show a balance for treasury stock. Does this mean the company has not repurchased any of its own stock? Explain.

ATC 8-2   Group Assignment   *Missing information*

Listed here are the stockholders' equity sections of three public companies for fiscal years ending in 2017 and 2016. (Note that for General Mills these data are for the fiscal years ended on May 27, 2018 and May 28, 2017.)

	2017	2016
The Wendy's Company (in thousands)		
Stockholders' equity		
Common stock, ?? stated value per share, authorized:		
1,500,000; 470,424 shares issued	$ 47,042	$ 47,042
Capital in excess of stated value	2,885,955	2,878,589
Retained earnings	(163,289)	(290,857)
Acc. other comp. income (loss)	(46,198)	(63,241)
Treasury stock, at cost: 229,912 in 2017 and 223,850 in 2016	(2,150,307)	(2,043,797)
Coca-Cola (in millions)		
Stockholders' equity		
Common stock, ?? par value per share, authorized:		
11,200; issued: 7,040 shares in 2017 and 2016	1,760	1,760
Capital surplus	15,864	14,993
Reinvested earnings	60,430	65,502
Acc. other comp. inc. (loss)	(10,305)	(11,205)
Treasury stock, at cost: 2,781 in 2017 and 2,752 in 2016	(50,677)	(47,988)
General Mills (in millions)		
Stockholders' equity		
Common stock, ?? par value per share, authorized:		
754.6 shares issued in 2017 and 2016	75.5	75.5
Additional paid-in capital	1,202.5	1,120.9
Retained earnings	14,459.6	13,138.9
Acc. other comp. inc. (loss)	(2,429.0)	(2,244.5)
Treasury stock, at cost: 161.5 in 2017 and 177.7 in 2016	(7,167.5)	(7,762.9)

Required

a. Divide the class in three sections and divide each section into groups of three to five students. Assign each section one of the companies.

Group Tasks

Based on the company assigned to your group, answer the following questions:

b. What is the per-share par or stated value of the common stock in 2017?

c. What was the average issue price of the common stock for each year?

d. How many shares of stock are outstanding at the end of each year?

e. What is the average cost per share of the treasury stock for 2017?

f. Do the data suggest that your company was profitable in 2017?

g. Can you determine the amount of net income from the information given? What is missing?

h. What is the total stockholders' equity of your company for each year?

Class Discussion

i. Have each group select a representative to present the information about its company. Compare the share issue price and the par or stated value of the companies.

j. Compare the average issue price to the current market price for each of the companies. Speculate about what might cause the difference.

ATC 8-3   Research Assignment   *Analyzing Bed Bath & Beyond's stockholders' equity structure*

Using either Bed Bath & Beyond, Inc.'s most current Form 10-K or the company's annual report, answer the following questions. To obtain the Form 10-K use either the EDGAR system following the instructions in Appendix A or the company's website. The company's annual report is available on its website.

Required

a. What is the *book value* of Bed Bath & Beyond's stockholders' equity that is shown on the company's balance sheet? What is the book value per share?

b. What is the par value of Bed Bath & Beyond's common stock?

c. Does Bed Bath & Beyond have any treasury stock? If so, how many shares of treasury stock does the company hold?

d. In recent years, the market price of Bed Bath & Beyond's stock has often been lower than its book value. What does this say about investors' opinion of the company's future prospects?

ATC 8-4   Writing Assignment   *Comparison of organizational forms*

Jim Baku and Scott Hanson are thinking about opening a new restaurant. Baku has extensive marketing experience but does not know that much about food preparation. However, Hanson is an excellent chef. Both will work in the business, but Baku will provide most of the funds necessary to start the business. At this time, they cannot decide whether to operate the business as a partnership or a corporation.

Required

Prepare a written memo to Baku and Hanson describing the advantages and disadvantages of each organizational form. Also, from the limited information provided, recommend the organizational form you think they should use.

ATC 8-5   Ethical Dilemma   *Bad news versus very bad news*

Louise Stinson, the chief financial officer of Bostonian Corporation, was on her way to the president's office. She was carrying the latest round of bad news. There would be no executive bonuses this year. Corporate profits were down. Indeed, if the latest projections held true, the company would report a small loss on the year-end income statement. Executive bonuses were tied to corporate profits. The executive compensation plan provided for 10 percent of net earnings to be set aside for bonuses. No profits meant no bonuses. While things looked bleak, Stinson had a plan that might help soften the blow.

After informing the company president of the earnings forecast, Stinson made the following suggestion: Because the company was going to report a loss anyway, why not report a big loss? She reasoned that the directors and stockholders would not be much more angry if the company reported a large loss than if it reported a small one. There were several questionable assets that could be written down in the current year. This would increase the current year's loss but would reduce expenses in subsequent accounting periods. For example, the company was carrying damaged inventory that was estimated to have a value of $2,500,000. If this estimate were revised to $500,000, the company would have to recognize a $2,000,000 loss in the current year. However, next year when the goods were sold, the expense for cost of goods sold would be $2,000,000 less and profits would be higher by that amount. Although the directors would be angry this year, they would certainly be happy next year. The strategy would also have the benefit of adding $200,000 to next year's executive bonus pool ($2,000,000 × 0.10). Furthermore, it could not hurt this year's bonus pool since there would be no pool this year because the company is going to report a loss.

Some of the other items that Stinson is considering include (1) converting from straight-line to accelerated depreciation, (2) increasing the percentage of receivables estimated to be uncollectible in the current year and lowering the percentage in the following year, and (3) raising the percentage of estimated warranty claims in the current period and lowering it in the following period. Finally, Stinson notes that two of the company's department stores have been experiencing losses. The company could sell these stores this year and thereby improve earnings next year. Stinson admits that the sale would result in significant losses this year, but she smiles as she thinks of next year's bonus check.

Required

a. Explain how each of the three numbered strategies for increasing the amount of the current year's loss would affect the stockholders' equity section of the balance sheet in the current year. How would the other elements of the balance sheet be affected?

b. If Stinson's strategy were effectively implemented, how would it affect the stockholders' equity in subsequent accounting periods?

c. Comment on the ethical implications of running the company for the sake of management (maximization of bonuses) versus the maximization of return to stockholders.

d. Formulate a bonus plan that will motivate managers to maximize the value of the firm instead of motivating them to manipulate the reporting process.

e. How would Stinson's strategy of overstating the amount of the reported loss in the current year affect the company's current P/E ratio?

CHAPTER 9

Financial Statement Analysis

LEARNING OBJECTIVES

After you have mastered the material in this chapter, you will be able to:

LO 9-1   Differentiate between horizontal and vertical analysis.

LO 9-2   Calculate ratios for assessing a company's liquidity.

LO 9-3   Calculate ratios for assessing a company's solvency.

LO 9-4   Calculate ratios for assessing a company's managerial effectiveness.

LO 9-5   Calculate ratios for assessing a company's position in the stock market.

  Video lectures and accompanying self-assessment quizzes are available in Connect *for all learning objectives.*

  Set B exercises and problems are available in Additional Student Resources.

CHAPTER OPENING

Expressing financial statement information in the form of ratios enhances its usefulness. Ratios permit comparisons over time and among companies, highlighting similarities, differences, and trends. Proficiency with common financial statement analysis techniques benefits both internal and external users. Before beginning detailed explanations of numerous ratios and percentages, however, we consider factors relevant to communicating useful information.

The Curious Accountant

Worawee Meepian/Shutterstock

On June 15, 2017, Amazon.com, Inc., announced that it had agreed to purchase Whole Foods Market for $42 per share, or $13.7 billion in total. The offering price of $42 per share was 27 percent higher than the stock was currently trading. This was by far the biggest acquisition Amazon.com had ever made. Although Whole Foods is more profitable than most grocery companies, its profitability percentages had been declining in recent years. For example, from 2014 to 2017 its return on investment had declined from 10.3 percent to 3.8 percent, its gross margin declined from 35.5 percent to 33.7 percent, and its net margin declined from 4.1 percent to 1.5 percent. Furthermore, Whole Foods was viewed as a high-priced "bricks and mortar" business, while Amazon is viewed as an online discount company.

NYCStock/Shutterstock

How do companies such as Amazon determine that a business they want to own is worth more than the current market price? What types of analysis would they use to make such decisions? Do you think the highly educated, experienced, and well-paid individuals involved in making these high-dollar acquisitions made the right decisions? (Answer on page 331.)

FACTORS IN COMMUNICATING USEFUL INFORMATION

The primary objective of accounting is to provide information useful for decision making. To provide information that supports this objective, accountants must consider the intended users, the types of decisions users make with financial statement information, and available means of analyzing the information.

The Users

maxuser/Shutterstock

Users of financial statement information include managers, creditors, stockholders, potential investors, and regulatory agencies. These individuals and organizations use financial statements for different purposes and bring varying levels of sophistication to understanding business activities. For example, investors range from private individuals who know little about financial statements to large investment brokers and institutional investors capable of using complex statistical analysis techniques. At what level of user knowledge should financial statements be aimed? Condensing and reporting complex business transactions at a level easily understood by nonprofessional investors is increasingly difficult. Current reporting standards target users that have a reasonably informed knowledge of business, though that level of sophistication is difficult to define.

The Types of Decisions

Just as the knowledge level of potential users varies, the information needs of users also vary, depending on the decision at hand. A supplier considering whether or not to sell goods on account to a particular company wants to evaluate the likelihood of getting paid; a potential investor in that company wants to predict the likelihood of increases in the market value of the company's common stock. Financial statements, however, are designed for general purposes; they are not aimed at any specific user group. Some disclosed information, therefore, may be irrelevant to some users but vital to others. Users must employ different forms of analysis to identify information most relevant to a particular decision.

Financial statements can provide only highly summarized economic information. The costs to a company of providing excessively detailed information would be prohibitive. In addition, too much detail leads to **information overload,** the problem of having so much data that important information becomes obscured by trivial information. Users faced with reams of data may become so frustrated attempting to use them that they lose the value of *key* information that is provided.

Information Analysis

Because of the diversity of users, their different levels of knowledge, the varying information needs for particular decisions, and the general nature of financial statements, a variety of analysis techniques have been developed. In the following sections, we explain several common methods of analysis. The choice of method depends on which technique appears to provide the most relevant information in a given situation.

METHODS OF ANALYSIS

LO 9-1

Differentiate between horizontal and vertical analysis.

Financial statement analysis should focus primarily on isolating information useful for making a particular decision. The information required can take many forms but usually involves comparisons, such as comparing changes in the same item for the same company over a number of years, comparing key relationships within the same year, or comparing the operations of several different companies in the same industry. This chapter discusses three categories of analysis methods: horizontal, vertical, and ratio. Exhibits 9.1 and 9.2 present comparative financial statements for Milavec Company. We refer to these statements in the examples of analysis techniques.

EXHIBIT 9.1

MILAVEC COMPANY
Income Statements and Statements of
Retained Earnings
For the Years Ending December 31

	Year 4	Year 3
Sales	$900,000	$800,000
Cost of goods sold		
Beginning inventory	43,000	40,000
Purchases	637,000	483,000
Goods available for sale	680,000	523,000
Ending inventory	70,000	43,000
Cost of goods sold	610,000	480,000
Gross margin	290,000	320,000
Operating expenses	248,000	280,000
Income before taxes	42,000	40,000
Income taxes	17,000	18,000
Net income	25,000	22,000
Plus: Retained earnings, beginning balance	137,000	130,000
Less: Dividends	0	15,000
Retained earnings, ending balance	$162,000	$137,000

EXHIBIT 9.2

MILAVEC COMPANY
Balance Sheets
As of December 31

	Year 4	Year 3
Assets		
Cash	$ 20,000	$ 17,000
Marketable securities	20,000	22,000
Notes receivable	4,000	3,000
Accounts receivable	50,000	56,000
Merchandise inventory	70,000	43,000
Prepaid expenses	4,000	4,000
Property, plant, and equipment (net)	340,000	310,000
Total assets	$508,000	$455,000
Liabilities and Stockholders' Equity		
Accounts payable	$ 40,000	$ 38,000
Salaries payable	2,000	3,000
Taxes payable	4,000	2,000
Bonds payable, 8%	100,000	100,000
Preferred stock, 6%, $100 par, cumulative	50,000	50,000
Common stock, $10 par	150,000	125,000
Retained earnings	162,000	137,000
Total liabilities and stockholders' equity	$508,000	$455,000

Horizontal Analysis

Horizontal analysis, also called **trend analysis,** refers to studying the behavior of individual financial statement items over several accounting periods. These periods may be several quarters within the same fiscal year or they may be several different years. The analysis of a given item may focus on trends in the absolute dollar amount of the item or trends in percentages. For example, a user may observe that revenue increased from one period to the next by $42 million (an absolute dollar amount) or that it increased by a percentage such as 15 percent.

Absolute Amounts

The **absolute amounts** of particular financial statement items have many uses. Various national economic statistics, such as gross domestic product and the amount spent to replace productive capacity, are derived by combining absolute amounts reported by businesses. Financial statement users with expertise in particular industries might evaluate amounts reported for research and development costs to judge whether a company is spending excessively or conservatively. Users are particularly concerned with how amounts change over time. For example, a user might compare a pharmaceutical company's revenue before and after the patent expired on one of its drugs.

Comparing only absolute amounts has drawbacks, however, because *materiality* levels differ from company to company or even from year to year for a given company. The **materiality** of information refers to its relative importance. An item is considered material if knowledge of it would influence the decision of a reasonably informed user. Generally accepted accounting principles permit companies to account for *immaterial* items in the most convenient way, regardless of technical accounting rules. For example, companies may expense, rather than capitalize and depreciate, relatively inexpensive long-term assets like pencil sharpeners or wastebaskets, even if the assets have useful lives of many years.

The concept of materiality, which has both quantitative and qualitative aspects, underlies all accounting principles.

It is difficult to judge the materiality of an absolute financial statement amount without considering the size of the company reporting it. For reporting purposes, Exxon Corporation's financial statements are rounded to the nearest million dollars. For Exxon, a $400,000 increase in sales is not material. For a small company, however, $400,000 could represent total sales, a highly material amount. Meaningful comparisons between the two companies' operating performance are impossible using only absolute amounts. Users can surmount these difficulties with percentage analysis.

Percentage Analysis

Percentage analysis involves computing the percentage relationship between two amounts. In horizontal percentage analysis, a financial statement item is expressed as a percentage of the previous balance for the same item. Percentage analysis sidesteps the materiality problems of comparing different size companies by measuring changes in percentages rather than absolute amounts. Each change is converted to a percentage of the base year. Exhibit 9.3 presents a condensed version of Milavec's income statement with horizontal percentages for each item.

The percentage changes disclose that, even though Milavec's net income increased slightly more than sales, products may be underpriced. Cost of goods sold increased much more than sales, resulting in a lower gross margin. Users would also want to investigate why operating expenses decreased substantially despite the increase in sales.

Whether basing their analyses on absolute amounts, percentages, or ratios, users must avoid drawing overly simplistic conclusions about the reasons for the results. Numerical relationships flag conditions requiring further study. Recall that a change that appears favorable on the surface may not necessarily be a good sign. Users must evaluate the underlying reasons for the change.

EXHIBIT 9.3

MILAVEC COMPANY
Comparative Income Statements
For the Years Ending December 31

	Year 4	Year 3	Percentage Difference
Sales	$900,000	$800,000	+12.5%*
Cost of goods sold	610,000	480,000	+27.1
Gross margin	290,000	320,000	−9.4
Operating expenses	248,000	280,000	−11.4
Income before taxes	42,000	40,000	+5.0
Income taxes	17,000	18,000	−5.6
Net income	$ 25,000	$ 22,000	+13.6

*($900,000 − $800,000) ÷ $800,000; all changes expressed as percentages of previous totals.

✓ CHECK YOURSELF 9.1

The following information was drawn from the annual reports of two retail companies (amounts are shown in millions). One company is an upscale department store; the other is a discount store. Based on this limited information, identify which company is the upscale department store.

	Jenkins Co.	Horn's, Inc.
Sales	$325	$680
Cost of goods sold	130	408
Gross margin	$195	$272

Answer   Jenkins' gross margin represents 60 percent ($195 ÷ $325) of sales. Horn's gross margin represents 40 percent ($272 ÷ $680) of sales. Because an upscale department store would have higher margins than a discount store, the data suggest that Jenkins is the upscale department store.

Answers to The Curious Accountant

Obviously, Amazon's acquisition of Whole Foods was based on a desire to make a profit on its investment. Of the $13.7 billion Amazon paid for Whole Foods, $9.0 billion was attributed to the intangible asset goodwill, indicating that Amazon believes Whole Foods had, and would continue to have, excess earnings power compared to the typical grocery retailer. But many analysts believe there were several ways Amazon expected it could use Whole Foods to make money other than just continuing to sell high-priced groceries in physical stores. Some analysts believe that Amazon saw Whole Foods as an opportunity to expand its distributions network. Whole Foods had 11 distribution centers and 440 retail stores that Amazon could use to get its goods to customers faster than with its existing 70 distribution centers. This could be especially helpful as Amazon was trying to expand its delivery of fresh foods to customers.

How do companies decide what another company is worth? Valuing a potential investment is the result of extensive financial analysis, as discussed in this chapter, along with capital budgeting techniques, which are discussed in Chapter 16. As you have seen in these chapters, such decision making is based on estimates about future events. Predicting the future is imperfect, no matter how well trained the forecaster might be.

How good are companies' decisions to acquire other businesses at a premium price? It is too early to say for the purchase of Whole Foods, but not all acquisitions turn out well. In 2013, Microsoft Corp. purchased Nokia Corp. for $7.2 billion. And in 2015, just two years after its acquisition, Microsoft announced it was writing down $7.6 billion related to its Nokia investment, and eliminating 7,800 jobs.

Does this mean that financial analysis is useless? No. Assume you were planning to drive across the United States. Would you prefer to take the trip with a map or without? Obviously, you would prefer to have a map or GPS, even though you know neither device is perfect. Financial analysis can be of great benefit when making business decisions, but there are always uncertainties about future events that mathematics cannot eliminate.

Sources: Hufford, Austen. 2017. Amazon Buys Whole Foods: What You Need to Know. *The Wall Street Journal.*

When comparing more than two periods, analysts use either of two basic approaches: (1) choosing one base year from which to calculate all increases or decreases or (2) calculating each period's percentage change from the preceding figure. To illustrate, assume Milavec's sales for Year 1 through Year 4 are as follows.

	Year 4	Year 3	Year 2	Year 1
Sales	$900,000	$800,000	$750,000	$600,000
Increase over Year 1 sales	50.0%	33.3%	25.0%	—
Increase over preceding year	12.5%	6.7%	25.0%	—

Analysis discloses that Milavec's Year 4 sales represented a 50 percent increase over Year 1 sales, and a large increase (25 percent) occurred in Year 2. From Year 2 to Year 3, sales increased only 6.7 percent, but, in the following year, sales increased much more (12.5 percent).

Vertical Analysis

Vertical analysis uses percentages to compare individual components of financial statements to a key statement figure. Horizontal analysis compares items over many time periods; vertical analysis compares many items within the same time period.

Vertical Analysis of the Income Statement

Vertical analysis of an income statement (also called a *common size* income statement) involves converting each income statement component to a percentage of sales. Although vertical analysis suggests examining only one period, it is useful to compare common size income statements for several years. Exhibit 9.4 presents Milavec's income statements, along with vertical percentages, for Year 4 and Year 3. This analysis discloses that cost of goods sold increased significantly as a percentage of sales. Operating expenses and income taxes, however, decreased in relation to sales. Each of these observations indicates a need for more analysis regarding possible trends for future profits.

EXHIBIT 9.4

MILAVEC COMPANY

Vertical Analysis of Comparative Income Statements

	Year 4		Year 3	
	Amount	Percentage* of Sales	Amount	Percentage* of Sales
Sales	$900,000	100.0%	$800,000	100.0%
Cost of goods sold	610,000	67.8	480,000	60.0
Gross margin	290,000	32.2	320,000	40.0
Operating expenses	248,000	27.6	280,000	35.0
Income before taxes	42,000	4.7	40,000	5.0
Income taxes	17,000	1.9	18,000	2.3
Net income	$ 25,000	2.8%	$ 22,000	2.8%

*Percentages may not add exactly due to rounding.

Vertical Analysis of the Balance Sheet

Vertical analysis of the balance sheet involves converting each balance sheet component to a percentage of total assets. The vertical analysis of Milavec's balance sheets in Exhibit 9.5 discloses few large percentage changes from the preceding year. Even small individual percentage changes, however, may represent substantial dollar increases. For example, inventory constituted 9.5 percent of total assets in Year 3 and 13.8 percent in Year 4. While this appears to be a small increase, it actually represents a 62.8 percent increase in the inventory account balance [($70,000 − $43,000) ÷ $43,000] from Year 3 to Year 4. Careful analysis requires considering changes in both percentages *and* absolute amounts.

RATIO ANALYSIS

Ratio analysis involves studying various relationships between different items reported in a set of financial statements. For example, net earnings (net income) reported on the income statement may be compared to total assets reported on the balance sheet. Analysts calculate many different ratios for a wide variety of purposes. The remainder of this chapter is devoted to discussing some of the more commonly used ratios.

Objectives of Ratio Analysis

As suggested earlier, various users approach financial statement analysis with many different objectives. Creditors are interested in whether a company will be able to repay its debts on time. Both creditors and stockholders are concerned with how the company is financed, whether through debt, equity, or earnings. Stockholders and potential investors analyze past earnings performance and dividend policy for clues to the future value of their investments. In addition to using internally generated data to analyze operations, company managers find much information prepared for external purposes useful for examining past operations and planning future policies. Although many of these objectives are interrelated, it is convenient to group ratios into categories such as measures of debt-paying ability and measures of profitability.

EXHIBIT 9.5

MILAVEC COMPANY Vertical Analysis of Comparative Balance Sheets				
	Year 4	Percentage* of Total	Year 3	Percentage* of Total
Assets				
Cash	$ 20,000	3.9%	$ 17,000	3.7%
Marketable securities	20,000	3.9	22,000	4.8
Notes receivable	4,000	0.8	3,000	0.7
Accounts receivable	50,000	9.8	56,000	12.3
Merchandise inventory	70,000	13.8	43,000	9.5
Prepaid expenses	4,000	0.8	4,000	0.9
Total current assets	168,000	33.1	145,000	31.9
Property, plant, and equipment	340,000	66.9	310,000	68.1
Total assets	$508,000	100.0%	$455,000	100.0%
Liabilities and Stockholders' Equity				
Accounts payable	$ 40,000	7.9%	$ 38,000	8.3%
Salaries payable	2,000	0.4	3,000	0.7
Taxes payable	4,000	0.8	2,000	0.4
Total current liabilities	46,000	9.1	43,000	9.4
Bonds payable, 8%	100,000	19.7	100,000	22.0
Total liabilities	146,000	28.8	143,000	31.4
Preferred stock 6%, $100 par	50,000	9.8	50,000	11.0
Common stock, $10 par	150,000	29.5	125,000	27.5
Retained earnings	162,000	31.9	137,000	30.1
Total stockholders' equity	362,000	71.2	312,000	68.6
Total liabilities and stockholders' equity	$508,000	100.0%	$455,000	100.0%

*Percentages may not add exactly due to rounding.

MEASURES OF DEBT-PAYING ABILITY

Liquidity Ratios

Liquidity ratios indicate a company's ability to pay short-term debts. They focus on current assets and current liabilities. The examples in the following section use the financial statement information reported by Milavec Company.

Working Capital

Working capital is current assets minus current liabilities. Current assets include assets most likely to be converted into cash in the current operating period. Current liabilities represent debts that must be satisfied in the current period. Working capital therefore measures the excess funds the company will have available for operations, excluding any new funds it generates during the year. Think of working capital as the cushion against short-term, debt-paying problems. Working capital at the end of Year 4 and Year 3 for Milavec Company was as follows.

	Year 4	Year 3
Current assets	$168,000	$145,000
− Current liabilities	46,000	43,000
Working capital	$122,000	$102,000

LO 9-2

 Calculate ratios for assessing a company's liquidity.

Milavec's working capital increased from Year 3 to Year 4, but the numbers themselves say little. Whether $122,000 is sufficient or not depends on such factors as the industry in which Milavec operates, its size, and the maturity dates of its current obligations. We can see, however, that the increase in working capital is primarily due to the increase in inventories.

Current Ratio

Working capital is an absolute amount. Its usefulness is limited by the materiality difficulties discussed earlier. It is hard to draw meaningful conclusions from comparing Milavec's working capital of $122,000 with another company that also has working capital of $122,000. By expressing the relationship between current assets and current liabilities as a ratio, however, we have a more useful measure of the company's debt-paying ability relative to other companies. The **current ratio,** also called the **working capital ratio,** is calculated as follows:

$$\text{Current ratio} = \frac{\text{Current assets}}{\text{Current liabilities}}$$

To illustrate using the current ratio for comparisons, consider Milavec's current position relative to that of Laroque's, a larger firm with current assets of $500,000 and current liabilities of $378,000.

	Milavec	Laroque
Current assets (a)	$168,000	$500,000
− Current liabilities (b)	46,000	378,000
Working capital	$122,000	$122,000
Current ratio (a ÷ b)	3.65:1	1.32:1

The current ratio is expressed as the number of dollars of current assets for each dollar of current liabilities. In the preceding example, both companies have the same amount of working capital. Milavec, however, appears to have a much stronger working capital position. Any conclusions from this analysis must take into account the circumstances of the particular companies; there is no single ideal current ratio that suits all companies. In recent years, the average current ratio of the nonfinancial companies that constitute the Dow Jones Industrial Average (DJIA) was around 1.46:1. The individual company ratios, however, ranged from 0.73:1 to 3.03:1. A current ratio can be too high. Money invested in factories and developing new products is usually more profitable than money held as large cash balances or invested in inventory.

Quick Ratio

The **quick ratio,** also known as the **acid-test ratio,** is a conservative variation of the current ratio. The quick ratio measures a company's *immediate* debt-paying ability. Only cash, receivables, and current marketable securities (*quick assets*) are included in the numerator. Less liquid current assets, such as inventories and prepaid expenses, are omitted. Inventories may take several months to sell; prepaid expenses reduce otherwise necessary expenditures but do not lead eventually to cash receipts. The quick ratio is computed as follows:

$$\text{Quick ratio} = \frac{\text{Quick assets}}{\text{Current liabilities}}$$

Milavec Company's current ratios and quick ratios for Year 4 and Year 3 follow.

	Year 4	Year 3
Current ratio	168,000 ÷ 46,000	145,000 ÷ 43,000
	3.65:1	3.37:1
Quick ratio	94,000 ÷ 46,000	98,000 ÷ 43,000
	2.04:1	2.28:1

The decrease in the quick ratio from Year 3 to Year 4 reflects both a decrease in quick assets and an increase in current liabilities. The result indicates that the company is less liquid (has less ability to pay its short-term debt) in Year 4 than it was in Year 3.

Accounts Receivable Ratios

Offering customers credit plays an enormous role in generating revenue, but it also increases expenses and delays cash receipts. To minimize bad debts expense and collect cash for use in current operations, companies want to collect receivables as quickly as possible without losing customers. Two relationships are often examined to assess a company's collection record: *accounts receivable turnover* and *average days to collect receivables (average collection period).*
  Accounts receivable turnover is calculated as follows:

$$\text{Accounts receivable turnover} = \frac{\text{Net credit sales}}{\text{Average accounts receivable}}$$

Net credit sales refers to total sales on account less sales discounts and returns. When most sales are credit sales or when a breakdown of total sales between cash sales and credit sales is not available, the analyst must use total sales in the numerator. The denominator is based on *net accounts receivable* (receivables after subtracting the allowance for doubtful accounts). Because the numerator represents a whole period, it is preferable to use average receivables in the denominator if possible. When comparative statements are available, the average can be based on the beginning and ending balances. Milavec Company's accounts receivable turnover is computed as follows.

	Year 4	Year 3
Net sales (assume all on account) (a)	$900,000	$800,000
Beginning receivables (b)	$ 56,000	$ 55,000*
Ending receivables (c)	50,000	56,000
Average receivables (d) = (b + c) ÷ 2	$ 53,000	$ 55,500
Accounts receivable turnover (a ÷ d)	16.98	14.41

*The Year 3 beginning receivables balance was drawn from the Year 2 financial statements, which are not included in the illustration.

The Year 4 accounts receivable turnover of 16.98 indicates Milavec collected its average receivables almost 17 times that year. The higher the turnover, the faster the collections. A company can have cash flow problems and lose substantial purchasing power if resources are tied up in receivables for long periods.
  Average days to collect accounts receivables, or the *average collection period,* is calculated as follows:

$$\text{Average days to collect receivables} = \frac{365 \text{ days}}{\text{Accounts receivable turnover}}$$

This ratio offers another way to look at turnover by showing the number of days, on average, it takes to collect a receivable. If receivables were collected 16.98 times in Year 4, the average collection period was 21 days, 365 ÷ 16.98 (the number of days in the year divided by accounts receivable turnover). For Year 3, it took an average of 25 days (365 ÷ 14.41) to collect a receivable.

Although the collection period improved, no other conclusions can be reached without considering the industry, Milavec's past performance, and the general economic environment. In recent years, the average time to collect accounts receivable for the 25 nonfinancial companies that make up the DJIA was around 49 days. (Financial firms are excluded because, by the nature of their business, they have very long collection periods.)

Inventory Ratios

A fine line exists between having too much and too little inventory in stock. Too little inventory can result in lost sales and costly production delays. Too much inventory can use needed space, increase financing and insurance costs, and become obsolete. To help analyze how efficiently a company manages inventory, we use two ratios similar to those used in analyzing accounts receivable.

Inventory turnover indicates the number of times, on average, that inventory is totally replaced during the year. The relationship is computed as follows:

$$\text{Inventory turnover} = \frac{\text{Cost of goods sold}}{\text{Average inventory}}$$

The average inventory is usually based on the beginning and ending balances that are shown in the financial statements. Inventory turnover for Milavec was as follows.

	Year 4	Year 3
Cost of goods sold (a)	$610,000	$480,000
Beginning inventory (b)	$ 43,000	$ 40,000*
Ending inventory (c)	70,000	43,000
Average inventory (d) = (b + c) ÷ 2	$ 56,500	$ 41,500
Inventory turnover (a ÷ d)	10.80	11.57

*The Year 3 beginning inventory balance was drawn from the company's Year 2 financial statements, which are not included in the illustration.

Generally, a higher turnover indicates that merchandise is being handled more efficiently. Trying to compare firms in different industries, however, can be misleading. Inventory turnover for grocery stores and many retail outlets is high. Because of the nature of the goods being sold, inventory turnover is much lower for appliance and jewelry stores. We look at this issue in more detail when we discuss return on investment.

Average days to sell inventory, or *average days in inventory,* is determined by dividing the number of days in the year by the inventory turnover as follows:

$$\text{Average days to sell inventory} = \frac{\text{365 days}}{\text{Inventory turnover}}$$

The result approximates the number of days the firm could sell inventory without purchasing more. For Milavec, this figure was 34 days in Year 4 (365 ÷ 10.80) and 32 days in Year 3 (365 ÷ 11.57). In recent years, it took around 93 days, on average, for the companies in the DJIA that have inventory to sell their inventory. The time it took individual companies to sell their inventory varied by industry, ranging from 5 days to 246 days.

Solvency Ratios

Solvency ratios are used to analyze a company's long-term debt-paying ability and its financing structure. Creditors are concerned with a company's ability to satisfy outstanding obligations. The larger a company's liability percentage, the greater the risk that the company could fall behind or default on debt payments. Stockholders, too, are concerned about a company's solvency. If a company is unable to pay its debts, the owners could lose their investment. Each user group desires that company financing choices minimize its investment risk, whether the investment is in debt or stockholders' equity.

Calculate ratios for assessing a company's solvency.

Debt Ratios

The following ratios represent two different ways to express the same relationship. Both are frequently used.

- **Debt-to-assets ratio.** This ratio measures the percentage of a company's assets that are financed by debt.

- **Debt-to-equity ratio.** As used in this ratio, *equity* means stockholders' equity. The debt-to-equity ratio compares creditor financing to owner financing. It is expressed as the dollar amount of liabilities for each dollar of stockholders' equity.

These ratios are calculated as follows:

$$\text{Debt to assets} = \frac{\text{Total liabilities}}{\text{Total assets}}$$

$$\text{Debt to equity} = \frac{\text{Total liabilities}}{\text{Total stockholders' equity}}$$

Applying these formulas to Milavec Company's results produces the following.

	Year 4	Year 3
Total liabilities (a)	$146,000	$143,000
Total stockholders' equity (b)	362,000	312,000
Total equities (Liabilities + Stockholders' equity) (c)	$508,000	$455,000
Debt to assets (a ÷ c)	29%	31%
Debt-to-equity ratio (a ÷ b)	0.40:1	0.46:1

Each year, less than one-third of the company's assets was financed with debt. The amount of liabilities per dollar of stockholders' equity declined by 0.06. It is difficult to judge whether the reduced percentage of liabilities is favorable. In general, a lower level of liabilities provides greater security because the likelihood of bankruptcy is reduced. Perhaps, however, the company is financially strong enough to incur more liabilities and benefit from financial leverage. The 25 nonfinancial companies that make up the DJIA report around 51 percent of their assets, on average, are financed through borrowing. The debt-to-assets ratios of these companies ranged from 19 to 110 percent.

Number of Times Interest Is Earned

This ratio measures the burden a company's interest payments represent. Users often consider the **number of times interest is earned** along with the debt ratios when evaluating financial risk. The numerator of this ratio uses *earnings before interest and taxes (EBIT)*, rather than net earnings, because the amount of earnings *before* interest and income taxes is available for paying interest.

$$\frac{\text{Number of times}}{\text{interest is earned}} = \frac{\text{Earnings before interest and taxes expense}}{\text{Interest expense}}$$

Dividing EBIT by interest expense indicates how many times the company could have made its interest payments. Obviously, interest is paid only once, but the more times it *could* be paid, the bigger the company's safety net. Although interest is paid from cash, not accrual earnings, it is standard practice to base this ratio on accrual-based EBIT, not a cash-based amount. For Milavec, this calculation is as follows.

	Year 4	Year 3
Income before taxes	$42,000	$40,000
Interest expense (b)	8,000	8,000*
Income before taxes and interest (a)	$50,000	$48,000
Times interest earned (a ÷ b)	6.25 times	6 times

*Interest on bonds: $100,000 × 0.08 = $8,000.

Any expense or dividend payment can be analyzed this way. Another frequently used calculation is the number of times the preferred dividend is earned. In that case, the numerator is net income (after taxes) and the denominator is the amount of the annual preferred dividend.

CHECK YOURSELF 9.2

Selected data for Riverside Corporation and Academy Company follow (amounts are shown in millions).

	Riverside Corporation	Academy Company
Total liabilities (a)	$650	$450
Stockholders' equity (b)	300	400
Total liabilities + Stockholders' equity (c)	$950	$850
Interest expense (d)	$ 65	$ 45
Income before taxes (e)	140	130
Income before taxes and interest (f)	$205	$175

Based on this information alone, which company would likely obtain the less favorable interest rate on additional debt financing?

Answer Interest rates vary with risk levels. Companies with less solvency (long-term, debt-paying ability) generally must pay higher interest rates to obtain financing. Two solvency measures for the two companies follow. Recall:

Total assets = Liabilities + Stockholders' equity

	Riverside Corporation	Academy Company
Debt-to-assets ratio (a ÷ c)	68.4%	52.9%
Times interest earned (f ÷ d)	3.15 times	3.89 times

Because Riverside has a higher percentage of debt and a lower times-interest-earned ratio, the data suggest that Riverside is less solvent than Academy. Riverside would therefore likely have to pay a higher interest rate to obtain additional financing.

Plant Assets to Long-Term Liabilities

Companies often pledge plant assets as collateral for long-term liabilities. Financial statement users may analyze a firm's ability to obtain long-term financing on the strength of its asset base. Effective financial management principles dictate that asset purchases should be financed over a time span about equal to the expected lives of the assets. Short-term assets should be financed with short-term liabilities; the current ratio, introduced earlier, indicates how well a company manages current debt. Long-lived assets should be financed with long-term liabilities, and the plant assets to **long-term liabilities** ratio shows the amount of assets per each dollar of long-term debt. All other things being equal, the larger the ratio the lower the financial risk. In other words, a company with a high plant assets to long-term liabilities could sell the larger amount of assets to obtain funds to pay off a relatively small amount of debt. The ratio is calculated as follows:

$$\text{Plant assets to long-term liabilities} = \frac{\text{Net plant assets}}{\text{Long-term liabilities}}$$

For Milavec Company, these ratios follow.

	Year 4	Year 3
Net plant assets (a)	$340,000	$310,000
Bonds payable (b)	100,000	100,000
Plant assets to long-term liabilities (a ÷ b)	3.4:1	3.1:1

MEASURES OF PROFITABILITY

Profitability refers to a company's ability to generate earnings. Both management and external users employ **profitability ratios** to assess a company's success in generating profits and how these profits are used to reward investors. Some of the many ratios available to measure different aspects of profitability are discussed in the following two sections.

LO 9-4

Calculate ratios for assessing a company's managerial effectiveness.

Measures of Managerial Effectiveness

The most common ratios used to evaluate managerial effectiveness measure what percentage of sales results in earnings and how productive assets are in generating those sales. As mentioned earlier, the *absolute amount* of sales or earnings means little without also considering company size.

Net Margin (or Return on Sales)

Gross margin and *gross profit* are alternate terms for the amount remaining after subtracting the expense cost of goods sold from sales. **Net margin,** sometimes called *operating margin, profit margin,* or the *return-on-sales ratio,* describes the percentage of each sales dollar remaining after subtracting other expenses, as well as cost of goods sold. Net margin can be calculated in several ways; some of the more common methods subtract only normal operating expenses or all expenses other than income tax expense. For simplicity, our calculation uses net income (we subtract all expenses). Net income divided by net sales expresses net income (earnings) as a percentage of sales:

$$\text{Net margin} = \frac{\text{Net income}}{\text{Net sales}}$$

For Milavec Company, the net margins for Year 4 and Year 3 were as follows.

	Year 4	Year 3
Net income (a)	$ 25,000	$ 22,000
Net sales (b)	900,000	800,000
Net margin (a ÷ b)	2.78%	2.75%

StockStudio/Shutterstock

Milavec has maintained approximately the same net margin. Obviously, the larger the percentage, the better; a meaningful interpretation, however, requires analyzing the company's history and comparing the net margin to other companies in the same industry. The average net margin for the 25 nonfinancial companies that make up the Dow Jones Industrial Average (DJIA) has been around 13 percent in recent years; some companies, such as Pfizer with 41 percent, have been much higher than the average. Of course, if a company has a net loss, its net margin for that year will be negative.

Asset Turnover Ratio

The **asset turnover ratio** (sometimes called *turnover-of-assets ratio*) measures how many sales dollars were generated for each dollar of assets invested. As with many ratios used in financial statement analysis, users may define the numerator and denominator of this ratio in different ways. For example, they may use total assets or only include operating assets. Because the numerator represents a whole period, it is preferable to use average assets in the denominator if possible, especially if the amount of assets changed significantly during the year. We use average total assets in our illustration.

$$\text{Asset turnover} = \frac{\text{Net sales}}{\text{Average total assets}}$$

For Milavec, the asset turnover ratios were as follows.

	Year 4	Year 3
Net sales (a)	$900,000	$800,000
Beginning assets (b)	$455,000	$420,000*
Ending assets (c)	508,000	455,000
Average assets (d) = (b + c) ÷ 2	$481,500	$437,500
Asset turnover (a ÷ d)	1.87	1.83

*The Year 3 beginning asset balance was drawn from the Year 2 financial statements, which are not included in the illustration.

As with most ratios, the implications of a given asset turnover ratio are affected by other considerations. Asset turnover will be high in an industry that requires only minimal investment to operate, such as real estate sales companies. On the other hand, industries that require large investments in plant and machinery, like the auto industry, are likely to have lower asset turnover ratios. The asset turnover ratios of the nonfinancial companies that make up the DJIA have averaged around 2.86 in recent years. This means that annual sales have averaged 286 percent of their assets.

Return on Investment

Return on investment (ROI), also called **return on assets** or *earning power,* is the ratio of wealth generated (net income) to the amount invested (average total assets) to generate the wealth. ROI can be calculated as follows:[1]

$$\text{ROI} = \frac{\text{Net income}}{\text{Average total assets}}$$

[1]Detailed coverage of the return on investment ratio is provided in introductory managerial accounting courses, which will explain how companies frequently manipulate the formula to improve managerial motivation and performance. For example, instead of using net income, companies frequently use operating income because net income may be affected by items that are not controllable by management such as loss on a plant closing, storm damage, and so on.

For Milavec, ROI was as follows:

Year 4

$25,000 ÷ $481,500* = 5.19%

Year 3

$22,000 ÷ $437,500* = 5.03%

*The computation of average assets is shown previously.

In general, higher ROIs suggest better performance. The return-on-investment ratios of the large nonfinancial companies that make up the DJIA have averaged around 8 percent in recent years. These data suggest that Milavec is performing below average and therefore signal a need for further evaluation.

Return on Equity

Return on equity (ROE) is often used to measure the profitability of the stockholders' investment. ROE is usually higher than ROI because of financial leverage. Financial leverage refers to using debt financing to increase the assets available to a business beyond the amount of assets financed by owners. As long as a company's ROI exceeds its cost of borrowing (interest expense), the owners will earn a higher return on their investment in the company by using borrowed money. For example, if a company borrows money at 8 percent and invests it at 10 percent, the owners will enjoy a return that is higher than 10 percent. ROE is computed as follows:

$$ROE = \frac{\text{Net income}}{\text{Average total stockholders' equity}}$$

	Year 4	Year 3
Net income (a)	$ 25,000	$ 22,000
Preferred stock, 6%, $100 par, cumulative	50,000	50,000
Common stock, $10 par	150,000	125,000
Retained earnings	162,000	137,000
Ending stockholders' equity (b)	$362,000	$312,000
Beginning stockholders' equity (c)	$312,000	$268,000*
Average stockholders' equity (d) = (b + c) ÷ 2	$337,000	$290,000
ROE (a ÷ d)	7.4%	7.6%

*The Year 3 beginning stockholders' equity balance was drawn from the Year 2 financial statements, which are not included in the illustration.

The slight decrease in ROE is due primarily to the increase in common stock. The effect of the increase in total stockholders' equity offsets the effect of the increase in earnings. It is interesting to note that Milavec's ROEs of 7.6 percent and 7.4 percent are low in relation to real-world companies that make up the DJIA. Recently, the average ROE for these companies was 27 percent. One contributing factor explaining this difference is that most companies in the DJIA are more highly leveraged.

STOCK MARKET RATIOS

LO 9-5

Calculate ratios for assessing a company's position in the stock market.

Existing and potential investors in a company's stock use many common ratios to analyze and compare the earnings and dividends of different-sized companies in different industries. Purchasers of stock can profit in two ways: through receiving dividends and through increases in stock value. Investors consider both dividends and overall earnings performance as indicators of the value of the stock they own.

Earnings per Share

Perhaps the most frequently quoted measure of earnings performance is **earnings per share (EPS)**. EPS calculations are among the most complex in accounting, and more advanced textbooks devote entire chapters to the subject. At this level, we use the following basic formula:

$$\text{Earnings per share} = \frac{\text{Net earnings available for common stock}}{\text{Average number of outstanding common shares}}$$

EPS pertains to shares of *common stock*. Limiting the numerator to earnings available for common stock eliminates the annual preferred dividend ($0.06 \times \$50,000 = \$3,000$) from the calculation. Exhibit 9.1 shows that Milavec did not pay the preferred dividends in Year 4. Because the preferred stock is cumulative, however, the preferred dividend is in arrears and not available to the common stockholders. The number of common shares outstanding is determined by dividing the book value of the common stock by its par value per share ($\$150,000 \div \$10 = 15,000$ for Year 4 and $\$125,000 \div \$10 = 12,500$ for Year 3). Using these data, Milavec's Year 4 EPS is calculated as follows:

$$\frac{\$25,000 \text{ (net income)} - \$3,000 \text{ (preferred dividend)}}{(15,000 + 12,500)/2 \text{(average outstanding common shares)}} = \$1.60 \text{ per share}$$

Investors attribute a great deal of importance to EPS figures. The amounts used in calculating EPS, however, have limitations. Many accounting choices, assumptions, and estimates underlie net income computations, including alternative depreciation methods, different inventory cost flow assumptions, and estimates of future bad debt or warranty expenses, to name only a few. The denominator is also inexact because various factors (discussed in intermediate accounting courses) affect the number of shares to include. Numerous opportunities therefore exist to manipulate EPS figures. Prudent investors consider these variables in deciding how much weight to attach to earnings per share.

Book Value

Book value per share is another frequently quoted measure of a share of stock. It is calculated as follows:

$$\text{Book value per share} = \frac{\text{Stockholders' equity} - \text{Preferred stock}}{\text{Outstanding common shares}}$$

Instead of describing the numerator as stockholders' equity, we could have used assets minus liabilities, the algebraic computation of a company's "net worth." Net worth is a misnomer. A company's accounting records reflect book values, not worth. Because assets are recorded at historical costs and different methods are used to transfer asset costs to expense, the book value of assets after deducting liabilities is difficult to interpret. Nevertheless, investors use the term *book value per share* frequently. Milavec's book value per share for Year 4 is calculated as follows:

$$\frac{\$362,000 - \$50,000}{15,000 \text{ shares}} = \$20.80 \text{ per share}$$

Price-Earnings Ratio

The **price-earnings (P/E) ratio** compares the earnings per share of a company to the market price for a share of the company's stock. Assume Avalanche Company and Brushfire Company each report earnings per share of $3.60. For the same year, Cyclone Company reports EPS of $4.10. Based on these data alone, Cyclone stock may seem to be the best investment. Suppose, however, that the price for one share of stock in each company is $43.20, $36.00, and $51.25, respectively. Which stock would you buy?

Cyclone's stock price is the highest, but so is its EPS. The P/E ratio provides a common base of comparison.

$$\text{Price-earnings ratio} = \frac{\text{Market price per share}}{\text{Earnings per share}}$$

The P/E ratios for the three companies are as follows.

Avalanche	Brushfire	Cyclone
12.0	10.0	12.5

Brushfire might initially seem to be the best buy for your money. Yet there must be some reason that Cyclone's stock is selling at 12½ times earnings. In general, a higher P/E ratio indicates the market is more optimistic about a company's growth potential than it is about a company with a lower P/E ratio. The market price of a company's stock reflects judgments about both the company's current results and expectations about future results. Investors cannot make informed use of these ratios for investment decisions without examining the reasons behind the ratios. In late April 2018, when the Dow Jones Industrial Average was around 24,500 points, the average P/E ratio for the companies included in the DJIA was around 25.

Dividend Yield

There are two ways to profit from a stock investment. One, investors can sell the stock for more than they paid to purchase it (if the stock price rises). Two, the company that issued the stock can pay cash dividends to the shareholders. Most investors view rising stock prices as the primary reward for investing in stock. The importance of receiving dividends, however, should not be overlooked. Evaluating dividend payments is more complex than simply comparing the dividends per share paid by one company to the dividends per share paid by another company. Receiving a $1 dividend on a share purchased for $10 is a much better return than receiving a $1.50 dividend on stock bought for $100. Computing the **dividend yield** simplifies comparing dividend payments. Dividend yield measures dividends received as a percentage of a stock's market price.

$$\text{Dividend yield} = \frac{\text{Dividends per share}}{\text{Market price per share}}$$

To illustrate, consider Dragonfly, Inc. and Elk Company. The information for calculating dividend yield follows.

	Dragonfly	Elk
Dividends per share (a)	$ 1.80	$ 3.00
Market price per share (b)	40.00	75.00
Dividend yield (a ÷ b)	4.5%	4.0%

Even though the dividend per share paid by Elk Company is higher, the yield is lower (4.0 percent versus 4.5 percent) because Elk's stock price is so high. The dividend yields for the companies included in the DJIA were averaging around 2.2 percent in April 2018.

Other Ratios

Investors can also use a wide array of other ratios to analyze profitability. Most *profitability ratios* use the same reasoning. For example, you can calculate the *yield* of a variety of financial investments. Yield is determined by dividing the amount of the return (the dividend or interest earned) by the amount of the investment. The dividend yield explained previously could be calculated for either common or preferred stock. Investors could measure the earnings yield by calculating earnings per share as a percentage of market price. Yield on a bond can be calculated the same way: interest received divided by the price of the bond.

The specific ratios presented in this chapter are summarized in Exhibit 9.6.

EXHIBIT 9.6

Summary of Key Relationships

Liquidity Ratios		
	1. Working capital	Current assets − Current liabilities
	2. Current ratio	Current assets ÷ Current liabilities
	3. Quick (acid-test) ratio	(Current assets − Inventory − Prepaids) ÷ Current liabilities
	4. Accounts receivable turnover	Net credit sales ÷ Average receivables
	5. Average days to collect receivables	365 ÷ Accounts receivable turnover
	6. Inventory turnover	Cost of goods sold ÷ Average inventory
	7. Average days to sell inventory	365 ÷ Inventory turnover
Solvency Ratios	8. Debt-to-assets ratio	Total liabilities ÷ Total assets
	9. Debt-to-equity ratio	Total liabilities ÷ Total stockholders' equity
	10. Number of times interest is earned	Earnings before interest and taxes ÷ Interest expense
	11. Plant assets to long-term liabilities	Net plant assets ÷ Long-term liabilities
Profitability Ratios	12. Net margin	Net income ÷ Net sales
	13. Asset turnover	Net sales ÷ Average total assets
	14. Return on investment (also: return on assets)	Net income ÷ Average total assets
	15. Return on equity	Net income ÷ Average total stockholders' equity
Stock Market Ratios	16. Earnings per share	Net earnings available for common stock ÷ Average outstanding common shares
	17. Book value per share	(Stockholders' equity − Preferred rights) ÷ Outstanding common shares
	18. Price-earnings ratio	Market price per share ÷ Earnings per share
	19. Dividend yield	Dividends per share ÷ Market price per share

LIMITATIONS OF FINANCIAL STATEMENT ANALYSIS

Analyzing financial statements is analogous to choosing a new car. Each car is different, and prospective buyers must evaluate and weigh myriad features: gas mileage, engine size, manufacturer's reputation, color, accessories, and price, to name a few. Just as it is difficult to compare a Toyota minivan to a Ferrari sports car, so it is difficult to compare a small textile firm to a giant oil company. To make a meaningful assessment, the potential car buyer must focus on key data that can be comparably expressed for each car, such as gas mileage. The superior gas mileage of the minivan may pale in comparison to the thrill of driving the sports car, but the price of buying and operating the sports car may be the characteristic that determines the ultimate choice.

External users can rely on financial statement analysis only as a general guide to the potential of a business. They should resist placing too much weight on any particular figure or trend. Many factors must be considered simultaneously before making any judgments. Furthermore, the analysis techniques discussed in this chapter are all based on historical information. Future events and unanticipated changes in conditions will also influence a company's operating results.

Different Industries

Different industries may be affected by unique social policies, special accounting procedures, or other individual industry attributes. Ratios of companies in different industries are not comparable without considering industry characteristics. A high debt-to-assets ratio is more

REALITY BYTES

The single most important source of financial information is a company's annual report, but decision makers should also consider other sources. Interested persons can access quarterly and annual reports through the SEC's EDGAR database and often from company websites as well. Many companies will provide printed versions of these reports upon request. Companies also post information on their websites that is not included in their annual reports. For example, some automobile companies provide very detailed production data through their corporate websites.

Users can frequently obtain information useful in analyzing a particular company from independent sources, as well as from the company itself. For example, the websites of popular news services, such as CNN (www.money.cnn.com) and CNBC (www.cnbc.com), provide archived news stories and independent financial information about many companies. The websites of brokerage houses like www.schwab.com offer free financial information about companies. Finally, libraries often subscribe to independent services that evaluate companies as potential investments. One example worth reviewing is *Value Line Investment Survey*.

Jim Pruitt/qingwa/123RF

---

acceptable in some industries than others. Even within an industry, a particular business may require more or less working capital than the industry average. If so, the working capital and quick ratios would mean little compared to those of other firms, but may still be useful for trend analysis.

Because of industry-specific factors, most professional analysts specialize in only one industry, or just a few. Financial institutions such as brokerage houses, banks, and insurance companies typically employ financial analysts who specialize in areas such as mineral or oil extraction, chemicals, banking, retail, insurance, bond markets, or automobile manufacturing.

Changing Economic Environment

When comparing firms, analysts must be alert to changes in general economic trends from year to year. Significant changes in fuel costs and interest rates in recent years make old rule-of-thumb guidelines for evaluating these factors obsolete. In addition, the presence or absence of inflation affects business prospects.

Accounting Principles

Financial statement analysis is only as reliable as the data on which it is based. Although most firms follow generally accepted accounting principles, a wide variety of acceptable accounting methods is available from which to choose, including different inventory and depreciation methods, different schedules for recognizing revenue, and different ways to account for oil and gas exploration costs. Analyzing statements of companies that seem identical may produce noncomparable ratios if the companies have used different accounting methods. Analysts may seek to improve comparability by trying to recast different companies' financial statements as if the same accounting methods had been applied.

Accrual accounting requires the use of many estimates; bad debt expense, warranty expense, asset lives, and salvage value are just a few. The reliability of the resulting financial reports depends on the expertise and integrity of the persons who make the estimates.

The quality and usefulness of accounting information are influenced by underlying accounting concepts. Two particular concepts, *conservatism* and *historical cost,* have a tremendous impact on financial reporting. Conservatism dictates recognizing estimated losses as soon as they occur, but gain recognition is almost always deferred until the gains are actually realized. Conservatism produces a negative bias in financial statements. There are persuasive arguments for the conservatism principle, but users should be alert to distortions it may cause in accounting information.

The pervasive use of the historical cost concept is probably the greatest single cause of distorted financial statement analysis results. The historical cost of an asset does not represent its current value. The asset purchased in Year 1 for $10,000 is not comparable in value to the asset purchased in Year 5 for $10,000 because of changes in the value of the dollar. Using historical cost produces financial statements that report dollars with differing purchasing power in the same statement. Combining these differing dollar values is akin to adding miles to kilometers. To get the most from analyzing financial statements, users should be cognizant of these limitations.

☑ CHECK YOURSELF 9.3

The return on equity for Gup Company and Hunn Company is 23.4 percent and 17 percent, respectively. Does this mean Gup Company is better managed than Hunn Company?

Answer No single ratio can adequately measure management performance. Even analyzing a wide range of ratios provides only limited insight. Any useful interpretation requires the analyst to recognize the limitations of ratio analysis. For example, ratio norms typically differ between industries and may be affected by temporary economic factors. In addition, companies' use of different accounting practices and procedures produces different ratio results even when underlying circumstances are comparable.

A Look Back

Financial statement analysis involves many factors, among them user characteristics, information needs for particular types of decisions, and how financial information is analyzed. Analytical techniques include *horizontal, vertical,* and *ratio analysis.* Users commonly calculate ratios to measure a company's liquidity, solvency, and profitability. The specific ratios presented in this chapter are summarized in Exhibit 9.6. Although ratios are easy to calculate and provide useful insights into business operations, when interpreting analytical results, users should consider limitations resulting from differing industry characteristics, differing economic conditions, and the fundamental accounting principles used to produce reported financial information.

A Look Forward

This chapter concludes the financial accounting portion of the text. Beginning with Chapter 10, we introduce various topics related to managerial accounting. Managerial accounting focuses on meeting the accounting information needs of decision makers inside, rather than outside, a company. In addition to financial statement data, inside users require detailed, forward-looking information that includes nonfinancial as well as financial components. We begin with a chapter that discusses the value management accounting adds to the decision-making process.

Video lectures and accompanying self-assessment quizzes are available in *Connect* for all learning objectives.

SELF-STUDY REVIEW PROBLEM

Financial statements for Stallings Company follow.

Income Statements For the Years Ended December 31		
	Year 4	Year 3
Revenues		
Net sales	$315,000	$259,000
Expenses		
Cost of goods sold	(189,000)	(154,000)
Selling, general, and administrative expenses	(54,000)	(46,000)
Interest expense	(4,000)	(4,500)
Income before taxes	68,000	54,500
Income tax expense (40%)	(27,200)	(21,800)
Net income	$ 40,800	$ 32,700

Balance Sheets As of December 31		
	Year 4	Year 3
Assets		
Current assets		
Cash	$ 6,500	$ 11,500
Accounts receivable	51,000	49,000
Inventories	155,000	147,500
Total current assets	212,500	208,000
Plant and equipment (net)	187,500	177,000
Total assets	$400,000	$385,000
Liabilities and Stockholders' Equity		
Liabilities		
Current liabilities		
Accounts payable	$ 60,000	$ 81,500
Other	25,000	22,500
Total current liabilities	85,000	104,000
Bonds payable	100,000	100,000
Total liabilities	185,000	204,000
Stockholders' equity		
Common stock (50,000 shares, $3 par)	150,000	150,000
Paid-in capital in excess of par	20,000	20,000
Retained earnings	45,000	11,000
Total stockholders' equity	215,000	181,000
Total liabilities and stockholders' equity	$400,000	$385,000

Required

a. Use horizontal analysis to determine which expense item increased by the highest percentage from Year 3 to Year 4.

b. Use vertical analysis to determine whether the inventory balance is a higher percentage of total assets in Year 3 or Year 4.

c. Calculate the following ratios for Year 3 and Year 4. When data limitations prohibit computing averages, use year-end balances in your calculations.

(1) Net margin

(2) Return on investment

(3) Return on equity

(4) Earnings per share

(5) Price-earnings ratio (market price per share at the end of Year 4 and Year 3 was $12.04 and $8.86, respectively)

(6) Book value per share of common stock

(7) Times interest earned

(8) Working capital

(9) Current ratio

(10) Acid-test ratio

(11) Accounts receivable turnover

(12) Inventory turnover

(13) Debt to equity

Solution to Requirement *a*

Income tax expense increased by the greatest percentage. Computations follow.

Cost of goods sold ($189,000 − $154,000) ÷ $154,000 = 22.73%

General, selling, and administrative ($54,000 − $46,000) ÷ $46,000 = 17.39%

Interest expense decreased.

Income tax expense ($27,200 − $21,800) ÷ $21,800 = 24.77%

Solution to Requirement *b*

Year 3: $147,500 ÷ $385,000 = 38.31%

Year 4: $155,000 ÷ $400,000 = 38.75%

Inventory is slightly larger relative to total assets in Year 4.

Solution to Requirement *c*

		Year 4	Year 3
1.	$\dfrac{\text{Net income}}{\text{Net sales}}$	$\dfrac{\$40,800}{\$315,000} = 12.95\%$	$\dfrac{\$32,700}{\$259,000} = 12.63\%$
2.	$\dfrac{\text{Net income}}{\text{Average total assets}}$	$\dfrac{\$40,800}{\$392,500} = 10.39\%$	$\dfrac{\$32,700}{\$385,000} = 8.49\%$
3.	$\dfrac{\text{Net income}}{\text{Average total stockholders' equity}}$	$\dfrac{\$40,800}{\$198,000} = 20.61\%$	$\dfrac{\$32,700}{\$181,000} = 18.07\%$
4.	$\dfrac{\text{Net income}}{\text{Average common shares outstanding}}$	$\dfrac{\$40,800}{50,000 \text{ shares}} = \$0.816$	$\dfrac{\$32,700}{50,000 \text{ shares}} = \$0.654$
5.	$\dfrac{\text{Market price per share}}{\text{Earnings per share}}$	$\dfrac{\$12.04}{\$0.816} = 14.75 \text{ times}$	$\dfrac{\$8.86}{\$0.654} = 13.55 \text{ times}$
6.	$\dfrac{\text{Stockholders' equity} - \text{Preferred rights}}{\text{Outstanding common shares}}$	$\dfrac{\$215,000}{50,000 \text{ shares}} = \$4.30$	$\dfrac{\$181,000}{50,000 \text{ shares}} = \$3.62$
7.	$\dfrac{\text{Net income} + \text{Taxes} + \text{Interest expense}}{\text{Interest expense}}$	$\dfrac{\$40,800 + \$27,200 + \$4,000}{\$4,000} = 18 \text{ times}$	$\dfrac{\$32,700 + \$21,800 + \$4,500}{\$4,500} = 13.1 \text{ times}$
8.	Current assets − Current liabilities	$\$212,500 - \$85,000 = \$127,500$	$\$208,000 - \$104,000 = \$104,000$
9.	$\dfrac{\text{Current assets}}{\text{Current liabilities}}$	$\dfrac{\$212,500}{\$85,000} = 2.5{:}1$	$\dfrac{\$208,000}{\$104,000} = 2{:}1$
10.	$\dfrac{\text{Quick assets}}{\text{Current liabilities}}$	$\dfrac{\$57,500}{\$85,000} = 0.68{:}1$	$\dfrac{\$60,500}{\$104,000} = 0.58{:}1$
11.	$\dfrac{\text{Net credit sales}}{\text{Average accounts receivable}}$	$\dfrac{\$315,000}{\$50,000} = 6.3 \text{ times}$	$\dfrac{\$259,000}{\$49,000} = 5.29 \text{ times}$
12.	$\dfrac{\text{Cost of goods sold}}{\text{Average inventory}}$	$\dfrac{\$189,000}{\$151,250} = 1.25 \text{ times}$	$\dfrac{\$154,000}{\$147,500} = 1.04 \text{ times}$
13.	$\dfrac{\text{Total liabilities}}{\text{Total stockholders' equity}}$	$\dfrac{\$185,000}{\$215,000} = 86.05\%$	$\dfrac{\$204,000}{\$181,000} = 112.71\%$

KEY TERMS

Absolute amounts 329
Accounts receivable
  turnover 335
Acid-test ratio 334
Asset turnover ratio 340
Average days to collect
  accounts receivables
  (average collection
  period) 335
Average days to sell inventory
  (average days in
  inventory) 336

Book value per
  share 342
Current ratio (working
  capital ratio) 334
Debt-to-assets ratio 337
Debt-to-equity ratio 337
Dividend yield 343
Earnings per share
  (EPS) 342
Horizontal analysis 329
Information overload 328
Inventory turnover 336

Liquidity ratios 333
Long-term
  liabilities 339
Materiality 329
Net margin 339
Number of times interest
  is earned 337
Percentage analysis 330
Price-earnings (P/E)
  ratio 342
Profitability ratios 339
Quick ratio 334

Ratio analysis 332
Return on assets 340
Return on equity
  (ROE) 340
Return on investment
  (ROI) 340
Solvency ratios 337
Trend analysis 329
Vertical analysis 331
Working capital 333
Working capital ratio 334

QUESTIONS

1. Why are ratios and trends used in financial analysis?

2. What do the terms *liquidity* and *solvency* mean?

3. What is apparent from a horizontal presentation of financial statement information? A vertical presentation?

4. What is the significance of inventory turnover, and how is it calculated?

5. What is the difference between the current ratio and the quick ratio? What does each measure?

6. Why are absolute amounts of limited use when comparing companies?

7. What is the difference between return on investment and return on equity?

8. Which ratios are used to measure long-term, debt-paying ability? How is each calculated?

9. What are some limitations of the earnings per share figure?

10. What is the formula for calculating return on investment (ROI)?

11. What is information overload?

12. What is the price-earnings ratio? Explain the difference between it and the dividend yield.

13. What environmental factors must be considered in analyzing companies?

14. How do accounting principles affect financial statement analysis?

EXERCISES—SERIES A

 An electronic auto-gradable version of the Series A Exercises is available in Connect. A PDF version of Series B Exercises is in Connect under the "Additional Student Resources" tab. Solutions to the Series B Exercises are available in Connect under the "Instructor Library" tab. Instructor and student Workpapers for the Series B Exercises are available in Connect under the "Instructor Library" and "Additional Student Resources" tabs respectively.

Exercise 9-1A *Horizontal analysis*   LO 9-1

Winthrop Corporation reported the following operating results for two consecutive years.

	Year 3	Year 2	Percentage Change
Sales	$1,200,000	$1,000,000	
Cost of goods sold	720,000	640,000	
Gross margin	480,000	360,000	
Operating expenses	200,000	160,000	
Income before taxes	280,000	200,000	
Income taxes	56,000	40,000	
Net income	$ 224,000	$ 160,000	

Required

a. Compute the percentage changes in Winthrop Corporation's income statement components between the two years. Round percentages to one decimal point.

b. Comment on apparent trends revealed by the percentage changes computed in Requirement *a*.

LO 9-1

Exercise 9-2A   *Vertical analysis*

Sharma Company reported the following operating results for two consecutive years.

Year 3	Amount	Percentage of Sales
Sales	$ 800,000	
Cost of goods sold	450,000	
Gross margin on sales	350,000	
Operating expenses	100,000	
Income before taxes	250,000	
Income taxes	50,000	
Net income	$ 200,000	

Year 4	Amount	Percentage of Sales
Sales	$1,000,000	
Cost of goods sold	590,000	
Gross margin on sales	410,000	
Operating expenses	120,000	
Income before taxes	290,000	
Income taxes	60,000	
Net income	$ 230,000	

Required

Express each income statement component for each of the two years as a percentage of sales. Round percentages to one decimal point.

LO 9-1

Exercise 9-3A   *Horizontal and vertical analysis*

Income statements for Burch Company for Year 3 and Year 4 follow.

	Year 4	Year 3
Sales	$240,000	$200,000
Cost of goods sold	180,000	124,000
Selling expenses	26,000	20,000
Administrative expenses	12,000	18,000
Interest expense	7,500	8,000
Total expenses	225,500	170,000
Income before taxes	14,500	30,000
Income taxes expense	1,200	3,000
Net income	$ 13,300	$ 27,000

Required

Round all percentages to one decimal point.

a. Perform a horizontal analysis, showing the percentage change in each income statement component between Year 3 and Year 4.

b. Perform a vertical analysis, showing each income statement component as a percentage of sales for each year.

LO 9-2

Exercise 9-4A   *Inventory turnover*

Selected financial information for Edwards Company for Year 4 follows.

Sales	$800,000
Cost of goods sold	500,000
Merchandise inventory	
Beginning of year	37,500
End of year	42,500

Required

Assuming that the merchandise inventory buildup was relatively constant, how many times did the merchandise inventory turn over during Year 4?

Exercise 9-5A   *Current ratio*

Swartz Corporation wrote off a $1,600 uncollectible account receivable against the $48,000 balance in its allowance account.

Required

Explain the effect of the write-off on Swartz's current ratio.

Exercise 9-6A   *Working capital and current ratio*

On June 30, Year 3, Franza Company's total current assets were $900,000 and its total current liabilities were $360,000. On July 1, Year 3, Franza issued a *short-term note* to a bank for $72,000 cash.

Required

a. Compute Franza's working capital before and after issuing the note.

b. Compute Franza's current ratio before and after issuing the note. Round ratios to two decimal points.

Exercise 9-7A   *Working capital and current ratio*

On June 30, Year 3, Franza Company's total current assets were $900,000 and its total current liabilities were $360,000. On July 1, Year 3, Franza issued a *long-term note* to a bank for $72,000 cash.

Required

Round computations to one decimal point.

a. Compute Franza's working capital before and after issuing the note.

b. Compute Franza's current ratio before and after issuing the note.

Exercise 9-8A   *Ratio analysis*

The balance sheet for Shankland Corporation follows.

Current assets	$ 600,000
Long-term assets (net)	1,900,000
Total assets	$2,500,000
Current liabilities	$ 400,000
Long-term liabilities	1,200,000
Total liabilities	1,600,000
Common stock and retained earnings	900,000
Total liabilities and stockholders' equity	$2,500,000

Required

Compute the following and round ratios to one decimal point.

Working capital	_____
Current ratio	_____
Debt-to-assets ratio	_____
Debt-to-equity ratio	_____

Exercise 9-9A   *Comprehensive analysis*

The December 31, Year 4, balance sheet for Burdette Corporation is presented here. These are the only accounts on Burdette's balance sheet. Amounts indicated by question marks (?) can be calculated using the following additional information.

Assets	
Cash	$ 30,000
Accounts receivable (net)	?
Inventory	?
Property, plant, and equipment (net)	352,800
	$ 518,400

Liabilities and Stockholders' Equity	
Accounts payable (trade)	$?
Income taxes payable (current)	30,000
Long-term debt	?
Common stock	360,000
Retained earnings	?
	$?

Additional Information	
Current ratio (at year end)	1.5 to 1.0
Total liabilities ÷ Total stockholders' equity	80%
Gross margin percentage	30%
Inventory turnover (Cost of goods sold ÷ Ending inventory)	10.5 times
Gross margin for Year 4	$ 378,000

Required

Determine the following:

a. The balance in trade accounts payable as of December 31, Year 4.

b. The balance in retained earnings as of December 31, Year 4.

c. The balance in the inventory account as of December 31, Year 4. (Assume that the level of inventory did not change from last year.)

LO 9-3

Exercise 9-10A   *Number of times interest earned*

The following data come from the financial records of Fargo Corporation for Year 3.

Sales	$640,000
Interest expense	6,000
Income tax expense	12,000
Net income	42,000

Required

How many times was interest earned in Year 3?

LO 9-2, 9-4

Exercise 9-11A   *Accounts receivable turnover, inventory turnover, and net margin*

Selected data from Emporia Company follow.

Balance Sheets As of December 31		
	Year 3	**Year 2**
Accounts receivable	$600,000	$480,000
Allowance for doubtful accounts	(40,000)	(20,000)
Net accounts receivable	$560,000	$460,000
Inventories, lower of cost or market	$500,000	$400,000

Income Statement For the Years Ended December 31		
	Year 3	**Year 2**
Net credit sales	$2,400,000	$1,950,000
Net cash sales	600,000	450,000
Net sales	3,000,000	2,400,000
Cost of goods sold	1,800,000	1,520,000
Selling, general, and administrative expenses	300,000	240,000
Other expenses	80,000	50,000
Total operating expenses	$2,180,000	$1,810,000

Required

Compute the following and round computations to two decimal points:

a. The accounts receivable turnover for Year 3.

b. The inventory turnover for Year 3.

c. The net margin for Year 2.

Exercise 9-12A   *Ratio analysis*   LO 9-5

During Year 3, Blue Ridge Corporation reported after-tax net income of $4,150,000. During the year, the number of shares of stock outstanding remained constant at 15,000 of $100 par, 9 percent preferred stock and 400,000 shares of common stock. The company's total stockholders' equity is $20,000,000 at December 31, Year 3. Blue Ridge Corporation's common stock was selling at $80 per share at the end of its fiscal year. All dividends for the year have been paid, including $4.80 per share to common stockholders.

Required

Compute the following by rounding to two decimal points:

a. Earnings per share.

b. Book value per share of common stock.

c. Price-earnings ratio.

d. Dividend yield.

Exercise 9-13A   *Ratio analysis*   LO 9-2, 9-3, 9-4, 9-5

Compute the specified ratios using Duluth Company's balance sheet for Year 3.

Assets	
Cash	$ 36,000
Marketable securities	24,000
Accounts receivable	50,000
Inventory	44,000
Property and equipment	320,000
Accumulated depreciation	(74,000)
Total assets	$400,000
Liabilities and Stockholders' Equity	
Accounts payable	$ 23,000
Current notes payable	7,000
Mortgage payable	8,000
Bonds payable	43,000
Common stock	200,000
Retained earnings	119,000
Total liabilities and stockholders' equity	$400,000

The average number of common stock shares outstanding during Year 3 was 880 shares. Net income for the year was $40,000.

Required

Compute each of the following and round computations to two decimal points:

a. Current ratio.
b. Earnings per share.
c. Quick (acid-test) ratio.
d. Return on investment.
e. Return on equity.
f. Debt-to-equity ratio.

LO 9-2, 9-3, 9-4, 9-5   **Exercise 9-14A** *Ratio analysis*

Required

Match each of the following ratios with the formula used to compute it:

_____ 1. Working capital	a. Net income ÷ Average total stockholders' equity
_____ 2. Current ratio	b. Cost of goods sold ÷ Average inventory
_____ 3. Quick ratio	c. Current assets − Current liabilities
_____ 4. Accounts receivable turnover	d. 365 ÷ Inventory turnover
_____ 5. Average days to collect	e. Net income ÷ Average total assets
_____ 6. Inventory turnover	f. (Net income − Preferred dividends) ÷ Average outstanding common shares
_____ 7. Average days to sell inventory	g. (Current assets − Inventory − Prepaid expenses) ÷ Current liabilities
_____ 8. Debt-to-assets ratio	h. Total liabilities ÷ Total assets
_____ 9. Debt-to-equity ratio	i. 365 ÷ Accounts receivable turnover
_____ 10. Return on investment	j. Total liabilities ÷ Total stockholders' equity
_____ 11. Return on equity	k. Net credit sales ÷ Average accounts receivable
_____ 12. Earnings per share	l. Current assets ÷ Current liabilities

LO 9-2, 9-3, 9-4, 9-5   **Exercise 9-15A** *Comprehensive analysis*

Required

Indicate the effect of each of the following transactions on (1) the current ratio, (2) working capital, (3) stockholders' equity, (4) book value per share of common stock, and (5) retained earnings. Assume that the current ratio is greater than 1:1.

a. Collected account receivable.
b. Wrote off account receivable.
c. Converted a short-term note payable to a long-term note payable.
d. Purchased inventory on account.
e. Declared cash dividend.
f. Sold merchandise on account at a profit.
g. Issued stock dividend.
h. Paid account payable.
i. Sold building at a loss.

PROBLEMS—SERIES A

An electronic auto-gradable version of the Series A Problems is available in Connect. A PDF version of Series B Problems is in Connect under the "Additional Student Resources" tab. Solutions to the Series B Problems are available in Connect under the "Instructor Library" tab. Instructor and student Workpapers for the Series B Problems are available in Connect under the "Instructor Library" and "Additional Student Resources" tabs respectively.

LO 9-1   **Problem 9-16A** *Vertical analysis*

The following percentages apply to Thornton Company for Year 3 and Year 4.

	Year 4	Year 3
Sales	100.0%	100.0%
Cost of goods sold	61.0	64.0
Gross margin	39.0	36.0
Selling and administrative expense	26.5	20.5
Interest expense	2.5	2.0
Total expenses	29.0	22.5
Income before taxes	10.0	13.5
Income tax expense	5.5	7.0
Net income	4.5%	6.5%

Required

Assuming that sales were $800,000 in Year 3 and $960,000 in Year 4, prepare income statements for the two years.

Problem 9-17A   *Horizontal analysis*

Financial statements for Allendale Company follow.

ALLENDALE COMPANY
Balance Sheets
As of December 31

	Year 4	Year 3
Assets		
Current assets		
Cash	$ 40,000	$ 36,000
Marketable securities	20,000	6,000
Accounts receivable (net)	54,000	46,000
Inventories	135,000	143,000
Prepaid items	25,000	10,000
Total current assets	274,000	241,000
Investments	27,000	20,000
Plant (net)	270,000	255,000
Land	29,000	24,000
Total assets	$600,000	$540,000
Liabilities and Stockholders' Equity		
Liabilities		
Current liabilities		
Notes payable	$ 17,000	$ 6,000
Accounts payable	113,800	100,000
Salaries payable	21,000	15,000
Total current liabilities	151,800	121,000
Noncurrent liabilities		
Bonds payable	100,000	100,000
Other	32,000	27,000
Total noncurrent liabilities	132,000	127,000
Total liabilities	283,800	248,000
Stockholders' equity		
Preferred stock (par value $10, 4% cumulative, nonparticipating; 8,000 shares authorized and issued)	80,000	80,000
Common stock (no par; 50,000 shares authorized; 10,000 shares issued)	80,000	80,000
Retained earnings	156,200	132,000
Total stockholders' equity	316,200	292,000
Total liabilities and stockholders' equity	$600,000	$540,000

ALLENDALE COMPANY		
Statements of Income and Retained Earnings		
For the Years Ended December 31		
	Year 4	Year 3
Revenues		
Sales (net)	$230,000	$210,000
Other revenues	8,000	5,000
Total revenues	238,000	215,000
Expenses		
Cost of goods sold	120,000	103,000
Selling, general, and administrative	55,000	50,000
Interest expense	8,000	7,200
Income tax expense	23,000	22,000
Total expenses	206,000	182,200
Net earnings (net income)	32,000	32,800
Retained earnings, January 1	132,000	107,000
Less: Preferred stock dividends	3,200	3,200
Common stock dividends	4,600	4,600
Retained earnings, December 31	$156,200	$132,000

Required

Prepare a horizontal analysis of the balance sheet and income statement for Year 4 and Year 3. Round percentages to one decimal point.

LO 9-1

CHECK FIGURE
Year 4 Retained earnings: 26.03%

Problem 9-18A *Vertical analysis*

Required

Use the financial statements for Allendale Company from Problem 9-17A to perform a vertical analysis of both the balance sheets and income statements for Year 4 and Year 3. Round computations to two decimal points.

LO 9-2

Problem 9-19A *Effect of transactions on current ratio and working capital*

Riley Manufacturing has a current ratio of 3:1 on December 31, Year 3. Indicate whether each of the following transactions would increase (+), decrease (−), or have no effect (NA) on Riley's current ratio and its working capital.

Required

a. Paid cash for a trademark.

b. Wrote off an uncollectible account receivable.

c. Sold equipment for cash.

d. Sold merchandise at a profit (cash).

e. Declared a cash dividend.

f. Purchased inventory on account.

g. Scrapped a fully depreciated machine (no gain or loss).

h. Issued a stock dividend.

i. Purchased a machine with a long-term note.

j. Paid a previously declared cash dividend.

k. Collected accounts receivable.

l. Invested in current marketable securities.

Problem 9-20A   *Supply missing balance sheet numbers*

The bookkeeper for Packard's Country Music Bar left this incomplete balance sheet. Packard's working capital is $90,000 and its debt-to-assets ratio is 40 percent.

Assets

Current assets	
Cash	$ 21,000
Accounts receivable	42,000
Inventory	(A)
Prepaid expenses	9,000
Total current assets	(B)
Long-term assets	
Building	(C)
Less: Accumulated depreciation	(39,000)
Total long-term assets	210,000
Total assets	$ (D)

Liabilities and Stockholders' Equity

Liabilities	
Current liabilities	
Accounts payable	$ (E)
Notes payable	12,000
Income tax payable	10,500
Total current liabilities	37,500
Long-term liabilities	
Mortgage payable	(F)
Total liabilities	(G)
Stockholders' equity	
Common stock	105,000
Retained earnings	(H)
Total stockholders' equity	(I)
Total liabilities and stockholders' equity	$ (J)

Required

Complete the balance sheet by supplying the missing amounts.

Problem 9-21A   *Ratio analysis*

Selected data for Dalton Company for Year 3 and additional information on industry averages follow.

Earnings (net income)		$ 97,800
Preferred stock (13,200 shares at $25 par, 4%)		$330,000
Common stock (45,000 shares no par, market value $28)		255,000
Retained earnings		281,250
		866,250
Less: Treasury stock		
Preferred (1,800 shares)	$27,000	
Common (1,800 shares)	12,000	39,000
Total stockholders' equity		$827,250

Industry averages	
Earnings per share	$2.60
Price-earnings ratio	9.50
Return on equity	11.20%

Required

a. Calculate Dalton Company's earnings per share ratio, price-earnings ratio, and return on equity ratio and compare them with the industry averages.

b. Discuss factors you would consider in deciding whether to invest in the company.

LO 9-3, 9-4, 9-5

Problem 9-22A *Ratio analysis*

Otis Company's income statement information follows.

	Year 3	Year 2
Net sales	$480,000	$320,000
Income before interest and taxes	120,000	98,000
Net income after taxes	81,000	72,000
Interest expense	9,000	8,000
Stockholders' equity, December 31 (Year 1: $200,000)	300,000	240,000
Common stock, December 31	240,000	200,000

The average number of shares outstanding was 9,600 for Year 3 and 8,000 for Year 2.

Required

Compute the following ratios for Otis for Year 3 and Year 2 and round the computation to two decimal points:

a. Number of times interest was earned.

b. Earnings per share based on the average number of shares outstanding.

c. Price-earnings ratio (market prices: Year 3, $64 per share; Year 2, $78 per share).

d. Return on average equity.

e. Net margin.

LO 9-2, 9-3, 9-4, 9-5

Problem 9-23A *Ratio analysis*

The following financial statements apply to Karl Company:

	Year 2	Year 1
Revenues	$436,000	$360,000
Expenses		
Cost of goods sold	252,000	206,000
Selling expenses	42,000	38,000
General and administrative expenses	22,000	20,000
Interest expense	6,000	6,000
Income tax expense	42,000	36,000
Total expenses	364,000	306,000
Net income	$ 72,000	$ 54,000

(*continued*)

	Year 2	Year 1
Assets		
Current assets		
Cash	$ 74,000	$ 84,000
Marketable securities	2,000	2,000
Accounts receivable	70,000	64,000
Inventories	200,000	192,000
Prepaid expenses	6,000	4,000
Total current assets	352,000	346,000
Plant and equipment (net)	210,000	210,000
Intangibles	40,000	0
Total assets	$602,000	$556,000
Liabilities and Stockholders' Equity		
Liabilities		
Current liabilities		
Accounts payable	$ 80,000	$108,000
Other	34,000	30,000
Total current liabilities	114,000	138,000
Bonds payable	132,000	134,000
Total liabilities	246,000	272,000
Stockholders' equity		
Common stock (100,000 shares)	230,000	230,000
Retained earnings	126,000	54,000
Total stockholders' equity	356,000	284,000
Total liabilities and stockholders' equity	$602,000	$556,000

Required

Calculate the following ratios for Year 1 and Year 2. When data limitations prohibit computing averages, use year-end balances in your calculations. Round computations to two decimal points.

a. Net margin.

b. Return on investment.

c. Return on equity.

d. Earnings per share.

e. Price-earnings ratio (market prices at the end of Year 1 and Year 2 were $11.88 and $9.54, respectively).

f. Book value per share of common stock.

g. Times interest earned.

h. Working capital.

i. Current ratio.

j. Quick (acid-test) ratio.

k. Accounts receivable turnover.

l. Inventory turnover.

m. Debt-to-equity ratio.

n. Debt-to-assets ratio.

Problem 9-24A   *Ratio analysis*

Required

Use the financial statements for Allendale Company from Problem 9-17A to calculate the following ratios for Year 4 and Year 3:

a. Working capital.

b. Current ratio.

LO 9-2, 9-3, 9-4, 9-5

CHECK FIGURES
k. Year 4: 2.05:1
p. Year 3: $2.96

c. Quick ratio.

d. Receivables turnover (beginning receivables at January 1, Year 3, were $47,000).

e. Average days to collect accounts receivable.

f. Inventory turnover (beginning inventory at January 1, Year 3, was $140,000).

g. Number of days to sell inventory.

h. Debt-to-assets ratio.

i. Debt-to-equity ratio.

j. Number of times interest was earned.

k. Plant assets to long-term debt.

l. Net margin.

m. Turnover of assets.

n. Return on investment.

o. Return on equity.

p. Earnings per share.

q. Book value per share of common stock.

r. Price-earnings ratio (market price per share: Year 3, $11.75; Year 4, $12.50).

s. Dividend yield on common stock.

ANALYZE, THINK, COMMUNICATE

ATC 9-1   Business Applications Case   *Analyzing Home Depot and Lowe's*

The following information relates to Home Depot, Inc., and Lowe's Companies, Inc. for their 2017 and 2016 fiscal years.

HOME DEPOT, INC. Selected Financial Information (amounts in millions, except per share amounts)		
	January 28, 2018	February 29, 2017
Total current assets	$ 18,933	$17,724
Merchandise inventory	12,748	12,549
Property and equipment, net of depreciation	22,075	21,914
Total assets	44,529	42,966
Total current liabilities	16,194	14,133
Total long-term liabilities	26,881	24,500
Total liabilities	43,075	38,633
Total shareholders' equity	1,454	4,333
Revenue	100,904	94,595
Cost of goods sold	66,548	62,282
Gross profit	34,356	32,313
Operating income	14,681	13,427
Earnings from continuing operations before income tax expense	13,698	12,491
Income tax expense	5,068	4,534
Net earnings	8,630	7,957
Basic earnings per share	$ 7.33	$ 6.47

LOWE'S COMPANIES, INC.
Selected Financial Information
(amounts in millions except per share data)

	February 2, 2018	February 3, 2017
Total current assets	$12,772	$12,000
Merchandise inventory	11,393	10,458
Property and equipment, net of depreciation	19,721	19,949
Total assets	35,291	34,408
Total current liabilities	12,096	11,974
Total long-term liabilities	17,322	16,000
Total liabilities	29,418	27,974
Total stockholders' equity	5,873	6,434
Revenues	68,619	65,017
Cost of goods sold	45,210	42,553
Gross profit	23,409	22,464
Operating income	6,586	5,846
Earnings from continuing operations before income taxes	5,489	5,201
Income tax expense	2,042	2,108
Net earnings	3,447	3,093
Basic earnings per share	$ 4.09	$ 3.48

Required

a. Compute the following ratios for the companies' 2017 fiscal years (years ending in January and February of 2018):

(1) Current ratio.

(2) Average days to sell inventory. (Use average inventory.)

(3) Debt-to-assets ratio.

(4) Return on investment. (Use average assets and use "earnings from continuing operations" rather than "net earnings.")

(5) Gross margin percentage.

(6) Asset turnover. (Use average assets.)

(7) Return on sales. (Use "earnings from continuing operations" rather than "net earnings.")

(8) Plant assets to long-term debt ratio.

b. Which company appears to be more profitable? Explain your answer and identify which ratio(s) from Requirement *a* you used to reach your conclusion.

c. Which company appears to have the higher level of financial risk? Explain your answer and identify which ratio(s) from Requirement *a* you used to reach your conclusion.

d. Which company appears to be charging higher prices for its goods? Explain your answer and identify which ratio(s) from Requirement *a* you used to reach your conclusion.

e. Which company appears to be the more efficient at using its assets? Explain your answer and identify which ratio(s) from Requirement *a* you used to reach your conclusion.

ATC 9-2   Group Assignment   *Ratios and basic logic*

Presented here is selected information from the 2016 fiscal-Year 10-K reports of four companies. The four companies, in alphabetical order, are:

AT&T, Inc., a company that provides communications and digital entertainment;

Deere & Company, a manufacturer of heavy machinery;

Starbucks, a company that sells coffee products; and

Tiffany & Company, a company that operates high-end jewelry and department stores.

The data for the companies, presented in the order of the amount of their sales in millions of dollars, are as follows.

	A	B	C	D
Sales	$163,786	$26,644.0	$21,315.9	$4,104.9
Cost of goods sold	76,884	18,248.9	8,511.1	1,613.6
Net earnings	12,976	1,523.9	2,817.7	463.9
Inventory	—	3,340.5	1,378.5	2,225.0
Accounts receivable	16,794	29,741.1	768.8	206.4
Total assets	403,821	57,981.4	14,329.5	5,129.7

Required

a. Divide the class into groups of four or five students per group and then organize the groups into four sections. Assign Task 1 to the first section of groups, Task 2 to the second section, Task 3 to the third section, and Task 4 to the fourth section.

Group Tasks

(1) Assume that you represent AT&T. Identify the set of financial data (Column A, B, C, or D) that relates to your company.

(2) Assume that you represent Deere. Identify the set of financial data (Column A, B, C, or D) that relates to your company.

(3) Assume that you represent Starbucks. Identify the set of financial data (Column A, B, C, or D) that relates to your company.

(4) Assume that you represent Tiffany. Identify the set of financial data (Column A, B, C, or D) that relates to your company.

Hint: In addition to the ratios presented in this chapter, you might also find it useful to compute a ratio from the first course of accounting, the gross margin percentage (Gross margin ÷ Sales).

b. Select a representative from each section. Have the representative explain the rationale for the group's selection. The explanation should include a set of ratios that support the group's conclusion.

ATC 9-3   Research Assignment   *Analyzing Kraft Food's merger with Heinz Company*

In July 2015, H. J. Heinz Company and Kraft Foods Group completed their merger. The new company, named The Kraft Heinz Company (KHC), became the fifth largest food and beverage company in the world. Prior to the merger, Kraft had been much larger than Heinz in terms of sales, $18 billion versus $6 billion, but Heinz was larger in terms of assets. To complete the requirements that follow you will need to obtain Kraft Foods Group, Inc.'s Form 10-K for 2014, the year before the acquisition, and KHC's Form 10-K 2017, two years after the deal was closed. The 2014 Form 10-K for Kraft Foods can only be found on the SEC's EDGAR website. Be sure to search and select Kraft Foods Group, not Kraft Heinz Company. The 2017 Form 10-K for Kraft Heinz Company can be found on the EDGAR website on the company's website, www.kraftheinzcompany.com, or through the EDGAR system.

Required

a. Compute the following ratios for 2014 and 2017. To make the computations simpler, use end-of-year amounts for total assets and total equity rather than averages. Also, changes to the federal income tax laws enacted in 2017 caused some unusual effects on KHC's 2017 net earnings. Therefore, for this problem, use "Earnings before income taxes" instead of net earnings for computing the following ratios. Show your calculations.

Net margin	Current ratio
Return on investment	Debt-to-assets ratio
Return on equity	

b. Based on the ratios computed in Requirement *a*, comment on the apparent effects of Kraft's merger with Heinz. Assume any significant change in these ratios was the result of the acquisition.

c. Based on this limited analysis, does it appear that the effects of the merger were good or bad for Kraft?

ATC 9-4   Writing Assignment   *Identifying companies based on financial statement information*

The following ratios are for four companies in different industries. Some of these ratios have been discussed in the textbook and others have not, but their names explain how the ratio was computed. These data are for the companies' 2016 fiscal years. The four sets of ratios, presented randomly, are as follows.

	Company 1	Company 2	Company 3	Company 4
Current assets ÷ Total assets	7%	18%	31%	19%
Average days to sell inventory	72 days	12 days	163 days	108 days
Average days to collect receivables	60 days	3 days	47 days	9 days
Return-on-assets	7%	8%	3%	5%
Gross margin	39%	22%	22%	50%
Sales ÷ Property, plant, and equipment	1.1 times	3.4 times	4.5 times	23.5 times
Sales ÷ Number of full-time employees	$279,980	$46,350	$397,743	$64,717

The four companies to which these ratios relate are:

Molson Coors Brewing Company, a company that produces beer and related products.

Darden Restaurants, Inc., which operates approximately 2,150 restaurants under 10 different names, including Olive Garden, Bahama Breeze, and LongHorn Steakhouse.

Deere & Company, a company that manufactures heavy construction equipment.

Weight Watchers International, Inc., a company that provides weight loss services and products. Its fiscal year-end was December 31, 2016, during which 81 percent of its revenues came from services and 19 percent from product sales.

Required

Determine which company should be matched with each set of ratios. Write a memorandum explaining the rationale for your decisions.

ATC 9-5   Ethical Dilemma   *Making the ratios look good*

J. Talbot is the accounting manager for Kolla Waste Disposal Corporation. Kolla is having its worst financial year since its inception. The company is expected to report a net loss. In the midst of such bad news, Ms. Talbot surprised the company president, Mr. Winston, by suggesting that the company write off approximately 25 percent of its garbage trucks. Mr. Winston responded by noting that the trucks could still be operated for another two or three years. Ms. Talbot replied, "We may use them for two or three more years, but you couldn't sell them on the street if you had to. Who wants to buy a bunch of old garbage trucks, and besides, it will make next year's financials so sweet. No one will care about the additional write-off this year. We are already showing a loss. Who will care if we lose a little bit more?"

Required

a.   How will the write-off affect the following year's return-on-assets ratio?

b.   How will the write-off affect the asset and income growth percentages?

c.   Explain how the components of the fraud triangle relate to this case.

CHAPTER 10

An Introduction to Management Accounting

LEARNING OBJECTIVES

After you have mastered the material in this chapter, you will be able to:

LO 10-1 Distinguish between managerial and financial accounting.

LO 10-2 Identify the cost of manufacturing a product.

LO 10-3 Show how manufacturing product costs affect financial statements.

LO 10-4 Compare the treatment of upstream, midstream, and downstream costs in manufacturing, service, and merchandising companies.

LO 10-5 Prepare a schedule of cost of goods manufactured and sold.

LO 10-6 Show how just-in-time inventory can increase profitability.

LO 10-7 Identify the standards contained in IMA's *Statement of Ethical Professional Practice*.

LO 10-8 Identify best practices in managerial accounting. (Appendix)

 Video lectures and accompanying self-assessment quizzes are available in Connect *for all learning objectives.*

 Set B exercises and problems are available in Additional Student Resources.

CHAPTER OPENING

Buffalo Burgers, Inc. is a restaurant chain that is growing rapidly. The vice president of operations (VPO) is concerned that the amount of salary expense has increased significantly more than other expense items. The VPO needs to know if the number of employees has increased, if employee salaries have increased, or if more people are working overtime.

Will the VPO find answers to these questions in the company's financial statements? No. **Financial accounting** is not designed to satisfy all the information needs of business managers. Its scope is limited to the needs of external users such as investors and creditors. The field of accounting designed to meet the needs of internal users is called **managerial accounting.**

The Curious Accountant

Mike Davies/Alamy Stock Photo

Earlier in this course you learned how retailers, such as Target, account for the cost of equipment that lasts more than one year. Recall that the equipment was recorded as an asset when purchased, and then it was depreciated over its expected useful life. The depreciation charge reduced the company's assets and increased its expenses. This approach was justified under the matching principle, which seeks to recognize costs as expenses in the same period that the cost (resource) is used to generate revenue.

Is depreciation always shown as an expense on the income statement? The answer may surprise you. Consider the following scenario. Skyrocket, LLC. manufactures the Sky Viper Streaming FPV Video Drone that it sells to Target. Assume that in order to produce the video drone, Skyrocket had to purchase a robotic machine that it expects can be used to produce 1,000,000 drones.

Do you think Skyrocket should account for depreciation on its manufacturing equipment the same way Target accounts for depreciation on its registers at the checkout counters? If not, how should Skyrocket account for its depreciation? Remember the matching principle when thinking of your answer. (Answer on page 374.)

DIFFERENCES BETWEEN MANAGERIAL AND FINANCIAL ACCOUNTING

LO 10-1

Distinguish between managerial and financial accounting.

While the information needs of internal and external users overlap, the needs of managers generally differ from those of investors or creditors. Some distinguishing characteristics are discussed in the following section.

Users and Types of Information

Financial accounting provides information used primarily by investors, creditors, and others *outside* a business. In contrast, managerial accounting focuses on information used by executives, managers, and employees who work *inside* the business. These two user groups need different types of information.

Internal users need information to *plan, direct,* and *control* business operations. The nature of information needed is related to an employee's job level. Lower-level employees use nonfinancial information such as work schedules, store hours, and customer service policies. Moving up the organizational ladder, financial information becomes increasingly important. Middle managers use a blend of financial and nonfinancial information, while senior executives concentrate on financial data. To a lesser degree, senior executives also use general economic data and nonfinancial operating information. For example, an executive may consider the growth rate of the economy before deciding to expand the company's workforce.

External users (investors and creditors) have greater needs for general economic information than do internal users. For example, an investor debating whether to purchase stock versus bond securities might be more interested in government tax policy than financial statement data. Exhibit 10.1 summarizes the information needs of different user groups.

Level of Aggregation

External users generally desire *global information* that reflects the performance of a company as a whole. For example, an investor is not so much interested in the performance of a particular Sears store as she is in the performance of Sears, Roebuck and Company versus that of JCPenney Company. In contrast, internal users focus on detailed information about specific subunits of the company. To meet the needs of the different user groups, financial accounting data are more aggregated than managerial accounting data.

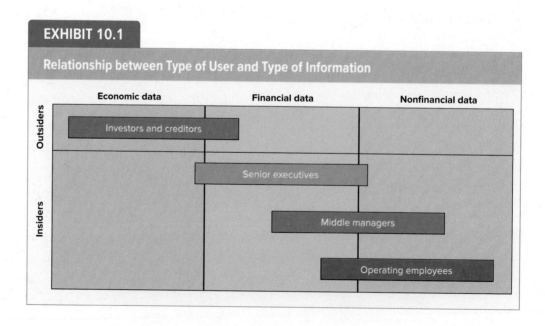

EXHIBIT 10.1

Relationship between Type of User and Type of Information

Regulation

Financial accounting is designed to generate information for the general public. In an effort to protect the public interest, Congress established the **Securities and Exchange Commission (SEC)** and gave it authority to regulate public financial reporting practices. The SEC has delegated much of its authority for developing accounting rules to the private sector **Financial Accounting Standards Board (FASB),** thereby allowing the accounting profession considerable influence over financial accounting reports. The FASB supports a broad base of pronouncements and practices known as **generally accepted accounting principles (GAAP).** GAAP severely restrict the accounting procedures and practices permitted in published financial statements.

Susan Walsh/AP Images

Beyond financial statement data, much of the information generated by management accounting systems is proprietary information not available to the public. Since this information is not distributed to the public, it need not be regulated to protect the public interest. Management accounting is restricted only by the **value-added principle.** Management accountants are free to engage in any information gathering and reporting activity so long as the activity adds value in excess of its cost. For example, management accountants are free to provide forecasted information to internal users. In contrast, financial accounting as prescribed by GAAP does not permit forecasting.

Information Characteristics

While financial accounting is characterized by its objectivity, reliability, consistency, and historical nature, managerial accounting is more concerned with relevance and timeliness. Managerial accounting uses more estimates and fewer facts than financial accounting. Financial accounting reports what happened yesterday; managerial accounting reports what is expected to happen tomorrow.

Time Horizon and Reporting Frequency

Financial accounting information is reported periodically, normally at the end of a year. Management cannot wait until the end of the year to discover problems. Planning, controlling, and directing require immediate attention. Managerial accounting information is delivered on a continuous basis.

Exhibit 10.2 summarizes significant differences between financial and managerial accounting.

EXHIBIT 10.2

Comparative Features of Managerial versus Financial Accounting Information

Features	Managerial Accounting	Financial Accounting
Users	Insiders, including executives, managers, and operators	Outsiders, including investors, creditors, government agencies, analysts, and reporters
Information type	Economic and physical data as well as financial data	Financial data
Level of aggregation	Local information on subunits of the organization	Global information on the company as a whole
Regulation	No regulation, limited only by the value-added principle	Regulation by SEC, FASB, and other determiners of GAAP
Information characteristics	Estimates that promote relevance and enable timeliness	Factual information that is characterized by objectivity, reliability, consistency, and accuracy
Time horizon	Past, present, and future	Past only, historically based
Reporting frequency	Continuous reporting	Delayed, with emphasis on annual reports

PRODUCT COSTING IN MANUFACTURING COMPANIES

A major focus for managerial accountants is determining **product cost.** Managers need to know the cost of their products for a variety of reasons. For example, **cost-plus pricing** is a common business practice. **Product costing** is also used to control business operations. It is useful in answering questions such as: Are costs higher or lower than expected? Who is responsible for the variances between expected and actual costs? What actions can be taken to control the variances?

Components of Product Cost

Generally accepted accounting principles (GAAP) recognize three types of cost that are incurred in the process of making products. Specifically, the company must pay for (1) the *materials* used to make the products, (2) the *labor* used to transform the materials into products, and (3) the **overhead** (other resources such as utilities and equipment consumed in the process of making the products). If the company stores its products, the costs of the materials, labor, and overhead used in making the products are maintained in an inventory account until the products are sold. For a detailed explanation of how product costs flow through the financial statements, refer to the following example of Tabor Manufacturing Company.

Tabor Manufacturing Company

Tabor Manufacturing Company makes wooden tables. The company spent $1,000 cash to build four tables: $390 for materials, $470 for a carpenter's labor, and $140 for tools used in making the tables. How much is Tabor's expense? The answer is zero. The $1,000 cash has been converted into products (four tables). The cash payments for materials, labor, and tools (overhead) were *asset exchange* transactions. One asset (cash) decreased while another asset (tables) increased. Tabor will not recognize any expense until the tables are sold; in the meantime, the cost of the tables is held in an asset account called **Finished Goods Inventory.** Exhibit 10.3 illustrates how cash is transformed into inventory.

EXHIBIT 10.3

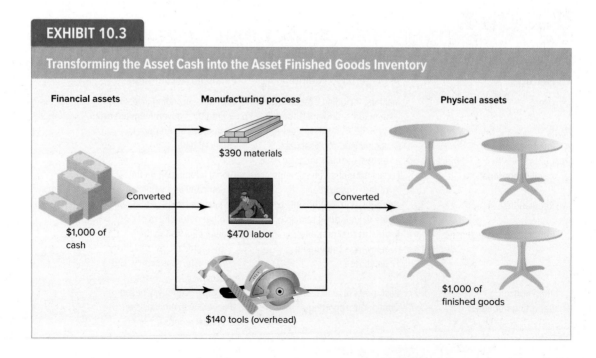

Transforming the Asset Cash into the Asset Finished Goods Inventory

Financial assets — Manufacturing process — Physical assets

$1,000 of cash — Converted — $390 materials / $470 labor / $140 tools (overhead) — Converted — $1,000 of finished goods

Average Cost per Unit

How much did each table made by Tabor cost? The *actual* cost of each of the four tables likely differs. The carpenter probably spent a little more time on some of the tables than others. Material and tool usage probably varied from table to table. Determining the exact cost of each table is virtually impossible. Minute details such as a second of labor time cannot be effectively measured. Even if Tabor could determine the exact cost of each table, the information would be of little use. Minor differences in the cost per table would make no difference in pricing or other decisions management needs to make. Accountants therefore normally calculate cost per unit as an *average*. In the case of Tabor Manufacturing, the **average cost** per table is $250 ($1,000 ÷ 4 units). Unless otherwise stated, assume *cost per unit* means *average cost per unit*.

☑ CHECK YOURSELF 10.1

All boxes of General Mills's Total Raisin Bran cereal are priced at exactly the same amount in your local grocery store. Does this mean that the actual cost of making each box of cereal was exactly the same?

Answer   No, making each box would not cost exactly the same amount. For example, some boxes contain slightly more or less cereal than other boxes. Accordingly, some boxes cost slightly more or less to make than others do. General Mills uses average cost rather than actual cost to develop its pricing strategy.

Costs Can Be Assets or Expenses

It might seem odd that wages paid to production workers are recorded as inventory instead of being expensed. Remember, however, that expenses are assets used in the process of *earning revenue*. The cash paid to production workers is not used to produce revenue. Instead, the cash is used to produce inventory. Revenue will be earned when the inventory is used (sold). So long as the inventory remains on hand, all product costs (materials, labor, and overhead) remain in an inventory account.

When a table is sold, the average cost of the table is transferred from the Inventory account to the Cost of Goods Sold (expense) account. If some tables remain unsold at the end of the accounting period, part of the *product cost* is reported as an asset (inventory) on the balance sheet while the other part is reported as an expense (cost of goods sold) on the income statement.

Costs that are not classified as product costs are normally expensed in the period in which they are incurred. These costs include *general operating costs, selling and administrative costs, interest costs,* and the *cost of income taxes.*

To illustrate, return to the Tabor Manufacturing example. Recall that Tabor made four tables at an average cost per unit of $250. Assume Tabor pays an employee who sells three of the tables a $200 sales commission. The sales commission is expensed immediately. The total product cost for the three tables (3 tables × $250 each = $750) is expensed on the income statement as cost of goods sold. The portion of the total product cost remaining in inventory is $250 (1 table × $250). Exhibit 10.4 shows the relationship between the costs incurred and the expenses recognized for Tabor Manufacturing Company.

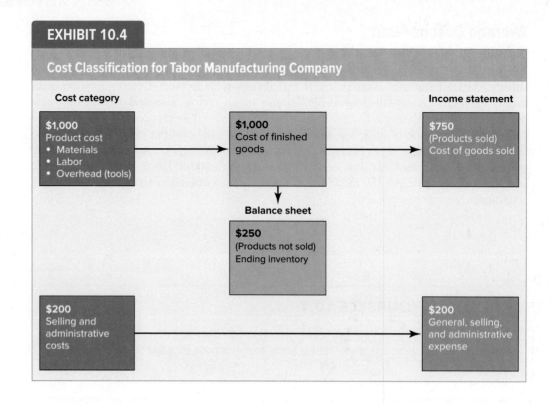

EXHIBIT 10.4

Cost Classification for Tabor Manufacturing Company

EFFECT OF MANUFACTURING PRODUCT COSTS ON FINANCIAL STATEMENTS

Show how manufacturing product costs affect financial statements.

We illustrate accounting for product costs in manufacturing companies with Patillo Manufacturing Company, a producer of ceramic pottery. Patillo, started on January 1, Year 1, experienced the following accounting events during its first year of operations. *Assume that all transactions except 6, 8, and 10 are cash transactions.*

1. Acquired $15,000 cash by issuing common stock.

2. Paid $2,000 for materials that were used to make products. All products started were completed during the period.

3. Paid $1,200 for salaries of selling and administrative employees.

4. Paid $3,000 for wages of production workers.

5. Paid $2,800 for furniture used in selling and administrative offices.

6. Recognized depreciation on the office furniture purchased in Event 5. The furniture was acquired on January 1, had a $400 estimated salvage value, and a four-year useful life. The annual depreciation charge is $600 [($2,800 − $400) ÷ 4].

7. Paid $4,500 for manufacturing equipment.

8. Recognized depreciation on the equipment purchased in Event 7. The equipment was acquired on January 1, had a $1,500 estimated salvage value, and a three-year useful life. The annual depreciation charge is $1,000 [($4,500 − $1,500) ÷ 3].

9. Sold inventory to customers for $7,500 cash.

10. The inventory sold in Event 9 cost $4,000 to make.

The effects of these transactions on the balance sheet and income statement are shown in Exhibit 10.5. Study each row in this exhibit, paying particular attention to how similar costs such as salaries for selling and administrative personnel and wages for production

EXHIBIT 10.5

Effect of Product versus Selling and Administrative Costs on Financial Statements

Event No.	Balance Sheet											Income Statement					Statement of Cash Flows
	Assets								Stk. Equity								
	Cash	+	Inventory	+	B.V. Office Furn.*	+	B.V. Manuf. Equip.*	=	Com. Stk.	+	Ret. Earn.	Rev.	−	Exp.	=	Net Inc.	
1	15,000							=	15,000								15,000 FA
2	(2,000)	+	2,000														(2,000) OA
3	(1,200)							=			(1,200)		−	1,200	=	(1,200)	(1,200) OA
4	(3,000)	+	3,000														(3,000) OA
5	(2,800)	+			2,800												(2,800) IA
6					(600)			=			(600)		−	600	=	(600)	
7	(4,500)	+					4,500										(4,500) IA
8			1,000	+			(1,000)										
9	7,500							=			7,500	7,500			=	7,500	7,500 OA
10			(4,000)					=			(4,000)		−	4,000	=	(4,000)	
Totals	9,000	+	2,000	+	2,200	+	3,500	=	15,000	+	1,700	7,500	−	5,800	=	1,700	9,000 NC

*Note: In the financial statements model the Book Value of the Office Furniture account is abbreviated as B.V. Office Furn. and the Book Value of the Manufacturing Equipment account is abbreviated as B.V. Manuf. Equip.

workers have radically different effects on the financial statements. The example illustrates the three elements of product costs—materials (Event 2), labor (Event 4), and overhead (Event 8). These events are discussed in more detail as follows.

Materials Costs (Event 2)

Materials used to make products are usually called **raw materials.** The cost of raw materials is first recorded in an asset account (Inventory). The cost is then transferred from the Inventory account to the Cost of Goods Sold account at the time the goods are sold. Remember that materials cost is only one component of total manufacturing costs. When inventory is sold, the combined cost of materials, labor, and overhead is expensed as *cost of goods sold.* The costs of materials that can be easily and conveniently traced to products are called **direct raw materials** costs.

Labor Costs (Event 4)

The salaries paid to selling and administrative employees (Event 3) and the wages paid to production workers (Event 4) are accounted for differently. Salaries paid to selling and administrative employees are expensed immediately, but the cost of production wages is added to inventory. Production wages are expensed as part of cost of goods sold at the time the inventory is sold. Labor costs that can be easily and conveniently traced to products are called **direct labor** costs. The cost flow of wages for production employees versus salaries for selling and administrative personnel is shown in Exhibit 10.6.

Overhead Costs (Event 8)

Although depreciation cost totaled $1,600 ($600 on office furniture and $1,000 on manufacturing equipment), only the $600 of depreciation on the office furniture is expensed directly on the income statement. The depreciation on the manufacturing equipment is split between the income statement (cost of goods sold) and the balance sheet (inventory). The depreciation cost flow for the manufacturing equipment versus the office furniture is shown in Exhibit 10.7.

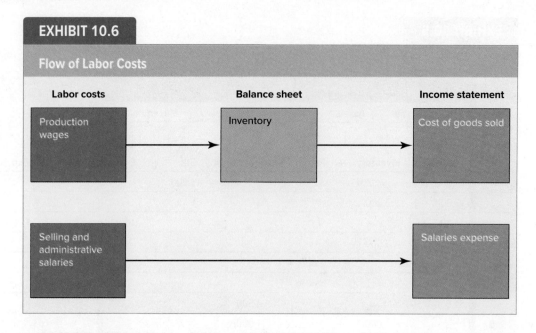

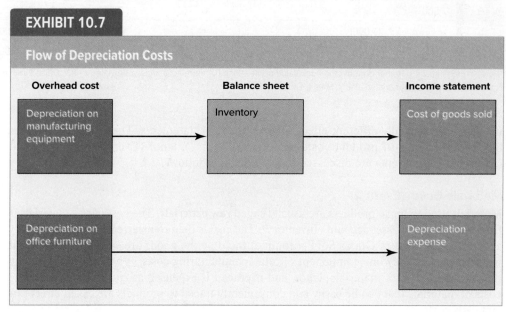

A summary of Patillo Manufacturing's **total product cost** is shown in Exhibit 10.8.

EXHIBIT 10.8

Schedule of Inventory Costs

Materials	$ 2,000
Labor	3,000
Manufacturing overhead*	1,000
Total product costs	6,000
Less: Cost of goods sold	(4,000)
Ending inventory balance	$ 2,000

*Depreciation [($4,500 − $1,500) ÷ 3].

Financial Statements

The GAAP-based income statement and balance sheet for Patillo Manufacturing are displayed in Exhibit 10.9.

Product Costs. The $4,000 cost of goods sold reported on the income statement includes a portion of the materials, labor, and overhead costs incurred by Patillo during the year. Similarly, the $2,000 of finished goods inventory on the balance sheet includes materials, labor, and overhead costs. These product costs will be recognized as an expense in the next accounting period when the goods are sold. Initially classifying a cost as a product cost delays, but does not eliminate, its recognition as an expense. All product costs are ultimately recognized as an expense (cost of goods sold).

EXHIBIT 10.9

PATILLO MANUFACTURING COMPANY
Financial Statements
Income Statement for Year 1

Sales revenue	$ 7,500
Cost of goods sold	(4,000)
Gross margin	3,500
SG&A expenses	
Salaries expense	(1,200)
Depreciation expense—office furniture	(600)
Net income	$ 1,700

Balance Sheet as of December 31, Year 1

Cash		$ 9,000
Finished goods inventory		2,000
Office furniture	$ 2,800	
Accumulated depreciation	(600)	
Book value		2,200
Manufacturing equipment	4,500	
Accumulated depreciation	(1,000)	
Book value		3,500
Total assets		$16,700
Stockholders' equity		
Common stock		$15,000
Retained earnings		1,700
Total stockholders' equity		$16,700

Selling, General, and Administrative Costs. Selling, general, and administrative costs (SG&A) are normally expensed *in the period* in which they are incurred. Because of this recognition pattern, nonproduct expenses are sometimes called **period costs.** In Patillo's case, the salaries expense for selling and administrative employees and the depreciation on office furniture are period costs reported directly on the income statement.

Overhead Costs: A Closer Look. Costs such as depreciation on manufacturing equipment cannot be easily traced to products. Suppose that Patillo Manufacturing makes both tables and chairs. What part of the depreciation is caused by manufacturing tables versus manufacturing chairs? Similarly, suppose a production supervisor oversees employees who work on both tables and chairs. How much of the supervisor's salary relates to tables and how much to chairs?

 CHECK YOURSELF 10.2

Lawson Manufacturing Company paid production workers wages of $100,000. It incurred materials costs of $120,000 and manufacturing overhead costs of $160,000. Selling and administrative salaries were $80,000. Lawson started and completed 1,000 units of product and sold 800 of these units. The company sets sales prices at $220 above the average per-unit production cost. Based on this information alone, determine the amount of gross margin and net income. What is Lawson's pricing strategy called?

Answer   Total product cost is $380,000 ($100,000 labor + $120,000 materials + $160,000 overhead). Cost per unit is $380 ($380,000 ÷ 1,000 units). The sales price per unit is $600 ($380 + $220). Cost of goods sold is $304,000 ($380 × 800 units). Sales revenue is $480,000 ($600 × 800 units). Gross margin is $176,000 ($480,000 revenue − $304,000 cost of goods sold). Net income is $96,000 ($176,000 gross margin − $80,000 selling and administrative salaries). Lawson's pricing strategy is called *cost-plus* pricing.

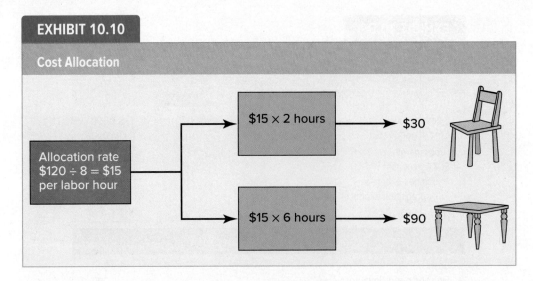

EXHIBIT 10.10

Cost Allocation

Allocation rate
$120 ÷ 8 = $15
per labor hour

$15 × 2 hours → $30

$15 × 6 hours → $90

Likewise, the cost of glue used in the production department would be difficult to trace to tables versus chairs. You could count the drops of glue used on each product, but the information would not be useful enough to merit the time and money spent collecting the data.

Costs that cannot be traced to products and services in a *cost-effective* manner are called **indirect costs.** The indirect costs incurred to make products are called **manufacturing overhead.** Some of the items commonly included in manufacturing overhead are indirect materials, indirect labor, factory utilities, rent of manufacturing facilities, and depreciation on manufacturing assets.

Since indirect costs cannot be effectively traced to products, they are normally assigned to products using **cost allocation**, a process of dividing a total cost into parts and assigning the parts to relevant cost objects. To illustrate, suppose that production workers spend an eight-hour day making a chair and a table. The chair requires two hours to complete and the table requires six hours. Now suppose that $120 of utilities cost is consumed during the day. How much of the $120 should be assigned to each piece of furniture? The utility cost cannot be directly traced to each specific piece of furniture, but the piece of furniture that required more labor also likely consumed more of the utility cost. Using this line of reasoning, it is rational to allocate the utility cost to the two pieces of furniture based on *direct labor hours* at a rate of $15 per hour ($120 ÷ 8 hours). The chair would be assigned $30 ($15 per hour × 2 hours) of the utility cost and the table would be assigned the remaining $90 ($15 × 6 hours) of utility cost. The allocation of the utility cost is shown in Exhibit 10.10.

We discuss the details of cost allocation in a later chapter. For now, recognize that overhead costs are normally allocated to products rather than traced directly to them.

Manufacturing Product Cost Summary

As explained, the cost of a product made by a manufacturing company is normally composed of three categories: direct materials, direct labor, and manufacturing overhead. Relevant information about these three cost components is summarized in Exhibit 10.11.

Answers to The Curious Accountant

As you have seen, accounting for depreciation related to manufacturing assets is different from accounting for depreciation for nonmanufacturing assets. Depreciation on the checkout equipment at Target is recorded as depreciation expense. Depreciation on manufacturing equipment at Skyrocket is considered a product cost. It is included first as part of the cost of inventory and eventually as part of the expense, cost of goods sold. Recording depreciation on manufacturing equipment as an inventory cost is simply another example of the matching principle, because the cost does not become an expense until revenue from the product sale is recognized.

EXHIBIT 10.11

Components of Manufacturing Product Cost

Component 1—Direct Raw Materials
Sometimes called *raw materials*. In addition to basic resources such as wood or metals, it can include manufactured parts. For example, engines, glass, and car tires can be considered as raw materials for an automotive manufacturer. If the amount of a material in a product is known, it can usually be classified as a direct material. The cost of direct materials can be easily traced to specific products.

Component 2—Direct Labor
The cost of wages paid to factory workers involved in hands-on contact with the products being manufactured. If the amount of time employees worked on a product can be determined, this cost can usually be classified as direct labor. Like direct materials, labor costs must be easily traced to a specific product in order to be classified as a direct cost.

Component 3—Manufacturing Overhead
Costs that cannot be easily traced to specific products. Accordingly, these costs are called *indirect costs*. They can include but are not limited to the following:

1. Indirect materials such as glue, nails, paper, and oil. Indeed, note that indirect materials used in the production process may not appear in the finished product. An example is a chemical solvent used to clean products during the production process but not a component material found in the final product.

2. Indirect labor such as the cost of salaries paid to production supervisors, inspectors, and maintenance personnel.

3. Rental cost for manufacturing facilities and equipment.

4. Utility costs.

5. Depreciation.

6. Security.

7. The cost of preparing equipment for the manufacturing process (i.e., setup costs).

8. Maintenance cost for the manufacturing facility and equipment.

UPSTREAM, MIDSTREAM, AND DOWNSTREAM COSTS IN MANUFACTURING, SERVICE, AND MERCHANDISING COMPANIES

Accountants frequently classify cost into three categories including (1) upstream, (2) midstream, and (3) downstream costs. The following section explains the treatment of these costs in manufacturing, service, and merchandising companies.

LO 10-4

 Compare the treatment of upstream, midstream, and downstream costs in manufacturing, service, and merchandising companies.

Cost Classification in Manufacturing Companies

For manufacturing companies, **midstream costs** are composed of the costs incurred in the process of making products including direct materials, direct labor, and manufacturing overhead. **Upstream costs** are costs that are incurred prior to manufacturing process including research and development costs and product design costs. **Downstream costs** are costs incurred after the manufacturing process including marketing, distribution, and customer services. A summary of this cost classification scheme as it relates to an automobile manufacturing company is shown in Exhibit 10.12.

Note that the upstream, midstream, and downstream costs of one company can become the midstream costs of another company. For example, the upstream, midstream, and downstream costs of a steel manufacturing company are passed on as a midstream cost (direct materials) to an auto parts manufacturing company when it purchases steel. Likewise, the upstream, midstream, and downstream costs of the auto parts company are passed on to an automobile manufacturing company as part of its midstream (direct materials) costs when it purchases auto parts. Also, note that the same type of cost can be classified as an upstream,

EXHIBIT 10.12

Upstream Costs:

- Research and development
- Product design

Midstream Costs:

- Direct materials
- Direct labor
- Manufacturing overhead

Downstream Costs:

- Marketing
- Distribution
- Customer service

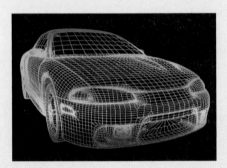

Alfred Pasieka/Science Photo Library/Getty Images

Monty Rakusen/Cultura/Getty Images

John Lund/Marc Romanelli/Blend Images LLC

midstream, or downstream cost. For example, salaries of a researcher may be classified as an upstream cost, while salaries of a production worker are classified as midstream costs, and salaries of a salesperson are classified as a downstream cost.

Generally accepted accounting principles (GAAP) require midstream costs to be reported separately from upstream and downstream costs on public financial statements. More specifically, the midstream costs (direct materials, direct labor, and manufacturing overhead) are classified as product costs and are expensed as cost of goods sold at the time goods are sold. In contrast, upstream and downstream cost are classified as general, selling, and administrative expenses and are expensed in the period they are incurred. In general, cost of goods sold is subtracted from sales revenue to determine the amount of gross margin and then upstream and downstream costs are subtracted from gross margin to determine the amount of net income. The format of a typical GAAP-based income statement is shown in Exhibit 10.13.

EXHIBIT 10.13

Sales revenue
— Cost of goods sold (midstream costs)
= Gross margin
— General, selling, and administrative costs (upstream and downstream costs)
= Net income

Cost Classification in Service and Merchandising Companies

Companies are frequently classified as being service, merchandising, or manufacturing businesses. As the name implies, service organizations provide services, rather than physical products, to consumers. For example, St. Jude Children's Hospital provides treatment programs aimed at healing patient diseases. Other common service providers include public accountants, lawyers, restaurants, dry cleaning establishments, and lawn care companies. Merchandising businesses are sometimes called retail or wholesale companies; they sell goods to other companies. The Home Depot, Inc., Costco Wholesale Corporation, and Best Buy Co., Inc. are merchandising companies. Manufacturing companies make the goods they sell to their customers. Toyota Motor Corporation, Texaco, Inc., and American Standard Companies, Inc. are manufacturing businesses.

Do service and merchandising companies incur materials, labor, and overhead costs? Yes; for example, Wendy's has materials costs (meat, potatoes, etc.), labor costs (cooks, packaging staff), and overhead (depreciation on equipment). Can the costs incurred by service and merchandising companies be classified as being upstream, midstream, and downstream? Yes. Continuing the Wendy's example, the company incurs research and development costs to produce its recipes and to find new locations (upstream costs); meat, labor, and overhead costs to make its food products (midstream costs); and sales staff and janitorial salaries and costs incurred to provide space for customers to consume their food (downstream costs).

So how do manufacturing companies differ from service and merchandising businesses? *The primary difference between manufacturing entities and service companies is that the finished products provided by service companies are consumed immediately.* For example, advice from a doctor is being consumed as it is being delivered to the patient. In contrast, products made by manufacturing companies can be held in the form of inventory until they are sold to consumers.

While merchandising companies frequently hold inventory, they differ from manufacturing companies in that they do not make the products they sell. Rather, they buy finished goods from suppliers and simply hold those products until they are delivered to customers. Indeed, most labor and overhead costs incurred by merchandising companies result from providing assistance to customers. These costs are normally treated as selling, general, and administrative expenses rather than accumulated in inventory accounts. This is why merchandising companies are often viewed as service companies rather than considered a separate business category.

The important point to remember is that all business managers are expected to control costs, improve quality, and increase productivity. Like managers of manufacturing companies, managers of service and merchandising businesses can benefit from the analysis of the cost of satisfying their customers. For example, Wendy's, a service company, can benefit from knowing how much a hamburger costs in the same manner that Bayer AG, a manufacturing company, benefits from knowing the cost of a bottle of aspirin.

☑ CHECK YOURSELF 10.3

The cost of making a Burger King hamburger includes the cost of materials, labor, and overhead. Does this mean that Burger King is a manufacturing company?

Answer   No, Burger King is not a manufacturing company. It is a service company because its products are consumed immediately. In contrast, there may be a considerable delay between the time the product of a manufacturing company is made and the time it is consumed. For example, it could be several months between the time Ford Motor Company makes an Explorer and the time the Explorer is ultimately sold to a customer. The primary difference between service and manufacturing companies is that manufacturing companies have inventories of products and service companies do not.

Managerial versus Financial Treatment of Upstream, Midstream, and Downstream Cost in Manufacturing Companies

To avoid having one system for external reporting and a different system for internal reporting, many companies use generally accepted accounting principles (GAAP) for internal as well as external reports. Unfortunately, the effort to maintain consistency between internal and external reporting systems can lead to mistakes in decision making. Specifically, managers may fail to include upstream and downstream costs when establishing sales prices and/or measuring product profitability. If upstream or downstream costs are not included in determining the cost of products, those products will be undercosted. This may lead managers to set prices that are below the total cost of producing and selling products, thereby leading to long-term losses rather than profitability.

☑ CHECK YOURSELF 10.4

To illustrate, Warm Zero, Inc. makes down jackets. The manufacturing costs per unit include $30 direct materials, $35 direct labor, and $15 manufacturing overhead. These costs are based on a production and sales volume of 4,000 units. Advertising costs amounted to $50,000. Research and development cost for the cloth materials used in the jackets amounted to $60,000. Companywide administrative costs amounted to $90,000. Fashion design costs amounted to $40,000. To be competitive, Warm Zero's management team used industry standards to establish the sales price at 160 percent of GAAP-defined product cost.

Required

a. Determine the total amount of upstream costs.

b. Determine the total amount of downstream costs.

c. Determine the total amount of midstream costs.

d. Determine the sales price per unit.

e. Prepare a GAAP-based income statement.

f. Provide a plausible explanation as to why the company incurred the loss shown on the income statement prepared to satisfy Requirement e. (*Hint:* Calculate the full cost of making and selling the jackets.)

Answer

a. Upstream costs = $60,000 R&D + $40,000 fashion design = $100,000

b. Downstream costs = $50,000 advertising + $90,000 administrative costs = $140,000

c. Midstream costs = ($30 direct materials + $35 direct labor + $15 manufacturing overhead) × 4,000 units = $320,000

d. Sales price = GAAP-defined product cost × 160% = [($30 direct materials + $35 direct labor + $15 manufacturing overhead) × 1.6] = $128

e.

Sales revenue ($128 price × 4,000 jackets)	$ 512,000
Cost of goods sold ($80 cost × 4,000)	(320,000)
Gross margin	192,000
General, selling, and administrative costs	
Upstream costs (R&D and design)	(100,000)
Downstream costs (administrative and advertising)	(140,000)
Net loss	$ (48,000)

f. It appears that management failed to give appropriate consideration to upstream and downstream costs when pricing the product. Only the GAAP-based product cost was used to determine the price. The total cost of making a down jacket is upstream cost + midstream cost + downstream cost. In this case, total cost per unit includes:

Midstream cost = ($30 direct materials + $35 direct labor + $15 manufacturing overhead) = $80

Upstream cost = ($100,000 R&D and design) ÷ 4,000 units = $25

Downstream cost = ($140,000 administrative and advertising) ÷ 4,000 units = $35

Total cost = $80 midstream + $25 upstream + $35 downstream = $140

Note that the selling price of $128 is below the total cost per unit of $140. This explains the loss incurred by the company.

SCHEDULE OF COST OF GOODS MANUFACTURED AND SOLD

LO 10-5

Prepare a schedule of cost of goods manufactured and sold.

To this point, we assumed all inventory started during an accounting period was also completed during that accounting period. All product costs (materials, labor, and manufacturing overhead) were either in inventory or expensed as cost of goods sold. At the end of an accounting period, however, most real-world companies have raw materials on hand, and manufacturing companies are likely to have in inventory items that have been started but are not completed. Most manufacturing companies accumulate product costs in three distinct inventory accounts: (1) **Raw Materials Inventory,** which includes lumber, metals, paints, and chemicals that will be used to make the company's products; (2) **Work in Process Inventory,** which includes partially completed products; and (3) Finished Goods Inventory, which includes completed products that are ready for sale.

The cost of materials is first recorded in the Raw Materials Inventory account. The cost of materials placed in production is then transferred from the Raw Materials Inventory account to the Work in Process Inventory account. The costs of labor and overhead are added to the Work in Process Inventory account. The cost of the goods completed during the period is transferred from the Work in Process Inventory account to the Finished Goods Inventory account. The cost of the goods that are sold during the accounting period is transferred from the Finished Goods Inventory account to the Cost of Goods Sold account. The balances that remain in the Raw Materials, Work in Process, and Finished Goods Inventory accounts are reported on the balance sheet. The amount of product cost transferred to the Cost of Goods Sold account is expensed on the income statement. Exhibit 10.14 shows the flow of manufacturing costs through the accounting records.

EXHIBIT 10.14

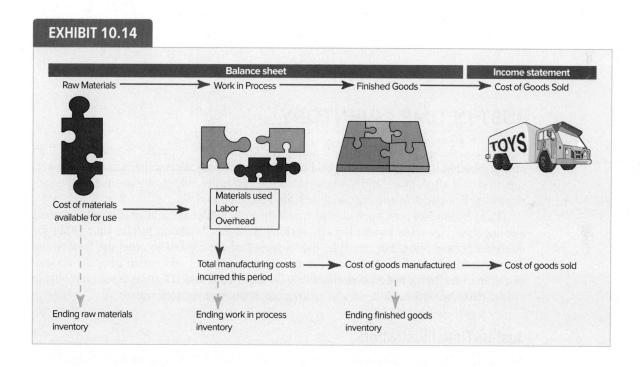

To help managers analyze manufacturing costs, companies frequently summarize product cost information in a report called a **schedule of cost of goods manufactured and sold.** To illustrate, assume that in Year 2 Patillo Manufacturing Company purchased $37,950 of raw materials inventory. During Year 2, Patillo used $37,000 of raw materials, incurred $34,600 of labor costs, and $26,700 of overhead costs in the process of making inventory. Also, during Year 2 the company completed work on products that cost $94,600. Recall that Patillo had zero balances in its Raw Materials and Work in Process Inventory accounts at the end of Year 1. It had a $2,000 balance in its Finished Goods Inventory account at the end of Year 1. The Year 1 ending balance becomes the Year 2 beginning balance for finished goods. The Year 2 ending balances for the inventory accounts were as follows: Raw Materials Inventory, $950; Work in Process Inventory, $3,700; Finished Goods Inventory, $3,200. Finally, during Year 2 Patillo had sales revenue of $153,000. Patillo's schedule of cost of goods manufactured and sold for Year 2 is shown in Exhibit 10.15.

The $93,400 of cost of goods sold would appear on Patillo's Year 2 income statement. A partial income statement for Patillo is shown in Exhibit 10.16.

EXHIBIT 10.15

PATILLO MANUFACTURING COMPANY
Schedule of Cost of Goods Manufactured and Sold
For the Year Ended December 31, Year 2

Beginning raw materials Inventory	$ 0
Plus: Raw materials purchases	37,950
Less: Ending raw materials inventory	(950)
Raw materials used	37,000
Labor	34,600
Overhead	26,700
Total manufacturing costs	98,300
Plus: Beginning work in process inventory	0
Total work in process inventory	98,300
Less: Ending work in process inventory	(3,700)
Cost of goods manufactured	94,600
Plus: Beginning finished goods inventory	2,000
Cost of goods available for sale	96,600
Less: Ending finished goods inventory	(3,200)
Cost of goods sold	$93,400

EXHIBIT 10.16

PATILLO MANUFACTURING COMPANY
Income Statement
For the Year Ended December 31, Year 2

Sales revenue	$153,000
Cost of goods sold	(93,400)
Gross margin	$ 59,600

JUST-IN-TIME INVENTORY

LO 10-6

Show how just-in-time inventory can increase profitability.

Companies attempt to minimize the amount of inventory they maintain because of the high cost of holding it. Many **inventory holding costs** are obvious: financing, warehouse space, supervision, theft, damage, and obsolescence. Other costs are hidden: diminished motivation, sloppy work, inattentive attitudes, and increased production time.

Many businesses have been able to simultaneously reduce their inventory holding costs and increase customer satisfaction by making products available **just in time (JIT)** for customer consumption. For example, hamburgers that are cooked to order are fresher and more individualized than those that are prepared in advance and stored until a customer places an order. Many fast-food restaurants have discovered that JIT systems lead not only to greater customer satisfaction but also to lower costs through reduced waste.

Just-in-Time Illustration

To illustrate the benefits of a JIT system, consider Paula Elliot, a student at a large urban university. She helps support herself by selling flowers. Three days each week, Paula drives to a florist, purchases 25 single-stem roses, returns to the school, and sells the flowers to individuals from a location on a local street corner. She pays $2 per rose and sells each one for $3. Some days she does not have enough flowers to meet customer demand. Other days, she must discard one or two unsold flowers; she believes quality is important and refuses to sell flowers that are not fresh. During May, she purchased 300 roses and sold 280. She calculated her driving cost to be $45. Exhibit 10.17 displays Paula's May income statement.

After studying just-in-time inventory systems in her managerial accounting class, Paula decided to apply the concepts to her small business. She *reengineered* her distribution system by purchasing her flowers from a florist within walking distance of her sales location. She had considered purchasing from this florist earlier but had rejected the idea because the florist's regular selling price of $2.25 per rose was too high. After learning about *most-favored customer status,* she developed a strategy to get a price reduction. By guaranteeing that she would buy at least 30 roses per week, she was able to convince the local florist to match her current cost of $2.00 per rose. The local florist agreed that she could make purchases in batches of any size so long as the total amounted to at least 30 per week. Under

EXHIBIT 10.17

Income Statement for May

Sales revenue (280 units × $3 per unit)	$840
Cost of goods sold (280 units × $2 per unit)	(560)
Gross margin	280
Driving expense	(45)
Excess inventory waste (20 units × 2)	(40)
Net income	$195

EXHIBIT 10.18

Income Statement for June

Sales revenue (310 units × $3 per unit)	$930
Cost of goods sold (310 units × $2 per unit)	(620)
Gross margin	310
Driving expense	0
Net income	$310

Ingram Publishing

this arrangement, Paula was able to buy roses *just in time* to meet customer demand. Each day she purchased a small number of flowers. When she ran out, she simply returned to the florist for additional ones.

The JIT system also enabled Paula to eliminate the cost of the *nonvalue-added activity* of driving to her former florist. Customer satisfaction actually improved because no one was ever turned away because of the lack of inventory. In June, Paula was able to buy and sell 310 roses with no waste and no driving expense. The June income statement is shown in Exhibit 10.18.

Paula was ecstatic about her $115 increase in profitability ($310 in June − $195 in May = $115 increase), but she was puzzled about the exact reasons for the change. She had saved $40 (20 flowers × $2 each) by avoiding waste and eliminated $45 of driving expenses. These two factors explained only $85 ($40 waste + $45 driving expense) of the $115 increase. What had caused the remaining $30 ($115 − $85) increase in profitability? Paula asked her accounting professor to help her identify the remaining $30 difference.

The professor explained that May sales had suffered from *lost opportunities*. Recall that under the earlier inventory system, Paula had to turn away some prospective customers because she sold out of flowers before all customers were served. Sales increased from 280 roses in May to 310 roses in June. A likely explanation for the 30-unit difference (310 − 280) is that customers who would have purchased flowers in May were unable to do so because of a lack of availability. May's sales suffered from the lost opportunity to earn a gross margin of $1 per flower on 30 roses, a $30 **opportunity cost.** This opportunity cost is the missing link in explaining the profitability difference between May and June. The total $115 difference consists of (1) $40 savings from waste elimination, (2) $45 savings from eliminating driving expense, and (3) opportunity cost of $30. The subject of opportunity cost has widespread application and is discussed in more depth in subsequent chapters of the text.

 CHECK YOURSELF 10.5

A strike at a General Motors brake plant caused an almost immediate shutdown of many of the company's assembly plants. What could have caused such a rapid and widespread shutdown?

Answer A rapid and widespread shutdown could have occurred because General Motors uses a just-in-time inventory system. With a just-in-time inventory system, there is no stockpile of inventory to draw on when strikes or other forces disrupt inventory deliveries. This illustrates a potential negative effect of using a just-in-time inventory system.

STATEMENT OF ETHICAL PROFESSIONAL PRACTICE

LO 10-7

Identify the standards contained in IMA's *Statement of Ethical Professional Practice.*

There are several conflicts of interest management accountants might face. It is tempting to misclassify a cost if doing so will significantly increase a manager's bonus. Management accountants must be prepared not only to make difficult choices between legitimate alternatives but also to face conflicts of a more troubling nature, such as pressure to:

1. Undertake duties they have not been trained to perform competently.
2. Disclose confidential information.
3. Compromise their integrity through falsification, embezzlement, bribery, and so on.
4. Issue biased, misleading, or incomplete reports.

To provide management accountants with guidance for ethical conduct, the Institute of Management Accountants (IMA) issued a *Statement of Ethical Professional Practice,* which is shown in Exhibit 10.19. Management accountants are also frequently required to abide by organizational codes of ethics. Failure to adhere to professional and organizational ethical standards can lead to personal disgrace, loss of employment, or imprisonment.

EXHIBIT 10.19

Statement of Ethical Professional Practice

Members of IMA shall behave ethically. A commitment to ethical professional practice includes overarching principles that express our values, and standards that guide our conduct. IMA's overarching ethical principles include: Honesty, Fairness, Objectivity, and Responsibility. Members shall act in accordance with these principles and shall encourage others within their organizations to adhere to them. A member's failure to comply with the following standards may result in disciplinary action.

Competence Each member has a responsibility to
- Maintain an appropriate level of professional expertise by continually developing knowledge and skills.
- Perform professional duties in accordance with relevant laws, regulations, and technical standards.
- Provide decision support information and recommendations that are accurate, clear, concise, and timely.
- Recognize and communicate professional limitations or other constraints that would preclude responsible judgment or successful performance of an activity.

Confidentiality Each member has a responsibility to
- Keep information confidential except when disclosure is authorized or legally required.
- Inform all relevant parties regarding appropriate use of confidential information. Monitor subordinates' activities to ensure compliance.
- Refrain from using confidential information for unethical or illegal advantage.

Integrity Each member has a responsibility to
- Mitigate actual conflicts of interest and avoid apparent conflicts of interest. Advise all parties of any potential conflicts.
- Refrain from engaging in any conduct that would prejudice carrying out duties ethically.
- Abstain from engaging in or supporting any activity that might discredit the profession.

Credibility Each member has a responsibility to
- Communicate information fairly and objectively.
- Disclose all relevant information that could reasonably be expected to influence an intended user's understanding of the reports, analyses, or recommendations.
- Disclose delays or deficiencies in information, timeliness, processing, or internal controls in conformance with organization policy and/or applicable law.

Resolution of Ethical Conflict In applying these standards, you may encounter problems identifying unethical behavior or resolving an ethical conflict. When faced with ethical issues, follow your organization's established policies on the resolution of such conflict. If these policies do not resolve the ethical conflict, consider the following courses of action:
- Discuss the issue with your immediate supervisor except when it appears that the supervisor is involved. In that case, present the issue to the next level. If you cannot achieve a satisfactory resolution, submit the issue to the next management level. Communication of such problems to authorities or individuals not employed or engaged by the organization is not considered appropriate, unless you believe there is a clear violation of the law.
- Clarify relevant ethical issues by initiating a confidential discussion with an IMA Ethics Counselor or other impartial advisor to obtain a better understanding of possible courses of action.
- Consult your own attorney as to legal obligations and rights concerning the ethical conflict.

Reprinted with permission of Institute of Management Accountants, Inc.

FOCUS ON INTERNATIONAL ISSUES

FINANCIAL ACCOUNTING VERSUS MANAGERIAL ACCOUNTING—AN INTERNATIONAL PERSPECTIVE

This chapter has already explained some of the conceptual differences between financial and managerial accounting, but these differences have implications for international businesses as well. With respect to financial accounting, publicly traded companies in most countries must follow the generally accepted accounting principles (GAAP) for their country, but these rules can vary from country to country. Generally, companies that are audited under the auditing standards of the United States follow the standards established by the Financial Accounting Standards Board. Most companies located outside the United States follow the standards established by the International Accounting Standards Board (IASB). For example, the United States is one of very few countries whose GAAP allow the use of the LIFO inventory cost flow assumption.

Adam Rountree/Bloomberg/Getty Images

Conversely, most of the managerial accounting concepts introduced in this course can be used by businesses in any country. For example, while accrual-based earnings can differ depending on whether a company uses U.S. GAAP or IFRS, cash flow will not. As you will learn, managerial accounting decisions often focus on cash flow versus accrual-based income. Therefore, managerial accounting concepts are more universal than financial accounting rules.

REALITY BYTES

Unethical behavior occurs in most large organizations, but some organizations seem to have fewer ethics problems than others. In its 2015 report, *The State of Ethics in Large Companies*, the Ethics Resource Center reported its findings of the occurrences and reporting of unethical behavior in large American corporations, based on a survey it conducts every two years.

Purestock/SuperStock

Forty-five percent of those surveyed reported having observed unethical conduct during the past year. This was the lowest level reported in the 17 years the survey has been conducted. Sixty-five percent of those who said they had observed misconduct went on to report it to their employer. However, fear of retaliation for reporting misconduct was a concern. Of respondents who said they had reported misconduct at their companies, 22 percent said they had experienced some form of retaliation, such as being excluded from decision making.

Overall, 51 percent of individuals surveyed reported having observed unethical conduct at their company. However, in companies that had an effective ethics program, only 33 percent reported seeing misconduct, while 61 percent of those in companies without such programs reported seeing misconduct. Employees in companies with effective programs were also much more likely to report what they saw than those in other companies, 87 percent versus 32 percent. Additionally, when misconduct was reported, only 4 percent of employees in companies with effective programs reported retaliation, compared to 59 percent of those in other companies.

The definition of ethical misconduct used in the study was quite broad, and included misusing company time, demonstrating abusive behavior, abusing company resources, lying to employees, and violating the company's policies for using the Internet.

For more information go to www.ethics.org.

A Look Back

Managerial accounting focuses on the information needs of *internal* users, while *financial accounting* focuses on the information needs of *external* users. Managerial accounting uses economic, operating, and nonfinancial, as well as financial, data. Managerial accounting information is local (pertains to the company's subunits), is limited by cost/benefit considerations, is more concerned with relevance and timeliness, and is future-oriented. Financial accounting information, on the other hand, is more global than managerial accounting information. It supplies information that applies to the whole company. Financial accounting is regulated by numerous authorities, is characterized by objectivity, is focused on reliability and accuracy, and is historical in nature.

Both managerial and financial accounting are concerned with product costing. Financial accountants need product cost information to determine the amount of inventory reported on the balance sheet and the amount of cost of goods sold reported on the income statement. Managerial accountants need to know the cost of products for pricing decisions and for control and evaluation purposes. When determining unit product costs, managers use the average cost per unit. Determining the actual cost of each product requires an unreasonable amount of time and record keeping and it makes no difference in product pricing and product cost control decisions.

Product costs are the costs incurred to make products: the costs of direct materials, direct labor, and overhead. *Overhead costs* are product costs that cannot be cost-effectively traced to a product; therefore, they are assigned to products using *cost allocation*. Overhead costs include indirect materials, indirect labor, depreciation, rent, and utilities for manufacturing facilities. Product costs are first accumulated in an asset account (Inventory). They are expensed as cost of goods sold in the period the inventory is sold. The difference between sales revenue and cost of goods sold is called *gross margin*.

Selling, general, and administrative costs are classified separately from product costs. They are subtracted from gross margin to determine net income. Selling, general, and administrative costs can be divided into two categories. Costs incurred before the manufacturing process begins (research and development costs) are *upstream costs*. Costs incurred after manufacturing is complete (transportation) are *downstream costs*.

Service companies, like manufacturing companies, incur materials, labor, and overhead costs, but the products provided by service companies are consumed immediately. Therefore, service company product costs are not accumulated in an Inventory account.

A *code of ethical conduct* is needed in the accounting profession because accountants hold positions of trust and face conflicts of interest. In recognition of the temptations that accountants face, the IMA has issued a *Statement of Ethical Professional Practice*, which provides accountants guidance in resisting temptations and in making difficult decisions.

Emerging trends such as *just-in-time inventory* and *activity-based management* are methods that many companies have used to reengineer their production and delivery systems to eliminate waste, reduce errors, and minimize costs. Activity-based management seeks to eliminate or reduce *nonvalue-added activities* and to create new *value-added activities*. Just-in-time inventory seeks to reduce inventory holding costs and to lower prices for customers by making inventory available just in time for customer consumption.

 A Look Forward

In addition to distinguishing costs by product versus SG&A classification, other classifications can be used to facilitate managerial decision making. In the next chapter, costs are classified according to the *behavior* they exhibit when the number of units of product increases or decreases (volume of activity changes). You will learn to distinguish between costs that vary with activity volume changes versus costs that remain fixed with activity volume changes. You will learn not only to recognize *cost behavior* but also how to use such recognition to evaluate business risk and opportunity.

APPENDIX

Best Practices in Managerial Accounting

Global competition has forced many companies to reengineer their production and delivery systems to eliminate waste, reduce errors, and minimize costs. A key ingredient of successful **reengineering** is benchmarking. **Benchmarking** involves identifying the **best practices** used by world-class competitors. By studying and mimicking these practices, a company uses benchmarking to implement highly effective and efficient operating methods. Best practices employed by world-class companies include total quality management (TQM), activity-based management (ABM), and value-added assessment.

Identify best practices in managerial accounting.

Total Quality Management

To promote effective and efficient operations, many companies practice **total quality management (TQM).** TQM is a two-dimensional management philosophy using (1) a systematic problem-solving philosophy that encourages frontline workers to achieve *zero defects* and (2) an organizational commitment to achieving *customer satisfaction*. A key component of TQM is **continuous improvement,** an ongoing process through which employees strive to eliminate waste, reduce response time, minimize defects, and simplify the design and delivery of products and services to customers.

Activity-Based Management

Simple changes in perspective can have dramatic results. For example, imagine how realizing the world is round instead of flat changed the nature of travel. A recent change in perspective developing in management accounting is the realization that an organization cannot manage *costs.* Instead, it manages the *activities* that cause costs to be incurred. **Activities** represent the measures an organization takes to accomplish its goals.

The primary goal of all organizations is to provide products (goods and services) their customers *value.* The sequence of activities used to provide products is called a **value chain. Activity-based management (ABM)** assesses the value chain to create new or refine existing **value-added activities** and to eliminate or reduce *nonvalue-added activities.* A value-added activity is any unit of work that contributes to a product's ability to satisfy customer needs. For example, cooking is an activity that adds value to food served to a hungry customer. **Nonvalue-added activities** are tasks undertaken that do not contribute to a product's ability to satisfy customer needs. Waiting for the oven to preheat so that food can be cooked does not add value. Most customers value cooked food, but they do not value waiting for it.

To illustrate, consider the value-added activities undertaken by a pizza restaurant. Begin with a customer who is hungry for pizza; certain activities must occur to satisfy that hunger. These activities are pictured in Exhibit 10.20. At a minimum, the restaurant

EXHIBIT 10.20

Value Chain

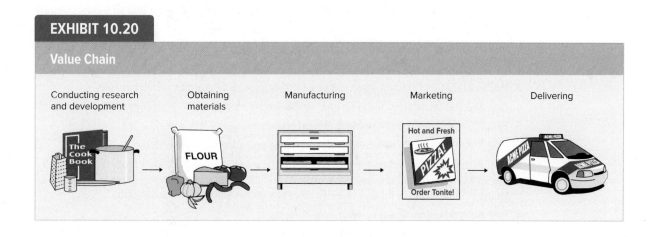

| Conducting research and development | Obtaining materials | Manufacturing | Marketing | Delivering |

must conduct research and development (devise a recipe), obtain raw materials (acquire the ingredients), manufacture the product (combine and bake the ingredients), market the product (advertise its availability), and deliver the product (transfer the pizza to the customer).

Businesses gain competitive advantages by adding activities that satisfy customer needs. For example, Domino's Pizza grew briskly by recognizing the value customers placed on the convenience of home pizza delivery. Alternatively, Little Caesars has been highly successful by satisfying customers who value low prices. Other restaurants capitalize on customer values pertaining to taste, ambience, or location. Businesses can also gain competitive advantages by identifying and eliminating nonvalue-added activities, providing products of comparable quality at lower cost than competitors.

Value Chain Analysis across Companies

Comprehensive value chain analysis extends from obtaining raw materials to the ultimate disposition of finished products. It encompasses the activities performed not only by a particular organization but also by that organization's suppliers and those who service its finished products. For example, PepsiCo must be concerned with the activities of the company that supplies the containers for its soft drinks as well as the retail companies that sell its products. If cans of Pepsi fail to open properly, the customer is more likely to blame PepsiCo than the supplier of the cans. Comprehensive value chain analysis can lead to identifying and eliminating nonvalue-added activities that occur between companies. For example, container producers could be encouraged to build manufacturing facilities near Pepsi's bottling factories, eliminating the nonvalue-added activity of transporting empty containers from the manufacturer to the bottling facility. The resulting cost savings benefit customers by reducing costs without affecting quality.

 Video lectures and accompanying self-assessment quizzes are available in *Connect* for all learning objectives.

SELF-STUDY REVIEW PROBLEM

Tuscan Manufacturing Company makes a unique headset for use with mobile phones. The company had the following amounts in its accounts at the beginning of Year 2: Cash, $795,000; Raw Materials Inventory, $5,000; Work in Process Inventory, $11,000; Finished Goods Inventory, $39,000; Common Stock, $650,000; and Retained Earnings, $200,000. Tuscan experienced the following accounting events during Year 2. Other than the adjusting entries for depreciation, assume that all transactions are cash transactions.

1. Paid $50,000 of research and development costs to create the headset.
2. Paid $139,000 for raw materials that will be used to make headsets.
3. Placed $141,000 of the raw materials cost into the process of manufacturing headsets.
4. Paid $82,200 for salaries of selling and administrative employees.
5. Paid $224,000 for wages of production workers.
6. Paid $48,000 to purchase furniture used in selling and administrative offices.
7. Recognized depreciation on the office furniture. The furniture was acquired January 1, Year 2. It has an $8,000 salvage value and a four-year useful life. The amount of depreciation is computed as [(cost − salvage) ÷ useful life]. Specifically, ($48,000 − $8,000) ÷ 4 = $10,000.
8. Paid $65,000 to purchase manufacturing equipment.

9. Recognized depreciation on the manufacturing equipment. The equipment was acquired January 1, Year 2. It has a $5,000 salvage value and a three-year useful life. The amount of depreciation is computed as [(cost − salvage) ÷ useful life]. Specifically, ($65,000 − $5,000) ÷ 3 = $20,000.

10. Paid $136,000 for rent and utility costs on the manufacturing facility.

11. Paid $41,000 for inventory holding expenses for completed headsets (rental of warehouse space, salaries of warehouse personnel, and other general storage costs).

12. Completed and transferred headsets that had a total cost of $520,000 from work in process inventory to finished goods.

13. Sold headsets for $738,200.

14. It cost Tuscan $517,400 to make the headsets sold in Event 13.

Required

a. Show how these events affect the balance sheet, income statement, and statement of cash flows by recording them in a horizontal financial statement model.

b. Explain why Tuscan's recognition of cost of goods sold expense had no impact on cash flow.

c. Prepare a schedule of costs of goods manufactured and sold, an income statement, and a balance sheet.

d. Distinguish between the product costs and the upstream and downstream costs that Tuscan incurred.

Solution to Requirement a

Event No.	Cash	Raw Mat. Inv.	WIP Inv.	Finished Goods Inv.	B.V. Office Furn.	B.V. Manuf. Equip.	Com. Stk.	Ret. Earn.	Rev.	Exp.	Net Inc.	Statement of Cash Flows
	795,000	5,000	11,000	39,000			650,000	200,000				
1	(50,000)							(50,000)		50,000	(50,000)	(50,000) OA
2	(139,000)	139,000										(139,000) OA
3		(141,000)	141,000									
4	(82,200)							(82,200)		82,200	(82,200)	(82,200) OA
5	(224,000)		224,000									(224,000) OA
6	(48,000)				48,000							(48,000) IA
7					(10,000)			(10,000)		10,000	(10,000)	
8	(65,000)					65,000						(65,000) IA
9			20,000			(20,000)						
10	(136,000)		136,000									(136,000) OA
11	(41,000)							(41,000)		41,000	(41,000)	(41,000) OA
12			(520,000)	520,000								
13	738,200							738,200	738,200		738,200	738,200 OA
14				(517,400)				(517,400)		517,400	(517,400)	
Totals	748,000	3,000	12,000	41,600	38,000	45,000	650,000	237,600	738,200	700,600	37,600	(47,000) NC

*Note: In the financial statements model the Book Value of the Office Furniture account is abbreviated as B.V. Office Furn. and the Book Value of the Manufacturing Equipment account is abbreviated as B.V. Manuf. Equip.

Solution to Requirement b

Tuscan does not recognize a cash outflow at the time the goods are sold because the cash is paid when the materials, labor, and overhead are acquired.

Solution to Requirement c

TUSCAN MANUFACTURING COMPANY	
Schedule of Cost of Goods Manufactured and Sold	
For the Year Ended December 31, Year 2	
Beginning raw materials inventory	$ 5,000
Plus: Raw materials purchases	139,000
Less: Ending raw materials inventory	(3,000)
Raw materials used	141,000
Labor	224,000
Overhead	156,000
Total manufacturing costs	521,000
Plus: Beginning work in process inventory	11,000
Total work in process inventory	532,000
Less: Ending work in process inventory	(12,000)
Cost of goods manufactured	520,000
Plus: Beginning finished goods inventory	39,000
Cost of goods available for sale	559,000
Less: Ending finished goods inventory	(41,600)
Cost of goods sold	$517,400

TUSCAN MANUFACTURING COMPANY	
Income Statement	
For the Year Ended December 31, Year 2	
Sales revenue	$738,200
Cost of goods sold	(517,400)
Gross margin	220,800
Research and development expenses	(50,000)
Selling and administrative salary expense	(82,200)
Selling and administrative depreciation expense	(10,000)
Inventory holding expenses	(41,000)
Net Income	$ 37,600

TUSCAN MANUFACTURING COMPANY	
Balance Sheet	
As of December 31, Year 2	
Assets	
Cash	$748,000
Raw materials inventory	3,000
Work in process inventory	12,000
Finished goods inventory	41,600
Manufacturing equipment less accumulated depreciation	45,000
Office furniture less accumulated depreciation	38,000
Total assets	$887,600
Stockholders' Equity	
Common stock	$650,000
Retained earnings	237,600
Total stockholders' equity	$887,600

Solution to Requirement *d*

Inventory product costs for manufacturing companies focus on the costs necessary to make the product. The cost of research and development (Event 1) occurs before the inventory is made and is therefore an upstream cost, not an inventory (product) cost. The inventory holding costs (Event 11) are incurred after the inventory has been made and are therefore downstream costs, not product costs. Selling costs (included in Events 4 and 7) are normally incurred after products have been made and are therefore usually classified as downstream costs. Administrative costs (also included in Events 4 and 7) are not related to making products and are therefore not classified as product costs. Administrative costs may be incurred before, during, or after products are made, so they may be classified as either upstream or downstream costs. Only the costs of materials, labor, and overhead that are actually incurred for the purpose of making goods (Events 3, 5, 9, and 10) are classified as product costs.

KEY TERMS

Activities 385
Activity-based management (ABM) 385
Average cost 369
Benchmarking 381
Best practices 381
Continuous improvement 385
Cost allocation 374
Cost-plus pricing 368
Direct labor 371
Direct raw materials 371
Downstream costs 375
Financial accounting 364

Financial Accounting Standards Board (FASB) 367
Finished Goods Inventory 368
Generally accepted accounting principles (GAAP) 367
Indirect costs 374
Inventory holding costs 380
Just in time (JIT) 380
Managerial accounting 364
Manufacturing overhead 374
Midstream costs 375

Nonvalue-added activity 385
Opportunity cost 381
Overhead 368
Period costs 373
Product costing 368
Product costs 373
Raw materials 371
Raw Materials Inventory 379
Reengineering 381
Schedule of cost of goods manufactured and sold 379

Securities and Exchange Commission (SEC) 367
Selling, general, and administrative costs (SG&A) 373
Total quality management (TQM) 385
Upstream costs 375
Value-added activity 385
Value-added principle 367
Value chain 385
Work in Process Inventory 379

QUESTIONS

1. What are some differences between financial and managerial accounting?

2. What does the value-added principle mean as it applies to managerial accounting information? Give an example of value-added information that may be included in managerial accounting reports but is not shown in publicly reported financial statements.

3. How does product costing used in financial accounting differ from product costing used in managerial accounting?

4. What does the statement "costs can be assets or expenses" mean?

5. Why are the salaries of production workers accumulated in an inventory account instead of being directly expensed on the income statement?

6. How do product costs affect the financial statements? How does the classification of product cost (as an asset vs. an expense) affect net income?

7. What is an indirect cost? Provide examples of product costs that would be classified as indirect.

8. How does a product cost differ from a general, selling, and administrative cost? Give examples of each.

9. Why is cost classification important to managers?

10. What is cost allocation? Give an example of a cost that needs to be allocated.

11. What are some of the common ethical conflicts that accountants encounter?

12. What costs should be considered in determining the sales price of a product?

13. What is a just-in-time (JIT) inventory system? Name some inventory costs that can be eliminated or reduced by its use.

14. What are the two dimensions of a total quality management (TQM) program? Why is TQM being used in business practice? (Appendix)

15. How has the Institute of Management Accountants responded to the need for high standards of ethical conduct in the accounting profession?

16. What does the term *reengineering* mean? Name some reengineering practices. (Appendix)

17. What does the term *activity-based management* mean? (Appendix)

18. What is a value chain? (Appendix)

19. What do the terms *value-added activity* and *nonvalue-added activity* mean? Provide an example of each type of activity. (Appendix)

EXERCISES—SERIES A

Mc Graw Hill connect An electronic auto-gradable version of the Series A Exercises is available in Connect. A PDF version of Series B Exercises is in Connect under the "Additional Student Resources" tab. Solutions to the Series B Exercises are available in Connect under the "Instructor Library" tab. Instructor and student Workpapers for the Series B Exercises are available in Connect under the "Instructor Library" and "Additional Student Resources" tabs respectively.

LO 10-1

Exercise 10-1A   *Identifying financial versus managerial accounting items*

Required

Indicate whether each of the following items is representative of managerial or of financial accounting:

a. Information is factual and is characterized by objectivity, reliability, consistency, and accuracy.

b. Information is reported continuously and has a current or future orientation.

c. Information is provided to outsiders, including investors, creditors, government agencies, analysts, and reporters.

d. Information is regulated by the SEC, FASB, and other sources of GAAP.

e. Information is based on estimates that are bounded by relevance and timeliness.

f. Information is historically based and usually reported annually.

g. Information is local and pertains to subunits of the organization.

h. Information includes economic and nonfinancial data as well as financial data.

i. Information is global and pertains to the company as a whole.

j. Information is provided to insiders, including executives, managers, and employees.

LO 10-2

Exercise 10-2A   *Identifying product versus selling, general, and administrative (SG&A) costs*

Required

Indicate whether each of the following costs should be classified as a product cost or as an SG&A cost in accordance with GAAP:

a. Direct materials used in a manufacturing company.

b. Indirect materials used in a manufacturing company.

c. Salaries of employees working in the accounting department.

d. Commissions paid to sales staff.

e. Interest on the mortgage for the company's corporate headquarters.

f. Indirect labor used to manufacture inventory.

g. Attorney's fees paid to protect the company from frivolous lawsuits.

h. Research and development costs incurred to create new drugs for a pharmaceutical company.

i. The cost of secretarial supplies used in a doctor's office.

j. Depreciation on the office furniture of the company president.

LO 10-2

Exercise 10-3A   *Classifying costs: Product or SG&A cost; asset or expense*

Required

Use the following table to classify each cost as a product cost or an SG&A cost. Also indicate whether the cost would be recorded as an asset or an expense. Assume product cost is defined by generally accepted accounting principles. The first item is shown as an example.

Cost Category	Product/SG&A	Asset/Expense
Wages of production workers	Product	Asset
Advertising costs		
Promotion costs		
Production supplies		
Depreciation on administration building		
Depreciation on manufacturing equipment		
Research and development costs		
Cost to set up manufacturing equipment		
Utilities used in manufacturing facility		
Cars for sales staff		
Real estate tax levied on a factory		
General office supplies		
Raw materials used in the manufacturing process		
Cost to rent office equipment		

Exercise 10-4A *Identifying the effect of product versus selling, general, and administrative costs on financial statements*

LO 10-3

Required

Finch Corporation recognized accrued compensation cost. Use the following model to show how this event would affect the company's financial statements under the following two assumptions: (1) the compensation is for office personnel and (2) the compensation is for production workers. Use the letter *I* for increase or the letter *D* for decrease to show the effect on each element. If an element is not affected, indicate so by placing the letters *NA* under the appropriate heading.

	Balance Sheet			Income Statement			Statement of Cash Flows
	Assets	=	Liab. + Stk. Equity	Rev.	− Exp.	= Net Inc.	
1.							
2.							

Exercise 10-5A *Identifying the effect of product versus selling, general, and administrative costs on financial statements*

LO 10-3

Required

Driscoll Industries recognized the annual cost of depreciation on its December 31, Year 1, financial statements. Using the following horizontal financial statements model, indicate how this event affected the company's financial statements under the following two assumptions: (1) the depreciation was on office furniture and (2) the depreciation was on manufacturing equipment. Indicate whether the event increases (*I*), decreases (*D*), or has no effect (*NA*) on each element of the financial statements. (Note: In the financial statements model the Book Value of the Manufacturing Equipment account is abbreviated as B.V. Manuf. Equip. and the Book Value of the Office Furniture account is abbreviated as B.V. Office Furn.)

	Balance Sheet							Income Statement			Statement of Cash Flows
	Assets				Stk. Equity						
Event No.	Cash	+ Inventory	+ B.V. Manuf. Equip.	+ B.V. Office Furn.	= Com. Stk.	+ Ret. Earn.		Rev.	− Exp.	= Net Inc.	
1.											
2.											

Exercise 10-6A *Identifying product versus SG&A costs*

A review of the accounting records of Baird Manufacturing indicated that the company incurred the following payroll costs during the month of March. Assume the company's financial statements are prepared in accordance with GAAP.

1. Salary of the company president–$75,000.
2. Salary of the vice president of manufacturing–$50,000.
3. Salary of the chief financial officer–$42,000.
4. Salary of the vice president of marketing–$40,000.
5. Salaries of middle managers (department heads, production supervisors) in manufacturing plant–$147,000.
6. Wages of production workers–$703,500.
7. Salaries of administrative secretaries–$60,000.
8. Salaries of engineers and other personnel responsible for maintaining production equipment–$133,500.
9. Commissions paid to sales staff–$146,000.

Required

a. What amount of payroll cost would be classified as SG&A expense?
b. Assuming that Baird made 5,000 units of product and sold 4,000 of them during the month of March, determine the amount of payroll cost that would be included in cost of goods sold.

LO 10-3

Exercise 10-7A *Recording product versus SG&A costs in a financial statements model*

Weib Manufacturing experienced the following events during its first accounting period:

1. Recognized revenue from cash sale of products.
2. Recognized cost of goods sold from sale referenced in Event 1.
3. Acquired cash by issuing common stock.
4. Paid cash to purchase raw materials that were used to make products.
5. Paid wages to production workers.
6. Paid salaries to administrative staff.
7. Recognized depreciation on manufacturing equipment.
8. Recognized depreciation on office furniture.

Required

Use the following horizontal financial statements model to show how each event affects the GAAP-based balance sheet and income statement. Indicate whether the event increases (*I*), decreases (*D*), or has no effect (*NA*) on each element of the financial statements. Also, for events that affect the statement of cash flow indicate whether the event is a financing activity (FA), an investing activity (IA), or an operating activity (OA). The first transaction has been recorded as an example. Show accumulated depreciation as a decrease in the book value of the appropriate asset account. (Note: In the financial statements model the Book Value of the Manufacturing Equipment account is abbreviated as B.V. Manuf. Equip. and the Book Value of the Office Furniture account is abbreviated as B.V. Office Furn.)

	Balance Sheet						Income Statement			Statement of Cash Flows
	Assets				Stk. Equity					
Event No.	Cash +	Inventory +	B.V. Manuf. Equip. +	B.V. Office Furn. =	Com. Stk. +	Ret. Earn.	Rev. −	Exp. =	Net Inc.	
1.	I	NA	NA	NA	NA	I	I	NA	I	I OA

LO 10-3

Exercise 10-8A *Allocating product costs between ending inventory and cost of goods sold*

Mustafa Manufacturing Company began operations on January 1. During the year, it started and completed 3,000 units of product. The financial statements are prepared in accordance with GAAP. The company incurred the following costs:

1. Raw materials purchased and used–$6,200.
2. Wages of production workers–$7,400.

3. Salaries of administrative and sales personnel–$3,000.
4. Depreciation on manufacturing equipment–$4,400.
5. Depreciation on administrative equipment–$2,200.

Mustafa sold 2,400 units of product.

Required

a. Determine the total product cost for the year.
b. Determine the total cost of the ending inventory.
c. Determine the total of cost of goods sold.

Exercise 10-9A   *Upstream, midstream, and downstream costs*

LO 10-4

Required

Identify each of the items shown in the left column of the following table as being an upstream, a midstream, or a downstream cost by placing an X in the one of the columns to the right of the items column. The first item is shown as an example.

Item	Upstream	Midstream	Downstream
Direct materials		X	
Research and development			
Product design			
Manufacturing overhead			
Sales salaries			
Cost of delivering merchandise to customers			
Cost to create a copyright			
Salaries of product engineers			
Salaries of production line workers			
Direct labor			
Cost to heat the manufacturing plant			
Advertising expenses			
Patent filing fees			
Salary of company president			
Depreciation on manufacturing equipment			
Depreciation on office equipment			

Exercise 10-10A   *Identifying upstream and downstream costs*

LO 10-4

During Year 2, Rooney Manufacturing Company incurred $8,000,000 of research and development (R&D) costs to create a long-life battery to use in computers. In accordance with FASB standards, the entire R&D cost was recognized as an expense in Year 2. Manufacturing costs (direct materials, direct labor, and overhead) are expected to be $45 per unit. Packaging, shipping, and sales commissions are expected to be $8 per unit. Rooney expects to sell 2,000,000 batteries before new research renders the battery design technologically obsolete. During Year 2, Rooney made 440,000 batteries and sold 400,000 of them.

Required

a. Identify the upstream and downstream costs.
b. Determine the Year 2 amount of cost of goods sold and the ending inventory balance that would appear on the financial statements that are prepared in accordance with GAAP.
c. Determine the sales price assuming that Rooney desires to earn a profit margin that is equal to 25 percent of the *total cost* of developing, making, and distributing the batteries.

d. Prepare a GAAP-based income statement for Year 2. Use the sales price developed in Requirement *c*.

e. Given that the price was properly established using total cost (upstream, midstream, and downstream costs), why does the GAAP-based income statement prepared in Requirement *d* show a loss?

LO 10-4

Exercise 10-11A *Identifying product costs in a manufacturing company*

Anne Wood was talking to another accounting student, Don Kirby. Upon discovering that the accounting department offered an upper-level course in cost measurement, Anne remarked to Don, "How difficult can it be? My parents own a toy store. All you have to do to figure out how much something costs is look at the invoice. Surely you don't need an entire course to teach you how to read an invoice."

Required

a. Identify the three main components of product cost as defined by GAAP for a manufacturing entity.

b. Explain why measuring product cost for a manufacturing entity is more complex than measuring product cost for a retail toy store.

c. Assume that Anne's parents rent a store for $6,000 per month. Different types of toys use different amounts of store space. For example, displaying a bicycle requires more store space than displaying a deck of cards. Also, some toys remain on the shelf longer than others. Fad toys sell rapidly, but traditional toys sell more slowly. Under these circumstances, how would you determine the amount of rental cost required to display each type of toy? Identify two other costs incurred by a toy store that may be difficult to allocate to individual toys.

LO 10-4

Exercise 10-12A *Financial statement effects for manufacturing versus service organizations*

The following financial statements model shows the effects of recognizing depreciation in two different circumstances. One circumstance represents recognizing depreciation on a machine used in a factory. The other circumstance recognizes depreciation on computers used in a consulting firm. The effects of each event have been recorded using the letter *I* for increase, *D* for decrease, and *NA* for no effect. (Note: In the financial statements model the book value of the machine and the book value of the computer are abbreviated as B.V. Asset.)

| Event No. | Balance Sheet | | | | | Income Statement | | | Statement of Cash Flows |
| | Assets | | | Stk. Equity | | | | | |
	Cash +	Inventory +	B.V. Asset =	Com. Stk. +	Ret. Earn.	Rev. −	Exp. =	Net Inc.	
1.	NA	NA	D	NA	D	NA	I	D	NA
2.	NA	I	D	NA	NA	NA	NA	NA	NA

Required

a. Identify the event that represents depreciation on the computers.

b. Explain why recognizing depreciation on equipment used in a manufacturing company affects financial statements differently than recognizing depreciation on equipment used in a service organization.

LO 10-5

Exercise 10-13A *Missing information in a schedule of cost of goods manufactured*

Required

Supply the missing information on the following schedule of cost of goods manufactured:

FISCHER CORPORATION
Schedule of Cost of Goods Manufactured
For the Year Ended December 31, Year 2

Raw materials		
Beginning inventory	$?	
Plus: Purchases	120,000	
Raw materials available for use	148,000	
Minus: Ending raw materials inventory	?	
Cost of direct raw materials used		$124,000
Direct labor		?
Manufacturing overhead		24,000
Total manufacturing costs		324,000
Plus: Beginning work in process inventory		?
Total work in process		?
Minus: Ending work in process inventory		46,000
Cost of goods manufactured		$320,000

Exercise 10-14A   *Cost of goods manufactured and sold*

LO 10-5

The following information pertains to Flaxman Manufacturing Company for April. Assume actual overhead equaled applied overhead.

April 1

Inventory balances	
Raw materials	$100,000
Work in process	120,000
Finished goods	78,000

April 30

Inventory balances	
Raw materials	$ 60,000
Work in process	145,000
Finished goods	80,000

During April

Costs of raw materials purchased	$120,000
Costs of direct labor	100,000
Costs of manufacturing overhead	63,000
Sales revenues	380,000

Required

a. Prepare a schedule of cost of goods manufactured and sold.
b. Calculate the amount of gross margin on the income statement.

Exercise 10-15A   *Identifying the effect of a just-in-time inventory system on financial statements*

LO 10-6

After reviewing the financial statements of Perez Company, Lou Brewer concluded that the company was a service company. Mr. Brewer based his conclusion on the fact that Perez's financial statements displayed no inventory accounts.

Required

Explain how Perez's implementation of a 100 percent effective just-in-time inventory system could have led Mr. Brewer to a false conclusion regarding the nature of Perez's business.

Exercise 10-16A   *Using JIT to minimize waste and lost opportunity*

Becky Shelton, a teacher at Kemp Middle School, is in charge of ordering the T-shirts to be sold for the school's annual fund-raising project. The T-shirts are printed with a special Kemp School logo. In some years, the supply of T-shirts has been insufficient to satisfy the number of sales orders. In other years, T-shirts have been left over. Excess T-shirts are normally donated to some charitable organization. T-shirts cost the school $5 each and are normally sold for $12 each. Ms. Shelton has decided to order 700 shirts.

Required

a. If the school receives actual sales orders for 600 shirts, what amount of profit will the school earn? What is the cost of waste due to excess inventory?

b. If the school receives actual sales orders for 800 shirts, what amount of profit will the school earn? What amount of opportunity cost will the school incur?

c. Explain how a JIT inventory system could maximize profitability by eliminating waste and opportunity cost.

Exercise 10-17A   *Using JIT to minimize holding costs*

Gwen Pet Supplies purchases its inventory from a variety of suppliers, some of which require a six-week lead time before delivering the goods. To ensure that she has a sufficient supply of goods on hand, Ms. Leblanc, the owner, must maintain a large supply of inventory. The cost of this inventory averages $67,000. She usually finances the purchase of inventory and pays a 5 percent annual finance charge. Ms. Leblanc's accountant has suggested that she establish a relationship with a single large distributor who can satisfy all of her orders within a two-week time period. Given this quick turnaround time, she will be able to reduce her average inventory balance to $17,000. Ms. Leblanc also believes that she could save $9,000 per year by reducing phone bills, insurance, and warehouse rental space costs associated with ordering and maintaining the larger level of inventory.

Required

a. Is the new inventory system available to Ms. Leblanc a pure or approximate just-in-time system?

b. Based on the information provided, how much of Ms. Leblanc's inventory holding cost could be eliminated by taking the accountant's advice?

Exercise 10-18A   *Ethical Professional Practice*

The CFO of the Jordan Microscope Corporation intentionally misclassified a downstream transportation expense in the amount of $575,000 as a product cost in an accounting period when the company made 5,000 microscopes and sold 4,000 microscopes. Jordan rewards its officers with bonuses that are based on net earnings.

Required

a. Indicate whether the elements on the financial statements (i.e., assets, liabilities, stockholders' equity, revenue, expense, and net income) would be overstated or understated as a result of the misclassification of the downstream transportation expense. Determine the amount of the overstatement or understatement for each element.

b. Suppose an employee who works for the CFO discovers that the CFO deliberately engaged in the fraudulent misclassification. What action should the employee take?

Exercise 10-19A   *Professional conduct and code of ethics*

In February 2006, former senator Warren Rudman of New Hampshire completed a 17-month investigation of an $11 billion accounting scandal at Fannie Mae (a major enterprise involved in home mortgage financing). The Rudman investigation concluded that Fannie Mae's CFO and controller used an accounting gimmick to manipulate financial statements in order to meet earnings-per-share (EPS) targets. Meeting the EPS targets triggered bonus payments for the executives. Fannie Mae's problems continued after 2006, and on September 8, 2008, it went into conservatorship under the control of the Federal Housing Financing Agency. The primary executives at the time of the Rudman investigation were replaced, and the enterprise reported a $59.8 billion loss in 2008. By June 2012, the federal government had spent $170 million to assist Fannie Mae as a result of mismanagement.

Required

Review the statement of ethical professional practice shown in Exhibit 10.19. Identify and comment on which of the ethical principles the CFO and controller violated.

Exercise 10-20A *Value chain analysis (Appendix)*

Soundwave Company manufactures and sells high-quality audio speakers. The speakers are encased in solid walnut cabinets supplied by Walton Cabinet, Inc. Walton packages the speakers in durable moisture-proof boxes and ships them by truck to Soundwave's manufacturing facility, which is located 40 miles from the cabinet factory.

Required

Identify the nonvalue-added activities that occur between the companies described in the given scenario. Provide a logical explanation as to how these nonvalue-added activities could be eliminated.

PROBLEMS—SERIES A

McGraw Hill connect   An electronic auto-gradable version of the Series A Problems is available in Connect. A PDF version of Series B Problems is in Connect under the "Additional Student Resources" tab. Solutions to the Series B Problems are available in Connect under the "Instructor Library" tab. Instructor and student Workpapers for the Series B Problems are available in Connect under the "Instructor Library" and "Additional Student Resources" tabs respectively.

Problem 10-21A *Characteristics of financial versus managerial accounting*

Required

Use the following table to indicate whether the information is more representative of managerial versus financial accounting. The first item is shown as an example.

Information Item	Financial Accounting	Managerial Accounting
Estimates of future revenue		X
GAAP-based product cost		
Salary of the manager of a particular branch of a bank		
Salary expense for all company employees shown in the income statement		
Historical-based information included in financial statements		
Reporting rules established by government authorities		
Reports designed for the company president		
Daily time clock reports		
A company's annual report to stockholders		
Budgets		
Information provided to investors and creditors		
Vacation schedules for key employees		
Customer satisfaction survey results		
Amount of total assets shown on the balance sheet		

Problem 10-22A *Product versus selling, general, and administrative (SG&A) costs*

Stuart Manufacturing Company was started on January 1, Year 1, when it acquired $89,000 cash by issuing common stock. Stuart immediately purchased office furniture and manufacturing equipment costing $32,000 and $40,000, respectively. The office furniture had an eight-year useful life and a zero salvage value. The manufacturing equipment had a $4,000 salvage value and an expected useful life of six years. The company paid $12,000 for salaries of administrative personnel and $21,000 for wages to production personnel. Finally, the company paid $26,000 for raw materials that were used to make inventory. All inventory was started and completed during the year. Stuart completed production on 10,000 units of product and sold 8,000 units at a price of $9 each in Year 1. (Assume that all transactions are cash transactions and that product costs are computed in accordance with GAAP.)

Required

a. Determine the total product cost and the average cost per unit of the inventory produced in Year 1.
b. Determine the amount of cost of goods sold that would appear on the Year 1 income statement.

c. Determine the amount of the ending inventory balance that would appear on the December 31, Year 1, balance sheet.

d. Determine the amount of net income that would appear on the Year 1 income statement.

e. Determine the amount of retained earnings that would appear on the December 31, Year 1, balance sheet.

f. Determine the amount of total assets that would appear on the December 31, Year 1, balance sheet.

Problem 10-23A   *Effect of product versus period costs on financial statements*

Sinclair Manufacturing Company experienced the following accounting events during its first year of operation. With the exception of the adjusting entries for depreciation, assume that all transactions are cash transactions and that financial statement data are prepared in accordance with GAAP.

1. Acquired $68,000 cash by issuing common stock.
2. Paid $8,700 for the materials used to make its products, all of which were started and completed during the year.
3. Paid salaries of $4,500 to selling and administrative employees.
4. Paid wages of $10,000 to production workers.
5. Paid $9,600 for furniture used in selling and administrative offices. The furniture was acquired on January 1. It had a $1,600 estimated salvage value and a four-year useful life.
6. Paid $16,000 for manufacturing equipment. The equipment was acquired on January 1. It had a $1,000 estimated salvage value and a five-year useful life.
7. Sold inventory to customers for $35,000 that had cost $14,000 to make.

Required

Explain how these events would affect the balance sheet and income statement by recording them in a horizontal financial statements model as indicated here. The first event is recorded as an example. (Note: In the financial statements model the Book Value of the Manufacturing Equipment account is abbreviated as B.V. Manuf. Equip. and the Book Value of the Office Furniture account is abbreviated as B.V. Office Furn.)

Event No.		Financial Statements Model									Income Statement				Statement of Cash Flows
		Assets						Stk. Equity							
	Cash	+	Inventory	+	B.V. Manuf. Equip.	+	B.V. Office Furn.	=	Com. Stk.	+	Ret. Earn.	Rev.	− Exp.	= Net Inc.	
1	68,000								68,000						68,000 FA

Problem 10-24A   *Product versus SG&A costs*

The following transactions pertain to Year 1, the first-year operations of Gibson Company. All inventory was started and completed during Year 1. Assume that all transactions are cash transactions.

1. Acquired $12,000 cash by issuing common stock.
2. Paid $4,700 for materials used to produce inventory.
3. Paid $2,400 to production workers.
4. Paid $900 rental fee for production equipment.
5. Paid $350 to administrative employees.
6. Paid $400 rental fee for administrative office equipment.
7. Produced 400 units of inventory of which 360 units were sold at a price of $25 each.

Required

Prepare an income statement and a balance sheet in accordance with GAAP.

Problem 10-25A   *Upstream, midstream, and downstream costs*

Power-To-Spare, Inc. makes a smartphone case that includes a battery that extends the operating life of an iPhone. The manufacturing costs per unit include $15 direct materials, $17 direct labor, and $8 manufacturing overhead. These costs are based on a production and sales volume of 4,000 units.

Advertising costs amounted to $25,000. Research and development cost for the materials used in the phone cases amounted $30,000. Companywide administrative costs amounted to $45,000. Fashion design costs amounted to $20,000. Power-To-Spare's management team established the sales price at 150 percent of GAAP-defined product cost.

Required

a. Determine the total amount of upstream costs.

b. Determine the total amount of downstream cost.

c. Determine the total amount of midstream cost.

d. Determine the sales price per unit.

e. Prepare a GAAP-based income statement.

f. Provide a plausible explanation as to why the company incurred the loss shown on the income statement prepared to satisfy Requirement e. (*Hint:* Calculate the full cost of making and selling the cases.)

Problem 10-26A   *Service versus manufacturing companies*

LO 10-4

Wang Company began operations on January 1, Year 1, by issuing common stock for $70,000 cash. During Year 1, Wang received $88,000 cash from revenue and incurred costs that required $65,000 of cash payments.

Required

Prepare a GAAP-based income statement and balance sheet for Wang Company for Year 1, under each of the following independent scenarios:

a. Wang is a promoter of rock concerts. The $65,000 was paid to provide a rock concert that produced the revenue.

b. Wang is in the car rental business. The $65,000 was paid to purchase automobiles. The automobiles were purchased on January 1, Year 1, and have five-year useful lives, with no expected salvage value. Wang uses straight-line depreciation. The revenue was generated by leasing the automobiles.

c. Wang is a manufacturing company. The $65,000 was paid to purchase the following items:

   (1) Paid $10,000 cash to purchase materials that were used to make products during the year.

   (2) Paid $20,000 cash for wages of factory workers who made products during the year.

   (3) Paid $5,000 cash for salaries of sales and administrative employees.

   (4) Paid $30,000 cash to purchase manufacturing equipment. The equipment was used solely to make products. It had a three-year life and a $6,000 salvage value. The company uses straight-line depreciation.

   (5) During Year 1, Wang started and completed 2,000 units of product. The revenue was earned when Wang sold 1,500 units of product to its customers.

d. Refer to Requirement c. Could Wang determine the actual cost of making the 500th unit of product? How likely is it that the actual cost of the 500th unit of product was exactly the same as the cost of producing the 501st unit of product? Explain why management may be more interested in average cost than in actual cost.

Problem 10-27A   *Schedule of cost of goods manufactured and sold*

LO 10-3

Antioch Company makes eBook readers. The company had the following amounts at the beginning of Year 2: Cash, $660,000; Raw Materials Inventory, $51,000; Work in Process Inventory, $18,000; Finished Goods Inventory, $43,000; Common Stock, $583,000; and Retained Earnings, $189,000. Antioch experienced the following accounting events during Year 2. Other than the adjusting entries for depreciation, assume that all transactions are cash transactions.

1. Paid $23,000 of research and development costs.

2. Paid $47,000 for raw materials that will be used to make eBook readers.

3. Placed $83,000 of the raw materials cost into the process of manufacturing eBook readers.

4. Paid $60,000 for salaries of selling and administrative employees.

5. Paid $91,000 for wages of production workers.

6. Paid $90,000 to purchase equipment used in selling and administrative offices.

7. Recognized depreciation on the office equipment. The equipment was acquired on January 1, Year 2. It has a $10,000 salvage value and a five-year life. The amount of depreciation is computed as [(Cost − salvage) ÷ useful life]. Specifically, ($90,000 − $10,000) ÷ 5 = $16,000.

8. Paid $165,000 to purchase manufacturing equipment.

9. Recognized depreciation on the manufacturing equipment. The equipment was acquired on January 1, Year 2. It has a $25,000 salvage value and a seven-year life. The amount of depreciation is computed as [(Cost − salvage) ÷ useful life]. Specifically, ($165,000 − $25,000) ÷ 7 = $20,000.

10. Paid $45,000 for rent and utility costs on the manufacturing facility.

11. Paid $70,000 for inventory holding expenses for completed eBook readers (rental of warehouse space, salaries of warehouse personnel, and other general storage cost).

12. Completed and transferred eBook readers that had total cost of $240,000 from work in process inventory to finished goods.

13. Sold 1,000 eBook readers for $420,000.

14. It cost Antioch $220,000 to make the eBook readers sold in Event 13.

Required

a. Show how these events affect the balance sheet, income statement, and statement of cash flows by recording them in a horizontal financial statements model.

b. Explain why Antioch's recognition of cost of goods sold had no impact on cash flow.

c. Prepare a schedule of cost of goods manufactured and sold, a formal income statement, and a balance sheet for the year.

d. Distinguish between the product costs and the upstream costs that Antioch incurred.

e. The company president believes that Antioch could save money by buying the inventory that it currently makes. The warehouse manager said that would not be a good idea because the purchase price of $230 per unit was above the $220 average cost per unit of making the product. Assuming the purchased inventory would be available on demand, explain how the company president could be correct and why the production manager could be biased in his assessment of the option to buy the inventory.

LO 10-6

CHECK FIGURE
a. $216,000

Problem 10-28A   *Using JIT to reduce inventory holding costs*

Kenta Manufacturing Company obtains its raw materials from a variety of suppliers. Kenta's strategy is to obtain the best price by letting the suppliers know that it buys from the lowest bidder. Approximately four years ago, unexpected increases in demand resulted in materials shortages. Kenta was unable to find the materials it needed even though it was willing to pay premium prices. Because of the lack of raw materials, Kenta was forced to close its manufacturing facility for two weeks. Its president vowed that her company would never again be at the mercy of its suppliers. She immediately ordered her purchasing agent to perpetually maintain a one-month supply of raw materials. Compliance with the president's orders resulted in a raw materials inventory amounting to approximately $1,200,000. Warehouse rental and personnel costs to maintain the inventory amounted to $8,000 per month. Kenta has a line of credit with a local bank that calls for a 10 percent annual rate of interest. Assume that Kenta finances the raw materials inventory with the line of credit.

Required

a. Based on the information provided, determine the annual holding cost of the raw materials inventory.

b. Explain how a JIT system could reduce Kenta's inventory holding cost.

c. Explain how most-favored-customer status could enable Kenta to establish a JIT inventory system without risking the raw materials shortages experienced in the past.

LO 10-6

CHECK FIGURES
a. $3,000
b. $37,000

Problem 10-29A   *Using JIT to minimize waste and lost opportunity*

CIA Review, Inc. provides review courses twice each year for students studying to take the CIA exam. The cost of textbooks is included in the registration fee. Text material requires constant updating and is useful for only one course. To minimize printing costs and ensure availability of books on the first day of class, CIA Review has books printed and delivered to its offices two weeks in advance of the first class. To ensure that enough books are available, CIA Review normally orders 10 percent more than expected enrollment. Usually there is an oversupply and books are thrown away. However, demand occasionally exceeds expectations by more than 10 percent and there are too few books available for student use. CIA Review has been forced to turn away students because of a lack of textbooks. CIA Review expects to enroll approximately 200 students per course. The tuition fee is $2,000 per student. The cost of teachers is $50,000 per course, textbooks cost $150 each, and other operating expenses are estimated to be $75,000 per course. Assume all financial statements data are prepared in accordance with GAAP.

Required

a. Prepare an income statement, assuming that 200 students enroll in a course. Determine the cost of waste associated with unused books.

b. Prepare an income statement, assuming that 240 students attempt to enroll in the course. Note that 20 students are turned away because of too few textbooks. Determine the amount of lost profit resulting from the inability to serve the 20 additional students.

c. Suppose that textbooks can be produced through a high-speed copying process that permits delivery *just in time* for class to start. The cost of books made using this process, however, is $160 each. Assume that all books must be made using the same production process. In other words, CIA Review cannot order some of the books using the regular copy process and the rest using the high-speed process. Prepare an income statement under the JIT system assuming that 200 students enroll in a course. Compare the income statement under JIT with the income statement prepared in Requirement *a*. Comment on how the JIT system would affect profitability.

d. Assume the same facts as in Requirement *c* with respect to a JIT system that enables immediate delivery of books at a cost of $160 each. Prepare an income statement under the JIT system, assuming that 240 students enroll in a course. Compare the income statement under JIT with the income statement prepared in Requirement *b*. Comment on how the JIT system would affect profitability.

e. Discuss the possible effect of the JIT system on the level of customer satisfaction.

Problem 10-30A *Importance of cost classification*

Campbell Manufacturing Company (CMC) was started when it acquired $80,000 by issuing common stock. During the first year of operations, the company incurred specifically identifiable product costs (materials, labor, and overhead) amounting to $75,000. CMC also incurred $60,000 of engineering design and planning costs. There was a debate regarding how the design and planning costs should be classified. Advocates of Option 1 believe that the costs should be classified as general, selling, and administrative costs. Advocates of Option 2 believe it is more appropriate to classify the design and planning costs as product costs. During the year, CMC made 5,000 units of product and sold 4,000 units at a price of $35 each. All transactions were cash transactions.

CHECK FIGURES
a. Option 1: NI = $20,000
Option 2: Total assets = $112,000

Required

a. Prepare a GAAP-based income statement and balance sheet under each of the two options.

b. Identify the option that results in financial statements that are more likely to leave a favorable impression on investors and creditors.

c. Assume that CMC provides an incentive bonus to the company president equal to 20 percent of net income. Compute the amount of the bonus under each of the two options. Identify the option that provides the president with the higher bonus.

d. Assume a 30 percent income tax rate. Determine the amount of income tax expense under each of the two options. Identify the option that minimizes the amount of the company's income tax expense.

e. Comment on the conflict of interest between the company president as determined in Requirement *c* and the owners of the company as indicated in Requirement *d*. Describe an incentive compensation plan that would avoid a conflict of interest between the president and the owners.

Problem 10-31A *Statement of Ethical Professional Practice*

The Chief Financial Officer (CFO) of Automation Company was aware that the company's controller was reporting fraudulent revenues. Upper-level executives are paid very large bonuses when the company meets the earnings goals established in the company's budgets. While the CFO had pushed the controller to "make the numbers," he had not told him to "make up the numbers" Besides, he could plead ignorance if the fraud was ever discovered. The CFO knew he should prohibit the fraudulent reporting but also knew the importance of making the numbers established in the budget. He told himself that it wasn't just for his bonus but for the stockholders as well. If the actual earnings were below the budgeted target numbers, the stock price would drop and the shareholders would suffer. Besides, he believed that the actual revenues would increase dramatically in the near future and they could cover for the fraudulent revenue by underreporting these future revenues. He concluded that no one would get hurt and everything would be straightened out in the near future. The company's Chief Executive Officer (CEO) was not aware of the fraud.

Required

a. Review the statement of ethical professional practice shown in Exhibit 1.19. Identify and comment on which of the ethical principles were violated by the CFO.

b. Suppose you are an accountant working is the controllers' office. What should you do if you become aware of the fraud and the fact that the CFO is complicit in the deception?

LO 10-8

Problem 10-32A   *Value Chain Analysis*

Vernon Company invented a new process for manufacturing ice cream. The ingredients are mixed in high-tech machinery that forms the product into small round beads. Like a bag of balls, the ice cream beads are surrounded by air pockets in packages. This design has numerous advantages. First, each bite of ice cream melts rapidly when placed in a person's mouth, creating a more flavorful sensation when compared to ordinary ice cream. Also, the air pockets mean that a typical serving includes a smaller amount of ice cream. This not only reduces materials cost but also provides the consumer with a low-calorie snack. A cup appears full of ice cream, but it is really half full of air. The consumer eats only half the ingredients that are contained in a typical cup of blended ice cream. Finally, the texture of the ice cream makes scooping it out of a large container a very easy task. The frustration of trying to get a spoon into a rock-solid package of blended ice cream has been eliminated. Vernon Company named the new product Sonic Cream.

Like many other ice cream producers, Vernon Company purchases its raw materials from a food wholesaler. The ingredients are mixed in Vernon's manufacturing plant. The packages of finished product are distributed to privately owned franchise ice cream shops that sell Sonic Cream directly to the public.

Vernon provides national advertising and is responsible for all research and development costs associated with making new flavors of Sonic Cream.

Required

a. Based on the information provided, draw a comprehensive value chain for Vernon Company that includes its suppliers and customers.

b. Identify the place in the chain where Vernon Company is exercising its opportunity to create added value beyond that currently being provided by its competitors.

ANALYZE, THINK, COMMUNICATE

ATC 10-1   Business Applications Case   *Financial versus managerial accounting*

The following information was taken from Starbucks Corporation's SEC filings.

	Fiscal Year Ended	
	October 1, 2017	**October 2, 2016**
Number of employees	277,000	254,000
Revenues (in millions)	$22,387	$21,316
Properties (in thousands)	6,322 square feet	6,277 square feet
Total assets (in millions)	$14,366	$14,313
Company-owned stores	13,275	12,711
Net earnings (in millions)	$2,885	$2,818

Required

a. Explain whether each line of information in the table would best be described as being primarily financial accounting or managerial accounting in nature.

b. Provide some additional examples of managerial and financial accounting information that could apply to Starbucks.

c. If you analyze only the data you identified as financial in nature, does it appear that Starbucks' 2017 fiscal year was better or worse than its 2016 fiscal year? Explain.

d. If you analyze only the data you identified as managerial in nature, does it appear that Starbucks' 2017 fiscal year was better or worse than its 2016 fiscal year? Explain.

e. Did Starbucks appear to be using its facilities more efficiently or less efficiently in 2017 than in 2016?

ATC 10-2   Group Assignment   *Product versus upstream and downstream costs*

Victor Holt, the accounting manager of Sexton, Inc., gathered the following information for Year 1. Some of it can be used to construct an income statement for Year 1. Ignore items that do not appear on an income statement. Some computation may be required. For example, the cost of manufacturing equipment would not appear on the income statement. However, the cost of manufacturing equipment is needed to compute the amount of depreciation. All units of product were started and completed in Year 1.

1. Issued $864,000 of common stock.

2. Paid engineers in the product design department $10,000 for salaries that were accrued at the end of the previous year.

3. Incurred advertising expenses of $70,000.

4. Paid $720,000 for materials used to manufacture the company's product.

5. Incurred utility costs of $160,000. These costs were allocated to different departments on the basis of square footage of floor space. Mr. Holt identified three departments and determined the square footage of floor space for each department to be as shown in the following table.

Department	Square Footage
Research and development	10,000
Manufacturing	60,000
Selling and administrative	30,000
Total	100,000

6. Paid $880,000 for wages of production workers.

7. Paid cash of $658,000 for salaries of administrative personnel. There was $16,000 of accrued salaries owed to administrative personnel at the end of Year 1. There was no beginning balance in the Salaries Payable account for administrative personnel.

8. Purchased manufacturing equipment two years ago at a cost of $10,000,000. The equipment had an eight-year useful life and a $2,000,000 salvage value.

9. Paid $390,000 cash to engineers in the product design department.

10. Paid a $258,000 cash dividend to owners.

11. Paid $80,000 to set up manufacturing equipment for production.

12. Paid a one-time $186,000 restructuring cost to redesign the production process to implement a just-in-time inventory system.

13. Prepaid the premium on a new insurance policy covering nonmanufacturing employees. The policy cost $72,000 and had a one-year term with an effective starting date of May 1. Four employees work in the research and development department and eight employees work in the selling and administrative department. Assume a December 31 closing date.

14. Made 69,400 units of product and sold 60,000 units at a price of $70 each.

Required

a. Divide the class into groups of four or five students per group, and then organize the groups into three sections. Assign Task 1 to the first section of groups, Task 2 to the second section of groups, and Task 3 to the third section of groups.

Group Tasks

(1) Identify the items that are classified as product costs and determine the amount of cost of goods sold reported on the Year 1 income statement.

(2) Identify the items that are classified as upstream costs and determine the amount of upstream cost expensed on the Year 1 income statement.

(3) Identify the items that are classified as downstream costs and determine the amount of downstream cost expensed on the Year 1 income statement.

b. Have the class construct an income statement in the following manner. Select a member of one of the groups assigned Group Task (1), identifying the product costs. Have that person go to the board and list the costs included in the determination of cost of goods sold. Anyone in the other groups who disagrees with one of the classifications provided by the person at the board should voice an objection and explain why the item should be classified differently. The instructor should lead the class to a consensus on the disputed items. After the amount of cost of goods sold is determined, the student at the board constructs the part of the income statement showing the determination of gross margin. The exercise continues in a similar fashion with representatives from the other sections explaining the composition of the upstream and downstream costs. These items are added to the income statement started by the first group representative. The final result is a completed income statement.

ATC 10-3   Research Assignment   *Identifying product costs at Snap-on Inc.*

Use the December 31, 2017, Form 10-K for Snap-on, Inc. to complete the following requirements. To obtain the Form 10-K, you can use the EDGAR system following the instructions in Appendix A, or it can be found under "Corporate Information" on the company's corporate website at www.snapon.com. Read carefully the following portions of the document:

■ "Products and services" on page 6.

■ "Consolidated Statement of Earnings" on page 68.

■ The following parts of Note 1 on page 74 and 75:

   • "Shipping and handling"

   • "Advertising and promotion"

■ "Note 4: Inventories" on page 85.

■ "Note 5: Property and equipment" on page 86.

Required

a. Does the level of detail that Snap-on provides regarding costs incurred to manufacture its products suggest the company's financial statements are designed primarily to meet the needs of external or internal users?

b. Does Snap-on treat shipping and handling costs as product or nonproduct costs?

c. Does Snap-on treat advertising and promotion costs as product or nonproduct costs?

d. Earlier in this course you learned about a class of inventory called merchandise inventory. What categories of inventory does Snap-on report in its annual report?

e. What is the cost of the land owned by Snap-on? What is the cost of its machinery, equipment, and software?

ATC 10-4   Writing Assignment   *Emerging practices in managerial accounting*

On January 4, 2017, Macy's Inc., faced with declining revenues and profits announced a series of actions it planned to implement to try to improve its operations. In its press release the company reported:

Macy's, Inc. today announced a series of actions to streamline its store portfolio, intensify cost efficiency efforts, and execute its real estate strategy. These actions bolster the company's strategy to further invest in omnichannel capabilities, improve customer experience and create shareholder value. The actions include:

   • *The closure of 68 stores and the reorganization of the field structure that supports the remaining stores, reinforcing the strategy of fewer stores with better customer experience. These store closures are part of the approximately 100 closings announced in August 2016.*

- *The significant restructuring of the Macy's, Inc. operations to focus resources on strategic priorities, improve organizational agility and reduce expense.*
- *The sale of properties consistent with the previously announced real estate strategy.*

The actions announced today are estimated to generate annual expense savings of approximately $550 million, beginning in 2017, enabling the company to invest an additional $250 million in growing the digital business, store-related growth strategies, Bluemercury, Macy's Backstage and China. These savings, combined with savings from initiatives implemented in early 2016, exceed the $500 million goal communicated in fall of 2015, one year earlier than expected.*

*2017. Macy's, Inc. Announces Actions to Streamline Store Portfolio, Intensify Cost Efficiency Efforts and Execute Real Estate Strategy. MarketWatch Inc.

Required

Assume that you are Macy's vice president of human relations. Write a letter to the employees who are affected by the restructuring. The letter should explain why it was necessary for the company to undertake the restructuring. Your explanation should refer to the ideas discussed in the section "Best Practices in Managerial Accounting" of this chapter (Appendix).

ATC 10-5   Ethical Dilemma   *Product cost versus selling and administrative expense*

Emma Emerson is a proud woman with a problem. Her daughter has been accepted into a prestigious law school. While Ms. Emerson beams with pride, she is worried sick about how to pay for the school; she is a single parent who has worked hard to support herself and her three children. She had to go heavily into debt to finance her own education. Even though she now has a good job, family needs have continued to outpace her income and her debt burden is staggering. She knows she will be unable to borrow the money needed for her daughter's law school.

Ms. Emerson is the chief financial officer (CFO) of a small manufacturing company. She has just accepted a new job offer. Indeed, she has not yet told her employer that she will be leaving in a month. She is concerned that her year-end incentive bonus may be affected if her boss learns of her plans to leave. She plans to inform the company immediately after receiving the bonus. She knows her behavior is less than honorable, but she believes that she has been underpaid for a long time. Her boss, a relative of the company's owner, makes twice what she makes and does half the work. Why should she care about leaving with a little extra cash? Indeed, she is considering an opportunity to boost the bonus.

Ms. Emerson's bonus is based on a percentage of net income. Her company recently introduced a new product line that required substantial production start-up costs. Ms. Emerson is fully aware that GAAP requires these costs to be expensed in the current accounting period, but no one else in the company has the technical expertise to know exactly how the costs should be treated. She is considering misclassifying the start-up costs as product costs. If the costs are misclassified, net income will be significantly higher, resulting in a nice boost in her incentive bonus. By the time the auditors discover the misclassification, Ms. Emerson will have moved on to her new job. If the matter is brought to the attention of her new employer, she will simply plead ignorance. Considering her daughter's needs, Ms. Emerson decides to classify the start-up costs as product costs.

Required

a. Based on this information, indicate whether Ms. Emerson believes the number of units of product sold will be equal to, less than, or greater than the number of units made. Write a brief paragraph explaining the logic that supports your answer.

b. Explain how the misclassification could mislead an investor or creditor regarding the company's financial condition.

c. Explain how the misclassification could affect income taxes.

d. Review the Statement of Ethical Professional Practice shown in Exhibit 10.19 and identify at least two ethical principles that Ms. Emerson's misclassification of the start-up costs violated.

Design Elements: Abstract texture: ©Ingram Publishing; Video Camera icon: ©McGraw-Hill Education; Check mark: ©McGraw-Hill Education; Look forward/backward icon: ©McGraw-Hill Education; Globe icon: ©McGraw-Hill Education; Globe with magnifying glass icon: ©McGraw-Hill Education; Pen and paper icon: ©McGraw-Hill Education; Group Assignment icon: ©McGraw-Hill Education; Ethics Cases icon: ©McGraw-Hill Education; Self-Study Review icon: © Design Pics/Don Hammond; and Point de la Coubre lighthouse near Roy, France: © Westend61/Getty Images.

CHAPTER 11

Cost Behavior, Operating Leverage, and Profitability Analysis

LEARNING OBJECTIVES

After you have mastered the material in this chapter, you will be able to:

LO 11-1   Identify and describe fixed, variable, and mixed cost behavior.

LO 11-2   Demonstrate the effects of operating leverage on profitability.

LO 11-3   Prepare an income statement using the contribution margin approach.

LO 11-4   Calculate the magnitude of operating leverage.

LO 11-5   Determine the sales volume necessary to break even or to earn a desired profit.

LO 11-6   Calculate and interpret the margin of safety measure.

 Video lectures and accompanying self-assessment quizzes are available in Connect *for all learning objectives.*

 Set B exercises and problems are available in Additional Student Resources.

CHAPTER OPENING

Three college students are planning a vacation. One of them suggests inviting a fourth person along, remarking that four can travel for the same cost as three. Certainly, some costs will be the same whether three or four people go on the trip. For example, the hotel room costs $800 per week, regardless of whether three or four people stay in the room. In accounting terms, the cost of the hotel room is a **fixed cost.** The total amount of a fixed cost does not change when volume changes. The total hotel room cost is $800 whether one, two, three, or four people use the room. In contrast, some costs vary in direct proportion with changes in volume. When volume increases, total variable cost increases; when volume decreases, total variable cost decreases. For example, the cost of tickets to a theme park is a **variable cost.** The total cost of tickets increases proportionately with each vacationer who goes to the theme park. Cost behavior (fixed versus variable) can significantly impact profitability. This chapter explains cost behavior and ways it can be used to increase profitability.

The Curious Accountant

chrisdorney/Shutterstock

News flash! For the third quarter of 2017, Best Buy, Inc.'s revenues increased 4.2 percent compared to those of the same quarter of 2016; however its operating earnings increased by 12.2 percent. For the third quarter of 2017, Conagra Brands, Inc. reported that its revenues for 2017 were 4.1 percent higher than revenues for 2016, but its earnings increased 78.3 percent. During the third quarter of 2017, The Walt Disney Company saw its revenues decrease 0.3 percent compared to the third quarter of 2016. Unfortunately, during this period its operating earnings fell 13.5 percent.

Can you explain why such relatively small changes in these companies' revenues resulted in such relatively large changes in their earnings or losses? In other words, if a company's sales increase 10 percent, why do its earnings not also increase 10 percent? (Answer on page 411.)

FIXED COST BEHAVIOR

LO 11-1

Identify and describe fixed, variable, and mixed cost behavior.

How much more will it cost to send one additional employee to a sales meeting? If more people buy our products, can we charge less? If sales increase by 10 percent, how will profits be affected? Managers seeking answers to such questions must consider **cost behavior.** Knowing how costs behave relative to the level of business activity enables managers to more effectively plan and control costs. To illustrate, consider the entertainment company Star Productions, Inc. (SPI).

SPI specializes in promoting rock concerts. It is considering paying a band $48,000 to play a concert. Obviously, SPI must sell enough tickets to cover this cost. In this example, the relevant activity base is the number of tickets sold. The cost of the band is a fixed cost because it does not change regardless of the number of tickets sold. Exhibit 11.1 illustrates the fixed cost behavior pattern, showing the *total cost* and the *cost per unit* at three different levels of activity.

Total versus *per-unit* fixed costs behave differently. The total cost for the band remains constant (fixed) at $48,000. In contrast, fixed cost per unit decreases as volume (number of tickets sold) increases. The term *fixed cost* is consistent with the behavior of *total cost.* Total fixed cost remains constant (fixed) when activity changes. However, there is a contradiction between the term *fixed cost per unit* and the *per-unit behavior pattern of a fixed cost.* Fixed cost per unit is *not* fixed. It changes with the number of tickets sold. This contradiction in terminology can cause untold confusion. Study carefully the fixed cost behavior patterns in Exhibit 11.2.

EXHIBIT 11.1

Fixed Cost Behavior

Number of tickets sold (a)	2,700	3,000	3,300
Total cost of band (b)	$48,000	$48,000	$48,000
Cost per ticket sold (b ÷ a)	$ 17.78	$ 16.00	$ 14.55

EXHIBIT 11.2

Fixed Cost Behavior

	When Activity Increases	When Activity Decreases
Total fixed cost	Remains constant	Remains constant
Fixed cost **per unit**	Decreases	Increases

The fixed cost data in Exhibit 11.1 help SPI's management decide whether to sponsor the concert. For example, the information influences potential pricing choices. The per-unit costs represent the minimum ticket prices required to cover the fixed cost at various levels of activity. SPI could compare these per-unit costs to the prices of competing entertainment events (such as the prices of movies, sporting events, or theater tickets). If the price is not competitive, tickets will not sell and the concert will lose money. Management must also consider the number of tickets to be sold. The volume data in Exhibit 11.1 can be compared to the band's track record of ticket sales at previous concerts. A proper analysis of these data can reduce the risk of undertaking an unprofitable venture.

OPERATING LEVERAGE

LO 11-2

Demonstrate the effects of operating leverage on profitability.

Heavy objects can be moved with little effort using *physical* leverage. Business managers apply **operating leverage** to magnify small changes in revenue into dramatic changes in profitability. The *lever* managers use to achieve disproportionate changes between revenue and profitability is fixed costs. The leverage relationships between revenue, fixed costs, and profitability are displayed in Exhibit 11.3.

When all costs are fixed, every sales dollar contributes one dollar toward the potential profitability of a project. Once sales dollars cover fixed costs, each additional sales dollar represents pure profit. As a result, a small change in sales volume can significantly

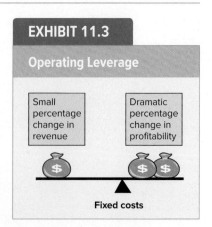

EXHIBIT 11.3

Operating Leverage

Small percentage change in revenue

Dramatic percentage change in profitability

Fixed costs

FOCUS ON INTERNATIONAL ISSUES

ANOTHER REASON FIXED COSTS AREN'T ALWAYS FIXED

Suppose that a company is renting a facility at an annual rental rate that does not change for the next five years *no matter what*. Is this a fixed cost? By now, you are aware that the proper response is to ask, fixed in relation to what? Is the rental cost of this facility fixed in relation to the activity at this facility? The answer seems to be yes, but it might be "not necessarily."

Consider the large multinational company Samsung Electronics Company, which has its headquarters in Suwon, South Korea. Although Samsung does a lot of business in Korea where the currency is the Korean won, it does 90 percent of its business in other countries. Suppose Samsung rents facilities in Japan. The annual rental fee is usually stated and paid in the currency of the local country, which in Japan is the yen. Even though Samsung may be paying the same number of yen in rent each year, Samsung's rental cost in won could vary greatly over time due to fluctuation in the exchange rate between the won and the yen. Such potential foreign currency exchange fluctuations cause companies to enter very complex hedging arrangements to add stability to transactions that must be paid in foreign currencies.

Lestertair/Shutterstock

The following information, taken from Samsung's 2016 financial statements, gives a perspective of the international dimensions of the company. Before a multinational company can answer the question, "Is a cost fixed?" it must determine what currency the person asking the question has in mind. Even though Samsung measures its activities using the Korean won, its financial transactions take place using dozens of different currencies, which have exchange rates that are constantly changing. The symbol for the Korean won is "₩."

Geographic Area	Segment Earnings*	Percentage of Total	Total Assets*	Percentage of Total
American	$ 68,728,575	34%	$ 7,041,731	7%
Asia and Africa	39,099,991	19	9,626,711	10
Europe	38,253,185	19	730,490	1
China	35,583,166	18	11,132,720	11
Korea	20,201,828	10	68,978,040	71
Totals	$201,866,745	100%	$97,509,692	100%

*Amounts in millions of won.

affect profitability. To illustrate, assume SPI estimates it will sell 3,000 tickets for $18 each. A 10 percent difference in actual sales volume will produce a 90 percent difference in profitability. Examine the data in Exhibit 11.4 to verify this result.[1]

EXHIBIT 11.4

Effect of Operating Leverage on Profitability

Number of tickets sold	2,700	⇐ −10% ⇐	3,000	⇒ +10% ⇒	3,300
Sales revenue ($18 per ticket)	$ 48,600		$ 54,000		$ 59,400
Cost of band (fixed cost)	(48,000)		(48,000)		(48,000)
Gross margin	$ 600	⇐ −90% ⇐	$ 6,000	⇒ +90% ⇒	$ 11,400

[1]Do not confuse operating leverage with financial leverage. Companies employ *financial leverage* when they use debt to profit from investing money at a higher rate of return than the rate they pay on borrowed money. Companies employ *operating leverage* when they use proportionately more fixed costs than variable costs to magnify the effect on earnings of changes in revenues.

Calculating Percentage Change

The percentages in Exhibit 11.4 are computed as follows:

$$\text{(Alternative measure − Base measure)} \div \text{Base measure} = \% \text{ change}$$

The base measure is the starting point. To illustrate, compute the percentage change in gross margin when moving from 3,000 units (base measure) to 3,300 units (the alternative measure).

$$\text{(Alternative measure − Base measure)} \div \text{Base measure} = \% \text{ change}$$
$$(\$11{,}400 − \$6{,}000) \div \$6{,}000 = 90\%$$

The percentage *decline* in profitability is similarly computed:

$$\text{(Alternative measure − Base measure)} \div \text{Base measure} = \% \text{ change}$$
$$(\$600 − \$6{,}000) \div \$6{,}000 = (90\%)$$

Risk and Reward Assessment

Risk refers to the possibility that sacrifices may exceed benefits. A fixed cost represents a commitment to an economic sacrifice. It represents the ultimate risk of undertaking a particular business project. If SPI pays the band but nobody buys a ticket, the company will lose $48,000. SPI can avoid this risk by substituting *variable costs* for the *fixed cost*.

Variable Cost Behavior

To illustrate variable cost behavior, assume SPI arranges to pay the band $16 per ticket sold instead of a fixed $48,000. Exhibit 11.5 shows the total cost of the band and the cost per ticket sold at three different levels of activity.

EXHIBIT 11.5

Variable Cost Behavior

Number of tickets sold (a)	2,700	3,000	3,300
Total cost of band (b)	$43,200	$48,000	$52,800
Cost per ticket sold (b ÷ a)	$ 16	$ 16	$ 16

Since SPI will pay the band $16 for each ticket sold, the *total* variable cost increases in direct proportion to the number of tickets sold. If SPI sells one ticket, total band cost will be $16 (1 × $16); if SPI sells two tickets, total band cost will be $32 (2 × $16); and so on. The total cost of the band increases proportionately as ticket sales move from 2,700 to 3,000 to 3,300. The variable cost *per ticket* remains $16, however, regardless of whether the number of tickets sold is 1, 2, 3, or 3,000. The behavior of variable cost *per unit* is contradictory to the word *variable*. Variable cost per unit remains *constant* regardless of how many tickets are sold. Study carefully the variable cost behavior patterns in Exhibit 11.6.

EXHIBIT 11.6

Variable Cost Behavior

	When Activity Increases	When Activity Decreases
Total variable cost	Increases proportionately	Decreases proportionately
Variable cost **per unit**	Remains constant	Remains constant

Risk and Reward Assessment

Shifting the cost structure from fixed to variable enables SPI to avoid the fixed cost risk. Recall that under the fixed cost structure, SPI was locked into a $48,000 cost for the band regardless of how many tickets are sold. If no tickets are sold, SPI will have to report a $48,000 loss on its income statement. The risk of incurring this loss is eliminated by the

EXHIBIT 11.7

Variable Cost Eliminates Operating Leverage						
Number of tickets sold	2,700	⇐ −10% ⇐	3,000	⇒ +10% ⇒	3,300	
Sales revenue ($18 per ticket)	$ 48,600		$ 54,000		$ 59,400	
Cost of band ($16 variable cost)	(43,200)		(48,000)		(52,800)	
Gross margin	$ 5,400	⇐ −10% ⇐	$ 6,000	⇒ +10% ⇒	$ 6,600	

variable cost structure that requires SPI to pay the band only $16 per ticket sold. If SPI sells zero tickets, then the cost of the band is zero. For each ticket sold, SPI earns a $2 profit ($18 ticket sales price − $16 fee paid to band).

Shifting the cost structure from fixed to variable reduces not only the level of risk but also the potential for profits. Managers cannot avoid the risk of fixed costs without also sacrificing the benefits. Variable costs do not offer operating leverage. Exhibit 11.7 shows that a variable cost structure produces a proportional relationship between sales and profitability. A 10 percent increase or decrease in sales results in a corresponding 10 percent increase or decrease in profitability.

 CHECK YOURSELF 11.1

Suppose that you are sponsoring a political rally at which Ralph Nader will speak. You estimate that approximately 2,000 people will buy tickets to hear Mr. Nader's speech. The tickets are expected to be priced at $12 each. Would you prefer a contract that agrees to pay Mr. Nader $10,000 or one that agrees to pay him $5 per ticket purchased?

Answer   Your answer would depend on how certain you are that 2,000 people will purchase tickets. If it were likely that many more than 2,000 tickets would be sold, you would be better off with a fixed cost structure, agreeing to pay Mr. Nader a flat fee of $10,000. If attendance numbers are highly uncertain, you would be better off with a variable cost structure, thereby guaranteeing a lower cost if fewer people buy tickets.

Answers to The Curious Accountant

The explanation for how a company's earnings can rise faster, as a percentage, than its revenue is operating leverage, and operating leverage is due entirely to fixed costs. As the chapter explains, when a company's output goes up, its fixed cost per unit goes down. As long as it can keep prices about the same, this lower unit cost will result in higher profit per unit sold. In real-world companies, the relationship between changing sales levels and changing earnings levels can be very complex, but the existence of fixed costs helps explain why a 4.2 percent rise in revenue can cause a 12.2 percent rise in net earnings.

 CHECK YOURSELF 11.2

If both The Kroger Co, and Delta Air Lines were to experience a 5 percent increase in revenues, which company would be more likely to experience a higher percentage increase in net income?

Answer   Delta would be more likely to experience a higher percentage increase in net income because a large portion of its cost (e.g., employee salaries and depreciation) is fixed, while a large portion of Kroger's cost is variable (e.g., cost of goods sold).

AN INCOME STATEMENT UNDER THE CONTRIBUTION MARGIN APPROACH

LO 11-3

Prepare an income statement using the contribution margin approach.

The impact of cost structure on profitability is so significant that managerial accountants frequently construct income statements that classify costs according to their behavior patterns. Such income statements first subtract variable costs from revenue; the resulting subtotal is called the **contribution margin.** The contribution margin represents the amount available to cover fixed expenses and thereafter to provide company profits. Net income is computed by subtracting the fixed costs from the contribution margin. A contribution margin style income statement cannot be used for public reporting (GAAP prohibits its use in external financial reports), but it is widely used for internal reporting purposes. Exhibit 11.8 illustrates income statements prepared using the contribution margin approach.

EXHIBIT 11.8

Income Statements

	Company Name	
	Bragg	**Biltmore**
Variable cost per unit (a)	$ 6	$ 12
Sales revenue (10 units × $20)	$200	$200
Variable cost (10 units × a)	(60)	(120)
Contribution margin	140	80
Fixed cost	(120)	(60)
Net income	$ 20	$ 20

MEASURING OPERATING LEVERAGE USING CONTRIBUTION MARGIN

LO 11-4

Calculate the magnitude of operating leverage.

A contribution margin income statement allows managers to easily measure operating leverage. The magnitude of operating leverage can be determined as follows:

$$\text{Magnitude of operating leverage} = \frac{\text{Contribution margin}}{\text{Net income}}$$

Applying this formula to the income statement data reported for Bragg Company and Biltmore Company in Exhibit 11.8 produces the following measures.

Bragg Company:

$$\text{Magnitude of operating leverage} = \frac{\$140}{\$20} = 7$$

Biltmore Company:

$$\text{Magnitude of operating leverage} = \frac{\$80}{\$20} = 4$$

The computations show that Bragg is more highly leveraged than Biltmore. Bragg's change in profitability will be seven times greater than a given percentage change in revenue. In contrast, Biltmore's profits change by only four times the percentage change in revenue. For example, a 10 percent increase in revenue produces a 70 percent increase (10 percent × 7) in profitability for Bragg Company and a 40 percent increase (10 percent × 4) in profitability for Biltmore Company. The income statements in Exhibits 11.9 and 11.10 confirm these expectations.

EXHIBIT 11.9

Comparative Income Statements for Bragg Company

Units (a)	10		11
Sales revenue ($20 × a)	$200	⇒ +10% ⇒	$220
Variable cost ($6 × a)	(60)		(66)
Contribution margin	140		154
Fixed cost	(120)		(120)
Net income	$ 20	⇒ +70% ⇒	$ 34

EXHIBIT 11.10

Comparative Income Statements for Biltmore Company

Units (a)	10		11
Sales revenue ($20 × a)	$200	⇒ +10% ⇒	$220
Variable cost ($12 × a)	(120)		(132)
Contribution margin	80		88
Fixed cost	(60)		(60)
Net income	$ 20	⇒ +40% ⇒	$ 28

Operating leverage itself is neither good nor bad; it represents a strategy that can work to a company's advantage or disadvantage, depending on how it is used. The next section explains how managers can use operating leverage to create a competitive business advantage.

☑ CHECK YOURSELF 11.3

Boeing Company's 2018 10-K annual report filed with the Securities and Exchange Commission refers to "operating margins in our Commercial Airplanes business." Is Boeing referring to gross margins or contribution margins?

Answer   Since the data come from the company's external annual report, the reference must be to gross margins (revenue − cost of goods sold), a product cost measure. The contribution margin (revenue − variable cost) is a measure used in internal reporting.

Cost Behavior Summarized

The term *fixed* refers to the behavior of *total* fixed cost. The cost *per unit* of a fixed cost *varies inversely* with changes in the level of activity. As activity increases, fixed cost per unit decreases. As activity decreases, fixed cost per unit increases. These relationships are graphed in Exhibit 11.11.

The term *variable* refers to the behavior of *total* variable cost. Total variable cost increases or decreases proportionately with changes in the volume of activity. In contrast, variable cost *per unit* remains *fixed* at all levels of activity. These relationships are graphed in Exhibit 11.12.

EXHIBIT 11.11

Graphical Presentation of Fixed Cost Behavior

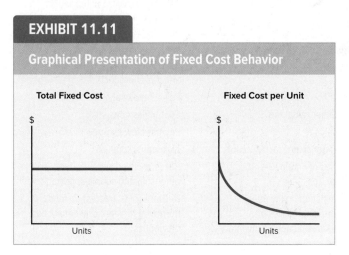

EXHIBIT 11.12

Graphical Presentation of Variable Cost Behavior

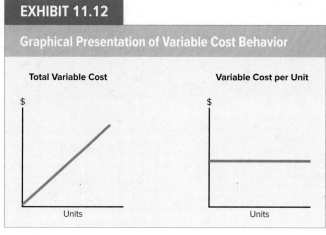

EXHIBIT 11.13

Fixed and Variable Cost Behavior

When Activity Level Changes	Total Cost	Cost per Unit
Fixed costs	Remains constant	Changes *inversely*
Variable costs	Changes in direct proportion	Remains constant

The relationships between fixed and variable costs are summarized in the chart in Exhibit 11.13. Study these relationships thoroughly.

Mixed Costs (Semivariable Costs)

Mixed costs (semivariable costs) include both fixed and variable components. For example, suppose Star Productions, Inc. has to pay for janitorial services. The charge for these services includes a base fee of $1,000 plus $20 per hour required to do a cleanup. The $1,000 base fee is fixed. It is the same no matter how many hours it takes to accomplish the cleanup. In contrast, the $20 hourly cost is a variable cost because the total cost increases with each additional hour it takes to complete the cleanup. Since the total janitorial cost is composed of fixed and variable components, it is frequently called a mixed cost. It may also be called a semivariable cost.

Given the $1,000 base plus $20 per hour cost components, the total janitorial cost for any cleanup can be easily computed as shown:

$$\text{Total cost} = \text{Fixed cost} + (\text{Variable cost per hour} \times \text{Number of hours})$$

If 60 hours are required to accomplish a cleanup, the total mixed cost is:

$$\text{Total cost} = \$1,000 + (\$20 \times 60) = \$2,200$$

If 90 hours are required to accomplish a cleanup, the total mixed cost is:

$$\text{Total cost} = \$1,000 + (\$20 \times 90) = \$2,800$$

Exhibit 11.14 illustrates a variety of mixed costs businesses commonly encounter.

EXHIBIT 11.14

Examples of Mixed Costs

Type of Cost	Fixed Cost Component(s)	Variable Cost Component(s)
Cost of sales staff	Monthly salary	Bonus based on sales volume
Truck rental	Monthly rental fee	Cost of gas, tires, and maintenance
Legal fees	Monthly retainer	Reimbursements to attorney for out-of-pocket costs (copying, postage, travel, filing fees)
Outpatient service cost	Salaries of doctors and nurses, depreciation of facility, utilities	Medical supplies such as bandages, sterilization solution, and paper products
Phone services	Monthly connection fee	Per-minute usage fee
LP gas utility cost	Container rental fee	Cost of gas consumed
Cable TV services	Monthly fee	Pay-per-view charges
Training cost	Instructor salary, facility cost	Textbooks, supplies
Shipping and handling	Salaries of employees who process packages	Boxes, packing supplies, tape, and other shipping supplies, postage
Inventory holding cost	Depreciation on inventory warehouse, salaries of employees managing inventory	Delivery costs, interest on funds borrowed to finance inventory, cost of supplies

The Relevant Range

Suppose SPI, the rock concert promoter mentioned earlier, must pay $5,000 to rent a concert hall with a seating capacity of 4,000 people. Is the cost of the concert hall fixed or variable? Since total cost remains unchanged regardless of whether one ticket, 4,000 tickets, or any number in between is sold, the cost is fixed relative to ticket sales. However, what if demand for tickets is significantly more than 4,000? In that case, SPI might rent a larger concert hall at a higher cost. In other words, *the cost is fixed only for a designated range of activity (1 to 4,000).*

A similar circumstance affects many variable costs. For example, a supplier may offer a volume discount to buyers who purchase more than a specified number of products. The point is that descriptions of cost behavior pertain to a specified range of activity. The range of activity over which the definitions of fixed and variable costs are valid is commonly called the **relevant range.**

Context-Sensitive Definitions of Fixed and Variable

The behavior pattern of a particular cost may be either fixed or variable, depending on the context. For example, the cost of the band was fixed at $48,000 when SPI was considering hiring it to play a single concert. Regardless of how many tickets SPI sold, the total band cost was $48,000. However, the band cost becomes variable if SPI decides to hire it to perform at a series of concerts. The total cost and the cost per concert for one, two, three, four, or five concerts are shown in Exhibit 11.15.

EXHIBIT 11.15

Cost Behavior Relative to Number of Concerts					
Number of concerts (a)	1	2	3	4	5
Cost per concert (b)	$48,000	$48,000	$ 48,000	$ 48,000	$ 48,000
Total cost (a × b)	$48,000	$96,000	$144,000	$192,000	$240,000

In this context, the total cost of hiring the band increases proportionately with the number of concerts while cost per concert remains constant. The band cost is therefore variable. The same cost can behave as either a fixed cost or a variable cost, depending on the **activity base.** When identifying a cost as fixed or variable, first ask, fixed or variable *relative to what activity base?* The cost of the band is fixed relative to *the number of tickets sold for a specific concert;* it is variable relative to *the number of concerts produced.*

 CHECK YOURSELF 11.4

Is the compensation cost for managers of Pizza Hut Restaurants a fixed cost or a variable cost?

Answer   The answer depends on the context. For example, since a store manager's salary remains unchanged regardless of how many customers enter a particular restaurant, it can be classified as a fixed cost relative to the number of customers at a particular restaurant. However, the more restaurants that Pizza Hut operates, the higher the total managers' compensation cost will be. Accordingly, managers' salary cost would be classified as a variable cost relative to the number of restaurants opened.

REALITY BYTES

As this chapter notes, CVP analysis for a particular set of data is valid only within the "relevant range" of the variables, such as fixed costs and variable costs. One important relevant range consideration is the maximum capacity at which a business can operate without having to add fixed costs. In academic settings, such as this course, theoretical examples are often presented showing a business doubling or tripling output with no change in fixed costs. Is this true in the real world?

A few years ago one of the coauthor's students asked him what the average operating capacity percentage for most businesses is. Though this seems like an obvious question, of the more than 10,000 students the instructor has taught, this was the only student to have asked the question. So, what is the answer? Some companies disclose operating capacity in their annual reports; examples from hotels and airlines are shown in the following table.

Image Source/Getty Images

	2017	2016
Marriott Hotels occupancy rate	73.2%	72.5%
Hilton Hotels occupancy rate	75.5	75.0
Delta Air Lines passenger load factor	85.6	84.6
Southwest Airlines passenger load factor	83.9	84.0

Although the annual reports of most companies do not report the percentage of plant capacity that is being used, the United States Census Bureau publishes these results for manufacturers, in great detail, in its *Quarterly Survey of Plant Capacity Utilization*. The average percentage of plant capacity utilized by all manufacturing entities surveyed for the third quarter of 2017 was 72.1 percent. Of course some specific industries were much higher and some much lower. Periodical publications reported a utilization rate of 99.4 percent while ready-mix concrete manufacturers reported a rate of 44.6 percent.

What does this mean for CVP analysis? Consider that if a company is operating at 80 percent of capacity, it can increase its output by only 25 percent before reaching full capacity (0.25 × 80 percent = 20 percent; 80 percent + 20 percent = 100 percent). Furthermore, a company cannot operate at 100 percent of capacity for very long without systems breaking down. Therefore, many businesses in the real world will need to add capacity, and thus fixed costs, if their output increases by more than 10 to 15 percent.

When doing real-world analysis, relevant range must be considered.

DETERMINING THE BREAK-EVEN POINT

LO 11-5

Determine the sales volume necessary to break even or to earn a desired profit.

Bright Day Distributors sells nonprescription health food supplements including vitamins, herbs, and natural hormones in the northwestern United States. Bright Day recently obtained the rights to distribute the new herb mixture Delatine. Recent scientific research found that Delatine delayed aging in laboratory animals. The researchers hypothesized that the substance would have a similar effect on humans. Their theory could not be confirmed because of the relatively long human life span. The news media reported the research findings; as stories turned up on television and radio news, talk shows, and in magazines, demand for Delatine increased.

Bright Day plans to sell the Delatine product at a price of $36 per bottle. Delatine costs $24 per bottle. Bright Day's management team suspects that enthusiasm for Delatine will abate quickly as the news media shift to other subjects. To attract customers immediately, the product managers consider television advertising. The marketing manager suggests running a campaign of several hundred cable channel ads at an estimated cost of $60,000.

Bright Day's first concern is whether it can sell enough units to cover its costs. The president made this position clear when he said, "We don't want to lose money on this product. We have to sell at least enough units to break even." In accounting terms, the **break-even point** is where profit (income) equals zero. So how many bottles of Delatine must be sold to produce a profit of zero? The break-even point is commonly computed using either the equation method or the contribution margin per unit method. Both of these approaches produce the same result. They are merely different ways to arrive at the same conclusion.

Equation Method

The **equation method** begins by expressing the income statement as follows:

$$\text{Sales} - \text{Variable costs} - \text{Fixed costs} = \text{Profit (Net income)}$$

As previously stated, profit at the break-even point is zero. Therefore, the break-even point for Delatine is computed as follows:

$$\text{Sales} - \text{Variable costs} - \text{Fixed costs} = \text{Profit}$$
$$\$36N - \$24N - \$60,000 = \$0$$
$$\$12N = \$60,000$$
$$N = \$60,000 \div \$12$$
$$N = 5,000 \text{ Units}$$

Where:
N = Number of units
$36 = Sales price per unit
$24 = Variable cost per unit
$60,000 = Fixed costs

 CHECK YOURSELF 11.5

B-Shoc is an independent musician who is considering whether to independently produce and sell a CD. B-Shoc estimates fixed costs of $5,400 and variable costs of $2.00 per unit. The expected selling price is $8.00 per CD. Use the equation method to determine B-Shoc's break-even point.

Answer

$$\text{Sales} - \text{Variable costs} - \text{Fixed costs} = \text{Profit}$$
$$\$8N - \$2N - \$5,400 = \$0$$
$$\$6N = \$5,400$$
$$N = \$5,400 \div \$6$$
$$N = 900 \text{ Units (CDs)}$$

Where:

N = Number of units
$8 = Sales price per unit
$2 = Variable cost per unit
$5,400 = Fixed costs

Contribution Margin per Unit Method

Recall that the *total contribution margin* is the amount of sales minus total variable cost. The **contribution margin per unit** is the sales price per unit minus the variable cost per unit. Therefore, the contribution margin per unit for Delatine is:

Sales price per unit	$ 36
Less: Variable cost per unit	(24)
Contribution margin per unit	$ 12

For every bottle of Delatine it sells, Bright Day earns a $12 contribution margin. In other words, every time Bright Day sells a bottle of Delatine, it receives enough money ($24) to cover the variable cost of the bottle of Delatine and still has $12 left to go toward paying the fixed cost. Bright Day will reach the break-even point when it sells enough bottles of Delatine to cover its fixed costs. Therefore the break-even point can be determined as follows:

$$\text{Break-even point in units} = \frac{\text{Fixed costs}}{\text{Contribution margin per unit}}$$

$$\text{Break-even point in units} = \frac{\$60,000}{\$12}$$

$$\text{Break-even point in units} = 5,000 \text{ Units}$$

This result is the same as that determined under the equation method. Indeed, the contribution margin per unit method formula is an abbreviated version of the income statement formula used in the equation method. In other words, both methods are simply different derivations of the same formula. The proof is provided in this footnote.[2]

Both the *equation method* and the *contribution margin per unit method* yield the amount of break-even sales measured *in units.* To determine the amount of break-even sales measured *in dollars,* multiply the number of units times the sales price per unit. For Delatine, the break-even point measured in dollars is $180,000 (5,000 units × $36 per unit). The following income statement confirms this result:

Sales revenue (5,000 units × $36)	$ 180,000
Total variable expenses (5,000 units × $24)	(120,000)
Total contribution margin (5,000 units × $12)	60,000
Fixed expenses	(60,000)
Net income	$ 0

Determining the Sales Volume Necessary to Reach a Desired Profit

Bright Day's president decides the ad campaign should produce a $40,000 profit. He asks the accountant to determine the sales volume that is required to achieve this level of profitability. Using the *equation method,* the sales volume in units required to attain the desired profit is computed as follows:

$$\text{Sales} - \text{Variable costs} - \text{Fixed costs} = \text{Profit}$$

$$\$36N - \$24N - \$60,000 = \$40,000$$

$$\$12N = \$60,000 + \$40,000$$

$$N = \$100,000 \div \$12$$

$$N = 8,333 \text{ Units}$$

Where:
N = Number of units
$36 = Sales price per unit
$24 = Variable cost per unit
$60,000 = Fixed costs
$40,000 = Desired profit

---

[2]The formula for the *contribution margin per unit method* is (where N is the number of units at the break-even point):

N = Fixed costs ÷ Contribution margin per unit

The income statement formula for the *equation method* produces the same result as shown (where N is the number of units at the break-even point):

Sales − Variable costs − Fixed costs = Profit
Sales price per unit (N) − Variable cost per unit (N) − Fixed costs = Profit
Contribution margin per unit (N) − Fixed costs = Profit
Contribution margin per unit (N) − Fixed costs = 0
Contribution margin per unit (N) = Fixed costs

N = Fixed costs ÷ Contribution margin per unit

The accountant used the *contribution margin per unit method* to confirm these computations as follows:

$$\text{Sales volume in units} = \frac{\text{Fixed costs} + \text{Desired profit}}{\text{Contribution margin per unit}}$$

$$= \frac{\$60,000 + \$40,000}{\$12} = 8,333.33 \text{ Units}$$

The required volume in sales dollars is this number of units multiplied by the sales price per unit (8,333.33 units × $36 = $300,000). The following income statement confirms this result; all amounts are rounded to the nearest whole dollar.

Sales revenue (8,333.33 units × $36)	$300,000
Total variable expenses (8,333.33 units × $24)	(200,000)
Total contribution margin (8,333.33 units × $12)	100,000
Fixed expenses	(60,000)
Net income	$ 40,000

In practice, the company will not sell partial bottles of Delatine, so the accountant rounds 8,333.33 bottles to 8,334 whole units. For planning and decision making, managers frequently make decisions using approximate data. Accuracy is desirable, but it is not as important as relevance. Do not be concerned when computations do not produce whole numbers. Rounding and approximation are common characteristics of managerial accounting data.

 CHECK YOURSELF 11.6

VolTech Company manufactures small engines that it sells for $130 each. Variable costs are $70 per unit. Fixed costs are expected to be $100,000. The management team has established a target profit of $188,000. Use the contribution margin per unit method to determine how many engines VolTech must sell to attain the target profit.

Answer

Contribution margin per unit approach:

$$\text{Sales volume in units} = \frac{\text{Fixed costs} + \text{Desired profit}}{\text{Contribution margin per unit}} = \frac{\$100,000 + \$188,000}{\$130 - \$70} = 4,800 \text{ Units}$$

CALCULATING THE MARGIN OF SAFETY

The final meeting of Bright Day's management team focused on the reliability of the data produced in the CVP analysis. The marketing manager was reasonably certain that the company could sell the 8,333.33 bottles ($300,000 of sales) required to earn the desired profit of $40,000. Even so, the company president wanted to know the risk of failing to earn a profit on the project. To quantify the risk, the accountant highlighted the large gap between the budgeted and break-even sales. The amount of this gap, called the *margin of safety,* can be measured in units or in sales dollars as shown here.

LO 11-6

 Calculate and interpret the margin of safety measure.

	In Units	In Dollars
Budgeted sales	8,333.33	$300,000
Break-even sales	(5,000.00)	(180,000)
Margin of safety	3,333.33	$120,000

The **margin of safety** measures the cushion between budgeted sales and the break-even point. It quantifies the amount by which actual sales can fall short of expectations before the company will begin to incur losses.

To help compare diverse products or companies of different sizes, the margin of safety can be expressed as a percentage. Divide the margin of safety by the budgeted sales volume[3] as shown here.

$$\text{Margin of safety} = \frac{\text{Budgeted sales} - \text{Break-even sales}}{\text{Budgeted sales}}$$

$$\text{Margin of safety} = \frac{\$300,000 - \$180,000}{\$300,000} = 40\%$$

This analysis suggests actual sales would have to fall short of expected sales by more than 40 percent before Bright Day would experience a loss on Delatine. The large margin of safety suggests the proposed television advertising program to market Delatine capsules has minimal risk. As a result, the project team recommends that Delatine be added to the company's line of products.

✓ CHECK YOURSELF 11.7

Suppose that Bright Day is considering the possibility of selling a protein supplement that will cost Bright Day $5 per bottle. Bright Day believes that it can sell 4,000 bottles of the supplement for $25 per bottle. Fixed costs associated with selling the supplement are expected to be $42,000. Does the supplement have a wider margin of safety than Delatine?

Answer   Calculate the break-even point for the protein supplement.

$$\text{Break-even volume in units} = \frac{\text{Fixed costs}}{\text{Contribution margin per unit}} = \frac{\$42,000}{\$25 - \$5} = 2,100 \text{ Units}$$

Calculate the margin of safety. Note that the margin of safety expressed as a percentage can be calculated using the number of units or sales dollars. Using either units or dollars yields the same percentage.

$$\text{Margin of safety} = \frac{\text{Budgeted sales} - \text{Break-even sales}}{\text{Budgeted sales}} = \frac{4,000 - 2,100}{4,000} = 47.5\%$$

The margin of safety for Delatine (40 percent) is less than that for the protein supplement (47.5 percent). This suggests that Bright Day is more likely to incur losses selling Delatine than selling the supplement.

 ## A Look Back

To plan and control business operations effectively, managers need to understand how different costs behave in relation to changes in the volume of activity. Total *fixed cost* remains constant when activity changes. Fixed cost per unit decreases with increases in activity and increases with decreases in activity. In contrast, total *variable cost* increases proportionately with increases in activity and decreases proportionately with decreases in activity. Variable cost per unit remains constant regardless of activity levels. The definitions of fixed and variable costs have meaning only within the context of a specified range of activity (the relevant range) for a defined period of time. In addition, cost behavior depends on the relevant volume measure (a store manager's salary is fixed relative to the number of customers visiting a particular store but is variable relative to the number of stores operated). A mixed cost has both fixed and variable cost components.

---

[3]The margin of safety percentage can be based on actual as well as budgeted sales. For example, an analyst could compare the margins of safety of two companies under current operating conditions by substituting actual sales for budgeted sales in the computation, as follows: [(Actual sales − Break-even sales) ÷ Actual sales].

Fixed costs allow companies to take advantage of *operating leverage*. With operating leverage, each additional sale decreases the cost per unit. This principle allows a small percentage change in volume of revenue to cause a significantly larger percentage change in profits. The *magnitude of operating leverage* can be determined by dividing the contribution margin by net income. When all costs are fixed and revenues have covered fixed costs, each additional dollar of revenue represents pure profit. Having a fixed cost structure (employing operating leverage) offers a company both risks and rewards. If sales volume increases, fixed costs do not increase, allowing profits to soar. Alternatively, if sales volume decreases, fixed costs do not decrease and profits decline significantly more than revenues. Companies with high variable costs in relation to fixed costs do not experience as great a level of operating leverage. Their costs increase or decrease in proportion to changes in revenue. These companies face less risk but fail to reap disproportionately higher profits when volume soars.

Under the contribution margin approach, variable costs are subtracted from revenue to determine the *contribution margin*. Fixed costs are then subtracted from the contribution margin to determine net income. The contribution margin represents the amount available to pay fixed costs and provide a profit. Although not permitted by GAAP for external reporting, many companies use the contribution margin format for internal reporting purposes.

The *break-even point* (the point where total revenue equals total cost) in units can be determined by dividing fixed costs by the contribution margin per unit. The break-even point in sales dollars can be determined by multiplying the number of break-even units by the sales price per unit. To determine sales in units to obtain a designated profit, the sum of fixed costs and desired profit is divided by the contribution margin per unit.

The *margin of safety* is the number of units or the amount of sales dollars by which actual sales can fall below expected sales before a loss is incurred. The margin of safety can also be expressed as a percentage to permit comparing different size companies. The margin of safety can be computed as a percentage by dividing the difference between budgeted sales and break-even sales by the amount of budgeted sales.

A Look Forward

The next chapter begins investigating cost measurement. Accountants seek to determine the cost of certain objects. A cost object may be a product, a service, a department, a customer, or any other thing for which the cost is being determined. Some costs can be directly traced to a cost object, while others are difficult to trace. Costs that are difficult to trace to cost objects are called *indirect costs,* or *overhead.* Indirect costs are assigned to cost objects through *cost allocation.* The next chapter introduces the basic concepts and procedures of cost allocation.

 Video lectures and accompanying self-assessment quizzes are available in *Connect* for all learning objectives.

 SELF-STUDY REVIEW PROBLEM 1

Mensa Mountaineering Company (MMC) provides guided mountain climbing expeditions in the Rocky Mountains. Its only major expense is guide salaries; it pays each guide $4,800 per climbing expedition. MMC charges its customers $1,500 per expedition and expects to take five climbers on each expedition.

Part 1

Base your answers on the preceding information.

Required

a. Determine the total cost of guide salaries and the cost of guide salaries per climber assuming that four, five, or six climbers are included in a trip. Relative to the number of climbers in a single expedition, is the cost of guides a fixed or a variable cost?

b. Relative to the number of expeditions, is the cost of guides a fixed or a variable cost?

c. Determine the profit of an expedition assuming that five climbers are included in the trip.

d. Determine the profit assuming a 20 percent increase (six climbers total) in expedition revenue. What is the percentage change in profitability?

e. Determine the profit assuming a 20 percent decrease (four climbers total) in expedition revenue. What is the percentage change in profitability?

f. Explain why a 20 percent shift in revenue produces more than a 20 percent shift in profitability. What term describes this phenomenon?

Part 2

Assume that the guides offer to make the climbs for a percentage of expedition fees. Specifically, MMC will pay guides $960 per climber on the expedition. Assume also that the expedition fee charged to climbers remains at $1,500 per climber.

Required

g. Determine the total cost of guide salaries and the cost of guide salaries per climber assuming that four, five, or six climbers are included in a trip. Relative to the number of climbers in a single expedition, is the cost of guides a fixed or a variable cost?

h. Relative to the number of expeditions, is the cost of guides a fixed or a variable cost?

i. Determine the profit of an expedition assuming that five climbers are included in the trip.

j. Determine the profit assuming a 20 percent increase (six climbers total) in expedition revenue. What is the percentage change in profitability?

k. Determine the profit assuming a 20 percent decrease (four climbers total) in expedition revenue. What is the percentage change in profitability?

l. Explain why a 20 percent shift in revenue does not produce more than a 20 percent shift in profitability.

Solution to Part 1, Requirement *a*

Number of climbers (a)	4	5	6
Total cost of guide salaries (b)	$4,800	$4,800	$4,800
Cost per climber (b ÷ a)	1,200	960	800

Because the total cost remains constant (fixed) regardless of the number of climbers on a particular expedition, the cost is classified as fixed. Note that the cost per climber decreases as the number of climbers increases. This is the *per unit* behavior pattern of a fixed cost.

Solution to Part 1, Requirement *b*

Because the total cost of guide salaries changes proportionately each time the number of expeditions increases or decreases, the cost of salaries is variable relative to the number of expeditions.

Solution to Part 1, Requirements *c*, *d*, and *e*

Number of Climbers	4	Percentage Change	5	Percentage Change	6
Revenue ($1,500 per climber)	$6,000	⇐ (20%) ⇐	$7,500	⇒ +20% ⇒	$9,000
Cost of guide salaries (fixed)	4,800		4,800		4,800
Profit	$1,200	⇐ (55.6%) ⇐	$2,700	⇒ +55.6% ⇒	$4,200

Percentage change in revenue: ±$1,500 ÷ $7,500 = ±20%

Percentage change in profit: ±$1,500 ÷ $2,700 = ±55.6%

Solution to Part 1, Requirement *f*

Because the cost of guide salaries remains fixed while volume (number of climbers) changes, the change in profit, measured in absolute dollars, exactly matches the change in revenue. More specifically, each time MMC increases the number of climbers by one, revenue and profit increase by $1,500. Because the base figure for profit ($2,700) is lower than the base figure for revenue ($7,500), the percentage change in profit ($1,500 ÷ $2,700 = 55.6%) is higher than percentage change in revenue ($1,500 ÷ $7,500). This phenomenon is called *operating leverage.*

Solution for Part 2, Requirement *g*

	4	5	6
Number of climbers (a)	4	5	6
Per climber cost of guide salaries (b)	$ 960	$ 960	$ 960
Cost per climber (b × a)	3,840	4,800	5,760

Because the total cost changes in proportion to changes in the number of climbers, the cost is classified as variable. Note that the cost per climber remains constant (stays the same) as the number of climbers increases or decreases. This is the *per unit* behavior pattern of a variable cost.

Solution for Part 2, Requirement *h*

Because the total cost of guide salaries changes proportionately with changes in the number of expeditions, the cost of salaries is also variable relative to the number of expeditions.

Solution for Part 2, Requirements *i, j,* and *k*

Number of climbers (a)	4	Percentage Change	5	Percentage Change	6
Revenue ($1,500 per climber)	$6,000	⇐ (20%) ⇐	$7,500	⇒ +20% ⇒	$9,000
Cost of guide salaries (variable)	3,840		4,800		5,760
Profit	$2,160	⇐ (20%) ⇐	$2,700	⇒ +20% ⇒	$3,240

Percentage change in revenue: ±$1,500 ÷ $7,500 = ±20%

Percentage change in profit: ±$540 ÷ $2,700 = ±20%

Solution for Part 2, Requirement *l*

Because the cost of guide salaries changes when volume (number of climbers) changes, the change in net income is proportionate to the change in revenue. More specifically, each time the number of climbers increases by one, revenue increases by $1,500 and net income increases by $540 ($1,500 − $960). Accordingly, the percentage change in net income will always equal the percentage change in revenue. This means that there is no operating leverage when all costs are variable.

 Video lectures and accompanying self-assessment quizzes are available in *Connect* for all learning objectives.

 ## SELF-STUDY REVIEW PROBLEM 2

Sharp Company makes and sells pencil sharpeners. The variable cost of each sharpener is $20. The sharpeners are sold for $30 each. Fixed operating expenses amount to $40,000.

Required

a. Determine the break-even point in units and sales dollars.

b. Determine the sales volume in units and dollars that is required to attain a profit of $12,000. Verify your answer by preparing an income statement using the contribution margin format.

c. Determine the margin of safety between sales required to attain a profit of $12,000 and break-even sales.

Solution to Requirement *a*

Formula for Computing Break-Even Point in Units
Sales − Variable costs − Fixed costs = Profit
Sales price per unit (N) − Variable cost per unit (N) − Fixed costs = Profit
Contribution margin per unit (N) − Fixed costs = Profit
N = (Fixed costs + Profit) ÷ Contribution margin per unit
N = ($40,000 + 0) ÷ ($30 − $20) = 4,000 Units

Break-Even Point in Sales Dollars	
Sales price	$ 30
× Number of units	4,000
Sales volume in dollars	$120,000

Solution to Requirement *b*

Formula for Computing Unit Sales Required to Attain Desired Profit
Sales − Variable costs − Fixed costs = Profit
Sales price per unit (N) − Variable cost per unit (N) − Fixed costs = Profit
Contribution margin per unit (N) − Fixed costs = Profit
N = (Fixed costs + Profit) ÷ Contribution margin per unit
N = ($40,000 + 12,000) ÷ ($30 − $20) = 5,200 Units

Sales Dollars Required to Attain Desired Profit	
Sales price	$ 30
× Number of units	5,200
Sales volume in dollars	$156,000

Income Statement	
Sales volume in units (a)	5,200
Sales revenue (a × $30)	$156,000
Variable costs (a × $20)	(104,000)
Contribution margin	52,000
Fixed costs	(40,000)
Net income	$ 12,000

Solution to Requirement *c*

Margin of Safety Computations	Units	Dollars
Budgeted sales	5,200	$ 156,000
Break-even sales	(4,000)	(120,000)
Margin of safety	1,200	$ 36,000

Percentage Computation
$\dfrac{\text{Margin of safety in \$}}{\text{Budgeted sales}} = \dfrac{\$36,000}{\$156,000} = 23.08\%$

KEY TERMS

Activity base 415
Break-even point 416
Contribution
   margin 412

Contribution margin
   per unit 417
Cost behavior 408
Equation method 417

Fixed cost 406
Margin of safety 420
Mixed costs (semivariable
   costs) 414

Operating leverage 408
Relevant range 415
Variable cost 406

QUESTIONS

1. Define *fixed cost* and *variable cost* and give an example of each.
2. How can knowing cost behavior relative to volume fluctuations affect decision making?
3. Define the term *operating leverage* and explain how it affects profits.
4. How is operating leverage calculated?
5. Explain the limitations of using operating leverage to predict profitability.
6. If volume is increasing, would a company benefit more from a pure variable or a pure fixed cost structure? Which cost structure would be advantageous if volume is decreasing?
7. Explain the risk and rewards to a company that result from having fixed costs.
8. Are companies with predominately fixed cost

structures likely to be most profitable?
9. How is the relevant range of activity related to fixed and variable cost? Give an example of how the definitions of these costs become invalid when volume is outside the relevant range.
10. Which cost structure has the greater risk? Explain.
11. The president of Bright Corporation tells you that he sees a dim future for his company. He feels that his hands are tied because fixed costs are too high. He says that fixed costs do not change and therefore the situation is hopeless. Do you agree? Explain.
12. All costs are variable because if a business ceases operations, its costs fall to zero. Do you agree with the statement? Explain.

13. Verna Salsbury tells you that she thinks the terms fixed cost and variable cost are confusing. She notes that fixed cost per unit changes when the number of units changes. Furthermore, variable cost per unit remains fixed regardless of how many units are produced. She concludes that the terminology seems to be backward. Explain why the terminology appears to be contradictory.
14. What does the term *break-even point* mean? Name the two ways it can be measured.
15. How does a contribution margin income statement differ from the income statement used in financial reporting?
16. If Company A has a projected margin of safety of 22 percent while Company B has a margin

of safety of 52 percent, which company is at greater risk when actual sales are less than budgeted?
17. Mary Hartwell and Jane Jamail, college roommates, are considering the joint purchase of a computer that they can share to prepare class assignments. Ms. Hartwell wants a particular model that costs $2,000; Ms. Jamail prefers a more economical model that costs $1,500. In fact, Ms. Jamail is adamant about her position, refusing to contribute more than $750 toward the purchase. If Ms. Hartwell is also adamant about her position, should she accept Ms. Jamail's $750 offer and apply that amount toward the purchase of the more expensive computer?

EXERCISES—SERIES A

Exercise 11-1   *Identifying cost behavior*   LO 11-1

Rachael's Restaurant, a fast-food restaurant company, operates a chain of restaurants across the nation. Each restaurant employs eight people; one is a manager paid a salary plus a bonus equal to 4 percent of sales. Other employees, two cooks, one dishwasher, and four servers, are paid salaries. Each manager is budgeted $3,000 per month for advertising costs.

Required

Classify each of the following costs incurred by Rachael's Restaurant as fixed, variable, or mixed:

a. Advertising costs relative to the number of customers for a particular restaurant.

b. Rental costs relative to the number of restaurants.

c. Cooks' salaries at a particular location relative to the number of customers.

d. Cost of supplies (cups, plates, spoons, etc.) relative to the number of customers.

e. Manager's compensation relative to the number of customers.

f. Servers' salaries relative to the number of restaurants.

LO 11-1

Exercise 11-2 *Identifying cost behavior*

At the various activity levels shown, Harper Company incurred the following costs.

	Units Sold	20	40	60	80	100
a.	Rental cost per unit of merchandise sold	$ 36.00	$ 18.00	$ 12.00	$ 9.00	$ 7.20
b.	Total phone expense	80.00	100.00	120.00	140.00	160.00
c.	Cost per unit of supplies	1.00	1.00	1.00	1.00	1.00
d.	Total insurance cost	480.00	480.00	480.00	480.00	480.00
e.	Total salary cost	1,200.00	1,600.00	2,000.00	2,400.00	2,800.00
f.	Total cost of goods sold	1,800.00	3,600.00	5,400.00	7,200.00	9,000.00
g.	Depreciation cost per unit	240.00	120.00	80.00	60.00	48.00
h.	Total rent cost	3,200.00	3,200.00	3,200.00	3,200.00	3,200.00
i.	Total cost of shopping bags	2.00	4.00	6.00	8.00	10.00
j.	Cost per unit of merchandise sold	90.00	90.00	90.00	90.00	90.00

Required

Identify each of these costs as fixed, variable, or mixed.

LO 11-1

Exercise 11-3 *Determining fixed cost per unit*

Fanning Corporation incurs the following annual fixed costs.

Item	Cost
Depreciation	$ 80,000
Officers' salaries	190,000
Long-term lease	42,000
Property taxes	48,000

Required

Determine the total fixed cost per unit of production, assuming that Fanning produces 4,000, 4,500, or 5,000 units.

LO 11-1

Exercise 11-4 *Determining total variable cost*

The following variable production costs apply to goods made by O'Brien Manufacturing Corporation.

Item	Cost per Unit
Materials	$ 6.00
Labor	3.00
Variable overhead	3.50
Total	$12.50

Required

Determine the total variable production cost, assuming that O'Brien makes 4,000, 8,000, or 12,000 units.

Exercise 11-5   *Fixed versus variable cost behavior*

Tanaka Company's cost and production data for two recent months included the following:

	March	April
Production (units)	300	600
Rent	$1,800	$1,800
Utilities	$ 600	$1,200

Required

a. Separately calculate the rental cost per unit and the utilities cost per unit for both March and April.
b. Identify which cost is variable and which is fixed. Explain your answer.

Exercise 11-6   *Fixed versus variable cost behavior*

Leach Trophies makes and sells trophies it distributes to little league ballplayers. The company normally produces and sells between 6,000 and 12,000 trophies per year. The following cost data apply to various activity levels.

Number of Trophies	6,000	8,000	10,000	12,000
Total costs incurred				
Fixed	$ 60,000			
Variable	60,000			
Total costs	$120,000			
Cost per unit				
Fixed	$ 10.00			
Variable	10.00			
Total cost per trophy	$ 20.00			

Required

a. Complete the preceding table by filling in the missing amounts for the levels of activity shown in the first row of the table. Round all cost-per-unit figures to the nearest whole penny.
b. Explain why the total cost per trophy decreases as the number of trophies increases.

Exercise 11-7   *Graphing fixed cost behavior*

The following graph setups depict the dollar amount of fixed cost on the vertical axes and the level of activity on the horizontal axes.

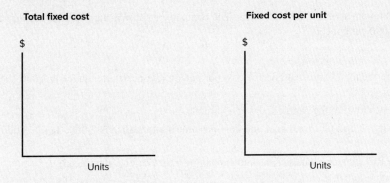

Total fixed cost   Fixed cost per unit

Required

a. Draw a line that depicts the relationship between total fixed cost and the level of activity.

b. Draw a line that depicts the relationship between fixed cost per unit and the level of activity.

LO 11-1

Exercise 11-8   *Graphing variable cost behavior*

The following graph setups depict the dollar amount of variable cost on the vertical axes and the level of activity on the horizontal axes.

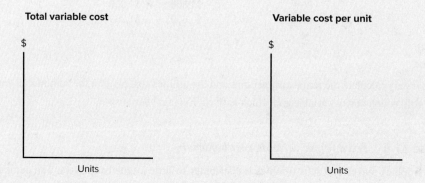

Required

a. Draw a line that depicts the relationship between total variable cost and the level of activity.

b. Draw a line that depicts the relationship between variable cost per unit and the level of activity.

LO 11-1

Exercise 11-9   *Mixed cost at different levels of activity*

Solomon Corporation paid one of its sales representatives $4,000 during the month of March. The rep is paid a base salary plus $10 per unit of product sold. During March, the rep sold 300 units.

Required

Calculate the total monthly cost of the sales representative's salary for each of the following months.

Month	April	May	June	July
Number of units sold	320	180	360	200
Total variable cost				
Total fixed cost				
Total salary cost				

LO 11-1, 11-2

Exercise 11-10   *Fixed versus variable cost behavior*

Bell Entertainment sponsors rock concerts. The company is considering a contract to hire a band at a cost of $84,000 per concert.

Required

a. What are the total band cost and the cost per person if concert attendance is 2,000, 2,500, 3,000, 3,500, or 4,000?

b. Is the cost of hiring the band a fixed or a variable cost?

c. Draw a graph and plot total cost and cost per unit if attendance is 2,000, 2,500, 3,000, 3,500, or 4,000.

d. Identify Bell's major business risks and explain how they can be minimized.

Exercise 11-11   *Fixed versus variable cost behavior*

Bell Entertainment sells souvenir T-shirts at each rock concert that it sponsors. The shirts cost $7 each. Any excess shirts can be returned to the manufacturer for a full refund of the purchase price. The sales price is $16 per shirt.

Required

a. What are the total cost of shirts and cost per shirt if sales amount to 2,000, 2,500, 3,000, 3,500, or 4,000?

b. Is the cost of T-shirts a fixed or a variable cost?

c. Draw two graphs. On one graph plot the total cost and on the other plot cost per shirt if sales amount to 2,000, 2,500, 3,000, 3,500, or 4,000.

d. Comment on Bell's likelihood of incurring a loss due to its operating activities.

Exercise 11-12   *Using fixed cost as a competitive business strategy*

The following income statements illustrate different cost structures for two competing companies.

Income Statements		
	Company Name	
	Hill	Creek
Number of customers (a)	200	200
Sales revenue (a × $200)	$40,000	$40,000
Variable cost (a × $140)	N/A	(28,000)
Variable cost (a × $0)	0	N/A
Contribution margin	40,000	12,000
Fixed cost	(28,000)	0
Net income	$12,000	$12,000

Required

a. Reconstruct Hill's income statement, assuming that it serves 400 customers when it lures 200 customers away from Creek by lowering the sales price to $120 per customer.

b. Reconstruct Creek's income statement, assuming that it serves 400 customers when it lures 200 customers away from Hill by lowering the sales price to $120 per customer.

c. Explain why the price-cutting strategy increased Hill Company's profits but caused a net loss for Creek Company.

Exercise 11-13   *Prepare an income statement using the contribution margin approach*

AJ Manufacturing Company incurred $50,000 of fixed product cost and $40,000 of variable product cost during its first year of operation. Also during its first year, AJ incurred $16,000 of fixed and $13,000 of variable selling and administrative costs. The company sold all of the units it produced for $160,000.

Required

a. Prepare an income statement using the format required by generally accepted accounting principles (GAAP).

b. Prepare an income statement using the contribution margin approach.

c. Explain why both statements have the same amount of net income.

Exercise 11-14   *Determining variable cost from incomplete cost data*

Estrada Corporation produced 300,000 watches that it sold for $35 each. The company determined that fixed manufacturing cost per unit was $14 per watch. The company reported a $2,700,000 gross margin on its financial statements.

Required

Determine the variable cost per unit, the total variable cost, and the total contribution margin.

Exercise 11-15   *Using contribution margin format income statement to measure the magnitude of operating leverage*

The following income statement was drawn from the records of Joel Company, a merchandising firm.

JOEL COMPANY	
Income Statement	
for the Year Ended December 31	
Sales revenue (2,000 units × $125)	$250,000
Cost of goods sold (2,000 units × $65)	(130,000)
Gross margin	120,000
Sales commissions (10% of sales)	(25,000)
Administrative salaries expense	(30,000)
Advertising expense	(20,000)
Depreciation expense	(24,000)
Shipping and handling expenses (2,000 units × $1.00)	(2,000)
Net income	$ 19,000

Required

a. Reconstruct the income statement using the contribution margin format.

b. Calculate the magnitude of operating leverage. Round the answer to two decimal places.

c. Use the measure of operating leverage to determine the amount of net income Joel will earn if sales increase by 10 percent.

Exercise 11-16   *Assessing the magnitude of operating leverage*

The following income statement applies to Kawai Company for the current year.

Income Statement	
Sales revenue (200 units × $60)	$12,000
Variable cost (200 units × $36)	(7,200)
Contribution margin	4,800
Fixed costs	(1,600)
Net income	$ 3,200

Required

a. Use the contribution margin approach to calculate the magnitude of operating leverage.

b. Use the operating leverage measure computed in Requirement *a* to determine the amount of net income that Kawai Company will earn if it experiences a 10 percent increase in revenue. The sales price per unit is not affected.

c. Verify your answer to Requirement *b* by constructing an income statement based on a 10 percent increase in sales revenue. The sales price is not affected. Calculate the percentage change in net income for the two income statements.

Exercise 11-17 *Break-even point* LO 11-5

Chang Corporation sells products for $120 each that have variable costs of $80 per unit. Chang's annual fixed cost is $720,000.

Required

Use the per-unit contribution margin approach to determine the break-even point in units and dollars.

Exercise 11-18 *Desired profit* LO 11-5

Santiago Company incurs annual fixed costs of $66,000. Variable costs for Santiago's product are $34 per unit, and the sales price is $50 per unit. Santiago desires to earn an annual profit of $34,000.

Required

Use the per unit contribution margin approach to determine the sales volume in units and dollars required to earn the desired profit.

Exercise 11-19 *Margin of safety* LO 11-6

Information concerning a product produced by Ender Company appears here:

Sales price per unit	$ 200
Variable cost per unit	$ 80
Total annual fixed manufacturing and operating costs	$600,000

Required

Determine the following:

a. Contribution margin per unit.
b. Number of units that Ender must sell to break even.
c. Sales level in units that Ender must reach to earn a profit of $240,000.
d. Determine the margin of safety in units, sales dollars, and as a percentage. Round the percentage to one decimal place.

Exercise 11-20 *Margin of safety* LO 11-6

Owen Company makes a product that sells for $61 per unit. The company pays $37 per unit for the variable costs of the product and incurs annual fixed costs of $360,000. Owen expects to sell 20,000 units of product.

Required

Determine Owen's margin of safety expressed as a percentage.

PROBLEMS—SERIES A

connect An electronic auto-gradable version of the Series A Problems is available in Connect. A PDF version of Series B Problems is in Connect under the "Additional Student Resources" tab. Solutions to the Series B Problems are available in Connect under the "Instructor Library" tab. Instructor and student Workpapers for the Series B Problems are available in Connect under the "Instructor Library" and "Additional Student Resources" tabs respectively.

Problem 11-21 *Identifying cost behavior* LO 11-1

Required

Identify the following costs as fixed or variable:

Costs related to plane trips between Boston, Massachusetts, and San Diego, California, follow. Pilots are paid on a per-trip basis.

a. Pilots' salaries relative to the number of trips flown.
b. Depreciation relative to the number of planes in service.

c. Cost of refreshments relative to the number of passengers.

d. Pilots' salaries relative to the number of passengers on a particular trip.

e. Cost of a maintenance check relative to the number of passengers on a particular trip.

f. Fuel costs relative to the number of trips.

Metro National Bank operates several branch offices in grocery stores. Each branch employs a supervisor and two tellers. Costs related to Metro's branch operations follow.

g. Tellers' salaries relative to the number of tellers in a particular district, which is composed of branches.

h. Supplies cost relative to the number of transactions processed in a particular branch.

i. Tellers' salaries relative to the number of customers served at a particular branch.

j. Supervisors' salaries relative to the number of branches operated.

k. Supervisors' salaries relative to the number of customers served in a particular branch.

l. Facility rental costs relative to the size of customer deposits.

Costs related to operating a fast-food restaurant follow.

m. Depreciation of equipment relative to the number of restaurants.

n. Building rental cost relative to the number of customers served in a particular restaurant.

o. Manager's salary of a particular store relative to the number of employees.

p. Food cost relative to the number of customers.

q. Utility cost relative to the number of restaurants in operation.

r. Company president's salary relative to the number of restaurants in operation.

s. Land costs relative to the number of hamburgers sold at a particular restaurant.

t. Depreciation of equipment relative to the number of customers served at a particular restaurant.

LO 11-1

CHECK FIGURES

c. Total supplies cost for cleaning 30 houses: $210

d. Total cost for 20 houses: $1,740

Problem 11-22   *Cost behavior and averaging*

Janice Huffman has decided to start Janice Cleaning, a residential housecleaning service company. She is able to rent cleaning equipment at a cost of $600 per month. Labor costs are expected to be $50 per house cleaned and supplies are expected to cost $7 per house.

Required

a. Determine the total expected cost of equipment rental and the average expected cost of equipment rental per house cleaned, assuming that Janice Cleaning cleans 10, 20, or 30 houses during one month. Is the cost of equipment a fixed or a variable cost?

b. Determine the total expected cost of labor and the average expected cost of labor per house cleaned, assuming that Janice Cleaning cleans 10, 20, or 30 houses during one month. Is the cost of labor a fixed or a variable cost?

c. Determine the total expected cost of supplies and the average expected cost of supplies per house cleaned, assuming that Janice Cleaning cleans 10, 20, or 30 houses during one month. Is the cost of supplies a fixed or a variable cost?

d. Determine the total expected cost of cleaning houses, assuming that Janice Cleaning cleans 10, 20, or 30 houses during one month.

e. Determine the average expected cost per house, assuming that Janice Cleaning cleans 10, 20, or 30 houses during one month. Why does the cost per unit decrease as the number of houses increases?

f. If Ms. Huffman tells you that she prices her services at 30 percent above cost, would you assume that she means average or actual cost? Why?

LO 11-1

CHECK FIGURE

b. Average teller cost for 60,000 transactions: $1.60

Problem 11-23   *Context-sensitive nature of cost behavior classifications*

Seattle Bank's start-up division establishes new branch banks. Each branch opens with three tellers. Total teller cost per branch is $96,000 per year. The three tellers combined can process up to 90,000 customer transactions per year. If a branch does not attain a volume of at least 60,000 transactions during its first year of operations, it is closed. If the demand for services exceeds 90,000 transactions, an additional teller is hired and the branch is transferred from the start-up division to regular operations.

Required

a. What is the relevant range of activity for new branch banks?

b. Determine the amount of teller cost in total and the average teller cost per transaction for a branch that processes 60,000, 70,000, 80,000, or 90,000 transactions. In this case (the activity base is the number of transactions for a specific branch), is the teller cost a fixed or a variable cost? Round your figures to two decimal points.

c. Determine the amount of teller cost in total and the average teller cost per branch for Seattle Bank, assuming that the start-up division operates 10, 15, 20, or 25 branches. In this case (the activity base is the number of branches), is the teller cost a fixed or a variable cost?

Problem 11-24   *Context-sensitive nature of cost behavior classifications*

LO 11-1

Rita Jekyll operates a sales booth in computer software trade shows, selling an accounting software package, *Abacus*. She purchases the package from a software company for $210 each. Booth space at the convention hall costs $8,400 per show.

CHECK FIGURES
a. Average cost at 400 units: $231
b. Average price at 250 units: $293.60

Required

a. Sales at past trade shows have ranged between 200 and 400 software packages per show. Determine the average cost of sales per unit if Ms. Jekyll sells 200, 250, 300, 350, or 400 units of *Abacus* at a trade show. Use the following chart to organize your answer. Is the cost of booth space fixed or variable? Round your computation to two decimal points.

	Sales Volume in Units (a)				
	200	250	300	350	400
Total cost of software (a × $210)	$42,000				
Total cost of booth rental	8,400				
Total cost of sales (b)	$50,400				
Average cost per unit (b ÷ a)	$ 252				

b. If Ms. Jekyll wants to earn a $50 profit on each package of software she sells at a trade show, what price must she charge at sales volumes of 200, 250, 300, 350, or 400 units?

c. Record the total cost of booth space if Ms. Jekyll attends one, two, three, four, or five trade shows. Record your answers in the following chart. Is the cost of booth space fixed or variable relative to the number of shows attended?

	Number of Trade Shows Attended				
	1	2	3	4	5
Total cost of booth rental	$8,400				

d. Ms. Jekyll provides decorative shopping bags to customers who purchase software packages. Some customers take the bags; others do not. Some customers stuff more than one software package into a single bag. The number of bags varies in relation to the number of units sold, but the relationship is not proportional. Assume that Ms. Jekyll uses $30 of bags for every 50 software packages sold. What is the additional cost per unit sold? Is the cost fixed or variable?

Problem 11-25   *Effects of operating leverage on profitability*

LO 11-2

Franklin Training Services (FTS) provides instruction on the use of computer software for the employees of its corporate clients. It offers courses in the clients' offices on the clients' equipment. The only major expense FTS incurs is instructor salaries; it pays instructors $6,000 per course taught. FTS recently agreed to offer a course of instruction to the employees of Novak Incorporated at a price of $700 per student. Novak estimated that 20 students would attend the course.

Base your answers on the preceding information.

Part 1:

Required

a. Relative to the number of students in a single course, is the cost of instruction a fixed or a variable cost?

b. Determine the profit, assuming that 20 students attend the course.

c. Determine the profit, assuming a 10 percent increase in enrollment (i.e., enrollment increases to 22 students). What is the percentage change in profitability?

d. Determine the profit, assuming a 10 percent decrease in enrollment (i.e., enrollment decreases to 18 students). What is the percentage change in profitability?

e. Explain why a 10 percent shift in enrollment produces more than a 10 percent shift in profitability. Use the term that identifies this phenomenon.

Part 2:

The instructor has offered to teach the course for a percentage of tuition fees. Specifically, she wants $300 per person attending the class. Assume that the tuition fee remains at $700 per student.

Required

f. Is the cost of instruction a fixed or a variable cost?

g. Determine the profit, assuming that 20 students take the course.

h. Determine the profit, assuming a 10 percent increase in enrollment (i.e., enrollment increases to 22 students). What is the percentage change in profitability?

i. Determine the profit, assuming a 10 percent decrease in enrollment (i.e., enrollment decreases to 18 students). What is the percentage change in profitability?

j. Explain why a 10 percent change in enrollment produces a proportional 10 percent change in profitability.

Part 3:

FTS sells a workbook with printed material unique to each course to each student who attends the course. Any workbooks that are not sold must be destroyed. Prior to the first class, FTS printed 20 copies of the books based on the client's estimate of the number of people who would attend the course. Each workbook costs $30 and is sold to course participants for $50. This cost includes a royalty fee paid to the author and the cost of duplication.

Required

k. Calculate the workbook cost in total and per student, assuming that 18, 20, or 22 students attempt to attend the course. Round your computation to two decimal points.

l. Classify the cost of workbooks as fixed or variable relative to the number of students attending the course.

m. Discuss the risk of holding inventory as it applies to the workbooks.

n. Explain how a just-in-time inventory system can reduce the cost and risk of holding inventory.

Problem 11-26 *Effects of fixed and variable cost behavior on the risk and rewards of business opportunities*

Kenton and Denton Universities offer executive training courses to corporate clients. Kenton pays its instructors $5,000 per course taught. Denton pays its instructors $250 per student enrolled in the class. Both universities charge executives a $450 tuition fee per course attended.

Required

a. Prepare income statements for Kenton and Denton, assuming that 20 students attend a course.

b. Kenton University embarks on a strategy to entice students from Denton by lowering its tuition to $240 per course. Prepare an income statement for Kenton assuming that the university is successful and enrolls 40 students in its course.

c. Denton University embarks on a strategy to entice students from Kenton University by lowering its tuition to $240 per course. Prepare an income statement for Denton, assuming that the university is successful and enrolls 40 students in its course.

d. Explain why the strategy described in Requirement *b* produced a profit but the same strategy described in Requirement *c* produced a loss.

e. Prepare income statements for Kenton and Denton Universities, assuming that 10 students attend a course, and assuming that both universities charge executives a $450 tuition fee per course attended.

f. It is always better to have fixed rather than variable cost. Explain why this statement is false.

g. It is always better to have variable rather than fixed cost. Explain why this statement is false.

Problem 11-27   *Analyzing operating leverage*

LO 11-3, 11-4

Arnold Vimka is a venture capitalist facing two alternative investment opportunities. He intends to invest $800,000 in a start-up firm. He is nervous, however, about future economic volatility. He asks you to analyze the following financial data for the past year's operations of the two firms he is considering and give him some business advice.

	Company Name	
	Larson	Benson
Variable cost per unit (a)	$ 16.00	$ 7.00
Sales revenue (8,000 units × $25)	$200,000	$200,000
Variable cost (8,000 units × a)	(128,000)	(56,000)
Contribution margin	72,000	144,000
Fixed cost	(24,000)	(96,000)
Net income	$ 48,000	$ 48,000

Required

Round your figures to two decimal points in all required computation.

a. Use the contribution margin approach to compute the operating leverage for each firm.

b. If the economy expands in coming years, Larson and Benson will both enjoy a 10 percent per year increase in sales, assuming that the selling price remains unchanged. Compute the change in net income for each firm in *dollar amount* and in *percentage*. (*Note:* Since the number of units increases, both revenue and variable cost will increase.)

c. If the economy contracts in coming years, Larson and Benson will both suffer a 10 percent decrease in sales volume, assuming that the selling price remains unchanged. Compute the change in net income for each firm in *dollar amount* and in *percentage*. (*Note:* Since the number of units decreases, both total revenue and total variable cost will decrease.)

d. Write a memo to Arnold Vimka with your analyses and advice.

CHECK FIGURES
b. % of change for Larson: 15.00
c. % of change for Benson: (30.00)

Problem 11-28   *Determining the break-even point and preparing a contribution margin income statement*

LO 11-3, 11-5

Ritchie Manufacturing Company makes a product that it sells for $150 per unit. The company incurs variable manufacturing costs of $60 per unit. Variable selling expenses are $18 per unit, annual fixed manufacturing costs are $480,000, and fixed selling and administrative costs are $240,000 per year.

Required

Determine the break-even point in units and dollars using each of the following approaches:

a. Use the equation method.

b. Use the contribution margin per unit approach.

c. Confirm your results by preparing a contribution margin income statement for the break-even sales volume.

CHECK FIGURE
a. 10,000 units

Problem 11-29 *Margin of safety and operating leverage*

Hampton Company is considering the addition of a new product to its cosmetics line. The company has three distinctly different options: a skin cream, a bath oil, or a hair coloring gel. Relevant information and budgeted annual income statements for each of the products follow.

Relevant Information	Skin Cream	Bath Oil	Color Gel
Budgeted sales in units (a)	120,000	216,000	72,000
Expected sales price (b)	$ 7.00	$ 4.00	$ 10.00
Variable costs per unit (c)	$ 2.00	$ 1.00	$ 6.00
Income statements			
Sales revenue (a × b)	$840,000	$864,000	$720,000
Variable costs (a × c)	(240,000)	(216,000)	(432,000)
Contribution margin	600,000	648,000	288,000
Fixed costs	(480,000)	(540,000)	(120,000)
Net income	$120,000	$108,000	$168,000

Required

a. Determine the margin of safety as a percentage for each product. Round your figures to two decimal points.

b. Prepare revised income statements for each product, assuming a 25 percent increase in the budgeted sales volume.

c. For each product, determine the percentage change in net income that results from the 25 percent increase in sales. Which product has the highest operating leverage? Round your figures to two decimal points.

d. Assuming that management is pessimistic and risk averse, which product should the company add to its cosmetics line? Explain your answer.

e. Assuming that management is optimistic and risk aggressive, which product should the company add to its cosmetics line? Explain your answer.

ANALYZE, THINK, COMMUNICATE

ATC 11-1   Business Applications   *Operating leverage*

Description of business for Facebook, Inc.

Our mission is to give people the power to share and make the world more open and connected. Our top priority is to build useful and engaging products that enable people to connect and share through mobile devices, personal computers, and other surfaces. We also help people discover and learn about what is going on in the world around them, enable people to share their opinions, ideas, photos and videos, and other activities with audiences ranging from their closest friends to the public at large, and stay connected everywhere by accessing our products.

Facebook, Inc.	2016	2015
Revenue	$27,638	$17,928
Operating earnings	12,427	6,225

Description of business for Lowe's Companies, Inc.

Lowe's Companies, Inc. and subsidiaries (the Company or Lowe's) is a Fortune® 50 company and the world's second largest home improvement retailer. As of February 3, 2017, Lowe's operated 2,129 home improvement and hardware stores, representing approximately 213 million square feet of retail selling space.

These operations were comprised of 1,820 stores located across 50 U.S. states, including 87 Orchard Supply Hardware (Orchard) stores, as well as 299 stores in Canada, and 10 stores in Mexico.

Lowe's, Inc.	2016	2015
Revenue	$65,017	$59,074
Operating earnings	5,846	4,971

Required

a. Determine which company appears to have the higher operating leverage.

b. Write a paragraph or two explaining why the company you identified in Requirement *a* might be expected to have the higher operating leverage.

c. If revenues for both companies increased by 5 percent, which company do you think would likely experience the greater percentage increase in operating earnings? Explain your answer.

ATC 11-2   Group Assignment   *Operating leverage*

The Parent Teacher Association (PTA) of Meadow High School is planning a fund-raising campaign. The PTA is considering the possibility of hiring Eric Logan, a world-renowned investment counselor, to address the public. Tickets would sell for $28 each. The school has agreed to let the PTA use Harville Auditorium at no cost. Mr. Logan is willing to accept one of two compensation arrangements. He will sign an agreement to receive a fixed fee of $10,000 regardless of the number of tickets sold. Alternatively, he will accept payment of $20 per ticket sold. In communities similar to that in which Meadow is located, Mr. Logan has drawn an audience of approximately 500 people.

Required

a. In front of the class, present a statement showing the expected net income assuming 500 people buy tickets.

b. The instructor will divide the class into groups and then organize the groups into four sections. The instructor will assign one of the following tasks to each section of groups.

Group Tasks

(1) Assume the PTA pays Mr. Logan a fixed fee of $10,000. Determine the amount of net income that the PTA will earn if ticket sales are 10 percent higher than expected. Calculate the percentage change in net income.

(2) Assume the PTA pays Mr. Logan a fixed fee of $10,000. Determine the amount of net income that the PTA will earn if ticket sales are 10 percent lower than expected. Calculate the percentage change in net income.

(3) Assume the PTA pays Mr. Logan $20 per ticket sold. Determine the amount of net income that the PTA will earn if ticket sales are 10 percent higher than expected. Calculate the percentage change in net income.

(4) Assume the PTA pays Mr. Logan $20 per ticket sold. Determine the amount of net income that the PTA will earn if ticket sales are 10 percent lower than expected. Calculate the percentage change in net income.

c. Have each group select a spokesperson. Have one of the spokespersons in each section of groups go to the board and present the results of the analysis conducted in Requirement *b*. Resolve any discrepancies between the computations presented at the board and those developed by the other groups.

d. Draw conclusions regarding the risks and rewards associated with operating leverage. At a minimum, answer the following questions:

(1) Which type of cost structure (fixed or variable) produces the higher growth potential in profitability for a company?

(2) Which type of cost structure (fixed or variable) faces the higher risk of declining profitability for a company?

(3) Under what circumstances should a company seek to establish a fixed cost structure?

(4) Under what circumstances should a company seek to establish a variable cost structure?

ATC 11-3 Research Assignment *Fixed versus variable cost*

Use the 2017 Form 10-K for Stanley Black & Decker, Inc. to complete the following requirements. To obtain the Form 10-K, you can use the EDGAR system (see Appendix A at the back of this text for instructions), or it can be found under "Corporate" and "Investor Information" on the company's corporate website at www.stanleyblackanddecker.com. Be sure to read carefully the following portions of the document:

- "Item 1. Business" on pages 3–4.
- "Consolidated Statement of Operations" on page 57.

Required

a. Calculate the percentage increase in Stanley's sales and its "earnings from continuing operations" from 2016 to 2017.

b. Would fixed costs or variable costs be more likely to explain why Stanley's operating earnings increased by a bigger percentage than its sales?

c. On page 99, Stanley reported that it incurred research and development costs of $252.3 million in 2017. If this cost is thought of in the context of the number of units of products sold, should it be considered as primarily fixed or variable in nature?

d. If the research and engineering costs are thought of in the context of the number of new products developed, should they be considered as primarily fixed or variable in nature?

ATC 11-4 Writing Assignment *Cost averaging*

Candice Sterling is a veterinarian. She has always been concerned for the pets of low-income families. These families love their pets but frequently do not have the means to provide them proper veterinary care. Dr. Sterling decides to open a part-time veterinary practice in a low-income neighborhood. She plans to volunteer her services free of charge two days per week. Clients will be charged only for the actual costs of materials and overhead. Dr. Sterling leases a small space for $300 per month. Utilities and other miscellaneous costs are expected to be approximately $180 per month. She estimates the variable cost of materials to be approximately $10 per pet served. A friend of Dr. Sterling who runs a similar type of clinic in another area of town indicates that she should expect to treat the following number of pets during her first year of operation.

Jan.	Feb.	Mar.	Apr.	May	June	July	Aug.	Sept.	Oct.	Nov.	Dec.
18	26	28	36	42	54	63	82	42	24	20	15

Dr. Sterling's friend has noticed that visits increase significantly in the summer because children who are out of school tend to bring their pets to the vet more often. Business tapers off during the winter and reaches a low point in December when people spend what little money they have on Christmas presents for their children. After looking at the data, Dr. Sterling becomes concerned that the people in the neighborhood will not be able to afford pet care during some months of operation even if it is offered at cost. For example, the cost of providing services in December would be approximately $42 per pet treated ($480 overhead ÷ 15 pets = $32 per pet, plus $10 materials cost). She is willing to provide her services free of charge, but she realizes that she cannot afford to subsidize the practice further by personally paying for the costs of materials and overhead in the months of low activity. She decides to discuss the matter with her accountant to find a way to cut costs even more. Her accountant tells her that her problem is cost *measurement* rather than cost *cutting*.

Required

Assume that you are Dr. Sterling's accountant. Write a memo describing a pricing strategy that resolves the apparent problem of high costs during months of low volume. Recommend in your memo the price to charge per pet treated during the month of December.

ATC 11-5 Ethical Dilemma *Profitability versus social conscience (effects of cost behavior)*

Advances in biological technology have enabled two research companies, Bio Labs, Inc. and Scientific Associates, to develop an insect-resistant corn seed. Neither company is financially strong enough to develop the distribution channels necessary to bring the product to world markets. World Agra

Distributors, Inc. has negotiated contracts with both companies for the exclusive right to market their seed. Bio Labs signed an agreement to receive an annual royalty of $1,000,000. In contrast, Scientific Associates chose an agreement that provides for a royalty of $0.50 per pound of seed sold. Both agreements have a 10-year term. During Year 1, World Agra sold approximately 1,600,000 pounds of the Bio Labs, Inc. seed and 2,400,000 pounds of the Scientific Associates seed. Both types of seed were sold for $1.25 per pound. By the end of Year 1, it was apparent that the seed developed by Scientific Associates was superior. Although insect infestation was virtually nonexistent for both types of seed, the seed developed by Scientific Associates produced corn that was sweeter and had consistently higher yields.

World Agra Distributors's chief financial officer, Roger Weatherstone, recently retired. To the astonishment of the annual planning committee, Mr. Weatherstone's replacement, Ray Borrough, adamantly recommended that the marketing department develop a major advertising campaign to promote the seed developed by Bio Labs, Inc. The planning committee reluctantly approved the recommendation. A $100,000 ad campaign was launched; the ads emphasized the ability of the Bio Labs seed to avoid insect infestation. The campaign was silent with respect to taste or crop yield. It did not mention the seed developed by Scientific Associates. World Agra's sales staff was instructed to push the Bio Labs seed and to sell the Scientific Associates seed only on customer demand. Although total sales remained relatively constant during Year 2, sales of the Scientific Associates seed fell to approximately 1,300,000 pounds while sales of the Bio Labs, Inc. seed rose to 2,700,000 pounds.

Required

a. Determine the amount of increase or decrease in profitability experienced by World Agra in Year 2 as a result of promoting the Bio Labs seed. Support your answer with appropriate commentary.

b. Did World Agra's customers in particular and society in general benefit or suffer from the decision to promote the Bio Labs seed?

c. Review the statement of ethical professional practice in Exhibit 10.19 of Chapter 10 and comment on whether Mr. Borrough's recommendation violated any of the standards in the code of ethical conduct.

d. Comment on your belief regarding the adequacy of the statement of ethical professional practice in terms of directing the conduct of management accountants.

Cost Accumulation, Tracing, and Allocation

CHAPTER OPENING

What does it cost? This is one of the questions most frequently asked by business managers. Managers must have reliable cost estimates to price products, evaluate performance, control operations, and prepare financial statements. As this discussion implies, managers need to know the cost of many different things. The things for which we are trying to determine the cost are commonly called **cost objects.** For example, if we are trying to determine the cost of operating a department, that department is the cost object. Cost objects may be products, processes, departments, services, activities, and so on. This chapter explains techniques managerial accountants use to determine the cost of a variety of cost objects.

The Curious Accountant

A former patient of a California hospital complained about being charged $7 for a single aspirin tablet. After all, an entire bottle of 100 aspirins can be purchased at the local pharmacy store for around $2.

Can you think of any reasons, other than shameless profiteering, that a hospital would need to charge $7 for an aspirin? Remember that the hospital is not just selling the aspirin; it is also delivering it to the patient. (Answer on page 450.)

Ariel Skelley/Blend Images

DETERMINE THE COST OF COST OBJECTS

Identify cost objects and distinguish between direct costs versus indirect costs.

Allen Donikowski/Moment/Getty Images

Accountants use **cost accumulation** to determine the cost of a particular object. Suppose the Atlanta Braves advertising manager wants to promote a Tuesday night ball game by offering free baseball caps to all children who attend. What would be the promotion cost? The team's accountant must *accumulate* many individual costs and add them together. For simplicity, consider only three cost components: (1) the cost of the caps, (2) the cost of advertising the promotion, and (3) the cost of an employee to work on the promotion.

Cost accumulation begins with identifying the cost objects. The primary cost object is the cost of the promotion. Three secondary cost objects are (1) the cost of caps, (2) the cost of advertising, and (3) the cost of labor. The costs of the secondary cost objects are combined to determine the cost of the primary cost object.

Determining the costs of the secondary cost objects requires identifying what *drives* those costs. A **cost driver** has a *cause-and-effect* relationship with a cost object. For example, the *number of caps* (cost driver) has an effect on the *cost of caps* (cost object). The *number of advertisements* is a cost driver for the *advertising cost* (cost object); the *number of labor hours* worked is a cost driver for the *labor cost* (cost object). Using the following assumptions about unit costs and cost drivers, the accumulated cost of the primary cost object (cost of the cap promotion) is:

Cost Object	Cost per Unit	×	Cost Driver	=	Total Cost of Object
Cost of caps	$ 2.50	×	4,000 Caps	=	$10,000
Cost of advertising	$100.00	×	50 Advertisements	=	5,000
Cost of labor	$ 8.00	×	100 Hours	=	800
Cost of cap promotion					$15,800

The Atlanta Braves should run the promotion if management expects it to produce additional revenues exceeding $15,800.

Estimated versus Actual Cost

The accumulated cost of the promotion—$15,800—is an *estimate.* Management cannot know *actual* costs and revenues until after running the promotion. While actual information is more accurate, it is not relevant for deciding whether to run the promotion because the decision must be made before the actual cost is known. Managers must accept a degree of inaccuracy in exchange for the relevance of timely information. Many business decisions are based on estimated rather than actual costs.

Managers use cost estimates to set prices, bid on contracts, evaluate proposals, distribute resources, plan production, and set goals. Certain circumstances, however, require actual cost data. For example, published financial reports and managerial performance evaluations use actual cost data. Managers frequently accumulate both estimated and actual cost data for the same cost object. For example, companies use cost estimates to establish goals and use actual costs to evaluate management performance in meeting those goals. The following discussion provides a number of business examples that use estimated data, actual data, or a combination of both.

Assignment of Costs to Objects in a Retail Business

Exhibit 12.1 displays the January income statement for In Style, Inc. (ISI), a retail clothing store. ISI subdivides its operations into women's, men's, and children's departments. To encourage the departmental managers to maximize sales, ISI began

paying the manager of each department a bonus based on a percentage of departmental sales revenue.

Although the bonus incentive increased sales revenue, it also provoked negative consequences. The departmental managers began to argue over floor space; each manager wanted more space to display merchandise. The managers reduced prices; they increased sales commissions. In the drive to maximize sales, the managers ignored the need to control costs. To improve the situation, the store manager decided to base future bonuses on each department's contribution to profitability rather than its sales revenue.

Identifying Direct and Indirect Costs

The new bonus strategy requires determining the cost of operating each department. Each department is a separate *cost object*. Assigning costs to the departments (cost objects) requires **cost tracing** and **cost allocation. Direct costs** can be easily traced to a cost object. **Indirect costs** cannot be easily traced to a cost object. Whether or not a cost is easily traceable requires *cost/benefit analysis.*

EXHIBIT 12.1	
Income Statement	
IN STYLE, INC.	
Income Statement	
For the Month Ended January 31	
Sales	$360,000
Cost of goods sold	(216,000)
Gross margin	144,000
Sales commissions	(18,000)
Dept. managers' salaries	(12,000)
Store manager's salary	(9,360)
Depreciation	(16,000)
Rental fee for store	(18,400)
Utilities	(2,300)
Advertising	(7,200)
Supplies	(900)
Net income	$ 59,840

Some of ISI's costs can be easily traced to the cost objects (specific departments). The cost of goods sold is an example of an easily traced cost. Price tags on merchandise can be coded so cash register scanners capture the departmental code for each sale. The cost of goods sold is not only easily traceable but also very useful information. Companies need cost of goods sold information for financial reporting (income statement and balance sheet) and for management decisions (determining inventory reorder points, pricing strategies, and cost control). Because the cost of tracing *cost of goods sold* is small relative to the benefits obtained, cost of goods sold is a *direct cost.*

In contrast, the cost of supplies (shopping bags, sales slips, pens, staples, price tags) used by each department is much more difficult to trace. How could the number of staples used to seal shopping bags be traced to any particular department? The sales staff could count the number of staples used, but doing so would be silly for the benefits obtained. Although tracing the cost of supplies to each department may be possible, it is not worth the effort of doing so. The cost of supplies is therefore an *indirect cost.* Indirect costs are also called **overhead costs.**

Direct and indirect costs can be described as follows.

> **Direct costs** can be traced to cost objects in a *cost-effective* manner.
> **Indirect costs** cannot be traced to objects in a *cost-effective* manner.

By analyzing the accounting records, ISI's accountant classified the costs from the income statement in Exhibit 12.1 as direct or indirect, as shown in Exhibit 12.2. The next paragraph explains the classifications.

All figures represent January costs. Items 1 through 4 are direct costs, traceable to the cost objects in a cost-effective manner. Cost of goods sold is traced to departments at the point of sale using cash register scanners. Sales commissions are based on a percentage of departmental sales and are therefore easy to trace to the departments. Departmental managers' salaries are also easily traceable to the departments. Equipment, furniture, and fixtures are tagged with department codes that permit tracing depreciation charges directly to specific departments. Items 5 through 8 are incurred on behalf of the company as a whole and are therefore not directly traceable to a specific department. Although Item 9 could be traced to specific departments, the cost of doing so would exceed the benefits. The cost of supplies is therefore also classified as indirect.

EXHIBIT 12.2

Income Statement Classification of Costs

Cost Item	Direct Costs			Indirect Costs
	Women's	Men's	Children's	
1. Cost of goods sold—$216,000	$120,000	$58,000	$38,000	
2. Sales commissions—$18,000	9,500	5,500	3,000	
3. Dept. managers' salaries—$12,000	5,000	4,200	2,800	
4. Depreciation—$16,000	7,000	5,000	4,000	
5. Store manager's salary				$ 9,360
6. Rental fee for store				18,400
7. Utilities				2,300
8. Advertising				7,200
9. Supplies				900
Totals	$141,500	$72,700	$47,800	$38,160

Cost Classifications—Independent and Context Sensitive

Whether a cost is direct or indirect is independent of whether it is fixed or variable. In the ISI example, both cost of goods sold and the cost of supplies vary relative to sales volume (both are variable costs), but cost of goods sold is direct and the cost of supplies is indirect. Furthermore, the cost of rent and the cost of depreciation are both fixed relative to sales volume, but the cost of rent is indirect and the cost of depreciation is direct. In fact, the very same cost can be classified as direct or indirect, depending on the cost object. The store manager's salary is not directly traceable to a specific department, but it is traceable to a particular store. As these examples demonstrate, cost classification depends on the context in which the costs occur.

ALLOCATING INDIRECT COSTS TO OBJECTS

LO 12-2

Allocate indirect costs to cost objects.

Common costs support multiple cost objects but cannot be directly traced to any specific object. In the case of In Style, Inc., the cost of renting the store (common cost) supports the women's, men's, and children's departments (cost objects). The departmental managers may shirk responsibility for the rental cost by claiming that others higher up the chain of command are responsible. Responsibility can be motivated at the departmental level by assigning (*allocating*) a portion of the total rental cost to each department.

To accomplish appropriate motivation, authority must accompany responsibility. In other words, the departmental managers should be held responsible for a portion of rental cost only if they are able to exercise some degree of control over that cost. For example, if managers are assigned a certain amount of the rental cost for each square foot of space they use, they should have the authority to establish the size of the space used by their departments. **Controllable costs** are costs that can be influenced by a manager's decisions and actions. The controllability concept is discussed in more detail later in the text.

Cost **allocation** involves dividing a total cost into parts and assigning the parts to designated cost objects. How should ISI allocate the $38,160 of indirect costs to each of the three departments? First, identify a cost driver for each cost to be allocated. For example, there is a cause-and-effect relationship between store size and rent cost; the larger the building, the higher the rent cost. This relationship suggests that the more floor space a department occupies, the more rent cost that department should bear. To illustrate, assume ISI's store

REALITY BYTES

How does Southwest Airlines know the cost of flying a passenger from Houston, Texas, to Los Angeles, California? The fact is that Southwest does not know the actual cost of flying particular passengers anywhere. There are many indirect costs associated with flying passengers. Some of these include the cost of planes, fuel, pilots, office buildings, and ground personnel. Indeed, besides insignificant food and beverage costs, there are few costs that could be traced directly to customers. Southwest and other airlines are forced to use allocation and averaging to determine the estimated cost of providing transportation services to customers. Estimated rather than actual cost is used for decision-making purposes.

Chris Parypa/Essentials/rypson/iStockphoto

Consider that in its 2017 annual report Southwest reported the average operating expenses of flying one passenger one mile (called a *passenger mile*) were 11.4¢. However, this number was based on 153.8 billion "available passenger miles." In 2017, Southwest operated at 83.9 percent of capacity, not 100 percent, so it was able to charge passengers only for 129.0 billion passenger miles. Thus, its average operating expenses were closer to 13.6¢ for each mile for which it was able to charge. Had it operated at a higher capacity, its average costs would have been lower.

---

capacity is 23,000 square feet and the women's, men's, and children's departments occupy 12,000, 7,000, and 4,000 square feet, respectively. ISI can achieve a rational allocation of the rent cost using the following two-step process.[1]

Step 1. Compute the *allocation rate* by dividing the *total cost to be allocated* ($18,400 rental fee) by the *cost driver* (23,000 square feet of store space). The cost driver is also called the **allocation base.** This computation produces the **allocation rate**, as follows:

Total cost to be allocated ÷ Cost driver (allocation base) = Allocation rate

$18,400 rental fee ÷ 23,000 square feet = $0.80 per square foot

Step 2. Multiply the *allocation rate* by the *weight of the cost driver* (weight of the base) to determine the allocation *per cost object,* as follows.

Cost Object	Allocation Rate	×	Number of Square Feet	=	Allocation per Cost Object
Women's department	$0.80	×	12,000	=	$ 9,600
Men's department	0.80	×	7,000	=	5,600
Children's department	0.80	×	4,000	=	3,200
Total			23,000		$18,400

It is also plausible to presume utilities cost is related to the amount of floor space a department occupies. Larger departments will consume more heating, lighting, air condition-

---

[1] Other mathematical approaches achieve the same result. This text consistently uses the two-step method described here. Specifically, the text determines allocations by (1) computing a *rate* and (2) multiplying the *rate* by the *weight of the base* (cost driver).

ing, and so on than smaller departments. Floor space is a reasonable cost driver for utility cost. Based on square footage, ISI can allocate utility cost to each department as follows.

Step 1. Compute the allocation rate by dividing the total cost to be allocated ($2,300 utility cost) by the cost driver (23,000 square feet of store space):

Total cost to be allocated ÷   Cost driver   =   Allocation rate

$2,300 utility cost   ÷ $23,000 square feet = $0.10 per square foot

Step 2. Multiply the *allocation rate* by the *weight of the cost driver* to determine the allocation *per cost object.*

Cost Object	Allocation Rate	×	Number of Square Feet	=	Allocation per Cost Object
Women's department	$0.10	×	12,000	=	$1,200
Men's department	0.10	×	7,000	=	700
Children's department	0.10	×	4,000	=	400
Total			23,000		$2,300

 CHECK YOURSELF 12.1

HealthCare, Inc. wants to estimate the cost of operating the three departments (Dermatology, Gynecology, and Pediatrics) that serve patients in its Health Center. Each department performed the following number of patient treatments during the most recent year of operation: Dermatology, 2,600; Gynecology, 3,500; and Pediatrics, 6,200. The annual salary of the Health Center's program administrator is $172,200. How much of the salary cost should HealthCare allocate to the Pediatrics department?

Answer

Step 1. Compute the *allocation rate.*

Total cost to be allocated ÷ Cost driver (patient treatments) =   Allocation rate

$172,200 salary cost ÷   (2,600 + 3,500 + 6,200)   = $14 per patient treatment

Step 2. Multiply the *allocation rate* by the *weight of the cost driver* (weight of the base) to determine the allocation per *cost object.*

Cost Object	Allocation Rate	×	No. of Treatments	=	Allocation per Cost Object
Pediatrics department	$14	×	6,200	=	$ 86,800

Determining the Cost to Be Allocated Using Cost Pools

Allocating *individually* every single indirect cost a company incurs would be tedious and not particularly useful relative to the benefit obtained. Instead, companies frequently accumulate many individual costs into a single **cost pool.** The total of the pooled cost is then allocated to the cost objects. For example, a company may accumulate costs for gas, water, electricity, and telephone service into a single utilities cost pool. It would then allocate the total cost in the utilities cost pool to the cost objects rather than individually allocating each of the four types of utility costs.

How far should pooling costs go? Why not pool utility costs with indirect labor costs? If the forces driving the utility costs are different from the forces driving the labor costs, pooling the costs will likely reduce the reliability of any associated cost allocations. To promote accuracy, pooling should be limited to costs with common cost drivers.

Costs that have been pooled for one purpose may require disaggregation for a different purpose. Suppose all overhead costs are pooled for the purpose of determining the cost of making a product. Further, suppose that making the product requires two processes that are performed in different departments. A cutting department makes heavy use of machinery to cut raw materials into product parts. An assembly department uses human labor to assemble the parts into a finished product. Now suppose the objective changes from determining the cost of making the product to determining the cost of operating each department. Under these circumstances, it may be necessary to disaggregate the total overhead cost into smaller pools such as a utility cost pool, an indirect labor cost pool, and so on so that different drivers can be used to allocate these costs to the two departments.

SELECTING THE COST DRIVER

Companies can frequently identify more than one cost driver for a particular indirect cost. For example, ISI's cost of shopping bags provided to customers can be linked to both the number of sales transactions and the total amount of sales. More specifically, since the store normally uses at least one shopping bag each time a sales transaction occurs, the number of sales transactions drives the cost of shopping bags. Likewise, a $500 sales transaction is likely to require the company to provide more shopping bags to a customer than would a $100 sales transaction. Therefore, the total amount of sales also drives the use of shopping bags. Given this scenario, should ISI use the *number of sales transactions* or the *total amount of sales* as the driver of the cost of shopping bags? The answer is, ISI should use the driver with the strongest cause-and-effect relationship.

Identify the most appropriate cost driver.

Cause and Effect versus Availability of Information

To illustrate, consider shopping bag usage for T-shirts sold in the children's department versus T-shirts sold in the men's department. Assume ISI studied T-shirt sales during the first week of June and found the following.

Department	Children's	Men's
Number of sales transactions	120	92
Amount of total sales	$1,440	$1,612

Given that every sales transaction uses a shopping bag, the children's department uses far more shopping bags than the men's department (120 versus 92) even though it has a lower amount of total sales ($1,440 versus $1,612). A reasonable explanation for this circumstance is that children's T-shirts sell for less than men's T-shirts. The number of sales transactions is the better cost driver because it has a stronger cause-and-effect relationship with shopping bag usage than does the amount of sales. Should ISI therefore use the number of sales transactions to allocate supply cost to the departments? Not necessarily.

The *availability of information* also influences cost driver selection. While the number of sales transactions is the more accurate cost driver, ISI could not use this allocation base unless it maintains records of the number of sales transactions per department. If the store tracks the amount of sales but not the number of transactions, it must use the amount of sales even if the number of transactions is the better cost driver. For ISI, total sales appears to be the best *available* cost driver for allocating supply cost.

Assuming that total sales for the women's, men's, and children's departments was $190,000, $110,000, and $60,000, respectively, ISI can allocate the supplies cost as follows.

Step 1. Compute the allocation rate by dividing the total cost to be allocated ($900 supplies cost) by the cost driver ($360,000 total sales).

Total cost to be allocated ÷   Cost driver   =   Allocation rate

$900 supplies cost   ÷ $360,000 total sales = $0.0025 per sales dollar

Step 2. Multiply the allocation rate by the weight of the cost driver to determine the allocation per cost object.

Cost Object	Allocation Rate	×	Total Sales	=	Allocation per Cost Object
Women's department	$0.0025	×	$190,000	=	$475
Men's department	0.0025	×	110,000	=	275
Children's department	0.0025	×	60,000	=	150
Total			$360,000		$900

ISI believes the amount of sales is also the appropriate allocation base for advertising cost. The sales generated in each department were likely influenced by the general advertising campaign. ISI can allocate advertising cost as follows.

Step 1. Compute the allocation rate by dividing the total cost to be allocated ($7,200 advertising cost) by the cost driver ($360,000 total sales).

Total cost to be allocated ÷   Cost driver   =   Allocation rate

$7,200 advertising cost ÷ $360,000 total sales = $0.02 per sales dollar

Step 2. Multiply the allocation rate by the weight of the cost driver to determine the allocation per cost object.

Cost Object	Allocation Rate	×	Total Sales	=	Allocation per Cost Object
Women's department	$0.02	×	$190,000	=	$3,800
Men's department	0.02	×	110,000	=	2,200
Children's department	0.02	×	60,000	=	1,200
Total			$360,000		$7,200

There is no strong cause-and-effect relationship between the store manager's salary and the departments. ISI pays the store manager the same salary regardless of sales level, square footage of store space, number of labor hours, or any other identifiable variable. Because no plausible cost driver exists, ISI must allocate the store manager's salary arbitrarily. Here the manager's salary is simply divided equally among the departments as follows:

Step 1. Compute the allocation rate by dividing the total cost to be allocated ($9,360 manager's monthly salary) by the allocation base (number of departments).

Total cost to be allocated   ÷   Cost driver   =   Allocation rate

$9,360 store manager's salary ÷ 3 departments = $3,120 per department

Step 2. Multiply the allocation rate by the weight of the cost driver to determine the allocation per cost object.

Cost Object	Allocation Rate	×	Number of Departments	=	Allocation per Cost Object
Women's department	$3,120	×	1	=	$3,120
Men's department	3,120	×	1	=	3,120
Children's department	3,120	×	1	=	3,120
Total			3		$9,360

As the allocation of the store manager's salary demonstrates, many allocations are arbitrary or based on a weak relationship between the allocated cost and the allocation base (cost driver). Managers must use care when making decisions using allocated costs.

Behavioral Implications

Using the indirect cost allocations just discussed, Exhibit 12.3 shows the profit each department generated in January. ISI paid the three departmental managers bonuses based on each department's contribution to profitability. The store manager noticed an immediate change in the behavior of the departmental managers. For example, the manager of the women's department offered to give up 1,000 square feet of floor space because she believed reducing the selection of available products would not reduce sales significantly. Customers would simply buy different brands. Although sales would not decline dramatically, rent and utility cost allocations to the women's department would decline, increasing the profitability of the department.

In contrast, the manager of the children's department wanted the extra space. He believed the children's department was losing sales because it did not have enough floor space to display a competitive variety of merchandise. Customers came to the store to shop at the women's department, but they did not come specifically for children's wear. With additional space, the children's department could carry items that would draw customers to the store specifically to buy children's clothing. He believed the extra space would increase sales enough to cover the additional rent and utility cost allocations.

EXHIBIT 12.3

Profit Analysis by Department

	Department			
	Women's	Men's	Children's	Total
Sales	$190,000	$110,000	$60,000	$360,000
Cost of goods sold	(120,000)	(58,000)	(38,000)	(216,000)
Sales commissions	(9,500)	(5,500)	(3,000)	(18,000)
Dept. managers' salary	(5,000)	(4,200)	(2,800)	(12,000)
Depreciation	(7,000)	(5,000)	(4,000)	(16,000)
Store manager's salary	(3,120)	(3,120)	(3,120)	(9,360)
Rental fee for store	(9,600)	(5,600)	(3,200)	(18,400)
Utilities	(1,200)	(700)	(400)	(2,300)
Advertising	(3,800)	(2,200)	(1,200)	(7,200)
Supplies	(475)	(275)	(150)	(900)
Departmental profit	$ 30,305	$ 25,405	$ 4,130	$ 59,840

Answers to the Curious Accountant

When we compare the cost that a hospital charges for an aspirin to the price we pay for an aspirin, we are probably not considering the full cost that we incur to purchase aspirin. If someone were to ask you what you pay for an aspirin, you would probably take the price of a bottle, say $2, and divide it by the number of pills in the bottle, say 100. This would suggest their cost is $0.02 each. Now, consider what it costs to buy an aspirin when all costs are considered. First, there is your time to drive to the store; what do you get paid per hour? Then, there is the cost of operating your automobile. You get the idea; in reality, the cost of an aspirin, from a business perspective, is much more than just the cost of the pill itself.

The following exhibit shows the income statement of Hospital Corporation of America (HCA), Inc. for three recent years. HCA claims to be "one of the leading health care services companies in the United States." In 2017, it operated 299 facilities in 20 states and England. As you can see, while it generated over $47.7 billion in revenue, it also incurred a lot of expenses. Look at its first two expense categories. Although it incurred $7.3 billion in supplies expenses, it incurred over two and a half times this amount in compensation expense. In other words, it costs a lot more to have someone deliver the aspirin to your bed than the aspirin itself costs.

In 2017, HCA earned $2.7 billion from its $47.1 billion in revenues. This is a return on sales percentage of 5.8 percent ($2,743 ÷ $47,653). Therefore, on a $7 aspirin, HCA would earn 40 cents of profit, which is still not a bad profit for selling one aspirin. As a comparison, in 2017, Walgreens, which also sells aspirin, had a return on sales of 3.4 percent.

HCA, INC.
Consolidated Income Statements
For the Years Ended December 31, 2017, 2016, and 2015
(dollars in millions)

	2017	2016	2015
Revenues before the provision for doubtful accounts	$47,653	$44,747	$43,591
Provision for doubtful accounts	4,039	3,257	3,913
Revenues	43,614	41,490	39,678
Salaries and benefits	20,059	18,897	18,115
Supplies	7,316	6,933	6,638
Other operating expenses	8,051	7,496	7,056
Equity in earnings of affiliates	(45)	(54)	(46)
Depreciation and amortization	2,131	1,966	1,904
Interest expense	1,690	1,707	1,665
Losses (gains) on sales of facilities	(8)	(23)	5
Losses on retirement of debt	39	4	135
Legal claim costs (benefits)	—	(246)	249
Total expenses	39,233	36,680	35,721
Income before income taxes	4,381	4,810	3,957
Provision for income taxes	1,638	1,378	1,261
Net income	2,743	3,432	2,696
Net income attributable to noncontrolling interests	527	542	567
Net income attributable to HCA, Inc.	$ 2,216	$ 2,890	$ 2,129

The store manager was pleased with the emphasis on profitability that resulted from tracing and assigning costs to specific departments.

Cost Drivers for Variable Overhead Costs

A *causal relationship* exists between variable overhead product costs (indirect materials, indirect labor, inspection costs, utilities, etc.) and the volume of production. For example, the cost of indirect materials such as glue, staples, screws, nails, and varnish will increase or decrease in proportion to the number of desks a furniture manufacturing company makes. *Volume measures are good cost drivers* for allocating variable overhead costs.

Volume can be expressed by such measures as the number of units produced, the number of labor hours worked, or the amount of *direct* materials used in production. Given the variety of possible volume measures, how does management identify the most appropriate cost driver (allocation base) for assigning particular overhead costs? Consider the case of Filmier Furniture Company.

Using Units as the Cost Driver

During the most recent year, Filmier Furniture Company produced 4,000 chairs and 1,000 desks. It incurred $60,000 of *indirect materials* cost during the period. How much of this cost should Filmier allocate to chairs versus desks? Using number of units as the cost driver produces the following allocation.

Step 1. Compute the allocation rate.

$$\text{Total cost to be allocated} \div \text{Cost driver} = \text{Allocation rate}$$

$$\$60,000 \text{ indirect materials cost} \div 5,000 \text{ units} = \$12 \text{ per unit}$$

Step 2. Multiply the allocation rate by the weight of the cost driver to determine the allocation per cost object.

Product	Allocation Rate	×	Number of Units Produced	=	Allocated Cost
Desks	$12	×	1,000	=	$12,000
Chairs	12	×	4,000	=	48,000
Total			5,000	=	$60,000

Using Direct Labor Hours as the Cost Driver

Using the number of units as the cost driver assigns an *equal amount* ($12) of indirect materials cost to each piece of furniture. However, if Filmier uses more indirect materials to make a desk than to make a chair, assigning the same amount of indirect materials cost to each is inaccurate. Assume Filmier incurs the following direct costs to make chairs and desks.

	Desks	Chairs	Total
Direct labor hours	3,500 hrs.	2,500 hrs.	6,000 hrs.
Direct materials cost	$1,000,000	$500,000	$1,500,000

Both direct labor hours and direct materials cost are volume measures that indicate Filmier uses more indirect materials to make a desk than a chair. It makes sense that the amount of direct labor used is related to the amount of indirect materials used. Because production workers use materials to make furniture, it is plausible to assume that the more hours they work, the more materials they use. Using this reasoning, Filmier could assign the indirect materials cost to the chairs and desks as follows.

Step 1.   Compute the allocation rate.

$$\text{Total cost to be allocated} \div \text{Cost driver} = \text{Allocation rate}$$
$$\$60,000 \text{ indirect materials cost} \div 6,000 \text{ hours} = \$10 \text{ per hour}$$

Step 2.   Multiply the allocation rate by the weight of the cost driver.

Product	Allocation Rate	×	Number of Labor Hours	=	Allocated Cost
Desks	$10.00	×	3,500	=	$35,000
Chairs	10.00	×	2,500	=	25,000
Total			6,000	=	$60,000

Basing the allocation on labor hours rather than number of units assigns a significantly larger portion of the indirect materials cost to desks ($35,000 versus $12,000). Is this allocation more accurate? Suppose the desks, but not the chairs, require elaborate, labor-intensive carvings. A significant portion of the labor is then not related to consuming indirect materials (glue, staples, screws, nails, and varnish). It would therefore be inappropriate to allocate the indirect materials cost based on direct labor hours.

Using Direct Material Dollars as the Cost Driver

If labor hours is an inappropriate allocation base, Filmier can consider direct materials usage, measured in material dollars, as the allocation base. It is likely that the more lumber (direct material) Filmier uses, the more glue, nails, and so forth (indirect materials) it uses. It is reasonable to presume direct materials usage drives indirect materials usage. Using direct materials dollars as the cost driver for indirect materials produces the following allocation.

Step 1.   Compute the allocation rate.

$$\text{Total cost to be allocated} \div \text{Cost driver} = \text{Allocation rate}$$
$$\$60,000 \text{ indirect materials cost} \div \$1,500,000 \text{ direct material dollars} = \$0.04 \text{ per direct material dollar}$$

Step 2.   Multiply the allocation rate by the weight of the cost driver.

Product	Allocation Rate	×	Number of Direct Material Dollars	=	Allocated Cost
Desks	$0.04	×	$1,000,000	=	$40,000
Chairs	0.04	×	500,000	=	20,000
Total			$1,500,000	=	$60,000

Selecting the Best Cost Driver

Which of the three volume-based cost drivers (units, labor hours, or direct material dollars) results in the most accurate allocation of the overhead cost? Management must use judgment to decide. In this case, direct material dollars appears to have the most convincing relationship to indirect materials usage. If the cost Filmier was allocating were fringe benefits, however, direct labor hours would be a more appropriate cost driver. If the cost Filmier was allocating were machine maintenance cost, a different volume-based cost driver, machine hours, would be an appropriate base. The most accurate allocations of indirect costs may actually require using multiple cost drivers.

☑ CHECK YOURSELF 12.2

Boston Boat Company builds custom sailboats for customers. During the current accounting period, the company built five different-sized boats that ranged in cost from $35,000 to $185,000. The company's manufacturing overhead cost for the period was $118,000. Would you recommend using the number of units (boats) or direct labor hours as the base for allocating the overhead cost to the five boats? Why?

Answer   Using the number of units as the allocation base would assign the same amount of overhead cost to each boat. Since larger boats require more overhead cost (supplies, utilities, equipment, etc.) than smaller boats, there is no logical link between the number of boats and the amount of overhead cost required to build a particular boat. In contrast, there is a logical link between direct labor hours used and overhead cost incurred. The more labor used, the more supplies, utilities, equipment, and so on used. Since larger boats require more direct labor than smaller boats, using direct labor hours as the allocation base would allocate more overhead cost to larger boats and less overhead cost to smaller boats, producing a logical overhead allocation. Therefore, Boston should use direct labor hours as the allocation base.

Cost Drivers for Fixed Overhead Costs

Fixed costs present a different cost allocation problem. By definition, the volume of production does not drive fixed costs. Suppose Lednicky Bottling Company rents its manufacturing facility for $28,000 per year. The rental cost is fixed regardless of how much product Lednicky bottles. However, Lednicky may still use a volume-based cost driver as the allocation base. The object of allocating fixed costs to products is to distribute a *rational share* of the overhead cost to each product. Selecting an allocation base that spreads total overhead cost equally over total production often produces a rational distribution. For example, assume Lednicky produced 2,000,000 bottles of apple juice during the current accounting period. If it sold 1,800,000 bottles of the juice during this period, how much of the $28,000 rental cost should Lednicky allocate to ending inventory and to cost of goods sold? A rational allocation follows.

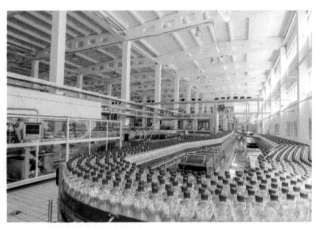
Albert Karimov/Shutterstock

Step 1.   Compute the allocation rate.

Total cost to be allocated ÷ Allocation base (cost driver) =   Allocation rate

$28,000 rental cost   ÷   2,000,000 units   = $0.014 per bottle of juice

Because the base (number of units) used to allocate the cost does not drive the cost, it is sometimes called an *allocation base* instead of a *cost driver*. However, many managers use the term cost driver in conjunction with fixed cost even though that usage is technically inaccurate. The terms allocation base and cost driver are frequently used interchangeably.

Step 2.   Multiply the allocation rate by the weight of the cost driver.

Financial Statement Item	Allocation Rate	×	Number of Bottles	=	Allocated Cost
Inventory	$0.014	×	200,000	=	$ 2,800
Cost of goods sold	0.014	×	1,800,000	=	25,200

Using number of units as the allocation base assigns equal amounts of the rental cost to each unit of product. Equal allocation is appropriate so long as the units are homogeneous. If the units are not identical, however, Lednicky may need to choose a different allocation base to rationally distribute the rental cost. For example, if some of the bottles are significantly larger than others, Lednicky may find using some physical measure, like liters of direct material used, to be a more appropriate allocation base. Whether an indirect cost is fixed or variable, selecting the most appropriate allocation base requires sound reasoning and judgment.

Allocating Fixed Costs When the Volume of Production Varies

Under certain circumstances products may be made before or after the costs associated with making them have been incurred. Suppose, for example, premiums for an annual insurance policy are paid in March. The insurance cost benefits the products made in the months before and after March as well as those produced in March. Allocation can be used to spread the insurance cost over products made during the entire accounting period rather than charging the total cost only to products made in March.

Monthly fluctuations in production volume complicate fixed cost allocations. To illustrate, assume Grave Manufacturing pays its production supervisor a monthly salary of $3,000. Furthermore, assume Grave makes 800 units of product in January and 1,875 in February. How much salary cost should Grave assign to the products made in January and February, respectively? The allocation seems simple. Just divide the $3,000 monthly salary cost by the number of units of product made each month as follows:

$$\text{January} \quad \$3,000 \div \quad 800 \text{ units} = \$3.75 \text{ cost per unit}$$

$$\text{February} \quad \$3,000 \div 1,875 \text{ units} = \$1.60 \text{ cost per unit}$$

If Grave Manufacturing based a cost-plus pricing decision on these results, it would price products made in January significantly higher than products made in February. It is likely such price fluctuations would puzzle and drive away customers. Grave needs an allocation base that will spread the annual salary cost evenly over annual production. A timing problem exists, however, because Grave must allocate the salary cost before the end of the year. In order to price its products, Grave needs to know the allocated amount before the actual cost information is available. Grave can manage the timing problem by using estimated rather than actual costs.

Grave Manufacturing can *estimate* the annual cost of the supervisor's salary (indirect labor) as $36,000 ($3,000 × 12 months). The *actual* cost of indirect labor may differ because the supervisor might receive a pay raise or be replaced with a person who earns less. Based on current information, however, $36,000 is a reasonable estimate of the annual indirect labor cost. Grave must also estimate total annual production volume. Suppose Grave produced 18,000 units last year and expects no significant change in the current year. It can allocate indirect labor cost for January and February as follows.

Step 1. Compute the allocation rate.

$$\text{Total cost to be allocated} \div \text{Allocation base (cost driver)} = \text{Allocation rate}$$

$$\$36,000 \quad \div \quad 18,000 \text{ units} \quad = \$2.00 \text{ per unit}$$

Step 2. Multiply the rate by the weight of the base (number of units per month) to determine how much of the salary cost to allocate to each month's production.

Month	Allocation Rate	×	Number of Units Produced	=	Allocation per Month
January	$2.00	×	800	=	$1,600
February	2.00	×	1,875	=	3,750

Grave Manufacturing will add these indirect cost allocations to other product costs to determine the total estimated product cost to use in cost-plus pricing or other managerial decisions.

Because the overhead allocation rate is determined *before* actual cost and volume data are available, it is called the **predetermined overhead rate.** Companies use predetermined overhead rates for product costing estimates and pricing decisions during a year, but they must use actual costs in published year-end financial statements. If necessary, companies adjust their accounting records at year-end when they have used estimated data on an interim basis. The procedures for making such adjustments are discussed in a later chapter.

THE HUMAN FACTOR: A COMPREHENSIVE EXAMPLE

Cost allocations significantly affect individuals. They may influence managers' performance evaluations and compensation. They may dictate the amount of resources various departments, divisions, and other organizational subunits receive. Control over resources usually offers managers prestige and influence over organization operations. The following scenario illustrates the emotional impact and perceptions of fairness of cost allocation decisions.

Recognize the effects of cost allocation on employee motivation.

Using Cost Allocations in a Budgeting Decision

Sharon Southport, dean of the School of Business at a major state university, is in dire need of a budgeting plan. Because of cuts in state funding, the money available to the School of Business for copying costs next year will be reduced substantially. Dean Southport supervises four departments: management, marketing, finance, and accounting. The dean knows the individual department chairpersons will be unhappy and frustrated with the deep cuts they face.

Using Cost Drivers to Make Allocations

To address the allocation of copying resources, Dean Southport decided to meet with the department chairs. She explained that the total budgeted for copying costs will be $36,000. Based on past usage, department allocations would be as follows: $12,000 for management, $10,000 for accounting, $8,000 for finance, and $6,000 for marketing.

Dr. Bill Thompson, the management department chair, immediately protested that his department could not operate on a $12,000 budget for copy costs. Management has more faculty members than any other department. Dr. Thompson argued that copy costs are directly related to the number of faculty members, so copy funds should be allocated based on the number of faculty members. Dr. Thompson suggested that number of faculty members rather than past usage should be used as the allocation base.

Since the School of Business has 72 faculty members (29 in management, 16 in accounting, 12 in finance, and 15 in marketing), the allocation should be as follows.

Step 1. Compute the allocation rate.

Total cost to be allocated ÷ Cost driver = Allocation rate

$36,000 ÷ 72 = $500 per faculty member

Step 2. Multiply the rate by the weight of the driver (the number of faculty per department) to determine the allocation per object (department).

Department	Allocation Rate	×	Number of Faculty	=	Allocation per Department	Allocation Based on Past Usage
Management	$500	×	29	=	$14,500	$12,000
Accounting	500	×	16	=	8,000	10,000
Finance	500	×	12	=	6,000	8,000
Marketing	500	×	15	=	7,500	6,000
Total					$36,000	$36,000

Seeing these figures, Dr. Bob Smethers, chair of the accounting department, questioned the accuracy of using the number of faculty members as the cost driver. Dr. Smethers suggested the number of *students* rather than the number of *faculty members* drives the cost of copying. He argued that most copying results from duplicating syllabi, exams, and handouts. The accounting department teaches mass sections of introductory accounting that have extremely high student/teacher ratios. Because his department teaches more students, it spends more on copying costs even though it has fewer faculty members. Dr. Smethers recomputed the copy cost allocation as follows.

Step 1. Compute the allocation rate based on number of students. University records indicate that the School of Business taught 1,200 students during the most recent academic year. The allocation rate (copy cost per student) follows.

$$\text{Total cost to be allocated} \div \text{Cost driver} = \text{Allocation rate}$$
$$\$36,000 \div 1,200 = \$30 \text{ per student}$$

Step 2. Multiply the rate by the weight of the driver (number of students taught by each department) to determine the allocation per object (department).

Department	Allocation Rate	×	Number of Students	=	Allocation per Department	Allocation Based on Past Usage
Management	$30	×	330	=	$ 9,900	$12,000
Accounting	30	×	360	=	10,800	10,000
Finance	30	×	290	=	8,700	8,000
Marketing	30	×	220	=	6,600	6,000
Total					$36,000	$36,000

Choosing the Best Cost Driver

Dr. Thompson objected vigorously to using the number of students as the cost driver. He continued to argue that the size of the faculty is a more appropriate allocation base. The chair of the finance department sided with Dr. Smethers, the chair of the marketing department kept quiet, and the dean had to settle the dispute.

Dean Southport recognized that the views of the chairpersons were influenced by self-interest. The allocation base affects the amount of resources available to each department. Furthermore, the dean recognized that the size of the faculty does drive some of the copying costs. For example, the cost of copying manuscripts that faculty submit for publication relates to faculty size. The more articles faculty submit, the higher the copying cost. Nevertheless, the dean decided the number of students has the most significant impact on copying costs. She also wanted to encourage faculty members to minimize the impact of funding cuts on student services. Dean Southport therefore decided to allocate copying costs based on the number of students taught by each department. Dr. Thompson stormed angrily out of the meeting. The dean developed a budget by assigning the available funds to each department using the number of students as the allocation base.

Controlling Emotions

Dr. Thompson's behavior may relieve his frustration but it doesn't indicate clear thinking. Dean Southport recognized that Dr. Thompson's contention that copy costs were related to faculty size had some merit. Had Dr. Thompson offered a compromise rather than an emotional outburst, he might have increased his department's share of the funds. Perhaps a portion of the allocation could have been based on the number of faculty members with the balance allocated based on the number of students. Had Dr. Thompson controlled his anger, the others might have agreed to compromise. Technical expertise in computing numbers is of little use without the interpersonal skills to persuade others. Accountants may provide numerical measurements, but they should never forget the impact of their reports on the people in the organization.

A Look Back

Managers need to know the costs of products, processes, departments, activities, and so on. The target for which accountants attempt to determine cost is a *cost object*. Knowing the cost of specific objects enables management to control costs, evaluate performance, and price products. *Direct costs* can be cost-effectively traced to a cost object. *Indirect costs* cannot be easily traced to designated cost objects.

The same cost can be direct or indirect, depending on the cost object to which it is traced. For example, the salary of a Burger King restaurant manager can be directly traced to a particular store but cannot be traced to particular food items made and sold in the store. Classifying a cost as direct or indirect is independent of whether the cost behaves as fixed or variable; it is also independent of whether the cost is relevant to a given decision. A direct cost could be either fixed or variable or either relevant or irrelevant, depending on the context and the designated cost object.

Indirect costs are assigned to cost objects using *cost allocation*. Allocation divides an indirect cost into parts and distributes the parts among the relevant cost objects. Companies frequently allocate costs to cost objects in proportion to the *cost drivers* that cause the cost to be incurred. The first step in allocating an indirect cost is to determine the allocation rate by dividing the total cost to be allocated by the chosen cost driver. The next step is to multiply the allocation rate by the amount of the cost driver for a particular object. The result is the amount of indirect cost to assign to the cost object.

A particular indirect cost may be related to more than one driver. The best cost driver is the one that most accurately reflects the amount of the resource used by the cost object. Objects that consume the most resources should be allocated a proportionately greater share of the costs. If no suitable cost driver exists, companies may use arbitrary allocations such as dividing a total cost equally among cost objects.

Cost allocations have behavioral implications. Using inappropriate cost drivers can distort allocations and lead managers to make choices that are detrimental to the company's profitability.

A Look Forward

The failure to accurately allocate indirect costs to cost objects can result in misinformation that impairs decision making. The next chapter explains how increased use of automation in production has caused distortion in allocations determined using traditional approaches. The chapter introduces the allocation of indirect costs using more recently developed activity-based costing and explains how activity-based management can improve efficiency and productivity. Finally, the chapter introduces total quality management, a strategy that seeks to minimize the costs of conforming to a designated standard of quality.

 Video lectures and accompanying self-assessment quizzes are available in *Connect* for all learning objectives.

 SELF-STUDY REVIEW PROBLEM

New budget constraints have pressured Body Perfect Gym to control costs. The owner of the gym, Mr. Ripple, has notified division managers that their job performance evaluations will be highly influenced by their ability to minimize costs. The gym has three divisions: weight lifting, aerobics, and spinning. The owner has formulated a report showing how much it cost to operate each of the three divisions last year. In preparing the report, Mr. Ripple identified several indirect costs that must be allocated among the divisions. These indirect costs are $4,200 of laundry expense, $48,000 of supplies, $350,000 of office rent, $50,000 of janitorial services, and $120,000 for administrative salaries. To provide a reasonably accurate cost allocation, Mr. Ripple has identified several potential cost drivers. These drivers and their association with each division follow.

Cost Driver	Weight Lifting	Aerobics	Spinning	Total
Number of participants	26	16	14	56
Number of instructors	10	8	6	24
Square feet of gym space	12,000	6,000	7,000	25,000
Number of staff	2	2	1	5

Required

a. Identify the appropriate cost objects.

b. Identify the most appropriate cost driver for each indirect cost, and compute the allocation rate for assigning each indirect cost to the cost objects.

c. Determine the amount of supplies expense that should be allocated to each of the three divisions.

d. The spinning manager wants to use the number of staff rather than the number of instructors as the allocation base for the supplies expense. Explain why the spinning manager would take this position.

e. Identify two cost drivers other than your choice for Requirement b that could be used to allocate the cost of the administrative salaries to the three divisions.

Solution to Requirement a

The objective is to determine the cost of operating each division. Therefore, the cost objects are the three divisions (weight lifting, aerobics, and spinning).

Solution to Requirement b

The costs, appropriate cost drivers, and allocation rates for assigning the costs to the departments follow.

Cost	Base	Computation	Allocation Rate
Laundry expense	Number of participants	$ 4,200 ÷ 56	$75 per participant
Supplies	Number of instructors	48,000 ÷ 24	$2,000 per instructor
Office rent	Square feet	350,000 ÷ 25,000	$14 per square foot
Janitorial service	Square feet	50,000 ÷ 25,000	$2 per square foot
Administrative salaries	Number of divisions	120,000 ÷ 3	$40,000 per division

There are other logical cost drivers. For example, the cost of supplies could be allocated based on the number of staff. It is also logical to use a combination of cost drivers. For example, the allocation for the cost of supplies could be based on the combined number of instructors and staff. For this problem, we assumed that Mr. Ripple chose the number of instructors as the base for allocating supplies expense.

Solution to Requirement c

Department	Cost to Be Allocated	Allocation Rate	×	Weight	=	Amount Allocated
Weight lifting	Supplies	$2,000	×	10	=	$20,000
Aerobics	Supplies	2,000	×	8	=	16,000
Spinning	Supplies	2,000	×	6	=	12,000
Total						$48,000

Solution to Requirement d

If the number of staff were used as the allocation base, the allocation rate for supplies would be as follows:

$$\$48,000 \div 5 \text{ staff} = \$9,600 \text{ per staff member}$$

Using this rate, the total cost of supplies would be allocated among the three divisions as follows.

Department	Cost to Be Allocated	Allocation Rate	×	Weight of Base	=	Amount Allocated
Weight lifting	Supplies	$9,600	×	2	=	$19,200
Aerobics	Supplies	9,600	×	2	=	19,200
Spinning	Supplies	9,600	×	1	=	9,600
Total						$48,000

By using the number of staff as the allocation base instead of the number of instructors, the amount of overhead cost allocated to the spinning division falls from $12,000 to $9,600. Since managers are evaluated based on minimizing costs, it is clearly in the spinning manager's self-interest to use the number of staff as the allocation base.

Solution to Requirement e

Among other possibilities, bases for allocating the administrative salaries include the number of participants, the number of lessons, or the number of instructors.

KEY TERMS

allocation 444
allocation base 445
allocation rate 445
common costs 444

controllable costs 444
cost accumulation 442
cost allocation 443
cost driver 442

cost objects 440
cost pool 446
cost tracing 443
direct cost 443

indirect cost 443
overhead costs 443
predetermined overhead rate 455

QUESTIONS

1. What is a cost object? Identify four different cost objects in which an accountant would be interested.

2. Why is cost accumulation imprecise?

3. If the cost object is a manufactured product, what are the three major cost categories to accumulate?

4. What is a direct cost? What criteria are used to determine whether a cost is a direct cost?

5. Why are the terms *direct cost* and *indirect cost* independent of the terms *fixed cost* and *variable cost*? Give an example to illustrate.

6. Give an example of why the statement "All direct costs are avoidable" is incorrect.

7. What are the important factors in determining the appropriate cost driver to use in allocating a cost?

8. How is an allocation rate determined? How is an allocation made?

9. In a manufacturing environment, which costs are direct and which are indirect in product costing?

10. Why are some manufacturing costs not directly traceable to products?

11. What is the objective of allocating indirect manufacturing overhead costs to the product?

12. On January 31, the managers of Integra, Inc. seek to determine the cost of producing their product during January for product pricing and control purposes. The company

can easily determine the costs of direct materials and direct labor used in January production, but many fixed indirect costs are not affected by the level of production activity and have not yet been incurred. The managers can reasonably estimate the overhead costs for the year based on the fixed indirect costs incurred in past periods. Assume the managers decide to allocate an equal amount of these estimated costs to the products produced each month. Explain why this practice may not provide a reasonable estimate of product costs in January.

13. Respond to the following statement: "The allocation base chosen is unimportant. What is important in prod-

uct costing is that overhead costs be assigned to production in a specific period by an allocation process."

14. Larry Kwang insists that the costs of his school's fund-raising project should be determined after the project is complete. He argues that only after the project is complete can its costs be determined accurately and that it is a waste of time to try to estimate future costs. Georgia Sundum counters that waiting until the project is complete will not provide timely information for planning expenditures. How would you arbitrate this discussion? Explain the trade-offs between accuracy and timeliness.

EXERCISES—SERIES A

LO 12-1

Exercise 12-1A *Direct versus indirect costs*

Ludmilla Construction Company is composed of two divisions: (1) Home Construction and (2) Commercial Construction. The Home Construction Division is in the process of building 12 houses and the Commercial Construction Division is working on three projects. Cost items of the company follow:

Wages of workers assigned to a specific construction project
Supplies used by the Commercial Construction Division
Labor on a particular house
Salary of the supervisor of commercial construction projects
Supplies, such as glue and nails, used by the Home Construction Division
Cost of building permits
Materials used in commercial construction projects
Depreciation on home building equipment (small tools such as hammers or saws)
Company president's salary
Depreciation on crane used in commercial construction
Depreciation on home office building
Salary of corporate office manager

Required

a. Identify each cost as being a direct or indirect cost assuming the cost objects are the individual products (houses or projects).
b. Identify each cost as being a direct or indirect cost, assuming the cost objects are the two divisions.
c. Identify each cost as being a direct or indirect cost, assuming the cost object is Ludmilla Construction Company as a whole.

LO 12-2

Exercise 12-2A *Allocating costs between divisions*

Beasley Services Company (BSC) has 50 employees, 28 of whom are assigned to Division A and 22 to Division B. BSC incurred $450,000 of fringe benefits cost during Year 2.

Required

Determine the amount of the fringe benefits cost to be allocated to Division A and to Division B.

LO 12-2

Exercise 12-3A *Allocating overhead cost to accomplish smoothing*

Rasmussen Corporation expects to incur indirect overhead costs of $80,000 per month and direct manufacturing costs of $12 per unit. The expected production activity for the first four months of the year are as follows.

	January	February	March	April
Estimated production in units	6,000	7,000	3,000	4,000

Required

a. Calculate a predetermined overhead rate based on the number of units of product expected to be made during the first four months of the year.
b. Allocate overhead costs to each month using the overhead rate computed in Requirement *a*.
c. Calculate the total cost per unit for each month using the overhead allocated in Requirement *b*.

Exercise 12-4A *Pooling overhead cost*

Ware Manufacturing Company produced 2,000 units of inventory in January, Year 2. It expects to produce an additional 14,000 units during the remaining 11 months of the year. In other words, total production for Year 2 is estimated to be 16,000 units. Direct materials and direct labor costs are $64 and $52 per unit, respectively. Ware expects to incur the following manufacturing overhead costs during the Year 2 accounting period.

Production supplies	$ 20,000
Supervisor salary	160,000
Depreciation on equipment	75,000
Utilities	20,000
Rental fee on manufacturing facilities	45,000

Required

a. Combine the individual overhead costs into a cost pool and calculate a predetermined overhead rate assuming the cost driver is number of units.

b. Determine the cost of the 2,000 units of product made in January.

c. Is the cost computed in Requirement *b* actual or estimated? Could Ware improve accuracy by waiting until December to determine the cost of products? Identify two reasons that a manager would want to know the cost of products in January. Discuss the relationship between accuracy and relevance as it pertains to this problem.

Exercise 12-5A *Cost pools*

Russell Department Stores, Inc. has three departments: women's, men's, and children's. The following are the indirect costs related to its operations:

Vacation pay	Payroll taxes
Sewer bill	Paper rolls for cash registers
Staples	Medical insurance
Natural gas bill	Salaries of secretaries
Pens	Water bill
Ink cartridges	

Required

a. Organize the costs in the following three pools: indirect materials, indirect labor, and indirect utilities, assuming that each department is a cost object.

b. Identify an appropriate cost driver for each pool.

c. Explain why accountants use cost pools.

Exercise 12-6A *Allocating overhead cost among products*

Tyson Hats Corporation manufactures three different models of hats: Vogue, Beauty, and Glamour. Tyson expects to incur $480,000 of overhead cost during the next fiscal year. Other budget information follows.

	Vogue	Beauty	Glamour	Total
Direct labor hours	2,000	4,000	6,000	12,000
Machine hours	1,200	1,400	1,400	4,000

Required

a. Use direct labor hours as the cost driver to compute the allocation rate and the budgeted overhead cost for each product.

b. Use machine hours as the cost driver to compute the allocation rate and the budgeted overhead cost for each product.

c. Describe a set of circumstances where it would be more appropriate to use direct labor hours as the allocation base.

d. Describe a set of circumstances where it would be more appropriate to use machine hours as the allocation base.

LO 12-3

Exercise 12-7A   *Allocating overhead costs among products*

Willey Company makes three products in its factory: plastic cups, plastic tablecloths, and plastic bottles. The expected overhead costs for the next fiscal year include the following.

Factory manager's salary	$210,000
Factory utility cost	70,000
Factory supplies	20,000
Total overhead costs	$300,000

Willey uses machine hours as the cost driver to allocate overhead costs. Budgeted machine hours for the products are as follows.

Cups	300 hours
Tablecloths	750
Bottles	950
Total machine hours	2,000

Required

a. Allocate the budgeted overhead costs to the products.

b. Provide a possible explanation as to why Willey chose machine hours, instead of labor hours, as the allocation base.

LO 12-3

Exercise 12-8A   *Allocating costs among products*

Fanya Construction Company expects to build three new homes during a specific accounting period. The estimated direct materials and labor costs are as follows.

Expected Costs	Home 1	Home 2	Home 3
Direct labor	$40,000	$60,000	$100,000
Direct materials	30,000	50,000	80,000

Assume Fanya needs to allocate two major overhead costs ($80,000 of employee fringe benefits and $40,000 of indirect materials costs) among the three jobs.

Required

Choose an appropriate cost driver for each of the overhead costs and determine the total cost of each house. Round your figures to three decimal points.

LO 12-3

Exercise 12-9A   *Allocating to smooth cost over varying levels of production*

Production workers for Essa Manufacturing Company provided 300 hours of labor in January and 600 hours in February. Essa expects to use 5,000 hours of labor during the year. The rental fee for the manufacturing facility is $6,000 per month.

Required

Explain why allocation is needed. Based on this information, how much of the rental cost should be allocated to the products made in January and to those made in February?

Exercise 12-10A *Allocating to solve a timing problem*

LO 12-3

Production workers for Chadwick Manufacturing Company provided 3,200 hours of labor in January and 2,800 hours in February. The company, whose operation is labor intensive, expects to use 48,000 hours of labor during the year. Chadwick paid a $120,000 annual premium on July 1 of the prior year for an insurance policy that covers the manufacturing facility for the following 12 months.

Required

Explain why allocation is needed. Based on this information, how much of the insurance cost should be allocated to the products made in January and to those made in February?

Exercise 12-11A *Allocating to solve a timing problem*

LO 12-3

Erickson Air is a large airline company that pays a customer relations representative $8,000 per month. The representative, who processed 3,000 customer complaints in January and 2,500 complaints in February, is expected to process 40,000 customer complaints during the year.

Required

a. Determine the total cost of processing customer complaints in January and in February.

b. Explain why allocating the cost of the customer relations representative would or would not be relevant to decision making.

Exercise 12-12A *How the allocation of fixed cost affects a pricing decision*

LO 12-3

Arrow Manufacturing Co. expects to make 50,000 chairs during the Year 1 accounting period. The company made 3,000 chairs in January. Materials and labor costs for January were $36,000 and $48,000, respectively. Arrow produced 4,000 chairs in February. Material and labor costs for February were $48,000 and $60,000, respectively. The company paid the $480,000 annual rental fee on its manufacturing facility on January 1, Year 1.

Required

Assuming that Arrow desires to sell its chairs for cost plus 40 percent of cost, what price should be charged for the chairs produced in January and February?

Exercise 12-13A *Human factor*

LO 12-4

Miriana Clinics provides medical care in three departments: internal medicine (IM), pediatrics (PD), and obstetrics gynecology (OB). The estimated costs to run each department follow.

	IM	PD	OB
Physicians	$600,000	$400,000	$500,000
Nurses	80,000	120,000	160,000

Miriana expects to incur $450,000 of indirect (overhead) costs in the next fiscal year.

Required

a. Name four allocation bases that could be used to assign the overhead cost to each department.

b. Assume the manager of each department is permitted to recommend how the overhead cost should be allocated to the departments. Which of the allocation bases named in Requirement *a* is the manager of OB most likely to recommend? Explain why. What argument may the manager of OB use to justify his choice of the allocation base?

c. Which of the allocation bases would result in the fairest allocation of the overhead cost from the perspective of the company president?

d. Explain how classifying overhead costs into separate pools could improve the fairness of the allocation of the overhead costs.

PROBLEMS—SERIES A

An electronic auto-gradable version of the Series A Problems is available in Connect. A PDF version of Series B Problems is in Connect under the "Additional Student Resources" tab. Solutions to the Series B Problems are available in Connect under the "Instructor Library" tab. Instructor and student Workpapers for the Series B Problems are available in Connect under the "Instructor Library" and "Additional Student Resources" tabs respectively.

LO 12-1, 12-2, 12-3

eXcel

CHECK FIGURE

c. Product N: $522.55

Problem 12-14A   *Cost accumulation and allocation*

Yalland Manufacturing Company makes two different products, M and N. The company's two departments are named after the products; for example, Product M is made in Department M. Yalland's accountant has identified the following annual costs associated with these two products.

Financial data	
Salary of vice president of production division	$160,000
Salary of supervisor Department M	80,000
Salary of supervisor Department N	60,000
Direct materials cost Department M	300,000
Direct materials cost Department N	420,000
Direct labor cost Department M	240,000
Direct labor cost Department N	680,000
Direct utilities cost Department M	120,000
Direct utilities cost Department N	24,000
General factorywide utilities	36,000
Production supplies	36,000
Fringe benefits	138,000
Depreciation	600,000
Nonfinancial data	
Machine hours Department M	5,000
Machine hours Department N	1,000

Required

a. Identify the costs that are (1) direct costs of Department M, (2) direct costs of Department N, and (3) indirect costs.

b. Select the appropriate cost drivers for the indirect costs and allocate these costs to Departments M and N.

c. Determine the total estimated cost of the products made in Departments M and N. Assume that Yalland produced 2,000 units of Product M and 4,000 units of Product N during the year. If Yalland prices its products at cost plus 40 percent of cost, what price per unit must it charge for Product M and for Product N?

LO 12-1, 12-2, 12-3

Problem 12-15A   *Selecting an appropriate cost driver (What is the base?)*

The Huffman School of Vocational Technology has organized the school training programs into three departments. Each department provides training in a different area as follows: nursing assistant, dental hygiene, and office technology. The school's owner, Amy Huffman, wants to know how much it costs to operate each of the three departments. To accumulate the total cost for each department, the accountant has identified several indirect costs that must be allocated to each. These costs are $12,000 of phone expense, $21,000 of office supplies, $900,000 of office rent, $144,000 of janitorial services, and $150,000 of salary paid to the dean of students. To provide a reasonably accurate allocation of costs, the accountant has identified several possible cost drivers. These drivers and their association with each department follow.

Cost Driver	Department 1	Department 2	Department 3
Number of telephones	20	30	50
Number of faculty members	20	16	24
Square footage of office space	14,000	8,000	14,000
Number of secretaries	2	2	2

Required

a. Identify the appropriate cost objects.

b. Identify the appropriate cost driver for each indirect cost and compute the allocation rate for assigning each indirect cost to the cost objects.

c. Determine the amount of telephone expense that should be allocated to each of the three departments.

d. Determine the amount of supplies expense that should be allocated to Department 3.

e. Determine the amount of office rent that should be allocated to Department 2.

f. Determine the amount of janitorial services cost that should be allocated to Department 1.

g. Identify two cost drivers not listed here that could be used to allocate the cost of the dean's salary to the three departments.

Problem 12-16A   *Cost allocation in a service industry*

LO 12-1, 12-2, 12-3

Eagle Airlines is a small airline that occasionally carries overload shipments for the overnight delivery company Never-Fail, Inc. Never-Fail is a multimillion-dollar company started by Wes Never immediately after he failed to finish his first accounting course. The company's motto is "We Never-Fail to Deliver Your Package on Time." When Never-Fail has more freight than it can deliver, it pays Eagle to carry the excess. Eagle contracts with independent pilots to fly its planes on a per-trip basis. Eagle recently purchased an airplane that cost the company $6,000,000. The plane has an estimated useful life of 20,000,000 miles and a zero salvage value. During the first week in January, Eagle flew two trips. The first trip was a round-trip flight from Chicago to San Francisco, for which Eagle paid $350 for the pilot and $500 for fuel. The second flight was a round-trip from Chicago to New York. For this trip, it paid $300 for the pilot and $300 for fuel. The round-trip between Chicago and San Francisco is approximately 4,400 miles and the round-trip between Chicago and New York is 1,600 miles.

CHECK FIGURE
b. To NY: $1,080

Required

a. Identify the direct and indirect costs that Eagle incurs for each trip.

b. Determine the total cost of each trip.

c. In addition to depreciation, identify three other indirect costs that may need to be allocated to determine the cost of each trip.

Problem 12-17A   *Cost allocation in a manufacturing company*

LO 12-1, 12-2, 12-3

Camp Manufacturing Company makes tents that it sells directly to camping enthusiasts through a mail-order marketing program. The company pays a quality control expert $80,000 per year to inspect completed tents before they are shipped to customers. Assume that the company completed 1,600 tents in January and 1,200 tents in February. For the entire year, the company expects to produce 20,000 tents.

CHECK FIGURE
d. Feb.: $4,800

Required

a. Explain how changes in the cost driver (number of tents inspected) affect the total amount of fixed inspection cost.

b. Explain how changes in the cost driver (number of tents inspected) affect the amount of fixed inspection cost per unit.

c. If the cost objective is to determine the cost per tent, is the expert's salary a direct or an indirect cost?

d. How much of the expert's salary should be allocated to tents produced in January and February?

Problem 12-18A   *Allocation to accomplish smoothing*

LO 12-1, 12-2, 12-3

Velez Corporation estimated its overhead costs would be $50,000 per month except for January when it pays the $30,000 annual insurance premium on the manufacturing facility. Accordingly, the January overhead costs were expected to be $80,000 ($30,000 + $50,000). The company expected to use 7,000 direct labor hours per month except during July, August, and September when the company expected 9,000 hours of direct labor each month to build inventories for high demand that normally occurs during the Christmas season. The company's actual direct labor hours were the same as the estimated hours. The company made 3,500 units of product in each month except July, August, and September, in which it produced 4,500 units each month. Direct labor costs were $30 per unit, and direct materials costs were $25 per unit.

CHECK FIGURES
a. $7
c. March: $69

Required

a.   Calculate a predetermined overhead rate based on direct labor hours.

b.   Determine the total allocated overhead cost for January, March, and August.

c.   Determine the cost per unit of product for January, March, and August.

d.   Determine the selling price for the product, assuming that the company desires to earn a gross margin of $20 per unit.

LO 12-2, 12-3

CHECK FIGURES
a. Cost/unit for EZRecords: $162.50
b. Cost/unit for ProOffice: $175

Problem 12-19A   *Allocating indirect costs between products*

Hannah Ortega is considering expanding her business. She plans to hire a salesperson to cover trade shows. Because of compensation, travel expenses, and booth rental, fixed costs for a trade show are expected to be $7,500. The booth will be open 30 hours during the trade show. Ms. Ortega also plans to add a new product line, ProOffice, which will cost $150 per package. She will continue to sell the existing product, EZRecords, which costs $100 per package. Ms. Garcia believes that the salesperson will spend approximately 20 hours selling EZRecords and 10 hours marketing ProOffice.

Required

a.   Determine the estimated total cost and cost per unit of each product, assuming that the salesperson is able to sell 80 units of EZRecords and 50 units of ProOffice.

b.   Determine the estimated total cost and cost per unit of each product, assuming that the salesperson is able to sell 200 units of EZRecords and 100 units of ProOffice.

c.   Explain why the cost per unit figures calculated in Requirement *a* are different from the amounts calculated in Requirement *b*. Also explain how the differences in estimated cost per unit will affect pricing decisions.

LO 12-1, 12-2, 12-3, 12-4

Problem 12-20A   *Fairness and cost pool allocations*

Clement Manufacturing Company uses two departments to make its products. Department I is a cutting department that is machine intensive and uses very few employees. Machines cut and form parts and then place the finished parts on a conveyor belt that carries them to Department II, where they are assembled into finished goods. The assembly department is labor intensive and requires many workers to assemble parts into finished goods. The company's manufacturing facility incurs two significant overhead costs: employee fringe benefits and utility costs. The annual costs of fringe benefits are $420,000 and utility costs are $300,000. The typical consumption patterns for the two departments are as follows.

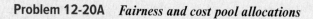

	Department I	Department II	Total
Machine hours used	20,000	4,000	24,000
Direct labor hours used	2,000	14,000	16,000

The supervisor of each department receives a bonus based on how well the department controls costs. The company's current policy requires using a single allocation base (machine hours or labor hours) to allocate the total overhead cost of $720,000.

Required

a.   Assume that you are the supervisor of Department I. Choose the allocation base that would minimize your department's share of the total overhead cost. Calculate the amount of overhead that would be allocated to both departments using the base that you selected.

b.   Assume that you are the supervisor of Department II. Choose the allocation base that would minimize your department's share of the total overhead cost. Calculate the amount of overhead that would be allocated to both departments using the base that you selected.

c.   Assume that you are the plant manager and have the authority to change the company's overhead allocation policy. Formulate an overhead allocation policy that would be fair to the supervisors of both Department I and Department II. Compute the overhead allocations for each department using your policy.

d.   Explain why it is necessary to disaggregate the overhead cost pool in order to accomplish fairness.

ANALYZE, THINK, COMMUNICATE

ATC 12-1   Business Applications Case   *Allocating fixed costs at HealthSouth Corporation*

HealthSouth Corporation claims to be "the nation's leading owner and operator of inpatient rehabilitation hospitals and a leader in home-based care (home health and hospice), offering services in 36 states and Puerto Rico." As of December 31, 2017, the company derived 96.7 percent of its hospital revenues from inpatient services. During 2017 it treated and discharged 171,922 patients, and the average length of a patient's stay was 12.7 days. If one patient occupying one bed for one day represents a "patient-day," then HealthSouth produced 2,183,409 patient-days of output during 2017 (171,922 × 12.7 = 2,183,409). During this period, HealthSouth incurred depreciation and amortization costs of $183,800,000. For the purpose of this problem, assume that all of this is depreciation related to the property, plant, and equipment of inpatient hospitals.

Required

a. Indicate whether the depreciation cost is a:
   (1) Product (i.e., patient) cost or a general, selling, and administrative cost.
   (2) Fixed or variable cost relative to the volume of production.
   (3) Direct or indirect cost if the cost object is the cost of patient services provided in 2017.

b. Assume that HealthSouth incurred depreciation of $15,320,000 during each month of the 2017 fiscal year, but that it produced 196,000 patient-days of service during February and 166,000 patient-days of service during March. Based on monthly costs and service levels, what was the average amount of depreciation cost per patient-day of service provided during each of these two months, assuming each patient-day of service was charged the same amount of depreciation?

c. If HealthSouth expected to produce 2,270,000 patient-days of service during 2017 and estimated its annual depreciation costs to be $190,000,000, what would have been its predetermined overhead charge per patient-day of service for depreciation? Explain the advantage of using this amount to determine the cost of providing one patient-day of service in February and March versus the amounts you computed in Requirement b.

d. If HealthSouth's management had estimated the profit per patient-day of service based on its budgeted production of 2,270,000 patient-days, would you expect its actual profit per patient-day of service to be higher or lower than expected? Explain.

ATC 12-2   Group Assignment   *Selection of the cost driver*

Vulcan College School of Business is divided into three departments: accounting, marketing, and management. Relevant information for each of the departments follows.

Cost Driver	Accounting	Marketing	Management
Number of students	1,400	800	400
Number of classes per semester	64	36	28
Number of professors	20	24	10

Vulcan is a private school that expects each department to generate a profit. It rewards departments for profitability by assigning 20 percent of each department's profits back to that department. Departments have free rein as to how to use these funds. Some departments have used them to supply professors with computer technology. Others have expanded their travel budgets. The practice has been highly successful in motivating the faculty to control costs. The revenues and direct costs for the year follow.

	Accounting	Marketing	Management
Revenue	$29,600,000	$16,600,000	$8,300,000
Direct costs	24,600,000	13,800,000	6,600,000

Vulcan allocates to the School of Business $4,492,800 of indirect overhead costs such as administrative salaries and the costs of operating the registrar's office and the bookstore.

Required

a. Divide the class into groups and organize the groups into three sections. Assign each section a department. For example, groups in Sections 1, 2, and 3 should represent the Accounting Department, the Marketing Department, and the Management Department, respectively. Assume that the dean of the school is planning to assign an equal amount of the college overhead to each department. Have the students in each group prepare a response to the dean's plan. Each group should select a spokesperson who is prepared to answer the following questions:

(1) Is your group in favor of or opposed to the allocation plan suggested by the dean?

(2) Does the plan suggested by the dean provide a fair allocation? Why?

The instructor should lead a discussion designed to assess the appropriateness of the dean's proposed allocation plan.

b. Have each group select the cost driver (allocation base) that best serves the self-interest of the department it represents.

c. Consensus on Requirement *c* should be achieved before completing Requirement *d*. Each group should determine the amount of the indirect cost to be allocated to each department using the cost driver that best serves the self-interest of the department it represents. Have a spokesperson from each section go to the board and show the resulting income statement for each department.

d. Discuss the development of a cost driver(s) that would promote fairness rather than self-interest in allocating the indirect costs.

ATC 12-3   Research Assignment   *Using real-world data from Coca-Cola Bottling Co. Consolidated*

Use the 2017 Form 10-K (year ended on December 31, 2017) for Coca-Cola Bottling Co. Consolidated to complete the following requirements. Be aware that Coca-Cola Bottling Co. Consolidated (COKE) is a separate company from The Coca-Cola Company (KO), so do not confuse them. To obtain the Form 10-K, you can use the EDGAR system (see Appendix A at the back of this text for instructions), or it can be found under the "Investor Relations" link on the company's corporate website at www.cokeconsolidated.com. The company's Form 10-K can be found under "SEC Filings." Be sure to read carefully the following sections of the document:

■ Under "Item 1. Business," read the subsection titled "Seasonality" on page 13.

■ Under "Item 2. Properties," on page 22.

■ In the footnotes section of the report, under "Note 1—Summary of Significant Accounting Policies," read the following subsections:

■ "Marketing Programs and Sales Incentives" on page 69.

■ "Cost of Sales"on page 70.

■ "Selling, Delivery and Administrative Expenses" on page 70.

■ "Shipping and Handling Costs" on page 70.

Required

a. Does COKE consider *shipping and handling costs* and *advertising costs* to be direct or indirect costs in relation to the manufacturing of its products? Explain.

b. Assume that when COKE ships orders of finished goods from manufacturing locations to sales distribution centers each shipment includes several different products such as Coca-Cola, Sprite, Dr Pepper, and Seagrams Ginger Ale. If COKE wanted to allocate the shipping costs among the various products, what would be an appropriate cost driver? Explain the rationale for your choice.

c. Based on COKE's discussion of the seasonality of its business, should the depreciation of production equipment recorded in a given month be based on the volume of drinks produced that month, or should the depreciation for each month be 1/12th of the estimated annual depreciation COKE expects to incur? Explain your answer.

d. As "Item 2. Properties" indicates, COKE appears to have significant excess capacity at its plants. Approximately what percentage of available production capacity was *not* being used by COKE in 2017? What are some possible reasons COKE might want to have this much excess capacity? Explain.

ATC 12-4   Writing Assignment   *Selection of the appropriate cost driver*

Bullions Enterprises, Inc. (BEI) makes gold, silver, and bronze medals used to recognize outstanding athletic performance in regional and national sporting events. The per-unit direct costs of producing the medals follow.

	Gold	Silver	Bronze
Direct materials	$300	$130	$ 35
Labor	120	120	120

During Year 6, BEI made 1,200 units of each type of medal for a total of 3,600 (1,200 × 3) medals. All medals are created through the same production process, and they are packaged and shipped in identical containers. Indirect overhead costs amounted to $324,000. BEI currently uses the number of units as the cost driver for the allocation of overhead cost. As a result, BEI allocated $90 ($324,000 ÷ 3,600 units) of overhead cost to each medal produced.

Required

The president of the company has questioned the wisdom of assigning the same amount of overhead to each type of medal. He believes that overhead should be assigned on the basis of the cost to produce the medals. In other words, more overhead should be charged to expensive gold medals, less to silver, and even less to bronze. Assume that you are BEI's chief financial officer. Write a memo responding to the president's suggestion.

ATC 12-5   Ethical Dilemma   *Allocation to achieve fairness*

The American Acupuncture Association offers continuing professional education courses for its members at its annual meeting. Instructors are paid a fee for each student attending their courses but are charged a fee for overhead costs that is deducted from their compensation. Overhead costs include fees paid to rent instructional equipment such as overhead projectors, provide supplies to participants, and offer refreshments during coffee breaks. The number of courses offered is used as the allocation base for determining the overhead charge. For example, if overhead costs amount to $5,000 and 25 courses are offered, each course is allocated an overhead charge of $200 ($5,000 ÷ 25 courses). Heidi McCarl, who taught one of the courses, received the following statement with her check in payment for her instructional services.

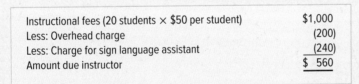

Instructional fees (20 students × $50 per student)	$1,000
Less: Overhead charge	(200)
Less: Charge for sign language assistant	(240)
Amount due instructor	$ 560

Although Ms. McCarl was well aware that one of her students was deaf and required a sign language assistant, she was surprised to find that she was required to absorb the cost of this service.

Required

a. Given that the Americans with Disabilities Act stipulates that the deaf student cannot be charged for the cost of providing sign language, who should be required to pay the cost of sign language services?

b. Explain how allocation can be used to promote fairness in distributing service costs to people with disabilities. Describe two ways to treat the $240 cost of providing sign language services that improve fairness.

CHAPTER 13

Relevant Information for Special Decisions

LEARNING OBJECTIVES

After you have mastered the material in this chapter, you will be able to:

LO 13-1   Identify the characteristics of relevant information.

LO 13-2   Make appropriate special order decisions.

LO 13-3   Make appropriate outsourcing decisions.

LO 13-4   Make appropriate segment elimination decisions.

LO 13-5   Make appropriate asset replacement decisions.

 Video lectures and accompanying self-assessment quizzes are available in Connect *for all learning objectives.*

 Set B exercises and problems are available in Additional Student Resources.

CHAPTER OPENING

Mary Daniels paid $25,000 to purchase a car that was used in her rental business. After one year, the car had a book value of $21,000. Ms. Daniels needs cash and is considering selling the car. After advertising the vehicle for sale, the best offer she received was $19,000. Ms. Daniels really needed the money, but ultimately decided not to sell because she did not want to incur a $2,000 loss ($21,000 book value − $19,000 market value). Did Ms. Daniels make the right decision?

Whether Ms. Daniels will be better off selling the car or keeping it is unknown. However, it is certain that she based her decision on irrelevant data. Ms. Daniels incurred a loss when the market value of the car dropped. She cannot avoid a loss that already exists. Past mistakes should not affect current decisions. The current value of the car is $19,000. Ms. Daniels' decision is whether to take the money or keep the car. The book value of the car is not relevant. This chapter explains how to isolate and focus on the variables that are relevant in the decision-making process.

The Curious Accountant

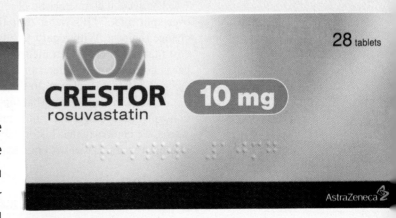

nattul/Shutterstock

In 2018, the authors compared the prices of 10 of the top-selling, nongeneric drugs at two large online pharmacies, one in the United States and one in Canada. The analysis showed the Canadian prices for these 10 prescription drugs, such as Advair and Crestor, were only 48 percent of prices charged in the United States.

Major pharmaceutical companies have earnings before tax that average around 18 percent of sales, indicating that their costs average about 82 percent of the prices they charge. In other words, it costs approximately $82 to generate $100 of revenue. Given that drugs are sold in Canada for 48 percent of the U.S. sales price, a drug that is sold in the United States for $100 would be sold in Canada for only $48.

How can drugs be sold in Canada for less ($48) than they cost to manufacture ($82)? (Answer on page 476.)

Source: goodrx.com and canadadrugonline.com.

RELEVANT INFORMATION

How can you avoid irrelevant information when making decisions? Two primary characteristics distinguish relevant from useless information. Specifically, **relevant information** (1) differs among the alternatives and (2) is future-oriented.

The first characteristic recognizes that relevant information differs for one or more of the alternatives being considered. Suppose the car Ms. Daniels is considering selling is due for a state-required safety inspection. Further assume that the inspection must be completed before the car can be sold or driven. Since the inspection fee must be paid regardless of whether Ms. Daniels keeps or sells the car, it does not differ among the alternatives and therefore is not relevant to her decision. In contrast, assume the car is due for an oil change that can be delayed until after the car is sold. Since Ms. Daniels can avoid the cost of the oil change if she sells the car but must pay for the oil change if she keeps the car, the cost of the oil change differs between the alternatives and is relevant to her decision.

The second characteristic of relevant information is that it impacts the future. "Don't cry over spilt milk." "It's water over the dam." These aphorisms remind people they cannot change the past. With regard to business decisions, the principle means you cannot avoid a cost that has already been incurred. In the Daniels example, the book value ($21,000) of the car is not relevant to a decision regarding whether to sell the car today. The current market value of $19,000 is relevant to the decision regarding whether to sell the car today.

It is interesting to note that the two characteristics are merely different views of the same concept because historical information does not differ between the alternatives. In other words, we could say that historical costs are not relevant because they do not differ between alternatives associated with current decisions.

Sunk Cost

Historical costs are frequently called *sunk costs.* Since **sunk costs** have been incurred in past transactions, they cannot be changed and are not relevant for making current decisions. The $21,000 book value of the car in the Daniels example is a sunk cost. Recall that the book value is the original cost minus accumulated depreciation. Accordingly, the original cost and the accumulated depreciation are also components of a sunk cost.

Why even bother to collect historical information if it is not relevant? Historical information may be useful in predicting the future. A company that earned $5 million last year is more likely to earn $5 million this year than a company that earned $5,000 last year. The predictive capacity is relevant because it provides insight into the future.

Opportunity Costs

An **opportunity cost** is the sacrifice that is incurred in order to obtain an alternative opportunity. For example, in the previous case, Ms. Daniels must give up the opportunity to obtain $19,000 in order to keep the car. So, the opportunity cost of owning the car is $19,000. Since this cost differs between the alternatives of owning the car versus selling it and since it affects the present or future, it is relevant to the decision regarding whether to keep or sell the car.

The best offer that Ms. Daniels received for the car was $19,000. Suppose Ms. Daniels also received a less favorable offer of $18,000. Does this mean that the opportunity cost of keeping the car is $37,000 ($18,000 + $19,000)? No. Opportunity costs are not cumulative. Ms. Daniels really has only one opportunity. If she accepts the $19,000 offer, she must reject the $18,000 offer or vice versa. Accountants normally measure opportunity cost as the highest value of the available alternatives. In this case, the opportunity cost of keeping the car is $19,000.

 CHECK YOURSELF 13.1

Aqua, Inc. makes statues for use in fountains. On January 1, Year 1, the company paid $13,500 for a mold to make a particular type of statue. The mold had an expected useful life of four years and a salvage value of $1,500. On December 31, Year 2, the mold had a market value of $3,000 and a salvage value of $1,200. The expected useful life did not change. What is the opportunity cost of continuing to use the mold as of December 31, Year 2?

Answer   The opportunity cost as of December 31, Year 2 is $1,800 ($3,000 Market value − $1,200 Salvage value). The original cost ($13,500) and the original estimate of the salvage value ($1,500) are historical measures that are not relevant to the current opportunity. You cannot go back in time. You can only seize the opportunities that are currently available.

Relevance Is an Independent Concept

The concept of relevance is independent from the concept of cost behavior. In a given circumstance, **relevant costs** could be either fixed or variable. Consider the following illustration. Executives of Better Bakery Products are debating whether to add a new product, either cakes or pies, to the company's line. Projected costs for the two options follow.

Cost of Cakes		Cost of Pies	
Materials (per unit)	$ 1.50	Materials (per unit)	$ 2.00
Direct labor (per unit)	1.00	Direct labor (per unit)	1.00
Supervisor's salary*	25,000.00	Supervisor's salary*	25,000.00
Franchise fee†	50,000.00	Advertising‡	40,000.00

*It will be necessary to hire a new production supervisor at a cost of $25,000 per year.

†Cakes will be distributed under a nationally advertised label. Better Bakery pays an annual franchise fee for the right to use the product label. Because of the established brand name, Better Bakery will not be required to advertise the product.

‡Better Bakery will market the pies under its own name and will advertise the product in the local market in which the product sells.

Which costs are relevant? Fifty cents per unit of the materials can be avoided by choosing cakes instead of pies. A portion of the materials cost is therefore relevant. Labor costs will be one dollar per unit whether Better Bakery makes cakes or pies. Labor cost is therefore not relevant. Although both materials and direct labor are variable costs, one is relevant but the other is not.

Since Better Bakery must hire a supervisor under either alternative, the supervisor's salary is not relevant. The franchise fee can be avoided if Better Bakery makes pies, and advertising costs can be avoided if it makes cakes. All three of these costs are fixed, but only two are relevant. Finally, all the costs (whether fixed or variable) could be avoided if Better Bakery rejects both products. Whether a cost is fixed or variable has no bearing on its relevance.

Relevance Is Context Sensitive

A particular cost that is relevant in one context may be irrelevant in another. Consider a store that carries men's, women's, and children's clothing. The store manager's salary could not be avoided by eliminating the children's department, but it could be avoided if the entire store were closed. The salary is not relevant to deciding whether to eliminate the children's department but is relevant with respect to deciding to close the store. In one context, the salary is not relevant. In the other context, it is relevant.

Relationship between Relevance and Accuracy

Information need not be exact to be relevant. You may decide to delay purchasing a laptop computer you want if you know its price is going to drop even if you don't know exactly how much the price decrease will be. You know part of the cost can be avoided by waiting; you are just not sure of the amount.

The most useful information is both relevant and precise. Totally inaccurate information is useless. Likewise, irrelevant information is useless regardless of its accuracy.

Quantitative versus Qualitative Characteristics of Decision Making

Relevant information can have both **quantitative** and **qualitative characteristics.** The previous examples focused on quantitative data. Now consider qualitative issues. Suppose you are deciding which of two laptop computers to purchase. Computer A costs $300 more than Computer B. Both computers satisfy your technical requirements; however, Computer A has a more attractive appearance. From a quantitative standpoint, you would select Computer B because you could avoid $300 of cost. However, if the laptop will be used in circumstances where clients need to be impressed, appearance—a qualitative characteristic—may be more important than minimizing cost. You might purchase Computer A even though quantitative factors favor Computer B. Both qualitative and quantitative data are relevant to decision making.

As with quantitative data, qualitative features must *differ* between the alternatives to be relevant. If the two computers were identical in appearance, attractiveness would not be relevant to making the decision.

Differential Revenue and Avoidable Cost

Since relevant revenue *differs* among the alternatives, it is sometimes called **differential revenue.** To illustrate, assume Pecks Department Stores sells men's, women's, and children's clothing and is considering eliminating the children's line. The revenue generated by the children's department is differential (relevant) revenue because Pecks' total revenue would be different if the children's department were eliminated.

Why would Pecks consider eliminating the children's department and thereby lose the differential (relevant) revenue? Pecks may be able to save more by eliminating the cost of operating the department than it loses in differential revenue. Some but not all of the costs associated with operating the children's department can be saved. For example, if Pecks Department Stores eliminates the children's department, the company can eliminate the cost of the department manager's salary but cannot get rid of the salary of the company president. The costs that stay the same are not relevant. The costs that can be *avoided* by closing the department are relevant. Indeed, relevant costs are frequently called *avoidable costs.*

Avoidable costs are the costs managers can eliminate by making specific choices. In the Pecks example, the cost of the department manager's salary is an avoidable (relevant) cost. The cost of the president's salary is not avoidable and is not relevant to the elimination decision.

Relationship of Cost Avoidance to a Cost Hierarchy

Classifying costs into one of four hierarchical levels helps identify avoidable costs.[1]

1. *Unit-level costs.* Costs incurred each time a company generates one unit of product are **unit-level costs.**[2] Examples include the cost of direct materials, direct labor, inspections, packaging, shipping, and handling. Incremental (additional) unit-level costs increase *with each additional unit of product generated. Unit-level costs can be avoided by eliminating the production of a single unit of product.*

2. *Batch-level costs.* Many products are generated in batches rather than individual units. For example, a heating and air conditioning technician may service a batch of air conditioners in an apartment complex. Some of the job costs apply only to individual units, and other costs relate to the entire batch. For instance, the labor to service each air conditioner is a unit-level cost, but the cost of driving to the site is a **batch-level cost.**

    Classifying costs as unit versus batch level frequently depends on the context rather than the type of cost. For example, shipping and handling costs to send 200 computers to a university are batch-level costs. In contrast, the shipping and handling cost to deliver a single computer to each of a number of individual customers is a unit-level cost. Elimi-

---

[1] R. Cooper and R. S. Kaplan, *The Design of Cost Management Systems* (Englewood Cliffs, NJ: Prentice-Hall, 1991). Our classifications are broader than those typically presented. They encompass service and merchandising companies as well as manufacturing businesses. The original cost hierarchy was developed as a platform for activity-based costing, a topic introduced in the previous chapter. These classifications are equally useful as a tool for identifying avoidable costs.

[2] Recall that we use the term *product* in a generic sense to represent producing goods or services.

nating a batch of work avoids both batch-level and unit-level costs. Similarly, adding a batch of work increases batch-level and unit-level costs. Increasing the number of units in a particular batch increases unit-level but not batch-level costs. Decreasing the number of units in a batch reduces unit-level costs but not batch-level costs.

3. *Product-level costs.* Costs incurred to support specific products or services are called **product-level costs.** Product-level costs include quality inspection costs, engineering design costs, the costs of obtaining and defending patents, the costs of regulatory compliance, and inventory holding costs such as interest, insurance, maintenance, and storage. *Product-level costs can be avoided by discontinuing a product line.* For example, suppose the Snapper Company makes the engines used in its lawn mowers. Buying engines from an outside supplier instead of making them would allow Snapper to avoid the product-level costs such as legal fees for patents, manufacturing supervisory costs of producing the engines, and the maintenance and inventory costs of holding engine parts.

4. *Facility-level costs.* **Facility-level costs** are incurred to support the entire company. They are not related to any specific product, batch, or unit of product. Because these costs maintain the facility as a whole, they are frequently called *facility-sustaining costs.* Facility-level costs include building rent or depreciation, personnel administration and training, property and real estate taxes, insurance, maintenance, administrative salaries, general selling costs, landscaping, utilities, and security. Total facility-level costs cannot be avoided unless the entire company is dissolved. However, eliminating a business segment (such as a division, department, or office) may enable a company to avoid some facility-level costs. For example, if a bank eliminates one of its branches, it can avoid the costs of renting, maintaining, and insuring that particular branch building. In general, *segment-level* facility costs can be avoided when a segment is eliminated. In contrast, *corporate-level* facility costs cannot be avoided unless the corporation is eliminated.

Ryan Pyle/Corbis/Getty Images

Precise distinctions between the various categories are often difficult to draw. One company may incur sales staff salaries as a facility-level cost while another company may pay sales commissions traceable to product lines or even specific units of a product line. Cost classifications cannot be memorized. Classifying specific cost items into the appropriate categories requires thoughtful judgment.

RELEVANT INFORMATION AND SPECIAL DECISIONS

Five types of special decisions are frequently encountered in business practice: (1) special order, (2) outsourcing, (3) segment elimination, (4) asset replacement, and (5) scarce resource allocation. The following sections discuss using relevant information in making the first four types of special decisions. The Appendix to this chapter discusses scarce resource decisions.

SPECIAL ORDER DECISIONS

Occasionally, a company receives an offer to sell its goods at a price significantly below its normal selling price. The company must make a **special order decision** to accept or reject the offer.

LO 13-2

 Make appropriate special order decisions.

Quantitative Analysis

Assume Premier Office Products manufactures printers. Premier expects to make and sell 2,000 printers in 10 batches of 200 units per batch during the coming year. Expected production costs are summarized in Exhibit 13.1.

Adding its normal markup to the total cost per unit, Premier set the selling price at $360 per printer.

Suppose Premier receives a *special order* from a new customer for 200 printers. If Premier accepts the order, its expected sales would increase from 2,000 units to 2,200 units.

EXHIBIT 13.1

Budgeted Cost for Expected Production of 2,000 Printers

Unit-level costs		
Materials costs (2,000 units × $90)	$180,000	
Labor costs (2,000 units × $82.50)	165,000	
Overhead (2,000 units × $7.50)	15,000	
Total unit-level costs (2,000 × $180)		$360,000
Batch-level costs		
Assembly setup (10 batches × $1,700)	17,000	
Materials handling (10 batches × $500)	5,000	
Total batch-level costs (10 batches × $2,200)		22,000
Product-level costs		
Engineering design	14,000	
Production manager salary	63,300	
Total product-level costs		77,300
Facility-level costs		
Segment-level costs:		
Division manager's salary	85,000	
Administrative costs	12,700	
Allocated—corporate-level costs:		
Company president's salary	43,200	
Building rental	27,300	
General expenses	31,000	
Total facility-level costs		199,200
Total expected cost		$658,500

Cost per unit: $658,500 ÷ 2,000 = $329.25

But the special order customer is willing to pay only $250 per printer. This price is well below not only Premier's normal selling price of $360 but also the company's expected per-unit cost of $329.25. Should Premier accept or reject the special order? At first glance, it seems Premier should reject the special order because the customer's offer is below the expected cost per unit. But analyzing relevant costs and revenue leads to a different conclusion.

Answers to the Curious Accountant

There are several factors that enable drug companies to reduce their prices to certain customers. One significant factor is the issue of relevant cost. Pharmaceutical manufacturers have a substantial amount of fixed cost, such as research and development. For example, in 2017 Merck & Co. had research and development expenses that were 25.4 percent of sales, while its cost of goods sold expense was 31.8 percent of sales. With respect to a special order decision, the research and development costs would not change and therefore would not be relevant. In contrast, the unit-level cost of goods sold would increase and therefore would be relevant. Many other costs at Merck, such as administrative and advertising expenses, are more fixed in nature than variable. Clearly, relevant costs are significantly less than the total cost. If Canadian prices are based on relevant costs, that is, if drug companies view Canadian sales as a special order opportunity, the lower prices may provide a contribution to profitability even though they are significantly less than the prices charged in the United States.

The quantitative analysis follows in three steps.

Step 1.   Determine the amount of the relevant (differential) revenue Premier will earn by accepting the special order. Premier's alternatives are (1) to accept or (2) to reject the special order. If Premier accepts the special order, additional revenue will be $50,000 ($250 × 200 units). If Premier rejects the special order, additional revenue will be zero. Since the amount of revenue differs between the alternatives, the $50,000 is relevant.

Step 2.   Determine the amount of the relevant (differential) cost Premier will incur by accepting the special order. Examine the costs in Exhibit 13.1. If Premier accepts the special order, it will incur additional unit-level costs (materials, labor, and overhead). It will also incur the cost of one additional 200-unit batch. The unit- and batch-level costs are relevant because Premier could avoid them by rejecting the special order. The other costs in Exhibit 13.1 are not relevant because Premier will incur them whether it accepts or rejects the special order.

Step 3.   Accept the special order if the relevant revenue exceeds the relevant (avoidable) cost. Reject the order if relevant cost exceeds relevant revenue. Exhibit 13.2 summarizes the relevant figures. Since the relevant revenue exceeds the relevant cost, Premier should accept the special order because profitability will increase by $11,800.

EXHIBIT 13.2

Relevant Information for Special Order of 200 Printers

Differential revenue ($250 × 200 units)	$50,000
Avoidable unit-level costs ($180 × 200 units)	(36,000)
Avoidable batch-level costs ($2,200 × 1 batch)	(2,200)
Contribution to income	$11,800

Opportunity Costs

Premier can consider the special order because it has enough excess productive capacity to make the additional units. Suppose Premier has the opportunity to lease its excess capacity (currently unused building and equipment) for $15,000. If Premier uses the excess capacity to make the additional printers, it must forgo the opportunity to lease the excess capacity to a third party. Sacrificing the potential leasing income represents an opportunity cost of accepting the special order. Adding this opportunity cost to the other relevant costs increases the cost of accepting the special order to $53,200 ($38,200 unit-level and batch-level costs + $15,000 opportunity cost). The avoidable costs would then exceed the differential revenue, resulting in a projected loss of $3,200 ($50,000 differential revenue − $53,200 avoidable costs). Under these circumstances Premier would be better off rejecting the special order and leasing the excess capacity.

Relevance and the Decision Context

Assume Premier does not have the opportunity to lease its excess capacity. Recall the original analysis indicated the company could earn an $11,800 contribution to profit by accepting a special order to sell 200 printers at $250 per unit (see Exhibit 13.2). Because Premier can earn a contribution to profit by selling printers for $250 each, can the company reduce its normal selling price (price charged to existing customers) to $250? The answer is no, as illustrated in Exhibit 13.3.

EXHIBIT 13.3

Projections Based on 2,200 Printers at a Sales Price of $250 per Unit		
Revenue ($250 × 2,200 units)		$ 550,000
Unit-level supplies and inspection ($180 × 2,200 units)	$396,000	
Batch-level costs ($2,200 × 11 batches)	24,200	
Product-level costs	77,300	
Facility-level costs	199,200	
Total cost		(696,700)
Projected loss		$(146,700)

If a company is to be profitable, it must ultimately generate revenue in excess of total costs. Although the facility-level and product-level costs are not relevant to the special order decision, they are relevant to the operation of the business as a whole.

Qualitative Characteristics

Should a company ever reject a special order if the relevant revenues exceed the relevant costs? Qualitative characteristics may be even more important than quantitative ones. If Premier's regular customers learn the company sold printers to another buyer at $250 per unit, they may demand reduced prices on future purchases. Exhibit 13.3 shows Premier cannot reduce the price for all customers. Special order customers should therefore come from outside Premier's normal sales territory. In addition, special order customers should be advised that the special price does not apply to repeat business. Cutting off a special order customer who has been permitted to establish a continuing relationship is likely to lead to ill-feelings and harsh words. A business's reputation can depend on how management handles such relationships. Finally, at full capacity, Premier should reject any special orders at reduced prices because filling those orders reduces its ability to satisfy customers who pay full price.

REALITY BYTES

Sometimes companies make special pricing decisions that appear to violate the rule of rejecting an offer when its relevant cost exceeds its relevant revenue. Consider companies that use the services of Groupon.

In these special pricing decisions, retail customers are offered a reduced price on goods or services if they make the purchase through Groupon. For example, a restaurant may offer to sell a customer $40 worth of food for only $20. This appears to be a deal where the restaurant is selling its food for 50 percent off, but actually it is probably selling the food for around 60 percent off. The restaurant will receive only around $15 of the $20 the customer pays to Groupon. Groupon keeps the remaining $5 for itself. Thus, the restaurant is selling $40 of food for $15.

At Darden Restaurants Inc., the company that owns several restaurant chains including LongHorn Steakhouse and Olive Garden, the cost of the food sold averages 30 percent of revenue, and restaurant labor costs average 34 percent. In other words, if a customer buys $40

Juan Camilo
Bernal/Shutterstock

worth of food, approximately $26 of those dollars are costs of providing the food to the customer. Not all of these costs are unit-level costs, but many of them are. Therefore, when a restaurant sells a customer $40 worth of food for only $15, as in the previous Groupon example, it appears to be selling the goods for much less than their relevant cost. Why would the restaurant do this?

Obviously, the restaurant is hoping that it will attract new customers with its special pricing offer and that these new customers will become repeat customers who pay full price for future meals. In this situation, the true relevant revenue is not the $15 received for the first meal, but includes the revenue from future meals the customer buys, along with alcoholic beverages that may not be included in the coupon deal. Of course there is no guarantee the customer will ever return, but as with most business decisions, managers must make decisions with less than perfect information.

OUTSOURCING DECISIONS

Companies can sometimes purchase products they need for less than it would cost to make them. This circumstance explains why automobile manufacturers purchase rather than make many of the parts in their cars or why a caterer might buy gourmet desserts from a specialty company. Buying goods and services from other companies rather than producing them internally is commonly called **outsourcing.**

Make appropriate outsourcing decisions.

Quantitative Analysis

Assume Premier Office Products is considering whether to outsource production of the printers it currently makes. A supplier has offered to sell an unlimited supply of printers to Premier for $240 each. The estimated cost of making the printers is $329.25 per unit (see Exhibit 13.1). The data suggest that Premier could save money by outsourcing. Analyzing relevant costs proves this presumption wrong.

A two-step quantitative analysis for the outsourcing decision follows.

Step 1. **Determine the production costs Premier can avoid if it outsources printer production.** A review of Exhibit 13.1 discloses the costs Premier could avoid by outsourcing. If Premier purchases the printers, it can avoid the unit-level costs (materials, labor, overhead) and the batch-level costs (assembly setup and materials handling). It can also avoid the product-level costs (engineering design costs and production manager salary). Deciding to outsource will not, however, affect the facility-level costs. Because Premier will incur them whether or not it outsources printer production, the facility-level costs are not relevant to the outsourcing decision. Exhibit 13.4 shows the avoidable (relevant) costs of outsourcing.

Step 2. **Compare the avoidable (relevant) production costs with the cost of buying the product and select the lower-cost option.** Because the relevant production cost is less than the purchase price of the printers ($229.65 per unit versus $240.00), the quantitative analysis suggests that Premier should continue to make the printers. Profitability would decline by $20,700 [$459,300 − ($240 × 2,000)] if printer production were outsourced.

EXHIBIT 13.4

Relevant Cost for Expected Production for Outsourcing 2,000 Printers

Unit-level costs ($180 × 2,000 units)	$360,000
Batch-level costs ($2,200 × 10 batches)	22,000
Product-level costs	77,300
Total relevant cost	$459,300

Cost per unit: $459,300 ÷ 2,000 = $229.65

Opportunity Costs

Suppose Premier's accountant determines that the space Premier currently uses to manufacture printers could be leased to a third party for $40,000 per year. By using the space to manufacture printers, Premier is *forgoing the opportunity* to earn $40,000. Because this *opportunity cost* can be avoided by purchasing the printers, it is relevant to the outsourcing decision. After adding the opportunity cost to the other relevant costs, the total relevant cost increases to $499,300 ($459,300 + $40,000) and the relevant cost per unit becomes $249.65 ($499,300 ÷ 2,000). Since Premier can purchase printers for $240, it should outsource printer production. It would be better off buying the printers and leasing the manufacturing space.

Evaluating the Effect of Growth on the Level of Production

The decision to outsource would change if expected production increased from 2,000 to 3,000 units. Because some of the avoidable costs are fixed relative to the level of production, cost per unit decreases as volume increases. For example, the product-level costs (engineering design, production manager's salary, and opportunity cost) are fixed relative to the level of production. Exhibit 13.5 shows the relevant cost per unit if Premier expects to produce 3,000 printers.

EXHIBIT 13.5

Relevant Cost for Expected Production for Outsourcing 3,000 Printers

Unit-level costs ($180 × 3,000 units)	$540,000
Batch-level costs ($2,200 × 15 batches)	33,000
Product-level costs	77,300
Opportunity cost	40,000
Total relevant cost	$690,300

Cost per unit: $690,300 ÷ 3,000 units = $230.10

At 3,000 units of production, the relevant cost of making printers is less than the cost of outsourcing ($230.10 versus $240.00). If management believes the company is likely to experience growth in the near future, it should reject the outsourcing option. Managers must consider potential growth when making outsourcing decisions.

Qualitative Features

A company that uses **vertical integration** controls the full range of activities from acquiring raw materials to distributing goods and services. Outsourcing reduces the level of vertical integration, passing some of a company's control over its products to outside suppliers. The reliability of the supplier is critical to an outsourcing decision. An unscrupulous supplier may lure an unsuspecting manufacturer into an outsourcing decision using **low-ball pricing.** Once the manufacturer is dependent on the supplier, the supplier raises prices. If a price sounds too good to be true, it probably is too good to be true. Other potential problems include product quality and delivery commitments. If the printers do not work properly or are not delivered on time, Premier's customers will be dissatisfied with Premier, not the supplier. Outsourcing requires that Premier depend on the supplier to deliver quality products at designated prices according to a specified schedule. Any supplier failures will become Premier's failures.

To protect themselves from unscrupulous or incompetent suppliers, many companies establish a select list of reliable **certified suppliers.** These companies seek to become the preferred customers of the suppliers by offering incentives such as guaranteed volume purchases with prompt payments. These incentives motivate the suppliers to ship high-quality products on a timely basis. The purchasing companies recognize that prices ultimately depend on the suppliers' ability to control costs, so the buyers and suppliers work together to minimize costs. For example, buyers may share confidential information about their production plans with suppliers if such information would enable the suppliers to more effectively control costs.

Companies must approach outsourcing decisions cautiously even when relationships with reliable suppliers are ensured. Outsourcing has both internal and external effects. It usually displaces employees. If the supplier experiences difficulties, reestablishing internal production capacity is expensive once a trained workforce has been released. Loyalty and trust are difficult to build but easy to destroy. In fact, companies must consider not only the employees who will be discharged but also the morale of those who remain. Cost reductions achieved through outsourcing are of little benefit if they are acquired at the expense of low morale and reduced productivity.

In spite of the potential pitfalls outsourcing entails, the vast majority of U.S. businesses engage in some form of it. Such widespread acceptance suggests that most companies believe the benefits achieved through outsourcing exceed the potential shortcomings.

☑ CHECK YOURSELF 13.2

Addison Manufacturing Company pays a production supervisor a salary of $48,000 per year. The supervisor manages the production of sprinkler heads that are used in water irrigation systems. Should the production supervisor's salary be considered a relevant cost to a special order decision? Should the production supervisor's salary be considered a relevant cost to an outsourcing decision?

Answer   The production supervisor's salary is not a relevant cost to a special order decision because Addison would pay the salary regardless of whether it accepts or rejects a special order. Since the cost does not differ for the alternatives, it is not relevant. In contrast, the supervisor's salary would be relevant to an outsourcing decision. Addison could dismiss the supervisor if it purchased the sprinkler heads instead of making them. Since the salary could be avoided by purchasing heads instead of making them, the salary is relevant to an outsourcing decision.

REALITY BYTES

In 2008, Georgia Power, a subsidiary of Southern Company, along with other investors, received approval to build two new nuclear power units at its Vogtle electric power plant. Original estimates put the cost of completing these units at around $12 billion, and the reactors were expected to begin operating in 2016. Westinghouse Electric Company, a subsidiary of Toshiba Corporation, was awarded the contract to build the reactors.

Things did not go as planned. By 2017 the revised cost to build the reactors had reached $25 billion, and the expected completion date was late 2021. These cost overruns were such that Westinghouse filed for Chapter 11 bankruptcy in March of 2017.

With construction cost nearly double the original estimate, and the completion date five years behind schedule, the investors faced the decision as to whether to complete the project or call it quits and accept their losses. As bad as the numbers were, the reality was that the previously incurred costs were sunk costs. At this point, the relevant question was would expected revenues cover the costs to complete the project plus future operating expenses.

A critical factor in the decision was how much, if any, of the cost overruns would the Georgia Public Utility Commission allow Georgia Power to pass on to its customers. The rates utilities charge customers are regulated by the states in which they operate. Late in 2017 Utility Commission voted to allow the project to continue, but not at rates that would generate as much profit as Georgia Power had originally expected. Based on the new guidelines, profits on the project would be $750 million less that hoped. Even so, it was deemed more profitable to continue the project than to cancel it.

hornyak/Shutterstock

Even when the amounts involved are in the billions, the bottom-line decision rule is, "will future revenues exceed future costs." Past costs are sunk costs.

Sources: SEC filings of Southern Company and news releases on Westinghouse's website.

SEGMENT ELIMINATION DECISIONS

Businesses frequently organize their operations into subcomponents called **segments**. Segment data are used to make comparisons among different products, departments, or divisions. For example, in addition to the companywide income statement provided for external users, JCPenney may prepare separate income statements for each retail store for internal users. Executives can then evaluate managerial performance by comparing profitability measures among stores. *Segment reports* can be prepared for products, services, departments, branches, centers, offices, or divisions. These reports normally show segment revenues and costs. The primary objective of segment analysis is to determine whether relevant revenues exceed relevant costs.

LO 13-4

Make appropriate segment elimination decisions.

Quantitative Analysis

Assume Premier Office Products makes copy equipment and computers as well as printers. Each product line is made in a separate division of the company. Division (segment) operating results for the most recent year are shown in Exhibit 13.6. Initial review of the results suggests the copier division should be eliminated because it is operating at a loss. However, analyzing the relevant revenues and expenses leads to a different conclusion.

A three-step quantitative analysis for the segment elimination decision follows.

Step 1. **Determine the amount of relevant (differential) revenue that pertains to eliminating the copier division.** The alternatives are (1) to eliminate or (2) to continue to operate the copier division. If Premier eliminates the copier line, it will lose the $550,000 of revenue the copier division currently produces. If the division continues to operate, Premier will earn the revenue. Since the revenue differs between the alternatives, it is relevant.

EXHIBIT 13.6

Projected Revenues and Costs by Segment

	Copiers	Computers	Printers	Total
Projected revenue	$550,000	$850,000	$720,000	$2,120,000
Projected costs				
Unit-level costs				
Materials costs	(120,000)	(178,000)	(180,000)	(478,000)
Labor costs	(160,000)	(202,000)	(165,000)	(527,000)
Overhead	(30,800)	(20,000)	(15,000)	(65,800)
Batch-level costs				
Assembly setup	(15,000)	(26,000)	(17,000)	(58,000)
Materials handling	(6,000)	(8,000)	(5,000)	(19,000)
Product-level costs				
Engineering design	(10,000)	(12,000)	(14,000)	(36,000)
Production manager salary	(52,000)	(55,800)	(63,300)	(171,100)
Facility-level costs				
Segment level				
Division manager salary	(82,000)	(92,000)	(85,000)	(259,000)
Administrative costs	(12,200)	(13,200)	(12,700)	(38,100)
Allocated—corporate-level				
Company president salary	(34,000)	(46,000)	(43,200)	(123,200)
Building rental	(19,250)	(29,750)	(27,300)	(76,300)
General facility expenses	(31,000)	(31,000)	(31,000)	(93,000)
Projected income (loss)	$ (22,250)	$136,250	$ 61,500	$ 175,500

Step 2. **Determine the amount of cost Premier can avoid if it eliminates the copier division.** If it eliminates copiers, Premier can avoid the unit-level, batch-level, product-level, and segment-level facility-sustaining costs. The relevant revenue and the avoidable costs are shown in Exhibit 13.7.

Premier will incur the corporate-level facility-sustaining costs whether it eliminates the copier segment or continues to operate it. Since these costs do not differ between the alternatives, they are not relevant to the elimination decision.

Step 3. **If the relevant revenue is less than the avoidable cost, eliminate the segment (division). If not, continue to operate it.** Because operating the segment is contributing $62,000 per year to company profitability (see Exhibit 13.7), Premier should not eliminate the copier division. Exhibit 13.8 shows Premier's estimated revenues and costs if the computer and printer divisions were operated without the copier division. Projected company profit declines by $62,000 ($175,500 − $113,500) without the copier segment, confirming that eliminating it would be detrimental to Premier's profitability.

EXHIBIT 13.7

Relevant Revenue and Cost Data for Copier Segment

Projected revenue	$550,000
Projected costs	
Unit-level costs	
Materials costs	(120,000)
Labor costs	(160,000)
Overhead	(30,800)
Batch-level costs	
Assembly setup	(15,000)
Materials handling	(6,000)
Product-level costs	
Engineering design	(10,000)
Production manager salary	(52,000)
Facility-level costs	
Segment level	
Division manager salary	(82,000)
Administrative costs	(12,200)
Projected income (loss)	$ 62,000

Qualitative Considerations in Decisions to Eliminate Segments

As with other special decisions, management should consider qualitative factors when determining whether to eliminate segments. Employee lives will be disrupted; some employees may be reassigned elsewhere in the company, but others will be discharged. As with outsourcing decisions, reestablishing internal production capacity is difficult once a trained workforce has been released. Furthermore, employees in other segments, suppliers, customers, and investors may believe that the elimination of a segment implies the company as a whole is experiencing financial difficulty. These individuals may lose

EXHIBIT 13.8

Projected Revenues and Costs without Copier Division

	Computers	Printers	Total
Projected revenue	$850,000	$720,000	$1,570,000
Projected costs			
Unit-level costs			
Materials costs	(178,000)	(180,000)	(358,000)
Labor costs	(202,000)	(165,000)	(367,000)
Overhead	(20,000)	(15,000)	(35,000)
Batch-level costs			
Assembly setup	(26,000)	(17,000)	(43,000)
Materials handling	(8,000)	(5,000)	(13,000)
Product-level costs			
Engineering design	(12,000)	(14,000)	(26,000)
Production manager salary	(55,800)	(63,300)	(119,100)
Facility-level costs			
Segment level			
Division manager salary	(92,000)	(85,000)	(177,000)
Administrative costs	(13,200)	(12,700)	(25,900)
Allocated—corporate-level*			
Company president salary	(63,000)	(60,200)	(123,200)
Building rental	(39,375)	(36,925)	(76,300)
General facility expenses	(46,500)	(46,500)	(93,000)
Projected income (loss)	$ 94,125	$ 19,375	$ 113,500

*The corporate-level facility costs that were previously *allocated* to the copier division have been reassigned on the basis of one-half to the computer division and one-half to the printer division.

confidence in the company and seek business contacts with other companies they perceive to be more stable.

Management must also consider the fact that sales of different product lines are frequently interdependent. Some customers prefer one-stop shopping; they want to buy all their office equipment from one supplier. If Premier no longer sells copiers, customers may stop buying its computers and printers. Eliminating one segment may reduce sales of other segments.

What will happen to the space Premier used to make the copiers? Suppose Premier decides to make telephone systems in the space it previously used for copiers. The contribution to profit of the telephone business would be an *opportunity cost* of operating the copier segment. As demonstrated in previous examples, adding the opportunity cost to the avoidable costs of operating the copier segment could change the decision.

As with outsourcing, volume changes can affect elimination decisions. Because many costs of operating a segment are fixed, the cost per unit decreases as production increases. Growth can transform a segment that is currently producing real losses into a segment that produces real profits. Managers must consider growth potential when making elimination decisions.

☑ CHECK YOURSELF 13.3

Capital Corporation is considering eliminating one of its operating segments. Capital employed a real estate broker to determine the marketability of the building that houses the segment. The broker obtained three bids for the building: $250,000, $262,000, and $264,000. The book value of the building is $275,000. Based on this information alone, what is the relevant cost of the building?

Answer The book value of the building is a sunk cost that is not relevant. There are three bids for the building, but only one is relevant because Capital could sell the building only once. The relevant cost of the building is the highest opportunity cost, which in this case is $264,000.

Summary of Relationships between Avoidable Costs and the Hierarchy of Business Activity

A relationship exists between the cost hierarchy and the different types of special decisions just discussed. A special order involves making additional units of an existing product. Deciding to accept a special order affects unit-level and possibly batch-level costs. In contrast, outsourcing a product stops the production of that product. Outsourcing can avoid many product-level as well as unit- and batch-level costs. Finally, if a company eliminates an entire business segment, it can avoid some of the facility-level costs. The more complex the decision level, the more opportunities there are to avoid costs. Moving to a higher category does not mean, however, that all costs at the higher level of activity are avoidable. For example, all product-level costs may not be avoidable if a company chooses to outsource a product. The company may still incur inventory holding costs or advertising costs whether it makes or buys the product. Understanding the relationship between decision type and level of cost hierarchy helps when identifying avoidable costs. The relationships are summarized in Exhibit 13.9. For each type of decision, look for avoidable costs in the categories marked with an *X*. Remember also that sunk costs cannot be avoided.

EXHIBIT 13.9

Relationship between Decision Type and Level of Cost Hierarchy

Decision Type	Unit Level	Batch Level	Product Level	Facility Level
Special order	X	X		
Outsourcing	X	X	X	
Elimination	X	X	X	X

ASSET REPLACEMENT DECISIONS

LO 13-5

Make appropriate asset replacement decisions.

Assets may become technologically obsolete long before they fail physically. Managers should base **asset replacement decisions** on profitability analysis rather than physical deterioration. Assume Premier Office Products is considering replacing an existing machine with a new one. The following table summarizes pertinent information about the two machines.

Old Machine		New Machine	
Original cost	$90,000	Cost of the new machine	$29,000
Accumulated depreciation	(33,000)	Salvage value (in 5 years)	4,000
Book value	$57,000	Operating expenses	
		($4,500 × 5 years)	22,500
Market value (now)	$14,000		
Salvage value (in 5 years)	2,000		
Annual depreciation expense	11,000		
Operating expenses			
($9,000 × 5 years)	45,000		

Quantitative Analysis

First determine what relevant costs Premier will incur if it keeps the *old machine.*

1. The *original cost* ($90,000), *current book value* ($57,000), *accumulated depreciation* ($33,000), and *annual depreciation expense* ($11,000) are different measures of a cost that was incurred in a prior period. They represent irrelevant sunk costs.

2. The $14,000 market value represents the current sacrifice Premier must make if it keeps using the existing machine. In other words, if Premier does not keep the machine, it can sell it for $14,000. In economic terms, *forgoing the opportunity* to sell the machine costs as much as buying it. The *opportunity cost* is therefore relevant to the replacement decision.

3. The salvage value of the old machine reduces the opportunity cost. Premier can sell the old machine now for $14,000 or use it for five more years and then sell it for $2,000. The opportunity cost of using the old machine for five more years is therefore $12,000 ($14,000 − $2,000).

4. Because the $45,000 ($9,000 × 5) of operating expenses will be incurred if the old machine is used but can be avoided if it is replaced, the operating expenses are relevant costs.

Next, determine what relevant costs will be incurred if Premier purchases and uses the *new machine.*

1. The cost of the new machine represents a future economic sacrifice Premier must incur if it buys the new machine. It is a relevant cost.

2. The salvage value reduces the cost of purchasing the new machine. Part ($4,000) of the $29,000 cost of the new machine will be recovered at the end of five years. The relevant cost of purchasing the new machine is $25,000 ($29,000 − $4,000).

3. The $22,500 ($4,500 × 5) of operating expenses will be incurred if the new machine is purchased; it can be avoided if the new machine is not purchased. The operating expenses are relevant costs.

The relevant costs for the two machines are summarized here.

Old Machine		New Machine	
Opportunity cost	$14,000	Cost of the new machine	$29,000
Salvage value	(2,000)	Salvage value	(4,000)
Operating expenses	45,000	Operating expenses	22,500
Total	$57,000	Total	$47,500

The analysis suggests that Premier should acquire the new machine because buying it produces the lower relevant cost. The $57,000 cost of using the old machine can be *avoided* by incurring the $47,500 cost of acquiring and using the new machine. Over the five-year period, Premier would save $9,500 ($57,000 − $47,500) by purchasing the new machine. One caution: This analysis ignores income tax effects and the time value of money, which are explained later. The discussion in this chapter focuses on identifying and using relevant costs in decision making.

A Look Back

Decision making requires managers to choose from alternative courses of action. Successful decision making depends on a manager's ability to identify *relevant information*. Information that is relevant for decision making differs among the alternatives and is future oriented. Relevant revenues are sometimes called *differential revenues* because they differ among the alternatives. Relevant costs are sometimes called *avoidable costs* because they can be eliminated or avoided by choosing a specific course of action.

Costs that do not differ among the alternatives are not avoidable and therefore not relevant. *Sunk costs* are not relevant in decision making because they have been incurred in past transactions and therefore cannot be avoided. *Opportunity costs* are relevant because they represent potential benefits that may or may not be realized, depending on the decision maker's choice. In other words, future benefits that differ among the alternatives are relevant. Opportunity costs are not recorded in the financial accounting records.

Cost behavior (fixed or variable) is independent from the concept of relevance. Furthermore, a cost that is relevant in one decision context may be irrelevant in another context. Decision making depends on qualitative as well as quantitative information. *Quantitative information refers to information that can be measured using numbers. Qualitative information* is nonquantitative information such as personal preferences or opportunities.

Classifying costs into one of four hierarchical levels facilitates identifying relevant costs. *Unit-level costs* such as materials and labor are incurred each time a single unit of product is made. These costs can be avoided by eliminating the production of a single unit of product. *Batch-level costs* are associated with producing a group of products. Examples include setup costs and inspection costs related to a batch (group) of work rather than a single unit. Eliminating a batch would avoid both batch-level costs and unit-level costs. *Product-level costs* are incurred to support specific products or services (design and regulatory compliance costs). Product-level costs can be avoided by discontinuing a product line. *Facility-level costs,* like the president's salary, are incurred on behalf of the whole company or a segment of the company. In segment elimination decisions, the facility-level costs related to a particular segment being considered for elimination are relevant and avoidable. Those applying to the company as a whole are not avoidable.

Four types of special decisions that are frequently encountered in business are (1) *special orders,* (2) *outsourcing,* (3) *elimination decisions,* and (4) *asset replacement.* The relevant costs in a special order decision are the unit-level and batch-level costs that will be incurred if the special order is accepted. If the differential revenues from the special order exceed the relevant costs, the order should be accepted. Outsourcing decisions determine whether goods and services should be purchased from other companies. The relevant costs are the unit-level, batch-level, and product-level costs that could be avoided if the company outsources the product or service. If these costs are more than the cost to buy and the qualitative characteristics are satisfactory, the company should outsource. Segment-related unit-level, batch-level, product-level, and facility-level costs that can be avoided when a segment is eliminated are relevant. If the segment's avoidable costs exceed its differential revenues, it should be eliminated, assuming favorable qualitative factors. Asset replacement decisions compare the relevant costs of existing equipment with the relevant costs of new equipment to determine whether replacing the old equipment would be profitable.

>> A Look Forward

The next chapter introduces key concepts associated with planning and cost control. It shows you how to develop a master budget including the preparation of four operating budgets: (1) a sales budget, (2) an inventory purchases budget, (3) a selling and administrative expense budget, and (4) a cash budget. The chapter explains how data from the operating budgets are used to prepare pro forma (budgeted) financial statements. In addition to the quantitative aspects, the chapter discusses the effect of the budgeting process on human behavior.

Video lectures and accompanying self-assessment quizzes are available in *Connect* for all learning objectives.

SELF-STUDY REVIEW PROBLEM

Flying High, Inc. (FHI) is a division of The Master Toy Company. FHI makes remote-controlled airplanes. During Year 5, FHI incurred the following costs in the process of making 5,000 planes.

Unit-level materials costs (5,000 units × $80)	$ 400,000
Unit-level labor costs (5,000 units × $90)	450,000
Unit-level overhead costs (5,000 × $70)	350,000
Depreciation cost on manufacturing equipment*	50,000
Other manufacturing overhead†	140,000
Inventory holding costs	240,000
Allocated portion of The Master Toy Company's facility-level costs	600,000
Total costs	$2,230,000

*The manufacturing equipment, which originally cost $250,000, has a book value of $200,000, a remaining useful life of four years, and a zero salvage value. If the equipment is not used in the production process, it can be leased for $30,000 per year.

†Includes supervisors' salaries and rent for the manufacturing building.

Required

a. FHI uses a cost-plus pricing strategy. FHI sets its price at product cost plus $100. Determine the price that FHI should charge for its remote-controlled airplanes.

b. Assume that a potential customer who operates a chain of high-end toy stores has approached FHI. A buyer for this chain has offered to purchase 1,000 planes from FHI at a price of $275 each. Ignoring qualitative considerations, should FHI accept or reject the order?

c. FHI has the opportunity to purchase the planes from Arland Manufacturing Company for $325 each. Arland maintains adequate inventories so that it can supply its customers with planes on demand. Should FHI accept the opportunity to outsource the making of its planes?

d. When completing this requirement, use the sales price computed in Requirement *a*. Use the contribution margin format to prepare an income statement based on historical cost data. Prepare a second income statement that reflects the relevant cost data that Master Toy should consider in a segment elimination decision. Based on a comparison of these two statements, indicate whether Master Toy should eliminate the FHI division.

e. FHI is considering replacing the equipment it currently uses to manufacture its planes. It could purchase replacement equipment for $480,000 that has an expected useful life of four years and a salvage value of $40,000. The new equipment would increase productivity substantially, reducing unit-level labor costs by 20 percent. Assume that FHI would maintain its production and sales at 5,000 planes per year. Prepare a schedule that shows the relevant costs of operating the old equipment versus the costs of operating the new equipment. Should FHI replace the equipment?

Solution to Requirement *a*

Product Cost for Remote-Controlled Airplanes	
Unit-level materials costs (5,000 units × $80)	$ 400,000
Unit-level labor costs (5,000 units × $90)	450,000
Unit-level overhead costs (5,000 units × $70)	350,000
Depreciation cost on manufacturing equipment	50,000
Other manufacturing overhead	140,000
Total product cost	$1,390,000

The cost per unit is $278 ($1,390,000 ÷ 5,000 units). The sales price per unit is $378 ($278 + $100). Depreciation expense is included because cost-plus pricing is usually based on historical cost rather than relevant cost. To be profitable in the long run, a company must ultimately recover the amount it paid for the equipment (the historical cost of the equipment).

Solution to Requirement b

The incremental (relevant) cost of making 1,000 additional airplanes follows. The depreciation expense is not relevant because it represents a sunk cost. The other manufacturing overhead costs are not relevant because they will be incurred regardless of whether FHI makes the additional planes.

Per-Unit Relevant Product Cost for Airplanes	
Unit-level materials costs	$ 80
Unit-level labor costs	90
Unit-level overhead costs	70
Total relevant product cost	$240

Since the relevant (incremental) cost of making the planes is less than the incremental revenue, FHI should accept the special order. Accepting the order will increase profits by $35,000 [($275 Incremental revenue − $240 Incremental cost) × 1,000 Units].

Solution to Requirement c

Distinguish this decision from the special order opportunity discussed in Requirement b. That special order (Requirement b) decision hinged on the cost of making additional units with the existing production process. In contrast, a make-or-buy decision compares current production with the possibility of making zero units (closing down the entire manufacturing process). If the manufacturing process were shut down, FHI could avoid the unit-level costs, the cost of the lost opportunity to lease the equipment, the other manufacturing overhead costs, and the inventory holding costs. Since the planes can be purchased on demand, there is no need to maintain any inventory. The allocated portion of the facility-level costs is not relevant because it would be incurred regardless of whether FHI manufactured the planes. The relevant cost of making the planes follows.

Relevant Manufacturing Cost for Airplanes	
Unit-level materials costs (5,000 units × $80)	$ 400,000
Unit-level labor costs (5,000 units × $90)	450,000
Unit-level overhead costs (5,000 units × $70)	350,000
Opportunity cost of leasing the equipment	30,000
Other manufacturing overhead costs	140,000
Inventory holding cost	240,000
Total product cost	$1,610,000

The relevant cost per unit is $322 ($1,610,000 ÷ 5,000 units). Since the relevant cost of making the planes ($322) is less than the cost of purchasing them ($325), FHI should continue to make the planes.

Solution to Requirement d

Income Statements		
	Historical Cost Data	Relevant Cost Data
Revenue (5,000 units × $378)	$1,890,000	$1,890,000
Less variable costs:		
Unit-level materials costs (5,000 units × $80)	(400,000)	(400,000)
Unit-level labor costs (5,000 units × $90)	(450,000)	(450,000)
Unit-level overhead costs (5,000 units × $70)	(350,000)	(350,000)
Contribution margin	690,000	690,000
Depreciation cost on manufacturing equipment	(50,000)	
Opportunity cost of leasing manufacturing equipment		(30,000)
Other manufacturing overhead costs	(140,000)	(140,000)
Inventory holding costs	(240,000)	(240,000)
Allocated facility-level administrative costs	(600,000)	
Net loss	$ (340,000)	
Contribution to Master Toy's profitability		$ 280,000

Master Toy should not eliminate the segment (FHI). Although it appears to be incurring a loss, the allocated facility-level administrative costs are not relevant because Master Toy would incur these costs regardless of whether it eliminated FHI. Also, the depreciation cost on the manufacturing equipment is not relevant because it is a sunk cost. However, since the company could lease the equipment if the segment were eliminated, the $30,000 potential rental fee represents a relevant opportunity cost. The relevant revenue and cost data show that FHI is contributing $280,000 to the profitability of The Master Toy Company.

Solution to Requirement e

The relevant costs of using the old equipment versus the new equipment are the costs that differ for the two alternatives. In this case, relevant costs include the purchase price of the new equipment, the opportunity cost of the old equipment, and the labor costs. These items are summarized in the following table. The data show the total cost over the four-year useful life of the replacement equipment.

Relevant Cost Comparison

	Old Equipment	New Equipment
Opportunity to lease the old equipment ($30,000 × 4 years)	$ 120,000	
Cost of new equipment ($480,000 − $40,000)		$ 440,000
Unit-level labor costs (5,000 units × $90 × 4 years)	1,800,000	
Unit-level labor costs (5,000 units × $90 × 4 years × 0.80)		1,440,000
Total relevant costs	$1,920,000	$1,880,000

Since the relevant cost of operating the new equipment is less than the cost of operating the old equipment, FHI should replace the equipment.

KEY TERMS

Asset replacement decisions 484
Avoidable costs 474
Batch-level costs 474
Certified suppliers 480
Differential revenue 474
Facility-level costs 475
Low-ball pricing 480
Opportunity cost 472
Outsourcing 479
Product-level costs 475
Qualitative characteristics 474
Quantitative characteristics 474
Relevant costs 473
Relevant information 472
Segment 481
Special order decisions 475
Sunk costs 472
Unit-level costs 474
Vertical integration 480

QUESTIONS

1. Identify the primary qualities of revenues and costs that are relevant for decision making.

2. Are variable costs always relevant? Explain.

3. Identify the four hierarchical levels used to classify costs. When can each of these levels of costs be avoided?

4. Describe the relationship between relevance and accuracy.

5. "It all comes down to the bottom line. The numbers never lie." Do you agree with this conclusion? Explain your position.

6. Carmon Company invested $300,000 in the equity securities of Mann Corporation. The current market value of Carmon's investment in Mann is $250,000. Carmon currently needs funds for operating purposes. Although interest rates are high, Carmon's president has decided to borrow the needed funds instead of selling the investment in Mann. He explains that his company cannot afford to take a $50,000 loss on the Mann stock. Evaluate the president's decision based on this information.

7. What is an opportunity cost? How does it differ from a sunk cost?

8. A local bank advertises that it offers a free noninterest-bearing checking account if the depositor maintains a $500 minimum balance in the account. Is the checking account truly free?

9. A manager is faced with deciding whether to replace Machine A or Machine B. The original cost of machine A was $20,000 and that of Machine B was $30,000. Because the two

cost figures differ, they are relevant to the manager's decision. Do you agree? Explain your position.

10. Are all fixed costs unavoidable?

11. Identify two qualitative considerations that could be associated with special order decisions.

12. Which of the following would not be relevant to a make-or-buy decision?

   (a) Allocated portion of depreciation expense on existing facilities.

   (b) Variable cost of labor used to produce products currently purchased from suppliers.

   (c) Warehousing costs for inventory of completed products (inventory levels will be constant regardless of whether products are purchased or produced).

   (d) Cost of materials used to produce the items currently purchased from suppliers.

   (e) Property taxes on the factory building.

13. What two factors should be considered in deciding how to allocate shelf space in a retail establishment?

14. What level(s) of costs is (are) relevant in special order decisions?

15. Why would a company consider outsourcing products or services?

16. Chris Sutter, the production manager of Satellite Computers, insists that the SSD drives used in the company's upper-end computers be outsourced since they can be purchased from a supplier at a lower cost per unit than the company is presently incurring to produce the drives. Jane Meyers, his assistant, insists that if sales growth continues at the current levels, the company will be able to produce the drives in the near future at a lower cost because of the company's predominately fixed cost structure. Does Ms. Meyers have a legitimate argument? Explain.

17. Identify some qualitative factors that should be considered in addition to quantitative costs in deciding whether to outsource.

18. The managers of Wilcox, Inc. are suggesting that the company president eliminate one of the company's segments that is operating at a loss. Why may this be a hasty decision?

19. Why would a supervisor choose to continue using a more costly old machine instead of replacing it with a less costly new machine?

EXERCISES—SERIES A

LO 13-1

Exercise 13-1A *Distinction between relevance and cost behavior*

Gayla Ojeda is trying to decide which of two different kinds of candy to sell in her retail candy store. One type is a name-brand candy that will practically sell itself. The other candy is cheaper to purchase but does not carry an identifiable brand name. Ms. Ojeda believes that she will have to incur significant advertising costs to sell this candy. Several cost items for the two types of candy are as follows.

Brandless Candy		Name-Brand Candy	
Cost per box	$ 4.00	Cost per box	$ 6.00
Sales commissions per box	1.00	Sales commissions per box	1.00
Rent of display space	900.00	Rent of display space	900.00
Advertising	3,000.00	Advertising	2,000.00

Required

Identify each cost as being relevant or irrelevant to Ms. Ojeda's decision and indicate whether it is fixed or variable relative to the number of boxes sold.

LO 13-1

Exercise 13-2A *Distinction between relevance and cost behavior*

Kilgore Company makes and sells a single product. Kilgore incurred the following costs in its most recent fiscal year.

Cost Items Appearing on the Income Statement	
Materials cost ($7 per unit)	Sales commissions (2% of sales)
Company president's salary	Salaries of administrative personnel
Depreciation on manufacturing equipment	Shipping and handling ($0.50 per unit)
Customer billing costs (1% of sales)	Depreciation on office furniture
Rental cost of manufacturing facility	Manufacturing supplies ($0.25 per unit)
Advertising costs ($200,000 per year)	Production supervisor's salary
Labor cost ($8 per unit)	

Kilgore could purchase the products that it currently makes. If it purchased the items, the company would continue to sell them using its own logo, advertising program, and sales staff.

Required

Identify each cost as relevant or irrelevant to the outsourcing decision and indicate whether the cost is fixed or variable relative to the number of products manufactured and sold.

Exercise 13-3A   *Distinction between avoidable costs and cost behavior*   LO 13-1

Boyle Company makes fine jewelry that it sells to department stores throughout the United States. Boyle is trying to decide which of two bracelets to manufacture. Cost data pertaining to the two choices follow.

	Bracelet A	Bracelet B
Cost of materials per unit	$ 10	$ 20
Cost of labor per unit	15	15
Advertising cost per year	5,000	3,000
Annual depreciation on existing equip.	5,000	4,000

Required

a. Identify the fixed costs and determine the amount of fixed cost for each product.
b. Identify the variable costs and determine the amount of variable cost per unit for each product.
c. Identify the avoidable costs and determine the amount of avoidable cost for each product.

Exercise 13-4A   *Cost hierarchy*   LO 13-1

Costs can be classified into one of four categories, including unit-level, batch-level, product-level, or facility-level costs.

Required

Classify each of the items listed below into one of the four categories listed previously. The first item has been categorized as an example.

Cost Description	Cost Classification
Salary of company president	Facility-level cost
Research and development cost	
Factory lawn care cost	
Cost of patent	
Startup cost to change color of a product	
Cost of resetting sewing machines to change shirt size	
Real estate tax for the factory	
Direct labor	

LO 13-1

Exercise 13-5A   *Opportunity costs*

Norman Dowd owns his own taxi, for which he bought a $10,000 permit to operate two years ago. Mr. Dowd earns $30,000 a year operating as an independent but has the opportunity to sell the taxi and permit for $36,500 and take a position as dispatcher for Carter Taxi Co. The dispatcher position pays $27,500 a year for a 40-hour week. Driving his own taxi, Mr. Dowd works approximately 55 hours per week. If he sells his business, he will invest the $36,500 and can earn a 10 percent return.

Required

a. Determine the opportunity cost of owning and operating the independent business.

b. Based solely on financial considerations, should Mr. Dowd sell the taxi and accept the position as dispatcher?

c. Discuss the qualitative as well as quantitative factors that Mr. Dowd should consider.

LO 13-2

Exercise 13-6A   *Special order decision*

Visburg Concrete Company pours concrete slabs for single-family dwellings. Lancing Construction Company, which operates outside Visburg's normal sales territory, asks Visburg to pour 40 slabs for Lancing's new development of homes. Visburg has the capacity to build 300 slabs and is presently working on 250 of them. Lancing is willing to pay only $3,300 per slab. Visburg estimates the cost of a typical job to include unit-level materials, $1,440; unit-level labor, $720; and an allocated portion of facility-level overhead, $1,200.

Required

Should Visburg accept or reject the special order to pour 40 slabs for $3,300 each? Support your answer with appropriate computations.

LO 13-2

Exercise 13-7A   *Special order decision*

Katzev Company manufactures a personal computer designed for use in schools and markets it under its own label. Katzev has the capacity to produce 40,000 units a year but is currently producing and selling only 32,000 units a year. The computer's normal selling price is $750 per unit with no volume discounts. The unit-level costs of the computer's production are $250 for direct materials, $225 for direct labor, and $62.50 for indirect unit-level manufacturing costs. The total product- and facility-level costs incurred by Katzev during the year are expected to be $2,000,000 and $500,000, respectively. Assume that Katzev receives a special order to produce and sell 6,000 computers at $562.50 each.

Required

Should Katzev accept or reject the special order? Support your answer with appropriate computations.

LO 13-2

Exercise 13-8A   *Identifying qualitative factors for a special order decision*

Required

Describe the qualitative factors that Katzev should consider before accepting the special order described in Exercise 13-7A.

LO 13-2

Exercise 13-9A   *Using the contribution margin approach for a special order decision*

Hensely Company, which produces and sells a small digital clock, bases its pricing strategy on a 25 percent markup on total cost. Based on annual production costs for 25,000 units of product, computations for the sales price per clock follow.

Unit-level costs	$240,000
Fixed costs	60,000
Total cost (a)	300,000
Markup (a × 0.25)	75,000
Total sales (b)	$375,000
Sales price per unit (b ÷ 25,000)	$ 15

Required

a. Hensely has excess capacity and receives a special order for 8,000 clocks for $12 each. Calculate the contribution margin per unit. Based on this, should Hensely accept the special order?

b. Support your answer by preparing a contribution margin income statement for the special order.

Exercise 13-10A   *Outsourcing decision*   LO 13-3

Steele Bicycle Manufacturing Company currently produces the handlebars used in manufacturing its bicycles, which are high-quality racing bikes with limited sales. Steele produces and sells only 10,000 bikes each year. Due to the low volume of activity, Steele is unable to obtain the economies of scale that larger producers achieve. For example, Steele could buy the handlebars for $31 each; they cost $34 each to make. The following is a detailed breakdown of current production costs.

Item	Unit Cost	Total
Unit-level costs		
Materials	$16	$160,000
Labor	12	120,000
Overhead	2	20,000
Allocated facility-level costs	4	40,000
Total	$34	$340,000

After seeing these figures, Steele's president remarked that it would be foolish for the company to continue to produce the handlebars at $34 each when it can buy them for $31 each.

Required

Do you agree with the president's conclusion? Support your answer with appropriate computations.

Exercise 13-11A   *Establishing price for an outsourcing decision*   LO 13-3

Levesque Company makes and sells lawn mowers for which it currently makes the engines. It has an opportunity to purchase the engines from a reliable manufacturer. The annual costs of making the engines are shown here.

Cost of materials (20,000 units × $26)	$ 520,000
Labor (20,000 units × $20)	400,000
Depreciation on manufacturing equipment*	42,000
Salary of supervisor of engine production	85,000
Rental cost of equipment used to make engines	23,000
Allocated portion of corporate-level facility-sustaining costs	80,000
Total cost to make 20,000 engines	$1,150,000

*The equipment has a book value of $90,000 but its market value is zero.

Required

a. Determine the maximum price per unit that Levesque would be willing to pay for the engines.

b. Would the price computed in Requirement *a* change if production increased to 24,000 units? Support your answer with appropriate computations.

Exercise 13-12A   *Outsourcing decision with qualitative factors*   LO 13-3

Kawai Corporation, which makes and sells 85,000 radios annually, currently purchases the radio speakers it uses for $8.00 each. Each radio uses one speaker. The company has idle capacity and is considering the possibility of making the speakers that it needs. Kawai estimates that the cost of materials and labor needed to make speakers would be a total of $6.50 for each speaker. In addition, supervisory salaries, rent, and other manufacturing costs would be $170,000. Allocated facility-level costs would be $75,000.

Required

a. Determine the change in net income Kawai would experience if it decides to make the speakers.

b. Discuss the qualitative factors that Kawai should consider.

LO 13-3

Exercise 13-13A   *Outsourcing decision affected by opportunity costs*

Omron Electronics currently produces the shipping containers it uses to deliver the electronics products it sells. The monthly cost of producing 10,000 containers follows.

Unit-level materials	$ 7,500
Unit-level labor	8,250
Unit-level overhead	5,250
Product-level costs*	13,500
Allocated facility-level costs	33,000

*One-third of these costs can be avoided by purchasing the containers.

Russo Container Company has offered to sell comparable containers to Omron for $3.00 each.

Required

a. Should Omron continue to make the containers? Support your answer with appropriate computations.

b. Omron could lease the space it currently uses in the manufacturing process. If leasing would produce $8,000 per month, would your answer to Requirement *a* be different? Explain.

LO 13-4

Exercise 13-14A   *Segment elimination decision*

Buckley Company operates three segments. Income statements for the segments imply that profitability could be improved if Segment A were eliminated.

BUCKLEY COMPANY			
Income Statements for Year 2			
Segment	**A**	**B**	**C**
Sales	$330,000	$480,000	$500,000
Cost of goods sold	(242,000)	(184,000)	(190,000)
Sales commissions	(30,000)	(44,000)	(44,000)
Contribution margin	58,000	252,000	266,000
General fixed oper. exp. (allocation of president's salary)	(92,000)	(92,000)	(92,000)
Advertising expense (specific to individual divisions)	(6,000)	(20,000)	0
Net income (loss)	$ (40,000)	$140,000	$174,000

Required

a. Explain the effect on profitability if Segment A is eliminated.

b. Prepare comparative income statements for the company as a whole under two alternatives: (1) the retention of Segment A and (2) the elimination of Segment A.

LO 13-4

Exercise 13-15A   *Segment elimination decision*

Dudley Transport Company divides its operations into four divisions. A recent income statement for its West Division follows.

DUDLEY TRANSPORT COMPANY

West Division
Income Statement for Year 3

Revenue	$300,000
Salaries for drivers	(210,000)
Fuel expenses	(30,000)
Insurance	(42,000)
Division-level facility-sustaining costs	(24,000)
Companywide facility-sustaining costs	(78,000)
Net loss	$ (84,000)

Required

a. Should West Division be eliminated? Support your answer by explaining how the division's elimination would affect the net income of the company as a whole. By how much would company-wide income increase or decrease?

b. Assume that West Division is able to increase its revenue to $324,000 by raising its prices. Would this change the decision you made in Requirement *a*? Determine the amount of the increase or decrease that would occur in companywide net income if the segment were eliminated if revenue were $324,000.

c. What is the minimum amount of revenue required to justify continuing the operation of West Division?

Exercise 13-16A   *Identifying avoidable cost of a segment*

LO 13-4

Lake Corporation is considering the elimination of one of its segments. The segment incurs the following fixed costs. If the segment is eliminated, the building it uses will be sold.

Advertising expense	$140,000
Supervisory salaries	300,000
Allocation of companywide facility-level costs	130,000
Original cost of building	220,000
Book value of building	100,000
Market value of building	160,000
Maintenance costs on equipment	112,000
Real estate taxes on building	12,000

Required

Based on this information, determine the amount of avoidable cost associated with the segment.

Exercise 13-17A   *Asset replacement decisions—opportunity cost*

LO 13-5

Roadrunner Freight Company owns a truck that cost $42,000. Currently, the truck's book value is $24,000, and its expected remaining useful life is four years. Roadrunner has the opportunity to purchase for $31,200 a replacement truck that is extremely fuel efficient. Fuel cost for the old truck is expected to be $6,000 per year more than fuel cost for the new truck. The old truck is paid for but, in spite of being in good condition, can be sold for only $14,400.

Required

Should Roadrunner replace the old truck with the new fuel-efficient model, or should it continue to use the old truck until it wears out? Explain.

Exercise 13-18A   *Asset replacement decision*

LO 13-5

A machine purchased three years ago for $720,000 has a current book value using straight-line depreciation of $400,000; its operating expenses are $60,000 per year. A replacement machine would cost $480,000, have a useful life of nine years, and would require $26,000 per year in operating expenses.

It has an expected salvage value of $130,000 after nine years. The current disposal value of the old machine is $170,000; if it is kept 9 more years, its residual value would be $20,000.

Required

Based on this information, should the old machine be replaced? Support your answer.

LO 13-5

Exercise 13-19A *Asset replacement decision*

Mead Company is considering the replacement of some of its manufacturing equipment. Information regarding the existing equipment and the potential replacement equipment follows.

Existing Equipment		Replacement Equipment	
Cost	$300,000	Cost	$250,000
Operating expenses*	240,000	Operating expenses*	160,000
Salvage value	40,000	Salvage value	40,000
Market value	120,000	Useful life	8 years
Book value	90,000		
Remaining useful life	8 years		

*The amounts shown for operating expenses are the cumulative total of all such expected expenses to be incurred over the useful life of the equipment.

Required

Based on this information, recommend whether to replace the equipment. Support your recommendation with appropriate computations.

LO 13-5

Exercise 13-20A *Asset replacement decision*

Kahn Company paid $240,000 to purchase a machine on January 1, Year 1. During Year 3, a technological breakthrough resulted in the development of a new machine that costs $300,000. The old machine costs $100,000 per year to operate, but the new machine could be operated for only $36,000 per year. The new machine, which will be available for delivery on January 1, Year 3, has an expected useful life of four years. The old machine is more durable and is expected to have a remaining useful life of four years. The current market value of the old machine is $80,000. The expected salvage value of both machines is zero.

Required

Based on this information, recommend whether to replace the machine. Support your recommendation with appropriate computations.

LO 13-5

Exercise 13-21A *Annual versus cumulative data for asset replacement decision*

Because of rapidly advancing technology, Chicago Publications Corporation is considering replacing its existing typesetting machine with leased equipment. The old machine, purchased two years ago, has an expected useful life of six years and is in good condition. Apparently, it will continue to perform as expected for the remaining four years of its expected useful life. A four-year lease for equipment with comparable productivity can be obtained for $40,000 per year. The following data apply to the old machine.

Original cost	$480,000
Accumulated depreciation	160,000
Current market value	190,000
Estimated salvage value	10,000

Required

a. Determine the annual opportunity cost of using the old machine. Based on your computations, recommend whether to replace it.

b. Determine the total cost of the lease over the four-year contract. Based on your computations, recommend whether to replace the old machine.

PROBLEMS—SERIES A

connect An electronic auto-gradable version of the Series A Problems is available in Connect. A PDF version of Series B Problems is in Connect under the "Additional Student Resources" tab. Solutions to the Series B Problems are available in Connect under the "Instructor Library" tab. Instructor and student Workpapers for the Series B Problems are available in Connect under the "Instructor Library" and "Additional Student Resources" tabs respectively.

Problem 13-22A   *Context-sensitive relevance*

LO 13-1

Required

Respond to each requirement independently.

a. Describe two decision-making contexts, one in which unit-level materials costs are avoidable and the other in which they are unavoidable.

b. Describe two decision-making contexts, one in which batch-level setup costs are avoidable and the other in which they are unavoidable.

c. Describe two decision-making contexts, one in which advertising costs are avoidable and the other in which they are unavoidable.

d. Describe two decision-making contexts, one in which rent paid for a building is avoidable and the other in which it is unavoidable.

e. Describe two decision-making contexts, one in which depreciation on manufacturing equipment is avoidable and the other in which it is unavoidable.

Problem 13-23A   *Context-sensitive relevance*

LO 13-1

Continent Construction Company is a building contractor specializing in small commercial buildings. The company has the opportunity to accept one of two jobs; it cannot accept both because they must be performed at the same time and Continent does not have the necessary labor force for both jobs. Indeed, it will be necessary to hire a new supervisor if either job is accepted. Furthermore, additional insurance will be required if either job is accepted. The revenue and costs associated with each job follow.

CHECK FIGURES
a. Contribution to profit for Job A: $224,000
b. Contribution to profit for Job B: $72,800

Cost Category	Job A	Job B
Contract price	$800,000	$750,000
Unit-level materials	250,000	220,000
Unit-level labor	260,000	310,000
Unit-level overhead	40,000	30,000
Supervisor's salary	70,000	70,000
Rental equipment costs	26,000	29,000
Depreciation on tools (zero market value)	19,900	19,900
Allocated portion of companywide facility-sustaining costs	10,400	8,600
Insurance cost for job	18,200	18,200

Required

a. Assume that Continent has decided to accept one of the two jobs. Identify the information relevant to selecting one job versus the other. Recommend which job to accept and support your answer with appropriate computations.

b. Assume that Job A is no longer available. Continent's choice is to accept or reject Job B alone. Identify the information relevant to this decision. Recommend whether to accept or reject Job B. Support your answer with appropriate computations.

Problem 13-24A   *Effect of order quantity on special order decision*

LO 13-2

Dalton Quilting Company makes blankets that it markets through a variety of department stores. It makes the blankets in batches of 1,000 units. Dalton made 20,000 blankets during the prior accounting period. The cost of producing the blankets is summarized here.

CHECK FIGURE
a. Relevant cost per unit: $24.50

Materials cost ($10 per unit × 20,000)	$200,000
Labor cost ($9 per unit × 20,000)	180,000
Manufacturing supplies ($1.50 × 20,000)	30,000
Batch-level costs (20 batches at $2,000 per batch)	40,000
Product-level costs	80,000
Facility-level costs	145,000
Total costs	$675,000
Cost per unit = $675,000 ÷ 20,000 = $33.75	

Required

a. Sunny Motels has offered to buy a batch of 500 blankets for $23.50 each. Dalton's normal selling price is $45 per unit. Based on the preceding quantitative data, should Dalton accept the special order? Support your answer with appropriate computations.

b. Would your answer to Requirement *a* change if Sunny offered to buy a batch of 1,000 blankets for $23.50 per unit? Support your answer with appropriate computations.

c. Describe the qualitative factors that Dalton Quilting Company should consider before accepting a special order to sell blankets to Sunny Motels.

LO 13-3

CHECK FIGURE
a. Total relevant cost: $150,000

Problem 13-25A *Effects of the level of production on an outsourcing decision*

Townsend Chemical Company makes a variety of cosmetic products, one of which is a skin cream designed to reduce the signs of aging. Townsend produces a relatively small amount (15,000 units) of the cream and is considering the purchase of the product from an outside supplier for $9 each. If Townsend purchases from the outside supplier, it would continue to sell and distribute the cream under its own brand name. Townsend's accountant constructed the following profitability analysis.

Revenue (15,000 units × $20)	$300,000
Unit-level materials costs (15,000 units × $2.50)	(37,500)
Unit-level labor costs (15,000 units × $1.80)	(27,000)
Unit-level overhead costs (15,000 × $0.70)	(10,500)
Unit-level selling expenses (15,000 × $1.00)	(15,000)
Contribution margin	210,000
Skin cream production supervisor's salary	(75,000)
Allocated portion of facility-level costs	(45,000)
Product-level advertising cost	(50,000)
Contribution to companywide income	$ 40,000

Required

a. Identify the cost items relevant to the make-or-outsource decision.

b. Should Townsend continue to make the product or buy it from the supplier? Support your answer by determining the change in net income if Townsend buys the cream instead of making it.

c. Suppose that Townsend is able to increase sales by 10,000 units (sales will increase to 25,000 units). At this level of production, should Townsend make or buy the cream? Support your answer by explaining how the increase in production affects the cost per unit.

d. Discuss the qualitative factors that Townsend should consider before deciding to outsource the skin cream. How can Townsend minimize the risk of establishing a relationship with an unreliable supplier?

Problem 13-26A   *Eliminating a segment*

Western Boot Co. sells men's, women's, and children's boots. For each type of boot sold, it operates a separate department that has its own manager. All departments are housed in a single store. In recent years, the children's department has operated at a net loss and is expected to continue to do so. Last year's income statements follow.

LO 13-4

CHECK FIGURE

a. Contribution to profit: $4,000

	Men's Department	Women's Department	Children's Department
Sales	$250,000	$300,000	$60,000)
Cost of goods sold	(105,000)	(125,000)	(35,000)
Gross margin	145,000	175,000	25,000
Department manager's salary	(26,000)	(30,000)	(12,000)
Sales commissions	(43,000)	(49,000)	(9,000)
Rent on store lease	(10,500)	(10,500)	(10,500)
Store utilities	(2,000)	(2,000)	(2,000)
Net income (loss)	$ 63,500	$ 83,500	$ (8,500)

Required

a. Determine whether to eliminate the children's department.

b. Confirm the conclusion you reached in Requirement *a* by preparing income statements for the company as a whole with and without the children's department.

c. Eliminating the children's department would increase space available to display men's and women's boots. Suppose management estimates that a wider selection of adult boots would increase the store's net earnings by $10,000. Would this information affect the decision that you made in Requirement *a*? Explain your answer.

Problem 13-27A   *Effect of activity level and opportunity cost on segment elimination decision*

LO 13-4

CHECK FIGURE

a. Contribution to profit: $(9,000)

Lenox Manufacturing Co. produces and sells specialized equipment used in the petroleum industry. The company is organized into three separate operating branches: Division A, which manufactures and sells heavy equipment; Division B, which manufactures and sells hand tools; and Division C, which makes and sells electric motors. Each division is housed in a separate manufacturing facility. Company headquarters is located in a separate building. In recent years, Division B has been operating at a net loss and is expected to continue to do so. Income statements for the three divisions for Year 2 follow.

	Division A	Division B	Division C
Sales	$1,000,000	$ 300,000	$1,250,000
Less: Cost of goods sold			
Unit-level manufacturing costs	(600,000)	(200,000)	(750,000)
Rent on manufacturing facility	(135,000)	(75,000)	(100,000)
Gross margin	265,000	25,000	400,000
Less: Operating expenses			
Unit-level selling and admin. expenses	(62,500)	(14,000)	(78,000)
Division-level fixed selling and admin. expenses	(80,000)	(20,000)	(100,000)
Headquarters facility-level costs	(50,000)	(50,000)	(50,000)
Net income (loss)	$ 72,500	$ (59,000)	$ 172,000

Required

a. Based on the preceding information, recommend whether to eliminate Division B. Support your answer by preparing companywide income statements before and after eliminating Division B.

b. During Year 2, Division B produced and sold 20,000 units of hand tools. Would your recommendation in response to Requirement *a* change if sales and production increase to 30,000 units in Year 3? Support your answer by comparing differential revenue and avoidable cost for Division B, assuming that it sells 30,000 units.

c. Suppose that Lenox could sublease Division B's manufacturing facility for $160,000. Would you operate the division at a production and sales volume of 30,000 units, or would you close it? Support your answer with appropriate computations.

LO 13-2, 13-3, 13-4

CHECK FIGURE
a. CM: $6,000

Problem 13-28A *Comprehensive problem including special order, outsourcing, and segment elimination decisions*

Bain Corporation makes and sells state-of-the-art electronics products. One of its segments produces The Math Machine, an inexpensive calculator. The company's chief accountant recently prepared the following income statement showing annual revenues and expenses associated with the segment's operating activities. The relevant range for the production and sale of the calculators is between 30,000 and 60,000 units per year.

Revenue (40,000 units × $10.80)	$432,000
Unit-level variable costs	
Materials cost (40,000 × $2.70)	(108,000)
Labor cost (40,000 × $1.20)	(48,000)
Manufacturing overhead (40,000 × $1.20)	(48,000)
Shipping and handling (40,000 × $0.30)	(12,000)
Sales commissions (40,000 × $1.20)	(48,000)
Contribution margin	168,000
Fixed expenses	
Advertising costs	(24,000)
Salary of production supervisor	(72,000)
Allocated companywide facility-level expenses	(96,000)
Net loss	$ (24,000)

Required (Consider each of the requirements independently.)

a. A large discount store has approached the owner of Bain about buying 5,000 calculators. It would replace The Math Machine's label with its own logo to avoid affecting Bain's existing customers. Because the offer was made directly to the owner, no sales commissions on the transaction would be involved, but the discount store is willing to pay only $6.60 per calculator. Based on quantitative factors alone, should Bain accept the special order? Support your answer with appropriate computations. Specifically, by what amount would the special order increase or decrease profitability?

b. Bain has an opportunity to buy the 40,000 calculators it currently makes from a reliable competing manufacturer for $6.72 each. The product meets Bain's quality standards. Bain could continue to use its own logo, advertising program, and sales force to distribute the products. Should Bain buy the calculators or continue to make them? Support your answer with appropriate computations. Specifically, how much more or less would it cost to buy the calculators than to make them? Would your answer change if the volume of sales were increased to 60,000 units?

c. Because the calculator division is currently operating at a loss, should it be eliminated from the company's operations? Support your answer with appropriate computations. Specifically, by what amount would the segment's elimination increase or decrease profitability?

LO 13-3, 13-5

Problem 13-29A *Outsourcing decision affected by equipment replacement*

Sturdy Bike Company makes the frames used to build its bicycles. During Year 2, Sturdy made 20,000 frames; the costs incurred follow.

Unit-level materials costs (20,000 units × $35.00)	$ 700,000
Unit-level labor costs (20,000 units × $42.50)	850,000
Unit-level overhead costs (20,000 × $10.00)	200,000
Depreciation on manufacturing equipment	120,000
Bike frame production supervisor's salary	70,000
Inventory holding costs	290,000
Allocated portion of facility-level costs	500,000
Total costs	$2,730,000

CHECK FIGURES

a. Avoidable cost per unit: $106.10

b. Avoidable cost per unit with new equipment: $27.50

Sturdy has an opportunity to purchase frames for $92.50 each.

Additional Information

1. The manufacturing equipment, which originally cost $550,000, has a book value of $450,000, a remaining useful life of four years, and a zero salvage value. If the equipment is not used to produce bicycle frames, it can be leased for $70,000 per year.

2. Sturdy has the opportunity to purchase for $910,000 new manufacturing equipment that will have an expected useful life of four years and a salvage value of $70,000. This equipment will increase productivity substantially, reducing unit-level labor costs by 60 percent. Assume that Sturdy will continue to produce and sell 20,000 frames per year in the future.

3. If Sturdy outsources the frames, the company can eliminate 80 percent of the inventory holding costs.

Required

a. Determine the avoidable cost per unit of making the bike frames, assuming that Sturdy is considering the alternatives of making the product using the existing equipment or outsourcing the product to the independent contractor. Based on the quantitative data, should Sturdy outsource the bike frames? Support your answer with appropriate computations.

b. Assuming that Sturdy is considering whether to replace the old equipment with the new equipment, determine the avoidable cost per unit to produce the bike frames using the new equipment and the avoidable cost per unit to produce the bike frames using the old equipment. Calculate the impact on profitability if the bike frames were made using the old equipment versus the new equipment.

c. Assuming that Sturdy is considering whether to either purchase the new equipment or outsource the bike frame, calculate the impact on profitability between the two alternatives.

d. Discuss the qualitative factors that Sturdy should consider before making a decision to outsource the bike frame. How can Sturdy minimize the risk of establishing a relationship with an unreliable supplier?

ANALYZE, THINK, COMMUNICATE

ATC 13-1   Business Application Case   *Analyzing inventory reductions at Procter & Gamble*

Real-world companies often seek to reduce the complexity of their operations in an attempt to increase profits. In 2012, Procter & Gamble (P&G) believed it could increase the company's profits by eliminating some product-lines. In 2017, P&G announced that it had "divested, discontinued, or consolidated 105 brands." As a result, even though its sales had *decreased* by 22 percent from 2012 to 2017, its profit as a percentage of sales had *increased* by 55 percent. Other companies have also tried to improve their financial performance by downsizing. In November 2017, General Electric announced it would begin a downsizing operation that would result in their exiting businesses using over $20 billion in assets in the next one to two years. In January 2018, Newell Brands, the company whose products include Tupperware, Sharpie pens, Elmer's Glue, and Rawlings sports products, announced it would be reducing its product offerings to the extent that it would close half of its facilities and reduce it revenues by 20 percent.

Required

a. Identify some costs savings these companies might realize by reducing the number of items they sell or use in production. Be as specific as possible, and use your imagination.

b. Consider the additional information presented as follows, which is hypothetical. All dollar amounts are in thousands, unit amounts are not. Assume that P&G decides to eliminate one shampoo product-line, Luster, for one of its segments that currently produces three products. As a result, the following are expected to occur:

(1) The number of units sold for the segment is expected to drop by only 125,000 because of the elimination of Luster, since most customers are expected to purchase an Anagen or Catagen product instead. The shift of sales from Luster to Anagen and Catagen is expected to be evenly split. In other words, the sales of Anagen and Catagen will each increase by 50,000 units.

(2) Rent is paid for the entire production facility, and the space used by Luster cannot be sublet.

(3) Utilities costs are expected to be reduced by $40,000.

(4) All of the supervisors for Luster were all terminated. No new supervisors will be hired for Anagen or Catagen.

(5) Half of the equipment being used to produce Luster is also used to produce the other two products and its depreciation cost must be absorbed by them. The remaining equipment has a remaining a book-value of $340,000 and can be sold for only $60,000.

(6) Facility-level costs will continue to be allocated between the product lines based on the number of units produced.

Product-Line Earnings Statements
(Dollar amounts are in thousands)

Annual Costs of Operating Each Product Line	Anagen	Catagen	Luster	Total
Sales in units	450,000	450,000	225,000	1,125,000
Sales in dollars	$900,000	$900,000	$450,000	$2,250,000
Unit-level costs:				
Cost of production	85,500	85,500	46,200	217,200
Sales commissions	11,700	11,700	6,000	29,400
Shipping and handling	20,250	18,000	9,000	47,250
Miscellaneous	6,750	4,500	2,250	13,500
Total unit-level costs	124,200	119,700	63,450	307,350
Product-level costs:				
Supervisors' salaries	9,600	7,200	2,400	19,200
Facility-level costs:				
Rent	100,000	100,000	50,000	250,000
Utilities	112,500	112,500	56,250	281,250
Depreciation on equipment	400,000	400,000	200,000	1,000,000
Allocated companywide expenses	22,500	22,500	11,250	56,250
Total facility-level costs	635,000	635,000	317,500	1,587,500
Total product cost	768,800	761,900	383,350	1,914,050
Profit on products	$131,200	$138,100	$ 66,650	$ 335,950

Prepare revised product-line earnings statements based on the elimination of Luster. (*Hint:* It will be necessary to calculate some per-unit data to accomplish this.)

ATC 13-2   Group Assignment   *Relevance and cost behavior*

Maccoa Soft, a division of Zayer Software Company, produces and distributes an automated payroll software system. A contribution margin format income statement for Maccoa Soft for the past year follows.

Revenue (12,000 units × $1,200)	$14,400,000
Unit-level variable costs	
Product materials cost (12,000 × $60)	(720,000)
Installation labor cost (12,000 × $200)	(2,400,000)
Manufacturing overhead (12,000 × $2)	(24,000)
Shipping and handling (12,000 × $25)	(300,000)
Sales commissions (12,000 × $300)	(3,600,000)
Nonmanufacturing miscellaneous costs (12,000 × $5)	(60,000)
Contribution margin (12,000 × $608)	7,296,000
Fixed costs	
Research and development	(2,700,000)
Legal fees to ensure product protection	(780,000)
Advertising costs	(1,200,000)
Rental cost of manufacturing facility	(600,000)
Depreciation on production equipment (zero market value)	(300,000)
Other manufacturing costs (salaries, utilities, etc.)	(744,000)
Division-level facility sustaining costs	(1,730,000)
Allocated companywide facility-level costs	(1,650,000)
Net loss	$ (2,408,000)

a. Divide the class into groups and then organize the groups into three sections. Assign Task 1 to the first section, Task 2 to the second section, and Task 3 to the third section. Each task should be considered independently of the others.

Group Tasks

(1) Assume that Maccoa has excess capacity. The sales staff has identified a large franchise company with 200 outlets that is interested in Maccoa's software system but is willing to pay only $800 for each system. Ignoring qualitative considerations, should Maccoa accept the special order?

(2) Maccoa has the opportunity to purchase a comparable payroll system from a competing vendor for $600 per system. Ignoring qualitative considerations, should Maccoa outsource producing the software? Maccoa would continue to sell and install the software if the manufacturing activities were outsourced.

(3) Given that Maccoa is generating a loss, should Zayer eliminate it? Would your answer change if Maccoa could increase sales by 1,000 units?

b. Have a representative from each section explain its respective conclusions. Discuss the following:

(1) Representatives from Section 1 should respond to the following: The analysis related to the special order (Task 1) suggests that all variable costs are always relevant. Is this conclusion valid? Explain your answer.

(2) Representatives from Section 2 should respond to the following: With respect to the outsourcing decision, identify a relevant fixed cost and a nonrelevant fixed cost. Discuss the criteria for determining whether a cost is or is not relevant.

(3) Representatives from Section 3 should respond to the following: Why did the segment elimination decision change when the volume of production and sales increased?

ATC 13-3   Research Assignment   *Challenging times at the USPS*

In recent years, the United States Postal Service (USPS) has experienced declining revenues, largely due to the increase in digital communications such as e-mail. These declining revenues have led the USPS to experience financial losses. On February 16, 2012, the USPS issued a report titled *Plan to Profitability: 5 Year Business Plan,* which outlined the problems facing the USPS and the actions needed to address them.

Financial performance at the USPS has improved since the report was issued. In its 2013 fiscal year, the USPS lost $5.5 billion, and in its 2017 fiscal year its losses were down to $2.7 billion; not a profit, but an improvement.

A copy of the report can be found at: https://about.usps.com/news/national-releases/2012/pr12_0217profitability.pdf. This should take you to a link where you can view and download the 28-page PDF document. You may want to review the entire document, but at a minimum you need to read the following pages: 3–5, 8–10, 12–14, and 26. (This is not as much as it seems as the print is large and there are lots of graphics.) *Note:* The report uses the acronym RHB, but does not define it. RHB stands for Retiree Health Benefits and represents money that Congress appropriated to help the USPS.

Required

a. Based on the information on page 4, summarize the basic factors contributing to the USPS's financial difficulties.

b. Based on the information on pages 8 and 9, in 2011 what percentage of the USPS mail *volume* resulted from delivery of first-class mail, and what percent of the USPS "*profit*" was derived from first-class mail?

c. What percentage of the USPS costs is due to compensation costs? From the USPS's point of view, are these costs more fixed or variable in nature, relative to the volume of mail delivered?

d. Page 26 of the report discusses "sensitivity analysis." Based on these data, if USPS's volume of activity were to increase by 1 percent, by how many dollars would revenues and profits be expected to increase? If USPS's *price* were to increase by 1 percent, by how many dollars would revenues and profits be expected to increase? With respect to the increase in *price*, how can the USPS expect that the dollar amount of increase in profit would be higher than the increase in revenue? (See the footnote.)

e. Based on the information on pages 12 through 14, summarize the proposals the USPS made to return to profitability. What percent of the proposals can be implemented without the approval of Congress? Do most of the proposals for cost reductions relate to reducing fixed costs or variable costs? Explain.

ATC 13-4   Writing Assignment   *Relevant versus full cost*

State law permits the State Department of Revenue to collect taxes for municipal governments that operate within the state's jurisdiction and allows private companies to collect taxes for municipalities. To promote fairness and to ensure the financial well-being of the state, the law dictates that the Department of Revenue must charge municipalities a fee for collection services that is above the cost of providing such services but does not define the term *cost*. Until recently, Department of Revenue officials have included a proportionate share of all departmental costs such as depreciation on buildings and equipment, supervisory salaries, and other facility-level overhead costs when determining the cost of providing collection services, a measurement approach known as *full costing*. The full costing approach has led to a pricing structure that places the Department of Revenue at a competitive disadvantage relative to private collection companies. Indeed, highly efficient private companies have been able to consistently underbid the Revenue Department for municipal customers. As a result, it has lost 30 percent of its municipal collection business over the last two years. The inability to be price competitive led the revenue commissioner to hire a consulting firm to evaluate the current practice of determining the cost to provide collection services.

The consulting firm concluded that the cost to provide collection services should be limited to the relevant costs associated with providing those services, defined as the difference between the costs that would be incurred if the services were provided and the costs that would be incurred if the services were not provided. According to this definition, the costs of depreciation, supervisory salaries, and other facility-level overhead costs are not included because they are the same regardless of whether the Department of Revenue provides collection services to municipalities. The Revenue Department adopted the relevant cost approach and immediately reduced the price it charges municipalities to collect their taxes and rapidly recovered the collection business it had lost. Indeed, several of the private collection companies were forced into bankruptcy. The private companies joined together and filed suit against the Revenue Department, charging that the new definition of cost violates the intent of the law.

Required

a. Assume that you are an accountant hired as a consultant for the private companies. Write a brief memo explaining why it is inappropriate to limit the definition of the costs of providing collection services to relevant costs.

b. Assume that you are an accountant hired as a consultant for the Department of Revenue. Write a brief memo explaining why it is appropriate to limit the definition of the costs of providing collection services to relevant costs.

c. Speculate on how the matter will be resolved.

ATC 13-5 Ethical Dilemma *Asset replacement clouded by self-interest*

John Dillworth is in charge of buying property used as building sites for branch offices of the National Bank of Commerce. Mr. Dillworth recently paid $110,000 for a site located in a growing section of the city. Shortly after purchasing this lot, Mr. Dillworth had the opportunity to purchase a more desirable lot at a significantly lower price. The traffic count at the new site is virtually twice that of the old site, but the price of the lot is only $80,000. It was immediately apparent that he had overpaid for the previous purchase. The current market value of the purchased property is only $75,000. Mr. Dillworth believes that it would be in the bank's best interest to buy the new lot, but he does not want to report a loss to his boss, Kelly Fullerton. He knows that Ms. Fullerton will severely reprimand him, even though she has made her share of mistakes. In fact, he is aware of a significant bad loan that Ms. Fullerton recently approved. When confronted with the bad debt by the senior vice president in charge of commercial lending, Ms. Fullerton blamed the decision on one of her former subordinates, Ira Sacks. Ms. Fullerton implied that Mr. Sacks had been dismissed for reckless lending decisions when, in fact, he had been an excellent loan officer with an uncanny ability to assess the creditworthiness of his customers. Indeed, Mr. Sacks had voluntarily resigned to accept a better position.

Required

a. Determine the amount of the loss that would be recognized on the sale of the existing branch site.

b. Identify the type of cost represented by the $110,000 original purchase price of the land. Also identify the type of cost represented by its current market value of $75,000. Indicate which cost is relevant to a decision as to whether the original site should be replaced with the new site.

c. Is Mr. Dillworth's conclusion that the old site should be replaced supported by quantitative analysis? If not, what facts do justify his conclusion?

d. Assuming that Mr. Dillworth is a certified management accountant (CMA), do you believe the failure to replace the land violates any of the standards of ethical professional practice in Exhibit 10.19 in Chapter 10? If so, which standards would be violated?

CHAPTER 14

Planning for Profit and Cost Control

LEARNING OBJECTIVES

After you have mastered the material in this chapter, you will be able to:

LO 14-1   Describe the budgeting process and the benefits it provides.

LO 14-2   Prepare a sales budget and related schedule of cash receipts.

LO 14-3   Prepare an inventory purchases budget and related schedule of cash payments.

LO 14-4   Prepare a selling and administrative expense budget and related schedule of cash payments.

LO 14-5   Prepare a cash budget.

LO 14-6   Prepare a pro forma income statement, balance sheet, and statement of cash flows.

 Video lectures and accompanying self-assessment quizzes are available in Connect *for all learning objectives.*

 Set B exercises and problems are available in Additional Student Resources.

CHAPTER OPENING

Planning is crucial to operating a profitable business. Expressing business plans in financial terms is commonly called **budgeting.** The budgeting process involves coordinating the financial plans of all areas of the business. For example, the production department cannot prepare a manufacturing plan until it knows how many units of product to produce. The number of units to produce depends on the marketing department's sales projection. The marketing department cannot project sales volume until it knows what products the company will sell. Product information comes from the research and development department. The point should be clear: A company's master budget results from combining numerous specific plans prepared by different departments.

Master budget preparation is normally supervised by a committee. The budget committee is responsible for settling disputes among various departments over budget matters. The committee also monitors reports on how various segments are progressing toward achieving their budget goals. The budgeting committee is not an accounting committee. It is a high-level committee that normally includes the company president, vice presidents of marketing, purchasing, production, and finance, and the controller.

The Curious Accountant

People in television commercials often say they shop at a particular store because "my family is on a budget." The truth is, most families do not have a formal budget. What these people mean is that they need to be sure their spending does not exceed their available cash.

When a family expects to spend more money in a given year than it will earn, it must plan on borrowing funds needed to make up the difference. However, even if a family's income for a year will exceed its spending, it may still need to borrow money because the timing of its cash inflows may not match the timing of its cash outflows. Whether a budget is being prepared for a family or a business, those preparing the budget must understand the specific issues facing that entity if potential financial problems are to be anticipated. There is no such thing as a "one size fits all" budget.

The United States Olympic Committee (USOC), like all large organizations, devotes considerable effort to budget planning.

Think about the Olympic Games and how the USOC generates revenues and incurs expenditures. Can you identify any unusual circumstances facing the USOC that complicate its budgeting efforts? (Answer on page 521.)

Tim Clayton/Corbis/Getty Images

THE PLANNING PROCESS

Planning normally addresses short, intermediate, and long-range time horizons. Short-term plans are more specific than long-term plans. Consider, for example, your decision to attend college. Long-term planning requires considering general questions such as:

■   Do I want to go to college?

■   How do I expect to benefit from the experience?

■   Do I want a broad knowledge base, or am I seeking to learn specific job skills?

■   In what field do I want to concentrate my studies?

Many students go to college before answering these questions. They discover the disadvantages of poor planning the hard way. While their friends are graduating, they are starting over in a new major.

Intermediate-range planning usually covers three to five years. In this stage, you consider which college to attend, how to support yourself while in school, and whether to live on or off campus.

Short-term planning focuses on the coming year. In this phase, you plan specific courses to take, decide which instructors to choose, schedule part-time work, and join a study group. Short-term plans are specific and detailed. Their preparation may seem tedious, but careful planning generally leads to efficient resource use and high levels of productivity.

Three Levels of Planning for Business Activity

Businesses describe the three levels of planning as *strategic planning, capital budgeting,* and *operations budgeting.* **Strategic planning** involves making long-term decisions such as defining the scope of the business, determining which products to develop or discontinue, and identifying the most profitable market niche. Upper-level management is responsible for these decisions. Strategic plans are descriptive rather than quantitative. Objectives such as "to have the largest share of the market" or "to be the best-quality producer" result from strategic planning. Although strategic planning is an integral component of managing a business, an in-depth discussion of it is beyond the scope of this text.

Capital budgeting focuses on intermediate range planning. It involves such decisions as whether to buy or lease equipment, whether to stimulate sales, or whether to increase the company's asset base. Capital budgeting is discussed in detail in a later chapter.

Operations budgeting concentrates on short-term plans. A key component of operations budgeting is the *master budget,* which describes short-term objectives in specific amounts of sales targets, production goals, and financing plans. The master budget describes how management intends to achieve its objectives and directs the company's short-term activities.

The master budget normally covers one year. It is frequently divided into quarterly projections and often subdivides quarterly data by month. Effective managers cannot wait until year-end to know whether operations conform to budget targets. Monthly data provide feedback to permit making necessary corrections promptly.

Many companies use **perpetual,** or **continuous, budgeting** covering a 12-month reporting period. As the current month draws to a close, an additional month is added at the end of the budget period, resulting in a continuous 12-month budget. A perpetual budget offers the advantage of keeping management constantly focused on thinking ahead to the next 12 months. The more traditional annual approach to budgeting invites a frenzied stop-and-go mentality, with managers preparing the budget in a year-end rush that is soon forgotten. Changing conditions may not be discussed until the next year-end budget is due. A perpetual budget overcomes these disadvantages.

Advantages of Budgeting

Budgeting is costly and time-consuming. The sacrifices, however, are more than offset by the benefits. Budgeting promotes planning and coordination; it enhances performance measurement and corrective action.

Planning

Almost everyone makes plans. Each morning, most people think about what they will do during the day. Thinking ahead is planning. Most business managers think ahead about how they will direct operations. Unfortunately, planning is frequently as informal as making a few mental notes. Informal planning cannot be effectively communicated. The business manager might know what her objectives are, but neither her superiors nor her subordinates know. Because it serves as a communication tool, budgeting can solve these problems. The budget formalizes and documents managerial plans, clearly communicating objectives to both superiors and subordinates.

Alistair Berg/Digital Vision/Getty Images

Coordination

Sometimes a choice benefits one department at the expense of another. For example, a purchasing agent may order large quantities of raw materials to obtain discounts from suppliers. But excessive quantities of materials pose a storage problem for the inventory supervisor who must manage warehouse costs. The budgeting process forces coordination among departments to promote decisions in the best interests of the company as a whole.

Performance Measurement

Budgets are specific, quantitative representations of management's objectives. Comparing actual results to budget expectations provides a way to evaluate performance. For example, if a company budgets sales of $10 million, it can judge the performance of the sales department against that level. If actual sales exceed $10 million, the company should reward the sales department; if actual sales fall below $10 million, the company should seek an explanation for the shortfall from the sales manager.

Corrective Action

Budgeting provides advance notice of potential shortages, bottlenecks, or other weaknesses in operating plans. For example, a cash budget alerts management to when the company can expect cash shortages during the coming year. The company can make borrowing arrangements well before it needs the money. Without knowing ahead of time, management might be unable to secure necessary financing on short notice, or it may have to pay excessively high interest rates to obtain funds. Budgeting advises managers of potential problems in time for them to carefully devise effective solutions.

Budgeting and Human Behavior

Effective budgeting requires genuine sensitivity on the part of upper management to the effect on employees of budget expectations. People are often uncomfortable with budgets. Budgets are constraining. They limit individual freedom in favor of an established plan. Many people find evaluation based on budget expectations stressful. Most students experience a similar fear about testing. Like examinations, budgets represent standards by which performance is evaluated. Employees worry about whether their performance will meet expectations.

The attitudes of high-level managers significantly impact budget effectiveness. Subordinates are keenly aware of management's expectations. If upper-level managers degrade, make fun of, or ignore the budget, subordinates will follow suit. If management uses budgets to humiliate, embarrass, or punish subordinates, employees will resent the treatment and the budgeting process. Upper-level managers must demonstrate that they view the budget as a sincere effort to express realistic goals employees are expected to meet. An honest, open, respectful atmosphere is essential to budgeting success.

Participative budgeting has frequently proved successful in creating a healthy atmosphere. This technique invites participation in the budget process by personnel at all levels of the organization, not just upper-level managers. Information flows from the bottom up as well as from the top down during budget preparation. Because they are directly responsible for meeting budget goals, subordinates can offer more realistic targets. Including them in budget preparation fosters development of a team effort. Participation fosters more cooperation and motivation, and less fear. With participative budgeting, subordinates cannot complain that the budget is management's plan. The budget is instead a self-imposed constraint. Employees can hold no one responsible but themselves if they fail to accomplish the budget objectives they established.

Upper management participates in the process to ensure that employee-generated objectives are consistent with company objectives. Furthermore, if subordinates were granted complete freedom to establish budget standards, they might be tempted to adopt lax standards to ensure they will meet them. Both managers and subordinates must cooperate if the participatory process is to produce an effective budget. If developed carefully, budgets can motivate employees to achieve superior performance. Normal human fears must be overcome, and management must create an honest budget atmosphere.

The Master Budget

The **master budget** is a group of detailed budgets and schedules representing the company's operating and financial plans for a future accounting period. The master budget usually includes (1) *operating budgets,* (2) *capital budgets,* and (3) *pro forma financial statements.* The budgeting process normally begins with preparing the **operating budgets,** which focus on detailed operating activities. This chapter illustrates operating budgets and pro forma statements for Hampton Hams, a retail sales company that uses (1) a sales budget, (2) an inventory purchases budget, (3) a selling and administrative (S&A) expense budget, and (4) a cash budget. As previously stated, capital budgets are discussed in a later chapter.

The sales budget includes a schedule of cash receipts from customers. The inventory purchases and S&A expense budgets include schedules of cash payments for inventory and expenses. Preparing the master budget begins with the sales forecast. Based on the sales forecast, the detailed budgets for inventory purchases and operating expenses are developed. The schedules of cash receipts and cash payments provide the foundation for preparing the cash budget.

The operating budgets are used to prepare *pro forma statements.* **Pro forma financial statements** are based on projected (budgeted) rather than historical information. Hampton Hams prepares a pro forma income statement, balance sheet, and statement of cash flows.

Exhibit 14.1 shows how information flows in a master budget.

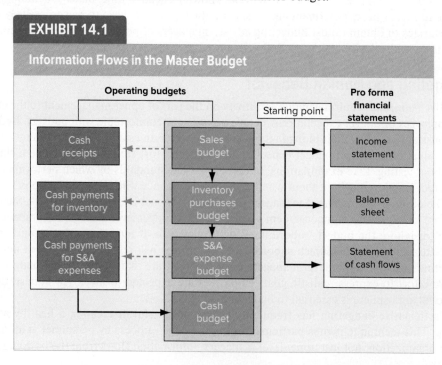

EXHIBIT 14.1

Information Flows in the Master Budget

HAMPTON HAMS BUDGETING ILLUSTRATION

HAMPTON HAMS

Hampton Hams (HH), a major corporation, sells cured hams nationwide through retail outlets in shopping malls. By focusing on a single product and standardized operations, the company controls costs stringently. As a result, it offers high-quality hams at competitive prices.

Hampton Hams has experienced phenomenal growth during the past five years. It opened two new stores in Indianapolis, Indiana, last month and plans to open a third new store in October. Hampton Hams finances new stores by borrowing on a line of credit arranged with National Bank. National's loan officer has requested monthly budgets for each of the first three months of the new store's operations. The accounting department is preparing the new store's master budget for October, November, and December. The first step is developing a sales budget.

SALES BUDGET

Preparing the master budget begins with the sales forecast. The accuracy of the sales forecast is critical because all the other budgets are derived from the sales budget. Normally, the marketing department coordinates the development of the sales forecast. Sales estimates frequently flow from the bottom up to the higher management levels. Sales personnel prepare sales projections for their products and territories and pass them up the line where they are combined with the estimates of other sales personnel to develop regional and national estimates. Using various information sources, upper-level sales managers adjust the estimates generated by sales personnel. Adjustment information comes from industry periodicals and trade journals, economic analysis, marketing surveys, historical sales figures, and changes in competition. Companies assimilate these data using sophisticated computer programs, statistical techniques, and quantitative methods, or, simply, professional judgment. Regardless of the technique, the senior vice president of sales ultimately develops a sales forecast for which she is held responsible.

To develop the sales forecast for HH's new store, the sales manager studied the sales history of existing stores operating in similar locations. He then adjusted for start-up conditions. October is an opportune time to open a new store because customers will learn the store's location before the holiday season. The sales manager expects significant growth in November and December as customers choose the company's hams as the centerpiece for many Thanksgiving and winter holiday dinner tables.

The new store's sales are expected to be $160,000 in October ($40,000 in cash and $120,000 on account). Sales are expected to increase 20 percent per month during November and December. Based on these estimates, the sales manager prepared the sales budget in Exhibit 14.2.

LO 14-2

 Prepare a sales budget and related schedule of cash receipts.

Projected Sales

The sales budget has two sections. Section 1 shows the projected sales for each month. The November sales forecast reflects a 20 percent increase over October sales. For example, November *cash sales* are calculated as $48,000 [$40,000 + ($40,000 × 0.20)], and December *cash sales* are calculated as $57,600 [$48,000 + ($48,000 × 0.20)]. *Sales on account* are similarly computed.

Schedule of Cash Receipts

Section 2 is a schedule of the cash receipts for the projected sales. This schedule is used later to prepare the cash budget. The accountant has assumed in this schedule that Hampton Hams will collect accounts receivable from credit sales *in full* in the month following the sale. In practice, collections may be spread over several months, and some receivables may become

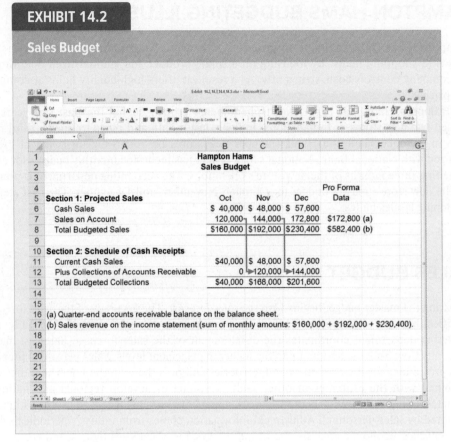

EXHIBIT 14.2

Sales Budget

Hampton Hams
Sales Budget

Section 1: Projected Sales	Oct	Nov	Dec	Pro Forma Data
Cash Sales	$ 40,000	$ 48,000	$ 57,600	
Sales on Account	120,000	144,000	172,800	$172,800 (a)
Total Budgeted Sales	$160,000	$192,000	$230,400	$582,400 (b)
Section 2: Schedule of Cash Receipts				
Current Cash Sales	$40,000	$ 48,000	$ 57,600	
Plus Collections of Accounts Receivable	0	120,000	144,000	
Total Budgeted Collections	$40,000	$168,000	$201,600	

(a) Quarter-end accounts receivable balance on the balance sheet.
(b) Sales revenue on the income statement (sum of monthly amounts: $160,000 + $192,000 + $230,400).

Source: Microsoft Corporation

bad debts that are never collected. Regardless of additional complexities, the objective is to estimate the amount and timing of expected cash receipts.

In the HH case, *total cash receipts* are determined by adding the current month's *cash sales* to the cash collected from the previous month's *credit sales* (accounts receivable balance). Cash receipts for each month are determined as follows:

- October receipts are projected to be $40,000. Because the store opens in October, no accounts receivable from September exist to be collected in October. Cash receipts for October equal the amount of October's cash sales.

- November receipts are projected to be $168,000 ($48,000 November cash sales + $120,000 cash collected from October sales on account).

- December receipts are projected to be $201,600 ($57,600 December cash sales + $144,000 cash collected from November sales on account).

Pro Forma Financial Statement Data

The Pro Forma Data column in the sales budget displays two figures HH will report on the quarter-end (December 31) budgeted financial statements. Since HH expects to collect December credit sales in January, the *accounts receivable balance* will be $172,800 on the December 31 pro forma balance sheet (shown later in Exhibit 14.7).

The $582,400 of *sales revenue* in the Pro Forma Data column will be reported on the budgeted income statement for the quarter (shown later in Exhibit 14.6). The sales revenue represents the sum of October, November, and December sales ($160,000 + $192,000 + $230,400 = $582,400).

FOCUS ON INTERNATIONAL ISSUES

CASH FLOW PLANNING IN BORDEAUX

The year 2015 was considered a great year for wine in the Bordeaux region of France, and the winemakers could look forward to selling their wines for high prices, but there was one catch: These wines would not be released to consumers until late in 2018. The winemakers had incurred most of their costs in 2015 when the vines were being tended and the grapes were being processed into wine. In many industries, this would mean the companies would have to finance their inventory for almost four years—not an insignificant cost. The company must finance the inventory by either borrowing the money, which results in out-of-pocket interest expense, or using its own funds. The second option generates an opportunity cost resulting from the interest revenue that could have been earned if these funds were not being used to finance the inventory.

FreeProd/Alamy Stock Photo

To address this potential cash flow problem, many of the winemakers in Bordeaux offer some of their wines for sale as "futures." That means the wines are purchased and paid for while they are still aging in barrels in France. Selling wine as futures reduces the time inventory must be financed from four years to only one to two years. Of course there are other types of costs in such deals. For one, the wines must be offered at lower prices than they are expected to sell for upon release. The winemakers have obviously decided this cost is less than the cost of financing inventory through borrowed money, or they would not do it.

Recently, one major Bordeaux winery announced a contrarian approach. Chateau Latour said that beginning with the 2012 vintage, not only would it no longer sell futures, but it would no longer sell its wines until it thinks they have aged sufficiently to be at their prime drinking age, which might be 12 years after the vintage. Obviously the winery believes this will allow it to sell its wine at a higher price, but it will need large sums of cash to finance many years of production while it waits. Clearly, this will complicate Chateau Latour's cash flow planning.

Companies in other industries use similar techniques to speed up cash flow, such as factoring of accounts receivable. A major reason entities prepare cash budgets is to be sure they will have enough cash on hand to pay bills as they come due. If the budget indicates a temporary cash-flow deficit, action must be taken to avoid the problem, and new budgets must be prepared based on these options. Budgeting is not a static process.

Source: Wine Spectator

INVENTORY PURCHASES BUDGET

The inventory purchases budget shows the amount of inventory HH must purchase each month to satisfy the demand projected in the sales budget. The *total inventory needed* each month equals the amount of inventory HH plans to sell that month plus the amount of inventory HH wants on hand at month-end. To the extent that total inventory needed exceeds the inventory on hand at the beginning of the month, HH will need to purchase additional inventory. The amount of inventory to purchase is computed as follows.

LO 14-3

Prepare an inventory purchases budget and related schedule of cash payments.

Cost of budgeted sales	XXX
Plus: Desired ending inventory	XXX
Total inventory needed	XXX
Less: Beginning inventory	(XXX)
Required purchases	XXX

It is HH's policy to maintain an ending inventory equal to 25 percent of the next month's *projected cost of goods sold.* HH's cost of goods sold normally equals 70 percent of *sales.* Using this information and the sales budget, the accounting department prepared the inventory purchases budget shown in Exhibit 14.3.

EXHIBIT 14.3

Inventory Purchases Budget

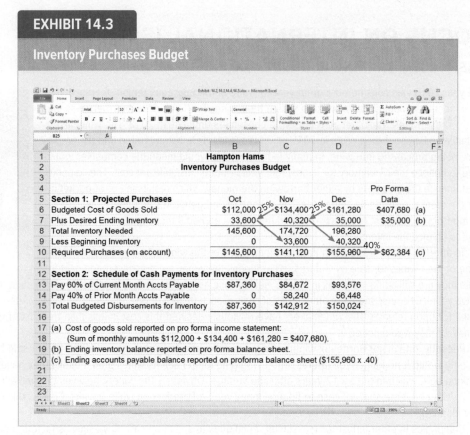

Source: Microsoft Corporation

Section 1 of the inventory purchases budget shows required purchases for each month. HH determined *budgeted cost of goods sold* for October by multiplying October *budgeted sales* by 70 percent ($160,000 × 0.70 = $112,000). Budgeted cost of goods sold for November and December were similarly computed. The October *desired ending inventory* was computed by multiplying November *budgeted cost of goods sold* by 25 percent ($134,400 × 0.25 = $33,600). Desired ending inventory for November is $40,320 ($161,280 × 0.25). Desired ending inventory for December is based on January projected cost of goods sold (not shown in the exhibit). HH expects ham sales to decline after the winter holidays. Because January projected cost of goods sold is only $140,000, the December desired ending inventory falls to $35,000 ($140,000 × 0.25).

Schedule of Cash Payments for Inventory Purchases

Section 2 is the schedule of cash payments for inventory purchases. HH makes all inventory purchases on account. The supplier requires that HH pay for 60 percent of inventory purchases in the month goods are purchased. HH pays the remaining 40 percent the month after purchase.

Cash payments are projected as follows (amounts are rounded to the nearest whole dollar):

- October cash payments for inventory are $87,360. Because the new store opens in October, no accounts payable balance from September remains to be paid in October. Cash payments for October equal 60 percent of October inventory purchases.

- November cash payments for inventory are $142,912 (40 percent of October purchases + 60 percent of November purchases).

- December cash payments for inventory are $150,024 (40 percent of November purchases + 60 percent of December purchases).

Pro Forma Financial Statement Data

The Pro Forma Data column in the inventory purchases budget displays three figures HH will report on the quarter-end budgeted financial statements. The $407,680 *cost of goods sold* reported on the pro forma income statement (shown later in Exhibit 14.6) is the sum of the monthly cost of goods sold amounts ($112,000 + $134,400 + $161,280 = $407,680).

The $35,000 *ending inventory* as of December 31 is reported on the pro forma balance sheet (shown later in Exhibit 14.7). December 31 is the last day of both the month of December and the three-month quarter represented by October, November, and December.

The $62,384 of *accounts payable* reported on the pro forma balance sheet (shown later in Exhibit 14.7) represents the 40 percent of December inventory purchases HH will pay for in January ($155,960 × 0.40).

 CHECK YOURSELF 14.1

Main Street Sales Company purchased $80,000 of inventory during June. Purchases are expected to increase by 2 percent per month in each of the next three months. Main Street makes all purchases on account. It normally pays cash to settle 70 percent of its accounts payable during the month of purchase and settles the remaining 30 percent in the month following purchase. Based on this information, determine the accounts payable balance Main Street would report on its July 31 balance sheet.

Answer   Purchases for the month of July are expected to be $81,600 ($80,000 × 1.02). Main Street will pay 70 percent of the resulting accounts payable in cash during July. The remaining 30 percent represents the expected balance in accounts payable as of July 31. Therefore, the balance would be $24,480 ($81,600 × 0.3).

SELLING AND ADMINISTRATIVE EXPENSE BUDGET

Section 1 of Exhibit 14.4 shows the selling and administrative (S&A) expense budget for Hampton Hams' new store. Most of the projected expenses are self-explanatory; depreciation and interest, however, merit comment. The depreciation expense is based on projections in the *capital expenditures budget.* Although not presented in this chapter, the capital budget calls for the cash purchase of $130,000 of store fixtures. The fixtures were purchased on October 1. The supplier allows a 30-day inspection period. As a result, payment for the fixtures was made at the end of October. The fixtures are expected to have a useful life of 10 years and a $10,000 salvage value. Using the straight-line method, HH estimates annual depreciation expense at $12,000 ([$130,000 − $10,000] ÷ 10). Monthly depreciation expense is $1,000 ($12,000 annual charge ÷ 12 months).

Interest expense is missing from the S&A expense budget. HH cannot estimate interest expense until it completes its borrowing projections. Expected borrowing (financing activities) and related interest expense are shown in the cash budget.

 LO 14-4

Prepare a selling and administrative expense budget and related schedule of cash payments.

Schedule of Cash Payments for Selling and Administrative Expenses

Section 2 of the S&A expense budget shows the schedule of cash payments. There are several differences between the S&A expenses recognized on the pro forma income statement and the cash payments for S&A expenses. First, Hampton Hams pays sales commissions and utilities expense the month following their incurrence. Since the store opens in October there are no payments due from September. Cash payments for sales commissions and utilities in October are zero. In November, HH will pay the October expenses for these items and in December it will pay the November sales commissions and utilities expenses. Depreciation expense does not affect the cash payments schedule. The cash outflow for the store fixtures occurs when the assets are purchased, not when they are depreciated. The cost of the investment in store fixtures is in the cash budget, not in the cash outflow for S&A expenses.

EXHIBIT 14.4

Selling and Administrative Expense Budget

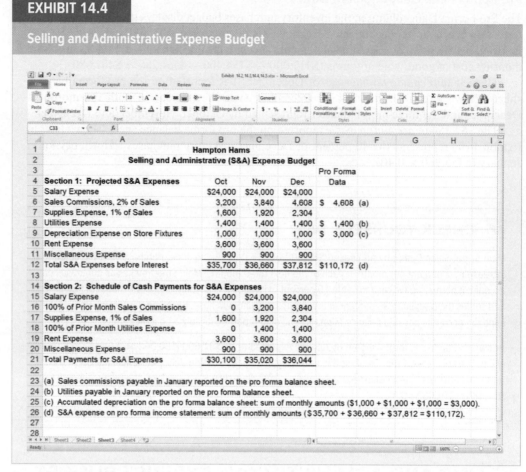

	A	B	C	D	E
1	**Hampton Hams**				
2	**Selling and Administrative (S&A) Expense Budget**				
3					Pro Forma
4	**Section 1: Projected S&A Expenses**	Oct	Nov	Dec	Data
5	Salary Expense	$24,000	$24,000	$24,000	
6	Sales Commissions, 2% of Sales	3,200	3,840	4,608	$ 4,608 (a)
7	Supplies Expense, 1% of Sales	1,600	1,920	2,304	
8	Utilities Expense	1,400	1,400	1,400	$ 1,400 (b)
9	Depreciation Expense on Store Fixtures	1,000	1,000	1,000	$ 3,000 (c)
10	Rent Expense	3,600	3,600	3,600	
11	Miscellaneous Expense	900	900	900	
12	Total S&A Expenses before Interest	$35,700	$36,660	$37,812	$110,172 (d)
13					
14	**Section 2: Schedule of Cash Payments for S&A Expenses**				
15	Salary Expense	$24,000	$24,000	$24,000	
16	100% of Prior Month Sales Commissions	0	3,200	3,840	
17	Supplies Expense, 1% of Sales	1,600	1,920	2,304	
18	100% of Prior Month Utilities Expense	0	1,400	1,400	
19	Rent Expense	3,600	3,600	3,600	
20	Miscellaneous Expense	900	900	900	
21	Total Payments for S&A Expenses	$30,100	$35,020	$36,044	
22					
23	(a) Sales commissions payable in January reported on the pro forma balance sheet.				
24	(b) Utilities payable in January reported on the pro forma balance sheet.				
25	(c) Accumulated depreciation on the pro forma balance sheet: sum of monthly amounts ($1,000 + $1,000 + $1,000 = $3,000).				
26	(d) S&A expense on pro forma income statement: sum of monthly amounts ($35,700 + $36,660 + $37,812 = $110,172).				
27					
28					

Source: Microsoft Corporation

REALITY BYTES

THE ULTIMATE CASH PLANNING

Most companies must spend money to buy inventory before they collect money from selling those goods. For example, if you sell building supplies, like The Home Depot, you need to purchase inventory before you sell it to customers. Home Depot receives payment from its customers relatively quickly; they usually pay with a credit card and the bank that issued the credit card usually pays Home Depot within a few days. If a company's customers are other businesses, however, it may take 30 to 60 days before receiving payment. At Home Depot, its accounts receivables are collected in an average of 8 days, but it takes 74 days, on average, to sell its inventory, so 82 days elapse from the time the inventory is bought until it is sold and the cash is collected. This does not mean that Home Depot has to finance its inventory for 82 days, because Home Depot buys its inventory using accounts payables, and it takes an average of 41 days to pay its suppliers. This means that Home Depot is financing its inventory for 41 days (82 days minus 41 days), and this increases the cost of doing business.

Rob Wilson/Shutterstock

Some companies are in the enviable position of being able to collect cash from their customers before they pay cash to their own suppliers for the goods they sell. Apple, Inc. takes only 13 days to sell its inventory, and 28 days to collect accounts receivables from those sales, for a total operating cycle of 41 days. However, it waits 127 days to pay its suppliers. Thus, Apple collects cash from its customers 86 days before it has to pay its suppliers.

Costco Wholesale Corporation also does a good job with cash management, but more from quick collection of its receivables than from slow payment to its suppliers, which is Apple's strategy. On average Costco sells its inventory in 32 days and collects the receivables from those sales in 4 days, for a total operating cycle of 36 days. It takes 31 days to pay its suppliers for the inventory that it sells. So, although not as efficient as Apple, Costco still manages to get its cash from customers within 5 days of the time it needs the cash to pay its suppliers, thus reducing its reliance on financing from sources such as bank loans.

Source: Companies' annual reports.

Pro Forma Financial Statement Data

The Pro Forma Data column of the S&A expense budget displays four figures HH will report on the quarter-end budgeted financial statements. The first and second figures are the sales commissions payable ($4,608) and utilities payable ($1,400) (shown later on the pro forma balance sheet in Exhibit 14.7). Because December sales commissions and utilities expense are not paid until January, these amounts represent liabilities as of December 31. The third figure in the column ($3,000) is the amount of accumulated depreciation on the pro forma balance sheet (shown later in Exhibit 14.7). Since depreciation accumulates, the $3,000 balance is the sum of the monthly depreciation amounts ($1,000 + $1,000 + $1,000 = $3,000). The final figure in the Pro Forma Data column ($110,172) is the total S&A expenses reported on the pro forma income statement (shown later in Exhibit 14.6). The total S&A expense is the sum of the monthly amounts ($35,700 + $36,660 + $37,812 = $110,172).

CASH BUDGET

Little is more important to business success than effective cash management. If a company experiences cash shortages, it will be unable to pay its debts and may be forced into bankruptcy. If excess cash accumulates, a business loses the opportunity to earn investment income or reduce interest costs by repaying debt. Preparing a **cash budget** alerts management to anticipated cash shortages or excess cash balances. Management can plan financing activities, making advance arrangements to cover anticipated shortages by borrowing and planning to repay past borrowings and making appropriate investments when excess cash is expected.

LO 14-5

Prepare a cash budget.

The cash budget is divided into three major sections: (1) a cash receipts section, (2) a cash payments section, and (3) a financing section. Much of the data needed to prepare the cash budget are included in the cash receipts and payment schedules previously discussed; however, further refinements to project financing needs and interest costs are sometimes necessary. The completed cash budget is shown in Exhibit 14.5.

EXHIBIT 14.5

Cash Budget

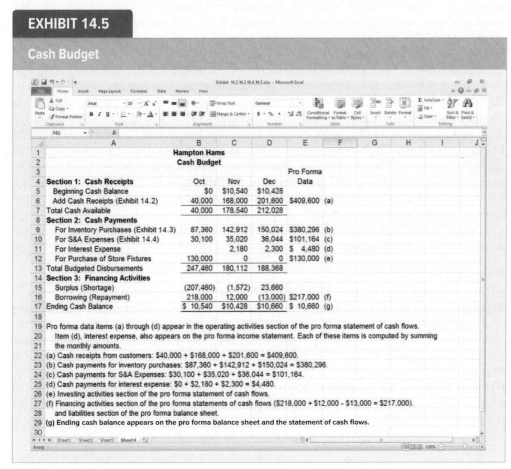

Source: Microsoft Corporation

REALITY BYTES

BUDGETING IN GOVERNMENTAL ENTITIES

This chapter has presented several reasons organizations should prepare budgets, but for governmental entities, budgets are not simply good planning tools—law requires them. If a manager at a commercial enterprise does not accomplish the budget objectives established for his or her part of the business, the manager may receive a poor performance evaluation. At worst, they may be fired. If managers of governmental agencies spend more than their budgets allow, they may have broken the law. In some cases, the manager could be required to personally repay the amount by which the budget was exceeded. Since governmental budgets are enacted by the relevant elected bodies, to violate the budget is to break the law.

Scott J. Ferrell/Congressional Quarterly/Getty Images

Because budgets are so important for governments and are not to be exceeded, government accounting practices require that budgeted amounts be formally entered into the bookkeeping system. As you learned in your first accounting course, companies do not make formal accounting entries when they order goods; they only make an entry when the goods are received. Governmental accounting systems are different. Each time goods or services are ordered by a government, an "encumbrance" is recorded against the budgeted amount so that agencies do not commit to spending more money than their budgets allow.

Cash Receipts Section

The total cash available (Exhibit 14.5, row 7) is determined by adding the beginning cash balance to the cash receipts from customers. There is no beginning cash balance in October because the new store is opening that month. The November beginning cash balance is the October ending cash balance. The December beginning cash balance is the November ending cash balance. Cash receipts from customers come from the *schedule of cash receipts* in the sales budget (Exhibit 14.2, section 2, row 13).

Cash Payments Section

Cash payments include expected cash outflows for inventory purchases, S&A expenses, interest expense, and investments. The cash payments for inventory purchases come from the *schedule of cash payments for inventory purchases* (Exhibit 14.3, section 2, row 15). The cash payments for S&A expenses come from the *schedule of cash payments for S&A expenses* (Exhibit 14.4, section 2, row 21).

HH borrows or repays principal and pays interest on the last day of each month. The cash payments for interest are determined by multiplying the loan balance for the month by the monthly interest rate. Since there is no outstanding debt during October, there is no interest payment at the end of October. HH expects an outstanding debt of $218,000 during the month of November. The bank charges interest at the rate of 12 percent per year, or 1 percent per month. The November interest expense and cash payment for interest is $2,180 ($218,000 × 0.01). The outstanding loan balance during December is $230,000. The December interest expense and cash payment for interest is $2,300 ($230,000 × 0.01). Determining the amount to borrow or repay at the end of each month is discussed in more detail in the next section of the text.

Finally, the cash payment for the store fixtures comes from the *capital expenditures budget* (not shown in this chapter).

Financing Section

HH has a line of credit under which it can borrow or repay principal in increments of $1,000 at the end of each month as needed. HH desires to maintain an ending cash balance of at least $10,000 each month. With the $207,460 projected cash shortage in row 15 of the cash budget ($40,000 cash balance in row 7 less $247,460 budgeted cash payments in row 13), HH must borrow $218,000 on October 31 to maintain an ending cash balance of at least $10,000. This $218,000 balance is outstanding during November. On November 30, HH must borrow an additional $12,000 to cover the November projected cash shortage of $1,572 plus the $10,000 desired ending cash balance. HH projects a surplus of $23,660 for the month of December. This surplus will allow HH to repay $13,000 of debt and still maintain the desired $10,000 cash balance.

Pro Forma Financial Statement Data

Figures in the Pro Forma Data column of the cash budget (Exhibit 14.5) are alphabetically referenced. The cash receipts from customers, item (a), and the cash payment items (b), (c), and (d) are reported in the operating activities section of the pro forma statement of cash flows (shown later in Exhibit 14.8). The interest expense, item (d), is also reported on the pro forma income statement (shown later in Exhibit 14.6). The figures are determined by summing the monthly amounts. The $130,000 purchase of store fixtures, item (e), is reported in the investing activities section of the pro forma statement of cash flows. The $217,000 net borrowings, item (f), is reported in the financing activities section of the pro forma statement of cash flows (shown later in Exhibit 14.8) and also as a liability on the pro forma balance sheet (shown later in Exhibit 14.7). The $10,660 ending cash balance, item (g), is reported as the ending balance on the pro forma statement of cash flows and as an asset on the pro forma balance sheet.

 CHECK YOURSELF 14.2

Astor Company expects to incur the following operating expenses during September: Salary Expense, $25,000; Utility Expense, $1,200; Depreciation Expense, $5,400; and Selling Expense, $14,000. In general, it pays operating expenses in cash in the month in which it incurs them. Based on this information alone, determine the total amount of cash outflow Astor would report in the Operating Activities section of the pro forma statement of cash flows.

Answer   Depreciation is not included in cash outflows because companies do not pay cash when they recognize depreciation expense. The total cash outflow is $40,200 ($25,000 + $1,200 + $14,000).

PRO FORMA FINANCIAL STATEMENTS

The information contained in the operating budgets is used to prepare pro forma financial statements. This section of the chapter shows how the pro forma income statement, balance sheet, and statement of cash flows are prepared using data from Hampton Hams' operating budgets.

 LO 14-6

 Prepare a pro forma income statement, balance sheet, and statement of cash flows.

Pro Forma Income Statement

Exhibit 14.6 shows the budgeted income statement for Hampton Hams' new store. The figures for this statement come from Exhibits 14.2, 14.3, 14.4, and 14.5. The budgeted income statement provides an advance estimate of the new store's expected profitability. If expected profitability is unsatisfactory, management could decide to abandon the project or modify planned activity. Perhaps HH could lease less costly store space, pay employees a lower rate, or reduce the number of employees hired. The pricing strategy could also be examined for possible changes.

Budgets are usually prepared using spreadsheets or computerized mathematical models that allow managers to easily undertake "what-if" analysis. What if the growth rate differs from expectations? What if interest rates increase or decrease? Exhibits 14.2 through 14.5 in this chapter were prepared using Microsoft Excel. When variables such as growth rate, collection assumptions, or interest rates are changed, the spreadsheet software instantly recalculates the budgets. Although managers remain responsible for data analysis and decision making, computer technology offers powerful tools to assist in those tasks.

EXHIBIT 14.6

HAMPTON HAMS Pro Forma Income Statement For the Quarter Ending December 31, Year 1		
		Data Source
Sales revenue	$582,400	Exhibit 14.2
Cost of goods sold	(407,680)	Exhibit 14.3
Gross margin	174,720	
Selling and administrative expenses	(110,172)	Exhibit 14.4
Operating income	64,548	
Interest expense	(4,480)	Exhibit 14.5
Net income	$ 60,068	

Pro Forma Balance Sheet

Most of the figures on the pro forma balance sheet in Exhibit 14.7 already have been explained. The new store has no contributed capital because its operations will be financed through debt and retained earnings. The amount of retained earnings equals the amount of net income because no earnings from prior periods exist and no distributions are planned.

EXHIBIT 14.7

HAMPTON HAMS
Pro Forma Balance Sheet
As of the Quarter Ending December 31, Year 1

			Data Source
Assets			
Cash		$ 10,660	Exhibit 14.5
Accounts receivable		172,800	Exhibit 14.2
Inventory		35,000	Exhibit 14.3
Store fixtures	$130,000		Exhibit 14.4 Discussion
Accumulated depreciation	(3,000)		Exhibit 14.4 Discussion
Book value of store fixtures		127,000	
Total assets		$345,460	
Liabilities			
Accounts payable		$ 62,384	Exhibit 14.3
Sales commissions payable		4,608	Exhibit 14.4
Utilities payable		1,400	Exhibit 14.4
Line of credit borrowings		217,000	Exhibit 14.5
Equity			
Retained earnings		60,068	
Total liabilities and equity		$345,460	

Pro Forma Statement of Cash Flows

Exhibit 14.8 shows the pro forma statement of cash flows for Hampton Hams. All information for this statement comes from the cash budget in Exhibit 14.5.

EXHIBIT 14.8

HAMPTON HAMS
Pro Forma Statement of Cash Flows
For the Quarter Ending December 31, Year 1

Cash flow from operating activities		
Cash receipts from customers	$409,600	
Cash payments for inventory	(380,296)	
Cash payments for S&A expenses	(101,164)	
Cash payments for interest expense	(4,480)	
Net cash flow for operating activities		$ (76,340)
Cash flow from investing activities		
Cash outflow to purchase fixtures		(130,000)
Cash flow from financing activities		
Inflow from borrowing on line of credit		217,000
Net change in cash		10,660
Plus beginning cash balance		0
Ending cash balance		$ 10,660

☑ **CHECK YOURSELF 14.3**

How do pro forma financial statements differ from the financial statements presented in a company's annual report to stockholders?

Answer   Pro forma financial statements are based on estimates and projections about business events that a company expects to occur in the future. The financial statements presented in a company's annual report to stockholders are based on historical events that occurred prior to the preparation of the statements.

Answers to The Curious Accountant

Budget preparation at the USOC is complicated by the fact that the timing of its revenues does not match the timing of its expenditures. The USOC spends a lot of money helping train athletes for the United States Olympic team. Training takes place year-round, every year, for many athletes. The USOC's training facilities in Colorado must also be maintained continuously.

Conversely, much of the USOC's revenues are earned in big batches, received every two years. This money comes from fees the USOC receives for the rights to broadcast the Olympic games on television in the United States. Most companies have a one-year budget cycle during which they attempt to anticipate the coming year's revenues and expenses. This model would not work well for the USOC. For example, in 2016, a year of summer Olympics, the USOC reported revenues of $351.4 million and a surplus of $78.7 million. The prior year, 2015, a year with no Olympic games, the USOC reported revenues of $147.9 million and a deficit of $72.0 million. In 2014, a year of winter Olympics, the USOC reported revenues of $270.3 million and a surplus of $47.9 million, while in 2013, the USOC reported revenues of $168.2 million and a deficit of $27.5 million.

Every business, like every family, faces its own set of circumstances. Those individuals responsible for preparing an entity's budget must have a thorough understanding of the environment in which the entity operates. This is the reason the budget process must be participatory if it is to be successful. No one person, or small group, can anticipate all the issues that a large organization will face in the coming budget period; input from employees at all levels is necessary.

Source: Audited Consolidated Financial Statements of the USOC

A Look Back

The planning of financial matters is called *budgeting*. The degree of detail in a company's budget depends on the budget period. Generally, the shorter the time period, the more specific the plans. *Strategic planning* involves long-term plans, such as the overall objectives of the business. Examples of strategic planning include which products to manufacture and sell and which market niches to pursue. Strategic plans are stated in broad, descriptive terms. Capital budgeting deals with intermediate investment planning. *Operations budgeting* focuses on short-term plans and is used to create the master budget.

A budgeting committee is responsible for consolidating numerous departmental budgets into a master budget for the whole company. The *master budget* has detailed objectives stated in specific amounts; it describes how management intends to achieve its objectives. The master budget usually covers one year. Budgeting supports planning, coordination, performance measurement, and corrective action.

Employees may be uncomfortable with budgets, which can be constraining. Budgets set standards by which performance is evaluated. To establish an effective budget system, management should recognize the effect on human behavior of budgeting. Upper-level management must set a positive atmosphere by taking budgets seriously and avoiding using them to humiliate subordinates. One way to create the proper atmosphere is to encourage subordinates' participation in the budgeting process; *participative budgeting* can lead to goals that are more realistic in terms of what can be accomplished and can help to establish a team effort in trying to reach those goals.

The primary components of the master budget are the *operating budgets,* the *capital budgets,* and the *pro forma financial statements.* The budgeting process begins with preparing the operating budgets, which consist of detailed schedules and budgets prepared by various company departments. The first operating budget to be prepared is the sales budget. The detailed operating budgets for inventory purchases and S&A expenses are based on the projected sales from the sales budget. The information in the schedules of cash receipts (prepared in conjunction with the sales budget) and cash payments (prepared in conjunction with the inventory purchases and S&A expense budgets) is used in preparing the cash budget. The cash budget subtracts cash payments from cash receipts; the resulting cash surplus or shortage determines the company's financing activities.

The capital budget describes the company's long-term plans regarding investments in facilities, equipment, new products, or other lines of business. The information from the capital budget is used as input to several of the operating budgets.

The pro forma financial statements are prepared from information in the operating budgets. The operating budgets for sales, inventory purchases, and S&A expenses contain information that is used to prepare the income statement and balance sheet. The cash budget includes the amount of interest expense reported on the income statement, the ending cash balance, the capital acquisitions reported on the balance sheet, and most of the information included in the statement of cash flows.

 ## A Look Forward

Once a company has completed its budget, it has defined its plans. Then the plans must be followed. The next chapter investigates the techniques used to evaluate performance. You will learn to compare actual results to budgets, calculate variances, and identify the parties who are normally accountable for deviations from expectations. Finally, you will learn about the human impact management must consider in taking corrective action when employees fail to accomplish budget goals.

 Video lectures and accompanying self-assessment quizzes are available in *Connect* for all learning objectives.

 ## SELF-STUDY REVIEW PROBLEM

The Getaway Gift Company operates a chain of small gift shops that are located in prime vacation towns. Getaway is considering opening a new store on January 1, Year 1. Getaway's president recently attended a business seminar that explained how formal budgets could be useful in judging the new store's likelihood of succeeding. Assume you are the company's accountant. The president has asked you to explain the budgeting process and to provide sample reports that show the new store's operating expectations for the first three months (January, February, and March). Respond to the following specific requirements.

Required

a. List the operating budgets and schedules included in a master budget.

b. Explain the difference between pro forma financial statements and the financial statements presented in a company's annual reports to shareholders.

c. Prepare a sample sales budget and a schedule of expected cash receipts using the following assumptions. Getaway estimates January sales will be $400,000, of which $100,000 will be cash and $300,000 will be credit. The ratio of cash sales to sales on account is expected to remain constant over the three-month period. The company expects sales to increase 10 percent per month. The company expects to collect 100 percent of the accounts receivable generated by credit sales in the month following the sale. Use this information to determine the amount of accounts receivable that Getaway would report on the March 31 pro forma balance sheet and the amount of sales it would report on the first quarter pro forma income statement.

d. Prepare a sample inventory purchases budget using the following assumptions. Cost of goods sold is 60 percent of sales. The company desires to maintain a minimum ending inventory equal to 25 percent of the following month's cost of goods sold. Getaway makes all inventory purchases on account. The company pays 70 percent of accounts payable in the month of purchase. It pays the remaining 30 percent in the following month. Prepare a schedule of expected cash payments for inventory purchases. Use this information to determine the amount of cost of goods sold Getaway would report on the first quarter pro forma income statement and the amounts of ending inventory and accounts payable it would report on the March 31 pro forma balance sheet.

Solution to Requirement a

A master budget would include (1) a sales budget and schedule of cash receipts, (2) an inventory purchases budget and schedule of cash payments for inventory, (3) a general, selling, and administrative expenses budget and a schedule of cash payments related to these expenses, and (4) a cash budget.

Solution to Requirement b

Pro forma statements result from the operating budgets listed in the response to Requirement *a*. Pro forma statements describe the results of expected future events. In contrast, the financial statements presented in a company's annual report reflect the results of events that have actually occurred in the past.

Solution to Requirement c

General Information				
				Pro Forma Statement Data
Sales growth rate 10%				
Sales Budget	January	February	March	
Sales				
Cash sales	$100,000	$110,000	$121,000	
Sales on account	300,000	330,000	363,000	$ 363,000*
Total sales	$400,000	$440,000	$484,000	$1,324,000†
Schedule of Cash Receipts				
Current cash sales	$100,000	$110,000	$121,000	
Plus 100% of previous month's credit sales	0	300,000	330,000	
Total budgeted collections	$100,000	$410,000	$451,000	

*Ending accounts receivable balance reported on March 31 pro forma balance sheet.

†Sales revenue reported on first quarter pro forma income statement (sum of monthly sales).

Solution to Requirement *d*

General Information

Cost of goods sold percentage 60%
Desired ending inventory percentage of CGS 25%

Pro Forma
Statement Data

Inventory Purchases Budget	January	February	March	Pro Forma Statement Data
Budgeted cost of goods sold	$240,000	$264,000	$290,400	$794,400*
Plus: Desired ending inventory	66,000	72,600	79,860	79,860†
Inventory needed	306,000	336,600	370,260	
Less: Beginning inventory	0	(66,000)	(72,600)	
Required purchases	$306,000	$270,600	$297,660	89,298‡
Schedule of Cash Payments for Inventory Purchases				
70% of current purchases	$214,200	$189,420	$208,362	
30% of prior month's purchases	0	91,800	81,180	
Total budgeted payments for inventory	$214,200	$281,220	$289,542	

*Cost of goods sold reported on first quarter pro forma income statement (sum of monthly amounts).

†Ending inventory balance ($484,000 × 1.10 × 0.60 × 0.25) reported on March 31 pro forma balance sheet.

‡Ending accounts payable balance reported on pro forma balance sheet ($297,660 × 0.3).

KEY TERMS

Budgeting 508
Capital
   budgeting 508
Cash budget 517

Master budget 510
Operating budgets 510
Operations
   budgeting 508

Participative
   budgeting 509
Perpetual (continuous)
   budgeting 508

Pro forma financial
   statements 510
Strategic planning 508

QUESTIONS

1. Budgets are useful only for small companies that can estimate sales with accuracy. Do you agree with this statement?

2. Why does preparing the master budget require a committee?

3. What are the three levels of planning? Explain each briefly.

4. What is the primary factor that distinguishes the three different levels of planning from each other?

5. What is the advantage of using a perpetual budget instead of the traditional annual budget?

6. What are the advantages of budgeting?

7. How may budgets be used as a measure of performance?

8. Ken Shilov, manager of the marketing department, tells you that "budgeting simply does not work." He says that he made budgets for his employees and when he reprimanded them for failing to accomplish budget goals, he got unfounded excuses. Suggest how Mr. Shilov could encourage employee cooperation.

9. What is a master budget?

10. What is the normal starting point in developing the master budget?

11. How does the level of inventory affect the production budget? Why is it important to manage the level of inventory?

12. What are the components of the cash budget? Describe each.

13. The primary reason for preparing a cash budget is to determine the amount of cash to include on the budgeted balance sheet. Do you agree or disagree with this statement? Explain.

14. What information does the pro forma income statement provide? How does its preparation depend on the operating budgets?

15. How does the pro forma statement of cash flows differ from the cash budget?

EXERCISES—SERIES A

Mc Graw Hill connect An electronic auto-gradable version of the Series A Exercises is available in Connect. A PDF version of Series B Exercises is in Connect under the "Additional Student Resources" tab. Solutions to the Series B Exercises are available in Connect under the "Instructor Library" tab. Instructor and student Workpapers for the Series B Exercises are available in Connect under the "Instructor Library" and "Additional Student Resources" tabs respectively.

Exercise 14-1A *Budget responsibility*

LO 14-1

Teresa Flanagan, the accountant, is a perfectionist. No one can do the job as well as she can. Indeed, she has found budget information provided by the various departments to be worthless. She must change everything they give her. She has to admit that her estimates have not always been accurate, but she shudders to think of what would happen if she used the information supplied by the marketing and operating departments. No one seems to care about accuracy. Indeed, some of the marketing staff have even become insulting. When Ms. Flanagan confronted one of the salespeople with the fact that he was behind in meeting his budgeted sales forecast, he responded by saying, "They're your numbers. Why don't you go out and make the sales? It's a heck of a lot easier to sit there in your office and make up numbers than it is to get out and get the real work done." Ms. Flanagan reported the incident, but, of course, nothing was done about it.

Required

Write a short report suggesting how the budgeting process could be improved.

Exercise 14-2A *Preparing a sales budget*

LO 14-2

Parliament Company, which expects to start operations on January 1, Year 2, will sell digital cameras in shopping malls. Parliament has budgeted sales as indicated in the following table. The company expects a 10 percent increase in sales per month for February and March. The ratio of cash sales to sales on account will remain stable from January through March.

Sales	January	February	March
Cash sales	$ 50,000	?	?
Sales on account	120,000	?	?
Total budgeted sales	$170,000	?	?

Required

a. Complete the sales budget by filling in the missing amounts.
b. Determine the amount of sales revenue Parliament will report on its first quarter pro forma income statement.

Exercise 14-3A *Preparing a schedule of cash receipts*

LO 14-2

The budget director of Heather's Florist has prepared the following sales budget. The company had $50,000 in accounts receivable on July 1. Heather's Florist normally collects 100 percent of accounts receivable in the month following the month of sale.

	July	August	September
Sales Budget			
Cash sales	$40,000	$42,500	$ 45,000
Sales on account	45,000	54,000	64,800
Total budgeted sales	$85,000	$96,500	$109,800
Schedule of Cash Receipts			
Current cash sales	?	?	?
Plus: Collections from accounts receivable	?	?	?
Total budgeted collections	$90,000	$87,500	$ 99,000

Required

a. Complete the schedule of cash receipts by filling in the missing amounts.
b. Determine the amount of accounts receivable the company will report on its third quarter pro forma balance sheet.

LO 14-2

Exercise 14-4A   *Preparing sales budgets with different assumptions*

Axon Corporation, which has three divisions, is preparing its sales budget. Each division expects a different growth rate because economic conditions vary in different regions of the country. The growth expectations per quarter are 4 percent for Cummings Division, 2 percent for Springfield Division, and 5 percent for Douglas Division.

Division	First Quarter	Second Quarter	Third Quarter	Fourth Quarter
Cummings Division	$ 75,000	?	?	?
Springfield Division	125,000	?	?	?
Douglas Division	100,000	?	?	?

Required

a. Complete the sales budget by filling in the missing amounts. (Round figures to the nearest dollar.)

b. Determine the amount of sales revenue that the company will report on its quarterly pro forma income statements.

LO 14-2

Exercise 14-5A   *Determining cash receipts from accounts receivable*

Carmen's Dress Delivery operates a mail-order business that sells clothes designed for frequent travelers. It had sales of $400,000 in December. Because Carmen's Dress Delivery is in the mail-order business, all sales are made on account. The company expects a 30 percent drop in sales for January. The balance in the Accounts Receivable account on December 31 was $60,000 and is budgeted to be $41,000 as of January 31.

Required

a. Determine the amount of cash Carmen's Dress Delivery expects to collect from accounts receivable during January.

b. Is it reasonable to assume that sales will decline in January for this type of business? Why or why not?

LO 14-2

Exercise 14-6A   *Using judgment in making a sales forecast*

Ozark Company operates a candy store located in a large shopping mall.

Required

Write a brief memo describing the sales pattern that you would expect Ozark to experience during the year. In which months will sales likely be high? In which months will sales likely be low? Explain why.

LO 14-3

Exercise 14-7A   *Preparing an inventory purchases budget*

Lumpkin Company sells lamps and other lighting fixtures. The purchasing department manager prepared the following inventory purchases budget. Lumpkin's policy is to maintain an ending inventory balance equal to 10 percent of the following month's cost of goods sold. April's budgeted cost of goods sold is $40,000.

	January	February	March
Budgeted cost of goods sold	$30,000	$32,000	$35,000
Plus: Desired ending inventory	3,200	?	?
Inventory needed	33,200	?	?
Less: Beginning inventory	6,000	?	?
Required purchases (on account)	$27,200	?	?

Required

a. Complete the inventory purchases budget by filling in the missing amounts.

b. Determine the amount of cost of goods sold the company will report on its first quarter pro forma income statement.

c. Determine the amount of ending inventory the company will report on its pro forma balance sheet at the end of the first quarter.

Exercise 14-8A   *Preparing a schedule of cash payments for inventory purchases*

LO 14-3

Dickey Books buys books and magazines directly from publishers and distributes them to grocery stores. The wholesaler expects to purchase the following inventory.

	April	May	June
Required purchases (on account)	$70,000	$80,000	$95,000

Dickey Books' accountant prepared the following schedule of cash payments for inventory purchases. Dickey Books' suppliers require that 90 percent of purchases on account be paid in the month of purchase; the remaining 10 percent are paid in the month following the month of purchase.

Schedule of Cash Payments for Inventory Purchases			
	April	May	June
Payment for current accounts payable	$63,000	?	?
Payment for previous accounts payable	4,000	?	?
Total budgeted payments for inventory	$67,000	?	?

Required

a. Complete the schedule of cash payments for inventory purchases by filling in the missing amounts.

b. Determine the amount of accounts payable the company will report on its pro forma balance sheet at the end of the second quarter.

Exercise 14-9A   *Determining the amount of expected inventory purchases and cash payments*

LO 14-3

Nunn Company, which sells electric razors, had $200,000 of cost of goods sold during the month of June. The company projects a 5 percent increase in cost of goods sold during July. The inventory balance as of June 30 is $15,000, and the desired ending inventory balance for July is $16,000. Nunn pays cash to settle 70 percent of its purchases on account during the month of purchase and pays the remaining 30 percent in the month following the purchase. The accounts payable balance as of June 30 was $18,000.

Required

a. Determine the amount of purchases budgeted for July.

b. Determine the amount of cash payments budgeted for inventory purchases in July.

Exercise 14-10A   *Preparing inventory purchases budgets with different assumptions*

LO 14-3

Executive officers of Stoneham Company are wrestling with their budget for the next year. The following are two different sales estimates provided by two difference sources.

Source of Estimate	First Quarter	Second Quarter	Third Quarter	Fourth Quarter
Sales manager	$225,000	$180,000	$160,000	$270,000
Marketing consultant	300,000	240,000	210,000	350,000

Stoneham's past experience indicates that cost of goods sold is about 60 percent of sales revenue. The company tries to maintain 10 percent of the next quarter's expected cost of goods sold as the current quarter's ending inventory. This year's ending inventory is $15,000. Next year's ending inventory is budgeted to be $18,000.

Required

a. Prepare an inventory purchases budget using the sales manager's estimate.

b. Prepare an inventory purchases budget using the marketing consultant's estimate.

LO 14-4

Exercise 14-11A *Preparing a schedule of cash payments for selling and administrative expenses*

The budget director for Kanosh Cleaning Services prepared the following list of expected selling and administrative expenses. All expenses requiring cash payments are paid for in the month incurred except salary expense and insurance. Salary is paid in the month following the month in which it is incurred. The insurance premium for six months is paid on October 1. October is the first month of operations; accordingly, there are no beginning account balances.

	October	November	December
Budgeted S&A Expenses			
Equipment lease expense	$ 7,500	$ 7,500	$ 7,500
Salary expense	8,200	8,700	9,000
Cleaning supplies	2,800	2,730	3,066
Insurance expense	1,200	1,200	1,200
Depreciation on computer	1,800	1,800	1,800
Rent	1,700	1,700	1,700
Miscellaneous expenses	700	700	700
Total operating expenses	$23,900	$24,330	$24,966
Schedule of Cash Payments for S&A Expenses			
Equipment lease expense	?	?	?
Prior month's salary expense, 100%	?	?	?
Cleaning supplies	?	?	?
Insurance premium	?	?	?
Depreciation on computer	?	?	?
Rent	?	?	?
Miscellaneous expenses	?	?	?
Total disbursements for operating expenses	$19,900	$20,830	$21,666

Required

a. Complete the schedule of cash payments for S&A expenses by filling in the missing amounts.

b. Determine the amount of salaries payable the company will report on its pro forma balance sheet at the end of the fourth quarter.

c. Determine the amount of prepaid insurance the company will report on its pro forma balance sheet at the end of the fourth quarter.

LO 14-4

Exercise 14-12A *Determining the amount of cash payments and pro forma statement data for selling and administrative expenses*

January budgeted selling and administrative expenses for the retail shoe store that Craig Shea plans to open on January 1, Year 1, are as follows: sales commissions, $50,000; rent, $30,000; utilities, $10,000; depreciation, $5,000; and miscellaneous, $2,500. Utilities are paid in the month after they are incurred. Other expenses are expected to be paid in cash in the month in which they are incurred.

Required

a. Determine the amount of budgeted cash payments for January selling and administrative expenses.

b. Determine the amount of utilities payable the store will report on the January 31 pro forma balance sheet.

c. Determine the amount of depreciation expense the store will report on the income statement for Year 1, assuming that monthly depreciation remains the same for the entire year.

Exercise 14-13A   *Preparing a cash budget*   LO 14-5

The accountant for Jean's Dress Shop prepared the following cash budget. Jean's desires to maintain a cash cushion of $10,000 at the end of each month. Funds are assumed to be borrowed and repaid on the last day of each month. Interest is charged at the rate of 1 percent per month.

Cash Budget	July	August	September
Section 1: Cash receipts			
Beginning cash balance	$ 25,000	$?	$?
Add cash receipts	90,000	100,000	120,300
Total cash available (a)	115,000	?	?
Section 2: Cash payments			
For inventory purchases	82,750	70,115	87,076
For S&A expenses	27,250	30,280	30,716
For interest expense	0	?	?
Total budgeted disbursements (b)	110,000	?	?
Section 3: Financing activities			
Surplus (shortage)	5,000	?	?
Borrowing (repayments) (c)	5,000	?	?
Ending cash balance (a − b + c)	$ 10,000	$ 10,000	$ 10,000

Required

a. Complete the cash budget by filling in the missing amounts. Round all computations to the nearest whole dollar.

b. Determine the amount of net cash flows from operating activities Jean's will report on the third quarter pro forma statement of cash flows.

c. Determine the amount of net cash flows from financing activities Jean's will report on the third quarter pro forma statement of cash flows.

Exercise 14-14A   *Determining amount to borrow and pro forma statement balances*   LO 14-5

Lois Bragg owns a small restaurant in Boston. Ms. Bragg provided her accountant with the following summary information regarding expectations for the month of June. The balance in accounts receivable as of May 31 is $40,000. Budgeted cash and credit sales for June are $100,000 and $250,000, respectively. Credit sales are made through Visa and MasterCard and are collected rapidly. Eighty percent of credit sales is collected in the month of sale, and the remainder is collected in the following month. Ms. Bragg's suppliers do not extend credit. Consequently, she pays suppliers on the last day of the month. Cash payments for June are expected to be $330,000. Ms. Bragg has a line of credit that enables the restaurant to borrow funds on demand; however, they must be borrowed on the last day of the month. Interest is paid in cash also on the last day of the month. Ms. Bragg desires to maintain a $15,000 cash balance before the interest payment. Her annual interest rate is 9 percent.

Required

a. Compute the amount of funds Ms. Bragg needs to borrow for June.

b. Determine the amount of interest expense the restaurant will report on the June pro forma income statement.

c. What amount will the restaurant report as interest expense on the July pro forma income statement?

Exercise 14-15A   *Preparing pro forma income statements with different assumptions*

Jacob Long, the controller of Arvada Corporation, is trying to prepare a sales budget for the coming year. The income statements for the last four quarters follow.

	First Quarter	Second Quarter	Third Quarter	Fourth Quarter	Total
Sales revenue	$90,000	$100,000	$105,000	$130,000	$425,000
Cost of goods sold	54,000	60,000	63,000	78,000	255,000
Gross profit	36,000	40,000	42,000	52,000	170,000
Selling & admin. expenses	8,500	10,000	10,500	13,000	42,000
Net income	$27,500	$ 30,000	$ 31,500	$ 39,000	$128,000

Historically, cost of goods sold is about 60 percent of sales revenue. Selling and administrative expenses are about 10 percent of sales revenue.

Fred Arvada, the chief executive officer, told Mr. Long that he expected sales next year to be 8 percent for each respective quarter above last year's level. However, Rita Banks, the vice president of sales, told Mr. Long that she believed sales growth would be only 5 percent.

Required

a. Prepare a pro forma income statement including quarterly budgets for the coming year using Mr. Arvada's estimate.

b. Prepare a pro forma income statement including quarterly budgets for the coming year using Ms. Banks' estimate.

c. Explain why two executive officers in the same company could have different estimates of future growth.

PROBLEMS—SERIES A

 An electronic auto-gradable version of the Series A Problems is available in Connect. A PDF version of Series B Problems is in Connect under the "Additional Student Resources" tab. Solutions to the Series B Problems are available in Connect under the "Instructor Library" tab. Instructor and student Workpapers for the Series B Problems are available in Connect under the "Instructor Library" and "Additional Student Resources" tabs respectively.

Problem 14-16A   *Behavioral impact of budgeting*

Amherst Corporation has three divisions, each operating as a responsibility center. To provide an incentive for divisional executive officers, the company gives divisional management a bonus equal to 15 percent of the excess of actual net income over budgeted net income. The following is Atlantic Division's current year's performance.

	Current Year
Sales revenue	$1,000,000
Cost of goods sold	625,000
Gross profit	375,000
Selling & admin. expenses	225,000
Net income	$ 150,000

The president has just received next year's budget proposal from the vice president in charge of Atlantic Division. The proposal budgets a 5 percent increase in sales revenue with an extensive explanation about stiff market competition. The president is puzzled. Atlantic has enjoyed revenue growth of around 10 percent for each of the past five years. The president had consistently approved the division's budget proposals based on 5 percent growth in the past. This time, the president wants to show that he is not a fool. "I will impose a 15 percent revenue increase to teach them a lesson!" the president says to himself smugly.

Assume that cost of goods sold and selling and administrative expenses remain stable in proportion to sales.

Required

a. Prepare the budgeted income statement based on Atlantic Division's proposal of a 5 percent increase.

b. If growth is actually 10 percent as usual, how much bonus would Atlantic Division's executive officers receive if the president had approved the division's proposal?

c. Prepare the budgeted income statement based on the 15 percent increase the president imposed.

d. If the actual results turn out to be a 10 percent increase as usual, how much bonus would Atlantic Division's executive officers receive since the president imposed a 15 percent increase?

e. Propose a better budgeting procedure for Amherst Corporation.

Problem 14-17A *Preparing a sales budget and schedule of cash receipts*

Spalding Pointers Corporation expects to begin operations on January 1, Year 1; it will operate as a specialty sales company that sells laser pointers over the Internet. Spalding expects sales in January Year 1 to total $120,000 and to increase 5 percent per month in February and March. All sales are on account. Spalding expects to collect 70 percent of accounts receivable in the month of sale, 20 percent in the month following the sale, and 10 percent in the second month following the sale.

Required

a. Prepare a sales budget for the first quarter of Year 1.

b. Determine the amount of sales revenue Spalding will report on the Year 1 first quarterly pro forma income statement.

c. Prepare a cash receipts schedule for the first quarter of Year 1.

d. Determine the amount of accounts receivable as of March 31, Year 1.

LO 14-2

CHECK FIGURE
c. Feb: $112,200
    March: $129,810

Problem 14-18A *Preparing an inventory purchases budget and schedule of cash payments*

Humboldt, Inc. sells fireworks. The company's marketing director developed the following cost of goods sold budget for April, May, June, and July.

LO 14-3

CHECK FIGURES
a. May: $33,600
c. June: $32,340

	April	May	June	July
Budgeted cost of goods sold	$37,500	$34,000	$30,000	$45,000

Humboldt had a beginning inventory balance of $1,800 on April 1 and a beginning balance in accounts payable of $7,400. The company desires to maintain an ending inventory balance equal to 10 percent of the next period's cost of goods sold. Humboldt makes all purchases on account. The company pays 60 percent of accounts payable in the month of purchase and the remaining 40 percent in the month following purchase.

Required

a. Prepare an inventory purchases budget for April, May, and June.

b. Determine the amount of ending inventory Humboldt will report on the end-of-quarter pro forma balance sheet.

c. Prepare a schedule of cash payments for inventory for April, May, and June.

d. Determine the balance in accounts payable Humboldt will report on the end-of-quarter pro forma balance sheet.

Problem 14-19A *Preparing a schedule of cash payments for selling and administrative expenses*

Malcolm is a retail company specializing in men's hats. Its budget director prepared the list of expected operating expenses that follows. All items are paid when incurred except sales commissions and utilities, which are paid in the month following their incurrence. July is the first month of operations, so there are no beginning account balances.

LO 14-4

CHECK FIGURE
a. Sept.: $17,405

	July	August	September
Salary expense	$12,000	$12,000	$12,000
Sales commissions (4 percent of sales)	1,000	1,000	1,000
Supplies expense	180	195	210
Utilities	550	550	550
Depreciation on store equipment	1,500	1,500	1,500
Rent	3,300	3,300	3,300
Miscellaneous	345	345	345
Total S&A expenses before interest	$18,875	$18,890	$18,905

Required

a. Prepare a schedule of cash payments for selling and administrative expenses.

b. Determine the amount of utilities payable as of September 30.

c. Determine the amount of sales commissions payable as of September 30.

LO 14-5

CHECK FIGURE

Feb. cash surplus before financing activities: $14,020

Problem 14-20A   *Preparing a cash budget*

Fayette Medical Clinic has budgeted the following cash flows.

	January	February	March
Cash receipts	$240,000	$232,000	$272,000
Cash payments			
For inventory purchases	220,000	164,000	190,000
For S&A expenses	62,000	64,000	54,000

Fayette Medical had a cash balance of $16,000 on January 1. The company desires to maintain a cash cushion of $10,000. Funds are assumed to be borrowed, in increments of $2,000, and repaid on the last day of each month; the interest rate is 1 percent per month. Repayments may be made in any amount available. Fayette pays its vendors on the last day of the month also. The company had a monthly $80,000 beginning balance in its line of credit liability account from last year's quarterly results.

Required

Prepare a cash budget. (Round all computations to the nearest whole dollar.)

LO 14-6

CHECK FIGURE

a. 13.59%

Problem 14-21A   *Preparing pro forma income statements with different assumptions*

Top executive officers of Tildon Company, a merchandising firm, are preparing the next year's budget. The controller has provided everyone with the current year's projected income statement.

	Current Year
Sales revenue	$1,600,000
Cost of goods sold	1,120,000
Gross profit	480,000
Selling & admin. expenses	190,000
Net income	$ 290,000

Cost of goods sold is usually 70 percent of sales revenue, and selling and administrative expenses are usually 10 percent of sales plus a fixed cost of $30,000. The president has announced that the company's goal is to increase net income by 15 percent.

Required

The following items are independent of each other:

a. What percentage increase in sales would enable the company to reach its goal? Support your answer with a pro forma income statement.

b. The market may become stagnant next year, and the company does not expect an increase in sales revenue. The production manager believes that an improved production procedure can cut cost of goods sold by 2 percent. What else can the company do to reach its goal? Prepare a pro forma income statement illustrating your proposal.

c. The company decides to escalate its advertising campaign to boost consumer recognition, which will increase selling and administrative expenses to $230,000. With the increased advertising, the company expects sales revenue to increase by 15 percent. Assume that cost of goods sold remains a constant proportion of sales. Can the company reach its goal?

Problem 14-22A *Preparing budgets with multiple products*

Jasper Fruits Corporation wholesales peaches and oranges. Barbara Jasper is working with the company's accountant to prepare next year's budget. Ms. Jasper estimates that sales will increase 5 percent for peaches and 10 percent for oranges. The current year's sales revenue data follow.

	First Quarter	Second Quarter	Third Quarter	Fourth Quarter	Total
Peaches	$ 80,000	$100,000	$160,000	$140,000	$ 480,000
Oranges	200,000	225,000	285,000	190,000	900,000
Total	$280,000	$325,000	$445,000	$330,000	$1,380,000

Based on the company's past experience, cost of goods sold is usually 60 percent of sales revenue. Company policy is to keep 10 percent of the next period's estimated cost of goods sold as the current period's ending inventory. (*Hint:* Use the cost of goods sold for the first quarter to determine the beginning inventory for the first quarter.)

Required

a. Prepare the company's sales budget for the next year for each quarter by individual product.

b. If the selling and administrative expenses are estimated to be $350,000, prepare the company's budgeted annual income statement.

c. Ms. Jasper estimates next year's ending inventory will be $10,000 for peaches and $20,000 for oranges. Prepare the company's inventory purchases budgets for the next year, showing quarterly figures by product.

Problem 14-23A *Preparing a master budget for retail company with no beginning account balances*

Camden Company is a retail company that specializes in selling outdoor camping equipment. The company is considering opening a new store on October 1, Year 1. The company president formed a planning committee to prepare a master budget for the first three months of operation. As budget coordinator, you have been assigned the following tasks.

Required

Round all computations to the nearest whole dollar.

a. October sales are estimated to be $125,000, of which 40 percent will be cash and 60 percent will be credit. The company expects sales to increase at the rate of 8 percent per month. Prepare a sales budget.

b. The company expects to collect 100 percent of the accounts receivable generated by credit sales in the month following the sale. Prepare a schedule of cash receipts.

c. The cost of goods sold is 60 percent of sales. The company desires to maintain a minimum ending inventory equal to 10 percent of the next month's cost of goods sold. However, ending inventory of December is expected to be $6,000. Assume that all purchases are made on account. Prepare an inventory purchases budget.

d. The company pays 70 percent of accounts payable in the month of purchase and the remaining 30 percent in the following month. Prepare a cash payments budget for inventory purchases.

LO 14-2, 14-3, 14-4, 14-6

CHECK FIGURE
c. 1st QTR purchases for peaches: $51,660
2nd QTR purchases for oranges: $152,460

LO 14-2, 14-3, 14-4, 14-5, 14-6

CHECK FIGURES
c. Dec. purchases: $84,732
g. Nov. surplus before financing activities: $30,486

e. Budgeted selling and administrative expenses per month follow.

Salary expense (fixed)	$9,000
Sales commissions	5% of Sales
Supplies expense	2% of Sales
Utilities (fixed)	$ 700
Depreciation on store fixtures (fixed)*	$2,000
Rent (fixed)	$2,400
Miscellaneous (fixed)	$ 600

*The capital expenditures budget indicates that Camden will spend $82,000 on October 1 for store fixtures, which are expected to have a $10,000 salvage value and a three-year (36-month) useful life.

Use this information to prepare a selling and administrative expenses budget.

f. Utilities and sales commissions are paid the month after they are incurred; all other expenses are paid in the month in which they are incurred. Prepare a cash payments budget for selling and administrative expenses.

g. Camden borrows funds, in increments of $1,000, and repays them on the last day of the month. Repayments may be made in any amount available. The company also pays its vendors on the last day of the month. It pays interest of 1 percent per month in cash on the last day of the month. To be prudent, the company desires to maintain a $6,000 cash cushion. Prepare a cash budget.

h. Prepare a pro forma income statement for the quarter.

i. Prepare a pro forma balance sheet at the end of the quarter.

j. Prepare a pro forma statement of cash flows for the quarter.

ANALYZE, THINK, COMMUNICATE

ATC 14-1   Business Applications Case   *Preparing and using pro forma statements*

Mary Helu and Jason Haynes recently graduated from the same university. After graduation they decided not to seek jobs at established organizations but, rather, to start their own small business hoping they could have more flexibility in their personal lives for a few years. Mary's family has operated Mexican restaurants and taco trucks for the past two generations, and Mary noticed there were no taco truck services in the town where their university was located. To reduce the amount they would need for an initial investment, they decided to start a business operating a taco cart rather than a taco truck, from which they would cook and serve traditional Mexican-style street food.

They bought a used taco cart for $18,000. This cost, along with the cost for supplies to get started, a business license, and street vendor license brought their initial expenditures to $22,000. They took $5,000 from personal savings they had accumulated by working part time during college, and they borrowed $17,000 from Mary's parents. They agreed to pay interest on the outstanding loan balance each month based on an annual rate of 5 percent. They will repay the principal over the next few years as cash becomes available. They were able to rent space in a parking lot near the campus they had attended, believing that the students would welcome their food as an alternative to the typical fast food that was currently available.

After two months in business, September and October, they had average monthly revenues of $25,000 and out-of-pocket costs of $22,000 for rent, ingredients, paper supplies, and so on, but not interest. Jason thinks they should repay some of the money they borrowed, but Mary thinks they should prepare a set of forecasted financial statements for their first year in business before deciding whether or not to repay any principal on the loan. She remembers a bit about budgeting from a survey of accounting course she took and thinks the results from their first two months in business can be extended over the next 10 months to prepare the budget they need. They estimate the cart will last at least four years, after which they expect to sell it for $6,000 and move on to something else in their lives. Mary agrees to prepare a forecasted (pro forma) income statement, balance sheet, and statement of cash flows for their first year in business, which includes the two months already passed.

Required

a. Prepare the annual pro forma financial statements that you would expect Mary to prepare based on her comments about her expectations for the business. Assume no principal will be repaid on the loan.

b. Review the statements you prepared for the first requirement and prepare a list of reasons why actual results for Mary and Jason's business probably will not match their budgeted statements.

ATC 14-2 Group Assignment *Master budget and pro forma statements*

The following trial balance was drawn from the records of Havel Company as of October 1, Year 2.

Cash	$ 16,000	
Accounts receivable	60,000	
Inventory	40,000	
Store equipment	200,000	
Accumulated depreciation		$ 76,800
Accounts payable		72,000
Line of credit loan		100,000
Common stock		50,000
Retained earnings		17,200
Totals	$316,000	$316,000

Required

a. Divide the class into groups, each with four or five students. Organize the groups into three sections. Assign Task 1 to the first section, Task 2 to the second section, and Task 3 to the third section.

Group Tasks

(1) Based on the following information, prepare a sales budget and a schedule of cash receipts for October, November, and December. Sales for October are expected to be $180,000, consisting of $40,000 in cash and $140,000 on credit. The company expects sales to increase at the rate of 10 percent per month. All accounts receivable are collected in the month following the sale.

(2) Based on the following information, prepare a purchases budget and a schedule of cash payments for inventory purchases for October, November, and December. The inventory balance as of October 1 was $40,000. Cost of goods sold for October is expected to be $72,000. Cost of goods sold is expected to increase by 10 percent per month. The company expects to maintain a minimum ending inventory equal to 20 percent of the current month cost of goods sold. Seventy-five percent of accounts payable is paid in the month that the purchase occurs; the remaining 25 percent is paid in the following month.

(3) Based on the following selling and administrative expenses budgeted for October, prepare a selling and administrative expenses budget for October, November, and December.

Sales commissions (10% increase per month)	$ 7,200
Supplies expense (10% increase per month)	1,800
Utilities (fixed)	2,200
Depreciation on store equipment (fixed)	1,600
Salary expense (fixed)	34,000
Rent (fixed)	6,000
Miscellaneous (fixed)	1,000

Cash payments for sales commissions and utilities are made in the month following the one in which the expense is incurred. Supplies and other operating expenses are paid in cash in the month in which they are incurred.

b. Select a representative from each section. Have the representatives supply the missing information in the following pro forma income statement and balance sheet for the fourth quarter of Year 2. The statements are prepared as of December 31, Year 2.

Income Statement	
Sales revenue	$?
Cost of goods sold	?
Gross margin	357,480
Operating expenses	?
Operating income	193,290
Interest expense	(2,530)
Net income	$190,760

Balance Sheet		
Assets		
Cash		$ 9,760
Accounts receivable		?
Inventory		?
Store equipment	$200,000	
Accumulated depreciation store equipment	?	
Book value of equipment		118,400
Total assets		$314,984
Liabilities		
Accounts payable		?
Utilities payable		?
Sales commissions payable		?
Line of credit		23,936
Equity		
Common stock		50,000
Retained earnings		?
Total liabilities and equity		$314,984

c. Indicate whether Havel will need to borrow money during October.

ATC 14-3   Research Assignment   *Analyzing budget data for the United States government*

The annual budget of the United States is very complex, but this case requires that you analyze only a small portion of the historical tables that are presented as a part of each year's budget. The fiscal year of the federal government ends on September 30. Obtain the budget documents needed at www.gpo .gov/fdsys/browse/collectionGPO.action?collectionCode=BUDGET and follow these steps:

■ Click on the "Fiscal Year 2018" link.

■ Scroll down and select "Historical Tables."

■ There are two options that can be used to download each historical data table. One is an XLS (Excel) file format. Click the "+" sign to access the Excel files. This option will make completing this assignment easier.

■ You will need to use Table 1.1, Table 1.2, and Table 4.2 to complete the following requirements.

Required

a. Table 1.2 shows the budget as a percentage of gross domestic product (GDP). Using the data in the third column, "Surplus or Deficit," determine how many years since 1960 the budget has shown a surplus and how many times it has shown a deficit. Ignore the "TQ" data between 1976 and 1977. This was a year that the government changed the ending date of its fiscal year.

b. Based on the data in Table 1.2, identify the three years with the highest deficits as a percentage of GDP. What were the deficit percentages for these years? Which year had the largest surplus and by what percentage?

c. Using your findings for Requirement *b* regarding the year with the highest deficit as a percentage of GDP, go to Table 1.1 and calculate the deficit for that year as a percentage of revenues. What percent of each dollar spent by the federal government in that year was paid for with tax revenues and what percent was paid for with borrowed funds?

d. The president of the United States from 2001 through 2009 was George W. Bush, a Republican. The president from 2009 through 2017 was Barack H. Obama, a Democrat. These men had significant input into the federal budget for the fiscal years 2002–2009 and 2010–2017, respectively. Table 4.2 shows what percentage of the total federal budget was directed toward each department within the government. Compare the data on Table 4.2 for 2002–2009, the Bush years, to the data for 2010–2017, the Obama years. Identify the five departments that appear to have changed the most from the Bush years to the Obama years. Ignore "Allowances" and "Undistributed offsetting receipts." Note, to approach this assignment more accurately, you should compute the average percentage for each department for the eight years each president served, and compare the two averages.

ATC 14-4   Writing Assignment   *Continuous budgeting*

The Curious Accountant in this chapter discussed some of the budgeting issues facing the United States Olympic Committee (USOC). First, to get a basic understanding of the sources of revenues and expenses of the USOC, review its "Audited Financial Statements." These may be accessed with the following link: www.teamusa.org/footer/finance/. You need to review the information on the "Consolidated statement of activities." Note that there are usually two of these, one for the current fiscal year and one for all the years since the year after last summer Olympic games. Either of these forms will provide additional insight into the sources of the USOC's revenues and expenses.

Required

Assume the USOC had not previously used continuous budgeting but was considering implementing a continuous budgeting system. Also assume you had been asked to identify some of the challenges the USOC would face in implementing this system. Write a memorandum explaining the challenges you identify.

ATC 14-5   Ethical Dilemma   *Bad budget system or unethical behavior?*

Clarence Cleaver is the budget director for the Harris County School District. Mr. Cleaver recently sent an urgent e-mail message to Sally Simmons, principal of West Harris County High. The message severely reprimanded Ms. Simmons for failing to spend the funds allocated to her to purchase computer equipment. Ms. Simmons responded that her school already has a sufficient supply of computers; indeed, the computer lab is never filled to capacity and usually is less than half filled. Ms. Simmons suggested that she would rather use the funds for teacher training. She argued that the reason the existing computers are not fully utilized is that the teachers lack sufficient computer literacy necessary to make assignments for their students.

Mr. Cleaver responded that it is not Ms. Simmons's job to decide how the money is to be spent; that is the school board's job. It is the principal's job to spend the money as the board directed. He informed Ms. Simmons that if the money is not spent by the fiscal closing date, the school board would likely reduce next year's budget allotment. To avoid a potential budget cut, Mr. Cleaver reallocated Ms. Simmons's computer funds to Jules Carrington, principal of East Harris County High. Mr. Carrington knows how to buy computers regardless of whether they are needed. Mr. Cleaver's final words were, "Don't blame me if parents of West High students complain that East High has more equipment. If anybody comes to me, I'm telling them that you turned down the money."

Required

a. Do Mr. Cleaver's actions violate the standards of ethical professional practice shown in Exhibit 10.19 of Chapter 10?

b. Explain how participative budgeting could improve the allocation of resources for the Harris County School District.

CHAPTER 15

Performance Evaluation

LEARNING OBJECTIVES

After you have mastered the material in this chapter, you will be able to:

LO 15-1   Describe the concept of decentralization.

LO 15-2   Distinguish between flexible and static budgets.

LO 15-3   Classify variances as being favorable or unfavorable.

LO 15-4   Compute and interpret sales and variable cost volume variances.

LO 15-5   Compute and interpret flexible budget variances.

LO 15-6   Evaluate investment opportunities using return on investment.

LO 15-7   Evaluate investment opportunities using residual income.

 Video lectures and accompanying self-assessment quizzes are available in Connect *for all learning objectives.*

 Set B exercises and problems are available in Additional Student Resources.

CHAPTER OPENING

Walter Keller, a production manager, complained to the accountant, Kelly Oberson, that the budget system failed to control his department's labor cost. Ms. Oberson responded, "People, not budgets, control costs." Budgeting is one of many tools management uses to control business operations. Managers are responsible for using control tools effectively. **Responsibility accounting** focuses on evaluating the performance of individual managers. For example, expenses controlled by a production department manager are presented in one report and expenses controlled by a marketing department manager are presented in a different report. This chapter discusses the development and use of a responsibility accounting system.

The Curious Accountant

Ken Wolter/Shutterstock

Gourmet Pizzas is located in an affluent section of a major metropolitan area. Its owner, Payten Flowers worked at a national-chain pizza restaurant while in college. He knew that there were more independent restaurants than chain restaurants, even though the national pizza chains, such as **Domino's** and **Papa John's**, had more sales in dollars than independent pizza restaurants. He also knew the popularity of pizza was growing. One survey showed pizza to be Americans' favorite comfort food, and another found that 41 percent of respondents said they ate pizza at least once each week.

Knowing it cannot beat the big guys on price, Gourmet Pizzas focuses on quality and service. Its pizza dough is made from scratch on the premises from organically grown flour, and, when possible, locally sourced ingredients. It offers a wide variety of unusual toppings, such as smoked salmon. He also knew he needed to offer online ordering, delivery, and a rewards program if he was going to compete successfully with the chains.

To determine a proper selling price for his pies, the owner estimated the cost of making the crusts, among other things. Knowing how much flour, yeast, etc., was needed to make the dough for one pizza and estimating the cost of these ingredients, he determined that the materials for the dough for each pizza should cost him 35 cents. However, after six months in business, he had spent $7,900 on materials needed for making his dough, and had sold 20,250 pizzas. This resulted in an actual price per pizza of 39 cents.

What are two general reasons that may explain why the materials cost for pizza dough was higher than Gourmet Pizzas' owner estimated? (Answer on page 547.)

DECENTRALIZATION CONCEPT

Describe the concept of decentralization.

Effective responsibility accounting requires clear lines of authority and responsibility. Divisions of authority and responsibility normally occur as a natural consequence of managing business operations. In a small business, one person can control everything: marketing, production, management, accounting. In contrast, large companies are so complex that authority and control must be divided among many people.

Consider the hiring of employees. A small business usually operates in a limited geographic area. The owner works directly with employees. She knows the job requirements, local wage rates, and the available labor pool. She is in a position to make informed hiring decisions. In contrast, a major corporation may employ thousands of employees throughout the world. The employees may speak different languages and have different social customs. Their jobs may require many different skills and pay a vast array of wage rates. The president of the corporation cannot make informed hiring decisions for the entire company. Instead, he delegates *authority* to a professional personnel manager and holds that manager *responsible* for hiring practices.

Decision-making authority is similarly delegated to individuals responsible for managing specific organization functions such as production, marketing, and accounting. Delegating authority and responsibility is referred to as **decentralization.**

Responsibility Centers

Decentralized businesses are usually subdivided into distinct reporting units called responsibility centers. A **responsibility center** is an organizational unit that controls identifiable revenue or expense items. The unit may be a division, a department, a subdepartment, or even a single machine. For example, a transportation company may identify a semitrailer truck as a responsibility center. The company holds the truck driver responsible for the revenues and expenses associated with operating the truck. Responsibility centers may be divided into three categories: cost, profit, and investment.

A **cost center** is an organizational unit that incurs expenses but does not generate revenue. Cost centers normally fall on the lower levels of an organization chart. The manager of a cost center is judged on his ability to keep costs within budget parameters.

A **profit center** differs from a cost center in that it not only incurs costs but also generates revenue. The manager of a profit center is judged on his ability to produce revenue in excess of expenses.

Investment center managers are responsible for revenues, expenses, and the investment of capital. Investment centers normally appear at the upper levels of an organization chart. Managers of investment centers are accountable for assets and liabilities as well as earnings.

Controllability Concept

The **controllability concept** is crucial to an effective responsibility accounting system. Managers should be evaluated based only on revenues or costs they control. Holding individuals responsible for things they cannot control is demotivating. Isolating control, however, may be difficult, as illustrated in the following case.

Dorothy Pasework, a buyer for a large department store chain, was criticized when stores could not resell the merchandise she bought at the expected price. Ms. Pasework countered that the sales staff caused the sluggish sales by not displaying the merchandise properly. The sales staff charged that the merchandise had too little sales potential to justify setting up more enticing displays. The division of influence between the buyer and the sales staff clouds the assignment of responsibility.

Because the exercise of control may be clouded, managers are usually held responsible for items over which they have *predominant* rather than *absolute* control. At times, responsibility accounting may be imperfect. Management must strive to ensure that praise or criticism is administered as fairly as possible.

PREPARING FLEXIBLE BUDGETS

A **flexible budget** is an extension of the *master budget* discussed previously. The master budget is based solely on the planned volume of activity. The master budget is frequently called a **static budget** because it remains unchanged even if the actual volume of activity differs from the planned volume. Flexible budgets differ from static budgets in that they show expected revenues and costs at a *variety* of volume levels.

To illustrate the differences between static and flexible budgets, consider Melrose Manufacturing Company, a producer of small, high-quality trophies used in award ceremonies. Melrose plans to make and sell 18,000 trophies during Year 1. Management's best estimates of the expected sales price and per-unit costs for the trophies are called *standard* prices and costs. The standard price and costs for the 18,000 trophies follow.

LO 15-2

Distinguish between flexible and static budgets.

Per-unit sales price and variable costs	
Expected sales price	$ 80.00
Standard materials cost	12.00
Standard labor cost	16.80
Standard overhead cost	5.60
Standard general, selling, and administrative cost	15.00
Total fixed costs	$291,600

The static budget is highlighted with red shading in Exhibit 15.1. Sales revenue is determined by multiplying the expected sales price per unit times the planned volume of activity ($80 × 18,000 = $1,440,000). Similarly, the variable costs are calculated by multiplying the standard cost per unit times the planned volume of activity. For example, the manufacturing materials cost is $216,000 ($12 × 18,000). The same computational procedures apply to the other variable costs. The variable costs are subtracted from the sales revenue to produce a contribution margin of $550,800. The fixed costs are subtracted from the contribution margin to produce a budgeted net income of $259,200.

EXHIBIT 15.1

Static and Flexible Budgets in Excel Spreadsheet

	Per Unit Standards	Static Budget	Flexible Budgets				
Number of Units		18,000	16,000	17,000	18,000	19,000	20,000
Sales Revenue	$80.00	$1,440,000	$1,280,000	$1,360,000	$1,440,000	$1,520,000	$1,600,000
Variable Manuf. Costs							
Materials	$12.00	216,000	192,000	204,000	216,000	228,000	240,000
Labor	16.80	302,400	268,800	285,600	302,400	319,200	336,000
Overhead	5.60	100,800	89,600	95,200	100,800	106,400	112,000
Variable G,S, &A	15.00	270,000	240,000	255,000	270,000	285,000	300,000
Contribution Margin		550,800	489,600	520,200	550,800	581,400	612,000
Fixed Costs		291,600	291,600	291,600	291,600	291,600	291,600
Net Income		$ 259,200	$ 198,000	$ 228,600	$ 259,200	$ 289,800	$ 320,400

Source: Microsoft Corporation

What happens if the number of units sold is different from the planned volume? In other words, *what* happens to net income *if* Melrose sells more or less than 18,000 units? Managers frequently use flexible budgets to examine such *what if* scenarios. Flexible budget income statements for Melrose at sales volumes of 16,000, 17,000, 18,000, 19,000, and 20,000 are shown in Exhibit 15.1.

The flexible budgets are prepared with the same per-unit standard amounts and fixed cost data used to produce the static budget. The only difference is the expected number of units sold. For example, the sales revenue at 16,000 units is $1,280,000 ($80 × 16,000), at 17,000 units it is $1,360,000 ($80 × 17,000), and so on. The variable materials cost at 16,000 units is $192,000 ($12 × 16,000), at 17,000 units it is $204,000 ($12 × 17,000), and so on. The other variable costs are computed in the same manner. Note that the fixed costs are the same at all levels of activity because, by definition, they are not affected by changes in volume.

Other flexible budgets are possible. Indeed, a flexible budget can be prepared for any number of units sold. You have probably noticed that Exhibit 15.1 was prepared using an Excel spreadsheet. Excel offers the opportunity to prepare an unlimited number of flexible budgets with minimal effort. For example, formulas can be created with cell references so that new budgets can be created simply by changing the number of units entered in a single cell.

Managers use flexible budgets for both planning and performance evaluation. For instance, managers may assess whether the company's cash position is adequate by assuming different levels of volume. They may judge if the number of employees, amounts of materials, and equipment and storage facilities are appropriate for a variety of different potential levels of volume. In addition to helping plan, flexible budgets are critical to implementing an effective performance evaluation system.

☑ CHECK YOURSELF 15.1

The static (master) budget of Parcel, Inc. called for a production and sales volume of 25,000 units. At that volume, total budgeted fixed costs were $150,000 and total budgeted variable costs were $200,000. Prepare a flexible budget for an expected volume of 26,000 units.

Answer   Budgeted fixed costs would remain unchanged at $150,000 because changes in the volume of activity do not affect budgeted fixed costs. Budgeted variable costs would increase to $208,000, computed as follows: Calculate the budgeted variable cost per unit ($200,000 ÷ 25,000 units = $8) and then multiply that variable cost per unit by the expected volume ($8 × 26,000 units = $208,000).

DETERMINING VARIANCES FOR PERFORMANCE EVALUATION

LO 15-3

Classify variances as being favorable or unfavorable.

One means of evaluating managerial performance is to compare *standard* amounts with *actual* results. The differences between the standard and actual amounts are called **variances;** variances can be either *favorable* or *unfavorable*. When actual sales revenue is greater than expected (planned) revenue, a company has a favorable sales variance because higher sales increase net income. When actual sales are less than expected, an unfavorable sales variance exists. When actual costs are *less* than standard costs, cost variances are favorable because lower costs increase net income. Unfavorable cost variances exist when actual costs are *more* than standard costs. These relationships are summarized as follows.

- When actual sales exceed expected sales, variances are favorable.
- When actual sales are less than expected sales, variances are unfavorable.
- When actual costs exceed standard costs, variances are unfavorable.
- When actual costs are less than standard costs, variances are favorable.

SALES AND VARIABLE COST VOLUME VARIANCES

The amount of a **sales volume variance** is the difference between the static budget (which is based on planned volume) and a flexible budget based on actual volume. Likewise, the **variable cost volume variances** are determined by calculating the differences between the static and flexible budget amounts. These variances measure management effectiveness in attaining the planned volume of activity. To illustrate, assume Melrose Manufacturing Company actually makes and sells 19,000 trophies during Year 1. The planned volume of activity was 18,000 trophies. Exhibit 15.2 shows Melrose's static budget, flexible budget, and volume variances.

Compute and interpret sales and variable cost volume variances.

EXHIBIT 15.2

Melrose Manufacturing Company's Volume Variances

	Static Budget	Flexible Budget	Volume Variances	
Number of units	18,000	19,000	1,000	Favorable
Sales revenue	$1,440,000	$1,520,000	$80,000	Favorable
Variable manufacturing costs				
Materials	216,000	228,000	12,000	Unfavorable
Labor	302,400	319,200	16,800	Unfavorable
Overhead	100,800	106,400	5,600	Unfavorable
Variable SG&A	270,000	285,000	15,000	Unfavorable
Contribution margin	550,800	581,400	30,600	Favorable
Fixed costs	291,600	291,600	0	
Net income	$ 259,200	$ 289,800	$30,600	Favorable

Interpreting the Sales and Variable Cost Volume Variances

Because the static and flexible budgets are based on the same standard sales price and per-unit variable costs, the variances are solely attributable to the difference between the planned and actual volume of activity. Marketing managers are usually responsible for the volume variances. Because the sales volume drives production levels, production managers have little control over volume. Exceptions occur; for example, if poor production quality control leads to inferior goods that are difficult to sell, the production manager is responsible. The production manager is responsible for production delays that affect product availability, which may restrict sales volume. Under normal circumstances, however, the marketing campaign determines the volume of sales. Upper-level marketing managers develop the promotional program and create the sales plan; they are in the best position to explain why sales goals are or are not met. When marketing managers refer to **making the numbers,** they usually mean reaching the sales volume in the static (master) budget.

Moodboard/Alamy Stock Photo

In the case of Melrose Manufacturing Company, the marketing manager not only achieved but also exceeded by 1,000 units the planned volume of sales. Exhibit 15.2 shows the activity variances resulting from the extra volume. At the standard price, the additional volume produces a favorable revenue variance of $80,000 (1,000 units × $80 per unit). The increase in volume also produces unfavorable variable cost variances. The net effect of producing and selling the additional 1,000 units is an increase of $30,600 in the contribution margin, a positive result. These preliminary results suggest that the marketing manager is to be commended. The analysis, however, is incomplete. For example, examining market share could reveal whether the manager won customers from competitors or whether the manager simply reaped the benefit of an unexpected industrywide increase in demand. The increase in sales volume could have been attained by reducing the sales price; the success of that strategy will be analyzed further in a later section of this chapter.

Since the variable costs in the flexible budget are higher than the variable costs in the static budget, the variable cost volume variances are *unfavorable*. The unfavorable classification may be misleading because it focuses solely on the cost component of the income statement. While costs are higher than expected, so too may be revenue. Indeed, as shown in Exhibit 15.2, the total of the unfavorable variable cost variances is more than offset by the favorable revenue variance, resulting in a higher contribution margin. Frequently, the assessment of variances requires a holistic perspective.

Fixed Cost Considerations

The fixed costs are the same in both the static and flexible budgets. By definition, the budgeted amount of fixed costs remains unchanged regardless of the volume of activity. However, this does not mean that there will be no fixed cost variances. Companies may certainly pay more or less than expected for a fixed cost. For example, a supervisor may receive an unplanned raise, causing actual salary costs to be more than the costs shown in the static budget. The difference between the *budgeted* fixed costs and the *actual* fixed costs is called a **spending variance.** At this point, it is important to note that the reason the fixed cost variances shown in Exhibit 15.2 are zero is because we are comparing two budgets (static versus flexible). Because total fixed cost is not affected by the level of activity, there will be no fixed cost variances associated with static versus flexible budgets.

While total fixed cost does not change in response to changes in the volume of activity, fixed cost per unit does change. Changes in the fixed cost per unit have important implications for decision making. For example, consider the impact on cost-plus pricing decisions. Because actual volume is unknown until the end of the year, selling prices must be based on planned volume. At the *planned volume* of activity of 18,000 units, Melrose's fixed cost per unit is expected to be $16.20 ($291,600 ÷ 18,000 units).

Based on the *actual volume* of 19,000 units, the fixed cost per unit is actually $15.35 per trophy ($291,600 ÷ 19,000 units). Because Melrose's prices were established using the $16.20 budgeted cost at planned volume rather than the $15.35 budgeted cost at actual volume, the trophies were overpriced, giving competitors a price advantage. Although Melrose sold more trophies than expected, sales volume might have been even greater if the trophies had been competitively priced.

Underpricing (not encountered by Melrose in this example) can also be detrimental. If planned volume is overstated, the estimated fixed cost per unit will be understated and prices will be set too low. When the higher amount of actual costs is subtracted from revenues, actual profits will be lower than expected. To monitor the effects of volume on fixed cost per unit, companies frequently calculate a **fixed cost volume variance.**

The fixed cost volume variance is *unfavorable* if actual volume is less than planned because cost per unit is higher than expected. Conversely, if actual volume is greater than planned, cost per unit is less than expected, resulting in a *favorable* variance. Both favorable and unfavorable variances can have negative consequences. Managers should strive for the greatest possible degree of accuracy.

FLEXIBLE BUDGET VARIANCES

LO 15-5

Compute and interpret flexible budget variances.

For performance evaluation, management compares actual results to a flexible budget based on the *actual* volume of activity. Because the actual results and the flexible budget reflect the same volume of activity, any variances in revenues and variable costs result from differences between standard and actual per-unit amounts. To illustrate computing and analyzing flexible budget variances, we assume that Melrose's *actual* per-unit amounts during Year 1 were those shown in the following table. The Year 1 per-unit *standard* amounts are repeated here for your convenience.

	Standard	Actual
Sales price	$80.00	$78.00
Variable materials cost	12.00	11.78
Variable labor cost	16.80	17.25
Variable manufacturing overhead cost	5.60	5.75
Variable G, S, & A	15.00	14.90

Actual and budgeted fixed costs are shown in Exhibit 15.3.

Exhibit 15.3 shows Melrose's Year 1 flexible budget, actual results, and flexible budget variances. The flexible budget is the same one compared to the static budget in Exhibit 15.2.

EXHIBIT 15.3

Flexible Budget Variances for Melrose Manufacturing Company

	Flexible Budget	Actual Results	Flexible Budget Variances	
Number of units	19,000	19,000	0	
Sales revenue	$1,520,000	$1,482,000	$38,000	Unfavorable
Variable manufacturing costs				
Materials	228,000	223,820	4,180	Favorable
Labor	319,200	327,750	8,550	Unfavorable
Overhead	106,400	109,250	2,850	Unfavorable
Variable SG&A	285,000	283,100	1,900	Favorable
Contribution margin	581,400	538,080	43,320	Unfavorable
Fixed costs	291,600	295,000	3,400	Unfavorable
Net income	$ 289,800	$ 243,080	$46,720	Unfavorable

Recall the flexible budget amounts come from multiplying the standard per-unit amounts by the actual volume of production. For example, the sales revenue in the flexible budget comes from multiplying the standard sales price by the actual volume ($80 × 19,000). The variable costs are similarly computed. The *actual results* are calculated by multiplying the actual per-unit sales price and cost figures from the preceding table by the actual volume of activity. For example, the sales revenue in the Actual Results column comes from multiplying the actual sales price by the actual volume ($78 × 19,000 = $1,482,000). The actual cost figures are similarly computed. The differences between the flexible budget figures and the actual results are the **flexible budget variances.**

Calculating the Sales Price Variance

Because both the flexible budget and actual results are based on the actual volume of activity, the flexible budget variance is attributable to sales price, not sales volume. In this case, the actual sales price of $78 per unit is less than the standard price of $80 per unit. Because Melrose sold its product for less than the standard sales price, the **sales price variance** is *unfavorable.* Even though the price variance is unfavorable, however, sales volume was 1,000 units more than expected. It is possible the marketing manager generated the additional volume by reducing the sales price. Whether the combination of lower sales price and higher sales volume is favorable or unfavorable depends on the amount of the unfavorable sales price variance versus the amount of the favorable sales volume variance. The *total* sales variance (price and volume) follows.

Actual sales (19,000 units × $78 per unit)	$1,482,000	
Expected sales (18,000 units × $80 per unit)	1,440,000	
Total sales variance	$ 42,000	Favorable

Alternatively:

Activity variance (sales volume)	$ 80,000	Favorable
Sales price variance	(38,000)	Unfavorable
Total sales variance	$ 42,000	Favorable

This analysis indicates that reducing the sales price had a favorable impact on the *total* amount of sales revenue. Use caution when interpreting variances as good or bad; in this instance, the favorable sales variance must be compared with the related cost variances to determine whether the price reduction strategy actually increased or decreased profitability. All unfavorable variances are not bad; all favorable variances are not good. Variances should not be considered the final answer, but instead be seen as a signal to investigate.

 CHECK YOURSELF 15.2

Scott Company's master budget called for a planned sales volume of 30,000 units. Budgeted direct materials cost was $4 per unit. Scott actually produced and sold 32,000 units with an actual materials cost of $3.90 per unit. Determine the volume variance for materials cost and identify the organizational unit most likely responsible for this variance. Determine the flexible budget variance for materials cost and identify the organizational unit most likely responsible for this variance.

Answer

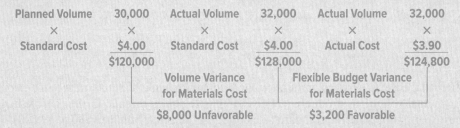

Planned Volume	30,000	Actual Volume	32,000	Actual Volume	32,000
×	×	×	×	×	×
Standard Cost	$4.00	Standard Cost	$4.00	Actual Cost	$3.90
	$120,000		$128,000		$124,800

Volume Variance for Materials Cost	Flexible Budget Variance for Materials Cost
$8,000 Unfavorable	$3,200 Favorable

The materials volume variance is unfavorable because the materials cost ($128,000) is higher than was expected ($120,000). However, this could actually be positive because higher volume was probably caused by increasing sales. Further analysis would be necessary to determine whether the overall effect on the company's profitability was positive or negative. The marketing department is most likely to be responsible for the volume variance.

The flexible budget materials cost variance is favorable because the cost of materials was less than expected at the actual volume of activity. Either the production department (used less than the expected amount of materials) or the purchasing department (obtained materials at a favorable price) is most likely to be responsible for this variance.

The Human Element Associated with Flexible Budget Variances

The flexible budget cost variances offer insight into management efficiency. For example, Melrose Manufacturing Company's favorable materials variance could mean purchasing agents were shrewd in negotiating price concessions, discounts, or delivery terms and therefore reduced the price the company paid for materials. Similarly, production employees may

Answers to the Curious Accountant

As this chapter demonstrates, there are two primary reasons a company spends more or less to produce a product than it estimated. First, the company may have paid more or less than estimated to purchase the inputs needed to produce the product. Second, the company may have used a greater or lesser quantity of these inputs than expected. In the case of Gourmet Pizzas, it may have had to pay more for flour, yeast, sugar, etc., than the owner estimated. Or, it may have used more flour, yeast, sugar, etc., than expected. For example, if pizza dough sits around too long before being used, it may have to be thrown out. This waste was not anticipated when computing the cost to make only one pizza. Of course, the higher than expected cost could have been a combination of price and quantity factors.

Gourmet Pizzas needs to determine if the difference between its expected costs and actual costs was because the estimates were faulty or because the production process was inefficient. If the estimates were to blame, the owner needs to revise them so he can charge customers the proper price. If the production process is inefficient, he needs to correct it if he is to earn an acceptable level of profit.

have used materials efficiently, using less than expected. The unfavorable labor variance could mean managers failed to control employee wages or motivate employees to work hard. As with sales variances, cost variances require careful analysis. A favorable variance may, in fact, mask unfavorable conditions. For example, the favorable materials variance might have been caused by paying low prices for inferior goods. Using substandard materials could have required additional labor in the production process, which would explain the unfavorable labor variance. Again, we caution that variances, whether favorable or unfavorable, alert management to investigate further.

Need for Standards

As the previous discussion suggests, standards are the building blocks for preparing the static and flexible budgets. Standard costs help managers plan and also establish benchmarks against which actual performance can be judged. Highlighting differences between standard (expected) and actual performance focuses management attention on the areas of greatest need. Because management talent is a valuable and expensive resource, businesses cannot afford to have managers spend large amounts of time on operations that are functioning normally. Instead, managers should concentrate on areas not performing as expected. In other words, management should attend to the exceptions; this management philosophy is known as **management by exception.**

Standard setting fosters using the management by exception principle. By reviewing performance reports that show differences between actual and standard costs, management can focus its attention on the items that show significant variances. Areas with only minor variances need little or no review.

MANAGERIAL PERFORMANCE MEASUREMENT

As previously discussed, managers are assigned responsibility for certain cost, profit, or investment centers. They are then evaluated based on how their centers perform relative to specific goals and objectives. The measurement techniques (variance analysis and contribution margin format income reporting) used for cost and profit centers have been discussed in this and previous chapters. The remainder of this chapter discusses performance measures for investment centers.

RETURN ON INVESTMENT

LO 15-6

Evaluate investment opportunities using return on investment.

Society confers wealth, prestige, and power upon those who have control of assets. Unsurprisingly, managers are motivated to increase the amount of assets employed by the investment centers they control. When companies have additional assets available to invest, how do upper-level managers decide which centers should get them? The additional assets are frequently allotted to the managers who demonstrate the greatest potential for increasing the company's wealth. Companies often assess managerial performance by comparing the return on investment ratios of various investment centers. The **return on investment (ROI)** is the ratio of wealth generated (operating income) to the amount invested (operating assets) to generate the wealth. ROI is commonly expressed with the following equation:

$$\text{ROI} = \frac{\text{Operating income}}{\text{Operating assets}}$$

To illustrate using ROI for comparative evaluations, assume Panther Holding Company's corporate (first-level) chief financial officer (CFO) determined the ROIs for the company's three divisions (second-level investment centers). The CFO used the following accounting data from the records of each division.

	Lumber Manufacturing Division	Home Building Division	Furniture Manufacturing Division
Operating income	$ 60,000	$ 46,080	$ 81,940
Operating assets	300,000	256,000	482,000

The ROI for each division is:

Lumber manufacturing: $\dfrac{\text{Operating income}}{\text{Operating assets}} = \$60,000 \div \$300,000 = 20\%$

Home building: $\dfrac{\text{Operating income}}{\text{Operating assets}} = \$46,080 \div \$256,000 = 18\%$

Furniture manufacturing: $\dfrac{\text{Operating income}}{\text{Operating assets}} = \$81,940 \div \$482,000 = 17\%$

All other things being equal, higher ROIs indicate better performance. In this case, the Lumber Manufacturing Division manager is the best performer. Assume Panther obtains additional funding for expanding the company's operations. Which investment center is most likely to receive the additional funds?

If the manager of the Lumber Manufacturing Division convinces the upper-level management team that his division would continue to outperform the other two divisions, the Lumber Manufacturing Division would most likely get the additional funding. The manager of the lumber division would then invest the funds in additional operating assets, which would in turn increase the division's operating income. As the division prospers, Panther would reward the manager for exceptional performance. Rewarding the manager of the lumber division would likely motivate the other managers to improve their divisional ROIs. Internal competition would improve the performance of the company as a whole.

Qualitative Considerations

Why do companies compute ROI using operating income and operating assets instead of using net income and total assets? Suppose Panther's corporate headquarters closes a furniture manufacturing plant because an economic downturn temporarily reduces the demand for furniture. It would be inappropriate to include these nonoperating plant assets in the denominator of the ROI computation. Similarly, if Panther sells the furniture plant and realizes a large gain on the sale, including the gain in the numerator of the ROI formula would distort the result. Since the manager of the Furniture Manufacturing Division does not control closing the plant or selling it, it is unreasonable to include the effects of these decisions in computing the ROI. These items would, however, be included in computing net income and total assets. Most companies use operating income and operating assets to compute ROI because those variables measure performance more accurately.

 CHECK YOURSELF 15.3

Green View is a lawn services company whose operations are divided into two districts. The District 1 manager controls $12,600,000 of operating assets. District 1 produced $1,512,000 of operating income during the year. The District 2 manager controls $14,200,000 of operating assets. District 2 reported $1,988,000 of operating income for the same period. Use return on investment to determine which manager is performing better.

Answer

District 1

   ROI = Operating income ÷ Operating assets = $1,512,000 ÷ $12,600,000 = 12%

District 2

   ROI = Operating income ÷ Operating assets = $1,988,000 ÷ $14,200,000 = 14%

Because the higher ROI indicates the better performance, the District 2 manager is the superior performer. This conclusion is based solely on quantitative results. In real-world practice, companies also consider qualitative factors.

Factors Affecting Return on Investment

Management can gain insight into performance by dividing the ROI formula into two separate ratios as follows:

$$\text{ROI} = \frac{\text{Operating income}}{\text{Sales}} \times \frac{\text{Sales}}{\text{Operating assets}}$$

The first ratio on the right side of the equation is called the margin. The **margin** is a measure of management's ability to control operating expenses relative to the level of sales. In general, high margins indicate superior performance. Management can increase the margin by reducing the level of operating expenses necessary to generate sales. Decreasing operating expenses increases profitability.

The second ratio in the expanded ROI formula is called turnover. **Turnover** is a measure of the amount of operating assets employed to support the achieved level of sales. Operating assets are scarce resources. To maximize profitability, they must be used wisely. Just as excessive expenses decrease profitability, excessive investments in operating assets also limit profitability.

Both the short and expanded versions of the ROI formula produce the same end result. To illustrate, we will use the ROI for the Lumber Manufacturing Division of Panther Holding

Company. Recall that the division employed $300,000 of operating assets to produce $60,000 of operating income, resulting in the following ROI:

$$\text{ROI} = \frac{\text{Operating income}}{\text{Operating assets}} = \frac{\$60,000}{\$300,000} = 20\%$$

Further analysis of the accounting records indicates the Lumber Manufacturing Division had sales of $600,000. The following computation demonstrates that the expanded ROI formula produces the same result as the short formula:

$$\text{ROI} = \text{Margin} \times \text{Turnover}$$

$$= \frac{\text{Operating income}}{\text{Sales}} \times \frac{\text{Sales}}{\text{Operating assets}}$$

$$= \frac{\$60,000}{\$600,000} \times \frac{\$600,000}{\$300,000}$$

$$= 0.10 \times 2$$

$$= 20\%$$

Dividing the ROI formula into a margin and a turnover computation encourages managers to examine the benefits of controlling assets as well as expenses.

Because ROI blends many aspects of managerial performance into a single ratio that enables comparisons between companies, comparisons between investment centers within companies, and comparisons between different investment opportunities within an investment center, ROI has gained widespread acceptance as a performance measure.

 CHECK YOURSELF 15.4

What three actions can a manager take to improve ROI?

Answer

1. Increase sales
2. Reduce expenses
3. Reduce the investment base

RESIDUAL INCOME

LO 15-7

Evaluate investment opportunities using residual income.

Suppose Panther Holding Company evaluates the manager of the Lumber Manufacturing Division (LMD) based on his ability to maximize ROI. The corporation's overall ROI is approximately 18 percent. LMD, however, has consistently outperformed the other investment centers. Its ROI is currently 20 percent. Now suppose the manager has an opportunity to invest additional funds in a project likely to earn a 19 percent ROI. Would the manager accept the investment opportunity?

These circumstances place the manager in an awkward position. The corporation would benefit from the project because the expected ROI of 19 percent is higher than the corporate average ROI of 18 percent. Personally, however, the manager would suffer from accepting the project because it would reduce the division ROI to less than the current 20 percent. The manager is forced to choose between his personal best interests and the best interests of the corporation. When faced with decisions such as these, many managers choose to benefit themselves at the expense of their corporations, a condition described as **suboptimization.**

To avoid *suboptimization,* many businesses base managerial evaluation on **residual income.** This approach measures a manager's ability to maximize earnings above some

FOCUS ON INTERNATIONAL ISSUES

DO MANAGERS IN DIFFERENT COMPANIES STRESS THE SAME PERFORMANCE MEASURES?

About the only ratio companies are required to disclose in their annual reports to stockholders is the earnings per share ratio. Nevertheless, many companies choose to show their performance as measured by other ratios, as well as providing nonratio data not required by GAAP. The types of ratio data companies choose to include in their annual reports provide a sense of what performance measure they consider most important.

A review of several publicly traded companies from the United Kingdom, Japan, and the United States will show that the most common ratios presented are variations of the return on sales percentage and the return on investment percentage, although they may be called by different names. The country in which the company is located does not seem to determine which ratio it will emphasize.

One nonratio performance measure that is popular with companies in all three countries is free cash flow, and it is usually reported in total pounds, yen, or dollars. Be sure to exercise caution before comparing one company's free cash flow, return on sales, or return on investment to those of other companies. There are no official rules governing how these data are calculated, and different companies make different interpretations about how to compute these measurements.

John Woodworth/Photodisc/Getty Images

targeted level. The targeted level of earnings is based on a minimum desired ROI. Residual income is calculated as follows.

$$\text{Residual income} = \text{Operating income} - (\text{Operating assets} \times \text{Desired ROI})$$

To illustrate, recall that LMD currently earns $60,000 of operating income with the $300,000 of operating assets it controls. ROI is 20 percent ($60,000 ÷ $300,000). Assume Panther's desired ROI is 18 percent. LMD's residual income is therefore:

$$\text{Residual income} = \text{Operating income} - (\text{Operating assets} \times \text{Desired ROI})$$
$$= \$60,000 - (\$300,000 \times 0.18)$$
$$= \$60,000 - \$54,000$$
$$= \$6,000$$

Now assume that Panther Holding Company has $50,000 of additional funds available to invest. Because LMD consistently performs at a high level, Panther's corporate management team offers the funds to the LMD manager. The manager believes he could invest the additional $50,000 at a 19 percent rate of return.

If the LMD manager's evaluation is based solely on ROI, he is likely to reject the additional funding because investing the funds at 19 percent would lower his overall ROI. If the LMD manager's evaluation is based on residual income, however, he is likely to accept the funds because an additional investment at 19 percent would increase his residual income as follows.

$$\text{Operating income} = \$50,000 \times 0.19$$
$$= \$9,500$$
$$\text{Residual income} = \text{Operating income} - (\text{Operating assets} \times \text{Desired ROI})$$
$$= \$9,500 - (\$50,000 \times 0.18)$$
$$= \$9,500 - \$9,000$$
$$= \$500$$

REALITY BYTES

Thinking about investments usually conjures up images of buildings and equipment, but investments typically include a much broader range of expenditures. For example, if Walmart plans to open a new store, it has to make an investment in inventory to stock the store that is as permanent as the building. But investment expenditures can be for items much less tangible than inventory. Consider the making of a movie.

While it is true that making a movie can require expenditures for items such as cameras and sets, the single highest cost can often be for actors' salaries. Although movie fans may focus on how much a movie grosses at the box office, from a business perspective it is the movie's ROI that matters.

From an ROI perspective the question is: Which actor generates the highest dollars of return for each dollar he or she is paid? To this end, for the past several years *Forbes* has calculated the "Best Actors for the Buck" list. Calculating the ROI for an actor in a movie, rather than for the entire investment in the movie, can be tricky and requires several

Jason LaVeris/FilmMagic/Getty Images

estimates. For example, should the credit for the spectacular success of the movie *Star Wars: The last Jedi* go to the main actor, Mark Hamill, or to the writer/director, Rian Johnson? Despite these challenges, *Forbes* reviews the financial performance of the highest-paid actors who had starred in at least three movies in the past five years and creates the list.

And the winner is . . . ? In 2017 the actor with the highest return per dollar paid was Jeremy Renner, who starred in *Captain America* and *Mission: Impossible*. According to *Forbes*, he returned $93.80 for each $1.00 of salary he was paid.

Source: Forbes.com.

Accepting the new project would add $500 to LMD's residual income. If the manager of LMD is evaluated based on his ability to maximize residual income, he would benefit by investing in any project that returns an ROI in excess of the desired 18 percent. The reduction in LMD's overall ROI does not enter into the decision. The residual income approach solves the problem of suboptimization.

The primary disadvantage of the residual income approach is that it measures performance in absolute dollars. As a result, a manager's residual income may be larger simply because her investment base is larger rather than because her performance is superior.

To illustrate, return to the example where Panther Holding Company has $50,000 of additional funds to invest. Assume the manager of the Lumber Manufacturing Division (LMD) and the manager of the Furniture Manufacturing Division (FMD) each have investment opportunities expected to earn a 19 percent return. Recall that Panther's desired ROI is 18 percent. If corporate headquarters allots $40,000 of the funds to the manager of LMD and $10,000 to the manager of FMD, the increase in residual income earned by each division is as follows.

$$\text{LMD's Residual income} = (\$40,000 \times 0.19) - (\$40,000 \times 0.18) = \$400$$

$$\text{FMD's Residual income} = (\$10,000 \times 0.19) - (\$10,000 \times 0.18) = \$100$$

Does LMD's higher residual income mean LMD's manager is outperforming FMD's manager? No. It means LMD's manager received more operating assets than FMD's manager received.

Calculating Multiple ROIs and/or RIs for the Same Company

You may be asked to calculate different ROI and RI measures for the same company. For example, ROI and/or RI may be calculated for the company as a whole, for segments of the company, for specific investment opportunities, and for individual managers. An example is shown in Check Yourself 15.5.

Responsibility Accounting and the Balanced Scorecard

Throughout the text, we have discussed many financial measures companies use to evaluate managerial performance. Examples include standard cost systems to evaluate cost center managers; the contribution margin income statement to evaluate profit center managers; and ROI or residual income to evaluate the performance of investment center managers. Many companies may have goals and objectives such as "satisfaction guaranteed" or "we try harder" that are more suitably evaluated using nonfinancial measures. To assess how well they accomplish the full range of their missions, many companies use a *balanced scorecard.*

 CHECK YOURSELF 15.5

Tambor Incorporated (TI) earned operating income of $4,730,400 on operating assets of $26,280,000 during Year 2. The Western Division earned $748,000 on operating assets of $3,400,000. TI has offered the Western Division $1,100,000 of additional operating assets. The manager of the Western Division believes he could use the additional assets to generate operating income amounting to $220,000. TI has a desired return on investment (ROI) of 17 percent. Determine the ROI and RI for TI, the Western Division, and the additional investment opportunity.

Answer

Return on investment (ROI) = Operating income ÷ Operating assets
ROI for TI = $4,730,400 ÷ $26,280,000 = 18%
ROI for Western Division = $748,000 ÷ $3,400,000 = 22%
ROI for investment opportunity = $220,000 ÷ $1,100,000 = 20%

Residual income (RI) = Operating income − (Operating assets × Desired ROI)
RI for TI = $4,730,400 − ($26,280,000 × 0.17) = $262,800
RI for Western Division = $748,000 − ($3,400,000 × 0.17) = $170,000
RI for investment opportunity = $220,000 − ($1,100,000 × 0.17) = $33,000

A **balanced scorecard** includes financial and nonfinancial performance measures. Standard costs, income measures, ROI, and residual income are common financial measures used in a balanced scorecard. Nonfinancial measures include defect rates, cycle time, on-time deliveries, number of new products or innovations, safety measures, and customer satisfaction surveys. Many companies compose their scorecards to highlight leading versus lagging measures. For example, customer satisfaction survey data are a leading indicator of sales growth, which is a lagging measure. The balanced scorecard is a holistic approach to evaluating managerial performance. It is gaining widespread acceptance among world-class companies.

A Look Back

The practice of delegating authority and responsibility is referred to as *decentralization.* Clear lines of authority and responsibility are essential in establishing a responsibility accounting system. In a responsibility accounting system, segment managers are held accountable for profits based on the amount of control they have over the profits in their segment.

A *responsibility center* is the point in an organization where control over revenue or expense is located. *Cost centers* are segments that incur costs but do not generate revenues. *Profit centers* incur costs and also generate revenues, producing a measurable profit. *Investment centers* incur costs, generate revenues, and use identifiable capital investments.

One of the primary purposes of responsibility accounting is to evaluate managerial performance. Comparing actual results with standards and budgets and calculating *return on investment* are used for this purpose. Because return on investment uses revenues, expenses, and investment, problems with measuring these parameters must be considered. The return on investment can be analyzed in terms of the margin earned on sales as well as the turnover (asset utilization) during the period. The *residual income approach* is sometimes used to avoid *suboptimization,* which occurs when managers choose to reject investment projects that would benefit their company's ROI but would reduce their investment center's ROI. The residual income approach evaluates managers based on their ability to generate earnings above some targeted level of earnings.

A Look Forward

The next chapter expands on the concepts in this chapter. You will see how managers select investment opportunities that will affect their future ROIs. You will learn to apply present value techniques to compute the net present value and the internal rate of return for potential investment opportunities. You will also learn to use less-sophisticated analytical techniques such as payback and the unadjusted rate of return.

Video lectures and accompanying self-assessment quizzes are available in *Connect* for all learning objectives.

SELF-STUDY REVIEW PROBLEM 1

Bugout Pesticides Inc. established the following standard price and costs for a termite control product that it sells to exterminators.

Variable price and cost data (per unit)	Standard	Actual
Sales price	$ 52.00	$ 49.00
Materials cost	10.00	10.66
Labor cost	12.00	11.90
Overhead cost	7.00	7.05
General, selling, and administrative (G, S, & A) cost	8.00	7.92
Expected fixed costs (in total)		
Manufacturing	$150,000	$140,000
General, selling, and administrative	60,000	64,000

The Year 1 master budget was established at an expected volume of 25,000 units. Actual production and sales volume for the year was 26,000 units.

Required

a. Prepare the pro forma income statement for Bugout's Year 1 master budget.

b. Prepare a flexible budget income statement at the actual volume.

c. Determine the sales activity (volume) variances and indicate whether they are favorable or unfavorable. Comment on how Bugout would use the variances to evaluate performance.

d. Determine the flexible budget variances and indicate whether they are favorable or unfavorable.

e. Identify the two variances Bugout is most likely to analyze further. Explain why you chose these two variances. Who is normally responsible for the variances you chose to investigate?

Solution to Requirements *a*, *b*, and *c*

Number of units		25,000	26,000	
	Per Unit Standards	Master Budget	Flexible Budget	Volume Variances
Sales revenue	$52	$1,300,000	$1,352,000	$52,000 F
Variable manufacturing costs				
Materials	10	(250,000)	(260,000)	10,000 U
Labor	12	(300,000)	(312,000)	12,000 U
Overhead	7	(175,000)	(182,000)	7,000 U
Variable G, S, & A	8	(200,000)	(208,000)	8,000 U
Contribution margin		375,000	390,000	15,000 F
Fixed costs				
Manufacturing		(150,000)	(150,000)	0
G, S, & A		(60,000)	(60,000)	0
Net income		$ 165,000	$ 180,000	$15,000 F

The sales activity variances are useful in determining how changes in sales volume affect revenues and costs. Because the flexible budget is based on standard prices and costs, the variances do not provide insight into differences between standard prices and costs versus actual prices and costs.

Solution to Requirement *d*

Number of units		26,000	26,000	
	Actual Unit Price/Cost	Flexible Budget*	Actual Results	Flexible Budget Variances
Sales revenue	$49.00	$1,352,000	$1,274,000	$78,000 U
Variable manufacturing costs				
Materials	10.66	(260,000)	(277,160)	17,160 U
Labor	11.90	(312,000)	(309,400)	2,600 F
Overhead	7.05	(182,000)	(183,300)	1,300 U
Variable G, S, & A	7.92	(208,000)	(205,920)	2,080 F
Contribution margin		390,000	298,220	91,780 U
Fixed costs				
Manufacturing		(150,000)	(140,000)	10,000 F
G, S, & A		(60,000)	(64,000)	4,000 U
Net income		$ 180,000	$ 94,220	$85,780 U

*The price and cost data for the flexible budget come from the previous table.

Solution to Requirement *e*

The management by exception doctrine focuses attention on the sales price variance and the materials variance. The two variances are material in size and are generally under the control of management. Upper-level marketing managers are responsible for the sales price variance. These managers are normally responsible for establishing the sales price. In this case, the actual sales price is less than the planned sales price, resulting in an unfavorable flexible budget variance. Mid-level production supervisors and purchasing agents are normally responsible for the materials cost variance. This variance could have been caused by waste or by paying more for materials than the standard price.

SELF-STUDY REVIEW PROBLEM 2

The following financial statements apply to Hola Division, one of three investment centers operated by Costa Corporation. Costa Corporation has a desired rate of return of 15 percent. Costa Corporation Headquarters has $80,000 of additional operating assets to assign to the investment centers.

HOLA DIVISION
Income Statement
For the Year Ended December 31, Year 2

Sales revenue	$ 78,695
Cost of goods sold	(50,810)
Gross margin	27,885
Operating expenses	
Selling expenses	(1,200)
Depreciation expense	(1,125)
Operating income	25,560
Nonoperating expense	
Loss on sale of land	(3,200)
Net income	$ 22,360

HOLA DIVISION
Balance Sheet
As of December 31, Year 2

Assets	
Cash	$ 8,089
Accounts receivable	22,870
Merchandise inventory	33,460
Equipment less acc. dep.	77,581
Nonoperating assets	8,250
Total assets	$150,250
Liabilities	
Accounts payable	$ 5,000
Notes payable	58,000
Stockholders' equity	
Common stock	55,000
Retained earnings	32,250
Total liab. and stk. equity	$150,250

Required

a. Should Costa use operating income or net income to determine the rate of return (ROI) for the Hola investment center? Explain.

b. Should Costa use operating assets or total assets to determine the ROI for the Hola investment center? Explain.

c. Calculate the ROI for Hola.

d. The manager of the Hola division has an opportunity to invest the funds at an ROI of 17 percent. The other two divisions have investment opportunities that yield only 16 percent. The manager of Hola rejects the additional funding. Why would the manager of Hola reject the funds under these circumstances?

e. Calculate the residual income from the investment opportunity available to Hola and explain how residual income could be used to encourage the manager to accept the additional funds.

Solution to Requirement *a*

Costa should use operating income because net income frequently includes items over which management has no control, such as the loss on sale of land.

Solution to Requirement *b*

Costa should use operating assets because total assets frequently include items over which management has no control, such as assets not currently in use.

Solution to Requirement *c*

$$\text{ROI} = \text{Operating income/Operating assets} = \$25,560/\$142,000 = 18\%$$

Solution to Requirement *d*

Since the rate of return on the investment opportunity (17 percent) is below Hola's current ROI (18 percent), accepting the opportunity would decrease Hola's average ROI, which would have a negative effect on the manager's performance evaluation. While it is to the advantage of the company as a whole for Hola to accept the investment opportunity, it will reflect negatively on the manager to do so. This phenomenon is called *suboptimization*.

Solution to Requirement *e*

Operating income from the investment opportunity is $13,600 ($80,000 × 0.17).

$$\text{Residual income} = \text{Operating income} - (\text{Operating assets} \times \text{Desired ROI})$$
$$\text{Residual income} = \$13,600 - (\$80,000 \times 0.15)$$
$$\text{Residual income} = \$13,600 - \$12,000$$
$$\text{Residual income} = \$1,600$$

Because the investment opportunity would increase Hola's residual income, the acceptance of the opportunity would improve the manager's performance evaluation, thereby motivating the manager to accept it.

KEY TERMS

Balanced scorecard 553
Controllability concept 540
Cost center 540
Decentralization 540
Fixed cost volume
 variance 544
Flexible budget 541
Flexible budget variance 545

Investment center 540
Making the
 numbers 543
Management by
 exception 547
Margin 549
Profit center 540
Residual income 550

Responsibility
 accounting 538
Responsibility center 540
Return on investment
 (ROI) 548
Sales price variance 545
Sales volume
 variance 543

Spending variance 544
Static budget 541
Suboptimization 550
Turnover 549
Variable cost volume
 variance 543
Variance 542

QUESTIONS

1. Pam Kelly says she has no faith in budgets. Her company, Kelly Manufacturing Corporation, spent thousands of dollars to install a sophisticated budget system. One year later the company's expenses are still out of control. She believes budgets simply do not work. How would you respond to Ms. Kelly's beliefs?

2. What is a responsibility center?

3. What are the three types of responsibility centers? Explain how each differs from the others.

4. What is the difference between a static budget and a flexible budget? When is each used?

5. When the operating costs for Bill Smith's production department were released, he was sure that he would be getting a raise. His costs were $20,000 less than the planned cost in the master budget. His supervisor informed him that the results look good but that a more in-depth analysis is necessary before raises can be assigned. What other considerations could Mr. Smith's supervisor be interested in before she rates his performance?

6. When are sales and cost variances favorable and unfavorable?

7. Joan Mason, the marketing manager for a large manufacturing company, believes her unfavorable sales volume variance is the responsibility of the production department.

What production circumstances that she does not control could have been responsible for her poor performance?

8. When would variable cost volume variances be expected to be unfavorable? How should unfavorable variable cost volume variances be interpreted?

9. What factors could lead to an increase in sales revenues that would not merit congratulations to the marketing manager?

10. With respect to fixed costs, what are the consequences of the actual volume of activity exceeding the planned volume?

11. How are flexible budget variances determined? What causes these variances?

12. Minnie Divers, the manager of the marketing department for one of the industry's leading retail businesses, has been notified by the accounting department that her department experienced an unfavorable sales volume variance in the preceding period but a favorable sales price variance. Based on these contradictory results, how would you interpret her overall performance as suggested by her variances?

13. How do variance reports promote the management by exception doctrine?

14. Carmen Douglas claims that her company's performance evaluation system is unfair. Her company uses return on investment (ROI) to evaluate performance. Ms. Douglas says that even though her ROI is lower than another manager's, her performance is far superior. Is it possible that Ms. Douglas is correct? Explain your position.

15. What two factors affect the computation of return on investment?

16. What three ways can a manager increase the return on investment?

17. How can a residual income approach to performance evaluation reduce the likelihood of suboptimization?

18. Is it true that the manager with the highest residual income is always the best performer?

EXERCISES—SERIES A

connect An electronic auto-gradable version of the Series A Exercises is available in Connect. A PDF version of Series B Exercises is in Connect under the "Additional Student Resources" tab. Solutions to the Series B Exercises are available in Connect under the "Instructor Library" tab. Instructor and student Workpapers for the Series B Exercises are available in Connect under the "Instructor Library" and "Additional Student Resources" tabs respectively.

LO 15-1

Exercise 15-1A *Evaluating a profit center*

Helen Kaito, the president of Gladstone Toys Corporation, is trying to determine this year's pay raises for the store managers. Gladstone Toys has seven stores in the southwestern United States. Corporate headquarters purchases all toys from different manufacturers globally and distributes them to individual stores. Additionally, headquarters makes decisions regarding location and size of stores. These practices allow Gladstone Toys to receive volume discounts from vendors and to implement coherent marketing strategies. Within a set of general guidelines, store managers have the flexibility to adjust product prices and hire local employees. Ms. Kaito is considering three possible performance measures for evaluating the individual stores: cost of goods sold, return on sales (net income divided by sales), and return on investment.

Required

a. Using the concept of controllability, advise Ms. Kaito about the best performance measure.

b. Explain how a balanced scorecard can be used to help Ms. Kaito.

LO 15-2

Exercise 15-2A *Preparing master and flexible budgets*

Cherokee Manufacturing Company established the following standard price and cost data:

Sales price	$12.00 per unit
Variable manufacturing cost	7.20 per unit
Fixed manufacturing cost	3,600 total
Fixed selling and administrative cost	1,200 total

Cherokee planned to produce and sell 2,000 units. Actual production and sales amounted to 2,200 units.

Required

a. Prepare the pro forma income statement in contribution format that would appear in a master budget.

b. Prepare the pro forma income statement in contribution format that would appear in a flexible budget.

Exercise 15-3A   *Using a flexible budget to accommodate market uncertainty*

LO 15-2

According to its original plan, Topeka Consulting Services Company plans to charge its customers for service at $120 per hour. The company president expects consulting services provided to customers to reach 45,000 hours at that rate. The marketing manager, however, argues that actual results may range from 40,000 hours to 50,000 hours because of market uncertainty. Topeka's standard variable cost is $45 per hour, and its standard fixed cost is $1,350,000.

Required

Develop flexible budgets based on the assumptions of service levels at 40,000 hours, 45,000 hours, and 50,000 hours.

Exercise 15-4A   *Classifying variances as favorable or unfavorable*

LO 15-3

Required

Indicate whether each of the following variances is favorable or unfavorable. The first one has been done as an example.

Item to Classify	Standard	Actual	Type of Variance
Sales volume	50,000 units	54,000 units	Favorable
Sales price	$4.00 per unit	$4.10 per unit	
Materials cost	$2.90 per pound	$3.00 per pound	
Materials usage	91,000 pounds	90,000 pounds	
Labor cost	$10.00 per hour	$9.60 per hour	
Labor usage	61,000 hours	61,800 hours	
Fixed cost spending	$400,000	$390,000	
Fixed cost per unit (volume)	$8.00 per unit	$7.22 per unit	

Exercise 15-5A   *Determining amount and type (favorable vs. unfavorable) of variance*

LO 15-3

Required

Compute variances for the following items and indicate whether each variance is favorable (F) or unfavorable (U).

Item	Budget	Actual	Variance	F or U
Sales price	$ 400	$ 390		
Sales revenue	$ 360,000	$ 390,000		
Cost of goods sold	$ 192,500	$ 180,000		
Material purchases at 5,000 pounds	$ 137,500	$ 140,000		
Materials usage	90,000 lbs	89,000 lbs		
Production volume	950 units	900 units		
Wages at 4,000 hours	$ 30,000	$ 29,350		
Labor usage at $12 per hour	$ 48,000	$ 48,500		
Research and development expense	$ 11,000	$ 12,500		
Selling and administrative expenses	$ 24,500	$ 20,000		

Exercise 15-6A *Income statement for internal use*

Dunlop Company has provided the following for the year.

Budget	
Sales	$400,000
Variable product costs	163,000
Variable selling expense	40,000
Other variable expenses	3,000
Fixed product costs	10,500
Fixed selling expense	20,000
Other fixed expenses	1,600
Interest expense	650
Variances	
Sales	3,200 U
Variable product costs	2,600 F
Variable selling expense	1,250 U
Other variable expenses	600 U
Fixed product costs	110 F
Fixed selling expense	195 F
Other fixed expenses	75 U
Interest expense	50 F

Required

a. Prepare in good form a budgeted and actual income statement for internal use. Separate operating income from net income in the statements.

Exercise 15-7A *Determining sales and variable cost volume variances*

Required

Use the information provided in Exercise 15-2.

a. Determine the sales and variable cost volume variances.

b. Classify the variances as favorable (F) or unfavorable (U).

c. Comment on the usefulness of the variances with respect to performance evaluation and identify the member of the management team most likely to be responsible for these variances.

d. Determine the amount of fixed cost that will appear in the flexible budget.

e. Determine the fixed cost per unit based on planned activity and the fixed cost per unit based on actual activity. Assuming Cherokee uses information in the master budget to price the company's product, comment on how the fixed cost volume variance could affect the company's profitability. Round computations to two decimal points.

Exercise 15-8A *Determining flexible budget variances*

Use the standard price and cost data provided in Exercise 15-2. Assume that the actual sales price is $11.76 per unit and that the actual variable cost is $6.90 per unit. The actual fixed manufacturing cost is $3,000, and the actual selling and administrative costs are $1,230.

Required

a. Determine the flexible budget variances.

b. Classify the variances as favorable (F) or unfavorable (U).

c. Provide another name for the fixed cost flexible budget variances.

d. Comment on the usefulness of the variances with respect to performance evaluation and identify the member(s) of the management team who is (are) most likely to be responsible for these variances.

Exercise 15-9A   *Responsibility for the fixed cost volume variance*

Roanoke Company expected to sell 400,000 of its dog tracking collars during the year. It set the standard sales price for the collar at $60 each. During June, it became obvious that the company would be unable to attain the expected volume of sales. Roanoke's chief competitor, Kenny Corporation, had lowered prices and was pulling market share from Roanoke. To be competitive, Roanoke matched Kenny's price, lowering its sales price to $56 per collar. Kenny responded by lowering its price even further to $48 per collar. In an emergency meeting of key personnel, Roanoke's accountant, Karen Velez, stated, "Our cost structure simply won't support a sales price in the $48 range." The production manager, Gene Cormier, said, "I don't understand why I'm here. The only unfavorable variance on my report is a fixed manufacturing overhead cost volume variance and that one is not my fault. We shouldn't be making the product if the marketing department isn't selling it."

Required

a. Describe a scenario in which the production manager is responsible for the fixed cost volume variance.
b. Describe a scenario in which the marketing manager is responsible for the fixed cost volume variance.
c. Explain how a decline in sales volume would affect Roanoke's ability to lower its sales price.

Exercise 15-10A   *Evaluating a cost center including flexible budgeting concepts*

Muskrat Medical Equipment Company makes a blood pressure measuring kit. Jason McCoy is the production manager. The production department's static budget and actual results for Year 3 follow.

	Static Budget	Actual Results
Production in units	*60,000 kits*	*64,000 kits*
Direct materials	$ 525,000	$ 655,000
Direct labor	450,000	464,000
Variable manufacturing overhead	120,000	135,000
Total variable costs	1,095,000	1,254,000
Fixed manufacturing overhead	525,000	512,500
Total manufacturing cost	$1,620,000	$1,766,500

Required

a. Convert the static budget into a flexible budget.
b. Use the flexible budget to evaluate Mr. McCoy's performance.
c. Explain why Mr. McCoy's performance evaluation does not include sales revenue and net income.

Exercise 15-11A   *Evaluating a decision to increase sales volume by lowering sales price*

Secor Educational Services had budgeted its training service charge at $120 per hour. The company planned to provide 30,000 hours of training services during the year. By lowering the service charge to $114 per hour, the company was able to increase the actual number of hours to 31,500.

Required

a. Determine the sales volume variance, and indicate whether it is favorable (F) or unfavorable (U).
b. Determine the flexible budget variance, and indicate whether it is favorable (F) or unfavorable (U).
c. Did lowering the price of training services increase revenue? Explain.

Exercise 15-12A   *Return on investment*

An investment center of Tribune Corporation shows an operating income of $7,500 on total operating assets of $125,000.

Required

Compute the return on investment. Round the computation to two decimal points.

LO 15-6

Exercise 15-13A *Return on investment*

Eastevan Company calculated its return on investment as 10 percent. Sales are now $300,000, and the amount of total operating assets is $320,000.

Required

a. If expenses are reduced by $28,000 and sales remain unchanged, what return on investment will result?

b. If both sales and expenses cannot be changed, what change in the amount of operating assets is required to achieve the same result? Round computation to whole dollar.

LO 15-7

Exercise 15-14A *Residual income*

Climax Corporation has a desired rate of return of 7.50 percent. William Tobin is in charge of one of Climax's three investment centers. His center controlled operating assets of $4,000,000 that were used to earn $480,000 of operating income.

Required

Compute Mr. Tobin's residual income.

LO 15-7

Exercise 15-15A *Residual income*

Gletchen Cough Drops operates two divisions. The following information pertains to each division for the year.

	Division A	Division B
Sales	$480,000	$300,000
Operating income	$ 32,000	$ 24,000
Average operating assets	$200,000	$160,000
Company's desired rate of return	10%	10%

Required

a. Compute each division's residual income.

b. Which division increased the company's profitability more?

LO 15-6, 15-7

Exercise 15-16A *Return on investment and residual income*

Required

Supply the missing information in the following table for Unify Company.

Sales	$605,000
ROI	?
Operating assets	?
Operating income	?
Turnover	2.2
Residual income	?
Operating profit margin	0.08
Desired rate of return	10%

LO 15-6, 15-7

Exercise 15-17A *Comparing return on investment with residual income*

The Monarch Division of Allgood Corporation has a current ROI of 12 percent. The company target ROI is 8 percent. The Monarch Division has an opportunity to invest $4,800,000 at 10 percent but is reluctant to do so because its ROI will fall to 11.25 percent. The present investment base for the division is $8,000,000.

Required

Demonstrate how Allgood can motivate the Monarch Division to make the investment by using the residual income method.

PROBLEMS—SERIES A

Mc Graw Hill connect An electronic auto-gradable version of the Series A Problems is available in Connect. A PDF version of Series B Problems is in Connect under the "Additional Student Resources" tab. Solutions to the Series B Problems are available in Connect under the "Instructor Library" tab. Instructor and student Workpapers for the Series B Problems are available in Connect under the "Instructor Library" and "Additional Student Resources" tabs respectively.

Problem 15-18A *Different types of responsibility centers*   **LO 15-1**

Yalaha National Bank is a large municipal bank with several branch offices. The bank's computer department handles all data processing for bank operations. In addition, the bank sells the computer department's expertise in systems development and excess machine time to several small business firms, serving them as a service bureau.

The bank currently treats the computer department as a cost center. The manager of the computer department prepares a cost budget annually for senior bank officials to approve. Monthly operating reports compare actual and budgeted expenses. Revenues from the department's service bureau activities are treated as other income by the bank and are not reflected on the computer department's operating reports. The costs of servicing these clients are included in the computer department reports, however.

The manager of the computer department has proposed that bank management convert the computer department to a profit or investment center.

Required

a. Describe the characteristics that differentiate a cost center, a profit center, and an investment center from each other.

b. Would the manager of the computer department be likely to conduct the operations of the department differently if the department were classified as a profit center or an investment center rather than as a cost center? Explain.

Problem 15-19A *Flexible budget planning*   **LO 15-2**

Howard Cooper, the president of Glacier Computer Services, needs your help. He wonders about the potential effects on the firm's net income if he changes the service rate that the firm charges its customers. The following basic data pertain to fiscal Year 1.

Standard rate and variable costs	
Service rate per hour	$ 60.00
Labor cost	32.00
Overhead cost	5.76
Selling, general, and administrative cost	3.44
Expected fixed costs	
Facility maintenance	$320,000
Selling, general, and administrative	120,000

Required

a. Prepare the pro forma income statement that would appear in the master budget if the firm expects to provide 30,000 hours of services in Year 1.

b. A marketing consultant suggests to Mr. Cooper that the service rate may affect the number of service hours that the firm can achieve. According to the consultant's analysis, if Glacier charges customers $56 per hour, the firm can achieve 38,000 hours of services. Prepare a flexible budget using the consultant's assumption.

c. The same consultant also suggests that if the firm raises its rate to $64 per hour, the number of service hours will decline to 25,000. Prepare a flexible budget using the new assumption.

d. Evaluate the three possible outcomes you determined in Requirements *a*, *b*, and *c* and recommend a pricing strategy.

Problem 15-20A *Determining sales and variable cost volume variances*   **LO 15-2, 15-3, 15-4**

Narcisco Publications established the following standard price and costs for a hardcover picture book that the company produces.

Standard price and variable costs	
Sales price	$ 90.00
Materials cost	18.00
Labor cost	9.00
Overhead cost	12.60
Selling, general, and administrative costs	14.40
Planned fixed costs	
Manufacturing overhead	$270,000
Selling, general, and administrative	108,000

Narcisco planned to make and sell 30,000 copies of the book.

Required

a. Prepare the pro forma income statement that would appear in the master budget.

b. Prepare flexible budget income statements, assuming production volumes of 29,000 and 31,000 units.

c. Determine the sales and variable cost volume variances, assuming volume is actually 31,000 units.

d. Indicate whether the variances are favorable (F) or unfavorable (U).

e. Comment on how Narcisco could use the variances to evaluate performance.

LO 15-5

Problem 15-21A *Determining and interpreting flexible budget variances*

Use the standard price and cost data supplied in Problem 15-20A. Assume that Narcisco actually produced and sold 32,000 books. The actual sales price and costs incurred follow.

Actual price and variable costs	
Sales price	$ 87.00
Materials cost	18.40
Labor cost	8.80
Overhead cost	12.70
Selling, general, and administrative costs	14.00
Actual fixed costs	
Manufacturing overhead	$250,000
Selling, general, and administrative	116,000

Required

a. Determine the flexible budget variances.

b. Indicate whether each variance is favorable (F) or unfavorable (U).

c. Identify the management position responsible for each variance. Explain what could have caused the variance.

LO 15-6

Problem 15-22A *Return on investment*

Sorrento Corporation's balance sheet indicates that the company has $500,000 invested in operating assets. During the year, Sorrento earned operating income of $50,000 on $1,000,000 of sales.

Required

a. Compute Sorrento's profit margin for the year.

b. Compute Sorrento's turnover for the year.

c. Compute Sorrento's return on investment for the year.

d. Recompute Sorrento's ROI under each of the following independent assumptions:

(1) Sales increase from $1,000,000 to $1,200,000, thereby resulting in an increase in operating income from $50,000 to $56,000.

(2) Sales remain constant, but Sorrento reduces expenses, resulting in an increase in operating income from $50,000 to $52,000.

(3) Sorrento is able to reduce its invested capital from $500,000 to $400,000 without affecting operating income.

Problem 15-23A *Comparing return on investment and residual income*

LO 15-6, 15-7

Helena Corporation operates three investment centers. The following financial statements apply to the investment center named Bowman Division.

CHECK FIGURE
c. 24.34%

BOWMAN DIVISION
Income Statement
For the Year Ended December 31, Year 2

Sales revenue	$138,000
Cost of goods sold	78,000
Gross margin	60,000
Operating expenses	
Selling expenses	(6,000)
Depreciation expense	(8,000)
Operating income	46,000
Nonoperating item	
Loss on sale of land	(16,000)
Net income	$ 30,000

BOWMAN DIVISION
Balance Sheet
As of December 31, Year 2

Assets	
Cash	$ 18,898
Accounts receivable	42,266
Merchandise inventory	37,578
Equipment less accum. dep.	90,258
Nonoperating assets	9,000
Total assets	$198,000
Liabilities	
Accounts payable	$ 9,637
Notes payable	72,000
Stockholders' equity	
Common stock	80,000
Retained earnings	36,363
Total liab. and stk. equity	$198,000

Required

a. Which should be used to determine the rate of return (ROI) for the Bowman investment center, operating income or net income? Explain your answer.

b. Which should be used to determine the ROI for the Bowman investment center, operating assets or total assets? Explain your answer.

c. Calculate the ROI for Bowman. Round the computation to two decimal points.

d. Helena has a desired ROI of 10 percent. Headquarters has $96,000 of funds to assign to its investment centers. The manager of the Bowman Division has an opportunity to invest the funds at an ROI of 12 percent. The other two divisions have investment opportunities that yield only 11 percent. Even so, the manager of Bowman rejects the additional funding. Explain why the manager of Bowman would reject the funds under these circumstances. Round the computation to two decimal points.

e. Explain how residual income could be used to encourage the manager to accept the additional funds. Round the computation to whole dollars.

LO 15-6, 15-7

Problem 15-24A *Comparing return on investment and residual income*

The manager of the Cranston Division of Wynn Manufacturing Corporation is currently producing a 20 percent return on invested capital. Wynn's desired rate of return is 16 percent. The Cranston Division has $6,000,000 of capital invested in operating assets and access to additional funds as needed. The manager is considering a new investment in operating assets that will require a $1,500,000 capital commitment and promises an 18 percent return.

Required

a. Would it be advantageous for Wynn Manufacturing Corporation if the Cranston Division makes the investment under consideration?

b. What effect would the proposed investment have on the Cranston Division's return on investment? Show computations.

c. What effect would the proposed investment have on the Cranston Division's residual income? Show computations.

d. Would return on investment or residual income be the better performance measure for the Cranston Division's manager? Explain.

ANALYZE, THINK, COMMUNICATE

ATC 15-1 **Business Applications Case** *Static versus flexible budget variances*

John Richardson is the manufacturing production supervisor for Torsion Tool Works (TTW), a company that manufactures hand tools for mechanics. Trying to explain why he did not get the year-end bonus that he had expected, he told his wife, "This is the dumbest place I've ever worked. Last year the company set up this budget assuming it would sell 250,000 units. Well, it sold only 240,000. The company lost money and gave me a bonus for not using as much materials and labor as was called for in the budget. This year, the company has the same 250,000 units goal and it sells 260,000. The company's making all kinds of money. You'd think I'd get this big fat bonus. Instead, management tells me I used more materials and labor than was budgeted. They said the company would have made a lot more money if I'd stayed within my budget. I guess I gotta wait for another bad year before I get a bonus. Like I said, this is the dumbest place I've ever worked."

TTW's master budget and the actual results for the most recent year of operating activity follow.

	Master Budget	Actual Results	Variances	F or U
Number of units	250,000	260,000	10,000	
Sales revenue	$ 3,750,000	$ 3,950,000	$ 200,000	F
Variable manufacturing costs				
Materials	(600,000)	(622,200)	22,200	U
Labor	(312,500)	(321,000)	8,500	U
Overhead	(337,500)	(354,700)	17,200	U
Variable selling, general,				
and admin. costs	(475,000)	(501,300)	26,300	U
Contribution margin	2,025,000	2,150,800	125,800	F
Fixed costs				
Manufacturing overhead	(1,275,000)	(1,273,100)	1,900	F
Selling, general, and admin. costs	(470,000)	(479,300)	9,300	U
Net income	$ 280,000	$ 398,400	$ 118,400	F

Required

a. Did TTW increase unit sales by cutting prices or by using some other strategy?

b. Is Mr. Richardson correct in his conclusion that something is wrong with the company's performance evaluation process? If so, what do you suggest be done to improve the system?

c. Prepare a flexible budget and recompute the budget variances.

d. Explain what might have caused the fixed costs to be different from the amount budgeted.

e. Assume that the company's materials price variance was favorable and its materials usage variance was unfavorable. Explain why Mr. Richardson may not be responsible for these variances. Now, explain why he may have been responsible for the materials usage variance.

f. Assume the labor price variance is unfavorable. Was the labor usage variance favorable or unfavorable?

g. Is the fixed cost volume variance favorable or unfavorable? Explain the effect of this variance on the cost of each unit produced.

ATC 15-2   Group Assignment   *Variable price and usage variances and fixed manufacturing overhead cost variances*

Kemp Tables, Inc. (KTI) makes picnic tables of 2 × 4 planks of treated pine. It sells the tables to large retail discount stores such as Walmart. After reviewing the following data generated by KTI's chief accountant, the company president, Arianne Darwin, expressed concern that the total manufacturing cost was more than $0.5 million above budget ($7,084,800 − $6,520,000 = $564,800).

	Actual Results	Master Budget
Cost of planks per table	$ 44.10	$ 40.00
Cost of labor per table	26.10	25.50
Total variable manufacturing cost per table (a)	$ 70.20	$ 65.50
Total number of tables produced (b)	82,000	80,000
Total variable manufacturing cost (a × b)	$5,756,400	$5,240,000
Total fixed manufacturing cost	1,328,400	1,280,000
Total manufacturing cost	$7,084,800	$6,520,000

Ms. Darwin asked Conrad Pearson, KTI's chief accountant, to explain what caused the increase in cost. Mr. Pearson responded that things were not as bad as they seemed. He noted that part of the cost variance resulted from making and selling more tables than had been expected. Making more tables naturally causes the cost of materials and labor to be higher. He explained that the flexible budget cost variance was less than $0.5 million. Specifically, he provided the following comparison.

	Actual Results	Flexible Budget
Cost of planks per table	$ 44.10	$ 40.00
Cost of labor per table	26.10	25.50
Total variable manufacturing cost per table (a)	$ 70.20	$ 65.50
Total number of tables produced (b)	82,000	82,000
Total variable manufacturing cost (a × b)	$5,756,400	$5,371,000
Total fixed manufacturing cost	1,328,400	1,280,000
Total manufacturing cost	$7,084,800	$6,651,000

Based on this information, he argued that the relevant variance for performance evaluation was only $433,800 ($7,084,800 − $6,651,000). Ms. Darwin responded, "*Only* $433,800! I consider that a very significant number. By the end of the day, I want a full explanation as to what is causing our costs to increase."

Required

a. Divide the class into groups of four or five students and divide the groups into three sections. Assign Task 1 to the first section, Task 2 to the second section, and Task 3 to the third section.

Group Tasks

(1) Based on the following information, determine the total materials cost variance and the price and usage variances. Assuming that the variances are an appropriate indicator of cause, explain what could have caused the variances. Identify the management position responsible.

	Actual Data	Standard Data
Number of planks per table	21	20
Price per plank	× $2.10	× $2.00
Material cost per table	$44.10	$40.00

(2) Based on the following information, determine the total labor cost variance and the price and usage variances. Assuming that the variances are an appropriate indicator of cause, explain what could have caused each variance. Identify the management position responsible.

	Actual Data	Standard Data
Number of hours per table	2.9	3.0
Price per hour	× $9.00	× $8.50
Labor cost per table	$26.10	$25.50

(3) Determine the amount of the fixed cost spending and volume variances. Explain what could have caused these variances. Based on the volume variance, indicate whether the actual fixed cost per unit would be higher or lower than the budgeted fixed cost per unit.

b. Select a spokesperson from each section to report the amount of the variances computed by the group. Reconcile any differences in the variances reported by the sections. Reconcile the individual variances with the total variance. Specifically, show that the total of the materials, labor, and overhead variances equals the total flexible budget variance ($433,800).

c. Discuss how Ms. Darwin should react to the variance information.

ATC 15-3   Research Assignment   *Using real-world data from Papa John's, Inc.*

Obtain the income statements for Papa John's, Inc. for 2014, 2015, 2016, and 2017. The 2015–2017 statements are included in Papa John's 2017 annual report and Form 10-K, and the 2014 statement is in its <u>2016</u> annual report and Form 10-K. (Obtain the 2014 numbers from the 2016 Form 10-K, not the 2014 Form 10-K.)

To obtain the Form 10-Ks, you can use the EDGAR system (see Appendix A at the back of this text for instructions), or they can be found under the "Investors Relations" link on the company's corporate website, www.papajohns.com.

Required

a. Compute the percentage change for each of the following categories of revenues and expenses for 2014 to 2015 and 2015 to 2016:

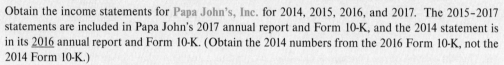

> Total revenues
> Domestic company-owned restaurant expenses
> North America commissary and other expenses
> International expenses
> General and administrative expenses
> Depreciation and amortization

Using an Excel spreadsheet will make this task much easier. After you have obtained these averages (you should have two averages for each of the six revenue and expense items), calculate an average of the changes for each item. The answer for the "Depreciation and amortization" item is shown as an example.

	Percentage Change
2014–2015	.9%
2015–2016	1.7%
Average of the changes	1.3%

b. Prepare a budgeted income statement, and compare the budgeted data to the actual results for 2017. To calculate budgeted amounts, multiply (1 + Average percentage change) in each revenue and expense item from Requirement *b* by the dollar amount of the corresponding revenue or expense item from 2016. This will represent the budgeted amount for that item for 2017. Don't forget to use decimal data and not percentage data. Subtract the actual 2017 results from the budgeted results. Finally, divide the actual versus budgeted difference by the budgeted amount to determine a percentage variance from the budget. The answer for the "Depreciation and amortization" item is shown as an example (dollar amounts are in millions).

	(1) 2016 Actual	(2) Average 2-year Change	(3) [1 + (1 × 2)] 2017 Budget	(4) 2017 Actual	(5) (3 − 4) Variance	(5 ÷ 3) Percentage Variance from Budget
Depreciation and amortization	$40,987	0.013	$41,520	$43,668	$2,148	0.052 [5.2%]

ATC 15-4   Business Applications Case   *Analyzing segments at Coca-Cola*

The following excerpt is from Coca-Cola Company's 2017 annual report filed with the SEC:

> *Management evaluates the performance of our operating segments separately to individually monitor the different factors affecting financial performance. Our Company manages income taxes and certain treasury-related items, such as interest income and expense, on a global basis within the Corporate operating segment. We evaluate segment performance based on income or loss before income taxes.**

> **2017. Investors Info: SEC Filings. Coca Cola Company.*

Selected segment data for Coca-Cola Company for the 2017 and 2016 fiscal years follow. Dollar amounts are in millions.

	Europe, Middle East, & Africa	Latin America	North America	Asia Pacific
2017 Fiscal Year				
Net operating revenues	$7,322	$3,956	$ 8,651	$4,767
Income before taxes	3,706	2,211	2,307	2,179
Identifiable operating assets	5,475	1,896	17,619	2,072
2016 Fiscal Year				
Net operating revenues	$7,041	$3,746	$ 6,437	$4,788
Income before taxes	3,749	1,966	2,560	2,238
Identifiable operating assets	4,067	1,785	16,566	2,024

Required

a. Compute the ROI for each of Coke's geographical segments for each fiscal year. Which segment appears to have the best performance during 2017 based on their ROIs? Which segment showed the most improvement from 2016 to 2017?

b. Assuming Coke's management expects a minimum return of 30 percent, calculate the residual income for each segment for each fiscal year. Which segment appears to have the best performance based on residual income? Which segment showed the most improvement from 2016 to 2017?

c. Explain why the segment with the highest ROI in 2017 was not the segment with the highest residual income.

d. Assume the management of Coke is considering a major expansion effort for the next five years. On which geographic segment would you recommend Coke focus its expansion efforts? Explain the rationale for your answer.

ATC 15-5   Ethics Dilemma   *Budget Games*

Melody Lovelady is the most highly rewarded sales representative at Swift Corporation. Her secret to success is always to understate her abilities. Ms. Lovelady is assigned to a territory in which her customer base is increasing at approximately 25 percent per year. Each year she estimates that her budgeted sales will be 10 percent higher than her previous year's sales. With little effort, she is able to double her budgeted sales growth. At Swift's annual sales meeting, she receives an award and a large bonus. Of course, Ms. Lovelady does not disclose her secret to her colleagues. Indeed, she always talks about how hard it is to continue to top her previous performance. She tells herself: "If they are dumb enough to fall for this rubbish, I'll milk it for all it's worth."

Required

a. What is the name commonly given to the budget game Ms. Lovelady is playing?

b. Does Ms. Lovelady's behavior violate any of the standards of ethical professional practice shown in Exhibit 10.19 of Chapter 10?

c. Recommend how Ms. Lovelady's budget game could be stopped.

CHAPTER 16

Planning for Capital Investments

LEARNING OBJECTIVES

After you have mastered the material in this chapter, you will be able to:

LO 16-1   Explain the time value of money concept.

LO 16-2   Determine and interpret the net present value of an investment opportunity.

LO 16-3   Determine and interpret the internal rate of return of an investment opportunity.

LO 16-4   Evaluate investment opportunities using the payback method and the unadjusted rate of return.

 Video lectures and accompanying self-assessment quizzes are available in Connect *for all learning objectives.*

 Set B exercises and problems are available in Additional Student Resources.

CHAPTER OPENING

The president of EZ Rentals (EZ) is considering expanding the company's rental service business to include projectors that can be used with notebook computers. A marketing study forecasts that renting projectors could generate revenue of $200,000 per year. The possibility of increasing revenue is alluring, but EZ's president has a number of unanswered questions. How much do the projectors cost? What is their expected useful life? Will they have a salvage value? Does EZ have the money to buy them? Does EZ have the technical expertise to support the product? How much will training cost? How long will customer demand last? What if EZ buys the projectors and they become technologically obsolete? How quickly will EZ be able to recover the investment? Are there more profitable ways to invest EZ's funds? This chapter discusses some of the analytical techniques companies use to evaluate major investment opportunities.

The Curious Accountant

The August 23, 2017, drawing for the **Powerball** multistate lottery had an advertised value of $758.7 million. This amount, however, was based on the assumption that the winner would take his or her prize as 30 equal annual payments of $25.29 million. If the winnings were taken in this manner, the first payment would be made immediately, and the others would be paid annually over the next 29 years. The winner also had the option of taking an immediate, lump-sum payment of $480.5 million.

Assume that you work as a personal financial planner and that one of your clients held the winning lottery ticket. If you think you could invest your client's winnings and earn an annual return of 7 percent, would you advise your client to take the lump-sum payment or the annual payments? Why? (Answer on page 585.)

Chris Althof/McGraw-Hill Education

CAPITAL INVESTMENT DECISIONS

Purchases of long-term operational assets are **capital investments.** Capital investments differ from stock and bond investments in an important respect. Investments in stocks and bonds can be sold in organized markets such as the New York Stock Exchange. In contrast, investments in capital assets normally can be recovered only by using those assets. Once a company purchases a capital asset, it is committed to that investment for an extended period of time. If the market turns sour, the company is stuck with the consequences. It may also be unable to seize new opportunities because its capital is committed. Business profitability ultimately hinges, to a large extent, on the quality of a few key capital investment decisions.

A capital investment decision is essentially a decision to exchange current cash outflows for the expectation of receiving future cash inflows. For EZ Rentals, purchasing projectors, cash outflows today, provides the opportunity to collect $200,000 per year in rental revenue, cash inflows in the future. Assuming the projectors have useful lives of four years and no salvage value, how much should EZ be willing to pay for the future cash inflows? If you were EZ's president, would you give up $700,000 today for the opportunity to receive $800,000 (4 × $200,000) in the future? What if you collect less than $200,000 per year? If revenue is only $160,000 per year, you would lose $60,000 [$700,000 − (4 × $160,000)]. Is $700,000 too much to pay for the opportunity to receive $200,000 per year for four years? If $700,000 is too much, would you spend $600,000? If not, how about $500,000? There is no one right answer to these questions. However, understanding the *time value of money* concept can help you develop a rational response.

C. Zachariasen/PhotoAlto

Time Value of Money

The **time value of money** concept recognizes that *the present value of a dollar received in the future is less than a dollar.* For example, you may be willing to pay only $0.90 today for a promise to receive $1.00 one year from today. The further into the future the receipt is expected to occur, the smaller is its present value. In other words, $1.00 to be received two years from today is worth less than $1.00 to be received one year from today. Likewise, $1.00 to be received three years from today is less valuable than $1.00 to be received two years from today, and so on.

The present value of cash inflows decreases as the time until expected receipt increases for several reasons. First, you could deposit today's dollar in a savings account to earn *interest* that increases its total value. If you wait for your money, you lose the opportunity to earn interest. Second, the expectation of receiving a future dollar carries an element of *risk*. Changed conditions may result in the failure to collect. Finally, *inflation* diminishes the buying power of the dollar. In other words, the longer you must wait to receive a dollar, the less you will be able to buy with it.

When a company invests in capital assets, it sacrifices present dollars in exchange for the opportunity to receive future dollars. Since trading current dollars for future dollars is risky, companies expect compensation before they invest in capital assets. The compensation a company expects is called *return on investment (ROI).* As discussed in Chapter 15, ROI is expressed as a percentage of the investment. For example, the ROI for a $1,000 investment that earns annual income of $100 is 10 percent ($100 ÷ $1,000 = 10%).

Determining the Minimum Rate of Return

To establish the minimum expected *return on investment* before accepting an investment opportunity, most companies consider their cost of capital. To attract capital, companies must provide benefits to their creditors and owners. Creditors expect interest payments; owners expect dividends and increased stock value. Companies that earn lower returns than their cost of capital eventually go bankrupt; they cannot continually pay out more than they collect. *The* **cost of capital** *represents the* **minimum rate of return** *on investments.* Calculating the cost of capital is a complex exercise that is beyond the scope of this text. It is addressed in finance courses. We discuss how management accountants *use* the cost of capital to evaluate investment opportunities. A variety of terms may be used to describe the minimum rate of return, including the *required rate of return,* the *hurdle rate,* the *cutoff rate,* or the *discount rate.* This text uses the term *desired rate of return* as a proxy for any of the common terms used as a label for the cost of capital. As used herein, the rate of return that a company aspires to attain is called the **desired rate of return**.

☑ CHECK YOURSELF 16.1

Study the following cash inflow streams expected from two different potential investments:

	Year 1	Year 2	Year 3	Total
Alternative 1	$2,000	$3,000	$4,000	$9,000
Alternative 2	4,000	3,000	2,000	9,000

Based on visual observation alone, which alternative has the higher present value? Why?

Answer   Alternative 2 has the higher present value. The size of the discount increases as the length of the time period increases. In other words, a dollar received in Year 3 has a lower present value (is worth less) than a dollar received in Year 1. Since most of the expected cash inflows from Alternative 2 are received earlier than those from Alternative 1, Alternative 2 has a higher present value even though the total expected cash inflows are the same.

Converting Future Cash Inflows to Their Equivalent Present Values

Given a desired rate of return and the amount of a future cash flow, the present value can be determined using algebra. To illustrate, refer to the $200,000 EZ expects to earn the first year it leases the projectors.[1] Assuming EZ desires a 12 percent rate of return, what amount of cash would EZ be willing to invest today (present value outflow) to obtain a $200,000 cash inflow at the end of the year (future value)? The answer follows:[2]

$$\text{Investment} + (0.12 \times \text{Investment}) = \text{Future cash inflow}$$

$$1.12 \times \text{Investment} = \$200{,}000$$

$$\text{Investment} = \$200{,}000 \div 1.12$$

$$\text{Investment} = \$178{,}571$$

The $178,571 is the *present value* of receiving $200,000 at the end of one year. In other words, if EZ invests $178,571 cash on January 1 and earns a 12 percent return on the

---

[1] The following computations assume the $200,000 cash inflow is received on the last day of each year. In actual practice, the timing of cash inflows is less precise and present value computations are recognized to be approximate, not exact.

[2] All computations in this chapter are rounded to the nearest whole dollar.

investment, EZ will have $200,000 on December 31. The two options are equal as shown in the following mathematical proof:

$$\text{Investment} + (0.12 \times \text{Investment}) = \$200,000$$
$$\$178,571 + (0.12 \times \$178,571) = \$200,000$$
$$\$178,571 + \$21,429 = \$200,000$$
$$\$200,000 = \$200,000$$

Present Value Table for Single-Amount Cash Inflows

The algebra illustrated above is used to convert a one-time future receipt of cash to its present value. One-time receipts of cash are frequently called **single-payment**, or **lump-sum**, cash flows. Because EZ desires a 12 percent rate of return, the present value of the first cash inflow is $178,571. We can also determine the present value of a $200,000 single amount (lump sum) at the end of the second, third, and fourth years. Instead of using cumbersome algebraic computations to convert these future values to their present value equivalents, financial analysts frequently use a table of conversion factors to convert future values to their present value equivalents. The table of conversion factors used to convert future values into present values is commonly called a **present value table.**[3] A typical present value table presents columns with different return rates and rows with different periods of time, like Appendix Table 1 located at the end of this chapter.

To illustrate using the present value table, locate the conversion factor in Table 1 at the intersection of the 12% column and the one-period row. The conversion factor is 0.892857. Multiplying this factor by the $200,000 expected cash inflow yields $178,571 ($200,000 × 0.892857). This is the same value determined algebraically in the previous section of this chapter. The conversion factors in the present value tables simplify converting future values to present values.

The conversion factors for the second, third, and fourth periods are 0.797194, 0.711780, and 0.635518, respectively. These factors are in the 12% column at rows 2, 3, and 4, respectively. Locate these factors in Appendix Table 1. Multiplying the conversion factors by the future cash inflow for each period produces their present value equivalents, shown in Exhibit 16.1. Exhibit 16.1 indicates that investing $607,470 today (present value) at a 12 percent rate of return is equivalent to receiving $200,000 per year for four years. Given that EZ Rentals desires to earn a 12 percent rate of return, the company should be willing to pay up to $607,470 to purchase the projectors.

Present Value Table for Annuities

The algebra described previously for converting equal lump-sum cash inflows to present value equivalents can be further simplified by adding the present value table factors together before

EXHIBIT 16.1

Present Value of a $200,000 Cash Inflow to Be Received for Four Years

PV	=	FV	×	Present Value Table Factor	=	Present Value Equivalent
Period 1	=	$200,000	×	0.892857	=	$178,571
Period 2	=	200,000	×	0.797194	=	159,439
Period 3	=	200,000	×	0.711780	=	142,356
Period 4	=	200,000	×	0.635518	=	127,104
Total						$607,470

[3]The present value table is based on the formula $[1 \div (1 + r)^n]$ where r equals the rate of return and n equals the number of periods.

multiplying them by the cash inflows. The total of the present value table factors in Exhibit 16.1 is 3.037349 (0.892857 + 0.797194 + 0.711780 + 0.635518). Multiplying this **accumulated conversion factor** by the expected annual cash inflow results in the same present value equivalent of $607,470 ($200,000 × 3.037349). As with lump-sum conversion factors, accumulated conversion factors can be calculated and organized in a table with *columns* for different rates of return and *rows* for different periods of time. Appendix Table 2 is a present value table of accumulated conversion factors. Locate the conversion factor at the intersection of the 12% column and the fourth time-period row. The factor at this intersection is 3.037349, confirming that the accumulated conversion factors represent the sum of the single-payment conversion factors.

The conversion factors in Appendix Table 2 apply to annuities. An **annuity** is a series of cash flows that meets three criteria: (1) equal payment amounts, (2) equal time intervals between payments, and (3) a constant rate of return. For EZ Rentals, the expected cash inflows from renting the projectors are all for equivalent amounts ($200,000); the expected intervals between cash inflows are equal lengths of time (one year); and the rate of return for each inflow is constant at 12 percent. The series of expected cash inflows from renting the projectors is therefore an annuity. The present value of an annuity table can be used only if all of these conditions are satisfied.

The present value of an annuity table (Appendix Table 2) simplifies converting future cash inflows to their present value equivalents. EZ Rentals can convert the cash inflows as shown in Exhibit 16.1, using four conversion factors, multiplying each conversion factor by the annual cash inflow (four multiplications), and adding the resulting products. In contrast, EZ can recognize that the series of payments is an annuity, which requires multiplying a single conversion factor from Appendix Table 2 by the amount of the annuity payment. Regardless of the conversion method, the result is the same (a present value of $607,470). Recall that EZ can also make the conversion using algebra. The table values are derived from algebraic formulas. The present value tables reduce the computations needed to convert future values to present values.

Software Programs That Calculate Present Values

Software programs offer an even more efficient means of converting future values into present value equivalents. These programs are frequently built into handheld financial calculators and computer spreadsheet programs. As an example, we demonstrate the procedures used in a Microsoft Excel spreadsheet.

An Excel spreadsheet offers a variety of financial functions, one of which converts a future value annuity into its present value equivalent. This present value function uses the syntax *PV(rate,nper,pmt)* in which *rate* is the desired rate of return, *nper* is the number of periods, and *pmt* is the amount of the payment (periodic cash inflow). To convert a future value annuity into its present value equivalent, provide the function with the appropriate amounts for the rate, number of periods, and amount of the annuity (cash inflows) into a spreadsheet cell. Press the Enter key and the present value equivalent appears in the spreadsheet cell.

The power of the spreadsheet to perform computations instantly is extremely useful for answering what-if questions. Exhibit 16.2 demonstrates this power by providing spreadsheet conversions for three different scenarios. The first scenario demonstrates the annuity assumptions for EZ Rentals, providing the present value equivalent ($607,470) of a four-year cash inflow of $200,000 per year at a 12 percent rate of interest. The present value is a *negative* number. This format indicates that an initial $607,470 *cash outflow* is required to obtain the four-year series of cash inflows. The present value equivalent in Scenario 2 shows the present value if the annuity assumptions reflect a 14 percent, rather than 12 percent, desired rate of return. The present value equivalent in Scenario 3 shows the present value if the annuity assumptions under Scenario 1 are changed to reflect annual cash inflows of $300,000, rather than $200,000. A wide range of scenarios could be readily considered by changing any or all of the variables in the spreadsheet function. In each case, the computer does the calculations, giving the manager more time to analyze the data rather than compute them.

Although software is widely used in business practice, the diversity of interfaces used by different calculators and spreadsheet programs makes it unsuitable for textbook presentations.

EXHIBIT 16.2

Microsoft Excel Spreadsheet Present Value Function

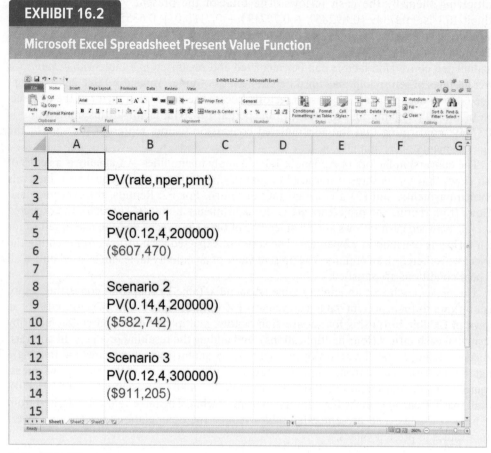

Source: Microsoft Corporation

This text uses the present value tables in the Appendix in the text illustrations and the end-of-chapter exercises and problems. If you use software to solve these problems, your answers will be the same. All of these tools—formulas, conversion tables, and software—are based on the same mathematical principles and will produce the same results.

Ordinary Annuity Assumption

All of the conversion methods described previously assume the cash inflows occur at the *end* of each accounting period. This distribution pattern is called an **ordinary annuity**.[4] In practice, cash inflows are likely to be received throughout the period, not just at the end. For example, EZ Rentals is likely to collect cash revenue from renting projectors each month rather than in a single lump-sum receipt at the end of each of the four years. Companies frequently use the ordinary annuity assumption in practice because it simplifies time value of money computations. Because capital investment decisions are necessarily based on uncertain projections about future cash inflows, the lives of investment opportunities, and the appropriate rates of return, achieving pinpoint accuracy is impossible. Sacrificing precision for simplicity by using the ordinary annuity assumption is a reasonable trade-off in the decision-making process.

Reinvestment Assumption

The present value computations in the previous sections show that investing $607,470 today at a 12 percent rate of return is equivalent to receiving four individual $200,000 payments at

---

[4]When equal cash inflows occur at the *beginning* of each accounting period, the distribution is called an *annuity due*. Although some business transactions are structured as annuities due, they are less common than ordinary annuities. This text focuses on the ordinary annuity assumption.

EXHIBIT 16.3

Cash Flow Classifications for EZ's Investment in Projectors

Time Period	(a) Investment Balance during the Year	(b) Annual Cash Inflow	(c) Return on Investment (a × 0.12)	(d) Recovered Investment (b − c)	(e) Year-End Investment Balance (a − d)
1	$607,470	$200,000	$ 72,896	$127,104	$480,366
2	480,366	200,000	57,644	142,356	338,010
3	338,010	200,000	40,561	159,439	178,571
4	178,571	200,000	21,429	178,571	0
Totals		$800,000	$192,530	$607,470	

the end of four successive years. Exhibit 16.3 illustrates that a cash inflow of $200,000 per year is equivalent to earning a 12 percent rate of return on a $607,470 investment.[5]

It is customary to assume that the desired rate of return includes the effects of *compounding*.[6] Saying an investment is "earning the desired rate of return," assumes the cash inflows generated by the investment are reinvested at the desired rate of return. In this case, we are assuming that EZ will reinvest the $200,000 annual cash inflows in other investments that will earn a 12 percent return.

ANALYZING CAPITAL INVESTMENT PROPOSALS

Managers can choose from among numerous analytical techniques to help them make capital investment decisions. Each technique has advantages and disadvantages. A manager may apply more than one technique to a particular proposal to take advantage of more information. Since most companies have computer capabilities that include a variety of standard capital budgeting programs, applying different techniques to the same proposal normally requires little extra effort. Limiting analysis to only one tool could produce biased results. Obtaining more than one perspective offers substantial benefit.

NET PRESENT VALUE

A variety of analytical techniques can be used to help make investment decisions. One frequently used technique is called the net present value method. The net present value is determined by subtracting the cost of an investment from its present value. To illustrate, return to the EZ Rental illustration. Recall that EZ Rentals' management determined it would be willing to invest $607,470 to purchase projectors today (present value) to obtain a $200,000 per year cash inflow from rent revenue for each of the next four years. The $607,470 investment is *not* the cost of the projectors; it is the amount EZ is willing to pay for them. The projectors may cost EZ Rentals more or less than their present value. To determine whether EZ should invest in the projectors, management must compare the present value of the future cash inflows ($607,470) to the cost of the projectors (the current cash outflow required to purchase them). Subtracting the cost of the investment from the present value of the future cash inflows determines the **net present value** of the investment opportunity. A positive net present value indicates the investment will yield a rate of return higher than 12 percent. A negative net present value means the return is less than 12 percent.

LO 16-2

Determine and interpret the net present value of an investment opportunity.

[5]Exhibit 16.3 is analogous to an amortization table for a long-term note with equal payments of principal and interest.

[6]*Compounding* refers to reinvesting investment proceeds so the total amount of invested capital increases, resulting in even higher returns. For example, assume $100 is invested at a 10 percent compounded annual rate of return. At the end of the first year, the investment yields a $10 return ($100 × 0.10). The $10 return plus any recovered investment is reinvested so that the total amount of invested capital at the beginning of the second year is $110. The return for the second year is $11 ($110 × 0.10). All funds are reinvested so that the return for the third year is $12.10 [($110 + $11) × 0.10].

To illustrate, assume EZ can purchase the projectors for $582,742. Assuming the desired rate of return is 12 percent, EZ should buy them. The net present value of the investment opportunity is computed as follows:

Present value of future cash inflows	$607,470
Cost of investment (required cash outflow)	(582,742)
Net present value	$ 24,728

The positive net present value suggests the investment will earn a rate of return in excess of 12 percent (if cash flows are indeed $200,000 each year). Because the projected rate of return is higher than the desired rate of return, this analysis suggests EZ should accept the investment opportunity. Based on the given analysis, we are able to establish the following decision rule:

Net present value decision rule: If the net present value is equal to or greater than zero, accept the investment opportunity.

CHECK YOURSELF 16.2

To increase productivity, Wald Corporation is considering the purchase of a new machine that costs $50,000. Wald expects using the machine to increase annual net cash inflows by $12,500 for each of the next five years. Wald desires a minimum annual rate of return of 10 percent on the investment. Determine the net present value of the investment opportunity and recommend whether Wald should acquire the machine.

Answer

Present value of future cash flows = Future cash flow × Table 2 factor ($n = 5, r = 10\%$)

Present value of future cash flows = $12,500 × 3.790787 = $47,385

Net present value = PV of future cash flows − Cost of machine

Net present value = $47,385 − $50,000 = ($2,615)

The negative net present value indicates the investment will yield a rate of return below the desired rate of return. Wald should not acquire the new machine.

Measuring Investment Cash Flows

The EZ Rentals example represents a simple capital investment analysis. The investment option involved only one cash outflow and a single annuity inflow. Investment opportunities often involve a greater variety of cash outflows and inflows. The following section of this chapter discusses different types of cash flows encountered in business practice.

Cash Inflows

Cash inflows generated from capital investments come from *four basic sources.* As in the case of EZ Rentals, the most common source of cash inflows is incremental revenue. **Incremental revenue** refers to the *additional* cash inflows from operating activities generated by using additional capital assets. For example, a taxi company expects revenues from taxi fares to increase if it purchases additional taxicabs. Similarly, investing in new apartments should increase rent revenue; opening a new store should result in additional sales revenue.

A second type of cash inflow results from *cost savings.* Decreases in cash outflows have the same beneficial effect as increases in cash inflows. Either way, a firm's cash position improves. For example, purchasing an automated computer system may enable a company to reduce cash outflows for salaries. Similarly, relocating a manufacturing facility closer to its raw materials source can reduce cash outflows for transportation costs.

An investment's *salvage value* provides a third source of cash inflows. Even when one company has finished using an asset, the asset may still be useful to another company. Many assets are sold after a company no longer wishes to use them. The salvage value represents a one-time cash inflow obtained when a company terminates an investment.

Companies can also experience a cash inflow through a *reduction in the amount of* **working capital** needed to support an investment. A certain level of working capital is required to support most business investments. For example, a new retail store outlet requires cash, receivables, and inventory to operate. When an investment is terminated, the decrease in the working capital commitment associated with the investment normally results in a cash inflow.

Cash Outflows

Cash outflows fall into *three primary categories.* One category consists of outflows for the *initial investment.* Managers must be alert to all the cash outflows connected with purchasing a capital asset. The purchase price, transportation costs, installation costs, and training costs are examples of typical cash outflows related to an initial investment.

A second category of cash outflows may result from *increases in operating expenses.* If a company increases output capacity by investing in additional equipment, it may experience higher utility bills, labor costs, and maintenance expenses when it places the equipment into service. These expenditures increase cash outflows.

Third, *increases in working capital* commitments result in cash outflows. Frequently, investments in new assets must be supported by a certain level of working capital. For example, investing in a copy machine requires spending cash to maintain a supply of paper and toner. Managers should treat an increased working capital commitment as a cash outflow in the period the commitment occurs.

Exhibit 16.4 lists the cash inflows and outflows discussed previously. The list is not exhaustive but does summarize the most common cash flows businesses experience.

EXHIBIT 16.4

Typical Cash Flows Associated with Capital Investments

Inflows	Outflows
1. Incremental revenue	1. Initial investment
2. Cost savings	2. Incremental expenses
3. Salvage values	3. Working capital commitments
4. Recovery of working capital	

Compare Alternative Capital Investment Opportunities

The management of Torres Transfer Company is considering two investment opportunities. One alternative, involving the purchase of new equipment for $80,000, would enable Torres to modernize its maintenance facility. The equipment has an expected useful life of five years and a $4,000 salvage value. It would replace existing equipment that had originally cost $45,000. The existing equipment has a current book value of $15,000 and a trade-in value of $5,000. The old equipment is technologically obsolete but can operate for an additional five years. On the day Torres purchases the new equipment, it would also pay the equipment manufacturer $3,000 for training costs to teach employees to operate the new equipment. The modernization has two primary advantages. One, it will improve management of the small parts inventory. The company's accountant believes that by the end of the first year, the carrying value of the small parts inventory could be reduced by $12,000. Second, the modernization is expected to increase efficiency, resulting in a $21,500 reduction in annual operating expenses.

The other investment alternative available to Torres is purchasing a truck. Adding another truck would enable Torres to expand its delivery area and increase revenue. The truck costs $115,000. It has a useful life of five years and a $30,000 salvage value. Operating the truck will require the company to increase its inventory of supplies, its petty cash account, and its accounts receivable and payable balances. These changes would add $5,000 to the company's working capital base immediately upon buying the truck. The working capital cash outflow is expected to be recovered at the end of the truck's useful life. The truck is expected to produce $69,000 per year in additional revenues. The driver's salary and other operating expenses are expected to be $32,000 per year. A major overhaul costing $20,000 is expected to be required at the end of the third year of operation. Assuming Torres desires to earn a rate of return of 14 percent, which of the two investment alternatives should it choose?

Determine the Net Present Value

Begin the analysis by calculating the net present value of the two investment alternatives. Exhibit 16.5 shows the computations. Study this exhibit. Each alternative is analyzed using three steps. Step 1 requires identifying all cash inflows; some may be annuities, and others may be lump-sum receipts. In the case of Alternative 1, the cost saving is an annuity, and the inflow from the salvage value is a lump-sum receipt. Once the cash inflows have been identified, the appropriate conversion factors are identified and the cash inflows are converted to their equivalent present values. Step 2 follows the same process to determine the present value of the cash outflows. Step 3 subtracts the present value of the outflows from the present value of the inflows to determine the net present value. The same three-step approach is used to determine the net present value of Alternative 2.

With respect to Alternative 1, the original cost and the book value of the existing equipment are ignored. As indicated in a previous chapter, these measures represent *sunk costs;*

EXHIBIT 16.5

Net Present Value Analysis

	Amount	×	Conversion Factor	=	Present Value
Alternative 1: Modernize Maintenance Facility					
Step 1: Cash inflows					
1. Cost savings	$ 21,500	×	3.433081*	=	$ 73,811
2. Salvage value	4,000	×	0.519369†	=	2,077
3. Working capital recovery	12,000	×	0.877193‡	=	10,526
Total					$ 86,414
Step 2: Cash outflows					
1. Cost of equipment					
($80,000 cost − $5,000 trade-in)	$ 75,000	×	1.000000§	=	$ 75,000
2. Training costs	3,000	×	1.000000§	=	3,000
Total					$ 78,000
Step 3: Net present value					
Total present value of cash inflows					$ 86,414
Total present value of cash outflows					(78,000)
Net present value					$ 8,414
Alternative 2: Purchase Delivery Truck					
Step 1: Cash inflows					
1. Incremental revenue	$ 69,000	×	3.433081*	=	$236,883
2. Salvage value	30,000	×	0.519369†	=	15,581
3. Working capital recovery	5,000	×	0.519369†	=	2,597
Total					$255,061
Step 2: Cash outflows					
1. Cost of truck	$115,000	×	1.000000§	=	$115,000
2. Working capital increase	5,000	×	1.000000§	=	5,000
3. Increased operating expense	32,000	×	3.433081*	=	109,859
4. Major overhaul	20,000	×	0.674972§§	=	13,499
Total					$243,358
Step 3: Net present value					
Total present value of cash inflows					$255,061
Total present value of cash outflows					(243,358)
Net present value					$ 11,703

*Present value of annuity Table 2, $n = 5$, $r = 14\%$.
†Present value of single payment Table 1, $n = 5$, $r = 14\%$.
‡Present value of single payment Table 1, $n = 1$, $r = 14\%$.
§Present value at beginning of period 1.
§§Present value of single payment Table 1, $n = 3$, $r = 14\%$.

they are not relevant to the decision. The concept of relevance applies to long-term capital investment decisions just as it applies to the short-term special decisions that were discussed in Chapter 13. To be relevant to a capital investment decision, costs or revenues must involve different present and future cash flows for each alternative. Since the historical cost of the old equipment does not differ between the alternatives, it is not relevant.

Since the *net present value* of each investment alternative is *positive,* either investment will generate a return in excess of 14 percent. Which investment is the more favorable? The data could mislead a careless manager. Alternative 2 might seem the better choice because it has a greater present value than Alternative 1 ($11,703 vs. $8,414). Net present value, however, is expressed in *absolute dollars.* The net present value of a more costly capital investment can be greater than the net present value of a smaller investment even though the smaller investment earns a higher rate of return.

To compare different size investment alternatives, management can compute a **present value index** by dividing the present value of cash inflows by the present value of cash outflows. *The higher the ratio, the higher the rate of return per dollar invested in the proposed project.* The present value indexes for the two alternatives Torres Transfer Company is considering are as follows:

$$\text{Present value index for Alternative 1} = \frac{\text{Present value of cash inflows}}{\text{Present value of cash outflows}} = \frac{\$86,414}{\$78,000} = 1.108$$

$$\text{Present value index for Alternative 2} = \frac{\text{Present value of cash inflows}}{\text{Present value of cash outflows}} = \frac{\$255,061}{\$243,358} = 1.048$$

Management can use the present value indexes to rank the investment alternatives. In this case, Alternative 1 yields a higher return than Alternative 2.

INTERNAL RATE OF RETURN

Managers may use multiple techniques to evaluate the same investment opportunity. Each technique has advantages and disadvantages. Computer technology makes applying different techniques to the same proposal fast and easy. Limiting analysis to only one tool could produce biased results. Accordingly, the benefits of multiple analysis usually exceed the sacrifices required. A second technique discussed here is called the *internal rate of return*.

LO 16-3

 Determine and interpret the internal rate of return of an investment opportunity.

Calculating the Internal Rate of Return when Expected Cash Flows Are Distributed Evenly

Recall that net present value analysis indicated that EZ's investment in the projectors would yield a return in excess of the *desired* rate of return. However, the analysis did not provide the *expected* rate of return that the investment would produce. If EZ's management team wants to know the rate of return to expect from investing in the projectors, it must use the *internal rate of return method.* The **internal rate of return** is the rate at which the present value of cash inflows equals the cash outflows. Generally, *the higher the internal rate of return, the more profitable the investment.*

The internal rate of return is the rate that will produce a zero net present value. For EZ Rentals, the internal rate of return can be determined as follows. First, compute the *present value table factor* for a $200,000 annuity that would yield a $582,742 present value cash outflow (cost of the projectors).

$$\text{Present value table factor} \times \$200,000 = \$582,742$$

$$\text{Present value table factor} = \$582,742 \div \$200,000$$

$$\text{Present value table factor} = 2.91371$$

Second, since the expected annual cash inflows represent a four-year annuity, scan Appendix Table 2 at period $n = 4$. Try to locate the table factor 2.91371. The rate listed at the top of the column in which the factor is located is the internal rate of return. Turn to Appendix Table 2 and determine the internal rate of return for EZ Rentals before you read further. The above factor is in the 14% column. The difference in the table value (2.913712) and the value computed here (2.91371) is not significant. This means that if EZ invests \$582,742 in the projectors and they produce a \$200,000 annual cash flow for four years, EZ will earn a 14 percent rate of return on the investment.

The *internal rate of return* may be compared to a *desired rate of return* to determine whether to accept or reject a particular investment project. If the internal rate of return is equal to or higher than the desired rate of return, the investment opportunity should be accepted. Accordingly, the preceding analysis suggests the EZ should accept the investment opportunity because the internal rate of return (14 percent) is higher than the desired rate of return (12 percent). An internal rate of return below the desired rate suggests management should reject a particular proposal. Based on the given analysis, we are able to establish the following decision rule:

> **Internal rate of return decision rule:** If the internal rate of return is equal to or greater than the desired rate of return, accept the investment opportunity.

Calculating the Internal Rate of Return when Expected Cash Flows Are Distributed Irregularly

We previously demonstrated how to calculate the internal rate of return for an investment that generates a simple, regular cash inflow annuity. The computations are significantly more complex for investments with uneven cash flows. Recall that the internal rate of return is the rate that produces a zero net present value. Manually computing the rate that produces a zero net present value is a tedious trial-and-error process. You must first estimate the rate of return for a particular investment, then calculate the net present value. If the calculation produces a negative net present value, you try a lower estimated rate of return and recalculate. If this calculation produces a positive net present value, the actual internal rate of return lies between the first and second estimates. Make a third estimate and once again recalculate the net present value, and so on. Eventually, you will determine the rate of return that produces a net present value of zero.

Many calculators and spreadsheet programs are designed to make these computations. We illustrate the process with a Microsoft Excel spreadsheet. Excel uses the syntax *IRR (values, guess)* in which *values* refers to cells that specify the cash flows for which you want to calculate the internal rate of return and *guess* is a number you estimate is close to the actual internal rate of return (IRR). The IRRs for the two investment alternatives available to Torres Transfer Company are shown in Exhibit 16.6. Study this exhibit. Excel requires netting cash outflows against cash inflows for each period in which both outflows and inflows are expected. For your convenience, we have labeled the net cash flows in the spreadsheet. Labeling is not necessary to execute the IRR function. The entire function, including values and guess, can be entered into a single cell of the spreadsheet. Persons familiar with spreadsheet programs learn to significantly simplify the input required.

The IRR results in Exhibit 16.6 confirm the ranking determined using the present value index. Alternative 1 (modernize maintenance facility), with an internal rate of return of 18.69 percent, ranks above Alternative 2 (purchase a truck) with an internal rate of return of 17.61 percent, even though Alternative 2 has a higher net present value (see Exhibit 16.5). Alternative 2, however, still may be the better investment option, depending on the amount available to invest. Suppose Torres has \$120,000 of available funds to invest. Because Alternative 1 requires an initial investment of only \$78,000, \$42,000 (\$120,000 − \$78,000) of capital will not be invested. If Torres has no other investment opportunities for this \$42,000, the company would be better off investing the entire \$120,000 in Alternative 2 (\$115,000 cost of truck + \$5,000 working capital increase). Earning 17.61 percent on a \$120,000 investment is better than earning 18.69 percent on a \$78,000 investment with no return on the remaining \$42,000. Management accounting requires exercising judgment when making decisions.

EXHIBIT 16.6

Microsoft Excel Spreadsheet Internal Rate of Return Function

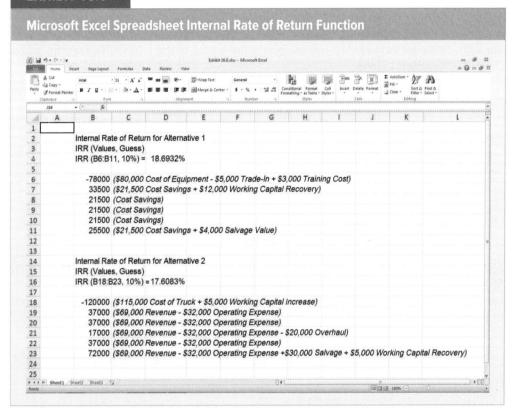

Source: Microsoft Corporation

REALITY BYTES

Developing proficiency with present value mathematics is usually the most difficult aspect of capital budgeting for students taking their first managerial accounting course. In real-world companies, the most difficult aspect of capital budgeting is forecasting cash flows for several years into the future. Consider the following capital budgeting project.

In 1965, representatives from the Georgia Power Company visited Ms. Taylor's fifth-grade class to tell her students about the Edwin I. Hatch Nuclear Plant that was going to be built nearby. One of the authors of this text was a student in that class.

In 1966, construction began on the first unit of the plant, and the plant started producing electricity in 1975. The next year, 10 years after hearing the presentation in his fifth-grade class, the author worked on construction of the second unit of the plant during the summer before his senior year of college. This second unit began operations in 1978.

Kristin Smith/Shutterstock

In its 2017 annual report, the Southern Company, which is now the major owner of the plant, stated that the Hatch plant is expected to operate until 2038, and that decommissioning of the plant will continue until 2075. The cost to construct both units of the plant was $934 million. The estimated cost to dismantle and decommission the plant is over $902 million.

It seems safe to assume that the students in Ms. Taylor's fifth-grade class were not among the first to hear about the power company's plans for the Hatch plant. Thus, we can reasonably conclude that the life of this capital project will be over 100 years, from around 1960 until 2068.

Try to imagine that you were assigned the task of predicting the cost inflows and outflows for a project that was expected to last 100 years. Clearly, mastering present value mathematics would not be your biggest worry.

Relevance and the Time Value of Money

Suppose you have the opportunity to invest in one of two capital projects. Both projects require an immediate cash outflow of $6,000 and will produce future cash inflows of $8,000. The only difference between the two projects is the timing of the inflows. The receipt schedule for both projects follows.

Year	Project 1	Project 2
1	$ 3,500	$2,000
2	3,000	2,000
3	1,000	2,000
4	500	2,000
Total	$8,000	$8,000

Because both projects cost the same and produce the same total cash inflows, they may appear to be equal. Whether you select Project 1 or Project 2, you pay $6,000 and receive $8,000. Because of the time value of money, however, Project 1 is preferable to Project 2. To see why, determine the net present value of both projects, assuming a 10 percent desired rate of return.

Computation of Net Present Value for Project 1 and Project 2

Net Present Value for Project 1

Period	Cash Inflow	×	Conversion Factor Table 1, $r = 10\%$	=	Present Value
1	$3,500	×	0.909091	=	$3,182
2	3,000	×	0.826446	=	2,479
3	1,000	×	0.751315	=	751
4	500	×	0.683013	=	342
Present value of future cash inflows					6,754
Present value of cash outflow					(6,000)
Net present value Project 1					$ 754

Net Present Value for Project 2

	Cash Inflow Annuity	×	Conversion Factor Table 2, $r = 10\%$, $n = 4$		
Present value of cash inflow	$2,000	×	3.169865		$6,340
Present value of cash outflow					(6,000)
Net present value Project 2					$ 340

The net present value of Project 1 ($754) exceeds the net present value of Project 2 ($340). The timing as well as the amount of cash flows has a significant impact on capital investment returns. Recall that to be relevant, costs or revenues must differ between alternatives. Differences in the timing of cash flow payments or receipts are also relevant for decision-making purposes.

Tax Considerations

The previous examples have ignored the effect of income taxes on capital investment decisions. Taxes affect the amount of cash flows generated by investments. To illustrate, assume

Answers to The Curious Accountant

One way to answer your client's question is to determine which option has the highest net present value. The present value of the lump-sum payment option is simple: it is the $480.5 million the lottery is prepared to pay the winner now. The present value of the annuity option must be calculated, and it consists of two parts. The first of the 30 payments of $25.29 million will be paid immediately, so it is worth $25.29 million today. The remaining 29 payments will occur at one-year intervals, so their present value is computed as:

$$\$25,290,000 \times 12.27767^* = \$310,502,274$$

Adding $25,290,000 to $310,502,274 yields a present value of $335,792,274, which is a lot less than $480.5 million. This suggests your client should take the lump-sum payment. Of course, the risk of the lottery not making its annual payments is very low. There is a greater risk that a financial planner may not find investments to earn a 7 percent annual return, so the winner would have to consider his or her tolerance for risk before making a final decision.

*This factor is not included in the tables at the end of the chapter, so it is provided here for the purposes of this illustration.

Wu Company purchases an asset that costs $240,000. The asset has a four-year useful life, no salvage value, and is depreciated on a straight-line basis. The asset generates cash revenue of $90,000 per year. Assume Wu's income tax rate is 40 percent. What is the net present value of the asset, assuming Wu's management desires to earn a 10 percent rate of return after taxes? The first step in answering this question is to calculate the annual cash flow generated by the asset, as shown in Exhibit 16.7.

Because recognizing depreciation expense does not require a cash payment (cash is paid when assets are purchased, not when depreciation is recognized), depreciation expense must be added back to after-tax income to determine the annual cash inflow. Once the cash flow is determined, the net present value is computed as shown here:

$$\frac{\text{Cash flow}}{\text{annuity}} \times \frac{\text{Conversion factor}}{\text{Table 2, } r = 10\%, n = 4} = \frac{\text{Present value}}{\text{cash inflows}} - \frac{\text{Present value}}{\text{cash outflows}} = \frac{\text{Net present}}{\text{value}}$$

$$\$78,000 \times 3.169865 = \$247,249 - \$240,000 = \$7,249$$

EXHIBIT 16.7

Determining Cash Flow from Investment

	Period 1	Period 2	Period 3	Period 4
Cash revenue	$90,000	$90,000	$90,000	$90,000
Depreciation expense (noncash)	(60,000)	(60,000)	(60,000)	(60,000)
Income before taxes	30,000	30,000	30,000	30,000
Income tax at 40%	(12,000)	(12,000)	(12,000)	(12,000)
Income after tax	18,000	18,000	18,000	18,000
Depreciation add back	60,000	60,000	60,000	60,000
Annual cash inflow	$78,000	$78,000	$78,000	$78,000

The depreciation sheltered some of the income from taxation. Income taxes apply to income after deducting depreciation expense. Without depreciation expense, income taxes each year would have been $36,000 ($90,000 × 0.40) instead of $12,000 ($30,000 × 0.40). The $24,000 difference ($36,000 − $12,000) is known as a *depreciation tax shield.* The amount of the depreciation tax shield can also be computed by multiplying the depreciation expense by the tax rate ($60,000 × 0.40 = $24,000).

Because of the time value of money, companies benefit by maximizing the depreciation tax shield early in the life of an asset. For this reason, most companies calculate depreciation expense for tax purposes using the *modified accelerated cost recovery system (MACRS)* permitted by tax law rather than using straight-line depreciation. MACRS recognizes depreciation on an accelerated basis, assigning larger amounts of depreciation in the early years of an asset's useful life. The higher depreciation charges result in lower amounts of taxable income and lower income taxes. In the later years of an asset's useful life, the reverse is true, and lower depreciation charges result in higher taxes. Accelerated depreciation does not allow companies to avoid paying taxes but to delay them. The longer companies can delay paying taxes, the more cash they have available to invest.

TECHNIQUES THAT IGNORE THE TIME VALUE OF MONEY

LO 16-4

Evaluate investment opportunities using the payback method and the unadjusted rate of return.

Several techniques for evaluating capital investment proposals ignore the time value of money. Although these techniques are less accurate, they are quick and simple. When investments are small or the returns are expected within a short time, these techniques are likely to result in the same decisions that more sophisticated techniques produce.

Payback Method

The **payback method** is simple to apply and easy to understand. It shows how long it will take to recover the initial cash outflow (the cost) of an investment. The formula for computing the payback period, measured in years, is as follows:

$$\text{Payback period} = \text{Net cost of investment} \div \text{Annual net cash inflow}$$

To illustrate, assume Winston Cleaners can purchase a new ironing machine that will press shirts in half the time of the one currently used. The new machine costs $100,000 and will reduce labor cost by $40,000 per year over a four-year useful life. The payback period is computed as follows:

$$\text{Payback period} = \$100,000 \div \$40,000 = 2.5 \text{ years}$$

Interpreting Payback

Generally, investments with shorter payback periods are considered better. Because the payback method measures only investment recovery, not profitability, however, this conclusion can be invalid when considering investment alternatives. To illustrate, assume Winston Cleaners also has the opportunity to purchase a different machine that costs $100,000 and provides an annual labor savings of $40,000. However, the second machine will last for 5 instead of 4 years. The payback period is still 2.5 years ($100,000 ÷ $40,000), but the second machine is a better investment because it improves profitability by providing an additional year of cost savings. The payback analysis does not measure this difference between the alternatives.

Unequal Cash Flows

The preceding illustration assumed Winston's labor cost reduction saved the same amount of cash each year for the life of the new machine. The payback method requires adjustment when cash flow benefits are unequal. Suppose a company purchases a machine for $6,000. The machine will be used sporadically and is expected to provide incremental revenue over the next five years as follows.

Year 1	Year 2	Year 3	Year 4	Year 5
$3,000	$1,000	$2,000	$1,000	$500

Based on this cash inflow pattern, what is the payback period? There are two acceptable solutions. One accumulates the incremental revenue until the sum equals the amount of the original investment.

	Annual Amount	Cumulative Total
Year 1	$3,000	$3,000
Year 2	1,000	4,000
Year 3	2,000	6,000

This approach indicates the payback period is three years.

A second solution uses an averaging concept. The average annual cash inflow is determined. This figure is then used in the denominator of the payback equation. Using the preceding data, the payback period is computed as follows:

1. Compute the average annual cash inflow.

$$\text{Year 1} + \text{Year 2} + \text{Year 3} + \text{Year 4} + \text{Year 5} = \text{Total} \div 5 = \text{Average}$$
$$\$3,000 + \$1,000 + \$2,000 + \$1,000 + \$500 = \$7,500 \div 5 = \$1,500$$

2. Compute the payback period.

$$\frac{\text{Net cost of investment}}{} \div \frac{\text{Average annual}}{\text{net cash inflow}} = 6,000 \div 1,500 = 4 \text{ years}$$

The average method is useful when a company purchases a number of similar assets with differing cash return patterns.

Unadjusted Rate of Return

The **unadjusted rate of return** method is another common evaluation technique. Investment cash flows are not adjusted to reflect the time value of money. The unadjusted rate of return is sometimes called the *simple rate of return*. It is computed as follows:

$$\frac{\text{Unadjusted}}{\text{rate of return}} = \frac{\text{Average incremental increase in annual net income}}{\text{Net cost of original investment}}$$

To illustrate computing the unadjusted rate of return, assume The Dining Table, Inc. is considering establishing a new restaurant that will require a $2,000,000 original investment. Management anticipates operating the restaurant for 10 years before significant renovations will be required. The restaurant is expected to provide an average after-tax return of $280,000 per year. The unadjusted rate of return is computed as follows:

$$\text{Unadjusted rate of return} = \$280,000 \div \$2,000,000 = 14\% \text{ per year}$$

The accuracy of the unadjusted rate of return suffers from the failure to recognize the recovery of invested capital. With respect to a depreciable asset, the capital investment is normally recovered through revenue over the life of the asset. To illustrate, assume we purchase a $1,000 asset with a two-year life and a zero salvage value. For simplicity, ignore income taxes. Assume the asset produces $600 of cash revenue per year. The income statement for the first year of operation appears as follows.

Revenue	$600
Depreciation expense	(500)
Net income	$100

What is the amount of invested capital during the first year? First, a $1,000 cash outflow was used to purchase the asset (the original investment). Next, we collected $600 of cash revenue of which $100 was a *return on investment* (net income) and $500 was a **recovery of investment**. As a result, $1,000 was invested in the asset at the beginning of the year and $500 was invested at the end of the year. Similarly, we will recover an additional $500 of capital during the second year of operation, leaving zero invested capital at the end of the second year. Given that the cash inflows from revenue are collected somewhat evenly over the life of the investment, the amount of invested capital will range from a beginning balance of $1,000 to an ending balance of zero. On average, we will have $500 invested in the asset (the midpoint between $1,000 and zero). The average investment can be determined by dividing the total original investment by 2 ($1,000 ÷ 2 = $500). The unadjusted rate of return based on average invested capital can be calculated as follows:

$$\text{Unadjusted rate of return (Based on average investment)} = \frac{\text{Average incremental increase in annual net income}}{\text{Net cost of original investment} \div 2}$$

$$= \frac{\$100}{\$1,000 \div 2} = 20\%$$

To avoid distortions caused by the failure to recognize the recovery of invested capital, the unadjusted rate of return should be based on the *average investment* when working with investments in depreciable assets.

 CHECK YOURSELF 16.3

EZ Rentals can purchase a van that costs $24,000. The van has an expected useful life of three years and no salvage value. EZ expects rental revenue from the van to be $12,000 per year. Determine the payback period and the unadjusted rate of return.

Answer

Payback = Cost of the investment ÷ Annual cash inflow

Payback = $24,000 ÷ $12,000 = 2 years

Unadjusted rate of return = Net income ÷ Average cost of the investment

Revenue	$12,000	
Depreciation expense	(8,000)	[$24,000 ÷ 3 years]
Net income	$ 4,000	

Unadjusted rate of return = $4,000 ÷ ($24,000 ÷ 2) = 33.33%

POSTAUDITS

The analytical techniques for evaluating capital investment proposals depend highly on estimates of future cash flows. Although predictions cannot be perfectly accurate, gross miscalculations can threaten the existence of an organization. For example, optimistic projections of future cash inflows that do not materialize will lead to investments that do not return the cost of capital. Managers must take their projections seriously. A postaudit policy can encourage managers to carefully consider their capital investment decisions. A **postaudit** is conducted at the completion of a capital investment project, using the same analytical technique that was used to justify the original investment. For example, if an internal rate of return was used to justify approving an investment project, the internal rate of return should be computed in the postaudit. In the postaudit computation, *actual* rather than estimated cash flows are used. Postaudits determine whether the expected results were achieved.

Postaudits should focus on continuous improvement rather than punishment. Managers who are chastised for failing to achieve expected results might become overly cautious when asked to provide estimates for future projects. Being too conservative can create problems as serious as those caused by being too optimistic. Managers can err two ways with respect to capital investment decisions. First, a manager might accept a project that should have been rejected. This mistake usually stems from excessively optimistic future cash flow projections. Second, a manager might reject a project that should have been accepted. These missed opportunities are usually the result of underestimating future cash flows. A too cautious manager can become unable to locate enough projects to fully invest the firm's funds.

Idle cash earns no return. If projects continue to outperform expectations, managers are probably estimating future cash flows too conservatively. If projects consistently fail to live up to expectations, managers are probably being too optimistic in their projections of future cash flows. Either way, the company suffers. The goal of a postaudit is to provide feedback that will help managers improve the accuracy of future cash flow projections, maximizing the quality of the firm's capital investments.

A Look Back

Capital expenditures have a significant, long-term effect on profitability. They usually involve major cash outflows that are recovered through future cash inflows. The most common cash inflows include incremental revenue, operating cost savings, salvage value, and working capital releases. The most common outflows are the initial investment, increases in operating expenses, and working capital commitments.

Several techniques for analyzing the cash flows associated with capital investments are available. The techniques can be divided into two categories: (1) techniques that use time value of money concepts and (2) techniques that ignore the time value of money. Generally, techniques that ignore the time value of money are less accurate but simpler and easier to understand. These techniques include the *payback method* and the *unadjusted rate of return method*.

The techniques that use time value of money concepts are the *net present value method* and the *internal rate of return method*. These methods offer significant improvements in accuracy but are more difficult to understand. They may involve tedious computations and require using experienced judgment. Computer software and programmed calculators that ease the tedious computational burden are readily available to most managers. Furthermore, the superiority of the techniques justifies learning how to use them. These methods should be used when investment expenditures are larger or when cash flows extend over a prolonged time period.

A Look Forward

We sincerely hope this text provided a meaningful learning experience that will serve you well as you progress through your academic training and, ultimately, your career. Good luck and best wishes.

APPENDIX

TABLE 1			Present Value of $1								
n	4%	5%	6%	7%	8%	9%	10%	12%	14%	16%	20%
1	0.961538	0.952381	0.943396	0.934579	0.925926	0.917431	0.909091	0.892857	0.877193	0.862069	0.833333
2	0.924556	0.907029	0.889996	0.873439	0.857339	0.841680	0.826446	0.797194	0.769468	0.743163	0.694444
3	0.888996	0.863838	0.839619	0.816298	0.793832	0.772183	0.751315	0.711780	0.674972	0.640658	0.578704
4	0.854804	0.822702	0.792094	0.762895	0.735030	0.708425	0.683013	0.635518	0.592080	0.552291	0.482253
5	0.821927	0.783526	0.747258	0.712986	0.680583	0.649931	0.620921	0.567427	0.519369	0.476113	0.401878
6	0.790315	0.746215	0.704961	0.666342	0.630170	0.596267	0.564474	0.506631	0.455587	0.410442	0.334898
7	0.759918	0.710681	0.665057	0.622750	0.583490	0.547034	0.513158	0.452349	0.399637	0.353830	0.279082
8	0.730690	0.676839	0.627412	0.582009	0.540269	0.501866	0.466507	0.403883	0.350559	0.305025	0.232568
9	0.702587	0.644609	0.591898	0.543934	0.500249	0.460428	0.424098	0.360610	0.307508	0.262953	0.193807
10	0.675564	0.613913	0.558395	0.508349	0.463193	0.422411	0.385543	0.321973	0.269744	0.226684	0.161506
11	0.649581	0.584679	0.526788	0.475093	0.428883	0.387533	0.350494	0.287476	0.236617	0.195417	0.134588
12	0.624597	0.556837	0.496969	0.444012	0.397114	0.355535	0.318631	0.256675	0.207559	0.168463	0.112157
13	0.600574	0.530321	0.468839	0.414964	0.367698	0.326179	0.289664	0.229174	0.182069	0.145227	0.093464
14	0.577475	0.505068	0.442301	0.387817	0.340461	0.299246	0.263331	0.204620	0.159710	0.125195	0.077887
15	0.555265	0.481017	0.417265	0.362446	0.315242	0.274538	0.239392	0.182696	0.140096	0.107927	0.064905
16	0.533908	0.458112	0.393646	0.338735	0.291890	0.251870	0.217629	0.163122	0.122892	0.093041	0.054088
17	0.513373	0.436297	0.371364	0.316574	0.270269	0.231073	0.197845	0.145644	0.107800	0.080207	0.045073
18	0.493628	0.415521	0.350344	0.295864	0.250249	0.211994	0.179859	0.130040	0.094561	0.069144	0.037561
19	0.474642	0.395734	0.330513	0.276508	0.231712	0.194490	0.163508	0.116107	0.082948	0.059607	0.031301
20	0.456387	0.376889	0.311805	0.258419	0.214548	0.178431	0.148644	0.103667	0.072762	0.051385	0.026084

TABLE 2			Present Value of an Annuity of $1								
n	4%	5%	6%	7%	8%	9%	10%	12%	14%	16%	20%
1	0.961538	0.952381	0.943396	0.934579	0.925926	0.917431	0.909091	0.892857	0.877193	0.862069	0.833333
2	1.886095	1.859410	1.833393	1.808018	1.783265	1.759111	1.735537	1.690051	1.646661	1.605232	1.527778
3	2.775091	2.723248	2.673012	2.624316	2.577097	2.531295	2.486852	2.401831	2.321632	2.245890	2.106481
4	3.629895	3.545951	3.465106	3.387211	3.312127	3.239720	3.169865	3.037349	2.913712	2.798181	2.588735
5	4.451822	4.329477	4.212364	4.100197	3.992710	3.889651	3.790787	3.604776	3.433081	3.274294	2.990612
6	5.242137	5.075692	4.917324	4.766540	4.622880	4.485919	4.355261	4.111407	3.888668	3.684736	3.325510
7	6.002055	5.786373	5.582381	5.389289	5.206370	5.032953	4.868419	4.563757	4.288305	4.038565	3.604592
8	6.732745	6.463213	6.209794	5.971299	5.746639	5.534819	5.334926	4.967640	4.638864	4.343591	3.837160
9	7.435332	7.107822	6.801692	6.515232	6.246888	5.995247	5.759024	5.328250	4.946372	4.606544	4.030967
10	8.110896	7.721735	7.360087	7.023582	6.710081	6.417658	6.144567	5.650223	5.216116	4.833227	4.192472
11	8.760477	8.306414	7.886875	7.498674	7.138964	6.805191	6.495061	5.937699	5.452733	5.028644	4.327060
12	9.385074	8.863252	8.383844	7.942686	7.536078	7.160725	6.813692	6.194374	5.660292	5.197107	4.439217
13	9.985648	9.393573	8.852683	8.357651	7.903776	7.486904	7.103356	6.423548	5.842362	5.342334	4.532681
14	10.563123	9.898641	9.294984	8.745468	8.244237	7.786150	7.366687	6.628168	6.002072	5.467529	4.610567
15	11.118387	10.379658	9.712249	9.107914	8.559479	8.060688	7.606080	6.810864	6.142168	5.575456	4.675473
16	11.652296	10.837770	10.105895	9.446649	8.851369	8.312558	7.823709	6.973986	6.265060	5.668497	4.729561
17	12.165669	11.274066	10.477260	9.763223	9.121638	8.543631	8.021553	7.119630	6.372859	5.748704	4.774634
18	12.659297	11.689587	10.827603	10.059087	9.371887	8.755625	8.201412	7.249670	6.467420	5.817848	4.812195
19	13.133939	12.085321	11.158116	10.335595	9.603599	8.905115	8.364920	7.365777	6.550369	5.877455	4.843496
20	13.590326	12.462210	11.469921	10.594014	9.818147	9.128546	8.513564	7.469444	6.623131	5.928841	4.869580

Video lectures and accompanying self-assessment quizzes are available in *Connect* for all learning objectives.

SELF-STUDY REVIEW PROBLEM

The CFO of Advo Corporation is considering two investment opportunities. The expected future cash inflows for each opportunity follow.

	Year 1	Year 2	Year 3	Year 4
Project 1	$144,000	$147,000	$160,000	$178,000
Project 2	204,000	199,000	114,000	112,000

Both investments require an initial payment of $400,000. Advo's desired rate of return is 16 percent.

Required

a. Compute the net present value of each project. Which project should Advo adopt based on the net present value approach?

b. Use the incremental revenue summation method to compute the payback period for each project. Which project should Advo adopt based on the payback approach?

Solution to Requirement *a*

Project 1

	Cash Inflows		Table Factor*		Present Value
Year 1	$144,000	×	0.862069	=	$124,138
Year 2	147,000	×	0.743163	=	109,245
Year 3	160,000	×	0.640658	=	102,505
Year 4	178,000	×	0.552291	=	98,308
PV of cash inflows					434,196
Cost of investment					(400,000)
Net present value					$ 34,196

*Table 1, $n = 1$ through 4, $r = 16\%$.

Project 2

	Cash Inflows		Table Factor*		Present Value
Year 1	$204,000	×	0.862069	=	$175,862
Year 2	199,000	×	0.743163	=	147,889
Year 3	114,000	×	0.640658	=	73,035
Year 4	112,000	×	0.552291	=	61,857
PV of cash inflows					458,643
Cost of investment					(400,000)
Net present value					$ 58,643

*Table 1, $n = 1$ through 4, $r = 16\%$.

Advo should adopt Project 2 since it has a greater net present value.

Solution to Requirement *b*

Cash Inflows	Project 1	Project 2
Year 1	$144,000	$204,000
Year 2	147,000	199,000
Total	$291,000	$403,000

By the end of the second year, Project 2's cash inflows have more than paid for the cost of the investment. In contrast, Project 1 still falls short of investment recovery by $109,000 ($400,000 − $291,000). Advo should adopt Project 2 since it has a shorter payback period.

KEY TERMS

Accumulated conversion
  factor 575
Annuity 575
Capital investments 572
Cost of capital 573
Desired rate of return 573

Incremental revenue 578
Internal rate of return 581
Minimum rate of return 573
Net present value 577
Ordinary annuity 576
Payback method 586

Postaudit 589
Present value index 581
Present value table 574
Recovery of investment 588
Single-payment
  (lump-sum) 574

Time value of
  money 572
Unadjusted rate of return
  (simple rate of
  return) 587
Working capital 579

QUESTIONS

1. What is a capital investment? How does it differ from an investment in stocks or bonds?

2. What are three reasons that cash is worth more today than cash to be received in the future?

3. "A dollar today is worth more than a dollar in the future." "The present value of a future dollar is worth less than one dollar." Are these two statements synonymous? Explain.

4. Define the term *return on investment*. How is the return normally expressed? Give an example of a capital investment return.

5. How does a company establish its minimum acceptable rate of return on investments?

6. If you wanted to have $100,000 one year from today and desired to earn a 6 percent return, what amount would you need to invest today? Which amount has more value, the amount today or the $100,000 a year from today?

7. Why are present value tables frequently used to convert future values to present values?

8. Define the term *annuity*. What is one example of an annuity receipt?

9. How can present value "what-if" analysis be enhanced by using software programs?

10. Receiving $100,000 per year for five years is equivalent to investing what amount today at 14 percent? Provide a mathematical formula to solve this problem, assuming use of a present value annuity table to convert the future cash flows to their present value equivalents. Provide the expression for the Excel spreadsheet function that would perform the present value conversion.

11. Maria Espinosa borrowed $15,000 from the bank and agreed to repay the loan at 8 percent annual interest over four years, making payments of $4,529 per year. Because part of the bank's payment from Ms. Espinosa is a recovery of the original investment, what assumption must the bank make to earn its desired 8 percent compounded annual return?

12. Two investment opportunities have positive net present values. Investment A's net present value amounts to $40,000 while B's is only $30,000. Does this mean that A is the better investment opportunity? Explain.

13. What criteria determine whether a project is acceptable under the net present value method?

14. Does the net present value method provide a measure of the rate of return on capital investments?

15. Which is the best capital investment evaluation technique for ranking investment opportunities?

16. Paul Henderson is a manager for Spark Company. He tells you that his company always maximizes profitability by accepting the investment opportunity with the highest internal rate of return. Explain to Mr. Henderson how his company may improve profitability by sometimes selecting investment opportunities with lower internal rates of return.

17. What is the relationship between desired rate of return and internal rate of return?

18. What typical cash inflow and outflow items are associated with capital investments?

19. "I always go for the investment with the shortest payback period." Is this a sound strategy? Why or why not?

20. "The payback method cannot be used if the cash inflows occur in unequal patterns." Do you agree or disagree? Explain.

21. What are the advantages and disadvantages associated with the unadjusted rate of return method for evaluating capital investments?

22. How do capital investments affect profitability?

23. What is a postaudit? How is it useful in capital budgeting?

EXERCISES—SERIES A

Exercise 16-1A   *Identifying cash inflows and outflows*   LO 16-1

Required

Indicate which of the following items will result in cash inflows and which will result in cash outflows. The first one is shown as an example.

Item	Type of Cash Flow
a. Initial investment	Outflow
b. Salvage value	
c. Recovery of working capital	
d. Incremental expenses	
e. Working capital commitments	
f. Cost savings	
g. Incremental revenue	

Exercise 16-2A   *Determining the present value of a lump-sum future cash receipt*   LO 16-1

Larry Mattingly turned 20 years old today. His grandfather had established a trust fund that will pay him $120,000 on his next birthday. However, Larry needs money today to start his college education, and his father is willing to help. Mr. Mattingly has agreed to give Larry the present value of the $120,000 future cash inflow, assuming a 6 percent rate of return.

Required

Round your figures to the nearest whole dollar.

a. Use a present value table to determine the amount of cash that Larry Mattingly's father should give him.

b. Use an algebraic formula to prove that the present value of the trust fund (the amount of cash computed in Requirement *a*) is equal to its $120,000 future value.

Exercise 16-3A   *Determining the present value of a lump-sum future cash receipt*   LO 16-1

Gail Trevino expects to receive a $500,000 cash benefit when she retires five years from today. Ms. Trevino's employer has offered an early retirement incentive by agreeing to pay her $325,000 today if she agrees to retire immediately. Ms. Trevino desires to earn a rate of return of 8 percent.

Required

Round your figures to the nearest whole dollar.

a. Assuming that the retirement benefit is the only consideration in making the retirement decision, should Ms. Trevino accept her employer's offer?

b. Identify the factors that cause the present value of the retirement benefit to be less than $500,000.

Exercise 16-4A   *Determining the present value of an annuity*   LO 16-1

The dean of the School of Fine Arts is trying to decide whether to purchase a copy machine to place in the lobby of the building. The machine would add to student convenience, but the dean feels compelled to earn an 8 percent return on the investment of funds. Estimates of cash inflows from copy machines that have been placed in other university buildings indicate that the copy machine would probably produce incremental cash inflows of approximately $25,000 per year. The machine is expected to have a three-year useful life with a zero salvage value.

Required

Round your figures to two decimal points.

a. Use Present Value Appendix Table 1 to determine the maximum amount of cash the dean should be willing to pay for a copy machine.

b. Use Present Value Appendix Table 2 to determine the maximum amount of cash the dean should be willing to pay for a copy machine.

c. Explain the consistency or lack of consistency in the answers to Requirements *a* and *b*.

LO 16-2

Exercise 16-5A   *Determining net present value*

Monterey Company is considering investing in two new vans that are expected to generate combined cash inflows of $30,000 per year. The vans' combined purchase price is $93,000. The expected life and salvage value of each are four years and $23,000, respectively. Monterey has an average cost of capital of 7 percent.

Required

Round your figures to two decimal points.

a. Calculate the net present value of the investment opportunity.

b. Indicate whether the investment opportunity is expected to earn a return that is above or below the cost of capital and whether it should be accepted.

LO 16-2

Exercise 16-6A   *Determining net present value*

Aaron Heath is seeking part-time employment while he attends school. He is considering purchasing technical equipment that will enable him to start a small training services company that will offer tutorial services over the Internet. Aaron expects demand for the service to grow rapidly in the first two years of operation as customers learn about the availability of the Internet assistance. Thereafter, he expects demand to stabilize. The following table presents the expected cash flows.

Year of Operation	Cash Inflow	Cash Outflow
Year 1	$25,000	$12,000
Year 2	29,000	16,000
Year 3	32,000	18,000
Year 4	32,000	18,000

In addition to these cash flows, Aaron expects to pay $25,000 for the equipment. He also expects to pay $4,000 for a major overhaul and updating of the equipment at the end of the second year of operation. The equipment is expected to have a $4,000 salvage value and a four-year useful life. Aaron desires to earn a rate of return of 8 percent.

Required

Round your computations to two decimal points.

a. Calculate the net present value of the investment opportunity.

b. Indicate whether the investment opportunity is expected to earn a return that is above or below the desired rate of return and whether it should be accepted.

LO 16-2

Exercise 16-7A   *Using the present value index*

Rolla Company has a choice of two investment alternatives. The present value of cash inflows and outflows for the first alternative is $125,000 and $100,000, respectively. The present value of cash inflows and outflows for the second alternative is $300,000 and $262,500, respectively.

Required

Round your computation to two decimal points.

a. Calculate the net present value of each investment opportunity.

b. Calculate the present value index for each investment opportunity.

c. Indicate which investment will produce the higher rate of return.

Exercise 16-8A   *Determining the cash flow annuity with income tax considerations*   LO 16-2

To open a new store, Enid Tire Company plans to invest $320,000 in equipment expected to have a four-year useful life and no salvage value. Enid expects the new store to generate annual cash revenues of $400,000 and to incur annual cash operating expenses of $240,000. Enid's average income tax rate is 30 percent. The company uses straight-line depreciation.

Required

Determine the expected annual net cash inflow from operations for each of the first four years after Enid opens the new store.

Exercise 16-9A   *Determining the internal rate of return*   LO 16-3

Gerty Manufacturing Company has an opportunity to purchase some technologically advanced equipment that will reduce the company's cash outflow for operating expenses by $640,000 per year. The cost of the equipment is $3,932,522.88. Gerty expects it to have a 10-year useful life and a zero salvage value. The company has established an investment opportunity hurdle rate of 9 percent and uses the straight-line method for depreciation.

Required

Round your computations to two decimal points.

a. Calculate the internal rate of return of the investment opportunity.
b. Indicate whether the investment opportunity should be accepted.

Exercise 16-10A   *Using the internal rate of return to compare investment opportunities*   LO 16-3

Velma and Keota (V&K) is a partnership that owns a small company. It is considering two alternative investment opportunities. The first investment opportunity will have a five-year useful life, will cost $19,680.96, and will generate expected cash inflows of $4,800 per year. The second investment is expected to have a useful life of three years, will cost $12,885.48, and will generate expected cash inflows of $5,000 per year. Assume that V&K has the funds available to accept only one of the opportunities.

Required

a. Calculate the internal rate of return of each investment opportunity.
b. Based on the internal rates of return, which opportunity should V&K select?
c. Discuss other factors that V&K should consider in the investment decision.

Exercise 16-11A   *Evaluating discounted cash flow techniques*   LO 16-2, 16-3

Barbara Harvey is angry with Martin Cochran. He is behind schedule developing supporting material for tomorrow's capital budget committee meeting. When she approached him about his apparent lackadaisical attitude in general and his tardiness in particular, he responded, "I don't see why we do this stuff in the first place. It's all a bunch of estimates. Who knows what future cash flows will really be? I certainly don't. I've been doing this job for five years, and no one has ever checked to see if I even came close at these guesses. I've been waiting for marketing to provide the estimated cash inflows on the projects being considered tomorrow. But, if you want my report now, I'll have it in a couple of hours. I can make up the marketing data as well as they can."

Required

Does Mr. Cochran have a point? Is there something wrong with the company's capital budgeting system? Write a brief response explaining how to improve the investment evaluation system.

Exercise 16-12A   *Determining the payback period*   LO 16-4

North Airline Company is considering expanding its territory. The company has the opportunity to purchase one of two different used airplanes. The first airplane is expected to cost $12,000,000; it will enable the company to increase its annual cash inflow by $4,000,000 per year. The plane is expected to have a useful life of five years and no salvage value. The second plane costs $24,000,000; it will enable the company to increase annual cash flow by $6,000,000 per year. This plane has an eight-year useful life and a zero salvage value.

Required

a. Determine the payback period for each investment alternative and identify the alternative North should accept if the decision is based on the payback approach.
b. Discuss the shortcomings of using the payback method to evaluate investment opportunities.

LO 16-4

Exercise 16-13A   *Determining the payback period with uneven cash flows*

Currie Company has an opportunity to purchase a forklift to use in its heavy equipment rental business. The forklift would be leased on an annual basis during its first two years of operation. Thereafter, it would be leased to the general public on demand. Currie would sell it at the end of the fifth year of its useful life. The expected cash inflows and outflows follow.

Year	Nature of Item	Cash Inflow	Cash Outflow
Year 1	Purchase price		$86,000
Year 1	Revenue	$30,000	
Year 2	Revenue	40,000	
Year 3	Revenue	28,000	
Year 3	Major overhaul		12,000
Year 4	Revenue	20,000	
Year 5	Revenue	14,400	
Year 5	Salvage value	9,600	

Required

a. Determine the payback period using the accumulated cash flows approach.

b. Determine the payback period using the average cash flows approach. Round your computation to one decimal point.

LO 16-4

Exercise 16-14A   *Determining the unadjusted rate of return*

Rainbow Painting Company is considering whether to purchase a new spray paint machine that costs $16,000. The machine is expected to save labor, increasing net income by $1,200 per year. The effective life of the machine is 15 years according to the manufacturer's estimate.

Required

a. Determine the unadjusted rate of return based on the average cost of the investment.

b. What is the predominant shortcoming of using the unadjusted rate of return to evaluate investment opportunities?

LO 16-4

Exercise 16-15A   *Computing the payback period and unadjusted rate of return for the same investment opportunity*

Garrison Rentals can purchase a van that costs $54,000; it has an expected useful life of three years and no salvage value. Garrison uses straight-line depreciation. Expected revenue is $36,000 per year. Assume that depreciation is the only expense associated with this investment.

Required

a. Determine the payback period.

b. Determine the unadjusted rate of return based on the average cost of the investment. Compute the percentage rate to one decimal point.

PROBLEMS—SERIES A

MC Graw Hill CONNECT   An electronic auto-gradable version of the Series A Problems is available in Connect. A PDF version of Series B Problems is in Connect under the "Additional Student Resources" tab. Solutions to the Series B Problems are available in Connect under the "Instructor Library" tab. Instructor and student Workpapers for the Series B Problems are available in Connect under the "Instructor Library" and "Additional Student Resources" tabs respectively.

LO 16-2

Problem 16-16A   *Using present value techniques to evaluate alternative investment opportunities*

Swift Delivery is a small company that transports business packages between New York and Chicago. It operates a fleet of small vans that moves packages to and from a central depot within each city and uses a common carrier to deliver the packages between the depots in the two cities. Swift Delivery recently acquired approximately $4 million of cash capital from its owners, and its president, George Hay, is trying to identify the most profitable way to invest these funds.

Todd Payne, the company's operations manager, believes that the money should be used to expand the fleet of city vans at a cost of $900,000. He argues that more vans would enable the company to expand its services into new markets, thereby increasing the revenue base. More specifically, he expects cash inflows to increase by $325,000 per year. The additional vans are expected to have an average useful life of four years and a combined salvage value of $100,000. Operating the vans will require additional working capital of $50,000, which will be recovered at the end of the fourth year.

In contrast, Oscar Vance, the company's chief accountant, believes that the funds should be used to purchase large trucks to deliver the packages between the depots in the two cities. The conversion process would produce continuing improvement in operating savings and reduce cash outflows as follows.

Year 1	Year 2	Year 3	Year 4
$175,000	$375,000	$450,000	$500,000

The large trucks are expected to cost $1,000,000 and to have a four-year useful life and a $81,250 salvage value. In addition to the purchase price of the trucks, up-front training costs are expected to amount to $20,000. Swift Delivery's management has established a 10 percent desired rate of return.

Required

Round your computations to two decimal points.

a. Determine the net present value of the two investment alternatives.
b. Calculate the present value index for each alternative.
c. Indicate which investment alternative you would recommend. Explain your choice.

Problem 16-17A *Applying the net present value approach with and without tax considerations*

LO 16-2

eXcel

CHECK FIGURE
a. $(2,960)

Antonio Melton, the chief executive officer of Melton Corporation, has assembled his top advisers to evaluate an investment opportunity. The advisers expect the company to pay $500,000 cash at the beginning of the investment and the cash inflow for each of the following four years to be the following.

Year 1	Year 2	Year 3	Year 4
$105,000	$120,000	$150,000	$225,000

Mr. Melton agrees with his advisers that the company should use a desired rate of return of 7 percent to compute net present value to evaluate the viability of the proposed project.

Required

Round your computation to the nearest whole dollar.

a. Compute the net present value of the proposed project. Should Mr. Melton approve the project?
b. Shawn Love, one of the advisers, is wary of the cash flow forecast, and she points out that the advisers failed to consider that the depreciation on equipment used in this project will be tax deductible. The depreciation is expected to be $100,000 per year for the four-year period. The company's income tax rate is 30 percent per year. Use this information to revise the company's expected cash flow from this project.
c. Compute the net present value of the project based on the revised cash flow forecast. Should Mr. Melton approve the project?

Problem 16-18A *Postaudit evaluation*

LO 16-2

CHECK FIGURE
b. NPV: $(523,338)

Brett Collins is reviewing his company's investment in a cement plant. The company paid $12,000,000 five years ago to acquire the plant. Now top management is considering an opportunity to sell it. The president wants to know whether the plant has met original expectations before he decides its fate. The company's desired rate of return for present value computations is 8 percent. Expected and actual cash flows follow.

	Year 1	Year 2	Year 3	Year 4	Year 5
Expected	$2,640,000	$3,936,000	$3,648,000	$3,984,000	$3,360,000
Actual	2,160,000	2,448,000	3,936,000	3,120,000	2,880,000

Required

Round your computations to the nearest whole dollar.

a. Compute the net present value of the expected cash flows as of the beginning of the investment.

b. Compute the net present value of the actual cash flows as of the beginning of the investment.

c. What do you conclude from this postaudit?

LO 16-2, 16-3

CHECK FIGURES
a. NPV of A: $17,328.00
b. Rate of return of B: 12%

Problem 16-19A   *Using net present value and internal rate of return to evaluate investment opportunities*

Dwight Donovan, the president of Donovan Enterprises, is considering two investment opportunities. Because of limited resources, he will be able to invest in only one of them. Project A is to purchase a machine that will enable factory automation; the machine is expected to have a useful life of four years and no salvage value. Project B supports a training program that will improve the skills of employees operating the current equipment. Initial cash expenditures for Project A are $400,000 and for Project B are $160,000. The annual expected cash inflows are $126,000 for Project A and $52,800 for Project B. Both investments are expected to provide cash flow benefits for the next four years. Donovan Enterprises' desired rate of return is 8 percent.

Required

a. Compute the net present value of each project. Which project should be adopted based on the net present value approach? Round your computations to two decimal points.

b. Compute the approximate internal rate of return of each project. Which one should be adopted based on the internal rate of return approach? Round your rates to six decimal points.

c. Compare the net present value approach with the internal rate of return approach. Which method is better in the given circumstances? Why?

LO 16-4

CHECK FIGURE
a. Payback period of the yogurt investment: 1.69 years; unadjusted rate of return of the cappuccino investment: 56.35%

Problem 16-20A   *Using the payback period and unadjusted rate of return to evaluate alternative investment opportunities*

Seth Fitch owns a small retail ice cream parlor. He is considering expanding the business and has identified two attractive alternatives. One involves purchasing a machine that would enable Mr. Fitch to offer frozen yogurt to customers. The machine would cost $16,200 and has an expected useful life of three years with no salvage value. Additional annual cash revenues and cash operating expenses associated with selling yogurt are expected to be $12,400 and $1,800, respectively.

Alternatively, Mr. Fitch could purchase for $20,160 the equipment necessary to serve cappuccino. That equipment has an expected useful life of four years and no salvage value. Additional annual cash revenues and cash operating expenses associated with selling cappuccino are expected to be $17,000 and $4,860, respectively.

Income before taxes earned by the ice cream parlor is taxed at an effective rate of 20 percent.

Required

Round your figures, including percentage rates, to two decimal points.

a. Determine the payback period and unadjusted rate of return (use average investment) for each alternative.

b. Indicate which investment alternative you would recommend. Explain your choice.

LO 16-2, 16-4

CHECK FIGURES
a. NPV of #1: $30,179.72
b. Payback period of #2: less than two years.

Problem 16-21A   *Using net present value and payback period to evaluate investment opportunities*

Daryl Kearns saved $240,000 during the 30 years that he worked for a major corporation. Now he has retired at the age of 60 and has begun to draw a comfortable pension check every month. He wants to ensure the financial security of his retirement by investing his savings wisely and is currently considering two investment opportunities. Both investments require an initial payment of $160,000. The following table presents the estimated cash inflows for the two alternatives.

	Year 1	Year 2	Year 3	Year 4
Opportunity #1	$44,000	$47,200	$63,200	$80,000
Opportunity #2	81,600	86,400	16,000	16,000

Mr. Kearns decides to use his past average return on mutual fund investments as the discount rate; it is 8 percent.

Required

Round your computation to two decimal points.

a. Compute the net present value of each opportunity. Which should Mr. Kearns adopt based on the net present value approach?

b. Compute the payback period for each project. Which should Mr. Kearns adopt based on the payback approach?

c. Compare the net present value approach with the payback approach. Which method is better in the given circumstances?

Problem 16-22A   *Effects of straight-line versus accelerated depreciation on an investment decision*

LO 16-2, 16-4

Harper Electronics is considering investing in manufacturing equipment expected to cost $250,000. The equipment has an estimated useful life of four years and a salvage value of $25,000. It is expected to produce incremental cash revenues of $125,000 per year. Harper has an effective income tax rate of 30 percent and a desired rate of return of 10 percent.

CHECK FIGURES
a. NPV = $97,930
d. Payback period: 2.40 years

Required

Round your financial figures to the nearest dollar and all other figures to two decimal points.

a. Determine the net present value and the present value index of the investment, assuming that Harper uses straight-line depreciation for financial and income tax reporting.

b. Determine the net present value and the present value index of the investment, assuming that Harper uses double-declining-balance depreciation for financial and income tax reporting.

c. Why do the net present values computed in Requirements *a* and *b* differ?

d. Determine the payback period and unadjusted rate of return (use average investment), assuming that Harper uses straight-line depreciation.

e. Determine the payback period and unadjusted rate of return (use average investment), assuming that Harper uses double-declining-balance depreciation. (*Note:* Use average annual cash flow when computing the payback period and average annual income when determining the unadjusted rate of return.)

f. Why are there no differences in the payback periods or unadjusted rates of return computed in Requirements *d* and *e*?

Problem 16-23A   *Comparing internal rate of return with unadjusted rate of return*

LO 16-3, 16-4

Barlae Auto Repair, Inc. is evaluating a project to purchase equipment that will not only expand the company's capacity but also improve the quality of its repair services. The board of directors requires all capital investments to meet or exceed the minimum requirement of a 10 percent rate of return. However, the board has not clearly defined the rate of return. The president and controller are pondering two different rates of return: unadjusted rate of return and internal rate of return. The equipment, which costs $200,000, has a life expectancy of five years. The increased net profit per year will be approximately $14,000, and the increased cash inflow per year will be approximately $55,400.

CHECK FIGURE
b. Internal rate of return: 12%

Required

Round rates to six decimal points.

a. If it uses the unadjusted rate of return (use average investment) to evaluate this project, should the company invest in the equipment?

b. If it uses the internal rate of return to evaluate this project, should the company invest in the equipment?

c. Which method is better for this capital investment decision?

ANALYZE, THINK, COMMUNICATE

ATC 16-1   Business Application Case   *Pension planning in state governments*

In recent years, there has been a lot of media coverage about the funding status of pension plans for state employees. In many states, the amount of money invested in employee pension plans is far less than the amount estimated to pay employees the retirement benefits they have been promised. Basically, pension plans work by investing enough money while employees are working so that the money invested, plus the investment income it earns over the years, will be sufficient to pay the workers their retirement incomes once they have retired.

There are many complicated assumptions, estimates, and calculations needed to determine how much money a state should invest in its pension fund each year. One of the most important assumptions is the rate of return the plan's investments will earn in the future. As you have seen in this chapter, the higher the rate of return used to calculate the present value of future cash flows, the lower the present value will be. To determine a pension plan's funded status, actuaries (1) estimate the future cash payments expected to be made to employees, (2) calculate the present value of those cash flows using an assumed rate of return (this present value is the gross liability of the fund), and (3) subtract the amount of money that has been invested from the gross liability calculated in step 2 (this amount is the funded status of the pension plan). Essentially, this is the same as calculating the net present value of an investment. If the plan has less money in its investments than the present value of its estimated future cash flows, it has a net liability and is considered to be underfunded by that amount.

Many states' pension plans have assumed they will earn 8 percent or more on their investments, even though many experts think a more appropriate assumption would be 6.5 percent. As an example, Virginia used an *assumed* rate of return of 7.5 percent in 2009 but reduced the rate to 7.0 percent in 2010. In 2014, Actual investment returns can vary widely. In 2016, Virginia's actual return on its pension assets was only 1.9 percent, but in 2017 it was 12.1 percent.

Virginia paid out approximately $4.5 billion in benefits to retirees in 2017.

Required

a. Assume Virginia's annual payments will continue to be $4.5 billion, and that retirees will receive benefits for 20 years on average. Using an assumed rate of return of 8 percent, calculate the liability of the state's pension plan. The liability is the present value of the future cash payments. (Be aware that the real-world calculation for a state's pension plan liability involves many more assumptions than just these two.)

b. Assume the annual payments will continue to be $4.5 billion, and that retirees will receive benefits for 20 years on average. Using an assumed rate of return of 6 percent, calculate the liability of the state's pension plan.

c. Reviewing your answers from Requirements *a* and *b*, provide an explanation as to why states may wish to assume a higher rate of return on their pension plan's investments than actuaries might recommend.

ATC 16-2   Group Assignment   *Net present value*

Espada Real Estate Investment Company (EREIC) purchases new apartment complexes, establishes a stable group of residents, and then sells the complexes to apartment management companies. The average holding time is three years. EREIC is currently investigating two alternatives.

1. EREIC can purchase Harding Properties for $4,500,000. The complex is expected to produce net cash inflows of $360,000, $502,500, and $865,000 for the first, second, and third years of operation, respectively. The market value of the complex at the end of the third year is expected to be $5,175,000.

2. EREIC can purchase Summit Apartments for $3,450,000. The complex is expected to produce net cash inflows of $290,000, $435,000, and $600,000 for the first, second, and third years of operation, respectively. The market value of the complex at the end of the third year is expected to be $4,050,000.

EREIC has a desired rate of return of 12 percent.

Required

a. Divide the class into groups of four or five students per group and then divide the groups into two sections. Assign Task 1 to the first section and Task 2 to the second section.

Group Tasks

(1) Calculate the net present value and the present value index for Harding Properties.
(2) Calculate the net present value and the present value index for Summit Apartments.

b. Have a spokesperson from one group in the first section report the amounts calculated by the group. Make sure that all groups in the section have the same result. Repeat the process for the second section. Have the class as a whole select the investment opportunity that EREIC should accept given that the objective is to produce the higher rate of return.

c. Assume that EREIC has $4,500,000 to invest and that any funds not invested in real estate properties must be invested in a certificate of deposit earning a 5 percent return. Would this information alter the decision made in Requirement *b*?

d. This requirement is independent of Requirement *c*. Assume there is a 10 percent chance that the Harding project will be annexed by the city of Hoover, which has an outstanding school district. The annexation would likely increase net cash flows by $37,500 per year and would increase the market value at the end of Year 3 by $300,000. Would this information change the decision reached in Requirement *b*?

ATC 16-3   Research Assignment   *Capital expenditures at Shake Shack, Inc.*

Obtain Shake Shack, Inc.'s Form 10-K for the fiscal year ending on December 27, 2017. To obtain the Form 10-K, you can use the EDGAR system (see Appendix A at the back of this text for instructions), or it can be found under the "Investor Relations" link on the company's website at www.shakeshack .com. Read the following sections of the 10-K: "Growth Strategies" on page 13, and the Consolidated Statements of Cash Flows on page 78.

Required

a. How many company-owned Shacks did Shake Shack plan to open during its 2017 fiscal year? By what percentage would these new Shacks increase the size of Shake Shack's company-owned Shacks?

b. How much cash did Shake Shack spend on investing activities during its 2015, 2016, and 2017 fiscal years? Do you think the amount spent on investing activities represents the full costs that Shake Shack incurred to open new Shacks? Explain your answer.

c. Where did Shake Shack get the cash used to make these investments?

ATC 16-4   Writing Assignment   *Limitations of capital investment techniques*

Webb Publishing Company is evaluating two investment opportunities. One is to purchase an Internet company with the capacity to open new marketing channels through which Webb can sell its books. This opportunity offers a high potential for growth but involves significant risk. Indeed, losses are projected for the first three years of operation. The second opportunity is to purchase a printing company that would enable Webb to better control costs by printing its own books. The potential savings are clearly predictable but would make a significant change in the company's long-term profitability.

Required

Write a response discussing the usefulness of capital investment techniques (net present value, internal rate of return, payback, and unadjusted rate of return) in making a choice between these two alternative investment opportunities. Your response should discuss the strengths and weaknesses of capital budgeting techniques in general. Furthermore, it should include a comparison between techniques based on the time value of money versus those that are not.

ATC 16-5   Ethical Dilemma   *Postaudit*

Gaines Company recently initiated a postaudit program. To motivate employees to take the program seriously, Gaines established a bonus program. Managers receive a bonus equal to 10 percent of the amount by which actual net present value exceeds the projected net present value. Victor Holt, manager of the North Western Division, had an investment proposal on his desk when the new system was implemented. The investment opportunity required a $250,000 initial cash outflow and was expected to return cash inflows of $90,000 per year for the next five years. Gaines' desired rate of return is 10 percent. Mr. Holt immediately reduced the estimated cash inflows to $70,000 per year and recommended accepting the project.

Required

a. Assume that actual cash inflows turn out to be $91,000 per year. Determine the amount of Mr. Holt's bonus if the original computation of net present value were based on $90,000 versus $70,000.

b. Is Mr. Holt's behavior in violation of any of the standards of ethical professional practice in Exhibit 10.19 of Chapter 10?

c. Speculate about the long-term effect the bonus plan is likely to have on the company.

d. Recommend how to compensate managers in a way that discourages gamesmanship.

Design Elements: Abstract texture: ©Ingram Publishing; Video Camera icon: ©McGraw-Hill Education; Check mark: ©McGraw-Hill Education; Look forward/backward icon: ©McGraw-Hill Education; Globe icon: ©McGraw-Hill Education; Globe with magnifying glass icon: ©McGraw-Hill Education; Pen and paper icon: ©McGraw-Hill Education; Group Assignment icon: ©McGraw-Hill Education; Ethics Cases icon: ©McGraw-Hill Education; Self-Study Review icon: © Design Pics/Don Hammond; and Point de la Coubre lighthouse near Roy, France: © Westend61/Getty Images.

APPENDIX A

Accessing the EDGAR Database through the Internet

Successful business managers need many different skills, including communication, interpersonal, computer, and analytical. Most business students become very aware of the data analysis skills used in accounting, but they may not be as aware of the importance of "data-finding" skills. There are many sources of accounting and financial data. The more sources you are able to use, the better.

One very important source of accounting information is the EDGAR database. Others are probably available at your school through the library or business school network. Your accounting instructor will be able to identify these for you and make suggestions regarding their use. By making the effort to learn to use electronic databases, you will enhance your abilities as a future manager and your marketability as a business graduate.

These instructions assume that you know how to access and use an Internet browser. Follow the instructions to retrieve data from the Securities and Exchange Commission's EDGAR database. Be aware that the SEC may have changed its interface since this appendix was written. Accordingly, be prepared for slight differences between the following instructions and what appears on your computer screen. Take comfort in the fact that changes are normally designed to simplify user access. If you encounter a conflict between the following instructions and the instructions provided in the SEC interface, remember that the SEC interface is more current and should take precedence over the following instructions.

Most companies provide links to their SEC filings from their corporate website. These links are often simpler to use and provide more choices regarding file formats than the SEC's EDGAR site. On company websites, links to SEC filings are usually found under one of the following links: "Investor Relations," "Company Info," or "About Us."

1. Connect to the EDGAR database through the following address: www.sec.gov/.
2. After the SEC home page appears, under the **Filings** dropdown heading, click on **Company Filings Search**.
3. On the screen that appears, click on **Company Name.**
4. On the screen that appears, enter the name of the company whose file you wish to retrieve in the "Company Name" window and click the **Search** button.
5. The following screen will present a list of companies that have the same, or similar, names as the one you entered. Identify the company you want and click on the CIK number beside it.
6. Enter the SEC form number that you want to retrieve in the window titled **Filling Type** that appears in the upper left portion of the screen. For example, if you want Form 10-K, which will usually be the case, enter **10-K** and click on the **Search** button.
7. A list of the forms you requested will be presented, along with the date they were filed. Click on the **Document** button next to the file you wish to retrieve.
8. You will be presented with a list of documents from which to select; usually you will want to choose the file **10k.**
9. Once the 10-K has been retrieved, you can search it online or save it on your computer.
10. Often the 10-K will have a table of contents that can help locate the part of the report you need. The financial statements are seldom located at the beginning of the Form 10-K. They are usually in either Section 8 or Section 15.

APPENDIX B

The Double-Entry Accounting System

INTRODUCTION

*To prepare financial statements, a company must have a system that captures the vast numbers of business transactions in which it engages each year. The most widely used system, **double-entry accounting**, is so effective it has been in use for hundreds of years! This appendix explains the rules for recording transactions using double-entry accounting.*

DEBIT/CREDIT TERMINOLOGY

An account form known as a **T-account** is a good starting point for learning double-entry recording procedures. A T-account looks like the letter T drawn on a piece of paper. The account title is written across the top of the horizontal bar of the T. The left side of the vertical bar is the **debit** side, and the right side is the **credit** side. An account has been *debited* when an amount is written on the left side and *credited* when an amount is written on the right side. For any given account, the difference between the total debit and credit amounts is the **account balance**.

The rules for using debits and credits to record transactions in T-accounts are as follows.

Assets			Claims				
			Liabilities		+	Equity	
Debit	Credit	=	Debit	Credit		Debit	Credit
+	−		−	+		−	+

Notice that a debit can represent an increase or a decrease. Likewise, a credit can represent an increase or a decrease. Whether a debit or credit is an increase or a decrease depends on the type of account (asset, liability, or stockholders' equity) in question. The rules of debits and credits are summarized as follows.

1. Debits increase asset accounts; credits decrease asset accounts.
2. Debits decrease liability and stockholders' equity accounts; credits increase liability and stockholders' equity accounts.

We now demonstrate the use of debits and credits in the double-entry accounting system.

The General Journal

Businesses find it impractical to record every individual transaction directly into accounts. Imagine the number of cash transactions a grocery store has each day. To simplify recordkeeping, businesses rely on **source documents** such as cash register tapes as the basis for

603

entering transaction data into the accounting system. Other source documents include invoices, time cards, check stubs, and deposit tickets.

Accountants further simplify recordkeeping by initially recording data from source documents into **journals.** Journals provide a chronological record of business transactions. *Transactions are recorded in journals before they are entered into ledger accounts.* Journals are therefore **books of original entry.** Companies may use different **special journals** to record specific types of recurring transactions. For example, a company may use one special journal to record sales on account, another to record purchases on account, a third to record cash receipts, and a fourth to record cash payments. Transactions that do not fall into any of these categories are recorded in the **general journal.** Although special journals can be useful, companies can keep records without them by recording all transactions in the general journal. For simplicity, this appendix illustrates a general journal only.

At a minimum, the general journal shows the dates, the account titles, and the amounts of each transaction. The date is recorded in the first column, followed by the title of the account to be debited. The title of the account to be credited is indented and written on the line directly below the account to be debited. The dollar amount of the transaction is recorded in the Debit and Credit columns. For example, providing services for $1,000 cash on August 1 would be recorded in general journal format as follows.

Date	Account Title	Debit	Credit
Aug. 1	Cash	1,000	
	Service Revenue		1,000

THE GENERAL LEDGER

The collection of all the accounts used by a particular business is called the **general ledger.** In a manual system, the ledger could be a book with pages for each account where entries are recorded by hand. In more sophisticated systems, the general ledger is maintained in electronic form. Data are entered into electronic ledgers using computer keyboards or scanners. Companies typically assign each ledger account a name and a number. A list of all ledger accounts and their account numbers is called the **chart of accounts.** As previously stated, accounting data are first recorded in journals. The data are then transferred to the ledger accounts through a process called **posting.** The posting process for the August 1, $1,000 revenue transaction is shown as follows.

Date	Account Title	Debit	Credit
Aug. 1	Cash	1,000	
	Service Revenue		1,000

	Cash			Service Revenue	
Aug. 1	1,000			Aug. 1	1,000

EXHIBIT B.1

Event No.	Account Title	Debit	Credit
1	Cash	28,000	
	Common Stock		28,000
2	Supplies	1,100	
	Accounts Payable		1,100
3	Prepaid Rent	12,000	
	Cash		12,000
4	Accounts Receivable	23,000	
	Consulting Revenue		23,000
5	General Operating Expenses	16,000	
	Accounts Payable		16,000
6	Cash	20,000	
	Accounts Receivable		20,000
7	Accounts Payable	13,000	
	Cash		13,000
8	Dividends	1,000	
	Cash		1,000
9	Supplies Expense	900	
	Supplies		900
10	Rent Expense	3,000	
	Prepaid Rent		3,000
11	Salaries Expense	1,200	
	Salaries Payable		1,200

ILLUSTRATION OF RECORDING PROCEDURES

We use the following transactions data to illustrate the process of recording transactions into a general journal and then posting them into a general ledger. The transactions data apply to the Mestro Financial Services Company. The journal entries are shown in Exhibit B.1. The general ledger after posting is shown in Exhibit B.2.

1. Acquired $28,000 cash by issuing common stock on January 1, Year 1.
2. Purchased $1,100 of supplies on account.
3. Paid $12,000 cash in advance for a one-year lease on office space.
4. Earned $23,000 of consulting revenue on account.
5. Incurred $16,000 of general operating expenses on account.
6. Collected $20,000 cash from receivables.
7. Paid $13,000 cash on accounts payable.
8. Paid a $1,000 cash dividend to stockholders.

Information for Adjusting Entries

9. There was $200 of supplies on hand at the end of the accounting period.
10. The one-year lease on the office space was effective beginning on October 1, Year 1.
11. There was $1,200 of accrued salaries at the end of Year 1.

EXHIBIT B.2

MESTRO FINANCIAL SERVICES COMPANY
T-Accounts, Year 1

Assets	=	Liabilities	+	Equity

Cash

1.	28,000	3.	12,000
6.	20,000	7.	13,000
		8.	1,000
Bal.	22,000		

Accounts Receivable

4.	23,000	6.	20,000
Bal.	3,000		

Supplies

2.	1,100	9.	900
Bal.	200		

Prepaid Rent

3.	12,000	10.	3,000
Bal.	9,000		

Accounts Payable

7.	13,000	2.	1,100
		5.	16,000
		Bal.	4,100

Salaries Payable

		11.	1,200
		Bal.	1,200

Common Stock

		1.	28,000
		Bal.	28,000

Dividends

8.	1,000

Consulting Revenue

		4.	23,000

General Operating Expenses

5.	16,000

Salaries Expense

11.	1,200

Supplies Expense

9.	900

Rent Expense

10.	3,000

Trial Balance

To test accuracy, accountants regularly prepare an internal accounting schedule called a **trial balance.** A trial balance lists every ledger account and its balance. Debit balances are listed in one column and credit balances are listed in an adjacent column. The columns are totaled and the totals are compared. Exhibit B.3 displays the trial balance for Mestro Financial Services Company after the adjusting entries have been posted to the ledger.

If the debit total does not equal the credit total, the accountant knows to search for an error. Even if the totals are equal, however, there may be errors in the accounting records. For example, equal trial balance totals would not disclose errors like the following: failure to record transactions; misclassifications, such as debiting the wrong account; or incorrectly recording the amount of a transaction, such as recording a $200 transaction as $2,000. Equal debits and credits in a trial balance provide evidence rather than proof of accuracy.

Financial Statements

Supplemented with details from the Cash and Common Stock ledger accounts, the trial balance (Exhibit B.3) provides the information to prepare the financial statements shown in Exhibit B.4.

EXHIBIT B.3

MESTRO FINANCIAL SERVICES COMPANY
Trial Balance
December 31, Year 1

Account Titles	Debit	Credit
Cash	$22,000	
Accounts receivable	3,000	
Supplies	200	
Prepaid rent	9,000	
Accounts payable		$ 4,100
Salaries payable		1,200
Common stock		28,000
Dividends	1,000	
Consulting revenue		23,000
General operating expenses	16,000	
Salaries expense	1,200	
Supplies expense	900	
Rent expense	3,000	
Totals	$56,300	$56,300

EXHIBIT B.4

MESTRO FINANCIAL SERVICES COMPANY
Financial Statements
For Year 1

Income Statement
For the Year Ended December 31, Year 1

Consulting revenue		$23,000
Expenses		
General operating expenses	$ 16,000	
Salaries expense	1,200	
Supplies expense	900	
Rent expense	3,000	
Total expenses		(21,100)
Net income		$ 1,900

Statement of Changes in Stockholders' Equity
For the Year Ended December 31, Year 1

Beginning common stock	$ 0	
Plus: Common stock issued	28,000	
Ending common stock		$28,000
Beginning retained earnings	0	
Plus: Net income	1,900	
Less: Dividends	(1,000)	
Ending retained earnings		900
Total stockholders' equity		$28,900

continued

Balance Sheet		
As of December 31, Year 1		
Assets		
Cash	$22,000	
Accounts receivable	3,000	
Supplies	200	
Prepaid rent	9,000	
Total assets		$34,200
Liabilities		
Accounts payable	$ 4,100	
Salaries payable	1,200	
Total liabilities		$ 5,300
Stockholders' equity		
Common stock	28,000	
Retained earnings	900	
Total stockholders' equity		28,900
Total liabilities and stockholders' equity		$34,200

Statement of Cash Flows		
For the Year Ended December 31, Year 1		
Cash flows from operating activities		
Inflow from customers	$20,000	
Outflow for expenses	(25,000)	
Net cash flow for operating activities		$ (5,000)
Cash flows from investing activities		0
Cash flows from financing activities		
Inflow from issue of common stock	28,000	
Outflow for dividends	(1,000)	
Net cash flow from financing activities		27,000
Net change in cash		22,000
Plus: Beginning cash balance		0
Ending cash balance		$22,000

KEY TERMS

Account balance 603	Debit 603	General ledger 604	Special journals 604
Books of original entry 604	Double-entry	Journal 604	T-account 603
Chart of accounts 604	accounting 603	Posting 604	Trial balance 606
Credit 603	General journal 604	Source documents 603	

EXERCISES

Appendix 1-1   *Debit/credit terminology*

Required

For each of the following independent events, identify the account that would be debited and the account that would be credited. The accounts for the first event are identified as an example.

Event	Account Debited	Account Credited
a	Cash	Common Stock

a. Received cash by issuing common stock.
b. Received cash for services to be performed in the future.
c. Provided services on account.
d. Paid accounts payable.
e. Paid cash in advance for one year's rent.
f. Paid cash for operating expenses.
g. Paid salaries payable.
h. Purchased supplies on account.
i. Paid cash dividends to the stockholders.
j. Recognized revenue for services completed; previously collected the cash in Event *b*.
k. Received cash in payment of accounts receivable.
l. Paid salaries expense.
m. Recognized expense for prepaid rent that had been used up by the end of the accounting period.

Appendix 1-2   *Recording transactions in general journal and T-accounts*

The following events apply to Pearson Service Co. for Year 1, its first year of operation:

1. Received cash of $50,000 from the issue of common stock.
2. Performed $90,000 worth of services on account.
3. Paid $64,000 cash for salaries expense.
4. Purchased supplies for $12,000 on account.
5. Collected $78,000 of accounts receivable.
6. Paid $8,500 of the accounts payable.
7. Paid a $5,000 dividend to the stockholders.
8. Had $1,500 of supplies on hand at the end of the period.

Required

a. Record these events in general journal form.
b. Post the entries to T-accounts and determine the ending balance in each account.
c. Determine the amount of total assets at the end of Year 1.
d. Determine the amount of net income for Year 1.

Appendix 1-3   *Recording events in the general journal, posting to T-accounts, and preparing a trial balance*

The following events apply to Complete Business Service in Year 1, its first year of operations:

1. Received $30,000 cash from the issue of common stock.
2. Earned $25,000 of service revenue on account.
3. Incurred $10,000 of operating expenses on account.
4. Received $20,000 cash for performing services.
5. Paid $8,000 cash to purchase land.
6. Collected $22,000 of cash from accounts receivable.
7. Received a $6,000 cash advance for services to be provided in the future.
8. Purchased $900 of supplies on account.
9. Made a $7,500 payment on accounts payable.
10. Paid a $5,000 cash dividend to the stockholders.
11. Recognized $500 of supplies expense.
12. Recognized $5,000 of revenue for services provided to the customer in Event 7.

Required

a. Record the events in the general journal.
b. Post the events to T-accounts and determine the ending account balances.
c. Test the equality of the debit and credit balances of the T-accounts by preparing a trial balance.

Appendix 1-4   *One complete accounting cycle*

The following events apply to Paradise Vacations's first year of operations:

1. Acquired $20,000 cash from the issue of common stock on January 1, Year 1.
2. Purchased $800 of supplies on account.
3. Paid $4,200 cash in advance for a one-year lease on office space.
4. Earned $28,000 of revenue on account.
5. Incurred $12,500 of other operating expenses on account.
6. Collected $24,000 cash from accounts receivable.
7. Paid $9,000 cash on accounts payable.
8. Paid a $3,000 cash dividend to the stockholders.

Information for Adjusting Entries

9. There was $150 of supplies on hand at the end of the accounting period.
10. The lease on the office space covered a one-year period beginning November 1.
11. There was $3,600 of accrued salaries at the end of the period.

Required

a. Record these transactions in general journal form.
b. Post the transaction data from the journal to ledger T-accounts.
c. Prepare a trial balance.
d. Prepare an income statement, statement of changes in stockholders' equity, a balance sheet, and a statement of cash flows.

APPENDIX C

Portion of the Form 10-K for Target Corporation

UNITED STATES
SECURITIES AND EXCHANGE COMMISSION
Washington, D.C. 20549
FORM 10-K

(Mark One)

☒   ANNUAL REPORT PURSUANT TO SECTION 13 OR 15(d) OF THE SECURITIES EXCHANGE ACT OF 1934

For the fiscal year ended February 2, 2019

OR

☐   TRANSITION REPORT PURSUANT TO SECTION 13 OR 15(d) OF THE SECURITIES EXCHANGE ACT OF 1934

For the transition period from   to

Commission file number **1-6049**

 **TARGET CORPORATION**

(Exact name of registrant as specified in its charter)

Minnesota	**41-0215170**
(State or other jurisdiction of incorporation or organization)	(I.R.S. Employer Identification No.)
1000 Nicollet Mall, Minneapolis, Minnesota	**55403**
(Address of principal executive offices)	(Zip Code)

Registrant's telephone number, including area code: 612/304-6073

Securities Registered Pursuant To Section 12(B) Of The Act:

Title of Each Class	**Name of Each Exchange on Which Registered**
Common Stock, par value $0.0833 per share	New York Stock Exchange

Securities registered pursuant to Section 12(g) of the Act: **None**

FORM 10-K. United States Securities and Exchange Commission

Indicate by check mark if the registrant is a well-known seasoned issuer, as defined in Rule 405 of the Securities Act. Yes ☒   No ☐

Indicate by check mark if the registrant is not required to file reports pursuant to Section 13 or Section 15(d) of the Act. Yes ☐   No ☒

Note – Checking the box above will not relieve any registrant required to file reports pursuant to Section 13 or 15(d) of the Exchange Act from their obligations under those Sections.

Indicate by check mark whether the registrant (1) has filed all reports required to be filed by Section 13 or 15(d) of the Securities Exchange Act of 1934 during the preceding 12 months (or for such shorter period that the registrant was required to file such reports), and (2) has been subject to such filing requirements for the past 90 days. Yes ☒   No ☐

Indicate by check mark whether the registrant has submitted electronically every Interactive Data File required to be submitted pursuant to Rule 405 of Regulation S-T (§232.405 of this chapter) during the preceding 12 months (or for such shorter period that the registrant was required to submit such files). Yes ☒   No ☐

Indicate by check mark if disclosure of delinquent filers pursuant to Item 405 of Regulation S-K (§229.405 of this chapter) is not contained herein, and will not be contained, to the best of registrant's knowledge, in definitive proxy or information statements incorporated by reference in Part III of this Form 10-K or any amendment to this Form 10-K. ☒

Indicate by check mark whether the registrant is a large accelerated filer, an accelerated filer, a non-accelerated filer, smaller reporting company, or an emerging growth company (as defined in Rule 12b-2 of the Exchange Act).

Large accelerated filer ☒   Accelerated filer ☐   Non-accelerated filer ☐

Smaller reporting company ☐   Emerging growth company ☐

If an emerging growth company, indicate by check mark if the registrant has elected not to use the extended transition period for complying with any new or revised financial accounting standards provided pursuant to Section 13(a) of the Exchange Act. ☐

Indicate by check mark whether the registrant is a shell company (as defined in Rule 12b-2 of the Act). Yes ☐ No ☒

The aggregate market value of the voting stock held by non-affiliates of the registrant as of August 4, 2018, was $42,763,636,334 based on the closing price of $81.45 per share of Common Stock as reported on the New York Stock Exchange Composite Index.

Indicate the number of shares outstanding of each of registrant's classes of Common Stock, as of the latest practicable date. Total shares of Common Stock, par value $0.0833, outstanding at March 7, 2019, were 516,333,213.

DOCUMENTS INCORPORATED BY REFERENCE

Portions of Target's Proxy Statement for the Annual Meeting of Shareholders to be held on June 12, 2019, are incorporated into Part III.

Item 8. Financial Statements and Supplementary Data

Report of Management on the Consolidated Financial Statements

Management is responsible for the consistency, integrity, and presentation of the information in the Annual Report. The consolidated financial statements and other information presented in this Annual Report have been prepared in accordance with accounting principles generally accepted in the United States and include necessary judgments and estimates by management.

To fulfill our responsibility, we maintain comprehensive systems of internal control designed to provide reasonable assurance that assets are safeguarded and transactions are executed in accordance with established procedures. The concept of reasonable assurance is based upon recognition that the cost of the controls should not exceed the benefit derived. We believe our systems of internal control provide this reasonable assurance.

The Board of Directors exercised its oversight role with respect to the Corporation's systems of internal control primarily through its Audit Committee, which is comprised of independent directors. The Committee oversees the Corporation's systems of internal control, accounting practices, financial reporting and audits to assess whether their quality, integrity, and objectivity are sufficient to protect shareholders' investments.

In addition, our consolidated financial statements have been audited by Ernst & Young LLP, independent registered public accounting firm, whose report also appears on this page.

/s/ Brian C. Cornell

Brian C. Cornell
Chairman and Chief Executive Officer
March 13, 2019

/s/ Cathy R. Smith

Cathy R. Smith
Executive Vice President and
Chief Financial Officer

Report of Independent Registered Public Accounting Firm

To the Shareholders and the Board of Directors of Target Corporation

Opinion on the Financial Statements

We have audited the accompanying consolidated statements of financial position of Target Corporation (the Corporation) as of February 2, 2019 and February 3, 2018, the related consolidated statements of operations, comprehensive income, cash flows and shareholders' investment for each of the three years in the period ended February 2, 2019, and the related notes (collectively referred to as the "consolidated financial statements"). In our opinion, the consolidated financial statements present fairly, in all material respects, the financial position of the Corporation at February 2, 2019 and February 3, 2018, and the results of its operations and its cash flows for each of the three years in the period ended February 2, 2019, in conformity with U.S. generally accepted accounting principles.

We also have audited, in accordance with the standards of the Public Company Accounting Oversight Board (United States) (PCAOB), the Corporation's internal control over financial reporting as of February 2, 2019, based on criteria established in *Internal Control-Integrated Framework* issued by the Committee of Sponsoring Organizations of the Treadway Commission (2013 framework) and our report dated March 13, 2019, expressed an unqualified opinion thereon.

Adoption of New Accounting Standards

ASU No. 2014-09
As discussed in Note 2 to the consolidated financial statements, the Corporation changed its method for recognizing revenue in 2018 due to the adoption of ASU No. 2014-09, Revenue from Contracts with Customers, as amended, effective February 4, 2018, using the full retrospective approach.

ASU No. 2016-02
As discussed in Note 2 to the consolidated financial statements, the Corporation changed its method of accounting for leases in 2018 due to the adoption of ASU No. 2016-02, Leases (Topic 842), as amended, effective February 4, 2018, using the modified retrospective approach.

Basis for Opinion

These financial statements are the responsibility of the Corporation's management. Our responsibility is to express an opinion on the Corporation's financial statements based on our audits. We are a public accounting firm registered with the PCAOB and are required to be independent with respect to the Corporation in accordance with the U.S. federal securities laws and the applicable rules and regulations of the Securities and Exchange Commission and the PCAOB.

We conducted our audits in accordance with the standards of the PCAOB. Those standards require that we plan and perform the audit to obtain reasonable assurance about whether the financial statements are free of material misstatement, whether due to error or fraud. Our audits included performing procedures to assess the risks of material misstatement of the financial statements, whether due to error or fraud, and performing procedures that respond to those risks. Such procedures included examining, on a test basis, evidence regarding the amounts and disclosures in the financial statements. Our audits also included evaluating the accounting principles used and significant estimates made by management, as well as evaluating the overall presentation of the financial statements. We believe that our audits provide a reasonable basis for our opinion.

/s/ Ernst & Young LLP

We have served as the Corporation's auditor since 1931.

Minneapolis, Minnesota
March 13, 2019

Report of Management on Internal Control over Financial Reporting

Our management is responsible for establishing and maintaining adequate internal control over financial reporting, as such term is defined in Exchange Act Rules 13a-15(f). Under the supervision and with the participation of our management, including our chief executive officer and chief financial officer, we assessed the effectiveness of our internal control over financial reporting as of February 2, 2019, based on the framework in *Internal Control—Integrated Framework (2013)*, issued by the Committee of Sponsoring Organizations of the Treadway Commission (2013 framework). Based on our assessment, we conclude that the Corporation's internal control over financial reporting is effective based on those criteria.

Our internal control over financial reporting as of February 2, 2019, has been audited by Ernst & Young LLP, the independent registered public accounting firm who has also audited our consolidated financial statements, as stated in their report which appears on this page.

/s/ Brian C. Cornell	/s/ Cathy R. Smith
Brian C. Cornell	Cathy R. Smith
Chairman and Chief Executive Officer	Executive Vice President and
March 13, 2019	Chief Financial Officer

Report of Independent Registered Public Accounting Firm

To the Shareholders and the Board of Directors of Target Corporation

Opinion on Internal Control over Financial Reporting

We have audited Target Corporation's internal control over financial reporting as of February 2, 2019, based on criteria established in Internal Control—Integrated Framework issued by the Committee of Sponsoring Organizations of the Treadway Commission (2013 framework) (the COSO criteria). In our opinion, Target Corporation (the Corporation) maintained, in all material respects, effective internal control over financial reporting as of February 2, 2019, based on the COSO criteria.

We also have audited, in accordance with the standards of the Public Company Accounting Oversight Board (United States) (PCAOB), the consolidated statements of financial position of the Corporation as of February 2, 2019 and February 3, 2018, the related consolidated statements of operations, comprehensive income, cash flows and shareholders' investment for each of the three years in the period ended February 2, 2019, and the related notes and our report dated March 13, 2019 expressed an unqualified opinion thereon.

Basis for Opinion

The Corporation's management is responsible for maintaining effective internal control over financial reporting and for its assessment of the effectiveness of internal control over financial reporting included in the accompanying Report of Management on Internal Control over Financial Reporting. Our responsibility is to express an opinion on the Corporation's internal control over financial reporting based on our audit. We are a public accounting firm registered with the PCAOB and are required to be independent with respect to the Corporation in accordance with the U.S. federal securities laws and the applicable rules and regulations of the Securities and Exchange Commission and the PCAOB.

We conducted our audit in accordance with the standards of the PCAOB. Those standards require that we plan and perform the audit to obtain reasonable assurance about whether effective internal control over financial reporting was maintained in all material respects.

Our audit included obtaining an understanding of internal control over financial reporting, assessing the risk that a material weakness exists, testing and evaluating the design and operating effectiveness of internal control based on the assessed risk, and performing such other procedures as we considered necessary in the circumstances. We believe that our audit provides a reasonable basis for our opinion.

Definition and Limitations of Internal Control Over Financial Reporting

A company's internal control over financial reporting is a process designed to provide reasonable assurance regarding the reliability of financial reporting and the preparation of financial statements for external purposes in accordance with generally accepted accounting principles. A company's internal control over financial reporting includes those policies and procedures that (1) pertain to the maintenance of records that, in reasonable detail, accurately and fairly reflect the transactions and dispositions of the assets of the company; (2) provide reasonable assurance that transactions are recorded as necessary to permit preparation of financial statements in accordance with generally accepted accounting principles, and that receipts and expenditures of the company are being made only in accordance with authorizations of management and directors of the company; and (3) provide reasonable assurance regarding prevention or timely detection of unauthorized acquisition, use, or disposition of the company's assets that could have a material effect on the financial statements.

Because of its inherent limitations, internal control over financial reporting may not prevent or detect misstatements. Also, projections of any evaluation of effectiveness to future periods are subject to the risk that controls may become inadequate because of changes in conditions, or that the degree of compliance with the policies or procedures may deteriorate.

/s/ Ernst & Young LLP

Minneapolis, Minnesota
March 13, 2019

Consolidated Statements of Operations

(millions, except per share data)	2018	2017 As Adjusted[a]	2016 As Adjusted[a]
Sales	$74,433	$71,786	$69,414
Other revenue	923	928	857
Total revenue	75,356	72,714	70,271
Cost of sales	53,299	51,125	49,145
Selling, general and administrative expenses	15,723	15,140	14,217
Depreciation and amortization (exclusive of depreciation included in cost of sales)	2,224	2,225	2,045
Operating income	4,110	4,224	4,864
Net interest expense	461	653	991
Net other (income)/expense	(27)	(59)	(88)
Earnings from continuing operations before income taxes	3,676	3,630	3,961
Provision for income taxes	746	722	1,295
Net earnings from continuing operations	2,930	2,908	2,666
Discontinued operations, net of tax	7	6	68
Net earnings	$ 2,937	$ 2,914	$ 2,734
Basic earnings per share			
Continuing operations	$ 5.54	$ 5.32	$ 4.61
Discontinued operations	0.01	0.01	0.12
Net earnings per share	$ 5.55	$ 5.32	$ 4.73
Diluted earnings per share			
Continuing operations	$ 5.50	$ 5.29	$ 4.58
Discontinued operations	0.01	0.01	0.12
Net earnings per share	$ 5.51	$ 5.29	$ 4.69
Weighted average common shares outstanding			
Basic	528.6	546.8	577.6
Diluted	533.2	550.3	582.5
Antidilutive shares	—	4.1	0.1

Note: Per share amounts may not foot due to rounding.
See accompanying Notes to Consolidated Financial Statements.
[a]Refer to Note 2 regarding the adoption of new accounting standards for revenue recognition, leases, and pensions.

Consolidated Statements of Comprehensive Income

(millions)	2018	2017 As Adjusted[a]	2016 As Adjusted[a]
Net earnings	$2,937	$2,914	$2,734
Other comprehensive (loss)/income, net of tax			
Pension and other benefit liabilities, net of tax	(52)	2	(13)
Currency translation adjustment and cash flow hedges, net of tax	(6)	6	4
Other comprehensive (loss)/income	(58)	8	(9)
Comprehensive income	$2,879	$2,922	$2,725

See accompanying Notes to Consolidated Financial Statements.
[a]Refer to Note 2 regarding the adoption of new accounting standards for revenue recognition, leases, and pensions.

Consolidated Statements of Financial Position

(millions, except footnotes)	February 2, 2019	February 3, 2018 As Adjusted[a]
Assets		
Cash and cash equivalents	$ 1,556	$ 2,643
Inventory	9,497	8,597
Other current assets	1,466	1,300
Total current assets	12,519	12,540
Property and equipment		
Land	6,064	6,095
Buildings and improvements	29,240	28,131
Fixtures and equipment	5,912	5,623
Computer hardware and software	2,544	2,645
Construction-in-progress	460	440
Accumulated depreciation	(18,687)	(18,398)
Property and equipment, net	25,533	24,536
Operating lease assets	1,965	1,884
Other noncurrent assets	1,273	1,343
Total assets	$ 41,290	$40,303
Liabilities and shareholders' investment		
Accounts payable	$ 9,761	$ 8,677
Accrued and other current liabilities	4,201	4,094
Current portion of long-term debt and other borrowings	1,052	281
Total current liabilities	15,014	13,052
Long-term debt and other borrowings	10,223	11,117
Noncurrent operating lease liabilities	2,004	1,924
Deferred income taxes	972	693
Other noncurrent liabilities	1,780	1,866
Total noncurrent liabilities	14,979	15,600
Shareholders' investment		
Common stock	43	45
Additional paid-in capital	6,042	5,858
Retained earnings	6,017	6,495
Accumulated other comprehensive loss	(805)	(747)
Total shareholders' investment	11,297	11,651
Total liabilities and shareholders' investment	$ 41,290	$40,303

Common Stock Authorized 6,000,000,000 shares, $0.0833 par value; 517,761,600 shares issued and outstanding at February 2, 2019; 541,681,670 shares issued and outstanding at February 3, 2018.
Preferred Stock Authorized 5,000,000 shares, $0.01 par value; no shares were issued or outstanding at February 2, 2019 or February 3, 2018.
See accompanying Notes to Consolidated Financial Statements.
[a]Refer to Note 2 regarding the adoption of new accounting standards for revenue recognition, leases, and pensions.

Consolidated Statements of Cash Flows

(millions)	2018	2017 As Adjusted[a]	2016 As Adjusted[a]
Operating activities			
Net earnings	$ 2,937	$ 2,914	$ 2,734
Earnings from discontinued operations, net of tax	7	6	68
Net earnings from continuing operations	2,930	2,908	2,666
Adjustments to reconcile net earnings to cash provided by operations:			
Depreciation and amortization	2,474	2,476	2,318
Share-based compensation expense	132	112	113
Deferred income taxes	322	(188)	40
Loss on debt extinguishment	—	123	422
Noncash losses/(gains) and other, net	95	208	(11)
Changes in operating accounts:			
Inventory	(900)	(348)	293
Other assets	(299)	(156)	56
Accounts payable	1,127	1,307	(166)
Accrued and other liabilities	89	419	(394)
Cash provided by operating activities—continuing operations	5,970	6,861	5,337
Cash provided by operating activities—discontinued operations	3	74	107
Cash provided by operations	5,973	6,935	5,444
Investing activities			
Expenditures for property and equipment	(3,516)	(2,533)	(1,547)
Proceeds from disposal of property and equipment	85	31	46
Cash paid for acquisitions, net of cash assumed	—	(518)	—
Other investments	15	(55)	28
Cash required for investing activities	(3,416)	(3,075)	(1,473)
Financing activities			
Additions to long-term debt	—	739	1,977
Reductions of long-term debt	(281)	(2,192)	(2,649)
Dividends paid	(1,335)	(1,338)	(1,348)
Repurchase of stock	(2,124)	(1,046)	(3,706)
Stock option exercises	96	108	221
Cash required for financing activities	(3,644)	(3,729)	(5,505)
Net (decrease)/increase in cash and cash equivalents	(1,087)	131	(1,534)
Cash and cash equivalents at beginning of period	2,643	2,512	4,046
Cash and cash equivalents at end of period	$ 1,556	$ 2,643	$ 2,512
Supplemental information			
Interest paid, net of capitalized interest	$ 476	$678	$ 999
Income taxes paid	373	934	1,514
Leased assets obtained in exchange for new finance lease liabilities	130	139	252
Leased assets obtained in exchange for new operating lease liabilities	246	212	148

See accompanying Notes to Consolidated Financial Statements.

[a]Refer to Note 2 regarding the adoption of new accounting standards for revenue recognition, leases, and pensions.

Consolidated Statements of Shareholders' Investment

(millions)	Common Stock Shares	Stock Par Value	Additional Paid-in Capital	Retained Earnings *As Adjusted*[a]	Accumulated Other Comprehensive (Loss) / Income	Total
January 30, 2016	602.2	$50	$5,348	$8,196	$(629)	$12,965
Adoption of ASC Topic 842 (Leases)	—	—	—	(43)	—	(43)
Net earnings	—	—	—	2,734	—	2,734
Other comprehensive loss	—	—	—	—	(9)	(9)
Dividends declared	—	—	—	(1,359)	—	(1,359)
Repurchase of stock	(50.9)	(4)	—	(3,682)	—	(3,686)
Stock options and awards	4.9	—	313	—	—	313
January 28, 2017	556.2	$46	$5,661	$5,846	$(638)	$10,915
Net earnings	—	—	—	2,914	—	2,914
Other comprehensive income	—	—	—	—	8	8
Dividends declared	—	—	—	(1,356)	—	(1,356)
Repurchase of stock	(17.6)	(1)	—	(1,026)	—	(1,027)
Stock options and awards	3.1	—	197	—	—	197
Reclassification of tax effects to retained earnings	—	—	—	117	(117)	—
February 3, 2018	541.7	$45	$5,858	$6,495	$(747)	$11,651
Net earnings	—	—	—	2,937	—	2,937
Other comprehensive loss	—	—	—	—	(58)	(58)
Dividends declared	—	—	—	(1,347)	—	(1,347)
Repurchase of stock	(27.2)	(2)	—	(2,068)	—	(2,070)
Stock options and awards	3.3	—	184	—	—	184
February 2, 2019	517.8	$43	$6,042	$6,017	$(805)	$11,297

We declared $2.54, $2.46, and $2.36 dividends per share for the twelve months ended February 2, 2019, February 3, 2018, and January 28, 2017, respectively.

See accompanying Notes to Consolidated Financial Statements.

[a]Refer to Note 2 regarding the adoption of new accounting standards for revenue recognition, leases, and pensions.

Big Data and Data Visualizations Overview

Over the last decade, big data has fundamentally transformed the managerial decision process and provided a new insightful way for managers to gauge company performance. *Big data* is a term that describes the large volume of information primarily captured by a variety of computerized systems. As a result of the Internet and advanced computerized devices, we have created more data in the last two years than in the history of the entire human race. This data is comprised of all types of information in both quantitative and qualitative form. Companies have begun collecting data in many forms including financial information, customer demographics, and geographical information, to name a few.

While the rate at which data is being created and captured has exploded over the last decade, it is how companies utilize this data to make informed business decisions that makes the real difference in company performance. As an example, we have all seen major companies such as Google and Facebook collect large amounts of personal data from its customers in order to generate personalized ads. These ads represent the major sources of revenue for these tech giants, making big data a key element to their success. Other companies such as Salesforce.com have relied on big data to retain employees by examining wage disparities between men and women serving in the same role. Results from their analysis revealed that wages were not consistent across genders, allowing the company to make the needed corrections to retain some of their top talent. The possibilities of using big data to improve enterprises are endless; however, companies require some powerful tools to analyze and process all this data to extract meaningful information.

Clive Humby is quoted as saying "Data is the new oil. It's valuable, but if unrefined it cannot really be used. It has to be changed into gas, plastic, chemicals, etc to create a valuable entity that drives profitable activity; so must data be broken down, analyzed for it to have value."* This quote exemplifies the importance of using analytical tools to extract the information an enterprise needs to make informed business decisions. Over the last decade, many software applications have been released to the market to assist managers in making use of big data. The tools perform a variety of functions in the big data environment including data crawlers that capture all types of information from a variety of websites, tools that convert unstructured data into a structured form that can be analyzed, and software that converts data into a visual form making interpretation of the data far easier to interpret. These examples represent only a small subset of the functions these tools perform. To provide an example of how big data can assist managers in making decisions, this appendix will focus on the third function, data visualizations.

We have all heard the quote that a picture is worth a thousand words, and this is certainly true when it comes to data visualizations. Data visualizations replace columns and rows of data with statistical graphics, plots, and information graphics. Examining data in visual form allows users to gain insights into their business far more efficiently than trying to make sense of raw data. One of the leading software tools for creating and analyzing data visualizations is called Tableau. The remainder of this appendix will give you the opportunity to learn more about Tableau by teaching you how to upload data into Tableau, create data visualizations from a raw dataset, and set up user dashboards that organize multiple data elements into a summary format.

Tableau Demonstration

In order to complete the exercise outlined in this appendix, you will need to download the student version of Tableau at the following URL: https://www.tableau.com/academic/students. We have provided a dataset (Super Store) for use in this exercise that can be

*Humby, Clive. 2006. ANA Senior marketer's summit, Kellogg School.

obtained through *Connect*. Once you have downloaded Tableau and the "Super Store" dataset to your computer, we recommend watching the introduction to Tableau training video included in *Connect*. This video will walk you through the basics of Tableau and demonstrate the Tableau procedures required to complete all assignments.

Conducting Financial Statement Analysis in Tableau

This demonstration involves analyzing a dataset for Super Store, a retailer of office supplies. The company was founded by Jim Rogers, who knows a lot about office supplies, but relies on his management team to help him understand vast amount of data supplied by the company's computer systems. Super Store has performed exceptionally well over the last three years due to its rapid expansion into new markets. One of the major changes at Super Store over the last year was its expansion into the international market by opening stores in India. India's rapidly growing economy compounded by the shortage of office supply stores has provided a prosperous opportunity for Super Store. However, the expansion into international markets has come with challenges resulting in Super Store management needing additional tools and expertise to understand how this new market is affecting its business.

Assume you were recently hired by Super Store management to assist the company in preparing data visualizations for financial statement analysis using Tableau. Historically, the company has relied on companywide ratios to gauge performance but would like you to dig deeper into these ratios to provide a more detailed picture of operations at Super Store.

Super Store management has asked you to analyze two companywide ratios: accounts receivable turnover and inventory turnover. Refer to Chapter 9 for descriptions of these ratios and equations for how they are calculated. The company has provided you with a dataset containing a large variety of company data for use in your analysis. Recall that the dataset is called "Super Store" and can be found on the *Connect* course website.

Accounts Receivable Turnover

Historically, Super Store has analyzed the companywide accounts receivable ratio to gauge the quality of its collection policies and procedures. The company calculates this ratio using the following equation:

$$\frac{\text{Net Credit Sales}}{\text{Average Accounts Receivable}}$$

For purposes of this example, we assume Super Store's prior year accounts receivable balance was $4,975,830. Using this balance and the current year balance from the Super Store dataset, the AR turnover ratio for the company would be calculated as follows:

$$\frac{\$52,267,354}{(\$4,975,830 + \$5,795,254) / 2} = 9.71$$

The ratio of 9.71 tells us that the company collects its accounts receivable balances a little under 10 times a year. To make more sense of this number, the company also calculates the average number of days that accounts receivable is outstanding using the following equation:

$$\frac{365 \text{ days}}{\text{Accounts Receivable Turnover}}$$

Using this equation, the company's average days outstanding is:

$$\frac{365}{9.71} = 38 \text{ days}$$

These companywide ratios tell management that, as a whole, the company collects its receivable a little under 10 times a year or every 38 days. Overall, these ratios would indicate that the company does a good job at collecting its outstanding receivable balances, indicating that its current policies and procedures for accounts receivable are effective. Relying solely on these companywide ratios would likely result in management making no changes to its current collection processes.

While the prior ratios are useful in gauging companywide performance, Super Store management has requested more detailed information analyzing collections across geographic regions. Specifically, management wants to know how collections differ between their stores in the United States compared to the stores in India. Jim Rogers, founder of Super Store, has asked you to prepare a data visualization that he can use for presentation purposes analyzing the turnover ratios.

In order to assist Mr. Rogers, you will be using Tableau to conduct analysis on the Super Store dataset. Begin by opening the Tableau program and adding the Super Store data file to Tableau. Refer to the Introduction to Tableau video for instructions on how to add a dataset to Tableau and complete the visualization for Mr. Rogers.

The following two visualizations illustrate the accounts receivable turnover ratio and average days outstanding for the United States and India.

Both of these visualizations clearly show that there are large differences between the United States and India accounts receivable ratios. For the average days outstanding ratio, the color green indicates lower values and red represents higher values. Since most people associate good news with green and bad news with red, this color scheme appropriately reflects how to interpret this ratio. For the AR turnover ratio, higher numbers would be representative of good news; therefore, the color green was assigned to higher values and red to lower values. Using a common color scheme such as red for negative news and green for positive news sends a clear indicator about which country is performing better. Using the legend in the top right of the visualization gives us number information that correspond to the colors. If you hover over each country, Tableau will display the exact numerical balance for each country.

Mr. Rogers could easily present these two visualizations to indicate to interested parties that the company is suffering collection problems in India as compared to the United States. These visualizations exemplify the importance of using visualizations to separate the ratios by country in order to better understand the differences between the two countries as compared to analyzing the ratios in total.

ASSIGNMENT

The following question pertains to the information provided in Appendix D. For additional practice using Tableau, a more detailed assignment is provided in *Connect*.

Required

Write a paragraph explaining the ratios for each country and what they mean in regards to the company's ability to collect its outstanding receivables in each country. Speculate as to the reasons for these differences and what the company could do to improve issues noted in the ratios.

2/10, n/30 Expression meaning the seller will allow the purchaser a 2 percent discount off the gross invoice price if the purchaser pays cash for the merchandise within 10 days from the date of purchase.

absolute amounts Dollar totals reported in accounts on financial reports that can be misleading because they make no reference to the relative size of the company being analyzed.

accelerated depreciation method Depreciation method that recognizes depreciation expense more rapidly in the early stages of an asset's life than in the later stages of its life.

account Record of classified and summarized transaction data; component of financial statement elements.

account balance Difference between total debits and total credits in an account.

account receivable Expected future cash receipt arising from permitting a customer to *buy now and pay later;* typically a relatively small balance due within a short time period.

accounting Service-based profession that provides reliable and relevant financial information useful in making decisions.

accounting equation Expression of the relationship between the assets and the claims on those assets.

accounting event Economic occurrence that changes a company's assets, liabilities, or equity.

accounting period Span of time covered by the financial statements, normally one year, but may be a quarter, a month, or some other time span.

accounts receivable turnover Financial ratio that measures how fast accounts receivable are turned into cash; computed by dividing sales by accounts receivable.

accrual Recognition of events before exchanging cash.

accrual accounting Accounting system that recognizes expenses or revenues when they occur regardless of when cash is exchanged.

accrued expenses Expenses that are recognized before cash is paid. An example is accrued salaries expense.

accrued interest Interest revenue or expense that is recognized before cash has been exchanged.

accumulated conversion factor Factor used to convert a series of future cash flows into their present value equivalent when applied to cash flows of equal amounts spread over equal interval time periods; this factor can be computed by adding the individual single factors applicable to each period.

accumulated depreciation Contra asset account that indicates the sum of all depreciation expense recognized for an asset since the date of acquisition.

acid-test ratio Measure of immediate debt-paying ability; calculated by dividing very liquid assets (cash, receivables, and marketable securities) by current liabilities.

activities The actions taken by an organization to accomplish its mission.

activity base Factor that causes changes in variable cost; is usually some measure of volume when used to define cost behavior.

activity-based management (ABM) Management of the activities of an organization to add the greatest value by developing products that satisfy the needs of that organization's customers.

adjusting entry Entry that updates account balances prior to preparing financial statements.

adverse opinion Opinion issued by a certified public accountant that means one or more departures from GAAP in a company's financial statements are so very material the auditors believe the financial statements do not fairly represent the company's status; contrast with *unqualified opinion.*

aging of accounts receivable Classifying each account receivable by the number of days it has been outstanding. The aging schedule is used to develop an estimate of the amount of the allowance for doubtful accounts.

allocation Process of dividing a total cost into parts and apportioning the parts among the relevant cost objects.

allocation base Cost driver used as the basis for the allocation process.

allocation rate Factor used to allocate or assign costs to a cost object; determined by taking the total cost to be allocated and dividing it by the appropriate cost driver.

allowance for doubtful accounts Contra asset account that contains an amount equal to the accounts receivable that are expected to be uncollectible.

allowance method of accounting for uncollectible accounts Method of accounting for uncollectible accounts in which uncollectible accounts are estimated and expensed in the same period in which the corresponding sales are recognized. The receivables are reported in the financial statements at net realizable value (the amount expected to be collected in cash).

American Institute of Certified Public Accountants (AICPA)
National association that serves the educational and professional interests of members of the public accounting profession; membership is voluntary.

amortization Method of systematically allocating the costs of intangible assets to expense over their useful lives; also term for converting the discount on a note or a bond to interest expense over a designated period.

annual report Document in which an organization provides information to stockholders, usually on an annual basis.

annuity Series of equal payments made over a specified number of periods.

appropriated retained earnings Retained earnings restricted by the board of directors for a specific purpose (e.g., to repay debt or for future expansion); although a part of total retained earnings, not available for distribution as dividends.

articles of incorporation Items on an application filed with a state agency for the formation of a corporation; contains such information as the corporation's name, its purpose, its location, its expected life, provisions for its capital stock, and a list of the members of its board of directors.

articulation Characteristic of financial statements that means they are interrelated. For example, the amount of net income reported on the income statement is added to beginning retained earnings as a component in calculating the ending retained earnings balance reported on the statement of changes in stockholders' equity.

asset Economic resource used to produce revenue that is expected to provide future benefit to the business.

asset exchange transaction Transaction that decreases one asset while increasing another asset so that total assets do not change; for example, the purchase of land with cash.

asset replacement decisions Decisions regarding whether existing assets should be replaced with newer assets based on identification and comparison of the avoidable costs of the old and new asset to determine which asset is more profitable to operate.

asset source transaction Transaction that increases an asset and a claim on assets; three types of asset source transactions are acquisitions from owners (equity), borrowings from creditors (liabilities), or earnings from operations (revenues).

asset turnover ratio   The amount of net sales divided by average total assets.

asset use transaction   A transaction that decreases both an asset and a claim on assets; the three types of asset use transactions are distributions (transfers to owners), liability payments (to creditors), or expenses (costs incurred to operate the business).

audit   Detailed examination of some aspect of a company's accounting records or operating procedures in order to report the results to interested parties.

authority manual   A document that outlines the chain of command for authority and responsibility. The authority manual provides guidelines for specific positions such as personnel officer as well as general authority, such as all vice presidents are authorized to spend up to a designated limit.

authorized stock   Number of shares that the corporation is approved by the state to issue.

average cost   The total cost of making products divided by the total number of products made.

average days to collect accounts receivable (average collection period)   Measure of how quickly, on average, a business collects its accounts receivable; calculated as 365 divided by the accounts receivable turnover.

average days to sell inventory (average days in inventory)   Financial ratio that measures the average number of days that inventory stays in stock before it is sold.

avoidable costs   Future costs that can be avoided by taking a specified course of action. To be avoidable in a decision-making context, costs must differ among the alternatives. For example, if the cost of material used to make two different products is the same for both products, that cost could not be avoided by choosing to produce one product over the other. Therefore, the material's cost would not be an avoidable cost.

bad debts expense   An expense resulting from a decrease in the amount of accounts receivable due to the inability to collect balances due from debtors. The term is a synonym for uncollectible accounts expense.

balance sheet   Financial statement that reports a company's assets and the corresponding claims (liabilities and equity) on those assets as of a specific date (usually as of the end of the accounting period).

balanced scorecard   A management evaluation tool that includes financial and nonfinancial measures.

bank reconciliation   Schedule that identifies and explains differences between the cash balance reported by the bank and the cash balance in the firm's accounting records.

bank statement   Statement issued by a bank (usually monthly) that denotes all activity in the bank account for that period.

bank statement credit memo   Memorandum that describes an increase in the account balance.

bank statement debit memo   Memorandum that describes a decrease in the account balance.

basket purchase   Acquisition of several assets in a single transaction with no specific cost attributed to each asset.

batch-level costs   The costs associated with producing a batch of products. For example, the cost of setting up machinery to produce 1,000 products is a batch-level cost. The classification of batch-level costs is context sensitive. Postage for one product would be classified as a unit-level cost. In contrast, postage for a large number of products delivered in a single shipment would be classified as a batch-level cost.

benchmarking   Identifying the best practices used by world-class competitors.

best practices   Practices used by world-class companies.

board of directors   Group of individuals elected by the stockholders of a corporation to oversee its operations.

bond certificate   Debt security used to obtain long-term financing in which a company borrows funds from a number of lenders, called *bondholders;* usually issued in denominations of $1,000.

bond discount   Difference between the selling price and the face amount of a bond sold for less than the face amount.

bond premium   Difference between the selling price and the face amount of a bond that is sold for more than the face amount.

bondholder   The party buying a bond (the lender or creditor).

book of original entry   A journal in which transactions are first recorded.

book value   Historical (original) cost of an asset minus the accumulated depreciation; alternatively, undepreciated amount to date.

book value per share   An accounting measure of a share of common stock, computed by dividing total stockholders' equity less preferred rights by the number of common shares outstanding.

break-even point   Point where total revenue equals total cost; can be expressed in units or sales dollars.

budgeting   Form of planning that formalizes a company's goals and objectives in financial terms.

capital budgeting   Financial planning activities that cover the intermediate range of time such as whether to buy or lease equipment, whether to purchase a particular investment, or whether to increase operating expenses to stimulate sales.

capital expenditures (on an existing asset)   Substantial amounts of funds spent to improve an asset's quality or to extend its life.

capital investments   Expenditures for the purchase of operational assets that involve a long-term commitment of funds that can be critically important to the company's ultimate success; normally recovered through the use of the assets.

carrying value   Face amount of a bond liability less any unamortized bond discount or plus any unamortized bond premium.

cash   Coins, currency, checks, balances in checking and certain savings accounts, money orders, bank drafts, certificates of deposit, and other items that are payable on demand.

cash budget   A budget that focuses on cash receipts and payments that are expected to occur in the future.

cash discount   Discount offered on merchandise sold to encourage prompt payment; offered by sellers of merchandise and represents sales discounts to the seller when they are used and purchase discounts to the purchaser of the merchandise.

certified check   Check guaranteed by a bank to be drawn on an account having funds sufficient to pay the check.

certified public accountant (CPA)   Accountant who, by meeting certain educational and experiential requirements, is licensed by the state government to provide audit services to the public.

certified suppliers   Suppliers who have gained the confidence of the buyer by providing quality goods and services at desirable prices and usually in accordance with strict delivery specifications; frequently provide the buyer with preferred customer status in exchange for guaranteed purchase quantities and prompt payment schedules.

chart of accounts   List of all ledger accounts and their corresponding account numbers.

checks   Prenumbered forms, sometimes multicopy, with the name of the business issuing them preprinted on the face, indicating to whom they are paid, the amount of the payment, and the transaction date.

claims   Owners' and creditors' interests in a business's assets.

claims exchange transaction   Transaction that decreases one claim and increases another so that total claims do not change. For example, the accrual of interest expense is a claims exchange transaction; liabilities increase, and the recognition of the expense causes retained earnings to decrease.

classified balance sheet   Balance sheet that distinguishes between current and noncurrent items.

closely held corporation   Corporation whose stock is exchanged between a limited number of individuals.

closing (the books)   Bookkeeping technique of transferring balances from the temporary accounts (Revenue, Expense, and Dividends) to the permanent account (Retained Earnings).

Code of Professional Conduct   A set of guidelines established by the American Institute of Certified Public Accountants (AICPA) to promote high ethical conduct among its membership.

collateral   Assets pledged as security for a loan.

common costs   Costs that are incurred to support more than one cost object but cannot be traced to any specific object.

common size financial statements   Financial statements in which amounts are converted to percentages to allow a better comparison of period-to-period and company-to-company financial data since all information is placed on a common basis.

common stock   Basic class of corporate stock that carries no preferences as to claims on assets or dividends; certificates that evidence ownership in a company.

confidentiality   Code of ethics requirement that prohibits CPAs from voluntarily disclosing information they acquire as a result of accountant–client relationships.

consistency   The generally accepted accounting principle that a company should, in most circumstances, continually use the same accounting method(s) so that its financial statements are comparable across time.

contingent liability   A potential obligation, the amount of which depends on the outcome of future events.

continuity   Concept that describes the fact that a corporation's life may extend well beyond the time at which any particular shareholder decides to retire or to sell his or her stock.

continuous improvement   Total quality management (TQM) feature that refers to an ongoing process through which employees learn to eliminate waste, reduce response time, minimize defects, and simplify the design and delivery of products and services to customers.

contra asset account   Account subtracted from another account with which it is associated; has the effect of reducing the asset account with which it is associated.

contribution margin   Difference between a company's sales revenue and total variable cost; represents the amount available to cover fixed cost and thereafter to provide a profit.

contribution margin per unit   The contribution margin per unit is equal to the sales price per unit minus the variable cost per unit.

controllability concept   Evaluating managerial performance based only on revenue and costs under the manager's direct control.

controllable costs   Costs that can be influenced by a particular manager's decisions and actions.

copyright   Legal protection of writings, musical compositions, and other intellectual property for the exclusive use of the creator or persons assigned the right by the creator.

corporation   Legal entity separate from its owners; formed when a group of individuals with a common purpose join together in an organization according to state laws.

cost   An amount paid to acquire a resource (asset) or to pay for a resource that has been consumed. Incurring a cost results in an asset exchange or expense recognition.

cost accumulation   Process of determining the cost of a particular object by accumulating many individual costs into a single total cost.

cost allocation   Process of dividing a total cost into parts and assigning the parts to relevant objects.

cost behavior   How a cost reacts (goes up, down, or remains the same) relative to changes in some measure of activity (e.g., the behavior pattern of the cost of raw materials is to increase as the number of units of product made increases).

cost center   Type of responsibility center that incurs costs but does not generate revenue.

cost driver   Any factor, usually some measure of activity, that causes cost to be incurred, sometimes referred to as *activity base* or *allocation base*.

Examples are labor hours, machine hours, or some other measure of activity whose change causes corresponding changes in the cost object.

cost method of accounting for treasury stock   Method of accounting for treasury stock in which the purchase of treasury stock is recorded at its cost to the firm but does not consider the original issue price or par value.

cost objects   Objects for which managers need to know the cost; can be products, processes, departments, services, activities, and so on.

cost of capital   Return paid to investors and creditors for the use of their assets (capital); usually represents a company's minimum rate of return.

cost of goods available for sale   Total costs paid to obtain goods and to make them ready for sale, including the cost of beginning inventory plus purchases and transportation-in costs, less purchase returns and allowances and purchase discounts.

cost of goods sold   Total cost incurred for the goods sold during a specific accounting period.

cost pool   A collection of costs organized around a common cost driver. The cost pool as opposed to individual costs is allocated to cost objects using the common cost driver, thereby promoting efficiency in the allocation process.

cost tracing   Relating specific costs to the objects that cause their incurrence.

cost-plus pricing   Pricing strategy that sets the price at cost plus a markup equal to a percentage of the cost.

credit   Entry that increases liability and equity accounts or decreases asset accounts.

creditor   Individual or organization that has loaned goods or services to a business.

cumulative dividends   Preferred dividends that accumulate from year to year until paid.

current (short-term) asset   Asset that will be converted to cash or consumed within one year or an operating cycle, whichever is longer.

current (short-term) liability   Obligation due within one year or an operating cycle, whichever is longer.

current ratio (working capital ratio)   Measure of liquidity; calculated by dividing current assets by current liabilities.

date of record   Date that establishes who will receive the dividend payment: shareholders who actually own the stock on the record date will be paid the dividend even if the stock is sold before the dividend is paid.

debit   Entry that increases asset accounts or decreases liability and equity accounts.

debt to assets ratio   Financial measure of a company's level of risk, calculated as total debt divided by total assets.

debt to equity ratio   Financial ratio that compares creditor financing to owner financing, expressed as the dollar amount of liabilities for each dollar of stockholder's equity.

decentralization   Practice of delegating authority and responsibility for the operation of business segments.

declaration date   Date on which the board of directors actually declares a dividend.

deferral   Recognition of revenue or expense in a period after the cash is exchanged.

depletion   Method of systematically allocating the costs of natural resources to expense as the resources are removed from the land.

deposit ticket   Bank form that accompanies checks and cash deposited into a bank account; normally specifies the account number, name of the account, and a record of the checks and cash being deposited.

deposits in transit   Deposits recorded in a depositor's books but not received and recorded by the bank.

depreciable cost   Original cost minus salvage value (of a long-term depreciable asset).

depreciation   Decline in value of long-term tangible assets such as buildings, furniture, or equipment. It is systematically recognized by accountants as depreciation expense over the useful lives of the affected assets.

depreciation expense   Portion of the original cost of a long-term tangible asset systematically allocated to an expense account in a given period.

desired rate of return   The rate of return that a company aspires to attain.

differential revenue   Revenues that are relevant to decision making because they differ among alternative courses of action.

direct cost   Cost that is easily traceable to a cost object and for which the sacrifice to trace is small in relation to the information benefits attained.

direct labor   Wages paid to production workers whose efforts can be easily and conveniently traced to products.

direct raw materials   Costs of raw materials used to make products that can be easily and conveniently traced to those products.

disclaimer of opinion   Report on financial statements issued when the auditor is unable to obtain enough information to determine if the statements conform to GAAP; is neither positive nor negative.

discount on bonds payable   Contra liability account used to record the amount of discount on a bond issue.

dividend   Transfer of wealth from a business to its owners.

dividend yield   Ratio for comparing stock dividends paid in relation to the market price; calculated as dividends per share divided by market price per share.

dividends in arrears   Cumulative dividends on preferred stock that have not been paid; must be paid prior to paying dividends to common stockholders.

double taxation   Policy to tax corporate profits distributed to owners twice, once when the income is reported on the corporation's income tax return and again when the dividends are reported on the individual's return.

double-declining-balance depreciation   Depreciation method that recognizes larger amounts of depreciation in the early stages of an asset's life and progressively smaller amounts as the asset ages.

double-entry accounting (double-entry bookkeeping)   Recordkeeping system that provides checks and balances by recording two sides for every transaction.

downstream costs   Costs, such as delivery costs and sales commissions, incurred after the manufacturing process is complete.

earnings (net income)   The difference between revenues and expenses. Sometimes called *profit*.

earnings per share   Measure of the value of a share of common stock in terms of company earnings; calculated as net income available to common stockholders divided by the average number of outstanding common shares.

effective interest rate   Yield rate of bonds, equal to the market rate of interest on the day the bonds are sold.

effective interest rate method   Method of amortizing bond discounts and premiums that bases interest computations on the carrying value of liability. As the liability increases or decreases, the amount of interest expense also increases or decreases.

elements   Key components of financials statements including assets, liabilities, stockholders' equity, common stock, retained earnings, revenue, expense, and net income.

entrenched management   Management that may have become ineffective but because of political implications may be difficult to remove.

equation method   Cost-volume-profit analysis technique that uses the algebraic relationship among sales, variable costs, fixed costs, and desired net income before taxes to solve for required sales volume.

estimated useful life   Time for which an asset is expected to be used by a business.

ex-dividend   Stock traded after the date of record but before the payment date; does not receive the benefit of the upcoming dividend.

expenses   Economic sacrifices (decreases in assets or increases in liabilities) that are incurred in the process of generating revenue.

face value   Amount of the bond to be paid back (to the bondholders) at maturity.

facility-level costs   Costs incurred on behalf of the whole company or a segment of the company; not related to any specific product, batch, or unit of production or service and unavoidable unless the entire company or segment is eliminated.

fidelity bond   Insurance policy that a company buys to insure itself against loss due to employee dishonesty.

financial accounting   Branch of accounting focused on the business information needs of external users (creditors, investors, governmental agencies, financial analysts, etc.); its objective is to classify and record business events and transactions to produce external financial reports (income statement, balance sheet, statement of cash flows, and statement of changes in equity).

Financial Accounting Standards Board (FASB)   Private, independent standard-setting body established by the accounting profession that has been delegated the authority by the SEC to establish most of the accounting rules and regulations for public financial reporting.

financial resources   Money or credit supplied to a business by investors (owners) and creditors.

financial statement audit   Detailed examination of a company's accounting records and the documents that support the information reported in the financial statements; includes testing the reliability of the underlying accounting system used to produce the financial reports.

financial statements   Primary means of communicating the financial information of an organization to the external users. The four general-purpose financial statements are the income statement, statement of changes in equity, balance sheet, and statement of cash flows.

financing activities   Cash inflows and outflows from transactions with investors and creditors (except interest), including cash receipts from issuing stock, borrowing activities, and cash disbursements to pay dividends; one of the three categories of cash inflows and outflows reported on the statement of cash flows. This category shows the amount of cash supplied by these resource providers and the amount of cash that is returned to them.

finished goods inventory   Asset account used to accumulate the product costs (direct materials, direct labor, and overhead) associated with completed products that have not yet been sold.

first-in, first-out (FIFO) cost flow method   Inventory cost flow method that treats the first items purchased as the first items sold for the purpose of computing cost of goods sold.

fixed cost   Cost that in total remains constant when activity volume changes; varies per unit inversely with changes in the volume of activity.

fixed cost volume variance   The difference between the budgeted fixed cost and the applied fixed cost.

fixed interest rate   Interest rate (charge for the use of money) that does not change over the life of the loan.

flexible budget   Budget that shows expected revenues and costs at a variety of different activity levels.

flexible budget variance   Difference between budgets based on standard amounts at the actual level of activity and actual results; caused by differences in standard and actual unit cost since the volume of activity is the same.

FOB (free on board) destination   Term that designates the seller as the responsible party for freight costs (transportation-in costs).

FOB (free on board) shipping point   Term that designates the buyer as the responsible party for freight costs (transportation-in costs).

franchise   Exclusive right to sell products or perform services in certain geographic areas.

full disclosure   The accounting principle that financial statements should include all information relevant to an entity's operations and financial condition. Full disclosure frequently requires adding footnotes to the financial statements.

gain   Increase in assets or decrease in liabilities that results from peripheral or incidental transactions.

general authority   Policies and procedures that apply across different levels of a company's management, such as everyone flies coach class.

general journal   Journal in which all types of accounting transactions can be entered but which is commonly used to record adjusting and closing entries and unusual types of transactions.

general ledger   The set of all accounts used in a given accounting system, typically organized in financial statement order.

general uncertainties   Uncertainties inherent in operating a business, such as competition and damage from storms. Unlike contingent liabilities, these uncertainties arise from future rather than past events.

generally accepted accounting principles (GAAP)   Rules and practices that accountants agree to follow in financial reports prepared for public distribution.

going concern (assumption)   Accounting presumption that a company will continue to operate indefinitely, benefiting from its assets and paying its obligations in full; justifies reporting assets and liabilities in the financial statements.

goodwill   Added value of a successful business that is attributable to factors—reputation, location, and superior products—that enable the business to earn above-average profits; stated differently, the excess paid for an existing business over the appraised value of the net assets.

gross margin (gross profit)   Difference between sales revenue and cost of goods sold; the amount a company makes from selling goods before subtracting operating expenses.

gross profit (gross margin)   Percentage difference between sales revenue and cost of goods sold; the amount a company makes from selling goods before subtracting operating expenses.

historical cost concept   Accounting practice of reporting assets at the actual price paid for them when purchased regardless of estimated changes in market value.

horizontal analysis   Analysis technique that compares amounts of the same item over several time periods.

horizontal statements model   Arrangement of a set of financial statements horizontally across a sheet of paper.

income   Added value created in transforming resources into more desirable states.

income statement   Financial report of profitability; measures the difference between revenues and expenses for the accounting period (whether or not cash has been exchanged).

incremental revenue   Additional cash inflows from operations generated by using an additional capital asset.

independent auditor   Licensed certified public accountant engaged to audit a company's financial statements; not an employee of the audited company.

indirect costs   Costs that cannot be easily traced to a cost object and for which the economic sacrifice to trace is not worth the informational benefits.

information overload   Situation in which the presentation of too much information confuses the user of the information.

installment note   Obligation that requires regular payments of principal and interest over the life of the loan.

intangible assets   Assets that may be represented by pieces of paper or contracts that appear tangible; however, the true value of an intangible asset lies in the rights and privileges extended to its owners.

interest   Fee paid for the use of funds; represents expense to the borrower and revenue to the lender.

internal controls   A company's policies and procedures designed to reduce the opportunity for fraud and to provide reasonable assurance that its objectives will be accomplished.

internal rate of return   Rate that will produce a present value of an investment's future cash inflows that equals cash outflows required to acquire the investment; alternatively, the rate that produces in a net present value of zero.

International Accounting Standards Board (IASB)
Private, independent body that establishes International Financial Reporting Standards (IFRS). The IASB's authority is established by various governmental institutions that require or permit companies in their jurisdiction to use IFRS. To date, over 100 countries require or permit companies to prepare their financial statements using IFRS. One notable exception is the United States of America.

International Financial Reporting Standards (IFRS)
Pronouncements established by the International Accounting Standards Board that provide guidance for the preparation of financial statements.

inventory cost flow methods   Methods used to allocate the cost of goods available for sale between cost of goods sold and inventory.

inventory holding costs   Costs associated with acquiring and retaining inventory including cost of storage space; lost, stolen, or damaged merchandise; insurance; personnel and management costs; and interest.

inventory turnover   A measure of sales volume relative to inventory levels; calculated as the cost of goods sold divided by average inventory; indicates how many times a year, on average, the inventory is sold (turned over).

investing activities   Cash inflows and outflows associated with buying or selling long-term assets and cash inflows and outflows associated with lending activities and investments in the debt and equity of other companies; one of the three categories of cash inflows and outflows reported on the statement of cash flows.

investment center   Type of responsibility center for which revenue, expense and capital investments can be measured.

investor   Company or individual who gives assets or services in exchange for security certificates representing ownership interests.

issued stock   Stock sold to the public.

issuer   Individual or business that issues a note payable, bonds payable, or stock (the party receiving cash). See also *maker*.

journal   Book (or electronic record) of original entry in which accounting data are entered chronologically before posting to the ledger accounts.

just in time (JIT)   Inventory flow system that minimizes the amount of inventory on hand by making inventory available for customer consumption on demand, therefore eliminating the need to store inventory. The system reduces explicit holding costs including financing, warehouse storage, supervision, theft, damage, and obsolescence. It also eliminates hidden opportunity costs such as lost revenue due to the lack of availability of inventory.

labor resources   The intellectual and physical efforts of individuals used in the process of providing goods and services to customers.

last-in, first-out (LIFO) cost flow method   Inventory cost flow method that treats the last items purchased as the first items sold for the purpose of computing cost of goods sold.

legal capital   Amount of assets that should be maintained as protection for creditors; the number of shares multiplied by the par value.

liabilities   Obligations of a business to relinquish assets, provide services, or accept other obligations.

limited liability   Concept that investors in a corporation may not be held personally liable for the actions of the corporation (the creditors cannot lay claim to the owners' personal assets as payment for the corporation's debts).

limited liability company (LLC)   Organization offering many of the best features of corporations and partnerships and with many legal benefits of corporations (e.g., limited liability and centralized management) but permitted by the Internal Revenue Service to be taxed as a partnership, thereby avoiding double taxation of profits.

line of credit   Preapproved credit arrangement with a lending institution in which a business can borrow money by simply writing a check up to the approved limit.

liquidation   Process of dividing up an organization's assets and returning them to the resource providers. In business liquidations, creditors normally have first priority; after creditor claims have been satisfied, any remaining assets are distributed to the company's owners (investors).

liquidity Ability to convert assets to cash quickly and meet short-term obligations.

liquidity ratios Measures of short-term debt-paying ability.

long-term liabilities Liabilities with maturity dates beyond one year or the company's operating cycle, whichever is longer; noncurrent liabilities.

long-term operational assets Assets used by a business to generate revenue; condition of being used distinguishes them from assets that are sold (inventory) and assets that are held (investments).

loss Decrease in assets or increase in liabilities that results from peripheral or incidental transactions.

low-ball pricing Pricing a product below competitors' price to lure customers away and then raising the price once customers depend on the supplier for the product.

maintenance costs Costs incurred for repair or maintenance of long-term operational assets; recorded as expenses and subtracted from revenue in the accounting period in which incurred.

maker The party issuing a note (the borrower).

making the numbers Expression that indicates marketing managers attained the planned master budget sales volume.

management by exception The philosophy of focusing management attention and resources only on those operations where performance deviates significantly from expectations.

managerial accounting Branch of accounting focused on the information needs of managers and others working within the business; its objective is to gather and report information that adds value to the business. Managerial accounting information is not regulated or reported to the public.

manufacturing businesses Companies that make the goods they sell to customers.

manufacturing overhead Production costs that cannot be traced directly to products.

margin Component in the determination of the return on investment. Computed by dividing operating income by sales.

margin of safety Difference between break-even sales and budgeted sales expressed in units, dollars, or as a percentage; the amount by which actual sales can fall below budgeted sales before a loss is incurred.

market Group of people or entities organized to buy and sell resources.

market rate of interest Interest rate currently available on a wide range of alternative investments with similar levels of risk.

market value The price at which securities sell in the secondary market: also called fair value.

master budget Composition of the numerous separate but interdependent departmental budgets that cover a wide range of operating and financial factors such as sales, production, manufacturing expenses, and administrative expenses.

matching concept Accounting principle of recognizing expenses in the same accounting period as the revenues they produce, using one of three methods: match expenses directly with revenues (e.g., cost of goods sold); match expenses to the period in which they are incurred (e.g., rent expense), and match expenses systematically with revenues (e.g., depreciation expense).

materiality The point at which knowledge of information would influence a user's decision; can be measured in absolute, percentage, quantitative, or qualitative terms. The concept allows nonmaterial matters to be handled in any convenient way, such as charging a pencil sharpener to expense rather than recording periodic depreciation over its useful life.

maturity date The date a liability is due to be settled (the date the borrower is expected to repay a debt).

merchandise inventory Supply of finished goods held for resale to customers.

merchandising businesses Companies that buy and resell merchandise inventory.

midstream costs Costs incurred in the process of making products including direct materials, direct labor, and manufacturing overhead.

minimum rate of return Minimum amount of profitability required to persuade a company to accept an investment opportunity; also known as *desired rate of return, required rate of return, hurdle rate, cutoff rate,* and *discount rate.*

mixed costs (semivariable costs) Costs composed of a mixture of fixed and variable components.

multistep income statement Income statement format that matches particular revenue items with related expense items and distinguishes between recurring operating activities and nonoperating items such as gains and losses.

natural resources Mineral deposits, oil and gas reserves, and reserves of timber, mines, and quarries are examples; sometimes called *wasting assets* because their value wastes away as the resources are removed.

net income Increase in equity resulting from operating the business.

net loss Decrease in equity resulting from operating the business.

net margin Profitability measurement that indicates the percentage of each sales dollar resulting in profit; calculated as net income divided by net sales.

net present value Evaluation technique that uses a desired rate of return to discount future cash flows back to their present value equivalents and then subtracts the cost of the investment from the present value equivalents to determine the net present value. A zero or positive net present value (present value of cash inflows equals or exceeds the present value of cash outflows) implies that the investment opportunity provides an acceptable rate of return.

net realizable value (NVR) Face amount of receivables less an allowance for accounts whose collection is doubtful (amount actually expected to be collected).

net sales Sales less returns from customers and allowances or cash discounts given to customers.

non-sufficient-funds (NSF) check Customer's check deposited but returned by the bank on which it was drawn because the customer did not have enough money in its account to pay the check.

nonvalue-added activity Task undertaken that does not contribute to a product's ability to satisfy customer needs.

not-for-profit entities Organizations (also called *nonprofit* or *nonbusiness organizations*) established primarily for motives other than making a profit, such as providing goods and services for the social good. Examples include state-supported universities and colleges, hospitals, public libraries, and public charities.

note payable A liability that results from executing a legal document called a *promissory note,* which describes the interest rate, maturity date, collateral, and so on.

notes receivable Notes that evidence rights to receive cash in the future from the maker of a *promissory note;* usually specify the maturity date, interest rate, and other credit terms.

number of times interest is earned Ratio that measures a company's ability to make its interest payments; calculated by dividing the amount of earnings available for interest payments (net income before interest and income taxes) by the amount of the interest payments.

operating activities Cash inflows from and outflows for routine, everyday business operations, normally resulting from revenue and expense transactions including interest; one of the three categories of cash inflows and outflows reported on the statement of cash flows.

operating budgets Budgets prepared by different departments within a company that will become a part of the company's master budget; typically include a sales budget, an inventory purchases budget, a selling and administrative budget, and a cash budget.

operating cycle Time required to turn cash into inventory, inventory into receivables, and receivables back to cash.

operating income (or loss)   Income statement subtotal representing the difference between operating revenues and operating expenses, but before recognizing gains and losses from peripheral activities which are added to or subtracted from operating income to determine net income or loss.

operating leverage   Operating condition in which a percentage change in revenue produces a proportionately larger percentage change in net income; measured by dividing the contribution margin by net income. The higher the proportion of fixed cost to total costs, the greater the operating leverage.

operations budgeting   Short-range planning activities such as the development and implementation of the master budget.

opportunity   An element of the fraud triangle that recognizes weaknesses in internal controls that enable the occurrence of fraudulent or unethical behavior.

opportunity cost   Cost of lost opportunities such as the failure to make sales due to an insufficient supply of inventory or the wage a working student forgoes to attend class.

ordinary annuity   Annuity whose cash inflows occur at the end of each accounting period.

outsourcing   The practice of buying goods and services from another company rather than producing them internally.

outstanding checks   Checks deducted from the depositor's cash account balance but not yet presented to the bank for payment.

outstanding stock   Stock owned by outside parties; normally the amount of stock issued less the amount of treasury stock.

overhead   Costs associated with producing products that cannot be cost effectively traced to products including indirect costs such as indirect materials, indirect labor, utilities, rent, and depreciation.

overhead costs   Indirect costs of doing business that cannot be directly traced to a product, department, or process, such as depreciation.

paid-in capital in excess of par (or stated) value   Any amount received above the par or stated value of stock when stock is issued.

par value   Arbitrary value assigned to stock by the board of directors.

participative budgeting   Budget technique that allows subordinates to participate with upper-level managers in setting budget objectives, thereby encouraging cooperation and support in the attainment of the company's goal.

partnership   Business entity owned by at least two people who share talents, capital, and the risks of the business.

partnership agreement   Legal document that defines the responsibilities of each partner and describes the division of income and losses.

patent   Legal right granted by the U.S. Patent Office ensuring a company or an individual the exclusive right to a product or process.

payback method   Technique that evaluates investment opportunities by determining the length of time necessary to recover the initial net investment through incremental revenue or cost savings; the shorter the period, the better the investment opportunity.

payee   The party collecting cash.

payment date   Date on which a dividend is actually paid.

percent of receivables method   Estimating the amount of the allowance for doubtful accounts as a percentage of the outstanding receivables balance. The percentage is typically based on a combination of factors such as historical experience, economic conditions, and the company's credit policies.

percent of revenue method   Estimating the amount of uncollectible accounts expense as a percentage of the revenue earned on account during the accounting period. The percentage is typically based on a combination of factors such as historical experience, economic conditions, and the company's credit policies.

percentage analysis   Analysis of relationships between two different items to draw conclusions or make decisions.

period costs   General, selling, and administrative costs that are expensed in the period in which the economic sacrifice is made.

periodic inventory system   Method of accounting for changes in the Inventory account only at the end of the accounting period.

permanent accounts   Balance sheet accounts; contain information carried forward from one accounting period to the next (ending account balance one period becomes beginning account balance next period).

perpetual (continuous) budgeting   Continuous budgeting activity normally covering a 12-month time span by replacing the current month's budget at the end of each month with a new budget; keeps management constantly involved in the budget process so that changing conditions are incorporated on a timely bases.

perpetual inventory system   Method of accounting for inventories that increases the Inventory account each time merchandise is purchased and decreases it each time merchandise is sold.

physical flow of goods   Physical movement of goods through the business; normally a FIFO flow so that the first goods purchased are the first goods delivered to customers, thereby reducing the likelihood of obsolete inventory.

physical resources   Natural resources businesses transform to create more valuable resources.

postaudit   Repeat calculation using the techniques originally employed to analyze an investment project; accomplished with the use of actual data available at the completion of the investment project so that the actual results can be compared with expected results based on estimated data at the beginning of the project. Its purpose is to provide feedback as to whether the expected results were actually accomplished in improving the accuracy of future analysis.

posting   Process of copying information from journals to ledgers.

predetermined overhead rate   Allocation rate calculated before actual costs or activity are known; determined by dividing the estimated overhead costs for the coming period by some measure of estimated total production activity for the period, such as the number of labor-hours or machine-hours. The base should relate rationally to overhead use. The rate is used throughout the accounting period to allocate overhead costs to work in process inventory based on actual production activity.

preferred stock   Stock that receives some form of preferential treatment (usually as to dividends) over common stock; normally has no voting rights.

premium on bonds payable   Difference between the selling price and the face amount of a bond that is sold for more than the face amount.

prepaid items   Deferred expenses. An example is prepaid insurance.

present value index   Present value of cash inflows divided by the present value of cash outflows. Higher index numbers indicate higher rates of return.

present value table   Table that consists of a list of factors to use in converting future values into their present value equivalents; composed of columns that represent different return rates and rows that depict different periods of time.

pressure   An element of the fraud triangle that recognizes conditions that motivate fraudulent or unethical behavior.

price-earnings (P/E) ratio   Measure that reflects the values of different stocks in terms of earnings; calculated as market price per share divided by earnings (net income) per share; a higher P/E ratio generally indicates that investors are optimistic about a company's future.

principal   Amount of cash actually borrowed.

pro forma financial statements   Budgeted financial statements prepared from the information in the master budget.

procedures manual   Manual that sets forth the accounting procedures to be followed.

product costing   Classification and accumulation of individual inputs (materials, labor, and overhead) for determining the cost of making a good or providing a service.

product costs   All costs related to obtaining or manufacturing a product intended for sale to customers; are accumulated in inventory accounts and expensed as cost of goods sold at the point of sale. For a manufacturing company, product costs include direct materials, direct labor, and manufacturing overhead.

product-level costs Costs incurred to support different kinds of products or services; can be avoided by the elimination of a product line or a type of service.

profit Value added by transforming resources into products or services desired by customers.

profit center Type of responsibility center for which both revenues and costs can be indentified.

profitability ratios Measurements of a firm's ability to generate earnings.

promissory note A legal document representing a credit agreement between a lender and a borrower. The note specifies technical details such as the maker, payee, interest rate, maturity date, payment terms, and any collateral.

property, plant, and equipment Category of assets, sometimes called *plant assets,* used to produce products or to carry on the administrative and selling functions of a business; includes machinery and equipment, buildings, and land.

purchase discount Reduction in the gross price of merchandise extended under the condition that the purchaser pay cash for the merchandise within a stated time (usually within 10 days of the date of the sale).

purchase returns and allowances A reduction in the cost of purchases resulting from dissatisfaction with merchandise purchased.

qualified opinion Opinion issued by a certified public accountant that means the company's financial statements are, for the most part, in compliance with GAAP, but there is some circumstance (explained in the auditor's report) about which the auditor has reservations; contrast with *unqualified opinion.*

qualitative characteristics Nonquantifiable features such as company reputation, welfare of employees, and customer satisfaction that can be affected by certain decisions.

quantitative characteristics Numbers in decision making subject to mathematical manipulation, such as the dollar amounts of revenues and expenses.

quick ratio Measure of immediate debt-paying ability; calculated by dividing very liquid assets (cash, receivables, and marketable securities) by current liabilities.

ratio analysis Analysis of relationships between two different items to draw conclusions or make decisions.

rationalization An element of the fraud triangle that recognizes a human tendency to justify fraudulent or unethical behavior.

raw materials Physical commodities (e.g., wood, metal, paint) used in the manufacturing process.

raw materials inventory Asset account used to accumulate the costs of materials (such as lumber, metals, paints, chemicals) that will be used to make a company's products.

recovery of investment Recovery of the funds used to acquire the original investment.

reengineering Business practices designed by companies to make production and delivery systems more competitive in world markets by eliminating or minimizing waste, errors, and costs.

reinstate Recording an account receivable previously written off back into the accounting records, generally when cash is collected long after the original due date.

relative fair market value method Method of assigning value to individual assets acquired in a basket purchase in which each asset is assigned a percentage of the total price paid for all assets. The percentage assigned equals the market value of a particular asset divided by the total of the market values of all assets acquired in the basket purchase.

relevant costs Future-oriented costs that differ between business alternatives; also known as *avoidable costs.*

relevant information Decision-making information about costs, costs savings, or revenues that have these features: (1) future-oriented information and (2) the information differs between the alternatives; decision-specific (information that is relevant in one decision may not be relevant in another decision).

relevant range Range of activity over which the definitions of fixed and variable costs are valid.

reporting entities Businesses or other organizations for which financial statements are prepared.

residual income Approach that evaluates managers on their ability to maximize the dollar value of earnings above some targeted level of earnings.

responsibility accounting Performance measure that evaluates managers based on how well they maximize the dollar value of earning above some target level of earnings.

responsibility center Point in an organization where the control over revenue or expense items is located.

restrictive covenants Special provisions specified in the loan contract that are designed to prohibit management from taking certain actions that place creditors at risk.

retail companies Companies that sell goods to consumers.

retained earnings Portion of stockholders' equity that includes all earnings retained in the business since inception (revenues minus expenses and distributions for all accounting periods).

return on assets Profitability measure based on earnings a company generates relative to its asset base; calculated as net income divided by average total assets.

return on equity Profitability measure based on earnings a company generates relative to its stockholders' equity; calculated as net income divided by average stockholders' equity.

return on investment (ROI) Measure of profitability based on the asset base of the firm. It is calculated as net income divided by average total assets. ROI is a product of net margin and asset turnover.

revenue The economic benefit (increase in assets or decrease in liabilities) gained by providing goods or services to customers.

salaries payable Amounts owed but not yet paid to employees for services they have already performed.

sales discount Cash discount extended by the seller of goods to encourage prompt payment. When the buyer of the goods takes advantage of the discount to pay less than the original selling price, the difference between the selling price and the cash collected is the sales discount.

sales price variance Difference between actual sales and expected sales based on the standard sales price per unit times the actual level of activity.

sales returns and allowances A reduction in sales revenue resulting from dissatisfaction with merchandise sold.

sales volume variance Difference between sales based on a static budget (standard sales price times standard level of activity) and sales based on a flexible budget (standard sales price times actual level of activity).

salvage value Expected selling price of an asset at the end of its useful life.

schedule of cost of goods manufactured and sold Internal accounting report that summarizes the manufacturing product costs for the period; its result, cost of goods sold, is reported as a single line item on the company's income statement.

schedule of cost of goods sold Schedule that reflects the computation of the amount of the cost of goods sold under the periodic inventory system; an internal report not shown in the formal financial statements.

Securities Act of 1933 and Securities Exchange Act of 1934 Acts passed after the stock market crash of 1929 designed to regulate the issuance of stock and govern the stock exchanges; created the Securities and Exchange Commission (SEC), which has the authority to establish accounting policies for companies registered on the stock exchanges.

Securities and Exchange Commission (SEC) Government agency responsible for overseeing the accounting rules to be followed by companies required to be registered with it.

segment Component part of an organization that is designated as a reporting entity.

selling and administrative costs Costs that cannot be directly traced to products that are recognized as expenses in the period in which they are incurred. Examples include advertising expense and rent expense.

selling, general, and administrative costs (SG&A) All costs not associated with obtaining or manufacturing a product; sometimes called *period costs* because they are normally expensed in the period in which the economic sacrifice is incurred.

separation of duties Internal control feature of, whenever possible, assigning the functions of authorization, recording, and custody to different individuals.

service businesses Organizations such as accounting and legal firms, dry cleaners, and insurance companies that provide services to consumers.

service charges Fees charged by a bank for services performed or a penalty for the depositor's failing to maintain a specified minimum cash balance throughout the period.

shrinkage A term that reflects decreases in inventory for reasons other than sales to customers.

signature card Bank form that records the bank account number and the signatures of the people authorized to write checks on an account.

single-payment (lump-sum) A one-time receipt of cash that can be converted to its present value using a conversion factor.

single-step income statement Single comparison between total revenues and total expenses.

sole proprietorship Business (usually small) owned by one person.

solvency ratios Measures of a firm's long-term debt-paying ability.

source documents Documents such as a cash register tape, invoice, time card, or check stub that provide accounting information to be recorded in the accounting journals and ledgers.

special journals Journals designed to improve the efficiency of recording specific types of repetitive transactions.

special order decision Decision of whether to accept orders from nonregular customers who want to buy goods or services significantly below the normal selling price. If the order's relevant revenues exceed its avoidable costs, the order should be accepted. Qualitative features such as the order's effect on the existing customer base if accepted must also be considered.

specific authorizations Policies and procedures that apply to designated levels of management, such as the policy that the right to approve overtime pay may apply only to the plant manager.

specific identification Inventory method that allocates costs between cost of goods sold and ending inventory using the cost of the specific goods sold or retained in the business.

spending variance The difference between the actual fixed overhead costs and the budgeted fixed overhead costs.

stakeholders Parties interested in the operations of a business, including owners, lenders, employees, suppliers, customers, and government agencies.

stated interest rate Rate of interest specified in the bond contract that will be paid at specified intervals over the life of the bond.

stated value Arbitrary value assigned to stock by the board of directors.

statement of cash flows The financial statement that reports a company's cash inflows and outflows for an accounting period, classifying them as operating, investing, or financing activities.

statement of changes in stockholders' equity Statement that summarizes the transactions that affected the owners' equity during the accounting period.

static budget Budget such as the master budget based solely on the level of planned activity; remains constant even when volume of activity changes.

stewardship Refers to a business's duty to protect and use the assets of the company for the benefit of the owners (the firm's stockholders).

stock certificate Evidence of ownership interest issued when an investor contributes assets to a corporation; describes the rights and privileges that accompany ownership.

stock dividend Proportionate distribution of additional shares of the declaring corporation's stock.

stock split Proportionate increase in the number of outstanding shares; designed to reduce the market value of the stock and its par value.

stockholders Owners of a corporation.

stockholders' equity Stockholders' equity represents the portion of the assets that is owned by the stockholders.

straight-line amortization Method of amortization in which equal amounts of the account being reduced (e.g., Bond Discount, Bond Premium, Patent) are transferred to the appropriate expense account over the relevant time period.

straight-line depreciation Method of computing depreciation that allocates the cost of an asset to expense in equal amounts over its life. The formula for calculating straight line depreciation is [(Cost 2 Salvage)/ Useful Life].

strategic planning Planning activities associated with long-range decisions such as defining the scope of the business, determining which products to develop, deciding whether to discontinue a business segment, and determining which market niche would be most profitable.

suboptimization Situation in which managers act in their own self-interests even though the organization as a whole suffers.

sunk costs Costs that have been incurred in past transactions and therefore are not relevant for decision making.

T-account Simplified account form, named for its shape, with the account title placed at the top of a horizontal bar, debit entries listed on the left side of the vertical bar, and credit entries shown on the right side.

tangible assets Assets that can be touched, such as equipment, machinery, natural resources, and land.

temporary accounts Accounts used to collect retained earnings data applicable to only the current accounting period (revenues, expenses and distributions); sometimes called *nominal accounts*.

time value of money Recognition that the present value of a promise to receive a dollar some time in the future is worth less than a dollar because of interest, risk, and inflation factors. For example, a person may be willing to pay $0.90 today for the right to receive $1.00 one year from today.

total quality management (TQM) Management philosophy that includes: (1) a continuous systematic problem-solving philosophy that engages personnel at all levels of the organization to eliminate waste, defects, and nonvalue-added activities; and (2) the effort to manage quality costs in a manner that leads to the highest level of customer satisfaction.

trademark Name or symbol that identifies a company or an individual product.

transaction Business event that involves transferring something of value between two entities.

transferability Concept referring to the practice of dividing the ownership of corporations into small units that are represented by shares of stock, which permits the easy exchange of ownership interests.

transportation-in (freight-in) Cost of freight on goods purchased under terms FOB shipping point that is usually added to the cost of inventory and is a product cost.

transportation-out (freight-out) Freight cost for goods delivered to customers under terms FOB destination; a period cost expensed when it is incurred.

treasury stock Stock first issued to the public and then bought back by the corporation.

trend analysis Study of the performance of a business over a period of time.

trial balance   List of ledger accounts and their balances that provides a check on the mathematical accuracy of the recording process.

true cash balance   Actual balance of cash owned by a company at the close of business on the date of the bank statement.

turnover   Component in the determination of the return on investment. Computed by dividing sales by operating assets.

unadjusted bank balance   Ending cash balance reported by the bank as of the date of the bank statement.

unadjusted book balance   Balance of the Cash account as of the date of the reconciliation before making any adjustments.

unadjusted rate of return (simple rate of return)   Measure of profitability computed by dividing the average incremental increase in annual net income by the average cost of the original investment (original cost divided by 2); does not account for the *time value of money*.

uncollectible accounts expense   Expense associated with uncollectible accounts receivable; the amount recognized may be estimated using the percent of revenue or the percent of receivables method, or actual losses may be recorded using the direct write-off method. In practice the *uncollectible account expense* is frequently called *bad debts expense*.

unearned revenue   Liability arising when customers pay cash in advance for services a business will perform in the future.

unit-level costs   Costs incurred each time a company makes a single product or performs a single service and that can be avoided by eliminating a unit of product or service. Likewise, unit-level costs increase with each additional product produced or service provided.

units-of-production depreciation   Depreciation method based on a measure of production rather than a measure of time; for example, an automobile may be depreciated based on the expected miles to be driven rather than on a specific number of years.

unqualified opinion   Opinion issued by a certified public accountant that means the company's financial statements are, in all material respects, in compliance with GAAP; the auditor has no reservations. Contrast with qualified opinion.

upstream costs   Costs incurred before the manufacturing process begins, for example, research and development costs.

users   Individuals or organizations that use financial information for decision making.

value chain   Linked sequence of activities that create value for the customer.

value-added activity   Any unit of work that contributes to a product's ability to satisfy customer needs.

value-added principle   The benefits attained (value added) from the process should exceed the cost of the process.

variable cost   Cost that in total changes in direct proportion to changes in volume of activity; remains constant per unit when volume of activity changes.

variable cost volume variance   The difference between a variable cost calculated at the planned volume of activity and the same variable cost calculated at the actual volume of activity.

variable interest rate   Interest rate that fluctuates (may change) from period to period over the life of the loan.

variance   Difference between standard and actual amounts.

vertical analysis   Analysis technique that compares items on financial statements to significant totals.

vertical integration   Attainment of control over the entire spectrum of business activity from production to sales; an example is a grocery store that owns farms.

vertical statements model   Concurrent representation of several financial statements shown vertically on a page.

warranties   Promises to correct deficiencies or dissatisfactions in quality, quantity, or performance of products or services sold.

weighted-average cost flow method   Inventory cost flow method in which the cost allocated between inventory and cost of goods sold is based on the average cost per unit, which is determined by dividing total costs of goods available for sale during the accounting period by total units available for sale during the period. If the average is recomputed each time a purchase is made, the result is called a *moving average*.

wholesale companies   Companies that sell goods to other businesses.

withdrawals   Distributions to the owners of proprietorships and partnerships.

work in process inventory   Asset account used to accumulate the product costs (direct materials, direct labor, and overhead) associated with incomplete products that have been started but are not yet completed.

working capital   Current assets minus current liabilities.

working capital ratio   Another term for the current ratio: calculated by dividing current assets by current liabilities.

INDEX